W9-CPC-921

Connect™ Accounting

Instructors...

Want to **streamline** lesson planning, student progress reporting, and assignment grading? (Less time planning means more time teaching...)

Need to **collect data and generate reports** required by accreditation organizations, such as AACSB and AICPA? (Say goodbye to manually tracking student learning outcomes...)

Want an **instant view** of student or class performance relative to learning objectives? (No more wondering if students understand...)

With **McGraw-Hill *Connect*™ Accounting,**

INSTRUCTORS GET

- The ability to **post assignments** and other communication between students and instructors.

- Simple **assignment management**, allowing you to spend more time teaching.

- **Auto-graded homework.**

- **Customized course gradebook** where grades are automatically posted.

- **Online testing capability**.

- A **progress-tracking** function that allows you to easily assign materials that conform to AACSB and AICPA standards.

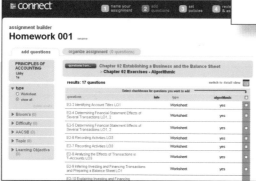

Q Want an online, **searchable version** of your textbook?

Wish your textbook could be available online while you're doing your homework?

A *Connect*™ **Plus Accounting eBook**

If your instructor has chosen to use *Connect*™ *Plus Accounting*, you have an affordable and searchable online version of your book integrated with your other online homework tools.

Connect™ **Plus Accounting eBook offers features like:**

- topic search
- adjustable text size
- jump to page number
- print by section

Q Want to get more **value** from your textbook purchase?

Think learning accounting should be a little bit more **interesting**?

A **Check out the companion website for this textbook www.mhhe.com/hoyle4e**

We put it there for you. Go online for test tips and practice problems whenever you study. The companion website for this book includes **quizzes, PowerPoints, Excel templates, check figures, and CPA simulations** to help you study. Get more from your textbook – use the Online Learning Center.

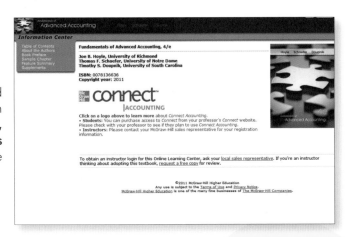

Fundamentals of Advanced Accounting

Fourth Edition

Joe B. Hoyle
Associate Professor of Accounting
Robins School of Business
University of Richmond

Thomas F. Schaefer
KPMG Professor of Accountancy
Mendoza College of Business
University of Notre Dame

Timothy S. Doupnik
Professor of Accounting
Moore School of Business
University of South Carolina

McGraw-Hill
Irwin

The McGraw·Hill Companies

McGraw-Hill
Irwin

FUNDAMENTALS OF ADVANCED ACCOUNTING

Published by McGraw-Hill/Irwin, a business unit of The McGraw-Hill Companies, Inc., 1221 Avenue of the Americas, New York, NY, 10020. Copyright © 2011, 2009, 2007, 2004 by The McGraw-Hill Companies, Inc. All rights reserved. No part of this publication may be reproduced or distributed in any form or by any means, or stored in a database or retrieval system, without the prior written consent of The McGraw-Hill Companies, Inc., including, but not limited to, in any network or other electronic storage or transmission, or broadcast for distance learning.

Some ancillaries, including electronic and print components, may not be available to customers outside the United States.

This book is printed on acid-free paper.

1 2 3 4 5 6 7 8 9 0 WDQ/WDQ 1 0 9 8 7 6 5 4 3 2 1 0

ISBN   978-0-07-813663-4
MHID   0-07-813663-6

Vice president and editor-in-chief: *Brent Gordon*
Editorial director: *Stewart Mattson*
Publisher: *Tim Vertovec*
Senior sponsoring editor: *Dana L. Woo*
Director of development: *Ann Torbert*
Development editor: *Katie Jones*
Vice president and director of marketing: *Robin J. Zwettler*
Marketing director: *Sankha Basu*
Associate marketing manager: *Dean Karampelas*
Vice president of editing, design and production: *Sesha Bolisetty*
Managing editor: *Lori Koetters*
Lead production supervisor: *Carol A. Bielski*
Interior and cover designer: *Pam Verros*
Media project manager: *Joyce J. Chappetto*
Cover credit: © *Adam Gault/Digital Vision/Getty Images*
Typeface: *10/12 Times New Roman*
Compositor: *Aptara®, Inc.*
Printer: *Worldcolor*

Library of Congress Cataloging-in-Publication Data

Hoyle, Joe Ben.
    Fundamentals of advanced accounting / Joe B. Hoyle, Thomas F. Schaefer,
Timothy S. Doupnik.—4th ed.
       p. cm.
    Includes index.
    ISBN-13: 978-0-07-813663-4 (alk. paper)
    ISBN-10: 0-07-813663-6 (alk. paper)
      1. Accounting. I. Schaefer, Thomas F. II. Doupnik, Timothy S. III. Title.
HF5636.H693 2011
657'.046—dc22   2010005433

www.mhhe.com

To our families

The real purpose of books is to trap the mind into doing its own thinking.
Christopher Morley

About the Authors

Joe B. Hoyle, *University of Richmond*

Joe B. Hoyle is Associate Professor of Accounting at the Robins School of Business at the University of Richmond, where he teaches Intermediate Accounting and Advanced Accounting. In 2009, he was named one of the 100 most influential people in the accounting profession by *Accounting Today.* He was named the 2007 Virginia Professor of the Year by the Carnegie Foundation for the Advancement of Teaching and the Center for Advancement and Support of Education. He has been named a Distinguished Educator five times at the University of Richmond and Professor of the Year on two occasions. Joe recently authored a book of essays titled *Tips and Thoughts on Improving the Teaching Process in College,* which is available without charge at http://oncampus.richmond.edu/~jhoyle/.

Thomas F. Schaefer, *University of Notre Dame*

Thomas F. Schaefer is the KPMG Professor of Accounting at the University of Notre Dame. He has written a number of articles in scholarly journals such as *The Accounting Review, Journal of Accounting Research, Journal of Accounting & Economics, Accounting Horizons,* and others. His primary teaching and research interests are in financial accounting and reporting. Tom is active with the Association for the Advancement of Collegiate Schools of Business International and is a past president of the American Accounting Association's Accounting Program Leadership Group. Tom received the 2007 Joseph A. Silvoso Faculty Merit Award from the Federation of Schools of Accountancy.

Timothy S. Doupnik, *University of South Carolina*

Timothy S. Doupnik is Professor of Accounting at the University of South Carolina, where he teaches Financial and International Accounting. Tim has published extensively in the area of international accounting in journals such as *Accounting, Organizations, and Society; Abacus; International Journal of Accounting;* and *Journal of International Business Studies.* Tim is a past president of the American Accounting Association's International Accounting Section, and he received the section's Outstanding International Accounting Educator Award in 2008.

The approach used by Hoyle, Schaefer, and Doupnik allows students to think critically about accounting, just as they will in their careers and as they prepare for the CPA exam. Read on to understand how students will succeed as accounting majors and as future CPAs by using *Fundamentals of Advanced Accounting,* 4e.

Thinking Critically

With this text, students gain a well-balanced appreciation of the accounting profession. As *Hoyle* 4e introduces them to the field's many aspects, it often focuses on past controversies and present resolutions. The text shows the development of financial reporting as a product of intense and considered debate that continues today and will in the future.

Readability

The writing style of the nine previous editions has been highly praised. **Students easily comprehend** chapter concepts because of the conversational tone used throughout the book. The authors have made every effort to ensure that the writing style remains engaging, lively, and consistent.

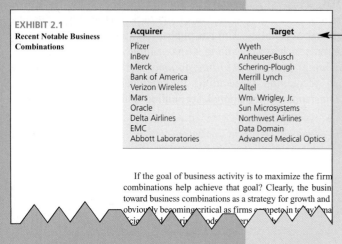

EXHIBIT 2.1
Recent Notable Business Combinations

Acquirer	Target
Pfizer	Wyeth
InBev	Anheuser-Busch
Merck	Schering-Plough
Bank of America	Merrill Lynch
Verizon Wireless	Alltel
Mars	Wm. Wrigley, Jr.
Oracle	Sun Microsystems
Delta Airlines	Northwest Airlines
EMC	Data Domain
Abbott Laboratories	Advanced Medical Optics

If the goal of business activity is to maximize the firm combinations help achieve that goal? Clearly, the busin toward business combinations as a strategy for growth and obviously becoming critical as firms compete in today' ma

Real-World Examples

Students are better able to relate what they learn to what they will encounter in the business world after reading these frequent examples. Quotations, articles, and illustrations from *Forbes, The Wall Street Journal, Time,* and *BusinessWeek* are incorporated throughout the text. Data have been pulled from business, not-for-profit, and government financial statements as well as official pronouncements.

Discussion Question

HOW DOES A COMPANY REALLY DECIDE W

Pilgrim Products, Inc., buys a controlling int poration. Shortly after the acquisition, a m convened to discuss the internal reporting subsidiary. Each member of the staff has method, initial value method, or partial equ issue, Pilgrim's chief financial officer outline

I already understand how each method

Discussion Questions

This feature **facilitates student understanding** of the underlying accounting principles at work in particular reporting situations. Similar to minicases, these questions help explain the issues at hand in practical terms. Many times, these cases are designed to demonstrate to students why a topic is problematic and worth considering.

with 4th Edition Features

CPA Simulations

Hoyle et al.'s CPA Simulations, powered by Kaplan, are found in Chapters 3, 5, 8, and 12 of the 4th edition. Simulations are set up in the text and completed online at the 4th edition Web site (mhhe.com/hoyle4e). This allows students to practice advanced accounting concepts in a Web-based interface identical to that used in the actual CPA exam. There will be no hesitation or confusion when students sit for the real exam; they will know exactly how to maneuver through the computerized test.

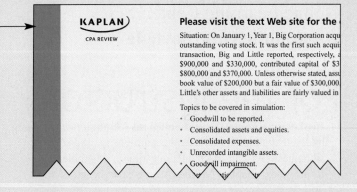

KAPLAN
CPA REVIEW

Please visit the text Web site for the

Situation: On January 1, Year 1, Big Corporation acqu
outstanding voting stock. It was the first such acqui
transaction, Big and Little reported, respectively, a
$900,000 and $330,000, contributed capital of $3
$800,000 and $370,000. Unless otherwise stated, assu
book value of $200,000 but a fair value of $300,000.
Little's other assets and liabilities are fairly valued in

Topics to be covered in simulation:
- Goodwill to be reported.
- Consolidated assets and equities.
- Consolidated expenses.
- Unrecorded intangible assets.
- Goodwill impairment.

End-of-Chapter Materials

As in previous editions, the end-of-chapter material remains a strength of the text. The sheer number of questions, problems, and Internet assignments tests, and therefore **expands, the students' knowledge** of chapter concepts.

Excel Spreadsheet Assignments extend specific problems and are located on the 4th edition Web site at mhhe.com/hoyle4e. An Excel icon appears next to those problems that have corresponding spreadsheet assignments.

"Develop Your Skills" asks questions that address the four skills students need to master to pass the CPA exam: Research, Analysis, Spreadsheet, and Communication. An icon indicates when these skills are tested.

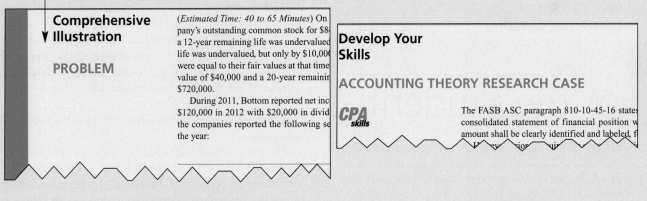

Comprehensive Illustration

PROBLEM

(*Estimated Time: 40 to 65 Minutes*) On
pany's outstanding common stock for $8
a 12-year remaining life was undervalued
life was undervalued, but only by $10,00
were equal to their fair values at that time
value of $40,000 and a 20-year remaining
$720,000.

During 2011, Bottom reported net inc
$120,000 in 2012 with $20,000 in divid
the companies reported the following se
the year:

Develop Your Skills

ACCOUNTING THEORY RESEARCH CASE

CPA skills

The FASB ASC paragraph 810-10-45-16 states
consolidated statement of financial position w
amount shall be clearly identified and labeled, f

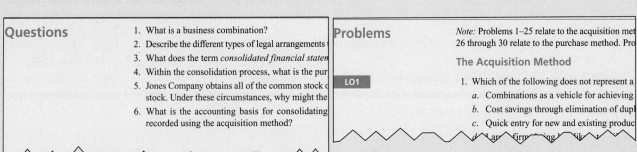

Questions

1. What is a business combination?
2. Describe the different types of legal arrangements
3. What does the term *consolidated financial statem*
4. Within the consolidation process, what is the pur
5. Jones Company obtains all of the common stock of
   stock. Under these circumstances, why might the
6. What is the accounting basis for consolidating
   recorded using the acquisition method?

Problems

Note: Problems 1–25 relate to the acquisition met
26 through 30 relate to the purchase method. Pro

The Acquisition Method

LO1

1. Which of the following does not represent a
   a. Combinations as a vehicle for achieving
   b. Cost savings through elimination of dupl
   c. Quick entry for new and existing produc
   d. an firm

Online Learning Center
www.mhhe.com/hoyle4e

For the Instructor

- **Instructor's Resource and Solutions Manual,** revised by the text authors, includes the solutions to all discussion questions, end-of-chapter questions, and problems. It provides chapter outlines to assist instructors in preparing for class.
- **Test Bank,** revised by Ilene Persoff, CW Post Campus/ Long Island University, has been significantly updated.
- **EZ Test Computerized Test Bank** can be used to make different versions of the same test, change the answer order, edit and add questions, and conduct online testing. Technical support for this software is available at (800) 331-5094 or visit www.mhhe.com/eztest.
- **PowerPoint® Presentations,** revised by Linda Hajec, Penn State Erie, deliver a complete set of slides covering many of the key concepts presented in each chapter.
- **Excel Template Problems and Solutions,** revised by Jack Terry of ComSource Associates, Inc., allow students to develop important spreadsheet skills by using Excel templates to solve selected assignments.
- **Connect Accounting** ⊞ connect |ACCOUNTING
  ISBN 9780077417345; MHID 0077417348.
- **Connect Plus Accounting** ⊞ connect(PLUS) |ACCOUNTING
  ISBN 9780077417369; MHID 0077417364.

For the Student

- **Study Guide/Working Papers** ISBN 9780077268046; MHID 0077268040. Revised by Sharon O'Reilly, Saint Mary's University of Minnesota, this combination of study guide and working papers reinforces the book's key concepts by providing students with chapter outlines, multiple-choice questions, and problems for each chapter in the text. In addition, this paperback contains all forms necessary for completing the end-of-chapter material.
- **Self-Grading Multiple-Choice Quizzes** (mhhe.com/ hoyle4e) for each chapter are available on the Student Center of the text's Online Learning Center.

- **Excel Template Problems** (mhhe.com/hoyle4e) are available on the Student Center of the text's Online Learning Center. The software includes innovatively designed Excel templates that may be used to solve many complicated problems found in the book. These problems are identified by a logo in the margin.
- **PowerPoint Presentations** (mhhe.com/hoyle4e) are available on the Student Center of the text's Online Learning Center. These presentations accompany each chapter of the text and contain the same slides that are available to the instructor.

Assurance of Learning Ready

Assurance of learning is an important element of many accreditation standards. Hoyle 4e is designed specifically to support your assurance of learning initiatives. Each chapter in the book begins with a list of numbered learning objectives that appear throughout the chapter, as well as in the end-of-chapter problems and exercises. Every test bank question is also linked to one of these objectives, in addition to level of difficulty, topic area, Bloom's Taxonomy level, AACSB, and AICPA skill area. *EZ Test,* McGraw-Hill's easy-to-use test bank software, can search the test bank by these and other categories, providing an engine for targeted Assurance of Learning analysis and assessment.

AACSB Statement

The McGraw-Hill Companies is a proud corporate member of AACSB International. Understanding the importance and value of AACSB accreditation, Hoyle 4e has sought to recognize the curricula guidelines detailed in the AACSB standards for business accreditation by connecting selected questions in the test bank to the general knowledge and skill guidelines found in the AACSB standards.

The statements contained in Hoyle 4e are provided only as a guide for the users of this text. The AACSB leaves content coverage and assessment within the purview of individual schools, the mission of the school, and the faculty. While Hoyle 4e and the teaching package make no claim of any specific AACSB qualification or evaluation, we have, within the test bank, labeled selected questions according to the six general knowledge and skills areas.

Technology

McGraw-Hill *Connect Accounting*

Less Managing. More Teaching. Greater Learning.

McGraw-Hill *Connect Accounting* is an online assignment and assessment solution that connects students with the tools and resources they'll need to achieve success. McGraw-Hill *Connect Accounting* helps prepare students for their future by enabling faster learning, more efficient studying, and higher retention of knowledge. *Connect Accounting* offers a number of powerful tools and features to make managing assignments easier, so faculty can spend more time teaching. *Connect Accounting* offers you the features described below.

Simple assignment management

With *Connect Accounting,* creating assignments is easier than ever. The assignment management function enables you to:

- Create and deliver assignments easily with selectable end-of-chapter questions and test bank items.
- Streamline lesson planning, student progress reporting, and assignment grading to make classroom management more efficient than ever.
- Go paperless with the eBook and online submission and grading of student assignments.

Smart grading

When it comes to studying, time is precious. *Connect Accounting* helps students learn more efficiently by providing feedback and practice material when they need it, where they need it. The grading function enables you to:

- Have assignments scored automatically, giving students immediate feedback on their work and side-by-side comparisons with correct answers.
- Access and review each response; manually change grades or leave comments for students to review.
- Reinforce classroom concepts with practice tests and instant quizzes.

Student progress tracking

Connect Accounting keeps instructors informed about how each student, section, and class is performing, allowing for more productive use of lecture and office hours. The progress-tracking function enables you to:

- View scored work immediately and track individual or group performance with assignment and grade reports.
- Access an instant view of student or class performance relative to learning objectives.
- Collect data and generate reports required by many accreditation organizations, such as AACSB and AICPA.

McGraw-Hill **Connect Plus Accounting**

McGraw-Hill reinvents the textbook learning experience for the modern student with *Connect Plus Accounting.* A seamless integration of an eBook and *Connect Accounting, Connect Plus Accounting* provides all of the *Connect Accounting* features plus an integrated eBook, allowing for anytime, anywhere access to the textbook; dynamic links between the problems or questions you assign to your students and the location in the eBook where that problem or question is covered; and a powerful search function to pinpoint and connect key concepts in a snap.

For more information about Connect, go to **www.mcgrawhillconnect.com,** or contact your local McGraw-Hill sales representative.

CPA Simulations

KAPLAN

CPA REVIEW

The McGraw-Hill Companies and Kaplan have teamed up to bring students CPA simulations to test their knowledge of the concepts discussed in various chapters, practice critical professional skills necessary for career success, and prepare for the computer-based CPA exam. Kaplan CPA Review provides a broad selection of Web-based simulations that were modeled after the AICPA format. Exam candidates become familiar with the item format, the research database, and the spreadsheet and word processing software used exclusively on the CPA exam (not Excel or Word), as well as the functionality of the simulations, including the tabs, icons, screens, and tools used on the exam. CPA simulations are found in the end-of-chapter material after the very last cases in Chapters 3, 5, 8, and 12.

Online Learning Center

www.mhhe.com/hoyle4e   For instructors, the book's Web site contains the Instructor's Resource and Solutions Manual, PowerPoint slides, Excel templates and solutions, Interactive Activities, Text and Supplement Updates, and links to professional resources. The student section of the site features online multiple-choice quizzes, a sample Study Guide chapter, PowerPoint presentations, Check Figures, and Excel template exercises.

ALEKS® for Financial Accounting

ALEKS®

ALEKS (Assessment and Learning in Knowledge Spaces) delivers precise, qualitative diagnostic assessments of students' knowledge, guides them in selecting appropriate new study material, and records their progress toward mastery of curricular goals in a robust classroom management system. ALEKS interacts with the student much as a skilled human tutor would, moving between explanation and practice as needed, correcting and analyzing errors, defining terms, and changing topics on request.

CourseSmart

CourseSmart

CourseSmart is a new way to find and buy eTextbooks. At CourseSmart you can save up to 40% off the cost of a print textbook, reduce your impact on the environment, and gain access to powerful Web tools for learning. Go to **www.coursesmart.com** to learn more.

Overall—this edition of the text provides updated accounting standards references to the new Financial Accounting Standards Board (FASB) *Accounting Standards Codification* **(ASC). Additionally, each chapter now includes Learning Objectives** that are designated in the margin at the point where the coverage of that particular learning objective begins. The end-of-chapter material has also been tagged by learning objectives.

Chapter Changes for *Fundamentals of Advanced Accounting,* 4th Edition:

Chapter 1

- Expanded coverage of the fair-value option for reporting investment of equity securities including a numerical example and four new/revised end-of-chapter problems.
- Provided new coverage of International Accounting Standard 28, "Investment in Associates," with comparisons to U.S. GAAP.
- Updated real-world examples for Coca-Cola and Citigroup.
- Included a new discussion question examining the relation between managerial compensation and historical use of the cost method for significant influence investments.

Chapter 2

- Added new business combinations discussions of Bank of America and Merrill Lynch, Inbev and Anheuser-Busch, and Pfizer and Wyeth.
- Added new real-world financial reporting examples for contingent consideration, gains on bargain purchases, and acquired in-process research and development under the acquisition method.
- Provided new coverage of convergence between U.S. GAAP and International Accounting Standard 3 (revised) related to acquisition-date accounting for business combinations.
- Streamlined the coverage of the legacy purchase and pooling of interests method for business combinations.
- Added several new end-of-chapter problems including three new research cases.

Chapter 3

- Updated annual report references including new citations for Berkshire Hathaway, Univision, and Pfizer.
- Included new coverage comparing U.S. GAAP and International Accounting Standards for goodwill recognition and accounting for goodwill impairment.
- Added and revised several end-of-chapter problems.
- Replaced Wendy's impairment case with a new, more recent case using the Sprint-Nextel business combination. The new case includes questions on comparisons with IFRS.

Chapter 4

- Revised for increased clarity the worksheet adjustments for allocating goodwill across the controlling and noncontrolling interests in the presence of a control premium.
- Included new coverage comparing U.S. GAAP and International Accounting Standard 3 (revised) for accounting for the noncontrolling interest.
- Added new real-world references to TicketMaster and Meade, International.
- Added and revised several end-of-chapter problems.

Chapter 5

- Replaced the term "intercompany" with "intra-entity" throughout as recommended by the FASB *Accounting Standards Codification.*
- Added and revised several end-of-chapter problems.

Chapter 6

- Updated and revised coverage of variable interest entities based on recent changes to the FASB *Accounting Standards Codification.*
- Provided new coverage comparing U.S. GAAP to the IFRS Standing Interpretation Committee Document No. 12 on consolidating special-purpose entities.
- Revised exposition extensively in the section on the consolidated statement of cash flows.

Chapter 7

- Provided additional explanation of the journal entries in the examples demonstrating the accounting for hedges of foreign currency-denominated assets and liabilities and foreign currency firm commitments.
- Added a section on IFRS—Foreign Currency Transactions and Hedges.

Chapter 8

- Updated references to international mergers and acquisitions.
- Added a section on IFRS—Translation of Foreign Currency Financial Statements.
- Replaced end-of-chapter FARS cases with two new Accounting Standards cases.

Chapter 9

- Updated real-world examples included in the chapter.
- Added and revised several end-of-chapter problems.

Chapter 10

- Updated references to the Uniform Partnership Act.
- Removed the discussion related to Marshaling of Assets.

Chapter 11

- Added extensive coverage of *GASB 54,* which impacts the reporting of fund balances and clarifies the definitions of the various fund types.
- Rewrote much of the introduction to the accounting for state and local governments to aid students in grasping the fundamental differences between this reporting and that of a for-profit business.
- Reworked a communication case.

Chapter 12

- Provided new financial statements from an actual city government as well as a public university.
- Included improved guidance to help students read and understand financial statements prepared by a state or local government entity.
- Updated virtually all of the real-world examples that are so prevalent in these chapters.
- Reworked a research case and an analysis case.

Acknowledgments

We could not produce a textbook of the quality and scope of *Fundamentals of Advanced Accounting* without the help of a great number of people. We would like to thank Ilene Persoff of CW Post Campus/Long Island University for revising and adding new material to the Test Bank; Marilynn Leathart of Concordia University, Texas, for updating and revising the online student quizzes and accuracy checking the PowerPoint presentations; Jack Terry of ComSource Associates for updating the Excel Template Exercises for students to use as they work the select end-of-chapter material; Sharon O'Reilly of Saint Mary's University of Minnesota for revising and adding new material to the Study Guide and Working Papers; Ilene Persoff of CW Post Campus/Long Island University and Beth Woods of Accuracy Counts for checking the text and Solutions Manual for accuracy; Beth Woods for checking the test bank for accuracy; and Linda Hajec of Penn State Erie, for revising the PowerPoints and checking the quizzes for accuracy.

We also want to thank the many people who completed questionnaires and reviewed the book. Our sincerest thanks to them all:

John Bildersee
New York University

Annhenrie Campbell
California State University

Fatma Cebenoyan
Hunter College/CUNY

Amy David
Queens College

Renu Desai
Florida International University

Desiree Elias
Florida International University

Steve Fabian
New Jersey City University

Jeff L. Harkins
University of Idaho

Coby Harmon
University of California, Santa Barbara

Alejandro Hazera
University of Rhode Island

Fred Heindl
Antonelli College

Philip Kintzele
Central Michigan University

Brian Laverty
University of Toledo

Li-Lin Liu
California State University, Dominguez Hills

Dan Mahoney
University of Scranton

Ronald M. Mano
Weber State University

Stephen R. Moehrle
University of Missouri–St. Louis

Dennis P. Moore
Worcester State College

Bernard H. Newman
Pace University

Dennis O'Reilly
East Carolina University

Sharon O'Reilly
Saint Mary's University of Minnesota

Abe Qastin
Lakeland College

William Ruland
Bernard M. Baruch College

Anwar Salimi
California State Polytechnic University, Pomona

Kendall Simmonds
University of Southern California

Nathan Slavin
Hofstra University

Christopher R. Smith
College of Staten Island (CUNY)

Karen Sneary
Northwestern Oklahoma State University

Kathleen Sobieralski
University of Maryland University College

Noemy Wachtel
Kean University

Hans Sprohge
Wright State University

Jan Williams
University of Baltimore

Roy Weatherwax
University of Wisconsin–Whitewater

Suzanne Wright
Penn State University

We also pass along a word of thanks to all the people at McGraw-Hill/Irwin who participated in the creation of this edition. In particular, Lori Koetters, Managing Editor; Carol Bielski, Production Supervisor; Pam Verros, Designer; Katie Jones, Developmental Editor; Dana Woo, Senior Sponsoring Editor; Tim Vertovec, Publisher; Joyce Chappetto, Media Project Manager; Dean Karampelas, Marketing Manager; and Stewart Mattson, Editorial Director, all contributed significantly to the project, and we appreciate their efforts.

Brief Contents

Contents

Chapter Four

Consolidated Financial Statements and Outside Ownership   139

Chapter Five

Consolidated Financial Statements—Intra-Entity Asset Transactions   195

Chapter Six

Variable Interest Entities, Intra-Entity Debt, Consolidated Cash Flows, and Other Issues   241

The Equity Method of Accounting for Investments

The first several chapters of this text present the accounting and reporting for investment activities of businesses. The focus is on investments when one firm possesses either significant influence or control over another through ownership of voting shares. When one firm owns enough voting shares to be able to affect the decisions of another, accounting for the investment can become challenging and complex. The source of such complexities typically stems from the fact that transactions among the firms affiliated through ownership cannot be considered independent, arm's-length transactions. As in many matters relating to financial reporting, we look to transactions with *outside parties* to provide a basis for accounting valuation. When firms are affiliated through a common set of owners, measurements that recognize the relationships among the firms help to provide objectivity in financial reporting.

THE REPORTING OF INVESTMENTS IN CORPORATE EQUITY SECURITIES

In a recent annual report, JB Hunt Transport Services describes the creation of Transplace, Inc. (TPI), an Internet-based global transportation logistics company. JB Hunt contributed all of its logistics segment business and all related intangible assets plus $5 million of cash in exchange for an approximate 27 percent initial interest in TPI, which it subsequently increased to 37 percent. JB Hunt accounts for its interest in TPI utilizing the equity method of accounting and stated, "The financial results of TPI are included on a one-line, nonoperating item included on the Consolidated Statements of Earnings entitled 'equity in earnings of associated companies.'"

Such information is hardly unusual in the business world; corporate investors frequently acquire ownership shares of both domestic and foreign businesses. These investments can range from the purchase of a few shares to the acquisition of 100 percent control. Although purchases of corporate equity securities (such as the one made by JB Hunt) are not uncommon, they pose a considerable number of financial reporting issues because a close relationship has been established without the investor gaining actual control. These issues are currently addressed by the **equity method.** This chapter deals with accounting for stock investments that fall under the application of this method.

LEARNING OBJECTIVES

After studying this chapter, you should be able to:

LO1 Describe in general the various methods of accounting for an investment in equity shares of another company.

LO2 Identify the sole criterion for applying the equity method of accounting and guidance in assessing whether the criterion is met.

LO3 Prepare basic equity method journal entries for an investor and describe the financial reporting for equity method investments.

LO4 Record the sale of an equity investment and identify the accounting method to be applied to any remaining shares that are subsequently held.

LO5 Allocate the cost of an equity method investment and compute amortization expense to match revenues recognized from the investment to the excess of investor cost over investee book value.

LO6 Describe the rationale and computations to defer unrealized gains on intra-entity transfers until the goods are either consumed or sold to outside parties.

LO7 Explain the rationale and reporting implications of the fair-value option for investments otherwise accounted for by the equity method.

LO1

Describe in general the various methods of accounting for an investment in equity shares of another company.

At present, generally accepted accounting principles (GAAP) recognize three different approaches to the financial reporting of investments in corporate equity securities:

- The fair-value method.
- The consolidation of financial statements.
- The equity method.

The financial statement reporting for a particular investment depends primarily on the degree of influence that the investor (stockholder) has over the investee, a factor typically indicated by the relative size of ownership.[1] Because voting power typically accompanies ownership of equity shares, influence increases with the relative size of ownership. The resulting influence can be very little, a significant amount, or, in some cases, complete control.

Fair-Value Method

In many instances, an investor possesses only a small percentage of an investee company's outstanding stock, perhaps only a few shares. Because of the limited level of ownership, the investor cannot expect to significantly affect the investee's operations or decision making. These shares are bought in anticipation of cash dividends or in appreciation of stock market values. Such investments are recorded at cost and periodically adjusted to fair value according to the Financial Accounting Standards Board (FASB) Accounting Standards Codification (ASC) Topic 320, Investments—Debt and Equity Securities.

Because a full coverage of limited ownership investments in equity securities is presented in intermediate accounting textbooks, only the following basic principles are noted here.

- Initial investments in equity securities are recorded at cost and subsequently adjusted to fair value if fair value is readily determinable; otherwise, the investment remains at cost.[2]
- Equity securities held for sale in the short term are classified as *trading securities* and reported at fair value, with unrealized gains and losses included in earnings.
- Equity securities not classified as trading securities are classified as *available-for-sale securities* and reported at fair value with unrealized gains and losses excluded from earnings and reported in a separate component of shareholders' equity as part of *other comprehensive income.*
- Dividends received are recognized as income for both trading and available-for-sale securities.

The above procedures are typically followed for equity security investments when neither significant influence nor control is present. However, as observed at the end of this chapter, FASB ASC Topic 825, Financial Instruments, allows a special fair-value reporting option for available-for-sale securities. Although the balance sheet amounts for the investments remain at fair value under this option, changes in fair values over time are recognized in the income statement (as opposed to other comprehensive income) as they occur.

Consolidation of Financial Statements

Many corporate investors acquire enough shares to gain actual control over an investee's operation. In financial accounting, such control is recognized whenever a stockholder accumulates more than 50 percent of an organization's outstanding voting stock. At that point, rather than simply influencing the investee's decisions, the investor clearly can direct

---

[1] The relative size of ownership is most often the key factor in assessing one company's degree of influence over another. However, other factors (e.g., contractual relationships between firms) can also provide influence or control over firms regardless of the percentage of shares owned.

[2] The FASB ASC (para. 325-20-35-1 and 2) notes two exceptions to the cost basis for reporting investments:
1. Dividends received in excess of earnings subsequent to the date of investment are considered returns of the investment and are recorded as reductions of cost of the investment.
2. A series of an investee's operating losses or other factors can indicate a decrease in value of the investment has occurred that is other than temporary and should be recognized accordingly.

the entire decision-making process. A review of the financial statements of America's largest organizations indicates that legal control of one or more subsidiary companies is an almost universal practice. PepsiCo, Inc., as just one example, holds a majority interest in the voting stock of literally hundreds of corporations.

Investor control over an investee presents a special accounting challenge. Normally, when a majority of voting stock is held, the investor-investee relationship is so closely connected that the two corporations are viewed as a single entity for reporting purposes. Hence, an entirely different set of accounting procedures is applicable. Control generally requires the consolidation of the accounting information produced by the individual companies. Thus, a single set of financial statements is created for external reporting purposes with all assets, liabilities, revenues, and expenses brought together.[3] The various procedures applied within this consolidation process are examined in subsequent chapters of this textbook.

The FASB ASC Section 810-10-05 on variable interest entities expands the use of consolidated financial statements to include entities that are financially controlled through special contractual arrangements rather than through voting stock interests. Prior to the accounting requirements for variable interest entities, many firms (e.g., Enron) avoided consolidation of entities in which they owned little or no voting stock but otherwise were controlled through special contracts. These entities were frequently referred to as "special purpose entities (SPEs)" and provided vehicles for some firms to keep large amounts of assets and liabilities off their consolidated financial statements.

Equity Method

Another investment relationship is appropriately accounted for using the equity method. In many investments, although control is not achieved, the degree of ownership indicates the ability for the investor to exercise *significant influence* over the investee. Recall JB Hunt's 37 percent investment in TPI's voting stock. Through its ownership, JB Hunt can undoubtedly influence TPI's decisions and operations.

To provide objective reporting for investments with significant influence, the FASB ASC Topic 323, Investments—Equity Method and Joint Ventures, describes the use of the equity method. The equity method employs the accrual basis for recognizing the investor's share of investee income. Accordingly, the investor recognizes income as it is earned by the investee. As noted in FASB ASC (para. 323-10-05-5), because of its significant influence over the investee, the investor

> . . . has a degree of responsibility for the return on its investment and it is appropriate to include in the results of operations of the investor its share of the earnings or losses of the investee.

Furthermore, under the equity method, dividends received from an investee are recorded as decreases in the investment account, not as income.

In today's business world, many corporations hold significant ownership interests in other companies without having actual control. The Coca-Cola Company alone owns between 20 and 50 percent of dozens of separate corporations. Many other investments represent joint ventures in which two or more companies form a new enterprise to carry out a specified operating purpose. For example, Microsoft and NBC formed MSNBC, a cable channel and online site to go with NBC's broadcast network. Each partner owns 50 percent of the joint venture. For each of these investments, the investors do not possess absolute control because they hold less than a majority of the voting stock. Thus, the preparation of consolidated financial statements is inappropriate. However, the large percentage of ownership indicates that each investor possesses some ability to affect the investee's decision-making process.

Finally, as discussed at the end of this chapter, firms are now allowed a fair-value option in their financial reporting for certain financial assets and financial liabilities. Among the qualifying financial assets for fair-value reporting are significant influence investments otherwise accounted for by the equity method.

---

[3] As is discussed in the next chapter, owning a majority of the voting shares of an investee does not always lead to consolidated financial statements.

Discussion **Question**

DID THE COST METHOD INVITE EARNINGS MANIPULATION?

Prior to GAAP for equity method investments, firms often used the cost method to account for their unconsolidated investments in common stock regardless of the presence of significant influence. The cost method employed the cash basis of income recognition. When the investee declared a dividend, the investor recorded "dividend income." The investment account typically remained at its original cost—hence the term *cost method*.

Many firms' compensation plans reward managers based on reported annual income. How might the cost method of accounting for significant investments have resulted in unintended wealth transfers from owners to managers? Do the equity or fair-value methods provide similar incentives?

INTERNATIONAL ACCOUNTING STANDARD 28— INVESTMENTS IN ASSOCIATES

The International Accounting Standards Board (IASB), similar to the FASB, recognizes the need to take into account the significant influence that can occur when one firm holds a certain amount of voting shares of another. The IASB defines significant influence as the power to participate in the financial and operating policy decisions of the investee, but it is not control or joint control over those policies. The following describes the basics of the equity method in International Accounting Standard (IAS) 28:[4]

> If an investor holds, directly or indirectly (e.g., through subsidiaries), 20 per cent or more of the voting power of the investee, it is presumed that the investor has significant influence, unless it can be clearly demonstrated that this is not the case. Conversely, if the investor holds, directly or indirectly (e.g., through subsidiaries), less than 20 per cent of the voting power of the investee, it is presumed that the investor does not have significant influence, unless such influence can be clearly demonstrated. A substantial or majority ownership by another investor does not necessarily preclude an investor from having significant influence.
>
> Under the equity method, the investment in an associate is initially recognised at cost and the carrying amount is increased or decreased to recognise the investor's share of the profit or loss of the investee after the date of acquisition. The investor's share of the profit or loss of the investee is recognised in the investor's profit or loss. Distributions received from an investee reduce the carrying amount of the investment.

As seen from the above excerpt from *IAS 28,* the equity method concepts and applications described are virtually identical to those prescribed by the FASB ASC.

APPLICATION OF THE EQUITY METHOD

An understanding of the equity method is best gained by initially examining the FASB's treatment of two questions:

1. What parameters identify the area of ownership for which the equity method is applicable?
2. How should the investor report this investment and the income generated by it to reflect the relationship between the two companies?

LO2

Identify the sole criterion for applying the equity method of accounting and guidance in assessing whether the criterion is met.

Criteria for Utilizing the Equity Method

The rationale underlying the equity method is that an investor begins to gain the ability to influence the decision-making process of an investee as the level of ownership rises. According to FASB ASC Topic 323 on equity method investments, achieving this "ability to exercise significant influence over operating and financial policies of an investee even though the

---

[4] International Accounting Standards Board, *IAS 28 Investments in Associates*, Technical Summary (www.iasb.org).

investor holds 50 percent or less of the voting stock" is the sole criterion for requiring application of the equity method [FASB ASC (para. 323-10-15-3)].

Clearly, a term such as *the ability to exercise significant influence* is nebulous and subject to a variety of judgments and interpretations in practice. At what point does the acquisition of one additional share of stock give an owner the ability to exercise significant influence? This decision becomes even more difficult in that only the *ability* to exercise significant influence need be present. There is no requirement that any actual influence must have ever been applied.

FASB ASC Topic 323 provides guidance to the accountant by listing several conditions that indicate the presence of this degree of influence:

- Investor representation on the board of directors of the investee.
- Investor participation in the policymaking process of the investee.
- Material intercompany transactions.
- Interchange of managerial personnel.
- Technological dependency.
- Extent of ownership by the investor in relation to the size and concentration of other ownership interests in the investee.

No single one of these guides should be used exclusively in assessing the applicability of the equity method. Instead, all are evaluated together to determine the presence or absence of the sole criterion: the ability to exercise significant influence over the investee.

These guidelines alone do not eliminate the leeway available to each investor when deciding whether the use of the equity method is appropriate. To provide a degree of consistency in applying this standard, the FASB provides a general ownership test: *If an investor holds between 20 and 50 percent of the voting stock of the investee, significant influence is normally assumed and the equity method is applied.*

> An investment (direct or indirect) of 20 percent or more of the voting stock of an investee should lead to a presumption that in the absence of evidence to the contrary an investor has the ability to exercise significant influence over an investee. Conversely, an investment of less than 20 percent of the voting stock of an investee should lead to a presumption that an investor does not have the ability to exercise significant influence unless such ability can be demonstrated.[5]

Limitations of Equity Method Applicability

At first, the 20 to 50 percent rule may appear to be an arbitrarily chosen boundary range established merely to provide a consistent method of reporting for investments. However, the essential criterion is still the ability to significantly influence (but not control) the investee, rather than 20 to 50 percent ownership. If the absence of this ability is proven (or control exists), the equity method should not be applied regardless of the percentage of shares held.

For example, the equity method is not appropriate for investments that demonstrate any of the following characteristics regardless of the investor's degree of ownership:[6]

- An agreement exists between investor and investee by which the investor surrenders significant rights as a shareholder.
- A concentration of ownership operates the investee without regard for the views of the investor.
- The investor attempts but fails to obtain representation on the investee's board of directors.

In each of these situations, because the investor is unable to exercise significant influence over its investee, the equity method is not applied.

Alternatively, if an entity can exercise *control* over its investee, regardless of its ownership level, consolidation (rather than the equity method) is appropriate. FASB ASC (para. 810-10-05-8) limits the use of the equity method by expanding the definition of a controlling financial interest and addresses situations in which financial control exists absent majority

---

[5] FASB ASC (para. 323-10-15-8).

[6] FASB ASC (para. 323-10-15-10). This paragraph deals specifically with limits to using the equity method for investments in which the owner holds 20 to 50 percent of the outstanding shares.

ownership interest. In these situations, control is achieved through contractual and other arrangements called *variable interests.*

To illustrate, one firm may create a separate legal entity in which it holds less than 50 percent of the voting interests, but nonetheless controls that entity through governance document provisions and/or contracts that specify decision-making power and the distribution of profits and losses. Entities controlled in this fashion are typically designated as *variable interest entities,* and their sponsoring firm may be required to include them in consolidated reports despite the fact that ownership is less than 50 percent. Many firms (e.g., The Walt Disney Company and Mills Corporation) reclassified former equity method investees as variable interest entities and now consolidate these investments.[7]

Extensions of Equity Method Applicability

For some investments that either fall short of or exceed 20 to 50 percent ownership, the equity method is nonetheless appropriately used for financial reporting. As an example, International Paper Company disclosed that it accounts for its investment in Scitex Corporation using the equity method despite holding only a 13 percent interest. In its annual report, International Paper cited its ability to exercise significant influence "because the Company is party to a shareowners' agreement with two other entities which together with the Company own just over 39% of Scitex."

Conditions can also exist where the equity method is appropriate despite a majority ownership interest. In some instances approval or veto rights granted to minority shareholders restrict the powers of the majority shareholder. Such minority rights may include approval over compensation, hiring, termination, and other critical operating and capital spending decisions of an entity. If the minority rights are so restrictive as to call into question whether control rests with the majority owner, the equity method is employed for financial reporting rather than consolidation. For example, prior to its acquisition of BellSouth, AT&T, Inc., stated in its financial reports "we account for our 60 percent economic investment in Cingular under the equity method of accounting because we share control equally with our 40 percent partner BellSouth."

To summarize, the following table indicates the method of accounting that is typically applicable to various stock investments:

Criterion	Normal Ownership Level	Applicable Accounting Method
Lack of ability to significantly influence	Less than 20%	Fair value or cost
Presence of ability to significantly influence	20%–50%	Equity method or fair value
Control through voting interests	More than 50%	Consolidated financial statements
Control through variable interests (governance documents, contracts)	Primary beneficiary status (no ownership required)	Consolidated financial statements

ACCOUNTING FOR AN INVESTMENT—THE EQUITY METHOD

Now that the criteria leading to the application of the equity method have been identified, a review of its reporting procedures is appropriate. Knowledge of this accounting process is especially important to users of the investor's financial statements because the equity method affects both the timing of income recognition as well as the carrying value of the investment account.

In applying the equity method, the accounting objective is to report the investor's investment and investment income reflecting the close relationship between the companies. After

---

[7] Chapters 2 and 6 provide further discussions of variable interest entities.

recording the cost of the acquisition, two equity method entries periodically record the investment's impact:

• The investor's investment account *increases as the investee earns and reports income.* Also, the investor recognizes investment income using the accrual method—that is, in the same time period as the investee earns it. If an investee reports income of $100,000, a 30 percent owner should immediately increase its own income by $30,000. This earnings accrual reflects the essence of the equity method by emphasizing the connection between the two companies; as the owners' equity of the investee increases through the earnings process, the investment account also increases. Although the investor initially records the acquisition at cost, upward adjustments in the asset balance are recorded as soon as the investee makes a profit. A reduction is necessary if a loss is reported.

• The investor's investment account is *decreased whenever a dividend is collected.* Because distribution of cash dividends reduces the book value of the investee company, the investor mirrors this change by recording the receipt as a decrease in the carrying value of the investment rather than as revenue. Once again, a parallel is established between the investment account and the underlying activities of the investee: The reduction in the investee's owners' equity creates a decrease in the investment. Furthermore, because the investor immediately recognizes income when the investee earns it, double counting would occur if the investor also recorded subsequent dividend collections as revenue. Importantly, the collection of a cash dividend is not an appropriate point for income recognition. Because the investor can influence the timing of investee dividend distributions, the receipt of a dividend is not an objective measure of the income generated from the investment.

Application of Equity Method	
Investee Event	**Investor Accounting**
Income is earned.	Proportionate share of income is recognized.
Dividends are distributed.	Dividends received are recorded as a reduction in investment.

Application of the equity method causes the investment account on the investor's balance sheet to vary directly with changes in the investee's equity. As an illustration, assume that an investor acquires a 40 percent interest in a business enterprise. If the investor has the ability to significantly influence the investee, the equity method may be utilized. If the investee subsequently reports net income of $50,000, the investor increases the investment account (and its own net income) by $20,000 in recognition of a 40 percent share of these earnings. Conversely, a $20,000 dividend paid by the investee necessitates a reduction of $8,000 in this same asset account (40 percent of the total payout).

In contrast, the fair-value method reports investments at fair value if it is readily determinable. Also, income is recognized only upon receipt of dividends. Consequently, financial reports can vary depending on whether the equity method or fair-value method is appropriate.

To illustrate, assume that Big Company owns a 20 percent interest in Little Company purchased on January 1, 2010, for $200,000. Little then reports net income of $200,000, $300,000, and $400,000, respectively, in the next three years while paying dividends of $50,000, $100,000, and $200,000. The fair values of Big's investment in Little, as determined by market prices, were $235,000, $255,000, and $320,000 at the end of 2010, 2011, and 2012, respectively.

Exhibit 1.1 compares the accounting for Big's investment in Little across the two methods. The fair-value method carries the investment at its market values, presumed to be readily available in this example. Because the investment is classified as an *available-for-sale security,* the excess of fair value over cost is reported as a separate component of stockholders' equity.[8] Income is recognized as dividends are received.

In contrast, under the equity method, Big recognizes income as it is earned by Little. As shown in Exhibit 1.1, Big recognizes $180,000 in income over the three years, and the carrying

---

[8] Fluctuations in the market values of *trading securities* are recognized in income in the period in which they occur.

EXHIBIT 1.1 Comparison of Fair-Value Method (ASC 320) and Equity Method (ASC 323)

Year	Income of Little Company	Dividends Paid by Little Company	Accounting by Big Company When Influence Is Not Significant (available-for-sale security)			Accounting by Big Company When Influence Is Significant (equity method)	
			Dividend Income	Carrying Value of Investment	Fair-Value Adjustment to Stockholders' Equity	Equity in Investee Income	Carrying Value of Investment
2010	$200,000	$ 50,000	$10,000	$235,000	$ 35,000	$ 40,000*	$230,000†
2011	300,000	100,000	20,000	255,000	55,000	60,000*	270,000†
2012	400,000	200,000	40,000	320,000	120,000	80,000*	310,000†
Total income recognized			$70,000			$180,000	

*Equity in investee income is 20 percent of the current year income reported by Little Company.
†The carrying value of an investment under the equity method is the original cost plus income recognized less dividends received. For 2010, as an example, the $230,000 reported balance is the $200,000 cost plus $40,000 equity income less $10,000 in dividends received.

value of the investment is adjusted upward to $310,000. Dividends received are not an appropriate measure of income because of the assumed significant influence over the investee. Big's ability to influence Little's decisions applies to the timing of dividend distributions. Therefore, dividends received do not objectively measure Big's income from its investment in Little. As Little earns income, however, under the equity method Big recognizes its share (20 percent) of the income and increases the investment account. The equity method reflects the accrual model: Income is recognized as it is earned, not when cash (dividend) is received.

Exhibit 1.1 shows that the carrying value of the investment fluctuates each year under the equity method. This recording parallels the changes occurring in the net asset figures reported by the investee. If the owner's equity of the investee rises through income, an increase is made in the investment account; decreases such as losses and dividends cause reductions to be recorded. Thus, the equity method conveys information that describes the relationship created by the investor's ability to significantly influence the investee.

ACCOUNTING PROCEDURES USED IN APPLYING THE EQUITY METHOD

LO3

Prepare basic equity method journal entries for an investor and describe the financial reporting for equity method investments.

Once guidelines for the application of the equity method have been established, the mechanical process necessary for recording basic transactions is quite straightforward. The investor accrues its percentage of the earnings reported by the investee each period. Dividend declarations reduce the investment balance to reflect the decrease in the investee's book value.

Referring again to the information presented in Exhibit 1.1, Little Company reported a net income of $200,000 during 2010 and paid cash dividends of $50,000. These figures indicate that Little's net assets have increased by $150,000 during the year. Therefore, in its financial records, Big Company records the following journal entries to apply the equity method:

Investment in Little Company	40,000	
Equity in Investee Income		40,000
To accrue earnings of a 20 percent owned investee ($200,000 × 20%).		
Cash	10,000	
Investment in Little Company		10,000
To record receipt of cash dividend from Little Company ($50,000 × 20%).		

In the first entry, Big accrues income based on the investee's reported earnings even though this amount greatly exceeds the cash dividend. The second entry reflects the actual receipt of the dividend and the related reduction in Little's net assets. The $30,000 net increment recorded here in Big's investment account ($40,000 − $10,000) represents 20 percent of the $150,000 increase in Little's book value that occurred during the year.

Although these two entries illustrate the basic reporting process used in applying the equity method, several other issues must be explored to obtain a full understanding of this approach. More specifically, special procedures are required in accounting for each of the following:

1. Reporting a change to the equity method.
2. Reporting investee income from sources other than continuing operations.
3. Reporting investee losses.
4. Reporting the sale of an equity investment.

Reporting a Change to the Equity Method

In many instances, an investor's ability to significantly influence an investee is not achieved through a single stock acquisition. The investor could possess only a minor ownership for some years before purchasing enough additional shares to require conversion to the equity method. Before the investor achieves significant influence, any investment should be reported by the fair-value method. After the investment reaches the point at which the equity method becomes applicable, a technical question arises about the appropriate means of changing from one method to the other.[9]

FASB ASC (para. 323-10-35-33) addresses this concern by stating that "the investment, results of operations (current and prior periods presented), and retained earnings of the investor should be adjusted retroactively." *Thus, all accounts are restated so that the investor's financial statements appear as if the equity method had been applied from the date of the first acquisition.* By mandating retrospective treatment, the FASB attempts to ensure comparability from year to year in the financial reporting of the investor company. For example, Frequency Electronics, a firm that specializes in designing, developing, and manufacturing satellite communications equipment, recently reported an increase in its stock ownership of Morion, Inc., a crystal oscillator manufacturer located in St. Petersburg, Russia. As reported in its 2006 annual report,

> the Company increased its investment from 19.8% to 36.2% of Morion's outstanding shares. Accordingly, the Company changed its method of carrying the Morion investment from cost to equity as required by generally accepted accounting principles. . . . The effect of the change in accounting method for the fiscal year ended April 30, 2005, was to increase income before provision for income taxes and net income by $315,000 ($0.04 per diluted share). The financial statements for the prior fiscal years were restated for the change in accounting method. . . . Retained earnings as of the beginning of fiscal year 2005 were increased by $207,000 for the effect of retroactive application of the equity method.

To further illustrate this restatement procedure, assume that Giant Company acquires a 10 percent ownership in Small Company on January 1, 2010. Officials of Giant do not believe that their company has gained the ability to exert significant influence over Small. Giant properly records the investment by using the fair-value method as an available-for-sale security. Subsequently, on January 1, 2012, Giant purchases an additional 30 percent of Small's outstanding voting stock, thereby achieving the ability to significantly influence the investee's decision making. From 2010 through 2012, Small reports net income, pays cash dividends, and has fair values at January 1 of each year as follows:

Year	Net Income	Cash Dividends	Fair Value at January 1
2010	$ 70,000	$20,000	$800,000
2011	110,000	40,000	840,000
2012	130,000	50,000	930,000

In Giant's 2010 and 2011 financial statements, as originally reported, dividend revenue of $2,000 and $4,000, respectively, would be recognized based on receiving 10 percent of these

---

[9] A switch to the equity method also can be required if the investee purchases a portion of its own shares as treasury stock. This transaction can increase the investor's percentage of outstanding stock.

DOES THE EQUITY METHOD REALLY APPLY HERE?

Abraham, Inc., a New Jersey corporation, operates 57 bakeries throughout the northeastern section of the United States. In the past, its founder, James Abraham, owned all the company's entire outstanding common stock. However, during the early part of this year, the corporation suffered a severe cash flow problem brought on by rapid expansion. To avoid bankruptcy, Abraham sought additional investment capital from a friend, Dennis Bostitch, who owns Highland Laboratories. Subsequently, Highland paid $700,000 cash to Abraham, Inc., to acquire enough newly issued shares of common stock for a one-third ownership interest.

At the end of this year, the accountants for Highland Laboratories are discussing the proper method of reporting this investment. One argues for maintaining the asset at its original cost: "This purchase is no more than a loan to bail out the bakeries. Mr. Abraham will continue to run the organization with little or no attention paid to us. After all, what does anyone in our company know about baking bread? I would be surprised if Abraham does not reacquire these shares as soon as the bakery business is profitable again."

One of the other accountants disagrees, stating that the equity method is appropriate. "I realize that our company is not capable of running a bakery. However, the official rules state that we must have only the *ability* to exert significant influence. With one-third of the common stock in our possession, we certainly have that ability. Whether we use it or not, this ability means that we are required to apply the equity method."

How should Highland Laboratories account for its investment in Abraham, Inc.?

distributions. The investment account is maintained at fair value because it is readily determinable. Also, the change in the investment's fair value results in a credit to an unrealized cumulative holding gain of $4,000 in 2010 and an additional credit of $9,000 in 2011 for a cumulative amount of $13,000 reported in Giant's 2011 stockholders' equity section. However, after changing to the equity method on January 1, 2012, Giant must restate these prior years to present the investment as if the equity method had always been applied. Subsequently, in comparative statements showing columns for previous periods, the 2010 statements should indicate equity income of $7,000 with $11,000 being disclosed for 2011 based on a 10 percent accrual of Small's income for each of these years.

The income restatement for these earlier years can be computed as follows:

Year	Equity in Investee Income (10%)	Income Reported from Dividends	Retrospective Adjustment
2010	$ 7,000	$2,000	$ 5,000
2011	11,000	4,000	7,000
Total adjustment to Retained Earnings			$12,000

Giant's reported earnings for 2010 will increase by $5,000 with a $7,000 increment needed for 2011. To bring about this retrospective change to the equity method, Giant prepares the following journal entry on January 1, 2012:

Investment in Small Company	12,000	
Retained Earnings—Prior Period Adjustment—		
Equity in Investee Income		12,000
To adjust 2010 and 2011 records so that investment is accounted for using the equity method in a consistent manner.		
Unrealized Holding Gain—Shareholders' Equity	13,000	
Fair Value Adjustment (Available-for-Sale)		13,000
To remove the investor's percentage of the increase in fair value (10% × $130,000) from stockholders' equity and the available-for-sale portfolio valuation account.		

The $13,000 adjustment removes the valuation accounts that pertain to the investment prior to obtaining significant influence. Because the investment is no longer part of the available-for-sale portfolio, it is carried under the equity method rather than at fair value. Accordingly, the fair-value adjustment accounts are reduced as part of the reclassification.

Continuing with this example, Giant makes two other journal entries at the end of 2012, but they relate solely to the operations and distributions of that period.

Investment in Small Company	52,000	
Equity in Investee Income		52,000
To accrue 40 percent of the year 2012 income reported by Small Company ($130,000 × 40%).		
Cash	20,000	
Investment in Small Company		20,000
To record receipt of year 2012 cash dividend from Small Company ($50,000 × 40%).		

Reporting Investee Income from Sources Other Than Continuing Operations

Traditionally, certain elements of income are presented separately within a set of financial statements. Examples include extraordinary items and discontinued operations. A concern that arises in applying the equity method is whether items appearing separately in the investee's income statement require similar treatment by the investor.

To examine this issue, assume that Large Company owns 40 percent of the voting stock of Tiny Company and accounts for this investment by means of the equity method. In 2010, Tiny reports net income of $200,000, a figure composed of $250,000 in income from continuing operations and a $50,000 extraordinary loss. Large Company accrues earnings of $80,000 based on 40 percent of the $200,000 net figure. However, for proper disclosure, the extraordinary loss incurred by the investee must also be reported separately on the financial statements of the investor. This handling is intended, once again, to mirror the close relationship between the two companies.

Based on the level of ownership, Large recognizes $100,000 as a component of operating income (40 percent of Tiny Company's $250,000 income from continuing operations) along with a $20,000 extraordinary loss (40 percent of $50,000). The overall effect is still an $80,000 net increment in Large's earnings, but this amount has been appropriately allocated between income from continuing operations and extraordinary items.

The journal entry to record Large's equity interest in the income of Tiny follows:

Investment in Tiny Company	80,000	
Extraordinary Loss of Investee	20,000	
Equity in Investee Income		100,000
To accrue operating income and extraordinary loss from equity investment.		

One additional aspect of this accounting should be noted. Even though the investee has already judged this loss as extraordinary, Large does not report its $20,000 share as a separate item unless that figure is considered to be material with respect to the investor's own operations.

Reporting Investee Losses

Although most of the previous illustrations are based on the recording of profits, accounting for losses incurred by the investee is handled in a similar manner. The investor recognizes the appropriate percentage of each loss and reduces the carrying value of the investment account. Even though these procedures are consistent with the concept of the equity method, they fail to take into account all possible loss situations.

Permanent Losses in Value

Investments can suffer permanent losses in fair value that are not evident through equity method accounting. Such declines can be caused by the loss of major customers, changes in economic conditions, loss of a significant patent or other legal right, damage to the company's reputation, and the like. Permanent reductions in fair value resulting from such adverse events might not be reported immediately by the investor through the normal equity entries discussed previously. Thus, FASB ASC (para. 323-10-35-32) provides the following guideline:

> A loss in value of an investment which is other than a temporary decline should be recognized the same as a loss in value of other long-term assets. Evidence of a loss in value might include, but would not necessarily be limited to, absence of an ability to recover the carrying amount of the investment or inability of the investee to sustain an earnings capacity which would justify the carrying amount of the investment.

Thus, when a permanent decline in an equity method investment's value occurs, the investor must recognize an impairment loss and reduce the asset to fair value. However, this loss must be permanent before such recognition becomes necessary. Under the equity method, a temporary drop in the fair value of an investment is simply ignored.

For example, Hess Corporation noted the following in its 2008 annual report:

> The Corporation reviews equity method investments for impairment whenever events or changes in circumstances indicate that an other than temporary decline in value has occurred. The amount of the impairment is based on quoted market prices, where available, or other valuation techniques.

Investment Reduced to Zero

Through the recognition of reported losses as well as any permanent drops in fair value, the investment account can eventually be reduced to a zero balance. This condition is most likely to occur if the investee has suffered extreme losses or if the original purchase was made at a low, bargain price. Regardless of the reason, the carrying value of the investment account could conceivably be eliminated in total.

As The Coca-Cola Company recently disclosed:

> The carrying value of our investment in CCE (Coca-Cola Enterprises) was reduced to zero as of December 31, 2008, primarily as a result of recording our proportionate share of impairment charges and items impacting AOCI (accumulated other comprehensive income) recorded by CCE.

When an investment account is reduced to zero, the investor should discontinue using the equity method rather than establish a negative balance. The investment retains a zero balance until subsequent investee profits eliminate all unrealized losses. Once the original cost of the investment has been eliminated, no additional losses can accrue to the investor (since the entire cost has been written off) *unless* some further commitment has been made on behalf of the investee.

Noise Cancellation Technologies, Inc., for example, explains in recent financial statements the discontinued use of the equity method when the investment account has been reduced to zero:

> When the Company's share of cumulative losses equals its investment and the Company has no obligation or intention to fund such additional losses, the Company suspends applying the equity method. . . . The Company will not be able to record any equity in income with respect to an entity until its share of future profits is sufficient to recover any cumulative losses that have not previously been recorded.

Reporting the Sale of an Equity Investment

LO4

Record the sale of an equity investment and identify the accounting method to be applied to any remaining shares that are subsequently held.

At any time, the investor can choose to sell part or all of its holdings in the investee company. If a sale occurs, the equity method continues to be applied until the transaction date, thus establishing an appropriate carrying value for the investment. The investor then reduces this balance by the percentage of shares being sold.

As an example, assume that Top Company owns 40 percent of the 100,000 outstanding shares of Bottom Company, an investment accounted for by the equity method. Although these 40,000 shares were acquired some years ago for $200,000, application of the equity method has increased the asset balance to $320,000 as of January 1, 2011. On July 1, 2011, Top elects to sell 10,000 of these shares (one-fourth of its investment) for $110,000 in cash, thereby reducing ownership in Bottom from 40 percent to 30 percent. Bottom Company reports income of $70,000 during the first six months of 2011 and distributes cash dividends of $30,000.

Top, as the investor, initially makes the following journal entries on July 1, 2010, to accrue the proper income and establish the correct investment balance:

Investment in Bottom Company	28,000	
Equity in Investee Income		28,000
To accrue equity income for first six months of 2011 ($70,000 × 40%).		
Cash	12,000	
Investment in Bottom Company		12,000
To record receipt of cash dividends from January through June 2011 ($30,000 × 40%).		

These two entries increase the carrying value of Top's investment by $16,000, creating a balance of $336,000 as of July 1, 2011. The sale of one-fourth of these shares can then be recorded as follows:

Cash	110,000	
Investment in Bottom Company		84,000
Gain on Sale of Investment		26,000
To record sale of one-fourth of investment in Bottom Company (¼ × $336,000 = $84,000).		

After the sale is completed, Top continues to apply the equity method to this investment based on 30 percent ownership rather than 40 percent. However, if the sale had been of sufficient magnitude to cause Top to lose its ability to exercise significant influence over Bottom, the equity method ceases to be applicable. For example, if Top Company's holdings were reduced from 40 percent to 15 percent, the equity method might no longer be appropriate after the sale. The shares still being held are reported according to the fair-value method with the remaining book value becoming the new *cost* figure for the investment rather than the amount originally paid.

If an investor is required to change from the equity method to the fair-value method, no retrospective adjustment is made. Although, as previously demonstrated, a change to the equity method mandates a restatement of prior periods, the treatment is not the same when the investor's change is to the fair-value method.

EXCESS OF INVESTMENT COST OVER BOOK VALUE ACQUIRED

LO5

Allocate the cost of an equity method investment and compute amortization expense to match revenues recognized from the investment to the excess of investor cost over investee book value.

After the basic concepts and procedures of the equity method are mastered, more complex accounting issues can be introduced. Surely one of the most common problems encountered in applying the equity method concerns investment costs that exceed the proportionate book value of the investee company.[10]

Unless the investor acquires its ownership at the time of the investee's conception, paying an amount equal to book value is rare. A number of possible reasons exist for a difference between the book value of a company and the price of its stock. A company's value at any time is based on a multitude of factors such as company profitability, the introduction of a new product, expected dividend payments, projected operating results, and general economic

---

[10] Although encountered less frequently, investments can be purchased at a cost that is less than the underlying book value of the investee. Accounting for this possibility is explored in later chapters.

conditions. Furthermore, stock prices are based, at least partially, on the perceived worth of a company's net assets, amounts that often vary dramatically from underlying book values. Asset and liability accounts shown on a balance sheet tend to measure historical costs rather than current value. In addition, these reported figures are affected by the specific accounting methods adopted by a company. Inventory costing methods such as LIFO and FIFO, for example, obviously lead to different book values as does each of the acceptable depreciation methods.

If an investment is acquired at a price in excess of book value, logical reasons should explain the additional cost incurred by the investor. The source of the excess of cost over book value is important. Income recognition requires matching the income generated from the investment with its cost. Excess costs allocated to fixed assets will likely be expensed over longer periods than costs allocated to inventory. In applying the equity method, the cause of such an excess payment can be divided into two general categories:

1. Specific investee assets and liabilities can have fair values that differ from their present book values. The excess payment can be identified directly with individual accounts such as inventory, equipment, franchise rights, and so on.
2. The investor could be willing to pay an extra amount because future benefits are expected to accrue from the investment. Such benefits could be anticipated as the result of factors such as the estimated profitability of the investee or the relationship being established between the two companies. In this case, the additional payment is attributed to an intangible future value generally referred to as *goodwill* rather than to any specific investee asset or liability. For example, in a recent annual report, Intel Corporation disclosed that its long-term investment in Clearwire, accounted for under the equity method, included goodwill of approximately $108 million.

As an illustration, assume that Big Company is negotiating the acquisition of 30 percent of the outstanding shares of Little Company. Little's balance sheet reports assets of $500,000 and liabilities of $300,000 for a net book value of $200,000. After investigation, Big determines that Little's equipment is undervalued in the company's financial records by $60,000. One of its patents is also undervalued, but only by $40,000. By adding these valuation adjustments to Little's book value, Big arrives at an estimated $300,000 worth for the company's net assets. Based on this computation, Big offers $90,000 for a 30 percent share of the investee's outstanding stock.

Book value of Little Company (assets minus liabilities [or stockholders' equity])	$200,000
Undervaluation of equipment	60,000
Undervaluation of patent	40,000
Value of net assets	$300,000
Portion being acquired	30%
Acquisition price	$ 90,000

Although Big's purchase price is in excess of the proportionate share of Little's book value, this additional amount can be attributed to two specific accounts: Equipment and Patents. No part of the extra payment is traceable to any other projected future benefit. Thus, the cost of Big's investment is allocated as follows:

Payment by investor		$90,000
Percentage of book value acquired ($200,000 × 30%)		60,000
Payment in excess of book value		30,000
Excess payment identified with specific assets:		
Equipment ($60,000 undervaluation × 30%)	$18,000	
Patent ($40,000 undervaluation × 30%)	12,000	30,000
Excess payment not identified with specific assets—goodwill		−0−

Of the $30,000 excess payment made by the investor, $18,000 is assigned to the equipment whereas $12,000 is traced to a patent and its undervaluation. No amount of the purchase price is allocated to goodwill.

To take this example one step further, assume that Little's owners reject Big's proposed $90,000 price. They believe that the value of the company as a going concern is higher than the fair value of its net assets. Because the management of Big believes that valuable synergies will be created through this purchase, the bid price is raised to $125,000 and accepted. This new acquisition price is allocated as follows:

Payment by investor		$125,000
Percentage of book value acquired ($200,000 × 30%)		60,000
Payment in excess of book value		65,000
Excess payment identified with specific assets:		
Equipment ($60,000 undervaluation × 30%)	$18,000	
Patent ($40,000 undervaluation × 30%)	12,000	30,000
Excess payment not identified with specific assets—goodwill		$ 35,000

As this example indicates, *any extra payment that cannot be attributed to a specific asset or liability is assigned to the intangible asset goodwill.* Although the actual purchase price can be computed by a number of different techniques or simply result from negotiations, goodwill is always the excess amount not allocated to identifiable asset or liability accounts.

Under the equity method, the investor enters total cost in a single investment account regardless of the allocation of any excess purchase price. If all parties accept Big's bid of $125,000, the acquisition is initially recorded at that amount despite the internal assignments made to equipment, patents, and goodwill. The entire $125,000 was paid to acquire this investment, and it is recorded as such.

The Amortization Process

The preceding extra payments were made in connection with specific assets (equipment, patents, and goodwill). Even though the actual dollar amounts are recorded within the investment account, a definite historical cost can be attributed to these assets. With a cost to the investor as well as a specified life, the payment relating to each asset (except land, goodwill, and other indefinite life intangibles) should be amortized over an appropriate time period.

Historically, goodwill implicit in equity method investments had been amortized over periods less than or equal to 40 years. However, in June 2001, a major and fundamental change in GAAP occurred for goodwill. The useful life for goodwill is now considered indefinite. Therefore, goodwill amortization expense no longer exists in financial reporting.[11] Any implicit goodwill is carried forward without adjustment until the investment is sold or a permanent decline in value occurs.

Goodwill can maintain its value and theoretically may even increase over time. The notion of an indefinite life for goodwill recognizes the argument that amortization of goodwill over an arbitrary period fails to reflect economic reality and therefore does not provide useful information. A primary reason for the presumption of an indefinite life for goodwill relates to the accounting for business combinations (covered in Chapters 2 through 7). Goodwill associated with equity method investments, for the most part, is accounted for in the same manner as goodwill arising from a business combination. One difference is that goodwill arising from a business combination is subject to annual impairment reviews, whereas goodwill implicit in equity investments is not. Equity method investments are tested in their entirety for permanent declines in value.[12]

---

[11] Other intangibles (such as certain licenses, trademarks) also can be considered to have indefinite lives and thus are not amortized unless and until their lives are determined to be limited. Further discussion of intangibles with indefinite lives appears in Chapter 3.

[12] Because equity method goodwill is not separable from the related investment, goodwill should not be separately tested for impairment. See also FASB ASC para. 350-20-35-59.

Assume, for illustrative purposes, that the equipment has a 10-year remaining life, the patent a 5-year life, and the goodwill an indefinite life. If the straight-line method is used with no salvage value, *the investor's cost* should be amortized initially as follows:[13]

Account	Cost Assigned	Useful Life	Annual Amortization
Equipment	$18,000	10 years	$1,800
Patent	12,000	5 years	2,400
Goodwill	35,000	Indefinite	−0−
Annual expense (for five years until patent cost is completely amortized)			$4,200

In recording this annual expense, Big is reducing a portion of the investment balance in the same way it would amortize the cost of any other asset that had a limited life. Therefore, at the end of the first year, the investor records the following journal entry under the equity method:

Equity in Investee Income	4,200	
Investment in Little Company		4,200
To record amortization of excess payment allocated to equipment and patent.		

Because this amortization relates to investee assets, the investor does not establish a specific expense account. Instead, as in the previous entry, the expense is recognized through a decrease in the equity income accruing from the investee company.

To illustrate this entire process, assume that Tall Company purchases 20 percent of Short Company for $200,000. Tall can exercise significant influence over the investee; thus, the equity method is appropriately applied. The acquisition is made on January 1, 2011, when Short holds net assets with a book value of $700,000. Tall believes that the investee's building (10-year life) is undervalued within the financial records by $80,000 and equipment with a 5-year life is undervalued by $120,000. Any goodwill established by this purchase is considered to have an indefinite life. During 2011, Short reports a net income of $150,000 and pays a cash dividend at year's end of $60,000.

Tall's three basic journal entries for 2011 pose little problem:

January 1, 2011		
Investment in Short Company	200,000	
Cash		200,000
To record acquisition of 20 percent of the outstanding shares of Short Company.		

December 31, 2011		
Investment in Short Company	30,000	
Equity in Investee Income		30,000
To accrue 20 percent of the 2011 reported earnings of investee ($150,000 × 20%).		
Cash	12,000	
Investment in Short Company		12,000
To record receipt of 2011 cash dividend ($60,000 × 20%).		

[13] Unless otherwise stated, all amortization computations are based on the straight-line method with no salvage value.

An allocation of Tall's $200,000 purchase price must be made to determine whether an additional adjusting entry is necessary to recognize annual amortization associated with the extra payment:

Payment by investor		$200,000
Percentage of 1/1/11 book value ($700,000 × 20%)		140,000
Payment in excess of book value		60,000
Excess payment identified with specific assets:		
Building ($80,000 × 20%)	$16,000	
Equipment ($120,000 × 20%)	24,000	40,000
Excess payment not identified with specific assets—goodwill		$ 20,000

As can be seen, $16,000 of the purchase price is assigned to a building, $24,000 to equipment, with the remaining $20,000 attributed to goodwill. For each asset with a definite useful life, periodic amortization is required.

Asset	Attributed Cost	Useful Life	Annual Amortization
Building	$16,000	10 years	$1,600
Equipment	24,000	5 years	4,800
Goodwill	20,000	Indefinite	–0–
Total for 2011			$6,400

At the end of 2011, Tall must also record the following adjustment in connection with these cost allocations:

Equity in Investee Income	6,400	
Investment in Short Company		6,400
To record 2011 amortization of extra cost of building ($1,600) and equipment ($4,800).		

Although these entries are shown separately here for better explanation, Tall would probably net the income accrual for the year ($30,000) and the amortization ($6,400) to create a single entry increasing the investment and recognizing equity income of $23,600. Thus, the first-year return on Tall Company's beginning investment balance (defined as equity earnings/beginning investment balance) is equal to 11.80 percent ($23,600/$200,000).

ELIMINATION OF UNREALIZED PROFITS IN INVENTORY[14]

LO6

Describe the rationale and computations to defer unrealized gains on intra-entity transfers until the goods are either consumed or sold to outside parties.

Many equity acquisitions establish ties between companies to facilitate the direct purchase and sale of inventory items. Such intra-entity transactions can occur either on a regular basis or only sporadically. For example, The Coca-Cola Company recently disclosed that it sold $6.3 billion of syrup, concentrate, and other finished products to its 35 percent-owned investee Coca-Cola Enterprises, Inc.

Regardless of their frequency, inventory sales between investor and investee necessitate special accounting procedures to ensure proper timing of revenue recognition. An underlying principle of accounting is that "revenues are not recognized until earned . . . and revenues are considered to have been earned when the entity has substantially accomplished what it must do to be entitled to the benefits represented by the revenues."[15] In the sale of

---

[14] Unrealized gains can involve the sale of items other than inventory. The intra-entity transfer of depreciable fixed assets and land is discussed in a later chapter.

[15] FASB, *Statement of Financial Accounting Concepts No. 6,* "Recognition and Measurement in Financial Statements of Business Enterprises" (Stamford, CT: December 1984), para. 83.

EXHIBIT 1.2
Downstream and
Upstream Sales

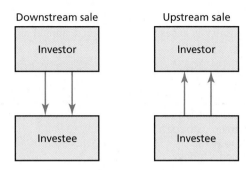

Downstream sale   Upstream sale

inventory to an unrelated party, recognition of revenue is normally not in question; substantial accomplishment is achieved when the exchange takes place unless special terms are included in the contract.

Unfortunately, the earning process is not so clearly delineated in sales made between related parties. *Because of the relationship between investor and investee, the seller of the goods is said to retain a partial stake in the inventory for as long as the buyer holds it.* Thus, the earning process is not considered complete at the time of the original sale. For proper accounting, income recognition must be deferred until substantial accomplishment is proven. Consequently, when the investor applies the equity method, reporting of the related profit on intra-entity transfers is delayed until the buyer's ultimate disposition of the goods. When the inventory is eventually consumed within operations or resold to an unrelated party, the original sale is culminated and the gross profit is fully recognized.

In accounting, transactions between related companies are identified as either *downstream* or *upstream*. *Downstream transfers* refer to the investor's sale of an item to the investee. Conversely, an *upstream sale* describes one that the investee makes to the investor (see Exhibit 1.2). *Although the direction of intra-entity sales does not affect reported equity method balances for investments when significant influence exists, it has definite consequences when financial control requires the consolidation of financial statements, as discussed in Chapter 5.* Therefore, these two types of intra-entity sales are examined separately even at this introductory stage.

Downstream Sales of Inventory

Assume that Big Company owns a 40 percent share of Little Company and accounts for this investment through the equity method. In 2011, Big sells inventory to Little at a price of $50,000. This figure includes a gross profit of 30 percent, or $15,000. By the end of 2011, Little has sold $40,000 of these goods to outside parties while retaining $10,000 in inventory for sale during the subsequent year.

The investor has made downstream sales to the investee. In applying the equity method, recognition of the related profit must be delayed until the buyer disposes of these goods. Although total intra-entity transfers amounted to $50,000 in 2011, $40,000 of this merchandise has already been resold to outsiders, thereby justifying the normal reporting of profits. For the $10,000 still in the investee's inventory, the earning process is not finished. In computing equity income, this portion of the intra-entity profit must be deferred until Little disposes of the goods.

The gross profit on the original sale was 30 percent of the transfer price; therefore, Big's profit associated with these remaining items is $3,000 ($10,000 × 30%). *However, because only 40 percent of the investee's stock is held, just $1,200 ($3,000 × 40%) of this profit is unearned.* Big's ownership percentage reflects the intra-entity portion of the profit. The total $3,000 gross profit within the ending inventory balance is not the amount deferred. Rather, 40 percent of that gross profit is viewed as the currently unrealized figure.

Remaining Ending Inventory	Gross Profit Percentage	Gross Profit in Ending Inventory	Investor Ownership Percentage	Unrealized Intra-entity Gross Profit
$10,000	30%	$3,000	40%	$1,200

Discussion **Question**

IS THIS REALLY ONLY SIGNIFICANT INFLUENCE?

The Coca-Cola Company accounts for its ownership of Coca-Cola Enterprises, Inc. (CCE), by the equity method as described in this chapter. In 2008, Coca-Cola held approximately 35 percent of CCE outstanding stock. According to the financial statements of CCE, the products of The Coca-Cola Company account for approximately 93 percent of total CCE revenues. Moreover, three CCE directors are executive officers of The Coca-Cola Company. CCE conducts its business primarily under agreements with The Coca-Cola Company. These agreements give the company the exclusive right to market, distribute, and produce beverage products of The Coca-Cola Company in authorized containers in specified territories. These agreements provide The Coca-Cola Company with the ability, in its sole discretion, to establish prices, terms of payment, and other terms and conditions for the purchase of concentrates and syrups from The Coca-Cola Company.

If Coca-Cola acquires approximately 16 percent more of CCE, it will hold a majority of the stock so that consolidation becomes a requirement. However, given the size of the present ownership and the dependence that CCE has on Coca-Cola for products and marketing, does Coca-Cola truly have no more than "the ability to exercise significant influence over the operating and financial policies" of CCE? Does the equity method fairly represent the relationship that exists? Or does Coca-Cola actually control CCE despite the level of ownership, and should consolidation be required? Should the FASB reexamine the boundary between the application of the equity method and consolidation? Should the rules be rewritten so that Coca-Cola must consolidate CCE rather than use the equity method? If so, at what level of ownership would the equity method no longer be appropriate?

After calculating the appropriate deferral, the investor decreases current equity income by $1,200 to reflect the unearned portion of the intra-entity profit. This procedure temporarily removes this portion of the profit from the investor's books in 2011 until the investee disposes of the inventory in 2012. Big accomplishes the actual deferral through the following year-end journal entry:

Deferral of Unrealized Gross Profit		
Equity in Investee Income	1,200	
Investment in Little Company		1,200
To defer unrealized gross profit on sale of inventory to Little Company.		

In the subsequent year, when this inventory is eventually consumed by Little or sold to unrelated parties, the deferral is no longer needed. The earning process is complete, and Big should recognize the $1,200. By merely reversing the preceding deferral entry, the accountant succeeds in moving the investor's profit into the appropriate time period. Recognition shifts from the year of transfer to the year in which the earning process is substantially accomplished.

Subsequent Realization of Intra-entity Gross Profit		
Investment in Little Company	1,200	
Equity in Investee Income		1,200
To recognize income on intra-entity sale that has now been earned through sales to outsiders.		

Upstream Sales of Inventory

Unlike consolidated financial statements (see Chapter 5), the equity method reports upstream sales of inventory in the same manner as downstream sales. Hence, unrealized profits remaining in ending inventory are deferred until the items are used or sold to unrelated parties. To illustrate, assume that Big Company once again owns 40 percent of Little Company. During the current year, Little sells merchandise costing $40,000 to Big for $60,000. At the end of the fiscal period, Big still retains $15,000 of these goods. Little reports net income of $120,000 for the year.

To reflect the basic accrual of the investee's earnings, Big records the following journal entry at the end of this year:

Income Accrual		
Investment in Little Company	48,000	
Equity in Investee Income		48,000
To accrue income from 40 percent owned investee ($120,000 × 40%).		

The amount of the gross profit remaining unrealized at year-end is computed using the 33⅓ gross profit percentage of the sales price ($20,000/$60,000):

Remaining Ending Inventory	Gross Profit Percentage	Gross Profit in Ending Inventory	Investor Ownership Percentage	Unrealized Intra-entity Gross Profit
$15,000	33⅓%	$5,000	40%	$2,000

Based on this calculation, a second entry is required of the investor at year-end. Once again, a deferral of the unrealized gross profit created by the intra-entity transfer is necessary for proper timing of income recognition. *Under the equity method for investments with significant influence, the direction of the sale between the investor and investee (upstream or downstream) has no effect on the final amounts reported in the financial statements.*

Deferral of Unrealized Gross Profit		
Equity in Investee Income	2,000	
Investment in Little Company		2,000
To defer recognition of intra-entity unrealized gross profit until inventory is used or sold to unrelated parties.		

After the adjustment, Big, the investor, reports earnings from this equity investment of $46,000 ($48,000 − $2,000). The income accrual is reduced because a portion of the intra-entity gross profit is considered unrealized. When the investor eventually consumes or sells the $15,000 in merchandise, the preceding journal entry is reversed. In this way, the effects of the transfer are reported in the proper accounting period when the profit is earned by sales to an outside party.

In an upstream sale, the investor's own inventory account contains the unrealized profit. The previous entry, though, defers recognition of this profit by decreasing Big's investment account rather than the inventory balance. An alternative treatment would be the direct reduction of the investor's inventory balance as a means of accounting for this unrealized amount. Although this alternative is acceptable, decreasing the investment remains the traditional approach for deferring unrealized gross profits, even for upstream sales.

Whether upstream or downstream, the investor's sales and purchases are still reported as if the transactions were conducted with outside parties. Only the unrealized gross profit is deferred, and that amount is adjusted solely through the equity income account. Furthermore, because the companies are not consolidated, the investee's reported balances are not altered at all to reflect the nature of these sales/purchases. Obviously, readers of the financial statements need to be made aware of the inclusion of these amounts in the income statement. Thus, reporting companies must disclose certain information about related-party transactions. These disclosures include the nature of the relationship, a description of the transactions, the dollar amounts of the transactions, and amounts due to or from any related parties at year-end.

Decision Making and the Equity Method

It is important to realize that business decisions, including equity investments, typically involve the assessment of a wide range of consequences. For example, managers frequently are very interested in how financial statements report the effects of their decisions. This attention to financial reporting effects of business decisions arises because measurements of financial performance often affect the following:

- The firm's ability to raise capital.
- Managerial compensation.
- The ability to meet debt covenants and future interest rates.
- Managers' reputations.

Managers are also keenly aware that measures of earnings per share can strongly affect investors' perceptions of the underlying value of their firms' publicly traded stock. Consequently, prior to making investment decisions, firms will study and assess the prospective effects of applying the equity method on the income reported in financial statements. Additionally, such analyses of prospective reported income effects can influence firms regarding the degree of influence they wish to have or even on the decision of whether to invest. For example, managers could have a required projected rate of return on an initial investment. In such cases, an analysis of projected income will be made to assist in setting an offer price.

For example, Investmor Co. is examining a potential 25 percent equity investment in Marco, Inc., that will provide a significant level of influence. Marco projects an annual income of $300,000 for the near future. Marco's book value is $450,000, and it has an unrecorded newly developed technology appraised at $200,000 with an estimated useful life of 10 years. In considering offer prices for the 25 percent investment in Marco, Investmor projects equity earnings as follows:

Projected income (25% × $300,000)	$75,000
Excess patent amortization ([25% × 200,000]/10 years)	(5,000)
Annual expected equity in Marco earnings	$70,000

Investmor's required first-year rate of return (before tax) on these types of investments is 20 percent. Therefore, to meet the first-year rate of return requirement involves a maximum price of $350,000 ($70,000/20% = $350,000). If the shares are publicly traded (leaving the firm a "price taker"), such income projections can assist the company in making a recommendation to wait for share prices to move to make the investment attractive.

Criticisms of the Equity Method

Over the past several decades, thousands of business firms have accounted for their investments using the equity method. Recently, however, the equity method has come under criticism for the following:

- Emphasizing the 20–50 percent of voting stock in determining significant influence versus control.
- Allowing off-balance sheet financing.
- Potentially biasing performance ratios.

The guidelines for the equity method suggest that a 20–50 percent ownership of voting shares indicates significant influence that falls short of control. But can one firm exert "control" over another firm absent an interest of more than 50 percent? Clearly, if one firm controls another, consolidation is the appropriate financial reporting technique. However, over the years, firms have learned ways to control other firms despite owning less than 50 percent of voting shares. For example, contracts across companies can limit one firm's ability to act without permission of the other. Such contractual control can be seen in debt arrangements, long-term sales and purchase agreements, and agreements concerning board membership. As a result, control is exerted through a variety of contractual arrangements. For financial reporting purposes, however, if ownership is 50 percent or less, a firm can argue that control technically does not exist.

In contrast to consolidated financial reports, when applying the equity method, the investee's assets and liabilities are not combined with the investor's amounts. Instead, the investor's balance sheet reports a single amount for the investment and the income statement reports a single amount for its equity in the earnings of the investee. If consolidated, the assets, liabilities, revenues, and expenses of the investee are combined and reported in the body of the investor's financial statements.

Thus, for those companies wishing to actively manage their reported balance sheet numbers, the equity method provides an effective means. By keeping its ownership of voting shares below 50 percent, a company can technically meet the rules for applying the equity method for its investments and at the same time report investee assets and liabilities "off balance sheet." As a result, relative to consolidation, a firm employing the equity method will report smaller values for assets and liabilities. Consequently, higher rates of return for its assets and sales, as well as lower debt-to-equity ratios, could result. For example, *Accounting Horizons* discussed Coca-Cola's application of the equity method as follows:

> Even today, if Coca-Cola consolidates its equity method investments in which it owns more than 40 percent of the outstanding voting stock, Coke's total liabilities increase by almost 300 percent, substantially raising its debt-to-equity ratio from 1.24 to 4.79. Media reports indicate that the debt-rating agencies actually calculate Coke's ratios on a pro forma basis assuming consolidation.[16]

On the surface, it appears that firms can avoid balance sheet disclosure of debts by maintaining investments at less than 50 percent ownership. However, the equity method requires summarized information as to assets, liabilities, and results of operations of the investees to be presented in the notes or in separate statements. Therefore, supplementary information could be available under the equity method that would not be separately identified in consolidation. Nonetheless, some companies have contractual provisions (e.g., debt covenants, managerial compensation agreements) based on ratios in the main body of the financial statements. Meeting the provisions of such contracts could provide managers strong incentives to maintain technical eligibility to use the equity method rather than full consolidation.

FAIR-VALUE REPORTING OPTION FOR EQUITY METHOD INVESTMENTS

LO7

Explain the rationale and reporting implications of the fair-value option for investments otherwise accounted for by the equity method.

In 2007, the FASB introduced a fair-value option under which an entity may irrevocably elect fair value as the initial and subsequent measurement attribute for certain financial assets and financial liabilities. Under the fair-value option, changes in the fair value of the elected financial items are included in earnings. Among the many financial assets available for the fair-value option are included investments accounted for under the equity method.

For example, Citigroup now reports at fair value certain of its investments that previously were reported using the equity method. In their 2008 annual report Citigroup noted that "certain investments that would otherwise be accounted for using the equity method are carried at fair value. Changes in fair value of such investments are recorded in earnings." Many other firms, however, appeared reluctant to elect the fair-value option for their equity method investments.[17]

Typically, the election date for the fair-value option is the date an investment first qualifies for equity method treatment—in other words, once significant influence is present.[18] However, such an election is irrevocable, leaving the firm no future option to apply the equity method for the investment. Any initial effect of the fair-value option election (e.g., adjusting an

---

[16] A. Hartgraves and G. Benston, "The Evolving Accounting Standards for Special Purpose Entities and Consolidations," *Accounting Horizons,* September 2002.

[17] "Fair Uptake on the Fair Value Option, Survey Says," *Treasury & Risk,* October 28, 2008, reports a Grant Thornton survey showing 31 percent of CFOs and controllers plan to adopt fair value for their equity method investments. In a similar survey by PricewaterhouseCoopers 15 percent of the respondents indicated they will likely adopt the fair-value option for their equity method investments ("PwC: CFOs Predict a Fair-Value Headache," CFO.com, May 30, 2007).

[18] Firms also had the opportunity to elect fair-value treatment for equity method investments existing in 2008, the first effective year for the fair-value option.

investment previously reported at cost or using a fair-value adjustment account) is reported as a cumulative-effect adjustment to the opening balance of retained earnings.

Under the fair-value option, firms simply report the investment's fair value as an asset and changes in fair value as earnings. As such, firms neither compute excess cost amortizations nor adjust earnings for intra-entity profits. Dividends received from an investee are included in earnings under the fair-value option. Because dividends typically reduce an investment's fair value, an increase in earnings from dividends received would be offset by a decrease in earnings from the decline in an investment's fair value.

To illustrate application of the fair-value option, on January 1, 2010, Westwind Co. pays $722,000 in exchange for 40,000 common shares of Armco, Inc. Armco has 100,000 common shares outstanding, the majority of which continue to trade on the New York Stock Exchange. During the next two years, Armco reports the following information:

Year	Net Income	Cash Dividends	Common Shares Total Fair Value at December 31
2010	$158,000	$25,000	$1,900,000
2011	125,000	25,000	1,870,000

Westwind elects to adopt the fair-value reporting option and accordingly makes the following journal entries for its investment in Armco over the next two years.

Investment in Armco, Inc.	722,000	
Cash		722,000
To record Westwind's initial 40 percent investment in Armco, Inc.		
Cash	10,000	
Dividend income		10,000
To recognize 2010 dividends received (40%) as investment income.		
Investment in Armco, Inc.	38,000	
Investment income		38,000
To recognize Westwind's 40 percent of the 2010 change in Armco's fair value.		
Cash	10,000	
Dividend income		10,000
To recognize 2011 dividends received (40%) as investment income.		
Investment loss	12,000	
Investment in Armco, Inc.		12,000
To recognize Westwind's 40 percent of the 2011 change in Armco's fair value.		

In its December 31, 2011, balance sheet, Westwind thus reports its Investment in Armco account at $748,000, equal to 40 percent of Armco's total fair value (or $722,000 initial cost adjusted for 2010–2011 fair-value changes of $38,000 less $12,000).

In addition to the increasing emphasis on fair values in financial reporting, the fair-value option also is motivated by a perceived need for consistency across various balance sheet items. In particular, the fair-value option is designed to limit volatility in earnings that occurs when some financial items are measured using cost-based attributes and others at fair value.

As FASB ASC (para. 825-10-10-1) observes, the objective of the fair value option is

> . . . to improve financial reporting by providing entities with the opportunity to mitigate volatility in reported earnings caused by measuring related assets and liabilities differently without having to apply complex hedge accounting provisions.

The fair-value reporting option is also available for available-for-sale and held-to-maturity securities. However, consolidated investments are specifically excluded from the statement's scope. The fair-value election for financial reporting began in 2008.

Summary

1. The equity method of accounting for an investment reflects the close relationship that could exist between an investor and an investee. More specifically, this approach is available when the owner achieves the ability to apply significant influence to the investee's operating and financial decisions. Significant influence is presumed to exist at the 20 to 50 percent ownership level. However, the accountant must evaluate each situation, regardless of the percentage of ownership, to determine whether this ability is actually present.

2. To mirror the relationship between the companies, the equity method requires the investor to accrue income when the investee earned it. In recording this profit or loss, the investor separately reports items such as extraordinary gains and losses as well as prior period adjustments to highlight their nonrecurring nature. Dividend payments decrease the owners' equity of the investee company; therefore, the investor reduces the investment account when collected.

3. When acquiring capital stock, an investor often pays an amount that exceeds the investee company's underlying book value. For accounting purposes, such excess payments must be either identified with specific assets and liabilities (such as land or buildings) or allocated to an intangible asset referred to as *goodwill*. The investor then amortizes each assigned cost (except for any amount attributed to land or goodwill) over the expected useful lives of the assets and liabilities. This amortization reduces the amount of equity income being reported.

4. If the investor sells the entire investment or any portion of it, the equity method is applied consistently until the date of disposal. A gain or loss is computed based on the adjusted book value at that time. Remaining shares are accounted for by means of either the equity method or the fair-value method, depending on the investor's subsequent ability to significantly influence the investee.

5. Inventory (or other assets) can be transferred between investor and investee. Because of the relationship between the two companies, the equity income accrual should be reduced to defer the intra-entity portion of any gross profit included on these transfers until the items are either sold to outsiders or consumed. Thus, the amount of intra-entity gross profit in ending inventory decreases the amount of equity income being recognized in the current period although this effect is subsequently reversed.

6. Since 2008, firms may elect to report significant influence investments at fair value with changes in fair value as earnings. Under the fair-value option, firms simply report the investment's fair value as an asset and changes in fair value as earnings.

Comprehensive Illustration

(*Estimated Time: 30 to 50 Minutes*) Every chapter in this textbook concludes with an illustration designed to assist students in tying together the essential elements of the material presented. After a careful reading of each chapter, attempt to work through the comprehensive problem. Then review the solution that follows the problem, noting the handling of each significant accounting issue.

PROBLEM

Part A

On January 1, 2010, Big Company pays $70,000 for a 10 percent interest in Little Company. On that date, Little has a book value of $600,000, although equipment, which has a five-year life, is undervalued by $100,000 on its books. Little Company's stock is closely held by a few investors and is traded only infrequently. Because fair values are not readily available on a continuing basis, the investment account is appropriately maintained at cost.

On January 1, 2011, Big acquires an additional 30 percent of Little Company for $264,000. This second purchase provides Big the ability to exert significant influence over Little and Big will now apply the equity method. At the time of this transaction, Little's equipment with a four-year life was undervalued by only $80,000.

During these two years, Little reported the following operational results:

Year	Net Income	Cash Dividends Paid
2010	$210,000	$110,000
2011	250,000	100,000

Additional Information

- Cash dividends are always paid on July 1 of each year.
- Any goodwill is considered to have an indefinite life.

Required

a. What income did Big originally report for 2010 in connection with this investment?

b. On comparative financial statements for 2010 and 2011, what figures should Big report in connection with this investment?

Part B (This Problem Is a Continuation of Part A)

In 2012, Little Company reports $400,000 in income from continuing operations plus a $60,000 extraordinary gain. The company pays a $120,000 cash dividend. During this fiscal year, Big sells inventory costing $80,000 to Little for $100,000. Little continues to hold 30 percent of this merchandise at the end of 2012. Big maintains 40 percent ownership of Little throughout the period.

Required

Prepare all necessary journal entries for Big for the year of 2012.

SOLUTION

Part A

a. Big Company accounts for its investment in Little Company at cost during 2010. Because Big held only 10 percent of the outstanding shares, significant influence was apparently not present. Because the stock is not actively traded, fair values are not available and the investment remains at cost. Therefore, the investor records only the $11,000 ($110,000 × 10%) received in dividends as income in the original financial reporting for that year.

b. To make comparative reports consistent, a change to the equity method is recorded retrospectively. Therefore, when the ability to exert significant influence over the operations of Little is established on January 1, 2011, both Big's 2010 and 2011 financial statements will reflect the equity method.

Big first evaluates the initial purchase of Little's stock to determine whether either goodwill or incremental asset values need to be reflected within the equity method procedures.

Purchase of 10 Percent of Voting Stock on January 1, 2010

Payment by investor	$70,000
Percentage of book value acquired ($600,000 × 10%)	60,000
Payment in excess of book value	10,000
Excess payment identified with specific assets:	
Equipment ($100,000 × 10%)	10,000
Excess payment not identified with specific assets—goodwill	–0–

As shown here, the $10,000 excess payment was made to recognize the undervaluation of Little's equipment. This asset had a useful life at that time of five years; thus, the investor records amortization expense of $2,000 each year.

A similar calculation must be carried out for Big's second stock purchase:

Purchase of 30 Percent of Voting Stock on January 1, 2011

Payment by investor	$264,000
Percentage of book value* acquired ($700,000 × 30%)	210,000
Payment in excess of book value	54,000
Excess payment identified with specific assets:	
Equipment ($80,000 × 30%)	24,000
Excess payment not identified with specific assets—goodwill	$ 30,000

*Little's book value on January 1, 2011, is computed by adding the 2010 net income of $210,000 less dividends paid of $110,000 to the previous book value of $600,000.

In this second acquisition, $24,000 of the payment is attributable to the undervalued equipment with $30,000 assigned to goodwill. Because the equipment now has only a four-year remaining life, annual amortization of $6,000 is appropriate ($24,000/4).

After the additional shares are acquired on January 1, 2011, Big's financial records for 2010 must be retrospectively restated as if the equity method had been applied from the date of the initial investment.

Financial Reporting—2010

Equity in Investee Income (income statement)	
Income reported by Little	$210,000
Big's ownership	10%
Accrual for 2010	$ 21,000
Less: Equipment amortization (first purchase)	(2,000)
Equity in investee income—2010	$ 19,000
Investment in Little (balance sheet)	
Cost of first acquisition	$ 70,000
2010 Equity in investee income (above)	19,000
Less: Dividends received ($110,000 × 10%)	(11,000)
Investment in Little—12/31/10	$ 78,000

Financial Reporting—2011

Equity in Investee Income (income statement)	
Income reported by Little	$250,000
Big's ownership	40%
Big's share of Little's reported income	$100,000
Less: Amortization expense:	
Equipment (first purchase)	(2,000)
Equipment (second purchase)	(6,000)
Equity in investee income—2011	$ 92,000
Investment in Little (balance sheet)	
Book value—12/31/10 (above)	$ 78,000
Cost of 2011 acquisition	264,000
Equity in investee income (above)	92,000
Less: Dividends received ($100,000 × 40%)	(40,000)
Investment in Little—12/31/11	$394,000

Part B

On July 1, 2012, Big receives a $48,000 cash dividend from Little (40% × $120,000). According to the equity method, receipt of this dividend reduces the carrying value of the investment account:

Cash	48,000	
Investment in Little Company		48,000
To record receipt of 2012 dividend from investee.		

Big records no other journal entries in connection with this investment until the end of 2012. At that time, the annual accrual of income as well as the adjustment to record amortization is made (see Part A for computation of expense). The investee's continuing income is reported separately from the extraordinary item.

Investment in Little Company	184,000	
Equity in Investee Income		160,000
Extraordinary Gain of Investee		24,000
To recognize reported income of investee based on a 40 percent ownership level of $400,000 operating income and $60,000 extraordinary gain.		
Equity in Investee Income	8,000	
Investment in Little Company		8,000
To record annual amortization on excess payment made in relation to equipment ($2,000 from first purchase and $6,000 from second).		

Big needs to make only one other equity entry during 2012. Intra-entity sales have occurred and Little continues to hold a portion of the inventory. Therefore, an unrealized profit exists that must be deferred. The gross profit rate from the sale was 20 percent ($20,000/$100,000). Because the investee still possesses $30,000 of this merchandise, the related gross profit is $6,000 ($30,000 × 20%). However, Big owns only 40 percent of Little's outstanding stock; thus, the unrealized intra-entity gross profit at year's end is $2,400 ($6,000 × 40%). That amount must be deferred until Little consumes or sells the inventory to unrelated parties in subsequent years.

Equity in Investee Company	2,400	
Investment in Little Company		2,400
To defer unrealized gross profit on intra-entity sale.		

Questions

1. A company acquires a rather large investment in another corporation. What criteria determine whether the investor should apply the equity method of accounting to this investment?

2. What indicates an investor's ability to significantly influence the decision-making process of an investee?

3. Why does the equity method record dividends received from an investee as a reduction in the investment account, not as dividend income?

4. Jones Company possesses a 25 percent interest in the outstanding voting shares of Sandridge Company. Under what circumstances might Jones decide that the equity method would not be appropriate to account for this investment?

5. Smith, Inc., has maintained an ownership interest in Watts Corporation for a number of years. This investment has been accounted for using the equity method. What transactions or events create changes in the Investment in Watts Corporation account being recorded by Smith?

6. Although the equity method is a generally accepted accounting principle (GAAP), recognition of equity income has been criticized. What theoretical problems can opponents of the equity method identify? What managerial incentives exist that could influence a firm's percentage ownership interest in another firm?

7. Because of the acquisition of additional investee shares, an investor can choose to change from the fair-value method to the equity method. Which procedures are applied to effect this accounting change?

8. Riggins Company accounts for its investment in Bostic Company using the equity method. During the past fiscal year, Bostic reported an extraordinary gain on its income statement. How would this extraordinary item affect the investor's financial records?

9. During the current year, Davis Company's common stock suffers a permanent drop in market value. In the past, Davis has made a significant portion of its sales to one customer. This buyer recently announced its decision to make no further purchases from Davis Company, an action that led to the loss of market value. Hawkins, Inc., owns 35 percent of the outstanding shares of Davis, an investment that is recorded according to the equity method. How would the loss in value affect this investor's financial reporting?

10. Wilson Company acquired 40 percent of Andrews Company at a bargain price because of losses expected to result from Andrews's failure in marketing several new products. Wilson paid only $100,000, although Andrews's corresponding book value was much higher. In the first year after acquisition, Andrews lost $300,000. In applying the equity method, how should Wilson account for this loss?

11. In a stock acquisition accounted for by the equity method, a portion of the purchase price often is attributed to goodwill or to specific assets or liabilities. How are these amounts determined at acquisition? How are these amounts accounted for in subsequent periods?

12. Princeton Company holds a 40 percent interest in the outstanding voting stock of Yale Company. On June 19 of the current year, Princeton sells part of this investment. What accounting should Princeton make on June 19? What accounting will Princeton make for the remainder of the current year?

13. What is the difference between downstream and upstream sales? How does this difference impact application of the equity method?

14. How is the unrealized gross profit on intra-entity sales calculated? What effect does an unrealized gross profit have on the recording of an investment if the equity method is applied?

15. How are intra-entity transfers reported in an investee's separate financial statements if the investor is using the equity method?

16. What is the fair-value option for reporting equity method investments? How do the equity method and the fair-value option differ in recognizing income from an investee?

Problems

LO3

1. When an investor uses the equity method to account for investments in common stock, cash dividends received by the investor from the investee should be recorded as
   a. A deduction from the investor's share of the investee's profits.
   b. Dividend income.
   c. A deduction from the stockholders' equity account, dividends to stockholders.
   d. A deduction from the investment account.
   (AICPA adapted)

LO2

2. Which of the following does not indicate an investor company's ability to significantly influence an investee?
   a. Material intra-entity transactions.
   b. The investor owns 30 percent of the investee but another owner holds the remaining 70 percent.
   c. Interchange of personnel.
   d. Technological dependency.

LO3

3. Sisk Company has owned 10 percent of Maust, Inc., for the past several years. This ownership did not allow Sisk to have significant influence over Maust. Recently, Sisk acquired an additional 30 percent of Maust and now will use the equity method. How will the investor report this change?
   a. A cumulative effect of an accounting change is shown in the current income statement.
   b. No change is recorded; the equity method is used from the date of the new acquisition.
   c. A retrospective adjustment is made to restate all prior years presented using the equity method.
   d. Sisk has the option to choose the method to show this change.

LO7

4. Under the fair-value option, which of the following affects the income the investor recognizes from its ownership of the investee?
   a. The investee's reported income adjusted for excess cost over book value amortizations.
   b. Changes in the fair value of the investor's ownership shares of the investee.
   c. Intra-entity profits from upstream sales.
   d. Extraordinary items reported by the investee.

LO7

5. When an investor elects the fair-value option for a significant influence investment, cash dividends received by the investor from the investee should be recorded as
   a. A deduction from the investor's share of the investee's reported income.
   b. A deduction from the investment account.
   c. A reduction from accumulated other comprehensive income reported in stockholders' equity.
   d. Dividend income.

LO3

6. On January 1, Puckett Company paid $1.6 million for 50,000 shares of Harrison's voting common stock, which represents a 40 percent investment. No allocation to goodwill or other specific account was made. Significant influence over Harrison is achieved by this acquisition and so Puckett applies the equity method. Harrison distributed a dividend of $2 per share during the year and reported net income of $560,000. What is the balance in the Investment in Harrison account found in Puckett's financial records as of December 31?
   a. $1,724,000.
   b. $1,784,000.
   c. $1,844,000.
   d. $1,884,000.

LO3, LO5

7. In January 2010, Wilkinson, Inc., acquired 20 percent of the outstanding common stock of Bremm, Inc., for $700,000. This investment gave Wilkinson the ability to exercise significant influence over Bremm. Bremm's assets on that date were recorded at $3,900,000 with liabilities of $900,000. Any excess of cost over book value of the investment was attributed to a patent having a remaining useful life of 10 years.

   In 2010, Bremm reported net income of $170,000. In 2011, Bremm reported net income of $210,000. Dividends of $70,000 were paid in each of these two years. What is the equity method balance of Wilkinson's Investment in Bremm, Inc., at December 31, 2011?
   a. $728,000.
   b. $748,000.
   c. $756,000.
   d. $776,000.

LO3, LO5

8. Ace purchases 40 percent of Baskett Company on January 1 for $500,000. Although Ace did not use it, this acquisition gave Ace the ability to apply significant influence to Baskett's operating and financing policies. Baskett reports assets on that date of $1,400,000 with liabilities of $500,000. One building with a seven-year life is undervalued on Baskett's books by $140,000. Also, Baskett's book value for its trademark (10-year life) is undervalued by $210,000. During the year, Baskett reports net income of $90,000 while paying dividends of $30,000. What is the Investment in Baskett Company balance (equity method) in Ace's financial records as of December 31?

   a. $504,000.

   b. $507,600.

   c. $513,900.

   d. $516,000.

LO3, LO5

9. Goldman Company reports net income of $140,000 each year and pays an annual cash dividend of $50,000. The company holds net assets of $1,200,000 on January 1, 2010. On that date, Wallace purchases 40 percent of the outstanding stock for $600,000, which gives it the ability to significantly influence Goldman. At the purchase date, the excess of Wallace's cost over its proportionate share of Goldman's book value was assigned to goodwill. On December 31, 2012, what is the Investment in Goldman Company balance (equity method) in Wallace's financial records?

   a. $600,000.

   b. $660,000.

   c. $690,000.

   d. $708,000.

LO6

10. Perez, Inc., applies the equity method for its 25 percent investment in Senior, Inc. During 2011, Perez sold goods with a 40 percent gross profit to Senior. Senior sold all of these goods in 2011. How should Perez report the effect of the intra-entity sale on its 2011 income statement?

   a. Sales and cost of goods sold should be reduced by the amount of intra-entity sales.

   b. Sales and cost of goods sold should be reduced by 25 percent of the amount of intra-entity sales.

   c. Investment income should be reduced by 25 percent of the gross profit on the amount of intra-entity sales.

   d. No adjustment is necessary.

LO6

11. Panner, Inc., owns 30 percent of Watkins and applies the equity method. During the current year, Panner buys inventory costing $54,000 and then sells it to Watkins for $90,000. At the end of the year, Watkins still holds only $20,000 of merchandise. What amount of unrealized gross profit must Panner defer in reporting this investment using the equity method?

   a. $2,400.

   b. $4,800.

   c. $8,000.

   d. $10,800.

LO3, LO5, LO6

12. Alex, Inc., buys 40 percent of Steinbart Company on January 1, 2010, for $530,000. The equity method of accounting is to be used. Steinbart's net assets on that date were $1.2 million. Any excess of cost over book value is attributable to a trade name with a 20-year remaining life. Steinbart immediately begins supplying inventory to Alex as follows:

Year	Cost to Steinbart	Transfer Price	Amount Held by Alex at Year-End (at Transfer Price)
2010	$70,000	$100,000	$25,000
2011	96,000	150,000	45,000

Inventory held at the end of one year by Alex is sold at the beginning of the next.

Steinbart reports net income of $80,000 in 2010 and $110,000 in 2011 while paying $30,000 in dividends each year. What is the equity income in Steinbart to be reported by Alex in 2011?

   a. $34,050.

   b. $38,020.

   c. $46,230.

   d. $51,450.

LO3, LO5

13. On January 3, 2011, Haskins Corporation acquired 40 percent of the outstanding common stock of Clem Company for $990,000. This acquisition gave Haskins the ability to exercise significant influence over the investee. The book value of the acquired shares was $790,000. Any excess cost over the underlying book value was assigned to a patent that was undervalued on Clem's balance sheet. This patent has a remaining useful life of 10 years. For the year ended December 31, 2011, Clem reported net income of $260,000 and paid cash dividends of $80,000. At December 31, 2011, what should Haskins report as its investment in Clem under the equity method?

LO3, LO5, LO7

14. On January 1, 2010, Alison, Inc., paid $60,000 for a 40 percent interest in Holister Corporation's common stock. This investee had assets with a book value of $200,000 and liabilities of $75,000. A patent held by Holister having a $5,000 book value was actually worth $20,000. This patent had a six-year remaining life. Any further excess cost associated with this acquisition was attributed to goodwill. During 2010, Holister earned income of $30,000 and paid dividends of $10,000. In 2011, it had income of $50,000 and dividends of $15,000. During 2011, the fair value of Allison's investment in Holister had risen from $68,000 to $75,000.

    a. Assuming Alison uses the equity method, what balance should appear in the Investment in Holister account as of December 31, 2011?

    b. Assuming Alison uses the fair-value option, what income from the investment in Holister should be reported for 2011?

LO6

15. On January 1, 2011, Ruark Corporation acquired a 40 percent interest in Batson, Inc., for $210,000. On that date, Batson's balance sheet disclosed net assets of $360,000. During 2011, Batson reported net income of $80,000 and paid cash dividends of $25,000. Ruark sold inventory costing $30,000 to Batson during 2011 for $40,000. Batson used all of this merchandise in its operations during 2011. Prepare all of Ruark's 2011 journal entries to apply the equity method to this investment.

LO1, LO2, LO3, LO5

16. Waters, Inc., acquired 10 percent of Denton Corporation on January 1, 2010, for $210,000 although Denton's book value on that date was $1,700,000. Denton held land that was undervalued by $100,000 on its accounting records. During 2010, Denton earned a net income of $240,000 while paying cash dividends of $90,000. On January 1, 2011, Waters purchased an additional 30 percent of Denton for $600,000. Denton's land is still undervalued on that date, but then by $120,000. Any additional excess cost was attributable to a trademark with a 10-year life for the first purchase and a 9-year life for the second. The initial 10 percent investment had been maintained at cost because fair values were not readily available. The equity method will now be applied. During 2011, Denton reported income of $300,000 and distributed dividends of $110,000. Prepare all of the 2011 journal entries for Waters.

LO6

17. Tiberand, Inc., sold $150,000 in inventory to Schilling Company during 2010 for $225,000. Schilling resold $105,000 of this merchandise in 2010 with the remainder to be disposed of during 2011. Assuming that Tiberand owns 25 percent of Schilling and applies the equity method, what journal entry is recorded at the end of 2010 to defer the unrealized gross profit?

LO3, LO5, LO6

18. Hager holds 30 percent of the outstanding shares of Jenkins and appropriately applies the equity method of accounting. Excess cost amortization (related to a patent) associated with this investment amounts to $9,000 per year. For 2010, Jenkins reported earnings of $80,000 and pays cash dividends of $30,000. During that year, Jenkins acquired inventory for $50,000, which it then sold to Hager for $80,000. At the end of 2010, Hager continued to hold merchandise with a transfer price of $40,000.

    a. What Equity in Investee Income should Hager report for 2010?

    b. How will the intra-entity transfer affect Hager's reporting in 2011?

    c. If Hager had sold the inventory to Jenkins, how would the answers to (a) and (b) have changed?

LO1, LO2, LO3

19. On January 1, 2009, Monroe, Inc., purchased 10,000 shares of Brown Company for $250,000, giving Monroe 10 percent ownership of Brown. On January 1, 2010, Monroe purchased an additional 20,000 shares (20 percent) for $590,000. This latest purchase gave Monroe the ability to apply significant influence over Brown. The original 10 percent investment was categorized as an available-for-sale security. Any excess of cost over book value acquired for either investment was attributed solely to goodwill.

    Brown reports net income and dividends as follows. These amounts are assumed to have occurred evenly throughout these years.

	Net Income	Cash Dividends (paid quarterly)
2009	$350,000	$100,000
2010	480,000	110,000
2011	500,000	120,000

On July 1, 2011, Monroe sells 2,000 shares of this investment for $46 per share, thus reducing its interest from 30 to 28 percent. However, the company retains the ability to significantly influence Brown. Using the equity method, what amounts appear in Monroe's 2011 income statement?

LO1, LO2, LO3

20. Collins, Inc., purchased 10 percent of Merton Corporation on January 1, 2010, for $345,000 and classified the investment as an available-for-sale security. Collins acquires an additional 15 percent of Merton on January 1, 2011, for $580,000. The equity method of accounting is now appropriate for this investment. No intra-entity sales have occurred.

    a. How does Collins initially determine the income to be reported in 2010 in connection with its ownership of Merton?

    b. What factors should have influenced Collins in its decision to apply the equity method in 2011?

    c. What factors could have prevented Collins from adopting the equity method after this second purchase?

    d. What is the objective of the equity method of accounting?

    e. What criticisms have been leveled at the equity method?

    f. In comparative statements for 2010 and 2011, how would Collins determine the income to be reported in 2010 in connection with its ownership of Merton? Why is this accounting appropriate?

    g. How is the allocation of Collins's acquisition made?

    h. If Merton pays a cash dividend, what impact does it have on Collins's financial records under the equity method? Why is this accounting appropriate?

    i. On financial statements for 2011, what amounts are included in Collins's Investment in Merton account? What amounts are included in Collins's Equity in Income of Merton account?

LO3, LO6

21. Parrot Corporation holds a 42 percent ownership of Sunrise, Inc. The equity method is being applied. Parrot assigned the entire original excess purchase price over book value to goodwill. During 2010, the two companies made intra-entity inventory transfers. A portion of this merchandise was not resold until 2011. During 2011, additional transfers were made.

    a. What is the difference between upstream transfers and downstream transfers?

    b. How does the direction of an intra-entity transfer (upstream versus downstream) affect the application of the equity method?

    c. How is the intra-entity unrealized gross profit computed in applying the equity method?

    d. How should Parrot compute the amount of equity income to be recognized in 2010? What entry is made to record this income?

    e. How should Parrot compute the amount of equity income to be recognized in 2011?

    f. If none of the transferred inventory had remained at the end of 2010, how would these transfers have affected the application of the equity method?

    g. How do these intra-entity transfers affect Sunrise's financial reporting?

LO1, LO4

22. Several years ago, Einstein, Inc., bought 40 percent of the outstanding voting stock of Brooks Company. The equity method is appropriately applied. On August 1 of the current year, Einstein sold a portion of these shares.

    a. How does Einstein compute the book value of this investment on August 1 to determine its gain or loss on the sale?

    b. How should Einstein account for this investment after August 1?

    c. If Einstein retains only a 2 percent interest in Brooks so that it holds virtually no influence over Brooks, what figures appear in the investor's income statement for the current year?

    d. If Einstein retains only a 2 percent interest in Brooks so that virtually no influence is held, does the investor have to retroactively adjust any previously reported figures?

LO3, LO5, LO6

23. Russell owns 30 percent of the outstanding stock of Thacker and has the ability to significantly influence the investee's operations and decision making. On January 1, 2011, the balance in the Investment in Thacker account is $335,000. Amortization associated with this acquisition is $9,000 per year. In 2011, Thacker earns an income of $90,000 and pays cash dividends of $30,000. Previously, in 2010, Thacker had sold inventory costing $24,000 to Russell for $40,000. Russell consumed all but 25 percent of this merchandise during 2010 and used the rest during 2011. Thacker sold additional inventory costing $28,000 to Russell for $50,000 in 2011. Russell did not consume 40 percent of these 2011 purchases from Thacker until 2012.

    a. What amount of equity method income would Russell recognize in 2011 from its ownership interest in Thacker?

    b. What is the equity method balance in the Investment in Thacker account at the end of 2011?

LO1, LO3, LO7

24. On January 1, 2010, Allan acquires 15 percent of Bellevue's outstanding common stock for $62,000. Allan classifies the investment as an available-for-sale security and records any unrealized holding gains or losses directly in owners' equity. On January 1, 2011, Allan buys an additional 10 percent of Bellevue for $43,800, providing Allan the ability to significantly influence Bellevue's decisions.

    During the next two years, the following information is available for Bellevue:

	Income	Dividends	Common Stock Fair Value (12/31)
2010	$ 80,000	$30,000	$438,000
2011	100,000	40,000	468,000

    In each purchase, Allan attributes any excess of cost over book value to Bellevue's franchise agreements that had a remaining life of 10 years at January 1, 2010. Also at January 1, Bellevue reports a net book value of $280,000.

    a. Assume Allan applies the equity method to its Investment in Bellevue account:

    1. On Allan's December 31, 2011, balance sheet, what amount is reported for the Investment in Bellevue account?

    2. What amount of equity income should Allan report for 2011?

    3. Prepare the January 1, 2011, journal entry to retrospectively adjust the Investment in Bellevue account to the equity method.

    b. Assume Allan elects the fair-value reporting option for its investment in Bellevue:

    1. On Allan's December 31, 2011, balance sheet, what amount is reported for the Investment in Bellevue account?

    2. What amount of income from its investment in Bellevue should Allan report for 2011?

LO1, LO3, LO4, LO5, LO6

25. Anderson acquires 10 percent of the outstanding voting shares of Barringer on January 1, 2009, for $92,000 and categorizes the investment as an available-for-sale security. An additional 20 percent of the stock is purchased on January 1, 2010, for $210,000, which gives Anderson the ability to significantly influence Barringer. Barringer has a book value of $800,000 at January 1, 2009, and records net income of $180,000 for that year. Barringer paid dividends of $80,000 during 2009. The book values of Barringer's asset and liability accounts are considered as equal to fair values except for a copyright whose value accounted for Anderson's excess cost in each purchase. The copyright had a remaining life of 16 years at January 1, 2009.

    Barringer reported $210,000 of net income during 2010 and $230,000 in 2011. Dividends of $100,000 are paid in each of these years. Anderson uses the equity method.

    a. On comparative income statements issued in 2011 by Anderson for 2009 and 2010, what amounts of income would be reported in connection with the company's investment in Barringer?

    b. If Anderson sells its entire investment in Barringer on January 1, 2012, for $400,000 cash, what is the impact on Anderson's income?

    c. Assume that Anderson sells inventory to Barringer during 2010 and 2011 as follows:

Year	Cost to Anderson	Price to Barringer	Year-End Balance (at Transfer Price)
2010	$35,000	$50,000	$20,000 (sold in following year)
2011	33,000	60,000	40,000 (sold in following year)

    What amount of equity income should Anderson recognize for the year 2011?

LO3, LO5

26. Smith purchased 5 percent of Barker's outstanding stock on October 1, 2009, for $7,475 and acquired an additional 10 percent of Barker for $14,900 on July 1, 2010. Both of these purchases were accounted for as available-for-sale investments. Smith purchases a final 20 percent on December 31, 2011, for $34,200. With this final acquisition, Smith achieves the ability to significantly influence Barker's decision-making process and employs the equity method.

    Barker has a book value of $100,000 as of January 1, 2009. Information follows concerning the operations of this company for the 2009–2011 period. Assume that all income was earned uniformly in each year. Assume also that one-fourth of the total annual dividends are paid at the end of each calendar quarter.

Year	Reported Income	Dividends
2009	$20,000	$ 8,000
2010	30,000	16,000
2011	24,000	9,000

On Barker's financial records, the book values of all assets and liabilities are the same as their fair values. Any excess cost from either purchase relates to identifiable intangible assets. For each purchase, the excess cost is amortized over 15 years. Amortization for a portion of a year should be based on months.

 a. On comparative income statements issued in 2012 for the years of 2009, 2010, and 2011, what would Smith report as its income derived from this investment in Barker?

 b. On a balance sheet as of December 31, 2011, what should Smith report as investment in Barker?

LO3, LO5, LO6

27. Hobson acquires 40 percent of the outstanding voting stock of Stokes Company on January 1, 2010, for $210,000 in cash. The book value of Stokes's net assets on that date was $400,000, although one of the company's buildings, with a $60,000 carrying value, was actually worth $100,000. This building had a 10-year remaining life. Stokes owned a royalty agreement with a 20-year remaining life that was undervalued by $85,000.

Stokes sold inventory with an original cost of $60,000 to Hobson during 2010 at a price of $90,000. Hobson still held $15,000 (transfer price) of this amount in inventory as of December 31, 2010. These goods are to be sold to outside parties during 2011.

Stokes reported a loss of $60,000 for 2010, $40,000 from continuing operations and $20,000 from an extraordinary loss. The company still manages to pay a $10,000 cash dividend during the year.

During 2011, Stokes reported a $40,000 net income and distributed a cash dividend of $12,000. It made additional inventory sales of $80,000 to Hobson during the period. The original cost of the merchandise was $50,000. All but 30 percent of this inventory had been resold to outside parties by the end of the 2011 fiscal year.

Prepare all journal entries for Hobson for 2010 and 2011 in connection with this investment. Assume that the equity method is applied.

LO3, LO5, LO6

28. Penston Company owns 40 percent (40,000 shares) of Scranton, Inc., which it purchased several years ago for $182,000. Since the date of acquisition, the equity method has been properly applied, and the book value of the investment account as of January 1, 2011, is $248,000. Excess patent cost amortization of $12,000 is still being recognized each year. During 2011, Scranton reports net income of $200,000, $320,000 in operating income earned evenly throughout the year, and a $120,000 extraordinary loss incurred on October 1. No dividends were paid during the year. Penston sold 8,000 shares of Scranton on August 1, 2011, for $94,000 in cash. However, Penston retains the ability to significantly influence the investee.

During the last quarter of 2010, Penston sold $50,000 in inventory (which it had originally purchased for only $30,000) to Scranton. At the end of that fiscal year, Scranton's inventory retained $9,000 (at sales price) of this merchandise, which was subsequently sold in the first quarter of 2011.

On Penston's financial statements for the year ended December 31, 2011, what income effects would be reported from its ownership in Scranton?

LO3, LO5, LO6

29. On July 1, 2009, Gibson Company acquired 75,000 of the outstanding shares of Miller Company for $12 per share. This acquisition gave Gibson a 35 percent ownership of Miller and allowed Gibson to significantly influence the investee's decisions.

As of July 1, 2009, the investee had assets with a book value of $2 million and liabilities of $400,000. At the time, Miller held equipment appraised at $150,000 above book value; it was considered to have a seven-year remaining life with no salvage value. Miller also held a copyright with a five-year remaining life on its books that was undervalued by $650,000. Any remaining excess cost was attributable to goodwill. Depreciation and amortization are computed using the straight-line method. Gibson applies the equity method for its investment in Miller.

Miller's policy is to pay a $1 per share cash dividend every April 1 and October 1. Miller's income, earned evenly throughout each year, was $550,000 in 2009, $575,000 in 2010, and $620,000 in 2011.

In addition, Gibson sold inventory costing $90,000 to Miller for $150,000 during 2010. Miller resold $80,000 of this inventory during 2010 and the remaining $70,000 during 2011.

a. Prepare a schedule computing the equity income to be recognized by Gibson during each of these years.

b. Compute Gibson's investment in Miller Company's balance as of December 31, 2011.

LO3, LO4, LO5

30. On January 1, 2009, Plano Company acquired 8 percent (16,000 shares) of the outstanding voting shares of the Sumter Company for $192,000, an amount equal to Sumter's underlying book and fair value. Sumter pays a cash dividend to its stockholders each year of $100,000 on September 15. Sumter reported net income of $300,000 in 2009, $360,000 in 2010, $400,000 in 2011, and $380,000 in 2012. Each income figure can be assumed to have been earned evenly throughout its respective year. In addition, the fair value of these 16,000 shares was indeterminate, and therefore the investment account remained at cost.

On January 1, 2011, Plano purchased an additional 32 percent (64,000 shares) of Sumter for $965,750 in cash and began to use the equity method. This price represented a $50,550 payment in excess of the book value of Sumter's underlying net assets. Plano was willing to make this extra payment because of a recently developed patent held by Sumter with a 15-year remaining life. All other assets were considered appropriately valued on Sumter's books.

On July 1, 2012, Plano sold 10 percent (20,000 shares) of Sumter's outstanding shares for $425,000 in cash. Although it sold this interest, Plano maintained the ability to significantly influence Sumter's decision-making process. Assume that Plano uses a weighted average costing system. Prepare the journal entries for Plano for the years of 2009 through 2012.

LO3, LO5, LO6

31. On January 1, 2010, Stream Company acquired 30 percent of the outstanding voting shares of Q-Video, Inc., for $770,000. Q-Video manufactures specialty cables for computer monitors. On that date, Q-Video reported assets and liabilities with book values of $1.9 million and $700,000, respectively. A customer list compiled by Q-Video had an appraised value of $300,000, although it was not recorded on its books. The expected remaining life of the customer list was five years with a straight-line depreciation deemed appropriate. Any remaining excess cost was not identifiable with any particular asset and thus was considered goodwill.

Q-Video generated net income of $250,000 in 2010 and a net loss of $100,000 in 2011. In each of these two years, Q-Video paid a cash dividend of $15,000 to its stockholders.

During 2010, Q-Video sold inventory that had an original cost of $100,000 to Stream for $160,000. Of this balance, $80,000 was resold to outsiders during 2010, and the remainder was sold during 2011. In 2011, Q-Video sold inventory to Stream for $175,000. This inventory had cost only $140,000. Stream resold $100,000 of the inventory during 2011 and the rest during 2012.

For 2010 and then for 2011, compute the amount that Stream should report as income from its investment in Q-Video in its external financial statements under the equity method.

Develop Your Skills

EXCEL CASE 1

On January 1, 2011, Acme Co. is considering purchasing a 40 percent ownership interest in PHC Co., a privately held enterprise, for $700,000. PHC predicts its profit will be $185,000 in 2011, projects a 10 percent annual increase in profits in each of the next four years, and expects to pay a steady annual dividend of $30,000 for the foreseeable future. Because PHC has on its books a patent that is undervalued by $375,000, Acme realizes that it will have an additional amortization expense of $15,000 per year over the next 10 years—the patent's estimated useful life. All of PHC's other assets and liabilities have book values that approximate market values. Acme uses the equity method for its investment in PHC.

Required

1. Using an Excel spreadsheet, set the following values in cells:
   - Acme's cost of investment in PHC.
   - Percentage acquired.
   - First-year PHC reported income.

- Projected growth rate in income.
- PHC annual dividends.
- Annual excess patent amortization.

2. Referring to the values in (1), prepare the following schedules using columns for the years 2011 through 2015.
    - Acme's equity in PHC earnings with rows showing these:
        - Acme's share of PHC reported income.
        - Amortization expense.
        - Acme's equity in PHC earnings.
    - Acme's Investment in PHC balance with rows showing the following:
        - Beginning balance.
        - Equity earnings.
        - Dividends.
        - Ending balance.
    - Return on beginning investment balance = Equity earnings/Beginning investment balance in each year.

3. Given the preceding values, compute the average of the projected returns on beginning investment balances for the first five years of Acme's investment in PHC. What is the maximum Acme can pay for PHC if it wishes to earn at least a 10 percent average return on beginning investment balance? (*Hint:* Under Excel's Tools menu, use the Solver or Goal Seek capability to produce a 10 percent average return on beginning investment balance by changing the cell that contains Acme's cost of investment in PHC. Excel's Solver should produce an exact answer while Goal Seek should produce a close approximation. You may need to first add in the Solver capability under Excel's Tools menu.)

EXCEL CASE 2

On January 1, Intergen, Inc., invests $200,000 for a 40 percent interest in Ryan, a new joint venture with two other partners each investing $150,000 for 30 percent interests. Intergen plans to sell all of its production to Ryan, which will resell the inventory to retail outlets. The equity partners agree that Ryan will buy inventory only from Intergen. Also, Intergen plans to use the equity method for financial reporting.

During the year, Intergen expects to incur costs of $850,000 to produce goods with a final retail market value of $1,200,000. Ryan projects that, during this year, it will resell three-fourths of these goods for $900,000. It should sell the remainder in the following year.

The equity partners plan a meeting to set the price Intergen will charge Ryan for its production. One partner suggests a transfer price of $1,025,000 but is unsure whether it will result in an equitable return across the equity holders. Importantly, Intergen agrees that its total rate of return (including its own operations and its investment in Ryan) should be equal to that of the other investors' return on their investments in Ryan. All agree that Intergen's value including its investment in Ryan is $1,000,000.

Required

1. Create an Excel spreadsheet analysis showing the following:
    - Projected income statements for Intergen and Ryan. Formulate the statements to do the following:
        - Link Ryan's cost of goods sold to Intergen's sales (use a starting value of $1,025,000 for Intergen's sales).
        - Link Intergen's equity in Ryan's earnings to Ryan's net income (adjusted for Intergen's gross profit rate × Ryan's ending inventory × 40 percent ownership percentage).
        - Be able to change Intergen's sales and see the effects throughout the income statements of Ryan and Intergen. Note that the cost of goods sold for Intergen is fixed.
    - The rate of return for the two 30 percent equity partners on their investment in Ryan.
    - The total rate of return for Intergen based on its $1,000,000 value.

2. What transfer price will provide an equal rate of return for each of the investors in the first year of operation? (*Hint:* Under Excel's Tools menu, use the Goal Seek or Solver capability to produce a zero difference in rates of return across the equity partners by changing the cell that contains Intergen's sales.)

ANALYSIS CASE

Refer to the Web sites www.cokecce.com and www.coca-cola.com.

Required

Address the following:

1. How does The Coca-Cola Company account for its investment in Coca-Cola Enterprises, Inc. (CCE)? What are the accounting implications of the method Coca-Cola uses?

2. What criterion does Coca-Cola use to choose the method of accounting for its investment in CCE?

3. Describe the relationship between Coca-Cola and CCE.

4. Calculate the debt-to-equity ratios in the most recent two years for both Coca-Cola and CCE. Does Coca-Cola have the ability to influence CCE's debt levels?

5. How are Coca-Cola's financials affected by its relationship with CCE? In general, how would Coca-Cola's financials change if it consolidated CCE?

RESEARCH AND ANALYSIS CASE—IMPAIRMENT

Wolf Pack Transport Co. has a 25 percent equity investment in Maggie Valley Depot (MVD), Inc., which owns and operates a warehousing facility used for the collection and redistribution of various consumer goods. Wolf Pack paid $1,685,000 for MVD several years ago, including a $300,000 allocation for goodwill as the only excess cost over book value acquired. Wolf Pack Transport has since appropriately applied the equity method to account for the investment in its internal and external financial reports. In its most recent balance sheet, because of recognized profits in excess of dividends since the acquisition, Wolf Pack reported a $2,350,000 amount for its Investment in Maggie Valley Depot, Inc., account.

However, competition in the transit warehousing industry has increased in the past 12 months. In the same area as the MVD facility, a competitor company opened two additional warehouses that are much more conveniently located near a major interstate highway. MVD's revenues declined 30 percent as customers shifted their business to the competitor's facilities and the prices for warehouse services declined. The market value of Wolf Pack's stock ownership in MVD fell to $1,700,000 from a high last year of $2,500,000. MVD's management is currently debating ways to respond to these events but has yet to formulate a firm plan.

Required

1. What guidance does the FASB ASC provide for equity method investment losses in value?

2. Should Wolf Pack recognize the decline in the value of its holdings in MVD in its current year financial statements?

3. Should Wolf Pack test for impairment of the value it had initially assigned to goodwill?

RESEARCH CASE—MINORITY SHAREHOLDER RIGHTS

Consolidated financial reporting is appropriate when one entity has a controlling financial interest in another entity. The usual condition for a controlling financial interest is ownership of a majority voting interest. But in some circumstances, control does not rest with the majority owner—especially when minority owners are contractually provided with approval or veto rights that can restrict the actions of the majority owner. In these cases, the majority owner employs the equity method rather than consolidation.

Required

Address the following by searching the FASB ASC Topic 810 on consolidation.

1. What are protective minority rights?

2. What are substantive participating minority rights?

3. What minority rights overcome the presumption that all majority-owned investees should be consolidated?

4. Zee Company buys 60 percent of the voting stock of Bee Company with the remaining 40 percent minority interest held by Bee's former owners, who negotiated the following minority rights:

   • Any new debt above $1,000,000 must be approved by the 40 percent minority shareholders.

   • Any dividends or other cash distributions to owners in excess of customary historical amounts must be approved by the 40 percent minority shareholders.

According to the FASB ASC, what are the issues in determining whether Zee should consolidate Bee or report its investment in Bee under the equity method?

Consolidation of Financial Information

Financial statements published and distributed to owners, creditors, and other interested parties appear to report the operations and financial position of a single company. In reality, these statements frequently represent a number of separate organizations tied together through common control (a *business combination*). When financial statements represent more than one corporation, we refer to them as *consolidated financial statements*.

Consolidated financial statements are typical in today's business world. Most major organizations, and many smaller ones, hold control over an array of organizations. For example, from 2000 through 2009, Cisco Systems, Inc., reported more than 60 business acquisitions that now are consolidated in its financial reports. PepsiCo, Inc., as another example, annually consolidates data from a multitude of companies into a single set of financial statements. By gaining control over these companies (often known as *subsidiaries*)—which include among others Pepsi-Cola Company, Tropicana Products, and Frito-Lay—PepsiCo (the *parent*) forms a single business combination and single reporting entity.

The consolidation of financial information as exemplified by Cisco Systems and PepsiCo is one of the most complex procedures in all of accounting. Comprehending this process completely requires understanding the theoretical logic that underlies the creation of a business combination. Furthermore, a variety of procedural steps must be mastered to ensure that proper accounting is achieved for this single reporting entity. The following coverage introduces both of these aspects of the consolidation process.

The FASB *Accounting Standards Codification* (ASC) contains the current accounting standards for business combinations under the following topics:

- Business Combinations (Topic 805).
- Consolidation (Topic 810).

Parent

Subsidiary

Business combination

LEARNING OBJECTIVES

After studying this chapter, you should be able to:

LO1   Discuss the motives for business combinations.

LO2   Recognize when consolidation of financial information into a single set of statements is necessary.

LO3   Define the term *business combination* and differentiate across various forms of business combinations.

LO4   Describe the valuation principles of the acquisition method.

LO5   Determine the total fair value of the consideration transferred for an acquisition and allocate that fair value to specific subsidiary assets acquired (including goodwill), and liabilities assumed, or a gain on bargain purchase.

LO6   Prepare the journal entry to consolidate the accounts of a subsidiary if dissolution takes place.

LO7   Prepare a worksheet to consolidate the accounts of two companies that form a business combination if dissolution does not take place.

LO8   Describe the two criteria for recognizing intangible assets apart from goodwill in a business combination.

LO9   Identify the general characteristics of the purchase method and the general characteristics of a pooling of interests. Also recognize that although the pooling of interests and purchase methods are no longer applicable for new business combinations their financial reporting effects will be evident for decades to come.

The Business Combinations topic provides guidance on the accounting and reporting for business combinations using the *acquisition method*. The acquisition method embraces a *fair value* measurement attribute. Adoption of this attribute reflects the FASB's increasing emphasis on fair value for measuring and assessing business activity. In the past, financial reporting standards embraced the cost principle to measure and report the financial effects of business combinations. This fundamental change from a cost-based to a fair-value model has transformed the way we account for and report business combinations in our society.

The Consolidation topic provides guidance on circumstances that require a firm to prepare consolidated financial reports and various other related reporting issues. Basically, consolidated financial reports must be prepared whenever one firm has a controlling financial interest in another. Although ownership of a majority voting interest is the usual condition for a controlling financial interest, the power to control may also exist with a lesser percentage of ownership through governance contracts, leases, or agreement with other stockholders.[1]

In this chapter, we first present expansion through corporate takeovers and present an overview of the consolidation process. Then we present the specifics of the acquisition method of accounting for business combinations where the acquirer obtains complete ownership of another firm. Later, beginning in Chapter 4, we introduce coverage of acquisitions with less than complete ownership.

Financial reporting for business combinations has experienced many changes over the past decade. Prior to the acquisition method requirement, accounting standards allowed either the purchase method or the earlier pooling of interests method of accounting for business combinations. Neither of these methods is now permitted for reporting the formation of new business combinations. However, because of the prospective application of the acquisition method beginning in 2009, legacy effects of these methods remain in many of today's financial statements. Therefore, at the end of this chapter we present coverage of the purchase and pooling of interests methods.

EXPANSION THROUGH CORPORATE TAKEOVERS

LO1

Discuss the motives for business combinations.

Reasons for Firms to Combine

A frequent economic phenomenon is the combining of two or more businesses into a single entity under common management and owner control. During recent decades, the United States and the rest of the world have experienced an enormous number of corporate mergers and takeovers, transactions in which one company gains control over another. According to Thomson Financial, the number of mergers and acquisitions globally in 2008 exceeded 39,597 with a total value of more than $2.9 trillion. Of these deals more than $1.5 trillion involved a U.S. firm. As indicated by Exhibit 2.1, the magnitude of recent combinations continues to be large.

As with any other economic activity, business combinations can be part of an overall managerial strategy to maximize shareholder value. Shareholders—the owners of the firm—hire managers to direct resources so that the firm's value grows over time. In this way, owners receive a return on their investment. Successful firms receive substantial benefits through enhanced share value. Importantly, the managers of successful firms also receive substantial benefits in salaries, especially if their compensation contracts are partly based on stock market performance of the firm's shares.

---

[1] We discuss entities controlled through contractual means (known as variable interest entities) in Chapter 6.

EXHIBIT 2.1
Recent Notable Business Combinations

Acquirer	Target	Deal Value (in billions)
Pfizer	Wyeth	$67.3
InBev	Anheuser-Busch	52.0
Merck	Schering-Plough	41.1
Bank of America	Merrill Lynch	29.1
Verizon Wireless	Alltel	28.1
Mars	Wm. Wrigley, Jr.	23.2
Oracle	Sun Microsystems	7.4
Delta Airlines	Northwest Airlines	3.4
EMC	Data Domain	2.4
Abbott Laboratories	Advanced Medical Optics	1.4

If the goal of business activity is to maximize the firm's value, in what ways do business combinations help achieve that goal? Clearly, the business community is moving rapidly toward business combinations as a strategy for growth and competitiveness. Size and scale are obviously becoming critical as firms compete in today's markets. If large firms can be more efficient in delivering goods and services, they gain a competitive advantage and become more profitable for the owners. Increases in scale can produce larger profits from enhanced sales volume despite smaller (more competitive) profit margins. For example, if a combination can integrate successive stages of production and distribution of products, coordinating raw material purchases, manufacturing, and delivery can result in substantial savings. As an example, Ford Motor Co.'s acquisition of Hertz Rental (one of its largest customers) enabled Ford not only to ensure demand for its cars but also to closely coordinate production with the need for new rental cars. Other cost savings resulting from elimination of duplicate efforts, such as data processing and marketing, can make a single entity more profitable than the separate parent and subsidiary had been in the past.

Although no two business combinations are exactly alike, many share one or more of the following characteristics that potentially enhance profitability:

- Vertical integration of one firm's output and another firm's distribution or further processing.
- Cost savings through elimination of duplicate facilities and staff.
- Quick entry for new and existing products into domestic and foreign markets.
- Economies of scale allowing greater efficiency and negotiating power.
- The ability to access financing at more attractive rates. As firm size increases, negotiating power with financial institutions can increase also.
- Diversification of business risk.

Business combinations also occur because many firms seek the continuous expansion of their organizations, often into diversified areas. Acquiring control over a vast network of different businesses has been a strategy utilized by a number of companies (sometimes known as *conglomerates*) for decades. Entry into new industries is immediately available to the parent without having to construct facilities, develop products, train management, or create market recognition. Many corporations have successfully employed this strategy to produce huge, highly profitable organizations. Unfortunately, others have discovered that the task of managing a widely diverse group of businesses can be a costly learning experience. Even combinations that purportedly take advantage of operating synergies and cost savings often fail if the integration is not managed carefully.[2]

Overall, the primary motivations for many business combinations can be traced to an increasingly competitive environment. Three recent examples of large business combinations provide interesting examples of some distinct motivations to combine: Bank of America and Merrill Lynch, InBev and Anheuser-Busch, and Pfizer and Wyeth. Each is discussed briefly in turn.

[2] Mark Sirower, "What Acquiring Minds Need to Know," *The Wall Street Journal—Manager's Journal,* February 22, 1999.

Bank of America and Merrill Lynch

On January 1, 2009, Bank of America completed its acquisition of Merrill Lynch in exchange for common and preferred stock valued at $29.1 billion.[3] At the time of the acquisition, Bank of America was the nation's largest retail bank, credit card company, and retail lender, while Merrill Lynch was a worldwide leader among investment banking and wealth management firms. Bank of America had made several previous attempts to establish its brokerage business but had struggled in doing so. Rather than continue to try and build this business internally, Bank of America determined that acquiring Merrill Lynch was a better option. With the addition of Merrill Lynch, Bank of America became the nation's largest brokerage firm. Merrill Lynch was also expected to help expand Bank of America's presence in the worldwide market.[4]

Merrill Lynch's motivation for accepting the deal was largely a matter of survival. During the third quarter of 2008, like almost all large investment banks, Merrill Lynch was hit hard by the credit crisis. Because of its large position in mortgage-backed securities, as the number of mortgage defaults rose dramatically, Merrill's stock decreased significantly and the company reported large losses. Most of the nation's top investment banks were also under duress and forced to make decisions affecting their survival. Some, like Lehman Brothers, were unable to secure government assistance and filed for bankruptcy, while others like Goldman Sachs shifted their business structures. Merrill Lynch opted for a takeover strategy and accepted Bank of America's offer.[5] Despite Merrill's 2008 large losses and stock price decline, Bank of America recorded $5 billion of goodwill from the combination.

While the two companies did not have a large overlap in services, Bank of America estimated annual pretax savings of $7 billion by the year 2012. These savings were expected to result primarily through the elimination of duplicate jobs within Bank of America's weak brokerage sector.

InBev and Anheuser-Busch

On July 13, 2008, the Belgian beer company InBev and the American company Anheuser-Busch announced their combination, creating the world's largest beer company and one of the world's top five consumer products companies. Under the terms of the deal, Anheuser-Busch shareholders received $70 in cash for each share held, and Anheuser-Busch became a wholly owned subsidiary of the newly named Anheuser-Busch InBev company. The total cost of the acquisition was $52 billion.[6]

From a geographical standpoint, the two firms complemented each other. In the United States, for example, InBev should be able to reduce costs by utilizing Busch's long-established distribution system for its own brands like Bass, Becks, and Stella Artois. Anheuser-Busch, on the other hand, may now be able to take advantage of InBev's established European presence to improve its product reception in Europe, where it had traditionally done poorly. The two companies also complemented each other in the Chinese market, where InBev brands were strong in the Northwest and Busch's Budweiser brand was strong in the Southeast.

In addition to creating a more globally integrated firm, InBev expects the combination to produce annual cost savings of $1.5 billion by 2011. Because there is not much overlap between the two firms geographically, the cost reductions are expected to come from economies of scale, combination of corporate functions, and knowledge sharing. Significant financial impacts from plant- and distribution-level layoffs are not anticipated given the complementary nature of the firms' mostly distinct operating locations.[7]

Pfizer and Wyeth

On January 26, 2009, pharmaceutical giant Pfizer announced that it would acquire its smaller competitor, Wyeth, for $68 billion in cash and stock. Wyeth shareholders were offered $33 in

---

[3] Some initial announcement date reports indicated a $50 billion price for Merrill Lynch. However, as revealed in Bank of America's March 31, 2009, 10-Q report, the final value assigned to the acquisition was $29.1 billion.

[4] Bank of America press release, September 18, 2008.

[5] Jonathan Stempel, "Bank of America/Merrill Merger Wins Shareholder OK," Reuters, December 8, 2008.

[6] Anheuser-Busch press release, July 14, 2008.

[7] AB InBev press release, November 18, 2008.

cash and 0.985 share of Pfizer for each share of Wyeth.[8] Pfizer had been looking to diversify its sales product portfolio, as the majority of its revenues were comprised of only a few key drugs. Wyeth was seen as a potential fit for Pfizer as its strengths in the vaccines and biologic drug markets were areas in which Pfizer lacked a strong presence. Additionally, the Wyeth acquisition was anticipated to solidify Pfizer's position atop the pharmaceutical industry.

The deal was expected to benefit both companies, as they each had patents expiring on many of their drugs. The patent on Pfizer's top-earning drug Lipitor is scheduled to expire in November of 2011 and, at the time of the acquisition announcement, Lipitor accounted for 25 percent of Pfizer's revenues. According to estimates, by 2015, 70 percent of Pfizer's revenue could be lost due to the expiration of drug patents. Wyeth was in a similar position, as patents for its two largest revenue-producing drugs, Effexor and Protonix, were set to expire in 2010 and 2011, respectively. With no new drug creation on the horizon, Pfizer's management determined that acquiring Wyeth would lessen its risks as well as aid in new drug development. Once the merger is completed, no one drug will account for more than 10 percent of the combined revenues.[9]

While Pfizer's management maintained that the motivation for the acquisition was to diversify its sales portfolio, Pfizer also expects to benefit from cost synergies. Upon completion of the acquisition, Pfizer planned to close 5 of its 46 manufacturing plants and eliminate 20,000, or 15 percent, of jobs between the two companies. As a result of these job cuts, Pfizer estimated savings of $4 billion by 2012.

THE CONSOLIDATION PROCESS

LO2

Recognize when consolidation of financial information into a single set of statements is necessary.

The consolidation of financial information into a single set of statements becomes necessary when the business combination of two or more companies creates a single economic entity. As stated in the FASB ASC (para. 810-10-10-1): "There is a presumption that consolidated statements are more meaningful than separate statements and that they are usually necessary for a fair presentation when one of the companies in the group directly or indirectly has a controlling financial interest in the other entities."

Thus, in producing financial statements for external distribution, the reporting entity transcends the boundaries of incorporation to encompass all companies for which control is present. Even though the various companies may retain their legal identities as separate corporations, the resulting information is more meaningful to outside parties when consolidated into a single set of financial statements.

To explain the process of preparing consolidated financial statements for a business combination, we address three questions:

- How is a business combination formed?
- What constitutes a controlling financial interest?
- How is the consolidation process carried out?

LO3

Define the term business combination *and differentiate across various forms of business combinations.*

Business Combinations—Creating a Single Economic Entity

A business combination refers to a transaction or other event in which an acquirer obtains control over one or more businesses.

Business combinations are formed by a wide variety of transactions or events with various formats. For example, each of the following is identified as a business combination although it differs widely in legal form. In every case, two or more enterprises are being united into a single economic entity so that consolidated financial statements are required.

1. One company obtains the assets, and often the liabilities, of another company in exchange for cash, other assets, liabilities, stock, or a combination of these. The second organization normally dissolves itself as a legal corporation. Thus, only the acquiring company remains in existence, having absorbed the acquired net assets directly into its own operations.

---

[8] Aaron Smith, "Pfizer to Buy Wyeth for $68 Billion," *CNN/Money,* January 30, 2009.

[9] Catherine Arnst, "Pfizer CEO: Wyeth Takeover Will Be Different," *BusinessWeek,* January 26, 2009.

Any business combination in which only one of the original companies continues to exist is referred to in legal terms as a *statutory merger*.

2. One company obtains all of the capital stock of another in exchange for cash, other assets, liabilities, stock, or a combination of these. After gaining control, the acquiring company can decide to transfer all assets and liabilities to its own financial records with the second company being dissolved as a separate corporation.[10] The business combination is, once again, a statutory merger because only one of the companies maintains legal existence. This statutory merger, however, is achieved by obtaining equity securities rather than by buying the target company's assets. Because stock is obtained, the acquiring company must gain 100 percent control of all shares before legally dissolving the subsidiary.

3. Two or more companies transfer either their assets or their capital stock to a newly formed corporation. Both original companies are dissolved, leaving only the new organization in existence. A business combination effected in this manner is a *statutory consolidation*. The use here of the term *consolidation* should not be confused with the accounting meaning of that same word. In accounting, *consolidation* refers to the mechanical process of bringing together the financial records of two or more organizations to form a single set of statements. A statutory consolidation denotes a specific type of business combination that has united two or more existing companies under the ownership of a newly created company.

4. One company achieves legal control over another by acquiring a majority of voting stock. *Although control is present, no dissolution takes place; each company remains in existence as an incorporated operation.* The Quaker Oats Company, as an example, continues to retain its legal status as a corporation after being acquired by PepsiCo. Separate incorporation is frequently preferred to take full advantage of any intangible benefits accruing to the acquired company as a going concern. Better utilization of such factors as licenses, trade names, employee loyalty, and the company's reputation can be possible when the subsidiary maintains its own legal identity. Moreover, maintaining an independent information system for a subsidiary often enhances its market value for an eventual sale or initial public offering as a stand-alone entity.

One important aspect of this type of business combination should be noted. Because the asset and liability account balances are not physically combined as in statutory mergers and consolidations, each company continues to maintain an independent accounting system. To reflect the combination, the acquiring company enters the takeover transaction into its own records by establishing a single investment asset account. However, the newly acquired subsidiary omits any recording of this event; its stock is simply transferred to the parent from the subsidiary's shareholders. Thus, the subsidiary's financial records are not directly affected by a takeover.

5. A final vehicle for control of another business entity does not involve a majority voting stock interest or direct ownership of assets. Control of a variable interest entity (VIE) by design often does not rest with its equity holders. Instead, control is exercised through contractual arrangements with a sponsoring firm that, although it technically does not own the VIE, may become its "primary beneficiary" with rights to its residual profits. These contracts can take the form of leases, participation rights, guarantees, or other residual interests. Past use of VIEs was often criticized in part because these structures provided sponsoring firms with off-balance sheet financing and sometimes questionable profits on sales to their VIEs. Prior to 2004, many sponsoring entities of VIEs did not technically meet the definition of a controlling financial interest (i.e., majority voting stock ownership) and thus did not consolidate their VIEs. Current GAAP, however, expands the notion of control and thus requires consolidation of VIEs by their primary beneficiary.

As you can see, business combinations are created in many distinct forms. Because the specific format is a critical factor in the subsequent consolidation of financial information, Exhibit 2.2 provides an overview of the various combinations.

---

[10] Although the acquired company has been legally dissolved, it frequently continues to operate as a separate division within the surviving company's organization.

EXHIBIT 2.2
Business Combinations

Type of Combination	Action of Acquiring Company	Action of Acquired Company
Statutory merger through asset acquisition	Acquires assets and often liabilities.	Dissolves and goes out of business.
Statutory merger through capital stock acquisition.	Acquires all stock and then transfers assets and liabilities to its own books.	Dissolves as a separate corporation, often remaining as a division of the acquiring company.
Statutory consolidation through capital stock or asset acquisition.	Newly created to receive assets or capital stock of original companies.	Original companies may dissolve while remaining as separate divisions of newly created company.
Acquisition of more than 50 percent of the voting stock.	Acquires stock that is recorded as an investment; controls decision making of acquired company.	Remains in existence as legal corporation, although now a subsidiary of the acquiring company.
Control through ownership of variable interests (see Chapter 6). Risks and rewards often flow to a sponsoring firm rather than the equity holders.	Establishes contractual control over a variable interest entity to engage in a specific activity.	Remains in existence as a separate legal entity—often a trust or partnership.

Control—An Elusive Quality

The definition of control is central to determining when two or more entities become one economic entity and therefore one reporting entity. Control of one firm by another is most often achieved through the acquisition of voting shares. By exercising majority voting power, one firm can literally dictate the financing and operating activities of another firm. Accordingly, U.S. GAAP traditionally has pointed to a majority voting share ownership as a controlling financial interest that requires consolidation.

However, both the FASB and the International Accounting Standards Board (IASB) have on their agendas a long-term project to develop comprehensive guidance on accounting for affiliations between entities. The two boards have agreed to work toward a common standard on consolidation policy that may include a new definition of financial control. According to the IASB:

> The Board has tentatively decided that a reporting entity controls another entity if it has the power to direct the activities of that other entity to generate returns for the reporting entity. A reporting entity has the power to direct the activities of another entity if it can determine that other entity's strategic operating and financing policies. Returns vary with an entity's activities and can be positive or negative. (IASB Projects: Consolidations).

Note that this tentative definition focuses on "power to direct" the activities of another entity. This power criterion defines control conceptually rather than operationally through "majority voting shares." The definition is thus much more expansive, and it implicitly recognizes that voting interests provide but one among several potential vehicles for controlling another firm. As the complexity of arrangements between companies increases, defining when one firm controls another firm remains a continuing challenge for financial reporting standard setters.

Nonetheless, the primary way U.S. firms exercise control remains through the acquisition of a majority of another firm's voting shares. Consequently, in this text, we largely focus on control relationships established through voting interests. In Chapter 6, however, we expand our coverage to include the consolidation of firms where control is exercised through variable interests.

Consolidation of Financial Information

When one company gains control over another, a business combination is established. Financial data gathered from the individual companies are then brought together to form a single set of consolidated statements. Although this process can be complicated, the objectives of a consolidation are straightforward—to report the financial position, results of operations, and cash flows for the combined entity. As a part of this process, reciprocal accounts and intra-entity transactions must be adjusted or eliminated to ensure that all reported balances truly represent the single entity.

Applicable consolidation procedures vary significantly depending on the legal format employed in creating a business combination. *For a statutory merger or a statutory consolidation, when the acquired company (or companies) is (are) legally dissolved, only one accounting consolidation ever occurs.* On the date of the combination, the surviving company simply records the various account balances from each of the dissolving companies. Because the accounts are brought together permanently in this manner, no further consolidation procedures are necessary. After the balances have been transferred to the survivor, the financial records of the acquired companies are closed out as part of the dissolution.

Conversely, in a combination when all companies retain incorporation, a different set of consolidation procedures is appropriate. Because the companies preserve their legal identities, each continues to maintain its own independent accounting records. *Thus, no permanent consolidation of the account balances is ever made. Rather, the consolidation process must be carried out anew each time that the reporting entity prepares financial statements for external reporting purposes.*

When separate record-keeping is maintained, the accountant faces a unique problem: The financial information must be brought together periodically without disturbing the accounting systems of the individual companies. Because these consolidations are produced outside the financial records, worksheets traditionally are used to expedite the process. Worksheets are a part of neither company's accounting records nor the resulting financial statements. Instead, they are an efficient structure for organizing and adjusting the information used to prepare externally reported consolidated statements.

Consequently, the legal characteristics of a business combination have a significant impact on the approach taken to the consolidation process:

What is to be consolidated?

- If dissolution takes place, appropriate account balances are physically consolidated in the surviving company's financial records.
- If separate incorporation is maintained, only the financial statement information (not the actual records) is consolidated.

When does the consolidation take place?

- If dissolution takes place, a permanent consolidation occurs at the date of the combination.
- If separate incorporation is maintained, the consolidation process is carried out at regular intervals whenever financial statements are to be prepared.

How are the accounting records affected?

- If dissolution takes place, the surviving company's accounts are adjusted to include appropriate balances of the dissolved company. The dissolved company's records are closed out.
- If separate incorporation is maintained, each company continues to retain its own records. Using worksheets facilitates the periodic consolidation process without disturbing the individual accounting systems.

FINANCIAL REPORTING FOR BUSINESS COMBINATIONS

LO4

Describe the valuation principles of the acquisition method.

The Acquisition Method: Change in Ownership

The fundamental characteristic of any asset acquisition—whether a single piece of property or a multibillion-dollar corporation—is a change in ownership. Following a business combination, accounting and financial reporting require that the new owner (the acquirer) record appropriate values for the items received in the transaction. As presented below, in a business combination, fair values for both the items exchanged and received can enter into the determination of the acquirer's accounting valuation of the acquired firm.

Current financial reporting standards require the acquisition method to account for business combinations. Applying the acquisition method typically involves recognizing and measuring

- the consideration transferred for the acquired business.
- the separately identified assets acquired, liabilities assumed, and any noncontrolling interest.
- goodwill or a gain from a bargain purchase.

Fair value is the measurement attribute used to recognize these and other aspects of a business combination. Therefore, prior to examining specific applications of the acquisition method, we present a brief discussion of the fair-value concept as applied to business combinations.

Consideration Transferred for the Acquired Business

The fair value of the consideration transferred to acquire a business from its former owners is the starting point in valuing and recording a business combination. In describing the acquisition method, the FASB ASC states

> The consideration transferred in a business combination shall be measured at fair value, which shall be calculated as the sum of the acquisition-date fair values of the assets transferred by the acquirer, the liabilities incurred by the acquirer to former owners of the acquiree, and the equity interests issued by the acquirer. (FASB ASC para. 805-30-30-7)

The acquisition method thus embraces the fair value of the consideration transferred in measuring the acquirer's interest in the acquired business.[11] Fair value is defined as the price that would be received to sell an asset or paid to transfer a liability in an orderly transaction between market participants at the measurement date. Thus, market values are often the best source of evidence of the fair value of consideration transferred in a business combination. Items of consideration transferred can include cash, securities (either stocks or debt), and other property or obligations.

Contingent consideration, when present in a business combination, also serves as an additional element of consideration transferred. Contingent consideration can be useful in negotiations when two parties disagree with each other's estimates of future cash flows for the target firm. Acquisition agreements often contain provisions to pay former owners upon achievement of specified future performance measures. For example, EMS Technologies of Norcross, Georgia, noted in its 2009 first-quarter 10-Q report that the arrangements for one of its 2009 acquisitions

> . . . includes contingent consideration of up to $15 million, which would be payable in cash, in part or in total, based upon the achievement of specified performance targets for 2009 and 2010. Management estimated that the fair value of the contingent consideration arrangement at the acquisition date was approximately $10.5 million, determined by applying the income approach, based on the probability-weighted projected payment amounts discounted to present value at a rate appropriate for the risk of achieving the milestones.

EMS Technologies included the fair value of the contingent consideration in the total consideration transferred for its acquisition as a negotiated component of the fair value of the consideration transferred.

The acquisition method treats contingent consideration obligations as a negotiated component of the fair value of the consideration transferred. Consistent with the disclosure by EMS Technologies, determining the fair value of any contingent future payments typically involves probability and risk assessments based on circumstances existing on the acquisition date.

In Chapters 2 and 3, we focus exclusively on combinations that result in complete ownership by the acquirer (i.e., no noncontrolling interest in the acquired firm). As described beginning in Chapter 4, in a less-than-100-percent acquisition, the noncontrolling interest also is measured initially at its fair value. Then, the combined fair values of the parent's consideration transferred and the noncontrolling interest comprise the valuation basis for the acquired firm in consolidated financial reports.

---

[11] An occasional exception occurs in a bargain purchase in which the fair value of the net assets acquired serves as the valuation basis for the acquired firm. Other exceptions include situations in which control is achieved without a transfer of consideration or determination of the fair value of the consideration transferred is less reliable than other measures of the business fair value.

Fair Values of the Assets Acquired and Liabilities Assumed

A fundamental principle of the acquisition method is that an acquirer must identify the assets acquired and the liabilities assumed in the business combination. Further, once these have been identified, the acquirer measures the assets acquired and the liabilities assumed at their acquisition-date fair values, with only a few exceptions.[12] As demonstrated in subsequent examples, the principle of recognizing and measuring assets acquired and liabilities assumed at fair value applies across all business combinations.

Deciding on the acquisition-date fair values of individual assets and liabilities can prove challenging for the acquirer because a business acquisition typically has only one overall valuation amount (e.g., the consideration transferred) but has many categories of assets acquired and liabilities assumed. Therefore, an allocation of the fair values of the entire acquired firms must be made across these assets and liabilities. As previously noted, the allocation principle is to use fair values—but such values are not always directly available. To estimate fair values for the individual assets acquired and liabilities assumed, three sets of valuation techniques are typically employed: the market approach, the income approach, and the cost approach.

Market Approach   The market approach recognizes that fair values can be estimated with other market transactions involving similar assets or liabilities. In a business combination, assets acquired such as marketable securities and some tangible assets may have established markets that can provide comparable market values for estimating fair values. Similarly, the fair values of many liabilities assumed can be determined by reference to market trades for similar debt instruments.

Income Approach   The income approach relies on multiperiod estimates of future cash flows projected to be generated by an asset. These projected cash flows are then discounted at a required rate of return that reflects the time value of money and the risk associated with realizing the future estimated cash flows. The multiperiod income approach is often useful for obtaining fair-value estimates of intangible assets and acquired in-process research and development.

Cost Approach   The cost approach estimates fair values by reference to the current cost of replacing an asset with another of comparable economic utility. Used assets can present a particular valuation challenge if active markets only exist for newer versions of the asset. Thus, the cost to replace a particular asset reflects both its estimated replacement cost and the effects of obsolescence. In this sense obsolescence is meant to capture economic declines in value including both technological obsolescence and physical deterioration. The cost approach is widely used to estimate fair values for many tangible assets acquired in business combinations such as property, plant, and equipment.

Goodwill, and Gains on Bargain Purchases

As discussed above, the parent records both the consideration transferred and the individual amounts of the identified assets acquired and liabilities assumed at their acquisition-date fair values. However, in many cases the respective collective amounts of these two values will differ. Current GAAP requires an asymmetrical accounting for the difference—in one situation the acquirer recognizes an asset, in the other a gain.

For combinations resulting in complete ownership by the acquirer, the acquirer recognizes the asset goodwill as the excess of the consideration transferred over the collective fair values of the net identified assets acquired and liabilities assumed. Goodwill is defined as an asset representing the future economic benefits arising in a business combination that are not individually identified and separately recognized. Essentially, goodwill embodies the expected synergies that the acquirer expects to achieve through control of the acquired firm's assets.

Conversely, if the collective fair value of the net identified assets acquired and liabilities assumed exceeds the consideration transferred, the acquirer recognizes a "gain on bargain purchase." In such cases, the fair value of the net assets acquired replaces the consideration transferred as the valuation basis for the acquired firm. Bargain purchases can result from business divestitures forced by regulatory agencies or other types of distress sales. Before recognizing

---

[12] Exceptions to the fair-value measurement principle include deferred taxes, certain employee benefits, indemnification assets, reacquired rights, share-based awards, and assets held for sale.

a gain on bargain purchase, however, the acquirer must reassess whether it has correctly identified and measured all of the acquired assets and liabilities. Illustrations and further discussions of goodwill and of bargain purchase gains follow in the next section.

PROCEDURES FOR CONSOLIDATING FINANCIAL INFORMATION

Legal as well as accounting distinctions divide business combinations into several separate categories. To facilitate the introduction of consolidation accounting, we present the various procedures utilized in this process according to the following sequence:

1. Acquisition method when dissolution takes place.
2. Acquisition method when separate incorporation is maintained.

As a basis for this coverage, assume that Smallport Company owns computers, telecommunications equipment, and software that allow its customers to implement billing and ordering systems through the Internet. Although the computers and equipment have a book value of $400,000, they have a current fair value of $600,000. The software developed by Smallport has only a $100,000 value on its books; the costs of developing it were primarily expensed as incurred. The software's observable fair value, however, is $1,200,000. Similarly, although not reflected in its financial records, Smallport has several large ongoing customer contracts. BigNet estimates the fair value of the customer contracts at $700,000. Smallport also has a $200,000 note payable incurred to help finance the software development. Because interest rates are currently low, this liability (incurred at a higher rate of interest) has a present value of $250,000.

BigNet Company owns Internet communications equipment and other business software applications that complement those of Smallport. BigNet wants to expand its operations and plans to acquire Smallport on December 31. Exhibit 2.3 lists the accounts reported by both BigNet and Smallport on that date. In addition, the estimated fair values of Smallport's assets and liabilities are included.

Smallport's net assets (assets less liabilities) have a book value of $600,000 but a fair value of $2,550,000. Only the assets and liabilities have been appraised here; the capital stock, retained earnings, dividend, revenue, and expense accounts represent historical measurements rather than any type of future values. Although these equity and income accounts can give some indication of the organization's overall worth, they are not property and thus not transferred in the combination.

EXHIBIT 2.3 **Basic Consolidation Information**

	BigNet Company Book Values December 31	Smallport Company Book Values December 31	Smallport Company Fair Values December 31
Current assets	$ 1,100,000	$ 300,000	$ 300,000
Computers and equipment (net).	1,300,000	400,000	600,000
Capitalized software (net)	500,000	100,000	1,200,000
Customer contracts	–0–	–0–	700,000
Notes payable	(300,000)	(200,000)	(250,000)
Net assets	**$ 2,600,000**	**$ 600,000**	**$2,550,000**
Common stock—$10 par value	$(1,600,000)		
Common stock—$5 par value		$(100,000)	
Additional paid-in capital	(40,000)	(20,000)	
Retained earnings, 1/1	(870,000)	(370,000)	
Dividends paid	110,000	10,000	
Revenues	(1,000,000)	(500,000)	
Expenses	800,000	380,000	
Owners' equity 12/31	**$(2,600,000)**	**$(600,000)**	
Retained earnings, 12/31	(960,000)*	(480,000)*	

*Retained earnings balance after closing out revenues, expenses, and dividends paid.
Parentheses indicate credit balances.

LO5

Determine the total fair value of the consideration transferred for an acquisition and allocate that fair value to specific subsidiary assets acquired (including goodwill), and liabilities assumed, or a gain on bargain purchase.

LO6

Prepare the journal entry to consolidate the accounts of a subsidiary if dissolution takes place.

Acquisition Method When Dissolution Takes Place

At the date control is obtained with complete ownership, the acquisition method typically records the combination recognizing

- the fair value of the consideration transferred by the acquiring firm to the former owners of the acquiree and
- the identified assets acquired and liabilities assumed at their individual fair values

However, the entry to record the combination further depends on the relation between the consideration transferred and the net amount of the fair values assigned to the identified assets acquired and liabilities assumed. Therefore, we initially provide three illustrations that demonstrate the procedures to record a business combination, each with different amounts of consideration transferred relative to the acquired asset and liability fair values. Each example assumes a merger takes place and, therefore, the acquired firm is dissolved.

Consideration Transferred Equals Net Fair Values of Identified Assets Acquired and Liabilities Assumed

Assume that after negotiations with the owners of Smallport, BigNet agrees to pay $2,550,000 (cash of $550,000 and 20,000 unissued shares of its $10 par value common stock that is currently selling for $100 per share) for all of Smallport's assets and liabilities. Smallport then dissolves itself as a legal entity. As is typical, the $2,550,000 fair value of the consideration transferred by BigNet represents the fair value of the acquired Smallport business.

The $2,550,000 consideration transferred will serve as the basis for recording the combination in total. BigNet also must record all of Smallport's identified assets and liabilities at their individual fair values. These two valuations present no difficulties because BigNet's consideration transferred exactly equals the $2,550,000 collective net fair values of the individual assets and liabilities acquired.

Because Smallport Company will be dissolved, BigNet (the surviving company) directly records a consolidation entry in its financial records. Under the acquisition method, BigNet records Smallport's assets and liabilities at fair value ignoring original book values. Revenue, expense, dividend, and equity accounts cannot be transferred to a parent and are omitted in recording the business combination.

Acquisition Method: Consideration Transferred Equals Net Identified Asset Fair Values—Subsidiary Dissolved

BigNet Company's Financial Records—December 31		
Current Assets	300,000	
Computers and Equipment	600,000	
Capitalized Software	1,200,000	
Customer Contracts	700,000	
Notes Payable		250,000
Cash (paid by BigNet)		550,000
Common Stock (20,000 shares issued by BigNet at $10 par value)		200,000
Additional Paid-In Capital		1,800,000
To record acquisition of Smallport Company. Assets acquired and liabilities assumed are recorded at fair value.		

BigNet's financial records now show $1,900,000 in the Computers and Equipment account ($1,300,000 former balance + $600,000 acquired), $1,700,000 in Capitalized Software ($500,000 + $1,200,000), and so forth. Note that the customer contracts, despite being unrecorded on Smallport's books, are nonetheless identified and recognized on BigNet's financial records as part of the assets acquired in the combination. These items have been added into BigNet's balances (see Exhibit 2.3) at their fair values. Conversely, BigNet's revenue balance continues to report the company's own $1,000,000 with expenses remaining at $800,000 and dividends of $110,000. Under the acquisition method, only the subsidiary's revenues, expenses, dividends, and equity transactions that occur subsequent to the takeover affect the business combination.

Consideration Transferred Exceeds Net Amount of Fair Values of Identified Assets Acquired and Liabilities Assumed

In this next illustration BigNet agrees to pay $3,000,000 in exchange for all of Smallport's assets and liabilities. BigNet transfers to the former owners of Smallport consideration of $1,000,000 in cash plus 20,000 shares of common stock with a fair value of $100 per share. The resulting consideration paid is $450,000 more than the $2,550,000 fair value of Smallport's net assets.

Several factors may have affected BigNet's $3,000,000 acquisition offer. First, BigNet may expect its assets to act in concert with those of Smallport, thus creating synergies that will produce profits beyond the total expected for the separate companies. In our earlier examples, Bank of America, InBev, and Pfizer all clearly expect substantial synergies from their acquisitions. Other factors such as Smallport's history of profitability, its reputation, the quality of its personnel, and the economic condition of the industry in which it operates may also enter into acquisition offers. In general, if a target company is projected to generate unusually high profits relative to its asset base, acquirers are frequently willing to pay a premium price.

When the consideration transferred in an acquisition exceeds total net fair value of the identified assets and liabilities, the excess is allocated to an unidentifiable asset known as goodwill.[13] Unlike other assets, we consider goodwill as unidentifiable because we presume it emerges from several other assets acting together to produce an expectation of enhanced profitability. Goodwill essentially captures all sources of profitability beyond what can be expected from simply summing the fair values of the acquired firm's assets and liabilities.

Returning to BigNet's $3,000,000 consideration, $450,000 is in excess of the fair value of Smallport's net assets. Thus, goodwill of that amount is entered into BigNet's accounting system along with the fair value of each individual asset and liability. BigNet makes the following journal entry at the date of acquisition:

Acquisition Method: Consideration Transferred Exceeds Net Identified Asset Fair Values—Subsidiary Dissolved

BigNet Company's Financial Records—December 31		
Current Assets	300,000	
Computers and Equipment	600,000	
Capitalized Software	1,200,000	
Customer Contracts	700,000	
Goodwill	450,000	
Notes Payable		250,000
Cash (paid by BigNet)		1,000,000
Common Stock (20,000 shares issued by BigNet at $10 par value)		200,000
Additional Paid-In Capital		1,800,000
To record acquisition of Smallport Company. Assets acquired and liabilities assumed are recorded at individual fair values with excess fair value attributed to goodwill.		

Once again, BigNet's financial records now show $1,900,000 in the Computers and Equipment account ($1,300,000 former balance + $600,000 acquired), $1,700,000 in Capitalized Software ($500,000 + $1,200,000), and so forth. As the only change, BigNet records goodwill of $450,000 for the excess consideration paid over the net identified asset fair values.[14]

[13] In business combinations, such excess payments are not unusual. When Oracle acquired PeopleSoft, it initially assigned $4.5 billion of its $11 billion purchase price to the fair value of the acquired identified net assets. It assigned the remaining $6.5 billion to goodwill.

[14] As discussed in Chapter 3, the assets and liabilities (including goodwill) acquired in a business combination are assigned to reporting units of the combined entity. A reporting unit is simply a line of business (often a segment) in which an acquired asset or liability will be employed. The objective of assigning acquired assets and liabilities to reporting units is to facilitate periodic goodwill impairment testing.

Bargain Purchase—Consideration Transferred Is Less Than Net Amount of Fair Values of Identified Assets Acquired and Liabilities Assumed

Occasionally, the fair value received in an acquisition will exceed the fair value of the consideration transferred by the acquirer. Such bargain purchases typically are considered anomalous. Businesses generally do not sell assets or businesses at prices below their fair values. Nonetheless, bargain purchases do occur—most often in forced or distressed sales.

For example, Westamerica Bank's February 2009 acquisition of County Bank (California) from the FDIC resulted in a $48.8 million dollar "bargain purchase" gain. The FDIC sold the failed County Bank to Westamerica for $0 and additional guarantees. As a result, Westamerica recorded the combination at the estimated fair value of the net assets acquired and recognized a gain of $48.8 million. This gain treatment is consistent with the view that the acquiring firm is immediately better off by the amount that the fair value acquired in the business combination exceeds the consideration transferred.

To demonstrate accounting for a bargain purchase, our third illustration begins with BigNet transferring consideration of $2,000,000 to the owners of Smallport in exchange for their business. BigNet conveys no cash and issues 20,000 shares of common stock having a $100 per share fair value.

In accounting for this acquisition, at least two competing fair values are present. First, the $2,000,000 consideration transferred for Smallport represents a negotiated transaction value for the business. Second, the net amount of fair values individually assigned to the identified assets acquired and liabilities assumed produces $2,550,000. Additionally, based on expected synergies with Smallport, BigNet's management may believe that the fair value of the business exceeds the net asset fair value. Nonetheless, because the consideration transferred is less than the net asset fair value, a bargain purchase has occurred.

The acquisition method records the identified assets acquired and liabilities assumed at their individual fair values. In a bargain purchase situation, this net asset fair value effectively replaces the consideration transferred as the acquired firm's valuation basis for financial reporting. The consideration transferred serves as the acquired firm's valuation basis only if the consideration equals or exceeds the net amount of fair values for the assets acquired and liabilities assumed (as in the first two examples). In this case, however, the $2,000,000 consideration paid is less than the $2,550,000 net asset fair value, indicating a bargain purchase. Thus, the $2,550,000 net asset fair value serves as the valuation basis for the combination. A $550,000 *gain on bargain purchase* results because the $2,550,000 recorded value is accompanied by a payment of only $2,000,000. The acquirer recognizes this gain on its income statement in the period the acquisition takes place.

Acquisition Method: Consideration Transferred Is Less Than Net Identified Asset Fair Values, Subsidiary Dissolved

BigNet Company's Financial Records—December 31		
Current Assets	300,000	
Computers and Equipment	600,000	
Capitalized Software	1,200,000	
Customer Contracts	700,000	
Notes Payable		250,000
Common Stock (20,000 shares issued by BigNet at $10 par value)		200,000
Additional Paid-In Capital		1,800,000
Gain on Bargain Purchase		550,000
To record acquisition of Smallport Company. Assets acquired and liabilities assumed are each recorded at fair value. Excess net asset fair value is attributed to a gain on bargain purchase.		

A consequence of implementing a fair-value concept to acquisition accounting is the recognition of an unrealized gain on the bargain purchase. A criticism of the gain recognition is that the acquirer recognizes profit from a buying activity that occurs prior to traditional accrual measures of earned income (i.e., selling activity). Nonetheless, an exception to the general rule

EXHIBIT 2.4
Acquisition Method—Accounting for Expenses Frequently Associated with Business Combinations

Direct combination expenses (e.g., accounting, legal, investment banking, appraisal fees, etc.)	Expense as incurred
Indirect combination expenses (e.g., internal costs such as allocated secretarial or managerial time)	Expense as incurred
Amounts incurred to register and issue securities	Reduce the value assigned to the fair value of the securities issued (typically a debit to additional paid-in capital)

of recording business acquisitions at fair value of the consideration transferred occurs in the rare circumstance of a bargain purchase. Thus, in a bargain purchase, the fair values of the assets received and all liabilities assumed in a business combination are considered more relevant for asset valuation than the consideration transferred.

Related Expenses of Business Combinations

Three additional categories of expenses typically accompany business combinations. First, firms often engage attorneys, accountants, investment bankers, and other professionals for services related to the business combination. The acquisition method does not consider such expenditures as part of the fair value received by the acquirer. Therefore, professional service fees are expensed in the period incurred. The second category of expenses concerns an acquiring firm's internal costs. Examples include secretarial and management time allocated to the acquisition activity. Such indirect expenditures are reported as current year expenses, too. Finally, amounts incurred to register and issue securities in connection with a business combination simply reduce the otherwise determinable fair value of the securities. Exhibit 2.4 summarizes the three categories of related payments that accompany a business combination and their respective accounting treatments.

To illustrate the accounting treatment of these expenditures that frequently accompany business combination, assume the following in connection with BigNet's acquisition of Smallport (also see Exhibit 2.3).

- BigNet issues 20,000 shares of its $10 par common stock with a fair value of $2,600,000 in exchange for all of Smallport's assets and liabilities.
- BigNet pays an additional $100,000 in accounting and attorney fees.
- Internal secretarial and administrative costs of $75,000 are indirectly attributable to BigNet's combination with Smallport
- Cost to register and issue BigNet's securities issued in the combination total $20,000.

Following the acquisition method, BigNet would record these transactions as follows:

BigNet Company's Financial Records		
Current Assets	300,000	
Computers and Equipment	600,000	
Capitalized Software	1,200,000	
Customer Contracts	700,000	
Goodwill	50,000	
Notes Payable		250,000
Common Stock (20,000 shares issued by BigNet at $10 par value)		200,000
Additional Paid-In Capital		2,400,000
To record Smallport acquisition for $2,600,000 consideration transferred.		
Professional services expense	100,000	
Cash		100,000
To record as expenses of the current period any direct combination costs.		
Salaries and Administrative Expenses	75,000	
Accounts Payable (or Cash)		75,000
To record as expenses of the current period any indirect combination costs.		

Additional Paid-In Capital	20,000	
Cash		20,000
To record costs to register and issue stock in connection with the Smallport acquisition.		

Summary of the Acquisition Method

For combinations resulting in complete ownership, the fair value of the consideration transferred by the acquiring firm provides the starting point for recording a business combination at the date of acquisition. With few exceptions, the separately identified assets acquired and liabilities assumed are recorded at their individual fair values. Goodwill is recognized if the fair value of the consideration transferred exceeds the net identified asset fair value. If the net identified asset fair value of the business acquired exceeds the consideration transferred, a gain on a bargain purchase is recognized and reported in current income of the combined entity. Exhibit 2.5 summarizes possible allocations using the acquisition method.

LO7

Prepare a worksheet to consolidate the accounts of two companies that form a business combination if dissolution does not take place.

The Acquisition Method When Separate Incorporation Is Maintained

When each company retains separate incorporation in a business combination, many aspects of the consolidation process are identical to those demonstrated in the previous section. Fair value, for example, remains the basis for initially consolidating the subsidiary's assets and liabilities.

However, several significant differences are evident in combinations in which each company remains a legally incorporated separate entity. Most noticeably, the consolidation of the financial information is only simulated; the acquiring company does not physically record the acquired assets and liabilities. Because dissolution does not occur, each company maintains independent record-keeping. To facilitate the preparation of consolidated financial statements, a worksheet and consolidation entries are employed using data gathered from these separate companies.

A worksheet provides the structure for generating financial reports for the single economic entity. An integral part of this process involves consolidation worksheet entries. *These adjustments and eliminations are entered on the worksheet and represent alterations that would be required if the financial records were physically united.* Because no actual union occurs, neither company ever records consolidation entries in its journals. Instead, they appear solely on the worksheet to derive consolidated balances for financial reporting purposes.

To illustrate using the Exhibit 2.3 information, assume that BigNet acquires Smallport Company on December 31 by issuing 26,000 shares of $10 par value common stock valued at $100 per share (or $2,600,000 in total). BigNet pays fees of $40,000 to a third party for its assistance in arranging the transaction. Then to settle a difference of opinion regarding Smallport's fair value, BigNet promises to pay an additional $83,200 to the former owners if Smallport's earnings exceed $300,000 during the next annual period. BigNet estimates a 25 percent

EXHIBIT 2.5
Consolidation Values—
The Acquisition Method

Consideration transferred equals the fair values of net identified assets acquired.	Identified assets acquired and liabilities assumed are recorded at their fair values.
Consideration transferred is greater than the fair values of net identified assets acquired.	Identified assets acquired and liabilities assumed are recorded at their fair values. The excess consideration transferred over the net identified asset fair value is recorded as goodwill.
Bargain purchase—consideration transferred is less than the fair values of net identified assets acquired. The total of the individual fair values of the net identified assets acquired effectively becomes the acquired business fair value.	Identified assets acquired and liabilities assumed are recorded at their fair values. The excess amount of net identified asset fair value over the consideration transferred is recorded as a gain on bargain purchase.

probability that the $83,200 contingent payment will be required. A discount rate of 4 percent (to represent the time value of money) yields an expected present value of $20,000 for the contingent liability ($83,200 $\times$ 25% $\times$ 0.961538). The fair-value approach of the acquisition method views such contingent payments as part of the consideration transferred. According to this view, contingencies have value to those who receive the consideration and represent measurable obligations of the acquirer. Therefore, the fair value of the consideration transferred in this example consists of the following two elements:

Fair value of securities issued by BigNet	$2,600,000
Fair value of contingent performance liability	20,000
Total fair value of consideration transferred	$2,620,000

To facilitate a possible future spinoff, BigNet maintains Smallport as a separate corporation with its independent accounting information system intact. Therefore, whenever financial statements for the combined entity are prepared, BigNet utilizes a worksheet in simulating the consolidation of these two companies. Although the assets and liabilities are not transferred, BigNet must still record the payment made to Smallport's owners. When the subsidiary remains separate, the parent establishes an investment account that initially reflects the acquired firm's acquisition-date fair value. Because Smallport maintains its separate identity, BigNet prepares the following journal entries on its books to record the business combination.

Acquisition Method—Subsidiary Is Not Dissolved

BigNet Company's Financial Records—December 31		
Investment in Smallport Company (consideration transferred)	2,620,000	
Contingent Performance Liability		20,000
Common Stock (26,000 shares issued by BigNet at $10 par value)		260,000
Additional Paid-In Capital (value of shares in excess of par value)		2,340,000
Professional Services Expense	40,000	
Cash (paid for third-party fees)		40,000
To record acquisition of Smallport Company, which maintains its separate legal identity.		

As demonstrated in Exhibit 2.6, a worksheet can be prepared on the date of acquisition to arrive at consolidated totals for this combination. The entire process consists of seven steps.

Step 1

Prior to constructing a worksheet, the parent prepares a formal allocation of the acquisition-date fair value similar to the equity method procedures presented in Chapter 1.[15] Thus, the following schedule is appropriate for BigNet's acquisition of Smallport:

Acquisition-Date Fair Value Allocation Schedule

Fair value of consideration transferred by BigNet		$2,620,000
Book value of Smallport (see Exhibit 2.3)		600,000
Excess of fair value over book value		$2,020,000
Allocations made to specific accounts based on acquisition-date fair and book value differences:		
Computers and equipment ($600,000 − $400,000)	$ 200,000	
Capitalized software ($1,200,000 − $100,000)	1,100,000	
Customer contracts ($700,000 − 0)	700,000	
Notes payable ($250,000 − $200,000)	(50,000)	1,950,000
Excess fair value not identified with specific items—Goodwill		$ 70,000

---

[15] This allocation procedure is helpful but not critical if dissolution occurs. The asset and liability accounts are simply added directly into the parent's books at their acquisition-date fair value with any excess assigned to goodwill as shown in the previous sections of this chapter.

EXHIBIT 2.6 Acquisition Method—Date of Acquisition

Accounts	BigNet	Smallport	Consolidation Entries		Consolidated Totals
			Debits	Credits	
Income Statement					
Revenues	(1,000,000)				(1,000,000)
Expenses	840,000*				840,000
Net income	(160,000)				(160,000)
Statement of Retained Earnings					
Retained earnings, 1/1	(870,000)				(870,000)
Net income (above)	(160,000)*				(160,000)
Dividends paid	110,000				110,000
Retained earnings, 12/31	(920,000)				(920,000)
Balance Sheet					
Current Assets	1,060,000*	300,000			1,360,000
Investment in Smallport Company	2,620,000*	–0–		(S) 600,000	–0–
				(A) 2,020,000	
Computers and equipment	1,300,000	400,000	(A) 200,000		1,900,000
Capitalized software	500,000	100,000	(A) 1,100,000		1,700,000
Customer contracts	–0–	–0–	(A) 700,000		700,000
Goodwill	–0–	–0–	(A) 70,000		70,000
Total assets	5,480,000	800,000			5,730,000
Note Payable	(300,000)	(200,000)		(A) 50,000	(550,000)
Contingent performance liability	(20,000)*				(20,000)
Common stock	(1,860,000)*	(100,000)	(S) 100,000		(1,860,000)
Additional paid-in capital	(2,380,000)*	(20,000)	(S) 20,000		(2,380,000)
Retained earnings, 12/31 (above)	(920,000)	(480,000)	(S) 480,000		(920,000)
Total liabilities and equities	(5,480,000)	(800,000)	2,670,000	2,670,000	(5,730,000)

Note: Parentheses indicate a credit balance
*Balances have been adjusted for consideration transferred and payment of consolidation costs. Also note follow-through effects to net income and retained earnings from the expensing of the direct acquisition costs.
(S) Elimination of Smallport's stockholders' equity accounts as of December 31 and book value portion of the investment account.
(A) Allocation of BigNet's consideration fair value in excess of book value.

Note that this schedule initially subtracts Smallport's acquisition-date book value. The resulting $2,020,000 difference represents the total amount needed on the Exhibit 2.6 worksheet to adjust Smallport's individual assets and liabilities from book value to fair value (and to recognize goodwill). Next, the schedule shows how this $2,020,000 total is allocated to adjust each individual item to fair value. The fair-value allocation schedule thus effectively serves as a convenient supporting schedule for the Exhibit 2.6 worksheet and is routinely prepared for every consolidation.

No part of the $2,020,000 excess fair value is attributed to the current assets because their book values equal their fair values. The Notes Payable account shows a negative allocation because the debt's present value exceeds its book value. An increase in debt decreases the fair value of the company's net assets.

Step 2

The first two columns of the worksheet (see Exhibit 2.6) show the separate companies' acquisition-date financial figures (see Exhibit 2.3). BigNet's accounts have been adjusted for the investment entry recorded earlier. As another preliminary step, Smallport's revenue, expense, and dividend accounts have been closed into its Retained Earnings account. The subsidiary's operations prior to the December 31 takeover have no direct bearing on the operating results of the business combination. These activities occurred before Smallport was acquired; thus, the new owner should not include any precombination subsidiary revenues or expenses in the consolidated statements.

Step 3

Consolidation Entry S eliminates Smallport's stockholders' equity accounts (S is a reference to beginning subsidiary Stockholders' equity). These balances (Common Stock, Additional Paid-In Capital, and Retained Earnings) represent ownership accounts held by the parent in their entirety and thus no longer are outstanding. By removing these accounts, only Smallport's assets and liabilities remain to be combined with the parent company figures.

Step 4

Consolidation Entry S also removes the $600,000 component of the Investment in Smallport Company account that equates to the book value of the subsidiary's net assets. For external reporting purposes, BigNet should include each of Smallport's assets and liabilities rather than a single investment balance. In effect, this portion of the Investment in Smallport Company account is deleted and replaced by the specific assets and liabilities that it represents.

Step 5

Entry A removes the $2,020,000 excess payment in the Investment in Smallport Company and assigns it to the specific accounts indicated by the fair-value allocation schedule. Consequently, Computers and Equipment is increased by $200,000 to agree with Smallport's fair value: $1,100,000 is attributed to Capitalized Software, $700,000 to Customer Contracts, and $50,000 to Notes Payable. The unidentified excess of $70,000 is allocated to goodwill. This entry is labeled Entry A to indicate that it represents the Allocations made in connection with Smallport's acquisition-date fair value. It also completes the Investment in Smallport account balance elimination.

Step 6

All accounts are extended into the Consolidated Totals column. For accounts such as Current Assets, this process simply adds Smallport and BigNet book values. However, when applicable, this extension also includes any allocations to establish the acquisition-date fair values of Smallport's assets and liabilities. Computers and Equipment, for example, is increased by $200,000. By increasing the subsidiary's book value to fair value, the reported balances are the same as in the previous examples when dissolution occurred. The use of a worksheet does not alter the consolidated figures but only the method of deriving those numbers.

Step 7

We subtract consolidated expenses from revenues to arrive at a $160,000 net income. Note that because this is an acquisition-date worksheet, we consolidate no amounts for Smallport's revenues and expenses. Having just been acquired, Smallport has not yet earned any income for BigNet owners. Consolidated revenues, expenses, and net income are identical to BigNet's balances. Subsequent to acquisition, of course, Smallport's income accounts will be consolidated with BigNet's (coverage of this topic begins in Chapter 3).

Worksheet Mechanics

In general, totals (such as Net Income and Ending Retained Earnings) are not directly consolidated across on the worksheet. Rather, the components (such as revenues and expenses) are extended across and then combined vertically to derive the appropriate figure. Net income is then carried down on the worksheet to the statement of retained earnings and used (along with beginning retained earnings and dividends paid) to compute the December 31 Retained Earnings balance. In the same manner, ending Retained Earnings of $920,000 is entered into the balance sheet to arrive at total liabilities and equities of $5,730,000, a number that reconciles with the total of consolidated assets.

The balances in the final column of Exhibit 2.6 are used to prepare consolidated financial statements for the business combination of BigNet Company and Smallport Company. The worksheet entries serve as a catalyst to bring together the two independent sets of financial information. The actual accounting records of both BigNet and Smallport remain unaltered by this consolidation process.

ACQUISITION-DATE FAIR-VALUE ALLOCATIONS—ADDITIONAL ISSUES

LO8

Describe the two criteria for recognizing intangible assets apart from goodwill in a business combination.

Intangibles

An important element of acquisition accounting is the acquirer's recognition and measurement of the assets acquired and liabilities assumed in the combination. In particular, the advent of the information age brings new measurement challenges for a host of intangible assets that provide value in generating future cash flows. Intangible assets often comprise the largest proportion of an acquired firm. For example, when AT&T acquired AT&T Broadband, it allocated approximately $19 billion of the $52 billion purchase price to franchise costs. These franchise costs form an intangible asset representing the value attributed to agreements with local authorities that allow access to homes.

Intangible assets include both current and noncurrent assets (not including financial instruments) that lack physical substance. In determining whether to recognize an intangible asset in a business combination, two specific criteria are essential.

1. Does the intangible asset arise from contractual or other legal rights?
2. Is the intangible asset capable of being sold or otherwise separated from the acquired enterprise?

Intangibles arising from contractual or legal rights are commonplace in business combinations. Often identified among the assets acquired are trademarks, patents, copyrights, franchise agreements, and a number of other intangibles that derive their value from governmental protection (or other contractual agreements) that allow a firm exclusive use of the asset. Most intangible assets recognized in business combinations meet the contractual-legal criterion.

Also seen in business combinations are intangible assets meeting the separability criterion. An acquired intangible asset is recognized if it is capable of being separated or divided from the acquiree and sold, transferred, licensed, rented, or exchanged individually or together with a related contract, identifiable asset, or liability. The acquirer is not required to have the intention to sell, license, or otherwise exchange the intangible in order to meet the separability criterion. For example, an acquiree may have developed internally a valuable customer list or other noncontractual customer relationships. Although the value of these items may not have arisen from a specific legal right, they nonetheless convey benefits to the acquirer that may be separable through sale, license, or exchange.

Exhibit 2.7 provides an extensive listing of intangible assets with indications of whether they typically meet the legal/contractual or separability criteria.

The FASB (Exposure Draft, *Business Combinations and Intangible Assets,* para. 271) recognized the inherent difficulties in estimating the separate fair values of many intangibles and stated that

> Difficulties may arise in assigning the acquisition cost to individual intangible assets acquired in a basket purchase such as a business combination. Measuring some of those assets is less difficult than measuring other assets, particularly if they are exchangeable and traded regularly in the marketplace. . . . Nonetheless, even those assets that cannot be measured on that basis may have more cash flow streams directly or indirectly associated with them than can be used as the basis for measuring them. While the resulting measures may lack the precision of other measures, they provide information that is more representationally faithful than would be the case if those assets were simply subsumed into goodwill on the grounds of measurement difficulties.

Undoubtedly, as our knowledge economy continues its rapid growth, asset allocations to items such as those identified in Exhibit 2.7 are expected to be frequent.

Preexisting Goodwill on Subsidiary's Books

In our examples of business combinations so far, the assets acquired and liabilities assumed have all been specifically identifiable (e.g., current assets, capitalized software, computers and equipment, customer contracts, and notes payable). However, in many cases, an acquired firm has an unidentifiable asset (i.e., goodwill recorded on its books in connection with a previous business combination of its own). A question arises as to the parent's treatment of this preexisting goodwill on the newly acquired subsidiary's books.

EXHIBIT 2.7   **Illustrative Examples of Intangible Assets That Meet the Criteria for Recognition Separately from Goodwill (FASB ASC paragraphs 805-20-55-11 through 45)**

The following are examples of intangible assets that meet the criteria for recognition as an asset apart from goodwill. The following illustrative list is not intended to be all-inclusive; thus, an acquired intangible asset could meet the recognition criteria of this statement but not be included on that list. Assets designated by the symbol [c] are those that would generally be recognized separately from goodwill because they meet the contractual-legal criterion. Assets designated by the symbol [s] do not arise from contractual or other legal rights but should nonetheless be recognized separately from goodwill because they meet the separability criterion. The determination of whether a specific acquired intangibile asset meets the criteria in this statement for recognition apart from goodwill should be based on the facts and circumstances of each individual business combination.*

Marketing-Related Intangible Assets

1. Trademarks, trade names.[c]
2. Service marks, collective marks, certification marks.[c]
3. Trade dress (unique color, shape, or package design).[c]
4. Newspaper mastheads.[c]
5. Internet domain names.[c]
6. Noncompetition agreements.[c]

Customer-Related Intangible Assets

1. Customer lists.[s]
2. Order or production backlog.[c]
3. Customer contracts and related customer relationships.[c]
4. Noncontractual customer relationships.[s]

Artistic-Related Intangible Assets

1. Plays, operas, and ballets.[c]
2. Books, magazines, newspapers, and other literary works.[c]
3. Musical works such as compositions, song lyrics, advertising jingles.[c]
4. Pictures and photographs.[c]
5. Video and audiovisual material, including motion pictures, music videos, and television programs.[c]

Contract-Based Intangible Assets

1. Licensing, royalty, standstill agreements.[c]
2. Advertising, construction, management, service, or supply contracts.[c]
3. Lease agreements.[c]
4. Construction permits.[c]
5. Franchise agreements.[c]
6. Operating and broadcast rights.[c]
7. Use rights such as landing, drilling, water, air, mineral, timber cutting, and route authorities.[c]
8. Servicing contracts such as mortgage servicing contracts.[c]
9. Employment contracts.[c]

Technology-Based Intangible Assets

1. Patented technology.[c]
2. Computer software and mask works.[c]
3. Unpatented technology.[s]
4. Databases, including title plants.[s]
5. Trade secrets, including secret formulas, processes, recipes.[c]

*The intangible assets designated by the symbol (c) also could meet the separability criterion. However, separability is not a necessary condition for an asset to meet the contractual-legal criterion.

By its very nature, such preexisting goodwill is not considered identifiable by the parent. Therefore, the new owner simply ignores it in allocating the acquisition-date fair value. The logic is that the total business fair value is first allocated to the identified assets and liabilities. Only if an excess amount remains after recognizing the fair values of the net identified assets is any goodwill recognized. Thus, in all business combinations, only goodwill reflected in the current acquisition is brought forward in the consolidated entity's financial reports.

Acquired In-Process Research and Development

The accounting for a business combination begins with the identification of the tangible and intangible assets acquired and liabilities assumed by the acquirer. The fair values of the individual assets and liabilities then provide the basis for financial statement valuations. Recently, many firms—especially those in pharmaceutical and high-tech industries—have allocated significant portions of acquired businesses to in-process research and development (IPR&D).

In a marked departure from past practice, current standards now require that acquired IPR&D be measured at acquisition-date fair value and recognized in consolidated financial statements as an asset. In commenting on the nature of IPR&D as an asset, Pfizer in an October 28, 2005, comment letter to the FASB observed that

> Board members know that companies frame business strategies around IPR&D, negotiate for it, pay for it, fair value it, and nurture it and they view those seemingly rational actions as inconsistent with the notion that IPR&D has no probable future economic benefit.

For example, ARCA Biopharma acquired a significant in-process research and development IPR&D asset through a merger with Nuvelo in early 2009. As ARCA Biopharma noted in its March 31, 2009, financial statements:

> A valuation firm was engaged to assist ARCA in determining the estimated fair values of these (IPR&D) assets as of the acquisition date. Discounted cash flow models are typically used in these valuations, and the models require the use of significant estimates and assumptions including but not limited to:
>
> • Projecting regulatory approvals.
> • Estimating future cash flows from product sales resulting from completed products and in-process projects.
> • Developing appropriate discount rates and probability rates by project.

The IPR&D asset is initially considered an indefinite-lived intangible asset and is not subject to amortization. IPR&D is then tested for impairment annually or more frequently if events or changes in circumstances indicate that the asset might be impaired.

Recognizing acquired IPR&D as an asset is clearly consistent with the FASB's fair-value approach to acquisition accounting. Similar to costs that result in goodwill and other internally generated intangibles (e.g., customer lists, trade names, etc.), IPR&D costs are expensed as incurred in ongoing business activities. However, a business combination is considered a significant recognition event for which all fair values transferred in the transaction should be fully accounted for, including any values assigned to IPR&D. Moreover, because the acquirer paid for the IPR&D, an expectation of future economic benefit is assumed and, therefore, the amount is recognized as an asset.

To illustrate further, assume that ClearTone Company pays $2,300,000 in cash for all assets and liabilities of Newave, Inc., in a merger transaction. ClearTone manufactures components for cell phones. The primary motivation for the acquisition is a particularly attractive research and development project under way at Newave that will extend a cell phone's battery life by up to 50 percent. ClearTone hopes to combine the new technology with its manufacturing process and projects a resulting substantial revenue increase. ClearTone is optimistic that Newave will finish the project in the next two years. At the acquisition date, ClearTone prepares the following schedule that recognizes the items of value it expects to receive from the Newave acquisition:

Consideration transferred		$2,300,000
Receivables	$ 55,000	
Patents	220,000	
In-process research and development	1,900,000	
Accounts payable	(175,000)	
Fair value of identified net assets acquired		2,000,000
Goodwill		$ 300,000

ClearTone records the transaction as follows:

Receivables	55,000	
Patents	220,000	
Research and development asset	1,900,000	
Goodwill	300,000	
Accounts payable		175,000
Cash		2,300,000

Research and development expenditures incurred subsequent to the date of acquisition will continue to be expensed. Acquired IPR&D assets should be considered initially indefinite-lived until the project is completed or abandoned. As with other indefinite-lived intangible assets, an acquired IPR&D asset is tested for impairment and is not amortized until its useful life is determined to be no longer indefinite.

CONVERGENCE BETWEEN U.S. AND INTERNATIONAL ACCOUNTING STANDARDS

The FASB ASC topics on Business Combinations (805) and Consolidations (810) represent outcomes of a joint project between the FASB and the International Accounting Standards Board (IASB). The primary objective of the project was stated as follows:

> to develop a single high-quality standard for business combinations that can be used for both domestic and cross-border financial reporting. The goal is to develop a standard that includes a common set of principles and related guidance that produces decision-useful information and minimizes exceptions to those principles. The standard should improve the completeness, relevance, and comparability of financial information about business combinations . . . (FASB Project Updates: *Business Combinations: Applying the Acquisition Method—Joint Project of the IASB and FASB:* October 25, 2007)

The IASB subsequently issued International Financial Reporting Standard 3 (*IFRS 3*) Revised (effective July 2009), which along with FASB ASC topics 805, Business Combinations, and 810, Consolidation, effectively converged the accounting for business combinations internationally. The two standards are identical in most important aspects of accounting for business combinations although differences can result in noncontrolling interest valuation and some other limited applications.[16] The joint project on business combinations represents one of the first successful implementations of the agreement between the two standard-setting groups to coordinate efforts on future work with the goal of developing high-quality comparable standards for both domestic and cross-border financial accounting.

LEGACY METHODS OF ACCOUNTING FOR BUSINESS COMBINATIONS

LO9

Identify the general characteristics of the purchase method and the general characteristics of a pooling of interests. Also recognize that although the pooling of interests and purchase methods are no longer applicable for new business combinations their financial reporting effects will be evident for decades to come.

The acquisition method provides the accounting for business combinations occurring in 2009 and thereafter. However, for decades, business combinations were accounted for using either the **purchase** or **pooling of interests** method. From 2002 through 2008, the purchase method was used exclusively for business combinations. Prior to 2002, financial reporting standards allowed two alternatives: the purchase method and the pooling of interests method. Because the FASB required prospective application of the acquisition method for 2009 and beyond, the purchase and pooling of interests methods continue to provide the basis for financial reporting for pre-2009 business combinations and thus will remain relevant for many years. Literally tens of thousands of past business combinations will continue to be reported in future financial statements under one of these legacy methods.

The Purchase Method: An Application of the Cost Principle

A basic principle of the purchase method was to record a business combination at the cost to the new owners. For example, several years ago MGM Grand, Inc., acquired Mirage Resorts, Inc., for approximately $6.4 billion. This purchase price continued to serve as the valuation basis for Mirage Resorts' assets and liabilities in the preparation of MGM Grand's consolidated financial statements.

Several elements of the purchase method reflect a strict application of the cost principle. The following items represent examples of how the cost-based purchase method differs from the fair-value-based acquisition method.

- Acquisition date allocations (including bargain purchases).
- Direct combination costs.
- Contingent consideration.
- In-process research and development.

We next briefly discuss the accounting treatment for these items across the current and previous financial reporting regimes.

---

[16] Chapter 4 of this text provides further discussion of noncontrolling interest accounting differences across U.S. GAAP and IFRS. Other differences are presented in chapters where the applicable topics are covered.

Purchase-Date Cost Allocations (Including Bargain Purchases)

In a business combination, the application of the cost principle often was complicated because literally hundreds of separate assets and liabilities were acquired. Accordingly, for asset valuation and future income determination, firms needed a basis to allocate the total cost among the various assets and liabilities received in the bargained exchange. Similar to the acquisition method, the purchase method based its cost allocations on the combination-date fair values of the acquired assets and liabilities. Also closely related to the acquisition method procedures, any excess of cost over the sum of the net identified asset fair values was attributed to goodwill.

But the purchase method stands in marked contrast to the acquisition method in bargain purchase situations. Under the purchase method, a bargain purchase occurred when the sum of the individual fair values of the acquired net assets exceeded the purchase cost. To record a bargain purchase at cost, however, the purchase method required that certain long-term assets be recorded at amounts below their assessed fair values.

For example, assume Adams Co. paid $520,000 for Brook Co. in 2008. Brook has the following assets with appraised fair values:

Accounts receivable	$ 15,000
Land	200,000
Building	400,000
Accounts payable	(5,000)
Total net fair value	$610,000

However, to record the combination at its $520,000 cost, Adams cannot use all of the above fair values. The purchase method solution was to require that Adams reduce the valuation assigned to the acquired long-term assets (land and building) proportionately by $90,000 ($610,000 − $520,000). The total fair value of the long-term assets, in this case $600,000, provided the basis for allocating the reduction. Thus, Adams would reduce the acquired land by (2/6 × $90,000) = $30,000 and the building by (4/6 × $90,000) = $60,000. Adams' journal entry to record the combination using the purchase method would then be as follows:

Accounts receivable	15,000	
Land ($200,000 − $30,000)	170,000	
Building ($400,000 − $60,000)	340,000	
Accounts payable		5,000
Cash		520,000

Note that the current assets and liabilities did not share in the proportionate reduction to cost. Long-term assets were subject to the reduction because their fair-value estimates were considered less reliable than current items and liabilities. Finally, in rare situations firms recognized an extraordinary gain on a purchase, but only in the very unusual case that the long-term assets were reduced to a zero valuation.

In contrast, the acquisition method embraces the fair-value concept and discards the consideration transferred as a valuation basis for the business acquired in a bargain purchase. Instead, the acquirer measures and recognizes the fair values of each of the assets acquired and liabilities assumed at the date of combination, regardless of the consideration transferred in the transaction. As a result, (1) no assets are recorded at amounts below their assessed fair values as is the case with bargain purchases accounted for by the purchase method and (2) a gain on bargain purchase is recognized at the acquisition date. Bargain purchases in acquisitions represent an exception to the general rule of valuing an acquisition at the consideration transferred by the acquirer.

Direct Combination Costs

Almost all business combinations employ professional services to assist in various phases of the transaction. Examples include target identification, due diligence regarding the value of an acquisition, financing, tax planning, and preparation of formal legal documents. Prior to 2009, under the purchase method, the investment cost basis included direct combination costs. In contrast, the acquisition method considers these costs as payments for services received, not part of the fair value exchanged for the business. Thus, under the acquisition method, direct combination costs are expensed as incurred.

Contingent Consideration

Often business combination negotiations result in agreements to provide additional payments to former owners if they meet specified future performance measures. The purchase method accounted for such contingent consideration obligations as post-combination adjustments to the purchase cost (or stockholders' equity if the contingency involved the parent's equity share value) upon resolution of the contingency. The acquisition method treats contingent consideration obligations as a negotiated component of the fair value of the consideration transferred, consistent with the fair value measurement attribute.

In-Process Research and Development (IPR&D)

Prior to 2009, financial reporting standards required the immediate expensing of acquired IPR&D if the project had not yet reached technological feasibility and the assets had no future alternative uses. Expensing acquired IPR&D was consistent with the accounting treatment for a firm's ongoing research and development costs. The acquisition method, however, requires tangible and intangible assets acquired in a business combination to be used in a particular research and development activity, including those that may have no alternative future use, to be recognized and measured at fair value at the acquisition date. These capitalized research and development costs are reported as intangible assets with indefinite lives subject to periodic impairment reviews. Moreover, because the acquirer identified and paid for the IPR&D, the acquisition method assumes an expectation of future economic benefit and therefore recognizes an asset.

The Pooling of Interests Method: Continuity of Previous Ownership

Historically, former owners of separate firms would agree to combine for their mutual benefit and continue as owners of a combined firm. It was asserted that the assets and liabilities of the former firms were never really bought or sold; former owners merely exchanged ownership shares to become joint owners of the combined firm. Combinations characterized by exchange of voting shares and continuation of previous ownership became known as pooling of interests. Rather than an exchange transaction with one ownership group replacing another, a pooling of interests was characterized by a continuity of ownership interests before and after the business combination. Prior to its elimination, this method was applied to a significant number of business combinations.[17] To reflect the continuity of ownership, two important steps characterized the pooling of interests method:

1. The book values of the assets and liabilities of both companies became the book values reported by the combined entity.
2. The revenue and expense accounts were combined retrospectively as well as prospectively. The idea of continuity of ownership gave support for the recognition of income accruing to the owners both before and after the combination.

Therefore, in a pooling, reported income was typically higher than under the contemporaneous purchase accounting. Under pooling, not only did the firms retrospectively combine incomes, but also the smaller asset bases resulted in smaller depreciation and amortization expenses. Because net income reported in financial statements often is used in a variety of contracts, including managerial compensation, managers considered the pooling method an attractive alternative to purchase accounting.

Prior to 2002, accounting and reporting standards allowed both the purchase and pooling of interest methods for business combinations. However, standard setters established strict criteria

---

[17] Past prominent business combinations accounted for by the pooling of interests method include ExxonMobil, Pfizer-Warner Lambert, Yahoo!-Broadcast.com, Pepsi-Quaker Oats, among thousands of others.

EXHIBIT 2.8
Precombination Information
for Baker Company

January 1	Book Values	Fair Values
Current assets	$ 30,000	$ 30,000
Internet domain name	160,000	300,000
Licensing agreements	0	500,000
In-process research and development	0	200,000
Notes payable	(25,000)	(25,000)
Total net assets	$165,000	$1,005,000

for use of the pooling method. The criteria were designed to prevent managers from engaging in purchase transactions and then reporting them as poolings of interests. Business combinations that failed to meet the pooling criteria had to be accounted for by the purchase method.

These criteria had two overriding objectives. First, to ensure the complete fusion of the two organizations, one company had to obtain substantially all (90 percent or more) of the voting stock of the other. The second general objective of these criteria was to prevent purchase combinations from being disguised as poolings. Past experience had shown that combination transactions were frequently manipulated so that they would qualify for pooling of interests treatment (usually to increase reported earnings). However, subsequent events, often involving cash being paid or received by the parties, revealed the true nature of the combination: One company was purchasing the other in a bargained exchange. A number of qualifying criteria for pooling of interests treatment were designed to stop this practice.

Comparisons across the Pooling of Interests, Purchase, and Acquisition Methods

To illustrate some of the differences across the purchase, pooling of interests, and acquisition methods, assume that on January 1, Archer, Inc., acquired Baker Company in exchange for 10,000 shares of its $1.00 par common stock having a fair value of $1,200,000 in a transaction structured as a merger. In connection with the acquisition, Archer paid $25,000 in legal and accounting fees. Also, Archer agreed to pay the former owners additional cash consideration contingent upon the completion of Baker's existing contracts at specified profit margins. The current fair value of the contingent obligation was estimated to be $150,000. Exhibit 2.8 provides Baker's combination-date book values and fair values.

Purchase Method Applied

Archer's valuation basis for its purchase of Baker is computed and allocated as follows:

Fair value of shares issued	$1,200,000
Direct combination costs (legal and accounting fees)	25,000
Cost of the Baker purchase	$1,225,000
Cost allocation:	
Current assets	$ 30,000
Internet domain name	300,000
Licensing agreements	500,000
Research and development expense	200,000
Notes payable	(25,000)
Total net fair value of items acquired	1,005,000
Goodwill	$ 220,000

Note the following characteristics of the purchase method from the above schedule.

- The valuation basis is cost and includes direct combination costs, but excludes the contingent consideration.

- The cost is allocated to the assets acquired and liabilities assumed based on their individual fair values (unless a bargain purchase occurs and then the long-term items may be recorded as amounts less than their fair values).

- Goodwill is the excess of cost of the fair values of the net assets purchase.
- Acquired in-process research and development is expensed immediately at the purchase date.

Pooling of Interests Method Applied

Because a purchase–sale was deemed not to occur, the pooling method relied on previously recorded values reflecting a continuation of previous ownership. Thus, the following asset values would be recorded by Archer in a business combination accounted for as a pooling of interests.

	Values Assigned
Current assets	$ 30,000
Internet domain name	160,000
Licensing agreements	–0–
In-process research and development	–0–
Notes payable	(25,000)
Total value assigned within the combination	$165,000

Note the following characteristics of the pooling of interests method from the above schedule.

- Because a pooling of interests was predicated on a continuity of ownership, the accounting incorporated a continuation of previous book values and ignored fair values exchanged in a business combination.
- Previously unrecognized (typically internally developed) intangibles continue to be reported at a zero value post-combination.
- Because the pooling of interests method values an acquired firm at its previously recorded book value, no new amount for goodwill was ever recorded in a pooling.

Acquisition Method Applied

According to the acquisition method, Archer's valuation basis for its acquisition of Baker is computed as follows:

Fair value of shares issued		$1,200,000
Fair value of contingent performance obligation		150,000
Total consideration transferred for the Baker acquisition		$1,350,000
Cost allocation:		
Current assets	$ 30,000	
Internet domain name	300,000	
Licensing agreements	500,000	
Research and development asset	200,000	
Notes payable	(25,000)	
Total net fair value of items acquired		1,005,000
Goodwill		$ 345,000

Note the following characteristics of the acquisition method from the above entry.

- The valuation basis is fair value of consideration transferred and includes the contingent consideration, but excludes direct combination costs.
- The assets acquired and liabilities assumed are recorded at their individual fair values.
- Goodwill is the excess of the consideration transferred over the fair values of the net assets acquired.
- Acquired in-process research and development is recognized as an asset.
- Professional service fees to help accomplish the acquisition are expensed.

The following table compares the amounts from Baker that Archer would include in its combination-date consolidated financial statements under the pooling of interests method, the purchase method, and the acquisition method.

**Values Incorporated in Archer's
Consolidated Balance Sheet Resulting
from the Baker Transaction**

	Pooling of Interests Method	Purchase Method	Acquisition Method
Current assets	$ 30,000	$ 30,000	$ 30,000
Internet domain name	160,000	300,000	300,000
Licensing agreements	–0–	500,000	500,000
In-process research and development asset*	–0–	–0–	200,000
Goodwill	–0–	220,000	345,000
Notes payable	(25,000)	(25,000)	(25,000)
Contingent performance obligation	–0–	–0–	(150,000)
Total net asset recognized by Archer	$165,000	$1,025,000	$1,200,000

*Acquired in-process research and development was expensed under the purchase method and not recognized at all under the pooling of interests method.

Several comparisons should be noted across these methods of accounting for business combinations:

- In consolidating Baker's assets and liabilities, the purchase and acquisition methods record fair values. In contrast, the pooling method uses previous book values and ignores fair values. Consequently, although a fair value of $1,350,000 is exchanged, only a net value of $165,000 (assets less liabilities) is reported in the pooling.

- The pooling method, as reflected in the preceding example, typically shows smaller asset values and consequently lowers future depreciation and amortization expenses. Thus, higher future net income was usually reported under the pooling method compared to similar situations that employed the purchase method.

- Under pooling, financial ratios such as Net Income/Total Assets were dramatically inflated. Not only was this ratio's denominator understated through failure to recognize internally developed assets acquired (and fair values in general), but the numerator was overstated through smaller depreciation and amortization expenses.

- Although not shown, the pooling method retrospectively combined the acquired firm's revenues, expenses, dividends, and retained earnings. The purchase and acquisition methods incorporate only post-combination values for these operational items. Also all costs of the combination (direct and indirect acquisition costs and stock issue costs) were expensed in the period of combination under the pooling of interests method.

- Finally, with adoption of the acquisition method, the FASB has moved clearly in the direction of increased management accountability for the fair values of all assets acquired and liabilities assumed in a business combination.

Summary

1. Consolidation of financial information is required for external reporting purposes when one organization gains control of another, thus forming a single economic entity. In many combinations, all but one of the companies is dissolved as a separate legal corporation. Therefore, the consolidation process is carried out fully at the date of acquisition to bring together all accounts into a single set of financial records. In other combinations, the companies retain their identities as separate enterprises and continue to maintain their own separate accounting systems. For these cases, consolidation is a periodic process necessary whenever the parent produces external financial statements. This periodic procedure is frequently accomplished through the use of a worksheet and consolidation entries.

2. Under the acquisition method, the fair value of the consideration transferred provides the starting point for valuing the acquired firm. The fair value of the consideration transferred by the acquirer includes the fair value of any contingent consideration. The acquired company assets and liabilities are consolidated at their individual acquisition-date fair values. If the consideration transferred exceeds the total fair value of the net assets, the residual amount is recognized in the consolidated financial statements as goodwill, an intangible asset. Direct combination costs are expensed as incurred because they are not part of the acquired business fair value. When a bargain purchase occurs, individual assets and liabilities acquired continue to be recorded at their fair values and a gain on bargain purchase

is recognized. Also, in contrast to past practice, the fair value of all acquired in-process research and development is recognized as an asset in business combinations subject to subsequent impairment reviews.

3. Particular attention should be paid to the recognition of intangible assets in business combinations. An intangible asset must be recognized in an acquiring firm's financial statement if the asset arises from a legal or contractual right (e.g., trademarks, copyrights, artistic materials, royalty agreements). If the intangible asset does not represent a legal or contractual right, the intangible will still be recognized if it is capable of being separated from the firm (e.g., customer lists, noncontractual customer relationships, unpatented technology).

4. Past financial reporting standards required either the purchase method or the pooling of interests method to account for business combinations. Because current GAAP prohibits retrospective treatment, vestiges of the earlier acquisition methods will remain in financial statements for many years to come.

5. The purchase method valued the acquired firm at cost including all direct consolidation costs unless expended to issue stock. The acquired assets and liabilities were consolidated at their fair values at the date of purchase. If the purchase cost exceeded the fair value of the net acquired assets, the residual was recognized in the consolidated financial statements as goodwill, an intangible asset. If the purchase price was less than total fair value, certain consolidated assets were reported at less than their individual fair values. Because of the bargain purchase, these noncurrent assets were consolidated at amounts less than their fair values. The total reduction was the difference between the acquisition cost and the net fair value of the subsidiary's assets and liabilities. This figure is prorated based on the fair value of the various noncurrent assets. An extraordinary gain was reported if the reduction exceeded the total value of the applicable noncurrent assets.

6. The pooling of interests method was criticized often because it relied on book values only and, therefore, ignored the exchange transaction that formed the economic entity. Poolings ignored unrecorded intangible assets even though they were some of the main value drivers among the target firm's assets. Poolings were also questioned because of the retroactive treatment of operating results. Consequently, companies were able to increase reported earnings by pooling with another company rather than by improving operating efficiency. Although firms needed to meet specific criteria to quality for pooling of interests treatment, many large firms were able to employ this method. After 2002, future use of the pooling method was prohibited.

Comprehensive Illustration

PROBLEM

(*Estimated Time: 45 to 65 Minutes*) Following are the account balances of Miller Company and Richmond Company as of December 31. The fair values of Richmond Company's assets and liabilities are also listed.

	Miller Company Book Values 12/31	Richmond Company Book Values 12/31	Richmond Company Fair Values 12/31
Cash.	$ 600,000	$ 200,000	$ 200,000
Receivables.	900,000	300,000	290,000
Inventory	1,100,000	600,000	820,000
Buildings and equipment (net)	9,000,000	800,000	900,000
Unpatented technology	–0–	–0–	500,000
In-process research and development	–0–	–0–	100,000
Accounts payable.	(400,000)	(200,000)	(200,000)
Notes payable.	(3,400,000)	(1,100,000)	(1,100,000)
Totals	$ 7,800,000	$ 600,000	$ 1,510,000
Common stock—$20 par value . . .	$ (2,000,000)		
Common stock—$5 par value		$ (220,000)	
Additional paid-in capital	(900,000)	(100,000)	
Retained earnings, 1/1	(2,300,000)	(130,000)	
Revenues	(6,000,000)	(900,000)	
Expenses	3,400,000	750,000	

Note: Parentheses indicate a credit balance.

Additional Information (not reflected in the preceding figures)

- On December 31, Miller issues 50,000 shares of its $20 par value common stock for all of the outstanding shares of Richmond Company.

- As part of the acquisition agreement, Miller agrees to pay the former owners of Richmond $250,000 if certain profit projections are realized over the next three years. Miller calculates the acquisition-date fair value of this contingency at $100,000.

- In creating this combination, Miller pays $10,000 in stock issue costs and $20,000 in accounting and legal fees.

Required

a. Miller's stock has a fair value of $32.00 per share. Using the acquisition method:

1. Prepare the necessary journal entries if Miller dissolves Richmond so it is no longer a separate legal entity.

2. Assume instead that Richmond will retain separate legal incorporation and maintain its own accounting systems. Prepare a worksheet to consolidate the accounts of the two companies.

b. If Miller's stock has a fair value of $26.00 per share, describe how the consolidated balances would differ from the results in requirement (*a*).

SOLUTION

a. 1. In a business combination, the accountant first determines the total fair value of the consideration transferred. Because Miller's stock is valued at $32 per share, the 50,000 issued shares are worth $1,600,000 in total. Included in the consideration transferred is the $100,000 acquisition-date fair value of the contingent performance obligation.

   This $1,700,000 total fair value is compared to the $1,510,000 fair value of Richmond's assets and liabilities (including the value of IPR&D). The $190,000 excess fair value ($1,700,000 − $1,510,000) is recognized as goodwill. Because dissolution will occur, Richmond's asset and liability accounts are transferred to Miller and entered at fair value with the excess recorded as goodwill.

   The $10,000 stock issue cost reduces Additional Paid-In Capital. The $20,000 direct combination costs (accounting and legal fees) are expensed when incurred.

Miller Company's Financial Records—December 31

Cash	200,000	
Receivables	290,000	
Inventory	820,000	
Buildings and Equipment	900,000	
Unpatented Technology	500,000	
In-Process Research and Development Asset	100,000	
Goodwill	190,000	
Accounts Payable		200,000
Notes Payable		1,100,000
Contingent Performance Obligation		100,000
Common Stock (Miller) (par value)		1,000,000
Additional Paid-In Capital (fair value in excess of par value)		600,000
To record acquisition of Richmond Company.		
Professional service expenses	20,000	
Cash (paid for combination costs)		20,000
To record legal and accounting fees related to the combination.		
Additional Paid-In Capital	10,000	
Cash (stock issuance costs)		10,000
To record payment of stock issuance costs.		

2. Under this scenario, the acquisition fair value is equal to that computed in part (*a*1).

50,000 shares of stock at $32.00 each	$1,600,000
Contingent performance obligation	100,000
Acquisition-date fair value of consideration transferred	$1,700,000

Because the subsidiary is maintaining separate incorporation, Miller establishes an investment account to reflect the $1,700,000 acquisition consideration:

Miller's Financial Records—December 31

Investment in Richmond Company	1,700,000	
Contingent Performance Obligation		100,000
Common Stock (Miller) (par value)		1,000,000
Additional Paid-In Capital (market value in excess of par value)		600,000
Professional service expenses	20,000	
Cash (paid for combination costs)		20,000
To record legal and accounting fees related to the combination.		
Additional Paid-In Capital	10,000	
Cash (stock issuance costs)		10,000
To record payment of stock issuance costs.		

Because Richmond maintains separate incorporation and its own accounting system, Miller prepares a worksheet for consolidation. To prepare the worksheet, Miller first allocates Richmond's fair value to assets acquired and liabilities assumed based on their individual fair values:

Fair value of consideration transferred by Miller	$1,700,000
Book value of Richmond	600,000
Excess fair value over book value	$1,100,000

Allocations are made to specific accounts based on differences in fair values and book values:

Receivables ($290,000 − $300,000)	$ (10,000)	
Inventory ($820,000 − $600,000)	220,000	
Buildings and equipment ($900,000 − $800,000)	100,000	
Unpatented technology ($500,000 − 0)	500,000	
In-process research and development	100,000	910,000
Goodwill		$ 190,000

The following steps produce consolidated financial statements totals in Exhibit 2.9:

- Miller's balances have been updated on this worksheet to include the effects of both the newly issued shares of stock, the recognition of the contingent performance liability, and the combination expenses.
- Richmond's revenue and expense accounts have been closed to Retained Earnings. The acquisition method consolidates only postacquisition revenues and expenses.
- Worksheet Entry S eliminates the $600,000 book value component of the Investment in Richmond account along with the subsidiary's stockholders' equity accounts.

Entry A adjusts all of Richmond's assets and liabilities to fair value based on the allocations determined earlier.

b. If the fair value of Miller's stock is $26.00 per share, then the fair value of the consideration transferred in the Richmond acquisition is recomputed as follows:

Fair value of shares issued ($26 × 50,000 shares)	$1,300,000
Fair value of contingent consideration	100,000
Total consideration transferred at fair value	$1,400,000

Because the consideration transferred is $110,000 less than the $1,510,000 fair value of the net assets received in the acquisition, a bargain purchase has occurred. In this situation, Miller continues to recognize each of the separately identified assets acquired and liabilities assumed at their fair values. Resulting differences in the consolidated balances relative to the Requirement (*a*) solution are as follows:

- The $110,000 excess fair value recognized over the consideration transferred is recognized as a "gain on bargain purchase."
- Consolidated net income increases by the $110,000 gain to $2,690,000.
- No goodwill is recognized.
- Miller's additional paid-in capital decreases by $300,000 to $1,190,000.
- Consolidated retained earnings increase by the $110,000 gain to $4,990,000.

EXHIBIT 2.9 **Comprehensive Illustration—Solution—Acquisition Method**

MILLER COMPANY AND RICHMOND COMPANY
Consolidation Worksheet
For Period Ending December 31

Accounts	Miller Company	Richmond Company	Consolidation Entries Debit	Consolidation Entries Credit	Consolidated Totals
Income Statement					
Revenues	(6,000,000)				(6,000,000)
Expenses	3,420,000*				3,420,000*
Net income	(2,580,000)				(2,580,000)
Statement of Retained Earnings					
Retained earnings, 1/1	(2,300,000)				(2,300,000)
Net income (above)	(2,580,000)				(2,580,000)
Retained earnings, 12/31	(4,880,000)				(4,880,000)
Balance Sheet					
Cash	570,000*	200,000			770,000
Receivables	900,000	300,000		(A) 10,000	1,190,000
Inventory	1,100,000	600,000	(A) 220,000		1,920,000
Investment in Richmond Company	1,700,000*	–0–		(A) 1,100,000 (S) 600,000	–0–
Buildings and equipment (net)	9,000,000	800,000	(A) 100,000		9,900,000
Goodwill	–0–	–0–	(A) 190,000		190,000
Unpatented technology	–0–	–0–	(A) 500,000		500,000
Research and development asset	–0–	–0–	(A) 100,000		100,000
Total assets	13,270,000	1,900,000			14,570,000
Accounts payable	(400,000)	(200,000)			(600,000)
Notes payable	(3,400,000)	(1,100,000)			(4,500,000)
Contingent performance obligation	(100,000)*	–0–			(100,000)
Common stock	(3,000,000)*	(220,000)	(S) 220,000		(3,000,000)
Additional paid-in capital	(1,490,000)*	(100,000)	(S) 100,000		(1,490,000)
Retained earnings, 12/31 (above)	(4,880,000)*	(280,000)†	(S) 280,000		(4,880,000)
Total liabilities and equities	(13,270,000)	(1,900,000)	1,710,000	1,710,000	(14,570,000)

Note: Parentheses indicate a credit balance.
*Balances have been adjusted for issuance of stock, payment of combination expenses, and recognition of contingent performance liability.
†Beginning retained earnings plus revenues minus expenses.

Also, because of the bargain purchase, the "Investment in Richmond" account balance on Miller's separate financial statements shows the $1,510,000 fair value of the net identified assets received. This valuation measure is an exception to the general rule of using the consideration transferred to provide the valuation basis for the acquired firm.

Questions

1. What is a business combination?
2. Describe the different types of legal arrangements that can take place to create a business combination.
3. What does the term *consolidated financial statements* mean?
4. Within the consolidation process, what is the purpose of a worksheet?
5. Jones Company obtains all of the common stock of Hudson, Inc., by issuing 50,000 shares of its own stock. Under these circumstances, why might the determination of an acquisition price be difficult?
6. What is the accounting basis for consolidating assets and liabilities in a business combination recorded using the acquisition method?

7. How are a subsidiary's revenues and expenses consolidated?

8. Morgan Company acquires all of the outstanding shares of Jennings, Inc., for cash. Morgan transfers consideration more than the fair value of the company's net assets. How should the payment in excess of fair value be accounted for in the consolidation process under the acquisition method?

9. Catron Corporation is having liquidity problems, and as a result, it sells all of its outstanding stock to Lambert, Inc., for cash. Because of Catron's problems, Lambert is able to acquire this stock at less than the fair value of the company's net assets. How is this reduction in price accounted for within the consolidation process under the acquisition method?

10. Sloane, Inc., issues 25,000 shares of its own common stock in exchange for all of the outstanding shares of Benjamin Company. Benjamin will remain a separately incorporated operation. How does Sloane record the issuance of these shares?

11. To obtain all of the stock of Molly, Inc., Harrison Corporation issued its own common stock. Harrison had to pay $98,000 to lawyers, accountants, and a stock brokerage firm in connection with services rendered during the creation of this business combination. In addition, Harrison paid $56,000 in costs associated with the stock issuance. How will these two costs be recorded under the acquisition method?

Problems

Note: Problems 1–25 relate to the acquisition method of accounting for business combinations. Problems 26 through 30 relate to the purchase method. Problems 31–33 relate to the pooling method.

The Acquisition Method

LO1

1. Which of the following does not represent a primary motivation for business combinations?
   a. Combinations as a vehicle for achieving rapid growth and competitiveness.
   b. Cost savings through elimination of duplicate facilities and staff.
   c. Quick entry for new and existing products into markets.
   d. Larger firms being less likely to fail.

LO2

2. Which of the following is the best theoretical justification for consolidated financial statements?
   a. In form the companies are one entity; in substance they are separate.
   b. In form the companies are separate; in substance they are one entity.
   c. In form and substance the companies are one entity.
   d. In form and substance the companies are separate.
      (AICPA)

LO3

3. What is a statutory merger?
   a. A merger approved by the Securities and Exchange Commission.
   b. An acquisition involving the purchase of both stock and assets.
   c. A takeover completed within one year of the initial tender offer.
   d. A business combination in which only one company continues to exist as a legal entity.

LO8

4. What is the appropriate accounting treatment for the value assigned to in-process research and development acquired in a business combination?
   a. Expense upon acquisition.
   b. Capitalize as an asset.
   c. Expense if there is no alternative use for the assets used in the research and development and technological feasibility has yet to be reached.
   d. Expense until future economic benefits become certain and then capitalize as an asset.

LO8

5. An acquired entity has a long-term operating lease for an office building used for central management. The terms of the lease are very favorable relative to current market rates. However, the lease prohibits subleasing or any other transfer of rights. In its financial statements, the acquiring firm should report the value assigned to the lease contract as
   a. An intangible asset under the contractual-legal criterion.
   b. A part of goodwill.
   c. An intangible asset under the separability criterion.
   d. A building.

LO4

6. When does gain recognition accompany a business combination?

    a. When a bargain purchase occurs.

    b. In a combination created in the middle of a fiscal year.

    c. In an acquisition when the value of all assets and liabilities cannot be determined.

    d. When the amount of a bargain purchase exceeds the value of the applicable noncurrent assets (other than certain exceptions) held by the acquired company.

LO4

7. According to the acquisition method of accounting for business combinations, costs paid to attorneys and accountants for services in arranging a merger should be

    a. Capitalized as part of the overall fair value acquired in the merger.

    b. Recorded as an expense in the period the merger takes place.

    c. Included in recognized goodwill.

    d. Written off over a five-year maximum useful life.

LO4

8. When negotiating a business acquisition, buyers sometimes agree to pay extra amounts to sellers in the future if performance metrics are achieved over specified time horizons. How should buyers account for such contingent consideration in recording an acquisition?

    a. The amount ultimately paid under the contingent consideration agreement is added to goodwill when and if the performance metrics are met.

    b. The fair value of the contingent consideration is expensed immediately at acquisition date.

    c. The fair value of the contingent consideration is included in the overall fair value of the consideration transferred, and a liability or additional owners' equity is recognized.

    d. The fair value of the contingent consideration is recorded as a reduction of the otherwise determinable fair value of the acquired firm.

LO5

9. On June 1, Cline Co. paid $800,000 cash for all of the issued and outstanding common stock of Renn Corp. The carrying values for Renn's assets and liabilities on June 1 follow:

Cash	$150,000
Accounts receivable	180,000
Capitalized software costs	320,000
Goodwill	100,000
Liabilities	(130,000)
Net assets	$620,000

On June 1, Renn's accounts receivable had a fair value of $140,000. Additionally, Renn's in-process research and development was estimated to have a fair value of $200,000. All other items were stated at their fair values. On Cline's June 1 consolidated balance sheet, how much is reported for goodwill?

    a. $320,000.

    b. $120,000.

    c. $80,000.

    d. $20,000.

LO5

10. Prior to being united in a business combination, Atkins, Inc., and Waterson Corporation had the following stockholders' equity figures:

	Atkins	Waterson
Common stock ($1 par value)	$180,000	$ 45,000
Additional paid-in capital	90,000	20,000
Retained earnings	300,000	110,000

Atkins issues 51,000 new shares of its common stock valued at $3 per share for all of the outstanding stock of Waterson. Assume that Atkins acquires Waterson. Immediately afterward, what are consolidated Additional Paid-In Capital and Retained Earnings, respectively?

    a. $104,000 and $300,000.

    b. $110,000 and $410,000.

    c. $192,000 and $300,000.

    d. $212,000 and $410,000.

Problems 11 and 12 are based on the following information:

Hill, Inc., obtains control over Loring, Inc., on July 1. The book value and fair value of Loring's accounts on that date (prior to creating the combination) follow, along with the book value of Hill's accounts:

	Hill Book Values	Loring Book Values	Loring Fair Values
Revenues	$(250,000)	$(130,000)	
Expenses	170,000	80,000	
Retained earnings, 1/1	(130,000)	(150,000)	
Cash and receivables	140,000	60,000	$ 60,000
Inventory	190,000	145,000	175,000
Patented technology (net)	230,000	180,000	200,000
Land	400,000	200,000	225,000
Buildings and equipment (net)	100,000	75,000	75,000
Liabilities.	(540,000)	(360,000)	(350,000)
Common stock	(300,000)	(70,000)	
Additional paid-in capital	(10,000)	(30,000)	

LO5

11. Assume that Hill issues 10,000 shares of common stock with a $5 par value and a $40 fair value to obtain all of Loring's outstanding stock. How much goodwill should be recognized?

   a. –0–.

   b. $15,000.

   c. $35,000.

   d. $100,000.

LO4

12. For the fiscal year ending December 31, how will consolidated net income of this business combination be determined if Hill acquires all of Loring's stock?

   a. Hill's income for the past year plus Loring's income for the past six months.

   b. Hill's income for the past year plus Loring's income for the past year.

   c. Hill's income for the past six months plus Loring's income for the past six months.

   d. Hill's income for the past six months plus Loring's income for the past year.

LO8

13. Prycal Co. merges with InterBuy, Inc., and acquires several different categories of intangible assets including trademarks, a customer list, copyrights on artistic materials, agreements to receive royalties on leased intellectual property, and unpatented technology.

   a. Describe the criteria for determining whether an intangible asset acquired in a business combination should be separately recognized apart from goodwill.

   b. For each of the acquired intangibles listed, identify which recognition criteria (separability and legal/contractual) may or may not apply in recognizing the intangible on the acquiring firm's financial statements.

LO6

14. The following book and fair values were available for Westmont Company as of March 1.

	Book Value	Fair Value
Inventory	$ 630,000	$ 600,000
Land	750,000	990,000
Buildings	1,700,000	2,000,000
Customer relationships	–0–	800,000
Accounts payable	(80,000)	(80,000)
Common stock	(2,000,000)	
Additional paid-in capital	(500,000)	
Retained earnings 1/1	(360,000)	
Revenues	(420,000)	
Expenses	280,000	

Arturo Company pays $4,000,000 cash and issues 20,000 shares of its $2 par value common stock (fair value of $50 per share) for all of Westmont's common stock in a merger, after which Westmont will cease to exist as a separate entity. Stock issue costs amount to $25,000 and Arturo pays $42,000 for legal fees to complete the transaction. Prepare Arturo's journal entry to record its acquisition of Westmont.

LO6

15. Use the same facts as in problem 14, but assume instead that Arturo pays cash of $4,200,000 to acquire Westmont. No stock is issued. Prepare Arturo's journal entry to record its acquisition of Westmont.

LO4, LO5, LO6, LO7

16. Following are preacquisition financial balances for Padre Company and Sol Company as of December 31. Also included are fair values for Sol Company accounts.

	Padre Company Book Values 12/31	Sol Company Book Values 12/31	Sol Company Fair Values 12/31
Cash	$ 400,000	$ 120,000	$ 120,000
Receivables	220,000	300,000	300,000
Inventory	410,000	210,000	260,000
Land	600,000	130,000	110,000
Building and equipment (net)	600,000	270,000	330,000
Franchise agreements	220,000	190,000	220,000
Accounts payable	(300,000)	(120,000)	(120,000)
Accrued expenses	(90,000)	(30,000)	(30,000)
Long-term liabilities	(900,000)	(510,000)	(510,000)
Common stock—$20 par value	(660,000)		
Common stock—$5 par value		(210,000)	
Additional paid-in capital	(70,000)	(90,000)	
Retained earnings, 1/1	(390,000)	(240,000)	
Revenues	(960,000)	(330,000)	
Expenses	920,000	310,000	

Note: Parentheses indicate a credit balance.

On December 31, Padre acquires Sol's outstanding stock by paying $360,000 in cash and issuing 10,000 shares of its own common stock with a fair value of $40 per share. Padre paid legal and accounting fees of $20,000 as well as $5,000 in stock issuance costs.

Determine the value that would be shown in Padre and Sol's consolidated financial statements for each of the accounts listed.

Accounts

Inventory	Revenues
Land	Additional paid-in capital
Buildings and equipment	Expenses
Franchise agreements	Retained earnings, 1/1
Goodwill	

LO4, LO5, LO6, LO7

17. On June 30, 2011, Wisconsin, Inc., issued $300,000 in debt and 15,000 new shares of its $10 par value stock to Badger Company owners in exchange for all of the outstanding shares of that company. Wisconsin shares had a fair value of $40 per share. Prior to the combination, the financial statements for Wisconsin and Badger for the six-month period ending June 30, 2011, were as follows:

	Wisconsin	Badger
Revenues	$ (900,000)	$ (300,000)
Expenses	660,000	200,000
Net income	$ (240,000)	$ (100,000)
Retained earnings, 1/1	$ (800,000)	$ (200,000)
Net income	(240,000)	(100,000)
Dividends paid	90,000	–0–
Retained earnings, 6/30	$ (950,000)	$ (300,000)
Cash	$ 80,000	$ 110,000
Receivables and inventory	400,000	170,000
Patented technology (net)	900,000	300,000
Equipment (net)	700,000	600,000
Total assets	$ 2,080,000	$ 1,180,000
Liabilities	$ (500,000)	$ (410,000)
Common stock	(360,000)	(200,000)
Additional paid-in capital	(270,000)	(270,000)
Retained earnings	(950,000)	(300,000)
Total liabilities and equities	$(2,080,000)	$(1,180,000)

Wisconsin also paid $30,000 to a broker for arranging the transaction. In addition, Wisconsin paid $40,000 in stock issuance costs. Badger's equipment was actually worth $700,000, but its patented technology was valued at only $280,000.

What are the consolidated balances for the following accounts?

a. Net income.

b. Retained earnings, 1/1/11.

c. Patented technology.

d. Goodwill.

e. Liabilities.

f. Common stock.

g. Additional paid-In capital.

LO4, LO7

18. On January 1, 2011, Pinnacle Corporation exchanged $3,200,000 cash for 100 percent of the outstanding voting stock of Strata Corporation. Pinnacle plans to maintain Strata as a wholly owned subsidiary with separate legal status and accounting information systems.

At the acquisition date, Pinnacle prepared the following fair-value allocation schedule:

Fair value of Strata (consideration transferred)		$3,200,000
Carrying amount acquired		2,600,000
Excess fair value		$ 600,000
to buildings (undervalued)	$ 300,000	
to licensing agreements (overvalued)	(100,000)	200,000
to goodwill (indefinite life)		$ 400,000

Immediately after closing the transaction, Pinnacle and Strata prepared the following post-acquisition balance sheets from their separate financial records.

	Pinnacle	Strata
Cash	$ 433,000	$ 122,000
Accounts receivable	1,210,000	283,000
Inventory	1,235,000	350,000
Investment in Strata	3,200,000	–0–
Buildings (net)	5,572,000	1,845,000
Licensing agreements	–0–	3,000,000
Goodwill	350,000	–0–
Total Assets	$ 12,000,000	$ 5,600,000
Accounts payable	(300,000)	(375,000)
Long-term debt	(2,700,000)	(2,625,000)
Common stock	(3,000,000)	(1,000,000)
APIC	–0–	(500,000)
Retained earnings	(6,000,000)	(1,100,000)
Total liabilities and equities	$(12,000,000)	$(5,600,000)

Prepare a January 1, 2011, consolidated balance sheet for Pinnacle Corporation and its subsidiary Strata Corporation.

LO4, LO5, LO7

eXcel

19. On January 1, 2011, Marshall Company acquired 100 percent of the outstanding common stock of Tucker Company. To acquire these shares, Marshall issued $200,000 in long-term liabilities and 20,000 shares of common stock having a par value of $1 per share but a fair value of $10 per share. Marshall paid $30,000 to accountants, lawyers, and brokers for assistance in the acquisition and another $12,000 in connection with stock issuance costs.

Prior to these transactions, the balance sheets for the two companies were as follows:

	Marshall Company Book Value	Tucker Company Book Value
Cash	$ 60,000	$ 20,000
Receivables	270,000	90,000
Inventory	360,000	140,000
Land	200,000	180,000
Buildings (net)	420,000	220,000

(continued)

	Marshall Company Book Value	Tucker Company Book Value
Equipment (net)	$ 160,000	$ 50,000
Accounts payable	(150,000)	(40,000)
Long-term liabilities	(430,000)	(200,000)
Common stock—$1 par value	(110,000)	
Common stock—$20 par value		(120,000)
Additional paid-in capital	(360,000)	–0–
Retained earnings, 1/1/11	(420,000)	(340,000)

Note: Parentheses indicate a credit balance.

In Marshall's appraisal of Tucker, it deemed three accounts to be undervalued on the subsidiary's books: Inventory by $5,000, Land by $20,000, and Buildings by $30,000. Marshall plans to maintain Tucker's separate legal identity and to operate Tucker as a wholly owned subsidiary.

a. Determine the amounts that Marshall Company would report in its postacquisition balance sheet. In preparing the postacquisition balance sheet, any required adjustments to income accounts from the acquisition should be closed to Marshall's retained earnings.

b. To verify the answers found in part (a), prepare a worksheet to consolidate the balance sheets of these two companies as of January 2011.

LO4, LO5, LO7, LO8

20. Pratt Company acquired all of Spider, Inc.'s outstanding shares on December 31, 2011, for $495,000 cash. Pratt will operate Spider as a wholly owned subsidiary with a separate legal and accounting identity. Although many of Spider's book values approximate fair values, several of its accounts have fair values that differ from book values. In addition, Spider has internally developed assets that remain unrecorded on its books. In deriving the acquisition price, Pratt assessed Spider's fair and book value differences as follows:

	Book Values	Fair Values
Computer software	$ 20,000	$ 70,000
Equipment	40,000	30,000
Client contracts	–0–	100,000
In-process research and development	–0–	40,000
Notes payable	(60,000)	(65,000)

At December 31, 2011, the following financial information is available for consolidation:

	Pratt	Spider
Cash	$ 36,000	$ 18,000
Receivables	116,000	52,000
Inventory	140,000	90,000
Investment in Spider	495,000	–0–
Computer software	210,000	20,000
Buildings (net)	595,000	130,000
Equipment (net)	308,000	40,000
Client contracts	–0–	–0–
Goodwill	–0–	–0–
Total assets	$ 1,900,000	$ 350,000
Accounts payable	$ (88,000)	$ (25,000)
Notes payable	(510,000)	(60,000)
Common stock	(380,000)	(100,000)
Additional paid-in capital	(170,000)	(25,000)
Retained earnings	(752,000)	(140,000)
Total liabilities and equities	$(1,900,000)	$(350,000)

Prepare a consolidated balance sheet for Pratt and Spider as of December 31, 2011.

LO4, LO5, LO6

21. Allerton Company acquires all Deluxe Company's assets and liabilities for cash on January 1, 2011, and subsequently formally dissolves Deluxe, At the acquisition date, the following book and fair values were available for the Deluxe Company accounts:

	Book Values	Fair Values
Current assets	$ 60,000	$ 60,000
Building	90,000	50,000
Land	10,000	20,000
Trademark	–0–	30,000
Goodwill	15,000	?
Liabilities	(40,000)	(40,000)
Common stock	(100,000)	
Retained earnings	(35,000)	

Using the acquisition method, prepare Allerton's entry to record its acquisition of Deluxe in its accounting records assuming the following cash exchange amounts:

(1) $145,000.

(2) $110,000.

LO4, LO6, LO9

22. On June 30, 2011, Sampras Company reported the following account balances:

Receivables	$ 80,000	Current liabilities	$ (10,000)
Inventory	70,000	Long-term liabilities	(50,000)
Buildings (net)	75,000	Common stock	(90,000)
Equipment (net)	25,000	Retained earnings	(100,000)
Total assets	$250,000	Total liabilities and equities	$(250,000)

On June 30, 2011, Pelham paid $300,000 cash for all assets and liabilities of Sampras, which will cease to exist as a separate entity. In connection with the acquisition, Pelham paid $10,000 in legal fees. Pelham also agreed to pay $50,000 to the former owners of Sampras contingent on meeting certain revenue goals during 2012. Pelham estimated the present value of its probability adjusted expected payment for the contingency at $15,000.

In determining its offer, Pelham noted the following pertaining to Sampras:

- It holds a building with a fair value $40,000 more than its book value.
- It has developed a customer list appraised at $22,000, although it is not recorded in its financial records.
- It has research and development activity in process with an appraised fair value of $30,000. However, the project has not yet reached technological feasibility and the assets used in the activity have no alternative future use.
- Book values for the receivables, inventory, equipment, and liabilities approximate fair values.

Prepare Pelham's accounting entry to record the combination with Sampras using the

a. Acquisition method.

b. Purchase method.

LO4, LO5

23. SafeData Corporation has the following account balances and respective fair values on June 30:

	Book Values	Fair Values
Receivables	$ 80,000	$ 80,000
Patented technology	100,000	700,000
Customer relationships	–0–	500,000
In-process research and development	–0–	300,000
Liabilities	(400,000)	(400,000)
Common stock	(100,000)	
Additional paid-in capital	(300,000)	
Retained earnings deficit, 1/1	700,000	
Revenues	(300,000)	
Expenses	220,000	

Privacy First, Inc., obtained all of the outstanding shares of SafeData on June 30 by issuing 20,000 shares of common stock having a $1 par value but a $75 fair market value. Privacy First incurred $10,000 in stock issuance costs and paid $75,000 to an investment banking firm for its assistance in arranging the combination. In negotiating the final terms of the deal, Privacy First also agrees to pay $100,000 to SafeData's former owners if it achieves certain revenue goals in the next two years.

Privacy First estimates the probability adjusted present value of this contingent performance obligation at $30,000. The transaction is to be accounted for using the acquisition method.

a. What is the fair value of the consideration transferred in this combination?

b. How should the stock issuance costs appear in Privacy First's postcombination financial statements?

c. How should Privacy First account for the fee paid to the investment bank?

d. How does the issuance of these shares affect the stockholders' equity accounts of Privacy First, the parent?

e. How is the fair value of the consideration transferred in the combination allocated among the assets acquired and the liabilities assumed?

f. What is the effect of SafeData's revenues and expenses on consolidated totals? Why?

g. What is the effect of SafeData's Common Stock and Additional Paid-In Capital balances on consolidated totals?

h. If Privacy First's stock had been worth only $50 per share rather than $75, how would the consolidation of SafeData's assets and liabilities have been affected?

LO4, LO5, LO6, LO7, LO8

24. On January 1, 2011, NewTune Company exchanges 15,000 shares of its common stock for all of the outstanding shares of On-the-Go, Inc. Each of NewTune's shares has a $4 par value and a $50 fair value. The fair value of the stock exchanged in the acquisition was considered equal to On-the-Go's fair value. NewTune also paid $25,000 in stock registration and issuance costs in connection with the merger.

Several of On-the-Go's accounts have fair values that differ from their book values on this date:

	Book Values	Fair Values
Receivables	$ 65,000	$ 63,000
Trademarks	95,000	225,000
Record music catalog	60,000	180,000
In-process research and development	–0–	200,000
Notes payable	(50,000)	(45,000)

Precombination January 1, 2011, book values for the two companies are as follows:

	NewTune	On-the-Go
Cash	$ 60,000	$ 29,000
Receivables	150,000	65,000
Trademarks	400,000	95,000
Record music catalog	840,000	60,000
Equipment (net)	320,000	105,000
Totals	$ 1,770,000	$ 354,000
Accounts payable	$ (110,000)	$ (34,000)
Notes payable	(370,000)	(50,000)
Common stock	(400,000)	(50,000)
Additional paid-in capital	(30,000)	(30,000)
Retained earnings	(860,000)	(190,000)
Totals	$(1,770,000)	$(354,000)

Required:

a. Assume that this combination is a statutory merger so that On-the-Go's accounts will be transferred to the records of NewTune. On-the-Go will be dissolved and will no longer exist as a legal entity. Using the acquisition method, prepare a postcombination balance sheet for NewTune as of the acquisition date.

b. Assume that no dissolution takes place in connection with this combination. Rather, both companies retain their separate legal identities. Using the acquisition method, prepare a worksheet to consolidate the two companies as of the combination date.

c. How do the balance sheet accounts compare across parts (a) and (b)?

LO4, LO5, LO7

25. On December 31, 2010, Pacifica, Inc., acquired 100 percent of the voting stock of Seguros Company. Pacifica will maintain Seguros as a wholly owned subsidiary with its own legal and accounting identity. The consideration transferred to the owner of Seguros included 50,000 newly issued Pacifica common shares ($20 market value, $5 par value) and an agreement to pay an additional $130,000 cash if Seguros meets certain project completion goals by December 31, 2011. Pacifica estimates a 50 percent probability that Seguros will be successful in meeting these goals and uses a 4 percent discount rate to represent the time value of money.

Immediately prior to the acquisition, the following data for both firms were available:

	Pacifica	Seguros Book Values	Seguros Fair Values
Revenues	$(1,200,000)		
Expenses	875,000		
Net income	$ (325,000)		
Retained earnings, 1/1/10	$ (950,000)		
Net income	(325,000)		
Dividends paid	90,000		
Retained earnings, 12/31/10	$(1,185,000)		
Cash	$ 110,000	$ 85,000	$ 85,000
Receivables and inventory	750,000	190,000	180,000
Property, plant, and equipment	1,400,000	450,000	600,000
Trademarks	300,000	160,000	200,000
Total assets	$ 2,560,000	$ 885,000	
Liabilities	$ (500,000)	$(180,000)	$(180,000)
Common stock	(400,000)	(200,000)	
Additional paid-in capital	(475,000)	(70,000)	
Retained earnings	(1,185,000)	(435,000)	
Total liabilities and equities	$(2,560,000)	$(885,000)	

In addition, Pacifica assessed a research and development project under way at Seguros to have a fair value of $100,000. Although not yet recorded on its books, Pacifica paid legal fees of $15,000 in connection with the acquisition and $9,000 in stock issue costs.

Using the acquisition method, prepare the following:

a. Pacifica's entries to account for the consideration transferred to the former owners of Seguros, the direct combination costs, and the stock issue and registration costs. (Use a 0.961538 present value factor where applicable.)

b. A postacquisition column of accounts for Pacifica.

c. A worksheet to produce a consolidated balance sheet as of December 31, 2010.

Purchase Method

LO9

26. Bakel Corporation has the following December 31 account balances:

Receivables	$ 80,000
Inventory	200,000
Land	600,000
Building	500,000
Liabilities	(400,000)
Common stock	(100,000)
Additional paid-in capital	(100,000)
Retained earnings, 1/1	(700,000)
Revenues	(300,000)
Expenses	220,000

Several of Bakel's accounts have fair values that differ from book value: land—$400,000; building—$600,000; inventory—$280,000; and liabilities—$330,000. Homewood, Inc., obtains all of Bakel's outstanding shares by issuing 20,000 shares of common stock having a $5 par value but a $55 fair value. Stock issuance costs amount to $10,000.

a. What is the purchase price in this combination?

b. What is the book value of Bakel's net assets on the date of the takeover?

c. How are the stock issuance costs handled?

d. How does the issuance of these shares affect the stockholders' equity accounts of Homewood, the parent?

e. What allocations are made of Homewood's purchase price to specific accounts and to goodwill?

f. If Bakel had in-process research and development assets (with no alternative future uses) valued at $60,000, how would the allocations in part (e) change? Where is acquired in-process research and development typically reported on consolidated financial statements?

g. How do Bakel's revenues and expenses affect consolidated totals? Why?

h. How do Bakel's common stock and additional paid-in capital balances affect consolidated totals?

i. In financial statements prepared immediately following the takeover, what impact will this acquisition have on the various consolidated totals?

j. If Homewood's stock had been worth only $40 per share rather than $55, how would the consolidation of Bakel's assets and liabilities have been affected?

LO9

27. Winston has the following account balances as of February 1.

Inventory	$ 600,000
Land	500,000
Buildings (net) (valued at $1,000,000)	900,000
Common stock ($10 par value)	(800,000)
Retained earnings, 1/1	(1,100,000)
Revenues	(600,000)
Expenses	500,000

Arlington pays $1.4 million cash and issues 10,000 shares of its $30 par value common stock (valued at $80 per share) for all of Winston's outstanding stock. Stock issuance costs amount to $30,000. Prior to recording these newly issued shares, Arlington reports a Common Stock account of $900,000 and Additional Paid-In Capital of $500,000. For each of the following accounts, determine what balance would be included in a February 1 consolidation.

a. Goodwill.

b. Expenses.

c. Retained Earnings, 1/1.

d. Buildings.

LO9

28. Use the same information as presented in problem 27 but assume that Arlington pays cash of $2.3 million. No stock is issued. An additional $40,000 is paid in direct combination costs. For each of the following accounts, determine what balance would be included in a February 1 consolidation.

a. Goodwill.

b. Expenses.

c. Retained Earnings, 1/1.

d. Buildings.

LO9

29. Use the same information as presented in problem 27 but assume that Arlington pays $2,020,000 in cash. An additional $20,000 is paid in direct combination costs. For each of the following accounts, determine what balance will be included in a February 1 consolidation.

a. Inventory.

b. Goodwill.

c. Expenses.

d. Buildings.

e. Land.

LO9

eXcel

30. Merrill acquires 100 percent of the outstanding voting shares of Harriss Company on January 1, 2008. To obtain these shares, Merrill pays $200,000 in cash and issues 10,000 shares of its own $10 par value common stock. On this date, Merrill's stock has a fair value of $18 per share. Merrill also pays $10,000 to a local investment company for arranging the acquisition. Merrill paid an additional $6,000 in stock issuance costs.

The book values for both Merrill and Harriss as of January 1, 2008, follow. The fair value of each of Harriss's accounts is also included. In addition, Harriss holds a fully amortized patent that still retains a $30,000 value.

	Merrill, Inc. Book Values	Harriss Company Book Values	Harriss Company Fair Values
Cash	$ 300,000	$ 40,000	$ 40,000
Receivables	160,000	90,000	80,000
Inventory	220,000	130,000	130,000
Land	100,000	60,000	60,000
Buildings (net)	400,000	110,000	140,000
Equipment (net)	120,000	50,000	50,000
Accounts payable	(160,000)	(30,000)	(30,000)
Long-term liabilities	(380,000)	(170,000)	(150,000)
Common stock	(400,000)	(40,000)	
Retained earnings	(360,000)	(240,000)	

a. Assume that this combination is a statutory merger so that Harriss's accounts are to be transferred to Merrill's records with Harriss subsequently being dissolved as a legal corporation. Prepare the journal entries for Merrill to record this merger.

b. Assume that no dissolution is to take place in connection with this combination. Rather, both companies retain their separate legal identities. Prepare a worksheet to consolidate the two companies as of January 1, 2008.

Pooling Method

LO9

31. How would equipment obtained in a business combination have been recorded under each of the following methods?

Pooling of Interests	Purchase
a. Recorded value	Recorded value
b. Recorded value	Fair value
c. Fair value	Fair value
d. Fair value	Recorded value

(AICPA adapted)

LO9

32. Flaherty Company entered into a business combination with Steeley Company in March 2001. The combination was accounted for as a pooling of interests. Registration fees were incurred in issuing common stock in this combination. Other costs, such as legal and accounting fees, were also paid.

a. In the business combination accounted for as a pooling of interests, how should the assets and liabilities of the two companies be included within consolidated statements? What was the rationale for accounting for a business combination as a pooling of interests?

b. In the business combination accounted for as a pooling of interests, how were the registration fees and the other direct costs recorded?

c. In the business combination accounted for as a pooling of interests, how were the results of the operations for 2001 reported?

(AICPA adapted)

LO9

33. On February 1, Piscina Corporation completed a combination with Swimwear Company accounted for as a pooling of interests. At that date, Swimwear's account balances were as follows:

	Book Values	Fair Values
Inventory	$ 600,000	$ 650,000
Land	450,000	750,000
Buildings	900,000	1,000,000
Unpatented technology	–0–	1,500,000
Common stock ($10 par value)	(750,000)	
Retained earnings, 1/1	(1,100,000)	
Revenues	(600,000)	
Expenses	500,000	

Piscina issued 30,000 shares of its common stock with a par value of $25 and a fair value of $150 per share to the owners of Swimwear for all of their Swimwear shares. Upon completion of the combination, Swimwear Company was formally dissolved.

Prior to 2002, business combinations were accounted for using either purchase or pooling of interests accounting. The two methods often produced substantially different financial statement effects. For the scenario above,

a. What are the respective consolidated values for Swimwear's assets under the pooling method and the purchase method?

b. Under each of the following methods, how would Piscina account for Swimwear's current year, but prior to acquisition, revenues and expenses?

• Pooling of interests method

• Purchase method

c. Explain the alternative impact of pooling versus purchase accounting on performance ratios such as return on assets and earnings per share in periods subsequent to the combination.

Develop Your Skills

FASB ASC RESEARCH AND ANALYSIS CASE—CONSIDERATION OR COMPENSATION?

NaviNow Company agrees to pay $20 million in cash to the four former owners of TrafficEye for all of its assets and liabilities. These four owners of TrafficEye developed and patented a technology for real-time monitoring of traffic patterns on the nation's top 200 frequently congested highways. NaviNow plans to combine the new technology with its existing global positioning systems and projects a resulting substantial revenue increase.

As part of the acquisition contract, NaviNow also agrees to pay additional amounts to the former owners upon achievement of certain financial goals. NaviNow will pay $8 million to the four former owners of TrafficEye if revenues from the combined system exceed $100 million over the next three years. NaviNow estimates this contingent payment to have a probability adjusted present value of $4 million.

The four former owners have also been offered employment contracts with NaviNow to help with system integration and performance enhancement issues. The employment contracts are silent as to service periods, have nominal salaries similar to those of equivalent employees, and specify a profit-sharing component over the next three years (if the employees remain with the company) that NaviNow estimates to have a current fair value of $2 million. The four former owners of TrafficEye say they will stay on as employees of NaviNow for at least three years to help achieve the desired financial goals.

Should NaviNow account for the contingent payments promised to the former owners of TrafficEye as consideration transferred in the acquisition or as compensation expense to employees?

RESEARCH CASE—ABBOTT'S ACQUISITION OF ADVANCED MEDICAL OPTICS

On February 25, 2009, Abbott Laboratories acquired 100 percent of the equity of Advanced Medical Optics Corporation in exchange for $1.4 billion cash. Referring to Abbott's 2009 financial statements, answer the following:

1. How did Abbott account for the Advanced Medical Optics acquisition?
2. What allocations did Abbott make to the assets acquired and liabilities assumed in the acquisition? Provide a calculation showing how Abbott determined the amount allocated to goodwill.
3. How will Abbott account for the in-process research and development acquired in the combination?
4. How will Abbott account for its acquisition-related expenses?
5. Why did Abbott acquire Advanced Medical Optics?

FASB ASC RESEARCH CASE—THE DOW CHEMICAL COMPANY'S ACQUIRED CONTINGENCIES

On April 1, 2009, The Dow Chemical Company completed its acquisition of Rohm and Haas Company. Dow Chemical paid $15,681 million cash consideration to Rohm and Haas stockholders in exchange for their ownership shares. Rohm and Haas continued as a wholly owned subsidiary of Dow Chemical.

Refer to Dow Chemical's 2009 second-quarter report, as well as related standards, to answer the following questions:

1. Did Dow Chemical recognize any acquired contingencies for its acquisition of Rohm and Haas? If it did, how were they measured? If not, why not?
2. Under what circumstances should a firm recognize an asset acquired or a liability assumed in a business combination that arises from a contingency?
3. How should Dow Chemical account for its acquired contingencies in periods after the acquisition date?
4. What is the disclosure requirement for Dow Chemical's acquired contingencies?
5. What are some potential concerns with authoritative accounting literature for acquired contingencies?

Consolidations— Subsequent to the Date of Acquisition

In 1996, Berkshire Hathaway, Inc. acquired all of the outstanding stock of Geico, Inc., an insurance company. Although this transaction involved well-known companies, it was not unique; mergers and acquisitions have long been common in the business world.

Berkshire Hathaway's current financial statements indicate that Geico is still a component of this economic entity. However, Geico, Inc., continues as a separate legally incorporated concern long after its purchase. As discussed in Chapter 2, a parent will often maintain separate legal status for a subsidiary corporation to better utilize its inherent value as a going concern.

For external reporting purposes, maintenance of incorporation creates an ongoing challenge for the accountant. In each subsequent period, consolidation must be simulated anew through the use of a worksheet and consolidation entries. Thus, for more than a decade, the financial data for Berkshire Hathaway and Geico (along with dozens of other subsidiaries) have been brought together periodically to provide figures for the financial statements that represent this business combination.

As also discussed in Chapter 2, the acquisition method governs the way we initially record a business combination. In periods subsequent to acquisition, the fair-value bases (established at the acquisition date) for subsidiary assets acquired and liabilities assumed will be amortized (or tested for possible impairment) for proper income recognition. Additionally, some combinations require accounting for the eventual disposition of contingent consideration, which, as presented later in this chapter, continues to follow a fair-value model.

In the next several sections of this chapter, we present the procedures to prepare consolidated financial statements in the years subsequent to acquisition. We start by analyzing the relation between the parent's internal accounting method for its subsidiary investment and the adjustments required in consolidation. We also examine the specific procedures for amortizing the acquisition-date fair-value adjustments to the subsidiary's assets and liabilities. We then cover testing for goodwill impairment, accounting for contingent consideration, and push-down accounting.

LEARNING OBJECTIVES

After studying this chapter, you should be able to:

LO1   Recognize the complexities in preparing consolidated financial reports that emerge from the passage of time.

LO2   Identify and describe the various methods available to a parent company in order to maintain its investment in subsidiary account in its internal records.

LO3   Understand that a parent's internal accounting method for its subsidiary investments has no effect on the resulting consolidated financial statements.

LO4   Prepare consolidated financial statements subsequent to acquisition when the parent has applied in its internal records:

    a. The equity method.
    b. The initial value method.
    c. The partial equity method.

LO5   Discuss the rationale for the goodwill impairment testing approach.

LO6   Describe the procedures for conducting a goodwill impairment test.

LO7   Understand the accounting and reporting for contingent consideration subsequent to a business acquisition.

LO8   Understand in general the requirements of push-down accounting and when its use is appropriate.

CONSOLIDATION—THE EFFECTS CREATED BY THE PASSAGE OF TIME

LO1

Recognize the complexities in preparing consolidated financial reports that emerge from the passage of time.

In Chapter 2, consolidation accounting is analyzed at the date that a combination is created. The present chapter carries this process one step further by examining the consolidation procedures that must be followed in subsequent periods whenever separate incorporation of the subsidiary is maintained.

Despite complexities created by the passage of time, the basic objective of all consolidations remains the same: to combine asset, liability, revenue, expense, and equity accounts of a parent and its subsidiaries. From a mechanical perspective, a worksheet and consolidation entries continue to provide structure for the production of a single set of financial statements for the combined business entity.

The time factor introduces additional complications into the consolidation process. For internal record-keeping purposes, the parent must select and apply an accounting method to monitor the relationship between the two companies. The investment balance recorded by the parent varies over time as a result of the method chosen, as does the income subsequently recognized. These differences affect the periodic consolidation process but not the figures to be reported by the combined entity. Regardless of the amount, the parent's investment account is eliminated on the worksheet so that the subsidiary's actual assets and liabilities can be consolidated. Likewise, the income figure accrued by the parent is removed each period so that the subsidiary's revenues and expenses can be included when creating an income statement for the combined business entity.

INVESTMENT ACCOUNTING BY THE ACQUIRING COMPANY

LO2

Identify and describe the various methods available to a parent company in order to maintain its investment in subsidiary account in its internal records.

For a parent company's external financial reporting, consolidation of a subsidiary becomes necessary whenever control exists. For internal record-keeping, though, the parent has a choice for monitoring the activities of its subsidiaries. Although several variations occur in practice, three methods have emerged as the most prominent: the equity method, the initial value method,[1] and the partial equity method.

At the acquisition date, each investment accounting method (equity, initial value, and partial equity) begins with an identical value recorded in an investment account. Typically the fair value of the consideration transferred by the parent will serve as the recorded valuation basis on the parent's books.[2]

LO3

Understand that a parent's internal accounting method for its subsidiary investments has no effect on the resulting consolidated financial statements.

Subsequent to the acquisition date, the three methods produce different account balances for the parent's investment in subsidiary, income recognized from the subsidiary's activities, and retained earnings accounts. *Importantly, the selection of a particular method does not affect the totals ultimately reported for the combined companies.* However, the parent's choice of an internal accounting method does lead to distinct procedures for consolidating the financial information from the separate organizations.

Internal Investment Accounting Alternatives—The Equity Method, Initial Value Method, and Partial Equity Method

The internal reporting philosophy of the acquiring company often determines the accounting method choice for its subsidiary investment. Depending on the measures a company uses to assess the ongoing performances of its subsidiaries, parent companies may choose their own preferred internal reporting method. Regardless of this choice, however, consolidated financial statements are required for external reporting.

The Equity Method

The equity method embraces full accrual accounting in maintaining the investment account and related income over time. Under the equity method, the acquiring company accrues

---

[1] The initial value method was formerly referred to as the cost method.

[2] In the unusual case of a bargain purchase, the valuation basis for the investment account is the fair value of the net amount of the assets acquired and liabilities assumed.

income when the subsidiary earns it. To match the additional fair value recorded in the combination against income, amortization expense stemming from the original excess fair-value allocations is recognized through periodic adjusting entries. Unrealized gains on intra-entity transactions are deferred; dividends paid by the subsidiary serve to reduce the investment balance. As discussed in Chapter 1, the equity method creates a parallel between the parent's investment accounts and changes in the underlying equity of the acquired company.[3]

When the parent has complete ownership, equity method earnings from the subsidiary, combined with the parent's other income sources, create a total income figure reflective of the entire combined business entity. Consequently, the equity method often is referred to as a single-line consolidation. The equity method is especially popular in companies where management periodically (e.g., monthly or quarterly) measures each subsidiary's profitability using accrual-based income figures.

The Initial Value Method (formerly known as the cost method)

Subsequent to acquisition, the initial value method uses the cash basis for income recognition. Dividends received by the parent from the subsidiary are recognized as income. No recognition is given to the income earned by the subsidiary. The investment balance remains permanently on the parent's financial records at the initial fair value assigned at the acquisition date.

The initial value method might be selected because the parent does not require an accrual-based income measure of subsidiary performance. For example, the parent may wish to assess subsidiary performance on its ability to generate cash flows, on revenues generated, or some other nonincome basis. Also, some firms may find the initial value method's ease of application attractive. Because the investment account is eliminated in consolidation, and the actual subsidiary revenues and expenses are eventually combined, firms may avoid the complexity of the equity method unless they need the specific information provided by the equity income measure for internal decision making.

The Partial Equity Method

A third method available to the acquiring company is a partial application of the equity method. Under this approach, the parent recognizes the reported income accruing from the subsidiary. Dividends that are collected reduce the investment balance. However, no other equity adjustments (amortization or deferral of unrealized gains) are recorded. Thus, in many cases, earnings figures on the parent's books approximate consolidated totals but without the effort associated with a full application of the equity method.

Exhibit 3.1 provides a summary of these three internal accounting techniques. The method adopted affects only the acquiring company's separate financial records. No changes are created in either the subsidiary's accounts or the consolidated totals.

Because specific worksheet procedures differ based on the investment method utilized by the parent, the consolidation process subsequent to the date of combination will be introduced twice. First, we review consolidations in which the acquiring company uses the equity method. Then we redevelop all procedures when the investment is recorded by one of the alternative methods.

Each acquiring company must decide for itself the appropriate approach in recording the operations of its subsidiaries. For example, Alliant Food Service, Inc., applies the equity method. According to Joe Tomczak, vice president and controller of Alliant Food Service, Inc., "We maintain the parent holding company books on an equity basis. This approach provides the best method of providing information for our operational decisions."[4]

---

[3] In Chapter 1, the equity method was introduced in connection with the external reporting of investments in which the owner held the ability to apply significant influence over the investee (usually by possessing 20 to 50 percent of the company's voting stock). Here, the equity method is utilized for the *internal* reporting of the parent for investments in which control is maintained. Although the accounting procedures are similar, the reason for using the equity method is different.

[4] Telephone conversation with Joe Tomczak.

EXHIBIT 3.1   Internal Reporting of Investment Accounts by Acquiring Company

Method	Investment Account	Income Account	Advantages
Equity	Continually adjusted to reflect ownership of acquired company.	Income accrued as earned; amortization and other adjustments are recognized.	Acquiring company totals give a true representation of consolidation figures.
Initial value	Remains at acquisition-date value assigned.	Cash received recorded as Dividend Income.	It is easy to apply; it measures cash flows.
Partial equity	Adjusted only for accrued income and dividends received from acquired company.	Income accrued as earned; no other adjustments recognized.	It usually gives balances approximating consolidation figures, but it is easier to apply than equity method.

In contrast, Reynolds Metals Corporation has chosen to utilize the partial equity method approach. Allen Earehart, director of corporate accounting for Reynolds, states, "We do adjust the carrying value of our investments annually to reflect the earnings of each subsidiary. We want to be able to evaluate the parent company on a stand-alone basis and a regular equity accrual is, therefore, necessary. However, we do separate certain adjustments such as the elimination of intra-entity gains and losses and record them solely within the development of consolidated financial statements."[5]

SUBSEQUENT CONSOLIDATION—INVESTMENT RECORDED BY THE EQUITY METHOD

LO4a

Prepare consolidated financial statements subsequent to acquisition when the parent has applied the equity method in its internal records.

Acquisition Made during the Current Year

As a basis for this illustration, assume that Parrot Company obtains all of the outstanding common stock of Sun Company on January 1, 2010. Parrot acquires this stock for $800,000 in cash.

The book values as well as the appraised fair values of Sun's accounts follow:

	Book Values 1/1/10	Fair Values 1/1/10	Difference
Current assets	$ 320,000	$ 320,000	–0–
Trademarks (indefinite life)	200,000	220,000	+ 20,000
Patented technology (10-year life)	320,000	450,000	+130,000
Equipment (5-year life)	180,000	150,000	(30,000)
Liabilities	(420,000)	(420,000)	–0–
Net book value	$ 600,000	$ 720,000	$120,000
Common stock—$40 par value	$(200,000)		
Additional paid-in capital	(20,000)		
Retained earnings, 1/1/10	(380,000)		

Parrot considers the economic life of Sun's trademarks as extending beyond the foreseeable future and thus having an indefinite life. Such assets are not amortized but are subject to periodic impairment testing.[6] For the definite lived assets acquired in the combination (patented technology and equipment), we assume that straight-line amortization with no salvage value is appropriate.[7]

[5] Telephone conversation with Allen Earehart.

[6] In other cases, trademarks can have a definite life and thus would be subject to regular amortization.

[7] Unless otherwise stated, all amortization expense computations in this textbook are based on the straight-line method with no salvage value.

EXHIBIT 3.2
Excess Fair
Value Allocation

PARROT COMPANY
100 Percent Acquisition of Sun Company
Allocation of Acquisition-Date Subsidiary Fair Value
January 1, 2011

Sun Company fair value (consideration transferred by Parrot Company) . .		$ 800,000
Book value of Sun Company:		
Common stock.	$200,000	
Additional paid-in capital	20,000	
Retained earnings, 1/1/11.	380,000	(600,000)
Excess of fair value over book value		200,000
Allocation to specific accounts based on fair values:		
Trademarks.	$ 20,000	
Patented technology.	130,000	
Equipment (overvalued)	(30,000)	120,000
Excess fair value not identified with specific accounts—goodwill		$ 80,000

Parrot paid $800,000 cash to acquire Sun Company, clear evidence of the fair value of the consideration transferred. As shown in Exhibit 3.2, individual allocations are used to adjust Sun's accounts from their book values to their acquisition-date fair values. Because the total value of these assets and liabilities was only $720,000, goodwill of $80,000 must be recognized for consolidation purposes.

Each of these allocated amounts (other than the $20,000 attributed to trademarks and the $80,000 for goodwill) represents a valuation associated with a definite life. As discussed in Chapter 1, Parrot must amortize each allocation over its expected life. The expense recognition necessitated by this fair value allocation is calculated in Exhibit 3.3.

One aspect of this amortization schedule warrants further explanation. The fair value of Sun's Equipment account was $30,000 *less* than book value. Therefore, instead of attributing an additional amount to this asset, the $30,000 allocation actually reflects a fair-value reduction. As such, the amortization shown in Exhibit 3.3 relating to Equipment is not an additional expense but an expense reduction.

Having determined the allocation of the acquisition-date fair value in the previous example as well as the associated amortization, the parent's separate record-keeping for its first year of Sun Company ownership can be constructed. Assume that Sun earns income of $100,000 during the year and pays a $40,000 cash dividend on August 1.

In this first illustration, Parrot has adopted the equity method. Apparently, this company believes that the information derived from using the equity method is useful in its evaluation of Sun.

EXHIBIT 3.3
Annual Excess
Amortization

PARROT COMPANY
100 Percent Acquisition of Sun Company
Excess Amortization Schedule—Allocation of Acquisition-Date Fair Values

Account	Allocation	Useful Life	Annual Excess Amortizations
Trademarks	$ 20,000	Indefinite	–0–
Patented technology	130,000	10 years	$13,000
Equipment	(30,000)	5 years	(6,000)
Goodwill	80,000	Indefinite	–0–
			$ 7,000*

*Total excess amortizations will be $7,000 annually for five years until the equipment allocation is fully removed. At the end of each asset's life, future amortizations will change.

Application of the Equity Method

	Parrot's Financial Records		
1/1/10	Investment in Sun Company	800,000	
	Cash		800,000
	To record the acquisition of Sun Company.		
8/1/10	Cash	40,000	
	Investment in Sun Company		40,000
	To record receipt of cash dividend from subsidiary under the equity method.		
12/31/10	Investment in Sun Company	100,000	
	Equity in Subsidiary Earnings		100,000
	To accrue income earned by 100 percent owned subsidiary.		
12/31/10	Equity in Subsidiary Earnings	7,000	
	Investment in Sun Company		7,000
	To recognize amortizations on allocations made in acquisition of subsidiary (see Exhibit 3.3).		

Parrot's application of the equity method, as shown in this series of entries, causes the Investment in Sun Company account balance to rise from $800,000 to $853,000 ($800,000 − $40,000 + $100,000 − $7,000). During the same period the parent recognizes a $93,000 equity income figure (the $100,000 earnings accrual less the $7,000 excess amortization expenses).

The consolidation procedures for Parrot and Sun one year after the date of acquisition are illustrated next. For this purpose, Exhibit 3.4 presents the separate 2010 financial statements for these two companies. Parrot recorded both investment-related accounts (the $853,000 asset balance and the $93,000 income accrual) based on applying the equity method.

Determination of Consolidated Totals

Before becoming immersed in the mechanical aspects of a consolidation, the objective of this process should be understood. As indicated in Chapter 2, in the preparation of consolidated financial reports, the subsidiary's revenue, expense, asset, and liability accounts are added to the parent company balances. Within this procedure, several important guidelines must be followed:

- Sun's assets and liabilities are adjusted to reflect the allocations originating from their acquisition-date fair values.

- Because of the passage of time, the income effects (e.g., amortizations) of these allocations must also be recognized within the consolidation process.

- Any reciprocal or intra-entity[8] accounts must be offset. If, for example, one of the companies owes money to the other, the receivable and the payable balances have no connection with an outside party. Both should be eliminated for external reporting purposes. When the companies are viewed as a single entity, the receivable and the payable are intra-entity balances to be removed.

A consolidation of the two sets of financial information in Exhibit 3.4 is a relatively uncomplicated task and can even be carried out without the use of a worksheet. Understanding the origin of each reported figure is the first step in gaining a knowledge of this process.

- *Revenues* = $1,900,000. The revenues of the parent and the subsidiary are added together.

- *Cost of goods sold* = $950,000. The cost of goods sold of the parent and subsidiary are added together.

[8] The FASB Accounting Standards Codification (ASC) recently began using the term *intra-entity* to describe transfers of assets across business entities affiliated though common stock ownership or other control mechanisms. The phrase indicates that although such transfers occur across separate legal entities, they are nonetheless made within a consolidated entity. Prior to the use of the term *intra-entity,* such amounts were routinely referred to as *intercompany* balances.

EXHIBIT 3.4
Separate Records—
Equity Method Applied

PARROT COMPANY AND SUN COMPANY
Financial Statements
For Year Ending December 31, 2010

	Parrot Company	Sun Company
Income Statement		
Revenues	$(1,500,000)	$ (400,000)
Cost of goods sold	700,000	250,000
Amortization expense	120,000	20,000
Depreciation expense	80,000	30,000
Equity in subsidiary earnings	(93,000)	–0–
Net income	$ (693,000)	$ (100,000)
Statement of Retained Earnings		
Retained earnings, 1/1/10	$ (840,000)	$ (380,000)
Net income (above)	(693,000)	(100,000)
Dividends paid	120,000	40,000
Retained earnings, 12/31/10	$(1,413,000)	$ (440,000)
Balance Sheet		
Current assets	$ 1,040,000	$ 400,000
Investment in Sun Company (at equity)	853,000	–0–
Trademarks	600,000	200,000
Patented technology	370,000	288,000
Equipment (net)	250,000	220,000
Total assets	$ 3,113,000	$ 1,108,000
Liabilities	$ (980,000)	$ (448,000)
Common stock	(600,000)	(200,000)
Additional paid-in capital	(120,000)	(20,000)
Retained earnings, 12/31/10 (above)	(1,413,000)	(440,000)
Total liabilities and equity	$(3,113,000)	$(1,108,000)

Note: Parentheses indicate a credit balance.

- *Amortization expense* = $153,000. The balances of the parent and of the subsidiary are combined along with the additional amortization from the recognition of the excess fair value over book value attributed to the subsidiary's patented technology.
- *Depreciation expense* = $104,000. The depreciation expenses of the parent and subsidiary are added together along with the $6,000 reduction in equipment depreciation, as indicated in Exhibit 3.3.
- *Equity in subsidiary earnings* = −0−. The investment income recorded by the parent is eliminated so that the subsidiary's revenues and expenses can be included in the consolidated totals.
- *Net income* = $693,000. Consolidated revenues less consolidated expenses.
- *Retained earnings, 1/1/10* = $840,000. The parent figure only because the subsidiary was not owned prior to that date.
- *Dividends paid* = $120,000. The parent company balance only because the subsidiary's dividends were paid intra-entity to the parent, not to an outside party.
- *Retained earnings, 12/31/10* = $1,413,000. Consolidated retained earnings as of the beginning of the year plus consolidated net income less consolidated dividends paid.
- *Current assets* = $1,440,000. The parent's book value plus the subsidiary's book value.
- *Investment in Sun Company* = −0−. The asset recorded by the parent is eliminated so that the subsidiary's assets and liabilities can be included in the consolidated totals.

- *Trademarks* = $820,000. The parent's book value plus the subsidiary's book value plus the $20,000 acquisition-date fair value allocation.
- *Patented technology* = $775,000. The parent's book value plus the subsidiary's book value plus the $130,000 acquisition-date fair value allocation less current year amortization of $13,000.
- *Equipment* = $446,000. The parent's book value plus the subsidiary's book value less the $30,000 fair value reduction allocation plus the current year expense reduction of $6,000.
- *Goodwill* = $80,000. The residual allocation shown in Exhibit 3.2. Note that goodwill is not amortized.
- *Total assets* = $3,561,000. A vertical summation of consolidated assets.
- *Liabilities* = $1,428,000. The parent's book value plus the subsidiary's book value.
- *Common stock* = $600,000. The parent's book value. Subsidiary shares are no longer outstanding.
- *Additional paid-in capital* = $120,000. The parent's book value. Subsidiary shares are no longer outstanding.
- *Retained earnings, 12/31/10* = $1,413,000. Computed previously.
- *Total liabilities and equities* = $3,561,000. A vertical summation of consolidated liabilities and equities.

Consolidation Worksheet

Although the consolidated figures to be reported can be computed as just shown, accountants normally prefer to use a worksheet. A worksheet provides an organized structure for this process, a benefit that becomes especially important in consolidating complex combinations.

For Parrot and Sun, only five consolidation entries are needed to arrive at the same figures previously derived for this business combination. As discussed in Chapter 2, *worksheet entries are the catalyst for developing totals to be reported by the entity but are not physically recorded in the individual account balances of either company.*

Consolidation Entry S

Common Stock (Sun Company)	200,000	
Additional Paid-In Capital (Sun Company)	20,000	
Retained Earnings, 1/1/10 (Sun Company)	380,000	
Investment in Sun Company		600,000

As shown in Exhibit 3.2, Parrot's $800,000 Investment account balance reflects two components: (1) a $600,000 amount equal to Sun's book value and (2) a $200,000 figure attributed to the difference, at January 1, 2010, between the book value and fair value of Sun's assets and liabilities (with a residual allocation made to goodwill). Entry **S** removes the $600,000 component of the Investment in Sun Company account so that the *book value* of each subsidiary asset and liability can be included in the consolidated figures. A second worksheet entry (Entry **A**) eliminates the remaining $200,000 portion of the January 1, 2010, Investment in Sun account, allowing the specific allocations to be included along with any goodwill.

Entry **S** also removes Sun's stockholders' equity accounts as of the beginning of the year. Subsidiary equity balances generated prior to the acquisition are not relevant to the business combination and should be deleted. The elimination is made through this entry because the equity accounts and the $600,000 component of the investment account represent reciprocal balances: Both provide a measure of Sun's book value as of January 1, 2010.

Before moving to the next consolidation entry, a clarification point should be made. In actual practice, worksheet entries are usually identified numerically. However, as in the previous chapter, the label "Entry **S**" used in this example refers to the elimination of Sun's beginning Stockholders' Equity. As a reminder of the purpose being served, all worksheet entries are identified in a similar fashion. Thus, throughout this textbook, "Entry **S**" always refers to the removal of the subsidiary's beginning stockholders' equity balances for the year against the book value portion of the investment account.

Consolidation Entry A

Trademarks	20,000	
Patented technology	130,000	
Goodwill	80,000	
Equipment		30,000
Investment in Sun Company		200,000

Consolidation entry **A** adjusts the subsidiary balances from their book values to acquisition-date fair values (see Exhibit 3.2). This entry is labeled "Entry **A**" to indicate that it represents the Allocations made in connection with the excess of the subsidiary's fair values over its book values. Sun's accounts are adjusted collectively by the $200,000 excess of Sun's $800,000 acquisition-date fair value over its $600,000 book value.

Consolidation Entry I

Equity in Subsidiary Earnings	93,000	
Investment in Sun Company		93,000

"Entry **I**" (for **I**ncome) removes the subsidiary income recognized by Parrot during the year so that Sun's underlying revenue and expense accounts (and the current amortization expense) can be brought into the consolidated totals. The $93,000 figure eliminated here represents the $100,000 income accrual recognized by Parrot, reduced by the $7,000 in excess amortizations. For consolidation purposes, the one-line amount appearing in the parent's records is not appropriate and is removed so that the individual revenues and expenses can be included. The entry originally recorded by the parent is simply reversed on the worksheet to remove its impact.

Consolidation Entry D

Investment in Sun Company	40,000	
Dividends Paid		40,000

The dividends distributed by the subsidiary during the year also must be eliminated from the consolidated totals. The entire $40,000 payment was made to the parent so that, from the viewpoint of the consolidated entity, it is simply an intra-entity transfer of cash. The distribution did not affect any outside party. Therefore, "Entry **D**" (for **D**ividends) is designed to offset the impact of this transaction by removing the subsidiary's Dividends Paid account. Because the equity method has been applied, Parrot's receipt of this money was recorded originally as a decrease in the Investment in Sun Company account. To eliminate the impact of this reduction, the investment account is increased.

Consolidation Entry E

Amortization Expense	13,000	
Equipment	6,000	
Patented Technology		13,000
Depreciation Expense		6,000

This final worksheet entry records the current year's excess amortization expenses relating to the adjustments of Sun's assets to acquisition-date fair values. Because the equity method amortization was eliminated within Entry **I**, "Entry **E**" (for **E**xpense) now records the current year expense attributed to each of the specific account allocations (see Exhibit 3.3). Note that we adjust depreciation expense for the tangible asset *equipment* and we adjust amortization expense for the intangible asset *patented technology*. As a matter of custom, we refer to the adjustments to all expenses resulting from excess acquisition-date fair value allocations collectively as *excess amortization expenses*.

Thus, the worksheet entries necessary for consolidation when the parent has applied the equity method are as follows:

Entry S—Eliminates the subsidiary's stockholders' equity accounts as of the beginning of the current year along with the equivalent book value component within the parent's investment account.

Entry A—Recognizes the unamortized allocations as of the beginning of the current year associated with the original adjustments to fair value.

Entry I—Eliminates the impact of intra-entity subsidiary income accrued by the parent.

Entry D—Eliminates the impact of intra-entity subsidiary dividends.

Entry E—Recognizes excess amortization expenses for the current period on the allocations from the original adjustments to fair value.

Exhibit 3.5 provides a complete presentation of the December 31, 2010, consolidation worksheet for Parrot Company and Sun Company. The series of entries just described brings

EXHIBIT 3.5

PARROT COMPANY AND SUN COMPANY
Consolidated Worksheet

Investment: Equity Method   **For Year Ending December 31, 2010**

Accounts	Parrot Company	Sun Company	Consolidation Entries Debit	Consolidation Entries Credit	Consolidated Totals
Income Statement					
Revenues	(1,500,000)	(400,000)			(1,900,000)
Cost of goods sold	700,000	250,000			950,000
Amortization expense	120,000	20,000	(E) 13,000		153,000
Depreciation expense	80,000	30,000		(E) 6,000	104,000
Equity in subsidiary earnings	(93,000)	–0–	(I) 93,000		–0–
Net income	(693,000)	(100,000)			(693,000)
Statement of Retained Earnings					
Retained earnings, 1/1/10	(840,000)	(380,000)	(S) 380,000		(840,000)
Net income (above)	(693,000)	(100,000)			(693,000)
Dividends paid	120,000	40,000		(D) 40,000	120,000
Retained earnings, 12/31/10	(1,413,000)	(440,000)			(1,413,000)
Balance Sheet					
Current assets	1,040,000	400,000			1,440,000
Investment in Sun Company	853,000	–0–	(D) 40,000	(S) 600,000	–0–
				(A) 200,000	
				(I) 93,000	
Trademarks	600,000	200,000	(A) 20,000		820,000
Patented technology	370,000	288,000	(A) 130,000	(E) 13,000	775,000
Equipment (net)	250,000	220,000	(E) 6,000	(A) 30,000	446,000
Goodwill	–0–	–0–	(A) 80,000		80,000
Total assets	3,113,000	1,108,000			3,561,000
Liabilities	(980,000)	(448,000)			(1,428,000)
Common stock	(600,000)	(200,000)	(S) 200,000		(600,000)
Additional paid-in capital	(120,000)	(20,000)	(S) 20,000		(120,000)
Retained earnings, 12/31/10 (above)	(1,413,000)	(440,000)			(1,413,000)
Total liabilities and equities	(3,113,000)	(1,108,000)	982,000	982,000	(3,561,000)

Note: Parentheses indicate a credit balance.

Consolidation entries:
(S) Elimination of Sun's stockholders' equity January 1 balances and the book value portion of the investment account.
(A) Allocation of Sun's acquisition-date excess fair values over book values.
(I) Elimination of parent's equity in subsidiary earnings accrual.
(D) Elimination of intra-entity dividend payment.
(E) Recognition of current year excess fair-value amortization and depreciation expenses.

together the separate financial statements of these two organizations. Note that the consolidated totals are the same as those computed previously for this combination.

Observe that Parrot separately reports net income of $693,000 as well as ending retained earnings of $1,413,000, figures that are identical to the totals generated for the consolidated entity. However, subsidiary income earned after the date of acquisition is to be *added* to that of the parent. Thus, a question arises in this example as to why the parent company figures alone equal the consolidated balances of both operations.

In reality, Sun's income for this period is contained in both Parrot's reported balances and the consolidated totals. Through the application of the equity method, the current year earnings of the subsidiary have already been accrued by Parrot along with the appropriate amortization expense. *The parent's Equity in Subsidiary Earnings account is, therefore, an accurate representation of Sun's effect on consolidated net income.* If the equity method is employed properly, the worksheet process simply replaces this single $93,000 balance with the specific revenue and expense accounts that it represents. *Consequently, when the parent employs the equity method, its net income and retained earnings mirror consolidated totals.*

Consolidation Subsequent to Year of Acquisition—Equity Method

In many ways, every consolidation of Parrot and Sun prepared after the date of acquisition incorporates the same basic procedures outlined in the previous section. However, the continual financial evolution undergone by the companies prohibits an exact repetition of the consolidation entries demonstrated in Exhibit 3.5.

As a basis for analyzing the procedural changes necessitated by the passage of time, assume that Parrot Company continues to hold its ownership of Sun Company as of December 31, 2013. This date was selected at random; any date subsequent to 2010 would serve equally well to illustrate this process. As an additional factor, assume that Sun now has a $40,000 liability that is payable to Parrot.

For this consolidation, assume that the January 1, 2013, Sun Company's Retained Earnings balance has risen to $600,000. Because that account had a reported total of only $380,000 on January 1, 2010, Sun's book value apparently has increased by $220,000 during the 2010–2012 period. Although knowledge of individual operating figures in the past is not required, Sun's reported totals help to clarify the consolidation procedures.

Year	Sun Company Net Income	Dividends Paid	Increase in Book Value	Ending Retained Earnings
2010	$100,000	$ 40,000	$ 60,000	$440,000
2011	140,000	50,000	90,000	530,000
2012	90,000	20,000	70,000	600,000
	$330,000	$110,000	$220,000	

For 2013, the current year, we assume that Sun reports net income of $160,000 and pays cash dividends of $70,000. Because it applies the equity method, Parrot recognizes earnings of $160,000. Furthermore, as shown in Exhibit 3.3, amortization expense of $7,000 applies to 2013 and must also be recorded by the parent. Consequently, Parrot reports an Equity in Subsidiary Earnings balance for the year of $153,000 ($160,000 − $7,000).

Although this income figure can be reconstructed with little difficulty, the current balance in the Investment in Sun Company account is more complicated. Over the years, the initial $800,000 acquisition price has been subjected to adjustments for

1. The annual accrual of Sun's income.
2. The receipt of dividends from Sun.
3. The recognition of annual excess amortization expenses.

Exhibit 3.6 analyzes these changes and shows the components of the Investment in Sun Company account balance as of December 31, 2013.

EXHIBIT 3.6

PARROT COMPANY
Investment in Sun Company Account
As of December 31, 2013
Equity Method Applied

Fair value of consideration transferred at date of acquisition		$ 800,000
Entries recorded in prior years:		
Accrual of Sun Company's income		
2010	$100,000	
2011	140,000	
2012	90,000	330,000
Sun Company—Dividends paid		
2010	$ (40,000)	
2011	(50,000)	
2012	(20,000)	(110,000)
Excess amortization expenses		
2010	$ (7,000)	
2011	(7,000)	
2012	(7,000)	(21,000)
Entries recorded in current year—2013		
Accrual of Sun Company's income	$160,000	
Sun Company—Dividends paid	(70,000)	
Excess amortization expenses	(7,000)	83,000
Investment in Sun Company, 12/31/13		$1,082,000

Following the construction of the Investment in Sun Company account, the consolidation worksheet developed in Exhibit 3.7 should be easier to understand. Current figures for both companies appear in the first two columns. The parent's investment balance and equity income accrual as well as Sun's income and stockholders' equity accounts correspond to the information given previously. Worksheet entries (lettered to agree with the previous illustration) are then utilized to consolidate all balances.

Several steps are necessary to arrive at these reported totals. The subsidiary's assets, liabilities, revenues, and expenses are added to those same accounts of the parent. The unamortized portion of the original acquisition-date fair-value allocations are included along with current excess amortization expenses. The investment and equity income balances are both eliminated as are the subsidiary's stockholders' equity accounts. Intra-entity dividends are removed with the same treatment required for the debt existing between the two companies.

Consolidation Entry S

Once again, this first consolidation entry offsets reciprocal amounts representing the subsidiary's book value as of the beginning of the current year. Sun's January 1, 2013, stockholders' equity accounts are eliminated against the book value portion of the parent's investment account. Here, though, the amount eliminated is $820,000 rather than the $600,000 shown in Exhibit 3.5 for 2010. Both balances have changed during the 2010–2012 period. Sun's operations caused a $220,000 increase in retained earnings. Parrot's application of the equity method created a parallel effect on its Investment in Sun Company account (the income accrual of $330,000 less dividends collected of $110,000).

Although Sun's Retained Earnings balance is removed in this entry, the income this company earned since the acquisition date is still included in the consolidated figures. Parrot accrues these profits annually through application of the equity method. Thus, elimination of the subsidiary's entire Retained Earnings is necessary; a portion was earned prior to the acquisition and the remainder has already been recorded by the parent.

Entry **S** removes these balances as of the first day of 2013 rather than at the end of the year. The consolidation process is made a bit simpler by segregating the effect of preceding

EXHIBIT 3.7

PARROT COMPANY AND SUN COMPANY
Consolidated Worksheet

Investment: Equity Method   **For Year Ending December 31, 2013**

Accounts	Parrot Company	Sun Company	Consolidation Entries Debit	Consolidation Entries Credit	Consolidated Totals
Income Statement					
Revenues	(2,100,000)	(600,000)			(2,700,000)
Cost of goods sold	1,000,000	380,000			1,380,000
Amortization expense	200,000	20,000	(E) 13,000		233,000
Depreciation expense	100,000	40,000		(E) 6,000	134,000
Equity in subsidiary earnings	(153,000)	–0–	(I) 153,000		–0–
Net income	(953,000)	(160,000)			(953,000)
Statement of Retained Earnings					
Retained earnings, 1/1/13	(2,044,000)	(600,000)	(S) 600,000		(2,044,000)
Net income (above)	(953,000)	(160,000)			(953,000)
Dividends paid	420,000	70,000		(D) 70,000	420,000
Retained earnings, 12/31/13	(2,577,000)	(690,000)			(2,577,000)
Balance Sheet					
Current assets	1,705,000	500,000		(P) 40,000	2,165,000
Investment in Sun Company	1,082,000	–0–	(D) 70,000	(S) 820,000	–0–
				(A) 179,000	
				(I) 153,000	
Trademarks	600,000	240,000	(A) 20,000		860,000
Patented technology	540,000	420,000	(A) 91,000	(E) 13,000	1,038,000
Equipment (net)	420,000	210,000	(E) 6,000	(A) 12,000	624,000
Goodwill	–0–	–0–	(A) 80,000		80,000
Total assets	4,347,000	1,370,000			4,767,000
Liabilities	(1,050,000)	(460,000)	(P) 40,000		(1,470,000)
Common stock	(600,000)	(200,000)	(S) 200,000		(600,000)
Additional paid-in capital	(120,000)	(20,000)	(S) 20,000		(120,000)
Retained earnings, 12/31/13 (above)	(2,577,000)	(690,000)			(2,577,000)
Total liabilities and equities	(4,347,000)	(1,370,000)	1,293,000	1,293,000	(4,767,000)

Note: Parentheses indicate a credit balance.
Consolidation entries:
   (S) Elimination of Sun's stockholders' equity January 1 balances and the book value portion of the investment account.
   (A) Allocation of Sun's acquisition-date excess fair values over book values, unamortized balance as of beginning of year.
   (I) Elimination of parent's equity in subsidiary earnings accrual.
   (D) Elimination of intra-entity dividend payment.
   (E) Recognition of current year excess fair-value amortization and depreciation expenses.
   (P) Elimination of intra-entity receivable/payable.

operations from the transactions of the current year. Thus, *all worksheet entries relate specifically to either the previous years (S and A) or the current period (I, D, E, and P)*.

Consolidation Entry A   In the initial consolidation (2010), fair-value allocations amounting to $200,000 were entered, but these balances have now undergone three years of amortization. As computed in Exhibit 3.8, expenses for these prior years totaled $21,000, leaving a balance of $179,000. Allocation of this amount to the individual accounts is also determined in Exhibit 3.8 and reflected in worksheet Entry **A.** As with Entry **S,** these balances are calculated as of January 1, 2013, so that the current year expenses can be included separately (in Entry **E**).

Consolidation Entry I   As before, this entry eliminates the equity income recorded currently by Parrot ($153,000) in connection with its ownership of Sun. The subsidiary's revenue and expense accounts are left intact so they can be included in the consolidated figures.

Accounts	Original Allocation	Annual Excess Amortizations			Balance 1/1/13
		2010	2011	2012	
Trademarks	$ 20,000	–0–	–0–	–0–	$ 20,000
Patented technology	130,000	$13,000	$13,000	$13,000	91,000
Equipment	(30,000)	(6,000)	(6,000)	(6,000)	(12,000)
Goodwill	80,000	–0–	–0–	–0–	80,000
	$200,000	$ 7,000	$ 7,000	$ 7,000	$179,000
			$21,000		

Consolidation Entry D   This worksheet entry offsets the $70,000 intra-entity dividend payment made by Sun to Parrot during the current period.

Consolidation Entry E   Excess amortization expenses relating to acquisition-date fair-value adjustments are individually recorded for the current period.

Before progressing to the final worksheet entry, note the close similarity of these entries with the five incorporated in the 2010 consolidation (Exhibit 3.5). Except for the numerical changes created by the passage of time, the entries are identical.

Consolidation Entry P   This last entry (labeled "Entry **P**" because it eliminates an intra-entity **P**ayable) introduces a new element to the consolidation process. As noted earlier, intra-entity debt transactions do not relate to outside parties. Therefore, Sun's $40,000 payable and Parrot's $40,000 receivable are reciprocals that must be removed on the worksheet because the companies are being reported as a single entity.

In reviewing Exhibit 3.7, note several aspects of the consolidation process:

- The stockholders' equity accounts of the subsidiary are removed.
- The Investment in Sun Company and the Equity in Subsidiary Earnings are both removed.
- The parent's Retained Earnings balance is not adjusted. Because the parent applies the equity method this account should be correct.
- The acquisition-date fair-value adjustments to the subsidiary's assets are recognized but only after adjustment for annual excess amortization expenses.
- Intra-entity transactions such as dividend payments and the receivable/payable are offset.

SUBSEQUENT CONSOLIDATIONS—INVESTMENT RECORDED USING INITIAL VALUE OR PARTIAL EQUITY METHOD

LO4b

*Prepare consolidated financial statements subsequent to acquisition when the parent has applied **the initial value method** in its internal records.*

LO4c

*Prepare consolidated financial statements subsequent to acquisition when the parent has applied **the partial equity method** in its internal records.*

Acquisition Made during the Current Year

As discussed at the beginning of this chapter, the parent company may opt to use the initial value method or the partial equity method for internal record-keeping rather than the equity method. Application of either alternative changes the balances recorded by the parent over time and, thus, the procedures followed in creating consolidations. However, *choosing one of these other approaches does not affect any of the final consolidated figures to be reported.*

When a company utilizes the equity method, it eliminates all reciprocal accounts, assigns unamortized fair-value allocations to specific accounts, and records amortization expense for the current year. Application of either the initial value method or the partial equity method has no effect on this basic process. For this reason, a number of the consolidation entries remain the same regardless of the parent's investment accounting method.

In reality, just three of the parent's accounts actually vary because of the method applied:

- The investment account.
- The income recognized from the subsidiary.
- The parent's retained earnings (in periods after the initial year of the combination).

EXHIBIT 3.9

PARROT COMPANY AND SUN COMPANY
Consolidated Worksheet
Investment: Initial Value Method — For Year Ending December 31, 2010

Accounts	Parrot Company	Sun Company	Consolidation Entries Debit	Consolidation Entries Credit	Consolidated Totals
Income Statement					
Revenues	(1,500,000)	(400,000)			(1,900,000)
Cost of goods sold	700,000	250,000			950,000
Amortization expense	120,000	20,000	(E) 13,000		153,000
Depreciation expense	80,000	30,000		(E) 6,000	104,000
Dividend income	(40,000)*	–0–	(I) 40,000*		–0–
Net income	(640,000)	(100,000)			(693,000)
Statement of Retained Earnings					
Retained earnings, 1/1/10	(840,000)	(380,000)	(S) 380,000		(840,000)
Net income (above)	(640,000)	(100,000)			(693,000)
Dividends paid	120,000	40,000		(I) 40,000*	120,000
Retained earnings, 12/31/10	(1,360,000)	(440,000)			(1,413,000)
Balance Sheet					
Current assets	1,040,000	400,000			1,440,000
Investment in Sun Company	800,000*	–0–		(S) 600,000	–0–
				(A) 200,000	
Trademarks	600,000	200,000	(A) 20,000		820,000
Patented technology	370,000	288,000	(A) 130,000	(E) 13,000	775,000
Equipment (net)	250,000	220,000	(E) 6,000	(A) 30,000	446,000
Goodwill	–0–	–0–	(A) 80,000		80,000
Total assets	3,060,000	1,108,000			3,561,000
Liabilities	(980,000)	(448,000)			(1,428,000)
Common stock	(600,000)	(200,000)	(S) 200,000		(600,000)
Additional paid-in capital	(120,000)	(20,000)	(S) 20,000		(120,000)
Retained earnings, 12/31/10 (above)	(1,360,000)	(440,000)			(1,413,000)
Total liabilities and equities	(3,060,000)	(1,108,000)	889,000	889,000	(3,561,000)

Note: Parentheses indicate a credit balance.
*Boxed items highlight differences with consolidation in Exhibit 3.5.
Consolidation entries:
  (S) Elimination of Sun's stockholders' equity January 1 balances and the book value portion of the investment account.
  (A) Allocation of Sun's acquisition-date excess fair values over book values.
  (I) Elimination of intra-entity dividend income and dividend paid by Sun.
  (E) Recognition of current year excess fair-value amortization and depreciation expenses.
Note: Consolidation entry (D) is not needed when the parent applies the initial value method because entry (I) eliminates the intra-entity dividend effects.

Only the differences found in these balances affect the consolidation process when another method is applied. Thus, any time after the acquisition date, accounting for these three balances is of special importance.

To illustrate the modifications required by the adoption of an alternative accounting method, the consolidation of Parrot and Sun as of December 31, 2010, is reconstructed. Only one differing factor is introduced: the method by which Parrot accounts for its investment. Exhibit 3.9 presents the 2010 consolidation based on Parrot's use of the initial value method. Exhibit 3.10 demonstrates this same process assuming that the parent applied the partial equity method. Each entry on these worksheets is labeled to correspond with the 2010 consolidation in which the parent used the equity method (Exhibit 3.5). Furthermore, differences

EXHIBIT 3.10

PARROT COMPANY AND SUN COMPANY
Consolidated Worksheet
Investment: Partial Equity Method   For Year Ending December 31, 2010

Accounts	Parrot Company	Sun Company	Consolidation Entries Debit	Consolidation Entries Credit	Consolidated Totals
Income Statement					
Revenues	(1,500,000)	(400,000)			(1,900,000)
Cost of goods sold	700,000	250,000			950,000
Amortization expense	120,000	20,000	(E) 13,000		153,000
Depreciation expense	80,000	30,000		(E) 6,000	104,000
Equity in subsidiary earnings	(100,000) *	–0–	(I) 100,000 *		–0–
Net income	(700,000)	(100,000)			(693,000)
Statement of Retained Earnings					
Retained earnings, 1/1/10	(840,000)	(380,000)	(S) 380,000		(840,000)
Net income (above)	(700,000)	(100,000)			(693,000)
Dividends paid	120,000	40,000		(D) 40,000	120,000
Retained earnings, 12/31/10	(1,420,000)	(440,000)			(1,413,000)
Balance Sheet					
Current assets	1,040,000	400,000			1,440,000
Investment in Sun Company	860,000 *	–0–	(D) 40,000	(S) 600,000	–0–
				(A) 200,000	
				(I) 100,000 *	
Trademarks	600,000	200,000	(A) 20,000		820,000
Patented technology	370,000	288,000	(A) 130,000	(E) 13,000	775,000
Equipment (net)	250,000	220,000	(E) 6,000	(A) 30,000	446,000
Goodwill	–0–	–0–	(A) 80,000		80,000
Total assets	3,120,000	1,108,000			3,561,000
Liabilities	(980,000)	(448,000)			(1,428,000)
Common stock	(600,000)	(200,000)	(S) 200,000		(600,000)
Additional paid-in capital	(120,000)	(20,000)	(S) 20,000		(120,000)
Retained earnings, 12/31/10 (above)	(1,420,000)	(440,000)			(1,413,000)
Total liabilities and equities	(3,120,000)	(1,108,000)			(3,561,000)

Note: Parentheses indicate a credit balance.
*Boxed items highlight differences with consolidation in Exhibit 3.5.
Consolidation entries:
  (S) Elimination of Sun's stockholders' equity January 1 balances and the book value portion of the investment account.
  (A) Allocation of Sun's acquisition-date excess fair values over book values.
  (I) Elimination of parent's equity in subsidiary earnings accrual.
  (D) Elimination of intra-entity dividend payment.
  (E) Recognition of current year excess fair-value amortization and depreciation expenses.

with the equity method (both on the parent company records and with the consolidation entries) are highlighted on each of the worksheets.

Initial Value Method Applied—2010 Consolidation

Although the initial value method theoretically stands in marked contrast to the equity method, few reporting differences actually exist. In the year of acquisition, Parrot's income and investment accounts relating to the subsidiary are the only accounts affected.

Under the initial value method, income recognition in 2010 is limited to the $40,000 dividend received by the parent; no equity income accrual is made. At the same time, the investment account retains its $800,000 initial value. Unlike the equity method, no adjustments are recorded in the parent's investment account in connection with the current year operations, subsidiary dividends, or amortization of any fair-value allocations.

After the composition of these two accounts has been established, worksheet entries can be used to produce the consolidated figures found in Exhibit 3.9 as of December 31, 2010.

Consolidation Entry S   As with the previous Entry **S** in Exhibit 3.5, the $600,000 component of the investment account is eliminated against the beginning stockholders' equity account of the subsidiary. Both are equivalent to Sun's net assets at January 1, 2010, and are, therefore, reciprocal balances that must be offset. This entry is not affected by the accounting method in use.

Consolidation Entry A   Sun's $200,000 excess acquisition-date fair value over book value is allocated to Sun's assets and liabilities based on their fair values at the date of acquisition. The $80,000 residual is attributed to goodwill. This procedure is identical to the corresponding entry in Exhibit 3.5 in which the equity method was applied.

Consolidation Entry I   Under the initial value method, the parent records dividend collections as income. Entry **I** removes this Dividend Income account along with Sun's Dividends Paid. From a consolidated perspective, these two $40,000 balances represent an intra-entity transfer of cash that had no financial impact outside of the entity. In contrast to the equity method, Parrot has not accrued subsidiary income, nor has amortization been recorded; thus, no further income elimination is needed.

Dividend Income	40,000	
Dividends Paid		40,000
To eliminate intra-entity income.		

Consolidation Entry D   When the initial value method is applied, the parent records intra-entity dividends as income. Because these distributions were already removed from the consolidated totals by Entry **I,** no separate Entry **D** is required.

Consolidation Entry E   Regardless of the parent's method of accounting, the reporting entity must recognize excess amortizations for the current year in connection with the original fair value allocations. Thus, Entry **E** serves to bring the current year expenses into the consolidated financial statements.

Consequently, using the initial value method rather than the equity method changes only Entries **I** and **D** in the year of acquisition. Despite the change in methods, reported figures are still derived by (1) eliminating all reciprocals, (2) allocating the excess portion of the acquisition-date fair values, and (3) recording amortizations on these allocations. As indicated previously, the consolidated totals appearing in Exhibit 3.9 are identical to the figures produced previously in Exhibit 3.5. Although the income and the investment accounts on the parent company's separate statements vary, the consolidated balances are not affected.

One significant difference between the initial value method and equity method does exist: The parent's separate statements do not reflect consolidated income totals when the initial value method is used. Because equity adjustments (such as excess amortizations) are ignored, neither Parrot's reported net income of $640,000 nor its retained earnings of $1,360,000 provides an accurate portrayal of consolidated figures.

Partial Equity Method Applied—2010 Consolidation

Exhibit 3.10 presents a worksheet to consolidate these two companies for 2010 (the year of acquisition) based on the assumption that Parrot applied the partial equity method. Again, the only changes from previous examples are found in (1) the parent's separate records for this investment and its related income and (2) worksheet Entries **I** and **D.**

As discussed earlier, under the partial equity approach, the parent's record-keeping is limited to two periodic journal entries: the annual accrual of subsidiary income and the receipt of dividends. Hence, within the parent's records, only a few differences exist when the partial equity method is applied rather than the initial value method. The entries recorded by Parrot in connection with Sun's 2010 operations illustrate both of these approaches.

Parrot Company Initial Value Method 2010			Parrot Company Partial Equity Method 2010		
Cash	40,000		Cash	40,000	
Dividend Income . . .		40,000	Investment in Sun		
Dividends collected			Company		40,000
from subsidiary.			Dividends collected		
			from subsidiary.		
			Investment in Sun		
			Company	100,000	
			Equity in		
			Subsidiary Earnings		100,000
			Accrual of subsidiary		
			income.		

Therefore, by applying the partial equity method, the investment account on the parent's balance sheet rises to $860,000 by the end of 2010. This total is composed of the original $800,000 acquisition-date fair value for Sun adjusted for the $100,000 income recognition and the $40,000 cash dividend payment. The same $100,000 equity income figure appears within the parent's income statement. These two balances are appropriately found in Parrot's records in Exhibit 3.10.

Because of the handling of income recognition and dividend payments, Entries **I** and **D** again differ on the worksheet. For the partial equity method, the $100,000 equity income is eliminated (Entry **I**) by reversing the parent's entry. Removing this accrual allows the individual revenue and expense accounts of the subsidiary to be reported without double-counting. The $40,000 intra-entity dividend payment must also be removed (Entry **D**). The Dividend Paid account is simply deleted. However, elimination of the dividend from the Investment in Sun Company actually causes an increase because receipt was recorded by Parrot as a reduction in that account. All other consolidation entries (Entries **S, A,** and **E**) are the same for all three methods.

Consolidation Subsequent to Year of Acquisition—Initial Value and Partial Equity Methods

By again incorporating the December 31, 2013, financial data for Parrot and Sun (presented in Exhibit 3.7), consolidation procedures for the initial value method and the partial equity method are examined for years subsequent to the date of acquisition. *In both cases, establishment of an appropriate beginning retained earnings figure becomes a significant goal of the consolidation.*

Conversion of the Parent's Retained Earnings to a Full-Accrual (Equity) Basis

Consolidated financial statements require a *full accrual-based measurement of both income and retained earnings.* The initial value method, however, employs the cash basis for income recognition. The partial equity method only partially accrues subsidiary income. Thus, neither provides a full-accrual-based measure of the subsidiary activities on the parent's income. As a result, over time the parent's retained earnings account fails to show a full accrual-based amount. Therefore, new worksheet adjustments are required to convert the parent's beginning of the year retained earnings balance to a full-accrual basis. These adjustments are made to *beginning of the year retained earnings* because current year earnings are readily converted to full-accrual basis by simply combining current year revenue and expenses. The resulting current year combined income figure is then added to the

EXHIBIT 3.11
Retained Earnings Differences

PARROT COMPANY AND SUN COMPANY Previous Years—2010–2012			
	Equity Method	Initial Value Method	Partial Equity Method
Equity accrual	$330,000	–0–	$330,000
Dividend income	–0–	$110,000	–0–
Excess amortization expenses	(21,000)	–0–	–0–
Increase in parent's retained earnings	$309,000	$110,000	$330,000

adjusted beginning of the year retained earnings to arrive at a full accrual ending retained earnings balance.

This concern was not faced previously when the equity method was adopted. Under that approach, the parent's Retained Earnings account balance already reflects a full-accrual basis so that no adjustment is necessary. In the earlier illustration, the $330,000 income accrual for the 2010–2012 period as well as the $21,000 amortization expense were recognized by the parent in applying the equity method (see Exhibit 3.6). Having been recorded in this manner, these two balances form a permanent part of Parrot's retained earnings and are included automatically in the consolidated total. Consequently, if the equity method is applied, the process is simplified; no worksheet entries are needed to adjust the parent's Retained Earnings account to record subsidiary operations or amortization for past years.

Conversely, if a method other than the equity method is used, a worksheet change must be made to the parent's beginning Retained Earnings account (in every subsequent year) to equate this balance with a full-accrual amount. To quantify this adjustment, the parent's recognized income for these past three years under each method is first determined (Exhibit 3.11). For consolidation purposes, the beginning retained earnings account must then be increased or decreased to create the same effect as the equity method.

Initial Value Method Applied—Subsequent Consolidation

As shown in Exhibit 3.11, if Parrot applied the initial value method during the 2010–2012 period, it recognizes $199,000 less income than under the equity method ($309,000 − $110,000). Two items cause this difference. First, Parrot has not accrued the $220,000 increase in the subsidiary's book value across the periods prior to the current year. Although the $110,000 in dividends was recorded as income, the parent never recognized the remainder of the $330,000 earned by the subsidiary.[9] Second, no accounting has been made of the $21,000 excess amortization expenses. Thus, the parent's beginning Retained Earnings account is $199,000 ($220,000 − $21,000) below the appropriate consolidated total and must be adjusted.[10]

To simulate the equity method so that the parent's beginning Retained Earnings account reflects a full-accrual basis, this $199,000 increase is recorded through a worksheet entry. The initial value method figures reported by the parent effectively are converted into equity method balances.

[9] Two different calculations are available for determining the $220,000 in nonrecorded income for prior years: (1) subsidiary income less dividends paid and (2) the change in the subsidiary's book value as of the first day of the current year. The second method works only if the subsidiary has had no other equity transactions such as the issuance of new stock or the purchase of treasury shares. Unless otherwise stated, the assumption is made that no such transactions have occurred.

[10] Because neither the income in excess of dividends nor excess amortization is recorded by the parent under the initial value method, its beginning Retained Earnings account is $199,000 less than the $2,044,000 reported under the equity method (Exhibit 3.7). Thus, a $1,845,000 balance is shown in Exhibit 3.12 ($2,044,000 − this $199,000). Conversely, if the partial equity method had been applied, Parrot's absence of amortization would cause the Retained Earnings account to be $21,000 higher than the figure derived by the equity method. For this reason, Exhibit 3.13 shows the parent with a beginning Retained Earnings account of $2,065,000 rather than $2,044,000.

Consolidation Entry *C

Investment in Sun Company	199,000	
Retained Earnings, 1/1/13 (Parrot Company)		199,000
To convert parent's beginning retained earnings from the initial value method to equity method.		

This adjustment is labeled Entry *C. The *C* refers to the conversion being made to equity method (full accrual) totals. The asterisk indicates that this equity simulation relates solely to transactions of prior periods. Thus, *Entry *C should be recorded before the other worksheet entries to align the beginning balances for the year.*

Exhibit 3.12 provides a complete presentation of the consolidation of Parrot and Sun as of December 31, 2013, based on the parent's application of the initial value method. After Entry *C has been recorded on the worksheet, the remainder of this consolidation follows the same pattern as previous examples. Sun's stockholders' equity accounts are eliminated (Entry S) while the allocations stemming from the $800,000 initial fair value are recorded (Entry A) at their unamortized balances as of January 1, 2013 (see Exhibit 3.8). Intra-entity dividend income is removed (Entry I) and current year excess amortization expenses are recognized (Entry E). To complete this process, the intra-entity debt of $40,000 is offset (Entry P).

In retrospect, the only new element introduced here is the adjustment of the parent's beginning Retained Earnings. For a consolidation produced after the initial year of acquisition, an Entry *C is required if the parent has not applied the equity method.

Partial Equity Method Applied—Subsequent Consolidation

Exhibit 3.13 demonstrates the worksheet consolidation of Parrot and Sun as of December 31, 2013, when the investment accounts have been recorded by the parent using the partial equity method. This approach accrues subsidiary income each year but records no other equity adjustments. Therefore, as of December 31, 2013, Parrot's Investment in Sun Company account has a balance of $1,110,000:

Fair value of consideration transferred for Sun Company 1/1/10 . . .		$800,000
Sun Company's 2010–2012 increase in book value:		
Accrual of Sun Company's income	$330,000	
Collection of Sun Company's dividends	(110,000)	220,000
Sun Company's 2013 operations:		
Accrual of Sun Company's income	$160,000	
Collection of Sun Company's dividends	(70,000)	90,000
Investment in Sun Company, 12/31/13 (Partial equity method)		$1,110,000

As indicated here and in Exhibit 3.11, Parrot has recognized the yearly equity income accrual but not amortization. Consequently, if the partial equity method is in use, the parent's beginning Retained Earnings Account must be adjusted to include this expense. The three-year total of $21,000 amortization is reflected through Entry *C to simulate the equity method and, hence, consolidated totals.

Consolidation Entry *C

Retained Earnings, 1/1/13 (Parrot Company)	21,000	
Investment in Sun Company		21,000
To convert parent's beginning Retained Earnings from partial equity method to equity method by including excess amortizations.		

EXHIBIT 3.12

PARROT COMPANY AND SUN COMPANY
Consolidated Worksheet
Investment: Initial Value Method   For Year Ending December 31, 2013

Accounts	Parrot Company	Sun Company	Consolidation Entries Debit	Consolidation Entries Credit	Consolidation Totals
Income Statement					
Revenues	(2,100,000)	(600,000)			(2,700,000)
Cost of goods sold	1,000,000	380,000			1,380,000
Amortization expense	200,000	20,000	(E) 13,000		233,000
Depreciation expense	100,000	40,000		(E) 6,000	134,000
Dividend income	(70,000)*	–0–	(I) 70,000 *		–0–
Net income	(870,000)	(160,000)			(953,000)
Statement of Retained Earnings					
Retained earnings, 1/1/13					
Parrot Company	(1,845,000)†*			(*C) 199,000 *	(2,044,000)
Sun Company		(600,000)	(S) 600,000		–0–
Net income (above)	(870,000)	(160,000)			(953,000)
Dividends paid	420,000	70,000		(I) 70,000 *	420,000
Retained earnings, 12/31/13	(2,295,000)	(690,000)			(2,577,000)
Balance Sheet					
Current assets	1,705,000	500,000		(P) 40,000	2,165,000
Investment in Sun Company	800,000 *	–0–	(*C) 199,000	(S) 820,000	–0–
				(A) 179,000	
Trademarks	600,000	240,000	(A) 20,000		860,000
Patented technology	540,000	420,000	(A) 91,000	(E) 13,000	1,038,000
Equipment (net)	420,000	210,000	(E) 6,000	(A) 12,000	624,000
Goodwill	–0–	–0–	(A) 80,000		80,000
Total assets	4,065,000	1,370,000			4,767,000
Liabilities	(1,050,000)	(460,000)	(P) 40,000		(1,470,000)
Common stock	(600,000)	(200,000)	(S) 200,000		(600,000)
Additional paid-in capital	(120,000)	(20,000)	(S) 20,000		(120,000)
Retained earnings, 12/31/13 (above)	(2,295,000)	(690,000)			(2,577,000)
Total liabilities and equities	(4,065,000)	(1,370,000)	1,339,000	1,339,000	(4,767,000)

Note: Parentheses indicate a credit balance.
*Boxed items highlight differences with consolidation in Exhibit 3.7.
†See footnote 9.
  Consolidation entries:
  (*C) To convert parent's beginning retained earnings to full accrual basis.
  (S)   Elimination of Sun's stockholders' equity January 1 balances and the book value portion of investment account.
  (A)   Allocation of Sun's excess acquisition-date fair value over book value, unamortized balance as of beginning of year.
  (I)   Elimination of intra-entity dividend income and dividend paid by Sun.
  (E)   Recognition of current year excess fair-value amortization and depreciation expenses.
  (P)   Elimination of intra-entity receivable/payable.
Note: Consolidation entry (D) is not needed when the parent applies the initial value method because entry (I) eliminates the intra-entity dividend effects.

By recording Entry ***C** on the worksheet, all of the subsidiary's operational results for the 2010–2012 period are included in the consolidation. As shown in Exhibit 3.13, the remainder of the worksheet entries follow the same basic pattern as that illustrated previously for the year of acquisition (Exhibit 3.10).

Summary of Investment Methods

Having three investment methods available to the parent means that three sets of entries must be understood to arrive at reported figures appropriate for a business combination. The

EXHIBIT 3.13

			Consolidation Entries		

PARROT COMPANY AND SUN COMPANY
Consolidated Worksheet
Investment: Partial Equity Method   For Year Ending December 31, 2013

Accounts	Parrot Company	Sun Company	Debit	Credit	Consolidation Totals
Income Statement					
Revenues	(2,100,000)	(600,000)			(2,700,000)
Cost of goods sold	1,000,000	380,000			1,380,000
Amortization expense	200,000	20,000	(E) 13,000		233,000
Depreciation expense	100,000	40,000		(E) 6,000	134,000
Equity in subsidiary earnings	(160,000) *	–0–	(I) 160,000 *		–0–
Net income	(960,000)	(160,000)			(953,000)
Statement of Retained Earnings					
Retained earnings, 1/1/13					
Parrot Company	(2,065,000)† *		(*C) 21,000 *		(2,044,000)
Sun Company		(600,000)	(S) 600,000		–0–
Net income (above)	(960,000)	(160,000)			(953,000)
Dividends paid	420,000	70,000		(D) 70,000 *	420,000
Retained earnings, 12/31/13	(2,605,000)	(690,000)			(2,577,000)
Balance Sheet					
Current assets	1,705,000	500,000		(P) 40,000	2,165,000
Investment in Sun Company	1,110,000 *	–0–	(D) 70,000	(*C) 21,000 *	–0–
				(S) 820,000	
				(A) 179,000	
				(I) 160,000 *	
Trademarks	600,000	240,000	(A) 20,000		860,000
Patented technology	540,000	420,000	(A) 91,000	(E) 13,000	1,038,000
Equipment (net)	420,000	210,000	(E) 6,000	(A) 12,000	624,000
Goodwill	–0–	–0–	(A) 80,000		80,000
Total assets	4,375,000	1,370,000			4,767,000
Liabilities	(1,050,000)	(460,000)	(P) 40,000		(1,470,000)
Common stock	(600,000)	(200,000)	(S) 200,000		(600,000)
Additional paid-in capital	(120,000)	(20,000)	(S) 20,000		(120,000)
Retained earnings, 12/31/13 (above)	(2,605,000)	(690,000)			(2,577,000)
Total liabilities and equities	(4,375,000)	(1,370,000)	1,321,000	1,321,000	(4,767,000)

Note: Parentheses indicate a credit balance.
*Boxed items highlight differences with consolidation in Exhibit 3.7.
†See footnote 8.
Consolidation entries:
  (*C) To convert parent's beginning retained earnings to full accrual basis.
  (S)   Elimination of Sun's stockholders' equity January 1 balances and the book value portion of investment account.
  (A)   Allocation of Sun's excess acquisition-date fair value over book value, unamortized balance as of beginning of year.
  (I)   Elimination of parent's equity in subsidiary earnings accrual.
  (D)   Elimination of intra-entity dividend payment.
  (E)   Recognition of current year excess fair-value amortization and depreciation expenses.
  (P)   Elimination of intra-entity receivable/payable.

process can initially seem to be a confusing overlap of procedures. However, at this point in the coverage, only three worksheet entries actually are affected by the choice of either the equity method, partial equity method, or initial value method: Entries ***C, I,** and **D.** Furthermore, accountants should never get so involved with a worksheet and its entries that they lose sight of the balances that this process is designed to calculate. These figures are never affected by the parent's choice of an accounting method.

Consolidated Totals Subsequent to Acquisition*

Current revenues	Parent revenues are included.
	Subsidiary revenues are included but only for the period since the acquisition.
Current expenses	Parent expenses are included.
	Subsidiary expenses are included but only for the period since the acquisition.
	Amortization expenses of the excess fair-value allocations are included by recognition on the worksheet.
Investment (or dividend) income	Income recognized by parent is eliminated and effectively replaced by the subsidiary's revenues and expenses.
Retained earnings, beginning balance	Parent balance is included.
	The change in the subsidiary balance since acquisition is included either as a regular accrual by the parent or through a worksheet entry to increase parent balance.
	Past amortization expenses of the excess fair-value allocations are included either as a part of parent balance or through a worksheet entry.
Assets and liabilities	Parent balances are included.
	Subsidiary balances are included after adjusting for acquisition-date fair values.
	Intra-entity receivable/payable balances are eliminated.
Goodwill	Original fair-value allocation is included.
Investment in subsidiary	Asset account recorded by parent is eliminated on the worksheet so that the balance is not included in consoliated figures.
Capital stock and additional paid-in capital	Parent balances only are included although they will have been adjusted at acquisition date if stock was issued.

*The next few chapters discuss the necessity of altering some of these balances for consolidation purposes. Thus, this table is not definitive but is included only to provide a basic overview of the consolidation process as it has been described to this point.

After the appropriate balance for each account is understood, worksheet entries assist the accountant in deriving these figures. To help clarify the consolidation process required under each of the three accounting methods, Exhibit 3.14 describes the purpose of each worksheet entry: first during the year of acquisition and second for any period following the year of acquisition.

GOODWILL IMPAIRMENT

LO5

Discuss the rationale for the goodwill impairment testing approach.

The FASB ASC Topic 350, Intangibles—Goodwill and Other, provides the accounting standards for reporting the income statement effects from either amortization or impairment of intangibles acquired in a business combination. In accounting for goodwill subsequent to the acquisition date, GAAP requires an impairment approach rather than amortization. The FASB reasoned that although goodwill can decrease over time, it does not do so in the "rational and systematic" manner that periodic amortization suggests.[11] Thus, amortization was not viewed as representationally faithful of the pattern of goodwill decline and the FASB decided that goodwill would no longer be subject to amortization. As a result, a consolidated balance sheet today can show acquisition-related goodwill at its original assigned value. Only upon the recognition of an impairment loss (or partial sale of a subsidiary) will goodwill decline from one period to the next.

Current financial reporting standards require an annual test for goodwill impairment. Additionally, if one or more indicators of a potential impairment are present, testing must be performed more frequently. Goodwill is considered impaired when its carrying amount exceeds

---

[11] L. Todd Johnson and Kimberly R. Petrone, "Why Did the Board Change Its Mind on Goodwill Amortization?" *FASB Viewpoints,* December 2000.

EXHIBIT 3.14   **Consolidation Worksheet Entries**

Equity Method Applied		Initial Value Method Applied	Partial Equity Method Applied
Any Time during Year of Acquisition			
Entry **S**	Beginning stockholders' equity of subsidiary is eliminated against book value portion of investment account.	Same as equity method.	Same as equity method.
Entry **A**	Excess fair value is allocated to assets and liabilities based on difference in book values and fair values; residual is assigned to goodwill.	Same as equity method.	Same as equity method.
Entry **I**	Equity income accrual (including amortization expense) is eliminated.	Dividend income is eliminated.	Equity income accrual is eliminated.
Entry **D**	Intra-entity dividends paid by subsidiary are eliminated.	No entry—intra-entity dividends are eliminated in Entry **I**.	Same as equity method.
Entry **E**	Current year excess amortization expenses of fair-value allocations are recorded.	Same as equity method.	Same as equity method.
Entry **P**	Intra-entity payable/receivable balances are offset.	Same as equity method.	Same as equity method.
Any Time Following Year of Acquisition			
Entry ***C**	No entry—equity income for prior years has already been recognized along with amortization expenses.	Increase in subsidiary's book value during prior years as well as excess amortization expenses are recognized (conversion is made to equity method).	Excess amortization expenses for prior years are recognized (conversion is made to equity method).
Entry **S**	Same as initial year.	Same as initial year.	Same as initial year.
Entry **A**	Unamortized excess fair value at beginning of year is allocated to specific accounts and to goodwill.	Same as equity method.	Same as equity method.
Entry **I**	Same as initial year.	Same as initial year.	Same as initial year.
Entry **D**	Same as initial year.	Same as initial year.	Same as initial year.
Entry **E**	Same as initial year.	Same as initial year.	Same as initial year.
Entry **P**	Same as initial year.	Same as initial year.	Same as initial year.

its implied fair value. Goodwill impairment losses are reported as operating items in the consolidated income statement.

Importantly, goodwill impairment testing is performed at the reporting unit level. As discussed shortly, all assets (including goodwill) acquired and liabilities assumed in a business combination must be assigned across reporting units within a consolidated enterprise. The goodwill residing in each reporting unit is then separately subjected to periodic impairment testing. For example, Univision, Inc., recently noted the following in its annual report:

> For purposes of performing the impairment test of goodwill, we established the following reporting units: Television, Radio, and Interactive Media. The Company compares the fair value of the reporting unit to its carrying amount on an annual basis to determine if there is potential goodwill impairment. If the fair value of the reporting unit is less than its carrying value, an impairment loss is recorded to the extent that the fair value of the goodwill within the reporting unit is less than its carrying value.

Recent evidence shows that goodwill impairment losses can be substantial. A study released in 2009 by KPMG showed a large increase in goodwill impairments in 2008. Based on financial information from 1,604 U.S. companies, total impairment charges were $340 billion in 2008,

Discussion Question

HOW DOES A COMPANY REALLY DECIDE WHICH INVESTMENT METHOD TO APPLY?

Pilgrim Products, Inc., buys a controlling interest in the common stock of Crestwood Corporation. Shortly after the acquisition, a meeting of Pilgrim's accounting department is convened to discuss the internal reporting procedures required by the ownership of this subsidiary. Each member of the staff has a definite opinion as to whether the equity method, initial value method, or partial equity method should be adopted. To resolve this issue, Pilgrim's chief financial officer outlines several of her concerns about the decision.

> I already understand how each method works. I know the general advantages and disadvantages of all three. I realize, for example, that the equity method provides more detailed information whereas the initial value method is much easier to apply. What I need to know are the factors specific to our situation that should be considered in deciding which method to adopt. I must make a recommendation to the president on this matter, and he will want firm reasons for my favoring a particular approach. I don't want us to select a method and then find out in six months that the information is not adequate for our needs or that the cost of adapting our system to monitor Crestwood outweighs the benefits derived from the data.

What are the factors that Pilgrim's officials should evaluate when making this decision?

---

up from $143 billion in 2007 and $87 billion in 2006.[12] Exhibit 3.15 provides examples of goodwill impairment losses recognized in 2002—the first year goodwill impairment testing was required.

LO6

Describe the procedures for conducting a goodwill impairment test.

Testing Goodwill for Impairment

The notion of an indefinite life for goodwill allows firms to report over time the original amount of goodwill acquired in a business combination at its assigned acquisition-date value. However, such goodwill can, at some point in time, become impaired, requiring loss recognition and a reduction in the amount reported in the consolidated balance sheet. Unlike amortization, which periodically reduces asset values, impairment must first be revealed before a write-down is justified. To detect when goodwill impairment has occurred, a two-step testing procedure is utilized.

Step 1—Goodwill Impairment Test: Is the Fair Value of a Reporting Unit Less Than Its Carrying Value?

In the first step of impairment testing, fair values of the consolidated entity's reporting units with allocated goodwill are compared with their carrying values (*including goodwill*). If an individual reporting unit's total fair value exceeds its carrying value, its goodwill is not considered impaired, and the second step in testing is not performed. Goodwill remains at the amount assigned at the date of the business combination. However, if the fair value of a reporting unit has fallen below its carrying value, a potential for goodwill impairment exists. In this case, a second step must be performed to determine whether goodwill has been impaired.

EXHIBIT 3.15
Goodwill Impairment Examples (in billions) 2002—First Year of Impairment Requirements

AOL Time Warner	$99.7 billion
Boeing	2.4
Blockbuster	1.8
SBC Communications	1.8
General Electric	1.0
Coca-Cola	926 million
AT&T	856
Safeway	700
Verizon Communications	500

[12] KPMG LLP, "Evaluation Impairment Risk: Goodwill Impairment Continues Its Upward Climb," 2009.

Step 2—Goodwill Impairment Test: Is Goodwill's Implied Value Less Than Its Carrying Value?

If Step 1 indicates a potential goodwill impairment for a reporting unit, goodwill's implied and carrying values are compared for that reporting unit. The second test requires determining the fair value of the related goodwill. If goodwill's fair value has declined below its carrying value, an impairment loss is recognized for the excess carrying value over fair value. However, determining fair values for reporting units and goodwill can be complex, making implementation of the necessary comparisons costly. These complexities are described in terms of three key attributes that govern the process of testing goodwill for impairment:

1. The assignment of acquisition values to reporting units.
2. The periodic determination of the fair values of reporting units.
3. The determination of goodwill implied fair value.

Assigning Values to Reporting Units

In deciding to forgo amortization in favor of impairment testing for goodwill, the FASB noted that goodwill is primarily associated with individual *reporting units* within the consolidated entity. Such goodwill is often considered "synergistic" because it arises from the interaction of the assets of the acquired company with those of the acquirer in specific ways. To better assess potential declines in value for goodwill (in place of amortization), the most specific business level at which goodwill is evident is deemed the appropriate level for impairment testing. This specific business level is referred to as the *reporting unit*. The FASB also noted that, in practice, goodwill is often assigned to reporting units either at the level of a reporting segment—as described in FASB ASC Topic 280, Segment Reporting—or at a lower level within a segment of a combined enterprise. Consequently, the reporting unit is the designated enterprise component for tests of goodwill impairment. Reporting units may thus include the following:

- A component of an operating segment at a level below the operating segment. Segment management should review and assess performance at this level. Also, the component should be a business in which discrete financial information is available and should differ economically from other components of the operating segment.
- The segments of an enterprise.
- The entire enterprise.

For example, Pfizer Inc. observed in its 2008 annual report:

> For goodwill, which includes amounts related to our Pharmaceutical and Animal Health segments, each year and whenever impairment indictors are present, we calculate the fair value of each business segment and calculate the implied fair value of goodwill by subtracting the fair value of the identifiable net assets other than goodwill and record an impairment loss for the excess of book value of goodwill over the implied fair value, if any.

In implementing impairment tests, it is essential first to identify the reporting units resulting from the acquisition. The assets and liabilities (including goodwill) acquired in a business combination are then assigned to these identified reporting units. The assignment should consider where the acquired assets and liabilities will be employed and whether they will be included in determining the reporting unit's fair value. The goodwill should be assigned to those reporting units that are expected to benefit from the synergies of the combination. Overall, the objective of the assignment of acquired assets and liabilities to reporting units is to facilitate the required fair value/carrying value comparisons for periodic impairment testing.

Determining Fair Values of Reporting Units Periodically

The necessary comparisons to determine whether goodwill is impaired depend first on the fair-value computation of the reporting unit and then, if necessary, the fair-value computation for goodwill—but how are such values computed? How can fair values be known if the subsidiary is wholly owned and thus not traded publicly?

Several alternative methods exist for determining the fair values of the reporting units that compose a consolidated entity. First, any quoted market prices that exist can provide a basis for assessing fair value—particularly for subsidiaries with actively traded noncontrolling interests. Second, comparable businesses may exist that can help indicate market values. Third, a variety of present value techniques assess the fair value of an identifiable set of future cash flow streams or profit projections discounted for the riskiness of the future flows. Clearly, portions of consolidated entities are frequently bought and sold. In these transactions, parties do derive fair values. However, the required periodic assessment of fair value is costly when applied to many firms.

Once a detailed determination of the fair value of a reporting unit is made, that fair value may be used in subsequent periods if *all* of the following criteria are met:

- The assets and liabilities that compose the reporting unit have not changed significantly since the most recent fair-value determination. (A recent acquisition or a reorganization of an entity's segment reporting structure are examples of events that might significantly change the composition of a reporting unit.)
- The most recent fair-value determination resulted in an amount that exceeded the carrying amount of the reporting unit by a substantial margin.
- Based on an analysis of events that have occurred and circumstances that have changed since the most recent fair-value determination, it is remote that a current fair-value determination would be less than the reporting unit's current carrying amount.

If any of these criteria are not met, an updated determination of the reporting unit's fair value is required.

Determining Goodwill's Implied Fair Value

If the fair value of a reporting unit, once determined, falls below its carrying value, the second step of the impairment test focuses on the possibility that goodwill could be impaired. Then the fair value of goodwill must be determined in order to make the relevant comparison to its carrying value. Because, by definition, goodwill is not separable from other assets, it is not possible to directly observe its market value. Therefore, an *implied* value for goodwill is calculated in a similar manner to the determination of goodwill in a business combination. The fair value of the reporting unit is treated as an acquisition-date fair value as if the reporting unit were being acquired in a business combination. Then this amount is allocated to all of the reporting unit's identifiable assets and liabilities with any remaining excess considered as the fair value of goodwill. This procedure is used only for assessing the fair value of goodwill. None of the other values allocated to assets and liabilities in the testing comparison are used to adjust their reported amounts.

Example—Accounting and Reporting for a Goodwill Impairment Loss

To illustrate the procedure for recognizing goodwill impairment, assume that on January 1, 2011, Newcall Corporation was formed to consolidate the telecommunications operations of DSM, Inc., Rocketel Company, and Visiontalk Company in a deal valued at $2.9 billion. Each of the three former firms is considered an operating segment, and each will be maintained as a subsidiary of Newcall. Additionally, DSM comprises two divisions—DSM Wired and DSM Wireless—that along with Rocketel and Visiontalk are treated as independent reporting units for internal performance evaluation and management reviews. Newcall recognized $221 million as goodwill at the merger date and allocated this entire amount to its reporting units. That information and each unit's acquisition fair value were as follows:

Newcall's Reporting Units	Goodwill	Acquisition Fair Value January 1, 2011
DSM Wired	$ 22,000,000	$950,000,000
DSM Wireless	155,000,000	748,000,000
Rocketel	38,000,000	492,000,000
Visiontalk	6,000,000	710,000,000

In December 2011, Newcall tested each of its four reporting units for goodwill impairment. Accordingly, Newcall compared the fair value of each of its reporting units to their respective carrying values. The comparisons revealed that the fair value of each reporting unit exceeded its carrying value except for DSM Wireless, whose market value had fallen to $600 million, well below its current carrying value. The decline in value was attributed to a failure to realize expected cost-saving synergies with Rocketel.

Newcall then compares the implied fair value of the DSM Wireless goodwill to its carrying value. Newcall derived the implied fair value of goodwill through the following allocation of the fair value of DSM Wireless:

DSM Wireless Dec. 31, 2011, fair value		$600,000,000
Fair values of DSM Wireless net assets at Dec. 31, 2011:		
Current assets	$ 50,000,000	
Property	125,000,000	
Equipment	265,000,000	
Subscriber list	140,000,000	
Patented technology	185,000,000	
Current liabilities	(44,000,000)	
Long-term debt	(125,000,000)	
Value assigned to identifiable net assets		596,000,000
Implied fair value of goodwill		4,000,000
Carrying value before impairment		155,000,000
Impairment loss		$151,000,000

Thus, $151,000,000 is reported as a separate line item in the operating section of Newcall's consolidated income statement as a goodwill impairment loss. Additional disclosures are required describing (1) the facts and circumstances leading to the impairment and (2) the method of determining the fair value of the associated reporting unit (e.g., market prices, comparable business, present value technique).

Although the amount reported for goodwill changes, the amounts for the other assets and liabilities of DSM Wireless do not change. The reported values for all of DSM Wireless's remaining assets and liabilities continue to be based on amounts assigned at the business combination date.

COMPARISONS WITH INTERNATIONAL ACCOUNTING STANDARDS

International Financial Reporting Standards (IFRS) and U.S. GAAP both require goodwill recognition in a business combination when the fair value of the consideration transferred exceeds the net fair values of the assets acquired and liabilities assumed. Subsequent to acquisition, both IFRS and U.S. GAAP require testing for goodwill impairment at least annually and more frequently in the presence of potential impairment indicators. Also for both sets of standards, goodwill impairments, once recognized, are not recoverable. However, differences exist across the two sets of standards in the way goodwill impairment is tested for and recognized. In particular, goodwill allocation, impairment testing, and determination of the impairment loss differ across the two reporting regimes and are discussed below.

Goodwill Allocation

- *U.S. GAAP.* Goodwill acquired in a business combination is allocated to reporting units expected to benefit from the goodwill. Reporting units are operating segments or a business component one level below an operating segment.
- *IFRS.* International Accounting Standard *(IAS) 36* requires goodwill acquired in a business combination to be allocated to cash-generating units or groups of cash-generating units that are expected to benefit from the synergies of the business combination. Cash-generating groups represent the lowest level within the entity at which the goodwill is monitored for internal management purposes and are not to be larger than an operating segment or determined in accordance with IFRS 8 *Operating Segments*.

Impairment Testing

- *U.S. GAAP.* A two-step testing procedure first requires a comparison between each reporting unit's total fair value and carrying value. If carrying value exceeds fair value, then a second step comparing goodwill's implied fair value to its carrying amount is performed.
- *IFRS.* A one-step approach compares the fair and carrying values of each cash-generating unit with goodwill. If the carrying amount exceeds the fair value of the cash-generating unit, then goodwill (and possibly other assets of the cash-generating unit) is considered impaired.

Determination of the Impairment Loss

- *U.S. GAAP.* In step two, a reporting unit's implied fair value for goodwill is computed as the excess of the reporting unit's fair value over the fair value of its identifiable net assets. If the carrying amount of goodwill is greater than its implied fair value, an impairment loss is recognized for the difference.
- *IFRS.* Any excess carrying amount over fair value for a cash-generating unit is first assigned to reduce goodwill. If goodwill is reduced to zero, then the other assets of the cash-generating unit are reduced pro-rata based on the carrying amounts of the assets.

Finally, the FASB and IASB have agreed to include impairment recognition and reporting as one of their future convergence projects.

AMORTIZATION AND IMPAIRMENT OF OTHER INTANGIBLES

As discussed in Chapter 2, the acquisition method governs how we initially consolidate the assets acquired and liabilities assumed in a business combination. In periods subsequent to acquisition, income determination becomes a regular part of the consolidation process. The fair value bases (established at the acquisition date) for definite-lived subsidiary assets acquired and liabilities assumed will be amortized over their remaining lives for income recognition. For indefinite-lived assets (e.g., goodwill, certain other intangibles), an impairment model is used to assess whether asset write-downs are appropriate.

Current accounting standards suggest categories of intangible assets for possible recognition when one business acquires another. Examples include noncompetition agreements, customer lists, patents, subscriber lists, databases, trademarks, lease agreements, licenses, and many others. All identified intangible assets should be amortized over their economic useful life unless such life is considered *indefinite.* The term *indefinite life* is defined as a life that extends beyond the foreseeable future. A recognized intangible asset with an indefinite life should not be amortized unless and until its life is determined to be finite. Importantly, *indefinite* does not mean "infinite." Also, the useful life of an intangible asset should not be considered indefinite because a precise finite life is not known.

For those intangible assets with finite lives, the amortization method should reflect the pattern of decline in the economic usefulness of the asset. If no such pattern is apparent, the straight-line method of amortization should be used. The amount to be amortized should be the value assigned to the intangible asset less any residual value. In most cases, the residual value is presumed to be zero. However, that presumption can be overcome if the acquiring enterprise has a commitment from a third party to purchase the intangible at the end of its useful life or an observable market exists for the intangible asset that provides a basis for estimating a terminal value.

The length of the amortization period for identifiable intangibles (i.e., those not included in goodwill) depends primarily on the assumed economic life of the asset. Factors that should be considered in determining the useful life of an intangible asset include

- Legal, regulatory, or contractual provisions.
- The effects of obsolescence, demand, competition, industry stability, rate of technological change, and expected changes in distribution channels.

- The enterprise's expected use of the intangible asset.
- The level of maintenance expenditure required to obtain the asset's expected future benefits.

Any recognized intangible assets considered to possess indefinite lives are not amortized but instead are tested for impairment on an annual basis.[13] To test for impairment, the carrying amount of the intangible asset is compared to its fair value. If the fair value is less than the carrying amount, then the intangible asset is considered impaired and an impairment loss is recognized. The asset's carrying value is reduced accordingly.

CONTINGENT CONSIDERATION

LO7

Understand the accounting and reporting for contingent consideration subsequent to a business acquisition.

Contingency agreements frequently accompany business combinations. In many cases, the target firm asks for consideration based on projections of its future performance. The acquiring firm, however, may not share the projections and, thus, may be unwilling to pay now for uncertain future performance. To close the deal, agreements for the acquirer's future payments to the former owners of the target are common. Alternatively, when the acquirer's stock comprises the consideration transferred, the sellers of the target firm may request a guaranteed minimum market value of the stock for a period of time to ensure a fair price.

Accounting for Contingent Consideration in Business Combinations

Under the acquisition method, contingent consideration obligations are recognized as part of the initial value assigned in a business combination, consistent with the fair-value concept. Therefore, the acquiring firm must estimate the fair value of the contingent portion of the total business fair value. The contingency's fair value is recognized as part of the acquisition regardless of whether it is based on future performance of the target firm or the future stock prices of the acquirer.[14]

As an illustration, assume that Skeptical, Inc., acquires 100 percent of the voting stock of Rosy Pictures Company on January 1, 2011, for the following consideration:

- $550,000 market value of 10,000 shares of its $5-par common stock.
- A contingent payment of $80,000 cash if Rosy Pictures generates cash flows from operations of $20,000 or more in 2011.
- A payment of sufficient shares of Skeptical common stock to ensure a total value of $550,000 if the price per share is less than $55 on January 1, 2012.

Under the acquisition method, each of the three elements of consideration represents a portion of the negotiated fair value of Rosy Pictures and therefore must be included in the recorded value entered on Skeptical's accounting records. For the cash contingency, Skeptical estimates that there is a 30 percent chance that the $80,000 payment will be required. For the stock contingency, Skeptical estimates that there is a 20 percent probability that the 10,000 shares issued will have a market value of $540,000 on January 1, 2012, and an 80 percent probability that the market value of the 10,000 shares will exceed $550,000. Skeptical uses an interest rate of 4 percent to incorporate the time value of money.

To determine the fair values of the contingent consideration, Skeptical computes the present value of the expected payments as follows:

- *Cash contingency* = $80,000 × 30% × (1/[1 + .04]) = $23,077
- *Stock contingency* = $10,000 × 20% × (1/[1 + .04]) = $1,923

---

[13] Impairment tests should also be conducted on an interim basis if an event or circumstance occurs between annual tests indicating that an intangible asset could be impaired.

[14] The FASB recommends that a probability weighted approach, such as the expected cash flow discussed in FASB *Concepts Statement No. 7,* "Using Cash Flow Information and Present Value in Accounting Measurements," may be useful in estimating the fair value of contingent consideration. This approach may include any or all of the following five elements:

1. An estimate of the future cash flow or, in more complex cases, series of future cash flows at different times.
2. Expectations about possible variations in the amount or timing of those cash flows.
3. The time value of money, represented by the risk-free rate of interest.
4. The price for bearing the uncertainty inherent in the asset or liability.
5. Other, sometimes unidentifiable, factors including illiquidity and market imperfections.

Skeptical then records in its accounting records the acquisition of Rosy Pictures as follows:

Investment in Rosy Pictures	575,000	
Common stock (5 par)		50,000
APIC		500,000
Contingent performance obligation		23,077
APIC—Contingent equity outstanding		1,923
To record acquisition of Rosy Pictures at fair value of consideration transferred including performance and stock contingencies.		

Skeptical will report the contingent cash payment under its liabilities and the contingent stock payment as a component of stockholders' equity. Subsequent to acquisition, obligations for contingent consideration that meet the definition of a liability will continue to be measured at fair value with adjustments recognized in income. Those obligations classified as equity are not subsequently remeasured at fair value, consistent with other equity issues (e.g., common stock).

To continue the preceding example, assume that in 2011 Rosy Pictures exceeds the cash flow from operations threshold of $20,000, thus requiring an additional payment of $80,000. Also, Skeptical's stock price had fallen to $54.45 at January 1, 2012, thus requiring Skeptical to issue another 101 shares of its $5 par common stock to the former owners of Rosy Pictures.

Contingent performance obligation	23,077	
Loss from revaluation of contingent performance obligation	56,923	
Cash		80,000
To record contingent cash payment required by original Rosy Pictures acquisition agreement.		
APIC—Contingent equity outstanding	1,923	
Common stock		505
APIC		1,418
To record contingent stock issue required by original Rosy Pictures acquisition agreement.		

The loss from revaluation of the contingent performance obligation is reported in Skeptical's consolidated income statement as a component of ordinary income. Regarding the additional required stock issue, note that Skeptical's total paid-in capital remains unchanged from the total $551,923 recorded at the acquisition date.

PUSH-DOWN ACCOUNTING

LO8

Understand in general the requirements of push-down accounting and when its use is appropriate.

External Reporting

In the analysis of business combinations to this point, discussion has focused on (1) the recording by the parent company and (2) required consolidation procedures. Unfortunately, official accounting pronouncements give virtually no guidance as to the impact of an acquisition on the separate financial statements of the subsidiary.

This issue has become especially significant in recent years because of acquisitions by private-equity firms. An organization, for example, might acquire a company and subsequently offer the shares back to the public in hopes of making a large profit. What should be reported in the subsidiary's financial statements being distributed with this offering? Such deals have reheated a long-standing debate over the merits of *push-down accounting,* the direct recording of fair-value allocations and subsequent amortization by a subsidiary.

For this reason, the FASB has explored various methods of reporting by a company that has been acquired or reorganized. To illustrate, assume that Yarrow Company owns one asset: a building with a book value of $200,000 but a fair value of $900,000. Mannen Corporation pays exactly $900,000 in cash to acquire Yarrow. Consolidation offers no real problem here: The building will be reported by the business combination at $900,000.

However, if Yarrow continues to issue separate financial statements (for example, to its creditors or potential stockholders), should the building be reported at $200,000 or $900,000? If adjusted, should the $700,000 increase be reported as a gain by the subsidiary or as an addition to contributed capital? Should depreciation be based on $200,000 or $900,000? If the subsidiary is to be viewed as a new entity with a new basis for its assets and liabilities, should Retained Earnings be returned to zero? If the parent acquires only 51 percent of Yarrow, does that change the answers to the previous questions? These questions represent just a few of the difficult issues currently being explored.

Proponents of push-down accounting argue that a change in ownership creates a new basis for subsidiary assets and liabilities. An unadjusted balance ($200,000 in the preceding illustration) is a cost figure applicable to previous stockholders. That total is no longer relevant information. Rather, according to this argument, it is the historical cost *paid by the current owner* that is important, a figure that is best reflected by the expenditure made in acquiring the subsidiary. Balance sheet accounts should be reported at the cost incurred by the present stockholders ($900,000 in the illustration) rather than the cost incurred by the company.

Currently, primary guidance concerning push-down accounting for external reporting purposes is provided by the Securities and Exchange Commission (SEC). Through *Staff Accounting Bulletin No. 54*, "Application of 'Push Down' Basis of Accounting in Financial Statements of Subsidiaries Acquired by Purchase," and *Staff Accounting Bulletin No. 73*, "'Push Down' Basis of Accounting for Parent Company Debt Related to Subsidiary Acquisitions," the SEC has indicated that

> push down accounting should be used in the separate financial statements of a "substantially wholly owned" subsidiary. . . . That view is based on the notion that when the form of ownership is within the control of the parent company, the accounting basis should be the same whether the entity continues to exist or is merged into the parent's operations. If a purchase of a "substantially wholly owned" subsidiary is financed by debt of the parent, that debt generally must be pushed down to the subsidiary. . . . As a general rule, the SEC requires push down accounting when the ownership change is greater than 95 percent and objects to push down accounting when the ownership change is less than 80 percent. However, if the acquired subsidiary has outstanding public debt or preferred stock, push down accounting is encouraged by the SEC but not required.

Thus, the SEC requires the use of push-down accounting for the separate financial statements of any subsidiary when no substantial outside ownership of the company's common stock, preferred stock, and publicly held debt exists. Apparently, the SEC believes that a change in ownership of that degree justifies a new basis of reporting for the subsidiary's assets and liabilities. Until the FASB takes action, though, application is required only when the subsidiary desires to issue securities (stock or debt) to the public as regulated by the SEC.

Internal Reporting

Although the use of push-down accounting for external reporting is limited, this approach has gained significant popularity in recent years for internal reporting purposes.

> Subsidiaries owned by the Chesapeake Corporation are recorded using push-down accounting. Under this theory, the subsidiary adjusts its assets and liabilities to current value at the time of the acquisition while also recording the necessary goodwill. The subsidiary's net assets, as adjusted, would equal the amount recorded by the parent as the investment in subsidiary.[15]

Push-down accounting has several advantages for internal reporting. For example, it simplifies the consolidation process. Because the allocations and amortization have already been entered into the records of the subsidiary, worksheet Entries **A** (to recognize the allocations originating from the fair-value adjustments) and **E** (amortization expense) are not needed. Therefore, except for eliminating the effects of intra-entity transactions, the assets, liabilities, revenues, and expenses of the subsidiary can be added directly to those of the parent to derive consolidated totals.

---

[15] Letter from Timothy M. Harhan, senior corporate accountant with Chesapeake Corporation.

More important, push-down accounting provides better information for internal evaluation. Because the subsidiary's separate figures include amortization expense, the net income reported by the company is a good representation of the impact that the acquisition has on the earnings of the business combination. As an example, assume that Ace Corporation owns 100 percent of Waxworth, Inc. Waxworth uses push-down accounting and reports net income of $500,000: $600,000 from operations less $100,000 in amortization expense resulting from fair-value allocations. Thus, Ace Corporation's officials know that this acquisition has added $500,000 to the consolidated net income of the business combination. They can then evaluate whether these earnings provide a sufficient return for the parent's investment.

However, the recording of amortization expense by the subsidiary can lead to dissension. Members of the subsidiary's management could argue that they are being forced to record a large expense over which they have no control or responsibility. This amortization comes directly from the consideration paid by the parent but is not a result of any action taken by the subsidiary. Chesapeake Corporation has considered this problem and resolved it in the following manner: "For internal reporting of income statement activity, earnings from operations are identified separately from amortization. This allows management to analyze the subsidiary's results without the effect of amortization."[16]

[16] Ibid.

Summary

1. The procedures used to consolidate financial information generated by the separate companies in a business combination are affected by both the passage of time and the method applied by the parent in accounting for the subsidiary. Thus, no single consolidation process that is applicable to all business combinations can be described.

2. The parent might elect to utilize the equity method to account for a subsidiary. As discussed in Chapter 1, the parent accrues income when earned by the subsidiary and dividend receipts are recorded as reductions in the investment account. The effects of excess fair-value amortizations or any intra-entity transactions also are reflected within the parent's financial records. The equity method provides the parent with accurate information concerning the subsidiary's impact on consolidated totals; however, it is usually somewhat complicated to apply.

3. The initial value method and the partial equity method are two alternatives to the equity method. The initial value method recognizes only the subsidiary's dividends as income while the asset balance remains at the acquisition-date fair value. This approach is simple and provides a measure of cash flows between the two companies. Under the partial equity method, the parent accrues the subsidiary's income as earned but does not record adjustments that might be required by excess fair-value amortizations or intra-entity transfers. The partial equity method is easier to apply than the equity method, and, in many cases, the parent's income is a reasonable approximation of the consolidated total.

4. For a consolidation in any subsequent period, all reciprocal balances must be eliminated. Thus, the subsidiary's equity accounts, the parent's investment balance, and intra-entity income, dividends, and liabilities are removed. In addition, the remaining unamortized portions of the fair-value allocations are recognized along with excess amortization expenses for the period. If the equity method has not been applied, the parent's beginning Retained Earnings account also must be adjusted for any previous income or excess amortizations that have not yet been recorded.

5. For each subsidiary acquisition, the parent must assign the acquired assets and liabilities (including goodwill) to individual reporting units of its combined operations. The reporting units should be at the level of operating segment or lower and must provide the basis for future assessments of fair value. Any value assigned to goodwill is not amortized but instead is tested annually for impairment. This test consists of two steps. First, if the fair values of any of the consolidated entity's reporting units fall below their carrying values, then the implied value of the associated goodwill must be recomputed. Second, the recomputed implied value of goodwill is compared to its carrying value. An impairment loss must then be recognized if the carrying value of goodwill exceeds its implied value.

6. The acquisition-date fair value assigned to a subsidiary can be based, at least in part, on the fair value of any contingent consideration. For contingent obligations that meet the definition of a liability, the obligation is adjusted for changes in fair value over time with corresponding recognition of gains or losses from the revaluation. For contingent obligations classified as equity, no remeasurement to fair value takes place. In either case the initial value recognized in the combination does not change regardless of whether the contingency is eventually paid or not.

7. Push-down accounting is the adjustment of the subsidiary's account balances to recognize allocations and goodwill stemming from the parent's acquisition. Subsequent amortization of these figures also is recorded by the subsidiary as an expense. At this time, push-down accounting is required by the SEC for the separate statements of the subsidiary only when no substantial outside ownership exists. The FASB is currently studying push-down accounting and may issue more specific rules on its application. However, for internal reporting purposes, push-down accounting is gaining popularity because it aids company officials in evaluating the impact that the subsidiary has on the business combination.

Comprehensive Illustration

PROBLEM

(*Estimated Time: 40 to 65 Minutes*) On January 1, 2011, Top Company acquired all of Bottom Company's outstanding common stock for $842,000 in cash. As of that date, one of Bottom's buildings with a 12-year remaining life was undervalued on its financial records by $72,000. Equipment with a 10-year life was undervalued, but only by $10,000. The book values of all of Bottom's other assets and liabilities were equal to their fair values at that time except for an unrecorded licensing agreement with an assessed value of $40,000 and a 20-year remaining useful life. Bottom's book value at the acquisition date was $720,000.

During 2011, Bottom reported net income of $100,000 and paid $30,000 in dividends. Earnings were $120,000 in 2012 with $20,000 in dividends distributed by the subsidiary. As of December 31, 2013, the companies reported the following selected balances, which include all revenues and expenses for the year:

	Top Company December 31, 2013		Bottom Company December 31, 2013	
	Debit	Credit	Debit	Credit
Buildings	$1,540,000		$460,000	
Cash and receivables	50,000		90,000	
Common stock		$ 900,000		$400,000
Dividends paid	70,000		10,000	
Equipment	280,000		200,000	
Cost of goods sold	500,000		120,000	
Depreciation expense	100,000		60,000	
Inventory	280,000		260,000	
Land	330,000		250,000	
Liabilities		480,000		260,000
Retained earnings, 1/1/13		1,360,000		490,000
Revenues		900,000		300,000

Required

a. If Top applies the equity method, what is its investment account balance as of December 31, 2013?

b. If Top applies the initial value method, what is its investment account balance as of December 31, 2013?

c. Regardless of the accounting method in use by Top, what are the consolidated totals as of December 31, 2013, for each of the following accounts?

Buildings	Revenues
Equipment	Net Income
Land	Investment in Bottom
Depreciation Expense	Dividends Paid
Amortization Expense	Cost of Goods Sold

d. Prepare the worksheet entries required on December 31, 2013, to consolidate the financial records of these two companies. Assume that Top applied the equity method to its investment account.

e. How would the worksheet entries in requirement (d) be altered if Top has used the initial value method?

SOLUTION

a. To determine the investment balances under the equity method, four items must be determined: the initial value assigned, the income accrual, dividend payments, and amortization of excess acquisition-date fair value over book value. Although the first three are indicated in the problem, amortizations must be calculated separately.

An allocation of Bottom's acquisition-date fair values as well as the related amortization expense follows.

Fair value of consideration transferred by Top Company	$ 842,000
Book value of Bottom Company, 1/1/11	(720,000)
Excess fair value over book value	$ 122,000

Adjustments to specific accounts based on fair values:

		Life (years)	Annual Amortization
Buildings	$ 72,000	12	$6,000
Equipment	10,000	10	1,000
Licensing agreement	40,000	20	2,000
Totals	$122,000		$9,000

Thus, if Top adopts the equity method to account for this subsidiary, the Investment in Bottom account shows a December 31, 2013, balance of $1,095,000, computed as follows:

Initial value (fair value of consideration transferred by Top)		$ 842,000
Bottom Company's 2011–2012 increase in book value (income less dividends)		170,000
Excess amortizations for 2011–2012 ($9,000 per year for two years)		(18,000)
Current year recognition (2013):		
Equity income accrual (Bottom's revenues less its expenses) . . .	$120,000	
Excess amortization expenses	(9,000)	
Dividend from Bottom	(10,000)	101,000
Investment in Bottom Company, 12/31/13		$1,095,000

The $120,000 income accrual and the $9,000 excess amortization expenses indicate that an Equity in Subsidiary Earnings balance of $111,000 appears in Top's income statement for the current period.

b. If Top Company applies the initial value method, the Investment in Bottom Company account permanently retains its original $842,000 balance, and the parent recognizes only the intra-entity dividend of $10,000 as income in 2013.

c. • The consolidated Buildings account as of December 31, 2013, has a balance of $2,054,000. Although the two book value figures total only $2 million, a $72,000 allocation was made to this account based on fair value at the date of acquisition. Because this amount is being depreciated at the rate of $6,000 per year, the original allocation will have been reduced by $18,000 by the end of 2013, leaving only a $54,000 increase.

• On December 31, 2013, the consolidated Equipment account amounts to $487,000. The book values found in the financial records of Top and Bottom provide a total of $480,000. Once again, the allocation ($10,000) established by the acquisition-date fair value must be included in the consolidated balance after being adjusted for three years of depreciation ($1,000 × 3 years, or $3,000).

• Land has a consolidated total of $580,000. Because the book value and fair value of Bottom's land were in agreement at the date of acquisition, no additional allocation was made to this account. Thus, the book values are simply added together to derive a consolidated figure.

• *Cost of goods sold* = $620,000. The cost of goods sold of the parent and subsidiary are added together.

- *Depreciation expense* = $167,000. The depreciation expenses of the parent and subsidiary are added together along with the $6,000 additional building depreciation and the $1,000 additional equipment depreciation as presented in the fair-value allocation schedule.

- *Amortization expense* = $2,000. An additional expense of $2,000 is recognized from the amortization of the licensing agreement acquired in the business combination.

- The Revenues account appears as $1.2 million in the consolidated income statement. None of the worksheet entries in this example affects the individual balances of either company. Consolidation results merely from the addition of the two book values.

- Net income for this business combination is $411,000: consolidated expenses of $789,000 subtracted from revenues of $1.2 million.

- The parent's Investment in Bottom account is removed entirely on the worksheet so that no balance is reported. For consolidation purposes, this account is always eliminated so that the individual assets and liabilities of the subsidiary can be included.

- Dividends paid by the combination should be reported as $70,000, the amount Top distributed. Because Bottom's dividend payments are entirely intra-entity, they are deleted in arriving at consolidated figures.

d. Consolidation Entries Assuming Equity Method Used by Parent

Entry S

Common Stock (Bottom Company)	400,000	
Retained Earnings, 1/1/13		
(Bottom Company)	490,000	
Investment in Bottom Company		890,000

Elimination of subsidiary's beginning stockholders' equity accounts against book value portion of investment account.

Entry A

Buildings	60,000	
Equipment	8,000	
Licensing Agreement	36,000	
Investment in Bottom Company		104,000

To recognize fair-value allocations to the subsidiary's assets in excess of book value. Balances represent original allocations less two years of amortization for the 2011–2013 period.

Entry I

Equity in Subsidiary Earnings	111,000	
Investment in Bottom Company		111,000

To eliminate parent's equity income accrual, balance is computed in requirement (*a*).

Entry D

Investment in Bottom	10,000	
Dividends Paid		10,000

To eliminate intra-entity dividend payment made by the subsidiary to the parent (and recorded as a reduction in the investment account because the equity method is in use).

Entry E

Depreciation expense	7,000	
Amortization expense	2,000	
Equipment		1,000
Buildings		6,000
Licensing Agreement		2,000

To recognize excess fair-value depreciation and amortization for 2013.

e. If Top utilizes the initial value method rather than the equity method, three changes are required in the development of consolidation entries:

(1) An Entry ***C** is required to update the parent's beginning Retained Earnings account as if the equity method had been applied. Both an income accrual as well as excess amortizations for the prior two years must be recognized because these balances were not recorded by the parent.

Entry *C

Investment in Bottom Company	152,000	
Retained Earnings, 1/1/13 (Top Company)		152,000

To convert to the equity method by accruing the net effect
of the subsidiary's operations (income less dividends) for the prior
two years ($170,000) along with excess amortization expenses
($18,000) for this same period.

(2) An alteration is needed in Entry **I** because, under the initial value method, only dividend payments are recorded by the parent as income.

Entry I

Dividend Income	10,000	
Dividends Paid		10,000

To eliminate intra-entity dividend payments recorded by parent as income.

(3) Finally, because the intra-entity dividends have been eliminated in Entry **I**, no separate Entry **D** is needed.

Questions

1. CCES Corporation acquires a controlling interest in Schmaling, Inc. CCES may utilize any one of three methods to internally account for this investment. Describe each of these methods, and indicate their advantages and disadvantages.

2. Maguire Company obtains 100 percent control over Williams Company in 2010. Several years after the takeover, consolidated financial statements are being produced. For each of the following accounts, briefly describe the values that should be included in consolidated totals.

   a. Equipment.
   b. Investment in Williams Company.
   c. Dividends Paid.
   d. Goodwill.
   e. Revenues.
   f. Expenses.
   g. Common Stock.
   h. Net Income.

3. When a parent company uses the equity method to account for an investment in a subsidiary, why do both the parent's Net Income and Retained Earnings account balances agree with the consolidated totals?

4. When a parent company uses the equity method to account for investment in a subsidiary, the amortization expense entry recorded during the year is eliminated on a consolidation worksheet as a component of Entry **I**. What is the necessity of removing this amortization?

5. When a parent company applies the initial value method or the partial equity method to an investment, worksheet adjustment must be made to the parent's beginning Retained Earnings account (Entry ***C**) in every period after the year of acquisition. What is the necessity for this entry? Why is no similar entry found when the parent utilizes the equity method?

6. Several years ago, Jenkins Company acquired a controlling interest in Lambert Company. Lambert recently borrowed $100,000 from Jenkins. In consolidating the financial records of these two companies, how will this debt be handled?

7. Benns adopts the equity method for its 100 percent investment in Waters. At the end of six years, Benns reports an investment in Waters of $920,000. What figures constitute this balance?

8. One company acquired another in a transaction in which $100,000 of the acquisition price is assigned to goodwill. Several years later, a worksheet is being produced to consolidate these two companies. How is the reported value of the goodwill determined at this date?

9. When should a parent consider recognizing an impairment loss for goodwill associated with a subsidiary? How should the loss be reported in the financial statements?

10. Reimers Company acquires Rollins Corporation on January 1, 2010. As part of the agreement, the parent states that an additional $100,000 payment to the former owners of Rollins will be made in 2012, depending on the achievement of certain income thresholds during the first two years following the acquisition. How should Reimers account for this contingency in its 2010 consolidated financial statements?

11. When is the use of push-down accounting required, and what is the rationale for its application?

12. How are the individual financial records of both the parent and the subsidiary affected when push-down accounting is being applied?

13. Why has push-down accounting gained popularity for internal reporting purposes?

Problems

LO2

1. A company acquires a subsidiary and will prepare consolidated financial statements for external reporting purposes. For internal reporting purposes, the company has decided to apply the initial value method. Why might the company have made this decision?
    a. It is a relatively easy method to apply.
    b. Operating results appearing on the parent's financial records reflect consolidated totals.
    c. GAAP now requires the use of this particular method for internal reporting purposes.
    d. Consolidation is not required when the parent uses the initial value method.

LO2

2. A company acquires a subsidiary and will prepare consolidated financial statements for external reporting purposes. For internal reporting purposes, the company has decided to apply the equity method. Why might the company have made this decision?
    a. It is a relatively easy method to apply.
    b. Operating results appearing on the parent's financial records reflect consolidated totals.
    c. GAAP now requires the use of this particular method for internal reporting purposes.
    d. Consolidation is not required when the parent uses the equity method.

LO5

3. When should a consolidated entity recognize a goodwill impairment loss?
    a. If both the market value of a reporting unit and its associated implied goodwill fall below their respective carrying values.
    b. Whenever the entity's market value declines significantly.
    c. If a reporting unit's market value falls below its original acquisition price.
    d. Annually on a systematic and rational basis.

LO1

4. Willkom Corporation bought 100 percent of Szabo, Inc., on January 1, 2010. On that date, Willkom's equipment (10-year life) has a book value of $300,000 but a fair value of $400,000. Szabo has equipment (10-year life) with a book value of $200,000 but a fair value of $300,000. Willkom uses the equity method to record its investment in Szabo. On December 31, 2012, Willkom has equipment with a book value of $210,000 but a fair value of $330,000. Szabo has equipment with a book value of $140,000 but a fair value of $270,000. What is the consolidated balance for the Equipment account as of December 31, 2012?
    a. $600,000.
    b. $490,000.
    c. $480,000.
    d. $420,000.

LO3

5. How would the answer to problem (4) have been affected if the parent had applied the initial value method rather than the equity method?
    a. No effect: The method the parent uses is for internal reporting purposes only and has no impact on consolidated totals.
    b. The consolidated Equipment account would have a higher reported balance.
    c. The consolidated Equipment account would have a lower reported balance.
    d. The balance in the consolidated Equipment account cannot be determined for the initial value method using the information given.

LO5

6. Goodwill recognized in a business combination must be allocated among a firm's identified reporting units. If the fair value of a particular reporting unit with recognized goodwill falls below its carrying amount, which of the following is true?
    a. No goodwill impairment loss is recognized unless the implied value for goodwill exceeds its carrying amount.

  b. A goodwill impairment loss is recognized if the carrying amount for goodwill exceeds its implied value.

  c. A goodwill impairment loss is recognized for the difference between the reporting unit's fair value and carrying amount.

  d. The reporting unit reduces the values assigned to its long-term assets (including any unrecognized intangibles) to reflect its fair value.

LO5

7. If no legal, regulatory, contractual, competitive, economic, or other factors limit the life of an intangible asset, the asset's assigned value is allocated to expense over which of the following?

  a. 20 years.

  b. 20 years with an annual impairment review.

  c. Infinitely.

  d. Indefinitely (no amortization) with an annual impairment review until its life becomes finite.

LO7

8. Dosmann, Inc., bought all outstanding shares of Lizzi Corporation on January 1, 2011, for $700,000 in cash. This portion of the consideration transferred results in a fair-value allocation of $35,000 to equipment and goodwill of $88,000. At the acquisition date, Dosmann also agrees to pay Lizzi's previous owners an additional $110,000 on January 1, 2013, if Lizzi earns a 10 percent return on the fair value of its assets in 2011 and 2012. Lizzi's profits exceed this threshold in both years. Which of the following is true?

  a. The additional $110,000 payment is a reduction in consolidated retained earnings.

  b. The fair value of the expected contingent payment increases goodwill at the acquisition date.

  c. Consolidated goodwill as of January 1, 2013, increases by $110,000.

  d. The $110,000 is recorded as an expense in 2013.

LO7

9. Kaplan Corporation acquired Star, Inc., on January 1, 2011, by issuing 13,000 shares of common stock with a $10 per share par value and a $23 market value. This transaction resulted in recognizing $62,000 of goodwill. Kaplan also agreed to compensate Star's former owners for any difference if Kaplan's stock is worth less than $23 on January 1, 2012. On January 1, 2012, Kaplan issues an additional 3,000 shares to Star's former owners to honor the contingent consideration agreement. Which of the following is true?

  a. The fair value of the number of shares issued for the contingency increases the Goodwill account balance at January 1, 2012.

  b. The parent's additional paid-in capital from the contingent equity recorded at the acquisition date is reclassified as a regular common stock issue on January 1, 2012.

  c. All of the subsidiary's asset and liability accounts must be revalued for consolidation purposes based on their fair values as of January 1, 2012.

  d. The additional shares are assumed to have been issued on January 1, 2011, so that a retrospective adjustment is required.

LO8

10. What is push-down accounting?

  a. A requirement that a subsidiary must use the same accounting principles as a parent company.

  b. Inventory transfers made from a parent company to a subsidiary.

  c. A subsidiary's recording of the fair-value allocations as well as subsequent amortization.

  d. The adjustments required for consolidation when a parent has applied the equity method of accounting for internal reporting purposes.

LO8

11. Treadway Corporation acquires Hooker, Inc. The parent pays more for it than the fair value of the subsidiary's net assets. On the acquisition date, Treadway has equipment with a book value of $420,000 and a fair value of $530,000. Hooker has equipment with a book value of $330,000 and a fair value of $390,000. Hooker is going to use push-down accounting. Immediately after the acquisition, what amounts in the Equipment account appear on Hooker's separate balance sheet and on the consolidated balance sheet?

  a. $330,000 and $750,000.

  b. $330,000 and $860,000.

  c. $390,000 and $810,000.

  d. $390,000 and $920,000.

LO4

12. Herbert, Inc., acquired all of Rambis Company's outstanding stock on January 1, 2011, for $574,000 in cash. Annual excess amortization of $12,000 results from this transaction. On the date of the takeover, Herbert reported retained earnings of $400,000, and Rambis reported a $200,000 balance. Herbert reported internal income of $40,000 in 2011 and $50,000 in 2012 and paid $10,000 in

dividends each year. Rambis reported net income of $20,000 in 2011 and $30,000 in 2012 and paid $5,000 in dividends each year.

a. Assume that Herbert's internal income figures above do not include any income from the subsidiary.
- If the parent uses the equity method, what is the amount reported as consolidated retained earnings on December 31, 2012?
- Would the amount of consolidated retained earnings change if the parent had applied either the initial value or partial equity method for internal accounting purposes?

b. Under each of the following situations, what is the Investment in Rambis account balance on Herbert's books on January 1, 2012?
- The parent uses the equity method.
- The parent uses the partial equity method.
- The parent uses the initial value method.

c. Under each of the following situations, what is Entry *C on a 2012 consolidation worksheet?
- The parent uses the equity method.
- The parent uses the partial equity method.
- The parent uses the initial value method.

LO3, LO4

13. Haynes, Inc., obtained 100 percent of Turner Company's common stock on January 1, 2011, by issuing 9,000 shares of $10 par value common stock. Haynes's shares had a $15 per share fair value. On that date, Turner reported a net book value of $100,000. However, its equipment (with a five-year remaining life) was undervalued by $5,000 in the company's accounting records. Also, Turner had developed a customer list with an assessed value of $30,000, although no value had been recorded on Turner's books. The customer list had an estimated remaining useful life of 10 years.

The following figures come from the individual accounting records of these two companies as of December 31, 2011:

	Haynes	Turner
Revenues	$(600,000)	$(230,000)
Expenses	440,000	120,000
Investment income	Not given	–0–
Dividends paid	80,000	50,000

The following figures come from the individual accounting records of these two companies as of December 31, 2012:

	Haynes	Turner
Revenues	$(700,000)	$(280,000)
Expenses	460,000	150,000
Investment income	Not given	–0–
Dividends paid	90,000	40,000
Equipment	500,000	300,000

a. What balance does Haynes's Investment in Turner account show on December 31, 2012, when the equity method is applied?

b. What is the consolidated net income for the year ending December 31, 2012?

c. What is the consolidated equipment balance as of December 31, 2012? How would this answer be affected by the investment method applied by the parent?

d. If Haynes has applied the initial value method to account for its investment, what adjustment is needed to the beginning of the Retained Earnings on a December 31, 2012, consolidation worksheet? How would this answer change if the partial equity method had been in use? How would this answer change if the equity method had been in use?

LO6

14. Francisco Inc. acquired 100 percent of the outstanding voting shares of Beltran Company on January 1, 2011. To obtain these shares, Francisco payed $450,000 in cash and issued 104,000 shares of its own $1 par value common stock. On this date, Francisco's stock had a fair value of $12 per share. The combination is a statutory merger with Beltran subsequently dissolved as a legal corporation. For internal accountability purposes, Beltran's assets and liabilities are assigned to a new reporting unit.

The following reports the fair values for the Beltran reporting unit for January 1, 2011, and December 31, 2012, along with their respective book values on December 31, 2012.

Beltran Reporting Unit	Fair Values 1/1/11	Fair Values 12/31/12	Book Values 12/31/12
Cash	$ 75,000	$ 50,000	$ 50,000
Receivables	193,000	225,000	225,000
Inventory	281,000	305,000	300,000
Patents	525,000	600,000	500,000
Customer relationships	500,000	480,000	450,000
Equipment (net)	295,000	240,000	235,000
Goodwill	?	?	400,000
Accounts payable	(121,000)	(175,000)	(175,000)
Long-term liabilities	(450,000)	(400,000)	(400,000)

a. Prepare Francisco's journal entry to record the assets acquired and the liabilities assumed in the Beltran merger on January 1, 2011.

b. On December 31, 2012, Francisco estimates that the total fair value of the entire Beltran reporting unit is $1,425,000. What amount of goodwill impairment, if any, should Francisco recognize on its 2012 income statement?

LO6

15. Acme Co., a consolidated enterprise, conducted an impairment review for each of its reporting units. One particular reporting unit, Martel, emerged as a candidate for possible goodwill impairment. Martel has recognized net assets of $780, including goodwill of $500. Martel's fair value is assessed at $650 and includes two internally developed unrecognized intangible assets (a patent and a customer list with fair values of $150 and $50, respectively). The following table summarizes current financial information for the Martel reporting unit:

	Carrying Amounts	Fair Values
Tangible assets, net	$ 80	$110
Recognized intangible assets, net	200	230
Goodwill	500	?
Unrecognized intangible assets	–0–	200
Total	$780	$650

a. Show the two steps to determine the amount of any goodwill impairment for Acme's Martel reporting unit.

b. After recognition of any goodwill impairment loss, what are the reported book values for the following assets of Acme's reporting unit Martel?
 • Tangible assets, net.
 • Goodwill.
 • Customer list.
 • Patent.

LO6

16. Destin Company recently acquired several businesses and recognized goodwill in each acquisition. Destin has allocated the resulting goodwill to its three reporting units: Sand Dollar, Salty Dog, and Baytowne.

In its annual review for goodwill impairment, Destin provides the following individual asset and liability values for each reporting unit:

	Carrying Values	Fair Values
Sand Dollar		
Tangible assets	$180,000	$190,000
Trademark	170,000	150,000
Customer list	90,000	100,000
Goodwill	120,000	?
Liabilities	(30,000)	(30,000)

(continued)

	Carrying Values	Fair Values
Salty Dog		
Tangible assets	$200,000	$200,000
Unpatented technology	170,000	125,000
Licenses	90,000	100,000
Goodwill	150,000	?
Baytowne		
Tangible assets	140,000	150,000
Unpatented technology	–0–	100,000
Copyrights	50,000	80,000
Goodwill	90,000	?

The overall valuations for the entire reporting units (including goodwill) are $510,000 for Sand Dollar, $580,000 for Salty Dog, and $560,000 for Baytowne. To date, Destin has reported no goodwill impairments.

a. Which of Destin's reporting units require both steps to test for goodwill impairment?

b. How much goodwill impairment should Destin report this year?

c. What changes to the valuations of Destin's tangible assets and identified intangible assets should be reported based on the goodwill impairment tests?

Problems 17 through 19 should be viewed as independent situations. They are based on the following data:

Chapman Company obtains 100 percent of Abernethy Company's stock on January 1, 2011. As of that date, Abernethy has the following trial balance:

	Debit	Credit
Accounts payable		$ 50,000
Accounts receivable	$ 40,000	
Additional paid-in capital		50,000
Buildings (net) (4-year life)	120,000	
Cash and short-term investments	60,000	
Common stock		250,000
Equipment (net) (5-year life)	200,000	
Inventory	90,000	
Land	80,000	
Long-term liabilities (mature 12/31/14)		150,000
Retained earnings, 1/1/11		100,000
Supplies	10,000	
Totals	$600,000	$600,000

During 2011, Abernethy reported income of $80,000 while paying dividends of $10,000. During 2012, Abernethy reported income of $110,000 while paying dividends of $30,000.

LO4a

17. Assume that Chapman Company acquired Abernethy's common stock for $490,000 in cash. As of January 1, 2011, Abernethy's land had a fair value of $90,000, its buildings were valued at $160,000, and its equipment was appraised at $180,000. Chapman uses the equity method for this investment. Prepare consolidation worksheet entries for December 31, 2011, and December 31, 2012.

LO4b

18. Assume that Chapman Company acquired Abernethy's common stock for $500,000 in cash. Assume that the equipment and long-term liabilities had fair values of $220,000 and $120,000, respectively, on the acquisition date. Chapman uses the initial value method to account for its investment. Prepare consolidation worksheet entries for December 31, 2011, and December 31, 2012.

LO4c

19. Assume that Chapman Company acquired Abernethy's common stock by paying $520,000 in cash. All of Abernethy's accounts are estimated to have a value approximately equal to present book values. Chapman uses the partial equity method to account for its investment. Prepare the consolidation worksheet entries for December 31, 2011, and December 31, 2012.

LO4a, LO4b

20. Adams, Inc., acquires Clay Corporation on January 1, 2010, in exchange for $510,000 cash. Immediately after the acquisition, the two companies have the following account balances. Clay's equipment (with a five-year life) is actually worth $440,000. Credit balances are indicated by parentheses.

	Adams	Clay
Current assets	$ 300,000	$ 220,000
Investment in Clay	510,000	–0–
Equipment	600,000	390,000
Liabilities	(200,000)	(160,000)
Common stock	(350,000)	(150,000)
Retained earnings, 1/1/10	(860,000)	(300,000)

In 2010, Clay earns a net income of $55,000 and pays a $5,000 cash dividend. In 2010, Adams reports income from its own operations (exclusive of any income from Clay) of $125,000 and declares no dividends. At the end of 2011, selected account balances for the two companies are as follows:

	Adams	Clay
Revenues	$(400,000)	$(240,000)
Expenses	290,000	180,000
Investment income	Not given	–0–
Retained earnings, 1/1/11	Not given	(350,000)
Dividends declared	–0–	8,000
Common stock	(350,000)	(150,000)
Current assets	580,000	262,000
Investment in Clay	Not given	–0–
Equipment	520,000	420,000
Liabilities	(152,000)	(130,000)

a. What are the December 31, 2011, Investment Income and Investment in Clay account balances assuming Adams uses the:
   1. Initial value method.
   2. Equity method.

b. How does the parent's internal investment accounting method choice affect the amount reported for expenses in its December 31, 2011, consolidated income statement?

c. How does the parent's internal investment accounting method choice affect the amount reported for equipment in its December 31, 2011, consolidated balance sheet?

d. What is Adams's January 1, 2011, Retained Earnings account balance assuming Adams accounts for its investment in Clay using the:
   1. Initial value method.
   2. Equity method.

e. What worksheet adjustment to Adams's January 1, 2011, Retained Earnings account balance is required if Adams accounts for its investment in Clay using the initial value method?

f. Prepare the worksheet entry to eliminate Clay's stockholders' equity.

g. What is consolidated net income for 2011?

LO1

21. Following are selected account balances from Penske Company and Stanza Corporation as of December 31, 2012:

	Penske	Stanza
Revenues	$(700,000)	$(400,000)
Cost of goods sold	250,000	100,000
Depreciation expense	150,000	200,000
Investment income	Not given	–0–
Dividends paid	80,000	60,000
Retained earnings, 1/1/12	(600,000)	(200,000)
Current assets	400,000	500,000
Copyrights	900,000	400,000
Royalty agreements	600,000	1,000,000
Investment in Stanza	Not given	–0–
Liabilities	(500,000)	(1,380,000)
Common stock	(600,000) ($20 par)	(200,000) ($10 par)
Additional paid-in capital	(150,000)	(80,000)

On January 1, 2012, Penske acquired all of Stanza's outstanding stock for $680,000 fair value in cash and common stock. Penske also paid $10,000 in stock issuance costs. At the date of acquisition copyrights (with a six-year remaining life) have a $440,000 book value but a fair value of $560,000.

a. As of December 31, 2012, what is the consolidated copyrights balance?

b. For the year ending December 31, 2012, what is consolidated Net Income?

c. As of December 31, 2012, what is the consolidated Retained Earnings balance?

d. As of December 31, 2012, what is the consolidated balance to be reported for goodwill?

LO2, LO3, LO4

22. Foxx Corporation acquired all of Greenburg Company's outstanding stock on January 1, 2011, for $600,000 cash. Greenburg's accounting records showed net assets on that date of $470,000, although equipment with a 10-year life was undervalued on the records by $90,000. Any recognized goodwill is considered to have an indefinite life.

Greenburg reports net income in 2011 of $90,000 and $100,000 in 2012. The subsidiary paid dividends of $20,000 in each of these two years.

Financial figures for the year ending December 31, 2013, follow. Credit balances are indicated by parentheses.

	Foxx	Greenburg
Revenues	$ (800,000)	$ (600,000)
Cost of goods sold	100,000	150,000
Depreciation expense	300,000	350,000
Investment income	(20,000)	–0–
Net income	$ (420,000)	$ (100,000)
Retained earnings, 1/1/13	$(1,100,000)	$ (320,000)
Net income	(420,000)	(100,000)
Dividends paid	120,000	20,000
Retained earnings, 12/31/13	$(1,400,000)	$ (400,000)
Current assets	$ 300,000	$ 100,000
Investment in subsidiary	600,000	–0–
Equipment (net)	900,000	600,000
Buildings (net)	800,000	400,000
Land	600,000	100,000
Total assets	$ 3,200,000	$ 1,200,000
Liabilities	$ (900,000)	$ (500,000)
Common stock	(900,000)	(300,000)
Retained earnings	(1,400,000)	(400,000)
Total liabilities and equity	$(3,200,000)	$(1,200,000)

a. Determine the December 31, 2013, consolidated balance for each of the following accounts:

Depreciation Expense	Buildings
Dividends Paid	Goodwill
Revenues	Common Stock
Equipment	

b. How does the parent's choice of an accounting method for its investment affect the balances computed in requirement (a)?

c. Which method of accounting for this subsidiary is the parent actually using for internal reporting purposes?

d. If the parent company had used a different method of accounting for this investment, how could that method have been identified?

e. What would be Foxx's balance for retained earnings as of January 1, 2013, if each of the following methods had been in use?

Initial value method

Partial equity method

Equity method

LO1, LO4a

23. Patrick Corporation acquired 100 percent of O'Brien Company's outstanding common stock on January 1, for $550,000 in cash. O'Brien reported net assets with a carrying value of $350,000 at that time. Some of O'Brien's assets either were unrecorded (having been internally developed) or had fair values that differed from book values as follows:

	Book Values	Fair Values
Trademarks (indefinite life)	$ 60,000	$160,000
Customer relationships (5-year life)	–0–	75,000
Equipment (10-year life)	342,000	312,000

Any goodwill is considered to have an indefinite life with no impairment charges during the year.

Following are financial statements at the end of the first year for these two companies prepared from their separately maintained accounting systems. Credit balances are indicated by parentheses.

	Patrick	O'Brien
Revenues	$ (1,125,000)	$ (520,000)
Cost of goods sold	300,000	228,000
Depreciation expense	75,000	70,000
Amortization expense	25,000	–0–
Income from O'Brien	(210,000)	–0–
Net Income	$ (935,000)	$ (222,000)
Retained earnings 1/1	(700,000)	(250,000)
Net Income	(935,000)	(222,000)
Dividends paid	142,000	80,000
Retained earnings 12/31	$ (1,493,000)	$ (392,000)
Cash	$ 185,000	$ 105,000
Receivables	225,000	56,000
Inventory	175,000	135,000
Investment in O'Brien	680,000	–0–
Trademarks	474,000	60,000
Customer relationships	–0–	–0–
Equipment (net)	925,000	272,000
Goodwill	–0–	–0–
Total assets	$ 2,664,000	$ 628,000
Liabilities	(771,000)	(136,000)
Common stock	(400,000)	(100,000)
Retained earnings 12/31	(1,493,000)	(392,000)
Total liabilities and equity	$ (2,664,000)	$ (628,000)

a. Show how Patrick computed the $210,000 Income of O'Brien balance. Discuss how you determined which accounting method Patrick uses for its investment in O'Brien.

b. Without preparing a worksheet or consolidation entries, determine and explain the totals to be reported for this business combination for the year ending December 31.

c. Verify the totals determined in part (*b*) by producing a consolidation worksheet for Patrick and O'Brien for the year ending December 31.

LO1, LO3, LO4a, LO4b

24. Following are separate financial statements of Michael Company and Aaron Company as of December 31, 2013 (credit balances indicated by parentheses). Michael acquired all of Aaron's outstanding voting stock on January 1, 2009, by issuing 20,000 shares of its own $1 par common stock. On the acquisition date, Michael Company's stock actively traded at $23.50 per share.

	Michael Company 12/31/13	Aaron Company 12/31/13
Revenues	$ (610,000)	$ (370,000)
Cost of goods sold	270,000	140,000
Amortizations expense	115,000	80,000
Dividend income	(5,000)	–0–
Net income	$ (230,000)	$ (150,000)
Retained earnings, 1/1/13	$ (880,000)	$ (490,000)
Net income (above)	(230,000)	(150,000)
Dividends paid	90,000	5,000
Retained earnings, 12/31/13	$(1,020,000)	$ (635,000)
Cash	$ 110,000	$ 15,000
Receivables	380,000	220,000
Inventory	560,000	280,000
Investment in Aaron Company	470,000	–0–
Copyrights	460,000	340,000
Royalty agreements	920,000	380,000
Total assets	$ 2,900,000	$ 1,235,000
Liabilities	$ (780,000)	$ (470,000)
Preferred stock	(300,000)	–0–
Common stock	(500,000)	(100,000)
Additional paid-in capital	(300,000)	(30,000)
Retained earnings, 12/31/13	(1,020,000)	(635,000)
Total liabilities and equity	$(2,900,000)	$(1,235,000)

On the date of acquisition, Aaron reported retained earnings of $230,000 and a total book value of $360,000. At that time, its royalty agreements were undervalued by $60,000. This intangible was assumed to have a six-year life with no residual value. Additionally, Aaron owned a trademark with a fair value of $50,000 and a 10-year remaining life that was not reflected on its books.

a. Using the preceding information, prepare a consolidation worksheet for these two companies as of December 31, 2013.

b. Assuming that Michael applied the equity method to this investment, what account balances would differ on the parent's individual financial statements?

c. Assuming that Michael applied the equity method to this investment, what changes would be necessary in the consolidation entries found on a December 31, 2013, worksheet?

d. Assuming that Michael applied the equity method to this investment, what changes would be created in the consolidated figures to be reported by this combination?

LO1, LO4, LO6

eXcel

25. Giant acquired all of Small's common stock on January 1, 2009. Over the next few years, Giant applied the equity method to the recording of this investment. At the date of the original acquisition, $90,000 of the fair-value price was attributed to undervalued land while $50,000 was assigned to equipment having a 10-year life. The remaining $60,000 unallocated portion of the acquisition-date excess fair value over book value was viewed as goodwill.

Following are individual financial statements for the year ending December 31, 2013. On that date, Small owes Giant $10,000. Credits are indicated by parentheses.

a. How was the $135,000 Equity in Income of Small balance computed?

b. Without preparing a worksheet or consolidation entries, determine and explain the totals to be reported by this business combination for the year ending December 31, 2013.

	Giant	Small
Revenues	$(1,175,000)	$ (360,000)
Cost of goods sold	550,000	90,000
Depreciation expense	172,000	130,000
Equity in income of Small	(135,000)	–0–
Net income	$ (588,000)	$ (140,000)

(*continued*)

	Giant	Small
Retained earnings, 1/1/13	$(1,417,000)	$ (620,000)
Net income (above)	(588,000)	(140,000)
Dividends paid	310,000	110,000
Retained earnings, 12/31/13	$(1,695,000)	$ (650,000)
Current assets	$ 398,000	$ 318,000
Investment in Small	995,000	–0–
Land	440,000	165,000
Buildings (net)	304,000	419,000
Equipment (net)	648,000	286,000
Goodwill	–0–	–0–
Total assets	$ 2,785,000	$ 1,188,000
Liabilities	$ (840,000)	$ (368,000)
Common stock	(250,000)	(170,000)
Retained earnings (above)	(1,695,000)	(650,000)
Total liabilities and equity	$(2,785,000)	$(1,188,000)

c. Verify the figures determined in part (*b*) by producing a consolidation worksheet for Giant and Small for the year ending December 31, 2013.

d. If Giant determined that the entire amount of goodwill from its investment in Small was impaired in 2013, how would the parent's accounts reflect the impairment loss? How would the worksheet process change? What impact does an impairment loss have on consolidated financial statements?

LO1, LO3, LO4

e**X**cel

26. Following are selected accounts for Mergaronite Company and Hill, Inc., as of December 31, 2013. Several of Mergaronite's accounts have been omitted. Credit balances are indicated by parentheses.

	Mergaronite	Hill
Revenues	$(600,000)	$(250,000)
Cost of goods sold	280,000	100,000
Depreciation expense	120,000	50,000
Investment income	Not given	NA
Retained earnings, 1/1/13	(900,000)	(600,000)
Dividends paid	130,000	40,000
Current assets	200,000	690,000
Land	300,000	90,000
Buildings (net)	500,000	140,000
Equipment (net)	200,000	250,000
Liabilities	(400,000)	(310,000)
Common stock	(300,000)	(40,000)
Additional paid-in capital	(50,000)	(160,000)

Assume that Mergaronite took over Hill on January 1, 2009, by issuing 7,000 shares of common stock having a par value of $10 per share but a fair value of $100 each. On January 1, 2009, Hill's land was undervalued by $20,000, its buildings were overvalued by $30,000, and equipment was undervalued by $60,000. The buildings had a 10-year life; the equipment had a 5-year life. A customer list with an appraised value of $100,000 was developed internally by Hill and was to be written off over a 20-year period.

a. Determine and explain the December 31, 2013, consolidated totals for the following accounts:

Revenues	Amortization Expense	Customer List
Cost of Goods Sold	Buildings	Common Stock
Depreciation Expense	Equipment	Additional Paid-In Capital

b. In requirement (*a*), why can the consolidated totals be determined without knowing which method the parent used to account for the subsidiary?

c. If the parent uses the equity method, what consolidation entries would be used on a 2013 worksheet?

LO3, LO4, LO6

27. On January 1, 2011, Peterson Corporation exchanged $1,090,000 fair-value consideration for all of the outstanding voting stock of Santiago, Inc. At the acquisition date, Santiago had a book value equal to $950,000. Santiago's individual assets and liabilities had fair values equal to their respective book values except for the patented technology account, which was undervalued by $240,000 with an estimated remaining life of six years. The Santiago acquisition was Peterson's only business combination for the year.

In case expected synergies did not materialize, Peterson Corporation wished to prepare for a potential future spin-off of Santiago, Inc. Therefore, Peterson had Santiago maintain its separate incorporation and independent accounting information system as elements of continuing value.

On December 31, 2011 each company submitted the following financial statements for consolidation.

	Peterson Corp.	Santiago, Inc.
Income Statement		
Revenues	(535,000)	(495,000)
Cost of goods sold	170,000	155,000
Gain on bargain purchase	(100,000)	–0–
Depreciation and amortization	125,000	140,000
Equity earnings from Santiago	(160,000)	–0–
Net income	(500,000)	(200,000)
Statement of Retained Earnings		
Retained earnings, 1/1	(1,500,000)	(650,000)
Net income (above)	(500,000)	(200,000)
Dividends paid	200,000	50,000
Retained earnings, 12/31	(1,800,000)	(800,000)
Balance Sheet		
Current assets	190,000	300,000
Investment in Santiago	1,300,000	–0–
Trademarks	100,000	200,000
Patented technology	300,000	400,000
Equipment	610,000	300,000
Total assets	2,500,000	1,200,000
Liabilities	(165,000)	(100,000)
Common stock	(535,000)	(300,000)
Retained earnings, 12/31	(1,800,000)	(800,000)
Total liabilities and equity	(2,500,000)	(1,200,000)

a. Show how Peterson determined the following account balances
   - Gain on bargain purchase
   - Earnings from Santiago
   - Investment in Santiago

b. Prepare a December 31, 2011, consolidated worksheet for Peterson and Santiago.

LO4a, LO4b, LO7

e**X**cel

28. Branson paid $465,000 cash for all of the outstanding common stock of Wolfpack, Inc., on January 1, 2011. On that date, the subsidiary had a book value of $340,000 (common stock of $200,000 and retained earnings of $140,000), although various unrecorded royalty agreements were assessed at a $100,000 fair value. The royalty agreements had an estimated 10-year remaining useful life.

In negotiating the acquisition price, Branson also promised to pay Wolfpack's former owners an additional $50,000 if Wolfpack's income exceeded $120,000 total over the first two years after the acquisition. At the acquisition date, Branson estimated the probability adjusted present value of this contingent consideration at $35,000. On December 31, 2011, based on Wolfpack's earnings to date, Branson increased the value of the contingency to $40,000.

During the subsequent two years, Wolfpack reported the following amounts for income and dividends:

	Net Income	Dividends Paid
2011	$65,000	$25,000
2012	75,000	35,000

In keeping with the original acquisition agreement, on December 31, 2012, Branson paid the additional $50,000 performance fee to Wolfpack's previous owners.

Using the acquisition method and assuming no goodwill impairment charges, prepare each of the following:

a. Branson's entry to record the acquisition of the shares of its Wolfpack subsidiary.

b. Branson's entries at the end of 2011 and 2012 to adjust its contingent performance obligation for changes in fair value and the December 31, 2012, payment.

    c. Consolidation worksheet entries as of December 31, 2012, assuming that Branson has applied the equity method.

    d. Consolidation worksheet entries as of December 31, 2012, assuming that Branson has applied the initial value method.

LO4, LO8

29. Palm Company acquired 100 percent of Storm Company's voting stock on January 1, 2009, by issuing 10,000 shares of its $10 par value common stock (having a fair value of $14 per share). As of that date, Storm had stockholders' equity totaling $105,000. Land shown on Storm's accounting records was undervalued by $10,000. Equipment (with a five-year life) was undervalued by $5,000. A secret formula developed by Storm was appraised at $20,000 with an estimated life of 20 years.

    Following are the separate financial statements for the two companies for the year ending December 31, 2013. Credit balances are indicated by parentheses.

	Palm Company	Storm Company
Revenues	$ (485,000)	$(190,000)
Cost of goods sold	160,000	70,000
Depreciation expense	130,000	52,000
Subsidiary earnings	(66,000)	–0–
Net income	$ (261,000)	$ (68,000)
Retained earnings, 1/1/13	$ (659,000)	$ (98,000)
Net income (above)	(261,000)	(68,000)
Dividends paid	175,500	40,000
Retained earnings, 12/31/13	$ (744,500)	$(126,000)
Current assets	$ 268,000	$ 75,000
Investment in Storm Company	216,000	–0–
Land	427,500	58,000
Buildings and equipment (net)	713,000	161,000
Total assets	$ 1,624,500	$ 294,000
Current liabilities	$ (110,000)	$ (19,000)
Long-term liabilities	(80,000)	(84,000)
Common stock	(600,000)	(60,000)
Additional paid-in capital	(90,000)	(5,000)
Retained earnings, 12/31/13	(744,500)	(126,000)
Total liabilities and equity	$(1,624,500)	$(294,000)

    a. Explain how Palm derived the $66,000 balance in the Subsidiary Earnings account.

    b. Prepare a worksheet to consolidate the financial information for these two companies.

    c. Explain how Storm's individual financial records would differ if the push-down method of accounting had been applied.

LO4a

30. Tyler Company acquired all of Jasmine Company's outstanding stock on January 1, 2009, for $206,000 in cash. Jasmine had a book value of only $140,000 on that date. However, equipment (having an eight-year life) was undervalued by $54,400 on Jasmine's financial records. A building with a 20-year life was overvalued by $10,000. Subsequent to the acquisition, Jasmine reported the following:

	Net Income	Dividends Paid
2009	$50,000	$10,000
2010	60,000	40,000
2011	30,000	20,000

    In accounting for this investment, Tyler has used the equity method. Selected accounts taken from the financial records of these two companies as of December 31, 2011, follow:

	Tyler Company	Jasmine Company
Revenues—operating	$(310,000)	$(104,000)
Expenses	198,000	74,000
Equipment (net)	320,000	50,000
Buildings (net)	220,000	68,000
Common stock	(290,000)	(50,000)
Retained earnings, 12/31/11 balance	(410,000)	(160,000)

Determine and explain the following account balances as of December 31, 2011:

    a. Investment in Jasmine Company (on Tyler's individual financial records).

    b. Equity in Subsidiary Earnings (on Tyler's individual financial records).

    c. Consolidated Net Income.

    d. Consolidated Equipment (net).

    e. Consolidated Buildings (net).

    f. Consolidated Goodwill (net).

    g. Consolidated Common Stock.

    h. Consolidated Retained Earnings, 12/31/11.

LO4

31. On January 1, 2010, Picante Corporation acquired 100 percent of the outstanding voting stock of Salsa Corporation for $1,765,000 cash. On the acquisition date, Salsa had the following balance sheet:

Cash	$ 14,000	Accounts payable	$ 120,000
Accounts receivable	100,000	Long-term debt	930,000
Land	700,000	Common stock	1,000,000
Equipment (net)	1,886,000	Retained earnings	650,000
	$2,700,000		$2,700,000

At the acquisition date, the following allocation was prepared:

Fair value of consideration transferred		$1,765,000
Book value acquired		1,650,000
Excess fair value over book value		115,000
To in-process research and development	$44,000	
To equipment (8-yr. remaining life)	56,000	100,000
To goodwill (indefinite life)		$ 15,000

Although at acquisition date Picante had expected $44,000 in future benefits from Salsa's in-process research and development project, by the end of 2010, it was apparent that the research project was a failure with no future economic benefits.

On December 31, 2011, Picante and Salsa submitted the following trial balances for consolidation:

	Picante	Salsa
Sales	$ (3,500,000)	$(1,000,000)
Cost of goods sold	1,600,000	630,000
Depreciation expense	540,000	160,000
Subsidiary income	(203,000)	–0–
Net income	$ (1,563,000)	$ (210,000)
Retained earnings 1/1/11	$ (3,000,000)	$ (800,000)
Net income	(1,563,000)	(210,000)
Dividends paid	200,000	25,000
Retained earnings 12/31/11	$ (4,363,000)	$ (985,000)
Cash	$ 228,000	$ 50,000
Accounts receivable	840,000	155,000
Inventory	900,000	580,000
Investment in Salsa	2,042,000	–0–
Land	3,500,000	700,000
Equipment (net)	5,000,000	1,700,000
Goodwill	290,000	–0–
Total assets	$ 12,800,000	$ 3,185,000
Accounts payable	$ (193,000)	$ (400,000)
Long-term debt	(3,094,000)	(800,000)
Common stock	(5,150,000)	(1,000,000)
Retained earnings 12/31/11	(4,363,000)	(985,000)
Total liabilities and equities	$(12,800,000)	$(3,185,000)

    a. Show how Picante derived its December 31, 2011, Investment in Salsa account balance.

    b. Prepare a consolidated worksheet for Picante and Salsa as of December 31, 2011.

LO4a, LO6

32. On January 1, Prine, Inc., acquired 100 percent of Lydia Company's common stock for a fair value of $120,000,000 in cash and stock. Lydia's assets and liabilities equaled their fair values except for its equipment, which was undervalued by $500,000 and had a 10-year remaining life.

    Prine specializes in media distribution and viewed its acquisition of Lydia as a strategic move into content ownership and creation. Prine expected both cost and revenue synergies from controlling Lydia's artistic content (a large library of classic movies) and its sports programming specialty video operation. Accordingly, Prine allocated Lydia's assets and liabilities (including $50,000,000 of goodwill) to a newly formed operating segment appropriately designated as a reporting unit.

    The fair values of the reporting unit's identifiable assets and liabilities through the first year of operations were as follows.

Account	Fair Values	
	1/1	12/31
Cash	$ 215,000	$ 109,000
Receivables (net)	525,000	897,000
Movie library (25-year life)	40,000,000	60,000,000
Broadcast licenses (indefinite life)	15,000,000	20,000,000
Equipment (10-year life)	20,750,000	19,000,000
Current liabilities	(490,000)	(650,000)
Long-term debt	(6,000,000)	(6,250,000)

   However, Lydia's assets have taken longer than anticipated to produce the expected synergies with Prine's operations. At year-end, Prine reduced its assessment of the Lydia reporting unit's fair value to $110,000,000.

   At December 31, Prine and Lydia submitted the following balances for consolidation:

	Prine, Inc.	Lydia Co.
Revenues	$ (18,000,000)	$(12,000,000)
Operating expenses	10,350,000	11,800,000
Equity in Lydia earnings	(150,000)	NA
Dividends paid	300,000	80,000
Retained earnings, 1/1	(52,000,000)	(2,000,000)
Cash	260,000	109,000
Receivables (net)	210,000	897,000
Investment in Lydia	120,070,000	NA
Broadcast licenses	350,000	14,014,000
Movie library	365,000	45,000,000
Equipment (net)	136,000,000	17,500,000
Current liabilities	(755,000)	(650,000)
Long-term debt	(22,000,000)	(7,250,000)
Common stock	(175,000,000)	(67,500,000)

   a. What is the relevant initial test to determine whether goodwill could be impaired?

   b. At what amount should Prine record an impairment loss for its Lydia reporting unit for the year?

   c. What is consolidated net income for the year?

   d. What is the December 31 consolidated balance for goodwill?

   e. What is the December 31 consolidated balance for broadcast licenses?

   f. Prepare a consolidated worksheet for Prine and Lydia (Prine's trial balance should first be adjusted for any appropriate impairment loss).

Develop Your Skills

RESEARCH CASE

Jonas Tech Corporation recently acquired Innovation + Company. The combined firm consists of three related businesses that will serve as reporting units. In connection with the acquisition, Jonas requests your help with the following asset valuation and allocation issues. Support your answers with references to FASB standards as appropriate.

Jonas recognizes several identifiable intangibles from its acquisition of Innovation +. It expresses the desire to have these intangible assets written down to zero in the acquisition period.

The price Jonas paid for Innovation + indicates that it paid a large amount for goodwill. However, Jonas worries that any future goodwill impairment may send the wrong signal to its investors about the wisdom of the Innovation + acquisition. Jonas thus wishes to allocate the combined goodwill of all of its reporting units to one account called *Enterprise Goodwill.* In this way, Jonas hopes to minimize the possibility of goodwill impairment because a decline in goodwill in one business unit could be offset by an increase in the value of goodwill in another business unit.

Required

1. Advise Jonas on the acceptability of its suggested immediate write-off of its identifiable intangibles.
2. Indicate the relevant factors to consider in allocating the value assigned to identifiable intangibles acquired in a business combination to expense over time.
3. Advise Jonas on the acceptability of its suggested treatment of goodwill.
4. Indicate the relevant factors to consider in allocating goodwill across an enterprise's business units.

SPRINT NEXTEL ANALYSIS CASE

In 2007 Sprint Nextel Corporation reported a large goodwill impairment loss. Referring to Sprint Nextel's 2007 financial statements and applicable financial reporting standards, answer the following questions:

1. How much goodwill impairment charge did Sprint Nextel report in 2007?
2. Why did Sprint Nextel write down their goodwill in 2007? What are some other indicators for goodwill impairment in general?
3. How did Sprint Nextel reflect this impairment in financial statements?
4. How often does Sprint Nextel test its goodwill for impairment and what are the testing steps?
5. Certain other indefinite-lived intangibles and other long-lived assets (including intangible assets with a finite life) are also subject to impairment assessment. Did Sprint Nextel incur any of these impairment charges in 2007? Explain briefly when and how Sprint Nextel tests these assets for impairment.
6. Is impairment of goodwill and other intangible assets reversible under U.S. GAAP? How about under IFRS? (Refer to FASB Topic 350 Intangibles—Goodwill and Other, and IAS 36 Impairment of Assets)
7. Is goodwill impaired in the same way under IFRS? Does IFRS also employ a two-step approach for goodwill impairment testing? If not, how is goodwill tested for impairment under IFRS? (Refer to *IAS 36 Impairment of Assets.*)

HISTORICAL ANALYSIS CASE

In July 2001, the FASB issued *SFAS 142,* which changed the accounting for goodwill and intangible assets. Upon adoption of *SFAS 142,* many companies recognized large goodwill impairment losses. For example, in 2002, AOL Time Warner (now Time Warner) recorded a $99 billion reduction in the carrying value of its goodwill—still one of the largest goodwill impairments. The *SFAS 142* requirements continue under ASC Topic 350, Intangibles—Goodwill and Other.

Use the AOL Time Warner, Inc., 2002 SEC Form 10-K Annual Report and *SFAS 142* to address the following issues and questions.

Required

1. How did AOL determine the initial amount of goodwill to recognize in its merger with Time Warner?
2. How did AOL Time Warner determine the $99 billion 2002 impairment charge to its goodwill? What procedures will Time Warner follow in the future to assess the value of its goodwill?
3. What business areas did AOL Time Warner designate as its reporting units? Why is it important to define the reporting units?
4. What effects did *SFAS 142* have on AOL Time Warner's earnings performance both in the short term and in the long term?
5. What is the rationale behind the accounting treatment for goodwill (initial recognition and subsequent allocation to income)?

EXCEL CASE 1

On January 1, 2010, Innovus, Inc., acquired 100 percent of the common stock of ChipTech Company for $670,000 in cash and other fair-value consideration. ChipTech's fair value was allocated among its net assets as follows:

Fair value of consideration transferred for ChipTech		$670,000
Book value of ChipTech:		
Common stock and APIC	$130,000	
Retained earnings	370,000	500,000
Excess fair value over book value to		170,000
Trademark (10-year remaining life)	40,000	
Existing technology (5-year remaining life)	80,000	120,000
Goodwill		$ 50,000

The December 31, 2011, trial balances for the parent and subsidiary follow:

	Innovus	ChipTech
Revenues	$ (990,000)	$(210,000)
Cost of goods sold	500,000	90,000
Depreciation expense	100,000	5,000
Amortization expense	55,000	18,000
Dividend income	(40,000)	–0–
Net income	$ (375,000)	$ (97,000)
Retained earnings 1/1/11	$(1,555,000)	$(450,000)
Net income	(375,000)	(97,000)
Dividends paid	250,000	40,000
Retained earnings 12/31/11	$(1,680,000)	$(507,000)
Current assets	$ 960,000	$ 355,000
Investment in ChipTech	670,000	
Equipment (net)	765,000	225,000
Trademark	235,000	100,000
Existing technology	–0–	45,000
Goodwill	450,000	–0–
Total assets	$ 3,080,000	$ 725,000
Liabilities	$ (780,000)	(88,000)
Common stock	(500,000)	(100,000)
Additional paid-in capital	(120,000)	(30,000)
Retained earnings 12/31/11	(1,680,000)	(507,000)
Total liabilities and equity	$(3,080,000)	$(725,000)

Required

a. Using Excel, compute consolidated balances for Innovus and ChipTech. Either use a worksheet approach or compute the balances directly.

b. Prepare a second spreadsheet that shows a 2011 impairment loss for the entire amount of goodwill from the ChipTech acquisition.

EXCEL CASE 2

On January 1, 2010, Hi-Speed.com acquired 100 percent of the common stock of Wi-Free Co. for cash of $730,000. The consideration transferred was allocated among Wi-Free's net assets as follows:

Wi-Free fair value (cash paid by Hi-Speed)		$730,000
Book value of Wi-Free:		
Common stock and APIC	$130,000	
Retained earnings	370,000	500,000

(*continued*)

Excess fair value over book value to		$230,000
In-process R&D	75,000	
Computer software (overvalued)	(30,000)	
Internet domain name	120,000	165,000
Goodwill		$ 65,000

At the acquisition date, the computer software had a 4-year remaining life, and the Internet domain name was estimated to have a 10-year life. By the end of 2010, it became clear that the acquired in-process research and development would yield no economic benefits and Hi-Speed.com recognized an impairment loss. At December 31, 2011, Wi-Free's accounts payable include a $30,000 amount owed to Hi-Speed.

The December 31, 2011, trial balances for the parent and subsidiary follow:

	Hi-Speed.com	Wi-Free Co.
Revenues	$(1,100,000)	$(325,000)
Cost of goods sold	625,000	122,000
Depreciation expense	140,000	12,000
Amortization expense	50,000	11,000
Equity in subsidiary earnings	(175,500)	–0–
Net income	$ (460,500)	$(180,000)
Retained earnings 1/1/11	$(1,552,500)	$(450,000)
Net income	(460,500)	(180,000)
Dividends paid	250,000	50,000
Retained earnings 12/31/11	$(1,763,000)	$(580,000)
Current assets	$ 1,034,000	$ 345,000
Investment in Wi-Free	856,000	–0–
Equipment (net)	713,000	305,000
Computer software	650,000	130,000
Internet domain name	–0–	100,000
Goodwill	–0–	–0–
Total assets	$ 3,253,000	$ 880,000
Liabilities	$ (870,000)	$(170,000)
Common stock	(500,000)	(110,000)
Additional paid-in capital	(120,000)	(20,000)
Retained earnings 12/31/11	(1,763,000)	(580,000)
Total liabilities and equity	$(3,253,000)	$(880,000)

Required

a. Using Excel, prepare calculations showing how Hi-Speed derived the $856,000 amount for its investment in Wi-Free.

b. Using Excel, compute consolidated balances for Hi-Speed and Wi-Free. Either use a worksheet approach or compute the balances directly.

Computer Project

Alternative Investment Methods, Goodwill Impairment, and Consolidated Financial Statements

In this project, you are to provide an analysis of alternative accounting methods for controlling interest investments and subsequent effects on consolidated reporting. The project requires the use of a computer and a spreadsheet software package (e.g., Microsoft Excel®, etc.). The use of these tools allows you to assess the sensitivity of alternative accounting methods on consolidated financial reporting without preparing several similar worksheets by hand. Also, by modeling a worksheet process, you can develop a better understanding of accounting for combined reporting entities.

Consolidated Worksheet Preparation

You will be creating and entering formulas to complete four worksheets. The first objective is to demonstrate the effect of different methods of accounting for the investments (equity, initial value, and partial equity) on the parent company's trial balance and on the consolidated worksheet subsequent to acquisition. The second objective is to show the effect on consolidated balances and key financial ratios of recognizing a goodwill impairment loss.

The project requires preparation of the following four separate worksheets:

a. Consolidated information worksheet (follows).
b. Equity method consolidation worksheet.
c. Initial value method consolidation worksheet.
d. Partial equity method consolidation worksheet.

If your spreadsheet package has multiple worksheet capabilities (e.g., Excel), you can use separate worksheets; otherwise, each of the four worksheets can reside in a separate area of a single spreadsheet.

In formulating your solution, each worksheet should link directly to the first worksheet. Also, feel free to create supplemental schedules to enhance the capabilities of your worksheet.

Project Scenario

Pecos Company acquired 100 percent of Suaro's outstanding stock for $1,450,000 cash on January 1, 2011, when Suaro had the following balance sheet:

Assets		Liabilities and Equity	
Cash	$ 37,000	Liabilities	$(422,000)
Receivables	82,000		
Inventory	149,000	Common stock	(350,000)
Land	90,000	Retained earnings	(126,000)
Equipment (net)	225,000		
Software	315,000		
Total assets	$898,000	Total liabilities and equity	$(898,000)

At the acquisition date, the fair values of each identifiable asset and liability that differed from book value were as follows:

Land	$ 80,000	
Brand name	60,000	(indefinite life—unrecognized on Suaro's books)
Software	415,000	(2-year estimated useful life)
In-Process R&D	300,000	

Additional Information

- Although at acquisition date Pecos expected future benefits from Suaro's in-process research and development (R&D), by the end of 2011, it became clear that the research project was a failure with no future economic benefits.
- During 2011, Suaro earns $75,000 and pays no dividends.
- Selected amounts from Pecos and Suaro's separate financial statements at December 31, 2012, are presented in the consolidated information worksheet. All consolidated worksheets are to be prepared as of December 31, 2012, two years subsequent to acquisition.
- Pecos's January 1, 2012, Retained Earnings balance—before any effect from Suaro's 2011 income— is $(930,000) (credit balance).
- Pecos has 500,000 common shares outstanding for EPS calculations and reported $2,943,100 for consolidated assets at the beginning of the period.

Following is the consolidated information worksheet.

	A	B	C	D
1	**December 31, 2012, trial balances**			
2				
3		**Pecos**	**Suaro**	
4	Revenues	($1,052,000)	($427,000)	
5	Operating expenses	$ 821,000	$262,000	
6	Goodwill impairment loss	?		
7	Income of Suaro	?		
8	Net income	?	($165,000)	
9				
10	Retained earnings—Pecos 1/1/12	?		
11	Retained earnings—Suaro 1/1/12		($201,000)	
12	Net income (above)	?	($165,000)	
13	Dividends paid	$ 200,000	$ 35,000	
14	Retained earnings 12/31/12	?	($331,000)	
15				
16	Cash	$ 195,000	$ 95,000	
17	Receivables	$ 247,000	$143,000	
18	Inventory	$ 415,000	$197,000	
19	Investment in Suaro	?		
20				
21				
22				
23	Land	$ 341,000	$ 85,000	
24	Equipment (net)	$ 240,100	$100,000	
25	Software		$312,000	
26	Other intangibles	$ 145,000		
27	Goodwill			
28	Total assets	?	$932,000	
29				
30	Liabilities	($1,537,100)	($251,000)	
31	Common stock	($ 500,000)	($350,000)	
32	Retained earnings (above)	?	($331,000)	
33	Total liabilities and equity	?	($932,000)	
34				
35	Fair value allocation schedule			
36	Price paid	$1,450,000		
37	Book value	$ 476,000		
38	Excess initial value	$ 974,000	Amortizations	
39	to land	($ 10,000)	2011	2012
40	to brand name	$ 60,000	?	?
41	to software	$ 100,000	?	?
42	to IPR&D	$ 300,000	?	?
43	to goodwill	$ 524,000	?	?
44				
45	Suaro's RE changes	Income	Dividends	
46	2011	$ 75,000	$ 0	
47	2012	$ 165,000	$ 35,000	

Project Requirements

Complete the four worksheets as follows:

1. Input the **consolidated information worksheet** provided and complete the fair value allocation schedule by computing the excess amortizations for 2011 and 2012.

2. Using separate worksheets, prepare Pecos's trial balances for each of the indicated accounting methods (equity, initial value, and partial equity). **Use only formulas for the Investment in Suaro, the Income of Suaro, and Retained Earnings accounts.**

3. **Using references to other cells only (either from the consolidated information worksheet or from the separate method sheets), prepare for each of the three consolidation worksheets:**
   * Adjustments and eliminations.
   * Consolidated balances.

4. Calculate and present the effects of a 2012 total goodwill impairment loss on the following ratios for the consolidated entity:
   * Earnings per share (EPS).
   * Return on assets.
   * Return on equity.
   * Debt to equity.

   Your worksheets should have the capability to adjust immediately for the possibility that all acquisition goodwill can be considered impaired in 2012.

5. **Prepare a word-processed report that describes and discusses the following worksheet results:**
   a. The effects of alternative investment accounting methods on the parent's trial balances and the final consolidation figures.
   b. The relation between consolidated retained earnings and the parent's retained earnings under each of the three (equity, initial value, partial equity) investment accounting methods.
   c. The effect on EPS, return on assets, return on equity, and debt-to-equity ratios of the recognition that all acquisition-related goodwill is considered impaired in 2012.

CPA REVIEW

Please visit the text Web site for the online CPA Simulation.

Situation: On January 1, Year 1, Big Corporation acquires for $700,000 in cash all of Little Corporation's outstanding voting stock. It was the first such acquisition for either company. On the day prior to the transaction, Big and Little reported, respectively, assets of $2 million and $800,000, liabilities of $900,000 and $330,000, contributed capital of $300,000 and $100,000, and retained earnings of $800,000 and $370,000. Unless otherwise stated, assume that Little Corporation holds a building with a book value of $200,000 but a fair value of $300,000. The building has a 10-year remaining life. All of Little's other assets and liabilities are fairly valued in its financial records.

Topics to be covered in simulation:

- Goodwill to be reported.
- Consolidated assets and equities.
- Consolidated expenses.
- Unrecorded intangible assets.
- Goodwill impairment.
- Determination of control.
- Unconsolidated subsidiaries.
- Application of the equity method.

Consolidated Financial Statements and Outside Ownership

Walmart, Inc., in its 2009 consolidated financial statements, includes the accounts of the company and all of its subsidiaries in which a controlling interest is maintained. For those consolidated subsidiaries where Walmart's ownership is less than 100 percent, the outside stockholders' interests are shown as *noncontrolling interests* in the stockholders' equity section of its consolidated balance sheet. On its consolidated income statement, Walmart also allocates a share of the consolidated net income to the noncontrolling interest.

Walmart includes *all of the financial figures* generated by both its wholly and majority-owned subsidiaries within consolidated financial statements. How does Walmart account for the partial ownership interest of the noncontrolling owners of its subsidiaries?

A number of reasons exist for one company to hold less than 100 percent ownership of a subsidiary. The parent might not have had sufficient resources available to obtain all of the outstanding stock. As a second possibility, a few stockholders of the subsidiary could have elected to retain their ownership, perhaps in hope of getting a better price at a later date.

Lack of total ownership is frequently encountered with foreign subsidiaries. The laws of some countries prohibit outsiders from maintaining complete control of domestic business enterprises. In other areas of the world, a parent can seek to establish better relations with a subsidiary's employees, customers, and local government by maintaining some percentage of native ownership.

Regardless of the reason for owning less than 100 percent, the parent consolidates the financial data of every subsidiary when control is present. As discussed in Chapter 2, *complete ownership is not a prerequisite for consolidation.* A single economic entity is formed whenever one company is able to control the decision-making process of another.

Although most parent companies do possess 100 percent ownership of their subsidiaries, a significant number, such as Walmart, establish control with a lesser amount of stock. The remaining outside owners are

LEARNING OBJECTIVES

After studying this chapter, you should be able to:

LO1 Understand that complete ownership is not a prerequisite for the formation of a business combination.

LO2 Describe the valuation principles underlying the acquisition method of accounting for the noncontrolling interest.

LO3 Allocate goodwill acquired in a business combination across the controlling and noncontrolling interests.

LO4 Allocate consolidated net income across the controlling and noncontrolling interests.

LO5 Identify and calculate the four noncontrolling interest figures that must be included within the consolidation process and prepare a consolidation worksheet in the presence of a noncontrolling interest.

LO6 Identify appropriate placements for the components of the noncontrolling interest in consolidated financial statements.

LO7 Determine the effect on consolidated financial statements of a control premium paid by the parent.

LO8 Understand the impact on consolidated financial statements of a midyear acquisition.

LO9 Understand the impact on consolidated financial statements when a step acquisition has taken place.

LO10 Record the sale of a subsidiary (or a portion of its shares).

LO11 Understand the principles of the legacy purchase method in accounting for a noncontrolling interest.

LO1

Understand that complete ownership is not a prerequisite for the formation of a business combination.

collectively referred to as *a noncontrolling interest,* which replaces the traditional term *minority interest.*[1] The presence of these other stockholders poses a number of reporting questions for the accountant. Whenever less than 100 percent of a subsidiary's voting stock is held, how should the subsidiary's accounts be valued within consolidated financial statements? How should the presence of these additional owners be acknowledged?

CONSOLIDATED FINANCIAL REPORTING IN THE PRESENCE OF A NONCONTROLLING INTEREST

Noncontrolling Interest Defined

The authoritative accounting literature defines a noncontrolling interest as follows:

> The ownership interests in the subsidiary that are held by owners other than the parent is a noncontrolling interest. The noncontrolling interest in a subsidiary is part of the equity of the consolidated group. [FASB ASC (para. 810-10-45-15)]

When a parent company acquires a controlling ownership interest with less than 100 percent of a subsidiary's voting shares, it must account for the noncontrolling shareholders' interest in its consolidated financial statements. The noncontrolling interest represents an additional set of owners who have legal claim to the subsidiary's net assets.

Exhibit 4.1 provides a framework for introducing two fundamental valuation challenges in accounting and reporting for a noncontrolling interest. The issues focus on how the parent, in its consolidated financial statements, should

- Assign values to the noncontrolling interest's share of the subsidiary's assets and liabilities?
- Value and disclose the presence of the other owners?

The answer to both of these questions involves fair value. The acquisition method captures the subsidiary's fair value as the relevant attribute for reporting the financial effects of a business combination. Fair values also provide for managerial accountability to investors and creditors for assessing the success or failure of the combination.

Control and Accountability

In acquiring a controlling interest, a parent company becomes responsible for managing all the subsidiary's assets and liabilities even though it may own only a partial interest. If a parent can control the business activities of its subsidiary, it directly follows that the parent is accountable to its investors and creditors for all of the subsidiary's assets, liabilities, and profits.

---

[1] The term *minority interest* had been used almost universally to identify the presence of other outside owners. However, current standards refer to these outside owners as the *noncontrolling interest.* Because this term is more descriptive, it is used throughout this textbook.

EXHIBIT 4.1
Noncontrolling Interest—
Date of Acquisition

PARENT AND 70% OWNED SUBSIDIARY COMPANIES
Consolidated Balance Sheet
Date of Acquisition

Parent's assets	Parent's liabilities
Subsidiary's assets	**Subsidiary's liabilities**
	Parent company owners' equity
	• 100% of parent's net assets
	• **70% of subsidiary's net assets**
	Noncontrolling owners' interest
	• **30% of subsidiary net assets**

To provide a complete picture of the acquired subsidiary requires fair-value measurements for both the subsidiary and the individual assets and liabilities. Thus, for business combinations involving less-than-100 percent ownership, the acquirer recognizes and measures at the acquisition date the

- Identifiable assets acquired and liabilities assumed at their full fair values.[2]
- Noncontrolling interest at fair value.
- Goodwill or a gain from a bargain purchase.

In concluding that consolidated statements involving a noncontrolling interest should initially show all of the subsidiary's assets and liabilities at their full fair values, the 2005 FASB exposure draft Business Combinations (para. B23.a.) observed

> The acquirer obtains control of the acquiree at the acquisition date and, therefore, becomes responsible and accountable for all of the acquiree's assets, liabilities, and activities, regardless of the percentage of its ownership in the investee.
> . . . an important purpose of financial statements is to provide users with relevant and reliable information about the performance of the entity and the resources under its control. That applies regardless of the extent of the ownership interest a parent holds in a particular subsidiary. The Boards concluded that measurement at fair value enables users to better assess the cash generating abilities of the identifiable net assets acquired in the business combination and the accountability of management for the resources entrusted to it.

Thus, even though a company acquires less than 100 percent of another firm, the acquisition method requires that the acquiring company include in its acquisition-date consolidated statements 100 percent of each of the assets acquired and each of the liabilities assumed at their full fair values. This requirement stands in marked contrast to the former purchase method that focused on cost accumulation and allocation. Under the former purchase method, the parent allocated the purchase cost only to the percentage acquired of each subsidiary asset and liability. Thus, prior to the acquisition method, subsidiary assets and liabilities were measured partially at fair value and partially at the subsidiary's carryover (book) value. The current requirements help ensure that managements are accountable for the entire fair value of their acquisitions. However, as discussed below, compared to situations where 100 percent of a firm is acquired, measuring subsidiary fair value when accompanied by a noncontrolling interest presents some special challenges.

LO2

Describe the valuation principles underlying the acquisition method of accounting for the noncontrolling interest.

Subsidiary Acquisition-Date Fair Value in the Presence of a Noncontrolling Interest

When a parent company acquires a less-than-100 percent controlling interest in another firm, the acquisition method requires a determination of the acquisition-date fair value of the acquired firm for consolidated financial reporting. The total acquired firm fair value in the presence of a partial acquisition is the sum of the following two components at the acquisition date:

- The fair value of the controlling interest.
- The fair value of the noncontrolling interest.

The sum of these two components then serves as the starting point for the parent in valuing and recording the subsidiary acquisition. If the sum exceeds the collective fair values of the net identifiable assets acquired and liabilities assumed, then goodwill is recognized. Conversely, if the collective fair values of the net identifiable assets acquired and liabilities assumed exceed the total fair value, the acquirer recognizes a gain on bargain purchase.

Measurement of the controlling interest fair value remains straightforward in the vast majority of cases—the consideration transferred by the parent typically provides the best evidence of fair value of the acquirer's interest. However, there is no parallel consideration transferred available to value the noncontrolling interest. Therefore, the parent must employ

---

[2] As noted in Chapter 2, exceptions to the fair value measurement principle include deferred taxes, certain employee benefits, indemnification assets, reacquired rights, share-based awards, and assets held for sale.

other valuation techniques to estimate the fair value of the noncontrolling interest at the acquisition date.

Usually, a parent can rely on readily available market trading activity to provide a fair valuation for its subsidiary's noncontrolling interest. Market trading prices for the noncontrolling interest shares in the weeks before and after the acquisition provide an objective measure of their fair value. The fair value of these shares then becomes the initial basis for reporting the noncontrolling interest in consolidated financial statements.

Acquirers frequently must pay a premium price per share to garner sufficient shares to ensure a controlling interest. A control premium, however, typically is needed only to acquire sufficient shares to obtain a controlling interest. The remaining (noncontrolling interest) shares no longer provide the added benefit of transferring control to the new owner, and, therefore, may sell at a price less than the shares that yielded control. Such control premiums are properly included in the fair value of the controlling interest, but usually do not affect the fair values of the remaining subsidiary shares. Therefore, separate independent valuations for the controlling and noncontrolling interests are typically best for measuring the total fair value of the subsidiary.

In the absence of fair value evidence based on market trades, firms must turn to less objective measures of noncontrolling interest fair value. For example, comparable investments may be available to estimate fair value. Alternatively, valuation models based on subsidiary discounted cash flows or residual income projections can be employed to estimate the acquisition-date fair value of the noncontrolling interest. Finally, if a control premium is unlikely, the consideration paid by the parent can be used to imply a fair value for the entire subsidiary. The noncontrolling interest fair value is then simply measured as its percentage of this implied subsidiary fair value.

Noncontrolling Interest Fair Value as Evidenced by Market Trades

In the majority of cases, direct evidence based on market activity in the outstanding subsidiary shares (not owned by the parent) will provide the best measure of acquisition-date fair value for the noncontrolling interest. For example, assume that Parker Corporation wished to acquire 9,000 of the 10,000 outstanding equity shares of Strong Company and projected substantial synergies from the proposed acquisition. Parker estimated that a 100 percent acquisition was not needed to extract these synergies. Also, Parker projected that financing more than a 90 percent acquisition would be too costly.

Parker then offered all of Strong's shareholders a premium price for up to 90 percent of the outstanding shares. To induce a sufficient number of shareholders to sell, Parker needed to offer $70 per share, even though the shares had been trading in the $59 to $61 range. During the weeks following the acquisition, the 10 percent noncontrolling interest in Strong Company continues to trade in the $59 to $61 range.

In this case, the $70 per share price paid by Parker does not appear representative of the fair value of all the shares of Strong Company. The fact that the noncontrolling interest shares continue to trade around $60 per share indicates a $60,000 fair value for the 1,000 shares not owned by Parker. Therefore, the valuation of the noncontrolling interest is best evidenced by the traded fair value of Strong's shares, not the price paid by Parker.

The $70 share price paid by Parker nonetheless represents a negotiated value for the 9,000 shares. In the absence of any evidence to the contrary, Parker's shares have a fair value of $630,000 incorporating the additional value Parker expects to extract from synergies with Strong. Thus the fair value of Strong is measured as the sum of the respective fair values of the controlling and noncontrolling interests as follows:

Fair value of controlling interest ($70 × 9,000 shares)	$630,000
Fair value of noncontrolling interest ($60 × 1,000 shares)	60,000
Total acquisition-date fair value of Strong Company	$690,000

At the acquisition date, Parker assessed the total fair value of Strong's net identifiable assets at $600,000. Therefore, we compute goodwill as the excess of the total fair value of the firm over the sum of the fair values of the identifiable net assets as follows:

Total acquisition-date fair value of Strong Company	$690,000
Fair value of net identifiable net assets acquired	600,000
Goodwill	$ 90,000

LO3

Allocate goodwill acquired in a business combination across the controlling and noncontrolling interests.

Allocating Acquired Goodwill to the Controlling and Noncontrolling Interests   To provide a basis for potential future allocations of goodwill impairment charges, acquisition-date goodwill should be apportioned across the controlling and noncontrolling interests. The parent first allocates goodwill to its controlling interest for the excess of the fair value of the parent's equity interest over its share of the fair value of the net identifiable assets. Any remaining goodwill is then attributed to the noncontrolling interest. As a result, goodwill allocated to the controlling and noncontrolling interests will not always be proportional to the percentages owned. Continuing the Parker and Strong example, all of the acquisition goodwill is allocated to the controlling interest as follows:

	Controlling Interest	Noncontrolling Interest
Fair value at acquisition date	$630,000	$60,000
Relative fair value of identifiable net		
assets acquired (90% and 10%)	540,000	60,000
Goodwill	$ 90,000	–0–

In the unlikely event that the noncontrolling interest's proportionate share of the subsidiary's net asset fair values exceeds its total fair value, such an excess would serve to reduce the goodwill recognized by the parent. For example, if Strong's 10 percent noncontrolling interest had a fair value of $55,000, Strong's total fair value would equal $685,000, and goodwill (all allocated to the controlling interest) would decrease to $85,000. Alternatively, if Strong's 10 percent noncontrolling interest had a fair value of $70,000, Strong's total fair value would equal $700,000. In this case, goodwill would equal $100,000 with $90,000 allocated to the controlling interest and $10,000 allocated to the noncontrolling interest. Finally, if the total fair value of the acquired firm is less than the collective sum of its net identifiable assets, a bargain purchase occurs. In such rare combinations, the parent recognizes the entire gain on bargain purchase in current income. In no case is any amount of the gain allocated to the noncontrolling interest.

Noncontrolling Interest Fair Value Implied by Parent's Consideration Transferred

In other cases, especially when a large percentage of the acquiree's voting stock is purchased, the consideration paid by the parent may be reflective of the acquiree's total fair value. For example, again assume Parker pays $70 per share for 9,000 shares of Strong Company representing a 90 percent equity interest. Also assume that the remaining 1,000 noncontrolling interest shares are not actively traded. If there was no compelling evidence that the $70 acquisition price was not representative of all of Strong's 10,000 shares, then it appears reasonable to estimate the fair value of the 10 percent noncontrolling interest using the price paid by Parker. The total fair value of Strong Company is then estimated at $700,000 and allocated as follows:

Fair value of controlling interest ($70 × 9,000 shares)	$630,000
Fair value of noncontrolling interest ($70 × 1,000 shares)	70,000
Total fair value of Strong Company	$700,000

Note that in this case, because the price per share paid by the parent equals the noncontrolling interest per share fair value, goodwill is recognized proportionately across the two ownership groups. Assuming again that the collective fair value of Strong's net identifiable assets equals $600,000, goodwill is recognized and allocated as follows:

	Controlling Interest	Noncontrolling Interest
Fair value at acquisition date	$630,000	$70,000
Relative fair value of net assets acquired (90% and 10%) . . .	540,000	60,000
Goodwill	$ 90,000	$10,000

ALLOCATING THE SUBSIDIARY'S NET INCOME TO THE PARENT AND NONCONTROLLING INTERESTS

LO4

Allocate consolidated net income across the controlling and noncontrolling interests.

Subsequent to acquisition, the subsidiary's net income must be allocated to its owners—the parent company and the noncontrolling interest—to properly measure their respective equity in the consolidated entity. Although current accounting standards require that net income and comprehensive income be attributed to the parent and the noncontrolling interest, they do not provide detailed guidance for making that attribution. Thus it is possible that certain acquired subsidiary assets may not benefit the parent and noncontrolling interest in a manner proportional to their interests. Nonetheless, we expect that such nonproportional benefits will be the exception rather than the rule.

In this text we will assume in all cases that the relative ownership percentages of the parent and noncontrolling interest represent an appropriate basis for attributing all elements (including excess acquisition-date fair-value amortizations for identifiable assets and liabilities) of a subsidiary's income across the ownership groups. Including the excess fair-value amortizations is based on the assumption that the noncontrolling interest represents equity in the subsidiary's net assets as remeasured on the acquisition date.

To illustrate, again assume that Parker acquires 90 percent of Strong Company. Further assume that $30,000 of annual excess fair-value amortization results from increasing Strong's acquisition-date book values to fair values. If Strong reports revenues of $280,000 and expenses of $200,000 based on its internal book values, then the noncontrolling interest share of Strong's income can be computed as follows:

Noncontrolling Interest in Strong Company Net Income

Revenues	$280,000
Expenses	200,000
Subsidiary Strong net income	$ 80,000
Excess acquisition-date fair-value amortization	30,000
Net income adjusted for excess amortizations	$ 50,000
Noncontrolling interest percentage	10%
Noncontrolling interest share of subsidiary net income	$ 5,000

As a procedural matter, the $5,000 noncontrolling interest in the subsidiary net income is then simply subtracted from the combined entity's consolidated net income to derive the parent's interest in consolidated net income. Note that the noncontrolling shareholders have a 10 percent interest in the subsidiary company, but no interest in the parent firm.

PARTIAL OWNERSHIP CONSOLIDATIONS (ACQUISITION METHOD)

LO5

Identify and calculate the four noncontrolling interest figures that must be included within the consolidation process and prepare a consolidation worksheet in the presence of a noncontrolling interest.

Having reviewed the basic concepts underlying the acquisition method of accounting for a noncontrolling interest, we now concentrate on the mechanical aspects of the consolidation process when an outside ownership is present. More specifically, we examine consolidations for time periods subsequent to the date of acquisition to analyze the full range of accounting complexities created by a noncontrolling interest. As indicated previously, this discussion centers on the acquisition method as required under generally accepted accounting principles.

Discussion **Question**

In considering its proposed statement of financial accounting standards on business combinations, the FASB received numerous comment letters. Many of these letters addressed the FASB's proposed adoption of the economic unit concept as a valuation basis for less-than-100 percent acquisitions. A sampling of these letters includes the following observations:

Bob Laux, Microsoft: Microsoft agrees with the Board that the principles underlying standards should strive to reflect the underlying economics of transactions and events. However, we do not believe the Board's conclusion that recognizing the entire economic value of the acquiree, regardless of the ownership interest in the acquiree at the acquisition date, reflects the underlying economics.

Patricia A. Little, Ford Motor Company: We agree that recognizing 100 percent of the fair value of the acquiree is appropriate. We believe that this is crucial in erasing anomalies which were created when only the incremental ownership acquired was fair valued and the minority interest was reflected at its carryover basis.

Sharilyn Gasaway, Alltell Corporation: One of the underlying principles . . . is that the acquirer should measure and recognize the fair value of the acquiree as a whole. If 100 percent of the ownership interests are acquired, measuring and recognizing 100 percent of the fair value is both appropriate and informative. However, if less than 100 percent of the ownership interests are acquired, recognizing the fair value of 100 percent of the business acquired is not representative of the value actually acquired. In the instance in which certain minority owners retain their ownership interest, recognizing the fair value of the minority interest does not provide sufficient benefit to financial statement users to justify the additional cost incurred to calculate that fair value.

PricewaterhouseCoopers: We agree that the noncontrolling interest should be recorded at its fair value when it is initially recorded in the consolidated financial statements. As such, when control is obtained in a single step, the acquirer would record 100 percent of the fair value of the assets acquired (including goodwill) and liabilities assumed.

Loretta Cangialosi, Pfizer: While we understand the motivation of the FASB to account for all elements of the acquisition transaction at fair value, we are deeply concerned about the practice issues that will result. The heavy reliance on expected value techniques, use of the hypothetical market participants, the lack of observable markets, and the obligation to affix values to "possible" and even "remote" scenarios, among other requirements, will all conspire to create a standard that will likely prove to be nonoperational, unauditable, representationally unfaithful, abuse-prone, costly, and of limited (and perhaps negative) shareholder value.

Do you think the FASB made the correct decision in requiring consolidated financial statements to recognize all subsidiary's assets and liabilities at fair value regardless of the percentage ownership acquired by the parent?

The acquisition method focuses on incorporating in the consolidated financial statements 100 percent of the subsidiary's assets and liabilities at their acquisition-date fair values. Note that subsequent to acquisition, changes in fair values for assets and liabilities are not recognized.[3] Instead, the subsidiary assets acquired and liabilities assumed are reflected in future consolidated financial statements using their acquisition-date fair values net of subsequent amortizations (or possibly reduced for impairment).

The presence of a noncontrolling interest does not dramatically alter the consolidation procedures presented in Chapter 3. The unamortized balance of the acquisition-date fair-value allocation must still be computed and included within the consolidated totals. Excess fair-value

---

[3] Exceptions common to all firms (whether subject to consolidation or not) include recognizing changing fair values for marketable equity securities and other financial instruments.

EXHIBIT 4.2
Subsidiary Accounts—
Date of Acquisition

PAWN COMPANY
Account Balances
January 1, 2011

	Book Value	Fair Value	Differences
Current assets	$ 440,000	$ 440,000	–0–
Trademarks (indefinite life)	260,000	320,000	$ 60,000
Patented technology (20-year life)	480,000	600,000	120,000
Equipment (10-year life)	110,000	100,000	(10,000)
Long-term liabilities (8 years to maturity)	(550,000)	(510,000)	40,000
Net assets	$ 740,000	$ 950,000	$210,000
Common stock	$(230,000)		
Retained earnings, 1/1/11	(510,000)		

Note: Parentheses indicate a credit balance.

amortization expenses of these allocations are recognized each year as appropriate. Reciprocal balances are eliminated. Beyond these basic steps, the valuation and recognition of four noncontrolling interest balances add a new dimension to the process of consolidating financial information. The parent company must determine and then enter each of these figures when constructing a worksheet:

- Noncontrolling interest in the subsidiary as of the beginning of the current year.
- Noncontrolling interest in the subsidiary's current year income.
- Noncontrolling interest in the subsidiary's dividend payments.
- Noncontrolling interest as of the end of the year (found by combining the three balances above).

To illustrate, assume that King Company acquires 80 percent of Pawn Company's 100,000 outstanding voting shares on January 1, 2011, for $9.75 per share or a total of $780,000 cash consideration. Further assume that the 20 percent noncontrolling interest shares traded both before and after the acquisition date at an average of $9.75 per share. The total fair value of Pawn to be used initially in consolidation is thus as follows:

Consideration transferred by King ($9.75 × 80,000 shares)	$780,000
Noncontrolling interest fair value ($9.75 × 20,000 shares)	195,000
Pawn's total fair value at January 1, 2011	$975,000

Exhibit 4.2 presents the book value of Pawn's accounts as well as the fair value of each asset and liability on the acquisition date. Pawn's total fair value is attributed to Pawn's assets and liabilities as shown in Exhibit 4.3. Annual amortization relating to these allocations also is included in this schedule. Although expense figures are computed for only the initial years, some amount of amortization is recognized in each of the 20 years following the acquisition (the life assumed for the patented technology).

Exhibit 4.3 shows first that all identifiable assets acquired and liabilities assumed are adjusted to their full individual fair values at the acquisition date. The noncontrolling interest will share proportionately in these fair-value adjustments. Exhibit 4.3 also shows that any excess fair value not attributable to Pawn's identifiable net assets is assigned to goodwill. Because the controlling and noncontrolling interests' acquisition-date fair values are identical at $9.75 per share, the resulting goodwill is allocated proportionately across these ownership interests.

Consolidated financial statements will be produced for the year ending December 31, 2012. This date is arbitrary. Any time period subsequent to 2011 could serve to demonstrate the applicable consolidation procedures. Having already calculated the acquisition-date fair-value allocations and related amortization, the accountant can construct a consolidation of these two companies along the lines demonstrated in Chapter 3. Only the presence of the 20 percent noncontrolling interest alters this process.

EXHIBIT 4.3
Excess Fair
Value Allocations

KING COMPANY AND 80% OWNED SUBSIDIARY PAWN COMPANY
Fair-Value Allocation and Amortization
January 1, 2011

	Allocation	Estimated Life (years)	Annual Excess Amortizations
Pawn's acquisition-date fair value (100%)	$975,000		
Pawn's acquisition date book value (100%) . .	(740,000)		
Fair value in excess of book value	$235,000		
Adjustments (100%) to			
Trademarks (indefinite life)	$ 60,000	indefinite	–0–
Patented technology (20-year life)	120,000	20	6,000
Equipment (10-year life)	(10,000)	10	(1,000)
Long-term liabilities (8 years to maturity) .	40,000	8	5,000
Goodwill (indefinite life)	$ 25,000	indefinite	–0–
Annual amortizations of excess fair value over book value (initial years)			$ 10,000

Goodwill Allocation to the Controlling and Noncontrolling Interests

	Controlling Interest	Noncontrolling Interest	Total
Fair value at acquisition date	$780,000	$195,000	$975,000
Relative fair value of Pawn's identifiable net assets (80% and 20%)	760,000	190,000	950,000
Goodwill	$ 20,000	$ 5,000	$ 25,000

To complete the information needed for this combination, assume that Pawn Company reports the following changes in retained earnings since King's acquisition:

Current year (2012)
Net income . . . . $ 90,000
Less: Dividends paid . . . .   (50,000)
Increase in retained earnings . . . . $ 40,000

Prior years (only 2011 in this illustration):
Increase in retained earnings . . . . $ 70,000

Assuming that King Company applies the equity method, the Investment in Pawn Company account as of December 31, 2012, can be constructed as shown in Exhibit 4.4. Note that the $852,000 balance is computed based on applying King's 80 percent ownership to Pawn's income (less amortization) and dividends. Although 100 percent of the subsidiary's assets and liabilities will be combined in consolidation, the internal accounting for King's investment in Pawn is based on its 80 percent ownership. This technique facilitates worksheet adjustments that allocate various amounts to the noncontrolling interest. Exhibit 4.5 presents the separate financial statements for these two companies as of December 31, 2012, and the year then ended, based on the information provided.

Consolidated Totals

Although the inclusion of a 20 percent outside ownership complicates the consolidation process, the 2012 totals to be reported by this business combination can nonetheless be determined without the use of a worksheet:

- *Revenues* = $1,340,000. The revenues of the parent and the subsidiary are added together. The acquisition method includes the subsidiary's revenues in total although King owns only 80 percent of the stock.

EXHIBIT 4.4
Equity Method
Investment Balance

KING COMPANY
Investment in Pawn Company
Equity Method
December 31, 2012

Acquisition price for 80% interest		$780,000
Prior year (2011):		
Increase in retained earnings (80% × $70,000)	$56,000	
Excess amortization expenses (80% × $10,000) (Exhibit 4.3) ..	(8,000)	48,000
Current year (2012):		
Income accrual (80% × $90,000)	72,000	
Excess amortization expense (80% × $10,000) (Exhibit 4.3) ...	(8,000)	
Equity in subsidiary earnings	64,000*	
Dividends received (80% × $50,000)	(40,000)	24,000
Balance, 12/31/12		$852,000

*This figure appears in King's 2012 income statement. See Exhibit 4.5.

EXHIBIT 4.5
Separate Financial
Records

KING COMPANY AND PAWN COMPANY
Separate Financial Statements
For December 31, 2012, and the Year Then Ended

	King	Pawn
Revenues	$ (910,000)	$ (430,000)
Cost of goods sold	344,000	200,000
Depreciation expense	60,000	20,000
Amortization expense	100,000	75,000
Interest expense	70,000	45,000
Equity in subsidiary earnings (see Exhibit 4.4)	(64,000)	–0–
Net income	$ (400,000)	$ (90,000)
Retained earnings, 1/1/12	$ (860,000)	$ (580,000)
Net income (above)	(400,000)	(90,000)
Dividends paid	60,000	50,000
Retained earnings, 12/31/12	$(1,200,000)	$ (620,000)
Current assets	$ 726,000	$ 445,000
Trademarks	304,000	295,000
Patented technology	880,000	540,000
Equipment (net)	390,000	160,000
Investment in Pawn Company (see Exhibit 4.4)	852,000	–0–
Total assets	$ 3,152,000	$ 1,440,000
Long-term liabilities	$(1,082,000)	$ (590,000)
Common stock	(870,000)	(230,000)
Retained earnings, 12/31/12	(1,200,000)	(620,000)
Total liabilities and equities	$(3,152,000)	$(1,440,000)

- *Cost of Goods Sold* = $544,000. The parent and subsidiary balances are added together.
- *Depreciation Expense* = $79,000. The parent and subsidiary balances are added together along with the $1,000 reduction in equipment depreciation as indicated in Exhibit 4.3.
- *Amortization Expense* = $181,000. The parent and subsidiary balances are added together along with the $6,000 additional patented technology amortization expense as indicated in Exhibit 4.3.
- *Interest Expense* = $120,000. The parent and subsidiary balances are added along with an additional $5,000. Exhibit 4.3 shows Pawn's long-term debt reduced by $40,000 to fair value. Because the maturity value remains constant, the $40,000 represents a discount amortized to interest expense over the remaining eight-year life of the debt.
- *Equity in Subsidiary Earnings* = −0−. The parent's investment income is eliminated so that the subsidiary's revenues and expenses can be included in the consolidated totals.
- *Consolidated Net Income* = $416,000. The consolidated entity's total earnings before allocation to the controlling and noncontrolling ownership interests.
- *Noncontrolling Interest in Subsidiary's Income* = $16,000. The outside owners are assigned 20 percent of Pawn's reported income of $90,000 less $10,000 total excess fair-value amortization. The acquisition method shows this amount as an allocation of consolidated net income.
- *Net Income to Controlling Interest* = $400,000. The acquisition method shows this amount as an allocation of consolidated net income.
- *Retained Earnings, 1/1* = $860,000. The parent company figure equals the consolidated total because the equity method was applied. If the initial value method or the partial equity method had been used, the parent's balance would require adjustment to include any unrecorded figures.
- *Dividends Paid* = $60,000. Only the parent company balance is reported. Eighty percent of the subsidiary's payments were made to the parent and are eliminated. The remaining distribution was made to the outside owners and serves to reduce the noncontrolling interest balance.
- *Retained Earnings, 12/31* = $1,200,000. The balance is found by adding the controlling interest's share of consolidated net income to the beginning Retained Earnings balance and then subtracting the dividends paid to the controlling interest. Because the equity method is utilized, the parent company figure reflects the total for the business combination.
- *Current Assets* = $1,171,000. The parent's and subsidiary's book values are added.
- *Trademarks* = $659,000. The parent's book value is added to the subsidiary's book value plus the $60,000 allocation of the acquisition-date fair value (see Exhibit 4.3).
- *Patented Technology* = $1,528,000. The parent's book value is added to the subsidiary's book value plus the $120,000 excess fair-value allocation less two years' excess amortizations of $6,000 per year (see Exhibit 4.3).
- *Equipment* = $542,000. The parent's book value is added to the subsidiary's book value less the $10,000 acquisition-date fair-value reduction plus two years' expense reductions of $1,000 per year (see Exhibit 4.3).
- *Investment in Pawn Company* = −0−. The balance reported by the parent is eliminated so that the subsidiary's assets and liabilities can be included in the consolidated totals.
- *Goodwill* = $25,000. The original allocation shown in Exhibit 4.3 is reported.
- *Total Assets* = $3,925,000. This balance is a summation of the consolidated assets.
- *Long-Term Liabilities* = $1,642,000. The parent's book value is added to the subsidiary's book value less the $40,000 acquisition-date fair-value allocation net of two years' amortizations of $5,000 per year (see Exhibit 4.3).
- *Noncontrolling Interest in Subsidiary* = $213,000. The outside ownership is 20 percent of the subsidiary's year-end book value adjusted for any unamortized excess fair value attributed to the noncontrolling interest:

Noncontrolling interest at 1/1/12
   20% of $810,000 beginning book value—common stock
     plus 1/1/12 retained earnings $162,000
     20% of unamortized excess fair-value allocations as of 1/1 45,000
Noncontrolling interest in subsidiary's income (from prior page) 16,000
Dividends paid to noncontrolling interest (20% of $50,000 total) . . . . (10,000)
Noncontrolling interest at 12/31/12 . . . . $213,000

- *Common Stock* = $870,000. Only the parent's balance is reported.
- *Retained Earnings, 12/31* = $1,200,000. Computed on prior page.
- *Total Liabilities and Equities* = $3,925,000. This total is a summation of consolidated liabilities, noncontrolling interest, and equities.

Alternative Calculation of Noncontrolling Interest at December 31, 2012

The acquisition method requires that the noncontrolling interest be measured at fair value at the date of acquisition. Subsequent to acquisition, however, the noncontrolling interest value is adjusted for its share of subsidiary income, excess fair-value amortizations, and dividends. The following schedule demonstrates how the noncontrolling interest's acquisition-date fair value is adjusted to show the ending consolidated balance sheet amount.

Fair value of 20% noncontrolling interest at acquisition date $195,000
   20% of $70,000 change in Pawn's 2011 retained earnings 14,000
   20% of excess fair-value amortizations . . . . (2,000)   12,000
2012 income allocation (20% × [90,000 − 10,000]) 16,000
2012 dividends (20% × $50,000) . . . . (10,000)
Noncontrolling interest at December 31, 2012 . . . . $213,000

As can be seen in the above schedule, the fair-value principle applies only to the initial noncontrolling interest valuation.

Worksheet Process—Acquisition Method

The consolidated totals for King and Pawn also can be determined by means of a worksheet as shown in Exhibit 4.6. Comparing this example with Exhibit 3.7 in Chapter 3 indicates that the presence of a noncontrolling interest does not create a significant number of changes in the consolidation procedures.

The worksheet still includes elimination of the subsidiary's stockholders' equity accounts (Entry **S**) although, as explained next, this entry is expanded to record the beginning noncontrolling interest for the year. The second worksheet entry (Entry **A**) recognizes the excess acquisition-date fair-value allocations at January 1 after one year of amortization with an additional adjustment to the beginning noncontrolling interest. Intra-entity income as well as dividend payments are removed also (Entries **I** and **D**) while current-year excess amortization expenses are recognized (Entry **E**). The differences with the Chapter 3 illustrations relate exclusively to the recognition of the three components of the noncontrolling interest. In addition, *a separate Noncontrolling Interest column is added to the worksheet to accumulate these components to form the year-end figure to be reported on the consolidated balance sheet.*

Noncontrolling Interest—Beginning of Year   Under the acquisition method, the noncontrolling interest shares proportionately in the fair values of the subsidiary's net identifiable assets as adjusted for excess fair-value amortizations. On the consolidated worksheet, this total net fair value is represented by two components:

1. Pawn's stockholders' equity accounts (common stock and beginning Retained Earnings) indicate a January 1, 2012, book value of $810,000.
2. The January 1, 2012, acquisition-date fair-value net of previous year's amortizations (in this case 2011 only).

EXHIBIT 4.6   Noncontrolling Interest Illustrated—Acquisition Method

KING COMPANY AND PAWN COMPANY

Consolidation: Acquisition Method
Investment: Equity Method

Consolidation Worksheet
For Year Ending December 31, 2012

Ownership: 80%

Accounts	King Company*	Pawn Company*	Consolidation Entries Debit	Consolidation Entries Credit	Noncontrolling Interest	Consolidated Totals
Revenues	(910,000)	(430,000)				(1,340,000)
Cost of goods sold	344,000	200,000				544,000
Depreciation expense	60,000	20,000		(E) 1,000		79,000
Amortization expense	100,000	75,000	(E) 6,000			181,000
Interest expense	70,000	45,000	(E) 5,000			120,000
Equity in Pawn's earnings (see Exhibit 4.4)	(64,000)	–0–	(I) 64,000			–0–
Separate company net income	(400,000)	(90,000)				
Consolidated net income						(416,000)
Noncontrolling interest in Pawn income					(16,000)	16,000
Net income to controlling interest						(400,000)
Retained earnings, 1/1	(860,000)	(580,000)	(S) 580,000			(860,000)
Net income (above)	(400,000)	(90,000)				(400,000)
Dividends paid	60,000	50,000		(D) 40,000	10,000	60,000
Retained earnings, 12/31	(1,200,000)	(620,000)				(1,200,000)
Current assets	726,000	445,000				1,171,000
Trademarks	304,000	295,000	(A) 60,000			659,000
Patented technology	880,000	540,000	(A) 114,000	(E) 6,000		1,528,000
Equipment (net)	390,000	160,000	(E) 1,000	(A) 9,000		542,000
Investment in Pawn Company (see Exhibit 4.4)	852,000	–0–	(D) 40,000	(S) 648,000 (A) 180,000 (I) 64,000		–0–
Goodwill	–0–	–0–	(A) 25,000			25,000
Total assets	3,152,000	1,440,000				3,925,000
Long-term liabilities	(1,082,000)	(590,000)	(A) 35,000	(E) 5,000		(1,642,000)
Common stock	(870,000)	(230,000)	(S) 230,000			(870,000)
				(S) 162,000		
Noncontrolling interest in Pawn 1/1				(A) 45,000	(207,000)	
Noncontrolling interest in Pawn 12/31					213,000	(213,000)
Retained earnings, 12/31	(1,200,000)	(620,000)				(1,200,000)
Total liabilities and equities	(3,152,000)	(1,440,000)	1,160,000	1,160,000		(3,925,000)

*See Exhibit 4.5.
Note: parentheses indicate credit balances.
Consolidation entries:
(S)   Elimination of subsidiary's stockholders' equity along with recognition of January 1 noncontrolling interest.
(A)   Allocation of subsidiary total fair value in excess of book value, unamortized balances as of January 1.
(I)   Elimination of intra-entity income (equity accrual less amortization expenses).
(D)   Elimination of intra-entity dividend payments.
(E)   Recognition of amortization expenses of fair-value allocations.

Therefore, the January 1, 2012, balance of the 20 percent outside ownership is computed as follows:

20% × $810,000 subsidiary book value at 1/1/12	162,000
20% × $225,000 unamortized excess fair-value allocation at 1/1/12	45,000
1/1/12 Noncontrolling interest in Pawn	$207,000

This balance is recognized on the worksheet through Entry **S** and Entry **A:**

Consolidation Entry S

Common Stock (Pawn)	230,000	
Retained Earnings, 1/1/12 (Pawn)	580,000	
Investment in Pawn Company (80%)		648,000
Noncontrolling Interest in Pawn Company, 1/1/12 (20%)		162,000
To eliminate beginning stockholders' equity accounts of subsidiary along with book value portion of investment (equal to 80 percent ownership). Noncontrolling interest of 20 percent is also recognized.		

Consolidation Entry A

Trademarks	60,000	
Patented technology	114,000	
Liabilities	35,000	
Goodwill	25,000	
Equipment		9,000
Investment in Pawn Company (80%)		180,000
Noncontrolling Interest in Subsidiary, 1/1/12 (20%)		45,000
To recognize unamortized excess fair value as of January 1, 2012, to Pawn's assets acquired and liabilities assumed in the combination. Also to allocate the unamortized fair value to the noncontrolling interest. Goodwill is attributable proportionately to controlling and noncontrolling interests.		

The total $207,000 balance assigned here to the outside owners at the beginning of the year is extended to the Noncontrolling Interest worksheet column (see Exhibit 4.6).

To complete the required worksheet adjustments, Entries **I, D,** and **E** are prepared as follows:

Consolidation Entry I

Equity in Pawn's earnings	64,000	
Investment in Pawn Company		64,000
To eliminate intra-entity income accrual comprising subsidiary income less excess acquisition-date fair-value amortizations.		

Consolidation Entry D

Investment in Pawn Company	40,000	
Dividends paid		40,000
To eliminate intra-entity dividend payments.		

Consolidation Entry E

Amortization expense	6,000	
Interest expense	5,000	
Equipment (net)	1,000	
Depreciation expense		1,000
Patented technology		6,000
Long-term liabilities		5,000
To recognize the current-income effects from excess acquisition-date fair-value allocations over their expected remaining lives.		

Noncontrolling Interest—Current Year Income Exhibit 4.6 shows the noncontrolling interest's share of current year earnings is $16,000. The amount is based on the subsidiary's $90,000 income (Pawn Company column) less excess acquisition-date fair-value amortizations. Thus, King assigns $16,000 to the outside owners computed as follows:

Noncontrolling Interest in Pawn Company Net Income

Pawn Company net income	$90,000
Excess acquisition-date fair-value amortization	10,000
Net income adjusted for excess amortizations	$80,000
Noncontrolling interest percentage	20%
Noncontrolling interest share of subsidiary net income	$16,000

In effect, 100 percent of each subsidiary revenue and expense account (including excess acquisition-date fair-value amortizations) is consolidated with an accompanying 20 percent allocation to the noncontrolling interest. The 80 percent net effect corresponds to King's ownership.

Because $16,000 of consolidated income accrues to the noncontrolling interest, this amount is added to the $207,000 beginning balance assigned (in Entries **S** and **A**) to these outside owners. The noncontrolling interest increases because the subsidiary generated a profit during the period.

Although we could record this allocation through an additional worksheet entry, the $16,000 is usually shown, as in Exhibit 4.6, by means of a columnar adjustment. The current year accrual is simultaneously entered in the Income Statement section of the consolidated column as an allocation of consolidated net income and in the Noncontrolling Interest column as an increase. This procedure assigns a portion of the combined earnings to the outside owners rather than to the parent company owners.

Noncontrolling Interest—Dividend Payments The $40,000 dividend paid to the parent company is eliminated routinely through Entry **D,** but the remainder of Pawn's dividend was paid to the noncontrolling interest. The impact of the dividend (20 percent of the subsidiary's total payment) distributed to the other owners must be acknowledged. As shown in Exhibit 4.6, this remaining $10,000 is extended directly into the Noncontrolling Interest column on the worksheet as a reduction. It represents the decrease in the underlying claim of the outside ownership that resulted from the subsidiary's asset distribution.

Noncontrolling Interest—End of Year The ending assignment for these other owners is calculated by a summation of

The beginning balance for the year	$207,000
Plus the appropriate share of the subsidiary's current income	16,000
Less the dividends paid to the outside owners	(10,000)
Noncontrolling interest end of year—credit balance	$213,000

The Noncontrolling Interest column on the worksheet in Exhibit 4.6 accumulates these figures. The $213,000 total is then transferred to the balance sheet, where it appears in the consolidated statements.

Consolidated Financial Statements

Having successfully consolidated the information for King and Pawn, the resulting financial statements for these two companies are produced in Exhibit 4.7. These figures are taken from the consolidation worksheet.

LO6

Identify appropriate placements for the components of the noncontrolling interest in consolidated financial statements.

Consolidated Financial Statement Presentations of Noncontrolling Interest

Prior to current reporting requirements, the placement of the noncontrolling interest on the consolidated balance sheet varied across reporting entities. Some firms reported their noncontrolling interests as "mezzanine" items between liabilities and equity. Others reported noncontrolling interest as liabilities or as stockholders' equity.

Noncontrolling interests in the equity of subsidiaries are now reported in the owners' equity section of the consolidated statement of financial position. The amount should be clearly

EXHIBIT 4.7
**Consolidated Statements
with Noncontrolling
Interest—Acquisition
Method**

KING COMPANY AND PAWN COMPANY
Consolidated Financial Statements

Income Statement
Year Ended December 31, 2012

Revenues	$1,340,000
Cost of goods sold	(544,000)
Depreciation expense	(79,000)
Amortization expense	(181,000)
Interest expense	(120,000)
Consolidated net income	$ 416,000
To noncontrolling interest	16,000
To controlling interest	$ 400,000

Statement of Changes in Owners' Equity
Year Ended December 31, 2012

	King Company Owners		Noncontrolling Interest
	Retained Earnings	Common Stock	
Balance, January 1	$ 860,000	$870,000	$ 207,000
Net income	400,000		16,000
Less: Dividends	(60,000)		(10,000)
Balance, December 31	$1,200,000	$870,000	$ 213,000

Statement of Financial Position
At December 31, 2012
Assets

Current assets	$1,171,000
Trademarks	659,000
Patented technology	1,528,000
Equipment (net)	542,000
Goodwill	25,000
Total assets	$3,925,000

Liabilities

Long-term liabilities	$1,642,000

Owners' Equity

Common stock—King Company	870,000
Noncontrolling interest in subsidiary	213,000
Retained earnings	1,200,000
Total liabilities and owners' equity	$3,925,000

identified, labeled, and distinguished from the parent's controlling interest in its subsidiaries. Also consolidated net income (or loss) and each component of other comprehensive income must be allocated to the controlling and noncontrolling interests.

Exhibit 4.7 shows first the consolidated statement of income. Consolidated net income is computed at the combined entity level as $416,000 and then allocated to the noncontrolling and controlling interests. The statement of changes in owners' equity provides details of the ownership changes for the year for both the controlling and noncontrolling interest shareholders.[4] Finally, note the placement of the noncontrolling interest in the subsidiary's equity squarely in the consolidated owners' equity section.

[4] If appropriate, this statement of changes in owners' equity would also provide an allocation of accumulated other comprehensive income elements across the controlling and noncontrolling interests.

ALTERNATIVE FAIR-VALUE SPECIFICATION—EVIDENCE OF A CONTROL PREMIUM

LO7

Determine the effect on consolidated financial statements of a control premium paid by the parent.

To illustrate the valuation implications for an acquisition involving a control premium, again assume that King Company acquires 80 percent of Pawn Company's 100,000 outstanding voting shares on January 1, 2011. We also again assume that Pawn's shares traded before the acquisition date at an average of $9.75 per share. In this scenario, however, we assume that to acquire sufficient shares to gain control King pays $11.00 per share or a total of $880,000 cash consideration for its 80 percent interest. King thus pays a control premium of $1.25 ($11.00 − $9.75) per share to acquire Pawn. King anticipates that synergies with Pawn will create additional value for King's shareholders. Finally, following the acquisition, the remaining 20 percent noncontrolling interest shares continue to trade at $9.75.

The total fair value of Pawn to be used initially in consolidation is thus recomputed as follows:

Consideration transferred by King ($11.00 × 80,000 shares)	$ 880,000
Noncontrolling interest fair value ($9.75 × 20,000 shares)	195,000
Pawn's total fair value at January 1, 2011	$1,075,000

In keeping with the acquisition method's requirement that identifiable assets acquired and liabilities assumed be adjusted to fair value, King allocates Pawn's total fair value as follows:

Fair value of Pawn at January 1, 2011		$1,075,000
Book value of Pawn at January 1, 2011		(740,000)
Fair value in excess of book value		$ 335,000
Adjustments to		
Trademarks	$ 60,000	
Patented technology	120,000	
Equipment	(10,000)	
Long-term liabilities	40,000	210,000
Goodwill		$ 125,000

Note that the *identifiable* assets acquired and liabilities assumed are again adjusted to their full individual fair values at the acquisition date. Only the amount designated as goodwill is changed to $125,000 from $25,000 in the original fair-value allocation example as shown in Exhibit 4.3. In this case, King allocates $120,000 of the $125,000 total goodwill amount to its own interest as follows:

	Controlling Interest	Noncontrolling Interest	Total
Fair value at acquisition date	$880,000	$195,000	$1,075,000
Relative fair value of Pawn's net identifiable			
assets (80% and 20%)	760,000	190,000	950,000
Goodwill	$120,000	$ 5,000	$ 125,000

The initial acquisition-date fair value of $195,000 for the noncontrolling interest includes only a $5,000 goodwill allocation from the combination. Because the parent paid an extra $1.25 per share more than the fair value of the noncontrolling interest shares, more goodwill is allocated to the parent.

Next we separate the familiar consolidated worksheet entry **A** into two components labeled **A1** and **A2**. The **A1** worksheet entry allocates the excess acquisition-date fair value to the *identifiable* assets acquired and liabilities assumed (trademarks, patented technology, equipment, and liabilities). Note that the relative ownership percentages of the parent and noncontrolling interest (80 percent and 20 percent) provide the basis for allocating the net $200,000 adjustment to the parent's Investment account and the 1/1/12 balance of the noncontrolling interest.

EXHIBIT 4.8   Consolidated Statements with Noncontrolling Interest—Acquisition Method, Parent Pays a Control Premium

KING COMPANY AND PAWN COMPANY
Consolidation Worksheet
For Year Ending December 31, 2012

Accounts	King Company	Pawn Company	Consolidation Entries Debit	Consolidation Entries Credit	Noncontrolling Interest	Consolidated Totals
Revenues	(910,000)	(430,000)				(1,340,000)
Cost of goods sold	344,000	200,000				544,000
Depreciation expense	60,000	20,000		(E) 1,000		79,000
Amortization expense	100,000	75,000	(E) 6,000			181,000
Interest expense	70,000	45,000	(E) 5,000			120,000
Equity in Pawn's earnings	(64,000)	–0–	(I) 64,000			–0–
Separate company net income	(400,000)	(90,000)				
Consolidated net income						(416,000)
Noncontrolling interest in Pawn income					(16,000)	16,000
Net income to controlling interest						(400,000)
Retained earnings, 1/1	(860,000)	(580,000)	(S) 580,000			(860,000)
Net income (above)	(400,000)	(90,000)				(400,000)
Dividends paid	60,000	50,000		(D) 40,000	10,000	60,000
Retained earnings, 12/31	(1,200,000)	(620,000)				(1,200,000)
Current assets	626,000	445,000				1,071,000
Trademarks	304,000	295,000	(A1) 60,000			659,000
Patented technology	880,000	540,000	(A1) 114,000	(E) 6,000		1,528,000
Equipment (net)	390,000	160,000	(E) 1,000	(A1) 9,000		542,000
Investment in Pawn Company	952,000	–0–	(D) 40,000	(S) 648,000		–0–
				(A1) 160,000		
				(A2) 120,000		
				(I) 64,000		
Goodwill	–0–	–0–	(A2) 125,000			125,000
Total assets	3,152,000	1,440,000				3,925,000
Long-term liabilities	(1,082,000)	(590,000)	(A1) 35,000	(E) 5,000		(1,642,000)
Common stock	(870,000)	(230,000)	(S) 230,000			(870,000)
Noncontrolling interest in Pawn 1/1				(S) 162,000		
				(A1) 40,000		
				(A2) 5,000	(207,000)	
Noncontrolling interest in Pawn 12/31					213,000	(213,000)
Retained earnings, 12/31	(1,200,000)	(620,000)				(1,200,000)
Total liabilities and equities	(3,152,000)	(1,440,000)	1,260,000	1,260,000		(3,925,000)

Consolidation entries:
(S)   Elimination of subsidiary's stockholders' equity along with recognition of January 1 noncontrolling interest.
(A1) Allocation of subsidiary identifiable net asset fair value in excess of book value, unamortized balances as of January 1.
(A2) Allocation of goodwill to parent and noncontrolling interest.
(I)   Elimination of intra-entity income (equity accrual less amortization expenses).
(D)   Elimination of intra-entity dividend payments.
(E)   Recognition of amortization expenses of fair-value allocations.

Next, consolidated worksheet entry **A2** provides the recognition and allocation of the goodwill balance taking into account the differing per share prices of the parent's consideration transferred and the noncontrolling interest fair value. Note that the presence of a control premium affects primarily the parents' shares, and thus goodwill is disproportionately (relative to the ownership percentages) allocated to the controlling and noncontrolling interests. Exhibit 4.8 shows the consolidated worksheet for this extension to the King and Pawn example.

Consolidation Entry A1

Trademarks	60,000	
Patented Technology	114,000	
Liabilities	35,000	
Equipment		9,000
Investment in Pawn Company (80%)		160,000
Noncontrolling Interest in Subsidiary 1/1/12 (20%)		40,000

Consolidation Entry A2

Goodwill	125,000	
Investment in Pawn Company		120,000
Noncontrolling Interest in Subsidiary 1/1/12		5,000

The worksheet calculates the December 31, 2012, noncontrolling balance as follows:

Pawn January 1, 2012: 20% book value	$162,000
January 1, 2012: 20% excess fair-value allocation for Pawn's net identifiable assets ($200,000 × 20%) + $5,000 goodwill allocation	45,000
Noncontrolling interest at January 1, 2012	$207,000
2012 Pawn income allocation	16,000
Noncontrolling interest share of Pawn dividends	(10,000)
December 31, 2012, balance	$213,000

Note that the $45,000 January 1 excess fair-value allocation to the noncontrolling interest includes the noncontrolling interest's full share of the *identifiable* assets acquired and liabilities assumed in the combination but only $5,000 for goodwill. Because King Company paid a $100,000 control premium (80,000 shares × $1.25), the additional $100,000 is allocated entirely to the controlling interest.

By comparing Exhibits 4.6 and 4.8 we can assess the effect of the separate acquisition-date valuations for the controlling and noncontrolling interests. As seen below, the presence of King's control premium affects the goodwill component in the consolidated financial statements and little else.

	Exhibit 4.6	Exhibit 4.8	Difference
On King's Separate Financial Statements			
Current assets	$ 726,000	$ 626,000	− $100,000
Investment in Pawn	$ 852,000	$ 952,000	+ $100,000
On the Consolidated Balances			
Current assets	$1,171,000	$1,071,000	− $100,000
Goodwill	$ 25,000	$ 125,000	+ $100,000

Because King paid an additional $100,000 for its 80 percent interest in Pawn, the initial value assigned to the Investment account increases and current assets (i.e., additional cash paid for the acquisition) decreases by $100,000. The extra $100,000 then simply increases goodwill on the consolidated balance sheet. Note that the noncontrolling interest fair value remains unchanged at $213,000 across Exhibits 4.6 and 4.8.

Effects Created by Alternative Investment Methods

In the King and Pawn illustrations, the parent uses the equity method and bases all worksheet entries on that approach. As discussed in Chapter 3, had King incorporated the initial value method or the partial equity method, a few specific changes in the consolidation process would be required although the reported figures would be identical.

Initial Value Method

Because it employs a cash basis for income recognition, the initial value method ignores two accrual-based adjustments. First, the parent recognizes dividend income rather than an equity income accrual. Thus, the parent does not accrue the percentage of the subsidiary's income earned in past years in excess of dividends (the increase in subsidiary retained earnings). Second, the parent does not record amortization expense under the initial value method and therefore must include it in the consolidation process if proper totals are to be achieved. Because neither of these figures is recognized in applying the initial value method, an Entry *C is added to the worksheet to convert the previously recorded balances to the equity method. The parent's beginning Retained Earnings is affected by this adjustment as well as the Investment in Subsidiary account. The exact amount is computed as follows.

*Conversion to Equity Method from Initial Value Method (Entry *C)*

Combine:

1. The increase (since acquisition) in the subsidiary's retained earnings during past years (income less dividends) times the parent's ownership percentage, and
2. The parent's percentage of total amortization expense for these same past years.

The parent's use of the initial value method requires an additional procedural change. Under this method, the parent recognizes income from its subsidiary only when it receives a dividend. Entry (**I**) removes both intra-entity dividend income and subsidiary dividends paid to the parent. Thus, when the initial value method is used, Entry **D** is unnecessary.

Partial Equity Method

Again, an Entry *C is needed to convert the parent's retained earnings as of January 1 to the equity method. In this case, however, only the amortization expense for the prior years must be included. Under the partial equity method, the income accrual is appropriately recognized each period by the parent company so that no further adjustment is necessary.

REVENUE AND EXPENSE REPORTING FOR MIDYEAR ACQUISITIONS

LO8

Understand the impact on consolidated financial statements of a midyear acquisition.

In virtually all of our previous examples, the parent gains control of the subsidiary on the first day of the fiscal year. How is the consolidation process affected if an acquisition occurs on a midyear (any other than the first day of the fiscal year) date?

When a company gains control at a midyear date, a few obvious changes are needed. The new parent must compute the subsidiary's book value as of that date to determine excess total fair value over book value allocations (e.g., intangibles). Excess amortization expenses as well as any equity accrual and dividend collections are recognized for a period of less than a year. Finally, because only income earned by the subsidiary after the acquisition date accrues to the new owners, it is appropriate to include only postacquisition revenues and expenses in consolidated totals.

Consolidating Postacquisition Subsidiary Revenue and Expenses

Following a midyear acquisition, a parent company excludes current year subsidiary revenue and expense amounts that have accrued prior to the acquisition date from its consolidated totals. For example, when Comcast acquired AT&T Broadband, its December 31 year-end income statement included AT&T Broadband revenues and expenses only subsequent to the acquisition date. Comcast reported $8.1 billion in revenues that year. However, in a pro forma schedule, Comcast noted that had it included AT&T Broadband's revenues from January 1, total revenue for the year would have been $16.8 billion. However, because the $8.7 billion additional revenue ($16.8 billion − $8.1 billion) was not earned by Comcast owners, Comcast excluded this preacquisition revenue from its consolidated total.

To further illustrate the complexities of accounting for a midyear acquisition, assume that Tyler Company acquires 90 percent of Steven Company on July 1, 2011, for $900,000 and prepares the following fair-value allocation schedule:

Steven Company fair value, 7/1/11		$1,000,000
Steven Company book value 7/1/11		
Common stock	$600,000	
Retained earnings, 7/1/11	200,000	800,000
Excess fair value over book value		$ 200,000
Adjust trademark to fair value (4-year life) . . .		200,000
Goodwill		–0–

The affiliates report the following 2011 income statement amounts from their own separate operations:

	Tyler	**Steven**
Revenues	$450,000	$300,000
Expenses	325,000	150,000
Dividends (paid quarterly)	100,000	20,000

Assuming that all revenues and expenses occurred evenly throughout the year, the December 31, 2011, consolidated income statement appears as follows:

TYLER COMPANY	
Consolidated Income Statement	
For the Year Ended December 31, 2011	
Revenues	$600,000
Expenses	425,000
Consolidated net income	$175,000
To noncontrolling interest	5,000
To controlling interest	$170,000

The consolidated income components are computed below:

- *Revenues* = $600,000. Combined balances of $750,000 less $150,000 (½ of Steven's revenues).
- *Expenses* = $425,000. Combined balances of $475,000 less $75,000 (½ of Steven's expenses) plus $25,000 excess amortization ($200,000 ÷ 4 years × ½ year).
- *Noncontrolling interest in Steven's income* = $5,000. 10% × ($150,000 Steven's income − $50,000 excess amortization) × ½ year.

In this example, preacquisition subsidiary revenue and expense accounts are eliminated from the consolidated totals. Note also that by excluding 100 percent of the preacquisition income accounts from consolidation, the noncontrolling interest is viewed as coming into being as of the parent's acquisition date.[5]

A midyear acquisition requires additional adjustments when preparing consolidating worksheets. The balances the subsidiary submits for consolidation typically include results for its entire fiscal period. Thus, in the December 31 financial statements, the book value of the firm acquired on a midyear date is reflected by a January 1 retained earnings balance plus revenues, expenses, and dividends paid from the beginning of the year to the acquisition date.

---

[5] Current practice provides comparability across fiscal years through pro forma disclosures of various categories of revenue and expense as if the combination had occurred at the beginning of the reporting period. With the advent of modern information systems, separate cutoffs for revenues and expenses are readily available.

To effectively eliminate subsidiary book value as of the acquisition date, Consolidation Entry **S** includes these items in addition to the other usual elements of book value (i.e., stock accounts). To illustrate, assuming that both affiliates submit fiscal year financial statements for consolidation, Tyler would make the following 2011 consolidation worksheet entry:

Consolidation Worksheet Entry S

Common stock—Steven	600,000	
Retained earnings—Steven (1/1/11)*	135,000	
Revenues	150,000	
Dividends paid—Steven		10,000
Expenses		75,000
Noncontrolling interest (7/1/11)		80,000
Investment in Steven		720,000

* July 1 balance of $200,000 less income from first six months of $75,000 (1/2 of $150,000 annual Steven income) plus $10,000 dividends paid.

Through Entry **S,** preacquisition subsidiary revenues, expenses, and dividends are effectively

- Included as part of the subsidiary book value elimination in the year of acquisition.
- Included as components of the beginning value of the noncontrolling interest.
- Excluded from the consolidated income statement and statement of retained earnings.

Acquisition Following an Equity Method Investment

In many cases, a parent company owns a noncontrolling equity interest in a firm prior to obtaining control. In such cases, as the preceding example demonstrates, the parent consolidates the postacquisition revenues and expenses of its new subsidiary. Because the parent owned an equity investment in the subsidiary prior to the control date, however, the parent reports on its income statement the "equity in earnings of the investee" that accrued up to the date control was obtained. In this case, in the year of acquisition, the consolidated income statement reports both combined revenues and expenses (postacquisition) of the subsidiary and equity method income (preacquisition).

In subsequent years, the need to separate pre- and postacquisition amounts is limited to ensuring that excess amortizations correctly reflect the midyear acquisition date. Finally, if the parent employs the initial value method of accounting for the investment in subsidiary on its books, the conversion to the equity method must also reflect only postacquisition amounts.

STEP ACQUISITIONS

LO9

Understand the impact on consolidated financial statements when a step acquisition has taken place.

In recent financial statements, Ticketmaster Entertainment Corporation reported an increase to its previous percentage ownership of Front Line Co., noting

> Ticketmaster Entertainment's investment in Front Line was consolidated beginning on October 29, 2008, when the Company increased its ownership interest from 39.4 percent to 82.3 percent . . . Prior to October 29, 2008, the investment in Front Line was accounted for using the equity method of accounting.

In all previous consolidation illustrations, control over a subsidiary was assumed to have been achieved through a single transaction. Obviously, Ticketmaster's takeover of Front Line shows that a combination also can be the result of a series of stock purchases. These step acquisitions further complicate the consolidation process. The financial information of the separate companies must still be brought together, but varying amounts of consideration have been transferred to former owners at several different dates. How do the initial acquisitions affect this process?

One area where the acquisition method provides a distinct departure from past reporting practices for business combinations is when control is achieved in a series of equity acquisitions, as opposed to a single transaction. Such acquisitions are frequently referred to as *step acquisitions* or *control achieved in stages.*

Past practice under the *purchase method* emphasized cost accumulation and allocation at each date that a parent acquired a block of subsidiary shares. The purchase method treated each acquisition of a firm's shares as a separate measurement event for reporting each acquisition's percentage of subsidiary assets and liabilities in consolidated financial statements. Thus, when a parent obtained control through, for example, three separate purchases of subsidiary shares, the resulting consolidated balance sheet might combine three different valuations for individual subsidiary assets acquired and/or liabilities assumed. Moreover, if a noncontrolling interest remained, a portion of each subsidiary asset and liability would remain at its original book value, further compromising the relevance and representational faithfulness of the consolidated financial statements.

Control Achieved in Steps—Acquisition Method

Attempting to increase both the relevance and representational faithfulness of consolidated reports, the FASB requires the acquisition method when a parent achieves control over another firm in stages. At the date control is first obtained, the acquisition method measures the acquired firm at fair value, including the noncontrolling interest. The acquisition of a controlling interest is considered an important economic, and therefore measurement, event. Consequently, the parent utilizes a single uniform valuation basis for all subsidiary assets acquired and liabilities assumed—fair value at the date control is obtained.

If the parent previously held a noncontrolling interest in the acquired firm, the parent remeasures that interest to fair value and recognizes a gain or loss. If after obtaining control, the parent increases its ownership interest in the subsidiary, no further remeasurement takes place. The parent simply accounts for the additional subsidiary shares acquired as an equity transaction—consistent with any transactions with other owners, as opposed to outsiders. Below we present first an example of consolidated reporting when the parent obtains a controlling interest in a series of steps. Then, we present an example of a parent's post-control acquisition of its subsidiary's shares.

Example: Step Acquisition Resulting in Control—Acquisition Method

To illustrate, assume that Arch Company obtains control of Zion Company through two cash acquisitions. The details of each acquisition are provided in Exhibit 4.9. Assuming that Arch has gained the ability to significantly influence Zion's decision-making process, the first investment, for external reporting purposes, is accounted for by means of the equity method as discussed in Chapter 1. Thus, Arch must determine any allocations and amortization associated with its purchase price (see Exhibit 4.10). A customer base with a 22-year life represented the initial excess payment.

Application of the equity method requires the accrual of investee income by the parent while any dividends received are recorded as a decrease in the Investment account. Arch must also reduce both the income and asset balances in recognition of the annual $2,000 amortization

EXHIBIT 4.9
Consolidation Information for a Step Acquisition

ARCH COMPANY'S ACQUISITIONS OF ZION COMPANY SHARES				
	Consideration Transferred	Percentage Acquired	Zion Company (100%)	
			Book Value	Fair Value
January 1, 2011	$164,000	30%	$400,000	$546,667
January 1, 2013	350,000	50	500,000	700,000
Zion Company's Income and Dividends for 2011–2013				
			Income	Dividends
	2011		$ 60,000	$20,000
	2012		80,000	20,000
	2013		100,000	20,000

EXHIBIT 4.10
**Allocation of First
Noncontrolling
Acquisition**

ARCH COMPANY AND ZION COMPANY	
Fair Value Allocation and Amortization	
January 1, 2011	
Fair value of consideration transferred	$ 164,000
Book value equivalent of Arch's ownership ($400,000 × 30%)	(120,000)
Customer base	$ 44,000
Assumed life	22 years
Annual amortization expense	$ 2,000

indicated in Exhibit 4.10. Following the information provided in Exhibits 4.9 and 4.10, over the next two years, Arch Company's Investment in Zion account grows to $190,000:

Price paid for 30% investment in Zion—1/1/11	$164,000
Accrual of 2011 equity income ($60,000 × 30 percent)	18,000
Dividends received 2011 ($20,000 × 30%)	(6,000)
Amortization	(2,000)
Accrual of 2012 equity income ($80,000 × 30 percent)	24,000
Dividends received 2012 ($20,000 × 30%)	(6,000)
Amortization	(2,000)
Investment in Zion—1/1/13	$190,000

On January 1, 2013, Arch's ownership is increased to 80 percent by the purchase of another 50 percent of Zion Company's outstanding common stock for $350,000. Although the equity method can still be utilized for internal reporting, this second acquisition necessitates the preparation of consolidated financial statements beginning in 2013. Arch now controls Zion; the two companies are viewed as a single economic entity for external reporting purposes.

Once Arch gains control over Zion on January 1, 2013, the acquisition method focuses exclusively on control-date fair values and considers any previous amounts recorded by the acquirer as irrelevant for future valuations. Thus, in a step acquisition all previous values for the investment, prior to the date control is obtained, are remeasured to fair value on the date control is obtained.

We add the assumption that the $350,000 consideration transferred by Arch in its second acquisition of Zion represents the best available evidence for measuring the fair value of Zion Company at January 1, 2013. Therefore, an estimated fair value of $700,000 ($350,000 ÷ 50%) is assigned to Zion Company as of January 1, 2013, and provides the valuation basis for the assets acquired, the liabilities assumed, and the 20 percent noncontrolling interest. Exhibit 4.11 shows Arch's allocation of Zion's $700,000 acquisition-date fair value.

Note that the acquisition method views a multiple-step acquisition as essentially the same as a single-step acquisition. In the Arch Company and Zion Company example, once control is evident, the only relevant values in consolidating the accounts of Zion are fair values at

EXHIBIT 4.11
**Allocation of Acquisition-
Date Fair Value**

ARCH COMPANY AND ZION COMPANY	
Fair Value Allocation and Amortization	
January 1, 2013	
Zion Company fair value	$ 700,000
Zion Company book value	(500,000)
Customer base	$ 200,000
Assumed life	20 years
Annual amortization expense	$ 10,000

January 1, 2013. A new basis of accountability arises for Zion Company on that single date because obtaining control of another firm is considered a significant remeasurement event. Previously owned noncontrolling blocks of stock are consequently revalued to fair value on the date control is obtained.

In revaluing a previous stock ownership in the acquired firm, the acquirer recognizes any resulting gain or loss in income. Therefore, on January 1, 2013, Arch increases the Investment in Zion account to $210,000 (30% × $700,000 fair value) and records the revaluation gain as follows:

Investment in Zion	20,000	
Gain on revaluation of Zion		20,000

Fair value of Arch's 30% investment in Zion at 1/1/13 (30% × $700,000)	$210,000
Book value of Arch's 30% investment in Zion at 1/1/13	190,000
Gain on revaluation of Zion to fair value	$ 20,000

Worksheet Consolidation for a Step Acquisition (Acquisition Method)

To continue the example, the amount in Arch Company's 80 percent Investment in Zion account is updated for 2013:

Investment in Zion (after revaluation on 1/1/13)	$210,000
January 1, 2013—Second acquisition price paid	350,000
Equity income accrual—2013 (80% × $100,000)	80,000
Amortization of customer base (80% × $10,000)	(8,000)
Dividends received—2013 (80% × $20,000)	(16,000)
Investment in Zion—12/31/13	$616,000

The worksheet for consolidating Arch Company and Zion Company is shown in Exhibit 4.12. Observe that

- The consolidation worksheet entries are essentially the same as if Arch had acquired its entire 80 percent ownership on January 1, 2013.
- The noncontrolling interest is allocated 20 percent of the excess fair-value allocation from the customer base.
- The noncontrolling interest is allocated 20 percent of Zion's 2013 income less its share of the excess amortization attributable to the customer base.
- The gain on revaluation of Arch's initial investment in Zion is recognized as income of the current period.

Example: Step Acquisition Resulting After Control Is Obtained

The previous example demonstrates a step acquisition with control achieved with the most recent purchase. Post-control acquisitions by a parent of a subsidiary's stock, however, often continue as well. Recall that the acquisition method measures an acquired firm at its fair value on the date control is obtained. A parent's subsequent subsidiary stock acquisitions do not affect these initially recognized fair values. Once the valuation basis for the acquired firm has been established, as long as control is maintained, this valuation basis remains the same. Any further purchases (or sales) of the subsidiary's stock are treated as equity transactions.

To illustrate a post-control step acquisition, assume that on January 1, 2011, Amanda Co. obtains 70 percent of Zoe, Inc., for $350,000 cash. We also assume that the $350,000

EXHIBIT 4.12   Step Acquisition Illustrated—Acquisition Method

ARCH COMPANY AND ZION COMPANY
Consolidation: Acquisition Method
Investment: Equity Method

Consolidated Worksheet
For Year Ending December 31, 2013

Accounts	Arch Company	Zion Company	Consolidation Entries Debit	Consolidation Entries Credit	Noncontrolling Interest	Consolidated Totals
Income Statement						
Revenues	(600,000)	(260,000)				(860,000)
Expenses	425,000	160,000	(E) 10,000			595,000
Equity in subsidiary earnings	(72,000)	–0–	(I) 72,000			–0–
Gain on revaluation of Zion	(20,000)					(20,000)
Separate company net income	(267,000)	(100,000)				
Consolidated net income						(285,000)
Noncontrolling interest in Zion Company's income					(18,000)	18,000
Controlling interest in consolidated net income						(267,000)
Statement of Retained Earnings						
Retained earnings, 1/1						
Arch Company	(758,000)					(758,000)
Zion Company		(230,000)	(S) 230,000			
Net income (above)	(267,000)	(100,000)				(267,000)
Dividends paid	125,000	20,000		(D) 16,000	4,000	125,000
Retained earnings, 12/31	(900,000)	(310,000)				(900,000)
Balance Sheet						
Current assets	509,000	280,000				789,000
Land	205,000	90,000				295,000
Buildings (net)	646,000	310,000				956,000
Investment in Zion Company	616,000	–0–	(D) 16,000	(A) 160,000		–0–
				(S) 400,000		
				(I) 72,000		
Customer base	–0–	–0–	(A) 200,000	(E) 10,000		190,000
Total assets	1,976,000	680,000				2,230,000
Liabilities	(461,000)	(100,000)				(561,000)
Noncontrolling interest in Zion Company, 1/1	–0–	–0–		(S) 100,000		
				(A) 40,000	(140,000)	
Noncontrolling interest in Zion Company, 12/31	–0–	–0–			154,000	(154,000)
Common stock	(355,000)	(200,000)	(S) 200,000			(355,000)
Additional paid-in capital	(260,000)	(70,000)	(S) 70,000			(260,000)
Retained earnings, 12/31 (above)	(900,000)	(310,000)				(900,000)
Total liabilities and equities	(1,976,000)	(680,000)	798,000	798,000		(2,230,000)

Consolidation entries:
(S)   Elimination of subsidiary's stockholders' equity along with recognition of 1/1 noncontrolling interest.
(A)   Allocation of subsidiary total fair value in excess of book value, unamortized balances as of 1/1.
(I)   Elimination of intra-entity income (equity accrual less amortization expenses).
(D)   Elimination of intra-entity dividend payments.
(E)   Recognition of amortization expenses on fair-value allocations.

consideration paid by Amanda also represents the best available evidence for measuring the fair value of the noncontrolling interest in Zoe Company. Therefore, Zoe Company's total fair value is assessed at $500,000 ($350,000 ÷ 70%). Because Zoe's net assets' book values equal their collective fair values of $400,000, Amanda recognizes goodwill of $100,000. Then, on January 1, 2012, when Zoe's book value has increased to $420,000, Amanda buys another 20 percent of Zoe for $95,000, bringing its total ownership to 90 percent. Under the acquisition method, the valuation basis for Zoe's net assets was established on January 1, 2011, the date Amanda obtained control. Subsequent transactions in the subsidiary's stock (purchases or sales) are now viewed as transactions in the combined entity's own stock. Therefore, when Amanda acquires Zoe's shares post-control, it recognizes the difference between the fair value of the consideration transferred and the underlying subsidiary valuation as an adjustment to Additional Paid-In Capital.

The difference between the $95,000 price and the underlying consolidated subsidiary value is computed as follows:

1/1/12 price paid for 20 percent interest		$ 95,000
Noncontrolling interest (NCI) acquired:		
Book value (20% of $420,000)	$84,000	
Goodwill (20% of $100,000)	20,000	
Noncontrolling interest book value (20%) 1/1/12		104,000
Additional paid-in capital from 20 percent NCI acquisition . .		$ 9,000

Amanda then prepares the following journal entry to record the acquisition of the 20 percent noncontrolling interest:

Investment in Zoe	104,000	
Cash		95,000
Additional paid-in capital		9,000

By purchasing 20 percent of Zoe for $95,000, the consolidated entity's owners have acquired a portion of their own firm at a price $9,000 less than consolidated book value. From a worksheet perspective, the $104,000 increase in the investment account simply replaces the 20 percent allocation to the noncontrolling interest. Importantly, the $95,000 exchanged for the 20 percent interest in Zoe's net assets does not affect consolidated asset valuation. The basis for the reported values in the consolidated financial statements was established on the date control was obtained.

LO10

Record the sale of a subsidiary (or a portion of its shares).

Parent Company Sales of Subsidiary Stock—Acquisition Method

Frequently, a parent company will sell a portion or all of the shares it owns of a subsidiary. For example, Meade, Inc., a consumer products company, reported the sale of one of its business units in its financial statements:

> In January 2009 we sold our Meade Europe subsidiary for gross proceeds of $12.4 million . . . Meade Europe qualified as a "Discontinued Operation" and is presented in that manner in our consolidated financial statements.

Once a parent gains control over a subsidiary, the combined firm becomes the basic accounting and reporting entity. Consistent with this view, transactions in the stock of the subsidiary, as long as the parent maintains control, are considered to be transactions in the equity of the consolidated entity.

To account for sales of subsidiary shares by a parent, the acquisition method maintains its valuation basis of acquisition-date fair value adjusted for subsequent changes in the subsidiary's net assets. The accounting effect of the sale of subsidiary shares depends on whether the parent continues to maintain control after the sale. If the parent maintains control, it recognizes no gains or losses when it sells a portion of its stock in the subsidiary. If the sale of the parent's ownership interest results in the loss of control of a subsidiary, it recognizes any resulting gain or loss in consolidated net income.

Sale of Subsidiary Shares with Control Maintained

To illustrate, assume Adams Company owns 100 percent of Smith Company's 25,000 voting shares and appropriately carries the investment on its books at January 1, 2011, at $750,000 using the equity method. Assuming Adams sells 5,000 shares to outside interests for $165,000 on January 1, 2011, the transaction is recorded as follows:

Cash	165,000	
Investment in Smith		150,000
Additional paid-in capital from noncontrolling interest transaction		15,000
To record sale of 5,000 Smith shares to noncontrolling interest with excess of sale proceeds over carrying value attributed to additional paid-in capital.		

The $15,000 "gain" on sale of the subsidiary shares is not recognized in income, but is reported as an increase in owner's equity. This equity treatment for the "gain" is consistent with the economic unit notion that as long as control is maintained, payments received from owners of the firm are considered contributions of capital. The ownership group of the consolidated entity specifically includes the noncontrolling interest. Therefore, the above treatment of sales to an ownership group is consistent with accounting for other stock transactions with owners.

Sale of Subsidiary Shares with Control Lost

The loss of control of a subsidiary is a remeasurement event that can result in gain or loss recognition. The gain or loss is computed as the difference between the sale proceeds and the carrying amount of the shares sold. Using the Adams and Smith example above, assume now that instead of selling 5,000 shares, Adams sells 20,000 of its shares in Smith to outside interests on January 1, 2011, and keeps the remaining 5,000 shares. Assuming sale proceeds of $675,000, we record the transaction as follows:

Cash	675,000	
Investment in Smith		600,000
Gain on sale of Smith investment		75,000
To record sale of 20,000 Smith shares, resulting in the loss of control over Smith Company.		

If the former parent retains any of its former subsidiary's shares, the retained investment should be remeasured to fair value on the date control is lost. Any resulting gain or loss from this remeasurement should be recognized in the parent's net income.

In our Adams and Smith example, Adams still retains 5,000 shares of Smith Company (25,000 original investment less 20,000 shares sold). Assuming further that the $675,000 sale price for the 20,000 shares sold represents a reasonable value for the remaining shares of $33.75, Adams's shares now have a fair value of $168,750 ($33.75 × 5,000 shares). Adams would thus record the revaluation of its retained 5,000 shares of Smith as follows:

Investment in Smith	18,750	
Gain on revaluation of retained Smith shares to fair value		18,750
To record the revaluation of Smith shares to a $33.75 per share fair value from their previous equity method January 1, 2011, carrying amount of $30.00 per share.		

The above revaluation of retained shares reflects the view that the loss of control of a subsidiary is a significant economic event that changes the fundamental relationship between the former parent and subsidiary. Also, the fair value of the retained investment provides the users of the parent's financial statements with more relevant information about the investment.

Cost-Flow Assumptions

If it sells less than an entire investment, the parent must select an appropriate cost-flow assumption when it has made more than one purchase. In the sale of securities, the use of specific identification based on serial numbers is acceptable, although averaging or FIFO assumptions often are applied. Use of the averaging method is especially appealing because all shares are truly identical, creating little justification for identifying different cost figures with individual shares.

Accounting for Shares That Remain

If Adams sells only a portion of the investment, it also must determine the proper method of accounting for the shares that remain. Three possible scenarios can be envisioned:

1. Adams could have so drastically reduced its interest that the parent no longer controls the subsidiary or even has the ability to significantly influence its decision making. For example, assume that Adams's ownership drops from 80 to 5 percent. In the current period prior to the sale, the 80 percent investment is reported by means of the equity method with the market-value method used for the 5 percent that remains thereafter. Consolidated financial statements are no longer applicable.

2. Adams could still apply significant influence over Smith's operations although it no longer maintains control. A drop in the level of ownership from 80 to 30 percent normally meets this condition. In this case, the parent utilizes the equity method for the entire year. Application is based on 80 percent until the time of sale and then on 30 percent for the remainder of the year. Again, consolidated statements cease to be appropriate because control has been lost.

3. The decrease in ownership could be relatively small so that the parent continues to maintain control over the subsidiary even after the sale. Adams's reduction of its ownership in Smith from 80 to 60 percent is an example of this situation. After the disposal, consolidated financial statements are still required, but the process is based on the *end-of-year ownership percentage.* Because only the retained shares (60 percent in this case) are consolidated, the parent must separately recognize any current year income accruing to it from its terminated interest. Thus, Adams shows earnings on this portion of the investment (a 20 percent interest in Smith for the time during the year that it is held) in the consolidated income statement as a single-line item computed by means of the equity method.

COMPARISONS WITH INTERNATIONAL ACCOUNTING STANDARDS

As observed in previous chapters of this text, the accounting and reporting for business combinations between U.S. and international standards has largely converged with FASB ASC Topic 805 and *IFRS 3R,* each of which carries the title *Business Combinations* and ASC topic 810, Consolidation. Each set of standards requires the acquisition method and embrace a fair-value model for the assets acquired and liabilities assumed in a business combination. Both sets of standards treat exchanges between the parent and the noncontrolling interest as equity transactions, unless control is lost. However, as seen below, the accounting for the noncontrolling interest can diverge across the two reporting regimes.

- *U.S. GAAP.* In reporting the noncontrolling interest in consolidated financial statements, U.S. GAAP requires a fair value measurement attribute, consistent with the overall valuation principles for business combinations. Thus, acquisition-date fair value provides a basis for reporting the noncontrolling interest, which is adjusted for its share of subsidiary income and dividends subsequent to acquisition.

- *IFRS.* In contrast, *IFRS 3R* allows an option for reporting the noncontrolling interest for each business combination. Under IFRS, the noncontrolling interest may be measured either at its acquisition-date fair value, which can include goodwill, or at a proportionate share of the acquiree's identifiable net asset fair value, which excludes goodwill. The IFRS proportionate-share option effectively assumes that any goodwill created through the business combination applies solely to the controlling interest.

THE LEGACY PURCHASE METHOD—CONSOLIDATED FINANCIAL REPORTING WITH A NONCONTROLLING INTEREST

LO11

Understand the principles of the legacy purchase method in accounting for a noncontrolling interest.

The current FASB ASC topics on Business Combinations (805) and Consolidation (810) represent a distinct departure from past consolidated reporting for subsidiary assets, liabilities, income, and noncontrolling interests. The acquisition method, which focuses on acquisition-date fair values, replaces the previous purchase method and its emphasis on cost accumulation and allocation. However, the acquisition method is applied prospectively, leaving intact long-lasting financial statement effects from past applications of the purchase method for business combinations occurring prior to January 1, 2009.

Under the purchase method, the parent recognized the fair values of acquired subsidiary assets and liabilities, but only to the extent of its percentage ownership interest. In the presence of a noncontrolling interest, subsidiary assets and liabilities were measured partially at fair value and partially at the subsidiary's carryover (book) value. This dual valuation for subsidiary assets and liabilities was viewed as being consistent with the cost principle. Because only the parent's percentage was purchased in the combination, only that percentage was adjusted to fair value. Therefore, the valuation principle for the noncontrolling interest under the purchase method was simply its share of the subsidiary's book value.

To illustrate the accounting for a business combination using the purchase method, assume that Ramsey Company purchased 80 percent of the outstanding shares of Santana Company for $1,435,000 cash on January 1, 2008. Exhibit 4.13 shows Santana's acquisition date balance sheet and Ramsey's cost allocation using the purchase method. Note that the parent allocates only its cost to the subsidiary's assets based on their fair values. Because the parent purchased only 80 percent of the subsidiary's shares, only 80 percent of the subsidiary's net assets are valued at the parent's cost. The 20 percent held by the noncontrolling interest is not part of the exchange transaction, and therefore no new basis of accountability arises. Thus, 20 percent of the net assets remains at the subsidiary's former book value (carryover basis), and 80 percent of the net assets is valued at cost to the parent.

EXHIBIT 4.13
Subsidiary Accounts and Cost Allocation–Date of 80 Percent Acquisition by Parent

SANTANA COMPANY
Account Balances for Consolidation—Purchase Method
January 1, 2008

	Book Value	Fair Value	Difference	80% Write-Up in Consolidation
Current assets	$ 239,000	$ 239,000	$ –0–	$ –0–
Land	575,000	610,000	35,000	28,000
Equipment (7-year life) . . .	1,886,000	1,956,000	70,000	56,000
Patent (8-year life)	–0–	20,000	20,000	16,000
Liabilities	(1,050,000)	(1,050,000)	–0–	–0–
Net assets	$ 1,650,000	$1,775,000	$125,000	$100,000
Common Stock	(900,000)			
Retained Earnings	(750,000)			

Allocation of Ramsey's Cost—Purchase Method

Purchase price for 80% of Santana Company		$1,435,000
Book value acquired (80% × $1,650,000)		1,320,000
Excess of parent's cost over 80% of subsidiary book value . . .		115,000
to land (80% × $35,000)	$28,000	
to equipment (80% × 70,000)	56,000	
to patent (80% × 20,000)	16,000	100,000
to goodwill		$ 15,000

For example, Santana's land account will appear on Ramsey's acquisition-date consolidated balance sheet at $603,000. This amount can be computed in either of two mathematically equivalent ways as follows:

Fair value × parent's ownership percentage = $610,000 × 80% = ... $488,000
+ Book value × noncontrolling interest percentage = $575,000 × 20% = ...   115,000
Consolidated value for subsidiary land $603,000

Book value of subsidiary land $575,000
+ (Fair value − book value) × parent's ownership percentage = $35,000 × 80% = . .   28,000
Consolidated value for subsidiary land $603,000

The subsidiary's book value is consolidated in total whereas any cost in excess of book value is assumed to be a parent company expenditure appropriately allocated based on fair values. By comparison, the acquisition method recognizes 100 percent of the fair values of the subsidiary's assets and liabilities regardless of the controlling interest's ownership percentage. Thus the acquisition method would show a full $610,000 fair value for the land.

To complete the illustration of the purchase method, assume that Ramsey and Santana submit December 31, 2011, financial statements as shown in the first two columns of Exhibit 4.14. Ramsey then prepares the following worksheet entries.

Consolidation Entry S

Common Stock (Santana)	900,000	
Retained Earnings, 1/1/11 (Santana)	800,000	
Investment in Santana Company (80%)		1,360,000
Noncontrolling Interest in Santana Company, 1/1/11 (20%)		340,000

To eliminate beginning stockholders' equity accounts of subsidiary along with book value portion of investment (equal to 80 percent ownership). Noncontrolling interest of 20 percent is also recognized.

Consolidation Entry A

Land	28,000	
Equipment	32,000	
Patent	10,000	
Goodwill	15,000	
Investment in Santana Company		85,000

To allocate the excess of Ramsey's cost over Santana's book value based on fair values net of 3 years amortization. Note that under the purchase method none of this excess allocation is attributed to the noncontrolling interest.

Consolidation Entry I

Subsidiary income	158,000	
Investment in Santana Company		158,000

To eliminate current year equity income recorded by Ramsey in connection with its ownership of Santana. The subsidiary's revenue and expense accounts are left intact and included in consolidated figures.

EXHIBIT 4.14   **Consolidated Worksheet with a Noncontrolling Interest—Legacy Purchase Method**

RAMSEY AND SUBSIDIARY SANTANA COMPANY
Consolidated Worksheet—Purchase Method
December 31, 2011

	Ramsey	Santana	Adjustments & Eliminations		Noncontrolling Interest	Consolidated
Revenues	(2,525,000)	(1,000,000)				(3,525,000)
Operating expenses	2,183,000	790,000	(E) 10,000			2,983,000
Subsidiary income	(158,000)	–0–	(I) 158,000		(42,000)	42,000
Net income	(500,000)	(210,000)				(500,000)
Retained earnings 1/1	(2,000,000)	(800,000)	(S) 800,000			(2,000,000)
Net income	(500,000)	(210,000)				(500,000)
Dividends declared	200,000	25,000		(D) 20,000	5,000	200,000
Retained earnings 12/31	(2,300,000)	(985,000)				(2,300,000)
Current assets	967,000	827,000				1,794,000
Investment in Santana	1,583,000		(D) 20,000	(S) 1,360,000		–0–
(equity method)				(A) 85,000		
				(I) 158,000		
Land	1,500,000	575,000	(A) 28,000			2,103,000
Buildings and equipment	3,090,000	1,726,000	(A) 32,000	(E) 8,000		4,840,000
Patent	–0–	–0–	(A) 10,000	(E) 2,000		8,000
Goodwill	200,000	–0–	(A) 15,000			215,000
Total assets	7,340,000	3,128,000				8,960,000
Liabilities	(1,890,000)	(1,243,000)				(3,133,000)
Common stock–Ramsey	(3,150,000)					(3,150,000)
Common stock–Santana		(900,000)	(S) 900,000			
Noncontrolling interest 1/1				(S) 340,000	(340,000)	
Noncontrolling interest 12/31					377,000	(377,000)
Retained earnings 12/31	(2,300,000)	(985,000)				(2,300,000)
Total liabilities and stockholders' equity	(7,340,000)	(3,128,000)	1,973,000	1,973,000		(8,960,000)

Consolidation entries:
(S) Elimination of subsidiary's stockholders' equity along with recognition of 1/1 noncontrolling interest.
(A) Allocation of excess cost over book value, unamortized balances as of 1/1.
(I) Elimination of intra-entity income (equity accrual less amortization expenses).
(D) Elimination of intra-entity dividend payments.
(E) Recognition of amortization expenses on excess cost allocations.

Consolidation Entry D

Investment in Santana Company	20,000	
Dividends declared		20,000

This worksheet entry offsets the $20,000 current year intra-entity dividend paid by Santana to Ramsey.

Consolidation Entry E

Operating expenses	10,000	
Equipment		8,000
Patent		2,000

To recognize excess cost amortization expenses for the current year based on Ramsey's percentage ownership of Santana's acquisition-date fair values.

The noncontrolling interest in Santana balance totals $377,000 at the end of the year. This valuation represents 20 percent of the subsidiary's year-end book value (common stock plus ending retained earnings) or 20% × ($900,000 + $985,000). This $377,000 total can also be seen on the worksheet with supporting details as follows:

Noncontrolling interest at 1/1/11 (20% of $1,700,000 beginning book value—common stock plus 1/1/11 retained earnings)	$340,000
Noncontrolling interest in subsidiary's income (20% × $210,000 subsidiary income)	42,000
Dividends paid to noncontrolling interest (20% of $25,000 total) . . .	(5,000)
Noncontrolling interest at 12/31/11	$377,000

Note that the noncontrolling interest's share of subsidiary income does not take into account any of the excess cost amortizations. This treatment is consistent with the noncontrolling interest valuation at subsidiary book value.

Criticisms of the Purchase Method in the Presence of a Noncontrolling Interest

Several criticisms were leveled at past practice for consolidated financial reporting in the presence of a noncontrolling interest. These include:

- Dual valuation of subsidiary balance sheet accounts.
- The "mezzanine" categorization of the noncontrolling interest in consolidated balance sheets.
- The valuation basis for the noncontrolling interest.
- Accounting for the parent's transactions in the ownership shares of its subsidiary.

We briefly discuss each of these criticisms below.

As shown in the Ramsey and Santana example above, the purchase method employed a mixed-attribute model to consolidate subsidiary assets whenever a noncontrolling interest was present. By recognizing the fair value of subsidiary assets only to the extent of the parent's ownership percentage, these assets were consolidated in part at fair value, and in part at the subsidiary's book value. Many considered this dual valuation in the presence of a noncontrolling interest as hindering the relevance of the resulting consolidated balances. Moreover, because book values tended to understate asset valuation, financial ratios such as return-on-assets were also overstated. The problem was compounded in step acquisitions when several purchase cost allocations were combined at various amounts through time.

Another criticism of past practice was the fact that most parent companies reported their noncontrolling interests between the liability and stockholder's equity sections in an area referred to as the "mezzanine." The 2005 FASB Exposure Draft, "Business Combinations and Consolidated Financial Statements, Including Accounting and Reporting of Noncontrolling Interests in Subsidiaries," argued for inclusion in equity (pages viii and ix):

> This proposed Statement would result in greater consistency with the Board's conceptual framework because it would require noncontrolling interests to be accounted for and reported as equity, separately from the parent shareholders' equity. In current practice, noncontrolling interests in the equity of subsidiaries are reported most commonly as "mezzanine" items between liabilities and equity in the consolidated financial statements of the parent, but also as liabilities or as equity. The display of noncontrolling interests as liabilities has no conceptual support because noncontrolling interests do not meet the definition of liabilities as defined in paragraph 35 of FASB Concepts Statement No. 6, Elements of Financial Statements. Not one of the entities involved—the parent, the subsidiary, or the consolidated entity—is obligated to transfer assets or provide services to the owners that hold equity interests in the subsidiary. Also, Concepts Statement 6 defines three elements of a statement of financial position: assets, liabilities, and equity (or net assets). The display of noncontrolling interests as mezzanine items would require that a new element—noncontrolling interests in consolidated subsidiaries—be created specifically for consolidated financial statements. The Board believes that no compelling reason exists to create such a new element. A view of consolidated financial statements as those of a single economic entity supports classification as equity because noncontrolling shareholders, partners, or other equity holders in subsidiaries are owners of a residual interest in a component of the consolidated entity.

Current GAAP requires that the noncontrolling interest be reported separately in the stockholders' equity section of the consolidated balance sheet.

Under the purchase method, the noncontrolling interest was valued at its percentage of the subsidiary's book value. To provide a consistent measurement attribute for the subsidiary, the acquisition method requires accounting for the noncontrolling interest at its acquisition-date fair value. Thus, the managers of the parent company are accountable for the entire fair values of their acquisitions.

Finally, past practice varied when the parent company sold or bought subsidiary shares while nonetheless maintaining control. In some cases, gains or losses were recognized on these transactions and in other cases they were treated as equity transactions. Current GAAP requires a consistent treatment for these economically similar events. Thus, all transactions by a parent in a subsidiary's ownership shares will be accounted for as equity transactions, as long as the parent maintains control.

Summary

1. A parent company need not acquire 100 percent of a subsidiary's stock to form a business combination. Only control over the decision-making process is necessary, a level that has historically been achieved by obtaining a majority of the voting shares. Ownership of any subsidiary stock that is retained by outside, unrelated parties is collectively referred to as a noncontrolling interest.

2. A consolidation takes on an added degree of complexity when a noncontrolling interest is present. The noncontrolling interest represents a group of subsidiary owners and their equity is recognized by the parent in its consolidated financial statements.

3. The valuation principle for the noncontrolling interest is acquisition-date fair value. The fair value of the noncontrolling interest is added to the consideration transferred by the parent to determine the acquisition-date fair value of the subsidiary. This fair value is then allocated to the subsidiary's assets acquired and liabilities assumed based on their individual fair values. At the acquisition date, each of the subsidiary's assets and liabilities is included in consolidation at its individual fair value regardless of the degree of parent ownership. Any remaining excess fair value beyond the total assigned to the net assets is recognized as goodwill.

4. Consolidated goodwill is allocated across the controlling and noncontrolling interests based on the excess of their respective acquisition-date fair values less their percentage share of the identifiable subsidiary net asset fair value. The goodwill allocation, therefore, does not necessarily correspond proportionately to the ownership interest of the parent and the noncontrolling interest.

5. This fair value is then adjusted through time for subsidiary income (less excess fair-value amortization) and subsidiary dividends.

6. Four noncontrolling interest figures appear in the annual consolidation process. First, a beginning-of-the-year balance is recognized on the worksheet (through Entry **S**) followed by the noncontrolling interest's share of the unamortized excess acquisition-date fair values of the subsidiary's assets and liabilities (including a separate amount for goodwill if appropriate). Next, the noncontrolling interest share of the subsidiary's income for the period (recorded by a columnar entry) is recognized. Subsidiary dividends paid to these unrelated owners are entered as a reduction of the noncontrolling interest. The final balance for the year is found as a summation of the Noncontrolling Interest column and is presented on the consolidated balance sheet, within the Stockholders' Equity section.

7. When a midyear business acquisition occurs, consolidated revenues and expenses should not include the subsidiary's current year preacquisition revenues and expenses. Only postacquisition subsidiary revenues and expenses are consolidated.

8. A parent can obtain control of a subsidiary by means of several separate purchases occurring over time, a process often referred to as a step acquisition. Once control is achieved, the acquisition method requires that the parent adjust to fair value all prior investments in the acquired firm and recognize any gain or loss. The fair values of these prior investments, along with the consideration transferred in the current investment that gave the parent control, and the noncontrolling interest fair value all comprise the total fair value of the acquired company.

9. When a parent sells some of its ownership shares of a subsidiary, it must establish an appropriate investment account balance to ensure an accurate accounting. If the equity method has not been used, the parent's investment balance is adjusted to recognize any income or amortization previously omitted. The resulting balance is then compared to the amount received for the stock to arrive at either an adjustment to additional paid-in capital (control maintained) or a gain or loss (control lost). Any shares still held will subsequently be reported through either consolidation, the equity method, or the fair-value method, depending on the influence retained by the parent.

Comprehensive Illustration

PROBLEM

(*Estimated Time: 60 to 75 Minutes*) On January 1, 2009, Father Company acquired an 80 percent interest in Sun Company for $425,000. The acquisition-date fair value of the 20 percent noncontrolling interest's ownership shares was $102,500. Also as of that date, Sun reported total stockholders' equity of $400,000: $100,000 in common stock and $300,000 in retained earnings. In setting the acquisition price, Father appraised four accounts at values different from the balances reported within Sun's financial records.

Buildings (8-year life)	Undervalued by $20,000
Land	Undervalued by $50,000
Equipment (5-year life)	Undervalued by $12,500
Royalty agreement (20-year life)	Not recorded, valued at $30,000

As of December 31, 2013, the trial balances of these two companies are as follows:

	Father Company	Sun Company
Debits		
Current assets	$ 605,000	$ 280,000
Investment in Sun Company	425,000	–0–
Land	200,000	300,000
Buildings (net)	640,000	290,000
Equipment (net)	380,000	160,000
Expenses	550,000	190,000
Dividends	90,000	20,000
Total debits	$2,890,000	$1,240,000
Credits		
Liabilities	$ 910,000	$ 300,000
Common stock	480,000	100,000
Retained earnings, 1/1/13	704,000	480,000
Revenues	780,000	360,000
Dividend income	16,000	–0–
Total credits	$2,890,000	$1,240,000

Included in these figures is a $20,000 debt that Sun owes to the parent company. No goodwill impairments have occurred since the Sun Company acquisition.

Required

a. Determine consolidated totals for Father Company and Sun Company for the year 2013.

b. Prepare worksheet entries to consolidate the trial balances of Father Company and Sun Company for the year 2013.

c. Assume instead that the acquisition-date fair value of the noncontrolling interest was $112,500. What balances in the December 31, 2013, consolidated statements would change?

SOLUTION

a. The consolidation of Father Company and Sun Company begins with the allocation of the subsidiary's acquisition-date fair value as shown in Exhibit 4.15. Because this consolidation is taking place after several years, the unamortized balances for the various allocations at the start of the current year also should be determined (see Exhibit 4.16).

Next, the parent's method of accounting for its subsidiary should be ascertained. The continuing presence of the original $425,000 acquisition price in the investment account indicates that Father is applying the initial value method. This same determination can be made from the Dividend Income account, which equals 80 percent of the subsidiary's dividends. Thus, Father's accounting records have ignored the increase in Sun's book value as well as the excess amortization expenses for the prior periods of ownership. These amounts have to be added to the parent's January 1, 2013, Retained Earnings account to arrive at a properly consolidated balance.

During the 2009–2012 period of ownership, Sun's Retained Earnings account increased by $180,000 ($480,000 − $300,000). Father's 80 percent interest necessitates an accrual of $144,000 ($180,000 × 80%) for these years. In addition, the acquisition-date fair value allocations require the

EXHIBIT 4.15
Excess Fair
Value Allocations

FATHER COMPANY AND SUN COMPANY
Acquisition-Date Fair-Value Allocation and Amortization
2009–2012

	Allocation	Estimated Life (years)	Annual Excess Amortization
Acquisition-date fair value	$527,500		
Sun book value (100%)	400,000		
Excess fair value	127,500		
Allocation to specific subsidiary accounts based on fair value:			
Buildings	$ 20,000	8	$ 2,500
Land	50,000		
Equipment	12,500	5	2,500
Royalty agreement	30,000	20	1,500
Goodwill	$ 15,000		
Annual excess amortization expenses			$ 6,500

Goodwill Allocation to the Controlling and Noncontrolling Interests

	Controlling Interest	Noncontrolling Interest	Total
Fair value at acquisition date	$425,000	$102,500	$527,500
Relative fair value of Sun's net identifiable assets (80% and 20%)	410,000	102,500	512,500
Goodwill	$ 15,000	$ –0–	$ 15,000

recognition of $20,800 in excess amortization expenses for this same period ($6,500 × 80% × 4 years). Thus, a net increase of $123,200 ($144,000 − $20,800) is needed to correct the parent's beginning Retained Earnings balance for the year.

Once the adjustment from the initial value method to the equity method is determined, the consolidated figures for 2013 can be calculated:

Current Assets = $865,000. The parent's book value is added to the subsidiary's book value. The $20,000 intra-entity balance is eliminated.

Investment in Sun Company = −0−. The intra-entity ownership is eliminated so that the subsidiary's specific assets and liabilities can be consolidated.

Land = $550,000. The parent's book value is added to the subsidiary's book value plus the $50,000 excess fair value allocation (see Exhibit 4.15).

EXHIBIT 4.16
Excess Fair Value
Allocation Balances

FATHER COMPANY AND SUN COMPANY
Unamortized Excess Fair over Book Value Allocation
January 1, 2013, Balances

Account	Excess Original Allocation	Excess Amortization 2009–2012	Balance 1/1/13
Buildings	$ 20,000	$10,000	$ 10,000
Land	50,000	–0–	50,000
Equipment	12,500	10,000	2,500
Royalty agreement	30,000	6,000	24,000
Goodwill	15,000	–0–	15,000
Total	$127,500	$26,000	$101,500

Buildings (net) = \$937,500. The parent's book value is added to the subsidiary's book value plus the \$20,000 fair-value allocation (see Exhibit 4.16) and less five years of amortization (2009 through 2013).

Equipment (net) = \$540,000. The parent's book value is added to the subsidiary's book value. The \$12,500 fair-value allocation has been completely amortized after five years.

Goodwill = \$15,000. Original acquisition-date value assigned.

Expenses = \$746,500. The parent's book value is added to the subsidiary's book value plus amortization expenses on the fair-value allocations for the year (see Exhibit 4.15).

Dividends Paid = \$90,000. Only parent company dividends are consolidated. Subsidiary dividends paid to the parent are eliminated; the remainder reduce the Noncontrolling Interest balance.

Royalty Agreement = \$22,500. The original residual allocation from the acquisition-date fair value is recognized after taking into account five years of amortization (see Exhibit 4.15).

Consolidated Net Income = \$393,500. The combined total of consolidated revenues and expenses.

Noncontrolling Interest in Subsidiary's Income = \$32,700. The outside owners are assigned a 20 percent share of the subsidiary's income less excess fair-value amortizations: 20% × (\$170,000 − \$6,500).

Controlling Interest in Consolidated Net Income = \$360,800. Consolidated net income less the amount allocated to the noncontrolling interest.

Liabilities = \$1,190,000. The parent's book value is added to the subsidiary's book value. The \$20,000 intra-entity balance is eliminated.

Common Stock = \$480,000. Only the parent company's balance is reported.

Retained Earnings, 1/1/13 = \$827,200. Only the parent company's balance after a \$123,200 increase to convert from the initial value method to the equity method.

Retained Earnings 12/31/13 = \$1,098,000. The parent's adjusted beginning balance of \$827,200, plus \$360,800 net income to the controlling interest, less \$90,000 dividends paid to the controlling interest.

Revenues = \$1,140,000. The parent's book value is added to the subsidiary's book value.

Dividend Income = –0–. The intra-entity dividend receipts are eliminated.

Noncontrolling Interest in Subsidiary, 12/31/13 = \$162,000.

NCI in Sun's 1/1/13 book value (20% × \$580,000)	\$116,000
NCI in unamortized excess fair-value allocations (20% × \$86,500)	17,300
January 1, 2013, NCI in Sun's fair value	133,300
NCI in Sun's net income [20% × (\$360,000 − 196,500)]	32,700
NCI dividend share (20% × \$20,000)	(4,000)
Total noncontrolling interest December 31, 2013	\$162,000

b. Six worksheet entries are necessary to produce a consolidation worksheet for Father Company and Sun Company.

Entry *C

Investment in Sun Company	123,200	
Retained Earnings, 1/1/13 (parent)		123,200

This increment is required to adjust the parent's Retained Earnings from the initial value method to the equity method. The amount is \$144,000 (80 percent of the \$180,000 increase in the subsidiary's book value during previous years) less \$20,800 in excess amortization over this same four-year period (\$6,500 × 80% × 4 years).

Entry S

Common Stock (subsidiary)	100,000	
Retained Earnings, 1/1/13 (subsidiary)	480,000	
Investment in Sun Company (80 percent)		464,000
Noncontrolling Interest in Sun Company (20 percent)		116,000

To eliminate beginning stockholders' equity accounts of the subsidiary and recognize the beginning balance book value attributed to the outside owners (20 percent).

Entry A1 and A2 Combined

Buildings	10,000	
Land	50,000	
Equipment	2,500	
Royalty Agreement	24,000	
Goodwill	15,000	
Investment in Sun Company		84,200
Noncontrolling Interest in Sun Company		17,300

To recognize unamortized excess fair over book value allocations as of the first day of the current year (see Exhibit 4.16). All goodwill is attributable to the controlling interest.

Entry I

Dividend Income	16,000	
Dividends Paid		16,000

To eliminate intra-entity dividend payments recorded by parent (using the initial value method) as income.

Entry E

Depreciation Expense	5,000	
Amortization Expense	1,500	
Buildings		2,500
Equipment		2,500
Royalty Agreement		1,500

To recognize excess amortization expenses for the current year (see Exhibit 4.15).

Entry P

Liabilities	20,000	
Current Assets		20,000

To eliminate the intra-entity debt.

c. If the acquisition-date fair value of the noncontrolling interest were $112,500, then Sun's fair value would increase by $10,000 to $537,500 and goodwill would increase by the same $10,000 to $25,000. The entire $10,000 increase in goodwill would be allocated to the noncontrolling interest as follows:

	Controlling Interest	Noncontrolling Interest	Total
Fair value at acquisition date	$425,000	$112,500	$537,500
Relative fair value of Sun's net identifiable assets (80% and 20%)	410,000	102,500	512,500
Goodwill	$ 15,000	$ 10,000	$ 25,000

Therefore, the consolidated balance sheet would show goodwill at $25,000 (instead of $15,000) and the noncontrolling interest balance would show $172,000 (instead of $162,000).

Questions

1. What does the term *noncontrolling interest* mean?
2. Atwater Company acquires 80 percent of the outstanding voting stock of Belwood Company. On that date, Belwood possesses a building with a $160,000 book value but a $220,000 fair value. Assuming that a bargain purchase has not been made, at what value would this building be consolidated under each of the following?
   a. Acquisition method
   b. Purchase method

3. What is a control premium and how does it affect consolidated financial statements?

4. Where should the noncontrolling interest's claims be reported in a consolidated set of financial statements?

5. How is the noncontrolling interest in a subsidiary company calculated as of the end of the current year?

6. December 31 consolidated financial statements are being prepared for Allsports Company and its new subsidiary acquired on July 1 of the current year. Should Allsports adjust its consolidated balances for the preacquisition subsidiary revenues and expenses?

7. Tree, Inc., has held a 10 percent interest in the stock of Limb Company for several years. Because of the level of ownership, this investment has been accounted for using the fair-value method. At the beginning of the current year, Tree acquires an additional 70 percent interest, which provides the company with control over Limb. In preparing consolidated financial statements for this business combination, how does Tree account for the previous 10 percent ownership interest?

8. Duke Corporation owns a 70 percent equity interest in UNCCH, a subsidiary corporation. During the current year, a portion of this stock is sold to an outside party. Before recording this transaction, Duke adjusts the book value of its investment account. What is the purpose of this adjustment?

9. In question (8), how would the parent record the sales transaction?

10. In question (8), how would Duke account for the remainder of its investment subsequent to the sale of this partial interest?

Problems

LO1

Note: Problems 1 through 37 assume the use of the acquisition method. Problems 38 through 40 assume the use of the purchase method.

1. What is a basic premise of the acquisition method regarding accounting for a noncontrolling interest?
   a. Consolidated financial statements should be primarily for the benefit of the parent company's stockholders.
   b. Consolidated financial statements should be produced only if both the parent and the subsidiary are in the same basic industry.
   c. A subsidiary is an indivisible part of a business combination and should be included in its entirety regardless of the degree of ownership.
   d. Consolidated financial statements should not report a noncontrolling interest balance because these outside owners do not hold stock in the parent company.

LO2

2. Bailey, Inc., buys 60 percent of the outstanding stock of Luebs, Inc. Luebs owns a piece of land that cost $200,000 but was worth $500,000 at the acquisition date. What value should be attributed to this land in a consolidated balance sheet at the date of takeover?
   a. $120,000.
   b. $300,000.
   c. $380,000.
   d. $500,000.

LO2

3. Jordan, Inc., holds 75 percent of the outstanding stock of Paxson Corporation. Paxson currently owes Jordan $400,000 for inventory acquired over the past few months. In preparing consolidated financial statements, what amount of this debt should be eliminated?
   a. −0−.
   b. $100,000.
   c. $300,000.
   d. $400,000.

LO2

4. On January 1, 2011, Brendan, Inc., reports net assets of $760,000 although equipment (with a four-year life) having a book value of $440,000 is worth $500,000 and an unrecorded patent is valued at $45,000. Hope Corporation pays $692,000 on that date for an 80 percent ownership in Brendan. If the patent is to be written off over a 10-year period, at what amount should it be reported on consolidated statements at December 31, 2012?
   a. $28,800.
   b. $32,400.
   c. $36,000.
   d. $40,500.

LO6

5. The noncontrolling interest represents an outside ownership in a subsidiary that is not attributable to the parent company. Where in the consolidated balance sheet is this outside ownership interest recognized?

   a. In the liability section.

   b. In a mezzanine section between liabilities and owners' equity.

   c. In the owners' equity section.

   d. The noncontrolling interest is not recognized in the consolidated balance sheet.

LO4

6. On January 1, 2011, Chamberlain Corporation pays $388,000 for a 60 percent ownership in Neville. Annual excess fair-value amortization of $15,000 results from the acquisition. On December 31, 2012, Neville reports revenues of $400,000 and expenses of $300,000 and Chamberlain reports revenues of $700,000 and expenses of $400,000. The parent figures contain no income from the subsidiary. What is consolidated net income attributable to the controlling interest?

   a. $231,000.

   b. $351,000.

   c. $366,000.

   d. $400,000.

LO8

7. James Company acquired 85 percent of Mark-Right Company on April 1. On its December 31 consolidated income statement, how should James account for Mark-Right's revenues and expenses that occurred before April 1?

   a. Include 100 percent of Mark-Right's revenues and expenses and deduct the preacquisition portion as noncontrolling interest in net income.

   b. Exclude 100 percent of the preacquisition revenues and 100 percent of the preacquisition expenses from their respective consolidated totals.

   c. Exclude 15 percent of the preacquisition revenues and 15 percent of the preacquisition expenses from consolidated expenses.

   d. Deduct 15 percent of the net combined revenues and expenses relating to the preacquisition period from consolidated net income.

LO9

8. Amie, Inc., has 100,000 shares of $2 par value stock outstanding. Prairie Corporation acquired 30,000 of Amie's shares on January 1, 2009, for $120,000 when Amie's net assets had a total fair value of $350,000. On July 1, 2012, Prairie agreed to buy an additional 60,000 shares of Amie from a single stockholder for $6 per share. Although Amie's shares were selling in the $5 range around July 1, 2012, Prairie forecasted that obtaining control of Amie would produce significant revenue synergies to justify the premium price paid. If Amie's net identifiable assets had a fair value of $500,000 at July 1, 2012, how much goodwill should Prairie report in its postcombination consolidated balance sheet?

   a. $60,000.

   b. $90,000.

   c. $100,000.

   d. $–0–.

LO9

9. A parent buys 32 percent of a subsidiary in one year and then buys an additional 40 percent in the next year. In a step acquisition of this type, the original 32 percent acquisition should be

   a. maintained at its initial value.

   b. adjusted to its equity method balance at the date of the second acquisition.

   c. adjusted to fair value at the date of the second acquisition with a resulting gain or loss recorded.

   d. adjusted to fair value at the date of the second acquisition with a resulting adjustment to additional paid-in capital.

LO4, LO8

10. On April 1, Pujols, Inc., exchanges $430,000 fair-value consideration for 70 percent of the outstanding stock of Ramirez Corporation. The remaining 30 percent of the outstanding shares continued to trade at a collective fair value of $165,000. Ramirez' identifiable assets and liabilities each had book values that equaled their fair values on April 1 for a net total of $500,000. During the remainder of the year, Ramirez generates revenues of $600,000 and expenses of $360,000 and paid no dividends. On a December 31 consolidated balance sheet, what amount should be reported as noncontrolling interest?

   a. $219,000.

   b. $237,000.

   c. $234,000.

   d. $250,500.

LO10

11. McKinley, Inc., owns 100 percent of Jackson Company's 45,000 voting shares. On June 30, McKinley's internal accounting records show a $192,000 equity method adjusted balance for its investment in

Jackson. McKinley sells 15,000 of its Jackson shares on the open market for $80,000 on June 30. How should McKinley record the excess of the sale proceeds over its carrying value for the shares?

a. Reduce goodwill by $64,000.

b. Recognize a gain on sale for $16,000.

c. Increase its additional paid-in capital by $16,000.

d. Recognize a revaluation gain on its remaining shares of $48,000.

Use the following information for Problems 12 through 14:

West Company acquired 60 percent of Solar Company for $300,000 when Solar's book value was $400,000. The newly comprised 40 percent noncontrolling interest had an assessed fair value of $200,000. Also at the acquisition date, Solar had a trademark (with a 10-year life) that was undervalued in the financial records by $60,000. Also, patented technology (with a 5-year life) was undervalued by $40,000. Two years later, the following figures are reported by these two companies (stockholders' equity accounts have been omitted):

	West Company Book Value	Solar Company Book Value	Solar Company Fair Value
Current assets	$620,000	$300,000	$320,000
Trademarks	260,000	200,000	280,000
Patented technology	410,000	150,000	150,000
Liabilities	(390,000)	(120,000)	(120,000)
Revenues	(900,000)	(400,000)	
Expenses	500,000	300,000	
Investment income	Not given		

LO2

12. What is the consolidated net income before allocation to the controlling and noncontrolling interests?

a. $400,000.

b. $486,000.

c. $491,600.

d. $500,000.

LO4, LO5

13. Assuming Solar Company has paid no dividends, what are the noncontrolling interest's share of the subsidiary's income and the ending balance of the noncontrolling interest in the subsidiary?

a. $26,000 and $230,000.

b. $28,800 and $252,000.

c. $34,400 and $240,800.

d. $40,000 and $252,000.

LO2

14. What is the consolidated trademarks balance?

a. $508,000.

b. $514,000.

c. $520,000.

d. $540,000.

LO2

Use the following information for Problems 15 through 19:

On January 1, Park Corporation and Strand Corporation had condensed balance sheets as follows:

	Park	Strand
Current assets	$ 70,000	$20,000
Noncurrent assets	90,000	40,000
Total assets	$160,000	$60,000
Current liabilities	$ 30,000	$10,000
Long-term debt	50,000	—
Stockholders' equity	80,000	50,000
Total liabilities and equities	$160,000	$60,000

On January 2, Park borrowed $60,000 and used the proceeds to obtain 80 percent of the outstanding common shares of Strand. The acquisition price was considered proportionate to Strand's total fair value. The $60,000 debt is payable in 10 equal annual principal payments, plus interest, beginning

December 31. The excess fair value of the investment over the underlying book value of the acquired net assets is allocated to inventory (60 percent) and to goodwill (40 percent). On a consolidated balance sheet as of January 2, what should be the amount for each of the following?

15. Current assets:
    a. $105,000.
    b. $102,000.
    c. $100,000.
    d. $ 90,000.

16. Noncurrent assets:
    a. $130,000.
    b. $134,000.
    c. $138,000.
    d. $140,000.

17. Current liabilities:
    a. $50,000.
    b. $46,000.
    c. $40,000.
    d. $30,000.

18. Noncurrent liabilities:
    a. $110,000.
    b. $104,000.
    c. $ 90,000.
    d. $ 50,000.

19. Stockholders' equity:
    a. $80,000.
    b. $90,000.
    c. $95,000.
    d. $130,000.

    (AICPA adapted)

LO4, LO5

20. On January 1, 2011, Harrison, Inc., acquired 90 percent of Starr Company in exchange for $1,125,000 fair-value consideration. The total fair value of Starr Company was assessed at $1,200,000. Harrison computed annual excess fair-value amortization of $8,000 based on the difference between Starr's total fair value and its underlying net asset fair value. The subsidiary reported earnings of $70,000 in 2011 and $90,000 in 2012 with dividend payments of $30,000 each year. Apart from its investment in Starr, Harrison had income of $220,000 in 2011 and $260,000 in 2012.

    a. What is the consolidated net income in each of these two years?
    b. What is the ending noncontrolling interest balance as of December 31, 2012?

LO4, LO5, LO7

21. On January 1, Patterson Corporation acquired 80 percent of the 100,000 outstanding voting shares of Soriano, Inc., in exchange for $31.25 per share cash. The remaining 20 percent of Soriano's shares continued to trade for $30.00 both before and after Patterson's acquisition.

    At January 1, Soriano's book and fair values were as follows:

	Book Values	Fair Values	Remaining Life
Current assets	80,000	80,000	
Buildings and equipment	1,250,000	1,000,000	5 years
Trademarks	700,000	900,000	10 years
Patented technology	940,000	2,000,000	4 years
	2,970,000		
Current liabilities	180,000	180,000	
Long-term notes payable	1,500,000	1,500,000	
Common stock	50,000		
Additional paid-in capital	500,000		
Retained earnings	740,000		
	2,970,000		

In addition, Patterson assigned a $600,000 value to certain unpatented technologies recently developed by Soriano. These technologies were estimated to have a 3-year remaining life.

During the year, Soriano paid a $30,000 dividend to its shareholders. The companies reported the following revenues and expenses from their separate operations for the year ending December 31.

	Patterson	Soriano
Revenues	3,000,000	1,400,000
Expenses	1,750,000	600,000

a. What total value should Patterson assign to its Soriano acquisition in its January 1 consolidated balance sheet?

b. What valuation principle should Patterson use to report each of Soriano's identifiable assets and liabilities in its January 1 consolidated balance sheet?

c. For years subsequent to acquisition, how will Soriano's identifiable assets and liabilities be valued in Patterson's consolidated reports?

d. How much goodwill resulted from Patterson's acquisition of Soriano?

e. What is the consolidated net income for the year and what amounts are allocated to the controlling and noncontrolling interests?

f. What is the noncontrolling interest amount reported in the December 31 consolidated balance sheet?

g. Assume instead that, based on its share prices, Soriano's January 1 total fair value was assessed at $2,250,000. How would the reported amounts for Soriano's assets change on Patterson's acquisition-date consolidated balance sheet?

LO2, LO7, LO8

22. Parker, Inc., acquires 70 percent of Sawyer Company for $420,000. The remaining 30 percent of Sawyer's outstanding shares continue to trade at a collective value of $174,000. On the acquisition date, Sawyer has the following accounts:

	Book Value	Fair Value
Current assets	$ 210,000	$ 210,000
Land	170,000	180,000
Buildings	300,000	330,000
Liabilities	(280,000)	(280,000)

The buildings have a 10-year life. In addition, Sawyer holds a patent worth $140,000 that has a five-year life but is not recorded on its financial records. At the end of the year, the two companies report the following balances:

	Parker	Sawyer
Revenues	$(900,000)	$(600,000)
Expenses	600,000	400,000

a. Assume that the acquisition took place on January 1. What figures would appear in a consolidated income statement for this year?

b. Assume that the acquisition took place on April 1. Sawyer's revenues and expenses occurred uniformly throughout the year. What amounts would appear in a consolidated income statement for this year?

LO2, LO4, LO5

23. On January 1, Beckman, Inc., acquires 60 percent of the outstanding stock of Calvin for $36,000. Calvin Co. has one recorded asset, a specialized production machine with a book value of $10,000 and no liabilities. The fair value of the machine is $50,000, and the remaining useful life is estimated to be 10 years. Any remaining excess fair value is attributable to an unrecorded process trade secret with an estimated future life of 4 years. Calvin's total acquisition-date fair value is $60,000.

At the end of the year, Calvin reports the following in its financial statements:

Revenues	$50,000	Machine	$ 9,000	Common stock	$10,000
Expenses	20,000	Other assets	26,000	Retained earnings	25,000
Net income	$30,000	Total assets	$35,000	Total equity	$35,000
Dividends paid	$ 5,000				

Determine the amounts that Beckman should report in its year-end consolidated financial statements for noncontrolling interest in subsidiary income, total noncontrolling interest, Calvin's machine (net of accumulated depreciation), and the process trade secret.

24. On January 1, 2011, Morey, Inc., exchanged $178,000 for 25 percent of Amsterdam Corporation. Morey appropriately applied the equity method to this investment. At January 1, the book values of Amsterdam's assets and liabilities approximated their fair values.

On June 30, 2011, Morey paid $560,000 for an additional 70 percent of Amsterdam, thus increasing its overall ownership to 95 percent. The price paid for the 70 percent acquisition was proportionate to Amsterdam's total fair value. At June 30, the carrying values of Amsterdam's assets and liabilities approximated their fair values. Any remaining excess fair value was attributed to goodwill.

Amsterdam reports the following amounts at December 31, 2011 (credit balances shown in parentheses):

Revenues	$(210,000)
Expenses	140,000
Retained earnings, January 1	(200,000)
Dividends, October 1	20,000
Common stock	(500,000)

Amsterdam's revenue and expenses were distributed evenly throughout the year and no changes in Amsterdam's stock have occurred.

Using the acquisition method, compute the following:

a. The acquisition-date fair value of Amsterdam to be included in Morey's consolidated financial statements.

b. The revaluation gain (or loss) reported by Morey for its 25 percent investment in Amsterdam on June 30.

c. The amount of goodwill recognized by Morey on its December 31 balance sheet (assume no impairments have been recognized).

d. The noncontrolling interest amount reported by Morey on its
   - June 30 consolidated balance sheet.
   - December 31 consolidated balance sheet.

25. Posada Company acquired 7,000 of the 10,000 outstanding shares of Sabathia Company on January 1, 2010, for $840,000. The subsidiary's total fair value was assessed at $1,200,000 although its book value on that date was $1,130,000. The $70,000 fair value in excess of Sabathia's book value was assigned to a patent with a 5-year remaining life.

On January 1, 2012, Posada reported a $1,085,000 equity method balance in the Investment in Sabathia Company account. On October 1, 2012, Posada sells 1,000 shares of the investment for $191,000. During 2012, Sabathia reported net income of $120,000 and paid dividends of $40,000. These amounts are assumed to have occurred evenly throughout the year.

a. How should Posada report the 2012 income that accrued to the 1,000 shares prior to their sale?

b. What is the effect on Posada's financial statements from this sale of 1,000 shares?

c. How should Posada report in its financial statements the 6,000 shares of Sabathia it continues to hold?

26. On January 1, 2009, Telconnect acquires 70 percent of Bandmor for $490,000 cash. The remaining 30 percent of Bandmor's shares continued to trade at a total value of $210,000. The new subsidiary reported common stock of $300,000 on that date, with retained earnings of $180,000. A patent was undervalued in the company's financial records by $30,000. This patent had a 5-year remaining life. Goodwill of $190,000 was recognized and allocated proportionately to the controlling and noncontrolling interests. Bandmor earns income and pays cash dividends as follows:

Year	Net Income	Dividends Paid
2009	$ 75,000	$39,000
2010	96,000	44,000
2011	110,000	60,000

On December 31, 2011, Telconnect owes $22,000 to Bandmor.

a. If Telconnect has applied the equity method, what consolidation entries are needed as of December 31, 2011?

b. If Telconnect has applied the initial value method, what Entry *C is needed for a 2011 consolidation?

c. If Telconnect has applied the partial equity method, what Entry *C is needed for a 2011 consolidation?

d. What noncontrolling interest balances will appear in consolidated financial statements for 2011?

LO2, LO3, LO5

27. Miller Company acquired an 80 percent interest in Taylor Company on January 1, 2009. Miller paid $664,000 in cash to the owners of Taylor to acquire these shares. In addition, the remaining 20 percent of Taylor shares continued to trade at a total value of $166,000 both before and after Miller's acquisition.

On January 1, 2009, Taylor reported a book value of $600,000 (Common Stock = $300,000; Additional Paid-In Capital = $90,000; Retained Earnings = $210,000). Several of Taylor's buildings that had a remaining life of 20 years were undervalued by a total of $80,000.

During the next three years, Taylor reported the following figures:

Year	Net Income	Dividends Paid
2009	$ 70,000	$10,000
2010	90,000	15,000
2011	100,000	20,000

Determine the appropriate answers for each of the following questions:

a. What amount of excess depreciation expense should be recognized in the consolidated financial statements for the initial years following this acquisition?

b. If a consolidated balance sheet is prepared as of January 1, 2009, what amount of goodwill should be recognized?

c. If a consolidation worksheet is prepared as of January 1, 2009, what Entry S and Entry A should be included?

d. On the separate financial records of the parent company, what amount of investment income would be reported for 2009 under each of the following accounting methods?
   (1) The equity method.
   (2) The partial equity method.
   (3) The initial value method.

e. On the parent company's separate financial records, what would be the December 31, 2011, balance for the Investment in Taylor Company account under each of the following accounting methods?
   (4) The equity method.
   (5) The partial equity method.
   (6) The initial value method.

f. As of December 31, 2010, Miller's Buildings account on its separate records has a balance of $800,000 and Taylor has a similar account with a $300,000 balance. What is the consolidated balance for the Buildings account?

g. What is the balance of consolidated goodwill as of December 31, 2011?

h. Assume that the parent company has been applying the equity method to this investment. On December 31, 2011, the separate financial statements for the two companies present the following information:

	Miller Company	Taylor Company
Common stock	$500,000	$300,000
Additional paid-in capital	280,000	90,000
Retained earnings, 12/31/11	620,000	425,000

What will be the consolidated balance of each of these accounts?

LO1, LO8

28. Following are several account balances taken from the records of Karson and Reilly as of December 31, 2011. A few asset accounts have been omitted here. All revenues, expenses, and dividends occurred evenly throughout the year. Annual tests have indicated no goodwill impairment.

	Karson	Reilly
Sales	$ (800,000)	$(500,000)
Cost of goods sold	400,000	280,000
Operating expenses	200,000	100,000
Investment income	not given	–0–
Retained earnings, 1/1	(1,400,000)	(700,000)
Dividends	80,000	20,000
Trademarks	600,000	200,000
Royalty agreements	700,000	300,000
Licensing agreements	400,000	400,000
Liabilities	(500,000)	(200,000)
Common stock ($10 par value)	(400,000)	(100,000)
Additional paid-in capital	(500,000)	(600,000)

On July 1, 2011, Karson acquired 80 percent of Reilly for $1,330,000 cash consideration. In addition, Karson agreed to pay additional cash to the former owners of Reilly if certain performance measures are achieved after three years. Karson assessed a $30,000 fair value for the contingent performance obligation as of the acquisition date and as of December 31, 2011.

On July 1, 2011, Reilly's assets and liabilities had book values equal to their fair value except for some trademarks (with 5-year remaining lives) that were undervalued by $150,000. Karson estimated Reilly's total fair value at $1,700,000 on July 1, 2011.

For a consolidation prepared at December 31, 2011, what balances would be reported for the following?

Sales	Consolidated Net Income
Expenses	Retained Earnings, 1/1
Noncontrolling Interest in	Trademarks
Subsidiary's Net Income	Goodwill

LO5

29. Nascent, Inc., acquires 60 percent of Sea-Breeze Corporation for $414,000 cash on January 1, 2009. The remaining 40 percent of the Sea-Breeze shares traded near a total value of $276,000 both before and after the acquisition date. On January 1, 2009, Sea-Breeze had the following assets and liabilities:

	Book Value	Fair Value
Current assets	$150,000	$150,000
Land	200,000	200,000
Buildings (net) (6-year life)	300,000	360,000
Equipment (net) (4-year life)	300,000	280,000
Patent (10-year life)	–0–	100,000
Liabilities	(400,000)	(400,000)

The companies' financial statements for the year ending December 31, 2012, follow:

	Nascent	Sea-Breeze
Revenues	$ (600,000)	$ (300,000)
Operating expenses	410,000	210,000
Investment income	(42,000)	–0–
Net income	$ (232,000)	$ (90,000)
Retained earnings, 1/1/12	$ (700,000)	$ (300,000)
Net income	(232,000)	(90,000)
Dividends paid	92,000	70,000
Retained earnings, 12/31/12	$ (840,000)	$ (320,000)
Current assets	$ 330,000	$ 100,000
Land	220,000	200,000
Buildings (net)	700,000	200,000
Equipment (net)	400,000	500,000
Investment in Sea-Breeze	414,000	–0–
Total assets	$ 2,064,000	$ 1,000,000
Liabilities	$ (500,000)	$ (200,000)
Common stock	(724,000)	(480,000)
Retained earnings, 12/31/12	(840,000)	(320,000)
Total liabilities and equities	$(2,064,000)	$(1,000,000)

Answer the following questions:

a. How can the accountant determine that the parent has applied the initial value method?

b. What is the annual excess amortization initially recognized in connection with this acquisition?

c. If the parent had applied the equity method, what investment income would the parent have recorded in 2012?

d. What is the parent's portion of consolidated retained earnings as of January 1, 2012?

e. What is consolidated net income for 2012 and what amounts are attributable to the controlling and noncontrolling interests?

f. Within consolidated statements at January 1, 2009, what balance is included for the subsidiary's Buildings account?

g. What is the consolidated Buildings reported balance as of December 31, 2012?

LO1, LO5, LO7

30. On January 1, 2010, Pierson Corporation exchanged $1,710,000 cash for 90 percent of the outstanding voting stock of Steele Company. The consideration transferred by Pierson provided a reasonable basis for assessing the total January 1, 2010, fair value of Steele Company. At the acquisition date, Steele reported the following owner's equity amounts in its balance sheet:

Common stock	$400,000
Additional paid-in capital	60,000
Retained earnings	265,000

In determining its acquisition offer, Pierson noted that the values for Steele's recorded assets and liabilities approximated their fair values. Pierson also observed that Steele had developed internally a customer base with an assessed fair value of $800,000 that was not reflected on Steele's books. Pierson expected both cost and revenue synergies from the combination.

At the acquisition date, Pierson prepared the following fair-value allocation schedule:

Fair value of Steele Company	$1,900,000
Book value of Steele Company	725,000
Excess fair value	1,175,000
to customer base (10-year remaining life)	800,000
to goodwill	$ 375,000

At December 31, 2011, the two companies report the following balances:

	Pierson	Steele
Revenues	(1,843,000)	(675,000)
Cost of goods sold	1,100,000	322,000
Depreciation expense	125,000	120,000
Amortization expense	275,000	11,000
Interest expense	27,500	7,000
Equity in income of Steele	(121,500)	
Net income	(437,000)	(215,000)
Retained earnings, 1/1	(2,625,000)	(395,000)
Net income	(437,000)	(215,000)
Dividends paid	350,000	25,000
Retained earnings, 12/31	(2,712,000)	(585,000)
Current assets	1,204,000	430,000
Investment in Steele	1,854,000	
Buildings and equipment	931,000	863,000
Copyrights	950,000	107,000
Total assets	4,939,000	1,400,000
Accounts payable	(485,000)	(200,000)
Notes payable	(542,000)	(155,000)
Common stock	(900,000)	(400,000)
Additional paid-in capital	(300,000)	(60,000)
Retained earnings, 12/31	(2,712,000)	(585,000)
Total liabilities and equities	(4,939,000)	(1,400,000)

a. Using the acquisition method, determine the consolidated balances for this business combination as of December 31, 2011.

b. If instead the noncontrolling interest's acquisition-date fair value is assessed at $152,500, what changes would be evident in the consolidated statements?

LO5, LO6, LO7

31. The Krause Corporation acquired 80 percent of the 100,000 outstanding voting shares of Leahy, Inc., for $6.30 per share on January 1, 2011. The remaining 20 percent of Leahy's shares also traded actively at $6.30 per share before and after Krause's acquisition. An appraisal made on that date

determined that all book values appropriately reflected the fair values of Leahy's underlying accounts except that a building with a 5-year life was undervalued by $45,000 and a fully amortized trademark with an estimated 10-year remaining life had a $60,000 fair value. At the acquisition date, Leahy reported common stock of $100,000 and a retained earnings balance of $280,000.

Following are the separate financial statements for the year ending December 31, 2012:

	Krause Corporation	Leahy, Inc.
Sales	$ (584,000)	$(250,000)
Cost of goods sold	194,000	95,000
Operating expenses	246,000	65,000
Dividend income	(16,000)	–0–
Net income	$ (160,000)	$ (90,000)
Retained earnings, 1/1/12	$ (700,000)	$(350,000)
Net income (above)	(160,000)	(90,000)
Dividends paid	70,000	20,000
Retained earnings, 12/31/12	$ (790,000)	$(420,000)
Current assets	$ 296,000	$ 191,000
Investment in Leahy, Inc.	504,000	–0–
Buildings and equipment (net)	680,000	390,000
Trademarks	100,000	144,000
Total assets	$ 1,580,000	$ 725,000
Liabilities	$ (470,000)	$(205,000)
Common stock	(320,000)	(100,000)
Retained earnings, 12/31/12 (above)	(790,000)	(420,000)
Total liabilities and equities	$(1,580,000)	$(725,000)

a. Prepare a worksheet to consolidate these two companies as of December 31, 2012.

b. Prepare a 2012 consolidated income statement for Krause and Leahy.

c. If instead the noncontrolling interest shares of Leahy had traded for $4.85 surrounding Krause's acquisition date, how would the consolidated statements change?

32. Father, Inc., buys 80 percent of the outstanding common stock of Sam Corporation on January 1, 2011, for $680,000 cash. At the acquisition date, Sam's total fair value was assessed at $850,000 although Sam's book value was only $600,000. Also, several individual items on Sam's financial records had fair values that differed from their book values as follows:

	Book Value	Fair Value
Land	$ 60,000	$ 225,000
Buildings and equipment (10-year remaining life)	275,000	250,000
Copyright (20-year life)	100,000	200,000
Notes payable (due in 8 years)	(130,000)	(120,000)

For internal reporting purposes, Father, Inc., employs the equity method to account for this investment.

The following account balances are for the year ending December 31, 2011, for both companies. Using the acquisition method, determine consolidated balances for this business combination (through either individual computations or the use of a worksheet).

	Father	Sam
Revenues	$(1,360,000)	$(540,000)
Cost of goods sold	700,000	385,000
Depreciation expense	260,000	10,000
Amortization expense	–0–	5,000
Interest expense	44,000	5,000
Equity in income of Sam	(105,000)	–0–
Net income	$ (461,000)	$(135,000)

(continued)

	Father	Sam
Retained earnings, 1/1/11	$(1,265,000)	$(440,000)
Net income (above)	(461,000)	(135,000)
Dividends paid	260,000	65,000
Retained earnings, 12/31/11	$(1,466,000)	$(510,000)
Current assets	$ 965,000	$ 528,000
Investment in Sam	733,000	–0–
Land	292,000	60,000
Buildings and equipment (net)	877,000	265,000
Copyright	–0–	95,000
Total assets	$ 2,867,000	$ 948,000
Accounts payable	$ (191,000)	$(148,000)
Notes payable	(460,000)	(130,000)
Common stock	(300,000)	(100,000)
Additional paid-in capital	(450,000)	(60,000)
Retained earnings (above)	(1,466,000)	(510,000)
Total liabilities and equities	$(2,867,000)	$(948,000)

Note: Credits are indicated by parentheses.

LO1, LO5

33. Adams Corporation acquired 90 percent of the outstanding voting shares of Barstow, Inc., on December 31, 2009. Adams paid a total of $603,000 in cash for these shares. The 10 percent non-controlling interest shares traded on a daily basis at fair value of $67,000 both before and after Adams's acquisition. On December 31, 2009, Barstow had the following account balances:

	Book Value	Fair Value
Current assets	$ 160,000	$ 160,000
Land	120,000	150,000
Buildings (10-year life)	220,000	200,000
Equipment (5-year life)	160,000	200,000
Patents (10-year life)	–0–	50,000
Notes payable (5-year life)	(200,000)	(180,000)
Common stock	(180,000)	—
Retained earnings, 12/31/09	(280,000)	—

December 31, 2011, adjusted trial balances for the two companies follow:

	Adams Corporation	Barstow, Inc.
Debits		
Current assets	$ 610,000	$ 250,000
Land	380,000	150,000
Buildings	490,000	250,000
Equipment	873,000	150,000
Investment in Barstow, Inc.	702,000	–0–
Cost of goods sold	480,000	90,000
Depreciation expense	100,000	55,000
Interest expense	40,000	15,000
Dividends paid	110,000	70,000
Total debits	$3,785,000	$1,030,000
Credits		
Notes payable	$ 860,000	$ 230,000
Common stock	510,000	180,000
Retained earnings, 1/1/11	1,367,000	340,000
Revenues	940,000	280,000
Investment income	108,000	–0–
Total credits	$3,785,000	$1,030,000

a. Prepare schedules for acquisition-date fair-value allocations and amortizations for Adams's investment in Barstow.

b. Determine Adams's method of accounting for its investment in Barstow. Support your answer with a numerical explanation.

c. Without using a worksheet or consolidation entries, determine the balances to be reported as of December 31, 2011, for this business combination.

d. To verify the figures determined in requirement (c), prepare a consolidation worksheet for Adams Corporation and Barstow, Inc., as of December 31, 2011.

LO1, LO4, LO8

34. Following are the individual financial statements for Gibson and Davis for the year ending December 31, 2011:

	Gibson	Davis
Sales	$ (600,000)	$ (300,000)
Cost of goods sold	300,000	140,000
Operating expenses	174,000	60,000
Dividend income	(24,000)	–0–
Net income	$ (150,000)	$ (100,000)
Retained earnings, 1/1/11	$ (700,000)	$ (400,000)
Net income	(150,000)	(100,000)
Dividends paid	80,000	40,000
Retained earnings, 12/31/11	$ (770,000)	$ (460,000)
Cash and receivables	$ 248,000	$ 100,000
Inventory	500,000	190,000
Investment in Davis	528,000	–0–
Buildings (net)	524,000	600,000
Equipment (net)	400,000	400,000
Total assets	$ 2,200,000	$ 1,290,000
Liabilities	(800,000)	(490,000)
Common stock	(630,000)	(340,000)
Retained earnings, 12/31/11	(770,000)	(460,000)
Total liabilities and stockholders' equity	$(2,200,000)	$(1,290,000)

Gibson acquired 60 percent of Davis on April 1, 2011, for $528,000. On that date, equipment owned by Davis (with a five-year remaining life) was overvalued by $30,000. Also on that date, the fair value of the 40 percent noncontrolling interest was $352,000. Davis earned income evenly during the year but paid the entire dividend on November 1, 2011.

a. Prepare a consolidated income statement for the year ending December 31, 2011.

b. Determine the consolidated balance for each of the following accounts as of December 31, 2011:

Goodwill	Buildings (net)
Equipment (net)	Dividends Paid
Common Stock	

LO2, LO3, LO6, LO7, LO8

35. On July 1, 2011, Truman Company acquired a 70 percent interest in Atlanta Company in exchange for consideration of $720,000 in cash and equity securities. The remaining 30 percent of Atlanta's shares traded closely near an average price that totaled $290,000 both before and after Truman's acquisition.

In reviewing its acquisition, Truman assigned a $100,000 fair value to a patent recently developed by Atlanta, even though it was not recorded within the financial records of the subsidiary. This patent is anticipated to have a remaining life of five years.

The following financial information is available for these two companies for 2011. In addition, the subsidiary's income was earned uniformly throughout the year. Subsidiary dividend payments were made quarterly.

	Truman	Atlanta
Revenues	$ (670,000)	$ (400,000)
Operating expenses	402,000	280,000
Income of subsidiary	(35,000)	
Net income	$ (303,000)	$ (120,000)

(continued)

	Truman	Atlanta
Retained earnings, 1/1/11	$ (823,000)	$ (500,000)
Net income (above)	(303,000)	(120,000)
Dividends paid	145,000	80,000
Retained earnings, 12/31/11	$ (981,000)	$ (540,000)
Current assets	$ 481,000	$ 390,000
Investment in Atlanta	727,000	
Land	388,000	200,000
Buildings	701,000	630,000
Total assets	$ 2,297,000	$ 1,220,000
Liabilities	$ (816,000)	$ (360,000)
Common stock	(95,000)	(300,000)
Additional paid-in capital	(405,000)	(20,000)
Retained earnings, 12/31/11	(981,000)	(540,000)
Total liabilities and stockholders' equity	$(2,297,000)	$(1,220,000)

Answer each of the following:

a. How did Truman allocate Atlanta's acquisition-date fair value to the various assets acquired and liabilities assumed in the combination?

b. How did Truman allocate the goodwill from the acquisition across the controlling and noncontrolling interests?

c. How did Truman derive the Investment in Atlanta account balance at the end of 2011?

d. Prepare a worksheet to consolidate the financial statements of these two companies as of December 31, 2011.

LO9

36. On January 1, 2011, Allan Company bought a 15 percent interest in Sysinger Company. The acquisition price of $184,500 reflected an assessment that all of Sysinger's accounts were fairly valued within the company's accounting records. During 2011, Sysinger reported net income of $100,000 and paid cash dividends of $30,000. Allan possessed the ability to influence significantly Sysinger's operations and, therefore, accounted for this investment using the equity method.

On January 1, 2012, Allan acquired an additional 80 percent interest in Sysinger and provided the following fair value assessments of Sysinger's ownership components:

Consideration transferred by Allan for 80% interest	$1,400,000
Fair value of Allan's 15% previous ownership	262,500
Noncontrolling interest's 5% fair value	87,500
Total acquisition-date fair value for Sysinger Company	$1,750,000

Also, as of January 1, 2012, Allan assessed a $400,000 value to an unrecorded customer contract recently negotiated by Sysinger. The customer contract is anticipated to have a remaining life of 4 years. Sysinger's other assets and liabilities were judged to have fair values equal to their book values. Allan elects to continue applying the equity method to this investment for internal reporting purposes.

At December 31, 2012, the following financial information is available for consolidation:

	Allan Company	Sysinger Company
Revenues	$ (931,000)	$ (380,000)
Operating expenses	615,000	230,000
Equity earnings of Sysinger	(47,500)	–0–
Gain on revaluation of Investment in Sysinger to fair value	(67,500)	–0–
Net income	$ 431,000	$ 150,000
Retained earnings, January 1	$ (965,000)	$ (600,000)
Net income (above)	(431,000)	(150,000)
Cash dividends paid to stockholders	140,000	40,000
Retained earnings, December 31	$ (1,256,000)	$ (710,000)

(continued)

	Allan Company	Sysinger Company
Current assets	$ 288,000	$ 540,000
Investment in Sysinger (equity method)	1,672,000	–0–
Property, plant, and equipment	826,000	590,000
Patented technology	850,000	370,000
Customer contract	–0–	–0–
Total assets	$ 3,636,000	$ 1,500,000
Liabilities	$ (1,300,000)	$ (90,000)
Common stock	(900,000)	(500,000)
Additional paid-in capital	(180,000)	(200,000)
Retained earnings, December 31	(1,256,000)	(710,000)
Total liabilities and equities	$ (3,636,000)	$(1,500,000)

a. How should Allan allocate Sysinger's total acquisition-date fair value (January 1, 2012) to the assets acquired and liabilities assumed for consolidation purposes?

b. Show how the following amounts on Allan's pre-consolidation 2012 statements were derived:
   • Equity in earnings of Sysinger.
   • Gain on revaluation of Investment in Sysinger to fair value.
   • Investment in Sysinger.

c. Prepare a worksheet to consolidate the financial statements of these two companies as of December 31, 2012.

LO9

37. On January 1, 2010, Bretz, Inc., acquired 60 percent of the outstanding shares of Keane Company for $573,000 in cash. The price paid was proportionate to Keane's total fair value although at the date of acquisition, Keane had a total book value of $810,000. All assets acquired and liabilities assumed had fair values equal to book values except for a copyright (six-year remaining life) that was undervalued in Keane's accounting records by $120,000. During 2010, Keane reported net income of $150,000 and paid cash dividends of $80,000. On January 1, 2011, Bretz bought an additional 30 percent interest in Keane for $300,000.

The following financial information is for these two companies for 2011. Keane issued no additional capital stock during either 2010 or 2011.

	Bretz, Inc.	Keane Company
Revenues	$ (402,000)	$ (300,000)
Operating expenses	200,000	120,000
Equity in Keane earnings	(144,000)	–0–
Net income	$ (346,000)	$ (180,000)
Retained earnings 1/1	$ (797,000)	$ (500,000)
Net income (above)	(346,000)	(180,000)
Dividends paid	143,000	60,000
Retained earnings 12/31	$(1,000,000)	$ (620,000)
Current assets	$ 224,000	$ 190,000
Investment in Keane Company	994,500	–0–
Trademarks	106,000	600,000
Copyrights	210,000	300,000
Equipment (net)	380,000	110,000
Total assets	$ 1,914,500	$ 1,200,000
Liabilities	$ (453,000)	$ (200,000)
Common stock	(400,000)	(300,000)
Additional paid-in capital	(60,000)	(80,000)
Additional paid-in capital—step acquisition	(1,500)	–0–
Retained earnings 12/31	(1,000,000)	(620,000)
Total liabilities and equities	$(1,914,500)	$(1,200,000)

a. Show the journal entry Bretz made to record its January 1, 2011, acquisition of an additional 30 percent of Keane Company shares.

b. Prepare a schedule showing how Bretz determined the Investment in Keane Company balance as of December 31, 2011.

c. Prepare a consolidated worksheet for Bretz, Inc., and Keane Company for December 31, 2011.

LO11

38. Bon Air, Inc., purchased 70 percent (2,800 shares) of the outstanding voting stock of Creedmoor Corporation on January 1, 2007, for $250,000 cash. Creedmoor's net assets on that date totaled $230,000, but this balance included three accounts having fair values that differed from their book values:

	Book Value	Fair Value
Land	$ 30,000	$ 40,000
Equipment (14-year life)	50,000	118,000
Liabilities (10-year life)	(70,000)	(50,000)

As of December 31, 2010, the two companies report the following balances:

	Bon Air	Creedmoor
Revenues	$ (694,800)	$(250,000)
Operating expenses	630,000	180,000
Investment income	(44,200)	–0–
Net income	$ (109,000)	$ (70,000)
Retained earnings, 1/1/10	$ (760,000)	$(260,000)
Net income	(109,000)	(70,000)
Dividends paid	68,000	10,000
Retained earnings, 12/31/10	$ (801,000)	$(320,000)
Current assets	$ 72,000	$ 120,000
Investment in Creedmoor Corp.	321,800	–0–
Land	241,000	50,000
Buildings (net)	289,000	200,000
Equipment (net)	165,200	40,000
Total assets	$ 1,089,000	$ 410,000
Liabilities	$ (180,000)	$ (50,000)
Common stock	(50,000)	(40,000)
Additional paid-in capital	(58,000)	–0–
Retained earnings, 12/31/10	(801,000)	(320,000)
Total liabilities and equities	$(1,089,000)	$(410,000)

Prepare a worksheet to consolidate these two companies as of December 31, 2010. Because Bon Air acquired Creedmoor before the effective date of the acquisition method (2009), the purchase method is appropriate.

LO11

39. Watson, Inc., purchased 60 percent of Houston, Inc., on January 1, 2008, for $400,000 in cash. On that date, assets and liabilities of the subsidiary had the following values:

	Book Value	Fair Value
Current assets	$ 320,000	$ 320,000
Equipment (net) (10-year life)	410,000	380,000
Buildings (net) (15-year life)	300,000	455,000
Current liabilities	(190,000)	(190,000)
Bonds payable (due in 10 years)	(370,000)	(350,000)

On December 31, 2011, these two companies report the following figures:

	Watson	Houston
Revenues	$ (640,000)	$ (280,000)
Operating expenses	480,000	210,000
Equity in subsidiary earnings	(36,400)	–0–
Net income	$ (196,400)	$ (70,000)

(continued)

	Watson	Houston
Retained earnings, 1/1/11	$ (683,400)	$ (380,000)
Net income	(196,400)	(70,000)
Dividends paid	60,200	40,000
Retained earnings, 12/31/11	$ (819,600)	$ (410,000)
Current assets	$ 215,000	$ 260,000
Investment in Houston	491,600	–0–
Equipment (net)	500,000	420,000
Buildings (net)	413,000	520,000
Total assets	$ 1,619,600	$ 1,200,000
Current liabilities	$ (390,000)	$ (170,000)
Bonds payable	(100,000)	(370,000)
Common stock	(310,000)	(250,000)
Retained earnings, 12/31/11	(819,600)	(410,000)
Total liabilities and equities	$(1,619,600)	$(1,200,000)

Answer each of the following questions using the purchase method:

a. The parent shows a $36,400 balance as its Equity in Subsidiary Earnings. How was this balance calculated?

b. Is an adjustment to the parent's Retained Earnings as of January 1, 2011, needed? Why or why not?

c. How much total amortization expense should be recognized for consolidation purposes in 2011?

d. What is the noncontrolling interest in the subsidiary's net income?

e. Prepare a consolidated income statement.

f. What allocations were made as a result of the purchase price? What amount of each allocation remains at the end of 2011?

g. What is the December 31, 2011, amount in Noncontrolling Interest in the Subsidiary? What three components make up this total?

h. Prepare a consolidated balance sheet as of December 31, 2011.

LO11

40. Good Corporation acquired 80 percent of the outstanding stock of Morning, Inc., on January 1, 2008, for $1,400,000 in cash, debt, and stock. One of Morning's buildings, with a 10-year remaining life, was undervalued on the company's accounting records by $80,000. Also, Morning's newly developed unpatented technology, with an estimated 10-year life, was assessed to have a fair value of $550,000.

During subsequent years, Morning reports the following:

	Net Income	Dividends Paid
2008	$180,000	$100,000
2009	200,000	100,000
2010	300,000	100,000
2011	400,000	120,000

The following trial balances are for these two companies as of December 31, 2011. Morning owes Good $100,000 as of this date.

	Good	Morning
Debits		
Cash	$ 300,000	$ 200,000
Receivables	700,000	400,000
Inventory	400,000	500,000
Investment in Morning	1,400,000	–0–
Land	700,000	600,000
Buildings (net)	300,000	700,000
Operating expenses	400,000	100,000
Dividends paid	380,000	120,000
Total debits	$4,580,000	$2,620,000

(continued)

		Good	Morning
Credits			
Liabilities		$ 200,000	$ 620,000
Common stock		1,000,000	460,000
Additional paid-in capital		600,000	40,000
Retained earnings, 1/1/11		1,800,000	1,000,000
Revenues		884,000	500,000
Dividend income		96,000	–0–
Total credits		$4,580,000	$2,620,000

Using the purchase method, prepare consolidated balances for this business combination for 2011.

Develop Your Skills

ACCOUNTING THEORY RESEARCH CASE

The FASB ASC paragraph 810-10-45-16 states: "The noncontrolling interest shall be reported in the consolidated statement of financial position within equity, separately from the parent's equity. That amount shall be clearly identified and labeled, for example, as noncontrolling interest in subsidiaries."

However, prior to issuing this current reporting requirement, the FASB considered several alternative display formats for the noncontrolling interest. Access the precodification standard, *SFAS 160,* "Noncontrolling Interest in Consolidated Financial Statements," at www.fasb.org to answer the following:

- What alternative financial statement display formats did the FASB consider for the noncontrolling interest?

- What criteria did the FASB use to evaluate the desirability of each alternative?

- In what specific ways did FASB Concept Statement 6 affect the FASB's evaluation of these alternatives?

Consolidated Financial Statements— Intra-Entity Asset Transactions

Chapter 1 analyzes the deferral and subsequent recognition of gains created by inventory transfers between two affiliated companies in connection with equity method accounting. The central theme of that discussion is that intra-entity[1] profits are not realized until the earning process culminates in a sale to an unrelated party. This same accounting logic applies to transactions between companies within a business combination. Such sales within a single economic entity create neither profits nor losses. In reference to this issue, FASB ASC paragraph 810-10-45-1 states,

> As consolidated financial statements are based on the assumption that they represent the financial position and operating results of a single economic entity, such statements should not include gain or loss on transactions among the entities in the consolidated group. Accordingly, any intra-entity income or loss on assets remaining within the consolidated group shall be eliminated; the concept usually applied for this purpose is gross profit or loss.

The elimination of the accounting effects created by intra-entity transactions is one of the most significant problems encountered in the consolidation process. The volume of transfers within many enterprises can be large. A recent annual report for the Ford Motor Company, for example, shows the elimination of intersegment revenues amounting to $2.461 billion.

Such transactions are especially common in companies organized as a vertically integrated chain of organizations. These entities reduce their

---

[1] The FASB Accounting Standards Codification (ASC) recently began using the term *intra-entity* to describe transfers of assets across business entities affiliated though common stock ownership or other control mechanisms. The phrase indicates that although such transfers occur across separate legal entities, they are nonetheless made within a consolidated entity. Prior to the use of the term *intra-entity*, such transfers were routinely referred to as *intercompany* transactions.

LEARNING OBJECTIVES

After studying this chapter, you should be able to:

LO1   Understand that intra-entity asset transfers often create accounting effects within the financial records of affiliated companies that must be eliminated or adjusted in preparing consolidated financial statements.

LO2   Prepare the consolidation entry to eliminate the sales and purchases balances that are created by the intra-entity transfer of inventory.

LO3   Prepare the consolidation entry to eliminate any intra-entity inventory gross profit that remains unrealized at (a) the end of the year of transfer and (b) the beginning of the subsequent period.

LO4   Understand that the consolidation process for inventory transfers is designed to defer the unrealized portion of an intra-entity gross profit from the year of transfer into the year of disposal or consumption.

LO5   Understand the difference between upstream and downstream intra-entity transfers and how each affects the computation of noncontrolling interest balances.

LO6   Prepare the consolidation entry to remove any unrealized gain created by the intra-entity transfer of land from the accounting records of the year of transfer and subsequent years.

LO7   Prepare the consolidation entries to remove the effects of upstream and downstream intra-entity fixed asset transfers across affiliated entities.

costs by developing affiliations in which one operation furnishes products to another. As *Mergers & Acquisitions* observed,

> Downstream acquisitions . . . are aimed at securing critical sources of materials and components, streamlining manufacturing and materials planning, gaining economies of scale, entering new markets, and enhancing overall competitiveness. Manufacturers that combine with suppliers are often able to assert total control over such critical areas as product quality and resource planning.[2]

Intra-entity asset transactions take several forms. In particular, inventory transfers are especially prevalent. However, the sale of land and depreciable assets also can occur between the parties within a combination. This chapter examines the consolidation procedures for each of these different types of intra-entity asset transfers.

INTRA-ENTITY INVENTORY TRANSACTIONS

LO1

Understand that intra-entity asset transfers often create accounting effects within the financial records of affiliated companies that must be eliminated or adjusted in preparing consolidated financial statements.

As previous chapters discussed, companies that make up a business combination frequently retain their legal identities as separate operating centers and maintain their own record-keeping. Thus, inventory sales between these companies trigger the independent accounting systems of both parties. The seller duly records revenue, and the buyer simultaneously enters the purchase into its accounts. For internal reporting purposes, recording an inventory transfer as a sale/purchase provides vital data to help measure the operational efficiency of each enterprise.[3]

Despite the internal information benefits of accounting for the transaction in this manner, from a consolidated perspective neither a sale nor a purchase has occurred. *An intra-entity transfer is merely the internal movement of inventory, an event that creates no net change in the financial position of the business combination taken as a whole.* Thus, in producing consolidated financial statements, the recorded effects of these transfers are eliminated so that consolidated statements reflect only transactions with outside parties. Worksheet entries serve this purpose; they adapt the financial information reported by the separate companies to the perspective of the consolidated enterprise. The entire impact of the intra-entity transactions must be identified and then removed. Deleting the effects of the actual transfer is described here first.

LO2

Prepare the consolidation entry to eliminate the sales and purchases balances that are created by the intra-entity transfer of inventory.

The Sales and Purchases Accounts

To account for related companies as a single economic entity requires eliminating all intra-entity sales/purchases balances. For example, if Arlington Company makes an $80,000 inventory sale to Zirkin Company, an affiliated party within a business combination, both parties record the transfer in their internal records as a normal sale/purchase. The following consolidation worksheet entry is then necessary to remove the resulting balances from the externally reported figures. Cost of Goods Sold is reduced here under the assumption that the Purchases account usually is closed out prior to the consolidation process.

Consolidation Entry TI		
Sales	80,000	
Cost of Goods Sold (purchases component)		80,000
To eliminate effects of intra-entity transfer of inventory. (Labeled **"TI"** in reference to the transferred inventory.)		

[2] "Acquiring along the Value Chain," *Mergers & Acquisitions,* June–July 1996, p. 8.

[3] For all intra-entity transactions, the two parties involved view the events from different perspectives. Thus, the transfer is both a sale and a purchase, often creating both a receivable and a payable. To indicate the dual nature of such transactions, these accounts are indicated within this text as sales/purchases, receivables/payables, and so on.

> *In the preparation of consolidated financial statements, the preceding elimination must be made for all intra-entity inventory transfers.* The total recorded (intra-entity) sales figure is deleted regardless of whether the transaction was downstream (from parent to subsidiary) or upstream (from subsidiary to parent). Furthermore, any gross profit included in the transfer price does not affect the elimination. Because the entire amount of the transfer occurred between related parties, the total effect must be removed in preparing the consolidated statements.[4]

UNREALIZED GROSS PROFIT—YEAR OF TRANSFER (YEAR 1)

Removal of the sale/purchase is often just the first in a series of consolidation entries necessitated by inventory transfers. Despite the previous elimination, unrealized gross profits created by such sales can still exist in the accounting records at year-end. These profits initially result when the merchandise is priced at more than historical cost. Actual transfer prices are established in several ways, including the normal sales price of the inventory, sales price less a specified discount, or at a predetermined markup above cost. In a footnote to recent financial statements, Ford Motor Company explains that

> Intercompany sales among geographic areas consist primarily of vehicles, parts, and components manufactured by the company and various subsidiaries and sold to different entities within the consolidated group; transfer prices for these transactions are established by agreement between the affected entities.

Regardless of the method used for this pricing decision, intra-entity profits that remain unrealized at year-end must be removed in arriving at consolidated figures.

LO3

Prepare the consolidation entry to eliminate any intra-entity inventory gross profit that remains unrealized at (a) the end of the year of transfer and (b) the beginning of the subsequent period.

All Inventory Remains at Year-End

In the preceding illustration, assume that Arlington acquired or produced this inventory at a cost of $50,000 and then sold it to Zirkin, an affiliated party, at the indicated $80,000 price. From a consolidated perspective, the inventory still has a historical cost of only $50,000. However, Zirkin's records now report it as an asset at the $80,000 transfer price. In addition, because of the markup, Arlington has recorded a $30,000 gross profit as a result of this intra-entity sale. Because the transaction did not occur with an outside party, recognition of this profit is not appropriate for the combination as a whole.

Thus, although the consolidation entry **TI** shown earlier eliminated the sale/purchase figures, the $30,000 inflation created by the transfer price still exists in two areas of the individual statements:

- Ending inventory remains overstated by $30,000.
- Gross profit is artificially overstated by this same amount.

Correcting the ending inventory requires only reducing the asset. However, before decreasing gross profit, the accounts affected by the incomplete earnings process should be identified. The ending inventory total serves as a negative component within the Cost of Goods Sold computation; it represents the portion of acquired inventory that was not sold. Thus, the $30,000 overstatement of the inventory that is still held incorrectly decreases this expense (the inventory that was sold). *Despite Entry TI, the inflated ending inventory figure causes cost of goods sold to be too low and, thus, profits to be too high by $30,000.* For consolidation purposes, the expense is increased by this amount through a worksheet adjustment that properly removes the unrealized gross profit from consolidated net income.

Consequently, if all of the transferred inventory is retained by the business combination at the end of the year, the following worksheet entry also must be included to eliminate

---

[4] Alternative theoretical approaches to consolidation that advocate removing only the parent's portion of intra-entity sales/purchases when a noncontrolling interest is present can be identified. In current practice, elimination of all intra-entity sales/purchases (as shown here) appears to predominate.

Discussion Question

EARNINGS MANAGEMENT

Enron Corporation's 2001 third-quarter 10-Q report disclosed the following transaction with LJM2, a nonconsolidated special purpose entity (SPE) that was formed by Enron:

> In June 2000, LJM2 purchased dark fiber optic cable from Enron for a purchase price of $100 million. LJM2 paid Enron $30 million in cash and the balance in an interest-bearing note for $70 million. Enron recognized $67 million in pretax earnings in 2000 related to the asset sale. Pursuant to a marketing agreement with LJM2, Enron was compensated for marketing the fiber to others and providing operation and maintenance services to LJM2 with respect to the fiber. LJM2 sold a portion of the fiber to industry participants for $40 million, which resulted in Enron recognizing agency fee revenue of $20.3 million.

As investigations later discovered Enron controlled LJM2 in many ways.

The FASB ASC now requires the consolidation of SPEs (variable interest entities) that are essentially controlled by their primary beneficiary.

By selling goods to SPEs that it controlled but did not consolidate, did Enron overstate its earnings? What effect does consolidation have on the financial reporting for transactions between a firm and its controlled entities?

the effects of the seller's gross profit that remains unrealized within the buyer's ending inventory:

Consolidation Entry G—Year of Transfer (Year 1) All Inventory Remains		
Cost of Goods Sold (ending inventory component)	30,000	
Inventory (balance sheet account)		30,000
To remove unrealized gross profit created by intra-entity sale.		

This entry (labeled **G** for gross profit) reduces the consolidated Inventory account to its original $50,000 historical cost. Furthermore, increasing Cost of Goods Sold by $30,000 effectively removes the unrealized amount from recognized gross profit. Thus, this worksheet entry resolves both reporting problems created by the transfer price markup.

Only a Portion of Inventory Remains

Obviously, a company does not buy inventory to hold it for an indefinite time. It either uses the acquired items within the company's operations or resells them to unrelated, outside parties. Intra-entity profits ultimately are realized by subsequently consuming or reselling these goods. Therefore, only the transferred inventory still held at year-end continues to be recorded in the separate statements at a value more than the historical cost. For this reason, *the elimination of unrealized gross profit (Entry G) is based not on total intra-entity sales but only on the amount of transferred merchandise retained within the business at the end of the year.*

To illustrate, assume that Arlington transferred inventory costing $50,000 to Zirkin, a related company, for $80,000, thus recording a gross profit of $30,000. Assume further that by year-end Zirkin has resold $60,000 of these goods to unrelated parties but retains the other $20,000 (for resale in the following year). From the viewpoint of the consolidated company, it has now earned the profit on the $60,000 portion of the intra-entity sale and need not make an adjustment for consolidation purposes.

Conversely, any gross profit recorded in connection with the $20,000 in merchandise that remains is still a component within Zirkin's Inventory account. Because the gross profit rate was 37½ percent ($30,000 gross profit/$80,000 transfer price), this retained inventory is stated at a value $7,500 more than its original cost ($20,000 × 37½%). The required reduction

(Entry **G**) is not the entire $30,000 shown previously but only the $7,500 unrealized gross profit that remains in ending inventory.

Consolidation Entry G—Year of Transfer (Year 1) 25% of Inventory Remains (replaces previous entry)		
Cost of Goods Sold (ending inventory component)	7,500	
Inventory		7,500
To remove portion of intra-entity gross profit that is unrealized in year of transfer.		

LO4

Understand that the consolidation process for inventory transfers is designed to defer the unrealized portion of an intra-entity gross profit from the year of transfer into the year of disposal or consumption.

Unrealized Gross Profit—Year Following Transfer (Year 2)

Whenever an unrealized intra-entity profit is present in ending inventory, one further consolidation entry is eventually required. Although Entry **G** removes the gross profit from the *consolidated* inventory balances in the year of transfer, the $7,500 overstatement remains within the separate financial records of the buyer and seller. The effects of this deferred gross profit are carried into their beginning balances in the subsequent year. Hence, a worksheet adjustment is necessary in the period following the transfer. For consolidation purposes, the unrealized portion of the intra-entity gross profit must be adjusted in two successive years (from ending inventory in the year of transfer and from beginning inventory of the next period).

Referring again to Arlington's sale of inventory to Zirkin, the $7,500 unrealized gross profit is still in Zirkin's Inventory account at the start of the subsequent year. Once again, the overstatement is removed within the consolidation process but this time from the beginning inventory balance (which appears in the financial statements only as a positive component of cost of goods sold). This elimination is termed *Entry ***G***. The asterisk indicates that a previous year transfer created the intra-entity gross profits.

Consolidation Entry *G—Year Following Transfer (Year 2)		
Retained Earnings (beginning balance of seller)	7,500	
Cost of Goods Sold (beginning inventory component)		7,500
To remove unrealized gross profit from beginning figures so that it is recognized currently in the period in which the earning process is completed.		

Reducing Cost of Goods Sold (beginning inventory) through this worksheet entry increases the gross profit reported for this second year. For consolidation purposes, the gross profit on the transfer is recognized in the period in which the items are actually sold to outside parties. As shown in the following diagram, Entry **G** initially deferred the $7,500 gross profit because this amount was unrealized in the year of transfer. Entry ***G** now increases consolidated net income (by decreasing cost of goods sold) to reflect the earning process in the current year.

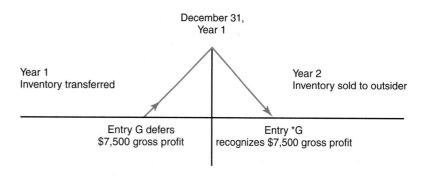

In Entry *G, removal of the $7,500 from beginning inventory (within Cost of Goods Sold) appropriately increases current income and should not pose a significant conceptual problem. However, the rationale for decreasing the seller's beginning Retained Earnings deserves further explanation. This reduction removes the unrealized gross profit (recognized by the seller in the year of transfer) so that the profit is reported in the period when it is earned. Despite the consolidation entries in Year 1, the $7,500 gain remained on this company's separate books and was closed to Retained Earnings at the end of the period. Recall that consolidation entries are never posted to the individual affiliate's books. Therefore, from a consolidated view, the buyer's Cost of Goods Sold (through the beginning inventory component) and the seller's Retained Earnings accounts as of the beginning of Year 2 contain the unrealized profit, and must both be reduced in Entry *G.[5]

Intra-Entity Beginning Inventory Profit Adjustment—Downstream Sales When Parent Uses Equity Method

The worksheet elimination of the sales/purchases balances (Entry TI) and the entry to remove the unrealized gross profit from ending Inventory in Year 1 (Entry G) are both standard, regardless of the circumstances of the consolidation. Conversely, in one specific situation, the procedure used to eliminate the intra-entity gross profit from Year 2's beginning account balances differs from the Entry *G just presented. If (1) the original transfer is downstream (made by the parent) and (2) the equity method has been applied for internal accounting purposes, the Equity in Subsidiary Earnings account replaces beginning Retained Earnings in Entry *G.

When using the equity method, the parent maintains appropriate income balances within its own individual financial records. Thus, the parent defers any unrealized gross profit at the end of Year 1 through an equity method adjustment that also decreases the Investment in Subsidiary account. With the profit deferred, the Retained Earnings of the parent/seller at the beginning of the following year is correctly stated. The parent's Retained Earnings does not contain the unrealized gross profit and needs no adjustment.

At the end of Year 2, both the Equity in Subsidiary Earnings and the Investment accounts are increased in recognition of the previously deferred intra-entity profit. The Investment account—having been decreased in Year 1 and increased in Year 2 for the intra-entity gross profit—thus no longer reflects any effects from the original deferral. For consolidation purposes, Entry *G simply transfers the income effect of the realized gross profit from the Equity in Subsidiary Earnings account to Cost of Goods Sold, appropriately increasing current consolidated income. The remaining balance in the Equity in Subsidiary Earnings account now reflects the same activity represented in the Investment account and is subsequently eliminated against the Investment account.

Consolidation Entry *G—Year Following Transfer (Year 2) (replaces previous Entry *G when transfers have been downstream and the equity method used)[6]		
Equity in Subsidiary Earnings	7,500	
Cost of Goods Sold (beginning inventory component)		7,500
To recognize the previously deferred unrealized downstream inventory gross profit as part of current year income. The Equity in Subsidiary Earnings account replaces the Retained Earnings account (used for upstream profit adjustments) when adjusting for downstream sales. The parent's Retained Earnings account has already been corrected by application of the equity method.		

---

[5] For upstream intra-entity profit in beginning inventory, the subsidiary's retained earnings remain overstated and must be adjusted through Entry *G.

[6] A widely accepted alternative to recognizing realized intra-entity inventory profits in the subsidiary's beginning inventory (downstream sale) when the parent uses the equity method (*G) is as follows:

Investment in Subsidiary	7,500	
Cost of Goods Sold		7,500

In this case, the full amount of the Equity in Subsidiary Earnings is eliminated against the Investment in Subsidiary account in Consolidation Adjustment I. In either alternative adjustment for recognizing realized intra-entity inventory profits, the final consolidated balances remain exactly the same: Equity in Subsidiary Earnings = 0, Investment in Subsidiary = 0, and Cost of Goods Sold is reduced by $7,500.

EXHIBIT 5.1
Relationship between Gross Profit Rate and Markup on Cost

In determining appropriate amounts of intra-entity profits for deferral and subsequent recognition in consolidated financial reports, two alternative—but mathematically related—profit percentages are often seen. Recalling that Gross Profit = Sales − Cost of Goods Sold, then

$$\textbf{Gross profit rate (GPR)} = \frac{\text{Gross profit}}{\text{Sales}} = \frac{MC}{1 + MC}$$

$$\textbf{Markup on cost (MC)} = \frac{\text{Gross profit}}{\text{Cost of goods sold}} = \frac{GPR}{1 - GPR}$$

Example:		
Sales (transfer price)	$1,000
Cost of goods sold	800
Gross profit	$ 200

Here the *GPR* = (200/1,000) = 20% and the *MC* = (200/800) = 25%. In most intra-entity purchases and sales, the sales (transfer) price is known and therefore the *GPR* is the simplest percentage to use to determine the amount of intra-entity profit.

Intra-entity profit = Transfer price × GPR

Instead, if the markup on cost is available, it readily converts to a *GPR* by the preceding formula. In this case (0.25/1.25) = 20%.

Finally, various markup percentages determine the dollar values for intra-entity profit deferrals. Exhibit 5.1 shows formulas for both the gross profit rate and markup on cost and the relation between the two.

· LO5

Understand the difference between upstream and downstream intra-entity transfers and how each affects the computation of noncontrolling interest balances.

Unrealized Gross Profits—Effect on Noncontrolling Interest Valuation

The worksheet entries just described appropriately account for the effects of intra-entity inventory transfers on business combinations. However, one question remains: What impact do these procedures have on the valuation of a noncontrolling interest? In regard to this issue, paragraph 810-10-45-6 of the FASB ASC states,

> The amount of intra-entity profit or loss to be eliminated in accordance with paragraph 810-10-45-1 is not affected by the existence of a noncontrolling interest. The complete elimination of the intra-entity profit or loss is consistent with the underlying assumption that consolidated financial statements represent the financial position and operating results of a single economic entity. The elimination of the intra-entity profit or loss may be allocated proportionately between the parent and noncontrolling interest.

The last sentence indicates that alternative approaches are available in computing the noncontrolling interest's share of a subsidiary's net income. According to this pronouncement, unrealized gross profits resulting from intra-entity transfers *may or may not* affect recognition of outside ownership. Because the amount attributed to a noncontrolling interest reduces consolidated net income, the handling of this issue can affect the reported profitability of a business combination.

To illustrate, assume that Large Company owns 70 percent of the voting stock of Small Company. To avoid extraneous complications, assume that no amortization expense resulted from this acquisition. Assume further that Large reports current net income (from separate operations) of $500,000 while Small earns $100,000. During the current period, intra-entity transfers of $200,000 occur with a total markup of $90,000. At the end of the year, an unrealized intra-entity gross profit of $40,000 remains within the inventory accounts.

Clearly, the consolidated net income prior to the reduction for the 30 percent noncontrolling interest is $560,000, the two income balances less the unrealized gross profit. The problem facing the accountant is the computation of the noncontrolling interest's share of Small's income. Because of the flexibility allowed by the FASB ASC, this figure may be reported as either $30,000 (30 percent of the $100,000 earnings of the subsidiary) or $18,000 (30 percent of reported income after that figure is reduced by the $40,000 unrealized gross profit).

To determine an appropriate valuation for this noncontrolling interest allocation, the relationship between an intra-entity transaction and the outside owners must be analyzed. If a transfer is downstream (the parent sells inventory to the subsidiary), a logical view would seem to be that the unrealized gross profit is that of the parent company. The parent made the original sale; therefore, the gross profit is included in its financial records. Because the subsidiary's income is unaffected, little justification exists for adjusting the noncontrolling interest to reflect the deferral of the unrealized gross profit. Consequently, in the example of Large and Small, if the transfers were downstream, the 30 percent noncontrolling interest would be $30,000 based on Small's reported income of $100,000.

In contrast, if the subsidiary sells inventory to the parent (an upstream transfer), the subsidiary's financial records would recognize the gross profit even though part of this income remains unrealized from a consolidation perspective. Because the outside owners possess their interest in the subsidiary, a reasonable conclusion would be that valuation of the noncontrolling interest is calculated on the income this company actually earned.

In this textbook, the noncontrolling interest's share of consolidated net income is computed based on *the reported income of the subsidiary after adjustment for any unrealized upstream gross profits*. Returning to Large Company and Small Company, if the $40,000 unrealized gross profit results from an upstream sale from subsidiary to parent, only $60,000 of Small's $100,000 reported income actually has been earned by the end of the year. The allocation to the noncontrolling interest is, therefore, reported as $18,000, or 30 percent of this realized income figure.

Although the noncontrolling interest figure is based here on the subsidiary's reported income adjusted for the effects of upstream intra-entity transfers, GAAP, as quoted earlier, does not require this treatment. Giving effect to upstream transfers in this calculation but not to downstream transfers is no more than an attempt to select the most logical approach from among acceptable alternatives.[7]

Intra-Entity Inventory Transfers Summarized

To assist in overcoming the complications created by intra-entity transfers, we demonstrate the consolidation process in three different ways:

- Before proceeding to a numerical example, review the impact of intra-entity transfers on consolidated figures. Ultimately, the accountant must understand how the balances reported by a business combination are derived when unrealized gross profits result from either upstream or downstream sales.

- Next, two different consolidation worksheets are produced: one for downstream transfers and the other for upstream. The various consolidation procedures used in these worksheets are explained and analyzed.

- Finally, several of the consolidation worksheet entries are shown side by side to illustrate the differences created by the direction of the transfers.

The Development of Consolidated Totals

The following summary discusses the accounts affected by intra-entity inventory transactions:

Revenues. The parent's balance is added to the subsidiary's balance, but all intra-entity transfers are then removed.

Cost of Goods Sold. The parent's balance is added to the subsidiary's balance, but all intra-entity transfers are removed. The resulting total is decreased by any beginning

---

[7] The 100 percent allocation of downstream profits to the parent affects its application of the equity method. As seen later in this chapter, in applying the equity method, the parent removes 100 percent of intra-entity profits resulting from downstream sales from its investment and equity earnings accounts rather than its percentage ownership in the subsidiary.

unrealized gross profit (thus raising net income) and increased by any ending unrealized gross profit (reducing net income).

Expenses. The parent's balance is added to the subsidiary's balance plus any amortization expense for the year recognized on the acquisition-date fair value allocations.[8]

Noncontrolling Interest in Subsidiary's Net Income. The subsidiary's reported net income is adjusted for any excess acquisition-date fair-value amortizations and the effects of unrealized gross profits on upstream transfers (but not downstream transfers) and then multiplied by the percentage of outside ownership.

Retained Earnings at the Beginning of the Year. As discussed in previous chapters, if the equity method is applied, the parent's balance mirrors the consolidated total. When any other method is used, the parent's beginning Retained Earnings must be converted to the equity method by Entry ***C.** Accruals for this purpose are based on the income actually earned by the subsidiary in previous years (reported income adjusted for any unrealized upstream gross profits).

Inventory. The parent's balance is added to the subsidiary's balance. Any unrealized gross profit remaining at the end of the current year is removed to adjust the reported balance to historical cost.

Land, Buildings, and Equipment. The parent's balance is added to the subsidiary's balance. This total is adjusted for any excess fair-value allocations and subsequent amortization.[9]

Noncontrolling Interest in Subsidiary at End of Year. The final total begins with the noncontrolling interest at the beginning of the year. This figure is based on the subsidiary's book value on that date plus its share of any unamortized acquisition-date excess fair value less any unrealized gross profits on upstream sales. The beginning balance is updated by adding the portion of the subsidiary's income assigned to these outside owners (as computed earlier) and subtracting the noncontrolling interest's share of the subsidiary's dividend payments.

Intra-Entity Inventory Transfers Illustrated

To examine the various consolidation procedures required by intra-entity inventory transfers, assume that Top Company acquires 80 percent of the voting stock of Bottom Company on January 1, 2010. The parent pays $400,000 and the acquisition-date fair value of the noncontrolling interest is $100,000. Top allocates the entire $50,000 excess fair value over book value to adjust a database owned by Bottom to fair value. The database has an estimated remaining life of 20 years.

The subsidiary reports net income of $30,000 in 2010 and $70,000 in 2011, the current year. Dividend payments are $20,000 in the first year and $50,000 in the second. Top applies the initial value method so that the parent records dividend income of $16,000 ($20,000 × 80%) and $40,000 ($50,000 × 80%) during these two years. Using the initial value method in this next example avoids the problem of computing the parent's investment account balances. However, this illustration is subsequently extended to demonstrate the changes necessary when the parent applies the equity method.

After the takeover, intra-entity inventory transfers between the two companies occurred as shown in Exhibit 5.2. A $10,000 intra-entity debt also exists as of December 31, 2011.

The 2011 consolidation of Top and Bottom is presented twice. First, the transfers are assumed to be downstream from parent to subsidiary (Exhibit 5.3). Second, consolidated figures are recomputed with the transfers being viewed as upstream (Exhibit 5.4). This distinction is significant only because of a noncontrolling interest.

---

[8] As discussed later in this chapter, worksheet adjustments remove excess depreciation following depreciable asset transfer between companies within a business combination at a price more than the book value.

[9] As discussed later in this chapter, if land, buildings, or equipment is transferred between parent and subsidiary, the separately reported balances must be returned to historical cost figures in deriving consolidated totals.

EXHIBIT 5.2
Intra-Entity Transfers

	2010	2011
Transfer prices	$80,000	$100,000
Historical cost	60,000	70,000
Gross profit	$20,000	$ 30,000
Inventory remaining at year-end (at transfer price)	$16,000	$ 20,000
Gross profit percentage	25%	30%
Gross profit remaining in year-end inventory	$ 4,000	$ 6,000

Downstream Sales

In the first example, all inventory transfers are assumed to be *downstream* from Top to Bottom. Based on that perspective, the worksheet to consolidate these two companies for the year ending December 31, 2011, is in Exhibit 5.3.

Most of the worksheet entries found in Exhibit 5.3 are described and analyzed in previous chapters of this textbook. Thus, only four of these entries are examined in detail along with the computation of the noncontrolling interests in the subsidiary's income.

Entry *G   Entry ***G** removes the unrealized gross profits carried over from the previous period. The gross profit on the $16,000 in transferred merchandise held by Bottom at the beginning of the current year was unearned and deferred in the 2010 consolidated statements. The gross profit rate (Exhibit 5.2) on these items was 25 percent ($20,000 gross profit/$80,000 transfer price), indicating an unrealized profit of $4,000 (25 percent of the remaining $16,000 in inventory). To recognize this gross profit in 2011, Entry ***G** reduces cost of goods sold (or the beginning inventory component of that expense) by that amount and Top's (as the seller of the goods) January 1, 2011, Retained Earnings. Essentially the $4,000 gross profit is removed from 2010 retained earnings and recognized in 2011 consolidated net income.

Entry ***G** creates two effects: First, last year's profits, as reflected in the seller's beginning Retained Earnings, are reduced because the $4,000 gross profit was not earned at that time. Second, the reduction in Cost of Goods Sold creates an increase in current year income. From a consolidation perspective, the gross profit is correctly recognized in 2011 when the inventory is sold to an outside party.

Entry *C   Chapter 3 introduced Entry ***C** as an initial consolidation adjustment required whenever the parent does not apply the equity method. Entry ***C** converts the parent's beginning Retained Earnings to a consolidated total. In the current illustration, Top did not accrue its portion of the 2010 increase in Bottom's book value [($30,000 income less $20,000 paid in dividends) × 80%, or $8,000] or record the $2,000 amortization expense for this same period. Because the parent recognized neither number in its financial records, the consolidation process adjusts the parent's beginning retained earnings by $6,000 (Entry ***C**). The intra-entity transfers do not affect this entry because they were downstream; the gross profits had no impact on the income the subsidiary recognized.

Entry TI   Entry **TI** eliminates the intra-entity sales/purchases for 2011. The entire $100,000 transfer recorded by the two parties during the current period is removed to arrive at consolidated figures for the business combination.

Entry G   Entry **G** defers the unrealized gross profit remaining at the end of 2011. The $20,000 in transferred merchandise (Exhibit 5.2) that Bottom has not yet sold has a gross profit rate of 30 percent ($30,000 gross profit/$100,000 transfer price); thus, the unrealized gross profit amounts to $6,000. On the worksheet, Entry **G** eliminates this overstatement in the Inventory asset balance as well as the ending inventory (negative) component of Cost of Goods Sold. Because the gross profit remains unrealized, the increase in this expense appropriately decreases consolidated income.

Noncontrolling Interest's Share of the Subsidiary's Income

In this first illustration, the intra-entity transfers are downstream. Thus, the unrealized gross profits are considered to relate solely to the parent company, creating no effect on the subsidiary or the outside ownership. For this reason, the noncontrolling interest's share of the subsidiary's

EXHIBIT 5.3   Downstream Inventory Transfers

TOP COMPANY AND BOTTOM COMPANY

Consolidation: Acquisition Method   **Consolidation Worksheet**
Investment: Initial Value Method   **For Year Ending December 31, 2011**   *Ownership: 80%*

Accounts	Top Company	Bottom Company	Consolidation Entries Debit	Consolidation Entries Credit	Noncontrolling Interest	Consolidated Totals
Income Statement						
Sales	(600,000)	(300,000)	(TI)100,000			(800,000)
Cost of goods sold	320,000	180,000	(G) 6,000	(*G) 4,000		402,000
				(TI)100,000		
Operating expenses	170,000	50,000	(E) 2,500			222,500
Dividend income	(40,000)		(I) 40,000			
Separate company net income	(150,000)	(70,000)				
Consolidated net income						(175,500)
Noncontrolling interest in Bottom Company's income					(13,500) †	13,500
Top's interest in consolidated net income						(162,000)
Statement of Retained Earnings						
Retained Earnings 1/1/11						
Top Company	(650,000)		(*G) 4,000	(*C) 6,000		(652,000)
Bottom Company		(310,000)	(S)310,000 ‡			
Net income (above)	(150,000)	(70,000)				(162,000)
Dividends paid	70,000	50,000		(I) 40,000	10,000	70,000
Retained earnings 12/31/11	(730,000)	(330,000)				(744,000)
Balance Sheet						
Cash and receivables	280,000	120,000		(P) 10,000		390,000
Inventory	220,000	160,000		(G) 6,000		374,000
Investment in Bottom	400,000		(*C) 6,000			–0–
				(S)368,000		
				(A) 38,000		
Land	410,000	200,000				610,000
Plant assets (net)	190,000	170,000				360,000
Database	–0–	–0–	(A) 47,500	(E) 2,500		45,000
Total assets	1,500,000	650,000				1,779,000
Liabilities	(340,000)	(170,000)	(P) 10,000			(500,000)
Noncontrolling interest in Bottom Company, 1/1/11				(S) 92,000		
				(A) 9,500	(101,500)	
Noncontrolling interest in Bottom Company, 12/31/11					105,000	(105,000)
Common stock	(430,000)	(150,000)	(S)150,000			(430,000)
Retained earnings 12/31/11 (above)	(730,000)	(330,000)				(744,000)
Total liabilities and equities	(1,500,000)	(650,000)	676,000	676,000		(1,779,000)

Note: Parentheses indicate a credit balance.

†Because intra-entity sales are made downstream (by the parent), the subsidiary's earned income is the $70,000 reported figure less $2,500 excess amortization with a 20% allocation to the noncontrolling interest (13,500).

‡Boxed items highlight differences with upstream transfers examined in Exhibit 5.4.

Consolidation entries:

(*G)   Removal of unrealized gross profit from beginning figures so that it can be recognized in current period. Downstream sales attributed to parent.

(*C)   Recognition of increase in book value and amortization relating to ownership of subsidiary for year prior to 2011.

(S)   Elimination of subsidiary's stockholders' equity accounts along with recognition of January 1, 2011, noncontrolling interest.

(A)   Allocation of subsidiary's fair value in excess of book value, unamortized balance as of January 1, 2011.

(I)   Elimination of intra-entity dividends recorded by parent as income.

(E)   Recognition of amortization expense for current year on database.

(P)   Elimination of intra-entity receivable/payable balances.

(TI)   Elimination of intra-entity sales/purchases balances.

(G)   Removal of unrealized gross profit from ending figures so that it can be recognized in subsequent period.

EXHIBIT 5.4   Upstream Inventory Transfers

TOP COMPANY AND BOTTOM COMPANY

Consolidation: Acquisition Method
Investment: Initial Value Method

Consolidation Worksheet
For Year Ending December 31, 2011

Ownership: 80%

Accounts	Top Company	Bottom Company	Consolidation Entries Debit	Consolidation Entries Credit	Noncontrolling Interest	Consolidated Totals
Income Statement						
Sales	(600,000)	(300,000)	(TI)100,000			(800,000)
Cost of goods sold	320,000	180,000	(G) 6,000	(*G) 4,000		402,000
				(TI)100,000		
Operating expenses	170,000	50,000	(E) 2,500			222,500
Dividend income	(40,000)		(I) 40,000			
Separate company net income	(150,000)	(70,000)				
Consolidated net income						(175,500)
Noncontrolling interest in Bottom Company's income					(13,100) †	13,100
Top's interest in consolidated net income						(162,400)
Statement of Retained Earnings						
Retained earnings 1/1/11						
Top Company	(650,000)			(*C) 2,800		(652,800)
Bottom Company		(310,000)	(*G) 4,000			
			(S)306,000 ‡			
Net income (above)	(150,000)	(70,000)				(162,400)
Dividends paid	70,000	50,000		(I) 40,000	10,000	70,000
Retained earnings 12/31/11	(730,000)	(330,000)				(745,200)
Balance Sheet						
Cash and receivables	280,000	120,000		(P) 10,000		390,000
Inventory	220,000	160,000		(G) 6,000		374,000
Investment in Bottom	400,000		(*C) 2,800			–0–
				(S)364,800		
				(A) 38,000		
Land	410,000	200,000				610,000
Plant assets (net)	190,000	170,000				360,000
Database	–0–	–0–	(A) 47,500	(E) 2,500		45,000
Total assets	1,500,000	650,000				1,779,000
Liabilities	(340,000)	(170,000)	(P) 10,000			(500,000)
Noncontrolling interest in Bottom Company, 1/1/11				(S) 91,200		
				(A) 9,500	(100,700)	
Noncontrolling interest in Bottom Company, 12/31/11					103,800	(103,800)
Common stock	(430,000)	(150,000)	(S)150,000			(430,000)
Retained earnings 12/31/11 (above)	(730,000)	(330,000)				(745,200)
Total liabilities and equities	(1,500,000)	(650,000)	668,800	668,800		(1,779,000)

Note: Parentheses indicate a credit balance.

†Because intra-entity sales were upstream, the subsidiary's $70,000 income is decreased for the $6,000 gross profit deferred into next year and increased for $4,000 gross profit deferred from the previous year. After further reduction for $2,500 excess amortization, the resulting $65,500 provides the noncontrolling interest with a $13,100 allocation (20%).

‡Boxed items highlight differences with downstream transfers examined in Exhibit 5.3.

Consolidation entries:

(*G) Removal of unrealized gross profit from beginning figures so that it can be recognized in current period. Upstream sales attributed to subsidiary.

(*C) Recognition of earned increase in book value and amortization relating to ownership of subsidiary for year prior to 2011.

(S) Elimination of adjusted stockholders' equity accounts along with recognition of January 1, 2011, noncontrolling interest.

(A) Allocation of subsidiary's fair value in excess of book value, unamortized balance as of January 1, 2011.

(I) Elimination of intra-entity dividends recorded by parent as income.

(E) Recognition of amortization expense for current year on fair value allocated to value of database.

(P) Elimination of intra-entity receivable/payable balances.

(TI) Elimination of intra-entity sales/purchases balances.

(G) Removal of unrealized gross profit from ending figures so that it can be recognized in subsequent period.

income is unaffected by the downstream intra-entity profit deferral and subsequent recognition. Therefore, Top allocates $13,500 of Bottom's income to the noncontrolling interest computed as 20 percent of $67,500 ($70,000 reported income less $2,500 current year database excess fair-value amortization).

By including these entries along with the other routine worksheet eliminations and adjustments, the accounting information generated by Top and Bottom is brought together into a single set of consolidated financial statements. However, this process does more than simply delete intra-entity transactions; it also affects reported income. A $4,000 gross profit is removed on the worksheet from 2010 figures and subsequently recognized in 2011 (Entry ***G**). A $6,000 gross profit is deferred in a similar fashion from 2011 (Entry **G**) and subsequently recognized in 2012. However, these changes do not affect the noncontrolling interest because the transfers were downstream.

Upstream Sales

A different set of consolidation procedures is necessary if the intra-entity transfers are upstream from Bottom to Top. As previously discussed, upstream gross profits are attributed to the subsidiary rather than to the parent company. Therefore, had these transfers been upstream, the $4,000 gross profit moved from 2010 into the current year (Entry ***G**) and the $6,000 unrealized gross profit deferred from 2011 into the future (Entry **G**) are both considered adjustments to Bottom's reported totals.

Tying upstream gross profits to Bottom's income complicates the consolidation process in several ways:

- Deferring the $4,000 gross profit from 2010 into 2011 dictates the adjustment of the subsidiary's beginning Retained Earnings balance (as the seller of the goods) to $306,000 rather than $310,000 found in the company's separate records on the worksheet.
- Because $4,000 of the income reported for 2010 was unearned at that time, Bottom's book value did not increase by $10,000 during the previous period (income less dividends as stated in the introduction) but only by an earned amount of $6,000.
- Bottom's earned income for the year 2011 is $65,500 rather than the $70,000 found within the company's separate financial statements. This $65,500 figure is based on adjusting the timing of the reported income to reflect the deferral and recognition of the intra-entity gross profits and excess fair-value amortization.

		Earned Income of Subsidiary—Upstream Transfers		
	Bottom's 2011 Income Less $2,500 Excess Amortization	Add: Gross Profit from Previous Period Realized in 2011	Less: Gross Profit Reported in 2011 to Be Realized in Later Period	2011 Income of Bottom Company from Consolidated Perspective
	$67,500	$4,000	$(6,000)	$65,500

Determinations of Bottom's beginning Retained Earnings (realized) to be $306,000 and its 2011 income as $65,500 are preliminary calculations made in anticipation of the consolidation process. These newly computed totals are significant because they serve as the basis for several worksheet entries. However, the subsidiary's financial records remain unaffected. In addition, because the initial value method has been applied, no change is required in any of the parent's accounts on the worksheet.

To illustrate the effects of upstream inventory transfers, in Exhibit 5.4, we consolidate the financial statements of Top and Bottom again. *The individual records of the two companies are unchanged from Exhibit 5.3: The only difference in this second worksheet is that the intra-entity transfers are assumed to have been made upstream from Bottom to Top.* This single change creates several important differences between Exhibits 5.3 and 5.4.

1. Because the intra-entity sales are made upstream, the $4,000 deferral of the beginning unrealized gross profit (Entry ***G**) is no longer a reduction in the parent company's retained

earnings, if Bottom sold the merchandise; thus, the elimination made in Exhibit 5.4 reduces that company's January 1, 2011, equity balance. Following this entry, Bottom's beginning Retained Earnings on the worksheet is $306,000, which is, as discussed earlier, the appropriate total from a consolidated perspective.

2. Because $4,000 of Bottom's 2010 income is deferred until 2011, the increase in the subsidiary's book value in the previous year is only $6,000 rather than $10,000 as reported. Consequently, conversion to the equity method (Entry *C) requires an increase of just $2,800:

$6,000 earned increase in subsidiary's book value during 2010 × 80%	$4,800
2010 amortization expense (80% × $2,500)	(2,000)
Increase in parent's beginning retained earnings (Entry *C)	$2,800

3. Within Entry S, the valuation of the initial noncontrolling interest and the portion of the parent's investment account to be eliminated differ from the previous example. This worksheet entry removes the stockholders' equity accounts of the subsidiary as of the beginning of the current year. Thus, the $4,000 reduction made to Bottom's Retained Earnings to remove the 2010 unrealized gross profit must be considered in developing Entry S. After posting Entry *G, only $456,000 remains as the subsidiary's January 1, 2011, book value (the total of Common Stock and beginning Retained Earnings accounts after adjustment for Entry *G). This figure forms the basis for the 20 percent noncontrolling interest ($91,200) and the elimination of the 80 percent parent company investment ($364,800).

4. Finally, to complete the consolidation, the noncontrolling interest's share of the subsidiary's net income is recorded on the worksheet as $13,100 computed as follows:

Bottom reported income for 2011	$70,000
Excess fair-value database amortization ($50,000/20 years)	(2,500)
2010 intra-entity gross profit recognized	4,000
2011 intra-entity gross profit deferred	(6,000)
Bottom 2011 net income adjusted	$65,500
Noncontrolling interest percentage	20%
Noncontrolling interest in Bottom's 2011 net income	$13,100

Upstream transfers affect this computation although the downstream sales in the previous example did not. Thus, the noncontrolling interest balance reported previously in the income statement in Exhibit 5.3 differs from the allocation in Exhibit 5.4.

Consolidations—Downstream versus Upstream Transfers

To help clarify the effect of downstream and upstream transfers, the worksheet entries that differ can be examined in more detail.

Downstream Transfers			Upstream Transfers		
(Exhibit 5.3)			(Exhibit 5.4)		
Entry *G			**Entry *G**		
Retained Earnings, 1/1/11—Top	4,000		Retained Earnings, 1/1/11—Bottom	4,000	
Cost of Goods Sold		4,000	Cost of Goods Sold		4,000
To remove 2010 unrealized gross profit from beginning balances of the seller.			To remove 2010 unrealized gross profit from beginning balances of the seller.		

Downstream Transfers			**Upstream Transfers**		

Entry *C

Investment in Bottom	6,000		Investment in Bottom	2,800	
Retained Earnings,			Retained Earnings,		
1/1/11—Top		6,000	1/1/11—Bottom		2,800

To convert 1/1/11 initial value figures to the equity method. Income accrual is 80% of $10,000 increase in Retained Earnings less $2,500 amortization.

To convert 1/1/11 initial value figures to the equity method. Income accrual is 80% of $6,000 increase in Retained Earnings after removal of unrealized gross profit and $2,500 amortization.

Entry S

Common stock—			Common stock—		
Bottom	150,000		Bottom	150,000	
Retained Earnings,			Retaining Earnings,		
1/1/11—Bottom	310,000		1/1/11—Bottom (as		
Investment in			adjusted)	306,000	
Bottom (80%)		368,000	Investment in		
Noncontrolling			Bottom (80%)		364,800
interest—1/1/11			Noncontrolling		
(20%)		92,000	interest—1/1/11		
			(20%)		91,200

To remove subsidiary's stockholders' equity accounts and portion of investment balance. Book value at beginning of year is appropriate.

To remove subsidiary's stockholders' equity accounts (as adjusted in Entry *G) and portion of investment balance. Adjusted book value at beginning of year is appropriate.

Noncontrolling Interest in Subsidiary's Income = $13,500. 20% of Bottom's reported income less excess database amortization.

Noncontrolling Interest in Subsidiary's Income = $13,100. 20% of Bottom's earned income (reported income after adjustment for unrealized gross profits and excess database amortization).

Effects of Alternative Investment Methods on Consolidation

Exhibits 5.3 and 5.4 utilized the initial value method. However, when using either the equity method or the partial equity method, consolidation procedures normally continue to follow the same patterns analyzed in the previous chapters of this textbook. As described earlier, though, a variation in Entry *G is required when the equity method is applied and downstream transfers have occurred. The equity in subsidiary earnings account is decreased rather than recording a reduction in the beginning retained earnings of the parent/seller with the remaining amount in equity in subsidiary earnings eliminated in Entry I. Otherwise, the specific accounting method in use creates no unique impact on the consolidation process for intra-entity transactions.

The major complication when the parent uses the equity method is not always related to a consolidation procedure. Frequently, the composition of the investment-related balances appearing on the parent's separate financial records proves to be the most complex element of the entire process. Under the equity method, the investment-related accounts are subjected to (1) income accrual, (2) amortization, (3) dividends, and (4) adjustments required by unrealized intra-entity gains. Thus, if Top Company applies the equity method and the transfers are downstream, the Investment in Bottom Company account increases from $400,000 to $414,000 by the end of 2011. For that year, the Equity in Earnings of Bottom Company account registers a $52,000 balance. Both of these totals result from the accounting shown in Exhibit 5.5.

Discussion **Question**

WHAT PRICE SHOULD WE CHARGE OURSELVES?

Slagle Corporation is a large manufacturing organization. Over the past several years, it has obtained an important component used in its production process exclusively from Harrison, Inc., a relatively small company in Topeka, Kansas. Harrison charges $90 per unit for this part:

Variable cost per unit	$40
Fixed cost assigned per unit	30
Markup	20
Total price	$90

In hope of reducing manufacturing costs, Slagle purchases all of Harrison's outstanding common stock. This new subsidiary continues to sell merchandise to a number of outside customers as well as to Slagle. Thus, for internal reporting purposes, Slagle views Harrison as a separate profit center.

A controversy has now arisen among company officials about the amount that Harrison should charge Slagle for each component. The administrator in charge of the subsidiary wants to continue the $90 price. He believes this figure best reflects the division's profitability: "If we are to be judged by our profits, why should we be punished for selling to our own parent company? If that occurs, my figures will look better if I forget Slagle as a customer and try to market my goods solely to outsiders."

In contrast, the vice president in charge of Slagle's production wants the price set at variable cost, total cost, or some derivative of these numbers. "We bought Harrison to bring our costs down. It only makes sense to reduce the transfer price; otherwise the benefits of acquiring this subsidiary are not apparent. I pushed the company to buy Harrison; if our operating results are not improved, I will get the blame."

Will the decision about the transfer price affect consolidated net income? Which method would be easiest for the company's accountant to administer? As the company's accountant, what advice would you give to these officials?

EXHIBIT 5.5
Investment Balances—
Equity Method—
Downstream Sales

Investment in Bottom Company Analysis 1/1/10 to 12/31/11		
Consideration paid (fair value) 1/1/10		$400,000
Bottom Co. reported income for 2010	$30,000	
Database amortization	(2,500)	
Bottom Co. adjusted 2010 net income	$27,500	
Top's ownership percentage	80%	
Top's share of Bottom income	$22,000	
Deferred profit from Top's 2010 downstream sales	(4,000)	
Equity in earnings of Bottom Company, 2010		$ 18,000
Top's share of Bottom Co. dividends, 2010 (80%)		(16,000)
Balance 12/31/10		$402,000
Bottom Co. reported income for 2011	$70,000	
Database amortization	(2,500)	
Bottom Co. adjusted 2011 net income	$67,500	
Top's ownership percentage	80%	
Top's share of Bottom income	$54,000	
Recognized profit from Top's 2010 downstream sales	4,000	
Deferred profit from Top's 2011 downstream sales	(6,000)	
Equity in earnings of Bottom Company, 2011		$ 52,000
Top's share of Bottom Company dividends, 2011 (80%)		(40,000)
Balance 12/31/11		$414,000

EXHIBIT 5.6
Investment Balances—
Equity Method—
Upstream Sales

Investment in Bottom Company Analysis 1/1/10 to 12/31/11		
Consideration paid (fair value) 1/1/10		$400,000
Bottom Co. reported income for 2010	$30,000	
Database amortization	(2,500)	
Deferred profit from Bottom's 2010 upstream sales	(4,000)	
Bottom Co. adjusted 2010 net income	$23,500	
Top's ownership percentage	80%	
Equity in earnings of Bottom Company, 2010		$ 18,800
Top's share of Bottom Company dividends, 2010 (80%)		(16,000)
Balance 12/31/10		$402,800
Bottom Co. reported income for 2011	$70,000	
Database amortization	(2,500)	
Recognized profit from Bottom's 2010 upstream sales	4,000	
Deferred profit from Bottom's 2011 upstream sales	(6,000)	
Bottom Co. adjusted 2011 net income	$65,500	
Top's ownership percentage	80%	
Equity in earnings of Bottom Company, 2011		$ 52,400
Top's share of Bottom Company dividends, 2011 (80%)		(40,000)
Balance 12/31/11		$415,200

If transfers are upstream, the individual investment-related accounts that the parent reports can be determined in the same manner as in Exhibit 5.5. Because of the change in direction, the gross profits are now attributed to the subsidiary. Thus, both accounts related to the investment in Bottom hold balances that vary from the totals computed earlier. The Investment in Bottom Company balance becomes $415,200, whereas the Equity in Earnings of Bottom Company account for the year is $52,400. The differences result from having upstream rather than downstream transfers. The components of these accounts are identified in Exhibit 5.6. Consolidated worksheets for downstream and upstream inventory transfers when Top uses the equity method are shown in Exhibit 5.7 and Exhibit 5.8.

Special Equity Method Procedures for Unrealized Intra-Entity Profits from Downstream Transfers

Exhibit 5.5 shows an analysis of the parent's equity method investment accounting procedures in the presence of unrealized intra-entity gross profits resulting from downstream inventory transfers. This application of the equity method differs from that presented in Chapter 1 for a significant influence (typically 20 to 50 percent ownership) investment. For significant influence investments, an investor company defers unrealized intra-entity gross profits only to the extent of its percentage ownership, regardless of whether the profits resulted from upstream or downstream transfers. In contrast, Exhibit 5.5 shows a 100 percent deferral in 2010, with a subsequent 100 percent recognition in 2011, for intra-entity gross profits resulting from Top's inventory transfers to Bottom, its 80 percent owned subsidiary.

Why the distinction? Because when control (rather than just significant influence) exists, 100 percent of all intra-entity gross profits are eventually removed from consolidated net income regardless of the direction of the underlying sale. The 100 percent intra-entity profit deferral on Top's books for downstream sales explicitly recognizes that none of the deferral will be allocated to the noncontrolling interest. As discussed previously, when the parent is the seller in an intra-entity transfer, little justification exists for it to allocate a portion of the gross profit deferral to the noncontrolling interest. In contrast, for an upstream sale, the subsidiary recognizes the gross profit on its books. Because the noncontrolling interest owns a portion of the subsidiary (but not of the parent), allocation of intra-entity gross profit deferrals and subsequent recognitions across the noncontrolling interest and the parent appear appropriate.

EXHIBIT 5.7   Downstream Inventory Transfers

TOP COMPANY AND BOTTOM COMPANY
Consolidation: Acquisition Method
Investment: Equity Method

Consolidation Worksheet
For Year Ending December 31, 2011

Ownership: 80%

Accounts	Top Company	Bottom Company	Consolidation Entries Debit	Consolidation Entries Credit	Noncontrolling Interest	Consolidated Totals
Income Statement						
Sales	(600,000)	(300,000)	(TI)100,000			(800,000)
Cost of goods sold	320,000	180,000	(G) 6,000	(*G) 4,000		402,000
				(TI) 100,000		
Operating expenses	170,000	50,000	(E) 2,500			222,500
Equity in earnings of Bottom	(52,000)		(*G) 4,000			
			(I) 48,000 ‡			–0–
Separate company net income	(162,000)	(70,000)				
Consolidated net income						(175,500)
Noncontrolling interest in Bottom Company's income					(13,500) †	13,500
Top's interest in consolidated income						(162,000)
Statement of Retained Earnings						
Retained earnings 1/1/11						
Top Company	(652,000)					(652,000)
Bottom Company		(310,000)	(S)310,000			
Net income (above)	(162,000)	(70,000)				(162,000)
Dividends paid	70,000	50,000		(D) 40,000	10,000	70,000
Retained earnings 12/31/11	(744,000)	(330,000)				(744,000)
Balance Sheet						
Cash and receivables	280,000	120,000		(P) 10,000		390,000
Inventory	220,000	160,000		(G) 6,000		374,000
Investment in Bottom	414,000		(D) 40,000	(I) 48,000		
				368,000		–0–
				(A) 38,000		
Land	410,000	200,000				610,000
Plant assets (net)	190,000	170,000				360,000
Database			(A) 47,500	(E) 2,500		45,000
Total assets	1,514,000	650,000				1,779,000
Liabilities	(340,000)	(170,000)	(P) 10,000			(500,000)
Noncontrolling interest in Bottom Company, 1/1/11				(S) 92,000		
				(A) 9,500	(101,500)	
Noncontrolling interest in Bottom Company, 12/31/11					105,000	(105,000)
Common stock	(430,000)	(150,000)	(S)150,000			(430,000)
Retained earnings 12/31/11 (above)	(744,000)	(330,000)				(744,000)
Total liabilities and equities	(1,514,000)	(650,000)	718,000	718,000		(1,779,000)

Note: Parentheses indicate a credit balance.

†Because intra-entity sales are made downstream (by the parent), the subsidiary's earned income is the $70,000 reported less $2,500 excess amortization figure with a 20% allocation to the noncontrolling interest ($13,500).

‡Boxed items highlight differences with upstream transfers examined in Exhibit 5.8.

Consolidation entries:
- (*G)   Removal of unrealized gross profit from beginning figures so that it can be recognized in current period. Downstream sales attributed to parent.
- (S)   Elimination of subsidiary's stockholders' equity accounts along with recognition of January 1, 2011, noncontrolling interest.
- (A)   Allocation of excess fair value over subsidiary's book value, unamortized balance as of January 1, 2011.
- (I)   Elimination of intra-entity income remaining after *G elimination.
- (D)   Elimination of intra-entity dividend.
- (E)   Recognition of amortization expense for current year on excess fair value allocated to database.
- (P)   Elimination of intra-entity receivable/payable balances.
- (TI)   Elimination of intra-entity sales/purchases balances.
- (G)   Removal of unrealized gross profit from ending figures so that it can be recognized in subsequent period.

EXHIBIT 5.8   **Upstream Inventory Transfers**

TOP COMPANY AND BOTTOM COMPANY

Consolidation: Acquisition Method   **Consolidation Worksheet**
Investment: Equity Method   **For Year Ending December 31, 2011**   *Ownership: 80%*

Accounts	Top Company	Bottom Company	Consolidation Entries Debit	Consolidation Entries Credit	Noncontrolling Interest	Consolidated Totals
Income Statement						
Sales	(600,000)	(300,000)	(TI)100,000			(800,000)
Cost of goods sold	320,000	180,000	(G) 6,000	(*G) 4,000		402,000
				(TI)100,000		
Operating expenses	170,000	50,000	(E) 2,500			222,500
Equity in earnings of Bottom	(52,400)			(I) 52,400 ‡		
Separate company net income	(162,400)	(70,000)				
Consolidated net income						(175,500)
Noncontrolling interest in Bottom Company's income					(13,100) †	13,100
Top's interest in consolidated net income						(162,400)
Statement of Retained Earnings						
Retained earnings 1/1/11						
Top Company	(652,800)					(652,800)
Bottom Company		(310,000)	(*G) 4,000			
			(S)306,000			
Net income (above)	(162,400)	(70,000)				(162,400)
Dividends paid	70,000	50,000		(D) 40,000	10,000	70,000
Retained earnings 12/31/11	(745,200)	(330,000)				(745,200)
Balance Sheet						
Cash and receivables	280,000	120,000		(P) 10,000		390,000
Inventory	220,000	160,000		(G) 6,000		374,000
Investment in Bottom	415,200		(D) 40,000	(I) 52,400		–0–
				(S)364,800		
				(A) 38,000		
Land	410,000	200,000				610,000
Plant assets (net)	190,000	170,000				360,000
Database			(A) 47,500	(E) 2,500		45,000
Total assets	1,515,200	650,000				1,779,000
Liabilities	(340,000)	(170,000)	(P) 10,000			(500,000)
Noncontrolling interest in Bottom Company, 1/1/11				(S) 91,200		
				(A) 9,500	(100,700)	
Noncontrolling interest in Bottom Company, 12/31/11					103,800	(103,800)
Common stock	(430,000)	(150,000)	(S)150,000			(430,000)
Retained earnings 12/31/11 (above)	(745,200)	(330,000)				(745,200)
Total liabilities and equities	(1,515,200)	(650,000)	718,400	718,400		(1,779,000)

Note: Parentheses indicate a credit balance.

†Because intra-entity sales were upstream, the subsidiary's $70,000 income is decreased for the $6,000 gross profit deferred into next year and increased for $4,000 gross profit deferred from the previous year. After further reduction for $2,500 excess amortization, the resulting $65,500 provides the noncontrolling interest with a $13,100 allocation (20%).

‡Boxed items highlight differences with downstream transfers examined in Exhibit 5.7.

Consolidation entries:

(*G)   Removal of unrealized gross profit from beginning figures so that it can be recognized in current period. Upstream sales attributed to subsidiary.

(S)   Elimination of adjusted stockholders' equity accounts along with recognition of January 1, 2011, noncontrolling interest.

(A)   Allocation of excess fair value over subsidiary's book value, unamortized balance as of January 1, 2011.

(I)   Elimination of intra-entity income.

(D)   Elimination of intra-entity dividends.

(E)   Recognition of amortization expense for current year on database.

(P)   Elimination of intra-entity receivable/payable balances.

(TI)   Elimination of intra-entity sales/purchases balances.

(G)   Removal of unrealized gross profit from ending figures so that it can be recognized in subsequent period.

INTRA-ENTITY LAND TRANSFERS

LO6

Prepare the consolidation entry to remove any unrealized gain created by the intra-entity transfer of land from the accounting records of the year of transfer and subsequent years.

Although not as prevalent as inventory transactions, intra-entity sales of other assets occur occasionally. The final two sections of this chapter examine the worksheet procedures that noninventory transfers necessitate. We first analyze land transactions and then discuss the effects created by the intra-entity sale of depreciable assets such as buildings and equipment.

Accounting for Land Transactions

The consolidation procedures necessitated by intra-entity land transfers partially parallel those for intra-entity inventory. As with inventory, the sale of land creates a series of effects on the individual records of the two companies. The worksheet process must then adjust the account balances to present all transactions from the perspective of a single economic entity.

By reviewing the sequence of events occurring in an intra-entity land sale, the similarities to inventory transfers can be ascertained as well as the unique features of this transaction.

1. The original seller of the land reports a gain (losses are rare in intra-entity asset transfers), even though the transaction occurred between related parties. At the same time, the acquiring company capitalizes the inflated transfer price rather than the land's historical cost to the business combination.
2. The gain the seller recorded is closed into Retained Earnings at the end of the year. From a consolidated perspective, this account has been artificially increased by a related party. Thus, both the buyer's Land account and the seller's Retained Earnings account continue to contain the unrealized profit.
3. The gain on the original transfer is actually earned only when the land is subsequently disposed of to an outside party. Therefore, appropriate consolidation techniques must be designed to eliminate the intra-entity gain each period until the time of resale.

Clearly, two characteristics encountered in inventory transfers also exist in intra-entity land transactions: inflated book values and unrealized gains subsequently culminated through sales to outside parties. Despite these similarities, significant differences exist. Because of the nature of the transaction, the individual companies do not use sales/purchases accounts when land is transferred. Instead, the seller establishes a separate gain account when it removes the land from its books. Because this gain is unearned, the balance has to be eliminated when preparing consolidated statements.

In addition, the subsequent resale of land to an outside party does not always occur in the year immediately following the transfer. Although inventory is normally disposed of within a relatively short time, the buyer often holds land for years if not permanently. Thus, the over-valued Land account can remain on the acquiring company's books indefinitely. As long as the land is retained, elimination of the effects of the unrealized gain (the equivalent of Entry *G in inventory transfers) must be made for each subsequent consolidation. By repeating this worksheet entry every year, the consolidated financial statements properly state both the Land and the Retained Earnings accounts.

Eliminating Unrealized Gains—Land Transfers

To illustrate these worksheet procedures, assume that Hastings Company and Patrick Company are related parties. On July 1, 2011, Hastings sold land that originally cost $60,000 to Patrick at a $100,000 transfer price. The seller reports a $40,000 gain; the buyer records the land at the $100,000 acquisition price. At the end of this fiscal period, the intra-entity effect of this transaction must be eliminated for consolidation purposes:

Consolidation Entry TL (year of transfer)		
Gain on Sale of Land	40,000	
Land		40,000
To eliminate effects of intra-entity transfer of land. (Labeled **"TL"** in reference to the transferred land.)		

This worksheet entry eliminates the unrealized gain from the 2011 consolidated statements and returns the land to its recorded value at date of transfer, for consolidated purposes. However, as with the transfer of inventory, the effects created by the original transaction remain in the financial records of the individual companies for as long as the property is held. The gain recorded by Hastings carries through to Retained Earnings while Patrick's Land account retains the inflated transfer price. *Therefore, for every subsequent consolidation until the land is eventually sold, the elimination process must be repeated.* Including the following entry on each subsequent worksheet removes the unrealized gain from the asset and from the earnings reported by the combination:

Consolidation Entry *GL (every year following transfer)		
Retained Earnings (beginning balance of seller)	40,000	
Land		40,000
To eliminate effects of intra-entity transfer of land made in a previous year. (Labeled "***GL**" in reference to the gain on a land transfer occurring in a prior year.)		

Note that the reduction in Retained Earnings is changed to an increase in the investment account when the original sale is downstream and the parent has applied the equity method. In that specific situation, equity method adjustments have already corrected the timing of the parent's unrealized gain. Removing the gain has created a reduction in the investment account that is appropriately allocated to the subsidiary's Land account on the worksheet. Conversely, if sales were upstream, the Retained Earnings of the seller (the subsidiary) continue to be overstated even if the parent applies the equity method.

One final consolidation concern exists in accounting for intra-entity transfers of land. If the property is ever sold to an outside party, the company making the sale records a gain or loss based on its recorded book value. However, this cost figure is actually the internal transfer price. The gain or loss being recognized is incorrect for consolidation purposes; it has not been computed by comparison to the land's historical cost. Again, the separate financial records fail to reflect the transaction from the perspective of the single economic entity.

Therefore, if the company eventually sells the land, it must recognize the gain deferred at the time of the original transfer. It has finally earned this profit by selling the property to outsiders. On the worksheet, the gain is removed one last time from beginning Retained Earnings (or the investment account, if applicable). In this instance, though, the entry is completed by reclassifying the amount as a realized gain. The timing of income recognition has been switched from the year of transfer into the fiscal period in which the land is sold to the unrelated party.

Returning to the previous illustration, Hastings acquired land for $60,000 and sold it to Patrick, a related party, for $100,000. Consequently, the $40,000 unrealized gain was eliminated on the consolidation worksheet in the year of transfer as well as in each succeeding period. However, if this land is subsequently sold to an outside party for $115,000, Patrick recognizes only a $15,000 gain. From the viewpoint of the business combination, the land (having been bought for $60,000) was actually sold at a $55,000 gain. To correct the reporting, the following consolidation entry must be made in the year that the property is sold to the unrelated party. This adjustment increases the $15,000 gain recorded by Patrick to the consolidated balance of $55,000:

Consolidation Entry *GL (year of sale to outside party)		
Retained Earnings (Hastings)	40,000	
Gain on Sale of Land		40,000
To remove intra-entity gain from year of transfer so that total profit can be recognized in the current period when land is sold to an outside party.		

As in the accounting for inventory transfers, the entire consolidation process demonstrated here accomplishes two major objectives:

1. Reports historical cost for the transferred land for as long as it remains within the business combination.
2. Defers income recognition until the land is sold to outside parties.

Recognizing the Effect on Noncontrolling Interest Valuation—Land Transfers

The preceding discussion of intra-entity land transfers ignores the possible presence of a non-controlling interest. In constructing financial statements for an economic entity that includes outside ownership, the guidelines already established for inventory transfers remain applicable.

If the original sale was a *downstream* transaction, neither the annual deferral nor the eventual recognition of the unrealized gain has any effect on the noncontrolling interest. The rationale for this treatment, as previously indicated, is that profits from downstream transfers relate solely to the parent company.

Conversely, if the transfer is made *upstream,* deferral and recognition of gains are attributed to the subsidiary and, hence, to the valuation of the noncontrolling interest. As with inventory, all noncontrolling interest balances are computed on the reported earnings of the subsidiary after adjustment for any upstream transfers.

To reiterate, the accounting consequences stemming from land transfers are these:

1. In the year of transfer, any unrealized gain is deferred and the Land account is reduced to historical cost. When an upstream sale creates the gain, the amount also is excluded in calculating the noncontrolling interest's share of the subsidiary's net income for that year.
2. Each year thereafter, the unrealized gain will be removed from the seller's beginning Retained Earnings. If the transfer was upstream, eliminating this earlier gain directly affects the balances recorded within both Entry ***C** (if conversion to the equity method is required) and Entry **S.** The additional equity accrual (Entry ***C,** if needed) as well as the elimination of beginning Stockholders' Equity (Entry **S**) must be based on the newly adjusted balance in the subsidiary's Retained Earnings. This deferral process also has an impact on the noncontrolling interest's share of the subsidiary's income, but only in the year of transfer and the eventual year of sale.
3. If the land is ever sold to an outside party, the original gain is earned and must be reported by the consolidated entity.

INTRA-ENTITY TRANSFER OF DEPRECIABLE ASSETS

LO7

Prepare the consolidation entries to remove the effects of upstream and downstream intra-entity fixed asset transfers across affiliated entities.

Just as related parties can transfer land, the intra-entity sale of a host of other assets is possible. Equipment, patents, franchises, buildings, and other long-lived assets can be involved. Accounting for these transactions resembles that demonstrated for land sales. However, the subsequent calculation of depreciation or amortization provides an added challenge in the development of consolidated statements.[10]

Deferral of Unrealized Gains

When faced with intra-entity sales of depreciable assets, the accountant's basic objective remains unchanged: *to defer unrealized gains to establish both historical cost balances and recognize appropriate income within the consolidated statements.* More specifically, accountants defer gains created by these transfers until such time as the subsequent use or resale of the asset consummates the original transaction. For inventory sales, the culminating disposal normally occurs currently or in the year following the transfer. In contrast, transferred land is quite often never resold, thus permanently deferring the recognition of the intra-entity profit.

For depreciable asset transfers, the ultimate realization of the gain normally occurs in a different manner; the property's use within the buyer's operations is reflected through depreciation. Recognition of this expense reduces the asset's book value every year and, hence, the overvaluation within that balance.

The depreciation systematically eliminates the unrealized gain not only from the asset account but also from Retained Earnings. For the buyer, excess expense results each year because the computation is based on the inflated transfer cost. This depreciation is then closed annually into Retained Earnings. *From a consolidated perspective, the extra expense gradually*

---

[10] To avoid redundancy within this analysis, all further references are made to depreciation expense alone, although this discussion is equally applicable to the amortization of intangible assets and the depletion of wasting assets.

offsets the unrealized gain within this equity account. In fact, over the life of the asset, the depreciation process eliminates all effects of the transfer from both the asset balance and the Retained Earnings account.

Depreciable Asset Transfers Illustrated

To examine the consolidation procedures required by the intra-entity transfer of a depreciable asset, assume that Able Company sells equipment to Baker Company at the current market value of $90,000. Able originally acquired the equipment for $100,000 several years ago; since that time, it has recorded $40,000 in accumulated depreciation. The transfer is made on January 1, 2010, when the equipment has a 10-year remaining life.

Year of Transfer

The 2010 effects on the separate financial accounts of the two companies can be quickly enumerated:

1. Baker, as the buyer, enters the equipment into its records at the $90,000 transfer price. However, from a consolidated view, the $60,000 book value ($100,000 cost less $40,000 accumulated depreciation) is still appropriate.
2. Able, as the seller, reports a $30,000 profit, although the combination has not yet earned anything. Able then closes this gain into its Retained Earnings account at the end of 2010.
3. Assuming application of the straight-line depreciation method with no salvage value, Baker records expense of $9,000 at the end of 2010 ($90,000 transfer price/10 years). The buyer recognizes this amount rather than the $6,000 depreciation figure applicable to the consolidated entity ($60,000 book value/10 years).

To report these events as seen by the business combination, both the $30,000 unrealized gain and the $3,000 overstatement in depreciation expense must be eliminated on the worksheet. For clarification purposes, two separate consolidation entries for 2010 follow. However, they can be combined into a single adjustment:

Consolidation Entry TA (year of transfer)

Gain on Sale of Equipment	30,000	
Equipment	10,000	
Accumulated Depreciation		40,000

To remove unrealized gain and return equipment accounts to balances based on original historical cost. (Labeled **"TA"** in reference to transferred asset.)

Consolidation Entry ED (year of transfer)

Accumulated Depreciation	3,000	
Depreciation Expense		3,000

To eliminate overstatement of depreciation expense caused by inflated transfer price. (Labeled **"ED"** in reference to excess depreciation.) *Entry must be repeated for all 10 years of the equipment's life.*

From the viewpoint of a single entity, these entries accomplish several objectives:[11]

- Reinstate the asset's historical cost of $100,000.
- Return the January 1, 2010, book value to the appropriate $60,000 figure by recognizing accumulated depreciation of $40,000.

[11] If the worksheet uses only one account for a net depreciated asset, this entry would have been

Gain on sale	30,000	
Equipment (net)		30,000

To reduce the 90,000 to original 60,000 book value at date of transfer rather than reinstating original balances.

- Eliminate the $30,000 unrealized gain recorded by Able so that this intra-entity profit does not appear in the consolidated income statement.
- Reduce depreciation for the year from $9,000 to $6,000, the appropriate expense based on historical cost.

In the year of the intra-entity depreciable asset transfer, the preceding consolidation entries **TA** and **ED** are applicable regardless of whether the transfer was upstream or downstream. They are likewise applicable regardless of whether the parent applies the equity method, initial value method, or partial equity method of accounting for its investment. As discussed subsequently, however, in the years following the intra-entity transfer, a slight modification must be made to the consolidation entry *TA when the equity method is applied and the transfer is downstream.

Years Following Transfer

Again, the preceding worksheet entries do not actually remove the effects of the intra-entity transfer from the individual records of these two organizations. Both the unrealized gain and the excess depreciation expense remain on the separate books and are closed into Retained Earnings of the respective companies at year-end. Similarly, the Equipment account with the related accumulated depreciation continues to hold balances based on the transfer price, not historical cost. *Thus, for every subsequent period, the separately reported figures must be adjusted on the worksheet to present the consolidated totals from a single entity's perspective.*

To derive worksheet entries at any future point, the balances in the accounts of the individual companies must be ascertained and compared to the figures appropriate for the business combination. As an illustration, the separate records of Able and Baker two years after the transfer (December 31, 2011) follow. Consolidated totals are calculated based on the original historical cost of $100,000 and accumulated depreciation of $40,000.

Account	Individual Records	Consolidated Perspective	Worksheet Adjustments
Equipment 12/31/11	$90,000	$100,000	$10,000
Accumulated Depreciation 12/31/11	(18,000)	(52,000)*	(34,000)
Depreciation Expense 12/31/11	9,000	6,000	(3,000)
1/1/11 Retained Earnings effect	(21,000)†	6,000	27,000

Note: Parentheses indicate a credit.
*Accumulated depreciation before transfer $(40,000) plus 2 years × $(6,000).
† Intra-entity transfer gain $(30,000) less one year's depreciation of $9,000.

Because the transfer's effects continue to exist in the separate financial records, the various accounts must be corrected in each succeeding consolidation. However, the amounts involved must be updated every period because of the continual impact that depreciation has on these balances. As an example, to adjust the individual figures to the consolidated totals derived earlier, the 2011 worksheet must include the following entries:

Consolidation Entry *TA (year following transfer)

Equipment	10,000	
Retained Earnings, 1/1/11 (Able)	27,000	
Accumulated Depreciation		37,000

To return the Equipment account to original historical cost and correct the 1/1/11 balances of Retained Earnings and Accumulated Depreciation.

Consolidation Entry ED (year following transfer)		
Accumulated Depreciation	3,000	
Depreciation Expense		3,000
To remove excess depreciation expense on the intra-entity transfer price and adjust Accumulated Depreciation to its correct 12/31/11 balance.		
Note that the $34,000 increase in 12/31/11 consolidated Accumulated Depreciation is accomplished by a $37,000 credit in Entry ***TA** and a $3,000 debit in Entry **ED.**		

Although adjustments of the asset and depreciation expense remain constant, the change in beginning Retained Earnings and Accumulated Depreciation varies with each succeeding consolidation. At December 31, 2010, the individual companies closed out both the unrealized gain of $30,000 and the initial $3,000 overstatement of depreciation expense. Therefore, as reflected in Entry ***TA,** the beginning Retained Earnings account for 2011 is overvalued by a net amount of only $27,000 rather than $30,000. *Over the life of the asset, the unrealized gain in retained earnings will be systematically reduced to zero as excess depreciation expense ($3,000) is closed out each year.* Hence, on subsequent consolidation worksheets, the beginning Retained Earnings account decreases by this amount: $27,000 in 2011, $24,000 in 2012, and $21,000 in the following period. This reduction continues until the effect of the unrealized gain no longer exists at the end of 10 years.

If this equipment is ever resold to an outside party, the remaining portion of the gain is considered earned. As in the previous discussion of land, the intra-entity profit that exists at that date must be recognized on the consolidated income statement to arrive at the appropriate amount of gain or loss on the sale.

Depreciable Intra-Entity Asset Transfers—Downstream Transfers When the Parent Uses the Equity Method

A slight modification to consolidation entry ***TA** is required when the intra-entity depreciable asset transfer is downstream and the parent uses the equity method. In applying the equity method, the parent adjusts its book income for both the original transfer gain and periodic depreciation expense adjustments. Thus, in downstream intra-entity transfers when the equity method is used, from a consolidated view, the book value of the parent's Retained Earnings balance has been already reduced for the gain. Therefore, continuing with the previous example, the following worksheet consolidation entries would be made for a downstream sale assuming that (1) Able is the parent and (2) Able has applied the equity method to account for its investment in Baker.

Consolidation Entry *TA (year following transfer)		
Equipment	10,000	
Investment in Baker	27,000	
Accumulated Depreciation		37,000

Consolidation Entry ED (year following transfer)		
Accumulated Depreciation	3,000	
Depreciation Expense		3,000

In Entry ***TA,** note that the Investment in Baker account replaces the parent's Retained Earnings. The debit to the investment account effectively allocates the write-down necessitated by the intra-entity transfer to the appropriate subsidiary equipment and accumulated depreciation accounts.

Effect on Noncontrolling Interest Valuation— Depreciable Asset Transfers

Because of the lack of official guidance, no easy answer exists as to the assignment of any income effects created within the consolidation process. Consistent with the previous sections of this chapter, all income is assigned here to the original seller. In Entry *TA, for example, the beginning Retained Earnings account of Able (the seller) is reduced. Both the unrealized gain on the transfer and the excess depreciation expense subsequently recognized are assigned to that party.

Thus, again, downstream sales are assumed to have no effect on any noncontrolling interest values. The parent rather than the subsidiary made the sale. Conversely, the impact on income created by upstream sales must be considered in computing the balances attributed to these outside owners. Currently, this approach is one of many acceptable alternatives. However, in its future deliberations on consolidation policies and procedures, the FASB could mandate a specific allocation pattern.

Summary

1. The transfer of assets, especially inventory, between the members of a business combination is a common practice. In producing consolidated financial statements, any effects on the separate accounting records created by such transfers must be removed because the transactions did not occur with an outside, unrelated party.

2. Inventory transfers are the most prevalent form of intra-entity asset transaction. Despite being only a transfer, one company records a sale while the other reports a purchase. These balances are reciprocals that must be offset on the worksheet in the process of producing consolidated figures.

3. Additional accounting problems result if inventory is transferred at a markup. Any portion of the merchandise still held at year-end is valued at more than historical cost because of the inflation in price. Furthermore, the gross profit that the seller reports on these goods is unrealized from a consolidation perspective. Thus, this gross profit must be removed from the ending Inventory account, a figure that appears as an asset on the balance sheet and as a negative component within cost of goods sold.

4. Unrealized inventory gross profits also create a consolidation problem in the year following the transfer. Within the separate accounting systems, the seller closes the gross profit to Retained Earnings. The buyer's ending Inventory balance becomes the next period's beginning balance (within Cost of Goods Sold). Therefore, the inflation must be removed again but this time in the subsequent year. The seller's beginning Retained Earnings is decreased to eliminate the unrealized gross profit while Cost of Goods Sold is reduced to remove the overstatement from the beginning inventory component. Through this process, the intra-entity profit is deferred from the year of transfer so that recognition can be made at the point of disposal or consumption.

5. The deferral and subsequent realization of intra-entity gross profits raise a question concerning the valuation of noncontrolling interest balances: Does the change in the period of recognition alter these calculations? Although the issue is currently under debate, no formal answer to this question is yet found in official accounting pronouncements. In this textbook, the deferral of profits from upstream transfers (from subsidiary to parent) is assumed to affect the noncontrolling interest whereas downstream transactions (from parent to subsidiary) do not. When upstream transfers are involved, noncontrolling interest values are based on the earned figures remaining after adjustment for any unrealized profits.

6. Inventory is not the only asset that can be sold between the members of a business combination. For example, transfers of land sometimes occur. Again, if the price exceeds original cost, the buyer's records state the asset at an inflated value while the seller recognizes an unrealized gain. As with inventory, the consolidation process must return the asset's recorded balance to cost while deferring the gain. Repetition of this procedure is necessary in every consolidation for as long as the land remains within the business combination.

7. The consolidation process required by the intra-entity transfer of depreciable assets differs somewhat from that demonstrated for inventory and land. Unrealized gain created by the transaction must still be eliminated along with the asset's overstatement. However, because of subsequent depreciation, these adjustments systematically change from period to period. Following the transfer, the buyer computes depreciation based on the new inflated transfer price. Thus, an expense that reduces the carrying value of the asset at a rate in excess of appropriate depreciation is recorded; the book value moves closer to the historical cost figure each time that depreciation is recorded. Additionally, because the

excess depreciation is closed annually to Retained Earnings, the overstatement of the equity account resulting from the unrealized gain is constantly reduced. To produce consolidated figures at any point in time, the remaining inflation in these figures (as well as in the current depreciation expense) must be determined and removed.

Comprehensive Illustration

PROBLEM

(*Estimated Time: 45 to 65 Minutes*) On January 1, 2009, Daisy Company acquired 80 percent of Rose Company for $594,000 in cash. Rose's total book value on that date was $610,000 and the fair value of the noncontrolling interest was $148,500. The newly acquired subsidiary possessed a trademark (10-year remaining life) that, although unrecorded on Rose's accounting records, had a fair value of $75,000. Any remaining excess acquisition-date fair value was attributed to goodwill.

Daisy decided to acquire Rose so that the subsidiary could furnish component parts for the parent's production process. During the ensuing years, Rose sold inventory to Daisy as follows:

Year	Cost to Rose Company	Transfer Price	Gross Profit Rate	Transferred Inventory Still Held at End of Year (at transfer price)
2009	$100,000	$140,000	28.6%	$20,000
2010	100,000	150,000	33.3	30,000
2011	120,000	160,000	25.0	68,000

Any transferred merchandise that Daisy retained at a year-end was always put into production during the following period.

On January 1, 2010, Daisy sold Rose several pieces of equipment that had a 10-year remaining life and were being depreciated on the straight-line method with no salvage value. This equipment was transferred at an $80,000 price, although it had an original $100,000 cost to Daisy and a $44,000 book value at the date of exchange.

On January 1, 2011, Daisy sold land to Rose for $50,000, its fair value at that date. The original cost had been only $22,000. By the end of 2011, Rose had made no payment for the land.

The following separate financial statements are for Daisy and Rose as of December 31, 2011. Daisy has applied the equity method to account for this investment.

	Daisy Company	Rose Company
Sales	$ (900,000)	$ (500,000)
Cost of goods sold	598,000	300,000
Operating expenses	210,000	80,000
Gain on sale of land	(28,000)	–0–
Income of Rose Company	(60,000)	–0–
Net income	$ (180,000)	$ (120,000)
Retained earnings, 1/1/11	$ (620,000)	$ (430,000)
Net income	(180,000)	(120,000)
Dividends paid	55,000	50,000
Retained earnings, 12/31/11	$ (745,000)	$ (500,000)
Cash and accounts receivable	$ 348,000	$ 410,000
Inventory	430,400	190,000
Investment in Rose Company	737,600	–0–
Land	454,000	280,000
Equipment	270,000	190,000
Accumulated depreciation	(180,000)	(50,000)
Total assets	$ 2,060,000	$ 1,020,000
Liabilities	(715,000)	(120,000)
Common stock	(600,000)	(400,000)
Retained earnings, 12/31/11	(745,000)	(500,000)
Total liabilities and equities	$(2,060,000)	$(1,020,000)

Required

Answer the following questions:

a. By how much did Rose's book value increase during the period from January 1, 2009, through December 31, 2010?

b. During the initial years after the takeover, what annual amortization expense was recognized in connection with the acquisition-date excess of fair value over book value?

c. What amount of unrealized gross profit exists within the parent's inventory figures at the beginning and at the end of 2011?

d. Equipment has been transferred between the companies. What amount of additional depreciation is recognized in 2011 because of this transfer?

e. The parent reports Income of Rose Company of $60,000 for 2011. How was this figure calculated?

f. Without using a worksheet, determine consolidated totals.

g. Prepare the worksheet entries required at December 31, 2011, by the transfers of inventory, land, and equipment.

SOLUTION

a. The subsidiary's book value on the date of purchase was given as $610,000. At the beginning of 2011, the company's common stock and retained earnings total is $830,000 ($400,000 and $430,000, respectively). In the previous years, Rose's book value has apparently increased by $220,000 ($830,000 − $610,000).

b. To determine amortization, an allocation of Daisy's acquisition-date fair value must first be made. The $75,000 allocation needed to show Daisy's equipment at fair value leads to additional annual expense of $7,500 for the initial years of the combination. The $57,500 assigned to goodwill is not subject to amortization.

Acquisition-Date Fair-Value Allocation and Excess Amortization Schedule	
Consideration paid by Daisy for 80% of Rose	$ 594,000
Noncontrolling interest (20%) fair value	148,500
Rose's fair value at acquisition date	$ 742,500
Book value of Rose Company	(610,000)
Excess fair value over book value	$ 132,500

		Life (Years)	Annual Excess Amortizations	Excess Amortizations 2009–2011	Unamortized Value, 12/31/11
Trademark	$ 75,000	10	$7,500	$22,500	$52,500
Goodwill	57,500		–0–	–0–	57,500
Totals	$132,500		$7,500	$22,500	

c. Of the inventory transferred to Daisy during 2010, $30,000 is still held at the beginning of 2011. This merchandise contains an unrealized gross profit of $10,000 ($30,000 × 33.3% gross profit rate for that year). At year-end, $17,000 ($68,000 remaining inventory × 25% gross profit rate) is viewed as an unrealized gross profit.

d. Additional depreciation for the net addition of 2011 is $3,600. Equipment with a book value of $44,000 was transferred at a price of $80,000. The net of $36,000 to this asset's account balances would be written off over 10 years for an extra $3,600 per year during the consolidation process.

e. According to the separate statements given, the subsidiary reports net income of $120,000. However, in determining the income allocation between the parent and the noncontrolling interest, this reported figure must be adjusted for the effects of *any upstream transfers*. Because Rose sold the inventory upstream to Daisy, the $10,000 net profit deferred in requirement (c) from 2010 into the current period is attributed to the subsidiary (as the seller). Likewise, the $17,000 unrealized net profit at year-end is viewed as a reduction in Rose's income.

All other transfers are downstream and not considered to have an effect on the subsidiary. Therefore, the Equity Income of Rose Company balance can be verified as follows:

Rose Company's reported income—2011	$120,000
Recognition of 2010 unrealized gross profit	10,000
Deferral of 2011 unrealized gross profit	(17,000)
Excess amortization expense—2011 (see requirement [b])	(7,500)
Earned income of subsidiary from consolidated perspective	105,500
Parent's ownership percentage	80%
Equity income accrual	$ 84,400
Adjustments attributed to parent's ownership	
Deferral of unrealized gain—land	(28,000)
Removal of excess depreciation (see requirement [d])	3,600
Equity income of Rose Company—2011	$ 60,000

f. Each of the 2011 consolidated totals for this business combination can be determined as follows:

Sales = $1,240,000. The parent's balance is added to the subsidiary's balance less the $160,000 in intra-entity transfers for the period.

Cost of Goods Sold = $745,000. The computation begins by adding the parent's balance to the subsidiary's balance less the $160,000 in intra-entity transfers for the period. The $10,000 unrealized gross profit from the previous year is deducted to recognize this income currently. Next, the $17,000 ending unrealized gross profit is added to cost of goods sold to defer the income until a later year when the goods are sold to an outside party.

Operating Expenses = $293,900. The parent's balance is added to the subsidiary's balance. Annual excess fair-value amortization of $7,500 (see requirement [b]) is also included. Excess depreciation of $3,600 resulting from the transfer of equipment (see requirement [e]) is removed.

Gain on Sale of Land = –0–. This amount is eliminated for consolidation purposes because the transaction was intra-entity.

Income of Rose Company = –0–. The equity income figure is removed so that the subsidiary's actual revenues and expenses can be included in the financial statements without double-counting.

Noncontrolling Interest in Subsidiary's Income = $21,100. Requirement (e) shows the subsidiary's earned income from a consolidated perspective as $105,500 after adjustments for unrealized upstream gains and excess fair-value amortization. Because outsiders hold 20 percent of the subsidiary, a $21,100 allocation ($105,500 × 20%) is made.

Consolidated Net Income = $201,100 computed as Sales less Cost of Goods Sold and Operating Expenses. The consolidated net income is then distributed: $21,100 to the noncontrolling interest and $180,000 to the parent company owners.

Retained Earnings, 1/1/11 = $620,000. The equity method has been applied; therefore, the parent's balance equals the consolidated total.

Dividends Paid = $55,000. Only the amount the parent paid is shown in the consolidated statements. Distributions from the subsidiary to the parent are eliminated as intra-entity transfers. Any payment to the noncontrolling interest reduces the ending balance attributed to these outside owners.

Cash and Accounts Receivable = $708,000. The two balances are added after removal of the $50,000 intra-entity receivable created by the transfer of land.

Inventory = $603,400. The two balances are added after removal of the $17,000 ending unrealized gross profit (see requirement [c]).

Investment in Rose Company = –0–. The investment balance is eliminated so that the actual assets and liabilities of the subsidiary can be included.

Land = $706,000. The two balances are added. The $28,000 unrealized gain created by the transfer is removed.

Equipment = $480,000. The two balances are added. Because of the intra-entity transfer, $20,000 must also be included to adjust the $80,000 transfer price to the original $100,000 cost of the asset.

Accumulated Depreciation = $278,800. The balances are combined and adjusted for $52,400 to reinstate the historical balance for the equipment transferred across affiliates ($56,000 written off at date of transfer less $3,600 for the previous year's depreciation on the intra-entity gain). Then, an additional $3,600 is removed for the current year's depreciation on the intra-entity gain.

Trademark = $52,500. The amount from the original $75,000 acquisition-date excess fair-value allocation less 3 years' amortization at $7,500 per year.

Goodwill = $57,500. The amount from the original allocation of the Rose's acquisition-date fair value.

Total Assets = $2,328,600. This figure is a summation of the preceding consolidated assets.

Liabilities = $785,000. The two balances are added after removal of the $50,000 intra-entity payable created by the transfer of land.

Noncontrolling Interest in Subsidiary, 12/31/11 = $198,600. This figure is composed of several different balances:

Rose 20% book value at 1/1/11	$164,000
20% of 1/1/11 unamortized excess fair-value allocation for Rose's net identifiable assets and goodwill ($117,500 × 20%)	23,500
Noncontrolling interest at 1/1/11	$187,500
2011 Rose income allocation	21,100
Noncontrolling interest share of Rose dividends	(10,000)
December 31, 2011, balance	$198,600

Common Stock = $600,000. Only the parent company balance is reported within the consolidated statements.

Retained Earnings, 12/31/11 = $745,000. The retained earnings amount is found by adding consolidated net income to the beginning Retained Earnings balance and then subtracting the dividends paid. All of these figures have been computed previously.

Total Liabilities and Equities = $2,328,600. This figure is the summation of all consolidated liabilities and equities.

g.

Consolidation Worksheet Entries
Intra-Entity Transactions
December 31, 2011

Inventory

Entry *G

Retained Earnings, 1/1/11—Subsidiary	10,000	
Cost of Goods Sold		10,000

To remove 2010 unrealized gross profit from beginning balances of the current year. Because transfers were upstream, retained earnings of the subsidiary (as the original seller) are being reduced. Balance is computed in requirement (c).

Entry TI

Sales	160,000	
Cost of Goods Sold		160,000

To eliminate current year intra-entity transfer of inventory.

Entry G

Cost of Goods Sold	17,000	
Inventory		17,000

To remove 2011 unrealized gross profit from ending accounts of the current year. Balance is computed in requirement (c).

Land

Entry TL

Gain on Sale of Land	28,000	
Land		28,000

To eliminate gross profit created on first day of current year by an intra-entity transfer of land.

Equipment

Entry *TA

Equipment	20,000	
Investment in Rose Company	32,400	
Accumulated Depreciation		52,400

To remove unrealized gross profit (as of January 1, 2011) created by intra-entity transfer of equipment and to adjust equipment and accumulated depreciation to historical cost figures.

Equipment is increased from the $80,000 transfer price to $100,000 cost.

Accumulated depreciation of $56,000 was eliminated at time of transfer. Excess depreciation of $3,600 per year has been recorded for the prior year ($3,600); thus, the accumulated depreciation is now only $52,400 less than the cost-based figure.

The unrealized gain on the transfer was $36,000 ($80,000 less $44,000). That figure has now been reduced by one year of excess depreciation ($3,600). Because the parent used the equity method and this transfer was downstream, the adjustment here is to the investment account rather than the parent's beginning Retained Earnings.

Entry ED

Accumulated Depreciation	3,600	
Operating Expenses (depreciation)		3,600

To eliminate the current year overstatement of depreciation created by inflated transfer price.

Questions

1. Intra-entity transfers between the component companies of a business combination are quite common. Why do these intra-entity transactions occur so frequently?

2. Barker Company owns 80 percent of the outstanding voting stock of Walden Company. During the current year, intra-entity sales amount to $100,000. These transactions were made with a gross profit rate of 40 percent of the transfer price. In consolidating the two companies, what amount of these sales would be eliminated?

3. Padlock Corp. owns 90 percent of Safeco, Inc. During the year, Padlock sold 3,000 locking mechanisms to Safeco for $900,000. By the end of the year, Safeco had sold all but 500 of the locking mechanisms to outside parties. Padlock marks up the cost of its locking mechanisms by 60 percent in computing its sales price to affiliated and nonaffiliated customers. How much intra-entity profit remains in Safeco's inventory at year-end?

4. How are unrealized inventory gross profits created, and what consolidation entries does the presence of these gains necessitate?

5. James, Inc., sells inventory to Matthews Company, a related party, at James's standard markup. At the current fiscal year-end, Matthews still holds some portion of this inventory. If consolidated financial statements are prepared, why are worksheet entries required in two different fiscal periods?

6. How do intra-entity profits present in any year affect the noncontrolling interest calculations?

7. A worksheet is being developed to consolidate Williams, Incorporated, and Brown Company. These two organizations have made considerable intra-entity transactions. How would the consolidation

process be affected if these transfers were downstream? How would the consolidation process be affected if these transfers were upstream?

8. King Company owns a 90 percent interest in the outstanding voting shares of Pawn Company. No excess fair-value amortization resulted from the acquisition. Pawn reports a net income of $110,000 for the current year. Intra-entity sales occur at regular intervals between the two companies. Unrealized gross profits of $30,000 were present in the beginning inventory balances, whereas $60,000 in similar gross profits were recorded at year-end. What is the noncontrolling interest's share of the subsidiary's net income?

9. When a subsidiary sells inventory to a parent, the intra-entity profit is removed from the subsidiary's income and reduces the income allocation to the noncontrolling interest. Is the profit permanently eliminated from the noncontrolling interest, or is it merely shifted from one period to the next? Explain.

10. The consolidation process applicable when intra-entity land transfers have occurred differs somewhat from that used for intra-entity inventory sales. What differences should be noted?

11. A subsidiary sells land to the parent company at a significant gain. The parent holds the land for two years and then sells it to an outside party, also for a gain. How does the business combination account for these events?

12. Why does an intra-entity sale of a depreciable asset (such as equipment or a building) require subsequent adjustments to depreciation expense within the consolidation process?

13. If a seller makes an intra-entity sale of a depreciable asset at a price above book value, the seller's beginning Retained Earnings is reduced when preparing each subsequent consolidation. Why does the amount of the adjustment change from year to year?

Problems

LO1

1. What is the primary reason we defer financial statement recognition of gross profits on intra-entity sales for goods that remain within the consolidated entity at year end?
    a. Revenues and COGS must be recognized for all intra-entity sales regardless of whether the sales are upstream or downstream.
    b. Intra-entity sales result in gross profit overstatements regardless of amounts remaining in ending inventory.
    c. Gross profits must be deferred indefinitely because sales among affiliates always remain in the consolidated group.
    d. When intra-entity sales remain in ending inventory, ownership of the goods has not changed.

LO3

2. King Corporation owns 80 percent of Lee Corporation's common stock. During October, Lee sold merchandise to King for $100,000. At December 31, 50 percent of this merchandise remains in King's inventory. Gross profit percentages were 30 percent for King and 40 percent for Lee. The amount of unrealized intra-entity profit in ending inventory at December 31 that should be eliminated in the consolidation process is
    a. $40,000.
    b. $20,000.
    c. $16,000.
    d. $15,000.
    (AICPA adapted)

LO5

3. In computing the noncontrolling interest's share of consolidated net income, how should the subsidiary's income be adjusted for intra-entity transfers?
    a. The subsidiary's reported income is adjusted for the impact of upstream transfers prior to computing the noncontrolling interest's allocation.
    b. The subsidiary's reported income is adjusted for the impact of all transfers prior to computing the noncontrolling interest's allocation.
    c. The subsidiary's reported income is not adjusted for the impact of transfers prior to computing the noncontrolling interest's allocation.
    d. The subsidiary's reported income is adjusted for the impact of downstream transfers prior to computing the noncontrolling interest's allocation.

LO2, LO3

4. Bellgrade, Inc., acquired a 60 percent interest in Hansen Company several years ago. During 2011, Hansen sold inventory costing $75,000 to Bellgrade for $100,000. A total of 16 percent of this inventory was not sold to outsiders until 2012. During 2012, Hansen sold inventory costing $96,000

to Bellgrade for $120,000. A total of 35 percent of this inventory was not sold to outsiders until 2013. In 2012, Bellgrade reported cost of goods sold of $380,000 while Hansen reported $210,000. What is the consolidated cost of goods sold in 2012?

    a. $465,600.

    b. $473,440.

    c. $474,400.

    d. $522,400.

LO2, LO3

5. Top Company holds 90 percent of Bottom Company's common stock. In the current year, Top reports sales of $800,000 and cost of goods sold of $600,000. For this same period, Bottom has sales of $300,000 and cost of goods sold of $180,000. During the current year, Top sold merchandise to Bottom for $100,000. The subsidiary still possesses 40 percent of this inventory at the current year-end. Top had established the transfer price based on its normal markup. What are the consolidated sales and cost of goods sold?

    a. $1,000,000 and $690,000.

    b. $1,000,000 and $705,000.

    c. $1,000,000 and $740,000.

    d. $970,000 and $696,000.

LO2, LO3, LO5

6. Use the same information as in problem 5 except assume that the transfers were from Bottom Company to Top Company. What are the consolidated sales and cost of goods sold?

    a. $1,000,000 and $720,000.

    b. $1,000,000 and $755,000.

    c. $1,000,000 and $696,000.

    d. $970,000 and $712,000.

LO3, LO5

7. Hardwood, Inc., holds a 90 percent interest in Pittstoni Company. During 2010, Pittstoni sold inventory costing $77,000 to Hardwood for $110,000. Of this inventory, $40,000 worth was not sold to outsiders until 2011. During 2011, Pittstoni sold inventory costing $72,000 to Hardwood for $120,000. A total of $50,000 of this inventory was not sold to outsiders until 2012. In 2011, Hardwood reported net income of $150,000 while Pittstoni earned $90,000 after excess amortizations. What is the noncontrolling interest in the 2011 income of the subsidiary?

    a. $8,000.

    b. $8,200.

    c. $9,000.

    d. $9,800.

LO7

8. Dunn Corporation owns 100 percent of Grey Corporation's common stock. On January 2, 2010, Dunn sold to Grey for $40,000 machinery with a carrying amount of $30,000. Grey is depreciating the acquired machinery over a five-year life by the straight-line method. The net adjustments to compute 2010 and 2011 consolidated net income would be an increase (decrease) of

	2010	2011
a.	$(8,000)	$2,000
b.	$(8,000)	–0–
c.	$(10,000)	$2,000
d.	$(10,000)	–0–

    (AICPA adapted)

LO7

9. Wallton Corporation owns 70 percent of the outstanding stock of Hastings, Incorporated. On January 1, 2009, Wallton acquired a building with a 10-year life for $300,000. Wallton anticipated no salvage value, and the building was to be depreciated on the straight-line basis. On January 1, 2011, Wallton sold this building to Hastings for $280,000. At that time, the building had a remaining life of eight years but still no expected salvage value. In preparing financial statements for 2011, how does this transfer affect the computation of consolidated net income?

    a. Income must be reduced by $32,000.

    b. Income must be reduced by $35,000.

    c. Income must be reduced by $36,000.

    d. Income must be reduced by $40,000.

Use the following data for problems 10–15:

On January 1, Jarel acquired 80 percent of the outstanding voting stock of Suarez for $260,000 cash consideration. The remaining 20 percent of Suarez had an acquisition-date fair value of $65,000. On January 1, Suarez possessed equipment (5-year life) that was undervalued on its books by $25,000. Suarez also had developed several secret formulas that Jarel assessed at $50,000. These formulas, although not recorded on Suarez's financial records, were estimated to have a 20-year future life.

As of December 31, the financial statements appeared as follows:

	Jarel	Suarez
Revenues	$ (300,000)	$(200,000)
Cost of goods sold	140,000	80,000
Expenses	20,000	10,000
Net income	$ (140,000)	$(110,000)
Retained earnings, 1/1	$ (300,000)	$(150,000)
Net income	(140,000)	(110,000)
Dividends paid	–0–	–0–
Retained earnings, 12/31	$ (440,000)	$(260,000)
Cash and receivables	$ 210,000	$ 90,000
Inventory	150,000	110,000
Investment in Suarez	260,000	–0–
Equipment (net)	440,000	300,000
Total assets	$ 1,060,000	$ 500,000
Liabilities	$ (420,000)	$(140,000)
Common stock	(200,000)	(100,000)
Retained earnings, 12/31	(440,000)	(260,000)
Total liabilities and equities	$(1,060,000)	$(500,000)

During the year, Jarel bought inventory for $80,000 and sold it to Suarez for $100,000. Of these goods, Suarez still owns 60 percent on December 31.

LO2

10. What is the total of consolidated revenues?
    a. $500,000.
    b. $460,000.
    c. $420,000.
    d. $400,000.

LO2, LO3

11. What is the total of consolidated cost of goods sold?
    a. $140,000.
    b. $152,000.
    c. $132,000.
    d. $145,000.

LO1

(Chapter 3)

12. What is the total of consolidated expenses?
    a. $30,000.
    b. $36,000.
    c. $37,500.
    d. $39,000.

LO5

13. What is the consolidated total of noncontrolling interest appearing on the balance sheet?
    a. $85,500.
    b. $83,100.
    c. $87,000.
    d. $70,500.

LO7

14. What is the consolidated total for equipment (net) at December 31?
    a. $740,000.
    b. $756,000.
    c. $760,000.
    d. $765,000.

LO3

15. What is the consolidated total for inventory at December 31?
    a. $240,000.
    b. $248,000.
    c. $250,000.
    d. $260,000.

LO2, LO3, LO5

16. Following are several figures reported for Preston and Sanchez as of December 31, 2011:

	Preston	Sanchez
Inventory	$400,000	$200,000
Sales	800,000	600,000
Investment income	not given	
Cost of goods sold	400,000	300,000
Operating expenses	180,000	250,000

Preston acquired 70 percent of Sanchez in January 2010. In allocating the newly acquired subsidiary's fair value at the acquisition date, Preston noted that Sanchez having developed a customer list worth $65,000 unrecorded on its accounting records and having a five-year remaining life. Any remaining excess fair value over Sanchez's book value was attributed to goodwill. During 2011, Sanchez sells inventory costing $120,000 to Preston for $160,000. Of this amount, 20 percent remains unsold in Preston's warehouse at year-end. For Preston's consolidated reports, determine the following amounts to be reported for the current year.

Inventory
Sales
Cost of Goods Sold
Operating Expenses
Noncontrolling Interest in the Subsidiary's Net Income

LO3, LO4, LO5

17. On January 1, 2010, Corgan Company acquired 80 percent of the outstanding voting stock of Smashing, Inc., for a total of $980,000 in cash and other consideration. At the acquisition date, Smashing had common stock of $700,000, retained earnings of $250,000, and a noncontrolling interest fair value of $245,000. Corgan attributed the excess of fair value over Smashing's book value to various covenants with a 20-year life. Corgan uses the equity method to account for its investment in Smashing.

During the next two years, Smashing reported the following:

	Net Income	Dividends	Inventory Purchases from Corgan
2010	$150,000	$35,000	$100,000
2011	130,000	45,000	120,000

Corgan sells inventory to Smashing using a 60 percent markup on cost. At the end of 2010 and 2011, 40 percent of the current year purchases remain in Smashing's inventory.

a. Compute the equity method balance in Corgan's Investment in Smashing, Inc., account as of December 31, 2011.

b. Prepare the worksheet adjustments for the December 31, 2011, consolidation of Corgan and Smashing.

LO1, LO3, LO4, LO5, LO6, LO7

18. Smith Corporation acquired 80 percent of the outstanding voting stock of Kane, Inc., on January 1, 2010, when Kane had a net book value of $400,000. Any excess fair value was assigned to intangible assets and amortized at a rate of $5,000 per year.

Reported net income for 2011 was $300,000 for Smith and $110,000 for Kane. Smith distributed $100,000 in dividends during this period; Kane paid $40,000. At year-end, selected figures from the two companies' balance sheets were as follows:

	Smith Corporation	Kane, Inc.
Inventory	$140,000	$ 90,000
Land	600,000	200,000
Equipment (net)	400,000	300,000
Common stock	400,000	200,000
Retained earnings, 12/31/11	600,000	400,000

During 2010, intra-entity sales of $90,000 (original cost of $54,000) were made. Only 20 percent of this inventory was still held at the end of 2010. In 2011, $120,000 in intra-entity sales were made with an original cost of $66,000. Of this merchandise, 30 percent had not been resold to outside parties by the end of the year.

Each of the following questions should be considered as an independent situation.

a. If the intra-entity sales were upstream, what is the noncontrolling interest's share of the subsidiary's 2011 net income?

b. What is the consolidated balance in the ending Inventory account?

c. If the intra-entity sales were downstream, what is the noncontrolling interest's share of the subsidiary's 2011 net income?

d. If the intra-entity sales were downstream, what is the consolidated net income? Assume that Smith uses the initial value method to account for this investment.

e. If the intra-entity sales were downstream, what is the consolidated balance of the Retained Earnings account as of the end of 2011? Assume that Smith uses the partial equity method to account for this investment.

f. If the intra-entity sales were upstream, what is the consolidated balance for Retained Earnings as of the end of 2011? Assume that Smith uses the partial equity method to account for this investment.

g. Assume that no intra-entity inventory sales occurred between Smith and Kane. Instead, in 2010, Kane sold land costing $30,000 to Smith for $50,000. On the 2011 consolidated balance sheet, what value should be reported for land?

h. Assume that no intra-entity inventory or land sales occurred between Smith and Kane. Instead, on January 1, 2010, Kane sold equipment (that originally cost $100,000 but had a $60,000 book value on that date) to Smith for $80,000. At the time of sale, the equipment had a remaining useful life of five years. What worksheet entries are made for a December 31, 2011, consolidation of these two companies to eliminate the impact of the intra-entity transfer? For 2011, what is the noncontrolling interest's share of Kane's net income?

LO2, LO3, LO4, LO5

19. On January 1, 2010, Doone Corporation acquired 60 percent of the outstanding voting stock of Rockne Company for $300,000 consideration. At the acquisition date, the fair value of the 40 percent noncontrolling interest was $200,000 and Rockne's assets and liabilities had a collective net fair value of $500,000. Doone uses the equity method in its internal records to account for its investment in Rockne. Rockne reports net income of $160,000 in 2011. Since being acquired, Rockne has regularly supplied inventory to Doone at 25 percent more than cost. Sales to Doone amounted to $250,000 in 2010 and $300,000 in 2011. Approximately 30 percent of the inventory purchased during any one year is not used until the following year.

a. What is the noncontrolling interest's share of Rockne's 2011 income?

b. Prepare Doone's 2011 consolidation entries required by the intra-entity inventory transfers.

LO3, LO4, LO5, LO7

20. Penguin Corporation acquired 80 percent of the outstanding voting stock of Snow Company on January 1, 2010, for $420,000 in cash and other consideration. At the acquisition date, Penguin assessed Snow's identifiable assets and liabilities at a collective net fair value of $525,000 and the fair value of the 20 percent noncontrolling interest was $105,000. No excess fair value over book value amortization accompanied the acquisition.

The following selected account balances are from the individual financial records of these two companies as of December 31, 2011:

	Penguin	Snow
Sales	$640,000	$360,000
Cost of goods sold	290,000	197,000
Operating expenses	150,000	105,000
Retained earnings, 1/1/11	740,000	180,000
Inventory	346,000	110,000
Buildings (net)	358,000	157,000
Investment income	Not given	–0–

Each of the following problems is an independent situation:

a. Assume that Penguin sells Snow inventory at a markup equal to 40 percent of cost. Intra-entity transfers were $90,000 in 2010 and $110,000 in 2011. Of this inventory, Snow retained and then sold $28,000 of the 2010 transfers in 2011 and held $42,000 of the 2011 transfers until 2012.

On consolidated financial statements for 2011, determine the balances that would appear for the following accounts:

Cost of Goods Sold
Inventory
Noncontrolling Interest in Subsidiary's Net Income

b. Assume that Snow sells inventory to Penguin at a markup equal to 40 percent of cost. Intra-entity transfers were $50,000 in 2010 and $80,000 in 2011. Of this inventory, $21,000 of the 2010 transfers were retained and then sold by Penguin in 2011, whereas $35,000 of the 2011 transfers were held until 2012.

On consolidated financial statements for 2011, determine the balances that would appear for the following accounts:

Cost of Goods Sold
Inventory
Noncontrolling Interest in Subsidiary's Net Income

c. Penguin sells Snow a building on January 1, 2010, for $80,000, although its book value was only $50,000 on this date. The building had a five-year remaining life and was to be depreciated using the straight-line method with no salvage value.

Determine the balances that would appear on consolidated financial statements for 2011 for

Buildings (net)
Operating Expenses
Noncontrolling Interest in Subsidiary's Net Income

LO3, LO4, LO5

21. Akron, Inc., owns all outstanding stock of Toledo Corporation. Amortization expense of $15,000 per year for patented technology resulted from the original acquisition. For 2011, the companies had the following account balances:

	Akron	Toledo
Sales	$1,100,000	$600,000
Cost of goods sold	500,000	400,000
Operating expenses	400,000	220,000
Investment income	Not given	–0–
Dividends paid	80,000	30,000

Intra-entity sales of $320,000 occurred during 2010 and again in 2011. This merchandise cost $240,000 each year. Of the total transfers, $70,000 was still held on December 31, 2010, with $50,000 unsold on December 31, 2011.

a. For consolidation purposes, does the direction of the transfers (upstream or downstream) affect the balances to be reported here?

b. Prepare a consolidated income statement for the year ending December 31, 2011.

LO7

22. On January 1, 2010, QuickPort Company acquired 90 percent of the outstanding voting stock of NetSpeed, Inc., for $810,000 in cash and stock options. At the acquisition date, NetSpeed had Common Stock of $800,000 and Retained Earnings of $40,000. The acquisition-date fair value of the 10 percent noncontrolling interest was $90,000. QuickPort attributed the $60,000 excess of NetSpeed's fair value over book value to a database with a 5-year remaining life.

During the next two years, NetSpeed reported the following:

	Income	Dividends
2010	$ 80,000	$8,000
2011	115,000	8,000

On July 1, 2010, QuickPort sold communication equipment to NetSpeed for $42,000. The equipment originally cost $48,000 and had accumulated depreciation of $9,000 and an estimated remaining life of three years at the date of the intra-entity transfer.

a. Compute the equity method balance in QuickPort's Investment in NetSpeed, Inc., account as of December 31, 2011.

b. Prepare the worksheet adjustments for the December 31, 2011, consolidation of QuickPort and NetSpeed.

LO7

23. Padre holds 100 percent of the outstanding shares of Sonora. On January 1, 2009, Padre transferred equipment to Sonora for $95,000. The equipment had cost $130,000 originally but had a $50,000 book value and five-year remaining life at the date of transfer. Depreciation expense is computed according to the straight-line method with no salvage value.

    Consolidated financial statements for 2011 currently are being prepared. What worksheet entries are needed in connection with the consolidation of this asset? Assume that the parent applies the partial equity method.

LO7

24. On January 1, 2011, Slaughter sold equipment to Bennett (a wholly owned subsidiary) for $120,000 in cash. The equipment had originally cost $100,000 but had a book value of only $70,000 when transferred. On that date, the equipment had a five-year remaining life. Depreciation expense is computed using the straight-line method.

    Slaughter earned $220,000 in net income in 2011 (not including any investment income) while Bennett reported $90,000. Slaughter attributed any excess acquisition-date fair value to Bennett's unpatented technology, which was amortized at a rate of $8,000 per year.

    a. What is the consolidated net income for 2011?

    b. What is the parent's share of consolidated net income for 2011 if Slaughter owns only 90 percent of Bennett?

    c. What is the parent's share of consolidated net income for 2011 if Slaughter owns only 90 percent of Bennett and the equipment transfer was upstream?

    d. What is the consolidated net income for 2012 if Slaughter reports $240,000 (does not include investment income) and Bennett $100,000 in income? Assume that Bennett is a wholly owned subsidiary and the equipment transfer was downstream.

LO2, LO3, LO4, LO7

25. Anchovy acquired 90 percent of Yelton on January 1, 2009. Of Yelton's total acquisition-date fair value, $60,000 was allocated to undervalued equipment (with a 10-year life) and $80,000 was attributed to franchises (to be written off over a 20-year period).

    Since the takeover, Yelton has transferred inventory to its parent as follows:

Year	Cost	Transfer Price	Remaining at Year-End
2009	$20,000	$ 50,000	$20,000 (at transfer price)
2010	49,000	70,000	30,000 (at transfer price)
2011	50,000	100,000	40,000 (at transfer price)

    On January 1, 2010, Anchovy sold Yelton a building for $50,000 that had originally cost $70,000 but had only a $30,000 book value at the date of transfer. The building is estimated to have a five-year remaining life (straight-line depreciation is used with no salvage value).

    Selected figures from the December 31, 2011, trial balances of these two companies are as follows:

	Anchovy	Yelton
Sales	$600,000	$500,000
Cost of goods sold	400,000	260,000
Operating expenses	120,000	80,000
Investment income	Not given	–0–
Inventory	220,000	80,000
Equipment (net)	140,000	110,000
Buildings (net)	350,000	190,000

    Determine consolidated totals for each of these account balances.

LO3, LO4, LO5, LO7

26. On January 1, 2011, Sledge had common stock of $120,000 and retained earnings of $260,000. During that year, Sledge reported sales of $130,000, cost of goods sold of $70,000, and operating expenses of $40,000.

    On January 1, 2009, Percy, Inc., acquired 80 percent of Sledge's outstanding voting stock. At that date, $60,000 of the acquisition-date fair value was assigned to unrecorded contracts (with a 20-year life) and $20,000 to an undervalued building (with a 10-year life).

    In 2010, Sledge sold inventory costing $9,000 to Percy for $15,000. Of this merchandise, Percy continued to hold $5,000 at year-end. During 2011, Sledge transferred inventory costing $11,000 to Percy for $20,000. Percy still held half of these items at year-end.

    On January 1, 2010, Percy sold equipment to Sledge for $12,000. This asset originally cost $16,000 but had a January 1, 2010, book value of $9,000. At the time of transfer, the equipment's remaining life was estimated to be five years.

Percy has properly applied the equity method to the investment in Sledge.

a. Prepare worksheet entries to consolidate these two companies as of December 31, 2011.

b. Compute the noncontrolling interest in the subsidiary's income for 2011.

LO1, LO2, LO3, LO5

27. Pitino acquired 90 percent of Brey's outstanding shares on January 1, 2009, in exchange for $342,000 in cash. The subsidiary's stockholders' equity accounts totaled $326,000 and the noncontrolling interest had a fair value of $38,000 on that day. However, a building (with a nine-year remaining life) in Brey's accounting records was undervalued by $18,000. Pitino assigned the rest of the excess fair value over book value to Brey's patented technology (six-year remaining life).

Brey reported net income from its own operations of $64,000 in 2009 and $80,000 in 2010. Brey paid dividends of $19,000 in 2009 and $23,000 in 2010.

Brey sells inventory to Pitino as follows:

Year	Cost to Brey	Transfer Price to Pitino	Inventory Remaining at Year-End (at transfer price)
2009	$69,000	$115,000	$25,000
2010	81,000	135,000	37,500
2011	92,800	160,000	50,000

At December 31, 2011, Pitino owes Brey $16,000 for inventory acquired during the period.

The following separate account balances are for these two companies for December 31, 2011, and the year then ended. Credits are indicated by parentheses.

	Pitino	Brey
Sales revenues	$ (862,000)	$(366,000)
Cost of goods sold	515,000	209,000
Expenses	185,400	67,000
Investment income—Brey	(68,400)	–0–
Net income	$ (230,000)	$ (90,000)
Retained earnings, 1/1/11	$ (488,000)	$(278,000)
Net income (above)	(230,000)	(90,000)
Dividends paid	136,000	27,000
Retained earnings, 12/31/11	$ (582,000)	$(341,000)
Cash and receivables	$ 146,000	$ 98,000
Inventory	255,000	136,000
Investment in Brey	450,000	–0–
Land, buildings, and equipment (net)	964,000	328,000
Total assets	$ 1,815,000	$ 562,000
Liabilities	$ (718,000)	$ (71,000)
Common stock	(515,000)	(150,000)
Retained earnings, 12/31/11	(582,000)	(341,000)
Total liabilities and equities	$(1,815,000)	$(562,000)

Answer each of the following questions:

a. What was the annual amortization resulting from the acquisition-date fair-value allocations?

b. Were the intra-entity transfers upstream or downstream?

c. What unrealized gross profit existed as of January 1, 2011?

d. What unrealized gross profit existed as of December 31, 2011?

e. What amounts make up the $68,400 Investment Income—Brey account balance for 2011?

f. What was the noncontrolling interest's share of the subsidiary's net income for 2011?

g. What amounts make up the $450,000 Investment in Brey account balance as of December 31, 2011?

h. Prepare the 2011 worksheet entry to eliminate the subsidiary's beginning owners' equity balances.

i. Without preparing a worksheet or consolidation entries, determine the consolidation balances for these two companies.

LO2, LO3, LO5

28. Bennett acquired 70 percent of Zeigler on June 30, 2010, for $910,000 in cash. Based on Zeigler's acquisition-date fair value, an unrecorded intangible of $400,000 was recognized and is being amortized at the rate of $10,000 per year. The noncontrolling interest fair value was assessed at $390,000 at the acquisition date. The 2011 financial statements are as follows:

	Bennett	Zeigler
Sales	$ (800,000)	$ (600,000)
Cost of goods sold	535,000	400,000
Operating expenses	100,000	100,000
Dividend income	(35,000)	–0–
Net income	$ (200,000)	$ (100,000)
Retained earnings, 1/1/11	$(1,300,000)	$ (850,000)
Net income	(200,000)	(100,000)
Dividends paid	100,000	50,000
Retained earnings, 12/31/11	$(1,400,000)	$ (900,000)
Cash and receivables	$ 400,000	$ 300,000
Inventory	290,000	700,000
Investment in Zeigler	910,000	–0–
Fixed assets	1,000,000	600,000
Accumulated depreciation	(300,000)	(200,000)
Totals	$ 2,300,000	$ 1,400,000
Liabilities	$ (600,000)	$ (400,000)
Common stock	(300,000)	(100,000)
Retained earnings	(1,400,000)	(900,000)
Totals	$(2,300,000)	$(1,400,000)

Bennett sold Zeigler inventory costing $72,000 during the last six months of 2010 for $120,000. At year-end, 30 percent remained. Bennett sells Zeigler inventory costing $200,000 during 2011 for $250,000. At year-end, 20 percent is left. With these facts, determine the consolidated balances for the accounts:

Sales
Cost of Goods Sold
Operating Expenses
Dividend Income
Noncontrolling Interest in Consolidated Income
Inventory
Noncontrolling Interest in Subsidiary, 12/31/11

LO2, LO3, LO4, LO5

29. Compute the balances in problem 28 again, assuming that all intra-entity transfers were made from Zeigler to Bennett.

LO1, LO2, LO3, LO4, LO5, LO7

30. Following are financial statements for Moore Company and Kirby Company for 2011:

	Moore	Kirby
Sales	$ (800,000)	$ (600,000)
Cost of goods sold	500,000	400,000
Operating and interest expenses	100,000	160,000
Net income	$ (200,000)	$ (40,000)
Retained earnings, 1/1/11	$ (990,000)	$ (550,000)
Net income	(200,000)	(40,000)
Dividends paid	130,000	–0–
Retained earnings, 12/31/11	$(1,060,000)	$ (590,000)
Cash and receivables	$ 217,000	$ 180,000
Inventory	224,000	160,000
Investment in Kirby	657,000	–0–

(continued)

	Moore	Kirby
Equipment (net)	600,000	420,000
Buildings	1,000,000	650,000
Accumulated depreciation—buildings	(100,000)	(200,000)
Other assets	200,000	100,000
Total assets	$ 2,798,000	$ 1,310,000
Liabilities	$(1,138,000)	$ (570,000)
Common stock	(600,000)	(150,000)
Retained earnings, 12/31/11	(1,060,000)	(590,000)
Total liabilities and equity	$(2,798,000)	$(1,310,000)

- Moore purchased 90 percent of Kirby on January 1, 2010, for $657,000 in cash. On that date, the 10 percent noncontrolling interest was assessed to have a $73,000 fair value. Also at the acquisition date, Kirby held equipment (4-year remaining life) undervalued on the financial records by $20,000 and interest-bearing liabilities (5-year remaining life) overvalued by $40,000. The rest of the excess fair value over book value was assigned to previously unrecognized brand names and amortized over a 10-year life.
- During 2010 Kirby earned a net income of $80,000 and paid no dividends.
- Each year Kirby sells Moore inventory at a 20 percent gross profit rate. Intra-entity sales were $145,000 in 2010 and $160,000 in 2011. On January 1, 2011, 30 percent of the 2010 transfers were still on hand and, on December 31, 2011, 40 percent of the 2011 transfers remained.
- Moore sold Kirby a building on January 2, 2010. It had cost Moore $100,000 but had $90,000 in accumulated depreciation at the time of this transfer. The price was $25,000 in cash. At that time, the building had a five-year remaining life.

Determine all consolidated balances either computationally or by using a worksheet.

LO2, LO3, LO4, LO5

31. On January 1, 2010, Woods, Inc., acquired a 60 percent interest in the common stock of Scott, Inc., for $672,000. Scott's book value on that date consisted of common stock of $100,000 and retained earnings of $220,000. Also, the January 1, 2010, fair value on the 40 percent noncontrolling interest was $248,000. The subsidiary held patents (with a 10-year remaining life) that were undervalued within the company's accounting records by $70,000 and an unrecorded customer list (15-year remaining life) assessed at a $45,000 fair value. Any remaining excess acquisition-date fair value was assigned to goodwill. Since acquisition, Woods has applied the equity method to its Investment in Scott account and no goodwill impairment has occurred.

    Intra-entity inventory sales between the two companies have been made as follows:

Year	Cost to Woods	Transfer Price to Scott	Ending Balance (at transfer price)
2010	120,000	150,000	50,000
2011	112,000	160,000	40,000

The individual financial statements for these two companies as of December 31, 2011, and the year then ended follow:

	Woods, Inc.	Scott, Inc.
Sales	$ (700,000)	$(335,000)
Cost of goods sold	460,000	205,000
Operating expenses	188,000	70,000
Equity earnings in Scott	(28,000)	–0–
Net income	$ (80,000)	$ (60,000)
Retained earnings, 1/1/11	$ (695,000)	$(280,000)
Net income (above)	(80,000)	(60,000)
Dividends paid	45,000	15,000
Retained earnings, 12/31/11	$ (730,000)	$(325,000)

(continued)

	Woods, Inc.	Scott, Inc.
Cash and receivables	$ 248,000	$ 148,000
Inventory	233,000	129,000
Investment in Scott	411,000	–0–
Buildings (net)	308,000	202,000
Equipment (net)	220,000	86,000
Patents (net)	–0–	20,000
Total assets	$ 1,420,000	$ 585,000
Liabilities	$ (390,000)	$(160,000)
Common stock	(300,000)	(100,000)
Retained earnings, 12/31/11	(730,000)	(325,000)
Total liabilities and equities	$(1,420,000)	$(585,000)

a. Show how Woods determined the $411,000 Investment in Scott account balance. Assume that Woods defers 100 percent of downstream intra-entity profits against its share of Scott's income.

b. Prepare a consolidated worksheet to determine appropriate balances for external financial reporting as of December 31, 2011.

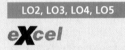

LO2, LO3, LO4, LO5

32. On January 1, 2009, Plymouth Corporation acquired 80 percent of the outstanding voting stock of Sander Company in exchange for $1,200,000 cash. At that time, although Sander's book value was $925,000, Plymouth assessed Sander's total business fair value at $1,500,000. Since that time, Sander has neither issued nor reacquired any shares of its own stock.

The book values of Sander's individual assets and liabilities approximated their acquisition-date fair values except for the patent account, which was undervalued by $350,000. The undervalued patents had a 5-year remaining life at the acquisition date. Any remaining excess fair value was attributed to goodwill. No goodwill impairments have occurred.

Sander regularly sells inventory to Plymouth. Below are details of the intra-entity inventory sales for the past three years:

Year	Intra-Entity Sales	Intra-Entity Ending Inventory at Transfer Price	Gross Profit Rate on Intra-Entity Inventory Transfers
2009	$125,000	$ 80,000	25%
2010	220,000	125,000	28%
2011	300,000	160,000	25%

Separate financial statements for these two companies as of December 31, 2011, follow:

	Plymouth	Sander
Revenues	$(1,740,000)	$ (950,000)
Cost of goods sold	820,000	500,000
Depreciation expense	104,000	85,000
Amortization expense	220,000	120,000
Interest expense	20,000	15,000
Equity in earnings of Sander	(124,000)	–0–
Net Income	$ (700,000)	$ (230,000)
Retained earnings 1/1/11	$(2,800,000)	$ (345,000)
Net Income	(700,000)	(230,000)
Dividends paid	200,000	25,000
Retained earnings 12/31/11	$(3,300,000)	$ (550,000)
Cash	$ 535,000	$ 115,000
Accounts receivable	575,000	215,000
Inventory	990,000	800,000
Investment in Sander	1,420,000	–0–
Buildings and equipment	1,025,000	863,000
Patents	950,000	107,000
Total assets	$ 5,495,000	$ 2,100,000

(continued)

	Plymouth	Sander
Accounts payable	$ (450,000)	$ (200,000)
Notes payable	(545,000)	(450,000)
Common stock	(900,000)	(800,000)
Additional paid-in capital	(300,000)	(100,000)
Retained earnings 12/31/11	(3,300,000)	(550,000)
Total liabilities and stockholders' equity	$(5,495,000)	$(2,100,000)

a. Prepare a schedule that calculates the Equity in Earnings of Sander account balance.

b. Prepare a worksheet to arrive at consolidated figures for external reporting purposes.

LO2, LO3, LO4, LO5, LO7

33. On January 1, 2009, Monica Company acquired 70 percent of Young Company's outstanding common stock for $665,000. The fair value of the noncontrolling interest at the acquisition date was $285,000. Young reported stockholders' equity accounts on that date as follows:

Common stock—$10 par value	$300,000
Additional paid-in capital	90,000
Retained earnings	410,000

In establishing the acquisition value, Monica appraised Young's assets and ascertained that the accounting records undervalued a building (with a five-year life) by $50,000. Any remaining excess acquisition-date fair value was allocated to a franchise agreement to be amortized over 10 years.

During the subsequent years, Young sold Monica inventory at a 30 percent gross profit rate. Monica consistently resold this merchandise in the year of acquisition or in the period immediately following. Transfers for the three years after this business combination was created amounted to the following:

Year	Transfer Price	Inventory Remaining at Year-End (at transfer price)
2009	$60,000	$10,000
2010	80,000	12,000
2011	90,000	18,000

In addition, Monica sold Young several pieces of fully depreciated equipment on January 1, 2010, for $36,000. The equipment had originally cost Monica $50,000. Young plans to depreciate these assets over a six-year period.

In 2011, Young earns a net income of $160,000 and distributes $50,000 in cash dividends. These figures increase the subsidiary's Retained Earnings to a $740,000 balance at the end of 2011. During this same year, Monica reported dividend income of $35,000 and an investment account containing the initial value balance of $665,000.

Prepare the 2011 consolidation worksheet entries for Monica and Young. In addition, compute the noncontrolling interest's share of the subsidiary's net income for 2011.

LO2, LO3, LO4, LO5, LO7

34. Assume the same basic information as presented in problem 33 except that Monica employs the equity method of accounting. Hence, it reports $102,740 investment income for 2011 with an Investment account balance of $826,220. Under these circumstances, prepare the worksheet entries required for the consolidation of Monica Company and Young Company.

LO2, LO3, LO4, LO5, LO6

35. The individual financial statements for Gibson Company and Keller Company for the year ending December 31, 2011, follow. Gibson acquired a 60 percent interest in Keller on January 1, 2010, in exchange for various considerations totaling $570,000. At the acquisition date, the fair value of the noncontrolling interest was $380,000 and Keller's book value was $850,000. Keller had developed internally a customer list that was not recorded on its books but had an acquisition-date fair value of $100,000. This intangible asset is being amortized over 20 years.

Gibson sold Keller land with a book value of $60,000 on January 2, 2010, for $100,000. Keller still holds this land at the end of the current year.

Keller regularly transfers inventory to Gibson. In 2010, it shipped inventory costing $100,000 to Gibson at a price of $150,000. During 2011, intra-entity shipments totaled $200,000, although the original cost to Keller was only $140,000. In each of these years, 20 percent of the merchandise was not resold to outside parties until the period following the transfer. Gibson owes Keller $40,000 at the end of 2011.

	Gibson Company	Keller Company
Sales	$ (800,000)	$ (500,000)
Cost of goods sold	500,000	300,000
Operating expenses	100,000	60,000
Income of Keller Company	(84,000)	–0–
Net income	$ (284,000)	$ (140,000)
Retained earnings, 1/1/11	$(1,116,000)	$ (620,000)
Net income (above)	(284,000)	(140,000)
Dividends paid	115,000	60,000
Retained earnings, 12/31/11	$(1,285,000)	$ (700,000)
Cash	$ 177,000	$ 90,000
Accounts receivable	356,000	410,000
Inventory	440,000	320,000
Investment in Keller Company	726,000	–0–
Land	180,000	390,000
Buildings and equipment (net)	496,000	300,000
Total assets	$ 2,375,000	$ 1,510,000
Liabilities	$ (480,000)	$ (400,000)
Common stock	(610,000)	(320,000)
Additional paid-in capital	–0–	(90,000)
Retained earnings, 12/31/11	(1,285,000)	(700,000)
Total liabilities and equities	$(2,375,000)	$(1,510,000)

a. Prepare a worksheet to consolidate the separate 2011 financial statements for Gibson and Keller.

b. How would the consolidation entries in requirement (a) have differed if Gibson had sold a building with a $60,000 book value (cost of $140,000) to Keller for $100,000 instead of land, as the problem reports? Assume that the building had a 10-year remaining life at the date of transfer.

LO2, LO3, LO4, LO6

36. On January 1, 2010, Parkway, Inc., issued securities with a total fair value of $450,000 for 100 percent of Skyline Corporation's outstanding ownership shares. Skyline has long supplied inventory to Parkway, which hopes to achieve synergies with production scheduling and product development with this combination.

Although Skyline's book value at the acquisition date was $300,000, the fair value of its trademarks was assessed to be $30,000 more than their carrying values. Additionally, Skyline's patented technology was undervalued in its accounting records by $120,000. The trademarks were considered to have indefinite lives, the estimated remaining life of the patented technology was eight years.

In 2010, Skyline sold Parkway inventory costing $30,000 for $50,000. As of December 31, 2010, Parkway had resold only 28 percent of this inventory. In 2011, Parkway bought from Skyline $80,000 of inventory that had an original cost of $40,000. At the end of 2011, Parkway held $28,000 of inventory acquired from Skyline, all from its 2011 purchases.

During 2011, Parkway sold Skyline a parcel of land for $95,000 and recorded a gain of $18,000 on the sale. Skyline still owes Parkway $65,000 related to the land sale.

At the end of 2011, Parkway and Skyline prepared the following statements in preparation for consolidation.

	Parkway, Inc.	Skyline Corporation
Revenues	$ (627,000)	$(358,000)
Cost of goods sold	289,000	195,000
Other operating expenses	170,000	75,000
Gain on sale of land	(18,000)	–0–
Equity in Skyline's earnings	(55,400)	–0–
Net income	$ (241,400)	$ (88,000)

(*continued*)

	Parkway, Inc.	Skyline Corporation
Retained earnings 1/1/11	$ (314,600)	$(292,000)
Net income	(241,400)	(88,000)
Dividends distributed	70,000	20,000
Retained earnings 12/31/11	$ (486,000)	$(360,000)
Cash and receivables	$ 134,000	$ 150,000
Inventory	281,000	112,000
Investment in Skyline	598,000	–0–
Trademarks	–0–	50,000
Land, buildings, and equip. (net)	637,000	283,000
Patented technology	–0–	130,000
Total assets	$ 1,650,000	$ 725,000
Liabilities	$ (463,000)	$(215,000)
Common stock	(410,000)	(120,000)
Additional paid-in capital	(291,000)	(30,000)
Retained earnings 12/31/11	(486,000)	(360,000)
Total liabilities and equity	$(1,650,000)	$(725,000)

a. Show how Parkway computed its $55,400 equity in Skyline's earnings balance.

b. Prepare a 2011 consolidated worksheet for Parkway and Skyline.

Develop Your Skills

EXCEL CASE

On January 1, 2010, Patrick Company purchased 100 percent of the outstanding voting stock of Shawn, Inc., for $1,000,000 in cash and other consideration. At the purchase date, Shawn had common stock of $500,000 and retained earnings of $185,000. Patrick attributed the excess of acquisition-date fair value over Shawn's book value to a trade name with a 25-year life. Patrick uses the equity method to account for its investment in Shawn.

During the next two years, Shawn reported the following:

	Income	Dividends	Inventory Transfers to Patrick at Transfer Price
2010	$78,000	$25,000	$190,000
2011	85,000	27,000	210,000

Shawn sells inventory to Patrick after a markup based on a gross profit rate. At the end of 2010 and 2011, 30 percent of the current year purchases remain in Patrick's inventory.

Required

Create an Excel spreadsheet that computes the following:

1. Equity method balance in Patrick's Investment in Shawn, Inc., account as of December 31, 2011.
2. Worksheet adjustments for the December 31, 2011, consolidation of Patrick and Shawn.

Formulate your solution so that Shawn's gross profit rate on sales to Patrick is treated as a variable.

ANALYSIS AND RESEARCH CASE: ACCOUNTING INFORMATION AND SALARY NEGOTIATIONS

Granger Eagles Players' Association and Mr. Doublecount, the CEO of Granger Eagles Baseball Company, ask your help in resolving a salary dispute. Mr. Doublecount presents the following income statement to the player representatives.

GRANGER EAGLES BASEBALL COMPANY
INCOME STATEMENT

Ticket revenues		$2,000,000
Stadium rent expense	$1,400,000	
Ticket expense	25,000	
Promotion	35,000	
Player salaries	400,000	
Staff salaries and miscellaneous	200,000	2,060,000
Net income (loss)		$ (60,000)

Mr. Doublecount argues that the Granger Eagles really lose money and, until things turn around, a salary increase is out of the question.

As a result of your inquiry, you discover that Granger Eagles Baseball Company owns 91 percent of the voting stock in Eagle Stadium, Inc. This venue is specifically designed for baseball and is where the Eagles play their entire home game schedule. However, Mr. Doublecount does not wish to consider the profits of Eagle Stadium in the negotiations with the players. He claims that "the stadium is really a separate business entity that was purchased separately from the team" and therefore does not concern the players. The Eagles Stadium income statement appears as follows:

EAGLES STADIUM, INC.
INCOME STATEMENT

Stadium rent revenue	$1,400,000	
Concession revenue	800,000	
Parking revenue	100,000	$2,300,000
Cost of goods sold	250,000	
Depreciation	80,000	
Staff salaries and miscellaneous	150,000	480,000
Net income (loss)		$1,820,000

Required

1. What advice would you provide the negotiating parties regarding the issue of considering the Eagles Stadium income statement in their discussions? What authoritative literature could you cite in supporting your advice?

2. What other pertinent information would you need to provide a specific recommendation regarding players' salaries?

Please visit the text Web site for the online CPA Simulation

Situation: Giant Company acquired all of Tiny Corporation's outstanding common stock 4 years ago for $240,000 more than book value. This excess was assigned equally to a building (10-year life), inventory (sold within 1 year), and goodwill. On its separate financial statements for the current year, Giant reported sales of $900,000, cost of goods sold of $500,000, and operating expenses of $200,000. No investment income was included in these figures. On its separate financial statements for the current year, Tiny reported sales of $500,000, cost of goods sold of $200,000, and operating expenses of $100,000. Both companies paid dividends of $20,000 this year. Both companies reported positive current ratios of above 1 to 1.

Topics to be covered in simulation:

- Intra-entity inventory transfers.
- Intra-entity equipment transfer.
- Intra-entity land transfer.
- Intra-entity debts.
- Equity method.
- Push-down accounting.
- Minority interest.
- Negative goodwill.

Variable Interest Entities, Intra-Entity Debt, Consolidated Cash Flows, and Other Issues

The consolidation of financial information can be a highly complex process often encompassing a number of practical challenges. This chapter examines the procedures required by several additional issues:

- Variable interest entities.
- Intra-entity debt.
- Subsidiary preferred stock.
- The consolidated statement of cash flows.
- Computation of consolidated earnings per share.
- Subsidiary stock transactions.

Variable interest entities emerged over the past two decades as a new type of business structure that provided effective control of one firm by another without overt ownership. In response to the evolving nature of control relationships among firms, the FASB expanded its definition of control beyond the long-standing criterion of a majority voting interest to include control exercised through variable interests. This topic and some of the more traditional advanced business combination subjects listed above provide for further exploration of the complexities faced by the financial reporting community in providing relevant and reliable information to users of consolidated financial reports.

CONSOLIDATION OF VARIABLE INTEREST ENTITIES

Starting in the late 1970s, many firms began establishing separate business structures to help finance their operations at favorable rates. These structures became commonly known as *special purpose entities* (SPEs), *special purpose vehicles,* or *off-balance sheet structures.* In this text, we refer to all such entities collectively as *variable interest entities* or VIEs. Many firms have routinely included their VIEs in their consolidated financial reports. However, others sought to avoid consolidation.

LEARNING OBJECTIVES

After studying this chapter, you should be able to:

LO1 Describe a variable interest entity, a primary beneficiary, and the factors used to decide when a variable interest entity is subject to consolidation.

LO2 Understand the consolidation procedures to eliminate all intra-entity debt accounts and recognize any associated gain or loss created whenever one company acquires an affiliate's debt instrument from an outside party.

LO3 Understand that subsidiary preferred stocks not owned by the parent are a component of the noncontrolling interest and are initially valued at acquisition-date fair value.

LO4 Prepare a consolidated statement of cash flows.

LO5 Compute basic and diluted earnings per share for a business combination.

LO6 Understand the accounting for subsidiary stock transactions that impact the underlying value recorded within the parent's Investment account and the consolidated financial statements.

LO1

Describe a variable interest entity, a primary beneficiary, and the factors used to decide when a variable interest entity is subject to consolidation.

VIEs can help accomplish legitimate business purposes. Nonetheless, their use was widely criticized in the aftermath of Enron Corporation's 2001 collapse. Because many firms avoided consolidation and used VIEs for off-balance sheet financing, such entities were often characterized as vehicles to hide debt and mislead investors. Other critics observed that firms with variable interests recorded questionable profits on sales to their VIEs that were not arm's-length transactions.[1] The FASB ASC Variable Interest Entities sections within the Consolidations Topic were issued in response to such financial reporting abuses.

Accounting standards for consolidating VIEs continue to evolve over time. In 2009, the FASB expanded consolidation requirements for entities previously known as qualifying special purpose entities (QSPEs). Such QSPEs are often established to transform financial assets such as trade receivables, loans, or mortgages into securities that are offered in equity markets. Additionally in 2009 the FASB adopted a new qualitative assessment for deciding whether a firm must consolidate a VIE. Consolidation criteria now focus on the power to direct the activities of the entity as well as the obligation to absorb losses and the right to receive benefits from the VIE.

What Is a VIE?

A VIE can take the form of a trust, partnership, joint venture, or corporation although sometimes it has neither independent management nor employees. Most are established for valid business purposes, and transactions involving VIEs have become widespread. Common examples of VIE activities include transfers of financial assets, leasing, hedging financial instruments, research and development, and other transactions. An enterprise often sponsors a VIE to accomplish a well-defined and limited business activity and to provide low-cost financing.

Low-cost financing of asset purchases is frequently a main benefit available through VIEs. Rather than engaging in the transaction directly, the business may sponsor a VIE to purchase and finance an asset acquisition. The VIE then leases the asset to the sponsor. This strategy saves the business money because the VIE is often eligible for a lower interest rate. This advantage is achieved for several reasons. First, the VIE typically operates with a very limited set of assets—in many cases just one asset. By isolating an asset in a VIE, the asset's risk is isolated from the sponsoring firm's overall risk. Thus the VIE creditors remain protected by the specific collateral in the asset. Second, the governing documents can strictly limit the business activities of a VIE. These limits further protect lenders by preventing the VIE from engaging in any activities not specified in its agreements. As a major public accounting firm noted,

> [t]he borrower/transferor gains access to a source of funds less expensive than would otherwise be available. This advantage derives from isolating the assets in an entity prohibited from undertaking any other business activity or taking on any additional debt, thereby creating a better security interest in the assets for the lender/investor.[2]

Because governing agreements limit activities and decision making in most VIEs, there is often little need for voting stock. In fact, a sponsoring enterprise may own very little, if any, of its VIE's voting stock. Prior to current consolidation requirements for VIEs, many businesses left such entities unconsolidated in their financial reports because technically they did not own a majority of the entity's voting stock. In utilizing the VIE as a conduit to provide financing, the related assets and debt were effectively removed from the enterprise's balance sheet.

Characteristics of Variable Interest Entities

Similar to most business entities, VIEs generally have assets, liabilities, and investors with equity interests. Unlike most businesses, because a VIE's activities can be strictly limited, the role of the equity investors can be fairly minor. The VIE may have been created specifically to benefit its sponsoring firm with low-cost financing. Thus, the equity investors may serve simply as a technical requirement to allow the VIE to function as a legal entity. Because they bear relatively low economic risk, equity investors are typically provided only a small rate of return.

---

[1] In its 2001 fourth quarter 10-Q, Enron recorded earnings restatements of more than $400 million related to its failure to properly consolidate several of its SPEs (e.g., Chewco and LMJ1). Enron also admitted an improper omission of $700 million of its SPE's debt. Within a month of the restatements, Enron filed for bankruptcy.

[2] KPMG, "Defining Issues: New Accounting for SPEs," March 1, 2002.

EXHIBIT 6.1
Examples of Variable
Interests

Variable interests in a variable interest entity are contractual, ownership, or other pecuniary interests in an entity that change with changes in the entity's net asset value. Variable interests absorb portions of a variable interest entity's expected losses if they occur or receive portions of the entity's expected residual returns if they occur.

The following are some examples of variable interests and the related potential losses or returns:

Variable interests	Potential losses or returns
• Participation rights	• Entitles holder to residual profits
• Asset purchase options	• Entitles holder to benefit from increases in asset fair values
• Guarantees of debt	• If a VIE cannot repay liabilities, honoring a debt guarantee will produce a loss
• Subordinated debt instruments	• If a VIE's cash flow is insufficient to repay all senior debt, subordinated debt may be required to absorb the loss
• Lease residual value guarantees	• If leased asset declines below the residual value, honoring the guarantee will produce a loss

The small equity investments normally are insufficient to induce lenders to provide a low-risk interest rate for the VIE. As a result, another party (often the sponsoring firm that benefits from the VIE's activities) must contribute substantial resources—often loans and/or guarantees—to enable the VIE to secure additional financing needed to accomplish its purpose. For example, the sponsoring firm may guarantee the VIE's debt, thus assuming the risk of default. Other contractual arrangements may limit returns to equity holders while participation rights provide increased profit potential and risks to the sponsoring firm. Risks and rewards such as these cause the sponsor's economic interest to vary depending on the created entity's success—hence the term *variable interest entity*. In contrast to a traditional entity, a VIE's risks and rewards are distributed not according to stock ownership but according to other variable interests. Exhibit 6.1 describes variable interests further and provides several examples.

Variable interests increase a firm's risk as the resources it provides (or guarantees) to the VIE increase. With increased risks come incentives to restrict the VIE's decision making. In fact, a firm with variable interests will regularly limit the equity investors' power through the VIE's governance documents. As noted by GAAP literature,

> [i]f the total equity investment at risk is not sufficient to permit the legal entity to finance its activities, the parties providing the necessary additional subordinated financial support most likely will not permit an equity investor to make decisions that may be counter to their interests. [FASB ASC (para. 810-10-05-13)]

Although the equity investors are technically the owners of the VIE, in reality they may retain little of the traditional responsibilities, risks, and benefits of ownership. In fact, the equity investors often cede financial control of the VIE to those with variable interest in exchange for a guaranteed rate of return.

Consolidation of Variable Interest Entities

Prior to current financial reporting standards, assets, liabilities, and results of operations for VIEs and other entities frequently were not consolidated with those of the firm that controlled the entity. These firms invoked a reliance on voting interests, as opposed to variable interests, to indicate a lack of a controlling financial interest. As legacy FASB standard *FIN 46R*[3] observed,

> . . . an enterprise's consolidated financial statements include subsidiaries in which the enterprise has a controlling financial interest. That requirement usually has been applied to subsidiaries in which an enterprise has a majority voting interest, but in many circumstances, the enterprise's consolidated financial statements do not include variable interest entities with which it has similar relationships. The voting interest approach is not effective in identifying controlling financial interests in entities that are not controllable through voting interests or in which the equity investors do not bear residual economic risk. (Summary, page 2)

[3] FASB *Interpretation No. 46R (FIN 46R),* "Consolidation of Variable Interest Entities," December 2003.

Companies must first identify a VIE that is not subject to control through voting ownership interests but is nonetheless subject to their control and therefore subject to consolidation. Each enterprise involved with a VIE must then determine whether the financial support it provides makes it the primary beneficiary of the VIE's activities. The VIE's primary beneficiary is then required to include the assets, liabilities, and results of the activities of the VIE in its consolidated financial statements.

Identification of a Variable Interest Entity

An entity qualifies as a VIE if either of the following conditions exists:

* The total equity at risk is not sufficient to permit the entity to finance its activities without additional subordinated financial support provided by any parties, including equity holders. In most cases, if equity at risk is less than 10 percent of total assets, the risk is deemed insufficient.[4]
* The equity investors in the VIE, as a group, lack any one of the following three characteristics of a controlling financial interest:
    1. The power, through voting rights or similar rights, to direct the activities of an entity that most significantly impact the entity's economic performance.
    2. The obligation to absorb the expected losses of the entity (e.g., the primary beneficiary may guarantee a return to the equity investors).
    3. The right to receive the expected residual returns of the entity (e.g., the investors' return may be capped by the entity's governing documents or other arrangements with variable interest holders).

Identification of the Primary Beneficiary of the VIE

Once it is established that a firm has a relationship with a VIE, the firm must determine whether it qualifies as the VIE's primary beneficiary. The primary beneficiary then must consolidate the VIE's assets, liabilities, revenues, expenses, and noncontrolling interest. An enterprise with a variable interest that provides it with a controlling financial interest in a variable interest entity will have both of the following characteristics:

* The power to direct the activities of a variable interest entity that most significantly impact the entity's economic performance.
* The obligation to absorb losses of the entity that could potentially be significant to the variable interest entity or the right to receive benefits from the entity that could potentially be significant to the variable interest entity.

Note that these characteristics mirror those that the equity investors lack in a VIE. Instead, the primary beneficiary will absorb a significant share of the VIE's losses or receive a significant share of the VIE's residual returns or both. The fact that the primary beneficiary may own no voting shares whatsoever becomes inconsequential because such shares do not effectively give the equity investors power to exercise control. Thus, a careful examination of the VIE's governing documents, contractual arrangements among parties involved, and who bears the risk is necessary to determine whether a reporting entity possesses control over a VIE.

The magnitude of the effect of consolidating an enterprise's VIEs can be large. For example, Walt Disney Company disclosed that two of its major investments qualified as VIEs and that it now will consolidate them. In its 2008 annual report, Disney stated the following:

> The Company has a 51 percent effective ownership interest in the operations of Euro Disney and a 43 percent ownership interest in the operations of Hong Kong Disneyland which are both consolidated as variable interest entities.

As a result of the 2008 consolidation of these two VIEs, Disney's total assets increased by $5.1 billion while its total debt increased by $3.4 billion.

---

[4] Alternatively, a 10 percent or higher equity interest may also be insufficient. According to GAAP, "Some entities may require an equity investment greater than 10 percent of their assets to finance their activities, especially if they engage in high-risk activities, hold high-risk assets, or have exposure to risks that are not reflected in the reported amounts of the entities' assets or liabilities." [FASB ASC (para. 810-10-25-46)]

Example of a Primary Beneficiary and Consolidated Variable Interest Entity

Assume that Twin Peaks Power Company seeks to acquire a generating plant for a negotiated price of $400 million from Ace Electric Company. Twin Peaks wishes to expand its market share and expects to be able to sell the electricity generated by the plant acquisition at a profit to its owners.

In reviewing financing alternatives, Twin Peaks observed that its general credit rating allowed for a 4 percent annual interest rate on a debt issue. Twin Peaks also explored the establishment of a separate legal entity whose sole purpose would be to own the electric generating plant and lease it back to Twin Peaks. Because the separate entity would isolate the electric generating plant from Twin Peaks's other risky assets and liabilities and provide specific collateral, an interest rate of 3 percent on the debt is available, producing before tax savings of $4 million per year. To obtain the lower interest rate, however, Twin Peaks must guarantee the separate entity's debt. Twin Peaks must also maintain certain of its own predefined financial ratios and restrict the amount of additional debt it can assume.

To take advantage of the lower interest rate, on January 1, 2011, Twin Peaks establishes Power Finance Co., an entity designed solely to own, finance, and lease the electric generating plant to Twin Peaks.[5] The documents governing the new entity specify the following:

- The sole purpose of Power Finance is to purchase the Ace electric generating plant, provide equity and debt financing, and lease the plant to Twin Peaks.
- An outside investor will provide $16 million in exchange for a 100 percent nonvoting equity interest in Power Finance.
- Power Finance will issue debt in exchange for $384 million. Because the $16 million equity investment by itself is insufficient to attract low-interest debt financing, Twin Peaks will guarantee the debt.
- Twin Peaks will lease the electric generating plant from Power Finance in exchange for payments of $12 million per year based on a 3 percent fixed interest rate for both the debt and equity investors for an initial lease term of five years.
- At the end of the five-year lease term (or any extension), Twin Peaks must do one of the following:
  - Renew the lease for five years subject to the approval of the equity investor.
  - Purchase the electric generating plant for $400 million.
  - Sell the electric generating plant to an independent third party. If the proceeds of the sale are insufficient to repay the equity investor, Twin Peaks must make a payment of $16 million to the equity investor.

Once the purchase of the electric generating plant is complete and the equity and debt are issued, Power Finance Company reports the following balance sheet:

POWER FINANCE COMPANY
Balance Sheet
January 1, 2011

Electric Generating Plant	$400M	Long-Term Debt	$384M
		Owner's Equity	16M
Total Assets	$400M	Total Liabilities and OE	$400M

Exhibit 6.2 shows the relationships between Twin Peaks, Power Finance, the electric generating plant, and the parties financing the asset purchase.

In evaluating whether Twin Peaks Electric Company must consolidate Power Finance Company, two conditions must be met. First, Power Finance must qualify as a VIE by either (1) an inability to secure financing without additional subordinated support or (2) a lack of either the

---

[5] This arrangement is similar to a "synthetic lease" commonly used in utility companies. Synthetic leases also can have tax advantages because the sponsoring firm accounts for them as capital leases for tax purposes.

EXHIBIT 6.2
**Variable Interest Entity
to Facilitate Financing**

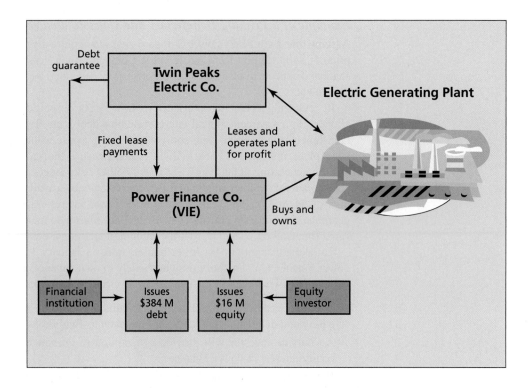

risk of losses or entitlement to residual returns (or both). Second, Twin Peaks must qualify as the primary beneficiary of Power Finance.

In assessing the first condition, several factors point to VIE status for Power Finance. Its owner's equity comprises only 4 percent of total assets, far short of the 10 percent benchmark. Moreover, Twin Peaks guarantees Power Finance's debt, suggesting insufficient equity to finance its operations without additional support. Finally, the equity investor appears to bear almost no risk with respect to the operations of the Ace electric plant. These characteristics indicate that Power Finance qualifies as a VIE.

In evaluating the second condition for consolidation, an assessment is made to determine whether Twin Peaks qualifies as Power Finance's primary beneficiary. Clearly, Twin Peaks has the power to direct Power Finance's activities. But to qualify for consolidation, Twin Peaks must also have the obligation to absorb losses or the right to receive returns from the Power Finance—either of which could potentially be significant to Power Finance. But what possible losses or returns would accrue to Twin Peaks? What are Twin Peaks's variable interests that rise and fall with the fortunes of Power Finance?

As stated in the VIE agreement, Twin Peaks will pay a fixed fee to lease the electric generating plant. It will then operate the plant and sell the electric power in its markets. If the business plan is successful, Twin Peaks will enjoy residual profits from operating while Power Finance's equity investors receive the fixed fee. On the other hand, if prices for electricity fall, Twin Peaks may generate revenues insufficient to cover its lease payments while Power Finance's equity investors are protected from this risk. Moreover, if the plant's fair value increases significantly, Twin Peaks can exercise its option to purchase the plant at a fixed price and either resell it or keep it for its own future use. Alternatively, if Twin Peaks were to sell the plant at a loss, it must pay the equity investors all of their initial investment, furthering the loss to Twin Peaks. Each of these elements points to Twin Peaks as the primary beneficiary of its VIE through variable interests. As the primary beneficiary, Twin Peaks must consolidate the assets, liabilities, and results of operations of Power Finance with its own.

Procedures to Consolidate Variable Interest Entities

As Power Finance's balance sheet exemplifies, VIEs typically possess only a few assets and liabilities. Also, their business activities usually are strictly limited. Thus, the actual procedures to consolidate VIEs are relatively uncomplicated.

Initial Measurement Issues

Just as in business combinations accomplished through voting interests, the financial reporting principles for consolidating variable interest entities require asset, liability, and noncontrolling interest valuations. These valuations initially, and with few exceptions, are based on fair values.

Recall that the acquisition method requires an allocation of the acquired business fair value based on the underlying fair values of its assets and liabilities. In determining the total amount to consolidate for a variable interest entity, the total business fair value of the entity is the sum of:

- Consideration transferred by the primary beneficiary.
- The fair value of the noncontrolling interest.

The fair value principle applies to consolidating VIEs in the same manner as business combinations accomplished through voting interests. If the total business fair value of the VIE exceeds the collective fair values of its net assets, goodwill is recognized.[6] Conversely, if the collective fair values of the net assets exceed the total business fair value, then the primary beneficiary recognizes a gain on bargain purchase.

In the previous example, assuming that the debt and noncontrolling interests are stated at fair values, Twin Peaks simply includes in its consolidated balance sheet the Electric Generating Plant at $400 million, the Long-Term Debt at $384 million, and a noncontrolling interest of $16 million.

As a further example, General Electric Company now consolidates Penske Truck Leasing Company as a VIE. GE recognizes an additional $1.055 billion in goodwill and more than $9 billion in property, plant, and equipment from the Penske consolidation. Previously, General Electric's investment in Penske was accounted for under the equity method.

To illustrate the initial measurement issues that a primary beneficiary faces, assume that Vax Company invests $5 million in TLH Property, a variable interest business entity. In agreements completed July 1, 2011, Vax establishes itself as the primary beneficiary of TLH Property. Previously, Vax had no interest in TLH. After Vax's investment, TLH presents the following financial information at assessed fair values:

Cash	$ 5 million
Land	20 million
Production facility	60 million
Long-term debt	(65 million)
Vax equity investment	(5 million)
Noncontrolling interest	(See following for alternative valuations.)

Vax will initially include each of TLH Property's assets and liabilities at their individual fair values in its acquisition-date consolidated financial reports. Any excess of TLH Property's acquisition-date business fair value over the collective fair values assigned to the acquired net assets must be recognized as goodwill. Conversely, if the collective fair values of the acquired net assets exceed the VIE's business fair value, a "gain on bargain purchase" is credited for the difference. To demonstrate these valuation principles, we use three brief examples, each with a different business fair value depending on alternative assessed fair values of the noncontrolling interest.

Total Business Fair Value of VIE Equals Assessed Net Asset Value

In this case, assume that the noncontrolling interest fair value equals $15 million. The VIE's total fair value is then $20 million ($5 million consideration paid + $15 million for the noncontrolling interest). Because the total fair value is identical to the $20 million collective amount of the individually assessed fair values for the net assets ($85 million total assets − $65 million long-term debt), neither goodwill nor a gain on bargain purchase is recognized. Vax simply consolidates all assets and liabilities at their respective fair values.

---

[6] The FASB ASC Glossary defines a business as an integrated set of activities and assets that is capable of being conducted and managed for the purpose of providing a return in the form of dividends, lower costs, or other economic benefits directly to investors or other owners, members, or participants. Alternatively, if the activities of the VIE are so restricted that it does not qualify as a business, the excess fair value is recognized as an acquisition loss, as opposed to goodwill.

Total Business Fair Value of VIE Is Less Than Assessed Net Asset Value

Alternatively, assume that the value of the noncontrolling interest was assessed at only $11 million. In this case, TLH Property's total fair value would be calculated at $16 million ($5 million consideration paid + $11 million for the noncontrolling interest). The $16 million total fair value compared to the $20 million assessed fair value of TLH Property's net assets (including cash) produces an excess of $4 million. In essence, the business combination receives a collective $20 million net identifiable asset fair value in exchange for $16 million. In this case, Vax recognizes a gain on bargain purchase of $4 million in its current year consolidated income statement.

Total Business Fair Value of VIE Is Greater Than Assessed Net Asset Value

Finally, assume that the value of the noncontrolling interest is assessed at $20 million. In this case, the total fair value of TLH Property would be calculated at $25 million ($5 million consideration paid + $20 million for the noncontrolling interest). The $25 million total fair value compared to the $20 million assessed fair value of TLH Property's net assets produces an excess total fair value of $5 million. Because TLH is a business entity, Vax Company reports the excess $5 million as goodwill in its consolidated statement of financial position.

Consolidation of VIEs Subsequent to Initial Measurement

After the initial measurement, consolidations of VIEs with their primary beneficiaries should follow the same process as if the entity were consolidated based on voting interests. Importantly, all intra-entity transactions between the primary beneficiary and the VIE (including fees, expenses, other sources of income or loss, and intra-entity inventory purchases) must be eliminated in consolidation. Finally, the VIE's income must be allocated among the parties involved (i.e., equity holders and the primary beneficiary). For a VIE, contractual arrangements, as opposed to ownership percentages, typically specify the distribution of its income. Therefore, a close examination of these contractual arrangements is needed to determine the appropriate allocation of VIE income to its equity owners and those holding variable interests.

Other Variable Interest Entity Disclosure Requirements

VIE disclosure requirements are designed to provide users of financial statements with more transparent information about an enterprise's involvement in a variable interest entity. The enhanced disclosures are required for any enterprise that holds a variable interest in a variable interest entity.

Included among the enhanced disclosures are requirements to show:

- The VIE's nature, purpose, size, and activities.
- The significant judgments and assumptions made by an enterprise in determining whether it must consolidate a variable interest entity and/or disclose information about its involvement in a variable interest entity.
- The nature of restrictions on a consolidated variable interest entity's assets and on the settlement of its liabilities reported by an enterprise in its statement of financial position, including the carrying amounts of such assets and liabilities.
- The nature of, and changes in, the risks associated with an enterprise's involvement with the variable interest entity.
- How an enterprise's involvement with the variable interest entity affects the enterprise's financial position, financial performance, and cash flows.

Enterprises that hold a significant variable interest in a VIE but are not the primary beneficiary must also disclose significant quantitative and qualitative information about the VIE and the enterprise's maximum exposure to loss as a result of its involvement with the VIE.

COMPARISONS WITH INTERNATIONAL ACCOUNTING STANDARDS

Although IFRS does not specifically mention variable interest entities, Standing Interpretations Committee (SIC) 12 addresses when a special purpose entity (SPE) should be consolidated. Similar to variable interest entities, SPEs may be controlled despite a lack of ownership interest. If a firm controls an SPE, then it must consolidate it. Control of an SPE by an entity is indicated by the following factors:

- The SPE conducts its activities for the benefit of the entity.
- The entity has decision-making power over the SPE.
- The entity can obtain the majority of the benefits of the SPE's activities.
- The entity has a majority of the ownership risks that arise from the SPE.

Examples of SPEs that should be consolidated include entities set up to conduct research and development activities, to provide a leasing arrangement, or to create securities from financial assets.

The International Accounting Standards Board has a project on its agenda to reconsider all of its consolidation guidance (including guidance for variable interest entities). The ultimate goal of both the FASB and the IASB is to work together to issue guidance that yields similar consolidation and disclosure results for special-purpose entities.

Clearly, the FASB wishes to enhance disclosures for all VIEs. Because in the past VIEs were often created in part to keep debt off a sponsoring firm's balance sheet, these enhanced disclosures are a significant improvement in financial reporting transparency.

INTRA-ENTITY DEBT TRANSACTIONS

LO2

Understand the consolidation procedures to eliminate all intra-entity debt accounts and recognize any associated gain or loss created whenever one company acquires an affiliate's debt instrument from an outside party.

The previous chapter explored the consolidation procedures required by the intra-entity transfer of inventory, land, and depreciable assets. In consolidating these transactions, all resulting gains were deferred until earned through either the use of the asset or its resale to outside parties. Deferral was necessary because these gains, although legitimately recognized by the individual companies, were unearned from the perspective of the consolidated entity. The separate financial information of each company was adjusted on the worksheet to be consistent with the view that the related companies actually composed a single economic concern.

This same objective applies in consolidating all other intra-entity transactions: The financial statements must represent the business combination as one enterprise rather than as a group of independent organizations. Consequently, in designing consolidation procedures for intra-entity transactions, the effects recorded by the individual companies first must be isolated. After the impact of each action is analyzed, worksheet entries recast these events from the vantage point of the business combination. Although this process involves a number of nuances and complexities, the desire for reporting financial information solely from the perspective of the consolidated entity remains constant.

We introduced the intra-entity sales of inventory, land, and depreciable assets together (in Chapter 5) because these transfers result in similar consolidation procedures. In each case, one of the affiliated companies recognizes a gain prior to the time the consolidated entity actually earned it. The worksheet entries required by these transactions simply realign the separate financial information to agree with the viewpoint of the business combination. The gain is removed and the inflated asset value is reduced to historical cost.

The next section of this chapter examines the intra-entity acquisition of bonds and notes. Although accounting for the related companies as a single economic entity continues to be the central goal, the consolidation procedures applied to intra-entity debt transactions are in diametric contrast to the process utilized in Chapter 5 for asset transfers.

Before delving into this topic, note that *direct* loans used to transfer funds between affiliated companies create no unique consolidation problems. Regardless of whether bonds or notes generate such amounts, the resulting receivable/payable balances are necessarily identical. Because no money is owed to or from an outside party, these reciprocal accounts must be eliminated in each subsequent consolidation. A worksheet entry simply offsets the two corresponding balances. Furthermore, the interest revenue/expense accounts associated with direct loans also agree and are removed in the same fashion.

Acquisition of Affiliate's Debt from an Outside Party

The difficulties encountered in consolidating intra-entity liabilities relate to a specific type of transaction: the purchase from an outside third party of an affiliate's debt instrument. A parent company, for example, could acquire a bond previously issued by a subsidiary on the open market. Despite the intra-entity nature of this transaction, the debt remains an outstanding obligation of the original issuer but is recorded as an investment by the acquiring company. Thereafter, even though related parties are involved, interest payments pass periodically between the two organizations.

Although the individual companies continue to report both the debt and the investment, from a consolidation viewpoint this liability is retired as of the acquisition date. From that time forward, the debt is no longer owed to a party outside the business combination. Subsequent interest payments are simply intra-entity cash transfers. To create consolidated statements, worksheet entries must be developed to adjust the various balances to report the debt's effective retirement.

Acquiring an affiliate's bond or note from an unrelated party poses no significant consolidation problems if the purchase price equals the corresponding book value of the liability. Reciprocal balances within the individual records would always be identical in value and easily offset in each subsequent consolidation.

Realistically, though, such reciprocity is rare when a debt is purchased from a third party. A variety of economic factors typically produce a difference between the price paid for the investment and the carrying amount of the obligation. The debt is originally sold under market conditions at a particular time. Any premium or discount associated with this issuance is then amortized over the life of the bond, creating a continuous adjustment to book value. The acquisition of this instrument at a later date is made at a price influenced by current economic conditions, prevailing interest rates, and myriad other financial and market factors.

Therefore, the cost paid to purchase the debt could be either more or less than the book value of the liability currently found within the issuing company's financial records. *To the business combination, this difference is a gain or loss because the acquisition effectively retires the bond; the debt is no longer owed to an outside party.* For external reporting purposes, this gain or loss must be recognized immediately by the consolidated entity.

Accounting for Intra-Entity Debt Transactions—Individual Financial Records

The accounting problems encountered in consolidating intra-entity debt transactions are fourfold:

1. Both the investment and debt accounts must be eliminated now and for each future consolidation despite containing differing balances.
2. Subsequent interest revenue/expense (as well as any interest receivable/payable accounts) must be removed although these balances also fail to agree in amount.
3. Changes in all of the preceding accounts occur constantly because of the amortization process.
4. The business combination must recognize the gain or loss on retirement of the debt, even though this balance does not appear within the financial records of either company.

To illustrate, assume that Alpha Company possesses an 80 percent interest in the outstanding voting stock of Omega Company. On January 1, 2009, Omega issued $1 million in 10-year bonds paying cash interest of 9 percent annually. Because of market conditions prevailing on that date, Omega sold the debt for $938,555 to yield an effective interest rate of 10 percent per year. Shortly thereafter, the prime interest rate began to fall, and by January 1, 2011, Omega made the decision to retire this debt prematurely and refinance it at the currently lower rates. To carry out this plan, Alpha purchased all of these bonds in the open market on January 1, 2011, for $1,057,466. This price was based on an effective yield of 8 percent, which is assumed to be in line with the interest rates at the time.

Many reasons could exist for having Alpha, rather than Omega, reacquire this debt. For example, company cash levels at that date could necessitate Alpha's role as the purchasing agent. Also, contractual limitations can prohibit Omega from repurchasing its own bonds.

In accounting for this business combination, an early extinguishment of the debt has occurred. Thus, the difference between the $1,057,466 payment and the January 1, 2011, book value of the liability must be recognized in the consolidated statements as a gain or loss. The exact account balance reported for the debt on that date depends on the amortization process. Although the issue was recorded initially at the $938,555 exchange price, after two years the carrying value increased to $946,651, calculated as follows:[7]

Bonds Payable—Book Value—January 1, 2011

Year	Book Value	Effective Interest (10 percent rate)	Cash Interest	Amortization	Year-End Book Value
2009	$938,555	$93,855	$90,000	$3,855	$942,410
2010	942,410	94,241	90,000	4,241	946,651

Because Alpha paid $110,815 in excess of the recorded liability ($1,057,466 − $946,651), the consolidated entity must recognize a loss of this amount. After the loss has been acknowledged, the bond is considered to be retired and no further reporting is necessary by the *business combination* after January 1, 2011.

Despite the simplicity of this approach, neither company accounts for the event in this manner. Omega retains the $1 million debt balance within its separate financial records and amortizes the remaining discount each year. Annual cash interest payments of $90,000 (9 percent) continue to be made. At the same time, Alpha records the investment at the historical cost of $1,057,466, an amount that also requires periodic amortization. Furthermore, as the owner of these bonds, Alpha receives the $90,000 interest payments made by Omega.

To organize the accountant's approach to this consolidation, a complete analysis of the subsequent financial recording made by each company should be produced. Omega records only two journal entries during 2011 assuming that interest is paid each December 31:

	Omega Company's Financial Records		
12/31/11	Interest Expense.	90,000	
	Cash.		90,000
	To record payment of annual cash interest on $1 million, 9 percent bonds payable.		
12/31/11	Interest Expense.	4,665	
	Bonds Payable (or Discount on Bonds Payable)		4,665
	To adjust interest expense to effective rate based on original yield rate of 10 percent ($946,651 book value for 2011 × 10% = $94,665). Book value increases to $951,316.		

Concurrently, Alpha journalizes entries to record its ownership of this investment:

	Alpha Company's Financial Records		
1/1/11	Investment in Omega Company Bonds	1,057,466	
	Cash		1,057,466
	To record acquisition of $1,000,000 in Omega Company bonds paying 9 percent cash interest, acquired to yield an effective rate of 8 percent.		

[7] The effective rate method of amortization is demonstrated here because this approach is theoretically preferable. However, the straight-line method can be applied if the resulting balances are not materially different than the figures computed using the effective rate method.

12/31/11	Cash.	90,000	
	Interest Income		90,000
	To record receipt of cash interest from Omega Company bonds ($1,000,000 × 9%).		
12/31/11	Interest Income.	5,403	
	Investment in Omega Company Bonds		5,403
	To reduce $90,000 interest income to effective rate based on original yield rate of 8 percent ($1,057,466 book value for 2011 × 8% = $84,597). Book value decreases to $1,052,063.		

Even a brief review of these entries indicates that the reciprocal accounts to be eliminated within the consolidation process do not agree in amount. You can see the dollar amounts appearing in each set of financial records in Exhibit 6.3. Despite the presence of these recorded balances, none of the four intra-entity accounts (the liability, investment, interest expense, and interest revenue) appears in the consolidated financial statements. *The only figure that the business combination reports is the $110,815 loss created by the extinguishment of this debt.*

Effects on Consolidation Process

As previous discussions indicated, consolidation procedures convert information generated by the individual accounting systems to the perspective of a single economic entity. A worksheet entry is therefore required on December 31, 2011, to eliminate the intra-entity balances shown in Exhibit 6.3 and to recognize the loss resulting from the repurchase. Mechanically, the differences in the liability and investment balances as well as the interest expense and interest income accounts stem from the $110,815 difference between the purchase price of the investment and the book value of the liability. Recognition of this loss, in effect, bridges the gap between the divergent figures.

Consolidation Entry B (December 31, 2011)

Bonds Payable	951,316	
Interest Income	84,597	
Loss on Retirement of Bond	110,815	
Investment in Omega Company Bonds		1,052,063
Interest Expense		94,665
To remove intra-entity bonds and related interest accounts and record loss on the early extinguishment of this debt. (Labeled **"B"** in reference to bonds.)		

EXHIBIT 6.3

ALPHA COMPANY AND OMEGA COMPANY
Effects of Intra-Entity Debt Transaction
2011

	Omega Company Reported Debt	Alpha Company Investment
2011 interest expense*	$ 94,665	$ –0–
2011 interest income†	–0–	(84,597)
Bonds payable*	(951,316)	–0–
Investment in bonds, 12/31/11†	–0–	1,052,063
Loss on retirement	–0–	–0–

Note: Parentheses indicate credit balances.
*Company total is adjusted for 2011 amortization of $4,665 (see journal entry).
†Adjusted for 2011 amortization of $5,403 (see journal entry).

The preceding entry successfully transforms the separate financial reporting of Alpha and Omega to that appropriate for the business combination. The objective of the consolidation process has been met: The statements present the bonds as having been retired on January 1, 2011. The debt and the corresponding investment are eliminated along with both interest accounts. Only the loss now appears on the worksheet to be reported within the consolidated financial statements.

Assignment of Retirement Gain or Loss

Perhaps the most intriguing issue in accounting for intra-entity debt transactions to be addressed concerns the assignment of any gains and losses created by the retirement. Should the $110,815 loss just reported be attributed to Alpha or to Omega? From a practical perspective, this assignment is important only in calculating and reporting noncontrolling interest figures. However, at least four different possible allocations can be identified, each of which demonstrates theoretical merit.

First, a strong argument can be made that the liability hypothetically extinguished is that of the issuing company and, thus, any resulting income relates solely to that party. This approach assumes that the retirement of any obligation affects only the debtor. Proponents of this position hold that the acquiring company is merely serving as a purchasing agent for the bonds' original issuer. Accordingly, in the previous illustration, the benefits derived from paying off the liability should accrue to Omega because refinancing reduced its interest rate. It incurred the loss solely to obtain these lower rates. Therefore, under this assumption, the entire $110,815 is assigned to Omega, the issuer of the debt. This assignment is usually considered to be consistent with the economic unit concept.

Second, other accountants argue that the loss should be assigned solely to the investor (Alpha). According to proponents of this approach, the acquisition of the bonds and the price negotiated by the buyer created the income effect.

A third hypothesis is that the resulting gain or loss should be split in some manner between the two companies. This approach is consistent with both the parent company concept and proportionate consolidation. Because both parties are involved with the debt, this proposition contends that assigning income to only one company is arbitrary and misleading. Normally, such a division is based on the original face value of the debt. Hence, $57,466 of the loss would be allocated to Alpha with the remaining $53,349 assigned to Omega:

Alpha		Omega	
Purchase price	$1,057,466	Book value	$ 946,651
Face value	1,000,000	Face value	1,000,000
Loss—Alpha	$ 57,466	Loss—Omega	$ 53,349

Allocating the loss in this manner is an enticing solution; the subsequent accounting process creates an identical division within the individual financial records. Because both Alpha's premium and Omega's discount must be amortized, the loss figures eventually affect the respective companies' reported earnings. Over the life of the bond, Alpha records the $57,466 as an interest income reduction, and Omega increases its own interest expense by $53,349 because of the amortization of the discount.

A fourth perspective takes a more practical view of intra-entity debt transactions: The parent company ultimately orchestrates all repurchases. As the controlling party in a business combination, the ultimate responsibility for retiring any obligation lies with the parent. The gain or loss resulting from the decision should thus be assigned solely to the parent regardless of the specific identity of the debt issuer or the acquiring company. In the current example, Alpha maintains control over Omega. Therefore, according to this theory, the financial consequences of reacquiring these bonds rest with Alpha so that the entire $110,815 loss must be attributed to it.

Each of these arguments has conceptual merit, and if the FASB eventually sets an official standard, any one approach (or possibly a hybrid) could be required. Unless otherwise stated, however, *all income effects in this textbook relating to intra-entity debt transactions are*

Discussion **Question**

WHO LOST THIS $300,000?

Several years ago, Penston Company purchased 90 percent of the outstanding shares of Swansan Corporation. Penston made the acquisition because Swansan produced a vital component used in Penston's manufacturing process. Penston wanted to ensure an adequate supply of this item at a reasonable price. The former owner, James Swansan, retained the remaining 10 percent of Swansan's stock and agreed to continue managing this organization. He was given responsibility for the subsidiary's daily manufacturing operations but not for any financial decisions.

Swansan's takeover has proven to be a successful undertaking for Penston. The subsidiary has managed to supply all of the parent's inventory needs and distribute a variety of items to outside customers.

At a recent meeting, Penston's president and the company's chief financial officer began discussing Swansan's debt position. The subsidiary had a debt-to-equity ratio that seemed unreasonably high considering the significant amount of cash flows being generated by both companies. Payment of the interest expense, especially on the subsidiary's outstanding bonds, was a major cost, one that the corporate officials hoped to reduce. However, the bond indenture specified that Swansan could retire this debt prior to maturity only by paying 107 percent of face value.

This premium was considered prohibitive. Thus, to avoid contractual problems, Penston acquired a large portion of Swansan's liability on the open market for 101 percent of face value. Penston's purchase created an effective loss of $300,000 on the debt, the excess of the price over the book value of the debt, as reported on Swansan's books.

Company accountants currently are computing the noncontrolling interest's share of consolidated net income to be reported for the current year. They are unsure about the impact of this $300,000 loss. The subsidiary's debt was retired, but officials of the parent company made the decision. Who lost this $300,000?

---

assigned solely to the parent company, as discussed in the final approach. Consequently, the results of extinguishing debt always are attributed to the party most likely to have been responsible for the action.

Intra-Entity Debt Transactions—Subsequent to Year of Acquisition

Even though the preceding Entry **B** correctly eliminates Omega's bonds in the year of retirement, the debt remains within the financial accounts of both companies until maturity. Therefore, in each succeeding time period, all balances must again be consolidated so that the liability is always reported as having been extinguished on January 1, 2011. Unfortunately, a simple repetition of Entry **B** is not possible. Developing the appropriate worksheet entry is complicated by the amortization process that produces continual change in the various account balances. Thus, as a preliminary step in each subsequent consolidation, current book values, as reported by the two parties, must be identified.

To illustrate, the 2012 journal entries for Alpha and Omega follow. Exhibit 6.4 (on the following page) shows the resulting account balances as of the end of that year.

Omega Company's Financial Records—December 31, 2012		
Interest Expense	90,000	
Cash		90,000
To record payment of annual cash interest on $1 million, 9 percent bonds payable.		
Interest Expense	5,132	
Bonds Payable (or Discount on Bonds Payable)		5,132
To adjust interest expense to effective rate based on an original yield rate of 10 percent ($951,316 book value for 2012 × 10% = $95,132). Book value increases to $956,448.		

EXHIBIT 6.4

ALPHA COMPANY AND OMEGA COMPANY
Effects of Intra-Entity Debt Transactions
2012

	Omega Company Reported Debt	Alpha Company Investment
2012 interest expense*	$ 95,132	–0–
2012 interest income†	–0–	$ (84,165)
Bonds payable*	(956,448)	–0–
Investment in bonds, 12/31/12†	–0–	1,046,228
Income effect within retained earnings, 1/1/12‡	94,665	(84,597)

Note: Parentheses indicate credit balances.
*Company total is adjusted for 2012 amortization of $5,132 (see journal entry).
†Adjusted for 2012 amortization of $5,835 (see journal entry).
‡The balance shown for the Retained Earnings account of each company represents the 2011 reported interest figures.

Alpha Company's Financial Records—December 31, 2012		
Cash	90,000	
Interest Income		90,000
To record receipt of cash interest from Omega Company bonds.		
Interest Income	5,835	
Investment in Omega Company Bonds		5,835
To reduce $90,000 interest income to effective rate based on an original yield rate of 8 percent ($1,052,063 book value for 2012 × 8% = $84,165). Book value decreases to $1,046,228.		

After the information in Exhibit 6.4 has been assembled, the necessary consolidation entry as of December 31, 2012, can be produced. This entry removes the balances reported at that date for the intra-entity bonds, as well as both of the interest accounts, to reflect the extinguishment of the debt on January 1, 2011. Because retirement occurred in a prior period, the worksheet adjustment must also create a $110,815 reduction in Retained Earnings to represent the original loss, but net of prior year's discount and premium amortizations.

Consolidation Entry *B (December 31, 2012)		
Bonds Payable	956,448	
Interest Income	84,165	
Retained Earnings, 1/1/12 (Alpha)	100,747	
Investment in Omega Company Bonds		1,046,228
Interest Expense		95,132
To eliminate intra-entity bond and related interest accounts and to adjust Retained Earnings from $10,068 (currently recorded net debit balance) to $110,815. (Labeled "*B" in reference to prior year bond transaction.)		

Analysis of this latest consolidation entry should emphasize several important factors:

1. The individual account balances change during the present fiscal period so that the current consolidation entry differs from Entry **B.** These alterations are a result of the amortization process. To ensure the accuracy of the worksheet entry, the adjusted balances are isolated in Exhibit 6.4.

2. As indicated previously, all income effects arising from intra-entity debt transactions are assigned to the parent company. For this reason, the adjustment to beginning Retained Earnings in Entry ***B** is attributed to Alpha as is the $10,967 increase in current income

($95,132 interest expense elimination less the $84,165 interest revenue elimination).[8] Consequently, the noncontrolling interest balances are not altered by Entry **B.**

3. The 2012 reduction to beginning Retained Earnings in Entry **B** ($100,747) does not agree with the original $110,815 retirement loss. The individual companies have recorded a net deficit balance of $10,068 (the amount by which previous interest expense exceeds interest revenue) at the start of 2012. To achieve the proper consolidated total, an adjustment of only $100,747 is required ($110,815 − $10,068).

Retained earnings balance—consolidation perspective (loss on retirement of debt)		$110,815
Individual retained earnings balances, 1/1/12:		
Omega Company (interest expense—2011).	$ 94,665	
Alpha Company (interest income—2011)	(84,597)	10,068
Adjustment to consolidated retained earnings, 1/1/12.		$100,747

Parentheses indicate a credit balance.

The periodic amortization of both the bond payable discount and the premium on the investment impacts the interest expense and revenue recorded by the two companies. As this schedule shows, these two interest accounts do not offset exactly; a $10,068 net residual amount remains in Retained Earnings after the first year. Because this balance continues to increase each year, the subsequent consolidation adjustments to record the loss decrease to $100,747 in 2012 and constantly lesser thereafter. *Over the life of the bond, the amortization process gradually brings the totals in the individual Retained Earnings accounts into agreement with the consolidated balance.*

4. Entry **B** as shown is appropriate for consolidations in which the parent has applied either the initial value or the partial equity method. However, a deviation is required if the parent uses the equity method for internal reporting purposes. Properly applying the equity method ensures that the parent's income and, hence, its retained earnings are correctly stated prior to consolidation. Alpha would have already recognized the loss in accounting for this investment. Consequently, when the parent applies the equity method, no adjustment to Retained Earnings is needed. In this one case, the $100,747 debit in Entry **B** is made to the Investment in Omega Company (instead of Retained Earnings) because the loss has become a component of that account.

SUBSIDIARY PREFERRED STOCK

LO3

Understand that subsidiary preferred stocks not owned by the parent are a component of the noncontrolling interest and are initially valued at acquisition-date fair value.

Although both small and large corporations routinely issue preferred shares, their presence within a subsidiary's equity structure adds a new dimension to the consolidation process. What accounting should be made of a subsidiary's preferred stock and the parent's payments that are made to acquire these shares?

Recall that preferred shares, although typically nonvoting, possess other "preferences" over common shares such as a cumulative dividend preference or participation rights. Preferred shares may even offer limited voting rights. Nonetheless, preferred shares are considered as a part of the subsidiary's stockholders' equity and their treatment in the parent's consolidated financial reports closely follows that for common shares.

The existence of subsidiary preferred shares does little to complicate the consolidation process. The acquisition method values all business acquisitions (whether 100 percent or less than 100 percent acquired) at their full fair values. In accounting for the acquisition of a subsidiary with preferred stock, the essential process of determining the acquisition-date business fair value of the subsidiary remains intact. Any preferred shares not owned by the parent

[8] Had the effects of the retirement been attributed solely to the original issuer of the bonds, the $10,967 addition to current income would have been assigned to Omega (the subsidiary), thus creating a change in the noncontrolling interest computations.

simply become a component of the noncontrolling interest and are included in the subsidiary business fair-value calculation. The acquisition-date fair value for any subsidiary common and/or preferred shares owned by outsiders becomes the basis for the noncontrolling interest valuation in the parent's consolidated financial reports.

To illustrate, assume that on January 1, 2011, High Company acquires control over Low Company by purchasing 80 percent of its outstanding common stock and 60 percent of its nonvoting, cumulative, preferred stock. Low owns land undervalued in its records by $100,000, but all other assets and liabilities have fair values equal to their book values. High paid a purchase price of $1 million for the common shares and $62,400 for the preferred. On the acquisition date, the 20 percent noncontrolling interest in the common shares had a fair value of $250,000 and the 40 percent preferred stock noncontrolling interest had a fair value of $41,600.

Low's capital structure immediately prior to the acquisition is shown below:

Common stock, $20 par value (20,000 shares outstanding)	$ 400,000
Preferred stock, 6% cumulative with a par value of $100	
(1,000 shares outstanding)	100,000
Additional paid-in capital	200,000
Retained earnings	516,000
Total stockholders' equity (book value)	$1,216,000

Exhibit 6.5 shows High's calculation of the acquisition-date fair value of Low and the allocation of the difference between the fair and book values to land and goodwill.

As seen in Exhibit 6.5, the subsidiary's ownership structure (i.e., comprising both preferred and common shares) does not affect the fair-value principle for determining the basis for consolidating the subsidiary. Moreover, the acquisition method follows the same procedure for calculating business fair value regardless of the various preferences the preferred shares may possess. Any cumulative or participating preferences (or any additional rights) attributed to the preferred shares are assumed to be captured by the acquisition-date fair value of the shares and thus automatically incorporated into the subsidiary's valuation basis for consolidation.

By utilizing the information above, we next construct a basic worksheet entry as of January 1, 2011 (the acquisition date). In the presence of both common and preferred subsidiary shares, combining the customary consolidation entries S and A avoids an unnecessary allocation of the subsidiary's retained earnings across these equity shares. The combined

EXHIBIT 6.5

LOW COMPANY
Acquisition-Date Fair Value
January 1, 2011

Consideration transferred for 80% interest in Low's common stock . .	$1,000,000
Consideration transferred for 60% interest in Low's preferred stock .	62,400
Noncontrolling interest in Low's common stock (20%)	250,000
Noncontrolling interest in Low's preferred stock (40%)	41,600
Total fair value of Low on 1/1/11	$1,354,000

HIGH'S ACQUISITION OF LOW
Excess Fair Value Over Book Value Allocation
January 1, 2011

Low Company business fair value		$1,354,000
Low Company book value		1,216,000
Excess acquisition-date fair value over book value		$ 138,000
Assigned to land	$100,000	
Assigned to goodwill	38,000	138,000
		–0–

consolidation entry also recognizes the allocations made to the undervalued land and goodwill. No other consolidation entries are needed because no time has passed since the acquisition took place.

Consolidation Entries S and A (combined)		
Common Stock (Low)	400,000	
Preferred Stock (Low)	100,000	
Additional Paid-In Capital (Low)	200,000	
Retained Earnings (Low)	516,000	
Land	100,000	
Goodwill	38,000	
Investment in Low's common stock		1,000,000
Investment in Low's preferred stock		62,400
Noncontrolling interest		291,600
To eliminate the subsidiary's common and preferred shares, recognize the fair values of the subsidiary's assets, and recognize the outside ownership.		

The above combined consolidation entry recognizes the noncontrolling interest as the total of
acquisition-date fair values of $250,000 for the common stock and $41,600 for the preferred
shares. Consistent with previous consolidation illustrations throughout the text, the entire
subsidiary's stockholders' equity section is eliminated along with the parent's investment
accounts—in this case for both the common and preferred shares.

Allocation of Subsidiary Income

The final factor influencing a consolidation that includes subsidiary preferred shares is the
allocation of the company's income between the two types of stock. A division must be made
for every period subsequent to the takeover (1) to compute the noncontrolling interest's share
and (2) for the parent's own recognition purposes. For a cumulative, nonparticipating preferred stock such as the one presently being examined, only the specified annual dividend is
attributed to the preferred stock with all remaining income assigned to common stock. Consequently, if we assume that Low reports earnings of $100,000 in 2011 while paying the an-
nual $6,000 dividend on its preferred stock, we allocate income for consolidation purposes
as follows:

	Income
Subsidiary total	$100,000
Preferred stock (6% dividend × $100,000 par value of the stock)	$ 6,000
Common stock (residual amount)	94,000

During 2011, High Company, as the parent, is entitled to $3,600 in dividends from Low's
preferred stock because of its 60 percent ownership. In addition, High holds 80 percent of
Low's common stock so that another $75,200 of the income ($94,000 × 80%) is attributed
to the parent. The noncontrolling interest in the subsidiary's income can be calculated in a
similar fashion:

		Percentage Outside Ownership	Noncontrolling Interest
Preferred stock dividend	$ 6,000	40%	$ 2,400
Income attributed to common stock	94,000	20	18,800
Noncontrolling interest in subsidiary's income ..			$21,200

CONSOLIDATED STATEMENT OF CASH FLOWS

LO4

Prepare a consolidated statement of cash flows.

Current accounting standards require that companies include a statement of cash flows among their consolidated financial reports. The main purpose of the statement of cash flows is to provide information about the entity's cash receipts and cash payments during a period. The statement is also designed to show why an entity's net income is different from its operating cash flows. For a consolidated entity, the cash flows relate to the entire business combination including the parent and all of its subsidiaries.

The statement of cash flows allocates the consolidated entity's overall change in cash during a period to three separate categories:

- Cash flows from operating activities.
- Cash flows from investing activities.
- Cash flows from financing activities.

The cash flows from operating activities can be shown using either the indirect approach or the direct approach. The indirect approach begins with consolidated net income and then adds and subtracts various items to adjust the accrual number to a cash flow amount. The direct approach examines cash flows directly from distinct sources that typically include revenues, purchases of inventory, and cash payments of other expenses. However, firms using the direct approach must also supplement the statement with the calculation of cash flows from operating activities using the indirect approach.

The consolidated statement of cash flows is not prepared from the individual cash flow statements of the separate companies. Instead, the consolidated income statements and balance sheets are first brought together on the worksheet. The cash flows statement is then based on the resulting consolidated figures. Thus, this statement is not actually produced by consolidation but is created from numbers generated by the process. Because special accounting procedures are needed in the period when the parent acquires a subsidiary, we first discuss preparation of the consolidated statement of cash flows for periods in which an acquisition takes place, followed by statement preparation in periods subsequent to acquisition.

Acquisition Period Statement of Cash Flows

If a business combination occurs during a particular reporting period, the consolidated cash flow statement must properly reflect several considerations. For many business combinations, the following issues frequently are present:

Business Acquisitions in Exchange for Cash

Cash purchases of businesses are an investing activity. The *net cash outflow* (cash paid less subsidiary cash acquired) is reported as the amount paid in a business acquisition.[9]

Operating Cash Flow Adjustments

Keeping in mind that the focus is on the consolidated entity's cash flows (not just the parent's), consolidated net income is the starting point for the indirect calculation of consolidated operating cash flows. Recall that consolidated net income includes only postacquisition subsidiary revenues and expenses. Therefore the adjustment to the accrual-based income number must also reflect only postacquisition amounts for the subsidiary. One important category of adjustments to consolidated net income to arrive at cash flows from operations involves changes in current operating accounts. Intraperiod acquisitions require special consideration in calculating changes in these current operating accounts.

For example, an increase in an accounts receivable balance typically indicates that a firm's accrual-based sales exceed the actual cash collections for sales during a period.

---

[9] For acquisitions that do not involve cash, or only partially involve cash, the details of the acquisitions should be provided in a supplemental section of the statement of cash flows for "significant noncash investing and financing activities."

Therefore, in computing operating cash flows, the increase in accounts receivable are deducted from the sales amount (direct method) or the net income (indirect method). However, when an acquisition takes place, the change in accounts receivable will often include amounts from the newly acquired subsidiary. Because the consolidated entity recognizes only postacquisition subsidiary revenues, such acquired receivables do not reflect sales that have been made by the consolidated entity. Therefore any subsidiary acquisition-date current operating account balances must be removed from the change in accounts receivable calculation.

In fact, any changes in operating balance sheet accounts (accounts receivable, inventory, accounts payable, etc.) must be computed net of the amounts acquired in the combination. Use of the direct approach of presenting operating cash flows also reports the separate computations of cash collected from customers and cash paid for inventory net of effects of any acquired businesses.

Excess Fair Value Amortizations

Any adjustments arising from the subsidiary's revenues or expenses (e.g., depreciation, amortization) must reflect only postacquisition amounts. Closing the subsidiary's books at the date of acquisition facilitates the determination of the appropriate current year postacquisition subsidiary effects on the consolidated entity's cash flows.

Subsidiary Dividends Paid

The cash outflow from dividends paid by a subsidiary only leaves the consolidated entity when paid to the noncontrolling interest. Thus dividends paid by a subsidiary to its parent do not appear as financing outflows. However, subsidiary dividends paid to the noncontrolling interest are a component of cash outflows from financing activities.

Intra-Entity Transfers

A significant volume of transfers between affiliated companies comprising a business combination often occurs. The resulting effects of intra-entity activities are eliminated in the preparation of consolidated statements. Likewise, the consolidated statement of cash flows does not include the impact of these transfers. Intra-entity sales and purchases do not change the amount of cash held by the business combination when viewed as a whole. Because the statement of cash flows is derived from the consolidated balance sheet and income statement, the impact of all transfers is already removed. Therefore, the proper presentation of cash flows requires no special adjustments for intra-entity transfers. The worksheet entries produce correct balances for the consolidated statement of cash flows.

Statement of Cash Flows in Periods Subsequent to Acquisition

The preparation of the consolidated statement of cash flows during periods of no acquisition is relatively uncomplicated. As before, consolidated net income is the starting point for the indirect calculation of consolidated operating cash flows. If the operating accounts are free from any effects of previous year's acquisitions, no further special adjustments are required. Because the consolidation process eliminates intra-entity balances, preparation of the operating activity section of the statement of cash flows typically proceeds in a straightforward manner using the already-available consolidated income statement and balance sheet amounts. Finally, subsidiary dividends paid to the noncontrolling interest are shown as a component of cash outflows from financing activities.

Consolidated Statement of Cash Flows Illustration

Assume that on July 1, 2011, Pinto Company acquires 90 percent of Salida Company's outstanding stock for $774,000 in cash. At the acquisition date, the 10 percent noncontrolling

EXHIBIT 6.6

SALIDA COMPANY
Book and Fair Values
July 1, 2011

Account	Book Value	Fair Value
Cash	$ 35,000	$ 35,000
Accounts receivable	145,000	145,000
Inventory	90,000	90,000
Land	100,000	120,000
Buildings	136,000	136,000
Equipment	259,000	299,000
Database	–0–	50,000
Accounts payable	(15,000)	(15,000)
Net book value	$750,000	$ 860,000

PINTO'S ACQUISITION OF SALIDA
Excess Fair Value over Book Value Allocation
July 1, 2011

Consideration transferred by Pinto		$ 774,000
Noncontrolling interest fair value		86,000
Salida's total fair value		$ 860,000
Salida's book value		750,000
Excess fair over book value		$ 110,000
To land	$ 20,000	
To equipment (five-year life)	40,000	
To database (25-year life)	50,000	110,000
		–0–

interest has a fair value of $86,000. Exhibit 6.6 shows book and fair values of Salida's assets and liabilities and Pinto's acquisition-date fair-value allocation schedule.

At the end of 2011, the following comparative balance sheets and consolidated income statement are available:

PINTO COMPANY AND SUBSIDIARY SALIDA COMPANY
Comparative Balance Sheets

	Pinto Co. January 1, 2011	Consolidated December 31, 2011
Cash	$ 170,000	$ 431,000
Accounts receivable (net)	118,000	319,000
Inventory	310,000	395,000
Land	250,000	370,000
Buildings (net)	350,000	426,000
Equipment (net)	1,145,000	1,380,000
Database	–0–	49,000
Total assets	$2,343,000	$3,370,000
Accounts payable	$ 50,000	$ 45,000
Long-term liabilities	18,000	522,000
Common stock	1,500,000	1,500,000
Noncontrolling interest	–0–	98,250
Retained earnings	775,000	1,204,750
Total liabilities and equities	$2,343,000	$3,370,000

PINTO COMPANY AND SUBSIDIARY SALIDA COMPANY
Consolidated Income Statement
For the Year Ended December 31, 2011

Revenues		$1,255,000
Cost of goods sold	$600,000	
Depreciation	124,000	
Database amortization	1,000	
Interest and other expenses	35,500	760,500
Consolidated net income		$ 494,500

Additional Information for 2011

- The consolidated income statement totals include Salida's postacquisition revenues and expenses.
- During the year, Pinto paid $50,000 in dividends. On August 1, Salida paid a $25,000 dividend.
- During the year, Pinto issued $504,000 in long-term debt at par value.
- No asset purchases or dispositions occurred during the year other than Pinto's acquisition of Salida.

In preparing the consolidated statement of cash flows, note that each adjustment derives from the consolidated income statement or changes from Pinto's January 1, 2011, balance sheet to the consolidated balance sheet at December 31, 2011.

Depreciation and Amortization   These expenses do not represent current operating cash outflows and thus are added back to convert accrual basis income to cash provided by operating activities.

Increases in Accounts Receivable, Inventory, and Accounts Payable (net of acquisition) Changes in balance sheet accounts affecting operating cash flows must take into account amounts acquired in business acquisitions. In this case, note that the changes in Accounts Receivable, Inventory, and Accounts Payable are computed as follows:

	Accounts Receivable	Inventory	Accounts Payable
Pinto's balance 1/1/11	$118,000	$310,000	$50,000
Increase from Salida acquisition	145,000	90,000	15,000
Adjusted beginning balance	263,000	400,000	65,000
Consolidated balance 12/31/11	319,000	395,000	45,000
Operating cash flow adjustment	$ 56,000	$ 5,000	$20,000

Acquisition of Salida Company   The Investing Activities section of the cash flow statement shows increases and decreases in assets purchased or sold involving cash. The cash outflow from the acquisition of Salida Company is determined as follows:

Cash paid for 90 percent interest in Salida	$774,000
Cash acquired	(35,000)
Net cash paid for Salida investment	$739,000

Note here that although Pinto acquires only 90 percent of Salida, 100 percent of Salida's cash is offset against the cash consideration paid in the acquisition in determining the investing cash outflow. Ownership divisions between the noncontrolling and controlling interests do not affect reporting for the entity's investing cash flows.

Issue of Long-Term Debt   Pinto Company's issuance of long-term debt represents a cash inflow from financing activities.

Dividends   The dividends paid to Pinto Company owners ($50,000) combined with the dividends paid to the noncontrolling interest ($2,500) represent cash outflows from financing activities.

Based on the consolidated totals from the comparative balance sheets and the consolidated income statement, the following consolidated statement of cash flows is then prepared. Pinto chooses to use the indirect method of reporting cash flows from operating activities.

PINTO COMPANY AND SUBSIDIARY SALIDA COMPANY
Consolidated Statement of Cash Flows
For the Year Ended December 31, 2011

Consolidated net income		$ 494,500
Depreciation expense	$ 124,000	
Amortization expense	1,000	
Increase in accounts receivable (net of acquisition effects)	(56,000)	
Decrease in inventory (net of acquisition effects)	5,000	
Decrease in accounts payable (net of acquisition effects)	(20,000)	54,000
Net cash provided by operations		$ 548,500
Purchase of Salida Company (net of cash acquired)		
Net cash used in investing activities	$(739,000)	(739,000)
Issue long-term debt	$ 504,000	
Dividends	(52,500)	
Net cash provided by financing activities		451,500
Increase in Cash 1/1/11 to 12/31/11		**$ 261,000**

CONSOLIDATED EARNINGS PER SHARE

LO5

Compute basic and diluted earnings per share for a business combination.

The consolidation process affects one other intermediate accounting topic, the computation of earnings per share (EPS). Publicly held companies must disclose EPS each period.

The following steps calculate such figures:

- Determine basic EPS by dividing the parent's share of consolidated net income (after reduction for preferred stock dividends) by the weighted average number of common stock shares outstanding for the period. If the reporting entity has no dilutive options, warrants, or other convertible items, only basic EPS is presented on the face of the income statement. However, diluted EPS also must be presented if any dilutive convertibles are present.

- Compute diluted EPS by combining the effects of *any dilutive securities* with basic earnings per share. Stock options, stock warrants, convertible debt, and convertible preferred stock often qualify as dilutive securities.[10]

In most instances, the computation of EPS for a business combination follows the same general pattern. Consolidated net income attributable to the parent company owners along with the number of outstanding parent shares provides the basis for calculating basic EPS. Any convertibles, warrants, or options for the parent's stock that can possibly dilute the reported figure must be included as described earlier in determining diluted EPS.

However, a problem arises if warrants, options, or convertibles that can dilute the subsidiary's earnings are outstanding. Although the parent company is not directly affected, the potential impact of these items on their share of consolidated net income must be given weight in computing diluted EPS for the consolidated income statement. Because of possible conversion,

---

[10] Complete coverage of the EPS computation can be found in virtually any intermediate accounting textbook. To adequately understand this process, a number of complex procedures must be mastered, including these:

- Calculation of the weighted average number of common shares outstanding.
- Understanding the method of including stock rights, convertible debt, and convertible preferred stock within the computation of diluted EPS.

the subsidiary earnings figure included in consolidated net income is not necessarily applicable to the diluted EPS computation. *Thus, the accountant must separately determine the parent's share of subsidiary income that should be used in deriving diluted EPS.*

Finally, the focus is on earnings per share for the parent company stockholders, even in the presence of a noncontrolling interest. As stated in the FASB ASC (para. 260-10-45-11A):

> For purposes of computing EPS in consolidated financial statements (both basic and diluted), if one or more less-than-wholly-owned subsidiaries are included in the consolidated group, income from continuing operations and net income shall exclude the income attributable to the noncontrolling interest in subsidiaries.

Thus, consolidated income attributable to the parent's interest forms the basis for the numerator in all EPS calculations for consolidated financial reporting.

Earnings per Share Illustration

Assume that Big Corporation has 100,000 shares of its common stock outstanding during the current year. The company also has issued 20,000 shares of nonvoting preferred stock, paying an annual cumulative preferred dividend of $5 per share ($100,000 total). Each of these preferred shares is convertible into two shares of Big's common stock.

Assume also that Big owns 90 percent of Little's common stock and 60 percent of its preferred stock (which pays $12,000 in preferred dividends per year). Annual amortization is $26,000 attributable to various intangibles. EPS computations currently are being made for 2011. During the year, Big reported separate income of $600,000 and Little earned $100,000. A simplified consolidation of the figures for the year indicates consolidated net income attributable to Big of $663,000:

Big's separate income for 2011		$600,000
Little's separate income for 2011	$100,000	
Amortization expense resulting from original fair-value allocation. . .	(26,000)	
Little's income after excess fair-value amortization		74,000
Consolidated net income.		$674,000
Noncontrolling interest in Little—common stock (10% of $74,000 income after $12,000 in preferred stock dividends)	$ (6,200)	
Noncontrolling interest in Little— preferred stock (40% of dividends).	(4,800)	
Total noncontrolling interest in consolidated net income		(11,000)
Consolidated net income attributable to Big (parent)		$663,000

Little has 20,000 shares of common stock and 4,000 shares of preferred stock outstanding. The preferred shares pay a $3 per year dividend, and each can be converted into two shares of common stock (or 8,000 shares in total). Because Big owns only 60 percent of Little's preferred stock, a $4,800 dividend is distributed each year to the outside owners (40 percent of $12,000 total payment).

Assume finally that the subsidiary also has $200,000 in convertible bonds outstanding that were originally issued at face value. This debt has a cash and an effective interest rate of 10 percent ($20,000 per year) and can be converted by the owners into 9,000 shares of Little's common stock. Big owns none of these bonds. Little's tax rate is 30 percent.

To better visualize these factors, the convertible items are scheduled as follows:

Company	Item	Interest or Dividend	Conversion	Big Owns
Big	Preferred stock	$100,000/year	40,000 shares	Not applicable
Little	Preferred stock	12,000/year	8,000 shares	60%
Little	Bonds	14,000/year*	9,000 shares	–0–

*Interest on the bonds is shown net of the 30 percent tax effect ($20,000 interest less $6,000 tax savings). No tax is computed for the preferred shares because distributed dividends do not create a tax impact.

EXHIBIT 6.7
Subsidiary's Diluted Earnings per Share

LITTLE COMPANY			
Diluted Earnings per Common Share			
For Year Ending December 31, 2011			
	Earnings	**Shares**	
Little's income after amortization	$74,000	20,000	
Preferred stock dividends	(12,000)		
Effect of possible preferred stock conversion:			
Dividends saved	12,000	New shares 8,000	$1.50 impact (12,000/8,000)
Effect of possible bond conversion:			
Interest saved (net of taxes)	14,000	9,000	$ 1.56 impact (14,000/9,000)
Diluted EPS	$88,000	37,000	$ 2.38 (rounded)

Because the subsidiary has convertible items that can affect the company's outstanding shares and net income, Little's diluted earnings per share must be derived *before* Big's diluted EPS can be determined. As shown in Exhibit 6.7, Little's diluted EPS are $2.38. Two aspects of this schedule should be noted:

- The individual impact of the convertibles ($1.50 for the preferred stock and $1.56 for the bonds) did not raise the EPS figures. Thus, neither the preferred stock nor the bonds are antidilutive, and both are properly included in these computations.
- Determining diluted EPS of the subsidiary is necessary only because of the possible dilutive impact. Without the subsidiary's convertible bonds and preferred stock, the parent's share of consolidated net income would form the basis for computing EPS, and only basic EPS would be reported.

According to Exhibit 6.7, Little's income is $88,000 for diluted EPS. The issue for the accountant is how much of this amount should be included in computing the parent's diluted EPS. This allocation is based on the percentage of shares controlled by the parent. Note that if the subsidiary's preferred stock and bonds are converted into common shares, Big's ownership falls from 90 to 62 percent. For diluted EPS, 37,000 shares are appropriate. Big's 62 percent ownership (22,800/37,000) is the basis for allocating the subsidiary's $88,000 income to the parent.

Supporting Calculations for Diluted Earnings per Share

	Little Company Shares	Big's Percentage	Big's Ownership
Common stock	20,000	90%	18,000
Possible new shares—preferred stock	8,000	60	4,800
Possible new shares—bonds	9,000	–0–	–0–
Total	37,000		22,800

Big's ownership (diluted): 22,800/37,000 = 62% (rounded)
Income assigned to Big (diluted earnings per share computation):
$88,000 × 62% = $54,560

We can now determine Big Company's EPS. Only $54,560 of subsidiary income is appropriate for the diluted EPS computation. Because two different income figures are utilized, basic and diluted calculations are made separately as in Exhibit 6.8. Consequently, these schedules determine that Big Company should report basic EPS of $5.63, with diluted earnings per share of $4.68.

EXHIBIT 6.8

BIG COMPANY AND CONSOLIDATED SUBSIDIARY
Basic Earnings per Common Share
For Year Ending December 31, 2011

	Earnings	Shares	
Consolidated net income (to Big)	$663,000		
Big's shares outstanding		100,000	
Preferred stock dividends (Big)	(100,000)		
Basic EPS	$563,000	100,000	$5.63

Diluted Earnings per Common Share
For Year Ending December 31, 2011

	Earnings	Shares	
Computed below	$654,560*		
Big's shares outstanding		100,000	
Preferred stock dividends (Big)	(100,000)		
Effect of possible preferred stock (Big) conversion:			
Dividends saved	100,000	New shares 40,000	$2.50 impact (100,000/40,000)
Diluted EPS	$654,560	140,000	$4.68 (rounded)

*Net income computation:

Big's separate income	$600,000
Portion of Little's income assigned to diluted earnings per share calculation	54,560 (computed in supporting calculations)
Earnings of the business combination applicable to diluted earnings per share	$654,560

SUBSIDIARY STOCK TRANSACTIONS

LO6

Understand the accounting for subsidiary stock transactions that impact the underlying value recorded within the parent's Investment account and the consolidated financial statements.

A footnote to the financial statements of Gerber Products Company disclosed a transaction carried out by one of the organization's subsidiaries: "The Company's wholly owned Mexican subsidiary sold previously unissued shares of common stock to Grupo Coral, S.A., a Mexican food company, at a price in excess of the shares' net book value." The footnote added that Gerber had increased consolidated Additional Paid-In Capital by $432,000 as a result of this stock sale.

As this illustration shows, subsidiary stock transactions can alter the level of parent ownership. A subsidiary, for example, can decide to sell previously unissued stock to raise needed capital. Although the parent company can acquire a portion or even all of these new shares, such issues frequently are marketed entirely to outsiders. A subsidiary could also be legally forced to sell additional shares of its stock. As an example, companies holding control over foreign subsidiaries occasionally encounter this problem because of laws in the individual localities. Regulations requiring a certain percentage of local ownership as a prerequisite for operating within a country can mandate issuance of new shares. Of course, changes in the level of parent ownership do not result solely from stock sales: A subsidiary also can repurchase its own stock. The acquisition, as well as the possible retirement, of such treasury shares serves as a means of reducing the percentage of outside ownership.

Changes in Subsidiary Value—Stock Transactions

When a subsidiary subsequently buys or sells its own stock, a nonoperational increase or decrease occurs in the company's fair and book value. Because the transaction need not involve the parent, the parent's investment account does not automatically reflect the effect of this change. *Thus, a separate adjustment must be recorded to maintain reciprocity between the subsidiary's stockholders' equity accounts and the parent's investment balance.* The accountant measures the impact the stock transaction has on the parent to ensure that this effect is appropriately recorded within the consolidation process.

An overall perspective of accounting for subsidiary stock transactions follows from the fundamental notion that the parent establishes the subsidiary's valuation basis at fair value as of the acquisition date. Over time, the parent adjusts this initial fair value for subsidiary income less excess amortization and subsidiary dividends. If the subsidiary issues (or buys) any of its own stock subsequent to acquisition, the effect on the parent will depend on whether the price received (or paid) is greater or less that the per share subsidiary adjusted fair value at that point in time.

An example demonstrates the mechanics of this issue. Assume that on January 1, 2010, Giant Company acquires in the open market 60,000 of Small Company's outstanding 80,000 shares and prepares the following fair-value allocation schedule.

Consideration transferred by Giant	$480,000	
Noncontrolling interest fair value	160,000	
Small Company acquisition-date fair value		$640,000
Small Company acquisition-date book value		
Common stock (80,000 shares outstanding)	$ 80,000	
Additional paid-in capital	200,000	
Retained earnings, 1/1/10	260,000	540,000
Excess fair value assigned to trademark (10-year life)		$100,000

Assuming Small reports earnings of $50,000 in 2010 and pays no dividends, Giant prepares the following routine consolidation entries for the December 31, 2010, worksheet. Giant uses the equity method to account for its 75 percent interest in Small.

December 31, 2010, Consolidation Worksheet Entries

Consolidation Entry S

Common Stock (Small Company)	80,000	
Additional Paid-In Capital (Small Company)	200,000	
Retained Earnings, 1/1/10 (Small Company)	260,000	
Investment in Small Company (75%)		405,000
Noncontrolling Interest in Small Company (25%)		135,000
To eliminate subsidiary's stockholders' equity accounts and recognize noncontrolling interest book value beginning balance.		

Consolidation Entry A

Trademark	100,000	
Investment in Small Company (75%)		75,000
Noncontrolling Interest in Small Company (25%)		25,000
To recognize the excess acquisition-date fair value assigned to Small's trademark with allocations to the controlling and noncontrolling interest.		

Consolidation Entry I

Equity in Small's Earnings	30,000	
Investment in Small Company		30,000
To eliminate Giant's equity in Small's earnings (75% × [$50,000 less $10,000 trademark excess amortization]).		

Consolidation Entry E

Amortization Expense	10,000	
Trademark		10,000
To recognize the excess trademark amortization ($100,000 ÷ 10 years).		

We now introduce a subsidiary stock transaction to demonstrate the effect created on the consolidation process. Assume that on January 1, 2011, Giant announces plans for expansion of Small's operations. To help finance the expansion, Small sells 20,000 previously unissued shares of its common stock to outside parties for $10 per share. After the stock issue, Small's book value is as follows:

Common stock ($1.00 par value with 100,000 shares issued and outstanding)	$100,000
Additional paid-in capital	380,000
Retained earnings, 1/1/11	310,000
Total stockholders' equity, 1/1/11	$790,000

Note that the common stock and additional paid-in capital balances reflect increases from the new stock issue. Retained earnings have also increased from Small's $50,000 income in 2010 (no dividends). Although Small's book value is now $790,000, its valuation for the consolidated entity is derived from its acquisition-date fair value as adjusted through time as follows:

Consideration transferred	$480,000
Noncontrolling interest acquisition-date fair value	160,000
2010 Small income less excess amortization	40,000
Adjusted subsidiary value, 1/1/11	$680,000
Stock issue proceeds ($10 × 20,000 shares)	200,000
Subsidiary valuation basis, 1/1/11	$880,000

Because of Small's stock issue, Giant no longer possesses a 75 percent interest. Instead, the parent now holds 60 percent (60,000 shares of a total of 100,000 shares) of Small Company. The effect on the parent's ownership can be computed as follows:

Small's valuation basis 1/1/11 (above)	$880,000
Giant's post-issue ownership (60,000 shares ÷ 100,000 shares)	60%
Giant's post-stock issue ownership balance	$528,000
Giant's equity-adjusted investment account ($480,000 + [75% × $40,000]) . . .	510,000
Required adjustment—increase in Giant's additional paid-in capital	$ 18,000

Independent of any action by the parent company, the assigned fair-value equivalency of this investment has risen from $510,000 to $528,000. Small's ability to sell shares of stock at more than the per share consolidated subsidiary value ($680,000 ÷ 80,000 shares = $8.50 per share) created an increased value for the parent. Therefore, Giant records the $18,000 increment as an adjustment to both its investment account (because the underlying value of the subsidiary has increased) and additional paid-in capital:

Giant Company's Financial Records—January 1, 2011		
Investment in Small Company	18,000	
Additional Paid-In Capital (Giant Company)		18,000
To recognize change in equity of business combination created by Small Company issuing 10,000 additional shares of common stock at above the previously assigned fair value.		

Note that the parent reports a change in stockholders' equity (i.e., Additional Paid-In Capital) for effects from subsidiary stock transactions. GAAP literature states that:

> [c]hanges in a parent's ownership interest while the parent retains its controlling financial interest in its subsidiary shall be accounted for as equity transactions (investments by owners and distributions to owners acting in their capacity as owners). Therefore, no gain or loss shall be recognized in consolidated net income or comprehensive income. The carrying amount of the noncontrolling interest shall be adjusted to reflect the change in its ownership interest in the subsidiary. Any difference between the fair value of the consideration received or paid and the amount by which the noncontrolling interest is adjusted shall be recognized in equity attributable to the parent. [FASB ASC (para. 810-10-45-23)]

Consistent with this view, this textbook treats the effects from subsidiary stock transactions on the consolidated entity as adjustments to Additional Paid-In Capital.

After the change in the parent's records has been made, the consolidation process can proceed in a normal fashion. Assuming Small reports earnings of $85,000 in 2011 and pays no dividends, Giant prepares the following routine consolidation entries for the December 31, 2011, worksheet. *Although the investment and subsidiary equity accounts are removed here, the change recorded earlier in Giant's Additional Paid-In Capital remains within the consolidated figures.*

December 31, 2011, Consolidation Worksheet Entries

Consolidation Entry S

Common Stock (Small Company)	100,000	
Additional Paid-In Capital (Small Company)	380,000	
Retained Earnings (Small Company)	310,000	
Investment in Small Company (60%)		474,000
Noncontrolling Interest in Small Company (40%)		316,000

To eliminate subsidiary's stockholders' equity accounts and recognize noncontrolling interest book value beginning balance. Small's capital accounts have been updated to reflect the issuance of 10,000 shares of $1 par value common stock at $10 per share.

Consolidation Entry A

Trademark	90,000	
Investment in Small Company (60%)		54,000
Noncontrolling Interest in Small Company (40%)		36,000

To recognize the unamortized excess acquisition-date fair value assigned to Small's trademark as of the beginning of the period with allocations to the controlling and noncontrolling interests' adjusted ownership percentages.

Consolidation Entry I

Equity in Small's Earnings	45,000	
Investment in Small Company		45,000

To eliminate Giant's equity in Small's earnings (60% × [$85,000 − $10,000 trademark excess amortization]).

Consolidation Entry E

Amortization expense	10,000	
Trademark		10,000

To recognize the excess trademark amortization ($100,000 ÷ 10 years).

The noncontrolling interest now stands at 40 percent ownership. Because these 40 percent owners will share in the profits generated by the subsidiary's trademark, they are allocated a 40 percent share to their overall equity balance in the consolidated financial statements. The noncontrolling interest is also assigned 40 percent of the excess fair-value trademark amortization.

Subsidiary Stock Transactions—Illustrated

No single example can demonstrate the many possible variations that different types of subsidiary stock transactions could create. To provide a working knowledge of this process, we analyze four additional cases briefly, each based on the following scenario:

Assume that Antioch Company acquires 90 percent of the common stock of Westminster Company on January 1, 2010, in exchange for $1,350,000 cash. The acquisition-date fair value of the 10 percent noncontrolling interest is $150,000. At that date, Westminster has the following stockholders' equity accounts:

Common stock—100,000 shares outstanding	$ 200,000
Additional paid-in capital	450,000
Retained earnings, 1/1/10	750,000
Total stockholders' equity	$1,400,000

The $100,000 excess acquisition-date fair over book value was allocated to a customer list with a five-year remaining life. In 2010, Westminster reports $190,000 in earnings and pays a $30,000 dividend. Antioch accrues its share of Westminster's income (less excess fair-value amortization related to the customer list) through application of the equity method. Antioch's equity method balance for its investment in Westminster is computed as follows:

Consideration transferred for 90% of Westminster	$1,350,000
Equity earnings of Westminster (90% × [$190,000 − $20,000 excess amortization])	153,000
Dividends received (90% × $30,000)	(27,000)
Equity method balance, 12/31/10	$1,476,000

View each of the following cases as an independent situation.

Case 1

Assume that on January 1, 2011, Westminster Company sells 25,000 shares of previously unissued common stock to outside parties for $14.40 per share. This stock issue changes both the parent's percentage interest in the subsidiary and the subsidiary's consolidated valuation basis. The parent's percentage ownership declines to 72 percent (90,000 shares ÷ 125,000 total shares). The subsidiary's valuation basis for consolidation becomes:

Consideration transferred	$1,350,000
Noncontrolling interest acquisition-date fair value	150,000
2010 Westminster income less excess amortization	170,000
Westminster dividends	(30,000)
Stock issue proceeds ($14.40 × 25,000 shares)	360,000
Subsidiary valuation basis 1/1/11	$2,000,000

Next, the effect on the parent's ownership can be computed as follows:

Westminster's valuation basis 1/1/11 (above)	$2,000,000
Antioch's post–stock issue ownership (90,000 shares ÷ 125,000 shares)	72%
Antioch's post–stock issue ownership balance	$1,440,000
Antioch's pre–stock issue equity-adjusted investment account (above)	1,476,000
Required adjustment—decrease in Antioch's additional paid-in capital	$ 36,000

To reflect this effect of the stock issue change on its valuation of the subsidiary, the parent makes the following journal entry on its financial records.

Antioch Company's Financial Records		
Additional Paid-In Capital (Antioch Company)	36,000	
Investment in Westminster Company		36,000
To recognize change in equity of business combination created by issuance of 25,000 additional shares of Westminster's common stock.		

Case 2

Assume that on January 1, 2011, Westminster issues 20,000 new shares of common stock for $16 per share. Of this total, Antioch acquires 18,000 shares to maintain its 90 percent level of ownership. Antioch pays a total of $288,000 (18,000 shares × $16) for this additional stock. Outside parties buy the remaining shares.

Under these circumstances, the stock transaction alters the consolidated valuation basis of the subsidiary but not the percentage owned by the parent. Thus, only the subsidiary value must be updated prior to determining the necessity of an equity revaluation:

Consideration transferred	$1,350,000
Noncontrolling interest acquisition-date fair value	150,000
2010 Westminster income less excess amortization	170,000
Westminster dividends	(30,000)
Stock issue proceeds ($16 × 20,000 shares)	320,000
Subsidiary valuation basis 1/1/11	$1,960,000

The effect on the parent's ownership is computed as follows:

Westminster's valuation basis 1/1/11 (above)		$1,960,000
Antioch's post–stock issue ownership (108,000 shares ÷ 120,000 shares)		90%
Antioch's post-stock issue ownership balance		$1,764,000
Antioch's equity-adjusted investment account before stock purchase	$1,476,000	
Additional payment for 18,000 shares of Westminster	288,000	1,764,000
Required adjustment		$ –0–

This case requires no adjustment because Antioch's underlying interest remains aligned with the subsidiary's consolidated valuation basis. Any purchase of new stock by the parent in the same ratio as previous ownership does not affect consolidated Additional Paid-In Capital. The transaction creates no proportionate increase or decrease.

Case 3

Assume that instead of issuing new stock, on January 1, 2011, Westminster reacquires all 10,000 shares owned by the noncontrolling interest. It pays $16 per share for this treasury stock.

This illustration presents another type of subsidiary stock transaction: the acquisition of treasury stock. In this case the effect on the parent can be computed by reference to the amount of noncontrolling interest that must be reduced to zero in the consolidated financial statements.

Noncontrolling interest (NCI) acquisition-date fair value	$ 150,000
NCI share of 2010 Westminster income less excess amortization ($170,000 × 10%)	17,000
NCI share of Westminster dividends ($30,000 × 10%)	(3,000)
Noncontrolling interest valuation basis at 1/1/11	$ 164,000
Treasury stock purchase ($16 × 10,000 shares)	(160,000)
Required adjustment—increase in Antioch's additional paid-in capital	$ 4,000

The consolidated entity paid $160,000 to reduce a $164,000 owners' equity interest (the noncontrolling interest) to zero, thus increasing its own equity by $4,000. As usual, the increase in equity is attributed to additional paid-in capital and is recorded on the parent's records.

Antioch Company's Financial Records		
Investment in Westminster Company	4,000	
Additional Paid-In Capital (Antioch Company)		4,000
To recognize change in equity of business combination created by acquisition of 10,000 treasury shares by Westminster.		

This third illustration represents a newly introduced subsidiary stock transaction, the purchase of treasury stock. Therefore, display of consolidation Entries **S** and **A** are also presented.

These entries demonstrate the worksheet eliminations required when the subsidiary holds treasury shares:

Consolidation Entry S		
Common Stock (Westminster Company)	200,000	
Additional Paid-In Capital (Westminster Company)	450,000	
Retained Earnings, 1/1/11 (Westminster Company)	910,000	
Treasury Stock		160,000
Investment in Westminster Company		1,400,000
To eliminate equity accounts of Westminster Company		

Consolidation Entry A		
Customer List	80,000	
Investment in Westminster Company		80,000
To recognize the beginning-of-year unamortized excess acquisition-date fair value allocated to the customer list.		

Note first the absence of a noncontrolling interest entry. Also note that the sum of the credits to the Investment in Westminster account is $1,480,000, which is the pretreasury stock purchase equity method balance of $1,476,000 plus the $4,000 addition from the acquisition of the noncontrolling interest.

Case 4

Assume that on January 1, 2011, Westminster issues a 10 percent stock dividend (10,000 new shares) to its owners when the stock's fair value is $15 per share.

This final case illustrates another example of a subsidiary stock transaction producing no effect on the parent's records. Stock dividends, whether large or small, capitalize a portion of the issuing company's retained earnings without altering total book value. Shareholders recognize the receipt of a stock dividend as a change in the per share value rather than as an adjustment to the investment balance. Because neither party perceives a net effect, the consolidation process proceeds in a routine fashion. Therefore, a subsidiary stock dividend requires no special treatment prior to development of a worksheet.

Consideration transferred	$1,350,000
Noncontrolling interest acquisition-date fair value	150,000
2010 Westminster income less excess amortization	170,000
Westminster dividends	(30,000)
Subsidiary valuation basis 1/1/11	$1,640,000
Antioch's ownership (adjusted for 10% stock dividend 99,000 ÷ 110,000 shares)	90%
Antioch's post–stock dividend ownership interest	$1,476,000
Antioch's equity-adjusted investment account	1,476,000
Adjustment required by stock dividend	$ –0–

The consolidation Entries **S** and **A** made just after the stock dividend follow. The $1,404,000 component of the investment account is offset against the stockholders' equity of the subsidiary. Although the stock dividend did not affect the parent's investment, the equity accounts of the subsidiary have been realigned in recognition of the $150,000 stock dividend (10,000 shares of $2 par value stock valued at $15 per share):

Consolidation Entry S		
Common Stock (Westminster Company)	220,000	
Additional Paid-In Capital (Westminster Company)	580,000	
Retained Earnings, 1/1/11 (Westminster Company)	760,000	
Investment in Westminster Company (90%)		1,404,000
Noncontrolling Interest (10%)		156,000
To eliminate the equity accounts of Westminster Company.		

Consolidation Entry A		
Customer List	80,000	
Investment in Westminster Company		72,000
Noncontrolling Interest		8,000
To recognize the beginning-of-year unamortized excess fair value attributable to customer list.		

Note here that the sum of the credits to the Investment in Westminster account is $1,476,000, which equals the pre-stock dividend equity method balance.

Summary

1. Variable interest entities (VIEs) typically take the form of a trust, partnership, joint venture, or corporation. In most cases, a sponsoring firm creates these entities to engage in a limited and well-defined set of business activities. Control of VIEs, by design, often does not rest with its equity holders. Instead, control is exercised through contractual arrangements with the sponsoring firm that becomes the entity's "primary beneficiary." These contracts can take the form of leases, participation rights, guarantees, or other residual interests. Through contracting, the primary beneficiary bears a significant portion of the risks and receives a significant portion of the rewards of the entity, often without owning any voting shares. Current accounting standards require a business that has a controlling financial interest in a VIE to consolidate the financial statements of the VIE with its own.

2. If one member of a business combination acquires an affiliate's debt instrument (e.g., a bond or note) from an outside party, the purchase price usually differs from the book value of the liability. Thus, a gain or loss has been incurred from the perspective of the business combination. However, both the debt and investment remain in the individual financial accounts of the two companies, but the gain or loss goes unrecorded. The consolidation process must adjust all balances to reflect the effective retirement of the debt.

3. Following a related party's acquisition of a company's debt, Interest Income and Expense are recognized. Because these accounts result from intra-entity transactions, they also must be removed in every subsequent consolidation along with the debt and investment figures. Retained Earnings also requires adjustment in each year after the purchase to record the impact of the gain or loss.

4. Amortization of intra-entity debt/investment balances often is necessary because of discounts and/or premiums. Consequently, the Interest Income and Interest Expense figures reported by the two parties will not agree. The closing of these two accounts into Retained Earnings each year gradually reduces the consolidation adjustment that must be made to this equity account.

5. When acquired, many subsidiaries have preferred stock outstanding as well as common stock. The existence of subsidiary preferred shares does little to complicate the consolidation process. The acquisition method values all business acquisitions at their full fair values. If a subsidiary has preferred stock, the essential process of determining its acquisition-date business fair value remains intact. Any preferred shares not owned by the parent simply become a component of the noncontrolling interest and are included in the acquisition-date measure of subsidiary fair value.

6. Every business combination must prepare a statement of cash flows. This statement is not created by consolidating the individual cash flows of the separate companies. Instead, both a consolidated income statement and balance sheet are produced, and the cash flows statement is developed from these figures. Dividends paid to the noncontrolling interest must be listed as a financing activity.

7. For most business combinations, the determination of earnings per share (EPS) follows the normal pattern presented in intermediate accounting textbooks. However, if the subsidiary has potentially dilutive items outstanding (stock warrants, convertible preferred stock, convertible bonds, etc.), a different process must be followed. The subsidiary's own diluted EPS are computed as a preliminary procedure. The parent and the outside owners then allocate the earnings used in each of these calculations based on the ownership levels of the subsidiary's shares and the dilutive items. The determination of the EPS figures to be reported for the business combination is based on the portion of consolidated net income assigned to the parent.

8. After the combination is created, a subsidiary may enter into stock transactions such as issuing additional shares or acquiring treasury stock. Such actions normally create a proportional increase

or decrease in the subsidiary's equity when compared with the parent's investment. The change is measured and then reflected in the consolidated statements through the Additional Paid-In Capital account. To achieve the appropriate accounting, the parent adjusts the Investment in Subsidiary account as well as its own Additional Paid-In Capital. Because the worksheet does not eliminate this equity balance, the required increase or decrease carries over to the consolidated figures.

Comprehensive Illustration

PROBLEM: CONSOLIDATED STATEMENT OF CASH FLOWS AND EARNINGS PER SHARE

(*Estimated Time: 35 to 45 Minutes*) Pop, Inc., acquires 90 percent of the 20,000 shares of Son Company's outstanding common stock on December 31, 2009. Of the acquisition-date fair value, it allocates $80,000 to covenants, a figure amortized at the rate of $2,000 per year. Comparative consolidated balance sheets for 2011 and 2010 are as follow:

	2011	2010
Cash	$ 210,000	$ 130,000
Accounts receivable	350,000	220,000
Inventory	320,000	278,000
Land, buildings, and equipment (net)	1,090,000	1,120,000
Covenants	78,000	80,000
Total assets	$2,048,000	$1,828,000
Accounts payable	$ 290,000	$ 296,000
Long-term liabilities	650,000	550,000
Noncontrolling interest	37,800	34,000
Preferred stock (10% cumulative)	100,000	100,000
Common stock (26,000 shares outstanding)	520,000	520,000
Retained earnings, 12/31	450,200	328,000
Total liabilities and stockholders' equity	$2,048,000	$1,828,000

Additional Information for 2011

- Consolidated net income (after adjustments for all intra-entity items) was $178,000.
- Consolidated depreciation and amortization equaled $52,000.
- On April 10, Son sold a building with a $40,000 book value, receiving cash of $50,000. Later that month, Pop borrowed $100,000 from a local bank and purchased equipment for $60,000. These transactions were all with outside parties.
- During the year, Pop paid $40,000 dividends on its common stock and $10,000 on its preferred stock, and Son paid a $20,000 dividend on its common stock.
- Son has long-term convertible debt of $180,000 outstanding included in consolidated liabilities. It recognized interest expense of $16,000 (net of taxes) on this debt during the year. This debt can be exchanged for 10,000 shares of the subsidiary's common stock. Pop owns none of this debt.
- Son recorded $60,000 net income from its own operations. Noncontrolling interest in Son's income was $5,800.
- Pop recorded $4,000 in profits on sales of goods to Son. These goods remain in Son's warehouse at December 31.
- Pop applies the equity method to account for its investment in Son. On its own books, Pop recognized $48,200 equity in earnings from Son (90% × [$60,000 less $2,000 amortization] and $4,000 unrealized intra-entity profit on its sales to Son).

Required

a. Prepare a consolidated statement of cash flows for Pop, Inc., and Son Company for the year ending December 31, 2011. Use the indirect approach for determining the amount of cash generated by normal operations.[11]

b. Compute basic earnings per share and diluted earnings per share for Pop. Inc.

SOLUTION

a. Consolidated Statement of Cash Flows

The problem specifies that the indirect approach should be used in preparing the consolidated statement of cash flows. Therefore, all items that do not represent cash flows from operations must be removed from the $178,000 consolidated net income. For example, both the depreciation and amortization are eliminated (noncash items) as well as the gain on the sale of the building (a nonoperational item). As the chapter discussed, the noncontrolling interest's share of Son's net income is another noncash reduction that also is removed. In addition, each of the changes in consolidated Accounts Receivable, Inventory, and Accounts Payable produces a noncash impact on net income. The increase in Accounts Receivable, for example, indicates that the sales figure for the period was larger than the amount of cash collected so that adjustment is required in producing this statement.

From the information given, several nonoperational changes in cash can be determined: the bank loan, the acquisition of equipment, the sale of a building, the dividend paid by Son to the noncontrolling interest, and the dividend paid by the parent. Each of these transactions is included in the consolidated statement of cash flows shown in Exhibit 6.9, which explains the $80,000 increase in cash experienced by the entity during 2011.

[11] Prior to attempting this problem, a review of an intermediate accounting textbook might be useful to obtain a complete overview of the production of a statement of cash flows.

EXHIBIT 6.9

POP, INC., AND SON COMPANY
Consolidated Statement of Cash Flows
Year Ending December 31, 2011

Cash flows from operating activities		
Consolidated net income		$ 178,000
Adjustments to reconcile consolidated net income to net cash provided by operating activities:		
Depreciation and amortization	$ 52,000	
Gain on sale of building	(10,000)	
Increase in accounts receivable	(130,000)	
Increase in inventory	(42,000)	
Decrease in accounts payable	(6,000)	(136,000)
Net cash provided by operations		$ 42,000
Cash flows from investing activities		
Purchase of equipment	$ (60,000)	
Sale of building	50,000	
Net cash used in investing activities		(10,000)
Cash flows from financing activities		
Payment of cash dividends—Pop	$ (50,000)	
Payment of cash dividend to noncontrolling owners of Son	(2,000)	
Borrowed from bank	100,000	
Net cash provided by financing activities		48,000
Net increase in cash		$ 80,000
Cash, January 1, 2011		130,000
Cash, December 31, 2011		$ 210,000

EXHIBIT 6.10

POP, INC., AND SON COMPANY
Earnings per Share
Year Ending December 31, 2011

	Earnings	Shares	
Basic Earnings per Share			
Pop's share of consolidated net income	$172,200		
Preferred dividend paid by Pop	(10,000)		
Basic EPS	162,200	26,000	$6.24 (rounded)
Diluted Earnings per Share			
Pop's share of consolidated net income	$172,200		
Remove equity income	(48,200)		
Remove unrealized gain	(4,000)		
Preferred stock dividend	(10,000)		
Common shares outstanding (Pop, Inc.)		26,000	
Common stock income—Pop (for EPS computations)	$110,000		
Income of Son (for diluted EPS)	44,400		
Diluted EPS	$154,400	26,000	$5.94 (rounded)

b. *Earnings per Share*

The subsidiary's convertible debt has a potentially dilutive effect on earnings per share. Therefore, diluted EPS cannot be determined for the business combination directly from consolidated net income. First, the diluted EPS figure must be calculated for the subsidiary. This information then is used in the computations made by the consolidated entity.

Diluted EPS of $2.47 for the subsidiary is determined as follows:

Son Company—Diluted Earnings per Share

	Earnings		Shares	
As reported less excess amortization	$58,000		20,000	$2.90
Effect of possible debt conversion:				
Interest saved (net of taxes)	16,000	New shares	10,000	$1.60 impact
				(16,000/10,000)
Diluted EPS	$74,000		30,000	$2.47 (rounded)

The parent owns none of the convertible debt included in computing diluted EPS. Pop holds only 18,000 (90 percent of the outstanding common stock) of the 30,000 shares used in this EPS calculation. Consequently, in determining diluted EPS for the parent company, only $44,400 of the subsidiary's income is applicable:

$$\$74,000 \times 18,000/30,000 = \$44,400$$

Exhibit 6.10 reveals basic EPS of $6.24 and diluted EPS of $5.94. Because the subsidiary's earnings figure is included separately in the computation of diluted EPS, the parent's individual income must be identified in the same manner. Thus, the effect of the equity income and intra-entity (downstream) transactions are taken into account in arriving at the parent's separate earnings.

Questions

1. What is a variable interest entity (VIE)?
2. What are variable interests in an entity and how might they provide financial control over an entity?
3. When is a sponsoring firm required to consolidate the financial statements of a VIE with its own financial statements?

4. A parent company acquires from a third party bonds that had been issued originally by one of its subsidiaries. What accounting problems are created by this purchase?

5. In question 4, why is the consolidation process simpler if the bonds had been acquired directly from the subsidiary than from a third party?

6. When a company acquires an affiliated company's debt instruments from a third party, how is the gain or loss on extinguishment of the debt calculated? When should this balance be recognized?

7. Several years ago, Bennett, Inc., bought a portion of the outstanding bonds of Smith Corporation, a subsidiary organization. The acquisition was made from an outside party. In the current year, how should these intra-entity bonds be accounted for within the consolidation process?

8. One company purchases the outstanding debt instruments of an affiliated company on the open market. This transaction creates a gain that is appropriately recognized in the consolidated financial statements of that year. Thereafter, a worksheet adjustment is required to correct the beginning balance of the consolidated Retained Earnings. Why is the amount of this adjustment reduced from year to year?

9. A parent acquires the outstanding bonds of a subsidiary company directly from an outside third party. For consolidation purposes, this transaction creates a gain of $45,000. Should this gain be allocated to the parent or the subsidiary? Why?

10. Perkins Company acquires 90 percent of the outstanding common stock of the Butterfly Corporation as well as 55 percent of its preferred stock. How should these preferred shares be accounted for within the consolidation process?

11. The income statement and the balance sheet are produced using a worksheet, but a consolidated statement of cash flows is not. What process is followed in preparing a consolidated statement of cash flows?

12. How do noncontrolling interest balances affect the consolidated statement of cash flows?

13. In many cases, EPS is computed based on the parent's portion of consolidated net income and parent company shares and convertibles. However, a different process must be used for some business combinations. When is this alternative approach required?

14. A subsidiary has (1) a convertible preferred stock and (2) a convertible bond. How are these items factored into the computation of earnings per share for the parent company?

15. Why might a subsidiary decide to issue new shares of common stock to parties outside the business combination?

16. Washburn Company owns 75 percent of Metcalf Company's outstanding common stock. During the current year, Metcalf issues additional shares to outside parties at a price more than its per share consolidated value. How does this transaction affect the business combination? How is this impact recorded within the consolidated statements?

17. Assume the same information as in question 16 except that Metcalf issues a 10 percent stock dividend instead of selling new shares of stock. How does this transaction affect the business combination?

Problems

LO1

1. An enterprise that holds a variable interest in a variable interest entity (VIE) is required to consolidate the assets, liabilities, revenues, expenses, and noncontrolling interest of that entity if:
   a. The VIE has issued no voting stock.
   b. The variable interest held by the enterprise involves a lease.
   c. The enterprise has a controlling financial interest in the VIE.
   d. Other equity interests in the VIE have the obligation to absorb the expected losses of the VIE.

LO2

2. A subsidiary has a debt outstanding that was originally issued at a discount. At the beginning of the current year, the parent company acquired the debt at a slight premium from outside parties. Which of the following statements is true?
   a. Whether the balances agree or not, both the subsequent interest income and interest expense should be reported in a consolidated income statement.
   b. The interest income and interest expense will agree in amount and should be offset for consolidation purposes.
   c. In computing any noncontrolling interest allocation, the interest income should be included but not the interest expense.
   d. Although subsequent interest income and interest expense will not agree in amount, both balances should be eliminated for consolidation purposes.

LO3

3. The parent company acquires all of a subsidiary's common stock but only 70 percent of its preferred shares. This preferred stock pays a 7 percent annual cumulative dividend. No dividends are in arrears at the current time. How is the noncontrolling interest's share of the subsidiary's income computed?

   a. As 30 percent of the subsidiary's preferred dividend.

   b. No allocation is made because the dividends have been paid.

   c. As 30 percent of the subsidiary's income after all dividends have been subtracted.

   d. Income is assigned to the preferred stock based on total par value and 30 percent of that amount is allocated to the noncontrolling interest.

LO4

4. Aceton Corporation owns 80 percent of the outstanding stock of Voctax, Inc. During the current year, Voctax made $140,000 in sales to Aceton. How does this transfer affect the consolidated statement of cash flows?

   a. The transaction should be included if payment has been made.

   b. Only 80 percent of the transfers should be included because the subsidiary made the sales.

   c. Because the transfers were from a subsidiary organization, the cash flows are reported as investing activities.

   d. Because of the intra-entity nature of the transfers, the amount is not reported in the consolidated cash flow statement.

LO4

5. Warrenton, Inc., owns 80 percent of Aminable Corporation. On a consolidated income statement, the Noncontrolling Interest in the Subsidiary's Income is reported as $37,000. Aminable paid a total cash dividend of $100,000 for the year. How does this impact the consolidated statement of cash flows?

   a. The dividends paid to the outside owners are reported as a financing activity, but the noncontrolling interest figure is not viewed as a cash flow.

   b. The noncontrolling interest figure is reported as an investing activity, but the dividends amount paid to the outside owners is omitted entirely.

   c. Neither figure is reported on the statement of cash flows.

   d. Both dividends paid and the noncontrolling interest are viewed as financing activities.

Problems 6 and 7 are based on the following information.

Comparative consolidated balance sheet data for Iverson, Inc., and its 80 percent–owned subsidiary Oakley Co. follow:

	2011	2010
Cash	$ 7,000	$ 20,000
Accounts receivable (net)	55,000	38,000
Merchandise inventory	85,000	45,000
Buildings and equipment (net)	95,000	105,000
Trademark	85,000	100,000
Totals	$327,000	$308,000
Accounts payable	$ 75,000	$ 63,000
Notes payable, long-term	–0–	25,000
Noncontrolling interest	39,000	35,000
Common stock, $10 par	200,000	200,000
Retained earnings (deficit)	13,000	(15,000)
Totals	$327,000	$308,000

Additional Information for Fiscal Year 2011

- Iverson and Oakley's consolidated net income was $45,000.
- Oakley paid $5,000 in dividends during the year. Iverson paid $12,000 in dividends.
- Oakley sold $11,000 worth of merchandise to Iverson during the year.
- There were no purchases or sales of long-term assets during the year.

In the 2011 consolidated statement of cash flows for Iverson Company:

LO4

6. Net cash flows from operating activities were

   a. $12,000.

   b. $20,000.

   c. $24,000.

   d. $25,000.

LO4

7. Net cash flows from financing activities were
   a. $(25,000).
   b. $(37,000).
   c. $(38,000).
   d. $(42,000).

LO5

8. Bensman Corporation is computing EPS. One of its subsidiaries has stock warrants outstanding. How do these convertible items affect Bensman's EPS computation?
   a. No effect is created because the stock warrants were for the subsidiary company's shares.
   b. The stock warrants are not included in the computation unless they are antidilutive.
   c. The effect of the stock warrants must be computed in deriving the amount of subsidiary income to be included in making the diluted EPS calculation.
   d. The stock warrants are included only in basic EPS but never in diluted EPS.

LO6

9. Arcola, Inc., acquires all 40,000 shares of Tuscola Company for $725,000. A year later, when Arcola's equity adjusted balance in its investment in Tuscola equals $800,000, Tuscola issues an additional 10,000 shares to outside investors for $25 per share. Which of the following best describes the effect of Tuscola's stock issue on Arcola's investment account?
   a. No effect because the shares were all sold to outside parties.
   b. The investment account is reduced because Arcola now owns a smaller percentage of Tuscola.
   c. The investment account is increased because Arcola's share of Tuscola's value has increased.
   d. No effect because Arcola maintains control over Tuscola despite the new stock issue.

LO2

10. Jordan, Inc., owns Fey Corporation. For 2011, Jordan reports net income (without consideration of its investment in Fey) of $200,000 and the subsidiary reports $80,000. The parent had a bond payable outstanding on January 1, 2011, with a book value of $212,000. The subsidiary acquired the bond on that date for $199,000. During 2011, Jordan reported interest expense of $22,000 while Fey reported interest income of $21,000. What is the consolidated net income?
    a. $266,000.
    b. $268,000.
    c. $292,000.
    d. $294,000.

LO5

11. Mattoon, Inc., owns 80 percent of Effingham Company. For the current year, this combined entity reported consolidated net income of $500,000. Of this amount $465,000 was attributable to Mattoon's controlling interest while the remaining $35,000 was attributable to the noncontrolling interest. Mattoon has 100,000 shares of common stock outstanding and Effingham has 25,000 shares outstanding. Neither company has issued preferred shares or has any convertible securities outstanding. On the face of the consolidated income statement, how much should be reported as Mattoon's earnings per share?
    a. $5.00
    b. $4.65
    c. $4.00
    d. $3.88

LO2

12. Ace Company reports current earnings of $400,000 while paying $40,000 in cash dividends. Byrd Company earns $100,000 in net income and distributes $10,000 in dividends. Ace has held a 70 percent interest in Byrd for several years, an investment with an acquisition-date fair value equal to the book value of its underlying net assets. Ace uses the initial value method to account for these shares.

    On January 1 of the current year, Byrd acquired in the open market $50,000 of Ace's 8 percent bonds. The bonds had originally been issued several years ago for 92, reflecting a 10 percent effective interest rate. On the date of purchase, the book value of the bonds payable was $48,300. Byrd paid $46,600 based on a 12 percent effective interest rate over the remaining life of the bonds.

    What is consolidated net income for this year?
    a. $492,160.
    b. $493,938.
    c. $499,160.
    d. $500,258.

LO2

13. Using the same information presented in problem 12, what is the noncontrolling interest's share of the subsidiary's net income?

    a. $27,000.

    b. $28,290.

    c. $28,620.

    d. $30,000.

LO2

14. Able Company possesses 80 percent of Baker Company's outstanding voting stock. Able uses the partial equity method to account for this investment. On January 1, 2007, Able sold 9 percent bonds payable with a $10 million face value (maturing in 20 years) on the open market at a premium of $600,000. On January 1, 2010, Baker acquired 40 percent of these same bonds from an outside party at 96.6 of face value. Both companies use the straight-line method of amortization. For a 2011 consolidation, what adjustment should be made to Able's beginning Retained Earnings as a result of this bond acquisition?

    a. $320,000 increase.

    b. $326,000 increase.

    c. $331,000 increase.

    d. $340,000 increase.

LO3

15. On January 1, Tesco Company spent a total of $4,384,000 to acquire control over Blondel Company. This price was based on paying $424,000 for 20 percent of Blondel's preferred stock and $3,960,000 for 90 percent of its outstanding common stock. At the acquisition date, the fair value of the 10 percent noncontrolling interest in Blondel's common stock was $440,000. The fair value of the 80 percent of Blondel's preferred shares not owned by Tesco was $1,696,000. Blondel's stockholders' equity accounts at January 1 were as follows:

Preferred stock—9%, $100 par value, cumulative and participating; 10,000 shares outstanding	$1,000,000
Common stock—$50 par value; 40,000 shares outstanding	2,000,000
Retained earnings	3,000,000
Total stockholders' equity	$6,000,000

   Tesco believes that all of Blondel's accounts approximate their fair values within the company's financial statements. What amount of consolidated goodwill should be recognized?

    a. $300,000.

    b. $316,000.

    c. $364,000.

    d. $520,000.

LO3

16. On January 1, Morgan Company has a net book value of $1,460,000 as follows:

1,000 shares of preferred stock; par value $100 per share; cumulative, nonparticipating, nonvoting; call value $108 per share	$ 100,000
20,000 shares of common stock; par value $40 per share	800,000
Retained earnings	560,000
Total	$1,460,000

   Leinen Company acquires all outstanding preferred shares for $106,000 and 60 percent of the common stock for $870,000. The acquisition-date fair value of the noncontrolling interest in Morgan's common stock was $580,000. Leinen believed that one of Morgan's buildings, with a 12-year life, was undervalued by $50,000 on the company's financial records.

   What amount of consolidated goodwill would be recognized from this acquisition?

    a. $40,000.

    b. $41,200.

    c. $42,400.

    d. $46,000.

LO4

17. Aedion Company owns control over Breedlove, Inc. Aedion reports sales of $300,000 during 2011 and Breedlove reports $200,000. Inventory costing $20,000 was transferred from Breedlove to

Aedion (upstream) during the year for $40,000. Of this amount, 25 percent is still in ending inventory at year-end. Total receivables on the consolidated balance sheet were $80,000 at the first of the year and $110,000 at year-end. No intra-entity debt existed at the beginning or ending of the year. Using the direct approach, what is the consolidated amount of cash collected by the business combination from its customers?

    a. $430,000.

    b. $460,000.

    c. $490,000.

    d. $510,000.

LO6

18. Aaron owns 100 percent of the 12,000 shares of Veritable, Inc. The Investment in Veritable account has a balance of $588,000, corresponding to the subsidiary's unamortized acquisition-date fair value of $49 per share. Veritable issues 3,000 new shares to the public for $50 per share. How does this transaction affect the Investment in Veritable account?

    a. It is not affected because the shares were sold to outside parties.

    b. It should be increased by $2,400.

    c. It should be increased by $3,000.

    d. It should be decreased by $117,600.

Problems 19 through 21 are based on the following information.

Neill Company purchases 80 percent of the common stock of Stamford Company on January 1, 2010, when Stamford has the following stockholders' equity accounts:

Common stock—40,000 shares outstanding	$100,000
Additional paid-in capital	75,000
Retained earnings, 1/1/10	540,000
Total stockholders' equity	$715,000

To acquire this interest in Stamford, Neill pays a total of $592,000. The acquisition-date fair value of the 20 percent noncontrolling interest was $148,000. Any excess fair value was allocated to goodwill, which has not experienced any impairment.

    On January 1, 2011, Stamford reports retained earnings of $620,000. Neill has accrued the increase in Stamford's retained earnings through application of the equity method.

    View the following problems as independent situations:

LO6

19. On January 1, 2011, Stamford issues 10,000 additional shares of common stock for $25 per share. Neill acquires 8,000 of these shares. How will this transaction affect the parent company's Additional Paid-In Capital account?

    a. Has no effect on it.

    b. Increases it by $20,500.

    c. Increases it by $36,400.

    d. Increases it by $82,300.

LO6

20. On January 1, 2011, Stamford issues 10,000 additional shares of common stock for $15 per share. Neill does not acquire any of this newly issued stock. How does this transaction affect the parent company's Additional Paid-In Capital account?

    a. Has no effect on it.

    b. Increases it by $44,000.

    c. Decreases it by $35,200.

    d. Decreases it by $55,000.

LO6

21. On January 1, 2011, Stamford reacquires 8,000 of the outstanding shares of its own common stock for $24 per share. None of these shares belonged to Neill. How does this transaction affect the parent company's Additional Paid-In Capital account?

    a. Has no effect on it.

    b. Decreases it by $55,000.

    c. Decreases it by $35,000.

    d. Decreases it by $28,000.

LO1

22. Hillsborough Country Outfitters, Inc., entered into an agreement for HCO Media LLC to exclusively conduct Hillsborough's e-commerce initiatives through a jointly owned (50 percent each) Internet site known as HCO.com. HCO Media receives 2 percent of all sales revenue generated through the site up to a maximum of $500,000 per year. Both Hillsborough and HCO Media pay 50 percent of the costs to maintain the Internet site. However, if HCO Media's fees are insufficient to cover its 50 percent share of the costs, Hillsborough absorbs the loss.

Assuming that HCO Media qualifies as a VIE, should Hillsborough consolidate HCO Media LLC?

LO1

23. The following describes a set of arrangements between TecPC Company and a variable interest entity (VIE) as of December 31, 2011. TecPC agrees to design and construct a new research and development (R&D) facility. The VIE's sole purpose is to finance and own the R&D facility and lease it to TecPC Company after construction is completed. Payments under the operating lease are expected to begin in the first quarter of 2013.

The VIE has financing commitments sufficient for the construction project from equity and debt participants (investors) of $4 million and $42 million, respectively. TecPC, in its role as the VIE's construction agent, is responsible for completing construction by December 31, 2012. TecPC has guaranteed a portion of the VIE's obligations during the construction and postconstruction periods.

TecPC agrees to lease the R&D facility for five years with multiple extension options. The lease is a variable rate obligation indexed to a three-month market rate. As market interest rates increase or decrease, the payments under this operating lease also increase or decrease, sufficient to provide a return to the investors. If all extension options are exercised, the total lease term is 35 years.

At the end of the first five-year lease term or any extension, TecPC may choose one of the following:

- Renew the lease at fair value subject to investor approval.
- Purchase the facility at its original construction cost.
- Sell the facility on the VIE's behalf, to an independent third party. If TecPC sells the project and the proceeds from the sale are insufficient to repay the investors their original cost, TecPC may be required to pay the VIE up to 85 percent of the project's cost.

a. What is the purpose of reporting consolidated statements for a company and the entities that it controls?

b. When should a VIE's financial statements be consolidated with those of another company?

c. Identify the risks of ownership of the R&D facility that (1) TecPC has effectively shifted to the VIE's owners and (2) remain with TecPC.

d. What characteristics of a primary beneficiary does TecPC possess?

LO1

24. On December 31, 2011, PanTech Company invests $20,000 in SoftPlus, a variable interest entity. In contractual agreements completed on that date, PanTech established itself as the primary beneficiary of SoftPlus. Previously, PanTech had no interest in SoftPlus. Immediately after PanTech's investment, SoftPlus presents the following balance sheet

Cash	$ 20,000	Long-term debt	$120,000
Marketing software	140,000	Noncontrolling interest	60,000
Computer equipment	40,000	PanTech equity interest	20,000
Total assets	$200,000	Total liabilities and equity	$200,000

Each of the above amounts represents an assessed fair market value at December 31, 2011, except for the marketing software.

a. If the marketing software was undervalued by $20,000, what amounts for SoftPlus would appear in PanTech's December 31, 2011, consolidated financial statements?

b. If the marketing software was overvalued by $20,000, what amounts for SoftPlus would appear in PanTech's December 31, 2011, consolidated financial statements?

LO2

25. Darges owns 51 percent of the voting stock of Walrus, Inc. The parent's interest was acquired several years ago on the date that the subsidiary was formed. Consequently, no goodwill or other allocation was recorded in connection with the acquisition.

On January 1, 2008, Walrus sold $1,000,000 in 10-year bonds to the public at 105. The bonds had a cash interest rate of 9 percent payable every December 31. Darges acquired 40 percent of these bonds on January 1, 2010. What consolidation entry would be recorded in connection with these intra-entity bonds for 96 percent of face value? Both companies utilize the straight-line method of amortization.

   a. December 31, 2010?

   b. December 31, 2011?

   c. December 31, 2012?

LO2

26. Highlight, Inc., owns all outstanding stock of Kiort Corporation. The two companies report the following balances for the year ending December 31, 2011:

	Highlight	Kiort
Revenues and interest income	$(670,000)	$(390,000)
Operating and interest expense	540,000	221,000
Other gains and losses	(120,000)	(32,000)
Net income	$(250,000)	$(201,000)

On January 1, 2011, Highlight acquired on the open market bonds for $108,000 originally issued by Kiort. This investment had an effective rate of 8 percent. The bonds had a face value of $100,000 and a cash interest rate of 9 percent. At the date of acquisition, these bonds were shown as liabilities by Kiort with a book value of $84,000 (based on an effective rate of 11 percent). Determine the balances that should appear on a consolidated income statement for 2011.

LO2

27. Several years ago Absalom, Inc., sold $800,000 in bonds to the public. Annual cash interest of 8 percent ($64,000) was to be paid on this debt. The bonds were issued at a discount to yield 10 percent. At the beginning of 2010, McDowell Corporation (a wholly owned subsidiary of Absalom) purchased $100,000 of these bonds on the open market for $121,655, a price based on an effective interest rate of 6 percent. The bond liability had a book value on that date of $668,778. What consolidation entry would be required for these bonds on

   a. December 31, 2010?

   b. December 31, 2012?

LO2

28. Opus, Incorporated, owns 90 percent of Bloom Company. On December 31, 2010, Opus acquires half of Bloom's $500,000 outstanding bonds. These bonds had been sold on the open market on January 1, 2008, at a 12 percent effective rate. The bonds pay a cash interest rate of 10 percent every December 31 and are scheduled to come due on December 31, 2018. Bloom issued this debt originally for $435,763. Opus paid $283,550 for this investment, indicating an 8 percent effective yield.

   a. Assuming that both parties use the effective rate method, what gain or loss from the retirement of this debt should be reported on the consolidated income statement for 2010?

   b. Assuming that both parties use the effective rate method, what balances should appear in the Investment in Bloom Bonds account on Opus's records and the Bonds Payable account of Bloom as of December 31, 2011?

   c. Assuming that both parties use the straight-line method, what consolidation entry would be required on December 31, 2011, because of these bonds? Assume that the parent is not applying the equity method.

LO3

29. Hepner Corporation has the following stockholders' equity accounts:

Preferred stock (6% cumulative dividend)	$500,000
Common stock	750,000
Additional paid-in capital	300,000
Retained earnings	950,000

The preferred stock is participating. Wasatch Corporation buys 80 percent of this common stock for $1,600,000 and 70 percent of the preferred stock for $630,000. The acquisition-date fair value of the noncontrolling interest in the common shares was $400,000 and was $270,000 for the preferred shares. All of the subsidiary's assets and liabilities are viewed as having fair values equal to their book values. What amount is attributed to goodwill on the date of acquisition?

LO3

30. Smith, Inc., has the following stockholders' equity accounts as of January 1, 2011:

Preferred stock—$100 par, nonvoting and nonparticipating, 8 percent cumulative dividend	$ 2,000,000
Common stock—$20 par value	4,000,000
Retained earnings	10,000,000

Haried Company purchases all of Smith's common stock on January 1, 2011, for $14,040,000. The preferred stock remains in the hands of outside parties. Any excess acquisition-date fair value will be assigned to franchise contracts with a 40-year life.

During 2011, Smith reports earning $450,000 in net income and pays $360,000 in cash dividends. Haried applies the equity method to this investment.

a. What is the noncontrolling interest's share of consolidated net income for this period?

b. What is the balance in the Investment in Smith account as of December 31, 2011?

c. What consolidation entries are needed for 2011?

LO3

31. Through the payment of $10,468,000 in cash, Drexel Company acquires voting control over Young Company. This price is paid for 60 percent of the subsidiary's 100,000 outstanding common shares ($40 par value) as well as all 10,000 shares of 8 percent, cumulative, $100 par value preferred stock. Of the total payment, $3.1 million is attributed to the fully participating preferred stock with the remainder paid for the common. This acquisition is carried out on January 1, 2011, when Young reports retained earnings of $10 million and a total book value of $15 million. The acquisition-date fair value of the noncontrolling interest in Young's common stock was $4,912,000. On this same date, a building owned by Young (with a 5-year remaining life) is undervalued in the financial records by $200,000, while equipment with a 10-year life is overvalued by $100,000. Any further excess acquisition-date fair value is assigned to a brand name with a 20-year life.

During 2011, Young reports net income of $900,000 while paying $400,000 in cash dividends. Drexel uses the initial value method to account for both of these investments.

Prepare appropriate consolidation entries for 2011.

LO4

32. The following information has been taken from the consolidation worksheet of Peak and its 90 percent–owned subsidiary, Valley:

- Peak reports a $12,000 gain on the sale of a building. The building had a book value of $32,000 but was sold for $44,000 cash.
- Intra-entity inventory transfers of $129,000 occurred during the current period.
- Valley paid a $30,000 dividend during the year with $27,000 of this amount going to Peak.
- Amortization of an intangible asset recognized by Peak's purchase was $16,000 for the current period.
- Consolidated accounts payable decreased by $11,000 during the year.

Indicate how to reflect each of these events on a consolidated statement of cash flows.

LO4

33. Alford Company and its 80 percent–owned subsidiary, Knight, have the following income statements for 2011:

	Alford	Knight
Revenues	$(500,000)	$(230,000)
Cost of goods sold	300,000	140,000
Depreciation and amortization	40,000	10,000
Other expenses	20,000	20,000
Gain on sale of equipment	(30,000)	–0–
Equity in earnings of Knight	(36,200)	–0–
Net income	$(206,200)	$ (60,000)

Additional Information for 2011

- Intra-entity inventory transfers during the year amounted to $90,000 and were downstream from Alford to Knight.
- Unrealized inventory gains at January 1 were $6,000, but at December 31, they are $9,000.
- Annual excess amortization expense resulting from the acquisition is $11,000.
- Knight paid dividends totaling $20,000.
- The noncontrolling interest's share of the subsidiary's income is $9,800.
- During the year, consolidated inventory rose by $11,000 while accounts receivable and accounts payable declined by $8,000 and $6,000, respectively.

Using either the direct or the indirect approach, determine the amount of cash generated from operations during the period by this business combination.

LO5

34. Porter Corporation owns all 30,000 shares of the common stock of Street, Inc. Porter has 60,000 shares of its own common stock outstanding. During the current year, Porter earns income (without any consideration of its investment in Street) of $150,000 while Street reports $130,000. Annual

amortization of $10,000 is recognized each year on the consolidation worksheet based on acquisition-date fair-value allocations. Both companies have convertible bonds outstanding. During the current year, interest expense (net of taxes) is $32,000 for Porter and $24,000 for Street. Porter's bonds can be converted into 8,000 shares of common stock; Street's bonds can be converted into 10,000 shares. Porter owns none of these bonds. What are the earnings per share amounts that Porter should report in its current year consolidated income statement?

LO5

35. Primus, Inc., owns all outstanding stock of Sonston, Inc. For the current year, Primus reports income (exclusive of any investment income) of $600,000. Primus has 100,000 shares of common stock outstanding. Sonston reports net income of $200,000 for the period with 40,000 shares of common stock outstanding. Sonston also has 10,000 stock warrants outstanding that allow the holder to acquire shares at $10 per share. The value of this stock was $20 per share throughout the year. Primus owns 2,000 of these warrants. What amount should Primus report for diluted earnings per share?

LO5

36. Garfun, Inc., owns all of the stock of Simon, Inc. For 2011, Garfun reports income (exclusive of any investment income) of $480,000. Garfun has 80,000 shares of common stock outstanding. It also has 5,000 shares of preferred stock outstanding that pay a dividend of $15,000 per year. Simon reports net income of $290,000 for the period with 80,000 shares of common stock outstanding. Simon also has a liability for 10,000 of $100 bonds that pay annual interest of $8 per bond. Each of these bonds can be converted into three shares of common stock. Garfun owns none of these bonds. Assume a tax rate of 30 percent. What amount should Garfun report as diluted earnings per share?

LO5

37. The following separate income statements are for Mason and its 80 percent–owned subsidiary, Dixon:

	Mason	Dixon
Revenues	$(400,000)	$(300,000)
Expenses	290,000	225,000
Gain on sale of equipment	–0–	(15,000)
Equity earnings of subsidiary	(52,000)	–0–
Net income	$(162,000)	$ (90,000)
Outstanding common shares	50,000	30,000

Additional Information

- Amortization expense resulting from Dixon's excess acquisition-date fair value is $25,000 per year.
- Mason has convertible preferred stock outstanding. Each of these 5,000 shares is paid a dividend of $4 per year. Each share can be converted into four shares of common stock.
- Stock warrants to buy 10,000 shares of Dixon are also outstanding. For $20, each warrant can be converted into a share of Dixon's common stock. The fair value of this stock is $25 throughout the year. Mason owns none of these warrants.
- Dixon has convertible bonds payable that paid interest of $30,000 (after taxes) during the year. These bonds can be exchanged for 20,000 shares of common stock. Mason holds 15 percent of these bonds, which it bought at book value directly from Dixon.

Compute Mason's basic and diluted EPS.

LO6

38. DeMilo, Inc., owns 100 percent of the 40,000 outstanding shares of Ricardo, Inc. DeMilo currently carries the Investment in Ricardo account at $490,000 using the equity method.

Ricardo issues 10,000 new shares to the public for $15.75 per share. How does this transaction affect the Investment in Ricardo account that appears on DeMilo's financial records?

LO6

39. Albuquerque, Inc., acquired 16,000 shares of Marmon Company several years ago for $600,000. At the acquisition date, Marmon reported a book value of $710,000, and Albuquerque assessed the fair value of the noncontrolling interest at $150,000. Any excess of acquisition-date fair value over book value was assigned to broadcast licenses with indefinite lives. Since the acquisition date and until this point, Marmon has issued no additional shares. No impairment has been recognized for the broadcast licenses.

At the present time, Marmon reports $800,000 as total stockholders' equity, which is broken down as follows:

Common stock ($10 par value)	$200,000
Additional paid-in capital	230,000
Retained earnings	370,000
Total	$800,000

View the following as independent situations:

a. Marmon sells 5,000 shares of previously unissued common stock to the public for $47 per share. Albuquerque purchased none of this stock. What journal entry should Albuquerque make to recognize the impact of this stock transaction?

b. Marmon sells 4,000 shares of previously unissued common stock to the public for $33 per share. Albuquerque purchased none of this stock. What journal entry should Albuquerque make to recognize the impact of this stock transaction?

LO6

40. On January 1, 2009, Aronsen Company acquired 90 percent of Siedel Company's outstanding shares. Siedel had a net book value on that date of $480,000: common stock ($10 par value) of $200,000 and retained earnings of $280,000.

Aronsen paid $584,100 for this investment. The acquisition-date fair value of the 10 percent noncontrolling interest was $64,900. The excess fair value over book value associated with the acquisition was used to increase land by $89,000 and to recognize copyrights (16-year remaining life) at $80,000. Subsequent to the acquisition, Aronsen applied the initial value method to its investment account.

In the 2009–2010 period, the subsidiary's retained earnings increased by $100,000. During 2011, Siedel earned income of $80,000 while paying $20,000 in dividends. Also, at the beginning of 2011, Siedel issued 4,000 new shares of common stock for $38 per share to finance the expansion of its corporate facilities. Aronsen purchased none of these additional shares and therefore recorded no entry. Prepare the appropriate 2011 consolidation entries for these two companies.

LO2

41. Pavin acquires all of Stabler's outstanding shares on January 1, 2009, for $460,000 in cash. Of this amount, $30,000 was attributed to equipment with a 10-year remaining life and $40,000 was assigned to trademarks expensed over a 20-year period. Pavin applies the partial equity method so that income is accrued each period based solely on the earnings reported by the subsidiary.

On January 1, 2012, Pavin reports $300,000 in bonds outstanding with a book value of $282,000. Stabler purchases half of these bonds on the open market for $145,500.

During 2012, Pavin begins to sell merchandise to Stabler. During that year, inventory costing $80,000 was transferred at a price of $100,000. All but $10,000 (at sales price) of these goods were resold to outside parties by year-end. Stabler still owes $33,000 for inventory shipped from Pavin during December.

The following financial figures are for the two companies for the year ending December 31, 2012. Prepare a worksheet to produce consolidated balances. (Credits are indicated by parentheses.)

	Pavin	Stabler
Revenues	$ (740,000)	$(505,000)
Cost of goods sold	455,000	240,000
Expenses	125,000	158,500
Interest expense—bonds	36,000	–0–
Interest income—bond investment	–0–	(16,500)
Loss on extinguishment of bonds	–0–	–0–
Equity in Stabler's income	(123,000)	–0–
Net income	$ (247,000)	$(123,000)
Retained earnings, 1/1/12	$ (345,000)	
Retained earnings, 1/1/12		$(361,000)
Net income (above)	(247,000)	(123,000)
Dividends paid	155,000	61,000
Retained earnings, 12/31/12	$ (437,000)	$(423,000)
Cash and receivables	$ 217,000	$ 35,000
Inventory	175,000	87,000
Investment in Stabler	613,000	–0–
Investment in Pavin bonds	–0–	147,000
Land, buildings, and equipment (net)	245,000	541,000
Trademarks	–0–	–0–
Total assets	$ 1,250,000	$ 810,000

(*continued*)

	Pavin	Stabler
Accounts payable	$ (225,000)	$(167,000)
Bonds payable	(300,000)	(100,000)
Discount on bonds	12,000	–0–
Common stock	(300,000)	(120,000)
Retained earnings (above)	(437,000)	(423,000)
Total liabilities and stockholders' equity	$(1,250,000)	$(810,000)

LO2

42. Fred, Inc., and Herman Corporation formed a business combination on January 1, 2009, when Fred acquired a 60 percent interest in Herman's common stock for $312,000 in cash. The book value of Herman's assets and liabilities on that day totaled $300,000 and the fair value of the noncontrolling interest was $208,000. Patents being held by Herman (with a 12-year remaining life) were undervalued by $90,000 within the company's financial records and a customer list (10-year life) worth $130,000 was also recognized as part of the acquisition-date fair value.

Intra-entity inventory transfers occur regularly between the two companies. Merchandise carried over from one year to the next is always sold in the subsequent period.

Year	Original Cost to Herman	Transfer Price to Fred	Ending Balance at Transfer Price
2009	80,000	100,000	20,000
2010	100,000	125,000	40,000
2011	90,000	120,000	30,000

Fred had not paid for half of the 2011 inventory transfers by year-end.

On January 1, 2010, Fred sold $15,000 in land to Herman for $22,000. Herman is still holding this land.

On January 1, 2011, Herman acquired $20,000 (face value) of Fred's bonds on the open market. These bonds had an 8 percent cash interest rate. On the date of repurchase, the liability was shown within Fred's records at $21,386, indicating an effective yield of 6 percent. Herman's acquisition price was $18,732 based on an effective interest rate of 10 percent.

Herman indicated earning a net income of $25,000 within its 2011 financial statements. The subsidiary also reported a beginning Retained Earnings balance of $300,000, dividends paid of $4,000, and common stock of $100,000. Herman has not issued any additional common stock since its takeover. The parent company has applied the equity method to record its investment in Herman.

a. Prepare consolidation worksheet adjustments for 2011.

b. Calculate the 2011 balance for the noncontrolling interest's share of consolidated net income. In addition, determine the ending 2011 balance for noncontrolling interest in the consolidated balance sheet.

c. Determine the consolidation worksheet adjustments needed in 2012 in connection with the intra-entity bonds.

LO2, LO3

43. On January 1, 2010, Mona, Inc., acquired 80 percent of Lisa Company's common stock as well as 60 percent of its preferred shares. Mona paid $65,000 in cash for the preferred stock, with a call value of 110 percent of the $50 per share par value. The remaining 40 percent of the preferred shares traded at a $34,000 fair value. Mona paid $552,800 for the common stock. At the acquisition date, the noncontrolling interest in the common stock had a fair value of $138,200. The excess fair value over Lisa's book value was attributed to franchise contracts of $40,000. This intangible asset is being amortized over a 40-year period. Lisa pays all preferred stock dividends (a total of $8,000 per year) on an annual basis. During 2010, Lisa's book value increased by $50,000.

On January 2, 2010, Mona acquired one-half of Lisa's outstanding bonds payable to reduce the business combination's debt position. Lisa's bonds had a face value of $100,000 and paid cash interest of 10 percent per year. These bonds had been issued to the public to yield 14 percent. Interest is paid each December 31. On January 2, 2010, these bonds had a total $88,350 book value. Mona paid $53,310, indicating an effective interest rate of 8 percent.

On January 3, 2010, Mona sold Lisa fixed assets that had originally cost $100,000 but had accumulated depreciation of $60,000 when transferred. The transfer was made at a price of $120,000. These assets were estimated to have a remaining useful life of 10 years.

The individual financial statements for these two companies for the year ending December 31, 2011, are as follows:

	Mona, Inc.	Lisa Company
Sales and other revenues	$ (500,000)	$ (200,000)
Expenses	220,000	120,000
Dividend income—Lisa common stock	(8,000)	–0–
Dividend income—Lisa preferred stock	(4,800)	–0–
Net income	$ (292,800)	$ (80,000)
Retained earnings, 1/1/11	$ (700,000)	$ (500,000)
Net income (above)	(292,800)	(80,000)
Dividends paid—common stock	92,800	10,000
Dividends paid—preferred stock	–0–	8,000
Retained earnings, 12/31/11	$ (900,000)	$ (562,000)
Current assets	$ 130,419	$ 500,000
Investment in Lisa—common stock	552,800	–0–
Investment in Lisa—preferred stock	65,000	–0–
Investment in Lisa—bonds	51,781	–0–
Fixed assets	1,100,000	800,000
Accumulated depreciation	(300,000)	(200,000)
Total assets	$ 1,600,000	$ 1,100,000
Accounts payable	$ (400,000)	$ (144,580)
Bonds payable	–0–	(100,000)
Discount on bonds payable	–0–	6,580
Common stock	(300,000)	(200,000)
Preferred stock	–0–	(100,000)
Retained earnings, 12/31/11	(900,000)	(562,000)
Total liabilities and equities	$(1,600,000)	$(1,100,000)

a. What consolidation worksheet adjustments would have been required as of January 1, 2010, to eliminate the subsidiary's common and preferred stocks?

b. What consolidation worksheet adjustments would have been required as of December 31, 2010, to account for Mona's purchase of Lisa's bonds?

c. What consolidation worksheet adjustments would have been required as of December 31, 2010, to account for the intra-entity sale of fixed assets?

d. Assume that consolidated financial statements are being prepared for the year ending December 31, 2011. Calculate the consolidated balance for each of the following accounts:

Franchises

Fixed Assets

Accumulated Depreciation

Expenses

LO4

44. Rodriguez Company holds 80 percent of the common stock of Molina, Inc., and 30 percent of this subsidiary's convertible bonds. The following consolidated financial statements are for 2010 and 2011:

Rodriguez Company and Consolidated Subsidiary Molina

	2010	2011
Revenues	$ (850,000)	$ (980,000)
Cost of goods sold	600,000	640,000
Depreciation and amortization	90,000	100,000
Gain on sale of building	–0–	(20,000)
Interest expense	30,000	30,000
Consolidated net income	(130,000)	(230,000)
to noncontrolling interest	9,000	11,000
to parent company	$ (121,000)	$ (219,000)

(continued)

Rodriguez Company and Consolidated Subsidiary Molina

Retained earnings, 1/1	$ (300,000)	$ (371,000)
Net income	(121,000)	(219,000)
Dividends paid	50,000	100,000
Retained earnings, 12/31	$ (371,000)	$ (490,000)
Cash	$ 80,000	$ 150,000
Accounts receivable	150,000	140,000
Inventory	200,000	340,000
Buildings and equipment (net)	640,000	690,000
Databases	150,000	145,000
Total assets	$ 1,220,000	$ 1,465,000
Accounts payable	$ (140,000)	$ (100,000)
Bonds payable	(400,000)	(500,000)
Noncontrolling interest in Molina	(32,000)	(41,000)
Common stock	(100,000)	(130,000)
Additional paid-in capital	(177,000)	(204,000)
Retained earnings	(371,000)	(490,000)
Total liabilities and equities	$(1,220,000)	$(1,465,000)

Additional Information for 2011

- The parent issued bonds during the year for cash.
- Amortization of databases amounts to $5,000 per year.
- The parent sold a building with a cost of $60,000 but a $30,000 book value for cash on May 11.
- The subsidiary purchased equipment on July 23 using cash.
- Late in November, the parent issued stock for cash.
- During the year, the subsidiary paid dividends of $10,000.

Prepare a consolidated statement of cash flows for this business combination for the year ending December 31, 2011. Either the direct or the indirect approach may be used.

LO5

45. Following are separate income statements for Austin, Inc., and its 80 percent owned subsidiary, Rio Grande Corporation as well as a consolidated statement for the business combination as a whole.

	Austin	Rio Grande	Consolidated
Revenues	$(700,000)	$(500,000)	$(1,200,000)
Cost of goods sold	400,000	300,000	700,000
Operating expenses	100,000	70,000	195,000
Equity in earnings of Rio Grande	(84,000)		
Individual company net income	$(284,000)	$(130,000)	
Consolidated net income			$ (305,000)
Noncontrolling interest in Rio Grande's income			(21,000)
Consolidated net income attributable to Austin			$ (284,000)

Additional Information

- Annual excess fair over book value amortization of $25,000 resulted from the acquisition.
- The parent applies the equity method to this investment.
- Austin has 50,000 shares of common stock and 10,000 shares of preferred stock outstanding. Owners of the preferred stock are paid an annual dividend of $40,000, and each share can be exchanged for two shares of common stock.
- Rio Grande has 30,000 shares of common stock outstanding. The company also has 5,000 stock warrants outstanding. For $10, each warrant can be converted into a share of Rio Grande's common stock. Austin holds half of these warrants. The price of Rio Grande's common stock was $20 per share throughout the year.

- Rio Grande also has convertible bonds, none of which Austin owned. During the current year, total interest expense (net of taxes) was $22,000. These bonds can be exchanged for 10,000 shares of the subsidiary's common stock.

Determine Austin's basic and diluted EPS.

LO3

46. On January 1, Paisley, Inc., paid $560,000 for all of Skyler Corporation's outstanding stock. This cash payment was based on a price of $180 per share for Skyler's $100 par value preferred stock and $38 per share for its $20 par value common stock. The preferred shares are voting, cumulative, and fully participating. At the acquisition date, the book values of Skyler's accounts equaled their fair values. Any excess fair value is assigned to an intangible asset and will be amortized over a 10-year period.

During the year, Skyler sold inventory costing $60,000 to Paisley for $90,000. All but $18,000 (measured at transfer price) of this merchandise has been resold to outsiders by the end of the year. At the end of the year, Paisley continues to owe Skyler for the last shipment of inventory priced at $28,000.

Also, on January 2, Paisley sold Skyler equipment for $20,000 although it had a book value of only $12,000 (original cost of $30,000). Both companies depreciate such property according to the straight-line method with no salvage value. The remaining life at this date was four years.

The following financial statements are for each company for the year ending December 31. Determine consolidated financial totals for this business combination.

	Paisley, Inc.	Skyler Corporation
Sales	$ (800,000)	$(400,000)
Costs of goods sold	528,000	260,000
Expenses	180,000	130,000
Gain on sale of equipment	(8,000)	–0–
Net income	$ (100,000)	$ (10,000)
Retained earnings, 1/1	$ (400,000)	$(150,000)
Net income	(100,000)	(10,000)
Dividends paid	60,000	–0–
Retained earnings, 12/31	$ (440,000)	$(160,000)
Cash	$ 30,000	$ 40,000
Accounts receivable	300,000	100,000
Inventory	260,000	180,000
Investment in Skyler Corporation	560,000	–0–
Land, buildings, and equipment	680,000	500,000
Accumulated depreciation	(180,000)	(90,000)
Total assets	$ 1,650,000	$ 730,000
Accounts payable	$ (140,000)	$ (90,000)
Long-term liabilities	(240,000)	(180,000)
Preferred stock	–0–	(100,000)
Common stock	(620,000)	(200,000)
Additional paid-in capital	(210,000)	–0–
Retained earnings, 12/31	(440,000)	(160,000)
Total liabilities and equity	$(1,650,000)	$(730,000)

Note: Parentheses indicate a credit balance.

LO4

47. On June 30, 2011, Plaster, Inc., paid $916,000 for 80 percent of Stucco Company's outstanding stock. Plaster assessed the acquisition-date fair value of the 20 percent noncontrolling interest at $229,000. At acquisition date, Stucco reported the following book values for its assets and liabilities:

Cash	$ 60,000
Accounts receivable	127,000
Inventory	203,000
Land	65,000
Buildings	175,000
Equipment	300,000
Accounts payable	(35,000)

On June 30, Plaster allocated the excess acquisition-date fair value over book value to Stucco's assets as follows:

Equipment (3-year life) . . . . $ 75,000
Database (10-year life) 175,000

At the end of 2011, the following comparative (2010 and 2011) balance sheets and consolidated income statement were available:

	Plaster, Inc. December 31, 2010	Consolidated December 31, 2011
Cash	$ 43,000	$ 242,850
Accounts receivable (net)	362,000	485,400
Inventory	415,000	720,000
Land	300,000	365,000
Buildings (net)	245,000	370,000
Equipment (net)	1,800,000	2,037,500
Database	–0–	166,250
Total assets	$3,165,000	$4,387,000
Accounts payable	$ 80,000	$ 107,000
Long-term liabilities	400,000	1,200,000
Common stock	1,800,000	1,800,000
Noncontrolling interest	–0–	255,500
Retained earnings	885,000	1,024,500
Total liabilities and equities	$3,165,000	$4,387,000

PLASTER, INC., AND SUBSIDIARY STUCCO COMPANY
Consolidated Income Statement
For the Year Ended December 31, 2011

Revenues		$1,217,500
Cost of goods sold	$737,500	
Depreciation	187,500	
Database amortization	8,750	
Interest and other expenses	9,750	943,500
Consolidated net income		$ 274,000

Additional Information for 2011

- On December 1, Stucco paid a $40,000 dividend. During the year, Plaster paid $100,000 in dividends.
- During the year, Plaster issued $800,000 in long-term debt at par.
- Plaster reported no asset purchases or dispositions other than the acquisition of Stucco.

Prepare a 2011 consolidated statement of cash flows for Plaster and Stucco. Use the indirect method of reporting cash flows from operating activities.

Develop Your Skills

EXCEL CASE: INTRA-ENTITY BONDS

Place Company owns a majority voting interest in Sassano, Inc. On January 1, 2009, Place issued $1,000,000 of 11 percent 10-year bonds at $943,497.77 to yield 12 percent. On January 1, 2011, Sassano purchased all of these bonds in the open market at a price of $904,024.59 with an effective yield of 13 percent.

Required

Using an Excel spreadsheet, do the following:

1. Prepare amortization schedules for the Place Company bonds payable and the Investment in Place Bonds for Sassano, Inc.

2. Using the values from the amortization schedules, compute the worksheet adjustment for a December 31, 2011, consolidation of Place and Sassano to reflect the effective retirement of the Place bonds. Formulate your solution to be able to accommodate various yield rates (and therefore prices) on the repurchase of the bonds.

Hints

Present value of $1 = 1/(1 + r)^n$

Present value of an annuity of $1 = (1 - 1/[1 + r]^n)/r$

Where r = effective yield and n = years remaining to maturity

RESEARCH CASE

Find a recent annual report for a firm with business acquisitions (e.g., Compaq, GE). Locate the firm's consolidated statement of cash flows and answer the following:

- Does the firm employ the direct or indirect method of accounting for operating cash flows?
- How does the firm account for the balances in balance sheet operating accounts (e.g., accounts receivable, inventory, accounts payable) in determining operating cash flows?
- Describe the accounting for cash paid for business acquisitions in the statement of cash flows.
- Describe the accounting for any noncontrolling subsidiary interest, acquired in-process research and development costs, and any other business combination–related items in the consolidated statement of cash flows.

FINANCIAL REPORTING RESEARCH AND ANALYSIS CASE

The FASB ASC Subtopic Variable Interest Entities affects thousands of business enterprises that now, as primary beneficiaries, consolidate entities that qualify as controlled VIEs. Retrieve the annual reports of one or more of the following companies (or any others you may find) that consolidate VIEs:

- The Walt Disney Company.
- General Electric.
- ConAgra Foods.
- Time Warner.
- Allegheny Energy.

Required

Write a brief report that describes

1. The reasons for consolidation of the company's VIE(s).
2. The effect of the consolidation of the VIE(s) on the company's financial statements.

Foreign Currency Transactions and Hedging Foreign Exchange Risk

Today, international business transactions are a regular occurrence. In its 2008 annual report, Lockheed Martin Corporation reported export sales of $5.9 billion, representing 14 percent of total sales. Even small businesses are significantly involved in transactions occurring throughout the world as evidenced by this excerpt from Cirrus Logic, Inc.'s 2008 Annual Report: "Export sales, principally to Asia, include sales to U.S.-based customers with manufacturing plants overseas and represented 62 percent, 62 percent, and 66 percent of our net sales in fiscal years 2008, 2007, and 2006, respectively." Collections from export sales or payments for imported items may be made not in U.S. dollars but in pesos, pounds, yen, and the like depending on the negotiated terms of the transaction. As the foreign currency exchange rates fluctuate, so does the U.S. dollar value of these export sales and import purchases. Companies often find it necessary to engage in some form of hedging activity to reduce losses arising from fluctuating exchange rates. At the end of fiscal year 2008 as part of its foreign currency hedging activities, Textron, Inc., reported having outstanding foreign currency forward contracts and options with a notional value of $1.0 billion.

This chapter covers accounting issues related to foreign currency transactions and foreign currency hedging activities. To provide background for subsequent discussions of the accounting issues, the chapter begins by describing foreign exchange markets. The chapter then discusses accounting for import and export transactions, followed by coverage of various hedging techniques. Because they are most popular, the discussion concentrates on forward contracts and options. Understanding how to account for these items is important for any company engaged in international transactions.

LEARNING OBJECTIVES

After studying this chapter, you should be able to:

LO1 Understand concepts related to foreign currency, exchange rates, and foreign exchange risk.

LO2 Account for foreign currency transactions using the two-transaction perspective, accrual approach.

LO3 Understand how foreign currency forward contracts and foreign currency options can be used to hedge foreign exchange risk.

LO4 Account for forward contracts and options used as hedges of foreign currency denominated assets and liabilities.

LO5 Account for forward contracts and options used as hedges of foreign currency firm commitments.

LO6 Account for forward contracts and options used as hedges of forecasted foreign currency transactions.

LO7 Prepare journal entries to account for foreign currency borrowings.

FOREIGN EXCHANGE MARKETS

LO1

Understand concepts related to foreign currency, exchange rates, and foreign exchange risk.

Each country uses its own currency as the unit of value for the purchase and sale of goods and services. The currency used in the United States is the U.S. dollar, the currency used in Mexico is the Mexican peso, and so on. If a U.S. citizen travels to Mexico and wishes to purchase local goods, Mexican merchants require payment to be made in Mexican pesos. To make a purchase, a U.S. citizen has to acquire pesos using U.S. dollars. The *foreign exchange rate* is the price at which the foreign currency can be acquired. A variety of factors determine the exchange rate between two currencies; unfortunately for those engaged in international business, the exchange rate can fluctuate over time.[1]

Exchange Rate Mechanisms

Exchange rates have not always fluctuated. During the period 1945–1973, countries fixed the par value of their currency in terms of the U.S. dollar, and the value of the U.S. dollar was fixed in terms of gold. Countries agreed to maintain the value of their currency within 1 percent of the par value. If the exchange rate for a particular currency began to move outside this 1 percent range, the country's central bank was required to intervene by buying or selling its currency in the foreign exchange market. Because of the law of supply and demand, a central bank's purchase of currency would cause the price of the currency to stop falling, and its sale of currency would cause the price to stop rising.

The integrity of the system hinged on the U.S. dollar maintaining its value in gold and the ability of foreign countries to convert their U.S. dollar holdings into gold at the fixed rate of $35 per ounce. As the United States began to incur balance of payment deficits in the 1960s, a glut of U.S. dollars arose worldwide, and foreign countries began converting their U.S. dollars into gold. This resulted in a decline in the U.S. government's gold reserve from a high of $24.6 billion in 1949 to a low of $10.2 billion in 1971. In that year, the United States suspended the convertibility of the U.S. dollar into gold, signaling the beginning of the end for the fixed exchange rate system. In March 1973, most currencies were allowed to float in value.

Today, several different currency arrangements exist. Some of the more important ones and the countries affected follow:

1. *Independent float:* The value of the currency is allowed to fluctuate freely according to market forces with little or no intervention from the central bank (Canada, Japan, Sweden, Switzerland, United States).

2. *Pegged to another currency:* The value of the currency is fixed (pegged) in terms of a particular foreign currency and the central bank intervenes as necessary to maintain the fixed value. For example, the Bahamas, Panama, and Saudi Arabia peg their currency to the U.S. dollar.

3. *European Monetary System (euro):* In 1998, the countries comprising the European Monetary System adopted a common currency called the *euro* and established a European Central Bank.[2] Until 2002, local currencies such as the German mark and French franc continued to exist but were fixed in value in terms of the euro. On January 1, 2002, local currencies disappeared, and the euro became the currency in 12 European countries. Today, 16 countries are part of the euro area. The value of the euro floats against other currencies such as the U.S. dollar.

Foreign Exchange Rates

Exchange rates between the U.S. dollar and many foreign currencies are published on a daily basis in *The Wall Street Journal* and major U.S. newspapers. Exchange rates also are available on the Internet at www.oanda.com and www.x-rates.com. To better illustrate exchange rates

---

[1] Several theories attempt to explain exchange rate fluctuations but with little success, at least in the short term. An understanding of the causes of exchange rate changes is not necessary to comprehend the concepts underlying the accounting for changes in exchange rates.

[2] Most longtime members of the European Union (EU) are "euro zone" countries. The major exception is the United Kingdom, which elected not to participate. Switzerland is another important European country not part of the euro zone because it is not a member of the EU.

EXHIBIT 7.1 *The Wall Street Journal* Foreign Exchange Quotes, Tuesday, March 31, 2009

Country/currency	Tues in US$	Tues per US$	US$ vs, YTD chg (%)	Country/currency	Tues in US$	Tues per US$	US$ vs, YTD chg (%)
Americas				**Europe**			
Argentina peso*	.2694	3.7120	**7.5**	**Czech Rep.** koruna** ..	.04855	20.597	**7.2**
Brazil real	.4310	2.3202	**0.3**	**Denmark** krone	.1784	5.6054	**5.2**
Canada dollar	.7931	1.2609	**3.6**	**Euro area** euro	1.3286	.7527	**5.1**
1-mos forward	.7932	1.2607	**3.6**	**Hungary** forint	.004314	231.80	**21.9**
3-mos forward	.7941	1.2593	**3.5**	**Norway** krone	.1488	6.7204	**−3.4**
6-mos forward	.7953	1.2574	**3.5**	**Poland** zloty	.2875	3.4783	**17.1**
Chile peso	.001716	582.75	**−8.7**	**Russia** ruble‡	.02949	33.910	**11.1**
Colombia peso	.0003938	2539.36	**12.9**	**Sweden** krona	.1217	8.2169	**5.0**
Ecuador US dollar	1	1	**unch**	**Switzerland** franc	.8785	1.1383	**6.7**
Mexico peso*	.0706	14.1623	**3.2**	1-mos forward	.8790	1.1377	**6.6**
Peru new sol	.3170	3.155	**0.6**	3-mos forward	.8803	1.1360	**6.6**
Uruguay peso† ··········	.04150	24.10	**−1.2**	6-mos forward	.8824	1.1333	**6.6**
Venezuela b. fuerte ...	.465701	2.1473	**unch**	**Turkey** lira**	.6014	1.6627	**7.9**
Asia-Pacific				**UK pound**	1.4347	.6970	**1.7**
				1-mos forward	1.4348	.6970	**1.6**
Australian dollar	.6952	1.4384	**2.3**	3-mos forward	1.4352	.6968	**1.5**
China yuan	.1463	6.8334	**0.2**	6-mos forward	1.4359	.6964	**1.4**
Hong Kong dollar	.1290	7.7504	**unch**	**Middle East/Africa**			
India rupee	.01977	50.582	**4.0**				
Indonesia rupiah	.0000865	11561	**6.0**	**Bahrain** dinar	2.6526	.3770	**unch**
Japan yen	.010106	98.95	**9.1**	**Egypt** pound*	.1775	5.6329	**2.4**
1-mos forward	.010110	98.91	**9.1**	**Israel** shekel	.2369	4.2212	**11.7**
3-mos forward	.010121	98.80	**9.1**	**Jordan** dinar	1.4129	.7078	**−0.1**
6-mos forward	.010142	98.60	**9.2**	**Kuwait** dinar	3.4305	.2915	**5.5**
Malaysia ringgits§	.2743	3.6456	**5.6**	**Lebanon** pound	.0006634	1507.39	**unch**
New Zealand dollar ...	.5696	1.7556	**2.9**	**Saudi Arabia** riyal	.2666	3.7509	**−0.1**
Pakistan rupee	.01243	80.451	**1.7**	**South Africa** rand	.1055	9.4787	**0.9**
Philippines peso	.0207	48.239	**1.6**	**UAE** dirham	.2722	3.6738	**unch**
Singapore dollar	.6575	1.5209	**6.2**				
South Korea won	.0007278	1374.00	**8.8**	**SDR††**	1.4951	.6689	**3.0**
Taiwan dollar	.02947	33.933	**3.5**				
Thailand baht	.02820	35.461	**2.0**				
Vietnam dong	.00005622	17786	**1.7**				

*Floating rate.
†Financial.
§Government rate.
‡Russian Central Bank rate.
**Rebased as of Jan 1, 2005.
††Special Drawing Rights (SDR); from the International Monetary Fund; based on exchange rates for U.S., British, and Japanese currencies.
Note: Based on trading among banks of $1 million and more, as quoted at 4 p.m. ET by Reuters.
Source: *The Wall Street Journal*, April 1, 2009, p. C2. Reprinted with permission of *The Wall Street Journal*, copyright © Dow Jones & Company, Inc. All Rights Reserved Worldwide.

and the foreign currency market, next we examine the exchange rates published in *The Wall Street Journal* for Tuesday, March 31, 2009, as shown in Exhibit 7.1.

These exchange rates were quoted in New York at 4:00 p.m. Eastern time (ET). The U.S. dollar price for one Argentinian peso on Tuesday, March 31, at 4:00 p.m. in New York was $0.2694. The U.S. dollar price for a peso at 4:01 p.m. Eastern time in New York was probably something different, as was the U.S. dollar price for a peso in Buenos Aires at 4:00 p.m. ET. These exchange rates are for trades between banks in amounts of $1 million or more; that is, these are interbank or wholesale prices. Prices charged to retail customers, such as companies engaged in international business, are higher. These are selling rates at which banks in New York will sell currency to one another. The prices that banks are willing to pay to buy foreign currency (buying rates) are somewhat less than the selling rates. The difference between the buying and selling rates is the spread through which the banks earn a profit on foreign exchange trades.

Two columns of information are published for each day's exchange rates. The first column, in US$, indicates the number of U.S. dollars needed to purchase one unit of foreign currency. These are known as *direct quotes*. The direct quote for the Swedish krona on March 31 was $0.1217; in other words, 1.0 krona could be purchased with $0.1217. The second column, per US$, indicates the number of foreign currency units that could be purchased with one U.S. dollar. These are called *indirect quotes,* which are simply the inverse of direct quotes. If one krona can be purchased with $0.1217, then 8.2169 kroner can be purchased with $1.00. (The arithmetic does not always work out perfectly because the direct quotes published in *The Wall Street Journal* are carried out to only four decimal points.) To avoid confusion, *direct quotes are used exclusively in this chapter*.

The third column indicates the year-to-date change in the value of each foreign currency. In the three months following January 1, 2009, the Canadian dollar increased in value relative to the U.S. dollar by 3.6 percent, whereas during the same time period, the Chilean peso decreased in value by 8.7 percent. Several currencies, such as the Bahraini dinar and the Hong Kong dollar, did not change in value because they were pegged to the U.S. dollar.

Spot and Forward Rates

Foreign currency trades can be executed on a spot or forward basis. The *spot rate* is the price at which a foreign currency can be purchased or sold today. In contrast, the *forward rate* is the price today at which foreign currency can be purchased or sold sometime in the future. Because many international business transactions take some time to be completed, the ability to lock in a price today at which foreign currency can be purchased or sold at some future date has definite advantages.

Most of the quotes published in *The Wall Street Journal* are *spot rates*. In addition, it publishes forward rates quoted by New York banks for several major currencies (British pound, Canadian dollar, Japanese yen, and Swiss franc) on a daily basis. This is only a partial listing of possible forward contracts. A firm and its bank can tailor forward contracts in other currencies and for other time periods to meet the firm's needs. Entering into a forward contract has no up-front cost.

The forward rate can exceed the spot rate on a given date, in which case the foreign currency is said to be selling at a *premium* in the forward market, or the forward rate can be less than the spot rate, in which case it is selling at a *discount*. Currencies sell at a premium or a discount because of differences in interest rates between two countries. When the interest rate in the foreign country exceeds the domestic interest rate, the foreign currency sells at a discount in the forward market. Conversely, if the foreign interest rate is less than the domestic rate, the foreign currency sells at a premium.[3] Forward rates are said to be unbiased predictors of the future spot rate.

The spot rate for British pounds on March 31, 2009, indicates that 1 pound could have been purchased on that date for $1.4347. On the same day, the one-month forward rate was $1.4348. By entering into a forward contract on March 31, it was possible to guarantee that pounds could be purchased on April 30 at a price of $1.4348, regardless of what the spot rate turned out to be on April 30. Entering into the forward contract to purchase pounds would have been beneficial if the spot rate on April 30 was more than $1.4348. On the other hand, such a forward contract would have been detrimental if the spot rate was less than $1.4348. In either case, the forward contract must be honored and pounds must be purchased on April 30 at $1.4348.

As it turned out, the spot rate for pounds on April 30, 2009, was $1.4789, so entering into a one-month forward contract on March 31, 2009, to purchase pounds at $1.4348 would have resulted in a gain.

Option Contracts

To provide companies more flexibility than exists with a forward contract, a market for *foreign currency options* has developed. A foreign currency option gives the holder of the option *the right but not the obligation* to trade foreign currency in the future. A *put* option is for the sale of foreign currency by the holder of the option; a *call* is for the purchase of foreign currency by the holder of the option. The *strike price* is the exchange rate at which the option will be

---

[3] This relationship is based on the theory of interest rate parity that indicates the difference in national interest rates should be equal to, but opposite in sign to, the forward rate discount or premium. This topic is covered in detail in international finance textbooks.

executed if the option holder decides to exercise the option. The strike price is similar to a forward rate. There are generally several strike prices to choose from at any particular time. Foreign currency options can be purchased on the Philadelphia Stock Exchange, on the Chicago Mercantile Exchange, or directly from a bank in the so-called over-the-counter market.

Unlike a forward contract, for which banks earn their profit through the spread between buying and selling rates, options must actually be purchased by paying an *option premium*, which is a function of two components: intrinsic value and time value. An option's *intrinsic value* is equal to the gain that could be realized by exercising the option immediately. For example, if a spot rate for a foreign currency is $1.00, a *call* option (to purchase foreign currency) with a strike price of $0.97 has an intrinsic value of $0.03, whereas a *put* option (to sell foreign currency) with a strike price of $0.97 has an intrinsic value of zero. An option with a positive intrinsic value is said to be "in the money." The *time value* of an option relates to the fact that the spot rate can change over time and cause the option to become in the money. Even though a 90-day call option with a strike price of $1.00 has zero intrinsic value when the spot rate is $1.00, it will still have a positive time value because there is a chance that the spot rate could increase over the next 90 days and bring the option into the money.

The value of a foreign currency option can be determined by applying an adaptation of the Black-Scholes option pricing formula. This formula is discussed in detail in international finance books. In very general terms, the value of an option is a function of the difference between the current spot rate and strike price, the difference between domestic and foreign interest rates, the length of time to expiration, and the potential volatility of changes in the spot rate. For purposes of this book, the premium originally paid for a foreign currency option and its subsequent fair value up to the date of expiration derived from applying the pricing formula will be given.

On June 9, 2009, the Chicago Mercantile Exchange indicated that a July 2009 call option in euros with a strike price of $1.39 could have been purchased by paying a premium of $0.0197 per euro. Thus, the right to purchase a standard contract of 62,500 euros in June 2009 at a price of $1.39 per euro could have been acquired by paying $1,231.25 ($0.0197 × 62,500 euros). If the spot rate for euros in July 2009 turned out to be more than $1.39, the option would be exercised and euros purchased at the strike price of $1.39. If, on the other hand, the July spot rate is less than $1.39, the option would not be exercised; instead, euros would be purchased at the lower spot rate. The call option contract establishes the maximum amount that would have to be paid for euros but does not lock in a disadvantageous price should the spot rate fall below the option strike price.

FOREIGN CURRENCY TRANSACTIONS

LO2

Account for foreign currency transactions using the two-transaction perspective, accrual approach.

Export sales and import purchases are international transactions; they are components of what is called *trade*. When two parties from different countries enter into a transaction, they must decide which of the two countries' currencies to use to settle the transaction. For example, if a U.S. computer manufacturer sells to a customer in Japan, the parties must decide whether the transaction will be denominated (payment will be made) in U.S. dollars or Japanese yen.

Assume that a U.S. exporter (Amerco) sells goods to a German importer that will pay in euros (€). In this situation, Amerco has entered into a foreign currency transaction. It must restate the euro amount that it actually will receive into U.S. dollars to account for this transaction. This happens because Amerco keeps its books and prepares financial statements in U.S. dollars. Although the German importer has entered into an international transaction, it does not have a foreign currency transaction (payment will be made in its currency) and no restatement is necessary.

Assume that, as is customary in its industry, Amerco does not require immediate payment and allows its German customer 30 days to pay for its purchases. By doing this, Amerco runs the risk that the euro might depreciate against the U.S. dollar between the sale date and the date of payment. If so, the sale would generate fewer U.S. dollars than it would have had the euro not decreased in value, and the sale is less profitable because it was made on a credit basis. In this situation Amerco is said to have an *exposure to foreign exchange risk.* Specifically, Amerco has a transaction exposure that can be summarized as follows:

- *Export sale:* A transaction exposure exists when the exporter allows the buyer to pay in a foreign currency and allows the buyer to pay sometime after the sale has been made. The exporter is exposed to the risk that the foreign currency might depreciate (decrease in value) between the date of sale and the date payment is received, thereby decreasing the U.S. dollars ultimately collected.
- *Import purchase:* A transaction exposure exists when the importer is required to pay in foreign currency and is allowed to pay sometime after the purchase has been made. The importer is exposed to the risk that the foreign currency might appreciate (increase in price) between the date of purchase and the date of payment, thereby increasing the U.S. dollars that have to be paid for the imported goods.

Accounting Issue

The major issue in accounting for foreign currency transactions is how to deal with the change in U.S. dollar value of the sales revenue and account receivable resulting from the export when the foreign currency changes in value. (The corollary issue is how to deal with the change in the U.S. dollar value of the account payable and goods being acquired in an import purchase.) For example, assume that Amerco, a U.S. company, sells goods to a German customer at the price of 1 million euros when the spot exchange rate is $1.32 per euro. If payment were received at the sale date, Amerco could have converted 1 million euros into $1,320,000; this amount clearly would be the amount at which the sales revenue would be recognized. Instead, Amerco allows the German customer 30 days to pay for its purchase. At the end of 30 days, the euro has depreciated to $1.30 and Amerco is able to convert the 1 million euros received on that date into only $1,300,000. How should Amerco account for this $20,000 decrease in value?

Accounting Alternatives

Conceptually, the two methods of accounting for changes in the value of a foreign currency transaction are the one-transaction perspective and the two-transaction perspective. The *one-transaction perspective* assumes that an export sale is not complete until the foreign currency receivable has been collected and converted into U.S. dollars. Any change in the U.S. dollar value of the foreign currency is accounted for as an adjustment to Accounts Receivable and to Sales. Under this perspective, Amerco would ultimately report Sales at $1,300,000 and an increase in the Cash account of the same amount. This approach can be criticized because it hides the fact that the company could have received $1,320,000 if the German customer had been required to pay at the date of sale. Amerco incurs a $20,000 loss because of the depreciation in the euro, but that loss is buried in an adjustment to Sales. This approach is not acceptable under U.S. GAAP.

Instead, U.S. GAAP requires companies to use a *two-transaction perspective* in accounting for foreign currency transactions.[4] This perspective treats the export sale and the subsequent collection of cash as two separate transactions. Because management has made two decisions—(1) to make the export sale and (2) to extend credit in foreign currency to the customer—the company should report the income effect from each of these decisions separately. The U.S. dollar value of the sale is recorded at the date the sale occurs. At that point, the sale has been completed; there are no subsequent adjustments to the Sales account. Any difference between the number of U.S. dollars that could have been received at the date of sale and the number of U.S. dollars actually received at the date of collection due to fluctuations in the exchange rate is a result of the decision to extend foreign currency credit to the customer. This difference is treated as a foreign exchange gain or loss that is reported separately from Sales in the income statement. Using the two-transaction

---

[4] Accounting for foreign currency transactions is covered in Topic 830 Foreign Currency Matters in the FASB Accounting Standards Codification (ASC).

perspective to account for its export sale to Germany, Amerco would make the following journal entries:

Date of Sale:	Accounts Receivable (€)	1,320,000	
	Sales		1,320,000
	To record the sale and euro receivable at the spot rate of $1.32.		
Date of Collection:	Foreign Exchange Loss	20,000	
	Accounts Receivable (€)		20,000
	To adjust the value of the euro receivable to the new spot rate of $1.30 and record a foreign exchange loss resulting from the depreciation in the euro.		
	Cash	1,300,000	
	Accounts Receivable (€)		1,300,000
	To record the receipt of 1 million euros and conversion at the spot rate of $1.30.		

Sales are reported in income at the amount that would have been received if the customer had not been given 30 days to pay the 1 million euros—that is, $1,320,000. A separate Foreign Exchange Loss of $20,000 is reported in income to indicate that because of the decision to extend foreign currency credit to the German customer and because the euro decreased in value, Amerco actually received fewer U.S. dollars.[5]

Note that Amerco keeps its Account Receivable (€) account separate from its U.S. dollar receivables. Companies engaged in international trade need to keep separate receivable and payable accounts in each of the currencies in which they have transactions. Each foreign currency receivable and payable should have a separate account number in the company's chart of accounts.

We can summarize the relationship between fluctuations in exchange rates and foreign exchange gains and losses as follows:

		Foreign Currency (FC)	
Transaction	**Type of Exposure**	**Appreciates**	**Depreciates**
Export sale	Asset	Gain	Loss
Import purchase	Liability	Loss	Gain

A foreign currency receivable arising from an export sale creates an *asset exposure* to foreign exchange risk. If the foreign currency appreciates, the foreign currency asset increases in U.S. dollar value and a foreign exchange gain arises; depreciation of the foreign currency causes a foreign exchange loss. A foreign currency payable arising from an import purchase creates a *liability exposure* to foreign exchange risk. If the foreign currency appreciates, the foreign currency liability increases in U.S. dollar value and a foreign exchange loss results; depreciation of the currency results in a foreign exchange gain.

Balance Sheet Date before Date of Payment

The question arises as to what adjustments should be made if a balance sheet date falls between the date of sale and the date of payment. For example, assume that Amerco shipped goods to its German customer on December 1, 2011, with payment to be received on March 1, 2012. Assume that at December 1, the spot rate for the euro was $1.32, but by December 31, the euro has appreciated to $1.33. Is any adjustment needed at December 31, 2011, when the books are closed to account for the fact that the foreign currency receivable has changed in U.S. dollar value since December 1?

---

[5] Note that the foreign exchange loss results because the customer is allowed to pay in euros and is given 30 days to pay. If the transaction were denominated in U.S. dollars, no loss would result, nor would there be a loss if the euros had been received at the date the sale was made.

The general consensus worldwide is that a foreign currency receivable or foreign currency payable should be revalued at the balance sheet date to account for the change in exchange rates. Under the two-transaction perspective, this means that a foreign exchange gain or loss arises at the balance sheet date. The next question then is what should be done with these foreign exchange gains and losses that have not yet been realized in cash. Should they be included in net income?

The two approaches to accounting for unrealized foreign exchange gains and losses are the deferral approach and the accrual approach. Under the *deferral approach,* unrealized foreign exchange gains and losses are deferred on the balance sheet until cash is actually paid or received. When cash is paid or received, a *realized* foreign exchange gain or loss is included in income. This approach is not acceptable under U.S. GAAP.

U.S. GAAP requires U.S. companies to use the *accrual approach* to account for unrealized foreign exchange gains and losses. Under this approach, a firm reports unrealized foreign exchange gains and losses in net income in the period in which the exchange rate changes. This is consistent with accrual accounting as it results in reporting the effect of a rate change that will have an impact on cash flow in the period when the event causing the impact takes place. Thus, any change in the exchange rate from the date of sale to the balance sheet date results in a foreign exchange gain or loss to be reported in income in that period. Any change in the exchange rate from the balance sheet date to the date of payment results in a second foreign exchange gain or loss that is reported in the second accounting period. Amerco makes the following journal entries under the accrual approach:

12/1/11	Accounts Receivable (€)	1,320,000	
	Sales		1,320,000
	To record the sale and euro receivable at the spot rate of $1.32.		
12/31/11	Accounts Receivable (€)	10,000	
	Foreign Exchange Gain		10,000
	To adjust the value of the euro receivable to the new spot rate of $1.33 and record a foreign exchange gain resulting from the appreciation in the euro since December 1.		
3/1/12	Foreign Exchange Loss	30,000	
	Accounts Receivable (€)		30,000
	To adjust the value of the euro receivable to the new spot rate of $1.30 and record a foreign exchange loss resulting from the depreciation in the euro since December 31.		
	Cash	1,300,000	
	Accounts Receivable (€)		1,300,000
	To record the receipt of 1 million euros and conversion at the spot rate of $1.30.		

The net impact on income in 2011 is a sale of $1,320,000 and a foreign exchange gain of $10,000; in 2012, Amerco records a foreign exchange loss of $30,000. This results in a net increase of $1,300,000 in Retained Earnings that is balanced by an equal increase in Cash over the two-year period. Over the two-year period Amerco recognizes a net foreign exchange loss of $20,000.

One criticism of the accrual approach is that it leads to a violation of conservatism when an unrealized foreign exchange gain arises at the balance sheet date. In fact, this is one of only two situations in U.S. GAAP in which it is acceptable to recognize an unrealized gain in income. (The other situation relates to trading marketable securities reported at fair value.)

Restatement at the balance sheet date is required for all foreign currency assets and liabilities carried on a company's books. In addition to foreign currency payables and receivables arising from import and export transactions, companies might have dividends receivable from foreign subsidiaries, loans payable to foreign lenders, or lease payments receivable from foreign customers that are denominated in a foreign currency and therefore must be restated at the balance sheet date. Each of these foreign currency denominated assets and liabilities is exposed to foreign exchange risk; therefore, fluctuation in the exchange rate results in foreign exchange gains and losses.

Many U.S. companies report foreign exchange gains and losses on the income statement in a line item often titled Other Income (Expense). Companies include other incidental gains and losses such as gains and losses on sales of assets in this line item as well. Companies are required to disclose the magnitude of foreign exchange gains and losses if material. For example, in the Notes to Financial Statements in its 2008 annual report, Merck indicated that the income statement item Other (Income) Expense, Net included an exchange loss of $147.4 million in 2008 and exchange gains of $54.3 million and $25.0 million in 2007 and 2006, respectively.

HEDGES OF FOREIGN EXCHANGE RISK

LO3

Understand how foreign currency forward contracts and foreign currency options can be used to hedge foreign exchange risk.

In the preceding example, Amerco has an asset exposure in euros when it sells goods to the German customer and allows the customer three months to pay for its purchase. If the euro depreciates over the next three months, Amerco will incur a net foreign exchange loss. For many companies, the uncertainty of not knowing exactly how many U.S. dollars an export sale will generate is of great concern. To avoid this uncertainty, companies often use foreign currency derivatives to hedge against the effect of unfavorable changes in the value of foreign currencies. The two most common derivatives used to hedge foreign exchange risk are *foreign currency forward contracts* and *foreign currency options*. Through a forward contract, Amerco can lock in the price at which it will sell the euros it receives in three months. An option establishes a price at which Amerco will be able, but is not required, to sell the euros it receives in three months. If Amerco enters into a forward contract or purchases a put option on the date the sale is made, the derivative is being used as a *hedge of a recognized foreign currency denominated asset* (the euro account receivable).

Companies engaged in foreign currency activities often enter into hedging arrangements as soon as they receive a noncancelable sales order or place a noncancelable purchase order. A noncancelable order that specifies the foreign currency price and date of delivery is known as a *foreign currency firm commitment*. Assume that on June 1, Amerco accepts an order to sell parts to a customer in South Korea at a price of 5 million Korean won. The parts will be delivered and payment will be received on August 15. On June 1, before the sale has been made, Amerco enters into a forward contract to sell 5 million Korean won on August 15. In this case, Amerco is using a foreign currency derivative as a *hedge of an unrecognized foreign currency firm commitment*.

Some companies have foreign currency transactions that occur on a regular basis and can be reliably forecasted. For example, Amerco regularly purchases materials from a supplier in Hong Kong for which it pays in Hong Kong dollars. Even if Amerco has no contract to make future purchases, it has an exposure to foreign currency risk if it plans to continue making purchases from the Hong Kong supplier. Assume that on October 1, Amerco forecasts that it will make a purchase from the Hong Kong supplier in one month. To hedge against a possible increase in the price of the Hong Kong dollar, Amerco acquires a call option on October 1 to purchase Hong Kong dollars in one month. The foreign currency option represents a *hedge of a forecasted foreign currency denominated transaction*.

DERIVATIVES ACCOUNTING

Topic 815, Derivatives and Hedging, of the FASB Accounting Standards Codification governs the accounting for derivatives, including those used to hedge foreign exchange risk. This authoritative literature provides guidance for hedges of the following sources of foreign exchange risk:

1. Recognized foreign currency denominated assets and liabilities.
2. Unrecognized foreign currency firm commitments.
3. Forecasted foreign currency denominated transactions.
4. Net investments in foreign operations.

Different accounting applies to each type of foreign currency hedge. This chapter demonstrates the accounting for the first three types of hedge. The next chapter covers hedges of net investments in foreign operations.

Fundamental Requirement of Derivatives Accounting

The fundamental requirement is that companies carry all derivatives on the balance sheet at their fair value. Derivatives are reported on the balance sheet as assets when they have a positive fair value and as liabilities when they have a negative fair value. The first issue in accounting for derivatives is the determination of fair value.

The fair value of derivatives can change over time, causing adjustments to be made to the carrying values of the assets and liabilities. The second issue in accounting for derivatives is the treatment of the gains and losses that arise from these adjustments.

Determination of Fair Value of Derivatives

The *fair value of a foreign currency forward contract* is determined by reference to changes in the forward rate over the life of the contract, discounted to the present value. Three pieces of information are needed to determine the fair value of a forward contract at any point in time:

1. The forward rate when the forward contract was entered into.
2. The current forward rate for a contract that matures on the same date as the forward contract entered into.
3. A discount rate—typically, the company's incremental borrowing rate.

Assume that Exim Company enters into a forward contract on December 1 to sell 1 million Mexican pesos on March 1 at a forward rate of $0.085 per peso, or a total of $85,000. Exim incurs no cost to enter into the forward contract, which has no value on December 1. On December 31, when Exim closes its books to prepare financial statements, the forward rate to sell Mexican pesos on March 1 has changed to $0.082. On that date, a forward contract for the delivery of 1 million pesos could be negotiated, resulting in a cash inflow of only $82,000 on March 1. This represents a favorable change in the value of Exim's forward contract of $3,000 ($85,000 − $82,000). The undiscounted fair value of the forward contract on December 31 is $3,000. Assuming that the company's incremental borrowing rate is 12 percent per annum, the undiscounted fair value of the forward contract must be discounted at the rate of 1 percent per month for two months (from the current date of December 31 to the settlement date of March 1). The fair value of the forward contract at December 31 is $2,940.90 ($3,000 × 0.9803).[6]

The manner in which the *fair value of a foreign currency option* is determined depends on whether the option is traded on an exchange or has been acquired in the over-the-counter market. The fair value of an exchange-traded foreign currency option is its current market price quoted on the exchange. For over-the-counter options, fair value can be determined by obtaining a price quote from an option dealer (such as a bank). If dealer price quotes are unavailable, the company can estimate the value of an option using the modified Black-Scholes option pricing model (briefly mentioned earlier). Regardless of who does the calculation, principles similar to those of the Black-Scholes pricing model can be used to determine the fair value of the option.

---

[6] The present value factor for two months at 1 percent per month is calculated as $1/1.01^2$, or 0.9803.

Accounting for Changes in the Fair Value of Derivatives

Changes in the fair value of derivatives must be included in *comprehensive income,* which is defined as all changes in equity from nonowner sources. It consists of two components: *net income* and *other comprehensive income.* Other comprehensive income consists of income items that current authoritative accounting literature require to be deferred in stockholders' equity such as gains and losses on available-for-sale marketable securities. Other comprehensive income is accumulated and reported as a separate line in the stockholders' equity section of the balance sheet. This book uses the account title *Accumulated Other Comprehensive Income* to describe this stockholders' equity line item.

In accordance with U.S. GAAP, gains and losses arising from changes in the fair value of derivatives are recognized initially either (1) on the income statement as a part of net income or (2) on the balance sheet in accumulated other comprehensive income. Recognition treatment depends partly on whether the company uses derivatives for hedging purposes or for speculation.[7] For speculative derivatives, the company recognizes the change in the fair value of the derivative (the gain or loss) immediately in net income. The accounting for changes in the fair value of derivatives used for hedging depends on the nature of the foreign exchange risk being hedged and on whether the derivative qualifies for *hedge accounting.*

HEDGE ACCOUNTING

Companies enter into hedging relationships to minimize the adverse effect that changes in exchange rates have on cash flows and net income. As such, companies would like to account for hedges in such a way to recognize the gain or loss from the hedge in net income in the same period as the loss or gain on the risk being hedged. This approach is known as *hedge accounting.* U.S. GAAP allows hedge accounting for foreign currency derivatives only if three conditions are satisfied:

1. The derivative is used to hedge either a fair-value exposure or cash flow exposure to foreign exchange risk.
2. The derivative is highly effective in offsetting changes in the fair value or cash flows related to the hedged item.
3. The derivative is properly documented as a hedge.

Each of these conditions is discussed in turn.

Nature of the Hedged Risk

A *fair-value exposure* exists if changes in exchange rates can affect the fair value of an asset or liability reported on the balance sheet. To qualify for hedge accounting, the fair-value risk must have the potential to affect net income if it is not hedged. For example, a fair-value risk is associated with a foreign currency account receivable. If the foreign currency depreciates, the receivable must be written down with an offsetting loss recognized in net income. The authoritative literature has determined that a fair-value exposure also exists for foreign currency firm commitments.

A *cash flow exposure* exists if changes in exchange rates can affect the amount of cash flow to be realized from a transaction with changes in cash flow reflected in net income. A foreign currency account receivable, for example, has both a fair-value exposure and a cash flow exposure. A cash flow exposure exists for (1) recognized foreign currency assets and liabilities, (2) foreign currency firm commitments, and (3) forecasted foreign currency transactions.

---

[7] Companies can acquire derivative financial instruments as investments for speculative purposes. For example, assume that the three-month forward rate for British pounds is $2.00, and a speculator believes the British pound spot rate in three months will be $1.97. In that case, the speculator would enter into a three-month forward contract to sell British pounds. At the future date, the speculator purchases pounds at the spot rate of $1.97 and sells them at the contracted forward rate of $2.00, reaping a gain of $0.03 per pound. Of course, such an investment might as easily generate a loss if the spot rate does not move as expected.

Derivatives for which companies wish to use hedge accounting must be designated as either a *fair value hedge* or a *cash flow hedge*. For hedges of recognized foreign currency assets and liabilities and hedges of foreign currency firm commitments, companies must choose between the two types of designation. Hedges of forecasted foreign currency transactions can qualify only as cash flow hedges. Accounting procedures differ for the two types of hedges. In general, gains and losses on fair value hedges are recognized immediately in net income, and gains and losses on cash flow hedges are included in other comprehensive income.

Hedge Effectiveness

For hedge accounting to be used initially, the hedge must be expected to be highly effective in generating gains and losses that offset losses and gains on the item being hedged. The hedge actually must be effective in generating offsetting gains and losses for hedge accounting to continue to be applied.

At inception, a foreign currency derivative can be considered an effective hedge if the critical terms of the hedging instrument match those of the hedged item. Critical terms include the currency type, currency amount, and settlement date. For example, a forward contract to purchase 100,000 Canadian dollars in 30 days would be an effective hedge of a 100,000 Canadian dollar liability that is payable in 30 days. Assessing hedge effectiveness on an ongoing basis can be accomplished using a cumulative dollar offset method.

Hedge Documentation

For hedge accounting to be applied, U.S. GAAP requires formal documentation of the hedging relationship at the inception of the hedge (i.e., on the date a foreign currency forward contract is entered into or a foreign currency option is acquired). The hedging company must prepare a document that identifies the hedged item, the hedging instrument, the nature of the risk being hedged, how the hedging instrument's effectiveness will be assessed, and the risk management objective and strategy for undertaking the hedge.

HEDGES OF FOREIGN CURRENCY DENOMINATED ASSETS AND LIABILITIES

LO4

Account for forward contracts and options used as hedges of foreign currency denominated assets and liabilities.

Hedges of foreign currency denominated assets and liabilities, such as accounts receivable and accounts payable, can qualify as either *cash flow hedges* or *fair value hedges*. To qualify as a cash flow hedge, the hedging instrument must completely offset the variability in the cash flows associated with the foreign currency receivable or payable. If the hedging instrument does not qualify as a cash flow hedge or if the company elects not to designate the hedging instrument as a cash flow hedge, the hedge is designated as a fair value hedge. The following summarizes the basic accounting for the two types of hedges.

Cash Flow Hedge

At each balance sheet date, the following procedures are required:

1. The hedged asset or liability is adjusted to fair value based on changes in the spot exchange rate, and a foreign exchange gain or loss is recognized in net income.
2. The derivative hedging instrument is adjusted to fair value (resulting in an asset or liability reported on the balance sheet) with the counterpart recognized as a change in Accumulated Other Comprehensive Income (AOCI).
3. An amount equal to the foreign exchange gain or loss on the hedged asset or liability is then transferred from AOCI to net income; the net effect is to offset any gain or loss on the hedged asset or liability.
4. An additional amount is removed from AOCI and recognized in net income to reflect (a) the current period's amortization of the original discount or premium on the forward contract (if a forward contract is the hedging instrument) or (b) the change in the *time value* of the option (if an option is the hedging instrument).

Fair Value Hedge

At each balance sheet date, the following procedures are required:

1. Adjust the hedged asset or liability to fair value based on changes in the spot exchange rate and recognize a foreign exchange gain or loss in net income.
2. Adjust the derivative hedging instrument to fair value (resulting in an asset or liability reported on the balance sheet) and recognize the counterpart as a gain or loss in net income.

FORWARD CONTRACT USED TO HEDGE A FOREIGN CURRENCY DENOMINATED ASSET

We now return to the Amerco example in which the company has a foreign currency account receivable to demonstrate the accounting for a hedge of a recognized foreign currency denominated asset.[8] In the preceding example, Amerco has an asset exposure in euros when it sells goods to the German customer and allows the customer three months to pay for its purchase. To hedge its exposure to a possible decline in the U.S. dollar value of the euro, Amerco enters into a forward contract.

Assume that on December 1, 2011, the three-month forward rate for euros is $1.305 and Amerco signs a contract with New Manhattan Bank to deliver 1 million euros in three months in exchange for $1,305,000. No cash changes hands on December 1, 2011. Because the spot rate on December 1 is $1.32, the euro (€) is selling at a discount in the three-month forward market (the forward rate is less than the spot rate). Because the euro is selling at a discount of $0.015 per euro, Amerco receives $15,000 less than it would had payment been received at the date the goods are delivered ($1,305,000 versus $1,320,000). This $15,000 reduction in cash flow can be considered as an expense; it is the cost of extending foreign currency credit to the foreign customer.[9] Conceptually, this expense is similar to the transaction loss that arises on the export sale. It exists only because the transaction is denominated in a foreign currency. The major difference is that Amerco knows the exact amount of the discount expense at the date of sale, whereas when it is left unhedged, Amerco does not know the size of the transaction loss until three months pass. (In fact, it is possible that the unhedged receivable could result in a transaction gain rather than a transaction loss.)

Because the future spot rate turns out to be only $1.30, selling euros at a forward rate of $1.305 is obviously better than leaving the euro receivable unhedged: Amerco will receive $5,000 more as a result of the hedge. This can be viewed as a gain resulting from the use of the forward contract. Unlike the discount expense, the exact size of this gain is not known until three months pass. (In fact, it is possible that use of the forward contract could result in an additional loss. This would occur if the spot rate on March 1, 2012, is more than the forward rate of $1.305.)

Amerco must account for its foreign currency transaction and the related forward contract simultaneously but separately. The process can be better understood by referring to the steps involving the three parties—Amerco, the German customer, and New Manhattan Bank—shown in Exhibit 7.2.

Because the settlement date, currency type, and currency amount of the forward contract match the corresponding terms of the account receivable, the hedge is expected to be highly effective. If Amerco properly designates the forward contract as a hedge of its euro account receivable position, it may apply hedge accounting. Because it completely offsets the variability in the cash flows related to the account receivable, Amerco may designate the forward contract as a cash flow hedge. Alternatively, because changes in the spot rate affect not only the cash

---

[8] The comprehensive illustration at the end of this chapter demonstrates the accounting for the hedge of a foreign currency denominated liability.

[9] This should not be confused with the cost associated with normal credit risk—that is, the risk that the customer will not pay for its purchase. That is a separate issue unrelated to the currency in which the transaction is denominated.

EXHIBIT 7.2

Hedge of a Foreign Currency Account Receivable with a Forward Contract

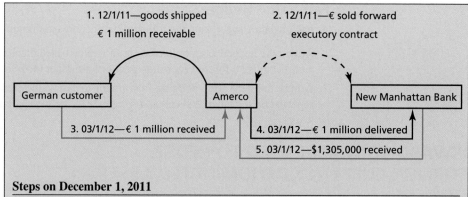

Steps on December 1, 2011

1. Amerco ships goods to the German customer, thereby creating an Account Receivable of € 1 million.
2. Amerco then sells € 1 million three months forward to New Manhattan Bank, creating an executory contract to pay € 1 million and receive $1,305,000.

Steps on March 1, 2012

3. The German customer remits € 1 million to Amerco—the € Account Receivable has been received and Amerco has € 1 million reflected in an account Foreign Currency (€).
4. Amerco delivers € 1 million to New Manhattan Bank.
5. New Manhattan Bank pays Amerco $1,305,000.

flows but also the fair value of the foreign currency receivable, Amerco may elect to account for this forward contract as a fair value hedge.

In either case, Amerco determines the fair value of the forward contract by referring to the change in the forward rate for a contract maturing on March 1, 2012. The relevant exchange rates, U.S. dollar value of the euro receivable, and fair value of the forward contract are determined as follows:

| | | Account Receivable (€) | | Forward | Forward Contract | |
| | | U.S. Dollar | Change in U.S. | Rate to | | Change in |
Date	Spot Rate	Value	Dollar Value	3/1/12	Fair Value	Fair Value
12/1/11	$1.32	$1,320,000	—	$1.305	–0–	—
12/31/11	1.33	1,330,000	+$10,000	1.316	$(10,783)*	−$10,783
3/1/12	1.30	1,300,000	−$30,000	1.30	5,000†	+ 15,783

*$1,305,000 − $1,316,000 = $(11,000) × 0.9803 = $(10,783), where 0.9803 is the present value factor for two months at an annual interest rate of 12 percent (1 percent per month) calculated as $1/1.01^2$.

†$1,305,000 − $1,300,000 = $5,000.

Amerco pays nothing to enter into the forward contract at December 1, 2011, and the forward contract has a fair value of zero on that date. At December 31, 2011, the forward rate for a contract to deliver euros on March 1, 2012, is $1.316. Amerco could enter into a forward contract on December 31, 2011, to sell 1 million euros for $1,316,000 on March 1, 2012. Because Amerco is committed to sell 1 million euros for $1,305,000, the nominal value of the forward contract is $(11,000). The fair value of the forward contract is the present value of this amount. Assuming that Amerco has an incremental borrowing rate of 12 percent per year (1 percent per month) and discounting for two months (from December 31, 2011, to March 1, 2012), the fair value of the forward contract at December 31, 2011, is $(10,783), a liability. On March 1, 2012, the forward rate to sell euros on that date is, by definition, the spot rate, $1.30. At that rate, Amerco could sell 1 million euros for $1,300,000. Because Amerco has a contract to sell euros for $1,305,000, the fair value of the forward contract on March 1, 2012, is $5,000. This represents an increase of $15,783 in fair value from December 31, 2011. The original discount on the forward contract is determined by the difference in the euro spot rate and three-month forward rate on December 1, 2011: ($1.305 − $1.32) × € 1 million = $15,000.

Forward Contract Designated as Cash Flow Hedge

Assume that Amerco designates the forward contract as a *cash flow hedge* of a foreign currency denominated asset. In this case, it allocates the original forward discount or premium to net income over the life of the forward contract using an effective interest method. The company prepares the following journal entries to account for the foreign currency transaction and the related forward contract:

2011 Journal Entries—Forward Contract Designated as a Cash Flow Hedge

12/1/11	Accounts Receivable (€)	1,320,000	
	Sales		1,320,000
	To record the sale and € 1 million account receivable at the spot rate of $1.32 (Step 1 in Exhibit 7.2).		

Amerco makes no formal entry for the forward contract because it is an executory contract (no cash changes hands) and has a fair value of zero (Step 2 in Exhibit 7.2).

Amerco prepares a memorandum designating the forward contract as a hedge of the risk of changes in the cash flow to be received on the foreign currency account receivable resulting from changes in the U.S. dollar–euro exchange rate. The company prepares the following journal entries on December 31:

12/31/11	Accounts Receivable (€)	10,000	
	Foreign Exchange Gain		10,000
	To adjust the value of the € receivable to the new spot rate of $1.33 and record a foreign exchange gain resulting from the appreciation of the € since December 1.		
	Accumulated Other Comprehensive Income (AOCI)	10,783	
	Forward Contract		10,783
	To record the forward contract as a liability at its fair value of $10,783 with a corresponding debit to AOCI.		
	Loss on Forward Contract	10,000	
	Accumulated Other Comprehensive Income (AOCI)		10,000
	To record a loss on forward contract to offset the foreign exchange gain on account receivable with a corresponding credit to AOCI.		
	Discount Expense	5,019	
	Accumulated Other Comprehensive Income (AOCI)		5,019
	To allocate the forward contract discount to net income over the life of the contract using the effective interest method with a corresponding credit to AOCI.		

The first entry at December 31, 2011, serves to revalue the foreign currency account receivable and recognize a foreign exchange gain of $10,000 in net income. The second entry recognizes the forward contract as a liability of $10,783 on the balance sheet. Because the forward contract has been designated as a cash flow hedge, the debit of $10,783 in the second entry is made to AOCI, which decreases stockholders' equity. The third entry achieves the objective of hedge accounting by transferring $10,000 from AOCI to a loss on forward contract. As a result of this entry, the loss on forward contract of $10,000 and the foreign exchange gain on the account receivable of $10,000 exactly offset one another, and the net impact on income is zero. As a result of the second and third entries, the forward contract is reported on the balance sheet as a liability at fair value of $(10,783); a loss on forward contract is recognized in the amount of $10,000 to offset the foreign exchange gain; and AOCI has a negative (debit) balance of $783. The second and third entries could be combined into one entry as follows:

Loss on Forward Contract	10,000	
Accumulated Other Comprehensive Income (AOCI)	783	
Forward Contract		10,783

The negative balance in AOCI of $783 can be viewed as that portion of the loss on the forward contract (decrease in fair value of the forward contract) that is not recognized in net income but instead is deferred in stockholders' equity. Under cash flow hedge accounting, a loss on the hedging instrument (forward contract) is recognized only to the extent that it offsets a gain on the item being hedged (account receivable).

The last entry uses the effective interest method to allocate a portion of the $15,000 forward contract discount as an expense to net income. The company calculates the implicit interest rate associated with the forward contract by considering the fact that the forward contract will generate cash flow of $1,305,000 from a foreign currency asset with an initial value of $1,320,000. Because the discount of $15,000 accrues over a three-month period, the effective interest rate is calculated as $[1 - \sqrt[3]{\$1,305,000/\$1,320,000}] = .0038023$. The amount of discount to be allocated to net income for the month of December 2011 is $1,320,000 × .0038023 = $5,019.

The impact on net income for the year 2011 follows:

Sales.		$1,320,000
Foreign exchange gain	$ 10,000	
Loss on forward contract	(10,000)	
Net gain (loss).		–0–
Discount expense		(5,019)
Impact on net income.		$1,314,981

The effect on the December 31, 2011, balance sheet is as follows:

Assets		Liabilities and Stockholders' Equity	
Accounts receivable (€)	$1,330,000	Forward contract . . . . $	10,783
		Retained earnings	1,314,981
		AOCI	4,236
			$1,330,000

2012 Journal Entries—Forward Contract Designated as Cash Flow Hedge

From December 31, 2011, to March 1, 2012, the euro account receivable decreases in value by $30,000 and the forward contract increases in value by $15,873. In addition, on March 1, 2012, the remaining discount on forward contract must be amortized to expense. The company prepares the following journal entries on March 1 to reflect these changes:

3/1/12	Foreign Exchange Loss	30,000	
	Accounts Receivable (€)		30,000
	To adjust the value of the € receivable to the new spot rate of $1.30 and record a foreign exchange loss resulting from the depreciation of the € since December 31.		
	Forward Contract	15,783	
	Accumulated Other Comprehensive Income (AOCI)		15,783
	To adjust the carrying value of the forward contract to its current fair value of $5,000 with a corresponding credit to AOCI.		

Accumulated Other Comprehensive Income (AOCI)	30,000	
Gain on Forward Contract		30,000
To record a gain on forward contract to offset the foreign exchange loss on account receivable with a corresponding debit to AOCI.		
Discount Expense	9,981	
Accumulated Other Comprehensive Income (AOCI)		9,981
To allocate the remaining forward contract discount to net income ($15,000 − 5,019 = $9,981) with a corresponding credit to AOCI.		

As a result of these entries, the balance in AOCI is zero: $4,236 + $15,783 − $30,000 + $9,981 = $0.

The next two journal entries recognize the receipt of euros from the customer, close out the euro account receivable, and record the settlement of the forward contract.

Foreign Currency (€)	1,300,000	
Accounts Receivable (€)		1,300,000
To record receipt of € 1 million from the German customer as an asset (Foreign Currency) at the spot rate of $1.30 (Step 3 in Exhibit 7.2).		
Cash	1,305,000	
Foreign Currency (€)		1,300,000
Forward Contract		5,000
To record settlement of the forward contract (i.e., record receipt of $1,305,000 in exchange for delivery of € 1 million) and remove the forward contract from the accounts (Steps 4 and 5 in Exhibit 7.2).		

The impact on net income for the year 2012 follows:

Foreign exchange loss	$(30,000)	
Gain on forward contract	30,000	
Net gain (loss) . . . . :		–0–
Discount expense		$(9,981)
Impact on net income		$(9,981)

The net effect on the balance sheet over the two years is a $1,305,000 increase in Cash with a corresponding increase in Retained Earnings of $1,305,000 ($1,314,981 − $9,981). The cumulative amount recognized as Discount Expense of $15,000 reflects the cost of extending credit to the German customer.

The net benefit from entering into the forward contract is $5,000. This "gain" is not directly reflected in net income. However, it can be calculated as the difference between the net gain on the forward contract and the cumulative amount of discount expense ($20,000 − $15,000 = $5,000) recognized over the two periods.

Effective Interest versus Straight-Line Methods

Use of the effective interest method results in allocating the forward contract discount $5,019 at the end of the first month and $9,981 at the end of the next two months. Straight-line allocation of the $15,000 discount on a monthly basis results in a reasonable approximation of these amounts:

$$12/31/11 \qquad \$15,000 \times {}^1\!/_3 = \$5,000$$
$$3/1/12 \qquad \$15,000 \times {}^2\!/_3 = \$10,000$$

Determining the effective interest rate is complex and provides no conceptual insights. For the remainder of this chapter, we use straight-line allocation of forward contract discounts and premiums. The important thing to keep in mind in this example is that with a cash flow hedge, an expense equal to the original forward contract discount is recognized in net income over the life of the contract.

What if the forward rate on December 1, 2011, had been $1.326 (i.e., the euro was selling at a premium in the forward market)? In that case, Amerco would receive $6,000 more through the forward sale of euros ($1,326,000) than had it received the euros at the date of sale ($1,320,000). Amerco would allocate the forward contract premium as an increase in net income at the rate of $2,000 per month: $2,000 at December 31, 2011, and $4,000 at March 1, 2012.

Forward Contract Designated as Fair Value Hedge

Assume that Amerco decides to designate the forward contract not as a cash flow hedge but as a fair value hedge. In that case, it takes the gain or loss on the forward contract directly to net income and does not separately amortize the original discount on the forward contract.

2011 Journal Entries—Forward Contract Designated as a Fair Value Hedge

12/1/11	Accounts Receivable (€)	1,320,000	
	Sales		1,320,000
	To record the sale and € 1 million account receivable at the spot rate of $1.32 (Step 1 in Exhibit 7.2).		

The forward contract requires no formal entry (Step 2 in Exhibit 7.2). A memorandum designates the forward contract as a hedge of the risk of changes in the fair value of the foreign currency account receivable resulting from changes in the U.S. dollar–euro exchange rate.

The company prepares the following entries on December 31:

12/31/11	Accounts Receivable (€)	10,000	
	Foreign Exchange Gain		10,000
	To adjust the value of the € receivable to the new spot rate of $1.33 and record a foreign exchange gain resulting from the appreciation of the € since December 1.		
	Loss on Forward Contract	10,783	
	Forward Contract		10,783
	To record the forward contract as a liability at its fair value of $10,783 and record a forward contract loss for the change in the fair value of the forward contract since December 1.		

The first entry at December 31, 2011, serves to revalue the foreign currency account receivable and recognize a foreign exchange gain of $10,000. The second entry recognizes the forward contract as a liability of $10,783 on the balance sheet. Because the forward contract has been designated as a fair value hedge, the debit in the second entry recognizes the entire change in fair value of the forward contract as a loss in net income; there is no deferral of loss in stockholders' equity. A net loss of $783 is reported in net income as a result of these two entries.

The impact on net income for the year 2011 is as follows:

Sales		$1,320,000
Foreign exchange gain	$ 10,000	
Loss on forward contract	(10,783)	
Net gain (loss)		(783)
Impact on net income		$1,319,217

DO WE HAVE A GAIN OR WHAT?

Ahnuld Corporation, a health juice producer, recently expanded its sales through exports to foreign markets. Earlier this year, the company negotiated the sale of several thousand cases of turnip juice to a retailer in the country of Tcheckia. The customer is unwilling to assume the risk of having to pay in U.S. dollars. Desperate to enter the Tcheckian market, the vice president for international sales agrees to denominate the sale in tchecks, the national currency of Tcheckia. The current exchange rate for 1 tcheck is $2.00. In addition, the customer indicates that it cannot pay until it sells all of the juice. Payment is scheduled for six months from the date of sale.

Fearful that the tcheck might depreciate in value over the next six months, the head of the risk management department at Ahnuld Corporation enters into a forward contract to sell tchecks in six months at a forward rate of $1.80. The forward contract is designated as a fair value hedge of the tcheck receivable. Six months later, when Ahnuld receives payment from the Tcheckian customer, the exchange rate for the tcheck is $1.70. The corporate treasurer calls the head of the risk management department into her office.

Treasurer: I see that your decision to hedge our foreign currency position on that sale to Tcheckia was a bad one.

Department head: What do you mean? We have a gain on that forward contract. We're $10,000 better off from having entered into that hedge.

Treasurer: That's not what the books say. The accountants have recorded a net loss of $20,000 on that particular deal. I'm afraid I'm not going to be able to pay you a bonus this year. Another bad deal like this one and I'm going to have to demote you back to the interest rate swap department.

Department head: Those bean counters have messed up again. I told those guys in international sales that selling to customers in Tcheckia was risky, but at least by hedging our exposure, we managed to receive a reasonable amount of cash on that deal. In fact, we ended up with a gain of $10,000 on the hedge. Tell the accountants to check their debits and credits again. I'm sure they just put a debit in the wrong place or some accounting thing like that.

Have the accountants made a mistake? Does the company have a loss, a gain, or both from this forward contract?

The effect on the December 31, 2011, balance sheet follows:

Assets		Liabilities and Stockholders' Equity	
Accounts receivable (€)	$1,330,000	Forward contract	$ 10,783
		Retained earnings	1,319,217
			$1,330,000

2012 Journal Entries—Forward Contract Designated as a Fair Value Hedge

The company prepares the following entries on March 1:

3/1/12	Foreign Exchange Loss	30,000	
	Accounts Receivable (€)		30,000
	To adjust the value of the € receivable to the new spot rate of $1.30 and record a foreign exchange loss resulting from the depreciation of the € since December 31.		

Forward Contract	15,783	
Gain on Forward Contract		15,783
To adjust the carrying value of the forward contract to its current fair value of $5,000 and record a forward contract gain for the change in the fair value since December 31.		
Foreign Currency (€)	1,300,000	
Accounts Receivable (€)		1,300,000
To record receipt of € 1 million from the German customer as an asset at the spot rate of $1.30 (Step 3 in Exhibit 7.2).		
Cash	1,305,000	
Foreign Currency (€)		1,300,000
Forward Contract		5,000
To record settlement of the forward contract (i.e., record receipt of $1,305,000 in exchange for delivery of € 1 million) and remove the forward contract from the accounts (Steps 4 and 5 in Exhibit 7.2).		

The impact on net income for the year 2012 follows:

Foreign exchange loss	$(30,000)
Gain on forward contract................	15,783
Impact on net income	$(14,217)

The net effect on the balance sheet for the two periods is an increase of $1,305,000 in Cash with a corresponding increase in Retained Earnings of $1,305,000 ($1,319,217 − $14,217).

Under fair value hedge accounting, the company does not amortize the original forward contract discount systematically over the life of the contract. Instead, it recognizes the discount in income as the difference between the foreign exchange Gain (Loss) on the account receivable and the Gain (Loss) on the forward contract—that is, $(783) in 2011 and $(14,217) in 2012. The net impact on net income over the two years is $(15,000), which reflects the cost of extending credit to the German customer. The net gain on the forward contract of $5,000 ($10,783 loss in 2011 and $15,783 gain in 2012) reflects the net benefit (i.e., increase in cash inflow) from Amerco's decision to hedge the euro receivable.

Companies often cannot or do not bother to designate as hedges the forward contracts they use to hedge foreign currency denominated assets and liabilities. In those cases, the company accounts for the forward contract in exactly the same way it would if it had designated it as a fair value hedge. The company reports an undesignated forward contract on the balance sheet at fair value as an asset or liability and immediately recognizes changes in the fair value of the forward contract in income. The only difference between a forward contract designated as a fair value hedge of a foreign currency denominated asset or liability and an undesignated forward contract is the manner in which the company discloses it in the notes to the financial statements. E.I. du Pont de Nemours and Company provided the following disclosure related to this in its 2008 Form 10-K (page F-44):

Derivatives Not Designated in Hedging Relationships

The company uses forward exchange contracts to reduce its net exposure, by currency, related to foreign currency-denominated monetary assets and liabilities. The netting of such exposures precludes the use of hedge accounting. However, the required revaluation of the forward contract and the associated foreign currency-denominated monetary assets and liabilities results in a minimal earnings impact, after taxes.

Cash Flow Hedge versus Fair Value Hedge

A forward contract used to hedge a foreign currency denominated asset or liability can be designated as either a cash flow hedge or a fair value hedge when it completely offsets the variability in cash flows associated with the hedged item. The total impact on income is the same regardless of whether the forward contract is designated as a fair value hedge or as a cash flow hedge. In our example, Amerco recognized an expense (or loss) of $15,000 in both cases, and the company knew what the total expense was going to be as soon as the contract was signed.

A benefit to designating a forward contract as a cash flow hedge is that the company knows the forward contract's effect on net income *each year* as soon as the contract is signed. The net impact on income is the periodic amortization of the forward contract discount or premium. In our example, Amerco knew on December 1, 2011, that it would recognize a discount expense of $5,000 in 2011 and $10,000 in 2012. The impact on each year's income is not as systematic when the forward contract is designated as a fair value hedge—loss of $783 in 2011 and $14,217 in 2012. Moreover, the company does not know what the net impact on 2011 income will be until December 31, 2011, when the euro account receivable and the forward contract are revalued. Because of the potential for greater volatility in periodic net income that results from a fair value hedge, companies may prefer to designate forward contracts used to hedge a foreign currency denominated asset or liability as cash flow hedges.

FOREIGN CURRENCY OPTION USED TO HEDGE A FOREIGN CURRENCY DENOMINATED ASSET

As an alternative to a forward contract, Amerco could hedge its exposure to foreign exchange risk arising from the euro account receivable by purchasing a foreign currency put option. A put option would give Amerco the right but not the obligation to sell 1 million euros on March 1, 2012, at a predetermined strike price. Assume that on December 1, 2011, Amerco purchases an over-the-counter option from its bank with a strike price of $1.32 when the spot rate is $1.32 and pays a premium of $0.009 per euro.[10] Thus, the purchase price for the option is $9,000 (€1 million × $0.009).

Because the strike price and spot rate are the same, no intrinsic value is associated with this option. The premium is based solely on time value; that is, it is possible that the euro will depreciate and the spot rate on March 1, 2012, will be less than $1.32, in which case the option will be "in the money." If the spot rate for euros on March 1, 2012, is less than the strike price of $1.32, Amerco will exercise its option and sell its 1 million euros at the strike price of $1.32. If the spot rate for euros in three months is more than the strike price of $1.32, Amerco will not exercise its option but will sell euros at the higher spot rate. By purchasing this option, Amerco is guaranteed a minimum cash flow from the export sale of $1,311,000 ($1,320,000 from exercising the option less the $9,000 cost of the option). There is no limit to the maximum number of U.S. dollars that Amerco could receive.

As is true for other derivative financial instruments, authoritative accounting literature requires foreign currency options to be reported on the balance sheet at fair value. The fair value of a foreign currency option at the balance sheet date is determined by reference to the premium quoted by banks on that date for an option with a similar expiration date. Banks (and other sellers of options) determine the current premium by incorporating relevant variables at the balance sheet date into the modified Black-Scholes option pricing model. Changes in value for the euro account receivable and the foreign currency option are summarized as follows:

Date	Spot Rate	Account Receivable (€)		Option Premium for 3/1/12	Foreign Currency Option	
		U.S. Dollar Value	Change in U.S. Dollar Value		Fair Value	Change in Fair Value
12/1/11	$1.32	$1,320,000	–0–	$0.009	$ 9,000	–0–
12/31/11	1.33	1,330,000	+ $10,000	0.006	6,000	– $ 3,000
3/1/12	1.30	1,300,000	– 30,000	0.020	20,000	+ 14,000

---

[10] The seller of the option determined the price of the option (the premium) by using a variation of the Black-Scholes option pricing formula.

The fair value of the foreign currency put option at December 1 is its cost of $9,000. The spot rate for the euro increases during December, which causes a decrease in the fair value of the put option; the right to sell euros at $1.32 is of even less value when the spot rate is $1.33 (on December 31) than when the spot rate was $1.32 (on December 1). The bank determines the fair value of the option at December 31 to be $6,000. By March 1, the euro spot rate has decreased to $1.30. By exercising its option on March 1 at the strike price of $1.32, Amerco will receive $1,320,000 from its export sale, rather than only $1,300,000 if it were required to sell euros in the spot market on March 1. Thus, the option has a fair value of $20,000 on March 1.

We can decompose the fair value of the foreign currency option into its intrinsic value and time value components as follows:

Date	Fair Value	Intrinsic Value	Time Value	Change in Time Value
12/1/11	$ 9,000	–0–	$9,000	–0–
12/31/11	6,000	–0–	6,000	– $3,000
3/1/12	20,000	$20,000	–0–	– 6,000

Because the option strike price is less than or equal to the spot rate at both December 1 and December 31, the option has no intrinsic value at those dates. The entire fair value is attributable to time value only. On March 1, the date of expiration, no time value remains, and the entire amount of fair value is attributable to intrinsic value.

Option Designated as Cash Flow Hedge

Assume that Amerco designates the foreign currency option as a *cash flow hedge* of a foreign currency denominated asset. In this case, Amerco recognizes the change in the option's time value immediately in net income. The company prepares the following journal entries to account for the foreign currency transaction and the related foreign currency option:

2011 Journal Entries—Option Designated as a Cash Flow Hedge

12/1/11	Accounts Receivable (€)	1,320,000	
	Sales		1,320,000
	To record the sale and € 1 million account receivable at the spot rate of $1.32.		
	Foreign Currency Option	9,000	
	Cash		9,000
	To record the purchase of the foreign currency option as an asset at its fair value of $9,000.		

From December 1 to December 31, the euro account receivable increases in value by $10,000 and the option decreases in value by $3,000. The company prepares the following journal entries on December 31 to reflect these changes:

12/31/11	Accounts Receivable (€)	10,000	
	Foreign Exchange Gain		10,000
	To adjust the value of the € receivable to the new spot rate of $1.33 and record a foreign exchange gain resulting from the appreciation of the € since December 1.		
	Accumulated Other Comprehensive Income (AOCI)	3,000	
	Foreign Currency Option		3,000
	To adjust the fair value of the option from $9,000 to $6,000 with a corresponding debit to AOCI.		

	Loss on Foreign Currency Option	10,000	
	Accumulated Other Comprehensive Income (AOCI)		10,000
	To record a loss on foreign currency option to offset the foreign exchange gain on the account receivable with a corresponding credit to AOCI.		
	Option Expense	3,000	
	Accumulated Other Comprehensive Income (AOCI)		3,000
	To recognize the change in the time value of the option as a decrease in net income with a corresponding credit to AOCI.		

The first three journal entries prepared on December 31 result in the euro account receivable and the foreign currency option being reported on the balance sheet at fair value with a net gain (loss) of zero reflected in net income, which is consistent with the concept of hedge accounting. The final entry serves to amortize a portion of the option cost to expense in net income. On March 1, the remaining $6,000 of option cost will be expensed.

The impact on net income for the year 2011 follows:

Sales		$1,320,000
Foreign exchange gain	$ 10,000	
Loss on foreign currency option	(10,000)	
Net gain (loss)		–0–
Option expense		(3,000)
Impact on net income		$1,317,000

The effect on the December 31, 2011, balance sheet is as follows:

Assets			**Liabilities and Stockholders' Equity**		
Cash	$	(9,000)	Retained earnings		$1,317,000
Accounts receivable (€)		1,330,000	AOCI		10,000
Foreign currency option		6,000			$1,327,000
		$1,327,000			

At March 1, 2012, the option has increased in fair value by $14,000—time value decreases by $6,000 and intrinsic value increases by $20,000. The accounting entries made in 2012 are presented next:

2012 Journal Entries—Option Designated as a Cash Flow Hedge

3/1/12	Foreign Exchange Loss	30,000	
	Accounts Receivable (€)		30,000
	To adjust the value of the € receivable to the new spot rate of $1.30 and record a foreign exchange loss resulting from the depreciation of the € since December 31.		
	Foreign Currency Option	14,000	
	Accumulated Other Comprehensive Income (AOCI)		14,000
	To adjust the fair value of the option from $6,000 to $20,000 with a corresponding credit to AOCI.		
	Accumulated Other Comprehensive Income (AOCI)	30,000	
	Gain on Foreign Currency Option		30,000
	To record a gain on foreign currency option to offset the foreign exchange gain on account receivable with a corresponding debit to AOCI.		

Option Expense	6,000	
Accumulated Other Comprehensive Income (AOCI)		6,000
To recognize the change in the time value of the option as a decrease in net income with a corresponding credit to AOCI.		

The first three entries above result in the euro account receivable and the foreign currency option being reported at their fair values, with a net gain (loss) of zero. The fourth entry amortizes the remaining cost of the option to expense. As a result of these entries, the balance in AOCI is zero: $10,000 + $14,000 − $30,000 + $6,000 = $0.

The next two journal entries recognize the receipt of euros from the customer, close out the euro account receivable, and record the exercise of the foreign currency option.

Foreign Currency (€)	1,300,000	
Accounts Receivable (€)		1,300,000
To record receipt of € 1 million from the German customer as an asset at the spot rate of $1.30.		
Cash	1,320,000	
Foreign Currency (€)		1,300,000
Foreign Currency Option		20,000
To record exercise of the option (i.e., record receipt of $1,320,000 in exchange for delivery of € 1 million) and remove the foreign currency option from the accounts.		

The impact on net income for the year 2012 follows:

Foreign exchange loss	$(30,000)	
Gain on foreign currency option	30,000	
Net gain (loss)		–0–
Option expense		(6,000)
Impact on net income		$(6,000)

Over the two accounting periods, Amerco reports Sales of $1,320,000 and a cumulative Option Expense of $9,000. The net effect on the balance sheet is an increase in the Cash account of $1,311,000 ($1,320,000 − $9,000) with a corresponding increase in the Retained Earnings account of $1,311,000 ($1,317,000 − $6,000).

The net benefit from having acquired the option is $11,000. Amerco reflects this "gain" in net income as the net Gain on Foreign Currency Option less the cumulative Option Expense ($20,000 − $9,000 = $11,000) recognized over the two accounting periods.

Option Designated as Fair Value Hedge

Assume that Amerco decides not to designate the foreign currency option as a cash flow hedge but to treat it as a fair value hedge. In that case, it takes the gain or loss on the option directly to net income and does not separately recognize the change in the time value of the option.

2011 Journal Entries—Option Designated as a Fair Value Hedge

12/1/11	Accounts Receivable (€)	1,320,000	
	Sales		1,320,000
	To record the sale and € 1 million account receivable at the spot rate of $1.32.		
	Foreign Currency Option	9,000	
	Cash		9,000
	To record the purchase of the foreign currency option as an asset at its fair value of $9,000.		

12/31/11	Accounts Receivable (€)	10,000	
	Foreign Exchange Gain		10,000
	To adjust the value of the € receivable to the new spot rate of $1.33 and record a foreign exchange gain resulting from the appreciation of the € since December 1.		
	Loss on Foreign Currency Option	3,000	
	Foreign Currency Option		3,000
	To adjust the fair value of the option from $9,000 to $6,000 and record a loss on foreign currency option for the change in the fair value of the option since December 1.		

The impact on net income for the year 2011 follows:

Sales		$1,320,000
Foreign exchange gain	$10,000	
Loss on foreign currency option	(3,000)	
Net gain (loss)		7,000
Impact on net income		$1,327,000

2012 Journal Entries—Option Designated as a Fair Value Hedge

3/1/12	Foreign Exchange Loss	30,000	
	Accounts Receivable (€)		30,000
	To adjust the value of the € receivable to the new spot rate of $1.30 and record a foreign exchange loss resulting from the depreciation of the € since December 31.		
	Foreign Currency Option	14,000	
	Gain on Foreign Currency Option		14,000
	To adjust the fair value of the option from $6,000 to $20,000 and record a gain on foreign currency option for the change in fair value since December 31.		
	Foreign Currency (€)	1,300,000	
	Accounts Receivable (€)		1,300,000
	To record receipt of € 1 million from the German customer as an asset at the spot rate of $1.30.		
	Cash	1,320,000	
	Foreign Currency (€)		1,300,000
	Foreign Currency Option		20,000
	To record exercise of the option (i.e., record receipt of $1,320,000 in exchange for delivery of € 1 million) and remove the foreign currency option from the accounts.		

The impact on net income for the year 2012 follows:

Foreign exchange loss	$(30,000)
Gain on foreign currency option	14,000
Impact on net income	$(16,000)

Over the two accounting periods, Amerco reports Sales of $1,320,000 and a cumulative net loss of $9,000 ($7,000 net gain in 2011 and $16,000 net loss in 2012). The net effect on the balance sheet is an increase in Cash of $1,311,000 ($1,320,000 − $9,000) with a corresponding increase in Retained Earnings of $1,311,000 ($1,327,000 − $16,000). The net benefit from having acquired the option is $11,000. Amerco reflects this in net income through the net Gain on Foreign Currency Option ($3,000 loss in 2011 and $14,000 gain in 2012) recognized over the two accounting periods.

The accounting for an option used as a fair value hedge of a foreign currency denominated asset or liability is the same as if the option had been considered a speculative derivative. The only advantage to designating the option as a fair value hedge relates to the disclosures made in the notes to the financial statements.

Spot Rate Exceeds Strike Price

If the spot rate at March 1, 2012, had been more than the strike price of $1.32, Amerco would allow its option to expire unexercised. Instead it would sell its foreign currency (€) at the spot rate. The fair value of the foreign currency option on March 1, 2012, would be zero. The journal entries for 2011 to reflect this scenario would be the same as the preceding ones. The option would be reported as an asset on the December 31, 2011, balance sheet at $6,000 and the € receivable would have a carrying value of $1,330,000. The entries on March 1, 2012, assuming a spot rate on that date of $1.325 (rather than $1.30), would be as follows:

3/1/12	Foreign Exchange Loss	5,000	
	Accounts Receivable (€)		5,000
	To adjust the value of the € receivable to the new spot rate of $1.325 and record a foreign exchange loss resulting from the depreciation of the € since December 31.		
	Loss on Foreign Currency Option	6,000	
	Foreign Currency Option		6,000
	To adjust the fair value of the option from $6,000 to $0 and record a loss on foreign currency option for the change in fair value since December 31.		
	Foreign Currency (€)	1,325,000	
	Accounts Receivable (€)		1,325,000
	To record receipt of € 1 million from the German customer as an asset at the spot rate of $1.325.		
	Cash	1,325,000	
	Foreign Currency (€)		1,325,000
	To record the sale of € 1 million at the spot rate of $1.325.		

The overall impact on net income for the year 2012 is as follows:

Foreign exchange loss	$ (5,000)
Loss on foreign currency option	(6,000)
Impact on net income	$(11,000)

HEDGES OF UNRECOGNIZED FOREIGN CURRENCY FIRM COMMITMENTS

LO5

Account for forward contracts and options used as hedges of foreign currency firm commitments.

In the examples thus far, Amerco does not enter into a hedge of its export sale until it actually makes the sale. Assume now that on December 1, 2011, Amerco receives and accepts an order from a German customer to deliver goods on March 1, 2012, at a price of 1 million euros. Assume further that under the terms of the sales agreement, Amerco will ship the goods to the German customer on March 1, 2012, and will receive immediate payment on delivery. In other words, Amerco will not allow the German customer time to pay. Although Amerco will not make the sale until March 1, 2012, it has a firm commitment to make the sale and receive 1 million euros in three months. This creates a euro asset exposure to foreign exchange risk as of December 1, 2011. On that date, Amerco wants to hedge against an adverse change in the value of the euro over the next three months. This is known as a *hedge of a foreign currency firm commitment*. Although prior U.S. GAAP originally indicated that only fair value hedge accounting is appropriate for hedges of foreign currency firm commitments, cash flow hedge accounting also now can be used. However, because the results of fair value hedge accounting are intuitively more appealing, we do not cover cash flow hedge accounting for firm commitments.

A firm commitment is an executory contract; the company has not delivered goods nor has the customer paid for them. Normally, executory contracts are not recognized in financial statements. However, when a firm commitment is hedged using a derivative financial instrument, hedge accounting requires explicit recognition on the balance sheet at fair value of both the derivative financial instrument (forward contract or option) and the firm commitment. The change in fair value of the firm commitment results in a gain or loss that offsets the loss or gain on the hedging instrument (forward contract or option), thus achieving the goal of hedge accounting. This raises the conceptual question of how to measure the fair value of the firm commitment. When a forward contract is used as the hedging instrument, the fair value of the firm commitment is determined through reference to changes in the forward exchange rate. Changes in the spot exchange rate are used to determine the fair value of the firm commitment when a foreign currency option is the hedging instrument.

Forward Contract Used as Fair Value Hedge of a Firm Commitment

To hedge its firm commitment exposure to a decline in the U.S. dollar value of the euro, Amerco decides to enter into a forward contract on December 1, 2011. Assume that on that date, the three-month forward rate for euros is $1.305 and Amerco signs a contract with New Manhattan Bank to deliver 1 million euros in three months in exchange for $1,305,000. No cash changes hands on December 1, 2011. Amerco measures the fair value of the firm commitment through changes in the forward rate. Because the fair value of the forward contract is also measured using changes in the forward rate, the gains and losses on the firm commitment and forward contract exactly offset. The fair value of the forward contract and firm commitment are determined as follows:

Date	Forward Rate to 3/1/12	Forward Contract		Firm Commitment	
		Fair Value	Change in Fair Value	Fair Value	Change in Fair Value
12/1/11	$1.305	–0–	–0–	–0–	–0–
12/31/11	1.316	$(10,783)*	– $10,783	$10,783*	+ $10,783
3/1/12	1.30 (spot)	5,000†	+ 15,783	(5,000)†	– 15,783

*($1,305,000 − $1,316,000) = $(11,000) × 0.9803 = $(10,783), where 0.9803 is the present value factor for two months at an annual interest rate of 12 percent (1 percent per month) calculated as 1/1.01².
†($1,305,000 − $1,300,000) = $5,000.

Amerco pays nothing to enter into the forward contract at December 1, 2011. Both the forward contract and the firm commitment have a fair value of zero on that date. At December 31, 2011, the forward rate for a contract to deliver euros on March 1, 2012, is $1.316. A forward contract could be entered into on December 31, 2011, to sell 1 million euros for $1,316,000 on March 1, 2012. Because Amerco is committed to sell 1 million euros for $1,305,000, the value of the forward contract is $(11,000); present value is $(10,783), a liability. The fair value of the firm commitment is also measured through reference to changes in the forward rate. As a result, the fair value of the firm commitment is equal in amount but of opposite sign to the fair value of the forward contract. At December 31, 2011, the firm commitment is an asset of $10,783.

On March 1, 2012, the forward rate to sell euros on that date, by definition, is the spot rate, $1.30. At that rate, Amerco could sell 1 million euros for $1,300,000. Because Amerco has a contract to sell euros for $1,305,000, the fair value of the forward contract on March 1, 2012, is $5,000 (an asset). The firm commitment has a value of $(5,000), a liability. The journal entries to account for the forward contract fair value hedge of a foreign currency firm commitment are as follows:

2011 Journal Entries—Forward Contract Fair Value Hedge of Firm Commitment

12/1/11	There is no entry to record either the sales agreement or the forward contract because both are executory contracts. A memorandum designates the forward contract as a hedge of the risk of changes in the fair value of the firm commitment resulting from changes in the U.S. dollar–euro forward exchange rate.		
12/31/11	Loss on Forward Contract	10,783	
	Forward Contract		10,783
	To record the forward contract as a liability at its fair value of $(10,783) and record a forward contract loss for the change in the fair value of the forward contract since December 1.		
	Firm Commitment	10,783	
	Gain on Firm Commitment		10,783
	To record the firm commitment as an asset at its fair value of $10,783 and record a firm commitment gain for the change in the fair value of the firm commitment since December 1.		

Consistent with the objective of hedge accounting, the gain on the firm commitment offsets the loss on the forward contract, and the impact on 2011 net income is zero. Amerco reports the forward contract as a liability and reports the firm commitment as an asset on the December 31, 2011, balance sheet. This achieves the objective of making sure that derivatives are reported on the balance sheet and ensures that there is no impact on net income.

On March 1, 2012, Amerco first recognizes changes in the fair value of the forward contract and firm commitment since December 31. The company then records the sale and the settlement of the forward contract. Finally, the $5,000 balance in the firm commitment account is closed as an adjustment to net income. The required journal entries are as follows:

2012 Journal Entries—Forward Contract Fair Value Hedge of Firm Commitment

3/1/12	Forward Contract	15,783	
	Gain on Forward Contract		15,783
	To adjust the fair value of the forward contract from $(10,783) to $5,000 and record a forward contract gain for the change in fair value since December 31.		
	Loss on Firm Commitment	15,783	
	Firm Commitment		15,783
	To adjust the fair value of the firm commitment from $10,783 to $(5,000) and record a firm commitment loss for the change in fair value since December 31.		
	Foreign Currency (€)	1,300,000	
	Sales		1,300,000
	To record the sale and the receipt of € 1 million as an asset at the spot rate of $1.30.		
	Cash	1,305,000	
	Foreign Currency (€)		1,300,000
	Forward Contract		5,000
	To record settlement of the forward contract (receipt of $1,305,000 in exchange for delivery of € 1 million) and remove the forward contract from the accounts.		
	Firm Commitment	5,000	
	Adjustment to Net Income–Firm Commitment		5,000
	To close the firm commitment as an adjustment to net income.		

Once again, the gain on forward contract and the loss on firm commitment offset. As a result of the last entry, the export sale increases 2012 net income by $1,305,000 ($1,300,000 in sales plus a $5,000 adjustment to net income). This exactly equals the amount of cash received. In practice, companies use a variety of account titles for the adjustment to net income that results from closing the firm commitment account.

The net gain on forward contract of $5,000 ($10,783 loss in 2011 plus $15,783 gain in 2012) measures the net benefit to the company from hedging its firm commitment. Without the forward contract, Amerco would have sold the 1 million euros received on March 1, 2012, at the spot rate of $1.30 generating cash flow of $1,300,000. Through the forward contract, Amerco is able to sell the euros for $1,305,000, a net gain of $5,000.

Option Used as Fair Value Hedge of Firm Commitment

Now assume that to hedge its exposure to a decline in the U.S. dollar value of the euro, Amerco purchases a put option to sell 1 million euros on March 1, 2012, at a strike price of $1.32. The premium for such an option on December 1, 2011, is $0.009 per euro. With this option, Amerco is guaranteed a minimum cash flow from the export sale of $1,311,000 ($1,320,000 from option exercise less $9,000 cost of the option).

Amerco measures the fair value of the firm commitment by referring to changes in the U.S. dollar–euro spot rate. In this case, Amerco must discount the fair value of the firm commitment to its present value. The fair value and changes in fair value for the firm commitment and foreign currency option are summarized here:

Date	Option Premium for 3/1/12	Foreign Currency Option		Spot Rate	Firm Commitment	
		Fair Value	Change in Fair Value		Fair Value	Change in Fair Value
12/1/11	$0.009	$ 9,000	–0–	$1.32	–0–	–0–
12/31/11	0.006	6,000	– $3,000	1.33	$ 9,803*	+ $ 9,803
3/1/12	0.020	20,000	+ 14,000	1.30	(20,000)†	– 29,803

*$1,330,000 − $1,320,000 = $10,000 × 0.9803 = $9,803, where 0.9803 is the present value factor for two months at an annual interest rate of 12 percent (1 percent per month) calculated as $1/1.01^2$.
†$1,300,000 − $1,320,000 = $(20,000).

At December 1, 2011, given the spot rate of $1.32, the firm commitment to receive 1 million euros in three months would generate a cash flow of $1,320,000. At December 31, 2011, the cash flow that the firm commitment could generate increases by $10,000 to $1,330,000. The fair value of the firm commitment at December 31, 2011, is the present value of $10,000 discounted at 1 percent per month for two months. Amerco determines the fair value of the firm commitment on March 1, 2012, by referring to the change in the spot rate from December 1, 2011, to March 1, 2012. Because the spot rate declines by $0.02 over that period, the firm commitment to receive 1 million euros has a fair value of $(20,000) on March 1, 2012. The journal entries to account for the foreign currency option and related foreign currency firm commitment are discussed next:

2011 Journal Entries—Option Fair Value Hedge of Firm Commitment

12/1/11	Foreign Currency Option	9,000	
	Cash		9,000
	To record the purchase of the foreign currency option as an asset.		

There is no entry to record the sales agreement because it is an executory contract. Amerco prepares a memorandum to designate the option as a hedge of the risk of changes in the fair value of the firm commitment resulting from changes in the spot exchange rate.

12/31/11	Loss on Foreign Currency Option	3,000	
	Foreign Currency Option		3,000
	To adjust the fair value of the option from $9,000 to $6,000 and record the change in the value of the option as a loss.		
	Firm Commitment	9,803	
	Gain on Firm Commitment		9,803
	To record the firm commitment as an asset at its fair value of $9,803 and record a firm commitment gain for the change in the fair value of the firm commitment since December 1.		

Because the fair value of the firm commitment is based on changes in the spot rate whereas the fair value of the option is based on a variety of factors, the gain on the firm commitment and loss on the option do not exactly offset.

The impact on net income for the year 2011 is as follows:

Gain on firm commitment	$ 9,803
Loss on foreign currency option	(3,000)
Impact on net income	$ 6,803

The effect on the December 31, 2011, balance sheet follows:

Assets		Liabilities and Stockholders' Equity	
Cash	$(9,000)	Retained earnings	$6,803
Foreign currency option	6,000		
Firm commitment	9,803		
	$ 6,803		

On March 1, 2012, Amerco first recognizes changes in the fair value of the option and of the firm commitment since December 31. The company then records the sale and the exercise of the option. Finally, the $20,000 balance in the firm commitment account is closed as an adjustment to net income. The required journal entries are as follows:

2012 Journal Entries—Option Fair Value Hedge of Firm Commitment

3/1/12	Foreign Currency Option	14,000	
	Gain on Foreign Currency Option		14,000
	To adjust the fair value of the foreign currency option from $6,000 to $20,000 and record a gain on foreign currency option for the change in fair value since December 31.		
	Loss on Firm Commitment	29,803	
	Firm Commitment		29,803
	To adjust the fair value of the firm commitment from $9,803 to $(20,000) and record a firm commitment loss for the change in fair value since December 31.		
	Foreign Currency (€)	1,300,000	
	Sales		1,300,000
	To record the sale and the receipt of € 1 million as an asset at the spot rate of $1.30.		
	Cash	1,320,000	
	Foreign Currency (€)		1,300,000
	Foreign Currency Option		20,000
	To record exercise of the foreign currency option (receipt of $1,320,000 in exchange for delivery of € 1 million) and remove the foreign currency option from the accounts.		
	Firm Commitment	20,000	
	Adjustment to Net Income		20,000
	To close the firm commitment as an adjustment to net income.		

The following is the impact on net income for the year 2012:

Sales	$1,300,000
Loss on firm commitment	(29,803)
Gain on foreign currency option	14,000
Adjustment to net income–firm commitment	20,000
Impact on net income	$1,304,197

The net increase in net income over the two accounting periods is $1,311,000 ($6,803 in 2011 plus $1,304,197 in 2012), which exactly equals the net cash flow realized on the export sale ($1,320,000 from exercising the option less $9,000 to purchase the option). The net gain on the option of $11,000 (loss of $3,000 in 2011 plus gain of $14,000 in 2012) reflects the net benefit from having entered into the hedge. Without the option, Amerco would have sold the 1 million euros received on March 1, 2012, at the spot rate of $1.30 for $1,300,000.

HEDGE OF FORECASTED FOREIGN CURRENCY DENOMINATED TRANSACTION

LO6

Account for forward contracts and options used as hedges of forecasted foreign currency transactions.

Cash flow hedge accounting also is used for foreign currency derivatives used to hedge the cash flow risk associated with a forecasted foreign currency transaction. For hedge accounting to apply, the forecasted transaction must be probable (likely to occur), the hedge must be highly effective in offsetting fluctuations in the cash flow associated with the foreign currency risk, and the hedging relationship must be properly documented.

Accounting for a hedge of a forecasted transaction differs from accounting for a hedge of a foreign currency firm commitment in two ways:

1. Unlike the accounting for a firm commitment, there is no recognition of the forecasted transaction or gains and losses on the forecasted transaction.
2. The company reports the hedging instrument (forward contract or option) at fair value, but because no gain or loss occurs on the forecasted transaction to offset against, the company does not report changes in the fair value of the hedging instrument as gains and losses in net income. Instead, it reports them in other comprehensive income. On the projected date of the forecasted transaction, the company transfers the cumulative change in the fair value of the hedging instrument from other comprehensive income (balance sheet) to net income (income statement).

Forward Contract Cash Flow Hedge of a Forecasted Transaction

To demonstrate the accounting for a hedge of a forecasted foreign currency transaction, assume that Amerco has a long-term relationship with its German customer and can reliably forecast that the customer will require delivery of goods costing 1 million euros in March 2012. Confident that it will receive 1 million euros on March 1, 2012, Amerco enters into a forward contract on December 1, 2011, to sell 1 million euros on March 1, 2012, at a rate of $1.30. The facts are essentially the same as those for the hedge of a firm commitment except that Amerco does not receive a sales order from the German customer until late February 2012. Relevant exchange rates and the fair value of the forward contract are as follows:

Date	Forward Rate to 3/31/12	Forward Contract Fair Value	Forward Contract Change in Fair Value
12/1/11	$1.305	–0–	–0–
12/31/11	1.316	$(10,783)*	– $10,783
3/1/12	1.30 (spot)	5,000	+ 15,783

* ($1,305,000 − $1,316,000) = $(11,000) × 0.9803 = $(10,783), where 0.9803 is the present value factor for two months at an annual interest rate of 12 percent (1 percent per month) calculated as $1/1.01^2$. The original discount on the forward contract is determined by the difference in the € spot rate and the three-month forward rate on December 1, 2011: ($1.305 − $1.32) × € 1 million = $15,000.

2011 Journal Entries—Forward Contract Hedge of a Forecasted Transaction

12/1/11	There is no entry to record either the forecasted sale or the forward contract. A memorandum designates the forward contract as a hedge of the risk of changes in the cash flows related to the forecasted sale resulting from changes in the spot rate.		
12/31/11	Accumulated Other Comprehensive Income (AOCI)	10,783	
	Forward Contract		10,783
	To record the forward contract as a liability at its fair value of $10,783 with a corresponding debit to AOCI.		
	Discount Expense	5,000	
	Accumulated Other Comprehensive Income (AOCI)		5,000
	To record straight-line allocation of the forward contract discount: $15,000 × ⅓ = $5,000.		

Discount expense reduces 2011 net income by $5,000. The impact on the December 31, 2011, balance sheet is as follows:

Assets	Liabilities and Stockholders' Equity	
No effect	Forward contract	$10,783
	Retained earnings	(5,000)
	AOCI	(5,783)
		$ 0

2012 Journal Entries—Forward Contract Hedge of a Forecasted Transaction

3/1/12	Forward Contract	15,783	
	Accumulated Other Comprehensive Income (AOCI)		15,783
	To adjust the carrying value of the forward contract to its current fair value of $5,000 with a corresponding credit to AOCI.		
	Discount Expense	10,000	
	Accumulated Other Comprehensive Income (AOCI)		10,000
	To record straight-line allocation of the forward contract discount: $15,000 × ⅔ = $10,000.		
	Foreign Currency (€)	1,300,000	
	Sales		1,300,000
	To record the sale and the receipt of € 1 million as an asset at the spot rate of $1.30.		
	Cash	1,305,000	
	Foreign Currency (€)		1,300,000
	Forward Contract		5,000
	To record settlement of the forward contract (receipt of $1,305,000 in exchange for delivery of € 1 million) and remove the forward contract from the accounts.		
	Accumulated Other Comprehensive Income (AOCI)	20,000	
	Adjustment to Net Income–Forecasted Transaction		20,000
	To close AOCI as an adjustment to net income.		

The impact on net income for the year 2012 follows:

Sales	$1,300,000
Discount expense	(10,000)
Adjustment to net income–forecasted transaction . .	20,000
Impact on net income	$1,310,000

Over the two accounting periods, the net impact on net income is $1,305,000, which equals the amount of net cash inflow realized from the sale.

Option Designated as a Cash Flow Hedge of a Forecasted Transaction

Now assume that Amerco hedges its forecasted foreign currency transaction by purchasing a 1 million euro put option on December 1, 2011. The option, which expires on March 1, 2012, has a strike price of $1.32 and a premium of $0.009 per euro. The fair value of the option at relevant dates is as follows (same as in previous examples):

Date	Option Premium for 3/1/12	Foreign Currency Option				
		Fair Value	Change in Fair Value	Intrinsic Value	Time Value	Change in Time Value
12/1/11	$0.009	$ 9,000	–0–	–0–	$9,000	–0–
12/31/11	0.006	6,000	–$ 3,000	–0–	6,000	–$ 3,000
3/1/12	0.020	20,000	+ 14,000	$20,000	–0–	– 6,000

2011 Journal Entries—Option Hedge of a Forecasted Transaction

12/1/11	Foreign Currency Option	9,000	
	Cash		9,000
	To record the purchase of the foreign currency option as an asset.		

There is no entry to record the forecasted sale. A memorandum designates the foreign currency option as a hedge of the risk of changes in the cash flows related to the forecasted sale.

At December 31, the carrying value of the option is decreased for the change in fair value since December 1, and the change in the time value of the option is recognized as option expense. The required journal entries are as follows:

12/31/11	Accumulated Other Comprehensive Income (AOCI)	3,000	
	Foreign Currency Option		3,000
	To adjust the carrying value of the option to its fair value with a corresponding debit to AOCI.		
	Option Expense	3,000	
	Accumulated Other Comprehensive Income (AOCI)		3,000
	To recognize the change in the time value of the option as a decrease in net income with a corresponding credit to AOCI.		

The impact on net income for the year 2011 follows:

Option expense	$(3,000)
Impact on net income	$(3,000)

A foreign currency option of $6,000 is reported as an asset on the December 31, 2011, balance sheet. Cash is decreased by $9,000, and Retained Earnings is decreased by $3,000.

On March 1, 2012, first the carrying value of the option is adjusted to fair value and the change in the time value of the option is recognized as option expense. Then, the sale and the exercise of the foreign currency option are recorded. Finally, the balance in AOCI related to the hedge of the forecasted transaction is closed as an adjustment to net income. The following entries are required:

2012 Journal Entries—Option Hedge of a Forecasted Transaction

3/1/12	Foreign Currency Option	14,000	
	Accumulated Other Comprehensive Income (AOCI)		14,000
	To adjust the carrying value of the option to its fair value with a corresponding credit to AOCI.		
	Option Expense	6,000	
	Accumulated Other Comprehensive Income (AOCI)		6,000
	To recognize the change in the time value of the option as a decrease in net income with a corresponding credit to AOCI.		
	Foreign Currency (€)	1,300,000	
	Sales		1,300,000
	To record the sale and the receipt of € 1 million as an asset at the spot rate of $1.30.		
	Cash	1,320,000	
	Foreign Currency (€)		1,300,000
	Foreign Currency Option		20,000
	To record the exercise of the foreign currency option (receipt of $1,320,000 in exchange for delivery of € 1 million) and remove the foreign currency option from the accounts.		
	Accumulated Other Comprehensive Income (AOCI)	20,000	
	Adjustment to Net Income–Forecasted Transaction		20,000
	To close AOCI as an adjustment to net income.		

The following is the impact on net income for the year 2012:

Sales	$1,300,000
Option expense	(6,000)
Adjustment to net income–forecasted transaction . .	20,000
Impact on net income	$1,314,000

Over the two periods, a total of $1,311,000 is recognized as net income, which is equal to the net cash inflow realized from the export sale ($1,320,000 from the sale less $9,000 for the option).

USE OF HEDGING INSTRUMENTS

There are probably as many different corporate strategies regarding hedging foreign exchange risk as there are companies exposed to that risk. Some companies simply require hedges of all foreign currency transactions. Others require the use of a forward contract hedge when the forward rate results in a larger cash inflow or smaller cash outflow than with the spot rate. Still other companies have proportional hedging policies that require hedging on some predetermined percentage (e.g., 50 percent, 60 percent, or 70 percent) of transaction exposure.

Companies are required to provide information on the use of derivative financial instruments to hedge foreign exchange risk in the notes to financial statements. Exhibit 7.3 presents disclosures made by Abbott Laboratories in its 2008 annual report. Abbott Labs uses forward contracts to hedge foreign exchange risk associated with anticipated foreign currency transactions, foreign currency denominated payables and receivables, and foreign currency borrowings. Much of its hedging activity relates to intercompany transactions involving foreign subsidiaries. The table in Exhibit 7.3 discloses that (1) Abbott's forward contracts primarily are to sell foreign currencies for U.S. dollars, (2) 47 percent of Abbott's $8.376 billion in forward

EXHIBIT 7.3 Disclosures Related to Hedging Foreign Exchange Risk in Abbott Laboratories' 2008 Annual Report

Foreign Currency Sensitive Financial Instruments

Abbott enters into foreign currency forward exchange contracts to manage its exposure to foreign currency denominated intercompany loans and trade payables and third-party trade payables and receivables. The contracts are marked-to-market, and resulting gains or losses are reflected in income and are generally offset by losses or gains on the foreign currency exposure being managed. At December 31, 2008 and 2007, Abbott held $8.3 billion and $5.5 billion, respectively, of such contracts, which all mature in the next twelve months.

In addition, certain Abbott foreign subsidiaries enter into foreign currency forward exchange contracts to manage exposures to changes in foreign exchange rates for anticipated intercompany purchases by those subsidiaries whose functional currencies are not the U.S. dollar. These contracts are designated as cash flow hedges of the variability of the cash flows due to changes in foreign exchange rates and are marked-to-market with the resulting gains or losses reflected in Accumulated other comprehensive income (loss). Gains or losses will be included in Cost of Products Sold at the time the products are sold, generally within the next calendar year. At December 31, 2008 and 2007, Abbott held $129 million and $281 million, respectively, of such contracts, which all mature in the following calendar year.

The following table reflects the total foreign currency forward contracts outstanding at December 31, 2008.

(dollars in millions)	Contract Amount	Average Exchange Rate	Fair and Carrying Value Receivable/ (Payable)
Receive primarily U.S. Dollars in exchange for the following currencies:			
Euro	$3,963	1.286	$ 3
British pound	1,208	1.553	(31)
Japanese yen	1,788	99.6	54
Canadian dollar	163	1.240	3
All other currencies	1,254	N/A	19
Total	$8,376		$48

contracts at December 31, 2008, was in euros, and (3) with the exception of contracts in British pounds, all of Abbott's forward contracts had a positive fair value and it reported these on the balance sheet as assets.

Abbott Labs uses forward contracts exclusively to manage its foreign exchange risk. In contrast, the Coca-Cola Company reported using a combination of forward contracts and currency options in its foreign exchange risk hedging strategy. In its 2008 annual report, Coca-Cola reported recording a decrease to AOCI of approximately $6 million, $59 million, and $31 million, respectively, in 2008, 2007, and 2006, on foreign currency cash flow hedges. The company had forward contracts and options with a fair value of $(112) million at December 31, 2008, which it reflected in accounts payable and accrued expenses on the consolidated balance sheet.

The Euro

The introduction of the euro as a common currency throughout much of Europe in 2002 reduced the need for hedging in that region of the world. For example, a German company purchasing goods from a Spanish supplier no longer has an exposure to foreign exchange risk because both countries use a common currency. This is also true for German subsidiaries of U.S. parent companies. However, any euro-denominated transactions between the U.S. parent and its German (or other euro zone) subsidiary continue to be exposed to foreign exchange risk.

One advantage of the euro for U.S. companies is that a euro account receivable from sales to a customer in, say, the Netherlands acts as a natural hedge of a euro account payable on purchases from, say, a supplier in Italy. Assuming that similar amounts and time periods are involved, any foreign exchange loss (gain) arising from the euro payable is offset by a foreign exchange gain (loss) on the euro receivable. A company does not need to hedge the euro account payable with a hedging instrument such as a foreign currency option.

FOREIGN CURRENCY BORROWING

LO7

Prepare journal entries to account for foreign currency borrowings.

In addition to the receivables and payables that arise from import and export activities, companies often must account for foreign currency borrowings, another type of foreign currency transaction. Companies borrow foreign currency from foreign lenders either to finance foreign operations or perhaps to take advantage of more favorable interest rates. The facts that both the principal and interest are denominated in foreign currency and both create an exposure to foreign exchange risk complicate accounting for a foreign currency borrowing.

To demonstrate the accounting for foreign currency debt, assume that on July 1, 2011, Multicorp International borrowed 1 billion Japanese yen (¥) on a one-year note at a per annum interest rate of 5 percent. Interest is payable and the note comes due on July 1, 2012. The following exchange rates apply:

Date	U.S. Dollars per Japanese Yen Spot Rate
July 1, 2011	$0.00921
December 31, 2011	0.00932
July 1, 2012	0.00937

On July 1, 2011, Multicorp borrows ¥ 1 billion and converts it into $9,210,000 in the spot market. On December 31, 2011, Mulitcorp must revalue the Japanese yen note payable with an offsetting foreign exchange gain or loss reported in income and must accrue interest expense and interest payable. Interest is calculated by multiplying the loan principal in yen by the relevant interest rate. The amount of interest payable in yen is then translated to U.S. dollars at the spot rate to record the accrual journal entry. On July 1, 2012, any difference between the amount of interest accrued at year-end and the actual U.S. dollar amount that must be spent to pay the accrued interest is recognized as a foreign exchange gain or loss. These journal entries account for this foreign currency borrowing:

7/1/11	Cash	9,210,000	
	Note Payable (¥)		9,210,000
	To record the ¥ note payable at the spot rate of $0.00921 and the conversion of ¥ 1 billion into U.S. dollars.		
12/31/11	Interest Expense	233,000	
	Accrued Interest Payable (¥)		233,000
	To accrue interest for the period July 1–December 31, 2011: ¥ 1 billion × 5% × ½ year = ¥ 25 million × $0.00932 = $233,000.		
	Foreign Exchange Loss	110,000	
	Note Payable (¥)		110,000
	To revalue the ¥ note payable at the spot rate of $0.00932 and record a foreign exchange loss of $110,000 [¥ 1 billion × ($0.00932 − $0.00921)].		
7/1/12	Interest Expense	234,250	
	Accrued Interest Payable (¥)	233,000	
	Foreign Exchange Loss	1,250	
	Cash		468,500
	To record the interest payment of ¥ 50 million acquired at the spot rate of $0.00937 for $468,500; interest expense for the period of January 1–July 1, 2012: ¥ 25 million × $0.00937; and a foreign exchange loss on the ¥ accrued interest payable: ¥ 25 million × ($0.00937 − $0.00932).		

| Foreign Exchange Loss . . . . | 50,000 | |
| Note Payable (¥) . . . . | | 50,000 |

To revalue the ¥ note payable at the spot rate of $0.00937
and record a foreign exchange loss of $50,000 [¥ 1 billion ×
($0.00937 − $0.00932)].

| Note Payable (¥) . . . . | 9,370,000 | |
| Cash . . . . | | 9,370,000 |

To record repayment of the ¥ 1 billion note through purchase
of ¥ at the spot rate of $0.00937.

Foreign Currency Loan

At times companies lend foreign currency to related parties, creating the opposite situation from a foreign currency borrowing. The accounting involves keeping track of a note receivable and interest receivable, both of which are denominated in foreign currency. Fluctuations in the U.S. dollar value of the principal and interest generally give rise to foreign exchange gains and losses that would be included in income. An exception arises when the foreign currency loan is made on a long-term basis to a foreign branch, subsidiary, or equity method affiliate. Foreign exchange gains and losses on "intra-entity foreign currency transactions that are of a long-term investment nature (that is, settlement is not planned or anticipated in the foreseeable future)" are deferred in accumulated other comprehensive income until the loan is repaid.[11] Only the foreign exchange gains and losses related to the interest receivable are recorded currently in net income.

IFRS—FOREIGN CURRENCY TRANSACTIONS AND HEDGES

Similar to U.S. GAAP, *IAS 21*, "The Effects of Changes in Foreign Exchange Rates," also requires the use of a two-transaction perspective in accounting for foreign currency transactions with unrealized foreign exchange gains and losses accrued in net income in the period of exchange rate change. There are no substantive differences between IFRS and U.S. GAAP in the accounting for foreign currency transactions.

IAS 39, "Financial Instruments: Recognition and Measurement," governs the accounting for hedging instruments including those used to hedge foreign exchange risk. Rules and procedures in *IAS 39* related to foreign currency hedge accounting generally are consistent with U.S. GAAP. Similar to current U.S. standards, *IAS 39* allows hedge accounting for recognized assets and liabilities, firm commitments, and forecasted transactions when documentation requirements and effectiveness tests are met, and requires hedges to be designated as cash flow or fair value hedges. One difference between the two sets of standards relates to the type of financial instrument that can be designated as a foreign currency cash flow hedge. Under U.S. GAAP, only derivative financial instruments can be used as a cash flow hedge, whereas IFRS also allows nonderivative financial instruments, such as foreign currency loans, to be designated as hedging instruments in a foreign currency cash flow hedge.

Summary

1. Several exchange rate mechanisms are used around the world. Most national currencies fluctuate in value against other currencies over time.

2. Exposure to foreign exchange risk exists when a payment to be made or to be received is denominated (stated) in terms of a foreign currency. Appreciation in a foreign currency results in a foreign exchange gain when the foreign currency is to be received and a foreign exchange loss when the foreign currency is to be paid. Conversely, a decrease in the value of a foreign currency results in a foreign exchange loss when the foreign currency is to be received and a foreign exchange gain when the foreign currency is to be paid.

---

[11] FASB ASC (para. 830-20-35-3b).

3. Companies must revalue foreign currency assets and liabilities to their current U.S. dollar value using current exchange rates when financial statements are prepared. The change in U.S. dollar value of foreign currency balances is recognized as a foreign exchange gain or loss in income in the period in which the exchange rate change occurs. This is known as the two-transaction perspective, accrual approach.

4. Exposure to foreign exchange risk can be eliminated through hedging. Hedging involves establishing a price today at which a foreign currency to be received in the future can be sold in the future or at which a foreign currency to be paid in the future can be purchased in the future.

5. The two most popular instruments for hedging foreign exchange risk are foreign currency forward contracts and foreign currency options. A *forward contract* is a binding agreement to exchange currencies at a predetermined rate. An *option* gives the buyer the right, but not the obligation, to exchange currencies at a predetermined rate.

6. Hedge accounting is appropriate if the derivative is used to hedge either a fair-value exposure or cash flow exposure to foreign exchange risk, the derivative is highly effective in offsetting changes in the fair value or cash flows related to the hedged item, and the derivative is properly documented as a hedge. Hedge accounting requires reporting gains and losses on the hedging instrument in net income in the same period as gains and loss on the item being hedged.

7. Companies must report all derivatives, including forward contracts and options, on the balance sheet at their fair value. Changes in fair value are included in accumulated other comprehensive income if the derivative is designated as a cash flow hedge and in net income if it is designated as a fair value hedge.

8. Current accounting standards provide guidance for hedges of (a) recognized foreign currency denominated assets and liabilities, (b) unrecognized foreign currency firm commitments, and (c) forecasted foreign currency denominated transactions. Cash flow hedge accounting can be used for all three types of hedge; fair value hedge accounting can be used only for (a) and (b).

9. If a company hedges a foreign currency firm commitment (fair value hedge), it should recognize gains and losses on the hedging instrument as well as on the underlying firm commitment in net income. The firm commitment account created to offset the gain or loss on firm commitment is treated as an adjustment to the underlying transaction when it takes place.

10. If a company hedges a forecasted transaction (cash flow hedge), it reports changes in the fair value of the hedging instrument in accumulated other comprehensive income. The cumulative change in fair value reported in other comprehensive income is included in net income in the period in which the forecasted transaction was originally anticipated to take place.

11. Borrowing foreign currency creates two exposures to foreign exchange risk. Foreign exchange gains and losses related to both the foreign currency note payable and accrued foreign currency interest payable are recognized in income over the life of the loan.

12. IFRS rules related to the accounting for foreign currency transactions and foreign currency hedges generally are consistent with U.S. GAAP. *IAS 21* requires a two-transaction, accrual approach in accounting for foreign currency transactions. *IAS 39* requires foreign currency hedging instruments to be designated either as a cash flow or fair value hedge; in either case the hedging instrument must be reported at fair value. Hedge accounting is allowed for hedges of foreign currency assets and liabilities, firm commitments, and forecasted transactions, provided that the hedge is properly documented and is effective.

Comprehensive Illustration

PROBLEM

(*Estimated Time: 60 to 75 minutes*) Zelm Company is a U.S. company that produces electronic switches for the telecommunications industry. Zelm regularly imports component parts from a supplier located in Guadalajara, Mexico, and makes payments in Mexican pesos. The following spot exchange rates, forward exchange rates, and call option premia for Mexican pesos exist during the period August to October.

		U.S. Dollar per Mexican Peso	
Date	Spot Rate	Forward Rate to October 31	Call Option Premium for October 31 (strike price $0.080)
August 1	$0.080	$0.085	$0.0052
September 30	0.086	0.088	0.0095
October 31	0.091	0.091	0.0110

Part A

On August 1, Zelm imports parts from its Mexican supplier at a price of 1 million Mexican pesos. It receives the parts on August 1 but does not pay for them until October 31. In addition, on August 1, Zelm enters into a forward contract to purchase 1 million pesos on October 31. It appropriately designates the forward contract as a *cash flow hedge* of the Mexican peso liability exposure. Zelm's incremental borrowing rate is 12 percent per annum (1 percent per month), and the company uses a straight-line method on a monthly basis for allocating forward discounts and premia.

Part B

The facts are the same as in Part A with the exception that Zelm designates the forward contract as a *fair value hedge* of the Mexican peso liability exposure.

Part C

On August 1, Zelm imports parts from its Mexican supplier at a price of 1 million Mexican pesos. It receives the parts on August 1 but does not pay for them until October 31. In addition, on August 1, Zelm purchases a three-month call option on 1 million Mexican pesos with a strike price of $0.080. The option is appropriately designated as a *cash flow hedge* of the Mexican peso liability exposure.

Part D

On August 1, Zelm orders parts from its Mexican supplier at a price of 1 million Mexican pesos. It receives the parts and pays for them on October 31. On August 1, Zelm enters into a forward contract to purchase 1 million Mexican pesos on October 31. It designates the forward contract as a *fair value hedge* of the Mexican peso firm commitment. Zelm determines the fair value of the firm commitment by referring to changes in the forward exchange rate.

Part E

On August 1, Zelm orders parts from its Mexican supplier at a price of 1 million Mexican pesos. It receives the parts and pays for them on October 31. On August 1, Zelm purchases a three-month call option on 1 million Mexican pesos with a strike price of $0.080. The option is appropriately designated as a *fair value hedge* of the Mexican peso firm commitment. The fair value of the firm commitment is by reference to changes in the spot exchange rate.

Part F

Zelm anticipates that it will import component parts from its Mexican supplier in the near future. On August 1, Zelm purchases a three-month call option on 1 million Mexican pesos with a strike price of $0.080. It appropriately designates the option as a *cash flow hedge* of a forecasted Mexican peso transaction. Zelm receives and pays for parts costing 1 million Mexican pesos on October 31.

Required

Prepare journal entries for each of these independent situations in accordance with U.S. GAAP standards and determine the impact each situation has on the September 30 and October 31 trial balances.

SOLUTION

Part A. Forward Contract Cash Flow Hedge of a Recognized Foreign Currency Liability

8/1	Parts Inventory	80,000	
	Accounts Payable (Mexican pesos)		80,000
	To record the purchase of parts and a Mexican peso account payable at the spot rate of $0.080.		

The forward contract requires no formal entry. Zelm prepares a memorandum to designate the forward contract as a hedge of the risk of changes in the cash flow to be paid on the foreign currency payable resulting from changes in the U.S. dollar–Mexican peso exchange rate.

9/30	Foreign Exchange Loss	6,000	
	Accounts Payable (Mexican pesos)		6,000
	To adjust the value of the Mexican peso payable to the new spot rate of $0.086 and record a foreign exchange loss resulting from the appreciation of the peso since August 1.		

Forward Contract	2,970	
Accumulated Other Comprehensive Income (AOCI)		2,970
To record the forward contract as an asset at its fair value of $2,970 with a corresponding credit to AOCI.		

Zelm determines the fair value of the forward contract by referring to the change in the forward rate for a contract that settles on October 31: ([$0.088 − $0.085] × 1 million pesos = $3,000. The present value of $3,000 discounted for one month [from October 31 to September 30] at an interest rate of 12 percent per year [1 percent per month] is calculated as follows: $3,000 × 0.9901 = $2,970.)

Accumulated Other Comprehensive Income (AOCI)	6,000	
Gain on Forward Contract		6,000
To record a gain on forward contract to offset the foreign exchange loss on account payable with a corresponding debit to AOCI.		
Premium Expense	3,333	
Accumulated Other Comprehensive Income (AOCI)		3,333
To allocate the forward contract premium to income over the life of the contract using a straight-line method on a monthly basis ($5,000 × 2/3 = $3,333).		

The original premium on the forward contract is determined by the difference in the peso spot rate and three-month forward rate on August 1: ($0.085 − $0.080) × 1 million pesos = $5,000.

Trial Balance—September 30	Debit	Credit
Parts Inventory	$80,000	–0–
Accounts Payable (Mexican pesos)		$86,000
Forward Contract (asset)	2,970	
AOCI		303
Foreign Exchange Loss	6,000	
Gain on Forward Contract		6,000
Premium Expense	3,333	–0–
	$92,303	$92,303

10/31	Foreign Exchange Loss	5,000	
	Accounts Payable (Mexican pesos)		5,000
	To adjust the value of the Mexican peso payable to the new spot rate of $0.091 and record a foreign exchange loss resulting from the appreciation of the peso since September 30.		
	Forward Contract	3,030	
	Accumulated Other Comprehensive Income (AOCI)		3,030
	To adjust the carrying value of the forward contract to its current fair value of $6,000 with a corresponding credit to AOCI.		

The current fair value of the forward contract is determined by referring to the difference in the spot rate on October 31 and the original forward rate: ($0.091 − $0.085) × 1 million pesos = $6,000. The forward contract adjustment on October 31 is calculated as the difference in the current fair value and the carrying value at September 30: $6,000 − $2,970 = $3,030.

Accumulated Other Comprehensive Income (AOCI)	5,000	
Gain on Forward Contract		5,000
To record a gain on forward contract to offset the foreign exchange loss on account payable with a corresponding debit to AOCI.		
Premium Expense	1,667	
Accumulated Other Comprehensive Income (AOCI)		1,667
To allocate the forward contract premium to income over the life of the contract using a straight-line method on a monthly basis ($5,000 × 1/3 = $1,667).		

Foreign Currency (Mexican pesos)	91,000	
Cash		85,000
Forward Contract		6,000

To record settlement of the forward contract: Record payment
of $85,000 in exchange for 1 million pesos, record the receipt of
1 million pesos as an asset at the spot rate of $0.091, and
remove the forward contract from the accounts.

Accounts Payable (pesos)	91,000	
Foreign Currency (pesos)		91,000

To record remittance of 1 million pesos to the Mexican supplier.

Trial Balance—October 31	Debit	Credit
Cash		$85,000
Parts Inventory	$80,000	–0–
Retained Earnings, 9/30	3,333	–0–
Foreign Exchange Loss	5,000	–0–
Gain on Forward Contract	–0–	5,000
Premium Expense	1,667	–0–
	$90,000	$90,000

Part B. Forward Contract Fair Value Hedge of a Recognized Foreign Currency Liability

8/1	Parts Inventory	80,000	
	Accounts Payable (Mexican pesos)		80,000

To record the purchase of parts and a peso account payable
at the spot rate of $0.080.

The forward contract requires no formal entry. A memorandum designates the forward contract as a
hedge of the risk of changes in the cash flow to be paid on the foreign currency payable resulting from
changes in the U.S. dollar–peso exchange rate.

9/30	Foreign Exchange Loss	6,000	
	Accounts Payable (Mexican pesos)		6,000

To adjust the value of the peso payable to the new spot rate
of $0.086 and record a foreign exchange loss resulting from
the appreciation of the peso since August 1.

	Forward Contract	2,970	
	Gain on Forward Contract		2,970

To record the forward contract as an asset at its fair value of
$2,970 and record a forward contract gain for the change in
the fair value of the forward contract since August 1.

Trial Balance—September 30	Debit	Credit
Parts Inventory	$80,000	–0–
Accounts Payable (Mexican pesos)		$86,000
Forward Contract (asset)	2,970	–0–
Foreign Exchange Loss	6,000	–0–
Gain on Forward Contract	–0–	2,970
	$88,970	$88,970

10/31	Foreign Exchange Loss	5,000	
	Accounts Payable (Mexican pesos)		5,000

To adjust the value of the peso payable to the new spot rate
of $0.091 and record a foreign exchange loss resulting from
the appreciation of the peso since September 30.

Forward Contract	3,030	
Gain on Forward Contract		3,030

To adjust the carrying value of the forward contract to its current fair value of $6,000 and record a forward contract gain for the change in fair value since September 30.

Foreign Currency (Mexican pesos)	91,000	
Cash		85,000
Forward Contract		6,000

To record settlement of the forward contract: Record payment of $85,000 in exchange for 1 million pesos, record the receipt of 1 million pesos as an asset at the spot rate of $0.091, and remove the forward contract from the accounts.

Accounts Payable (pesos)	91,000	
Foreign Currency (pesos)		91,000

To record remittance of 1 million pesos to the Mexican supplier.

Trial Balance—October 31	Debit	Credit
Cash	–0–	$85,000
Parts Inventory	$80,000	–0–
Retained Earnings, 9/30	3,030	–0–
Foreign Exchange Loss	5,000	–0–
Gain on Forward Contract	–0–	3,030
	$88,030	$88,030

Part C. Option Cash Flow Hedge of a Recognized Foreign Currency Liability

The following schedule summarizes the changes in the components of the fair value of the peso call option with a strike price of $0.080:

Date	Spot Rate	Option Premium	Fair Value	Change in Fair Value	Intrinsic Value	Time Value	Change in Time Value
8/1	$0.080	$0.0052	$ 5,200	–0–	–0–	$5,200*	–0–
9/30	0.086	0.0095	9,500	+$ 4,300	$ 6,000†	3,500†	–$1,700
10/31	0.091	0.0110	11,000	+ 1,500	11,000	–0–‡	– 3,500

*Because the strike price and spot rate are the same, the option has no intrinsic value. Fair value is attributable solely to the time value of the option.
† With a spot rate of $0.086 and a strike price of $0.08, the option has an intrinsic value of $6,000. The remaining $3,500 of fair value is attributable to time value.
‡ The time value of the option at maturity is zero.

8/1	Parts Inventory	80,000	
	Accounts Payable (Mexican pesos)		80,000

   To record the purchase of parts and a peso account payable at the spot rate of $0.080.

	Foreign Currency Option	5,200	
	Cash		5,200

   To record the purchase of a foreign currency option as an asset.

9/30	Foreign Exchange Loss	6,000	
	Accounts Payable (pesos)		6,000

   To adjust the value of the peso payable to the new spot rate of $0.086 and record a foreign exchange loss resulting from the appreciation of the peso since August 1.

	Foreign Currency Option	4,300	
	Accumulated Other Comprehensive Income (AOCI)		4,300

   To adjust the fair value of the option from $5,200 to $9,500 with a corresponding credit to AOCI.

	Accumulated Other Comprehensive Income (AOCI)	6,000	
	Gain on Foreign Currency Option		6,000

To record a gain on forward currency option to offset the foreign exchange loss on account payable with a corresponding debit to AOCI.

Option Expense 1,700

    Accumulated Other Comprehensive Income (AOCI)   1,700

To recognize the change in the time value of the foreign currency option as an expense with a corresponding credit to AOCI.

Trial Balance—September 30	Debit	Credit
Cash		$ 5,200
Parts Inventory	$80,000	–0–
Foreign Currency Option (asset)	9,500	–0–
Accounts Payable (Mexican pesos)	–0–	86,000
Foreign Exchange Loss	6,000	–0–
Gain on Foreign Currency Option	–0–	6,000
Option Expense	1,700	–0–
	$97,200	$97,200

10/31   Foreign Exchange Loss 5,000

        Accounts Payable (Mexican pesos)   5,000

To adjust the value of the peso payable to the new spot rate of $0.091 and record a foreign exchange loss resulting from the appreciation of the peso since September 30.

Foreign Currency Option 1,500

        Accumulated Other Comprehensive Income (AOCI)   1,500

To adjust the carrying value of the foreign currency option to its current fair value of $11,000 with a corresponding credit to AOCI.

Accumulated Other Comprehensive Income (AOCI) 5,000

        Gain on Foreign Currency Option   5,000

To record a gain on foreign currency option to offset the foreign exchange loss on account payable with a corresponding debit to AOCI.

Option Expense 3,500

        Accumulated Other Comprehensive Income (AOCI)   3,500

To recognize the change in the time value of the foreign currency option as an expense with a corresponding credit to AOCI.

Foreign Currency (Mexican pesos) 91,000

        Cash   80,000

        Foreign Currency Option   11,000

To record exercise of the foreign currency option: Record payment of $80,000 in exchange for 1 million pesos, record the receipt of 1 million pesos as an asset at the spot rate of $0.091, and remove the option from the accounts.

Accounts Payable (pesos) 91,000

        Foreign Currency (pesos)   91,000

To record remittance of 1 million pesos to the Mexican supplier.

Trial Balance—October 31	Debit	Credit
Cash ($5,200 credit balance + $80,000 credit) . . .	–0–	$85,200
Parts Inventory	$80,000	–0–
Retained Earnings, 9/30	1,700	–0–
Foreign Exchange Loss	5,000	–0–
Gain on Foreign Currency Option	–0–	5,000
Option Expense	3,500	–0–
	$90,200	$90,200

Part D. Forward Contract Fair Value Hedge of a Foreign Currency Firm Commitment

8/1	The forward contract or the purchase order requires no formal entry. A memorandum would be prepared designating the forward contract as a fair value hedge of the foreign currency firm commitment.		
9/30	Forward Contract	2,970	
	Gain on Forward Contract		2,970
	To record the forward contract as an asset at its fair value of $2,970 and record a forward contract gain for the change in the fair value of the forward contract since August 1.		
	Loss on Firm Commitment	2,970	
	Firm Commitment		2,970
	To record the firm commitment as a liability at its fair value of $2,970 based on changes in the forward rate and record a firm commitment loss for the change in fair value since August 1.		

Trial Balance—September 30	Debit	Credit
Forward Contract (asset)	$2,970	–0–
Firm Commitment (liability)	–0–	$2,970
Gain on Forward Contract	–0–	2,970
Loss on Firm Commitment	2,970	–0–
	$5,940	$5,940

10/31	Forward Contract	3,030	
	Gain on Forward Contract		3,030
	To adjust the carrying value of the forward contract to its current fair value of $6,000 and record a forward contract gain for the change in fair value since September 30.		
	Loss on Firm Commitment	3,030	
	Firm Commitment		3,030
	To adjust the value of the firm commitment to $6,000 based on changes in the forward rate and record a firm commitment loss for the change in fair value since September 30.		
	Foreign Currency (Mexican pesos)	91,000	
	Cash		85,000
	Forward Contract		6,000
	To record settlement of the forward contract: Record payment of $85,000 in exchange for 1 million pesos, record the receipt of 1 million pesos as an asset at the spot rate of $0.091, and remove the forward contract from the accounts.		
	Parts Inventory	91,000	
	Foreign Currency (Mexican pesos)		91,000
	To record the purchase of parts through the payment of 1 million pesos to the Mexican supplier.		
	Firm Commitment	6,000	
	Adjustment to Net Income–Firm Commitment		6,000
	To close the firm commitment account as an adjustment to net income.		

(*Note:* The final entry to close the Firm Commitment account to Adjustment to Net Income must be made *only* in the period in which Parts Inventory affects net income through Cost of Goods Sold. The Firm Commitment account remains on the books as a liability until that point in time.)

Trial Balance—October 31	Debit	Credit
Cash	–0–	$85,000
Parts Inventory (Cost of Goods Sold)	$91,000	–0–
Gain on Forward Contract	–0–	3,030
Loss on Firm Commitment	3,030	–0–
Adjustment to Net Income–Firm Commitment	–0–	6,000
	$94,030	$94,030

Part E. Option Fair Value Hedge of a Foreign Currency Firm Commitment

8/1	Foreign Currency Option	5,200	
	Cash		5,200

To record the purchase of a foreign currency option as an asset.

9/30	Foreign Currency Option	4,300	
	Gain on Foreign Currency Option		4,300

To adjust the fair value of the option from $5,200 to $9,500 and record an option gain for the change in fair value since August 1.

	Loss on Firm Commitment	5,940	
	Firm Commitment		5,940

To record the firm commitment as a liability at its fair value of $5,940 based on changes in the spot rate and record a firm commitment loss for the change in fair value since August 1.

The fair value of the firm commitment is determined by referring to changes in the spot rate from August 1 to September 30: ($0.080 − $0.086) × 1 million pesos = $(6,000). This amount must be discounted for one month at 12 percent per annum (1 percent per month): $(6,000) × 0.9901 = $(5,940).

Trial Balance—September 30	Debit	Credit
Cash	–0–	$ 5,200
Foreign Currency Option (asset)	$ 9,500	–0–
Firm Commitment (liability)	–0–	5,940
Gain on Foreign Currency Option	–0–	4,300
Loss on Firm Commitment	5,940	–0–
	$15,440	$15,440

10/31	Foreign Currency Option	1,500	
	Gain on Foreign Currency Option		1,500

To adjust fair value of the option from $9,500 to $11,000 and record an option gain for the change in fair value since September 30.

	Loss on Firm Commitment	5,060	
	Firm Commitment		5,060

To adjust the fair value of the firm commitment from $5,940 to $11,000 and record a firm commitment loss for the change in fair value since September 30.

The fair value of the firm commitment is determined by referring to changes in the spot rate from August 1 to October 31: ($0.080 − $0.091) × 1 million pesos = $(11,000).

Foreign Currency (Mexican pesos)	91,000	
Cash		80,000
Foreign Currency Option		11,000

To record exercise of the foreign currency option: Record payment of $80,000 in exchange for 1 million pesos, record the receipt of 1 million pesos as an asset at the spot rate of $0.091, and remove the option from the accounts.

Parts Inventory	91,000	
Foreign Currency (pesos)		91,000

To record the purchase of parts through the payment of 1 million pesos to the Mexican supplier.

Firm Commitment	11,000	
Adjustment to Net Income–Firm Commitment		11,000

To close Firm Commitment account to Adjustment to Net Income.

(*Note:* The final entry to close the Firm Commitment to Adjustment to Net Income is made *only* in the period in which Parts Inventory affects net income through Cost of Goods Sold. The Firm Commitment account remains on the books as a liability until that point in time.)

Trial Balance—October 31	Debit	Credit
Cash ($5,200 credit balance + $80,000 credit)...	–0–	$85,200
Parts Inventory (Cost of Goods Sold)	$91,000	–0–
Retained Earnings, 9/30	1,640	–0–
Gain on Foreign Currency Option	–0–	1,500
Loss on Firm Commitment	5,060	–0–
Adjustment to Net Income–Firm Commitment ...	–0–	11,000
	$97,700	$97,700

Part F. Option Cash Flow Hedge of a Forecasted Foreign Currency Transaction

8/1	Foreign Currency Option	5,200	
	Cash		5,200

To record the purchase of a foreign currency option as an asset.

9/30	Foreign Currency Option	4,300	
	Accumulated Other Comprehensive Income (AOCI)		4,300

To adjust the fair value of the option from $5,200 to $9,500 with a corresponding adjustment to AOCI.

	Option Expense	1,700	
	Accumulated Other Comprehensive Income (AOCI)		1,700

To recognize the change in the time value of the foreign currency option as an expense with a corresponding credit to AOCI.

Trial Balance—September 30	Debit	Credit
Cash	–0–	$ 5,200
Foreign Currency Option (asset)	$ 9,500	–0–
Accumulated Other Comprehensive Income ...	–0–	6,000
Option Expense	1,700	–0–
	$11,200	$11,200

10/31	Foreign Currency Option	1,500	
	Accumulated Other Comprehensive Income (AOCI)		1,500
	To adjust the fair value of the option from $9,500 to $11,000 with a corresponding adjustment to AOCI.		
	Option Expense	3,500	
	Accumulated Other Comprehensive Income (AOCI)		3,500
	To recognize the change in the time value of the foreign currency option as an expense with a corresponding credit to AOCI.		
	Foreign Currency (Mexican pesos)	91,000	
	Cash		80,000
	Foreign Currency Option		11,000
	To record exercise of the foreign currency option: Record payment of $80,000 in exchange for 1 million pesos, record the receipt of 1 million pesos as an asset at the spot rate of $0.091, and remove the option from the accounts.		
	Parts Inventory	91,000	
	Foreign Currency (Mexican pesos)		91,000
	To record the purchase of parts through the payment of 1 million pesos to the Mexican supplier.		
	Accumulated Other Comprehensive Income (AOCI)	11,000	
	Adjustment to Net Income–Forecasted Transaction		11,000
	To close AOCI as an adjustment to net income.		

(*Note:* The final entry to close AOCI to Adjustment to Net Income is made at the date that the forecasted transaction was expected to occur, regardless of when the parts inventory affects net income.)

Trial Balance—October 31	Debit	Credit
Cash ($5,200 credit balance + $80,000 credit)	–0–	$85,200
Parts Inventory (Cost of Goods Sold)	$91,000	–0–
Retained Earnings, 9/30.	1,700	–0–
Foreign Currency Option expense	3,500	–0–
Adjustment to Net Income–Forecasted Transaction . . .	–0–	11,000
	$96,200	$96,200

Questions

1. What concept underlies the two-transaction perspective in accounting for foreign currency transactions?
2. A company makes an export sale denominated in a foreign currency and allows the customer one month to pay. Under the two-transaction perspective, accrual approach, how does the company account for fluctuations in the exchange rate for the foreign currency?
3. What factors create a foreign exchange gain on a foreign currency transaction? What factors create a foreign exchange loss?
4. What does the term *hedging* mean? Why do companies elect to follow this strategy?
5. How does a foreign currency option differ from a foreign currency forward contract?
6. How does the timing of hedges of (*a*) foreign currency denominated assets and liabilities, (*b*) foreign currency firm commitments, and (*c*) forecasted foreign currency transactions differ?
7. Why would a company prefer a foreign currency option over a forward contract in hedging a foreign currency firm commitment? Why would a company prefer a forward contract over an option in hedging a foreign currency asset or liability?
8. How do companies report foreign currency derivatives, such as forward contracts and options, on the balance sheet?
9. How does a company determine the fair value of a foreign currency forward contract? How does it determine the fair value of an option?
10. What is hedge accounting?
11. Under what conditions can companies use hedge accounting to account for a foreign currency option used to hedge a forecasted foreign currency transaction?

12. What are the differences in accounting for a forward contract used as (*a*) a cash flow hedge and (*b*) a fair value hedge of a foreign currency denominated asset or liability?

13. What are the differences in accounting for a forward contract used as a fair value hedge of (*a*) a foreign currency denominated asset or liability and (*b*) a foreign currency firm commitment?

14. What are the differences in accounting for a forward contract used as a cash flow hedge of (*a*) a foreign currency denominated asset or liability and (*b*) a forecasted foreign currency transaction?

15. How are changes in the fair value of an option accounted for in a cash flow hedge? In a fair value hedge?

16. In what way is the accounting for a foreign currency borrowing more complicated than the accounting for a foreign currency account payable?

Problems

LO1

1. Which of the following combinations correctly describes the relationship between foreign currency transactions, exchange rate changes, and foreign exchange gains and losses?

	Type of Transaction	Foreign Currency	Foreign Exchange Gain or Loss
a.	Export sale	Appreciates	Loss
b.	Import purchase	Appreciates	Gain
c.	Import purchase	Depreciates	Gain
d.	Export sale	Depreciates	Gain

LO2

2. In accounting for foreign currency transactions, which of the following approaches is used in the United States?

   a. One-transaction perspective; accrue foreign exchange gains and losses.

   b. One-transaction perspective; defer foreign exchange gains and losses.

   c. Two-transaction perspective; defer foreign exchange gains and losses.

   d. Two-transaction perspective; accrue foreign exchange gains and losses.

LO2

3. On October 1, 2011, Mud Co., a U.S. company, purchased parts from Terra, a Portuguese company, with payment due on December 1, 2011. If Mud's 2011 operating income included no foreign exchange gain or loss, the transaction could have

   a. Resulted in an extraordinary gain.

   b. Been denominated in U.S. dollars.

   c. Generated a foreign exchange gain to be reported as a deferred charge on the balance sheet.

   d. Generated a foreign exchange loss to be reported as a separate component of stockholders' equity.

LO2

4. Post, Inc., had a receivable from a foreign customer that is payable in the customer's local currency. On December 31, 2011, Post correctly included this receivable for 200,000 local currency units (LCU) in its balance sheet at $110,000. When Post collected the receivable on February 15, 2012, the U.S. dollar equivalent was $95,000. In Post's 2012 consolidated income statement, how much should it report as a foreign exchange loss?

   a. $–0–.

   b. $10,000.

   c. $15,000.

   d. $25,000.

LO2, LO7

5. On July 1, 2011, Houghton Company borrowed 200,000 euros from a foreign lender evidenced by an interest-bearing note due on July 1, 2012. The note is denominated in euros. The U.S. dollar equivalent of the note principal is as follows:

Date	Amount
July 1, 2011 (date borrowed)	$195,000
December 31, 2011 (Houghton's year-end)	220,000
July 1, 2012 (date repaid)	230,000

In its 2012 income statement, what amount should Houghton include as a foreign exchange gain or loss on the note?

   a. $35,000 gain.

   b. $35,000 loss.

   c. $10,000 gain.

   d. $10,000 loss.

LO1, LO2

6. Slick Co. had a Swiss franc receivable resulting from exports to Switzerland and a Mexican peso payable resulting from imports from Mexico. Slick recorded foreign exchange gains related to both its franc receivable and peso payable. Did the foreign currencies increase or decrease in dollar value from the date of the transaction to the settlement date?

	Franc	Peso
a.	Increase	Increase
b.	Decrease	Decrease
c.	Decrease	Increase
d.	Increase	Decrease

LO2

7. Grete Corp. had the following foreign currency transactions during 2011:
   - Purchased merchandise from a foreign supplier on January 20, 2011, for the U.S. dollar equivalent of $60,000 and paid the invoice on April 20, 2011, at the U.S. dollar equivalent of $68,000.
   - On September 1, 2011, borrowed the U.S. dollar equivalent of $300,000 evidenced by a note that is payable in the lender's local currency on September 1, 2012. On December 31, 2011, the U.S. dollar equivalent of the principal amount was $320,000.

   In Grete's 2011 income statement, what amount should be included as a foreign exchange loss?
   a. $4,000.
   b. $20,000.
   c. $22,000.
   d. $28,000.

LO4

8. A U.S. exporter has a Thai baht account receivable resulting from an export sale on April 1 to a customer in Thailand. The exporter signed a forward contract on April 1 to sell Thai baht and designated it as a cash flow hedge of a recognized Thai baht receivable. The spot rate was $0.022 on that date, and the forward rate was $0.023. Which of the following did the U.S. exporter report in net income?
   a. Discount expense.
   b. Discount revenue.
   c. Premium expense.
   d. Premium revenue.

LO5

9. Lawrence Company ordered parts costing FC100,000 from a foreign supplier on May 12 when the spot rate was $0.20 per FC. A one-month forward contract was signed on that date to purchase FC100,000 at a forward rate of $0.21. The forward contract is properly designated as a fair value hedge of the FC100,000 firm commitment. On June 12, when the company receives the parts, the spot rate is $0.23. At what amount should Lawrence Company carry the parts inventory on its books?
   a. $20,000.
   b. $21,000.
   c. $22,000.
   d. $23,000.

LO3

10. On December 1, 2011, Barnum Company (a U.S.-based company) entered into a three-month forward contract to purchase 1,000,000 ringgits on March 1, 2012. The following U.S. dollar per ringgit exchange rates apply:

Date	Spot Rate	Forward Rate (to March 1, 2012)
December 1, 2011	$0.044	$0.042
December 31, 2011	0.040	0.037
March 1, 2012	0.038	N/A

Barnum's incremental borrowing rate is 12 percent. The present value factor for two months at an annual interest rate of 12 percent (1 percent per month) is 0.9803.

Which of the following correctly describes the manner in which Barnum Company will report the forward contract on its December 31, 2011, balance sheet?
   a. As an asset in the amount of $1,960.60.
   b. As an asset in the amount of $3,921.20.
   c. As a liability in the amount of $6,862.10.
   d. As a liability in the amount of $4,901.50.

Use the following information for Problems 11 and 12.

MNC Corp. (a U.S.-based company) sold parts to a South Korean customer on December 1, 2011, with payment of 10 million South Korean won to be received on March 31, 2012. The following exchange rates apply:

Date	Spot Rate	Forward Rate (to March 31, 2012)
December 1, 2011	$0.0035	$0.0034
December 31, 2011	0.0033	0.0032
March 31, 2012	0.0038	N/A

MNC's incremental borrowing rate is 12 percent. The present value factor for three months at an annual interest rate of 12 percent (1 percent per month) is 0.9706.

LO2

11. Assuming that MNC did not enter into a forward contract, how much foreign exchange gain or loss should it report on its 2011 income statement with regard to this transaction?

    a. $5,000 gain.

    b. $3,000 gain.

    c. $2,000 loss.

    d. $1,000 loss.

LO4

12. Assuming that MNC entered into a forward contract to sell 10 million South Korean won on December 1, 2011, as a fair value hedge of a foreign currency receivable, what is the net impact on its net income in 2011 resulting from a fluctuation in the value of the won?

    a. No impact on net income.

    b. $58.80 decrease in net income.

    c. $2,000 decrease in net income.

    d. $1,941.20 increase in net income.

LO6

13. On March 1, Pimlico Corporation (a U.S.-based company) expects to order merchandise from a supplier in Sweden in three months. On March 1, when the spot rate is $0.10 per Swedish krona, Pimlico enters into a forward contract to purchase 500,000 Swedish kroner at a three-month forward rate of $0.12. At the end of three months, when the spot rate is $0.115 per Swedish krona, Pimlico orders and receives the merchandise, paying 500,000 kroner. What amount does Pimlico report in net income as a result of this cash flow hedge of a forecasted transaction?

    a. $10,000 Premium Expense plus a $7,500 positive Adjustment to Net Income when the merchandise is purchased.

    b. $10,000 Discount Expense plus a $5,000 positive Adjustment to Net Income when the merchandise is purchased.

    c. $2,500 Premium Expense plus a $5,000 negative Adjustment to Net Income when the merchandise is purchased.

    d. $2,500 Premium Expense plus a $2,500 positive Adjustment to Net Income when the merchandise is purchased.

LO6

14. Palmer Corporation, operating as a U.S. corporation, expects to order goods from a foreign supplier at a price of 200,000 pounds, with delivery and payment to be made on April 15. On January 15, Palmer purchased a three-month call option on 200,000 pounds and designated this option as a cash flow hedge of a forecasted foreign currency transaction. The option has a strike price of $0.25 per pound and costs $2,000. The spot rate for pounds is $0.25 on January 15 and $0.22 on April 15. What amount will Palmer Corporation report as an option expense in net income during the period January 15 to April 15?

    a. $600.

    b. $1,000.

    c. $2,000.

    d. $4,400.

Use the following information for Problems 15 through 17.

On September 1, 2011, Jensen Company received an order to sell a machine to a customer in Canada at a price of 100,000 Canadian dollars. Jensen shipped the machine and received payment on March 1, 2012. On September 1, 2011, Jensen purchased a put option giving it the right to sell 100,000 Canadian dollars on March 1, 2012, at a price of $80,000. Jensen properly designated the option as a fair value hedge of the Canadian dollar firm commitment. The option cost $2,000 and had a fair value of $2,300 on

December 31, 2011. The fair value of the firm commitment was measured by referring to changes in the spot rate. The following spot exchange rates apply:

Date	U.S. Dollar per Canadian Dollar
September 1, 2011	$0.80
December 31, 2011	0.79
March 1, 2012	0.77

Jensen Company's incremental borrowing rate is 12 percent. The present value factor for two months at an annual interest rate of 12 percent (1 percent per month) is 0.9803.

LO5

15. What was the net impact on Jensen Company's 2011 income as a result of this fair value hedge of a firm commitment?
    a. $–0–.
    b. $680.30 decrease in income.
    c. $300 increase in income.
    d. $980.30 increase in income.

LO5

16. What was the net impact on Jensen Company's 2012 income as a result of this fair value hedge of a firm commitment?
    a. $–0–.
    b. $1,319.70 decrease in income.
    c. $77,980.30 increase in income.
    d. $78,680.30 increase in income.

LO5

17. What was the net increase or decrease in cash flow from having purchased the foreign currency option to hedge this exposure to foreign exchange risk?
    a. $–0–.
    b. $1,000 increase in cash flow.
    c. $1,500 decrease in cash flow.
    d. $3,000 increase in cash flow.

Use the following information for Problems 18 through 20.
On March 1, 2011, Werner Corp. received an order for parts from a Mexican customer at a price of 500,000 Mexican pesos with a delivery date of April 30, 2011. On March 1, when the U.S. dollar–Mexican peso spot rate is $0.115, Werner Corp. entered into a two-month forward contract to sell 500,000 pesos at a forward rate of $0.12 per peso. It designates the forward contract as a fair value hedge of the firm commitment to receive pesos, and the fair value of the firm commitment is measured by referring to changes in the peso forward rate. Werner delivers the parts and receives payment on April 30, 2011, when the peso spot rate is $0.118. On March 31, 2011, the Mexican peso spot rate is $0.123, and the forward contract has a fair value of $1,250.

LO5

18. What is the net impact on Werner's net income for the quarter ended March 31, 2011, as a result of this forward contract hedge of a firm commitment?
    a. $–0–.
    b. $1,250 increase in net income.
    c. $1,500 decrease in net income.
    d. $1,500 increase in net income.

LO5

19. What is the net impact on Werner's net income for the quarter ended June 30, 2011, as a result of this forward contract hedge of a firm commitment?
    a. $–0–.
    b. $59,000 increase in net income.
    c. $60,000 increase in net income.
    d. $61,500 increase in net income.

LO5

20. What is the net increase or decrease in cash flow from having entered into this forward contract hedge?
    a. $–0–.
    b. $1,000 increase in cash flow.
    c. $1,500 decrease in cash flow.
    d. $2,500 increase in cash flow.

Use the following information for Problems 21 and 22.

On November 1, 2011, Dos Santos Company forecasts the purchase of raw materials from a Brazilian supplier on February 1, 2012, at a price of 200,000 Brazilian reals. On November 1, 2011, Dos Santos pays $1,500 for a three-month call option on 200,000 reals with a strike price of $0.40 per real. Dos Santos properly designates the option as a cash flow hedge of a forecasted foreign currency transaction. On December 31, 2011, the option has a fair value of $1,100. The following spot exchange rates apply:

Date	U.S. Dollar per Brazilian Real
November 1, 2011	$0.40
December 31, 2011	0.38
February 1, 2012	0.41

LO6

21. What is the net impact on Dos Santos Company's 2011 net income as a result of this hedge of a forecasted foreign currency transaction?

a. $–0–.

b. $400 decrease in net income.

c. $1,000 decrease in net income.

d. $1,400 decrease in net income.

LO6

22. What is the net impact on Dos Santos Company's 2012 net income as a result of this hedge of a forecasted foreign currency transaction? Assume that the raw materials are consumed and become a part of the cost of goods sold in 2012.

a. $80,000 decrease in net income.

b. $80,600 decease in net income.

c. $81,100 decrease in net income.

d. $83,100 decrease in net income.

LO2

23. Rabato Corporation acquired merchandise on account from a foreign supplier on November 1, 2011, for 60,000 LCU (local currency units). It paid the foreign currency account payable on January 15, 2012. The following exchange rates for 1 LCU are known:

November 1, 2011	$0.345
December 31, 2011	0.333
January 15, 2012	0.359

a. How does the fluctuation in exchange rates affect Rabato's 2011 income statement?

b. How does the fluctuation in exchange rates affect Rabato's 2012 income statement?

LO2

24. On December 20, 2011, Butanta Company (a U.S. company headquartered in Miami, Florida) sold parts to a foreign customer at a price of 50,000 ostras. Payment is received on January 10, 2012. Currency exchange rates for 1 ostra are as follows:

December 20, 2011	$1.05
December 31, 2011	1.02
January 10, 2012	0.98

a. How does the fluctuation in exchange rates affect Butanta's 2011 income statement?

b. How does the fluctuation in exchange rates affect Butanta's 2012 income statement?

LO2

25. New Colony Corporation (a U.S. company) made a sale to a foreign customer on September 15, 2011, for 100,000 foreign currency units (FCU). It received payment on October 15, 2011. The following exchange rates for 1 FCU apply:

September 15, 2011	$0.40
September 30, 2011	0.42
October 15, 2011	0.37

Prepare all journal entries for New Colony in connection with this sale, assuming that the company closes its books on September 30 to prepare interim financial statements.

LO2

26. On December 1, 2011, Dresden Company (a U.S. company located in Albany, New York) purchases inventory from a foreign supplier for 60,000 local currency units (LCU). Dresden will pay in

90 days after it sells this merchandise. It makes sales rather quickly and pays this entire obligation on January 28, 2012. Currency exchange rates for 1 LCU are as follows:

December 1, 2011	$0.88
December 31, 2011	0.82
January 28, 2012	0.90

Prepare all journal entries for Dresden Company in connection with the purchase and payment.

LO2

27. Acme Corporation (a U.S. company located in Sarasota, Florida) has the following import/export transactions in 2011:

March 1	Bought inventory costing 50,000 pesos on credit.
May 1	Sold 60 percent of the inventory for 45,000 pesos on credit.
August 1	Collected 40,000 pesos from customers.
September 1	Paid 30,000 pesos to creditors.

Currency exchange rates for 1 peso for 2011 are as follows:

March 1	$0.17
May 1	0.18
August 1	0.19
September 1	0.20
December 31	0.21

For each of the following accounts, how much will Acme report on its 2011 financial statements?
a. Inventory.
b. Cost of Goods Sold.
c. Sales.
d. Accounts Receivable.
e. Accounts Payable.
f. Cash.

LO2

28. Bartlett Company, headquartered in Cincinnati, Ohio, has occasional transactions with companies in a foreign country whose currency is the lira. Prepare journal entries for the following transactions in U.S. dollars. Also prepare any necessary adjusting entries at December 31 caused by fluctuations in the value of the lira. Assume that the company uses a perpetual inventory system.

Transactions in 2011

February 1	Bought equipment for 40,000 lira on credit.
April 1	Paid for the equipment purchased February 1.
June 1	Bought inventory for 30,000 lira on credit.
August 1	Sold 70 percent of inventory purchased June 1 for 40,000 lira on credit.
October 1	Collected 30,000 lira from the sales made on August 1, 2011.
November 1	Paid 20,000 lira on the debts incurred on June 1, 2011.

Transactions in 2012

February 1	Collected remaining 10,000 lira from August 1, 2011, sales.
March 1	Paid remaining 10,000 lira on the debts incurred on June 1, 2011.

Currency exchange rates for 1 lira for 2011

February 1	$0.44
April 1	0.45
June 1	0.47
August 1	0.48
October 1	0.49
November 1	0.50
December 31	0.52

Currency exchange rates for 1 lira for 2012

February 1	$0.54
March 1	0.55

LO2

29. Benjamin, Inc., operates an export/import business. The company has considerable dealings with companies in the country of Camerrand. The denomination of all transactions with these companies

is alaries (AL), the Camerrand currency. During 2011, Benjamin acquires 20,000 widgets at a price of 8 alaries per widget. It will pay for them when it sells them. Currency exchange rates for 1 AL are as follows:

September 1, 2011	$0.46
December 1, 2011	0.44
December 31, 2011	0.48
March 1, 2012	0.45

a. Assume that Benjamin acquired the widgets on December 1, 2011, and made payment on March 1, 2012. What is the effect of the exchange rate fluctuations on reported income in 2011 and in 2012?

b. Assume that Benjamin acquired the widgets on September 1, 2011, and made payment on December 1, 2011. What is the effect of the exchange rate fluctuations on reported income in 2011?

c. Assume that Benjamin acquired the widgets on September 1, 2011, and made payment on March 1, 2012. What is the effect of the exchange rate fluctuations on reported income in 2011 and in 2012?

LO7

30. On September 30, 2011, Ericson Company negotiated a two-year, 1,000,000 dudek loan from a foreign bank at an interest rate of 2 percent per year. It makes interest payments annually on September 30 and will repay the principal on September 30, 2013. Ericson prepares U.S.-dollar financial statements and has a December 31 year-end.

a. Prepare all journal entries related to this foreign currency borrowing assuming the following exchange rates for 1 dudek:

September 30, 2011	$0.100
December 31, 2011	0.105
September 30, 2012	0.120
December 31, 2012	0.125
September 30, 2013	0.150

b. Determine the effective cost of borrowing in dollars in each of the three years 2011, 2012, and 2013.

LO4

31. Brandlin Company of Anaheim, California, sells parts to a foreign customer on December 1, 2011, with payment of 20,000 korunas to be received on March 1, 2012. Brandlin enters into a forward contract on December 1, 2011, to sell 20,000 korunas on March 1, 2012. Relevant exchange rates for the koruna on various dates are as follows:

Date	Spot Rate	Forward Rate (to March 1, 2012)
December 1, 2011	$2.00	$2.075
December 31, 2011	2.10	2.200
March 1, 2012	2.25	N/A

Brandlin's incremental borrowing rate is 12 percent. The present value factor for two months at an annual interest rate of 12 percent (1 percent per month) is 0.9803. Brandlin must close its books and prepare financial statements at December 31.

a. Assuming that Brandlin designates the forward contract as a cash flow hedge of a foreign currency receivable and recognizes any premium or discount using the straight-line method, prepare journal entries for these transactions in U.S. dollars. What is the impact on 2011 net income? What is the impact on 2012 net income? What is the impact on net income over the two accounting periods?

b. Assuming that Brandlin designates the forward contract as a fair value hedge of a foreign currency receivable, prepare journal entries for these transactions in U.S. dollars. What is the impact on 2011 net income? What is the impact on 2012 net income? What is the impact on net income over the two accounting periods?

LO4

32. Use the same facts as in Problem 31 except that Brandlin Company purchases parts from a foreign supplier on December 1, 2011, with payment of 20,000 korunas to be made on March 1, 2012. On December 1, 2011, Brandlin enters into a forward contract to purchase 20,000 korunas on March 1, 2012.

a. Assuming that Brandlin designates the forward contract as a cash flow hedge of a foreign currency payable and recognizes any premium or discount using the straight-line method, prepare journal entries for these transactions in U.S. dollars. What is the impact on 2011 net income? What is the impact on 2012 net income? What is the impact on net income over the two accounting periods?

b. Assuming that Brandlin designates the forward contract as a fair value hedge of a foreign currency payable, prepare journal entries for these transactions in U.S. dollars. What is the impact on net income in 2011 and in 2012? What is the impact on net income over the two accounting periods?

LO4

33. On June 1, Alexander Corporation sold goods to a foreign customer at a price of 1,000,000 pesos. It will receive payment in three months on September 1. On June 1, Alexander acquired an option to sell 1,000,000 pesos in three months at a strike price of $0.045. Relevant exchange rates and option premiums for the peso are as follows:

Date	Spot Rate	Call Option Premium for September 1 (strike price $0.045)
June 1	$0.045	$0.0020
June 30	0.048	0.0018
September 1	0.044	N/A

Alexander must close its books and prepare its second-quarter financial statements on June 30.

a. Assuming that Alexander designates the foreign currency option as a cash flow hedge of a foreign currency receivable, prepare journal entries for these transactions in U.S. dollars. What is the impact on net income over the two accounting periods?

b. Assuming that Alexander designates the foreign currency option as a fair value hedge of a foreign currency receivable, prepare journal entries for these transactions in U.S. dollars. What is the impact on net income over the two accounting periods?

LO4

34. On June 1, Hamilton Corporation purchased goods from a foreign supplier at a price of 1,000,000 markkas. It will make payment in three months on September 1. On June 1, Hamilton acquired an option to purchase 1,000,000 markkas in three months at a strike price of $0.085. Relevant exchange rates and option premiums for the markka are as follows:

Date	Spot Rate	Call Option Premium for September 1 (strike price $0.085)
June 1	$0.085	$0.002
June 30	0.088	0.004
September 1	0.090	N/A

Hamilton must close its books and prepare its second-quarter financial statements on June 30.

a. Assuming that Hamilton designates the foreign currency option as a cash flow hedge of a foreign currency payable, prepare journal entries for these transactions in U.S. dollars. What is the impact on net income over the two accounting periods?

b. Assuming that Hamilton designates the foreign currency option as a fair value hedge of a foreign currency payable, prepare journal entries for these transactions in U.S. dollars. What is the impact on net income over the two accounting periods?

LO4

35. On November 1, 2011, Ambrose Company sold merchandise to a foreign customer for 100,000 FCUs with payment to be received on April 30, 2012. At the date of sale, Ambrose entered into a six-month forward contract to sell 100,000 LCUs. It properly designates the forward contract as a cash flow hedge of a foreign currency receivable. The following exchange rates apply:

Date	Spot Rate	Forward Rate (to April 30, 2012)
November 1, 2011	$0.53	$0.52
December 31, 2011	0.50	0.48
April 30, 2012	0.49	N/A

Ambrose's incremental borrowing rate is 12 percent. The present value factor for four months at an annual interest rate of 12 percent (1 percent per month) is 0.9610.

a. Prepare all journal entries, including December 31 adjusting entries, to record the sale and forward contract.

b. What is the impact on net income in 2011?

c. What is the impact on net income in 2012?

LO4

36. Eximco Corporation (based in Champaign, Illinois) has a number of transactions with companies in the country of Mongagua, where the currency is the mong. On November 30, 2011, Eximco sold equipment at a price of 500,000 mongs to a Mongaguan customer that will make payment on January 31, 2012. In addition, on November 30, 2011, Eximco purchased raw materials from a Mongaguan supplier at a price of 300,000 mongs; it will make payment on January 31, 2012. To hedge its net exposure in mongs, Eximco entered into a two-month forward contract on November 30, 2011, to deliver 200,000 mongs to the foreign currency broker in exchange for $104,000. Eximco properly designates its forward contract as a fair value hedge of a foreign currency receivable. The following rates for the mong apply:

Date	Spot Rate	Forward Rate (to January 31, 2012)
November 30, 2011	$0.53	$0.52
December 31, 2011	0.50	0.48
January 31, 2012	0.49	N/A

Eximco's incremental borrowing rate is 12 percent. The present value factor for one month at an annual interest rate of 12 percent (1 percent per month) is 0.9901.

a. Prepare all journal entries, including December 31 adjusting entries, to record these transactions and the forward contract.

b. What is the impact on net income in 2011?

c. What is the impact on net income in 2012?

LO4, LO5

37. On October 1, 2011, Hanks Company entered into a forward contract to sell 100,000 LCUs in four months (on January 31, 2012) and receive $65,000 in U.S. dollars. Exchange rates for the LCU follow:

Date	Spot Rate	Forward Rate (to January 31, 2012)
October 1, 2011	$0.69	$0.65
December 31, 2011	0.71	0.74
January 31, 2012	0.72	N/A

Hanks' incremental borrowing rate is 12 percent. The present value factor for one month at an annual interest rate of 12 percent (1 percent per month) is 0.9901. Hanks must close its books and prepare financial statements on December 31.

a. Prepare journal entries, assuming that Hanks entered into the forward contract as a fair value hedge of a 100,000 LCU receivable arising from a sale made on October 1, 2011. Include entries for both the sale and the forward contract.

b. Prepare journal entries, assuming that Hanks entered into the forward contract as a fair value hedge of a firm commitment related to a 100,000 LCU sale that will be made on January 31, 2012. Include entries for both the firm commitment and the forward contract. The fair value of the firm commitment is measured referring to changes in the forward rate.

LO5

38. On August 1, Jackson Corporation (a U.S.-based importer) placed an order to purchase merchandise from a foreign supplier at a price of 200,000 rupees. Jackson will receive and make payment for the merchandise in three months on October 31. On August 1, Jackson entered into a forward contract to purchase 200,000 rupees in three months at a forward rate of $0.30. It properly designates the forward contract as a fair value hedge of a foreign currency firm commitment. The fair value of the firm commitment is measured by referring to changes in the forward rate. Relevant exchange rates for the rupee are as follows:

Date	Spot Rate	Forward Rate (to October 31)
August 1	$0.300	$0.300
September 30	0.305	0.325
October 31	0.320	N/A

Jackson's incremental borrowing rate is 12 percent. The present value factor for one month at an annual interest rate of 12 percent (1 percent per month) is 0.9901. Jackson must close its books and prepare its third-quarter financial statements on September 30.

a. Prepare journal entries for the forward contract and firm commitment.

b. What is the impact on net income over the two accounting periods?

c. What net cash outflow results from the purchase of merchandise from the foreign customer?

LO5

39. On June 1, Vandervelde Corporation (a U.S.-based manufacturing firm) received an order to sell goods to a foreign customer at a price of 500,000 leks. Vandervelde will ship the goods and receive payment in three months on September 1. On June 1, Vandervelde purchased an option to sell 500,000 leks in three months at a strike price of $1.00. It properly designated the option as a fair value hedge of a foreign currency firm commitment. The fair value of the firm commitment is measured by referring to changes in the spot rate. Relevant exchange rates and option premiums for the lek are as follows:

Date	Spot Rate	Call Option Premium for September 1 (strike price $1.00)
June 1	$1.00	$0.010
June 30	0.99	0.016
September 1	0.97	N/A

Vandervelde's incremental borrowing rate is 12 percent. The present value factor for two months at an annual interest rate of 12 percent (1 percent per month) is 0.9803. Vandervelde Corporation must close its books and prepare its second-quarter financial statements on June 30.

a. Prepare journal entries for the foreign currency option and firm commitment.

b. What is the impact on net income over the two accounting periods?

c. What is the net cash inflow resulting from the sale of goods to the foreign customer?

LO5

40. Big Arber Company ordered parts from a foreign supplier on November 20 at a price of 50,000 pijios when the spot rate was $0.20 per pijio. Delivery and payment were scheduled for December 20. On November 20, Big Arber acquired a call option on 50,000 pijios at a strike price of $0.20, paying a premium of $0.008 per pijio. It designates the option as a fair value hedge of a foreign currency firm commitment. The fair value of the firm commitment is measured by referring to changes in the spot rate. The parts arrive and Big Arber makes payment according to schedule. Big Arber does not close its books until December 31.

a. Assuming a spot rate of $0.21 per pijio on December 20, prepare all journal entries to account for the option and firm commitment.

b. Assuming a spot rate of $0.18 per pijio on December 20, prepare all journal entries to account for the option and firm commitment.

LO6

41. Based on past experience, Leickner Company expects to purchase raw materials from a foreign supplier at a cost of 1,000,000 marks on March 15, 2012. To hedge this forecasted transaction, the company acquires a three-month call option to purchase 1,000,000 marks on December 15, 2011. Leickner selects a strike price of $0.58 per mark, paying a premium of $0.005 per unit, when the spot rate is $0.58. The spot rate increases to $0.584 at December 31, 2011, causing the fair value of the option to increase to $8,000. By March 15, 2012, when the raw materials are purchased, the spot rate has climbed to $0.59, resulting in a fair value for the option of $10,000.

a. Prepare all journal entries for the option hedge of a forecasted transaction and for the purchase of raw materials, assuming that December 31 is Leickner's year-end and that the raw materials are included in the cost of goods sold in 2012.

b. What is the overall impact on net income over the two accounting periods?

c. What is the net cash outflow to acquire the raw materials?

LO2, LO4, LO5

42. Vino Veritas Company, a U.S.-based importer of wines and spirits, placed an order with a French supplier for 1,000 cases of wine at a price of 200 euros per case. The total purchase price is 200,000 euros. Relevant exchange rates for the euro are as follows:

Date	Spot Rate	Forward Rate to October 31, 2011	Call Option Premium for October 31, 2011 (strike price $1.00)
September 15, 2011	$1.00	$1.06	$0.035
September 30, 2011	1.05	1.09	0.070
October 31, 2011	1.10	1.10	0.100

Vino Veritas Company has an incremental borrowing rate of 12 percent (1 percent per month) and closes the books and prepares financial statements at September 30.

a. Assume that the wine arrived on September 15, 2011, and the company made payment on October 31, 2011. There was no attempt to hedge the exposure to foreign exchange risk. Prepare journal entries to account for this import purchase.

b. Assume that the wine arrived on September 15, 2011, and the company made payment on October 31, 2011. On September 15, Vino Veritas entered into a 45-day forward contract to purchase 200,000 euros. It properly designated the forward contract as a fair value hedge of a foreign currency payable. Prepare journal entries to account for the import purchase and foreign currency forward contract.

c. Vino Veritas ordered the wine on September 15, 2011. The wine arrived and the company paid for it on October 31, 2011. On September 15, Vino Veritas entered into a 45-day forward contract to purchase 200,000 euros. The company properly designated the forward contract as a fair value hedge of a foreign currency firm commitment. The fair value of the firm commitment is measured by referring to changes in the forward rate. Prepare journal entries to account for the foreign currency forward contract, firm commitment, and import purchase.

d. The wine arrived on September 15, 2011, and the company made payment on October 31, 2011. On September 15, Vino Veritas purchased a 45-day call option for 200,000 euros. It properly designated the option as a cash flow hedge of a foreign currency payable. Prepare journal entries to account for the import purchase and foreign currency option.

e. The company ordered the wine on September 15, 2011. It arrived on October 31, 2011, and the company made payment on that date. On September 15, Vino Veritas purchased a 45-day call option for 200,000 euros. It properly designated the option as a fair value hedge of a foreign currency firm commitment. The fair value of the firm commitment is measured by referring to changes in the spot rate. Prepare journal entries to account for the foreign currency option, firm commitment, and import purchase.

Develop Your Skills

RESEARCH CASE—INTERNATIONAL FLAVORS AND FRAGRANCES

Many companies make annual reports available on their corporate Internet home page. Annual reports also can be accessed through the SEC's EDGAR system at www.sec.gov (under Filing Type, search for 10-K). Access the most recent annual report for International Flavors and Fragrances (IFF).

Required

1. Identify the location(s) in the annual report where IFF provides disclosures related to its management of foreign exchange risk.
2. Determine the types of hedging instruments the company uses and the types of hedges in which it engages.
3. Determine the manner in which the company discloses the fact that its foreign exchange hedges are effective in offsetting gains and losses on the underlying items being hedged.

ACCOUNTING STANDARDS CASE—FORECASTED TRANSACTIONS

Fergusson Corporation, a U.S. company, manufactures components for the automobile industry. In the past, Fergusson purchased actuators used in its products from a supplier in the United States. The company plans to shift its purchases to a supplier in Portugal. Fergusson's CFO expects to place an order with the Portuguese supplier in the amount of 200,000 euros in three months. In contemplation of this future import, the CFO purchased a euro call option to hedge the cash flow risk that the euro might appreciate against the U.S. dollar over the next three months. The CFO is aware that a foreign currency option used to hedge the cash flow risk associated with a forecasted foreign currency transaction may be designated as a hedge for accounting purposes only if the forecasted transaction is probable. However, he is unsure how he should demonstrate that the anticipated import purchase from Portugal is likely to occur. He wonders whether management's intention to make the purchase is sufficient.

Required

Search current U.S. authoritative accounting literature to determine whether management's intent is sufficient to assess that a forecasted foreign currency transaction is likely to occur. If not, what additional evidence must be considered? Identify the source of guidance for answering these questions.

EXCEL CASE—DETERMINE FOREIGN EXCHANGE GAINS AND LOSSES

Import/Export Company, a U.S. company, made a number of import purchases and export sales denominated in foreign currency in 2008. Information related to these transactions is summarized in the following table. The company made each purchase or sale on the date in the Transaction Date column and made payment in foreign currency or received payment on the date in the Settlement Date column.

Foreign Currency	Type of Transaction	Amount in Foreign Currency	Transaction Date	Settlement Date
Brazilian real (BRL)	Import purchase	(89,000)	1/1/2008	5/1/2008
Swiss franc (CHF)	Export sale	56,700	1/1/2008	4/1/2008
Swiss franc (CHF)	Import purchase	(50,600)	4/1/2008	10/1/2008
Euro	Export sale	32,250	4/1/2008	7/1/2008
Euro	Export sale	32,250	4/1/2008	9/1/2008
South African rand (ZAR)	Export sale	402,000	4/1/2008	8/1/2008
Chinese yuan (CNY)	Import purchase	(360,000)	2/1/2008	8/1/2008
South Korean won (KRW)	Import purchase	(47,300,000)	2/1/2008	8/1/2008

Required

1. Create an electronic spreadsheet with the information from the preceding table. Label columns as follows:

    Foreign Currency

    Type of Transaction

    Amount in Foreign Currency

    Transaction Date

    Exchange Rate at Transaction Date

    $ Value at Transaction Date

    Settlement Date

    Exchange Rate at Settlement Date

    $ Value at Settlement Date

    Foreign Exchange Gain (Loss)

2. Use historical exchange rate information available on the Internet at www.x-rates.com, Historic Lookup, to find the 2008 exchange rates between the U.S. dollar and each foreign currency on the relevant transaction and settlement dates.

3. Complete the electronic spreadsheet to determine the foreign exchange gain (loss) on each transaction. Determine the total net foreign exchange gain (loss) reported in Import/Export Company's 2008 income statement.

ANALYSIS CASE—CASH FLOW HEDGE

On February 1, 2011, Linber Company forecasted the purchase of component parts on May 1, 2011, at a price of 100,000 euros. On that date, Linber entered into a forward contract to purchase 100,000 euros on May 1, 2011. It designated the forward contract as a cash flow hedge of the forecasted transaction. The spot rate for euros on February 1, 2011, is $1 per euro. On May 1, 2011, the forward contract was settled, and the component parts were received and paid for. The parts were consumed in the second quarter of 2011.

Linber's financial statements reported the following amounts related to this cash flow hedge (credit balances in parentheses):

Income Statement	First Quarter 2011	Second Quarter 2011
Premium expense	$4,000	$ 2,000
Cost of goods sold	–0–	103,000
Adjustment to net income	–0–	3,000

Balance Sheet	3/31/11	5/1/11
Forward contract (liability)	$(1,980)*	–0–
AOCI (credit)	(2,020)	–0–
Change in cash	–0–	$(106,000)

*$2,000 × 0.9901 = $1,980, where 0.9901 is the present value factor for one month at an annual interest rate of 12 percent calculated as 1/1.01.

Required

1. On January 15, 2011, what was the U.S. dollar per euro forward rate to May 1, 2011?

2. On March 31, 2011, what was the U.S. dollar per euro forward rate to May 1, 2011?

3. Was Linber better off or worse off as a result of having entered into this cash flow hedge of a fore-casted transaction? By what amount?

4. What does the total premium expense of $6,000 reflect?

INTERNET CASE—HISTORICAL EXCHANGE RATES

The Pier Ten Company, a U.S. company, made credit sales to four customers in Asia on December 15, 2008, and received payment on January 15, 2009. Information related to these sales is as follows:

Customer	Location	Invoice Price
Balihasa Properties Group	Jakarta	218,000,000 Indonesian rupiah (IDR)
Daewon Commercial Ltd.	Seoul	27,350,000 South Korean won (KRW)
Mishima Industrial Ltd.	Tokyo	1,825,000 Japanese yen (JPY)
Singapore Trading Company	Singapore	29,800 Singapore dollar (SGD)

The Pier Ten Company's fiscal year ends December 31.

Required

1. Use historical exchange rate information available on the Internet at www.oanda.com, FX Daily, to find exchange rates between the U.S. dollar and each foreign currency for December 15, 2008, December 31, 2008, and January 15, 2009.

2. Determine the foreign exchange gains and losses that Pier Ten would have recognized in net income in 2008 and 2009, and the overall foreign exchange gain or loss for each transaction. Determine for which transaction it would have been most important for Pier Ten to hedge its foreign exchange risk.

3. Pier Ten could have acquired a one-month put option on December 15, 2008, to hedge the foreign exchange risk associated with each of the four export sales. In each case, the put option would have cost $100 with the strike price equal to the December 15, 2008, spot rate. Determine for which hedges, if any, Pier Ten would have recognized a net gain on the foreign currency option.

COMMUNICATION CASE—FORWARD CONTRACTS AND OPTIONS

Palmetto Bug Extermination Corporation (PBEC), a U.S. company, regularly purchases chemicals from a supplier in Switzerland with the invoice price denominated in Swiss francs. PBEC has experienced several foreign exchange losses in the past year due to increases in the U.S. dollar price of the Swiss currency. As a result, Dewey Nukem, PBEC's CEO, has asked you to investigate the possibility of using derivative financial instruments, specifically foreign currency forward contracts and foreign currency options, to hedge the company's exposure to foreign exchange risk.

Required

Draft a memo to CEO Nukem comparing the advantages and disadvantages of using forward contracts and options to hedge foreign exchange risk. Recommend the type of hedging instrument you believe the company should employ and justify this recommendation.

Translation of Foreign Currency Financial Statements

- Anheuser-Busch agreed on Sunday night to sell itself to the Belgian brewer InBev for about $52 billion, putting control of the nation's largest beermaker and a fixture of American culture into a European rival's hands.[1]

- On March 3, 2008, we completed the acquisition of 100 percent of the outstanding shares of Umbro Plc ("Umbro"), a leading United Kingdom–based global soccer brand, for a purchase price of £290.5 million in cash (approximately $576.4 million), inclusive of direct transaction costs.[2]

- In Fiscal 2009, cash paid for acquisitions, net of divestitures, required $281 million, primarily related to the acquisitions of Benedicta, a sauce business in France; Golden Circle Limited, a fruit and juice business in Australia; La Bonne Cuisine, a chilled dip business in New Zealand; and Papillon, a small chilled products business in South Africa.[3]

Recent announcements such as these have become more the norm than the exception in today's global economy. Companies establish operations in foreign countries for a variety of reasons including to develop new markets for their products, take advantage of lower production costs, or gain access to raw materials. Some multinational companies have reached a stage in their development in which domestic operations are no longer considered to be of higher priority than international operations. For example, in 2008, U.S.-based International Flavors and Fragrances, Inc., had operations in 43 countries and 75 percent of its net sales outside North America; The Coca-Cola Company generated 75 percent of its sales and had 62 percent of its property, plant, and equipment outside of the United States.

[1] "Anheuser-Busch Agrees to Be Sold to InBev," *New York Times* online edition, July 15, 2008, www.nytimes.com.
[2] Nike, Inc., 2008 Form 10-K, p. 33.
[3] H.J. Heinz Company and Subsidiaries 2009 Annual Report, p. 22.

LEARNING OBJECTIVES

After studying this chapter, you should be able to:

LO1 Explain the theoretical underpinnings and the limitations of the current rate and temporal methods.

LO2 Describe guidelines as to when foreign currency financial statements are to be translated using the current rate method and when they are to be translated using the temporal method.

LO3 Translate a foreign subsidiary's financial statements into its parent's reporting currency using the current rate method and calculate the related translation adjustment.

LO4 Remeasure a foreign subsidiary's financial statements using the temporal method and calculate the associated remeasurement gain or loss.

LO5 Understand the rationale for hedging a net investment in a foreign operation and describe the treatment of gains and losses on hedges used for this purpose.

LO6 Prepare a consolidation worksheet for a parent and its foreign subsidiary.

Foreign operations create numerous managerial problems for the parent company that do not exist for domestic operations. Some of these problems arise from cultural differences between the home and foreign countries. Other problems exist because foreign operations generally are required to comply with the laws and regulations of the foreign country. For example, most countries require companies to prepare financial statements in the local currency using local accounting rules.

To prepare worldwide consolidated financial statements, a U.S. parent company must (1) convert the foreign GAAP financial statements of its foreign operations into U.S. GAAP and (2) translate the financial statements from the foreign currency into U.S. dollars. This conversion and translation process must be carried out regardless of whether the foreign operation is a branch, joint venture, majority-owned subsidiary, or affiliate accounted for under the equity method. This chapter deals with the issue of translating foreign currency financial statements into the parent's reporting currency.

Two major theoretical issues are related to the translation process: (1) which *translation method* should be used and (2) where the resulting *translation adjustment* should be reported in the consolidated financial statements. In this chapter, these two issues are examined first from a conceptual perspective and second by the manner in which the FASB in the United States has resolved these issues. The chapter concludes with a discussion of IFRS on this topic.

EXCHANGE RATES USED IN TRANSLATION

Two types of exchange rates are used in translating financial statements:

1. *Historical exchange rate:* the exchange rate that exists when a transaction occurs.
2. *Current exchange rate:* the exchange rate that exists at the balance sheet date.

Translation methods differ as to which balance sheet and income statement accounts to translate at historical exchange rates and which to translate at current exchange rates.

Assume that the company described in the discussion question on the next page began operations in Gualos on December 31, 2010, when the exchange rate was $0.20 per vilsek. When Southwestern Corporation prepared its consolidated balance sheet at December 31, 2010, it had no choice about the exchange rate used to translate the Land account into U.S. dollars. It translated the Land account carried on the foreign subsidiary's books at 150,000 vilseks at an exchange rate of $0.20; $0.20 was both the *historical* and *current* exchange rate for the Land account at December 31, 2010.

Consolidated Balance Sheet: 12/31/10

Land (150,000 vilseks × $0.20) $30,000

During the first quarter of 2011, the vilsek appreciates relative to the U.S. dollar by 15 percent; the exchange rate at March 31, 2011, is $0.23 per vilsek. In preparing its balance sheet at the end of the first quarter of 2011, Southwestern must decide whether the Land account carried on the subsidiary's balance sheet at 150,000 vilseks should be translated into dollars using the *historical exchange rate* of $0.20 or the *current exchange rate* of $0.23.

If the historical exchange rate is used at March 31, 2011, Land continues to be carried on the consolidated balance sheet at $30,000 with no change from December 31, 2010.

Historical Rate—Consolidated Balance Sheet: 3/31/11

Land (150,000 vilseks × $0.20) $30,000

Discussion **Question**

HOW DO WE REPORT THIS?

Southwestern Corporation operates throughout Texas buying and selling widgets. To expand into more profitable markets, the company recently decided to open a small subsidiary in the nearby country of Gualos. The currency in Gualos is the vilsek. For some time, the government of that country held the exchange rate constant: 1 vilsek equaled $0.20 (or 5 vilseks equaled $1.00). Initially, Southwestern invested cash in this new operation; its $90,000 was converted into 450,000 vilseks ($90,000 × 5). Southwestern used one-third of this money (150,000 vilseks, or $30,000) to purchase land to hold for the possible construction of a plant, invested one-third in short-term marketable securities, and spent one-third in acquiring inventory for future resale.

Shortly thereafter, the Gualos government officially revalued the currency so that 1 vilsek was worth $0.23. Because of the strength of the local economy, the vilsek gained buying power in relation to the U.S. dollar. The vilsek then was considered more valuable than in the past. Southwestern's accountants realized that a change had occurred; each of the assets was now worth more in U.S. dollars than the original $30,000 investment: 150,000 vilseks × $0.23 = $34,500. Two of the company's top officers met to determine the appropriate method for reporting this change in currency values.

Controller: Nothing has changed. Our cost is still $30,000 for each item. That's what we spent. Accounting uses historical cost wherever possible. Thus, we should do nothing.

Finance director: Yes, but the old rates are meaningless now. We would be foolish to report figures based on a rate that no longer exists. The cost is still 150,000 vilseks for each item. You are right, the cost has not changed. However, the vilsek is now worth $0.23, so our reported value must change.

Controller: The new rate affects us only if we take money out of the country. We don't plan to do that for many years. The rate will probably change 20 more times before we remove money from Gualos. We've got to stick to our $30,000 historical cost. That's our cost and that's good, basic accounting.

Finance director: You mean that for the next 20 years we will be translating balances for external reporting purposes using an exchange rate that has not existed for years? That doesn't make sense. I have a real problem using an antiquated rate for the investments and inventory. They will be sold for cash when the new rate is in effect. These balances have no remaining relation to the original exchange rate.

Controller: You misunderstand the impact of an exchange rate fluctuation. Within Gualos, no impact occurs. One vilsek is still one vilsek. The effect is realized only when an actual conversion takes place into U.S. dollars at a new rate. At that point, we will properly measure and report the gain or loss. That is when realization takes place. Until then our cost has not changed.

Finance director: I simply see no value at all in producing financial information based entirely on an exchange rate that does not exist. I don't care when realization takes place.

Controller: You've got to stick with historical cost, believe me. The exchange rate today isn't important unless we actually convert vilseks to dollars.

How should Southwestern report each of these three assets on its current balance sheet? Does the company have a gain because the value of the vilsek has increased relative to the U.S. dollar?

If the current exchange rate is used, Land is carried on the consolidated balance sheet at $34,500, an increase of $4,500 from December 31, 2010.

Current Rate—Consolidated Balance Sheet: 3/31/11	
Land (150,000 vilseks × $0.23)	$34,500

Translation Adjustments

To keep the accounting equation (A = L + OE) in balance, the increase of $4,500 on the asset (A) side of the consolidated balance sheet when the current exchange rate is used must be offset by an equal $4,500 *increase* in owners' equity (OE) on the other side of the balance sheet. The increase in owners' equity is called a *positive translation adjustment.* It has a *credit* balance.

The increase in dollar value of the Land due to the vilsek's appreciation creates a positive translation adjustment. This is true for any asset on the Gualos subsidiary's balance sheet that is translated at the *current* exchange rate. *Assets translated at the current exchange rate when the foreign currency has appreciated generate a positive (credit) translation adjustment.*

Liabilities on the Gualos subsidiary's balance sheet that are translated at the current exchange rate also increase in dollar value when the vilsek appreciates. For example, Southwestern would report Notes Payable of 10,000 vilseks at $2,000 on the December 31, 2010, balance sheet and at $2,300 on the March 31, 2011, balance sheet. To keep the accounting equation in balance, the increase in liabilities (L) must be offset by a *decrease* in owners' equity (OE), giving rise to a *negative translation adjustment.* This has a *debit* balance. *Liabilities translated at the current exchange rate when the foreign currency has appreciated generate a negative (debit) translation adjustment.*

Balance Sheet Exposure

Balance sheet items (assets and liabilities) translated at the *current* exchange rate change in dollar value from balance sheet to balance sheet as a result of the change in exchange rate. These items are *exposed* to translation adjustment. Balance sheet items translated at *historical* exchange rates do not change in dollar value from one balance sheet to the next. These items are *not* exposed to translation adjustment. Exposure to translation adjustment is referred to as *balance sheet, translation,* or *accounting exposure. Balance sheet exposure* can be contrasted with the *transaction exposure* discussed in Chapter 7 that arises when a company has foreign currency receivables and payables in the following way: *Transaction exposure gives rise to foreign exchange gains and losses that are ultimately realized in cash; translation adjustments arising from balance sheet exposure do not directly result in cash inflows or outflows.*

Each item translated at the current exchange rate is exposed to translation adjustment. In effect, a separate translation adjustment exists for each of these exposed items. However, negative translation adjustments on liabilities offset positive translation adjustments on assets when the foreign currency appreciates. If total exposed assets equal total exposed liabilities throughout the year, the translation adjustments (although perhaps significant on an individual basis) net to a zero balance. The *net* translation adjustment needed to keep the consolidated balance sheet in balance is based solely on the *net asset* or *net liability* exposure.

A foreign operation has a *net asset balance sheet exposure* when assets translated at the current exchange rate are higher in amount than liabilities translated at the current exchange rate. A *net liability balance sheet exposure* exists when liabilities translated at the current exchange rate are higher than assets translated at the current exchange rate. The following summarizes the relationship between exchange rate fluctuations, balance sheet exposure, and translation adjustments:

Balance Sheet Exposure	Foreign Currency (FC)	
	Appreciates	**Depreciates**
Net asset	Positive translation adjustment	Negative translation adjustment
Net liability	Negative translation adjustment	Positive translation adjustment

Exactly how to handle the translation adjustment in the consolidated financial statements is a matter of some debate. The major issue is whether the translation adjustment should be treated as a *translation gain or loss reported in net income* or whether the translation adjustment should be treated as a *direct adjustment to owners' equity without affecting net income.* We consider this issue in more detail later after examining methods of translation.

TRANSLATION METHODS

LO1

Explain the theoretical underpinnings and the limitations of the current rate and temporal methods.

Two major translation methods are currently used: (1) the current rate (or closing rate) method and (2) the temporal method. We discuss each method from the perspective of a U.S.-based multinational company translating foreign currency financial statements into U.S. dollars.

Current Rate Method

The basic assumption underlying the *current rate method* is that a company's *net investment* in a foreign operation is *exposed* to foreign exchange risk. In other words, a foreign operation represents a foreign currency net asset and if the foreign currency *decreases* in value against the U.S. dollar, a *decrease in the U.S. dollar value of the foreign currency net asset* occurs. This decrease in U.S. dollar value of the net investment will be reflected by reporting a *negative* (debit balance) translation adjustment in the consolidated financial statements. If the foreign currency *increases* in value, an *increase in the U.S. dollar value of the net asset* occurs and will be reflected through a *positive* (credit balance) translation adjustment.

To measure the net investment's exposure to foreign exchange risk, *all assets and all liabilities* of the foreign operation are translated at the *current* exchange rate. Stockholders' equity items are translated at historical rates. *The balance sheet exposure under the current rate method is equal to the foreign operation's net asset (total assets minus total liabilities) position.*[4]

$$\text{Total assets} > \text{Total liabilities} \rightarrow \text{Net asset exposure}$$

A positive translation adjustment arises when the foreign currency appreciates, and a negative translation adjustment arises when the foreign currency depreciates.

As mentioned, the major difference between the translation adjustment and a foreign exchange gain or loss is that the translation adjustment is not necessarily realized through inflows and outflows of cash. The translation adjustment that arises when using the current rate method is unrealized. It can become a realized gain or loss only if the foreign operation is sold (for its book value) and the foreign currency proceeds from the sale are converted into U.S. dollars.

The current rate method requires translation of all income statement items at the exchange rate in effect at the date of accounting recognition. In most cases, an assumption can be made that the revenue or expense is incurred evenly throughout the accounting period and a weighted average-for-the-period exchange rate can be used for translation. However, when an income account, such as a gain or loss, occurs at a specific point in time, the exchange rate at that date should be used for translation.[5]

Temporal Method

The basic objective underlying the *temporal method* of translation is to produce a set of U.S. dollar–translated financial statements as if the foreign subsidiary had actually used U.S. dollars in conducting its operations. Continuing with the Gualos subsidiary example, Southwestern, the U.S. parent, should report the Land account on the consolidated balance sheet at the amount of U.S. dollars that it would have spent if it had sent dollars to the subsidiary to purchase land. Because the land cost 150,000 vilseks at a time when one vilsek could be acquired with $0.20, the parent would have sent $30,000 to the subsidiary to acquire the land; this is the land's historical cost *in U.S. dollar terms*. The following rule is consistent with the temporal method's underlying objective:

1. Assets and liabilities carried on the foreign operation's balance sheet at *historical cost* are translated at *historical* exchange rates to yield an equivalent historical cost in U.S. dollars.
2. Conversely, assets and liabilities carried at a *current or future value* are translated at the *current* exchange rate to yield an equivalent current value in U.S. dollars.

---

[4] In rare cases, a foreign subsidiary could have liabilities higher than assets (negative stockholders' equity). In those cases, a net liability exposure exists under the current rate method.

[5] Alternatively, all income statement items may be translated at the current exchange rate. Later we demonstrate that translation at the current rate has a slight advantage over translation at the average-for-the-period rate.

Application of this rule maintains the underlying valuation method (current value or historical cost) that the foreign subsidiary uses in accounting for its assets and liabilities. In addition, stockholders' equity accounts are translated at historical exchange rates.

Cash, marketable securities, receivables, and most liabilities are carried at current or future value and translated at the *current* exchange rate under the temporal method.[6] The temporal method generates either a net asset or a net liability balance sheet exposure, depending on whether cash plus marketable securities plus receivables are more than or less than liabilities.

Cash + Marketable securities + Receivables > Liabilities → Net asset exposure

Cash + Marketable securities + Receivables < Liabilities → Net liability exposure

Because liabilities (current plus long term) usually are more than assets translated at the current exchange rate, *a net liability exposure generally exists when the temporal method is used.*

One way to understand the concept of exposure underlying the temporal method is to pretend that the parent actually carries on its balance sheet the foreign operation's cash, marketable securities, receivables, and payables. For example, consider the Japanese subsidiary of a U.S. parent company. The Japanese subsidiary's yen receivables that result from sales in Japan may be thought of as Japanese yen receivables of the U.S. parent that result from export sales to Japan. If the U.S. parent had yen receivables on its balance sheet, a decrease in the yen's value would result in a *foreign exchange loss*. A foreign exchange loss also occurs on the Japanese yen held in cash by the U.S. parent and on the Japanese yen denominated marketable securities. A foreign exchange gain on the parent's Japanese yen payables resulting from foreign purchases would offset these foreign exchange losses. Whether a net gain or a net loss exists depends on the relative amount of yen cash, marketable securities, and receivables versus yen payables. Under the temporal method, the translation adjustment measures the "net foreign exchange gain or loss" on the foreign operation's cash, marketable securities, receivables, and payables, *as if those items were actually carried on the parent's books.*

Again, the major difference between the translation adjustment resulting from the use of the temporal method and a foreign exchange gain or loss is that the translation adjustment is not necessarily realized through inflows or outflows of cash. The U.S. dollar translation adjustment in this case *is realized* only if (1) the parent sends U.S. dollars to the Japanese subsidiary to pay all of its yen liabilities and (2) the subsidiary converts its yen receivables and marketable securities into yen cash and then sends this amount plus the amount in its yen cash account to the U.S. parent, which converts it into U.S. dollars.

The temporal method translates income statement items at exchange rates that exist when the revenue is generated or the expense is incurred. For most items, an assumption can be made that the revenue or expense is incurred evenly throughout the accounting period and an average-for-the-period exchange rate can be used for translation. However, some expenses are related to assets carried at historical cost—for example, cost of goods sold, depreciation of fixed assets, and amortization of intangibles. Because the related assets are translated at historical exchange rates, these expenses must be translated at historical rates as well.

The current rate method and temporal method are the two methods currently used in the United States. They are also the predominant methods used worldwide. A summary of the appropriate exchange rate for selected financial statement items under these two methods is presented in Exhibit 8.1.

Translation of Retained Earnings

Stockholders' equity items are translated at historical exchange rates under both the temporal and current rate methods. This creates somewhat of a problem in translating retained earnings. This figure is actually a composite of many previous transactions: all revenues,

---

[6] Under current authoritative literature, all marketable equity securities and marketable debt securities that are classified as "trading" or "available for sale" are carried at current market value. Marketable debt securities classified as "held to maturity" are carried at amortized cost. Throughout the remainder of this chapter, we will assume that all marketable securities are reported at current value.

EXHIBIT 8.1
Exchange Rates for Selected Financial Statement Items

	Temporal Method Exchange Rate	Current Rate Method Exchange Rate
Balance Sheet		
Assets		
Cash and receivables	Current	Current
Marketable securities	Current*	Current
Inventory at market	Current	Current
Inventory at cost	Historical	Current
Prepaid expenses	Historical	Current
Property, plant, and equipment	Historical	Current
Intangible assets	Historical	Current
Liabilities		
Current liabilities	Current	Current
Deferred income	Historical	Current
Long-term debt	Current	Current
Stockholders' equity		
Capital stock	Historical	Historical
Additional paid-in capital	Historical	Historical
Retained earnings	Composite	Composite
Dividends	Historical	Historical
Income Statement		
Revenues	Average	Average
Most expenses	Average	Average
Cost of goods sold	Historical	Average
Depreciation of property, plant, and equipment	Historical	Average
Amortization of intangibles	Historical	Average

*Marketable debt securities classified as held to maturity are carried at cost and translated at the historical exchange rate under the temporal method.

expenses, gains, losses, and declared dividends occurring over the company's life. At the end of the first year of operations, foreign currency (FC) retained earnings (R/E) is translated as follows:

Net income in FC	[translated per method used to translate income statement items]	= Net income in $
− Dividends in FC	× historical exchange rate when declared	= − Dividends in $
Ending R/E in FC		Ending R/E in $

The ending dollar amount of retained earnings in Year 1 becomes the beginning dollar retained earnings for Year 2, and the translated retained earnings in Year 2 (and subsequent years) are then determined as follows:

Beginning R/E in FC	(from last year's translation)	= Beginning R/E in $
+ Net income in FC	[translated per method used to translate income statement items]	= + Net income in $
− Dividends in FC	× historical exchange rate when declared	= − Dividends in $
Ending R/E in FC		Ending R/E in $

The same approach translates retained earnings under both the current rate and the temporal methods. The only difference is that translation of the current period net income is calculated differently under the two methods.

COMPLICATING ASPECTS OF THE TEMPORAL METHOD

Under the temporal method, keeping a record of the exchange rates is necessary when acquiring inventory, prepaid expenses, fixed assets, and intangible assets because these assets, carried at historical cost, are translated at historical exchange rates. Keeping track of the historical rates for these assets is not necessary under the current rate method. Translating these assets at historical rates makes the application of the temporal method more complicated than the current rate method.

Calculation of Cost of Goods Sold

Under the *current rate method,* the account Cost of Goods Sold (COGS) in foreign currency (FC) is simply translated using the average-for-the-period exchange rate (ER):

$$\text{COGS in FC} \times \text{Average ER} = \text{COGS in \$}$$

Under the *temporal method,* COGS must be decomposed into beginning inventory, purchases, and ending inventory, and each component of COGS must then be translated at its appropriate historical rate. For example, if a company acquires beginning inventory (FIFO basis) in the year 2011 evenly throughout the fourth quarter of 2010, then it uses the average exchange rate in the fourth quarter of 2010 to translate beginning inventory. Likewise, it uses the fourth quarter (4thQ) 2011 exchange rate to translate ending inventory. When purchases can be assumed to have been made evenly throughout 2011, the average 2011 exchange rate is used to translate purchases:

Beginning inventory in FC	×	Historical ER (4thQ 2010)	=	Beginning inventory in $
+ Purchases in FC	×	Average ER (2011)	=	+ Purchases in $
− Ending inventory in FC	×	Historical ER (4thQ 2011)	=	− Ending inventory in $
COGS in FC				COGS in $

No single exchange rate can be used to directly translate COGS in FC into COGS in dollars.

Application of the Lower-of-Cost-or-Market Rule

Under the *current rate method,* the ending inventory reported on the foreign currency balance sheet is translated at the current exchange rate regardless of whether it is carried at cost or a lower market value. Application of the *temporal method* requires the inventory's foreign currency cost and foreign currency market value to be translated into U.S. dollars at appropriate exchange rates, and the *lower of the dollar cost and dollar market value* is reported on the consolidated balance sheet. As a result, inventory can be carried at cost on the foreign currency balance sheet and at market value on the U.S. dollar consolidated balance sheet, and vice versa.

Fixed Assets, Depreciation, and Accumulated Depreciation

The *temporal method* requires translating fixed assets acquired at different times at different (historical) exchange rates. The same is true for depreciation of fixed assets and accumulated depreciation related to fixed assets.

For example, assume that a company purchases a piece of equipment on January 1, 2010, for FC 1,000 when the exchange rate is $1.00 per FC. It purchases another item of equipment on January 1, 2011, for FC 5,000 when the exchange rate is $1.20 per FC. Both pieces of equipment have a five-year useful life. The temporal method reports the amount of the equipment on the consolidated balance sheet on December 31, 2012, when the exchange rate is $1.50 per FC, as follows:

$$
\begin{array}{rcl}
\text{FC } 1{,}000 \times \$1.00 & = & \$1{,}000 \\
5{,}000 \times 1.20 & = & 6{,}000 \\
\hline
\text{FC } 6{,}000 & & \$7{,}000
\end{array}
$$

Depreciation expense for 2012 under the temporal method is calculated as shown here:

$$
\begin{array}{lrl}
FC & 200 \times \$1.00 = & \$\ \ 200 \\
& \underline{1{,}000 \times\ \ \ 1.20 =} & \underline{\ \ 1{,}200} \\
FC\ \underline{\underline{1{,}200}} & & \underline{\underline{\$1{,}400}}
\end{array}
$$

Accumulated depreciation under the temporal method is calculated as shown:

$$
\begin{array}{lrl}
FC & 600 \times \$1.00 = & \$\ \ 600 \\
& \underline{2{,}000 \times\ \ \ 1.20 =} & \underline{\ \ 2{,}400} \\
FC\ \underline{\underline{2{,}600}} & & \underline{\underline{\$3{,}000}}
\end{array}
$$

Similar procedures apply for intangible assets as well.

The *current rate method* reports equipment on the December 31, 2012, balance sheet at FC 6,000 × $1.50 = $9,000. Depreciation expense is translated at the average exchange rate of $1.40, FC 1,200 × $1.40 = $1,680, and accumulated depreciation is FC 2,600 × $1.50 = $3,900.

In this example, the foreign subsidiary has only two fixed assets requiring translation. In comparison with the current rate method, the temporal method can require substantial additional work for subsidiaries that own hundreds and thousands of fixed assets.

Gain or Loss on the Sale of an Asset

Assume that a foreign subsidiary sells land that cost FC 1,000 at a selling price of FC 1,200. The subsidiary reports an FC 200 gain on the sale of land on its income statement. It acquired the land when the exchange rate was $1.00 per FC; it made the sale when the exchange rate was $1.20 per FC; and the exchange rate at the balance sheet date is $1.50 per FC.

The *current rate method* translates the gain on sale of land at the exchange rate in effect at the date of sale:

$$FC\ 200 \times \$1.20 = \$240$$

The *temporal method* cannot translate the gain on the sale of land directly. Instead, it requires translating the cash received and the cost of the land sold into U.S. dollars separately, with the difference being the U.S. dollar value of the gain. In accordance with the rules of the temporal method, the Cash account is translated at the exchange rate on the date of sale, and the Land account is translated at the historical rate:

$$
\begin{array}{llr}
\text{Cash} & FC\ 1{,}200 \times \$1.20 = & \$1{,}440 \\
\text{Land} & \underline{1{,}000 \times\ \ \ 1.00 =} & \underline{\ 1{,}000} \\
\text{Gain} & FC\ \underline{\underline{\ \ 200}} & \underline{\underline{\$\ \ \ 440}}
\end{array}
$$

DISPOSITION OF TRANSLATION ADJUSTMENT

The *first issue* related to the translation of foreign currency financial statements is selecting the appropriate method. The *second issue* in financial statement translation relates to deciding *where to report the resulting translation adjustment in the consolidated financial statements.* There are two prevailing schools of thought with regard to this issue:

1. *Translation gain or loss:* This treatment considers the translation adjustment to be a gain or loss analogous to the gains and losses arising from foreign currency transactions and reports it in net income in the period in which the fluctuation in the exchange rate occurs.

The first of two conceptual problems with treating translation adjustments as gains or losses in income is that the gain or loss is unrealized; that is, no cash inflow or outflow accompanies it. The second problem is that the gain or loss could be inconsistent with economic reality. For example, the depreciation of a foreign currency can have a *positive* impact on the foreign operation's export sales and income, but the particular translation method used gives rise to a translation *loss*.

2. *Cumulative translation adjustment in other comprehensive income:* The alternative to reporting the translation adjustment as a gain or loss in net income is to include it in Other Comprehensive Income. In effect, this treatment defers the gain or loss in stockholders' equity until it is realized in some way. As a balance sheet account, the cumulative translation adjustment is not closed at the end of an accounting period and fluctuates in amount over time.

The two major translation methods and the two possible treatments for the translation adjustment give rise to these four possible combinations:

Combination	Translation Method	Treatment of Translation Adjustment
A	Temporal	Gain or loss in Net Income
B	Temporal	Deferred in Other Comprehensive Income
C	Current rate	Gain or loss in Net Income
D	Current rate	Deferred in Other Comprehensive Income

U.S. RULES

Prior to 1975, the United States had no authoritative rules about which translation method to use or where to report the translation adjustment in the consolidated financial statements. Different companies used different combinations. As an indication of the importance of this particular accounting issue, the first official pronouncement issued by the newly created FASB in 1974 was *SFAS 1*, "Disclosure of Foreign Currency Translation Information." It did not express a preference for any particular combination but simply required disclosure of the method used and the treatment of the translation adjustment.

The use of different combinations by different companies created a lack of comparability across companies. To eliminate this noncomparability, in 1975 the FASB issued *SFAS 8*, "Accounting for the Translation of Foreign Currency Transactions and Foreign Currency Financial Statements." It mandated use of the *temporal method* with all companies reporting *translation gains or losses* in net income for all foreign operations (Combination A in the preceding table).

U.S. multinational companies (MNCs) strongly opposed *SFAS 8*. Specifically, they considered reporting translation gains and losses in income to be inappropriate because they are unrealized. Moreover, because currency fluctuations often reversed themselves in subsequent quarters, artificial volatility in quarterly earnings resulted.

After releasing two exposure drafts proposing new translation rules, the FASB finally issued *SFAS 52*, "Foreign Currency Translation," in 1981. This resulted in a complete overhaul of U.S. GAAP with regard to foreign currency translation. A narrow four-to-three vote of the board approving *SFAS 52* indicates how contentious the issue of foreign currency translation has been. Despite the narrow vote, *SFAS 52* has stood the test of time and was incorporated into the FASB Accounting Standards Codification (ASC) in 2009 as part of Topic 830 Foreign Currency Matters.

LO2

Describe guidelines as to when foreign currency financial statements are to be translated using the current rate method and when they are to be translated using the temporal method.

Two Translation Combinations

Implicit in the *temporal method* is the assumption that foreign subsidiaries of U.S. MNCs have very close ties to their parent companies and that they would actually carry out their day-to-day operations and keep their books in the U.S. dollar if they could. To reflect the integrated nature of the foreign subsidiary with its U.S. parent, the translation process should create a set of U.S. dollar–translated financial statements as if the foreign subsidiary had actually used the dollar in carrying out its activities. This is the *U.S. dollar perspective* to translation.

In developing the current rules, the FASB recognized two types of foreign entities. First, some foreign entities are so closely integrated with their parents that they conduct much of their business in U.S. dollars. *Second, other foreign entities are relatively self-contained and integrated with the local economy; primarily, they use a foreign currency in their daily operations.* For the first type of entity, the FASB determined that the U.S. dollar perspective still applies and, therefore, Combination A is still relevant.

For the second relatively independent type of entity, a *local currency perspective* to translation is applicable. For this type of entity, the FASB determined that a different translation methodology, namely the *current rate method,* should be used for translation and that translation adjustments should be reported as a *separate component in other comprehensive income* (Combination D on the previous page). In addition, the FASB requires using the *average-for-the-period* exchange rate to translate income when the current rate method is used.

In rationalizing the placement of the translation adjustment in stockholders' equity rather than net income, the FASB offered two contrasting positions on the conceptual nature of the translation adjustment. One view is that the "change in the dollar equivalent of the net investment is an unrealized enhancement or reduction, having no effect on the functional currency net cash flow generated by the foreign entity which may be currently reinvested or distributed to the parent." Philosophically, this position holds that even though changes in the exchange rate create gains and losses, they are unrealized in nature and should, therefore, not be included within net income.

The alternative perspective put forth by the FASB "regards the translation adjustment as merely a mechanical by-product of the translation process." This second contention argues that exchange rate fluctuation creates no meaningful effect; the resulting translation adjustment merely serves to keep the balance sheet in equilibrium.

Interestingly enough, the FASB chose not to express preference for either of these theoretical views. The board felt no need to offer a hint of guidance as to the essential nature of the translation adjustment because both explanations point to its exclusion from net income. Thus, a balance sheet figure that can amount to millions of dollars is basically undefined by the FASB.

Functional Currency

To determine whether a specific foreign operation is integrated with its parent or self-contained and integrated with the local economy, the FASB created the concept of the *functional currency.* The functional currency is the primary currency of the foreign entity's operating environment. It can be either the parent's currency (U.S.$) or a foreign currency (generally the local currency). The functional currency orientation results in the following rule:

Functional Currency	Translation Method	Translation Adjustment
U.S. dollar	Temporal method	Gain (loss) in Net Income
Foreign currency	Current rate method	Separate component of Other Comprehensive Income (Stockholders' Equity)

In addition to introducing the concept of the *functional currency,* the FASB introduced some new terminology. The *reporting currency* is the currency in which the entity prepares its financial statements. For U.S.-based corporations, this is the U.S. dollar. If a foreign operation's functional currency is the U.S. dollar, foreign currency balances must be *remeasured* into U.S. dollars using the temporal method with translation adjustments reported as *remeasurement gains and losses* in income. When a foreign currency is the functional currency, foreign currency balances are *translated* using the current rate method and a *translation adjustment* is reported on the balance sheet.

The functional currency is essentially a matter of fact. However, in some cases the facts will not clearly indicate a single functional currency. Management's judgment is essential in assessing the facts to determine the functional currency. Indicators to guide parent company management in its determination of a foreign entity's functional currency are presented in Exhibit 8.2. Current authoritative literature provides no guidance as to how to weight these indicators in determining the functional currency. Leaving the decision about identifying the functional currency up to management allows some leeway in this process. Different companies approach this selection in different ways:

> "For us it was intuitively obvious" versus "It was quite a process. We took the six criteria and developed a matrix. We then considered the dollar amount and the related percentages in developing a point scheme. Each of the separate criteria was given equal weight (in the analytical methods applied)."[7]

[7] Jerry L. Arnold and William W. Holder, *Impact of Statement 52 on Decisions, Financial Reports and Attitudes* (Morristown, NJ: Financial Executives Research Foundation, 1986), p. 89.

EXHIBIT 8.2
Indicators for Determining the Functional Currency

	Indication That Functional Currency Is the	
Indicator	**Foreign Currency**	**Parent's Currency**
Cash flow	Primarily in FC and does not affect parent's cash flows	Directly impacts parent's cash flows on a current basis
Sales price	Not affected on short-term basis by changes in exchange rate	Affected on short-term basis by changes in exchange rate
Sales market	Active local sales market	Sales market mostly in parent's country or sales denominated in parent's currency
Expenses	Primarily local costs	Primarily costs for components obtained from parent's country
Financing	Primarily denominated in foreign currency and FC cash flows adequate to service obligations	Primarily from parent or denominated in parent currency or FC cash flows not adequate to service obligations
Intra-entity transactions	Low volume of intra-entity transactions, not extensive interrelationship with parent's operations	High volume of intra-entity transactions and extensive interrelationship with parent's operations

Research has shown that the weighting schemes used by U.S. multinationals to determine the functional currency might be biased toward selection of the *foreign currency* as the functional currency.[8] This would be rational behavior for multinationals because, when the foreign currency is the functional currency, the translation adjustment is reported in stockholders' equity and does not affect net income.

Highly Inflationary Economies

Multinationals do not need to determine the functional currency of those foreign entities located in a *highly inflationary economy.* In those cases, entities must use the *temporal method with remeasurement gains or losses reported in income.*

A country is defined as having a *highly inflationary economy* when its cumulative three-year inflation exceeds 100 percent. With compounding, this equates to an average of approximately 26 percent per year for three years in a row. Countries that have met this definition at some time include Argentina, Brazil, Israel, Mexico, and Turkey. In any given year, a country may or may not be classified as highly inflationary, depending on its most recent three-year experience with inflation.

One reason for this rule is to avoid a "disappearing plant problem" caused by using the current rate method in a country with high inflation. Remember that under the current rate method, all assets (including fixed assets) are translated at the current exchange rate. To see the problem this creates in a highly inflationary economy, consider the following hypothetical example.

The Brazilian subsidiary of a U.S. parent purchased land at the end of 1984 for 10,000,000 cruzeiros (Cr$) when the exchange rate was $0.001 per Cr$. Under the *current rate method,* the land is reported in the parent's consolidated balance sheet (B.S.) at $10,000:

	Historical Cost		**Current ER**		**Consolidated B.S.**
1984	Cr$ 10,000,000	×	$0.001	=	$10,000

In 1985, Brazil experienced roughly 200 percent inflation. Accordingly, with the forces of purchasing power parity at work, the cruzeiro plummeted against the U.S. dollar to a value of

---

[8] Timothy S. Doupnik and Thomas G. Evans, "Functional Currency as a Strategy to Smooth Income," *Advances in International Accounting,* 1988.

$0.00025 at the end of 1985. Under the current rate method, the parent's consolidated balance sheet reports land at $2,500, and a negative translation adjustment of $7,500 results:

$$1985 \quad \text{Cr\$ } 10,000,000 \times \$0.00025 = \$2,500$$

Using the current rate method, the land has lost 75 percent of its U.S. dollar value in one year—and land is not even a depreciable asset!

High rates of inflation continued in Brazil and reached the high point of roughly 1,800 percent in 1993. As a result of applying the current rate method, the land originally reported on the 1984 consolidated balance sheet at $10,000 was carried on the 1993 balance sheet at less than $1.00.

In the exposure draft leading to the current authoritative guidance on translation, the FASB proposed requiring companies with operations in highly inflationary countries to first *restate* the historical costs for inflation and then *translate* using the current rate method. For example, with 200 percent inflation in 1985, the Land account would have been written up to Cr$ 40,000,000 and then translated at the current exchange rate of $0.00025, producing a translated amount of $10,000, the same as in 1984.

Companies objected to making inflation adjustments, however, because of a lack of reliable inflation indices in many countries. The FASB backed off from requiring the *restate/translate* approach; instead it requires using the temporal method in highly inflationary countries. In the previous example, under the *temporal method,* a firm uses the historical rate of $0.001 to translate the land value year after year. The firm carries land on the consolidated balance sheet at $10,000 each year, thereby avoiding the disappearing plant problem.

THE PROCESS ILLUSTRATED

To provide a basis for demonstrating the translation and remeasurement procedures prescribed by current authoritative literature, assume that USCO (a U.S.-based company) forms a wholly owned subsidiary in Switzerland (SWISSCO) on December 31, 2010. On that date, USCO invested $300,000 in exchange for all of the subsidiary's common stock. Given the exchange rate of $0.60 per Swiss franc (CHF), the initial capital investment was CHF 500,000, of which CHF 150,000 was immediately invested in inventory and the remainder held in cash. Thus, SWISSCO began operations on January 1, 2011, with stockholders' equity (net assets) of CHF 500,000 and net monetary assets of CHF 350,000.

SWISSCO
Opening Balance Sheet
January 1, 2011

Assets	CHF	Liabilities and Equity	CHF
Cash	CHF 350,000	Common stock	CHF 100,000
Inventory	150,000	Additional paid-in capital	400,000
	CHF 500,000		CHF 500,000

During 2011, SWISSCO purchased property and equipment, acquired a patent, and purchased additional inventory, primarily on account. It negotiated a five-year loan to help finance the purchase of equipment. It sold goods, primarily on account, and incurred expenses. It generated income after taxes of CHF 470,000 and declared dividends of CHF 150,000 on October 1, 2011.

As a company incorporated in Switzerland, SWISSCO must account for its activities using Swiss accounting rules, which differ from U.S. GAAP in many respects. As noted in the introduction to this chapter, to prepare consolidated financial statements, USCO must first convert SWISSCO's financial statements to a U.S. GAAP basis. SWISSCO's U.S. GAAP financial statements for the year 2011 in Swiss francs appear in Exhibit 8.3.

EXHIBIT 8.3
Foreign Currency
Financial Statements

SWISSCO
Income Statement
For Year Ending December 31, 2011

	CHF
Sales	4,000,000
Cost of goods sold	(3,000,000)
Gross profit	1,000,000
Depreciation expense	(100,000)
Amortization expense	(10,000)
Other expenses	(220,000)
Income before income taxes	670,000
Income taxes	(200,000)
Net income	470,000

Statement of Retained Earnings
For Year Ending December 31, 2011

	CHF
Retained earnings, 1/1/11	–0–
Net income, 2011	470,000
Less: Dividends, 10/1/11	(150,000)
Retained earnings, 12/31/11	320,000

Balance Sheet
December 31, 2011

Assets	CHF	Liabilities and Equity	CHF
Cash	130,000	Accounts payable	600,000
Accounts receivable	200,000	Total current liabilities	600,000
Inventory*	400,000	Long-term debt	250,000
Total current assets	730,000	Total liabilities	850,000
Property and equipment	1,000,000	Common stock	100,000
Accumulated depreciation	(100,000)	Additional paid-in capital	400,000
Patents, net	40,000	Retained earnings	320,000
Total assets	1,670,000	Total equity	820,000
		Total liabilities and equity	1,670,000

*Inventory is valued at FIFO cost under the lower-of-cost-or-market-value rule; ending inventory was acquired evenly throughout the fourth quarter.

Statement of Cash Flows
For Year Ending December 31, 2011

	CHF
Operating activities:	
Net income	470,000
Add: Depreciation expense	100,000
Amortization expense	10,000
Increase in accounts receivable	(200,000)
Increase in inventory	(250,000)
Increase in accounts payable	600,000
Net cash from operations	730,000
Investing activities:	
Purchase of property and equipment	(1,000,000)
Acquisition of patent	(50,000)
Net cash from investing activities	(1,050,000)
Financing activities:	
Proceeds from long-term debt	250,000
Payment of dividends	(150,000)
Net cash from financing activities	100,000
Decrease in cash	(220,000)
Cash at 12/31/10	350,000
Cash at 12/31/11	130,000

To properly translate the Swiss franc financial statements into U.S. dollars, USCO must gather exchange rates between the Swiss franc and U.S. dollar at various points in time. Relevant exchange rates (in U.S. dollars) are as follows:

January 1, 2011	$0.60
Rate when property and equipment were acquired and long-term debt was incurred, March 15, 2011	0.61
Rate when patent was acquired, April 10, 2011	0.62
Average 2011	0.65
Rate when dividends were declared, October 1, 2011	0.67
Average fourth quarter 2011	0.68
December 31, 2011	0.70

As you can see, the Swiss franc steadily appreciated against the dollar during the year.

TRANSLATION OF FINANCIAL STATEMENTS—CURRENT RATE METHOD

LO3

Translate a foreign subsidiary's financial statements into its parent's reporting currency using the current rate method and calculate the related translation adjustment.

The first step in translating foreign currency financial statements is to determine the functional currency. Assuming that the Swiss franc is the functional currency, the income statement and statement of retained earnings are translated into U.S. dollars using the current rate method as shown in Exhibit 8.4.

All revenues and expenses are translated at the exchange rate in effect at the date of accounting recognition. We utilize the weighted average exchange rate for 2011 here because each revenue and expense in this illustration would have been recognized evenly throughout the year. However, when an income account, such as a gain or loss, occurs at a specific point in time, the exchange rate as of that date is applied. Depreciation and amortization expenses also are translated at the average rate for the year. These expenses accrue evenly throughout the year even though the journal entry could have been delayed until year-end for convenience.

EXHIBIT 8.4

Translation of Income Statement and Statement of Retained Earnings— Current Rate Method

SWISSCO
Income Statement
For Year Ending December 31, 2011

	CHF	Translation Rate*	US$
Sales	CHF 4,000,000	0.65 A	$ 2,600,000
Cost of goods sold	(3,000,000)	0.65 A	(1,950,000)
Gross profit	1,000,000		650,000
Depreciation expense	(100,000)	0.65 A	(65,000)
Amortization expense	(10,000)	0.65 A	(6,500)
Other expenses	(220,000)	0.65 A	(143,000)
Income before income taxes	670,000		435,500
Income taxes	(200,000)	0.65 A	(130,000)
Net income	CHF 470,000		$ 305,500

Statement of Retained Earnings
For Year Ending December 31, 2011

	CHF	Translation Rate*	US$
Retained earnings, 1/1/11	CHF –0–		$ –0–
Net income, 2011	470,000	Above	305,500
Dividends, 10/1/11	(150,000)	0.67 H	(100,500)
Retained earnings, 12/31/11	CHF 320,000		$ 205,000

*Indicates the exchange rate used and whether the rate is the current (C), average (A), or a historical (H) rate.

EXHIBIT 8.5
Translation of Balance Sheet—Current Rate Method

	SWISSCO Balance Sheet December 31, 2011		
	CHF	Translation Rate	US$
Assets			
Cash	CHF 130,000	0.70 C	$ 91,000
Accounts receivable	200,000	0.70 C	140,000
Inventory	400,000	0.70 C	280,000
Total current assets	730,000		511,000
Property and equipment	1,000,000	0.70 C	700,000
Less: Accumulated depreciation	(100,000)	0.70 C	(70,000)
Patents, net	40,000	0.70 C	28,000
Total assets	CHF 1,670,000		$1,169,000
Liabilities and Equities			
Accounts payable	CHF 600,000	0.70 C	$ 420,000
Total current liabilities	600,000		420,000
Long-term debt	250,000	0.70 C	175,000
Total liabilities	850,000		595,000
Common stock	100,000	0.60 H	60,000
Additional paid-in capital	400,000	0.60 H	240,000
Retained earnings	320,000	Above	205,000
Cumulative translation adjustment		To balance	69,000
Total equity	820,000		574,000
Total liabilities and equity	CHF 1,670,000		$1,169,000

The translated amount of net income for 2011 is brought down from the income statement into the statement of retained earnings. Dividends are translated at the exchange rate on the date of declaration.

Translation of the Balance Sheet

Looking at SWISSCO's translated balance sheet in Exhibit 8.5, note that all assets and liabilities are translated at the current exchange rate. Common stock and additional paid-in capital are translated at the exchange rate on the day the common stock was originally sold. Retained earnings at December 31, 2011, is brought down from the statement of retained earnings. Application of these procedures results in total assets of $1,169,000 and total liabilities and equities of $1,100,000. The balance sheet is brought into balance by creating a positive translation adjustment of $69,000 that is treated as an increase in Stockholders' Equity.

Note that the translation adjustment for 2011 is a *positive* $69,000 (credit balance). The sign of the translation adjustment (positive or negative) is a function of two factors: (1) the nature of the balance sheet exposure (asset or liability) and (2) the change in the exchange rate (appreciation or depreciation). In this illustration, SWISSCO has a *net asset exposure* (total assets translated at the current exchange rate are more than total liabilities translated at the current exchange rate), and the Swiss franc has *appreciated*, creating a *positive translation adjustment.*

The translation adjustment can be derived as the amount needed to bring the balance sheet back into balance. The translation adjustment also can be calculated by considering the impact of exchange rate changes on the beginning balance and subsequent changes in the net asset position summarized as follows:

1. Translate the net asset balance of the subsidiary at the beginning of the year at the exchange rate in effect on that date (*a*).

2. Translate individual increases and decreases in the net asset balance during the year at the rates in effect when those increases and decreases occurred (b). Only a few events, such as net income, dividends, stock issuance, and the acquisition of treasury stock, actually change net assets. Transactions such as the acquisition of equipment or the payment of a liability have no effect on total net assets.

3. Combine the translated beginning net asset balance (a) and the translated value of the individual changes (b) to arrive at the relative value of the net assets being held prior to the impact of any exchange rate fluctuations during the year (c).

4. Translate the ending net asset balance at the current exchange rate to determine the reported value after all exchange rate changes have occurred (d).

5. Compare the translated value of the net assets prior to any rate changes (c) with the ending translated value (d). The difference is the result of exchange rate changes during the period. If (c) is higher than (d), a negative (debit) translation adjustment arises. If (d) is higher than (c), a positive (credit) translation adjustment results.

Computation of Translation Adjustment

Based on the process just described, the translation adjustment for SWISSCO in this example is calculated as follows:

Net asset balance, 1/1/11	CHF	500,000	× 0.60 =	$ 300,000	(a)
Change in net assets:					
Net income, 2011		470,000	× 0.65 =	305,500	(b)
Dividends declared, 10/1/11		(150,000)	× 0.67 =	(100,500)	(b)
Net asset balance, 12/31/11	CHF	820,000		$ 505,000	(c)
Net asset balance, 12/31/11					
at current exchange rate	CHF	820,000	× 0.70 =	574,000	(d)
Translation adjustment, 2011 (positive). . . .				$ (69,000)	

The process described and demonstrated above is used to calculate the current period's translation adjustment. Because SWISSCO began operations at the beginning of the current year, the $69,000 translation adjustment is the only amount that will be needed to keep the U.S. dollar consolidated balance sheet in balance. In subsequent years, a cumulative translation adjustment comprised of the current year's translation adjustment plus translation adjustments from prior years will be included in stockholders' equity on the U.S. dollar consolidated balance sheet. Most companies report the cumulative translation adjustment in Accumulated Other Comprehensive Income, along with unrealized foreign exchange gains and losses, gains and losses on cash flow hedges, unrealized gains and losses on available-for-sale marketable securities, and adjustments for pension accounting.

The cumulative translation adjustment is carried in accumulated other comprehensive income only until the foreign operation is sold or liquidated. In the period in which sale or liquidation occurs, the cumulative translation adjustment related to the particular entity is removed from accumulated other comprehensive income and included as part of the gain or loss on the sale of the investment. In effect, the accumulated unrealized foreign exchange gain or loss that has been deferred in accumulated other comprehensive income becomes realized when the entity is disposed of.

Translation of the Statement of Cash Flows

The current rate method requires translating all operating items in the statement of cash flows at the average-for-the-period exchange rate (see Exhibit 8.6). This is the same rate used for translating income statement items. Although the ending balances in Accounts Receivable, Inventory, and Accounts Payable on the balance sheet are translated at the current exchange rate, the average rate is used for the *changes* in these accounts because those changes are caused by operating activities (such as sales and purchases) that are translated at the average rate.

Investing and financing activities are translated at the exchange rate on the day the activity took place. Although long-term debt is translated in the balance sheet at the current rate, in the statement of cash flows, it is translated at the historical rate when the debt was incurred.

EXHIBIT 8.6
Translated Statement of Cash Flows—Current Rate Method

SWISSCO Statement of Cash Flows For Year Ending December 31, 2011			
	CHF	Translation Rate	US$
Operating activities:			
Net income	CHF 470,000	0.65 A	$ 305,500
Add: Depreciation	100,000	0.65 A	65,000
Amortization	10,000	0.65 A	6,500
Increase in accounts receivable	(200,000)	0.65 A	(130,000)
Increase in inventory	(250,000)	0.65 A	(162,500)
Increase in accounts payable	600,000	0.65 A	390,000
Net cash from operations	730,000		474,500
Investing activities:			
Purchase of property and equipment	(1,000,000)	0.61 H	(610,000)
Acquisition of patent	(50,000)	0.62 H	(31,000)
Net cash from investing activities	(1,050,000)		(641,000)
Financing activities:			
Proceeds from long-term debt	250,000	0.61 H	152,500
Payment of dividends	(150,000)	0.67 H	(100,500)
Net cash from financing activities	100,000		52,000
Decrease in cash	(220,000)		(114,500)
Effect of exchange rate change on cash		To balance	(4,500)
Cash at December 31, 2010	CHF 350,000	0.60 H	210,000
Cash at December 31, 2011	CHF 130,000	0.70 C	$ 91,000

The $(4,500) "effect of exchange rate change on cash" is a part of the overall translation adjustment of $69,000. It represents that part of the translation adjustment attributable to a decrease in Cash and is derived as a balancing amount.

REMEASUREMENT OF FINANCIAL STATEMENTS—TEMPORAL METHOD

LO4

Remeasure a foreign subsidiary's financial statements using the temporal method and calculate the associated remeasurement gain or loss.

Now assume that a careful examination of the functional currency indicators in Exhibit 8.2 leads USCO's management to conclude that SWISSCO's functional currency is the U.S. dollar. In that case, the Swiss franc financial statements must be remeasured into U.S. dollars using the temporal method and the remeasurement gain or loss reported in income. To ensure that the remeasurement gain or loss is reported in income, it is easiest to remeasure the balance sheet first (as shown in Exhibit 8.7).

According to the procedures outlined in Exhibit 8.1, the temporal method remeasures cash, receivables, and liabilities into U.S. dollars using the current exchange rate of $0.70. Inventory (carried at FIFO cost), property and equipment, patents, and the contributed capital accounts (Common Stock and Additional Paid-In Capital) are remeasured at historical rates. These procedures result in total assets of $1,076,800 and liabilities and contributed capital of $895,000. To balance the balance sheet, Retained Earnings must total $181,800. We verify the accuracy of this amount later.

Remeasurement of the Income Statement

Exhibit 8.8 shows the remeasurement of SWISSCO's income statement and statement of retained earnings. Revenues and expenses incurred evenly throughout the year (sales, other expenses, and income taxes) are remeasured at the average exchange rate of $0.65. Expenses related to assets remeasured at historical exchange rates (depreciation expense and amortization expense) are remeasured at relevant historical rates.

EXHIBIT 8.7
Remeasurement of Balance Sheet—Temporal Method

SWISSCO
Balance Sheet
December 31, 2011

	CHF	Remeasurement Rate	US$
Assets			
Cash	CHF 130,000	0.70 C	$ 91,000
Accounts receivable	200,000	0.70 C	140,000
Inventory	400,000	0.68 H	272,000
Total current assets	730,000		503,000
Property and equipment	1,000,000	0.61 H	610,000
Less: Accumulated depreciation	(100,000)	0.61 H	(61,000)
Patents, net	40,000	0.62 H	24,800
Total assets	CHF 1,670,000		$1,076,800
Liabilities and Equities			
Accounts payable	CHF 600,000	0.70 C	$ 420,000
Total current liabilities	600,000		420,000
Long-term debt	250,000	0.70 C	175,000
Total liabilities	850,000		595,000
Common stock	100,000	0.60 H	60,000
Additional paid-in capital	400,000	0.60 H	240,000
Retained earnings	320,000	To balance	181,800
Total equity	820,000		481,800
Total liabilities and equity	CHF 1,670,000		$1,076,800

EXHIBIT 8.8
Remeasurement of Income Statement and Statement of Retained Earnings— Temporal Method

SWISSCO
Income Statement
For Year Ending December 31, 2011

	CHF	Remeasurement Rate	US$
Sales	CHF 4,000,000	0.65 A	$ 2,600,000
Cost of goods sold	(3,000,000)	Calculation	(1,930,500)
Gross profit	1,000,000		669,500
Depreciation expense	(100,000)	0.61 H	(61,000)
Amortization expense	(10,000)	0.62 H	(6,200)
Other expenses	(220,000)	0.65 A	(143,000)
Income before income taxes	670,000		459,300
Income taxes	(200,000)	0.65 A	(130,000)
Remeasurement Loss		To balance	(47,000)
Net income	CHF 470,000	Below	$ 282,300

Statement of Retained Earnings
For Year Ending December 31, 2011

	CHF	Remeasurement Rate	US$
Retained earnings, 1/1/11	CHF –0–		$ –0–
Net income, 2011	470,000	To balance	282,300
Dividends	(150,000)	0.67 H	(100,500)
Retained earnings, 12/31/11	CHF 320,000	Above	$ 181,800

The following procedure remeasures cost of goods sold at historical exchange rates. Beginning inventory acquired on January 1 is remeasured at the exchange rate on that date ($0.60). Purchases made evenly throughout the year are remeasured at the average rate for the year ($0.65). Ending inventory (at FIFO cost) is purchased evenly throughout the fourth quarter of 2011 and the average exchange rate for the quarter ($0.68) is used to remeasure that component of cost of goods sold. These procedures result in Cost of Goods Sold of $1,930,500, calculated as follows:

Beginning inventory, 1/1/11	CHF	150,000	×	0.60	=	$	90,000
Plus: Purchases, 2011		3,250,000	×	0.65	=		2,112,500
Less: Ending inventory, 12/31/11		(400,000)	×	0.68	=		(272,000)
Cost of goods sold, 2011	CHF	3,000,000				$	1,930,500

The ending balances in Retained Earnings on the balance sheet and on the statement of retained earnings must reconcile with one another. Because dividends are remeasured into a U.S. dollar equivalent of $100,500 and the ending balance in Retained Earnings on the balance sheet is $181,800, net income must be $282,300.

Reconciling the amount of income reported in the statement of retained earnings and in the income statement requires a remeasurement loss of $47,000 in calculating net income. Without this remeasurement loss, the income statement, statement of retained earnings, and balance sheet are not consistent with one another.

The remeasurement loss can be calculated by considering the impact of exchange rate changes on the subsidiary's balance sheet exposure. Under the temporal method, SWISSCO's balance sheet exposure is defined by its net monetary asset or net monetary liability position. SWISSCO began 2011 with net monetary assets (cash) of CHF 350,000. During the year, however, expenditures of cash and the incurrence of liabilities caused monetary liabilities (accounts payable + long-term debt = CHF 850,000) to exceed monetary assets (cash + accounts receivable = CHF 330,000). A net monetary liability position of CHF 520,000 exists at December 31, 2011. The remeasurement loss is computed by translating the beginning net monetary asset position and subsequent changes in monetary items at appropriate exchange rates and then comparing this with the dollar value of net monetary liabilities at year-end based on the current exchange rate:

Computation of Remeasurement Loss

Net monetary assets, 1/1/11	CHF	350,000	× 0.60 =	$	210,000
Increase in monetary assets:					
Sales, 2011		4,000,000	× 0.65 =		2,600,000
Decreases in monetary assets and increases in monetary liabilities:					
Purchases, 2011		(3,250,000)	× 0.65 =		(2,112,500)
Other expenses, 2011		(220,000)	× 0.65 =		(143,000)
Income taxes, 2011		(200,000)	× 0.65 =		(130,000)
Purchase of property and equipment, 3/15/11		(1,000,000)	× 0.61 =		(610,000)
Acquisition of patent, 4/10/11		(50,000)	× 0.62 =		(31,000)
Dividends, 10/1/11		(150,000)	× 0.67 =		(100,500)
Net monetary liabilities, 12/31/11	CHF	(520,000)		$	(317,000)
Net monetary liabilities, 12/31/11 at the current exchange rate	CHF	(520,000)	× 0.70 =		(364,000)
Remeasurement loss				$	47,000

Had SWISSCO maintained its net monetary asset position of CHF 350,000 for the entire year, a $35,000 remeasurement gain would have resulted. The CHF held in cash was worth $210,000 (CHF 350,000 × $0.60) at the beginning of the year and $245,000 (CHF 350,000 × $0.70) at year-end. However, the net monetary asset position is not maintained because of changes during the year in monetary items other than the original cash balance. Indeed, a net

EXHIBIT 8.9
Remeasurement of Statement of Cash Flows—Temporal Method

		SWISSCO Statement of Cash Flows For Year Ending December 31, 2011		
		CHF	Remeasurement Rate	US$
Operating activities:				
Net income	CHF	470,000	From I/S	$ 282,300
Add: Depreciation expense		100,000	0.61 H	61,000
Amortization expense		10,000	0.62 H	6,200
Remeasurement loss			From I/S	47,000
Increase in accounts receivable		(200,000)	0.65 A	(130,000)
Increase in inventory		(250,000)	*	(182,000)
Increase in accounts payable		600,000	0.65 A	390,000
Net cash from operations		730,000		474,500
Investing activities:				
Purchase of property and equipment		(1,000,000)	0.61 H	(610,000)
Acquisition of patent		(50,000)	0.62 H	(31,000)
Net cash from investing activities		(1,050,000)		(641,000)
Financing activities:				
Proceeds from long-term debt		250,000	0.61 H	152,500
Payment of dividends		(150,000)	0.67 H	(100,500)
Net cash from financing activities		100,000		52,000
Decrease in cash		(220,000)		(114,500)
Effect of exchange rate changes on cash			To balance	(4,500)
Cash at December 31, 2010	CHF	350,000	0.6 H	$ 210,000
Cash at December 31, 2011	CHF	130,000	0.7 C	$ 91,000

*In remeasuring cost of goods sold earlier, beginning inventory was remeasured as $90,000 and ending inventory was remeasured as $272,000: an increase of $182,000.

monetary liability position arises. The foreign currency *appreciation* coupled with an increase in *net monetary liabilities* generates a *remeasurement loss* for the year.

Remeasurement of the Statement of Cash Flows

In remeasuring the statement of cash flows (shown in Exhibit 8.9), the U.S. dollar value for net income comes directly from the remeasured income statement. Depreciation and amortization are remeasured at the rates used in the income statement, and the remeasurement loss is added back to net income because it is a noncash item. The increases in accounts receivable and accounts payable relate to sales and purchases and therefore are remeasured at the average rate. The U.S. dollar value for the increase in inventory is determined by referring to the remeasurement of the cost of goods sold.

The resulting U.S. dollar amount of "net cash from operations" ($474,500) is exactly the same as when the current rate method was used in translation. In addition, the investing and financing activities are translated in the same manner under both methods. This makes sense; the amount of cash inflows and outflows is a matter of fact and is not affected by the particular translation methodology employed.

Nonlocal Currency Balances

One additional issue related to the translation of foreign currency financial statements needs to be considered. If any of the accounts of the Swiss subsidiary are denominated in a currency other than the Swiss franc, those balances would first have to be restated into francs in accordance with the rules discussed in Chapter 7. Both the foreign currency balance and any related foreign exchange gain or loss would then be translated (or remeasured) into U.S. dollars. For example, a note payable of 10,000 British pounds first would be remeasured into Swiss francs before the translation process could commence.

COMPARISON OF THE RESULTS FROM APPLYING THE TWO DIFFERENT METHODS

LO1

Explain the theoretical under-pinnings and the limitations of the current rate and temporal methods.

The determination of the foreign subsidiary's functional currency (and the use of different translation methods) can have a significant impact on consolidated financial statements. The following chart shows differences for SWISSCO in several key items under the two different translation methods:

| Item | Translation Method | | Difference |
	Current Rate	Temporal	
Net income	$ 305,500	$ 282,300	+ 8.2%
Total assets	1,169,000	1,076,800	+ 8.6
Total equity	574,000	481,800	+ 19.1
Return on equity	53.2%	58.6%	− 9.2

In this illustration, if the Swiss franc is determined to be SWISSCO's functional currency (and the current rate method is applied), net income reported in the consolidated income statement would be 8.2 percent more than if the U.S. dollar is the functional currency (and the temporal method is applied). In addition, total assets would be 8.6 percent more and total equity would be 19.1 percent more using the current rate method. Because of the larger amount of equity, return on equity using the current rate method is 9.2 percent less.

Note that the current rate method does not always result in higher net income and a higher amount of equity than the temporal method. For example, had SWISSCO maintained its net monetary asset position, it would have computed a remeasurement gain under the temporal method leading to higher income than under the current rate method. Moreover, if the Swiss franc had depreciated during 2011, the temporal method would have resulted in higher net income.

The important point is that determining the functional currency and resulting translation method can have a significant impact on the amounts a parent company reports in its consolidated financial statements. The appropriate determination of the functional currency is an important issue.

> "Within rather broad parameters," says Peat, Marwick, Mitchell partner James Weir, choosing the functional currency is basically a management call. So much so, in fact, that Texaco, Occidental, and Unocal settled on the dollar as the functional currency for most of their foreign operations, whereas competitors Exxon, Mobil, and Amoco chose primarily the local currencies as the functional currencies for their foreign businesses.[9]

Different functional currencies selected by different companies in the same industry could have a significant impact on the comparability of financial statements within that industry. Indeed, one concern that those FASB members dissenting on the current standard raised was that the functional currency rules might not result in similar accounting for similar situations.

In addition to differences in amounts reported in the consolidated financial statements, the results of the SWISSCO illustration demonstrate several conceptual differences between the two translation methods.

Underlying Valuation Method

Using the temporal method, SWISSCO remeasured its property and equipment as follows:

$$\text{Property and equipment CHF } 1,000,000 \times \$0.61 \text{ H} = \$610,000$$

By multiplying the historical cost in Swiss francs by the historical exchange rate, $610,000 represents the U.S. dollar–equivalent historical cost of this asset. It is the amount of U.S. dollars that the parent company would have had to pay to acquire assets having a cost of CHF 1,000,000 when the exchange rate was $0.61 per Swiss franc.

---

[9] John Heins, "Plenty of Opportunity to Fool Around," *Forbes*, June 2, 1986, p. 139.

Property and equipment were translated under the current rate method as follows:

Property and equipment CHF 1,000,000 $\times$ $0.70 C = $700,000

The $700,000 amount is not readily interpretable. It does not represent the U.S. dollar equivalent historical cost of the asset; that amount is $610,000. Nor does it represent the U.S. dollar equivalent current cost of the asset because CHF 1,000,000 is not the current cost of the asset in Switzerland. The $700,000 amount is simply the product of multiplying two numbers together!

Underlying Relationships

The following table reports the values for selected financial ratios calculated from the original foreign currency financial statements and from the U.S. dollar–translated statements using the two different translation methods:

Ratio	CHF	US$ Temporal	US$ Current Rate
Current ratio (current assets/current liabilities)	1.22	1.20	1.22
Debt/equity ratio (total liabilities/total equities)	1.04	1.23	1.04
Gross profit ratio (gross profit/sales)	25%	25.8%	25%
Return on equity (net income/total equity)	57.3%	58.6%	53.2%

The temporal method distorts all of the ratios measured in the foreign currency. The subsidiary appears to be less liquid, more highly leveraged, and more profitable than it does in Swiss franc terms.

The current rate method maintains the first three ratios but distorts return on equity. The distortion occurs because income was translated at the average-for-the-period exchange rate whereas total equity was translated at the current exchange rate. In fact, the use of the average rate for income and the current rate for assets and liabilities distorts any ratio combining balance sheet and income statement figures, such as turnover ratios.

Conceptually, when the current rate method is employed, income statement items can be translated at either the average or the current exchange rate. U.S. GAAP requires using the average exchange rate. In this illustration, if revenues and expenses had been translated at the current exchange rate, net income would have been $329,000 (CHF 470,000 $\times$ $0.70), and the return on equity would have been 57.3 percent ($329,000/$574,000), exactly the amount reflected in the Swiss franc financial statements.

HEDGING BALANCE SHEET EXPOSURE

LO5

Understand the rationale for hedging a net investment in a foreign operation and describe the treatment of gains and losses on hedges used for this purpose.

When the U.S. dollar is the functional currency or when a foreign operation is located in a highly inflationary economy, remeasurement gains and losses are reported in the consolidated income statement. Management of U.S. multinational companies could wish to avoid reporting remeasurement losses in net income because of the perceived negative impact this has on the company's stock price. Likewise, when the foreign currency is the functional currency, management could wish to avoid negative translation adjustments because of the adverse impact on the debt to equity ratio.

> More and more corporations are hedging their translation exposure—the recorded value of international assets such as plant, equipment and inventory—to prevent gyrations in their quarterly accounts. Though technically only paper gains or losses, translation adjustments can play havoc with balance-sheet ratios and can spook analysts and creditors alike.[10]

---

[10] Ida Picker, "Indecent Exposure," *Institutional Investor,* September 1991, p. 82.

Translation adjustments and remeasurement gains or losses are functions of two factors: (1) changes in the exchange rate and (2) balance sheet exposure. Although a company can do little if anything to influence exchange rates, parent companies can use several techniques to hedge the balance sheet exposures of their foreign operations.

Parent companies can hedge balance sheet exposure by using a derivative financial instrument, such as a forward contract or foreign currency option, or a nonderivative hedging instrument, such as a foreign currency borrowing. To illustrate, assume that SWISSCO's functional currency is the Swiss franc; this creates a net asset balance sheet exposure. USCO believes that the Swiss franc will depreciate, thereby generating a negative translation adjustment that will reduce consolidated stockholders' equity. USCO could hedge this balance sheet exposure by borrowing Swiss francs for a period of time, thus creating an offsetting Swiss franc liability exposure. As the Swiss franc depreciates, the U.S. dollar value of the Swiss franc borrowing decreases and USCO will be able to repay the Swiss franc borrowing using fewer U.S. dollars. This generates a foreign exchange gain, which offsets the negative translation adjustment arising from the translation of SWISSCO's financial statements. As an alternative to the Swiss franc borrowing, USCO might have acquired a Swiss franc put option to hedge its balance sheet exposure. A put option gives the company the right to sell Swiss francs at a predetermined strike price. As the Swiss franc depreciates, the fair value of the put option should increase, resulting in a gain. Current standards provide that the gain or loss on a hedging instrument designated and effective as a *hedge of the net investment in a foreign operation* should be reported in the same manner as the translation adjustment being hedged. Thus, the foreign exchange gain on the Swiss franc borrowing or the gain on the foreign currency option would be included in Accumulated Other Comprehensive Income along with the negative translation adjustment arising from the translation of SWISSCO's financial statements. In the event that the gain on the hedging instrument is larger than the translation adjustment being hedged, the excess is taken to net income.

The paradox of hedging a balance sheet exposure is that in the process of avoiding an unrealized translation adjustment, realized foreign exchange gains and losses can result. Consider USCO's foreign currency borrowing to hedge a Swiss franc balance sheet exposure. At the initiation of the loan, USCO converts the borrowed Swiss francs into U.S. dollars at the spot exchange rate. When the liability matures, USCO purchases Swiss francs at the spot rate prevailing at that date to repay the loan. The change in exchange rate over the life of the loan generates a *realized* gain or loss. If the Swiss franc depreciates as expected, a realized foreign exchange gain that offsets the negative translation adjustment in Accumulated Other Comprehensive Income results. Although the net effect on Accumulated Other Comprehensive Income is zero, a net increase in cash occurs as a result of the hedge. If the Swiss franc unexpectedly appreciates, a realized foreign exchange loss occurs. This is offset by a positive translation adjustment in Accumulated Other Comprehensive Income, but a net decrease in cash exists. While a hedge of a net investment in a foreign operation eliminates the possibility of reporting a negative translation adjustment in Accumulated Other Comprehensive Income, gains and losses realized in cash can result.

DISCLOSURES RELATED TO TRANSLATION

Current standards require firms to present an analysis of the change in the cumulative translation adjustment account in the financial statements or notes thereto. Many companies comply with this requirement by including an Accumulated Other Comprehensive Income column in their statement of stockholders' equity. Other companies provide separate disclosure in the notes; see Exhibit 8.10 for an example of this disclosure for Sonoco Products Company.

An analysis of the Foreign Currency Translation Adjustments column indicates a positive translation adjustment of $95,449 in 2007 and a negative translation adjustment of $141,556 in 2008. From the signs of these adjustments, one can infer that, in aggregate, the foreign currencies in which Sonoco has operations appreciated against the U.S. dollar in 2007 and depreciated against the U.S. dollar in 2008.

EXHIBIT 8.10
Sonoco Products Company, 2008 Annual Report

18 Accumulated Other Comprehensive Loss

The following table summarizes the components of accumulated other comprehensive loss and the changes in accumulated comprehensive loss, net of tax as applicable, for the years ended December 31, 2008, and 2007:

	Foreign Currency Translation Adjustments	Defined Benefit Plans	Derivative Financial Instruments	Accumulated Other Comprehensive Loss
Balance at December 31, 2006	$ (22,630)	$(237,616)	$ (2,059)	$(262,305)
Change during 2007	95,449	58,958	524	154,931
Balance at December 31, 2007	72,819	(178,658)	(1,535)	(107,374)
Change during 2008	(141,556)	(194,149)	(11,600)	(347,305)
Balance at December 31, 2008	$ (68,737)	$(372,807)	$(13,135)	$(454,679)

Although not specifically required to do so, many companies describe their translation procedures in their "summary of significant accounting policies" in the notes to the financial statements. The following excerpt from International Business Machines Corporation's 2008 annual report illustrates this type of disclosure:

Translation of Non-U.S. Currency Amounts—Assets and liabilities of non-U.S. subsidiaries that have a local functional currency are translated to U.S. dollars at year-end exchange rates. Translation adjustments are recorded in Accumulated gains and losses not affecting retained earnings in the Consolidated Statement of Stockholders' Equity. Income and expense items are translated at weighted-average rates of exchange prevailing during the year.

Inventories, plant, rental machines and other properties—net, and other non-monetary assets and liabilities of non-U.S. subsidiaries and branches that operate in U.S. dollars are translated at approximate exchange rates prevailing when the company acquired the assets or liabilities. All other assets and liabilities denominated in a currency other than U.S. dollars are translated at year-end exchange rates with the transaction gain or loss recognized in other (income) and expense. Cost of sales and depreciation are translated at historical exchange rates. All other income and expense items are translated at the weighted-average rates of exchange prevailing during the year. These translation gains and losses are included in net income for the period in which exchange rates change.

CONSOLIDATION OF A FOREIGN SUBSIDIARY

LO6

Prepare a consolidation worksheet for a parent and its foreign subsidiary.

This section of the chapter demonstrates the procedures used to consolidate a foreign subsidiary's financial statements with those of its parent. The treatment of the excess of fair value over book value requires special attention. As an item denominated in foreign currency, translation of the excess gives rise to a translation adjustment recorded on the consolidation worksheet.

On January 1, 2010, Altman, Inc., a U.S.-based manufacturing firm, acquired 100 percent of Bradford Ltd. in Great Britain. Altman paid £25,000,000, which was equal to Bradford's fair value. Bradford's balance sheet on January 1, 2010, was as follows:

Cash	£ 925,000	Accounts payable	£ 675,000
Accounts receivable	1,400,000	Long-term debt	4,000,000
Inventory	6,050,000	Common stock	20,000,000
Plant and equipment (net)	19,000,000	Retained earnings	2,700,000
Total	£27,375,000	Total	£27,375,000

The £2,300,000 excess of fair value over book value resulted from undervalued land (part of plant and equipment) and therefore is not subject to amortization. Altman uses the equity method to account for its investment in Bradford.

On December 31, 2011, two years after the acquisition date, Bradford submitted the following trial balance for consolidation (credit balances are in parentheses):

Cash	£ 600,000
Accounts Receivable	2,700,000
Inventory	9,000,000
Plant and Equipment (net)	17,200,000
Accounts Payable	(500,000)
Long-Term Debt	(2,000,000)
Common Stock	(20,000,000)
Retained Earnings, 1/1/11	(3,800,000)
Sales	(13,900,000)
Cost of Goods Sold	8,100,000
Depreciation Expense	900,000
Other Expenses	950,000
Dividends Declared, 6/30/11	750,000
	£ –0–

Although Bradford generated net income of £1,100,000 in 2010, it declared or paid no dividends that year. Other than the payment of dividends in 2011, no intra-entity transactions occurred between the two affiliates. Altman has determined the British pound to be Bradford's functional currency.

Relevant exchange rates for the British pound were as follows:

	January 1	June 30	December 31	Average
2010	$1.51	–0–	$1.56	$1.54
2011	1.56	$1.58	1.53	1.55

Translation of Foreign Subsidiary Trial Balance

The initial step in consolidating the foreign subsidiary is to translate its trial balance from British pounds into U.S. dollars. Because the British pound has been determined to be the functional currency, this translation uses the current rate method. The historical exchange rate for translating Bradford's common stock and January 1, 2010, retained earnings is the exchange rate that existed at the acquisition date—$1.51.

	British Pounds	Rate	U.S. Dollars
Cash	£ 600,000	1.53 C	$ 918,000
Accounts Receivable	2,700,000	1.53 C	4,131,000
Inventory	9,000,000	1.53 C	13,770,000
Plant and Equipment (net)	17,200,000	1.53 C	26,316,000
Accounts Payable	(500,000)	1.53 C	(765,000)
Long-Term Debt	(2,000,000)	1.53 C	(3,060,000)
Common Stock	(20,000,000)	1.51 H	(30,200,000)
Retained Earnings, 1/1/11	(3,800,000)	*	(5,771,000)
Sales	(13,900,000)	1.55 A	(21,545,000)
Cost of Goods Sold	8,100,000	1.55 A	12,555,000
Depreciation Expense	900,000	1.55 A	1,395,000
Other Expenses	950,000	1.55 A	1,472,500
Dividends Declared, 6/30/11	750,000	1.58 H	1,185,000
Cumulative translation adjustment			(401,500)
	£ –0–		$ –0–
*Retained Earnings, 1/1/10	£2,700,000	1.51 H	$4,077,000
Net Income, 2010	1,100,000	1.54 A	1,694,000
Retained Earnings, 12/31/10	£3,800,000		$5,771,000

A positive (credit balance) cumulative translation adjustment is required to make the trial balance actually balance. The cumulative translation adjustment is calculated as follows:

Net assets, 1/1/10	£22,700,000	1.51 H	$34,277,000
Change in net assets, 2010			
Net income, 2010	1,100,000	1.54 A	1,694,000
Net assets, 12/31/10	£23,800,000		$35,971,000

Net assets, 12/31/10, at			
current exchange rate	£23,800,000	1.56 C	37,128,000

Translation adjustment,

2010 (positive)				$ (1,157,000)
Net assets, 1/1/11	£23,800,000	1.56 H	$37,128,000	
Change in net assets, 2011				
Net income, 2011	3,950,000	1.55 A	6,122,500	
Dividends 6/30/11	(750,000)	1.58 H	(1,185,000)	
Net assets, 12/31/11	£27,000,000		$42,065,500	

Net assets, 12/31/11, at			
current exchange rate	£27,000,000	1.53 C	41,310,000

Translation adjustment, 2011 (negative)	755,500

Cumulative translation adjustment,	
12/31/11 (positive)	$ (401,500)

The translation adjustment in 2010 is positive because the British pound appreciated against the U.S. dollar that year; the translation adjustment in 2011 is negative because the British pound depreciated.

Determination of Balance in Investment Account—Equity Method

The original value of the investment in Bradford, the net income earned by Bradford, and the dividends paid by Bradford are all denominated in British pounds. Relevant amounts must be translated from pounds into U.S. dollars so Altman can account for its investment in Bradford under the equity method. In addition, the translation adjustment calculated each year is included in the Investment in Bradford account to update the foreign currency investment to its U.S. dollar equivalent. The counterpart is recorded as a translation adjustment on Altman's books:

12/31/10	Investment in Bradford	$1,157,000	
	Cumulative Translation Adjustment		$1,157,000
	To record the positive translation adjustment related to the investment in a British subsidiary when the British pound appreciated.		
12/31/11	Cumulative Translation Adjustment	$ 755,500	
	Investment in Bradford		$ 755,500
	To record the negative translation adjustment related to the investment in a British subsidiary when the British pound depreciated.		

As a result of these two journal entries, Altman has a Cumulative Translation Adjustment of $401,500 on its separate balance sheet.

The carrying value of the investment account in U.S. dollar terms at December 31, 2011, is determined as follows:

Investment in Bradford	British Pounds	Exchange Rate	U.S. Dollars
Original value	£25,000,000	1.51 H	$37,750,000
Bradford net income, 2010	1,100,000	1.54 A	1,694,000
Translation adjustment, 2010			1,157,000
Balance, 12/31/10	£26,100,000		$40,601,000
Bradford net income, 2011	3,950,000	1.55 A	6,122,500
Bradford dividends, 6/30/11	(750,000)	1.58 H	(1,185,000)
Translation adjustment, 2011			(755,500)
Balance, 12/31/11	£29,300,000		$44,783,000

In addition to Altman's $44,783,000 investment in Bradford, it has equity income on its December 31, 2011, trial balance in the amount of $6,122,500.

Consolidation Worksheet

Once the subsidiary's trial balance has been translated into dollars and the carrying value of the investment is known, the consolidation worksheet at December 31, 2011, can be prepared. As is true in the consolidation of domestic subsidiaries, the investment account, the subsidiary's equity accounts, and the effects of intra-entity transactions must be eliminated. The excess of fair value over book value at the date of acquisition also must be allocated to the appropriate accounts (in this example, plant and equipment).

Unique to the consolidation of foreign subsidiaries is the fact that the excess of fair value over book value, denominated in foreign currency, also must be translated into the parent's reporting currency. When the foreign currency is the functional currency, the excess is translated at the current exchange rate with a resulting translation adjustment. The excess is not carried on either the parent's or the subsidiary's books but is recorded only in the consolidation worksheet. *Neither the parent nor the subsidiary has recognized the translation adjustment related to the excess, and it must be recorded in the consolidation worksheet.* Exhibit 8.11 presents the consolidation worksheet of Altman and Bradford at December 31, 2011.

EXHIBIT 8.11   Consolidation Worksheet—Parent and Foreign Subsidiary

ALTMAN, INC., AND BRADFORD LTD.
Consolidation Worksheet
For Year Ending December 31, 2011

Accounts	Altman	Bradford	Consolidated Entries Debits	Consolidated Entries Credits	Consolidated Totals
Income Statement					
Sales	$ (32,489,000)	$(21,545,000)			$ (54,034,000)
Cost of goods sold	16,000,000	12,555,000			28,555,000
Depreciation expense	9,700,000	1,395,000			11,095,000
Other expenses	2,900,000	1,472,500			4,372,500
Equity income	(6,122,500)		(I) 6,122,500		–0–
Net income	$ (10,011,500)	$ (6,122,500)			$ (10,011,500)
Statement of Retained Earnings					
Retained earnings, 1/1/11	$ (25,194,000)	$ (5,771,000)	(S) 5,771,000		$ (25,194,000)
Net income (above)	(10,011,500)	(6,122,500)			(10,011,500)
Dividends paid	1,500,000	1,185,000		(D) 1,185,000	1,500,000
Retained earnings, 12/31/11	$ (33,705,500)	$(10,708,500)			$ (33,705,500)
Balance Sheet					
Cash	$ 3,649,800	$ 918,000			$ 4,567,800
Accounts receivable	3,100,000	4,131,000			7,231,000
Inventory	11,410,000	13,770,000			25,180,000
Investment in Bradford	44,783,000			(S) 35,971,000	–0–
				(A) 3,473,000	
			(D) 1,185,000	(I) 6,122,500	
				(T) 401,500	
Plant and equipment (net)	39,500,000	26,316,000	(A) 3,473,000		69,335,000
			(E) 46,000		
Total assets	$ 102,442,800	$ 45,135,000			$ 106,313,800
Accounts payable	$ (2,500,000)	$ (765,000)			$ (3,265,000)
Long-term debt	(22,728,800)	(3,060,000)			(25,788,800)
Common stock	(43,107,000)	(30,200,000)	(S) 30,200,000		(43,107,000)
Retained earnings, 12/31/11 (above)	(33,705,500)	(10,708,500)			(33,705,500)
Cumulative translation adjustment	(401,500)	(401,500)	(T) 401,500	(E) 46,000	(447,500)
Total liabilities and equities	$(102,422,800)	$(45,135,000)	$47,199,000	$47,199,000	$(106,313,800)

Explanation of Consolidation Entries

S—Eliminates the subsidiary's stockholders' equity accounts as of the beginning of the current year along with the equivalent book value component within the original value of the Investment in Bradford account.

A—Allocates the excess of fair value over book value at the date of acquisition to land (plant and equipment) and eliminates that amount within the original value of the Investment in Bradford account.

I—Eliminates the amount of equity income recognized by the parent in the current year and included in the Investment in Bradford account under the equity method.

D—Eliminates the subsidiary's dividend payment that was a reduction in the Investment in Bradford account under the equity method.

T—Eliminates the cumulative translation adjustment included in the Investment in Bradford account under the equity method and eliminates the cumulative translation adjustment carried on the parent's books.

E—Revalues the excess of fair value over book value for the change in exchange rate since the date of acquisition with the counterpart recognized as an increase in the consolidated cumulative translation adjustment. The revaluation is calculated as follows:

Excess of Fair Value over Book Value

U.S. dollar equivalent at 12/31/11	£2,300,000 × $1.53	=	$3,519,000
U.S. dollar equivalent at 1/1/10	2,300,000 × $1.51	=	3,473,000
Cumulative translation adjustment related to excess, 12/31/11			$ 46,000

IFRS—TRANSLATION OF FOREIGN CURRENCY FINANCIAL STATEMENTS

IAS 21, "The Effects of Changes in Foreign Exchange Rates," provides guidance in IFRS with respect to the translation of foreign currency financial statements. *IAS 21* generally follows the functional currency approach introduced by the FASB. Under *IAS 21,* as is true under U.S. GAAP, a foreign subsidiary's financial statements are translated using the current rate method when a foreign currency is the functional currency and using the temporal method when the parent company's currency is the functional currency. Significant differences between IFRS and U.S. GAAP relate to (*a*) the hierarchy of factors used to determine the functional currency and (*b*) the method used to translate the foreign currency statements of a subsidiary located in a hyperinflationary country.

Although stated differently, the factors to be considered in determining the functional currency of a foreign subsidiary in *IAS 21* generally are consistent with U.S. GAAP functional currency indicators. Specifically, *IAS 21* indicates that the *primary* factors to be considered are:

1. The currency that mainly influences sales price.
2. The currency of the country whose competitive forces and regulations mainly determine sales price.
3. The currency that mainly influences labor, material, and other costs of providing goods and services.

Other factors to be considered are:

1. The currency in which funds from financing activities are generated.
2. The currency in which receipts from operating activities are retained.
3. Whether the foreign operation carries out its activities as an extension of the parent or with a significant degree of autonomy.
4. The volume of transactions with the parent.
5. Whether cash flows generated by the foreign operation directly affect the cash flows of the parent.
6. Whether cash flows generated by the foreign operation are sufficient to service its debt.

IAS 21 states that when the above indicators are mixed and the functional currency is not obvious, the parent must give priority to the primary indicators in determining the foreign entity's functional currency.

As noted earlier, U.S. GAAP is silent with respect to weights to be assigned to various indicators to determine the functional currency and there is no hierarchy provided. Because of this difference in the functional currency determination process, it is possible that a foreign subsidiary could be determined to have a functional currency under IFRS that would be different from the functional currency determined under U.S. GAAP.

Under *IAS 21,* the financial statements of a foreign subsidiary located in a hyperinflationary economy are translated into the parent's currency using a two-step process. First, the financial statements are restated for local inflation in accordance with *IAS 29,* "Financial Reporting in Hyperinflationary Economies." Second, each financial statement line item, which has now been restated for local inflation, is translated using the current exchange rate. In effect, neither the temporal method nor the current rate method is used when the subsidiary is located in a country experiencing hyperinflation. Because all balance sheet accounts, including stockholders' equity, are translated at the current exchange rate, a translation adjustment does not exist. Unlike U.S. GAAP, IFRS does not provide a bright-line threshold to identify a hyperinflationary economy. Instead, *IAS 29* provides a list of characteristics that indicate hyperinflation, including (*a*) the general population prefers to keep its wealth in a relatively stable foreign currency; (*b*) interest rates, wages, and other prices are linked to a price index; and (*c*) the cumulative rate of inflation over three years is approaching, or exceeds, 100 percent. As noted earlier in this chapter, under current U.S. GAAP, the financial statements of a foreign subsidiary located in a highly inflationary economy must be translated using the temporal method, and high inflation is defined as a cumulative three-year inflation of 100 percent or more.

As noted in Chapter 7, there is considerable similarity between IFRS and U.S. GAAP with respect to the accounting for derivative financial instruments used to hedge foreign exchange risk. Similar to U.S. GAAP, *IAS 39* also allows hedge accounting for hedges of net investments in a foreign operation. The gain or loss on the hedging instrument is recognized in Accumulated Other Comprehensive Income (AOCI) along with the translation adjustment that is being hedged. Under both IFRS and U.S. GAAP, the cumulative translation adjustment and cumulative net gain or loss on the net investment hedge are transferred from AOCI to net income when the foreign subsidiary is sold or otherwise disposed of.

Summary

1. Because many companies have significant financial involvement in foreign countries, the process by which foreign currency financial statements are translated into U.S. dollars has special accounting importance. The two major issues related to the translation process are (1) which method to use and (2) where to report the resulting translation adjustment in the consolidated financial statements.

2. Translation methods differ on the basis of which accounts are translated at the current exchange rate and which are translated at historical rates. Accounts translated at the current exchange rate are exposed to translation adjustment. Different translation methods give rise to different concepts of balance sheet exposure and translation adjustments of differing signs and magnitude.

3. The temporal method translates assets carried at current value (cash, marketable securities, receivables) and liabilities at the current exchange rate. This method translates assets carried at historical cost and stockholders' equity at historical exchange rates. When liabilities are more than the sum of cash, marketable securities, and receivables, a net liability balance sheet exposure exists. Foreign currency appreciation results in a negative translation adjustment (remeasurement loss). Foreign currency depreciation results in a positive translation adjustment (remeasurement gain). By translating assets carried at historical cost at historical exchange rates, the temporal method maintains the underlying valuation method used by the foreign operation but distorts relationships in the foreign currency financial statements.

4. The current rate method translates all assets and liabilities at the current exchange rate, giving rise to a net asset balance sheet exposure. Foreign currency appreciation results in a positive translation adjustment. Foreign currency depreciation results in a negative translation adjustment. By translating assets carried at historical cost at the current exchange rate, the current rate method maintains relationships in the foreign currency financial statements but distorts the underlying valuation method used by the foreign operation.

5. Current U.S. accounting procedures require two separate procedures for translating foreign currency financial statements into the parent's reporting currency. *Translation* through use of the current rate

method is appropriate when the foreign operation's functional currency is a foreign currency. In this case, the translation adjustment is reported in Accumulated Other Comprehensive Income and reflected on the balance sheet as a separate component of stockholders' equity. *Remeasurement* by using the temporal method is appropriate when the operation's functional currency is the U.S. dollar. Remeasurement also is applied when the operation is in a country with a highly inflationary economy. In these situations, the translation adjustment is treated as a remeasurement gain or loss in net income.

6. Some companies hedge their balance sheet exposures to avoid reporting remeasurement losses in net income and/or negative translation adjustments in Accumulated Other Comprehensive Income. Gains and losses on derivative or nonderivative instruments used to hedge net investments in foreign operations are reported in the same manner as the translation adjustment being hedged.

7. IFRS and U.S. GAAP have broadly similar rules with regard to the translation of foreign currency financial statements. Differences exist with respect to the determination of functional currency, with *IAS 21* establishing a hierarchy of functional currency indicators, and in translating financial statements of foreign entities located in high inflation countries. For these entities, *IAS 21* requires financial statements to first be restated for local inflation and then translated into the parent's currency using the current exchange rate for all financial statement items.

Comprehensive Illustration

PROBLEM

(*Estimated Time: 55 to 65 Minutes*) Arlington Company is a U.S.-based organization with numerous foreign subsidiaries. As a preliminary step in preparing consolidated financial statements for 2011, it must translate the financial information from each foreign operation into its reporting currency, the U.S. dollar.

Arlington owns a Swedish subsidiary that has been in business for several years. On December 31, 2010, this entity's balance sheet was translated from Swedish kroner (SEK) (its functional currency) into U.S. dollars as prescribed by U.S. GAAP. Equity accounts at that date follow (all credit balances):

Common stock	SEK 110,000	=	$21,000
Retained earnings	194,800	=	36,100
Cumulative translation adjustment			3,860

At the end of 2011, the Swedish subsidiary produced the following trial balance. These figures include all of the entity's transactions for the year except for the results of several transactions related to sales made to a Chinese customer. A separate ledger has been maintained for these transactions denominated in Chinese renminbi (RMB). This ledger follows the company's trial balance.

Trial Balance—Swedish Subsidiary
December 31, 2011

	Debit	Credit
Cash	SEK 41,000	
Accounts Receivable	126,000	
Inventory	128,000	
Land	160,000	
Fixed Assets	228,000	
Accumulated Depreciation		SEK 98,100
Accounts Payable		39,000
Notes Payable		56,000
Bonds Payable		125,000
Common Stock		110,000
Retained Earnings, 1/1/11		194,800
Sales		350,000
Cost of Goods Sold	165,000	
Depreciation Expense	10,900	
Salary Expense	36,000	
Rent Expense	12,000	
Other Expenses	41,000	
Dividends Paid, 7/1/11	25,000	
Totals	SEK 972,900	SEK 972,900

Ledger—Transactions in Chinese Renminbi
December 31, 2011

	Debit	Credit
Cash	RMB 10,000	
Accounts Receivable	28,000	
Fixed Assets	20,000	
Accumulated Depreciation		RMB 4,000
Notes Payable		15,000
Sales		44,000
Depreciation Expense	4,000	
Interest Expense	1,000	
Totals	RMB 63,000	RMB 63,000

Additional Information

- The Swedish subsidiary began selling to the Chinese customer at the beginning of the current year. At that time, it borrowed 20,000 RMB to acquire a truck for delivery purposes. It paid one-fourth of that debt before the end of the year. The subsidiary made sales to China evenly during the period.
- The U.S. dollar exchange rates for 1 SEK are as follows:

January 1, 2011	$0.200 = 1.00 SEK
Weighted average rate for 2011	0.192 = 1.00
July 1, 2011	0.190 = 1.00
December 31, 2011	0.182 = 1.00

- The exchange rates applicable for the remeasurement of 1 RMB into Swedish kroner are as follows:

January 1, 2011	1.25 SEK = 1.00 RMB
Weighted average rate for 2011	1.16 = 1.00
December 1, 2011	1.10 = 1.00
December 31, 2011	1.04 = 1.00

- The Swedish subsidiary expended SEK 10,000 during the year on development activities. In accordance with IFRS, this cost has been capitalized within the Fixed Assets account. This expenditure had no effect on the depreciation recognized for the year.

Required

Prepare financial statements for the year ending December 31, 2011, for the Swedish subsidiary. Translate these statements into U.S. dollars in accordance with U.S. accounting standards to facilitate the preparation of consolidated statements. The Swedish krona is the subsidiary's functional currency.

SOLUTION

Remeasurement of Foreign Currency Balances

A portion of the Swedish subsidiary's operating results are presently stated in Chinese renminbi. These balances must be remeasured into the functional currency, the Swedish krona, before the translation process can begin. In remeasuring these accounts using the temporal method, the krona value of the monetary assets and liabilities is determined by using the current (C) exchange rate (1.04 SEK per RMB) whereas all other accounts are remeasured at historical (H) or average (A) rates.

Remeasurement of Foreign Currency Balances

	Renminbi	Rate		Kroner
Sales	RMB 44,000	× 1.16 A	=	SEK 51,040
Interest Expense	(1,000)	× 1.16 A	=	(1,160)
Depreciation Expense	(4,000)	× 1.25 H	=	(5,000)
Income from renminbi transactions	39,000			44,880

(continued)

Remeasurement of Foreign Currency Balances (Continued)

	Renminbi	Rate			Kroner
Cash	10,000	×	1.04 C	=	10,400
Accounts Receivable	28,000	×	1.04 C	=	29,120
Fixed Assets	20,000	×	1.25 H	=	25,000
Accumulated Depreciation	(4,000)	×	1.25 H	=	(5,000)
Total assets	54,000				59,520
Notes Payable	15,000	×	1.04 C	=	15,600
Income from renminbi transactions	39,000	From above			44,880
	54,000				60,480
Remeasurement Loss					(960)
Total					59,520

Remeasurement Loss for 2011

Net monetary asset balance, 1/1/11	–0–				–0–
Increases in net monetary items:					
Operations (sales less interest expense)	RMB 43,000	×	1.16	=	SEK 49,880
Decreases in net monetary items:					
Purchased truck, 1/1/11	(20,000)	×	1.25	=	(25,000)
Net monetary assets, 12/31/11	RMB 23,000				SEK 24,880
Net monetary assets, 12/31/11, at current exchange rate	RMB 23,000	×	1.04	=	SEK 23,920
Remeasurement loss (gain)					SEK 960

The net monetary asset exposure (cash and accounts receivable > notes payable) and depreciation of the Chinese renminbi create a remeasurement loss of SEK 960.

The remeasured figures from the Chinese operation must be combined in some manner with the subsidiary's trial balance denominated in Swedish kroner. For example, the accounts can simply be added together on a worksheet. As an alternative, a year-end adjustment can be recorded in the Swedish subsidiary's accounting system to add the remeasured balances for financial reporting purposes, as follows:

12/31/11 Adjustment	Debit	Credit
Cash	10,400	
Accounts receivable	29,120	
Fixed assets	25,000	
Depreciation expense	5,000	
Interest expense	1,160	
Remeasurement loss	960	
Accumulated depreciation		5,000
Notes payable		15,600
Sales		51,040

To record in Swedish kroner the foreign currency transactions originally denominated in renminbi.

One more adjustment is necessary before translating the subsidiary's Swedish krona financial statements into the parent's reporting currency. The development costs incurred by the Swedish entity should be reclassified as an expense as required by U.S. authoritative literature. After this adjustment, the Swedish subsidiary's statements conform with U.S. GAAP.

12/31/11 Adjustment	Debit	Credit
Other expenses	10,000	
Fixed assets		10,000

To adjust fixed assets and expenses in Swedish kroner to be in compliance with U.S. GAAP.

Combining all remeasured and adjusted balances with the Swedish subsidiary's trial balance allows totals to be derived. For example, total sales for the subsidiary are SEK 401,040 (350,000 + 51,040), cash is SEK 51,400 (41,000 + 10,400), and so on. Having established all account balances in the functional currency (Swedish kroner), the subsidiary's statements now can be translated into U.S. dollars. Under the current rate method, the dollar values to be reported for income statement items are based on the average exchange rate for the current year. All assets and liabilities are translated at the current exchange rate at the balance sheet date, and equity accounts are translated at historical rates in effect at the date of accounting recognition.

Swedish Subsidiary
Income Statement for Year Ending December 31, 2011

Sales	SEK 401,040	× 0.192 A =	$ 76,999.68
Cost of goods sold	(165,000)	× 0.192 A =	(31,680.00)
Gross profit	236,040		45,319.68
Depreciation expense	(15,900)	× 0.192 A =	(3,052.80)
Salary expense	(36,000)	× 0.192 A =	(6,912.00)
Rent expense	(12,000)	× 0.192 A =	(2,304.00)
Other expenses	(51,000)	× 0.192 A =	(9,792.00)
Interest expense	(1,160)	× 0.192 A =	(222.72)
Remeasurement loss	(960)	× 0.192 A =	(184.32)
Net income	SEK 119,020		$ 22,851.84

Statement of Retained Earnings for Year Ending December 31, 2011

Retained earnings, 1/1/11	SEK 194,800	Given above	$ 36,100.00
Net income, 2011	119,020		22,851.84
Dividends paid, 7/1/11	(25,000)	× 0.190 H =	(4,750.00)
Retained earnings, 12/31/11	SEK 288,820		$ 54,201.84

Balance Sheet
December 31, 2011

Cash	SEK 51,400	× 0.182 C =	$ 9,354.80
Accounts receivable	155,120	× 0.182 C =	28,231.84
Inventory	128,000	× 0.182 C =	23,296.00
Land	160,000	× 0.182 C =	29,120.00
Fixed assets	243,000	× 0.182 C =	44,226.00
Accumulated depreciation	(103,100)	× 0.182 C =	(18,764.20)
Total	SEK 634,420		$115,464.44
Accounts payable	SEK 39,000	× 0.182 C =	$ 7,098.00
Notes payable	71,600	× 0.182 C =	13,031.20
Bonds payable	125,000	× 0.182 C =	22,750.00
Common stock	110,000	Given above	21,000.00
Retained earnings	288,820		54,201.84
Cumulative translation adjustment			(2,616.60)
Total	SEK 634,420		$115,464.44

The cumulative translation adjustment at 12/31/11 comprises the beginning balance (given) plus the translation adjustment for the current year:

Cumulative Translation Adjustment

Balance, 1/1/11	$ 3,860.00
Translation adjustment for 2011	(6,476.60)
Balance, 12/31/11	$(2,616.60)

The negative translation adjustment for 2011 of $6,476.60 is calculated by considering the effect of exchange rate changes on net assets:

Translation Adjustment for 2011

Net assets, 1/1/11	SEK 304,800*	×	0.200	=	$60,960.00
Increase in net assets:					
Net income, 2011	119,020	×	0.192	=	22,851.84
Decrease in net assets:					
Dividends, 7/1/11	(25,000)	×	0.190	=	(4,750.00)
Net assets, 12/31/11	SEK 398,820†				$79,061.84
Net assets, 12/31/11, at					
current exchange rate	SEK 398,820	×	0.182	=	72,585.24
Translation adjustment, 2011—negative					$ 6,476.60

*Indicated by January 1, 2011, stockholders' equity balances—Common Stock, SEK 110,000; Retained Earnings, SEK 194,800.
†Indicated by December 31, 2011, stockholders' equity balances—Common Stock, SEK 110,000; Retained Earnings, SEK 288,820.

Questions

1. What are the two major issues related to the translation of foreign currency financial statements?
2. What causes balance sheet (or translation) exposure to foreign exchange risk? How does balance sheet exposure compare with transaction exposure?
3. Why might a company want to hedge its balance sheet exposure? What is the paradox associated with hedging balance sheet exposure?
4. How are gains and losses on financial instruments used to hedge the net investment in a foreign operation reported in the consolidated financial statements?
5. What concept underlies the temporal method of translation? What concept underlies the current rate method of translation? How does balance sheet exposure differ under these two methods?
6. In translating the financial statements of a foreign subsidiary, why is the value assigned to retained earnings especially difficult to determine? How is this problem normally resolved?
7. What are the major procedural differences in applying the current rate and temporal methods of translation?
8. Clarke Company has a subsidiary operating in a foreign country. In relation to this subsidiary, what does the term *functional currency* mean? How is the functional currency determined?
9. A translation adjustment must be calculated and disclosed when financial statements of a foreign subsidiary are translated into the parent's reporting currency. How is this figure computed, and where is the amount reported in the financial statements?
10. The FASB put forth two theories about the underlying nature of a translation adjustment. What are these theories, and which one did the FASB consider correct?
11. When is remeasurement rather than translation appropriate? How does remeasurement differ from translation?
12. Which translation method does U.S. GAAP require for operations in highly inflationary countries? What is the rationale for mandating use of this method?
13. In what ways does IFRS differ from U.S. GAAP with respect to the translation of foreign currency financial statements?

Problems

LO2

1. What is a subsidiary's functional currency?
   - a. The parent's reporting currency.
   - b. The currency in which transactions are denominated.
   - c. The currency in which the entity primarily generates and expends cash.
   - d. Always the currency of the country in which the company has its headquarters.

LO3, LO4

2. In comparing the translation and the remeasurement process, which of the following is true?
   - a. The reported balance of inventory is normally the same under both methods.
   - b. The reported balance of equipment is normally the same under both methods.
   - c. The reported balance of sales is normally the same under both methods.
   - d. The reported balance of depreciation expense is normally the same under both methods.

LO3

3. Which of the following statements is true for the translation process (as opposed to remeasurement)?

   a. A translation adjustment can affect consolidated net income.

   b. Equipment is translated at the historical exchange rate in effect at the date of its purchase.

   c. A translation adjustment is created by the change in the relative value of a subsidiary's net assets caused by exchange rate fluctuations.

   d. A translation adjustment is created by the change in the relative value of a subsidiary's monetary assets and monetary liabilities caused by exchange rate fluctuations.

LO2, LO3

4. A subsidiary of Byner Corporation has one asset (inventory) and no liabilities. The functional currency for this subsidiary is the peso. The inventory was acquired for 100,000 pesos when the exchange rate was $0.16 = 1 peso. Consolidated statements are to be produced, and the current exchange rate is $0.19 = 1 peso. Which of the following statements is true for the consolidated financial statements?

   a. A remeasurement gain must be reported.

   b. A positive translation adjustment must be reported.

   c. A negative translation adjustment must be reported.

   d. A remeasurement loss must be reported.

LO3

5. At what rates should the following balance sheet accounts in foreign statements be translated (rather than remeasured) into U.S. dollars?

	Accumulated Depreciation—Equipment	Equipment
a.	Current	Current
b.	Current	Average for year
c.	Historical	Current
d.	Historical	Historical

Problems 6 and 7 are based on the following information.

Certain balance sheet accounts of a foreign subsidiary of Rose Company have been stated in U.S. dollars as follows:

	Stated at	
	Current Rates	Historical Rates
Accounts receivable, current	$200,000	$220,000
Accounts receivable, long term	100,000	110,000
Prepaid insurance	50,000	55,000
Goodwill	80,000	85,000
	$430,000	$470,000

LO2, LO3

6. This subsidiary's functional currency is a foreign currency. What total should Rose's balance sheet include for the preceding items?

   a. $430,000.

   b. $435,000.

   c. $440,000.

   d. $450,000.

LO2, LO4

7. This subsidiary's functional currency is the U.S. dollar. What total should Rose's balance sheet include for the preceding items?

   a. $430,000.

   b. $435,000.

   c. $440,000.

   d. $450,000.

Problems 8 and 9 are based on the following information.

A subsidiary of Salisbury, Inc., is located in a foreign country whose functional currency is the schweikart (SWK). The subsidiary acquires inventory on credit on November 1, 2010, for SWK 100,000 that is sold on January 17, 2011, for SWK 130,000. The subsidiary pays for the inventory on January 31, 2011. Currency exchange rates for 1 SWK are as follows:

November 1, 2010	$0.16 = 1 SWK
December 31, 2010	0.17 = 1
January 17, 2011	0.18 = 1
January 31, 2011	0.19 = 1
Average for 2011	0.20 = 1

LO2, LO3

8. What amount does Salisbury's consolidated balance sheet report for this inventory at December 31, 2010?
   a. $16,000.
   b. $17,000.
   c. $18,000.
   d. $19,000.

LO2, LO3

9. What amount does Salisbury's consolidated income statement report for cost of goods sold for the year ending December 31, 2011?
   a. $16,000.
   b. $17,000.
   c. $18,000.
   d. $19,000.

Problems 10 and 11 are based on the following information.

A Clarke Corporation subsidiary buys marketable equity securities and inventory on April 1, 2011, for 100,000 pesos each. It pays for both items on June 1, 2011, and they are still on hand at year-end. Inventory is carried at cost under the lower-of-cost-or-market rule. Currency exchange rates for 1 peso follow:

January 1, 2011	$0.15 = 1 peso
April 1, 2011	0.16 = 1
June 1, 2011	0.17 = 1
December 31, 2011	0.19 = 1

LO2, LO4

10. Assume that the peso is the subsidiary's functional currency. What balances does a consolidated balance sheet report as of December 31, 2011?
    a. Marketable equity securities = $16,000 and Inventory = $16,000.
    b. Marketable equity securities = $17,000 and Inventory = $17,000.
    c. Marketable equity securities = $19,000 and Inventory = $16,000.
    d. Marketable equity securities = $19,000 and Inventory = $19,000.

LO2, LO4

11. Assume that the U.S. dollar is the subsidiary's functional currency. What balances does a consolidated balance sheet report as of December 31, 2011?
    a. Marketable equity securities = $16,000 and Inventory = $16,000.
    b. Marketable equity securities = $17,000 and Inventory = $17,000.
    c. Marketable equity securities = $19,000 and Inventory = $16,000.
    d. Marketable equity securities = $19,000 and Inventory = $19,000.

LO2, LO4

12. A U.S. company's foreign subsidiary had these amounts in foreign currency units (FCU) in 2011:

Cost of goods sold	FCU 10,000,000
Ending inventory	500,000
Beginning inventory	200,000

The average exchange rate during 2011 was $0.80 = FCU 1. The beginning inventory was acquired when the exchange rate was $1.00 = FCU 1. Ending inventory was acquired when the exchange rate was $0.75 = FCU 1. The exchange rate at December 31, 2011, was $0.70 = FCU 1. Assuming that the foreign country is highly inflationary, at what amount should the foreign subsidiary's cost of goods sold be reflected in the U.S. dollar income statement?

a. $7,815,000.

b. $8,040,000.

c. $8,065,000.

d. $8,090,000.

LO3

13. Ace Corporation starts a subsidiary in a foreign country; the subsidiary has the peso as its functional currency. On January 1, Ace buys all of the subsidiary's common stock for 20,000 pesos. On April 1, the subsidiary purchases inventory for 20,000 pesos with payment made on May 1, and sells this inventory on August 1 for 30,000 pesos, which it collects on October 1. Currency exchange rates for 1 peso are as follows:

January 1	$0.15 = 1 peso
April 1	0.17 = 1
May 1	0.18 = 1
August 1	0.19 = 1
October 1	0.20 = 1
December 31	0.21 = 1

In preparing consolidated financial statements, what translation adjustment will Ace report at the end of the current year?

a. $400 positive (credit).

b. $600 positive (credit).

c. $1,400 positive (credit).

d. $1,800 positive (credit).

LO1

14. In the translated financial statements, which method of translation maintains the underlying valuation methods used in the foreign currency financial statements?

a. Current rate method; income statement translated at average exchange rate for the year.

b. Current rate method; income statement translated at exchange rate at the balance sheet date.

c. Temporal method.

d. Monetary/nonmonetary method.

LO4

15. Houston Corporation operates a branch operation in a foreign country. Although this branch deals in pesos, the U.S. dollar is viewed as its functional currency. Thus, a remeasurement is necessary to produce financial information for external reporting purposes. The branch began the year with 100,000 pesos in cash and no other assets or liabilities. However, the branch immediately used 60,000 pesos to acquire equipment. On May 1, it purchased inventory costing 30,000 pesos for cash that it sold on July 1 for 50,000 pesos cash. The branch transferred 10,000 pesos to the parent on October 1 and recorded depreciation on the equipment of 6,000 pesos for the year. Currency exchange rates for 1 peso follow:

January 1	$0.16 = 1 peso
May 1	0.18 = 1
July 1	0.20 = 1
October 1	0.21 = 1
December 31	0.22 = 1
Average for the year	0.19 = 1

What is the remeasurement gain to be recognized in the consolidated income statement?

a. $2,100.

b. $2,400.

c. $2,700.

d. $3,000.

LO4

16. Which of the following items is *not* remeasured using historical exchange rates under the temporal method?

a. Accumulated depreciation on equipment.

b. Cost of goods sold.

c. Marketable equity securities.

d. Retained earnings.

LO2

17. In accordance with U.S. generally accepted accounting principles, which translation combination is appropriate for a foreign operation whose functional currency is the U.S. dollar?

	Method	Treatment of Translation Adjustment
a.	Temporal	Other comprehensive income
b.	Temporal	Gain or loss in net income
c.	Current rate	Other comprehensive income
d.	Current rate	Gain or loss in net income

LO3

18. A foreign subsidiary's functional currency is its local currency, which has not experienced significant inflation. The weighted average exchange rate for the current year is the appropriate exchange rate for translating

	Wages Expense	Wages Payable
a.	Yes	Yes
b.	Yes	No
c.	No	Yes
d.	No	No

LO5

19. The functional currency of DeZoort, Inc.'s British subsidiary is the British pound. DeZoort borrowed pounds as a partial hedge of its investment in the subsidiary. In preparing consolidated financial statements, DeZoort's negative translation adjustment on its investment in the subsidiary exceeded its foreign exchange gain on its borrowing. How should DeZoort report the effects of the negative translation adjustment and foreign exchange gain in its consolidated financial statements?

    a. Report the translation adjustment in Other Comprehensive Income on the balance sheet and the foreign exchange gain in the income statement.

    b. Report the translation adjustment in the income statement and defer the foreign exchange gain in Other Comprehensive Income on the balance sheet.

    c. Report the translation adjustment less the foreign exchange gain in Other Comprehensive Income on the balance sheet.

    d. Report the translation adjustment less the foreign exchange gain in the income statement.

LO4

20. Gains from remeasuring a foreign subsidiary's financial statements from the local currency, which is not the functional currency, into the parent's currency should be reported as a(n)

    a. Deferred foreign exchange gain.

    b. Translation adjustment in Other Comprehensive Income.

    c. Extraordinary item, net of income taxes.

    d. Part of continuing operations.

LO3

21. The foreign currency is the functional currency for a foreign subsidiary. At what exchange rate should each of the following accounts be translated?

    a. Rent Expense.

    b. Dividends Paid.

    c. Equipment.

    d. Notes Payable.

    e. Sales.

    f. Depreciation Expense.

    g. Cash.

    h. Accumulated Depreciation.

    i. Common Stock.

LO3

22. On January 1, Dandu Corporation started a subsidiary in a foreign country. On April 1, the subsidiary purchased inventory at a cost of 120,000 local currency units (LCU). One-fourth of this inventory remained unsold at the end of the year while 40 percent of the liability from the purchase had not yet been paid. The exchange rates for $1 were as follows:

January 1	$1 = LCU 2.5
April 1	1 = 2.8
Average for the current year	1 = 2.7
December 31	1 = 3.0

What should be the December 31 Inventory and Accounts Payable balances for this foreign subsidiary as translated into U.S. dollars using the current rate method?

LO3, LO4

23. The following accounts are denominated in pesos as of December 31, 2011. For reporting purposes, these amounts need to be stated in U.S. dollars. For each balance, indicate the exchange rate that would be used if a translation is made under the current rate method. Then, again for each account, provide the exchange rate that would be necessary if a remeasurement is being made using the temporal method. The company was started in 2000. The buildings were acquired in 2002 and the patents in 2003.

	Translation	**Remeasurement**
Accounts payable		
Accounts receivable		
Accumulated depreciation		
Advertising expense		
Amortization expense (patents)		
Buildings		
Cash		
Common stock		
Depreciation expense		
Dividends paid (10/1/11)		
Notes payable—due in 2014		
Patents (net)		
Salary expense		
Sales		

Exchange rates for 1 peso are as follows:

2000	1 peso = $0.28
2002	1 = 0.26
2003	1 = 0.25
January 1, 2011	1 = 0.24
April 1, 2011	1 = 0.23
July 1, 2011	1 = 0.22
October 1, 2011	1 = 0.20
December 31, 2011	1 = 0.16
Average for 2011	1 = 0.19

LO1, LO3, LO4

24. On December 18, 2011, Stephanie Corporation acquired 100 percent of a Swiss company for 3.7 million Swiss francs (CHF), which is indicative of fair value. At the acquisition date, the exchange rate was $0.70 = CHF 1. On December 18, 2011, the fair values of the subsidiary's assets and liabilities were:

Cash	CHF 500,000
Inventory	1,000,000
Fixed assets	3,000,000
Notes payable	(800,000)

Stephanie prepares consolidated financial statements on December 31, 2011. By that date, the Swiss franc has appreciated to $0.75 = CHF 1. Because of the year-end holidays, no transactions took place prior to consolidation.

a. Determine the translation adjustment to be reported on Stephanie's December 31, 2011, consolidated balance sheet, assuming that the Swiss franc is the Swiss subsidiary's functional currency. What is the economic relevance of this translation adjustment?

b. Determine the remeasurement gain or loss to be reported in Stephanie's 2011 consolidated net income, assuming that the U.S. dollar is the functional currency. What is the economic relevance of this remeasurement gain or loss?

LO3

25. Fenwicke Company began operating a subsidiary in a foreign country on January 1, 2011, by acquiring all of its common stock for LCU 40,000, which was equal to fair value. This subsidiary immediately borrowed LCU 100,000 on a five-year note with 10 percent interest payable annually beginning on January 1, 2012. The subsidiary then purchased for LCU 140,000 a building that had a 10-year anticipated life and no salvage value and is to be depreciated using the straight-line method. The subsidiary rents the building for three years to a group of local doctors for LCU 5,000 per month. By year-end, payments totaling LCU 50,000 had been received. On October 1, LCU

4,000 was paid for a repair made on that date. The subsidiary transferred a cash dividend of LCU 5,000 back to Fenwicke on December 31, 2011. The functional currency for the subsidiary is the LCU. Currency exchange rates for 1 LCU follow:

January 1, 2011	$2.00 = LCU 1
October 1, 2011	1.85 = 1
Average for 2011	1.90 = 1
December 31, 2011	1.80 = 1

Prepare an income statement, statement of retained earnings, and balance sheet for this subsidiary in LCU and then translate these amounts into U.S. dollars.

26. Refer to the information in problem 25. Prepare a statement of cash flows in LCU for Fenwicke's foreign subsidiary and then translate these amounts into U.S. dollars.

27. Watson Company has a subsidiary in the country of Alonza where the local currency unit is the kamel (KM). On December 31, 2010, the subsidiary has the following balance sheet:

Cash	KM 16,000	Notes payable (due 2012)	KM 19,000
Inventory	10,000	Common stock	20,000
Land	4,000	Retained earnings	10,000
Building	40,000		
Accumulated depreciation	(21,000)		
	KM 49,000		KM 49,000

The subsidiary acquired the inventory on August 1, 2010, and the land and buildings in 2000. It issued the common stock in 1998. During 2011, the following transactions took place:

2011
Feb. 1	Paid 5,000 KM on the note payable.
May 1	Sold entire inventory for 15,000 KM on account.
June 1	Sold land for 5,000 KM cash.
Aug. 1	Collected all accounts receivable.
Sept. 1	Signed long-term note to receive 6,000 KM cash.
Oct. 1	Bought inventory for 12,000 KM cash.
Nov. 1	Bought land for 4,000 KM on account.
Dec. 1	Paid 3,000 KM cash dividend to parent.
Dec. 31	Recorded depreciation for the entire year of 2,000 KM.

The exchange rates for 1 KM are as follows:

1998	1 KM = $0.24
2000	1 = 0.21
August 1, 2010	1 = 0.31
December 31, 2010	1 = 0.32
February 1, 2011	1 = 0.33
May 1, 2011	1 = 0.34
June 1, 2011	1 = 0.35
August 1, 2011	1 = 0.37
September 1, 2011	1 = 0.38
October 1, 2011	1 = 0.39
November 1, 2011	1 = 0.40
December 1, 2011	1 = 0.41
December 31, 2011	1 = 0.42
Average for 2011	1 = 0.37

a. If this is a translation, what is the translation adjustment determined solely for 2011?

b. If this is a remeasurement, what is the remeasurement gain or loss determined solely for 2011?

28. Aerkion Company starts 2011 with two assets: cash of 22,000 LCU (local currency units) and land that originally cost 60,000 LCU when acquired on April 4, 2005. On May 1, 2011, Aerkion rendered services to a customer for 30,000 LCU, an amount immediately paid in cash. On October 1, 2011,

the company incurred an 18,000 LCU operating expense that was immediately paid. No other transactions occurred during the year. Currency exchange rates for 1 LCU follow:

April 4, 2005	1 LCU = $0.23
January 1, 2011	1 = 0.24
May 1, 2011	1 = 0.25
October 1, 2011	1 = 0.26
Average for 2011	1 = 0.27
December 31, 2011	1 = 0.29

  a. Assume that Aerkion is a foreign subsidiary of a U.S. multinational company that uses the U.S. dollar as its reporting currency. Assume also that the LCU is the subsidiary's functional currency. What is the translation adjustment for this subsidiary for the year 2011?

  b. Assume that Aerkion is a foreign subsidiary of a U.S. multinational company that uses the U.S. dollar as its reporting currency. Assume also that the U.S. dollar is the subsidiary's functional currency. What is the remeasurement gain or loss for 2011?

  c. Assume that Aerkion is a foreign subsidiary of a U.S. multinational company. On the December 31, 2011, balance sheet, what is the translated value of the Land account? On the December 31, 2011, balance sheet, what is the remeasured value of the Land account?

LO3, LO4

29. Lancer, Inc., starts a subsidiary in a foreign country on January 1, 2010. The following account balances for the year ending December 31, 2011, are stated in kanquo (KQ), the local currency:

Sales	KQ 200,000
Inventory (bought on 3/1/11)	100,000
Equipment (bought on 1/1/10)	80,000
Rent expense	10,000
Dividends (paid on 10/1/11)	20,000
Notes receivable (to be collected in 2014)	30,000
Accumulated depreciation—equipment	24,000
Salary payable	5,000
Depreciation expense	8,000

The following exchange rates for $1 are applicable:

January 1, 2010	13 KQ
January 1, 2011	18
March 1, 2011	19
October 1, 2011	21
December 31, 2011	22
Average for 2010	14
Average for 2011	20

Lancer is preparing account balances to produce consolidated financial statements.

  a. Assuming that the kanquo is the functional currency, what exchange rate would be used to report each of these accounts in U.S. dollar consolidated financial statements?

  b. Assuming that the U.S. dollar is the functional currency, what exchange rate would be used to report each of these accounts in U.S. dollar consolidated financial statements?

LO3, LO5

30. Board Company has a foreign subsidiary that began operations at the start of 2011 with assets of 132,000 kites (the local currency unit) and liabilities of 54,000 kites. During this initial year of operation, the subsidiary reported a profit of 26,000 kites. It distributed two dividends, each for 5,000 kites with one dividend paid on March 1 and the other on October 1. Applicable exchange rates for 1 kite follow:

January 1, 2011 (start of business)	$0.80
March 1, 2011	0.78
Weighted average rate for 2011	0.77
October 1, 2011	0.76
December 31, 2011	0.75

a. Assume that the kite is this subsidiary's functional currency. What translation adjustment would Board report for the year 2011?

b. Assume that on October 1, 2011, Board entered into a forward exchange contract to hedge the net investment in this subsidiary. On that date, Board agreed to sell 200,000 kites in three months at a forward exchange rate of $0.76/1 kite. Prepare the journal entries required by this forward contract.

c. Compute the net translation adjustment for Board to report in Accumulated Other Comprehensive Income for the year 2011 under this second set of circumstances.

LO3, LO4

31. Kingsfield starts a subsidiary operation in a foreign country on January 1, 2011. The country's currency is the kumquat (KQ). To start this business, Kingsfield invests 10,000 kumquats. Of this amount, it spends 3,000 kumquats immediately to acquire equipment. Later, on April 1, 2011, it also purchases land. All subsidiary operational activities occur at an even rate throughout the year. The currency exchange rates for the kumquat for this year follow:

January 1, 2011	$1.71
April 1, 2011	1.59
June 1, 2011	1.66
Weighted average—2011	1.64
December 31, 2011	1.62

As of December 31, 2011, the subsidiary reports the following trial balance:

	Debits	Credits
Cash	KQ 8,000	
Accounts Receivable	9,000	
Equipment	3,000	
Accumulated Depreciation		KQ 600
Land	5,000	
Accounts Payable		3,000
Notes Payable (due 2014)		5,000
Common Stock		10,000
Dividends Paid (6/1/11)	4,000	
Sales		25,000
Salary Expense	5,000	
Depreciation Expense	600	
Miscellaneous Expenses	9,000	
Totals	KQ 43,600	KQ 43,600

A corporation based in East Lansing, Michigan, Kingsfield uses the U.S. dollar as its reporting currency.

a. Assume that the subsidiary's functional currency is the kumquat. Prepare a trial balance for it in U.S. dollars so that consolidated financial statements can be prepared.

b. Assume that the subsidiary's functional currency is the U.S. dollar. Prepare a trial balance for it in U.S. dollars so that consolidated financial statements can be prepared.

LO3

32. Livingston Company is a wholly owned subsidiary of Rose Corporation. Livingston operates in a foreign country with financial statements recorded in goghs (GH), the company's functional currency. Financial statements for the year of 2011 are as follows:

Income Statement
For Year Ending December 31, 2011

Sales	GH 270,000
Cost of goods sold	(155,000)
Gross profit	115,000
Less: Operating expenses	(54,000)
Gain on sale of equipment	10,000
Net income	GH 71,000

(*continued*)

Statement of Retained Earnings
For Year Ending December 31, 2011

Retained earnings, 1/1/11	GH 216,000
Net income	71,000
Less: Dividends paid	(26,000)
Retained earnings, 12/31/11	GH 261,000

Balance Sheet
December 31, 2011

Assets

Cash	GH 44,000
Receivables	116,000
Inventory	58,000
Fixed assets (net)	339,000
Total assets	GH 557,000

Liabilities and Equities

Liabilities	GH 176,000
Common stock	120,000
Retained earnings, 12/31/11	261,000
Total liabilities and equities	GH 557,000

Additional Information

- The common stock was issued in 2004 when the exchange rate was $1.00 = 0.48 GH; fixed assets were acquired in 2005 when the rate was $1.00 = 0.50 GH.
- As of January 1, 2011, the Retained Earnings balance was translated as $395,000.
- The currency exchange rates for $1 for the current year follow:

January 1, 2011	0.60 GH
April 1, 2011	0.62
September 1, 2011	0.58
December 31, 2011	0.65
Weighted average rate for 2011	0.63

- Inventory was acquired evenly throughout the year.
- The December 31, 2010, balance sheet reported a translation adjustment with a $85,000 debit balance.
- Dividends were paid on April 1, 2011, and a piece of equipment was sold on September 1, 2011.

  Translate the foreign currency statements into the parent's reporting currency, the U.S. dollar.

LO3, LO4

33. The following account balances are for the Agee Company as of January 1, 2011, and December 31, 2011. All figures are denominated in kroner (Kr).

	January 1, 2011	December 31, 2011
Accounts payable	(18,000)	(24,000)
Accounts receivable	35,000	79,000
Accumulated depreciation—buildings	(20,000)	(25,000)
Accumulated depreciation—equipment	–0–	(5,000)
Bonds payable—due 2014	(50,000)	(50,000)
Buildings	118,000	97,000
Cash	35,000	8,000
Common stock	(70,000)	(80,000)
Depreciation expense	–0–	15,000
Dividends (10/1/11)	–0–	32,000
Equipment	–0–	30,000
Gain on sale of building	–0–	(6,000)
Rent expense	–0–	14,000
Retained earnings	(30,000)	(30,000)
Salary expense	–0–	20,000
Sales	–0–	(80,000)
Utilities expense	–0–	5,000

Additional Information

- Agee issued additional shares of common stock during the year on April 1, 2011. Common stock at January 1, 2011, was sold at the start of operations in 2004.
- It purchased buildings in 2005 and sold one building with a book value of Kr 16,000 on July 1 of the current year.
- Equipment was acquired on April 1, 2011.

Relevant exchange rates for 1 Kr were as follows:

2004	$2.40
2005	2.20
January 1, 2011	2.50
April 1, 2011	2.60
July 1, 2011	2.80
October 1, 2011	2.90
December 31, 2011	3.00
Average for 2011	2.70

   a. Assuming the U.S. dollar is the functional currency and retained earnings at January 1, 2011, was $52,600, what is the remeasurement gain or loss for 2011?

   b. Assuming the foreign currency is the functional currency and retained earnings at January 1, 2011, was $62,319, what is the translation adjustment for 2011?

LO3, LO4

34. Sendelbach Corporation is a U.S.-based organization with operations throughout the world. One of its subsidiaries is headquartered in Toronto. Although this wholly owned company operates primarily in Canada, it engages in some transactions through a branch in Mexico. Therefore, the subsidiary maintains a ledger denominated in Mexican pesos (Ps) and a general ledger in Canadian dollars (C$). As of December 31, 2011, the subsidiary is preparing financial statements in anticipation of consolidation with the U.S. parent corporation. Both ledgers for the subsidiary are as follows:

Main Operation—Canada

	Debit	Credit
Accounts payable		C$ 35,000
Accumulated depreciation		27,000
Buildings and equipment	C$167,000	
Cash	26,000	
Common stock		50,000
Cost of goods sold	203,000	
Depreciation expense	8,000	
Dividends paid, 4/1/11	28,000	
Gain on sale of equipment, 6/1/11		5,000
Inventory	98,000	
Notes payable—due in 2014		76,000
Receivables	68,000	
Retained earnings, 1/1/11		135,530
Salary expense	26,000	
Sales		312,000
Utility expense	9,000	
Branch operation	7,530	
Totals	C$640,530	C$640,530

Branch Operation—Mexico

	Debit	Credit
Accounts payable		Ps 49,000
Accumulated depreciation		19,000
Building and equipment	Ps 40,000	
Cash	59,000	
Depreciation expense	2,000	
Inventory (beginning—income statement)	23,000	
Inventory (ending—income statement)		28,000
Inventory (ending—balance sheet)	28,000	
Purchases	68,000	
Receivables	21,000	

(continued)

Salary expense	9,000	
Sales		124,000
Main office		30,000
Totals	Ps 250,000	Ps 250,000

Additional Information

- The Canadian subsidiary's functional currency is the Canadian dollar, and Sendelbach's reporting currency is the U.S. dollar. The Canadian and Mexican operations are not viewed as separate accounting entities.
- The building and equipment used in the Mexican operation were acquired in 2005 when the currency exchange rate was C$0.25 = Ps 1.
- Purchases should be assumed as having been made evenly throughout the fiscal year.
- Beginning inventory was acquired evenly throughout 2010; ending inventory was acquired evenly throughout 2011.
- The Main Office account on the Mexican records should be considered an equity account. This balance was remeasured into C$7,530 on December 31, 2011.
- Currency exchange rates for 1 Ps applicable to the Mexican operation follow:

Weighted average, 2010	C$0.30
January 1, 2011	0.32
Weighted average rate for 2011	0.34
December 31, 2011	0.35

- The December 31, 2010, consolidated balance sheet reported a cumulative translation adjustment with a $36,950 credit (positive) balance.
- The subsidiary's common stock was issued in 2004 when the exchange rate was $0.45 = C$1.
- The subsidiary's December 31, 2010, Retained Earnings balance was C$135,530, a figure that has been translated into US$70,421.
- The applicable currency exchange rates for 1 C$ for translation purposes are as follows:

January 1, 2011	US$0.70
April 1, 2011	0.69
June 1, 2011	0.68
Weighted average rate for 2011	0.67
December 31, 2011	0.65

a. Remeasure the Mexican operation's figures into Canadian dollars. (*Hint:* Back into the beginning net monetary asset or liability position.)

b. Prepare financial statements (income statement, statement of retained earnings, and balance sheet) for the Canadian subsidiary in its functional currency.

c. Translate the Canadian dollar functional currency financial statements into U.S. dollars so that Sendelbach can prepare consolidated financial statements.

LO3, LO6

eXcel

35. On January 1, 2010, Cayce Corporation acquired 100 percent of Simbel Company for consideration paid of $126,000, which was equal to fair value. Cayce is a U.S.-based company headquartered in Buffalo, New York, and Simbel is in Cairo, Egypt. Cayce accounts for its investment in Simbel under the cost method. Any excess of fair value over book value is attributable to undervalued land on Simbel's books. Simbel had no retained earnings at the date of acquisition. Following are the 2011 financial statements for the two operations. Information for Cayce is in U.S. dollars ($) and for Simbel is in Egyptian pounds (£E).

	Cayce Corporation	Simbel Company
Sales	$200,000	£E 800,000
Cost of goods sold	(93,800)	(420,000)
Salary expense	(19,000)	(74,000)
Rent expense	(7,000)	(46,000)
Other expenses	(21,000)	(59,000)
Dividend income—from Simbel	13,750	–0–
Gain on sale of fixed asset, 10/1/11	–0–	30,000
Net income	$ 72,950	£E 231,000
Retained earnings, 1/1/11	$318,000	£E 133,000
Net income	72,950	231,000
Dividends paid	(24,000)	(50,000)
Retained earnings, 12/31/11	$366,950	£E 314,000

(continued)

	Cayce Corporation	Simbel Company
Cash and receivables	$110,750	£E 146,000
Inventory	98,000	297,000
Prepaid expenses	30,000	–0–
Investment in Simbel (cost)	126,000	–0–
Fixed assets (net)	398,000	455,000
Total assets	$762,750	£E 898,000
Accounts payable	$ 60,800	£E 54,000
Notes payable—due in 2013	132,000	140,000
Common stock	120,000	240,000
Additional paid-in capital	83,000	150,000
Retained earnings, 12/31/11	366,950	314,000
Total liabilities and equities	$762,750	£E 898,000

Additional Information

- During 2010, the first year of joint operation, Simbel reported income of £E 163,000 earned evenly throughout the year. Simbel paid a dividend of £E 30,000 to Cayce on June 1 of that year. Simbel also paid the 2011 dividend on June 1.
- On December 9, 2011, Simbel classified a £E 10,000 expenditure as a rent expense, although this payment related to prepayment of rent for the first few months of 2012.
- The exchange rates for 1 £E are as follows:

January 1, 2010	$0.300
June 1, 2010	0.290
Weighted average rate for 2010	0.288
December 31, 2010	0.280
June 1, 2011	0.275
October 1, 2011	0.273
Weighted average rate for 2011	0.274
December 31, 2011	0.270

Translate Simbel's 2011 financial statements into U.S. dollars and prepare a consolidation worksheet for Cayce and its Egyptian subsidiary. Assume that the Egyptian pound is the subsidiary's functional currency.

LO1, LO3, LO4

36. Diekmann Company, a U.S.-based company, acquired a 100 percent interest in Rakona A.S. in the Czech Republic on January 1, 2010, when the exchange rate for the Czech koruna (Kčs) was $0.05. Rakona's financial statements as of December 31, 2011, two years later, follow:

Balance Sheet
December 31, 2011

Assets

Cash	Kčs 2,000,000
Accounts receivable (net)	3,300,000
Inventory	8,500,000
Equipment	25,000,000
Less: Accumulated depreciation	(8,500,000)
Building	72,000,000
Less: Accumulated depreciation	(30,300,000)
Land	6,000,000
Total assets	Kčs 78,000,000

Liabilities and Stockholders' Equity

Accounts payable	Kčs 2,500,000
Long-term debt	50,000,000
Common stock	5,000,000
Additional paid-in capital	15,000,000
Retained earnings	5,500,000
Total liabilities and stockholders' equity	Kčs 78,000,000

Income Statement
For Year Ending December 31, 2011

Sales	Kčs 25,000,000
Cost of goods sold	(12,000,000)
Depreciation expense—equipment	(2,500,000)
Depreciation expense—building	(1,800,000)
Research and development expense	(1,200,000)
Other expenses (including taxes)	(1,000,000)
Net income	Kčs 6,500,000
Plus: Retained earnings, 1/1/11	500,000
Less: Dividends, 2011	(1,500,000)
Retained earnings, 12/31/11	Kčs 5,500,000

Additional Information

- The January 1, 2011, beginning inventory of Kčs 6,000,000 was acquired on December 18, 2010, when the exchange rate was $0.043. Purchases of inventory were acquired uniformly during 2011. The December 31, 2011, ending inventory of Kčs 8,500,000 was acquired in the latter part of 2011 when the exchange rate was $0.032. All fixed assets were on the books when the subsidiary was acquired except for Kčs 5,000,000 of equipment acquired on January 3, 2011, when the exchange rate was $0.036, and Kčs 12,000,000 in buildings acquired on March 5, 2011, when the exchange rate was $0.034. Straight-line depreciation is 10 years for equipment and 40 years for buildings. A full year's depreciation is taken in the year of acquisition.

- Dividends were declared and paid on December 15, 2011, when the exchange rate was $0.031.

- Other exchange rates for 1 Kčs follow:

January 1, 2011	$0.040
Average 2011	0.035
December 31, 2011	0.030

Part I. Translate the Czech koruna financial statements at December 31, 2011, in the following three situations:

    a. The Czech koruna is the functional currency. The December 31, 2010, U.S. dollar–translated balance sheet reported retained earnings of $22,500. The December 31, 2010, cumulative translation adjustment was negative $202,500 (debit balance).

    b. The U.S. dollar is the functional currency. The December 31, 2010, Retained Earnings account in U.S. dollars (including a 2010 remeasurement gain) that appeared in Rakona's remeasured financial statements was $353,000.

    c. The U.S. dollar is the functional currency. Rakona has no long-term debt. Instead, it has common stock of Kčs 20,000,000 and additional paid-in capital of Kčs 50,000,000. The December 31, 2010, U.S. dollar–translated balance sheet reported a negative balance in retained earnings of $147,000 (including a 2010 remeasurement loss).

Part II. Explain the positive or negative sign of the translation adjustment in Part I(*a*) and explain why a remeasurement gain or loss exists in Parts I(*b*) and I(*c*).

Develop Your Skills

RESEARCH CASE 1—FOREIGN CURRENCY TRANSLATION AND HEDGING ACTIVITIES

Many companies make annual reports available on their corporate Internet home page. Annual reports also can be accessed through the SEC's EDGAR system at www.sec.gov (under Filing Type, search for 10-K).

Access the most recent annual report for a U.S.-based multinational company with which you are familiar.

Required

a. Identify the location(s) in the annual report that provides disclosures related to the translation of foreign currency financial statements and foreign currency hedging.

b. Determine whether the company's foreign operations have a predominant functional currency.

c. Determine the amount of remeasurement gain or loss, if any, reported in net income in each of the three most recent years.

d. Determine the amount of translation adjustment, if any, reported in other comprehensive income in each of the three most recent years. Explain the sign (positive or negative) of the translation adjustment in each of the three most recent years.

e. Determine whether the company hedges net investments in foreign operations. If so, determine the type(s) of hedging instrument used.

RESEARCH CASE 2—FOREIGN CURRENCY TRANSLATION DISCLOSURES IN THE COMPUTER INDUSTRY

Many companies make annual reports available on their corporate Internet home page. Annual reports also can be accessed through the SEC's EDGAR system at www.sec.gov (under Filing Type, search for 10-K).

Access the most recent annual report for the following U.S.-based multinational corporations:
International Business Machines Corporation.
Dell Computer Company.

Required

a. Identify the location(s) in the annual report that provide disclosures related to foreign currency translation and foreign currency hedging.

b. Determine whether the company's foreign operations have a predominant functional currency. Discuss the implication this has for the comparability of financial statements of the two companies.

c. Determine the amount of translation adjustment, if any, reported in other comprehensive income in each of the three most recent years. Explain the sign (positive or negative) of the translation adjustment in each of the three most recent years. Compare the relative magnitude of these translation adjustments for the two companies.

d. Determine whether each company hedges the net investment in foreign operations. If so, determine the type(s) of hedging instrument used.

e. Prepare a brief report comparing and contrasting the foreign currency translation and foreign currency hedging policies of these two companies.

ACCOUNTING STANDARDS CASE 1—MORE THAN ONE FUNCTIONAL CURRENCY

Lynch Corporation has a wholly owned subsidiary in Mexico (Lynmex) with two distinct and unrelated lines of business. Lynmex's Small Appliance Division manufactures small household appliances such as toasters and coffeemakers at a factory in Monterrey, Nuevo Leon, and sells them directly to retailers such as Gigantes throughout Mexico. Lynmex's Electronics Division imports finished products produced by Lynch Corporation in the United States and sells them to a network of distributors operating throughout Mexico.

Lynch's CFO believes that the two divisions have different functional currencies. The functional currency of the Small Appliance division is the Mexican peso, whereas the functional currency of the Electronics Division is the U.S. dollar. The CFO is unsure whether to designate the Mexican peso or the U.S. dollar as Lynmex's functional currency, or whether the subsidiary can be treated as two separate foreign operations with different functional currencies.

Required

Search current U.S. authoritative accounting literature to determine how the functional currency should be determined for a foreign entity that has more than one distinct and separable operation. Identify the source of guidance for answering this question.

ACCOUNTING STANDARDS CASE 2—CHANGE IN FUNCTIONAL CURRENCY

Hughes Inc. has a wholly owned subsidiary in Canada that previously had been determined as having the Canadian dollar as its functional currency. Due to a recent restructuring, Hughes Inc.'s CFO believes that the functional currency of the Canadian company has changed to the U.S. dollar. A large cumulative translation adjustment related to the Canadian subsidiary is included in Accumulated Other Comprehensive Income on Hughes Inc.'s balance sheet. The CFO is unsure whether the cumulative translation adjustment should be removed from equity, and if so, to what other account it should be transferred. He also questions whether the change in functional currency qualifies as a change in accounting principle, which would require retrospective application of the temporal method in translating the Canadian subsidiary's financial statements. He wonders, for example, whether the Canadian subsidiary's nonmonetary assets need to be restated as if the temporal method had been applied in previous years.

Required

Search current U.S. authoritative accounting literature for guidance on how to handle a change in functional currency from a foreign currency to the U.S. dollar. Summarize that guidance to answer the CFO's questions. Identify the source of guidance for answering these questions.

ANALYSIS CASE—BELLSOUTH CORPORATION

BellSouth Corporation invested in two wireless communications operations in Brazil in the mid-1990s that it accounted for under the equity method. The following note is taken from BellSouth Corporation's interim report for the quarter ended March 31, 1999:

> *Note E—Devaluation of Brazilian Currency*
>
> *We hold equity interests in two wireless communications operations in Brazil. During January 1999, the government of Brazil allowed its currency to trade freely against other currencies. As a result, the Brazilian Real experienced a devaluation against the U.S. Dollar. The devaluation resulted in the entities recording exchange losses related to their net U.S. Dollar–denominated liabilities. Our share of the foreign exchange rate losses for the first quarter was $280.*
>
> *These exchange losses are subject to further upward or downward adjustment based on fluctuations in the exchange rates between the U.S. Dollar and the Brazilian Real.*

In a press release announcing first quarter 1999 results, BellSouth Corporation provided the following information (on its Web site):

> *BellSouth Corporation (NYSE: BLS) reported a 15 percent increase in first quarter earnings per share (EPS) before special items. EPS was 46 cents before a noncash expense of 14 cents related to Brazil's currency devaluation.*

BELLSOUTH CORPORATION:
Normalized Earnings Summary ($ in millions, except per share amounts)
(unaudited)

	Quarter Ended		
	3/31/99	3/31/98	%Change
Reported Net Income	$615	$892	(31.1%)
Foreign currency loss (a)	280	—	
Gain on sale of ITT World Directories (b)	—	(96)	
Normalized Net Income	$895	$796	12.4%

	Quarter Ended		
	3/31/99	3/31/98	%Change
Reported Diluted Earnings per Share	$0.32	$0.45	(28.9%)
Foreign currency loss (a)	0.14	—	
Gain on sale of ITT World Directories (b)	—	(0.05)	
Normalized Diluted Earnings per Share	$0.46	$0.40	15.0%

(a) Represents our share of foreign currency losses recorded during first quarter 1999 as a result of the devaluation of the Brazilian Real during January 1999.

(b) Represents the after-tax gain associated with additional proceeds received in first quarter 1998 on the July 1997 sale of ITT World Directories.

Required

Based on the disclosure provided by BellSouth Corporation presented here, answer these questions:

a. Why did the company report a foreign currency loss as a result of the devaluation of the Brazilian real?

b. What does the company mean when it states, "These exchange losses are subject to further upward or downward adjustment based on fluctuations in the exchange rates between the U.S. Dollar and the Brazilian Real"?

c. What is the company's objective in reporting Normalized Net Income?

d. Do you agree with the company's assessment that it had a 15 percent increase in first-quarter earnings per share?

EXCEL CASE—TRANSLATING FOREIGN CURRENCY FINANCIAL STATEMENTS

Charles Edward Company established a subsidiary in a foreign country on January 1, 2011, by investing FC 3,200,000 when the exchange rate was $0.50/FC. Charles Edward negotiated a bank loan of FC 3,000,000 on January 5, 2011, and purchased plant and equipment in the amount of FC 6,000,000 on January 8, 2011. It depreciated plant and equipment on a straight-line basis over a 10-year useful life. It purchased its beginning inventory of FC 1,000,000 on January 10, 2011, and acquired additional inventory of FC 4,000,000 at three points in time during the year at an average exchange rate of $0.43/FC. It uses the first-in, first-out (FIFO) method to determine cost of goods sold. Additional exchange rates per FC 1 during the year 2011 follow:

January 1–31, 2011	$0.50
Average 2011	0.45
December 31, 2011	0.38

The foreign subsidiary's income statement for 2011 and balance sheet at December 31, 2011, follow:

INCOME STATEMENT
For the Year Ended December 31, 2011
FC (in thousands)

Sales	FC 5,000
Cost of goods sold	3,000
Gross profit	2,000
Selling expense	400
Depreciation expense	600
Income before tax	1,000
Income taxes	300
Net income	700
Retained earnings, 1/1/11	–0–
Retained earnings, 12/31/11	FC 700

BALANCE SHEET
At December 31, 2011
FC (in thousands)

Cash	FC 1,000
Inventory	2,000
Fixed assets	6,000
Less: Accumulated depreciation	(600)
Total assets	FC 8,400
Current liabilities	FC 1,500
Long-term debt	3,000
Contributed capital	3,200
Retained earnings	700
Total liabilities and stockholders' equity	FC 8,400

As the controller for Charles Edward Company, you have evaluated the characteristics of the foreign subsidiary to determine that the FC is the subsidiary's functional currency.

Required

a. Use an electronic spreadsheet to translate the foreign subsidiary's FC financial statements into U.S. dollars at December 31, 2011, in accordance with U.S. GAAP. Insert a row in the spreadsheet after retained earnings and before total liabilities and stockholders' equity for the cumulative translation adjustment. Calculate the translation adjustment separately to verify the amount obtained as a balancing figure in the translation worksheet.

b. Use an electronic spreadsheet to remeasure the foreign subsidiary's FC financial statements in U.S. dollars at December 31, 2011, assuming that the U.S. dollar is the subsidiary's functional currency. Insert a row in the spreadsheet after depreciation expense and before income before taxes for the remeasurement gain (loss).

c. Prepare a report for James Edward, CEO of Charles Edward, summarizing the differences that will be reported in the company's 2011 consolidated financial statements because the FC, rather than the U.S. dollar, is the foreign subsidiary's functional currency. In your report, discuss the relationship between the current ratio, the debt-to-equity ratio, and profit margin calculated from the FC financial statements and from the translated U.S. dollar financial statements. Also discuss the meaning of the translated U.S. dollar amounts for inventory and for fixed assets.

EXCEL AND ANALYSIS CASE—PARKER, INC., AND SUFFOLK PLC

On January 1, 2010, Parker, Inc., a U.S.-based firm, acquired 100 percent of Suffolk PLC located in Great Britain for consideration paid of 52,000,000 British pounds (£), which was equal to fair value. The excess of fair value over book value is attributable to land (part of property, plant, and equipment) and is not subject to depreciation. Parker accounts for its investment in Suffolk at cost. On January 1, 2010, Suffolk reported the following balance sheet:

Cash	£ 2,000,000	Accounts payable	£ 1,000,000
Accounts receivable	3,000,000	Long-term debt	8,000,000
Inventory	14,000,000	Common stock	44,000,000
Property, plant, and		Retained earnings	6,000,000
equipment (net)	40,000,000		£59,000,000
	£ 59,000,000		

Suffolk's 2010 income was recorded at £2,000,000. It declared and paid no dividends in 2010.

On December 31, 2011, two years after the date of acquisition, Suffolk submitted the following trial balance to Parker for consolidation:

Cash	£ 1,500,000
Accounts Receivable	5,200,000
Inventory	18,000,000
Property, Plant, and Equipment (net)	36,000,000
Accounts Payable	(1,450,000)
Long-Term Debt	(5,000,000)
Common Stock	(44,000,000)
Retained Earnings (1/1/11)	(8,000,000)
Sales	(28,000,000)
Cost of Goods Sold	16,000,000
Depreciation	2,000,000
Other Expenses	6,000,000
Dividends Paid (1/30/11)	1,750,000
	–0–

Other than paying dividends, no intra-entity transactions occurred between the two companies. Relevant exchange rates for the British pound follow:

	January 1	January 30	Average	December 31
2010	$1.60	$1.61	$1.62	$1.64
2011	1.64	1.65	1.66	1.68

The December 31, 2011, financial statements (before consolidation with Suffolk) follow. Dividend income is the U.S. dollar amount of dividends received from Suffolk translated at the $1.65/£ exchange rate at January 30, 2011. The amounts listed for dividend income and all affected accounts (i.e., net income, December 31 retained earnings, and cash) reflect the $1.65/£ exchange rate at January 30, 2011. Credit balances are in parentheses.

Parker	
Sales	$ (70,000,000)
Cost of goods sold	34,000,000
Depreciation	20,000,000
Other expenses	6,000,000
Dividend income	(2,887,500)
Net income	$ (12,887,500)
Retained earnings, 1/1/11	$ (48,000,000)
Net income, 2011	(12,887,500)
Dividends, 1/30/11	4,500,000
Retained earnings, 12/31/11	$ (56,387,500)
Cash	$ 3,687,500
Accounts receivable	10,000,000
Inventory	30,000,000
Investment in Suffolk	83,200,000
Plant and equipment (net)	105,000,000
Accounts payable	(25,500,000)
Long-term debt	(50,000,000)
Common stock	(100,000,000)
Retained earnings, 12/31/11	(56,387,500)
	–0–

Parker's chief financial officer (CFO) wishes to determine the effect that a change in the value of the British pound would have on consolidated net income and consolidated stockholders' equity. To help assess the foreign currency exposure associated with the investment in Suffolk, the CFO requests assistance in comparing consolidated results under actual exchange rate fluctuations with results that would have occurred had the dollar value of the pound remained constant or declined during the first two years of Parker's ownership.

Required

Use an electronic spreadsheet to complete the following four parts:

Part I. Given the relevant exchange rates presented,

a. Translate Suffolk's December 31, 2011, trial balance from British pounds to U.S. dollars. The British pound is Suffolk's functional currency.

b. Prepare a schedule that details the change in Suffolk's cumulative translation adjustment (beginning net assets, income, dividends, etc.) for 2010 and 2011.

c. Prepare the December 31, 2011, consolidation worksheet for Parker and Suffolk.

d. Prepare the 2011 consolidated income statement and the December 31, 2011, consolidated balance sheet.

Note: Worksheets should possess the following qualities:

- Each spreadsheet should be programmed so that all relevant amounts adjust appropriately when different values of exchange rates (subsequent to January 1, 2010) are entered into it.
- Be sure to program Parker's dividend income, cash, and retained earnings to reflect the dollar value of alternative January 30, 2011, exchange rates.

Part II. Repeat tasks (*a*), (*b*), (*c*), and (*d*) from Part I to determine consolidated net income and consolidated stockholders' equity if the exchange rate had remained at $1.60/£ over the period 2010 to 2011.

Part III. Repeat tasks (*a*), (*b*), (*c*), and (*d*) from Part I to determine consolidated net income and consolidated stockholders' equity if the following exchange rates had existed:

	January 1	January 30	Average	December 31
2010	$1.60	$1.59	$1.58	$1.56
2011	1.56	1.55	1.54	1.52

Part IV. Prepare a report that provides Parker's CFO the risk assessments requested. Focus on profitability, cash flow, and the debt-to-equity ratio.

KAPLAN

CPA REVIEW

Please visit the text Web site for the online CPA Simulation

Situation: Texas Corporation, located in San Antonio, has transactions both in the United States and in Mexico although the U.S. dollar is its functional currency. In addition, Texas has a wholly owned subsidiary (Mexico, Inc.) located in Mexico. Consolidated financial statements are being prepared for Year 1. The currency exchange rates are as follows for the current year (Year 1):

- January 1, Year 1: 1 peso equals $0.088.
- Average for Year 1: 1 peso equals $0.090.
- November 1, Year 1: 1 peso equals $0.092.
- December 1, Year 1: 1 peso equals $0.094.
- December 31, Year 1: 1 peso equals $0.095.
- January 31, Year 2: 1 peso equals $0.098.

Topics to be covered in simulation:

- Remeasurement process.
- Translation process.
- Foreign currency balances—impact on net income.
- Foreign currency balances—impact on comprehensive income.
- Translation adjustment.
- Functional currency.
- Forward exchange contracts as a cash flow hedge.
- Forward exchange contracts as a fair value hedge.

Partnerships: Formation and Operation

A reader of college accounting textbooks might well conclude that business activity is carried out exclusively by corporations. Because most large companies are legally incorporated, a vast majority of textbook references and illustrations concern corporate organizations. Contrary to the perception being relayed, partnerships (as well as sole proprietorships) make up a vital element of the business community. The Internal Revenue Service projects that by 2012, nearly 3.6 million partnership income tax returns will be filed (as compared to nearly 7.3 million corporation income tax returns).[1]

The partnership form serves a wide range of business activities, from small local operations to worldwide enterprises. The following examples exist in the U.S. economy:

- Individual proprietors often join together to form a partnership as a way to reduce expenses, expand services, and add increased expertise. As will be discussed, partnerships also provide important tax benefits.

- A partnership is a common means by which friends and relatives can easily create and organize a business endeavor.

- Historically doctors, lawyers, and other professionals have formed partnerships because of legal prohibitions against the incorporation of their practices. Although most states now permit alternative forms for such organizations, operating as a partnership or sole proprietorship is still necessary in many areas.

Over the years, some partnerships have grown to enormous sizes. Connell Limited Partnership, for example, recycles and manufactures metal products; in 2008 it had revenues of more than $1 billion. The international accounting firm of PriceWaterhouseCoopers reported revenues of more than $28 billion.[2] In 2009, Deloitte Touche Tohmatsu indicated operations in nearly 140 countries,[3] and Ernst & Young reported having more than 135,000 employees.[4]

---

[1] www.irs.gov.

[2] "America's Largest Private Companies," *Forbes,* 2008.

[3] www.deloitte.com.

[4] "America's Largest Private Companies," *Forbes,* 2008.

LEARNING OBJECTIVES

After studying this chapter, you should be able to:

LO1 Discuss the advantages and disadvantages of the partnership versus the corporate form of business.

LO2 Describe the purpose of the articles of partnership and list specific items that should be included in this agreement.

LO3 Prepare the journal entry to record the initial capital investment made by a partner.

LO4 Use both the bonus method and the goodwill method to record a partner's capital investment.

LO5 Understand the impact that the allocation of partnership income has on the partners' individual capital balances.

LO6 Allocate income to partners when interest and/or salary factors are included.

LO7 Discuss the meaning of partnership dissolution and understand that a dissolution will often have little or no effect on the operations of the partnership business.

LO8 Prepare journal entries to record the acquisition by a new partner of either all or a portion of a current partner's interest.

LO9 Prepare journal entries to record a new partner's admission by a contribution made directly to the partnership.

LO10 Prepare journal entries to record the withdrawal of a current partner.

PARTNERSHIPS—ADVANTAGES AND DISADVANTAGES

LO1

Discuss the advantages and disadvantages of the partnership versus the corporate form of business.

The popularity of partnerships derives from several advantages inherent to this type of organization. An analysis of these attributes explains why nearly 3.6 million enterprises in the United States are partnerships rather than corporations.

One of the most common motives is the ease of formation. Only an oral agreement is necessary to create a legally binding partnership. In contrast, depending on specific state laws, incorporation requires filing a formal application and completing various other forms and documents. Operators of small businesses may find the convenience and reduced cost involved in creating a partnership to be an especially appealing characteristic. As the American Bar Association noted:

> The principal advantage of partnerships is the ability to make virtually any arrangements defining their relationship to each other that the partners desire. There is no necessity, as there is in a corporation, to have the ownership interest in capital and profits proportionate to the investment made; and losses can be allocated on a different basis from profits. It is also generally much easier to achieve a desirable format for control of the business in a partnership than in a corporation, since the control of a corporation, which is based on ownership of voting stock, is much more difficult to alter.
>
> Partnerships are taxed on a conduit or flow-through basis under subchapter K of the Internal Revenue Code. This means that the partnership itself does not pay any taxes. Instead the net income and various deductions and tax credits from the partnership are passed through to the partners based on their respective percentage interest in the profits and losses of the partnership, and the partners include the income and deductions in their individual tax returns.[5]

Thus, partnership revenue and expense items (as defined by the tax laws) must be assigned directly each year to the individual partners who pay the income taxes. Passing income balances through to the partners in this manner avoids double taxation of the profits that are earned by a business and then distributed to its owners. A corporation's income is taxed twice: when earned and again when conveyed as a dividend. A partnership's income is taxed only at the time that the business initially earns it.

For example, assume that a business earns $100. After paying any income taxes, the remainder is immediately conveyed to its owners. An income tax rate of 30 percent is assumed for both individuals and corporations. Corporate dividends paid to owners, however, are taxed at a 15 percent rate.[6] As the following table shows, if this business is a partnership rather than a corporation, the owners have $10.50 more expendable income, which is 10.5 percent of the business income. Although significant in amount, this difference narrows as tax rates are lowered.

	Partnership	Corporation
Income before income taxes	$100.00	$100.00
Income taxes paid by business (30%)	–0–	(30.00)
Income distributed to owners	$100.00	$ 70.00
Income taxes paid by owners*	(30.00)	(10.50)
Expendable income	$ 70.00	$ 59.50

* 30% assumed rate on ordinary income.
  15% assumed rate on dividend income.

Historically, a second tax advantage has long been associated with partnerships. Because income is taxable to the partners as the business earns it, any operating losses can be used to reduce their personal taxable income directly. In contrast, a corporation is viewed as legally separate from its owners, so losses cannot be passed through to them. A corporation has the ability to carry back any net operating losses and reduce previously taxed income (usually for

[5] American Bar Association, *Family Legal Guide,* 3rd ed. (New York: Random House Reference, 2004).

[6] The Tax Increase Prevention and Reconciliation Act of 2005 limits the top tax rate on both dividend income and capital gains to 15 percent through 2010.

the two prior years) and carry forward remaining losses to decrease future taxable income (for up to 20 years). However, if a corporation is newly formed or has not been profitable, operating losses provide no immediate benefit to a corporation or its owners as losses do for a partnership.

The tax advantage of deducting partnership losses is limited however. For tax purposes, ownership of a partnership is labeled as a passive activity unless the partner materially participates in the actual business activities. Passive activity losses thus serve only to offset other passive activity profits. In most cases, these partnership losses cannot be used to reduce earned income such as salaries. Thus, unless a taxpayer has significant passive activity income (from rents, for example), losses reported by a partnership create little or no tax advantage unless the partner materially participates in the actual business activity.

The partnership form of business also has certain significant disadvantages. Perhaps the most severe problem is the unlimited liability that each partner automatically incurs. Partnership law specifies that any partner can be held personally liable for *all* debts of the business. The potential risk is especially significant when coupled with the concept of *mutual agency.* This legal term refers to the right that each partner has to incur liabilities in the name of the partnership. Consequently, partners acting within the normal scope of the business have the power to obligate the company for any amount. If the partnership fails to pay these debts, creditors can seek satisfactory remuneration from any partner that they choose.

Such legal concepts as unlimited liability and mutual agency describe partnership characteristics that have been defined and interpreted over a number of years. To provide consistent application across state lines in regard to these terms as well as many other legal aspects of a partnership, the Uniform Partnership Act (UPA) was created. This act, which was first proposed in 1914 (and revised in 1997), now has been adopted by all states in some form. It establishes uniform standards in such areas as the nature of a partnership, the relationship of the partners to outside parties, and the dissolution of the partnership. For example, Section 6 of the act provides the most common legal definition of a partnership: "an association of two or more persons to carry on a business as co-owners for profit."

ALTERNATIVE LEGAL FORMS

Because of the possible owner liability, partnerships often experience difficulty in attracting large amounts of capital. Potential partners frequently prefer to avoid the risk that is a basic characteristic of a partnership. However, the tax benefits of avoiding double taxation still provide a strong pull toward the partnership form. Hence, in recent years, a number of alternative types of organizations have been developed. The availability of these legal forms depends on state laws as well as applicable tax laws. In each case, however, the purpose is to limit the owners' personal liability while providing the tax benefits of a partnership.[7]

Subchapter S Corporation

A Subchapter S Corporation (often referred to as an *S corporation*) is created as a corporation and, therefore, has all of the legal characteristics of that form.[8] According to the U.S. tax laws, if the corporation meets certain regulations, it will be taxed in virtually the same way as a partnership. Thus, the Subchapter S corporation pays no income taxes although any income (and losses) pass directly through to the taxable income of the individual owners. This form avoids double taxation, and the owners do not face unlimited liability. To qualify, the business can have only one class of stock and is limited to 100 stockholders. All owners must be individuals, estates, certain tax-exempt entities, or certain types of trusts. The most significant problem associated with this business form is that its growth potential is limited because of the restriction on the number and type of owners.

---

[7] Many factors should be considered in choosing a specific legal form for an organization. The information shown here is merely an overview. For more information, consult a tax guide or a business law textbook.

[8] Unless a corporation qualifies as a Subchapter S corporation or some other legal variation, it is referred to as a *Subchapter C corporation*. Therefore, a vast majority of all businesses are C corporations.

Limited Partnership (LPs)

A *limited partnership* is a type of investment designed primarily for individuals who want the tax benefits of a partnership but who do not wish to work in a partnership or have unlimited liability. In such organizations, a number of limited partners invest money as owners but are not allowed to participate in the company's management. These partners can still incur a loss on their investment, but the amount is restricted to what has been contributed. To protect the creditors of a limited partnership, one or more general partners must be designated to assume responsibility for all obligations created in the name of the business.

Buckeye Partners, L.P. (with annual revenues of more than $1.8 billion), is an example of a limited partnership that trades on the New York Stock Exchange. Buckeye's December 31, 2008, balance sheet reported capital of $1.2 billion for its limited partners.

Many limited partnerships were originally formed as tax shelters to create immediate losses (to reduce the taxable income of the partners) with profits spread out into the future. As mentioned earlier, tax laws limit the deduction of passive activity losses, and this significantly reduced the formation of limited partnerships.

Limited Liability Partnerships (LLPs)

The *limited liability partnership* has most of the characteristics of a general partnership except that it significantly reduces the partners' liability. Partners may lose their investment in the business and are responsible for the contractual debts of the business. The advantage here is created in connection with any liability resulting from damages. In such cases, the partners are responsible for only their own acts or omissions plus the acts and omissions of individuals under their supervision.

As Section 306(c) of the Uniform Partnership Act notes

> An obligation of a partnership incurred while the partnership is a limited liability partnership, whether arising in contract, tort, or otherwise, is solely the obligation of the partnership. A partner is not personally liable, directly or indirectly, by way of contribution or otherwise, for such an obligation solely by reason of being or so acting as a partner.

Thus, a partner in the Houston office of a public accounting firm would probably not be held liable for a poor audit performed by that firm's San Francisco office. Not surprisingly, limited liability partnerships have become very popular with professional service organizations that have multiple offices. For example, all of the four largest accounting firms are LLPs.

Limited Liability Companies (LLCs)

The limited liability company is a new type of organization in the United States although it has long been used in Europe and other areas of the world. It is classified as a partnership for tax purposes. However, depending on state laws, the owners risk only their own investments. In contrast to a Subchapter S corporation, the number of owners is not usually restricted so that growth is easier to accomplish.

PARTNERSHIP ACCOUNTING—CAPITAL ACCOUNTS

Despite legal distinctions, questions should be raised as to the need for an entirely separate study of partnership accounting:

- Does an association of two or more persons require accounting procedures significantly different from those of a corporation?
- Does proper accounting depend on the legal form of an organization?

The answers to these questions are both yes and no. Accounting procedures are normally standardized for assets, liabilities, revenues, and expenses regardless of the legal form of a business. *Partnership accounting, though, does exhibit unique aspects that warrant study, but they lie primarily in the handling of the partners' capital accounts.*

The stockholders' equity accounts of a corporation do not correspond directly with the capital balances found in a partnership's financial records. The various equity accounts reported by an incorporated enterprise display a greater range of information. This characteristic reflects the wide variety of equity transactions that can occur in a corporation as well as the influence of state and federal laws. Government regulation has had enormous effect on the accounting for corporate equity transactions in that extensive disclosure is required to protect stockholders and other outside parties such as potential investors.

To provide adequate information and to meet legal requirements, corporate accounting must provide details about numerous equity transactions and account balances. For example, the amount of a corporation's paid-in capital is shown separately from earned capital and other comprehensive income; the par value of each class of stock is disclosed; treasury stock, stock options, stock dividends, and other capital transactions are reported based on prescribed accounting principles.

In comparison, partnerships provide only a limited amount of equity disclosure primarily in the form of individual capital accounts that are accumulated for every partner or every class of partners. These balances measure each partner or group's interest in the book value of the net assets of the business. Thus, the equity section of a partnership balance sheet is composed solely of capital accounts that can be affected by many different events: contributions from partners as well as distributions to them, earnings, and any other equity transactions.

However, partnership accounting makes no differentiation between the various sources of ownership capital. Disclosing the composition of the partners' capital balances has not been judged necessary because partnerships have historically tended to be small with equity transactions that were rarely complex. Additionally, absentee ownership is not common, a factor that minimizes both the need for government regulation and outside interest in detailed information about the capital balances.

Articles of Partnership

LO2

Describe the purpose of the articles of partnership and list specific items that should be included in this agreement.

Because the demand for information about capital balances is limited, accounting principles specific to partnerships are based primarily on traditional approaches that have evolved over the years rather than on official pronouncements. These procedures attempt to mirror the relationship between the partners and their business especially as defined by the partnership agreement. This legal covenant, which may be either oral or written, is often referred to as the *articles of partnership* and forms the central governance for a partnership's operation. The financial arrangements spelled out in this contract establish guidelines for the various capital transactions. Therefore, the articles of partnership, rather than either laws or official rules, provide much of the underlying basis for partnership accounting.

Because the articles of partnership are a negotiated agreement that the partners create, an unlimited number of variations can be encountered in practice. Partners' rights and responsibilities frequently differ from business to business. Consequently, firms often hire accountants in an advisory capacity to participate in creating this document to ensure the equitable treatment of all parties. Although the articles of partnership may contain a number of provisions, an explicit understanding should always be reached in regard to the following:

- Name and address of each partner.
- Business location.
- Description of the nature of the business.
- Rights and responsibilities of each partner.
- Initial contribution to be made by each partner and the method to be used for valuation.
- Specific method by which profits and losses are to be allocated.
- Periodic withdrawal of assets by each partner.
- Procedure for admitting new partners.
- Method for arbitrating partnership disputes.
- Life insurance provisions enabling remaining partners to acquire the interest of any deceased partner.
- Method for settling a partner's share in the business upon withdrawal, retirement, or death.

Discussion **Question**

WHAT KIND OF BUSINESS IS THIS?

After graduating from college, Shelley Williams held several different jobs but found that she did not enjoy working for other people. Finally, she and Yvonne Hargrove, her college roommate, decided to start a business of their own. They rented a small building and opened a florist shop selling cut flowers such as roses and chrysanthemums that they bought from a local greenhouse.

Williams and Hargrove agreed orally to share profits and losses equally, although they also decided to take no money from the operation for at least four months. No other arrangements were made, but the business did reasonably well and, after the first four months had passed, each began to draw out $500 in cash every week.

At year-end, they took their financial records to a local accountant so that they could get their income tax returns completed. He informed them that they had been operating as a partnership and that they should draw up a formal articles of partnership agreement or consider incorporation or some other legal form of organization. They confessed that they had never really considered the issue and asked for his advice on the matter.

What advice should the accountant give to these clients?

LO3

Prepare the journal entry to record the initial capital investment made by a partner.

Accounting for Capital Contributions

Several types of capital transactions occur in a partnership: allocation of profits and losses, retirement of a current partner, admission of a new partner, and so on. The initial transaction, however, is the contribution the original partners make to begin the business. In the simplest situation, the partners invest only cash amounts. For example, assume that Carter and Green form a business to be operated as a partnership. Carter contributes $50,000 in cash and Green invests $20,000. The initial journal entry to record the creation of this partnership follows:

Cash	70,000	
Carter, Capital		50,000
Green, Capital		20,000
To record cash contributed to start new partnership.		

The assumption that only cash was invested avoids complications in this first illustration. Often, though, one or more of the partners transfers noncash assets such as inventory, land, equipment, or a building to the business. Although fair value is used to record these assets, a case could be developed for initially valuing any contributed asset at the partner's current book value. According to the concept of unlimited liability (as well as present tax laws), a partnership does not exist as an entity apart from its owners. A logical extension of the idea is that the investment of an asset is not a transaction occurring between two independent parties such as would warrant revaluation. This contention holds that the semblance of an arm's-length transaction is necessary to justify a change in the book value of any account.

Although retaining the recorded value for assets contributed to a partnership may seem reasonable, this method of valuation proves to be inequitable to any partner investing appreciated property. A $50,000 capital balance always results from a cash investment of that amount, but recording other assets depends entirely on the original book value.

For example, should a partner who contributes a building having a recorded value of $18,000 but a fair value of $50,000 be credited with only an $18,000 interest in the partnership? Because $50,000 in cash and $50,000 in appreciated property are equivalent contributions, a $32,000 difference in the partners' capital balances cannot be justified. To prevent such inequities, each item transferred to a partnership is initially recorded for external reporting purposes at current value.[9]

---

[9] For federal income tax purposes, the $18,000 book value is retained as the basis for this building, even after transfer to the partnership. Within the tax laws, no difference is seen between partners and their partnership so that no adjustment to fair value is warranted.

Requiring revaluation of contributed assets can, however, be advocated for reasons other than just the fair treatment of all partners. Despite some evidence to the contrary, a partnership can be viewed legitimately as an entity standing apart from its owners. As an example, a partnership maintains legal ownership of its assets and (depending on state law) can initiate lawsuits. For this reason, accounting practice traditionally has held that the contribution of assets (and liabilities) to a partnership is an exchange between two separately identifiable parties that should be recorded based on fair values.

The determination of an appropriate valuation for each capital balance is more than just an accounting exercise. Over the life of a partnership, these figures serve in a number of important capacities:

1. The totals in the individual capital accounts often influence the assignment of profits and losses to the partners.
2. The capital account balance is usually one factor in determining the final distribution that will be received by a partner at the time of withdrawal or retirement.
3. Ending capital balances indicate the allocation to be made of any assets that remain following the liquidation of a partnership.

To demonstrate, assume that Carter invests $50,000 in cash to begin the previously discussed partnership and Green contributes the following assets:

	Book Value to Green	Fair Value
Inventory	$ 9,000	$10,000
Land	14,000	11,000
Building	32,000	46,000
Totals	$55,000	$67,000

As an added factor, Green's building is encumbered by a $23,600 mortgage that the partnership has agreed to assume.

Green's net investment is equal to $43,400 ($67,000 less $23,600). The following journal entry records the formation of the partnership created by these contributions:

Cash	50,000	
Inventory	10,000	
Land	11,000	
Building	46,000	
Mortgage Payable		23,600
Carter, Capital		50,000
Green, Capital		43,400
To record properties contributed to start partnership. Assets and liabilities are recorded at fair value.		

We should make one additional point before leaving this illustration. Although having contributed inventory, land, and a building, Green holds no further right to these individual assets; they now belong to the partnership. The $43,400 capital balance represents an ownership interest in the business as a whole but does not constitute a specific claim to any asset. Having transferred title to the partnership, Green has no more right to these assets than does Carter.

LO4

Use both the bonus method and the goodwill method to record a partner's capital investment.

Intangible Contributions

In forming a partnership, the contributions made by one or more of the partners may go beyond assets and liabilities. A doctor, for example, can bring a particular line of expertise to a partnership, and a practicing dentist might have already developed an established clientele.

These attributes, as well as many others, are frequently as valuable to a partnership as cash and fixed assets. *Hence, formal accounting recognition of such special contributions may be appropriately included as a provision of any partnership agreement.*

To illustrate, assume that James and Joyce plan to open an advertising agency and decide to organize the endeavor as a partnership. James contributes cash of $70,000, and Joyce invests only $10,000. Joyce, however, is an accomplished graphic artist, a skill that is considered especially valuable to this business. Therefore, in producing the articles of partnership, the partners agree to start the business with equal capital balances. Often such decisions result only after long, and sometimes heated, negotiations. Because the value assigned to an intangible contribution such as artistic talent is arbitrary at best, proper reporting depends on the partners' ability to arrive at an equitable arrangement.

In recording this agreement, James and Joyce have two options: (1) the bonus method and (2) the goodwill method. Each of these approaches achieves the desired result of establishing equal capital account balances. Recorded figures can vary significantly, however, depending on the procedure selected. Thus, the partners should reach an understanding prior to beginning business operations as to the method to be used. The accountant can help avoid conflicts by assisting the partners in evaluating the impact created by each of these alternatives.

The Bonus Method   The bonus method assumes that a specialization such as Joyce's artistic abilities does *not* constitute a recordable partnership asset with a measurable cost. Hence, this approach recognizes only the assets that are physically transferred to the business (such as cash, patents, inventory). Although these contributions determine total partnership capital, the establishment of specific capital balances is viewed as an independent process based solely on the partners' agreement. Because the initial equity figures result from negotiation, they do not need to correspond directly with the individual investments.

James and Joyce have contributed a total of $80,000 in identifiable assets to their partnership and have decided on equal capital balances. According to the bonus method, this agreement is fulfilled simply by splitting the $80,000 capital evenly between the two partners. The following entry records the formation of this partnership under this assumption:

Cash	80,000	
James, Capital		40,000
Joyce, Capital.		40,000
To record cash contributions with bonus to Joyce because of artistic abilities.		

Joyce received a *capital bonus* here of $30,000 (the $40,000 recorded capital balance in excess of the $10,000 cash contribution) from James in recognition of the artistic abilities she brought into the business.

The Goodwill Method   The goodwill method is based on the assumption that an implied value can be calculated mathematically and recorded for any intangible contribution made by a partner. In the present illustration, Joyce invested $60,000 less cash than James but receives an equal amount of capital according to the partnership agreement. Proponents of the goodwill method argue that Joyce's artistic talent has an apparent value of $60,000, a figure that should be included as part of this partner's capital investment. If not recorded, Joyce's primary contribution to the business is ignored completely within the accounting records.

Cash	80,000	
Goodwill	60,000	
James, Capital		70,000
Joyce, Capital		70,000
To record cash contributions with goodwill attributed to Joyce in recognition of artistic abilities.		

Comparison of Methods   Both approaches achieve the intent of the partnership agreement: to record equal capital balances despite a difference in the partners' cash contributions. The bonus method allocates the $80,000 invested capital according to the percentages designated by the partners, whereas the goodwill method capitalizes the implied value of Joyce's intangible contribution.

Although nothing prohibits the use of either technique, the recognition of goodwill poses definite theoretical problems. In previous discussions of both the equity method (Chapter 1) and business combinations (Chapter 2), goodwill was recognized but only as a result of an acquisition made by the reporting entity. Consequently, this asset had a historical cost in the traditional accounting sense. Partnership goodwill has no such cost; the business recognizes an asset even though no funds have been spent.

The partnership of James and Joyce, for example, is able to record $60,000 in goodwill without any expenditure. Furthermore, the value attributed to this asset is based solely on a negotiated agreement between the partners; the $60,000 balance has no objectively verifiable basis. Thus, although partnership goodwill is sometimes encountered in actual practice, this "asset" should be viewed with a strong degree of professional skepticism.

Additional Capital Contributions and Withdrawals

Subsequent to forming a partnership, the owners may choose to contribute additional capital amounts during the life of the business. These investments can be made to stimulate expansion or to assist the business in overcoming working capital shortages or other problems. Regardless of the reason, the contribution is again recorded as an increment in the partner's capital account based on fair value. For example, in the previous illustration, assume that James decides to invest another $5,000 cash in the partnership to help finance the purchase of new office furnishings. The partner's capital account balance is immediately increased by this amount to reflect the transfer to the partnership.

The partners also may reverse this process by withdrawing assets from the business for their own personal use. For example, one partnership, Andersons, reported recently in its financial statements partner withdrawals of $1,759,072 for the year as well as increases in invested capital of $733,675. To protect the interests of the other partners, the articles of partnership should clearly specify the amount and timing of such withdrawals.

In many instances, the articles of partnership allow withdrawals on a regular periodic basis as a reward for ownership or as compensation for work performed for the business. Often such distributions are recorded initially in a separate drawing account that is closed into the individual partner's capital account at year-end. Assume, for illustration purposes, that James and Joyce take out $1,200 and $1,500, respectively, from their business. The journal entry to record these payments is as follows:

James, Drawing	1,200	
Joyce, Drawing	1,500	
Cash		2,700
To record withdrawal of cash by partners.		

Larger amounts might also be withdrawn from a partnership on occasion. A partner may have a special need for money or just desire to reduce the basic investment that has been made in the business. Such transactions are usually sporadic occurrences and entail amounts significantly higher than the partner's periodic drawing. The articles of partnership may require prior approval by the other partners.

LO5

Understand the impact that the allocation of partnership income has on the partners' individual capital balances.

Allocation of Income

At the end of each fiscal period, partnership revenues and expenses are closed out, accompanied by an allocation of the resulting net income or loss to the partners' capital accounts. Because a separate capital balance is maintained for each partner, a method must be devised for this assignment of annual income. Because of the importance of the process, the articles of partnership should always stipulate the procedure the partners established. If no arrangement has been

Discussion **Question**

HOW WILL THE PROFITS BE SPLIT?

James J. Dewars has been the sole owner of a small CPA firm for the past 20 years. Now 52 years old, Dewars is concerned about the continuation of his practice after he retires. He would like to begin taking more time off now although he wants to remain active in the firm for at least another 8 to 10 years. He has worked hard over the decades to build up the practice so that he presently makes a profit of $180,000 annually.

Lewis Huffman has been working for Dewars for the past four years. He now earns a salary of $68,000 per year. He is a very dedicated employee who generally works 44 to 60 hours per week. In the past, Dewars has been in charge of the larger, more profitable audit clients whereas Huffman, with less experience, worked with the smaller clients. Both Dewars and Huffman do some tax work although that segment of the business has never been emphasized.

Sally Scriba has been employed for the past seven years with another CPA firm as a tax specialist. She has no auditing experience but has a great reputation in tax planning and preparation. She currently earns an annual salary of $80,000.

Dewars, Huffman, and Scriba are negotiating the creation of a new CPA firm as a partnership. Dewars plans to reduce his time in this firm although he will continue to work with many of the clients that he has served for the past two decades. Huffman will begin to take over some of the major audit jobs. Scriba will start to develop an extensive tax practice for the firm.

Because of the changes in the firm, the three potential partners anticipate earning a total net income in the first year of operations of between $130,000 and $260,000. Thereafter, they hope that profits will increase at the rate of 10 to 20 percent annually for the next five years or so.

How should this new partnership allocate its future net income among these partners?

specified, state partnership law normally holds that all partners receive an equal allocation of any income or loss earned by the business. If the partnership agreement specifies only the division of profits, then losses must be divided in the same manner as directed for profit allocation.

An allocation pattern can be extremely important to the success of an organization because it can help emphasize and reward outstanding performance.

> The goal of a partner compensation plan is to inspire each principal's most profitable performance— and make a firm grow. When a CPA firm's success depends on partner contributions other than accounting expertise—such as bringing in business, developing a specialty or being a good manager—its compensation plan has to encourage those qualities, for both fairness and firm health.[10]

Actual procedures for allocating profits and losses can range from the simple to the elaborate.

> Our system is as follows: a base draw to all partners, which grows over an eight-year period from 0.63x to a maximum of x, to which is added a 7 percent return on our accrual capital and our intangible capital. (Intangible capital is defined as the goodwill of the firm valued at 75 percent of gross revenues.) A separate pool of funds (about 20 percent of our compensation) is reserved for the performance pool. Each partner assesses how his or her goals helped firm goals for the year, reviews the other partners' assessment reports and then prepares an allocation schedule. Bonus pool shares are based on a group vote.[11]

Partnerships can avoid all complications by assigning net income on an equal basis among all partners. Other organizations attempt to devise plans that reward such factors as the expertise of the individuals, number of years with the organization, or the amount of time that each works. Some agreements also consider the capital invested in the business as an element that should be recognized within the allocation process.

As an initial illustration, assume that Tinker, Evers, and Chance form a partnership by investing cash of $120,000, $90,000, and $75,000, respectively. The articles of partnership

---

[10] Michael Hayes, "Pay for Performance," *Journal of Accountancy*, June 2002, p. 24.
[11] Richard Kretz, "You Want to Minimize the Pain," *Journal of Accountancy*, June 2002, p. 28.

agreement specifies that Evers will be allotted 40 percent of all profits and losses because of previous business experience. Tinker and Chance are to divide the remaining 60 percent equally. This agreement also stipulates that each partner is allowed to withdraw $10,000 in cash annually from the business. The amount of this withdrawal does not directly depend on the method utilized for income allocation. *From an accounting perspective, the assignment of income and the setting of withdrawal limits are two separate decisions.*

At the end of the first year of operations, the partnership reports net income of $60,000. To reflect the changes made in the partners' capital balances, the closing process consists of the following two journal entries. The assumption is made here that each partner has taken the allowed amount of drawing during the year. In addition, for convenience, all revenues and expenses already have been closed into the Income Summary account.

Tinker, Capital	10,000	
Evers, Capital.	10,000	
Chance, Capital	10,000	
Tinker, Drawing		10,000
Evers, Drawing		10,000
Chance, Drawing		10,000
To close out drawing accounts recording payments made to the three partners.		

Income Summary	60,000	
Tinker, Capital (30%)		18,000
Evers, Capital (40%)		24,000
Chance, Capital (30%)		18,000
To allocate net income based on provisions of partnership agreement.		

Statement of Partners' Capital

Because a partnership does not separately disclose a retained earnings balance, the statement of retained earnings usually reported by a corporation is replaced by a statement of partners' capital. The following financial statement is based on the data presented for the partnership of Tinker, Evers, and Chance. The changes made during the year in the individual capital accounts are outlined along with totals representing the partnership as a whole:

TINKER, EVERS, AND CHANCE
Statement of Partners' Capital
For Year Ending December 31, Year 1

	Tinker, Capital	Evers, Capital	Chance, Capital	Totals
Capital balances beginning of year	$120,000	$ 90,000	$ 75,000	$285,000
Allocation of net income	18,000	24,000	18,000	60,000
Drawings	(10,000)	(10,000)	(10,000)	(30,000)
Capital balances end of year	$128,000	$104,000	$ 83,000	$315,000

LO6

Allocate income to partners when interest and/or salary factors are included.

Alternative Allocation Techniques—Example 1

Assigning net income based on a ratio may be simple, but this approach is not necessarily equitable to all partners. For example, assume that Tinker does not participate in the partnership's operations but is the contributor of the highest amount of capital. Evers and Chance both work full-time in the business, but Evers has considerably more experience in this line of work.

Under these circumstances, no single ratio is likely to reflect properly the various contributions made by each partner. Indeed, an unlimited number of alternative allocation plans could be devised in hope of achieving fair treatment for all parties. For example, because of the different levels of capital investments, consideration should be given to including interest within the allocation process to reward the contributions. A compensation allowance is also a possibility, usually in an amount corresponding to the number of hours worked or the level of a partner's business expertise.

To demonstrate one possible option, assume that Tinker, Evers, and Chance begin their partnership based on the original facts except that they arrive at a more detailed method of allocating profits and losses. After considerable negotiation, an articles of partnership agreement credits each partner annually for interest in an amount equal to 10 percent of that partner's beginning capital balance for the year. Evers and Chance also will be allotted $15,000 each as a compensation allowance in recognition of their participation in daily operations. Any remaining profit or loss will be split 4:3:3, with the largest share going to Evers because of the work experience that this partner brings to the business. As with any appropriate allocation, this pattern attempts to provide fair treatment for all three partners.

Under this arrangement, the $60,000 net income earned by the partnership in the first year of operation would be prorated as follows. The sequential alignment of the various provisions is irrelevant except that the ratio, which is used to assign the remaining profit or loss, must be calculated last.

	Tinker	Evers	Chance	Totals
Interest (10% of beginning capital)	$12,000	$ 9,000	$ 7,500	$28,500
Compensation allowance . . .	–0–	15,000	15,000	30,000
Remaining income:				
$ 60,000				
(28,500)				
(30,000)				
$ 1,500	450 (30%)	600 (40%)	450 (30%)	1,500
Totals	$12,450	$24,600	$22,950	$60,000

For the Tinker, Evers, and Chance partnership, the allocations just calculated lead to the following year-end closing entry:

Income Summary	60,000	
Tinker, Capital		12,450
Evers, Capital		24,600
Chance, Capital		22,950
To allocate income for the year to the individual partner's capital accounts based on partnership agreement.		

Alternative Allocation Techniques—Example 2

As the preceding illustration indicates, the assignment process is no more than a series of mechanical steps reflecting the change in each partner's capital balance resulting from the provisions of the partnership agreement. The number of different allocation procedures that could be employed is limited solely by the partners' imagination. Although interest, compensation allowances, and various ratios are the predominant factors encountered in practice, other possibilities exist. Therefore, another approach to the allocation process is presented to further illustrate some of the variations that can be utilized. A two-person partnership is used here to simplify the computations.

Assume that Webber and Rice formed a partnership in 2005 to operate a bookstore. Webber contributed the initial capital, and Rice manages the business. With the assistance of their accountant, they wrote an articles of partnership agreement that contains the following provisions:

1. Each partner is allowed to draw $1,000 in cash from the business every month. Any withdrawal in excess of that figure will be accounted for as a direct reduction to the partner's capital balance.

2. Partnership profits and losses will be allocated each year according to the following plan:

   a. Each partner will earn 15 percent interest based on the monthly average capital balance for the year (calculated without regard for normal drawings or current income).

   b. As a reward for operating the business, Rice is to receive credit for a bonus equal to 20 percent of the year's net income. However, no bonus is earned if the partnership reports a net loss.

   c. The two partners will divide any remaining profit or loss equally.

   Assume that Webber and Rice subsequently begin the year 2011 with capital balances of $150,000 and $30,000, respectively. On April 1 of that year, Webber invests an additional $8,000 cash in the business, and on July 1, Rice withdraws $6,000 in excess of the specified drawing allowance. Assume further that the partnership reports income of $30,000 for 2011.

   Because the interest factor established in this allocation plan is based on a monthly average figure, the specific amount to be credited to each partner is determined by means of a preliminary calculation:

Webber—Interest Allocation

Beginning balance:	$150,000 × 3 months =	$ 450,000
Balance, 4/1/11:	$158,000 × 9 months =	1,422,000
		1,872,000
		× 1/12
Monthly average capital balance		156,000
Interest rate		× 15%
Interest credited to Webber		$ 23,400

Rice—Interest Allocation

Beginning balance:	$30,000 × 6 months =	$180,000
Balance, 7/1/11:	$24,000 × 6 months =	144,000
		324,000
		× 1/12
Monthly average capital balance		27,000
Interest rate		× 15%
Interest credited to Rice		$ 4,050

Following this initial computation, the actual income assignment can proceed according to the provisions specified in the articles of partnership. The stipulations drawn by Webber and Rice must be followed exactly, even though the business's $30,000 profit in 2011 is not sufficient to cover both the interest and the bonus. Income allocation is a mechanical process that should always be carried out as stated in the articles of partnership without regard to the specific level of income or loss.

Based on the plan that was created, Webber's capital increases by $21,675 during 2011 but Rice's account increases by only $8,325:

	Webber	Rice	Totals
Interest (above)	$23,400	$ 4,050	$27,450
Bonus (20% × $30,000)	–0–	6,000	6,000
Remaining income (loss):			
$ 30,000			
(27,450)			
(6,000)			
$ (3,450)	(1,725) (50%)	(1,725) (50%)	(3,450)
Totals	$21,675	$ 8,325	$30,000

ACCOUNTING FOR PARTNERSHIP DISSOLUTION

LO7

Discuss the meaning of partnership dissolution and understand that a dissolution will often have little or no effect on the operations of the partnership business.

Many partnerships limit capital transactions almost exclusively to contributions, drawings, and profit and loss allocations. Normally, though, over any extended period, changes in the members who make up a partnership occur. Employees may be promoted into the partnership or new owners brought in from outside the organization to add capital or expertise to the business. Current partners eventually retire, die, or simply elect to leave the partnership. Large operations may even experience such changes on a routine basis.

Regardless of the nature or the frequency of the event, any alteration in the specific individuals composing a partnership automatically leads to legal dissolution. In many instances, the breakup is merely a prerequisite to the formation of a new partnership. For example, if Abernethy and Chapman decide to allow Miller to become a partner in their business, the legally recognized partnership of Abernethy and Chapman has to be dissolved first. The business property as well as the right to future profits can then be conveyed to the newly formed partnership of Abernethy, Chapman, and Miller. The change is a legal one. Actual operations of the business would probably continue unimpeded by this alteration in ownership.

Conversely, should the partners so choose, dissolution can be a preliminary step in the termination and liquidation of the business. The death of a partner, lack of sufficient profits, or internal management differences can lead the partners to break up the partnership business. Under this circumstance, the partnership sells properties, pays debts, and distributes any remaining assets to the individual partners. Thus, in liquidations (which are analyzed in detail in the next chapter), both the partnership and the business cease to exist.

Dissolution—Admission of a New Partner

One of the most prevalent changes in the makeup of a partnership is the addition of a new partner. An employee may have worked for years to gain this opportunity, or a prospective partner might offer the new investment capital or business experience necessary for future business success. An individual can gain admittance to a partnership in one of two ways: (1) by purchasing an ownership interest from a current partner or (2) by contributing assets directly to the business.

In recording either type of transaction, the accountant has the option, once again, to retain the book value of all partnership assets and liabilities (as exemplified by the bonus method) or revalue these accounts to their present fair values (the goodwill method). The decision as to a theoretical preference between the bonus and goodwill methods hinges on one single question: *Should the dissolved partnership and the newly formed partnership be viewed as two separate reporting entities?*

If the new partnership is merely an extension of the old, no basis exists for restatement. The transfer of ownership is a change only in a legal sense and has no direct impact on business assets and liabilities. However, if the continuation of the business represents a legitimate transfer of property from one partnership to another, revaluation of all accounts and recognition of goodwill can be justified.

Because both approaches are encountered in practice, this textbook presents each. However, the concerns previously discussed in connection with partnership goodwill still exist: Recognition is not based on historical cost and no objective verification of the capitalized amount can be made. One alternative revaluation approach that attempts to circumvent the problems involved with partnership goodwill has been devised. This hybrid method revalues all partnership assets and liabilities to fair value without making any corresponding recognition of goodwill.

LO8

Prepare journal entries to record the acquisition by a new partner of either all or a portion of a current partner's interest.

Admission through Purchase of a Current Interest

As mentioned, one method of gaining admittance to a partnership is by the purchase of a current interest. One or more partners can choose to sell their portion of the business to an outside party. This type of transaction is most common in operations that rely primarily on monetary capital rather than on the business expertise of the partners.

In making a transfer of ownership, a partner can actually convey only three rights:

1. *The right of co-ownership in the business property.* This right justifies the partner's periodic drawings from the business as well as the distribution settlement paid at liquidation or at the time of a partner's withdrawal.
2. *The right to share in profits and losses as specified in the articles of partnership.*
3. *The right to participate in the management of the business.*

Unless restricted by the articles of partnership, every partner has the power to sell or assign the first two of these rights at any time. Their transfer poses no threat of financial harm to the remaining partners. In contrast, partnership law states that the right to participate in the management of the business can be conveyed only with the consent of all partners. This particular right is considered essential to the future earning power of the enterprise as well as the maintenance of business assets. Therefore, current partners are protected from the intrusion of parties who might be considered detrimental to the management of the company.

As an illustration, assume that Scott, Thompson, and York formed a partnership several years ago. Subsequently, York decides to leave the partnership and offers to sell his interest to Morgan. Although York may transfer the right of property ownership as well as the specified share of future profits and losses, the partnership does not automatically admit Morgan. York legally remains a partner until such time as both Scott and Thompson agree to allow Morgan to participate in the management of the business.

To demonstrate the accounting procedures applicable to the transfer of a partnership interest, assume that the following information is available relating to the partnership of Scott, Thompson, and York:

Partner	Capital Balance	Profit and Loss Ratio
Scott	$ 50,000	20%
Thompson	30,000	50
York	20,000	30
Total capital	$100,000	

As often happens, the relationship of the capital accounts to one another does not correspond with the partners' profit and loss ratio. Capital balances are historical cost figures. They result from contributions and withdrawals made throughout the life of the business as well as from the allocation of partnership income. Therefore, any correlation between a partner's recorded capital at a particular point in time and the profit and loss percentage would probably be coincidental. Scott, for example, has 50 percent of the current partnership capital ($50,000/$100,000) but is entitled to only a 20 percent allocation of income.

Instead of York selling his interest to Morgan, assume that each of these three partners elects to transfer a 20 percent interest to Morgan for a total payment of $30,000. According to the sales contract, *the money is to be paid directly to the owners.*

One approach to recording this transaction is that, because Morgan's purchase is carried out between the individual parties, the acquisition has no impact on the assets and liabilities the partnership holds. Because the business is not involved directly, the transfer of ownership requires a simple capital reclassification without any accompanying revaluation. Book value is retained. This approach is similar to the bonus method; only a legal change in ownership is occurring so that revaluation of neither assets or liabilities nor goodwill is appropriate.

Book Value Approach		
Scott, Capital (20% of capital balance)	10,000	
Thompson, Capital (20%)	6,000	
York, Capital (20%)	4,000	
Morgan, Capital (20% of total)		20,000
To reclassify capital to reflect Morgan's acquisition. Money is paid directly to partners.		

An alternative for recording Morgan's acquisition relies on a different perspective of the new partner's admission. Legally, the partnership of Scott, Thompson, and York is transferring all assets and liabilities to the partnership of Scott, Thompson, York, and Morgan. Therefore, according to the logic underlying the goodwill method, a transaction is occurring between two separate reporting entities, an event that necessitates the complete revaluation of all assets and liabilities.

Because Morgan is paying $30,000 for a 20 percent interest in the partnership, the implied value of the business as a whole is $150,000 ($30,000/20%). However, the book value is only $100,000; thus, a $50,000 upward revaluation is indicated. This adjustment is reflected by restating specific partnership asset and liability accounts to fair value with any remaining balance recorded as goodwill. After the implied value of the partnership is established, the reclassification of ownership can be recorded based on the new capital balances.

Goodwill (Revaluation) Approach

Goodwill (or specific accounts)	50,000	
Scott, Capital (20% of goodwill)		10,000
Thompson, Capital (50%)		25,000
York, Capital (30%)		15,000
To recognize goodwill and revaluation of assets and liabilities based on value of business implied by size of Morgan's purchase price.		
Scott, Capital (20% of new capital balance)	12,000	
Thompson, Capital (20%)	11,000	
York, Capital (20%)	7,000	
Morgan, Capital (20% of new total)		30,000
To reclassify capital to reflect Morgan's acquisition. Money is paid directly to partners.		

As this entry indicates, the $50,000 revaluation is credited to the original partners based on the profit and loss ratio rather than on their percentages of capital. Recognition of goodwill (or an increase in the book value of specific accounts) indicates that unrecorded gains have accrued to the business during the previous years of operation. Therefore, the equitable treatment is to allocate this increment among the partners according to their profit and loss percentages.

LO9

Prepare journal entries to record a new partner's admission by a contribution made directly to the partnership.

Admission by a Contribution Made to the Partnership

Entrance into a partnership is not limited solely to the purchase of a current partner's interest. An outsider may be admitted to the ownership by contributing cash or other assets directly to the business rather than to the partners. For example, assume that King and Wilson maintain a partnership and presently report capital balances of $80,000 and $20,000, respectively. According to the articles of partnership, King is entitled to 60 percent of all profits and losses with the remaining 40 percent credited each year to Wilson. By agreement of the partners, Goldman is allowed to enter the partnership for a payment of $20,000 *with this money going into the business.* Based on negotiations that preceded the acquisition, all parties have agreed that Goldman receives an initial 10 percent interest in partnership property.

Bonus Credited to Original Partners   The bonus (or no revaluation) method maintains the same recorded value for all partnership assets and liabilities despite Goldman's admittance. The capital balance for this new partner is simply set at the appropriate 10 percent level based on the total book value of the partnership after the payment is recorded. Because $20,000 is invested, total reported capital increases to $120,000. Thus, Goldman's 10 percent interest is computed as $12,000. *The $8,000 difference between the amount contributed and this allotted capital balance is viewed as a bonus.* Because Goldman is willing to accept a capital balance that is less than his investment, this bonus is attributed to the original partners (again based on their profit and loss ratio). As a result of the nature of the transaction, no need exists to recognize goodwill or revalue any of the assets or liabilities.

Cash	20,000	
Goldman, Capital (10% of total capital)		12,000
King, Capital (60% of bonus)		4,800
Wilson, Capital (40% of bonus)		3,200
To record Goldman's entrance into partnership with $8,000 extra payment recorded as a bonus to the original partners.		

Goodwill Credited to Original Partners The goodwill method views Goldman's payment as evidence that the partnership as a whole possesses an actual value of $200,000 ($20,000/10%). Because, even with the new partner's investment, only $120,000 in net assets is reported, a valuation adjustment of $80,000 is implied.[12] Over the previous years, unrecorded gains have apparently accrued to the business. This $80,000 figure might reflect the need to revalue specific accounts such as inventory or equipment, although the entire amount, or some portion of it, may simply be recorded as goodwill.

Goodwill (or specific accounts)	80,000	
King, Capital (60% of goodwill)		48,000
Wilson, Capital (40%)		32,000
To recognize goodwill based on Goldman's purchase price.		
Cash	20,000	
Goldman, Capital		20,000
To record Goldman's admission into partnership.		

Comparison of Bonus Method and Goodwill Method Completely different capital balances as well as asset and liability figures result from these two approaches. In both cases, however, the new partner is credited with the appropriate 10 percent of total partnership capital.

	Bonus Method	Goodwill Method
Assets less liabilities (as reported)	$100,000	$100,000
Goldman's contribution	20,000	20,000
Goodwill	–0–	80,000
Total	$120,000	$200,000
Goldman's capital	$ 12,000	$ 20,000

Because Goldman contributed an amount more than 10 percent of the partnership's resulting book value, this business is perceived as being worth more than the recorded accounts indicate. Therefore, the bonus in the first instance and the goodwill in the second were both assumed as accruing to the two original partners. Such a presumption is not unusual in an established business, especially if profitable operations have developed over a number of years.

Hybrid Method of Recording Admission of New Partner One other approach to Goldman's admission can be devised. Assume that the assets and liabilities of the King and Wilson partnership have a book value of $100,000 as stated earlier. Also assume that a piece of land held by the business is actually worth $30,000 more than its currently recorded book value. Thus, the identifiable assets of the partnership are worth $130,000. Goldman pays $20,000 for a 10 percent interest.

[12] In this example, because $20,000 is invested in the business, total capital to be used in the goodwill computation has increased to $120,000. If, as in the previous illustration, payment had been made directly to the partners, the original capital of $100,000 is retained in determining goodwill.

In this approach, the identifiable assets (such as land) are revalued but no goodwill is recognized.

Land	30,000	
King, Capital (60% of revaluation)		18,000
Wilson, Capital (40%)		12,000
To record current fair value of land in preparation for admission of new partner.		

The admission of Goldman and the payment of $20,000 bring the total capital balance to $150,000. Because Goldman is acquiring a 10 percent interest, a capital balance of $15,000 is recorded. The extra $5,000 payment ($20,000 − $15,000) is attributed as a bonus to the original partners. In this way, asset revaluation and a capital bonus are both used to align the accounts.

Cash	20,000	
Goldman, Capital (10% of total capital)		15,000
King, Capital (60% of bonus)		3,000
Wilson, Capital (40% of bonus)		2,000
To record entrance of Goldman into partnership and bonus assigned to original partners.		

Bonus or Goodwill Credited to New Partner   As previously discussed, Goldman also may be contributing some attribute other than tangible assets to this partnership. Therefore, the articles of partnership may be written to credit the new partner, rather than the original partners, with either a bonus or goodwill. Because of an excellent professional reputation, valuable business contacts, or myriad other possible factors, Goldman might be able to negotiate a beginning capital balance in excess of the $20,000 cash contribution. This same circumstance may also result if the business is desperate for new capital and is willing to offer favorable terms as an enticement to the potential partner.

To illustrate, assume that Goldman receives a 20 percent interest in the partnership (rather than the originally stated 10 percent) in exchange for the $20,000 cash investment. The specific rationale for the higher ownership percentage need not be identified.

The bonus method sets Goldman's initial capital at $24,000 (20 percent of the $120,000 book value). To achieve this balance, a capital bonus of $4,000 must be credited to Goldman and taken from the present partners:

Cash	20,000	
King, Capital (60% of bonus)	2,400	
Wilson, Capital (40% of bonus)	1,600	
Goldman, Capital		24,000
To record Goldman's entrance into partnership with reduced payment reported as a bonus from original partners.		

If goodwill rather than a bonus is attributed to the *entering partner,* a mathematical problem arises in determining the implicit value of the business as a whole. In the current illustration, Goldman paid $20,000 for a 20 percent interest. Therefore, the value of the company is calculated as only $100,000 ($20,000/20%), a figure that is less than the $120,000 in net assets reported after the new contribution. Negative goodwill appears to exist. One possibility is that individual partnership assets are overvalued and require reduction. As an alternative, the cash contribution might not be an accurate representation of the new partner's investment. Goldman could be bringing an intangible contribution (goodwill) to the business along with the $20,000. This additional amount must be determined algebraically:

$$\text{Goldman's capital} = 20 \text{ percent of partnership capital}$$

Therefore:

$$\$20,000 + \text{Goodwill} = 0.20\,(\$100,000 + \$20,000 + \text{Goodwill})$$

$$\$20,000 + \text{Goodwill} = \$20,000 + \$4,000 + 0.20\,\text{Goodwill}$$

$$0.80\,\text{Goodwill} = \$4,000$$

$$\text{Goodwill} = \$5,000$$

If the partners determine that Goldman is, indeed, making an intangible contribution (a particular skill, for example, or a loyal clientele), Goldman should be credited with a $25,000 capital investment: $20,000 cash and $5,000 goodwill. When added to the original $100,000 in net assets reported by the partnership, this contribution raises the total capital for the business to $125,000. As the articles of partnership specified, Goldman's interest now represents a 20 percent share of the partnership ($25,000/$125,000).

Recognizing $5,000 in goodwill has established the proper relationship between the new partner and the partnership. Therefore, the following journal entry reflects this transaction:

Cash	20,000	
Goodwill	5,000	
Goldman, Capital		25,000
To record Goldman's entrance into partnership with goodwill attributed to this new partner.		

Dissolution—Withdrawal of a Partner

LO10

Prepare journal entries to record the withdrawal of a current partner.

Admission of a new partner is not the only method by which a partnership can undergo a change in composition. Over the life of the business, partners might leave the organization. Death or retirement can occur, or a partner may simply elect to withdraw from the partnership. The articles of partnership also can allow for the expulsion of a partner under certain conditions. Again, any change in membership legally dissolves the partnership, although its operations usually continue uninterrupted under the remaining partners' ownership.

Regardless of the reason for dissolution, some method of establishing an equitable settlement of the withdrawing partner's interest in the business is necessary. Often, the partner (or the partner's estate) may simply sell the interest to an outside party, with approval, or to one or more of the remaining partners. As an alternative, the business can distribute cash or other assets as a means of settling a partner's right of co-ownership. Consequently, many partnerships hold life insurance policies solely to provide adequate cash to liquidate a partner's interest upon death.

Whether death or some other reason caused the withdrawal, a final distribution will not necessarily equal the book value of the partner's capital account. A capital balance is only a recording of historical transactions and rarely represents the true value inherent in a business. Instead, payment is frequently based on the value of the partner's interest as ascertained by either negotiation or appraisal. Because a settlement determination can be derived in many ways, the articles of partnership should contain exact provisions regulating this procedure.

The withdrawal of an individual partner and the resulting distribution of partnership property can, as before, be accounted for by either the bonus (no revaluation) method or the goodwill (revaluation) method. Again, a hybrid option is also available.

As in earlier illustrations, if a bonus is recorded, the amount can be attributed to either of the parties involved: the withdrawing partner or the remaining partners. Conversely, any revaluation of partnership property (as well as the establishment of a goodwill balance) is allocated among all partners to recognize possible unrecorded gains. The hybrid approach restates assets and liabilities to fair value but does not record goodwill. This last alternative reflects the legal change in ownership but avoids the theoretical problems associated with partnership goodwill.

Accounting for the Withdrawal of a Partner—Illustration

To demonstrate the various approaches that can be taken to account for a partner's withdrawal, assume that the partnership of Duncan, Smith, and Windsor has existed for a number of years. At the present time, the partners have the following capital balances as well as the indicated profit and loss percentages:

Partner	Capital Balance	Profit and Loss Ratio
Duncan	$ 70,000	50%
Smith	20,000	30
Windsor	10,000	20
Total capital	$100,000	

Windsor decides to withdraw from the partnership, but Duncan and Smith plan to continue operating the business. As per the original partnership agreement, a final settlement distribution for any withdrawing partner is computed based on the following specified provisions:

1. An independent expert will appraise the business to determine its estimated fair value.
2. Any individual who leaves the partnership will receive cash or other assets equal to that partner's current capital balance after including an appropriate share of any adjustment indicated by the previous valuation. The allocation of unrecorded gains and losses is based on the normal profit and loss ratio.

Following Windsor's decision to withdraw from the partnership, its property is immediately appraised. Total fair value is estimated at $180,000, a figure $80,000 in excess of book value. According to this valuation, land held by the partnership is currently worth $50,000 more than its original cost. In addition, $30,000 in goodwill is attributed to the partnership based on its value as a going concern. *Therefore, Windsor receives $26,000 on leaving the partnership: the original $10,000 capital balance plus a 20 percent share of this $80,000 increment.* The amount of payment is not in dispute, but the method of recording the withdrawal is.

Bonus Method Applied

If the partnership used the bonus method to record this transaction, the extra $16,000 paid to Windsor is simply assigned as a decrease in the remaining partners' capital accounts. Historically, Duncan and Smith have been credited with 50 percent and 30 percent of all profits and losses, respectively. This same relative ratio is used now to allocate the reduction between these two remaining partners on a ⅝ and ⅜ basis:

Bonus Method		
Windsor, Capital (to remove account balance)	10,000	
Duncan, Capital (⅝ of excess distribution)	10,000	
Smith, Capital (⅜ of excess distribution)	6,000	
Cash		26,000
To record Windsor's withdrawal with $16,000 excess distribution taken from remaining partners.		

Goodwill Method Applied

This same transaction can also be accounted for by means of the goodwill (or revaluation) approach. The appraisal indicates that land is undervalued on the partnership's records by $50,000 and that goodwill of $30,000 has apparently accrued to the business over the years. The first of the following entries recognizes these valuations. This adjustment properly equates

Windsor's capital balance with the $26,000 cash amount to be distributed. Windsor's equity balance is merely removed in the second entry at the time of payment.

Goodwill Method		
Land	50,000	
Goodwill	30,000	
Duncan, Capital (50%)		40,000
Smith, Capital (30%)		24,000
Windsor, Capital (20%)		16,000
To recognize land value and goodwill as a preliminary step to Windsor's withdrawal.		
Windsor, Capital (to remove account balance)	26,000	
Cash		26,000
To distribute cash to Windsor in settlement of partnership interest.		

The implied value of a partnership as a whole cannot be determined directly from the amount distributed to a withdrawing partner. For example, paying Windsor $26,000 did not indicate that total capital should be $130,000 ($26,000/20%). This computation is appropriate only when (1) a new partner is admitted or (2) the percentage of capital is the same as the profit and loss ratio. Here, an outside valuation of the business indicated that it was worth $80,000 more than book value. As a 20 percent owner, Windsor was entitled to $16,000 of that amount, raising the partner's capital account from $10,000 to $26,000, the amount of the final payment.

Hybrid Method Applied

As indicated previously, a hybrid approach also can be adopted to record a partner's withdrawal. It also recognizes asset and liability revaluations but ignores goodwill. A bonus must then be recorded to reconcile the partner's adjusted capital balance with the final distribution.

The following journal entry, for example, does not record goodwill. However, the book value of the land is increased by $50,000 in recognition of present worth. This adjustment increases Windsor's capital balance to $20,000, a figure that is still less than the $26,000 distribution. The $6,000 difference is recorded as a bonus taken from the remaining two partners according to their relative profit and loss ratio.

Hybrid Method		
Land	50,000	
Duncan, Capital (50%)		25,000
Smith, Capital (30%)		15,000
Windsor, Capital (20%)		10,000
To adjust Land account to fair value as a preliminary step in Windsor's withdrawal.		
Windsor, Capital (to remove account balances)	20,000	
Duncan, Capital (⅝ of bonus)	3,750	
Smith, Capital (⅜ of bonus)	2,250	
Cash		26,000
To record final distribution to Windsor with $6,000 bonus taken from remaining partners.		

Summary

1. A partnership is defined as "an association of two or more persons to carry on a business as co-owners for profit." This form of business organization exists throughout the U.S. economy ranging in size from small, part-time operations to international enterprises. The partnership format is popular for many reasons, including the ease of creation and the avoidance of the double taxation that is

inherent in corporate ownership. However, the unlimited liability incurred by each general partner normally restricts the growth potential of most partnerships. Thus, although the number of partnerships in the United States is large, the size of each tends to be small.

2. Over the years, a number of different types of organizations have been developed to take advantage of both the single taxation of partnerships and the limited liability afforded to corporate stockholders. Such legal forms include S corporations, limited partnerships, limited liability partnerships, and limited liability companies.

3. The unique elements of partnership accounting are found primarily in the capital accounts accumulated for each partner. The basis for recording these balances is the articles of partnership, a document that should be established as a prerequisite to the formation of any partnership. One of the principal provisions of this agreement is each partner's initial investment. Noncash contributions such as inventory or land are entered into the partnership's accounting records at fair value.

4. In forming a partnership, the partners' contributions need not be limited to tangible assets. A particular line of expertise possessed by a partner and an established clientele are attributes that can have a significant value to a partnership. Two methods of recording this type of investment are found in practice. The bonus method recognizes only identifiable assets. The capital accounts are then aligned to indicate the balances negotiated by the partners. According to the goodwill approach, all contributions (even those of a nebulous nature such as expertise) are valued and recorded, often as goodwill.

5. Another accounting issue to be resolved in forming a partnership is the allocation of annual net income. In closing out the revenue and expense accounts at the end of each period, some assignment must be made to the individual capital balances. Although an equal division can be used to allocate any profit or loss, partners frequently devise unique plans in an attempt to be equitable. Such factors as time worked, expertise, and invested capital should be considered in creating an allocation procedure.

6. Over time, changes occur in the makeup of a partnership because of death or retirement or because of the admission of new partners. Such changes dissolve the existing partnership, although the business frequently continues uninterrupted through a newly formed partnership. If, for example, a new partner is admitted by the acquisition of a present interest, the capital balances can simply be reclassified to reflect the change in ownership. As an alternative, the purchase price may be viewed as evidence of the underlying value of the organization as a whole. Based on this calculation, asset and liability balances are adjusted to fair value, and any residual goodwill is recognized.

7. Admission into an existing partnership also can be achieved by a direct capital contribution from the new partner. Because of the parties' negotiations, the amount invested will not always agree with the beginning capital balance attributed to the new partner. The bonus method resolves this conflict by simply reclassifying the various capital accounts to align the balances with specified totals and percentages. No revaluation is carried out under this approach. Conversely, according to the goodwill method, all asset and liability accounts are adjusted first to fair value. The price the new partner paid is used to compute an implied value for the partnership, and any excess over fair value is recorded as goodwill.

8. The composition of a partnership also can undergo changes because of the death or retirement of a partner. Individuals may decide to withdraw. Such changes legally dissolve the partnership, although business operations frequently continue under the remaining partners' ownership. In compensating the departing partner, the final asset distribution may differ from the ending capital balance. This disparity can, again, be accounted for by means of the bonus method, which adjusts the remaining capital accounts to absorb the bonus. The goodwill approach by which all assets and liabilities are restated to fair value with any goodwill being recognized also can be applied. Finally, a hybrid method revalues the assets and liabilities but ignores goodwill. Under this last approach, any amount paid to the departing partner in excess of the newly adjusted capital balance is accounted for by means of the bonus method.

Comprehensive Illustration

PROBLEM

(*Estimated Time: 30 to 55 Minutes*) Heyman and Mullins begin a partnership on January 1, 2010. Heyman invests $40,000 cash and inventory costing $15,000 but with a current appraised value of only $12,000. Mullins contributes a building with a $40,000 book value and a $48,000 fair value. The partnership also accepts responsibility for a $10,000 note payable owed in connection with this building.

The partners agree to begin operations with equal capital balances. The articles of partnership also provide that at each year-end, profits and losses are allocated as follows:

1. For managing the business, Heyman is credited with a bonus of 10 percent of partnership income after subtracting the bonus. No bonus is accrued if the partnership records a loss.

2. Both partners are entitled to interest equal to 10 percent of the average monthly capital balance for the year without regard for the income or drawings of that year.

3. Any remaining profit or loss is divided 60 percent to Heyman and 40 percent to Mullins.

4. Each partner is allowed to withdraw $800 per month in cash from the business.

On October 1, 2010, Heyman invested an additional $12,000 cash in the business. For 2010, the partnership reported income of $33,000.

Lewis, an employee, is allowed to join the partnership on January 1, 2011. The new partner invests $66,000 directly into the business for a one-third interest in the partnership property. The revised partnership agreement still allows for both the bonus to Heyman and the 10 percent interest, but all remaining profits and losses are now split 40 percent each to Heyman and Lewis with the remaining 20 percent to Mullins. Lewis is also entitled to $800 per month in drawings.

Mullins chooses to withdraw from the partnership a few years later. After negotiations, all parties agree that Mullins should be paid a $90,000 settlement. The capital balances on that date were as follows:

Heyman, capital.	$88,000
Mullins, capital	78,000
Lewis, capital.	72,000

Required

a. Assuming that this partnership uses the bonus method exclusively, make all necessary journal entries. Entries for the monthly drawings of the partners are not required.

b. Assuming that this partnership uses the goodwill method exclusively, make all necessary journal entries. Again, entries for the monthly drawings are not required.

SOLUTION

a. **Bonus Method**

2010

Jan. 1 All contributed property is recorded at fair value. Under the bonus method, total capital is then divided as specified between the partners.

Cash	40,000	
Inventory	12,000	
Building	48,000	
Note Payable		10,000
Heyman, Capital (50%)		45,000
Mullins, Capital (50%)		45,000
To record initial contributions to partnership along with equal capital balances.		

Oct. 1

Cash	12,000	
Heyman, Capital		12,000
To record additional investment by partner.		

Dec. 31 Both the bonus assigned to Heyman and the interest accrual must be computed as preliminary steps in the income allocation process. Because the bonus is based on income after subtracting the bonus, the amount must be calculated algebraically:

$$\begin{aligned} \text{Bonus} &= 0.10\,(\$33,000 - \text{Bonus}) \\ \text{Bonus} &= \$3,300 - 0.10\ \text{Bonus} \\ 1.10\ \text{Bonus} &= \$3,300 \\ \text{Bonus} &= \$3,000 \end{aligned}$$

According to the articles of partnership, the interest allocation is based on a monthly average figure. Mullins's capital balance of $45,000 did not change during the year; therefore $4,500 (10 percent) is the appropriate interest accrual for that partner. However, because of the October 1, 2010, contribution, Heyman's interest must be determined as follows:

Beginning balance:	$45,000 × 9 months =	$405,000
New balance:	$57,000 × 3 months =	171,000
		576,000
		× 1/12
Monthly average—capital balance		48,000
Interest rate		× 10%
Interest credited to Heyman		$ 4,800

Following the bonus and interest computations, the $33,000 income earned by the business is allocated according to the previously specified arrangement:

	Heyman	Mullins	Totals
Bonus	$ 3,000	–0–	$ 3,000
Interest	4,800	$ 4,500	9,300
Remaining income:			
$33,000			
(3,000)			
(9,300)			
$20,700	12,420 (60%)	8,280 (40%)	20,700
Income allocation	$20,220	$12,780	$33,000

The partnership's closing entries for the year would be recorded as follows:

Heyman, Capital	9,600	
Mullins, Capital	9,600	
Heyman, Drawing		9,600
Mullins, Drawing		9,600
To close out $800 per month drawing accounts for the year.		
Income Summary	33,000	
Heyman, Capital		20,220
Mullins, Capital		12,780
To close out profit for year to capital accounts as computed above.		

At the end of this initial year of operation, the partners' capital accounts hold these balances:

	Heyman	Mullins	Totals
Beginning balance	$45,000	$45,000	$ 90,000
Additional investment	12,000	–0–	12,000
Drawing	(9,600)	(9,600)	(19,200)
Net income (above)	20,220	12,780	33,000
Total capital	$67,620	$48,180	$115,800

2011
Jan. 1 Lewis contributed $66,000 to the business for a one-third interest in the partnership property. Combined with the $115,800 balance previously computed, the partnership now has total capital of $181,800. Because no revaluation is recorded under the bonus approach, a one-third interest in the partnership equals $60,600 ($181,800 × 1/3). Lewis has invested $5,400 in excess of this amount, a balance viewed as a bonus accruing to the original partners:

Cash	66,000	
Lewis, Capital		60,600
Heyman, Capital (60% of bonus)		3,240
Mullins, Capital (40% of bonus)		2,160
To record Lewis's entrance into partnership with bonus to original partners.		

Several years later	The final event in this illustration is Mullins's withdrawal from the partnership. Although this partner's capital balance reports only $78,000, the final distribution is set at $90,000.

The extra $12,000 payment represents a bonus assigned to Mullins, an amount that decreases the capital of the remaining two partners. Because Heyman and Lewis have previously accrued equal 40 percent shares of all profits and losses, the reduction is split evenly between the two.

Mullins, Capital	78,000	
Heyman, Capital (½ of bonus payment)	6,000	
Lewis, Capital (½ of bonus payment)	6,000	
Cash		90,000
To record withdrawal of Mullins with a bonus from remaining partners.		

b. Goodwill Method

2010

Jan. 1	The fair value of Heyman's contribution is $52,000, whereas Mullins is investing only a net $38,000 (the value of the building less the accompanying debt). Because the capital accounts are initially to be equal, Mullins is presumed to be contributing goodwill of $14,000.

Cash	40,000	
Inventory	12,000	
Building	48,000	
Goodwill	14,000	
Note payable		10,000
Heyman, Capital		52,000
Mullins, Capital		52,000
Creation of partnership with goodwill attributed to Mullins.		

Oct. 1

Cash	12,000	
Heyman, Capital		12,000
To record additional contribution by partner		

Dec. 31	Although Heyman's bonus is still $3,000 as derived in requirement (*a*), the interest accruals must be recalculated because the capital balances are different. Mullins's capital for the entire year was $52,000; thus, interest of $5,200 (10 percent) is appropriate. However, Heyman's balance changed during the year so that a monthly average must be determined as a basis for computing interest:

Beginning balance:	$52,000 × 9 months =	$468,000
New balance:	$64,000 × 3 months =	192,000
		660,000
		× ¹⁄₁₂
Monthly average—capital balance	......	55,000
Interest rate	....	× 10%
Interest credited to Heyman	....	$5,500

The $33,000 partnership income is allocated as follows:

	Heyman	**Mullins**	**Totals**
Bonus (above)	$ 3,000	–0–	$ 3,000
Interest (above)	5,500	$ 5,200	10,700
Remaining income:			
$33,000			
(3,000)			
(10,700)			
$19,300	11,580 (60%)	7,720 (40%)	19,300
Income allocation	$20,080	$12,920	$33,000

The closing entries made under the goodwill approach would be as follows:

Heyman, Capital	9,600	
Mullins, Capital	9,600	
Heyman, Drawing		9,600
Mullins, Drawing		9,600
To close out drawing accounts for the year.		
Income Summary	33,000	
Heyman, Capital		20,080
Mullins, Capital		12,920
To assign profits per allocation schedule.		

After the closing process, the capital balances are composed of the following items:

	Heyman	Mullins	Totals
Beginning balance	$52,000	$52,000	$104,000
Additional investment	12,000	–0–	12,000
Drawing	(9,600)	(9,600)	(19,200)
Net income	20,080	12,920	33,000
Total capital	$74,480	$55,320	$129,800

2011

Jan. 1   Lewis's investment of $66,000 for a one-third interest in the partnership property implies that the business as a whole is worth $198,000 ($66,000 divided by ⅓). After adding Lewis's contribution to the present capital balance of $129,800, the business reports total net assets of only $195,800. Thus, a $2,200 increase in value ($198,000 − $195,800) is indicated and will be recognized at this time. Under the assumption that all partnership assets and liabilities are valued appropriately, this entire balance is attributed to goodwill.

Goodwill	2,200	
Heyman, Capital (60%)		1,320
Mullins, Capital (40%)		880
To recognize goodwill based on Lewis's acquisition price.		
Cash	66,000	
Lewis, Capital		66,000
To admit Lewis to the partnership		

Several years later   To conclude this illustration, Mullins's withdrawal must be recorded. This partner is to receive a distribution that is $12,000 more than the corresponding capital balance of $78,000. Because Mullins is entitled to a 20 percent share of profits and losses, the additional $12,000 payment indicates that the partnership as a whole is undervalued by $60,000 ($12,000/20%). Only in that circumstance would the extra payment to Mullins be justified. Therefore, once again, goodwill is recognized and is followed by the final distribution.

Goodwill	60,000	
Heyman, Capital (40%)		24,000
Mullins, Capital (20%)		12,000
Lewis, Capital (40%)		24,000
Recognition of goodwill based on withdrawal amount paid to Mullins.		
Mullins, Capital	90,000	
Cash		90,000
To distribute money to partner.		

Questions

1. What are the advantages of operating a business as a partnership rather than as a corporation? What are the disadvantages?

2. How does partnership accounting differ from corporate accounting?

3. What information do the capital accounts found in partnership accounting convey?

4. Describe the differences between a Subchapter S corporation and a Subchapter C corporation.

5. A company is being created and the owners are trying to decide whether to form a general partnership, a limited liability partnership, or a limited liability company. What are the advantages and disadvantages of each of these legal forms?

6. What is an articles of partnership agreement, and what information should this document contain?

7. What valuation should be recorded for noncash assets transferred to a partnership by one of the partners?

8. If a partner is contributing attributes to a partnership such as an established clientele or a particular expertise, what two methods can be used to record the contribution? Describe each method.

9. What is the purpose of a drawing account in a partnership's financial records?

10. At what point in the accounting process does the allocation of partnership income become significant?

11. What provisions in a partnership agreement can be used to establish an equitable allocation of income among all partners?

12. If no agreement exists in a partnership as to the allocation of income, what method is appropriate?

13. What is a partnership dissolution? Does dissolution automatically necessitate the cessation of business and the liquidation of partnership assets?

14. By what methods can a new partner gain admittance into a partnership?

15. When a partner sells an ownership interest in a partnership, what rights are conveyed to the new owner?

16. A new partner enters a partnership and goodwill is calculated and credited to the original partners. How is the specific amount of goodwill assigned to these partners?

17. Under what circumstance might goodwill be allocated to a new partner entering a partnership?

18. When a partner withdraws from a partnership, why is the final distribution often based on the appraised value of the business rather than on the book value of the capital account balance?

Problems

LO1

1. Which of the following is not a reason for the popularity of partnerships as a legal form for businesses?
   a. Partnerships may be formed merely by an oral agreement.
   b. Partnerships can more easily generate significant amounts of capital.
   c. Partnerships avoid the double taxation of income that is found in corporations.
   d. In some cases, losses may be used to offset gains for tax purposes.

LO1

2. How does partnership accounting differ from corporate accounting?
   a. The matching principle is not considered appropriate for partnership accounting.
   b. Revenues are recognized at a different time by a partnership than is appropriate for a corporation.
   c. Individual capital accounts replace the contributed capital and retained earnings balances found in corporate accounting.
   d. Partnerships report all assets at fair value as of the latest balance sheet date.

LO2

3. Which of the following best describes the articles of partnership agreement?
   a. The purpose of the partnership and partners' rights and responsibilities are required elements of the articles of partnership.
   b. The articles of partnership are a legal covenant and must be expressed in writing to be valid.
   c. The articles of partnership are an agreement that limits partners' liability to partnership assets.
   d. The articles of partnership are a legal covenant that may be expressed orally or in writing, and forms the central governance for a partnership's operations.

LO9

4. Pat, Jean Lou, and Diane are partners with capital balances of $50,000, $30,000, and $20,000, respectively. These three partners share profits and losses equally. For an investment of $50,000 cash (paid to the business), MaryAnn will be admitted as a partner with a one-fourth interest in capital and profits. Based on this information, which of the following best justifies the amount of MaryAnn's investment?
   a. MaryAnn will receive a bonus from the other partners upon her admission to the partnership.
   b. Assets of the partnership were overvalued immediately prior to MaryAnn's investment.
   c. The book value of the partnership's net assets was less than the fair value immediately prior to MaryAnn's investment.
   d. MaryAnn is apparently bringing goodwill into the partnership, and her capital account will be credited for the appropriate amount.

LO9

5. A partnership has the following capital balances:

Albert (50% of gains and losses)	$ 80,000
Barrymore (20%)	60,000
Candroth (30%)	140,000

Danville is going to invest $70,000 into the business to acquire a 30 percent ownership interest. Goodwill is to be recorded. What will be Danville's beginning capital balance?

   a. $70,000.

   b. $90,000.

   c. $105,000.

   d. $120,000.

LO8

6. A partnership has the following capital balances:

Elgin (40% of gains and losses)	$100,000
Jethro (30%)	200,000
Foy (30%)	300,000

Oscar is going to pay a total of $200,000 to these three partners to acquire a 25 percent ownership interest from each. Goodwill is to be recorded. What is Jethro's capital balance after the transaction?

   a. $150,000.

   b. $175,000.

   c. $195,000.

   d. $200,000.

LO9

7. The capital balance for Bolcar is $110,000 and for Neary is $40,000. These two partners share profits and losses 70 percent (Bolcar) and 30 percent (Neary). Kansas invests $50,000 in cash into the partnership for a 30 percent ownership. The bonus method will be used. What is Neary's capital balance after Kansas's investment?

   a. $35,000.

   b. $37,000.

   c. $40,000.

   d. $43,000.

LO9

8. Bishop has a capital balance of $120,000 in a local partnership, and Cotton has a $90,000 balance. These two partners share profits and losses by a ratio of 60 percent to Bishop and 40 percent to Cotton. Lovett invests $60,000 in cash in the partnership for a 20 percent ownership. The goodwill method will be used. What is Cotton's capital balance after this new investment?

   a. $99,600.

   b. $102,000.

   c. $112,000.

   d. $126,000.

LO9

9. The capital balance for Messalina is $210,000 and for Romulus is $140,000. These two partners share profits and losses 60 percent (Messalina) and 40 percent (Romulus). Claudius invests $100,000 in cash in the partnership for a 20 percent ownership. The bonus method will be used. What are the capital balances for Messalina, Romulus, and Claudius after this investment is recorded?

   a. $216,000, $144,000, $90,000.

   b. $218,000, $142,000, $88,000.

   c. $222,000, $148,000, $80,000.

   d. $240,000, $160,000, $100,000.

LO6

10. A partnership begins its first year with the following capital balances:

Arthur, Capital	$ 60,000
Baxter, Capital	80,000
Cartwright, Capital	100,000

The articles of partnership stipulate that profits and losses be assigned in the following manner:

- Each partner is allocated interest equal to 10 percent of the beginning capital balance.
- Baxter is allocated compensation of $20,000 per year.
- Any remaining profits and losses are allocated on a 3:3:4 basis, respectively.
- Each partner is allowed to withdraw up to $5,000 cash per year.

Assuming that the net income is $50,000 and that each partner withdraws the maximum amount allowed, what is the balance in Cartwright's capital account at the end of that year?

a. $105,800.

b. $106,200.

c. $106,900.

d. $107,400.

LO4, LO5, LO6

11. A partnership begins its first year of operations with the following capital balances:

Winston, Capital	$110,000
Durham, Capital	80,000
Salem, Capital	110,000

According to the articles of partnership, all profits will be assigned as follows:

- Winston will be awarded an annual salary of $20,000 with $10,000 assigned to Salem.
- The partners will be attributed interest equal to 10 percent of the capital balance as of the first day of the year.
- The remainder will be assigned on a 5:2:3 basis, respectively.
- Each partner is allowed to withdraw up to $10,000 per year.

Assume that the net loss for the first year of operations is $20,000 and that net income for the subsequent year is $40,000. Assume also that each partner withdraws the maximum amount from the business each period. What is the balance in Winston's capital account at the end of the second year?

a. $102,600.

b. $104,400.

c. $108,600.

d. $109,200.

LO10

12. A partnership has the following capital balances:

Allen, Capital	$60,000
Burns, Capital	30,000
Costello, Capital	90,000

Profits and losses are split as follows: Allen (20%), Burns (30%), and Costello (50%). Costello wants to leave the partnership and is paid $100,000 from the business based on provisions in the articles of partnership. If the partnership uses the bonus method, what is the balance of Burns's capital account after Costello withdraws?

a. $24,000.

b. $27,000.

c. $33,000.

d. $36,000.

LO10

13. At year-end, the Cisco partnership has the following capital balances:

Montana, Capital	$130,000
Rice, Capital	110,000
Craig, Capital	80,000
Taylor, Capital	70,000

Profits and losses are split on a 3:3:2:2 basis, respectively. Craig decides to leave the partnership and is paid $90,000 from the business based on the original contractual agreement. If the goodwill method is to be applied, what is the balance of Montana's capital account after Craig withdraws?

a. $133,000.

b. $137,500.

c. $140,000.

d. $145,000.

Problems 14 and 15 are *independent* problems based on the following capital account balances:

William (40% of gains and losses)	$220,000
Jennings (40%)	160,000
Bryan (20%)	110,000

LO8

14. Darrow invests $270,000 in cash for a 30 percent ownership interest. The money goes to the original partners. Goodwill is to be recorded. How much goodwill should be recognized, and what is Darrow's beginning capital balance?

    a. $410,000 and $270,000.

    b. $140,000 and $270,000.

    c. $140,000 and $189,000.

    d. $410,000 and $189,000.

LO9

15. Darrow invests $250,000 in cash for a 30 percent ownership interest. The money goes to the business. No goodwill or other revaluation is to be recorded. After the transaction, what is Jennings's capital balance?

    a. $160,000.

    b. $168,000.

    c. $170,200.

    d. $171,200.

LO9

16. Lear is to become a partner in the WS partnership by paying $80,000 in cash to the business. At present, the capital balance for Hamlet is $70,000 and for MacBeth is $40,000. Hamlet and MacBeth share profits on a 7:3 basis. Lear is acquiring 40 percent of the new partnership.

    a. If the goodwill method is applied, what will the three capital balances be following the payment by Lear?

    b. If the bonus method is applied, what will the three capital balances be following the payment by Lear?

LO9

17. The Distance Plus partnership has the following capital balances at the beginning of the current year:

Tiger (50% of profits and losses)	$85,000
Phil (30%)	60,000
Ernie (20%)	55,000

    Each of the following questions should be viewed independently.

    a. If Sergio invests $100,000 in cash in the business for a 25 percent interest, what journal entry is recorded? Assume that the bonus method is used.

    b. If Sergio invests $60,000 in cash in the business for a 25 percent interest, what journal entry is recorded? Assume that the bonus method is used.

    c. If Sergio invests $72,000 in cash in the business for a 25 percent interest, what journal entry is recorded? Assume that the goodwill method is used.

LO9

18. A partnership has the following account balances: Cash $50,000; Other Assets $600,000; Liabilities $240,000; Nixon, Capital (50% of profits and losses) $200,000; Hoover, Capital (20%) $120,000; and Polk, Capital (30%) $90,000. Each of the following questions should be viewed as an independent situation:

    a. Grant invests $80,000 in the partnership for an 18 percent capital interest. Goodwill is to be recognized. What are the capital accounts thereafter?

    b. Grant invests $100,000 in the partnership to get a 20 percent capital balance. Goodwill is not to be recorded. What are the capital accounts thereafter?

LO9

19. The C-P partnership has the following capital account balances on January 1, 2011:

Com, Capital	$150,000
Pack, Capital	110,000

    Com is allocated 60 percent of all profits and losses with the remaining 40 percent assigned to Pack after interest of 10 percent is given to each partner based on beginning capital balances.

    On January 2, 2011, Hal invests $76,000 cash for a 20 percent interest in the partnership. This transaction is recorded by the goodwill method. After this transaction, 10 percent interest is still to go to each partner. Profits and losses will then be split as follows: Com (50%), Pack (30%), and Hal (20%). In 2011, the partnership reports a net income of $36,000.

    a. Prepare the journal entry to record Hal's entrance into the partnership on January 2, 2011.

    b. Determine the allocation of income at the end of 2011.

LO6

20. The partnership agreement of Jones, King, and Lane provides for the annual allocation of the business's profit or loss in the following sequence:
    - Jones, the managing partner, receives a bonus equal to 20 percent of the business's profit.
    - Each partner receives 15 percent interest on average capital investment.
    - Any residual profit or loss is divided equally.

    The average capital investments for 2011 were as follows:

Jones	$100,000
King	200,000
Lane	300,000

    How much of the $90,000 partnership profit for 2011 should be assigned to each partner?

LO4, LO5, LO6

21. Purkerson, Smith, and Traynor have operated a bookstore for a number of years as a partnership. At the beginning of 2011, capital balances were as follows:

Purkerson	$60,000
Smith	40,000
Traynor	20,000

    Due to a cash shortage, Purkerson invests an additional $8,000 in the business on April 1, 2011.
    Each partner is allowed to withdraw $1,000 cash each month.
    The partners have used the same method of allocating profits and losses since the business's inception:
    - Each partner is given the following compensation allowance for work done in the business: Purkerson, $18,000; Smith, $25,000; and Traynor, $8,000.
    - Each partner is credited with interest equal to 10 percent of the average monthly capital balance for the year without regard for normal drawings.
    - Any remaining profit or loss is allocated 4:2:4 to Purkerson, Smith, and Traynor, respectively. The net income for 2011 is $23,600. Each partner withdraws the allotted amount each month.

    What are the ending capital balances for 2011?

LO4, LO5, LO6

22. On January 1, 2010, the dental partnership of Left, Center, and Right was formed when the partners contributed $20,000, $60,000, and $50,000, respectively. Over the next three years, the business reported net income and (loss) as follows:

2010	$(30,000)
2011	20,000
2012	40,000

    During this period, each partner withdrew cash of $10,000 per year. Right invested an additional $12,000 in cash on February 9, 2011.
    At the time that the partnership was created, the three partners agreed to allocate all profits and losses according to a specified plan written as follows:
    - Each partner is entitled to interest computed at the rate of 12 percent per year based on the individual capital balances at the beginning of that year.
    - Because of prior work experience, Left is entitled to an annual salary allowance of $12,000, and Center is credited with $8,000 per year.
    - Any remaining profit will be split as follows: Left, 20 percent; Center, 40 percent; and Right, 40 percent. If a loss remains, the balance will be allocated: Left, 30 percent; Center, 50 percent; and Right, 20 percent.

    Determine the ending capital balance for each partner as of the end of each of these three years.

LO10

23. The HELP partnership has the following capital balances as of the end of the current year:

Lennon	$230,000
McCartney	190,000
Harrison	160,000
Starr	140,000
Total capital	$720,000

Answer each of the following *independent* questions:

a. Assume that the partners share profits and losses 3:3:2:2, respectively. Harrison retires and is paid $190,000 based on the terms of the original partnership agreement. If the goodwill method is used, what is the capital balance of the remaining three partners?

b. Assume that the partners share profits and losses 4:3:2:1, respectively. Lennon retires and is paid $280,000 based on the terms of the original partnership agreement. If the bonus method is used, what is the capital balance of the remaining three partners?

LO2, LO4, LO6, LO9

24. In the early part of 2011, the partners of Page, Childers, and Smith sought assistance from a local accountant. They had begun a new business in 2010 but had never used an accountant's services.

Page and Childers began the partnership by contributing $80,000 and $30,000 in cash, respectively. Page was to work occasionally at the business, and Childers was to be employed full-time. They decided that year-end profits and losses should be assigned as follows:

- Each partner was to be allocated 10 percent interest computed on the beginning capital balances for the period.
- A compensation allowance of $5,000 was to go to Page with a $20,000 amount assigned to Childers.
- Any remaining income would be split on a 4:6 basis to Page and Childers, respectively.

In 2010, revenues totaled $90,000, and expenses were $64,000 (not including the compensation allowance assigned to the partners). Page withdrew cash of $8,000 during the year, and Childers took out $11,000. In addition, the business paid $5,000 for repairs made to Page's home and charged it to repair expense.

On January 1, 2011, the partnership sold a 20 percent interest to Smith for $43,000 cash. This money was contributed to the business with the bonus method used for accounting purposes.

Answer the following questions:

a. Why was the original profit and loss allocation, as just outlined, designed by the partners?

b. Why did the drawings for 2010 not agree with the compensation allowances provided for in the partnership agreement?

c. What journal entries should the partnership have recorded on December 31, 2010?

d. What journal entry should the partnership have recorded on January 1, 2011?

LO3, LO9, LO10

25. Following is the current balance sheet for a local partnership of doctors:

Cash and current		Liabilities	$ 40,000
assets	$ 30,000	A, capital	20,000
Land	180,000	B, capital	40,000
Building and		C, capital	90,000
equipment (net)	100,000	D, capital	120,000
Totals	$310,000	Totals	$310,000

The following questions represent *independent* situations:

a. E is going to invest enough money in this partnership to receive a 25 percent interest. No goodwill or bonus is to be recorded. How much should E invest?

b. E contributes $36,000 in cash to the business to receive a 10 percent interest in the partnership. Goodwill is to be recorded. Profits and losses have previously been split according to the following percentages: A, 30 percent; B, 10 percent; C, 40 percent; and D, 20 percent. After E makes this investment, what are the individual capital balances?

c. E contributes $42,000 in cash to the business to receive a 20 percent interest in the partnership. Goodwill is to be recorded. The four original partners share all profits and losses equally. After E makes this investment, what are the individual capital balances?

d. E contributes $55,000 in cash to the business to receive a 20 percent interest in the partnership. No goodwill or other asset revaluation is to be recorded. Profits and losses have previously been split according to the following percentages: A, 10 percent; B, 30 percent; C, 20 percent; and D, 40 percent. After E makes this investment, what are the individual capital balances?

e. C retires from the partnership and, as per the original partnership agreement, is to receive cash equal to 125 percent of her final capital balance. No goodwill or other asset revaluation is to be recognized. All partners share profits and losses equally. After the withdrawal, what are the individual capital balances of the remaining partners?

LO5, LO6, LO9

26. Boswell and Johnson form a partnership on May 1, 2009. Boswell contributes cash of $50,000; Johnson conveys title to the following properties to the partnership:

	Book Value	Fair Value
Land	$15,000	$28,000
Building and equipment	35,000	36,000

The partners agree to start their partnership with equal capital balances. No goodwill is to be recognized.

According to the articles of partnership written by the partners, profits and losses are allocated based on the following formula:

- Boswell receives a compensation allowance of $1,000 per month.
- All remaining profits and losses are split 60:40 to Johnson and Boswell, respectively.
- Each partner can make annual cash drawings of $5,000 beginning in 2010.

Net income of $11,000 is earned by the business during 2009.

Walpole is invited to join the partnership on January 1, 2010. Because of her business reputation and financial expertise, she is given a 40 percent interest for $54,000 cash. The bonus approach is used to record this investment, made directly to the business. The articles of partnership are amended to give Walpole a $2,000 compensation allowance per month and an annual cash drawing of $10,000. Remaining profits are now allocated:

Johnson	48%
Boswell	12
Walpole	40

All drawings are taken by the partners during 2010. At year-end, the partnership reports an earned net income of $28,000.

On January 1, 2011, Pope (previously a partnership employee) is admitted into the partnership. Each partner transfers 10 percent to Pope, who makes the following payments directly to the partners:

Johnson	$5,672
Boswell	7,880
Walpole	8,688

Once again, the articles of partnership must be amended to allow for the entrance of the new partner. This change entitles Pope to a compensation allowance of $800 per month and an annual drawing of $4,000. Profits and losses are now assigned as follows:

Johnson	40.5%
Boswell	13.5
Walpole	36.0
Pope	10.0

For the year of 2011, the partnership earned a profit of $46,000, and each partner withdrew the allowed amount of cash.

Determine the capital balances for the individual partners as of the end of each year: 2009 through 2011.

LO4, LO5, LO6, LO9

27. Gray, Stone, and Lawson open an accounting practice on January 1, 2009, in San Diego, California, to be operated as a partnership. Gray and Stone will serve as the senior partners because of their years of experience. To establish the business, Gray, Stone, and Lawson contribute cash and other properties valued at $210,000, $180,000, and $90,000, respectively. An articles of partnership agreement is drawn up. It has the following stipulations:

- Personal drawings are allowed annually up to an amount equal to 10 percent of the beginning capital balance for the year.
- Profits and losses are allocated according to the following plan:
  (1) A salary allowance is credited to each partner in an amount equal to $8 per billable hour worked by that individual during the year.

(2) Interest is credited to the partners' capital accounts at the rate of 12 percent of the average monthly balance for the year (computed without regard for current income or drawings).

(3) An annual bonus is to be credited to Gray and Stone. Each bonus is to be 10 percent of net income after subtracting the bonus, the salary allowance, and the interest. Also included in the agreement is the provision that the bonus cannot be a negative amount.

(4) Any remaining partnership profit or loss is to be divided evenly among all partners.

Because of monetary problems encountered in getting the business started, Gray invests an additional $9,100 on May 1, 2009. On January 1, 2010, the partners allow Monet to buy into the partnership. Monet contributes cash directly to the business in an amount equal to a 25 percent interest in the book value of the partnership property subsequent to this contribution. The partnership agreement as to splitting profits and losses is not altered upon Monet's entrance into the firm; the general provisions continue to be applicable.

The billable hours for the partners during the first three years of operation follow:

	2009	2010	2011
Gray	1,710	1,800	1,880
Stone	1,440	1,500	1,620
Lawson	1,300	1,380	1,310
Monet	–0–	1,190	1,580

The partnership reports net income for 2009 through 2011 as follows:

2009	$ 65,000
2010	(20,400)
2011	152,800

Each partner withdraws the maximum allowable amount each year.

a. Determine the allocation of income for each of these three years (to the nearest dollar).

b. Prepare in appropriate form a statement of partners' capital for the year ending December 31, 2011.

LO8, LO9, LO10

28. A partnership of attorneys in the St. Louis, Missouri, area has the following balance sheet accounts as of January 1, 2011:

Assets	$320,000	Liabilities	$120,000
		Athos, capital	80,000
		Porthos, capital	70,000
		Aramis, capital	50,000

According to the articles of partnership, Athos is to receive an allocation of 50 percent of all partnership profits and losses while Porthos receives 30 percent and Aramis, 20 percent. The book value of each asset and liability should be considered an accurate representation of fair value.

For each of the following *independent* situations, prepare the journal entry or entries to be recorded by the partnership. (Round to nearest dollar.)

a. Porthos, with permission of the other partners, decides to sell half of his partnership interest to D'Artagnan for $50,000 in cash. No asset revaluation or goodwill is to be recorded by the partnership.

b. All three of the present partners agree to sell 10 percent of each partnership interest to D'Artagnan for a total cash payment of $25,000. Each partner receives a negotiated portion of this amount. Goodwill is recorded as a result of the transaction.

c. D'Artagnan is allowed to become a partner with a 10 percent ownership interest by contributing $30,000 in cash directly into the business. The bonus method is used to record this admission.

d. Use the same facts as in requirement (c) except that the entrance into the partnership is recorded by the goodwill method.

e. D'Artagnan is allowed to become a partner with a 10 percent ownership interest by contributing $12,222 in cash directly to the business. The goodwill method is used to record this transaction.

f. Aramis decides to retire and leave the partnership. An independent appraisal of the business and its assets indicates a current fair value of $280,000. Goodwill is to be recorded. Aramis will then be given the exact amount of cash that will close out his capital account.

LO2, LO3, LO5,
LO6, LO8, LO10

29. Steve Reese is a well-known interior designer in Fort Worth, Texas. He wants to start his own business and convinces Rob O'Donnell, a local merchant, to contribute the capital to form a partnership. On January 1, 2009, O'Donnell invests a building worth $52,000 and equipment valued at $16,000 as well as $12,000 in cash. Although Reese makes no tangible contribution to the partnership, he will operate the business and be an equal partner in the beginning capital balances.

To entice O'Donnell to join this partnership, Reese draws up the following profit and loss agreement:
- O'Donnell will be credited annually with interest equal to 20 percent of the beginning capital balance for the year.
- O'Donnell will also have added to his capital account 15 percent of partnership income each year (without regard for the preceding interest figure) or $4,000, whichever is larger. All remaining income is credited to Reese.
- Neither partner is allowed to withdraw funds from the partnership during 2009. Thereafter, each can draw $5,000 annually or 20 percent of the beginning capital balance for the year, whichever is larger.

The partnership reported a net loss of $10,000 during the first year of its operation. On January 1, 2010, Terri Dunn becomes a third partner in this business by contributing $15,000 cash to the partnership. Dunn receives a 20 percent share of the business's capital. The profit and loss agreement is altered as follows:
- O'Donnell is still entitled to (1) interest on his beginning capital balance as well as (2) the share of partnership income just specified.
- Any remaining profit or loss will be split on a 6:4 basis between Reese and Dunn, respectively.

Partnership income for 2010 is reported as $44,000. Each partner withdraws the full amount that is allowed.

On January 1, 2011, Dunn becomes ill and sells her interest in the partnership (with the consent of the other two partners) to Judy Postner. Postner pays $46,000 directly to Dunn. Net income for 2011 is $61,000 with the partners again taking their full drawing allowance.

On January 1, 2012, Postner withdraws from the business for personal reasons. The articles of partnership state that any partner may leave the partnership at any time and is entitled to receive cash in an amount equal to the recorded capital balance at that time plus 10 percent.

a. Prepare journal entries to record the preceding transactions on the assumption that the bonus (or no revaluation) method is used. Drawings need not be recorded, although the balances should be included in the closing entries.

b. Prepare journal entries to record the previous transactions on the assumption that the goodwill (or revaluation) method is used. Drawings need not be recorded, although the balances should be included in the closing entries.

(Round all amounts to the nearest dollar.)

Develop Your Skills

RESEARCH CASE

Go to the Web site www.sec.gov where forms filed with the SEC are available. Look for a section entitled "Filings & Forms (EDGAR)," and click on "Search for Company Filings" within that section. On the next screen that appears, click on "Search Companies and Filings." On the next screen, enter the following company name: Buckeye Partners. A list of SEC filings made by that company will appear; scroll down to the first 10–K (annual report) filing from Buckeye Partners. Click on that 10–K. This path will provide the latest financial information available for Buckeye Partners. Scroll through the statement information until the actual financial statements, followed by the notes, appear.

Required

Review this set of financial statements as well as the accompanying notes. List information included for this partnership that would typically not appear in financial statements produced for a corporation.

ANALYSIS CASE

Brenda Wilson, Elizabeth Higgins, and Helen Poncelet form a partnership as a first step in creating a business. Wilson invests most of the capital but does not plan to be actively involved in the day-to-day operations. Higgins has had some experience and is expected to do a majority of the daily work. Poncelet has been in this line of business for some time and has many connections. Therefore, she will devote a majority of her time to getting new clients.

Required

Write a memo to these three partners suggesting at least two different ways in which the profits of the partnership can be allocated each year in order to be fair to all parties.

COMMUNICATION CASE 1

Heidi Birmingham and James T. Roberts have decided to create a business. They have financing available and have a well-developed business plan. However, they have not yet decided which type of legal business structure would be best for them.

Required

Write a report for these two individuals outlining the types of situations in which the corporate form of legal structure would be the best choice.

COMMUNICATION CASE 2

Use the information in Communication Case 1.

Required

Write a report for these two individuals outlining the types of situations in which the partnership form of legal structure would be the best choice.

EXCEL CASE

The Red and Blue partnership has been created to operate a law firm. The partners have been attempting to devise a fair system to allocate profits and losses. Red plans to work more billable hours each year than Blue. However, Blue has more experience and can charge a higher hourly rate. Red expects to invest more money in the business than Blue.

Required

Build a spreadsheet that can be used to allocate profits and losses to these two partners each year. The spreadsheet should be constructed so that the following variables can be entered:

Net income for the year.
Number of billable hours for each partner.
Hourly rate for each partner.
Capital investment by each partner.
Interest rate on capital investment.
Profit and loss ratio.

Use this spreadsheet to determine the allocation if partnership net income for the current year is $200,000, the number of billable hours is 2,000 for Red and 1,500 for Blue, the hourly rate for Red is $20 and for Blue is $30, and investment by Red is $80,000 and by Blue is $50,000. Interest on capital will be accrued each year at 10 percent of the beginning balance. Any remaining income amount will be split 50–50.

Use the spreadsheet a second time but make these changes: Blue reports 1,700 billable hours, Red invests $100,000, and interest will be recognized at a 12 percent annual rate. How do these three changes impact the allocation of the $200,000?

Partnerships: Termination and Liquidation

Partnerships can be rather frail organizations. Termination of business activities followed by the liquidation of partnership property can take place for a variety of reasons, both legal and personal.

> In any firm, unless there is continuous open and candid communication among equity partners, and acceptance and buy-in for the business plan chosen by the firm, sooner or later there will be a dissolution of the firm.
>
> The form of the dissolution is irrelevant, whether by withdrawal of individual partners or wholesale departure and formal liquidation. The end result will be the same: The original dream of harmonious and collegial growth of the firm will come to an end.[1]

Although a business organized as a partnership can exist indefinitely through periodic changes within the ownership, the actual cessation of operations is not an uncommon occurrence. "Sooner or later, all partnerships end, whether a partner dies, moves to Hawaii, or gets into a different line of business."[2] The partners simply may be incompatible and choose to cease operations. The same decision could be made if profits fail to reach projected levels. "In the best of times, partnerships are fragile."[3]

The death of a partner is an event that dissolves a partnership and frequently leads to the termination of business operations. Rather than continuing under a new partnership arrangement, the remaining owners could discover that liquidation is necessary to settle the claims of the deceased partner's estate. A similar action could be required if one or more partners elect to change careers or retire. Under that circumstance, liquidation is often the most convenient method for winding up the financial affairs of the business.

As a final possibility, bankruptcy can legally force a partnership into selling its noncash assets. Laventhol & Horwath, the seventh largest public accounting firm in the United States at the time, filed for bankruptcy protection after the firm came under intense financial pressure from numerous lawsuits. "Laventhol said that at least 100 lawsuits are pending in state and federal courts. Bankruptcy court protection 'is absolutely

LEARNING OBJECTIVES

After studying this chapter, you should be able to:

LO1 Determine amounts to be paid to partners in a liquidation.

LO2 Prepare journal entries to record the transactions incurred in the liquidation of a partnership.

LO3 Determine the distribution of available cash when one or more partners have a deficit capital balance or become personally insolvent.

LO4 Prepare a proposed schedule of liquidation from safe capital balances to determine an equitable preliminary distribution of available partnership assets.

LO5 Develop a predistribution plan to guide the distribution of assets in a partnership liquidation.

[1] Edward Poll, "Commentary: Coach's Corner: Reuniting a Firm Divided," *Massachusetts Lawyers Weekly*, pNA. Retrieved July 11, 2007, from *InfoTrac OneFile* via Thomson Gale.

[2] Camilla Cornell, "Breaking Up (with a Business Partner) Is Hard to Do," *Profit*, November 2004, p. 69.

[3] Sue Shellenbarger, "Cutting Losses When Partners Face a Breakup," *The Wall Street Journal*, May 21, 1991, p. B1.

necessary in order to protect the debtor and its creditors from the devastating results a destructive race for assets will cause,' the firm said."[4]

The bankruptcy of Laventhol & Horwath was not an isolated incident. During the period 1998–2004, a study conducted by Hildebrandt International identified 80 U.S. law firms with more than 10 lawyers that dissolved. In investigating the reasons for failure, the researcher identified internal dysfunction, the inability to pay market compensation levels, and a weak competitive market position as major factors leading to law firms going out of business.[5]

TERMINATION AND LIQUIDATION—PROTECTING THE INTERESTS OF ALL PARTIES

Accounting for the termination and liquidation of a business can prove to be a delicate task. Losses are commonly incurred. For example, "[f]ormer partners in Keck, Mahin and Cate have pledged to pay slightly over $3 million to general unsecured creditors to settle the bankrupt firm's debts . . . this figure represents about 36 percent of the money owed."[6] Here, both the partners and the creditors suffered heavy losses.

Other partnerships have experienced a similar fate.

In 1990, prior to the advent of limited-liability partnerships, the accounting firm of Laventhol & Horwath filed for Chapter 11 bankruptcy-court protection, in part due to lawsuits over questionable accounting. The firm's assets were insufficient to cover the claims of creditors and litigants. Under a plan negotiated with the firm's creditors, the 360 partners and former partners who had spent time at the firm since 1984 were required to dig into their own pockets to share a $46 million liability. Under a formula hammered out by partner Jacob Brandzel, now an executive at American Express Co. in Chicago, they were obligated to contribute between about $5,000 and $450,000, depending on factors including seniority. Managers were levied a 5 percent to 10 percent surcharge on top. Everyone was given 10 years to pay.[7]

Consequently, throughout any liquidation, both creditors and partners demand continuous accounting information that enables them to monitor and assess their financial risks. In generating these data for a partnership, the accountant must record the following:

- The conversion of partnership assets into cash.
- The allocation of the resulting gains and losses.
- The payment of liabilities and expenses.
- Any remaining unpaid debts to be settled or the distribution of any remaining assets to the partners based on their final capital balances.

Beyond the goal of merely reporting these transactions, the accountant must work to ensure the equitable treatment of all parties involved in the liquidation. The accounting records, for example, are the basis for allocating available assets to creditors and to the individual partners. If assets are limited, the accountant also may have to make recommendations as to the appropriate method for distributing any remaining funds. Protecting the interests of partnership creditors is an especially significant duty because the Uniform Partnership Act specifies that they have first priority to the assets held by the business at dissolution. The accountant's desire for an

---

[4] Peter Pae, "Laventhol Bankruptcy Filing Indicates Liabilities May Be as Much as $2 Billion," *The Wall Street Journal*, November 23, 1990, p. A4.

[5] William G. Johnston, "Anatomy of Law Firm Failures: A Look at US Law Firm Dissolutions from 1998–2004," Hildebrandt International, March 2004, p. 16. Retrieved July 11, 2007, from www.hildebrandt.com/publicdocs/doc_id_1739_492004850218.pdf.

[6] Chicago *Daily Law Bulletin*, August 13, 1999, p. 3.

[7] Mitchell Pacelle and Ianthe Jeanne Dugan, "Partners Forever? Within Andersen, Personal Liability May Bring Ruin," *The Wall Street Journal*, April 2, 2002, p. C1.

equitable settlement is enhanced, no doubt, in that any party to a liquidation who is not treated fairly can seek legal recovery from the responsible party.

Not only the creditors but also the partners themselves have a great interest in the financial data produced during the period of liquidation. They must be concerned, as indicated, by the possibility of incurring substantial monetary losses. The potential for loss is especially significant because of the unlimited liability to which the partners are exposed.

Even the new legal formats that have been developed do not necessarily provide safety.

> Because it is unclear how much protection the LLP structure will provide Andersen partners, partnership and bankruptcy lawyers are expected to be following the matter closely. "As far as I know, there has never been a litigation test of the extent of the LLP shield, and there have been very few LLP cases about liability at all," said Larry Ribstein, a law professor at George Mason University.[8]

As long as a partnership can meet all of its obligations, a partner's risk is normally no more than that of a corporate stockholder. However, should the partnership become insolvent, each partner faces the possibility of having to satisfy *all* remaining obligations personally. Although any partner suffering more than a proportionate share of these losses can seek legal retribution from the other partners, this process is not always an effective remedy. The other partners may themselves be insolvent, or anticipated legal costs might discourage the damaged party from seeking recovery. Therefore, each partner usually has a keen interest in monitoring the progress of a liquidation as it transpires.

LO1

Determine amounts to be paid to partners in a liquidation.

Termination and Liquidation Procedures Illustrated

The procedures involved in terminating and liquidating a partnership are basically mechanical. Partnership assets are converted into cash that is then used to pay business obligations as well as liquidation expenses. *Any remaining assets are distributed to the individual partners based on their final capital balances.* Once assets have been distributed, the partnership's books are permanently closed. If each partner has a capital balance large enough to absorb all liquidation losses, the accountant should experience little difficulty in recording this series of transactions.

To illustrate the typical process, assume that Morgan and Houseman have been operating an art gallery as a partnership for a number of years. Morgan and Houseman allocate all profits and losses on a 6:4 basis, respectively. On May 1, 2011, the partners decide to terminate business activities, liquidate all noncash assets, and dissolve their partnership. Although they give no specific explanation for this action, any number of reasons could exist. The partners, for example, could have come to a disagreement so that they no longer believe they can work together. Another possibility is that business profits have become inadequate to warrant the continuing investment of their time and capital.

Following is a balance sheet for the partnership of Morgan and Houseman as of the termination date. The revenue, expense, and drawing accounts have been closed as a preliminary step in terminating the business. A separate reporting of the gains and losses that occur during the final winding-down process will subsequently be made.

MORGAN AND HOUSEMAN
Balance Sheet
May 1, 2011

Assets		Liabilities and Capital	
Cash	$ 45,000	Liabilities	$ 32,000
Accounts receivable	12,000	Morgan, capital	50,000
Inventory	22,000	Houseman, capital	38,000
Land, building, and equipment (net)	41,000		
Total assets	$120,000	Total liabilities and capital	$120,000

[8] Ibid.

We assume here that the liquidation of Morgan and Houseman proceeds in an orderly fashion through the following events:

2011

June 1	The inventory is sold at auction for $15,000.
July 15	Of the total accounts receivable, the partnership collected $9,000 and wrote off the remainder as bad debts.
Aug. 20	The fixed assets are sold for a total of $29,000.
Aug. 25	All partnership liabilities are paid.
Sept. 10	A total of $3,000 in liquidation expenses is paid to cover costs such as accounting and legal fees as well as the commissions incurred in disposing of partnership property.
Oct. 15	All remaining cash is distributed to the owners based on their final capital account balances.

Accordingly, the partnership of Morgan and Houseman incurred a number of losses in liquidating its property. Such losses are almost anticipated because the need for immediate sale usually holds a high priority in a liquidation. Furthermore, a portion of the assets used by any business, such as its equipment and buildings, could have a utility that is strictly limited to a particular type of operation. If the property is not easily adaptable, disposal at any reasonable price often proves to be a problem.

LO2

Prepare journal entries to record the transactions incurred in the liquidation of a partnership.

To record the liquidation of Morgan and Houseman, the following journal entries would be made. Rather than report specific income and expense balances, gains and losses are traditionally recorded directly to the partners' capital accounts. Because operations have ceased, determination of a separate net income figure for this period would provide little informational value. *Instead, a primary concern of the parties involved in any liquidation is the continuing changes in each partner's capital balance.*

6/1/11	Cash	15,000	
	Morgan, Capital (60% of loss)	4,200	
	Houseman, Capital (40% of loss)	2,800	
	Inventory		22,000
	To record sale of partnership inventory at a $7,000 loss.		
7/15/11	Cash	9,000	
	Morgan, Capital	1,800	
	Houseman, Capital	1,200	
	Accounts Receivable		12,000
	To record collection of accounts receivable with write-off of remaining $3,000 in accounts as bad debts.		
8/20/11	Cash	29,000	
	Morgan, Capital	7,200	
	Houseman, Capital	4,800	
	Land, Building, and Equipment (net)		41,000
	To record sale of fixed assets and allocation of $12,000 loss.		
8/25/11	Liabilities	32,000	
	Cash		32,000
	To record payment made to settle the liabilities of the partnership.		
9/10/11	Morgan, Capital	1,800	
	Houseman, Capital	1,200	
	Cash		3,000
	To record payment of liquidation expenses with the amounts recorded as direct reductions to the partners' capital accounts.		

After liquidating the partnership assets and paying off all obligations, the cash that remains can be divided between Morgan and Houseman personally. The following schedule is utilized to determine the partners' ending capital account balances and, thus, the appropriate distribution for this final payment:

Cash and Capital Account Balances

	Cash	Morgan, Capital	Houseman, Capital
Beginning balances*	$ 45,000	$50,000	$38,000
Sold inventory	15,000	(4,200)	(2,800)
Collected accounts receivable	9,000	(1,800)	(1,200)
Sold fixed assets	29,000	(7,200)	(4,800)
Paid liabilities	(32,000)	–0–	–0–
Paid liquidation expenses	(3,000)	(1,800)	(1,200)
Final totals	$ 63,000	$35,000	$28,000

* Because of the presence of other assets as well as liabilities, the beginning balances in Cash and in the capital accounts are not equal.

After the ending capital balances have been calculated, the remaining cash can be distributed to the partners to close out the financial records of the partnership:

10/15/11	Morgan, Capital	35,000	
	Houseman, Capital	28,000	
	Cash		63,000
	To record distribution of cash to partners in accordance with final capital balances.		

Schedule of Liquidation

Liquidation can take a considerable length of time to complete. Because the various parties involved seek continually updated financial information, the accountant should produce frequent reports summarizing the transactions as they occur. Consequently, a statement (often referred to as the *schedule of liquidation*) can be prepared at periodic intervals to disclose

- Transactions to date.
- Property still being held by the partnership.
- Liabilities remaining to be paid.
- Current cash and capital balances.

Although the preceding Morgan and Houseman example has been condensed into a few events occurring during a relatively brief period of time, partnership liquidations usually require numerous transactions that transpire over months and, perhaps, even years. By receiving frequent schedules of liquidation, both the creditors and the partners are able to stay apprised of the results of this lengthy process.

See Exhibit 10.1 for the final schedule of liquidation for the partnership of Morgan and Houseman. The accountant should have distributed previous statements at each important juncture of this liquidation to meet the informational needs of the parties involved. The example here demonstrates the stair-step approach incorporated in preparing a schedule of liquidation. The effects of each transaction (or group of transactions) are outlined in a horizontal fashion so that current account balances and all prior transactions are evident. This structuring also facilitates the preparation of future statements: A new layer summarizing recent events can simply be added at the bottom each time a new schedule is to be produced.

EXHIBIT 10.1

	Cash	Noncash Assets	Liabilities	Morgan, Capital (60%)	Houseman, Capital (40%)
MORGAN AND HOUSEMAN Schedule of Partnership Liquidation Final Balances					
Beginning balances, 5/1/11	$ 45,000	$ 75,000	$ 32,000	$ 50,000	$ 38,000
Sold inventory, 6/1/11	15,000	(22,000)	–0–	(4,200)	(2,800)
Updated balances	60,000	53,000	32,000	45,800	35,200
Collected receivables, 7/15/11	9,000	(12,000)	–0–	(1,800)	(1,200)
Updated balances	69,000	41,000	32,000	44,000	34,000
Sold fixed assets, 8/20/11	29,000	(41,000)	–0–	(7,200)	(4,800)
Updated balances	98,000	–0–	32,000	36,800	29,200
Paid liabilities, 8/25/11	(32,000)		(32,000)	–0–	–0–
Updated balances	66,000	–0–	–0–	36,800	29,200
Paid liquidation expenses, 9/10/11	(3,000)			(1,800)	(1,200)
Updated balances	63,000	–0–	–0–	35,000	28,000
Distributed remaining cash, 10/15/11	(63,000)			(35,000)	(28,000)
Closing balances	–0–	–0–	–0–	–0–	–0–

LO3

Determine the distribution of available cash when one or more partners have a deficit capital balance or become personally insolvent.

Deficit Capital Balance—Contribution by Partner

In Exhibit 10.1, the liquidation process ended with both partners continuing to report positive capital balances. Thus, each partner was able to share in the remaining $63,000 cash. Unfortunately, such an outcome is not always possible. At the end of a liquidation, one or more partners could have a negative capital account, or the partnership could be unable to generate even enough cash to satisfy all of its creditors' claims. Such deficits are most likely to occur when the partnership is already insolvent at the start of the liquidation or when the disposal of noncash assets results in material losses. Under these circumstances, the accounting procedures to be applied depend on legal regulations as well as the individual actions of the partners.

To illustrate, assume that the partnership of Holland, Dozier, and Ross was dissolved at the beginning of the current year. Business activities were terminated and all noncash assets were subsequently converted into cash. During the liquidation process, the partnership incurred a number of large losses that have been allocated to the partners' capital accounts on a 4:4:2 basis, respectively. A portion of the resulting cash is then used to pay all partnership liabilities and liquidation expenses.

Following these transactions, assume that only the following four account balances remain open within the partnership's records:

Cash	$20,000	Holland, Capital	$ (6,000)
		Dozier, Capital	15,000
		Ross, Capital	11,000
		Total	$20,000

Holland has a negative capital balance of $6,000; the assigned share of partnership losses has exceeded this partner's net contribution. In such cases, the Uniform Partnership Act (Section 807[b]) stipulates that the partner "shall contribute to the partnership an amount equal to any excess charges over the credits in the partner's account . . ." Therefore, Holland legally is required to convey an additional $6,000 to the partnership to eliminate the deficit balance. This contribution raises the cash balance to $26,000, which allows a complete distribution to be made to Dozier ($15,000) and Ross ($11,000) in line with their capital accounts. The journal entry for this final payment closes out the partnership records:

Cash	6,000	
Holland, Capital		6,000
To record contribution made by Holland to extinguish negative capital balance.		
Dozier, Capital	15,000	
Ross, Capital	11,000	
Cash		26,000
To record distribution of remaining cash to partners in accordance with their ending capital balances.		

Deficit Capital Balance—Loss to Remaining Partners

Unfortunately, an alternative scenario can easily be conceived for the previous partnership liquidation. Although Holland's capital account shows a $6,000 deficit balance, this partner could resist any attempt to force an additional investment, especially because the business is in the process of being terminated. The possibility of such recalcitrance is enhanced if the individual is having personal financial difficulties. Thus, the remaining partners may eventually have to resort to formal litigation to gain Holland's contribution. Until that legal action is concluded, the partnership records remain open although inactive.

Distribution of Safe Payments

While awaiting the final resolution of this matter, no compelling reason exists for the partnership to continue holding $20,000 in cash. These funds will eventually be paid to Dozier and Ross regardless of any action that Holland takes. An immediate transfer should be made to these two partners to allow them the use of their money. However, because Dozier has a $15,000 capital account balance and Ross currently reports $11,000, a complete distribution is not possible. A method must be devised, therefore, to allow for a fair allocation of the available $20,000.

To ensure the equitable treatment of all parties, this initial distribution is based on the assumption that the $6,000 capital deficit will prove to be a total loss to the partnership. Holland may, for example, be completely insolvent so that no additional payment will ever be forthcoming. By making this conservative presumption, the accountant is able to calculate the lowest possible amounts (or *safe balances*) that Dozier and Ross must retain in their capital accounts to be able to absorb all future losses.

Should Holland's $6,000 deficit (or any portion of it) prove uncollectible, the loss will be written off against the capital accounts of Dozier and Ross. Allocation of this amount is based on the relative profit and loss ratio specified in the articles of partnership. According to the information provided, Dozier and Ross are credited with 40 percent and 20 percent of all partnership income, respectively. This 40:20 ratio equates to a 2:1 relationship (or $\frac{2}{3}:\frac{1}{3}$) between the two. Thus, if no part of the $6,000 deficit balance is ever recovered from Holland, $4,000 (two-thirds) of the loss will be assigned to Dozier and $2,000 (one-third) to Ross:

Allocation of Potential $6,000 Loss

Dozier . . . . $\frac{2}{3}$ of $(6,000) = $(4,000)
Ross . . . . $\frac{1}{3}$ of $(6,000) = $(2,000)

These amounts represent the maximum potential reductions that the two remaining partners could still incur. Depending on Holland's actions, Dozier could be forced to absorb an additional

$4,000 loss, and Ross's capital account could decrease by as much as $2,000. These balances must therefore remain in the respective capital accounts until the issue is resolved. Hence, Dozier is entitled to receive $11,000 in cash at the present time; this distribution reduces that partner's capital account from $15,000 to the minimum $4,000 level. Likewise, a $9,000 payment to Ross decreases the $11,000 capital balance to the $2,000 limit. These $11,000 and $9,000 amounts represent safe payments that can be distributed to the partners without fear of creating new deficits in the future.

Dozier, Capital	11,000	
Ross, Capital	9,000	
Cash		20,000
To record distribution of cash to Dozier and Ross based on safe capital balances, using the assumption that Holland will not contribute further to the partnership.		

After this $20,000 cash distribution, only a few other events can occur during the remaining life of the partnership. Holland, either voluntarily or through legal persuasion, may contribute the entire $6,000 needed to eradicate the capital deficit. If so, the money should be immediately turned over to Dozier ($4,000) and Ross ($2,000) based on their remaining capital balances. This final distribution effectively closes the partnership records.

A second possibility is that Dozier and Ross could be unable to recover any part of the deficit from Holland. These two remaining partners must then absorb the $6,000 loss themselves. Because adequate safe capital balances have been maintained, recording a complete default by Holland serves to close out the partnership books.

Dozier, Capital (⅔ of loss)	4,000	
Ross, Capital (⅓ of loss)	2,000	
Holland, Capital		6,000
To record allocation of deficit capital balance of insolvent partner.		

Deficit Is Partly Collectible

One other ending to this partnership liquidation is conceivable. The partnership could recover a portion of the $6,000 from Holland, but the remainder could prove to be uncollectible. This partner could become bankrupt, or the other partners could simply give up trying to collect. The partners could also negotiate this settlement to avoid protracted legal actions.

To illustrate, assume that Holland manages to contribute $3,600 to the partnership but subsequently files for relief under the provisions of the bankruptcy laws. In a later legal arrangement, $1,000 additional cash goes to the partnership, but the final $1,400 will never be collected. This series of events creates the following effects within the liquidation process:

1. The $3,600 contribution is distributed to Dozier and Ross based on a new computation of their safe capital balances.
2. The $1,400 default is charged against the two positive capital balances in accordance with the relative profit and loss ratio.
3. The final $1,000 contribution is then paid to Dozier and Ross in amounts equal to their ending capital accounts, a transaction that closes the partnership's financial records.

The distribution of the first $3,600 depends on a recalculation of the minimum capital balances that Dozier and Ross must maintain to absorb all potential losses. Each of these computations is necessary because of a basic realization: Holland's remaining deficit balance ($2,400 at this time) could prove to be a total loss. This approach guarantees that the other two partners will continue to report sufficient capital until the liquidation is ultimately resolved.

	Current Capital	Allocation of Potential Loss	Safe Capital Payments
Dozier	$4,000	⅔ of $(2,400) = $(1,600)	$2,400
Ross	2,000	⅓ of (2,400) = (800)	1,200

Thus, the $3,600 in cash that is now available is distributed immediately to Dozier and Ross based on their safe balances:

Cash	3,600	
Holland, Capital		3,600
Dozier, Capital	2,400	
Ross, Capital	1,200	
Cash		3,600
To record capital contribution by Holland and subsequent distribution of funds to Dozier and Ross based on safe capital balances.		

After recording this $3,600 contribution from Holland and the subsequent disbursement, the partnership's capital accounts stay open, registering the following individual balances:

Holland, Capital (deficit)	$(2,400)
Dozier, Capital (safe balance)	1,600
Ross, Capital (safe balance)	800

These accounts continue to remain on the partnership books until the final resolution of Holland's obligation.

In this illustration, the $1,000 legal settlement and the remaining $1,400 loss ultimately allow the parties to close out the records:

Cash	1,000	
Dozier, Capital (⅔ of loss)	933	
Ross, Capital (⅓ of loss)	467	
Holland, Capital		2,400
To record final $1,000 cash settlement of Holland's interest and resulting $1,400 loss.		
Dozier, Capital	667	
Ross, Capital	333	
Cash		1,000
To record distribution of final cash balance based upon remaining capital account totals.		

In the previous example, one partner (Holland) became insolvent during the liquidation process. Personal bankruptcy is not uncommon and raises questions as to the legal right that damaged partners have to proceed against an insolvent partner. We now consider another example in which two partners are insolvent.

The following balance sheet is presented for the partnership of Morris, Newton, Olsen, and Prince and indicates the applicable profit and loss percentages. Both Morris and Prince are personally insolvent. Morris's creditors have brought an $8,000 claim against the partnership's assets, and Prince's creditors are seeking $15,000. These claims have forced the partnership to terminate operations so that the business property can be liquidated and the insolvent partners can settle their personal obligations. The question as to which partner is entitled to any cash balance that remains is again raised.

Cash	$ 10,000	Liabilities		$ 70,000
Noncash assets	140,000	Morris, capital (40%)		15,000
		Newton, capital (20%)		10,000
		Olsen, capital (20%)		23,000
		Prince, capital (20%)		32,000
Total assets	$150,000	Total liabilities and capital		$150,000

Assume that the partnership sells the noncash assets for a total of $80,000, creating a $60,000 loss, and pays all its liabilities. The partnership's accounting system records these two events as follows:

Cash	80,000	
Morris, Capital (40% of loss)	24,000	
Newton, Capital (20% of loss)	12,000	
Olsen, Capital (20% of loss)	12,000	
Prince, Capital (20% of loss)	12,000	
Noncash Assets (or specific accounts)		140,000
To record sale of noncash assets and allocation of resulting $60,000 loss.		
Liabilities	70,000	
Cash		70,000
To record extinguishment of partnership obligations.		

Because of these two transactions, the partnership's cash has increased from $10,000 to $20,000.

After the allocation of this loss, the capital accounts for Morris and Newton report deficit balances of $9,000 ($15,000 − $24,000) and $2,000 ($10,000 − $12,000), respectively. Although Newton is solvent and would be expected to compensate the partnership, Morris's personal financial condition does not allow for any further contribution. Therefore, Newton, Olsen, and Prince must absorb Morris's $9,000 deficit. Because these three partners have historically shared profits evenly (20:20:20), they continue to do so in recording this additional capital loss:

Newton, Capital (⅓ of loss)	3,000	
Olsen, Capital (⅓ of loss)	3,000	
Prince, Capital (⅓ of loss)	3,000	
Morris, Capital		9,000
To record write-off of deficit capital balance of insolvent partner.		

This last allocation increases Newton's deficit to a $5,000 balance ($2,000 + $3,000), an amount that the partner should now contribute in accordance with partnership law:

Cash	5,000	
Newton, Capital		5,000
To record contribution from solvent partner necessitated by negative capital balance.		

Following this series of transactions, only the cash balance (now $25,000) and Olsen's and Prince's capital accounts remain open within the partnership records:

	Cash	Morris, Capital	Newton, Capital	Olsen, Capital	Prince, Capital
Beginning balances	$10,000	$15,000	$10,000	$23,000	$32,000
Sold assets	80,000	(24,000)	(12,000)	(12,000)	(12,000)
Paid liabilities	(70,000)	–0–	–0–	–0–	–0–
Default by Morris	–0–	9,000	(3,000)	(3,000)	(3,000)
Contribution by Newton	5,000	–0–	5,000	–0–	–0–
Current balances	$25,000	–0–	–0–	$ 8,000	$17,000

Although $8,000 of the partnership's remaining cash goes directly to Olsen, the $17,000 attributed to Prince is first subjected to the claims of the partner's personal creditors. Because of their claims, $15,000 of this amount must be used to satisfy these obligations, with only the final $2,000 being paid to Prince. Because Morris receives no distribution of cash from the partnership, no assets become available to settle claims of this partner's personal creditors.

Insolvent Partnership

The two previous illustrations analyzed liquidations in which one or more of the partners is personally insolvent. Another possibility is that the partnership itself is insolvent. In an active partnership, insolvency can occur if losses, partner drawings, or litigation deplete the operation's working capital. A bankruptcy petition could follow if the partnership cannot meet its debts as they come due. Liquidation of business assets could be necessary unless the partnership can generate additional capital quickly. Even a financially sound partnership can become insolvent if it incurs material losses during a voluntary liquidation.

To serve as a basis for examining the accounting and legal ramifications of an insolvent partnership, assume that the law firm of Keller, Lewis, Monroe, and Norris is in the final stages of liquidation. The firm has sold all noncash assets and has used available cash to pay a portion of the business's liabilities. After these transactions, the following account balances remain open within the partnership's records. The four partners share profits and losses equally.

Liabilities	$ 20,000
Keller, capital	(30,000)
Lewis, capital	(5,000)
Monroe, capital	5,000
Norris, capital	10,000

Note: Parentheses indicate deficit.

This partnership is insolvent; it continues to owe creditors $20,000, even after liquidation and distribution of all assets. However, additional money should be forthcoming from two of the partners. Because of their deficit capital accounts, Keller and Lewis are legally required to contribute an additional $30,000 and $5,000, respectively, to the business. With these newly available funds, the partnership will be able to pay all $20,000 of its remaining liabilities as well as make cash distributions to Monroe ($5,000) and Norris ($10,000) in accordance with their capital account balances. This final payment would close the partnership books.

Once again, the possibility exists that one or more of the partners who are reporting a negative capital balance will not step forward to make any further investment. Assume, for example, that Keller is personally insolvent and cannot contribute, whereas Lewis simply refuses to supply additional funds in hope of avoiding the obligation. *At this point, the remaining creditors can initiate legal recovery proceedings against any or all of the partners regardless of their capital balances.* Any action, however, against the insolvent partner could prove to be a futile effort.

Discussion **Question**

WHAT HAPPENS IF A PARTNER BECOMES INSOLVENT?

In 2001, three dentists—Ben Rogers, Judy Wilkinson, and Henry Walker—formed a partnership to open a practice in Toledo, Ohio. The partnership's primary purpose was to reduce expenses by sharing building and equipment costs, supplies, and the services of a clerical staff. Each contributed $70,000 in cash and, with the help of a bank loan, constructed a building and acquired furniture, fixtures, and equipment. Because the partners maintained their own separate clients, annual net income has been allocated as follows: Each partner receives the specific amount of revenues that he or she generated during the period less one-third of all expenses. From the beginning, the partners did not anticipate expansion of the practice; consequently, they could withdraw cash each year up to 90 percent of their share of income for the period.

The partnership had been profitable for a number of years. Over the years, Rogers has used much of his income to speculate in real estate in the Toledo area. By 2010 he was spending less time with the dental practice so that he could concentrate on his investments. Unfortunately, a number of these deals proved to be bad decisions and he incurred significant losses. On November 8, 2010, while Rogers was out of town, his personal creditors filed a $97,000 claim against the partnership assets. Unbeknownst to Wilkinson and Walker, Rogers had become insolvent.

Wilkinson and Walker hurriedly met to discuss the problem because Rogers could not be located. Rogers's capital account was currently at $105,000, but the partnership had only $27,000 in cash and liquid assets. The partners knew that Rogers's equipment had been used for a number of years and could be sold for relatively little. In contrast, the building had appreciated in value, and the claim could be satisfied by selling the property. However, this action would have a tremendously adverse impact on the dental practices of the remaining two partners.

What alternatives are available to Wilkinson and Walker, and what are the advantages and disadvantages of each?

Predicting the exact outcome of litigation is rarely possible. Thus, we assume here that Norris is forced to contribute $20,000 cash to settle the remaining liabilities. The following journal entries would then be required for this partnership:

Cash	20,000	
Norris, Capital		20,000
Liabilities	20,000	
Cash		20,000
To record capital contribution by Norris and payment to remaining partnership creditors.		

After all liabilities have been extinguished, the partners who still maintain positive capital accounts can demand remuneration from any partner with a negative balance. Despite this legal obligation, the chances of a significant recovery from the insolvent Keller is not likely. Thus, the partners could choose to write off this deficit as a step toward closing the partnership's financial records. Legal recovery proceedings can still continue against Keller regardless of the accounting treatment. As equal partners, Lewis, Monroe, and Norris absorb the $30,000 loss evenly.

Lewis, Capital ($1/3$ of loss)	10,000	
Monroe, Capital ($1/3$ of loss)	10,000	
Norris, Capital ($1/3$ of loss)	10,000	
Keller, Capital		30,000
To record write-off of deficit capital balance of insolvent partner.		

The partners' capital accounts now have the following balances:

	Keller, Capital	Lewis, Capital	Monroe, Capital	Norris, Capital
Beginning balances	$(30,000)	$ (5,000)	$ 5,000	$10,000
Capital contribution	–0–	–0–	–0–	20,000
Write-off of deficit balance	30,000	(10,000)	(10,000)	(10,000)
Current balances	–0–	$(15,000)	$(5,000)	$20,000

Both Lewis and Monroe now have a legal obligation to reimburse the partnership to offset their deficit capital balances. Upon their payment of $15,000 and $5,000, respectively, the entire $20,000 will be distributed to Norris (the only partner with a positive balance), and the partnership's books will be closed. Should either Lewis or Monroe fail to make the appropriate contribution, the additional loss must be allocated between the two remaining partners.

Preliminary Distribution of Partnership Assets

Prepare a proposed schedule of liquidation from safe capital balances to determine an equitable preliminary distribution of available partnership assets.

In all of the illustrations analyzed in this chapter, distributions were made to the partners only after all assets were sold and all liabilities paid. As previously mentioned, a liquidation can take an extended time to complete. During this lengthy process, the partnership need not retain any assets that will eventually be disbursed to the partners. If the business is safely solvent, waiting until all affairs have been settled before transferring property to the owners is not warranted. The partners should be allowed to use their own funds at the earliest possible time.

The objective in making any type of preliminary distribution is to ensure that the partnership maintains enough capital to absorb all future losses. Any capital in excess of this maximum requirement is a safe balance, an amount that can be immediately conveyed to the partner. To determine safe capital balances at any time, the accountant assumes that all subsequent events will result in maximum losses: No cash will be received in liquidating remaining noncash assets and each partner is personally insolvent. Any positive capital balance that would remain even after the inclusion of all potential losses can be paid to the partner without delay. Although the assumption that no further funds will be generated could be unrealistic, it does ensure that negative capital balances are not created by premature payments being made to any of the partners.

Preliminary Distribution Illustrated

To demonstrate the computation of safe capital distributions, assume that a liquidating partnership reports the following balance sheet:

Cash	$ 60,000	Liabilities	$ 40,000
Noncash assets	140,000	Mason, loan	20,000
		Mason, capital (50%)	60,000
		Lee, capital (30%)	30,000
		Dixon, capital (20%)	50,000
Total assets	$200,000	Total liabilities and capital	$200,000

Assume also that the partners estimate that $6,000 will be the maximum expense incurred in carrying out this liquidation. Consequently, the partnership needs $46,000 to meet all obligations: $40,000 to satisfy partnership liabilities and $6,000 for these final expenses. Because the partnership holds $60,000 in cash, it can transfer the extra $14,000 to the partners immediately without fear of injuring any participants in the liquidation. However, the appropriate allocation of this money is not readily apparent; safe capital balances must be computed to guide the actual distribution.

Before demonstrating the allocation of this $14,000, we examine the appropriate handling of a partner's loan balance. According to the balance sheet, Mason has conveyed $20,000 to the business at some point in the past, an amount that was considered a loan rather than additional capital. Perhaps the partnership was in desperate need of funds and Mason was willing to contribute only if the contribution was structured as a loan. Regardless of the reason, the question as to the status of this account remains: Is the $20,000 to be viewed as a liability to the partner or as a capital balance? The answer becomes especially significant during the liquidation process because available funds often are limited. In this regard, the Uniform Partnership Act (UPA) (Section 807[a]) indicates that the assets of the partnership must be applied to pay obligations to creditors, including partners who are creditors; any surplus is distributed to partners based on their capital balances.

Although the UPA indicates that the debt to Mason should be repaid entirely before any distribution of capital can be made to the other partners, actual accounting practice takes a different view. "In preparing predistribution schedules, accountants typically offset partners' loans with the partners' capital accounts and then distribute funds accordingly."[9]

In other words, the loan is merged with the partner's capital account balance at the beginning of liquidation. Thus, accounting practice and the UPA seem to differ in the handling of a loan from a partner.

To illustrate the potential problem with this conflict, assume that a partnership has $20,000 in cash left after liquidation. Partner A has a positive capital balance of $20,000 whereas Partner B has a negative capital balance of $20,000. In addition, Partner B has previously loaned the partnership $20,000. If Partner B is insolvent, a distribution problem arises.[10] If the provisions of the UPA are followed literally, the $20,000 cash should be given to Partner B (probably to the creditors of Partner B) to repay the loan. Because Partner B is insolvent, no more assets can be expected from this individual. Thus, Partner A would have to absorb the entire $20,000 deficit capital balance and will get no portion of the $20,000 in cash that the business holds.

However, despite the UPA, common practice appears to be that the loan from Partner B will be used to offset that partner's negative capital balance. Using that approach, Partner B is left with a zero capital balance so that the entire $20,000 goes to Partner A; neither Partner B nor the creditors of Partner B get anything. Thus, when a loan comes from a partner who later becomes insolvent and reports a negative capital balance, the handling of the loan becomes significant. Unfortunately, further legal guidance does not exist at this time because "no reported state or federal opinion has directly ruled on the right of offset of potential capital deficits."[11]

To follow common practice, this textbook accounts for a loan from a partner in liquidation as if the balance were a component of the partner's capital. By this offset, the accountant can reduce the amount accumulated as a negative capital balance for any insolvent partner. Any such loan can be transferred into the corresponding capital account at the start of the liquidation process. Similarly, any loans due from a partner should be shown as a reduction in the appropriate capital balance.

Proposed Schedule of Liquidation

Returning to the current illustration, the accountant needs to determine an equitable distribution for the $14,000 cash presently available. To structure this computation, a proposed schedule of liquidation is developed *based on the underlying assumption that all future events will result in total losses.* Exhibit 10.2 presents this statement for the Mason, Lee, and Dixon partnership. To expedite coverage, the $20,000 loan has already been transferred into Mason's capital account. Thus, regardless of whether this partner arrives at a deficit or a safe capital balance, the loan figure already has been included.

The preparation of Exhibit 10.2 forecasts complete losses ($140,000) in connection with the disposition of all noncash assets and anticipates liquidation expenses at maximum amounts

[9] Robert E. Whitis and Jeffrey R. Pittman, "Inconsistencies between Accounting Practices and Statutory Law in Partnership Liquidations," *Accounting Educators' Journal,* Fall 1996, p. 99.

[10] The same problem should not exist if the partner is solvent. The partner is legally required to contribute enough funds to delete any capital deficit. Thus, in this case, Partner B would be entitled to the $20,000 loan repayment but then must contribute $20,000 because of the negative capital balance. That cash amount would go to Partner A because of that partner's positive capital balance.

[11] Whitis and Pittman, "Inconsistencies between Accounting Practices," p. 93.

EXHIBIT 10.2

MASON, LEE, AND DIXON
Proposed Schedule of Liquidation—Initial Safe Capital Balances

	Cash	Noncash Assets	Liabilities	Mason, Capital (50%)	Lee, Capital (30%)	Dixon, Capital (20%)
Beginning balances	$ 60,000	$140,000	$40,000	$80,000	$ 30,000	$ 50,000
Maximum loss on noncash assets	-0-	(140,000)	-0-	(70,000)	(42,000)	(28,000)
Maximum liquidation expenses	(6,000)	-0-	-0-	(3,000)	(1,800)	(1,200)
Payment of liabilities	(40,000)	-0-	(40,000)	-0-	-0-	-0-
Potential balances	14,000	-0-	-0-	7,000	(13,800)	20,800
Assume Lee to be insolvent	-0-	-0-	-0-	(9,857) (5/7)	13,800	(3,943) (2/7)
Potential balances	14,000	-0-	-0-	(2,857)	-0-	16,857
Assume Mason to be insolvent	-0-	-0-	-0-	2,857	-0-	(2,857)
Safe balances	$ 14,000	-0-	-0-	-0-	-0-	$ 14,000

($6,000). Following the projected payment of liabilities, any partner reporting a negative capital account is assumed to be personally insolvent. These potential deficit balances are written off and the losses are assigned to the remaining solvent partners based on their relative profit and loss ratio. Lee, with a negative $13,800, is eliminated first. This allocation creates a deficit of $2,857 for Mason, an amount that Dixon alone must absorb. After this series of maximum losses is simulated, any positive capital balance that still remains is considered safe; a cash distribution of that amount can be made to the specific partners.

Exhibit 10.2 indicates that only Dixon has a large enough capital balance at the present time to absorb all possible future losses. Thus, the entire $14,000 can be distributed to this partner with no fear that the capital account will ever report a deficit. Based on current practice, Mason, despite having made a $20,000 loan to the partnership, is entitled to no part of this initial distribution. The loan is of insufficient size to prevent potential deficits from occurring in Mason's capital account.

One series of computations found in this proposed schedule of liquidation merits additional attention. The simulated losses initially create a $13,800 negative balance in Lee's capital account while the other two partners continue to report positive figures. Mason and Dixon must then absorb Lee's projected deficit according to their relative profit and loss percentages. Previously, Mason was allocated 50 percent of net income with 20 percent recorded to Dixon. These figures equate to a 50/70:20/70, or a 5/7:2/7 ratio. Based on this realigned relationship, the $13,800 potential deficit is allocated between Mason (5/7, or $9,857) and Dixon (2/7, or $3,943), reducing Mason's own capital account to a negative balance as shown in Exhibit 10.2.

Continuing with the assumption that maximum losses occur in all cases, Mason's $2,857 deficit is accounted for as if that partner were also personally insolvent. Therefore, the entire negative balance is assigned to Dixon, the only partner still in a positive capital position. Because all potential losses have been recognized at this point, the remaining $14,000 capital is a safe balance that should be paid to Dixon. Even after the money is distributed, Dixon's capital account will still be large enough to absorb all future losses.

Liquidation in Installments

In practice, complete losses are not likely to occur in the liquidation of any business. Thus, at various points during this process, additional cash amounts can become available as partnership property is sold. If the assets are disposed of in a piecemeal fashion, cash can actually flow into the company on a regular basis for an extended period of time. As needed, updated safe capital schedules must be developed to determine the recipients of newly available funds. Because numerous capital distributions could be required, this process is often referred to as a *liquidation made in installments.*

EXHIBIT 10.3 **Liquidation for Installments**

MASON, LEE, AND DIXON
Proposed Schedule of Liquidation—Subsequent Safe Capital Balances

	Cash	Noncash Assets	Liabilities	Mason, Capital (50%)	Lee, Capital (30%)	Dixon, Capital (20%)
Beginning balances	$ 60,000	$140,000	$ 40,000	$ 80,000	$ 30,000	$ 50,000
Capital distribution—safe balances	(14,000)	–0–	–0–	–0–	–0–	(14,000)
Disposal of noncash assets	20,000	(50,000)	–0–	(15,000)	(9,000)	(6,000)
Liabilities paid	(40,000)	–0–	(40,000)	–0–	–0–	–0–
Liquidation expenses	(2,000)	–0–	–0–	(1,000)	(600)	(400)
Current balances	24,000	90,000	–0–	64,000	20,400	29,600
Maximum loss on remaining noncash assets	–0–	(90,000)	–0–	(45,000)	(27,000)	(18,000)
Maximum liquidation expenses	(3,000)	–0–	–0–	(1,500)	(900)	(600)
Potential balances	21,000	–0–	–0–	17,500	(7,500)	11,000
Assume Lee to be insolvent	–0–	–0–	–0–	(5,357) (⅝)	7,500	(2,143) (⅖)
Safe balances—current	$ 21,000	–0–	–0–	$ 12,143	–0–	$ 8,857

To illustrate, assume that the partnership of Mason, Lee, and Dixon actually undergoes the following events in connection with its liquidation:

- As the proposed schedule of liquidation in Exhibit 10.2 indicates, Dixon receives $14,000 in cash as a preliminary capital distribution.
- Noncash assets with a book value of $50,000 are sold for $20,000.
- All $40,000 in liabilities are settled.
- Liquidation expenses of $2,000 are paid; the partners now believe that only a maximum of $3,000 more will be expended in this manner. The original estimation of $6,000 was apparently too high.

As a result of these transactions, the partnership has an additional $21,000 in cash now available to distribute to the partners: $20,000 received from the sale of noncash assets and another $1,000 because of the reduced estimation of liquidation expenses. Once again, the accountant must assume maximum future losses as a means of determining the appropriate distribution of these funds. The accountant produces a second proposed schedule of liquidation (Exhibit 10.3), indicating that $12,143 of this amount should go to Mason with the remaining $8,857 to Dixon. To facilitate a better visual understanding, actual transactions are recorded first on this schedule, followed by the assumed losses. *A dotted line separates the real from the potential occurrences.*

LO5

Develop a predistribution plan to guide the distribution of assets in a partnership liquidation.

Predistribution Plan

The liquidation of a partnership can require numerous transactions occurring over a lengthy period of time. The continual production of proposed schedules of liquidation could become a burdensome chore. The previous illustration already has required two separate statements, and the partnership still possesses $90,000 in noncash assets awaiting conversion to cash. *Therefore, at the start of a liquidation, most accountants produce a single predistribution plan to serve as a guideline for all future payments.* Thereafter, whenever cash becomes available, this plan indicates the appropriate recipient(s) without the necessity of drawing up ever-changing proposed schedules of liquidation.

A predistribution plan is developed by simulating a series of losses, each of which is just large enough to eliminate, one at a time, all of the partners' claims to partnership property.

This approach recognizes that the individual capital accounts exhibit differing degrees of sensitivity to losses. Capital accounts possess varying balances and could be charged with losses at different rates. Consequently, a predistribution plan is based on calculating the losses (the "maximum loss allowable") that would eliminate each of these capital balances in a sequential pattern. This series of absorbed losses then forms the basis for the predistribution plan.

To demonstrate the creation of a predistribution plan, assume that the following partnership is to be liquidated:

Cash	–0–	Liabilities	$100,000
Noncash assets	$221,000	Rubens, capital (50%)	30,000
		Smith, capital (20%)	40,000
		Trice, capital (30%)	51,000
Total assets	$221,000	Total liabilities and capital	$221,000

The partnership capital reported by this organization totals $121,000. However, the individual balances for the partners range from $30,000 to $51,000, and profits and losses are assigned according to three different percentages. Thus, differing losses would reduce each partner's current capital balance to zero. *As a prerequisite to developing a predistribution plan, the sensitivity to losses exhibited by each of these capital accounts must be measured:*

Partner	Capital Balance/ Loss Allocation	Maximum Loss That Can Be Absorbed
Rubens	$30,000/50%	$ 60,000 ✔
Smith	40,000/20%	200,000
Trice	51,000/30%	170,000

According to this initial computation, Rubens is the partner in the most vulnerable position at the present time. Based on a 50 percent share of income, a loss of only $60,000 would reduce this partner's capital account to a zero balance. If the partnership does incur a loss of this amount, Rubens can no longer hope to recover any funds from the liquidation process. Thus, the following schedule simulates the potential effects of this loss (referred to as a *Step 1 loss*):

	Rubens, Capital	Smith, Capital	Trice, Capital
Beginning balances	$ 30,000	$ 40,000	$ 51,000
Assumed $60,000 loss	(30,000) (50%)	(12,000) (20%)	(18,000) (30%)
Step 1 balances	–0–	$ 28,000	$ 33,000

As previously discussed, the predistribution plan is based on describing the series of losses that would eliminate each partner's capital in turn and, thus, all claims to cash. In the previous Step 1 schedule, the $60,000 loss did reduce Rubens's capital account to zero. Assuming, as a precautionary step, that Rubens is personally insolvent, all further losses would have to be allocated between Smith and Trice. Because these two partners have previously shared partnership profits and losses on a 20 percent and 30 percent basis, a 20/50:30/50 (or 40%:60%) relationship exists between them. Therefore, these realigned percentages must now be utilized in calculating a *Step 2 loss,* the amount just large enough to exclude another of the remaining partners from sharing in any future cash distributions:

Partner	Capital Balance/ Loss Allocation	Maximum Loss That Can Be Absorbed
Smith	$28,000/40%	$70,000
Trice	33,000/60%	55,000 ✔

Because Rubens's capital balance already has been eliminated, Trice is now in the most vulnerable position: Only a $55,000 Step 2 loss is required to reduce this partner's capital account to a zero balance.

	Rubens, Capital	Smith, Capital	Trice, Capital
Beginning balances	$ 30,000	$ 40,000	$ 51,000
Assumed $60,000 loss	(30,000) (50%)	(12,000) (20%)	(18,000) (30%)
Step 1 balances	–0–	$ 28,000	$ 33,000
Assumed $55,000 loss	–0–	(22,000) (40%)	(33,000) (60%)
Step 2 balances	–0–	$ 6,000	–0–

According to this second schedule, a total loss of $115,000 ($60,000 from Step 1 plus $55,000 from Step 2) leaves capital of only $6,000, a balance attributed entirely to Smith. At this final point in the simulation, an additional loss of this amount also ends Smith's right to receive any funds from the liquidation process. Having the sole positive capital account remaining, this partner would have to absorb the entire amount of the final loss.

	Rubens, Capital	Smith, Capital	Trice, Capital
Beginning balances	$ 30,000	$ 40,000	$ 51,000
Assumed $60,000 loss	(30,000) (50%)	(12,000) (20%)	(18,000) (30%)
Step 1 balances	–0–	$ 28,000	$ 33,000
Assumed $55,000 loss	–0–	(22,000) (40%)	(33,000) (60%)
Step 2 balances	–0–	6,000	–0–
Assumed $6,000 loss	–0–	(6,000) (100%)	–0–
Final balances	–0–	–0–	–0–

Once this series of simulated losses has reduced each partner's capital account to zero, a predistribution plan for the liquidation can be devised. *This procedure requires working backward through the preceding final schedule to determine the effects that will result if the assumed losses do not occur.* Without these losses, cash becomes available for the partners; therefore, a direct relationship exists between the volume of losses and the distribution pattern. For example, Smith will entirely absorb the last $6,000 loss. Should that loss fail to materialize, Smith is left with a positive safe capital balance of this amount. Thus, as cash becomes available, the first $6,000 received (in excess of partnership obligations and anticipated liquidation expenses) should be distributed solely to Smith.

Similarly, the preceding $55,000 Step 2 loss was divided between Smith and Trice on a 4:6 basis. Again, if such losses do not occur, these balances need not be retained to protect the partnership against capital deficits. Therefore, after Smith has received the initial $6,000, any additional cash that becomes available (up to $55,000) will be split between Smith (40 percent) and Trice (60 percent). For example, if the partnership holds exactly $61,000 in cash in excess of liabilities and possible liquidation expenses, this distribution should be made:

	Rubens	Smith	Trice
First $6,000	–0–	$ 6,000	–0–
Next $55,000	–0–	22,000 (40%)	$33,000 (60%)
Cash distribution	–0–	$28,000	$33,000

The predistribution plan can be completed by including the Step 1 loss, an amount that was to be absorbed by the partners on a 5:2:3 basis. Thus, all money that becomes available to the partners after the initial $61,000 is to be distributed according to the original profit and loss ratio. At this point in the liquidation, enough cash would have been generated to ensure that each partner has a safe capital balance: No possibility exists that a future deficit can occur. Any additional increases in the projected capital balances will be allocated by the 5:2:3 allocation pattern. *For this reason, once all partners begin to receive a portion of the cash disbursements, any remaining funds are divided based on the original profit and loss percentages.*

To inform all parties of the pattern by which available cash will be disbursed, the predistribution plan should be formally prepared in a schedule format prior to beginning liquidation. Following is the predistribution plan for the partnership of Rubens, Smith, and Trice. To complete this illustration, liquidation expenses of $12,000 have been estimated. Because these expenses have the same effect on the capital accounts as losses, they do not change the sequential pattern by which assets eventually will be distributed.

RUBENS, SMITH, AND TRICE
Predistribution Plan

Available Cash		Recipient
First	$112,000	Creditors ($100,000) and liquidation expenses (estimated at $12,000)
Next	6,000	Smith
Next	55,000	Smith (40%) and Trice (60%)
All further cash balances		Rubens (50%), Smith (20%), and Trice (30%)

Summary

1. Although a partnership can exist indefinitely through the periodic admission of new partners, termination of business activities and liquidation of property can take place for a number of reasons. A partner's death or retirement and the insolvency of a partner or even the partnership itself can trigger this process. Because of the risk that the partnership will incur large losses during liquidation, all parties usually seek frequent and timely information describing ongoing developments. The accountant is expected to furnish these data while also working to ensure the equitable treatment of all parties.

2. The liquidation process entails (*a*) converting partnership property into cash, (*b*) paying off liabilities and liquidation expenses, and (*c*) conveying any remaining property to the partners based on their final capital balances. As a means of reporting these transactions, a schedule of liquidation should be produced at periodic intervals. This statement discloses all recent transactions, the assets and liabilities still being held, and the current capital balances. Distribution of this schedule on a regular basis allows the various parties involved in the liquidation to monitor the progress being made.

3. During a liquidation, negative capital balances can arise for one or more of the partners, especially if the partnership incurs material losses in disposing of its property. In such cases, the specific partner or partners should contribute enough additional assets to eliminate their deficits. If payment is slow in coming, the partners who have safe capital balances can immediately divide any cash still held by the partnership. A *safe balance* is the amount of capital that would remain even if maximum future losses occur: Noncash assets are lost in total and all partners with deficits fail to fulfill their legal obligations. In making these computations, the remaining partners absorb negative capital balances based on their relative profit and loss ratio.

4. Completion of the actual liquidation of a partnership can take an extended period. Often, cash is generated during the early stages of this process in excess of the amount needed to cover liabilities and liquidation expenses. The accountant should propose a fair and immediate distribution of these available funds. A proposed schedule of liquidation can be created as a guide for such cash distributions. This statement is based on a *simulated* series of transactions: sale of all noncash assets, payment of liquidation expenses, and so on. At every point, maximum losses are assumed: Noncash assets have no resale value, liquidation expenses are set at the maximum level, and all partners are personally insolvent. Any safe capital balance remaining after incurring such losses represents a distribution that can be made at the present time. Even after this payment, the capital account will still be large enough to absorb all potential losses.

5. A partnership liquidation can require numerous transactions over a lengthy time period. Thus, the accountant could discover that the continual production of proposed schedules of liquidation becomes burdensome. For this reason, at the start of the liquidation process the accountant usually produces a single predistribution plan that serves as a definitive guideline for all payments to be made to the partners. To create this plan, the accountant simulates a series of losses with each loss, in turn, exactly eliminating a partner's capital balance. After these assumed losses have reduced all capital accounts to zero, the accountant devises the predistribution plan by working backward through the series. In effect, the accountant is measuring the cash that will become available if such losses do not occur.

Comprehensive Illustration

PROBLEM

(*Estimated Time: 30 to 40 Minutes*) For the past several years, the Andrews, Caso, Quinn, and Sheridan partnership has operated a local department store. Based on the provisions of the original articles of partnership, all profits and losses have been allocated on a 4:3:2:1 ratio, respectively. Recently, both Caso and Quinn have undergone personal financial problems and, as a result, are now insolvent. Caso's creditors have filed a $20,000 claim against the partnership's assets, and $22,000 is being sought to repay Quinn's personal debts. To satisfy these legal obligations, the partnership property must liquidate. The partners estimate that they will incur $12,000 in expenses to dispose of all noncash assets.

At the time that active operations cease and the liquidation begins, the following partnership balance sheet is produced. All measurement accounts have been closed out to arrive at the current capital balances.

Cash	$ 20,000	Liabilities	$140,000
Noncash assets	280,000	Caso, loan	10,000
		Andrews, capital (40%)	76,000
		Caso, capital (30%)	14,000
		Quinn, capital (20%)	51,000
		Sheridan, capital (10%)	9,000
Total assets	$300,000	Total liabilities and capital	$300,000

During the lengthy liquidation process, the following transactions take place:

* Sale of noncash assets with a book value of $190,000 for $140,000 cash.
* Payment of $14,000 liquidation expenses. No further expenses are expected.
* Distribution of safe capital balances to the partners.
* Payment of all business liabilities.
* Sale of the remaining noncash assets for $10,000.
* Determination of deficit capital balances for any insolvent partners as uncollectible.
* Receipt of appropriate cash contributions from any solvent partner who is reporting a negative capital balance.
* Distribution of final cash.

Required

a. Using the information available prior to the start of the liquidation process, develop a predistribution plan for this partnership.
b. Prepare journal entries to record the actual liquidation transactions.

SOLUTION

a. This partnership begins the liquidation process with capital amounting to $160,000. This total includes the $10,000 loan from Caso because the partnership must retain the liability as a possible offset against any eventual deficit capital balance. Therefore, the predistribution plan is based on the assumption that $160,000 in losses will be incurred, entirely eliminating all partnership capital. As discussed in this chapter, these simulated losses are arranged in a series so that each capital account is sequentially reduced to a zero balance.

At the start of the liquidation, Caso's capital position is the most vulnerable.

Partner	Capital Balance/ Loss Allocation	Maximum Loss That Can Be Absorbed
Andrews	$76,000/40%	$190,000
Caso	24,000/30%	80,000 ✔
Quinn	51,000/20%	255,000
Sheridan	9,000/10%	90,000

As this schedule indicates, an $80,000 loss would eradicate both Caso's $14,000 capital balance and the $10,000 loan. Therefore, to start the development of a predistribution plan, this loss is assumed to have occurred.

	Andrews, Capital	Caso, Loan and Capital	Quinn, Capital	Sheridan, Capital
Beginning balances	$ 76,000	$ 24,000	$ 51,000	$ 9,000
Assumed $80,000 loss	(32,000) (40%)	(24,000) (30%)	(16,000) (20%)	(8,000) (10%)
Step 1 balances	$ 44,000	–0–	$ 35,000	$ 1,000

With Caso's capital account eliminated, further losses are to be split among the remaining partners in the ratio of 4:2:1 (or $^4/_7:^2/_7:^1/_7$). Because only an additional $7,000 loss (the preceding $1,000 Step 1 capital balance divided by $^1/_7$) is now needed to reduce Sheridan's account to zero, this partner is in the second most vulnerable position.

	Andrews	Caso	Quinn	Sheridan
Step 1 balances (above)	$44,000	–0–	$35,000	$ 1,000
Assumed $7,000 loss	(4,000) (4/7)	–0–	(2,000) (2/7)	(1,000) (1/7)
Step 2 balances	$40,000	–0–	$33,000	–0–

Following these two simulated losses, only Andrews and Quinn continue to report positive capital balances. Thus, they divide any additional losses on a 4:2 basis, or $^2/_3:^1/_3$. Based on these realigned percentages, Andrews's position has become the more vulnerable. An additional loss of $60,000 ($40,000/$^2/_3$) reduces this partner's remaining capital to zero whereas a $99,000 loss ($33,000/$^1/_3$) is required to eliminate Quinn's balance.

	Andrews	Caso	Quinn	Sheridan
Step 2 balances (above)	$ 40,000	–0–	$33,000	–0–
Assumed $60,000 loss	(40,000) (2/3)	–0–	(20,000) (1/3)	–0–
Step 3 balances	–0–	–0–	$13,000	–0–

The final $13,000 capital balance belongs to Quinn; an additional loss of this amount is necessary to remove the last element of partnership capital.

Based on the results of this series of simulated losses, the accountant can create a predistribution plan. However, the $140,000 in liabilities owed by the partnership still retains first priority to any available cash. Additionally, $12,000 must be held to cover the anticipated liquidation expenses.

ANDREWS, CASO, QUINN, AND SHERIDAN
Predistribution Plan

Available Cash		Recipient
First	$152,000	Creditors and anticipated liquidation expenses
Next	13,000	Quinn
Next	60,000	Andrews ($^2/_3$) and Quinn ($^1/_3$)
Next	7,000	Andrews ($^4/_7$), Quinn ($^2/_7$), and Sheridan ($^1/_7$)
All further cash		Andrews (40%), Caso (30%), Quinn (20%), and Sheridan (10%)

b. Journal entries for the liquidation:

Caso, Loan	10,000	
Caso, Capital		10,000
To record offset of loan against capital balance in anticipation of liquidation.		
Cash	140,000	
Andrews, Capital (40% of loss)	20,000	
Caso, Capital (30% of loss)	15,000	
Quinn, Capital (20% of loss)	10,000	
Sheridan, Capital (10% of loss)	5,000	
Noncash Assets		190,000
To record sale of noncash assets and allocation of $50,000 loss.		
Andrews, Capital (40%)	5,600	
Caso, Capital (30%)	4,200	
Quinn, Capital (20%)	2,800	
Sheridan, Capital (10%)	1,400	
Cash		14,000
To record payment of liquidation expenses.		

- The partnership now holds $146,000 in cash, $6,000 more than is needed to satisfy all liabilities and estimated expenses. According to the predistribution plan drawn up in requirement (*a*), this entire amount can be safely distributed to Quinn (or to Quinn's creditors).

Quinn, Capital	6,000	
Cash		6,000
To record distribution of available cash based on safe capital balance.		
Liabilities	140,000	
Cash		140,000
To record extinguishment of all partnership debts.		
Cash	10,000	
Andrews, Capital (40% of loss)	32,000	
Caso, Capital (30% of loss)	24,000	
Quinn, Capital (20% of loss)	16,000	
Sheridan, Capital (10% of loss)	8,000	
Noncash Assets		90,000
To record sale of remaining noncash assets and allocation of $80,000 loss.		

- At this point in the liquidation, only the cash and the capital accounts remain open on the partnership books.

	Cash	Andrews, Capital	Caso, Capital	Quinn, Capital	Sheridan, Capital
Beginning balances	$ 20,000	$ 76,000	$ 14,000	$ 51,000	$ 9,000
Loan offset	–0–	–0–	10,000	–0–	–0–
Sale of noncash assets	140,000	(20,000)	(15,000)	(10,000)	(5,000)
Liquidation expenses	(14,000)	(5,600)	(4,200)	(2,800)	(1,400)
Cash distribution	(6,000)	–0–	–0–	(6,000)	–0–
Payment of liabilities	(140,000)	–0–	–0–	–0–	–0–
Sale of noncash assets	10,000	(32,000)	(24,000)	(16,000)	(8,000)
Current balances	$ 10,000	$ 18,400	$ (19,200)	$ 16,200	$(5,400)

Because Caso is personally insolvent, the $19,200 deficit balance will not be repaid, and the remaining three partners must absorb it on a 4:2:1 basis.

Andrews, Capital (⁴/₇ of loss)	10,971	
Quinn, Capital (²/₇ of loss)	5,486	
Sheridan, Capital (¹/₇ of loss)	2,743	
Caso, Capital		19,200

To record write-off of deficit capital balance of insolvent partner.

- This last allocation decreases Sheridan's capital account to an $8,143 negative total. Because this partner is personally solvent, that amount should be contributed to the partnership in accordance with regulations of the Uniform Partnership Act.

Cash	8,143	
Sheridan, Capital		8,143

To record contribution made to eliminate deficit capital balance.

- Sheridan's contribution brings the final cash total for the partnership to $18,143. This amount is distributed to the two partners who continue to maintain positive capital balances: Andrews and Quinn (or Quinn's creditors).

	Andrews, Capital	Quinn, Capital
Balances above	$18,400	$16,200
Caso deficit	(10,971)	(5,486)
Final balances	$ 7,429	$10,714

Andrews, Capital	7,429	
Quinn, Capital	10,714	
Cash		18,143

To record distribution of remaining cash according to final capital balances.

Questions

1. What is the difference between the dissolution of a partnership and the liquidation of partnership property?
2. Why would the members of a partnership elect to terminate business operations and liquidate all noncash assets?
3. Why are liquidation gains and losses usually recorded as direct adjustments to the partners' capital accounts?
4. After liquidating all property and paying partnership obligations, what is the basis for allocating remaining cash among the partners?
5. What is the purpose of a schedule of liquidation? What information does it convey to its readers?
6. According to the Uniform Partnership Act, what events should occur if a partner incurs a negative capital balance during the liquidation process?
7. How are safe capital balances computed when preliminary distributions of cash are to be made during a partnership liquidation?
8. How do loans from partners affect the distribution of assets in a partnership liquidation? What alternatives can affect the handling of such loans?
9. What is the purpose of a proposed schedule of liquidation, and how is it developed?
10. How is a predistribution plan created for a partnership liquidation?

Problems

1. If a partnership is liquidated, how is the final allocation of business assets made to the partners?
    a. Equally.
    b. According to the profit and loss ratio.
    c. According to the final capital account balances.
    d. According to the initial investment made by each of the partners.

2. Which of the following statements is true concerning the accounting for a partnership going through liquidation?
    a. Gains and losses are reported directly as increases and decreases in the appropriate capital account.
    b. A separate income statement is created to measure only the profit or loss generated during liquidation.
    c. Because gains and losses rarely occur during liquidation, no special accounting treatment is warranted.
    d. Within a liquidation, all gains and losses are divided equally among the partners.

3. During a liquidation, if a partner's capital account balance drops below zero, what *should* happen?
    a. The other partners file a legal suit against the partner with the deficit balance.
    b. The partner with the highest capital balance contributes sufficient assets to eliminate the deficit.
    c. The deficit balance is removed from the accounting records with only the remaining partners sharing in future gains and losses.
    d. The partner with a deficit contributes enough assets to offset the deficit balance.

4. A local partnership is liquidating and is currently reporting the following capital balances:

    Angela, capital (50% share of all profits and losses) . . . . $ 19,000
    Woodrow, capital (30%)   18,000
    Cassidy, capital (20%) . . . .   (12,000)

    Cassidy has indicated that a forthcoming contribution will cover the $12,000 deficit. However, the two remaining partners have asked to receive the $25,000 in cash that is presently available. How much of this money should each of the partners be given?
    a. Angela, $13,000; Woodrow, $12,000.
    b. Angela, $11,500; Woodrow, $13,500.
    c. Angela, $12,000; Woodrow, $13,000.
    d. Angela, $12,500; Woodrow, $12,500.

5. A local partnership is considering possible liquidation because one of the partners (Bell) is insolvent. Capital balances at the current time are as follows. Profits and losses are divided on a 4:3:2:1 basis, respectively.

    Bell, capital $50,000
    Hardy, capital   56,000
    Dennard, capital   14,000
    Suddath, capital   80,000

    Bell's creditors have filed a $21,000 claim against the partnership's assets. The partnership currently holds assets reported at $300,000 and liabilities of $100,000. If the assets can be sold for $190,000, what is the minimum amount that Bell's creditors would receive?
    a. –0–
    b. $2,000.
    c. $2,800.
    d. $6,000.

6. What is a predistribution plan?
    a. A guideline for the cash distributions to partners during a liquidation.
    b. A list of the procedures to be performed during a liquidation.

    c. A determination of the final cash distribution to the partners on the settlement date.

    d. A detailed list of the transactions that will transpire in the reorganization of a partnership.

LO3, LO4

7. A partnership has the following balance sheet just before final liquidation is to begin:

Cash	$ 26,000	Liabilities		$ 50,000
Inventory	31,000	Art, capital (40% of		
Other assets	62,000	profits and losses)		18,000
		Raymond, capital (30%)		25,000
		Darby, capital (30%)		26,000
Total	$119,000	Total		$119,000

Liquidation expenses are estimated to be $12,000. The other assets are sold for $40,000. What distribution can be made to the partners?

    a. –0– to Art, $1,500 to Raymond, $2,500 to Darby.

    b. $1,333 to Art, $1,333 to Raymond, $1,334 to Darby.

    c. –0– to Art, $1,200 to Raymond, $2,800 to Darby.

    d. $600 to Art, $1,200 to Raymond, $2,200 to Darby.

LO1, LO3, LO4

8. A partnership has the following capital balances: A (20% of profits and losses) = $100,000; B (30% of profits and losses) = $120,000; C (50% of profits and losses) = $180,000. If the partnership is to be liquidated and $30,000 becomes immediately available, who gets that money?

    a. $6,000 to A, $9,000 to B, $15,000 to C.

    b. $22,000 to A, $3,000 to B, $5,000 to C.

    c. $22,000 to A, $8,000 to B, –0– to C.

    d. $24,000 to A, $6,000 to B, –0– to C.

LO5

9. A partnership is currently holding $400,000 in assets and $234,000 in liabilities. The partnership is to be liquidated, and $20,000 is the best estimation of the expenses that will be incurred during this process. The four partners share profits and losses as shown. Capital balances at the start of the liquidation follow:

Kevin, capital (40%)	$59,000
Michael, capital (30%)	39,000
Brendan, capital (10%)	34,000
Jonathan, capital (20%)	34,000

The partners realize that Brendan will be the first partner to start receiving cash. How much cash will Brendan receive before any of the other partners collect any cash?

    a. $12,250.

    b. $14,750.

    c. $17,000.

    d. $19,500.

LO5

10. Carney, Pierce, Menton, and Hoehn are partners who share profits and losses on a 4:3:2:1 basis, respectively. They are beginning to liquidate the business. At the start of this process, capital balances are as follows:

Carney, capital	$60,000
Pierce, capital	27,000
Menton, capital	43,000
Hoehn, capital	20,000

Which of the following statements is true?

    a. The first available $2,000 will go to Hoehn.

    b. Carney will be the last partner to receive any available cash.

    c. The first available $3,000 will go to Menton.

    d. Carney will collect a portion of any available cash before Hoehn receives money.

LO3, LO4

11. A partnership has gone through liquidation and now reports the following account balances:

Cash	$16,000
Loan from Jones	3,000
Wayman, capital	(2,000) (deficit)
Jones, capital	(5,000) (deficit)
Fuller, capital	13,000
Rogers, capital	7,000

Profits and losses are allocated on the following basis: Wayman, 30 percent; Jones, 20 percent; Fuller, 30 percent; and Rogers, 20 percent. Which of the following events should occur now?

a. Jones should receive $3,000 cash because of the loan balance.

b. Fuller should receive $11,800 and Rogers $4,200.

c. Fuller should receive $10,600 and Rogers $5,400.

d. Jones should receive $3,000, Fuller $8,800, and Rogers $4,200.

LO1, LO3, LO4

12. A partnership has the following account balances: Cash, $70,000; Other Assets, $540,000; Liabilities, $260,000; Nixon (50% of profits and losses), $170,000; Cleveland (30%), $110,000; Pierce (20%), $70,000. The company liquidates, and $8,000 becomes available to the partners. Who gets the $8,000?

LO1, LO3

13. A local partnership has only two assets (cash of $10,000 and land with a cost of $35,000). All liabilities have been paid and the following capital balances are currently being recorded. The partners share profits and losses as follows. All partners are insolvent.

Brown, capital (40%)	$25,000
Fish, capital (30%)	15,000
Stone, capital (30%)	5,000

a. If the land is sold for $25,000, how much cash does each partner receive in a final settlement?

b. If the land is sold for $15,000, how much cash does each partner receive in a final settlement?

c. If the land is sold for $5,000, how much cash does each partner receive in a final settlement?

LO3

14. A local dental partnership has been liquidated and the final capital balances are as follows:

Atkinson, capital (40% of all profits and losses)	$ 60,000
Kaporale, capital (30%)	20,000
Dennsmore, capital (20%)	(30,000)
Rasputin, capital (10%)	(50,000)

If Rasputin contributes additional cash of $20,000 to the partnership, what should happen to it?

LO4

15. A partnership currently holds three assets: cash, $10,000; land, $35,000; and a building, $50,000. The partners anticipate that expenses required to liquidate their partnership will amount to $5,000. Capital balances are as follows:

Ace, capital	$25,000
Ball, capital	28,000
Eaton, capital	20,000
Lake, capital	22,000

The partners share profits and losses as follows: Ace (30%), Ball (30%), Eaton (20%), and Lake (20%). If a preliminary distribution of cash is to be made, how much will each partner receive?

LO4

16. The following condensed balance sheet is for the partnership of Hardwick, Saunders, and Ferris, who share profits and losses in the ratio of 4:3:3, respectively:

Cash	$ 90,000	Accounts payable	$210,000
Other assets	820,000	Ferris, loan	40,000
Hardwick, loan	30,000	Hardwick, capital	300,000
		Saunders, capital	200,000
		Ferris, capital	190,000
Total assets	$940,000	Total liabilities and capital	$940,000

The partners decide to liquidate the partnership. Forty percent of the other assets are sold for $200,000. Prepare a proposed schedule of liquidation.

LO5

17. The following condensed balance sheet is for the partnership of Miller, Tyson, and Watson, who share profits and losses in the ratio of 6:2:2, respectively:

Cash	$ 40,000	Liabilities		$ 70,000
Other assets	140,000	Miller, capital		50,000
		Tyson, capital		50,000
		Watson, capital		10,000
Total assets	$180,000	Total liabilities and capital		$180,000

For how much money must the other assets be sold so that each partner receives some amount of cash in a liquidation?

LO4

18. A partnership's balance sheet is as follows:

Cash	$ 60,000	Liabilities		$ 50,000
Noncash assets	120,000	Babb, capital		60,000
		Whitaker, capital		20,000
		Edwards, capital		50,000
Total assets	$180,000	Total liabilities and capital		$180,000

Babb, Whitaker, and Edwards share profits and losses in the ratio of 4:2:4, respectively. This business is to be terminated, and the partners estimate that $8,000 in liquidation expenses will be incurred. How should the $2,000 in safe cash that is presently held be disbursed?

LO3

19. A partnership has liquidated all assets but still reports the following account balances:

Loan from White	$ 6,000
Black, capital	3,000
White, capital	(9,000) (deficit)
Green, capital	(3,000) (deficit)
Brown, capital	15,000
Blue, capital	(12,000) (deficit)

The partners split profits and losses as follows: Black, 30 percent; White, 30 percent; Green, 10 percent; Brown, 20 percent; and Blue, 10 percent.

Assuming that all partners are personally insolvent except for Green and Brown, how much cash must Green now contribute to this partnership?

LO4, LO5

20. The following balance sheet is for a local partnership in which the partners have become very unhappy with each other.

Cash	$ 40,000	Liabilities		$ 30,000
Land	130,000	Adams, capital		80,000
Building	120,000	Baker, capital		30,000
		Carvil, capital		60,000
		Dobbs, capital		90,000
Total assets	$290,000	Total liabilities and capital		$290,000

To avoid more conflict, the partners have decided to cease operations and sell all assets. Using this information, answer the following questions. Each question should be viewed as an *independent* situation related to the partnership's liquidation.

a. The $10,000 cash that exceeds the partnership liabilities is to be disbursed immediately. If profits and losses are allocated to Adams, Baker, Carvil, and Dobbs on a 2:3:3:2 basis, respectively, how will the $10,000 be divided?

b. The $10,000 cash that exceeds the partnership liabilities is to be disbursed immediately. If profits and losses are allocated on a 2:2:3:3 basis, respectively, how will the $10,000 be divided?

    c. The building is immediately sold for $70,000 to give total cash of $110,000. The liabilities are then paid, leaving a cash balance of $80,000. This cash is to be distributed to the partners. How much of this money will each partner receive if profits and losses are allocated to Adams, Baker, Carvil, and Dobbs on a 1:3:3:3 basis, respectively?

    d. Assume that profits and losses are allocated to Adams, Baker, Carvil, and Dobbs on a 1:3:4:2 basis, respectively. How much money must the firm receive from selling the land and building to ensure that Carvil receives a portion?

LO5

21. The partnership of Larson, Norris, Spencer, and Harrison has decided to terminate operations and liquidate all business property. During this process, the partners expect to incur $8,000 in liquidation expenses. All partners are currently solvent.

    The balance sheet reported by this partnership at the time that the liquidation commenced follows. The percentages indicate the allocation of profits and losses to each of the four partners.

Cash	$ 28,250		Liabilities	$ 47,000
Accounts receivable	44,000		Larson, capital (20%)	15,000
Inventory	39,000		Norris, capital (30%)	60,000
Land and buildings	23,000		Spencer, capital (20%)	75,000
Equipment	104,000		Harrison, capital (30%)	41,250
Total assets	$238,250		Total liabilities and capital	$238,250

    Based on the information provided, prepare a predistribution plan for liquidating this partnership.

LO5

22. The following partnership is being liquidated:

Cash	$ 36,000		Liabilities	$50,000
Noncash assets	174,000		Able, loan	10,000
			Able, capital (20%)	40,000
			Moon, capital (30%)	60,000
			Yerkl, capital (50%)	50,000

    a. Liquidation expenses are estimated to be $12,000. Prepare a predistribution schedule to guide the distribution of cash.

    b. Assume that assets costing $28,000 are sold for $40,000. How is the available cash to be divided?

LO5

23. A local partnership is to be liquidated. Commissions and other liquidation expenses are expected to total $19,000. The business's balance sheet prior to the commencement of liquidation is as follows:

Cash	$ 27,000		Liabilities	$ 40,000
Noncash assets	254,000		Simpson, capital (20%)	18,000
			Hart, capital (40%)	40,000
			Bobb, capital (20%)	48,000
			Reidl, capital (20%)	135,000
Total assets	$281,000		Total liabilities and capital	$281,000

    Prepare a predistribution plan for this partnership.

LO3

24. The following information concerns two different partnerships. These problems should be viewed as independent situations.

Part A

The partnership of Ross, Milburn, and Thomas has the following account balances:

Cash	$ 36,000		Liabilities	$17,000
Noncash assets	100,000		Ross, capital	69,000
			Milburn, capital	(8,000) (deficit)
			Thomas, capital	58,000

This partnership is being liquidated. Ross and Milburn are each entitled to 40 percent of all profits and losses with the remaining 20 percent to Thomas.

a. What is the maximum amount that Milburn might have to contribute to this partnership because of the deficit capital balance?

b. How should the $19,000 cash that is presently available in excess of liabilities be distributed?

c. If the noncash assets are sold for a total of $41,000, what is the minimum amount of cash that Thomas could receive?

Part B

The partnership of Sampson, Klingon, Carton, and Romulan is being liquidated. It currently holds cash of $9,000 but no other assets. Liabilities amount to $24,000. The capital balances are as follows:

Sampson	$ 9,000
Klingon	(17,000)
Carton	5,000
Romulan	(12,000)

Profits and losses are allocated on the following basis: Sampson, 40 percent, Klingon, 20 percent, Carton, 30 percent, and Romulan, 10 percent.

a. If both Klingon and Romulan are personally insolvent, how much money must Carton contribute to this partnership?

b. If only Romulan is personally insolvent, how much money must Klingon contribute? How will these funds be disbursed?

c. If only Klingon is personally insolvent, how much money should Sampson receive from the liquidation?

25. March, April, and May have been in partnership for a number of years. The partners allocate all profits and losses on a 2:3:1 basis, respectively. Recently, each partner has become personally insolvent and, thus, the partners have decided to liquidate the business in hope of remedying their personal financial problems. As of September 1, the partnership's balance sheet is as follows:

Cash	$ 11,000	Liabilities		$ 61,000
Accounts receivable	84,000	March, capital		25,000
Inventory	74,000	April, capital		75,000
Land, building, and				
equipment (net)	38,000	May, capital		46,000
Total assets	$207,000	Total liabilities and capital		$207,000

Prepare journal entries for the following transactions:

a. Sold all inventory for $56,000 cash.

b. Paid $7,500 in liquidation expenses.

c. Paid $40,000 of the partnership's liabilities.

d. Collected $45,000 of the accounts receivable.

e. Distributed safe cash balances; the partners anticipate no further liquidation expenses.

f. Sold remaining accounts receivable for 30 percent of face value.

g. Sold land, building, and equipment for $17,000.

h. Paid all remaining liabilities of the partnership.

i. Distributed cash held by the business to the partners.

26. The partnership of W, X, Y, and Z has the following balance sheet:

Cash	$ 30,000	Liabilities	$42,000
Other assets	220,000	W, capital (50% of	
		profits and losses)	60,000
		X, capital (30%)	78,000
		Y, capital (10%)	40,000
		Z, capital (10%)	30,000

Z is personally insolvent, and one of his creditors is considering suing the partnership for the $5,000 that is currently due. The creditor realizes that liquidation could result from this litigation and does not wish to force such an extreme action unless the creditor is reasonably sure of getting the money that is due. If the partnership sells the other assets, how much money must it receive to ensure that $5,000 would be available from Z's portion of the business? Liquidation expenses are expected to be $15,000.

LO4

27. On January 1, the partners of Van, Bakel, and Cox (who share profits and losses in the ratio of 5:3:2, respectively) decide to liquidate their partnership. The trial balance at this date follows:

	Debit	Credit
Cash	$ 18,000	
Accounts receivable	66,000	
Inventory	52,000	
Machinery and equipment, net	189,000	
Van, loan	30,000	
Accounts payable		$ 53,000
Bakel, loan		20,000
Van, capital		118,000
Bakel, capital		90,000
Cox, capital		74,000
Totals	$355,000	$355,000

The partners plan a program of piecemeal conversion of the business's assets to minimize liquidation losses. All available cash, less an amount retained to provide for future expenses, is to be distributed to the partners at the end of each month. A summary of the liquidation transactions follows:

January	Collected $51,000 of the accounts receivable; the balance is deemed uncollectible.
	Received $38,000 for the entire inventory.
	Paid $2,000 in liquidation expenses.
	Paid $50,000 to the outside creditors after offsetting a $3,000 credit memorandum received by the partnership on January 11.
	Retained $10,000 cash in the business at the end of January to cover any unrecorded liabilities and anticipated expenses. The remainder is distributed to the partners.
February	Paid $3,000 in liquidation expenses.
	Retained $6,000 cash in the business at the end of the month to cover unrecorded liabilities and anticipated expenses.
March	Received $146,000 on the sale of all machinery and equipment.
	Paid $5,000 in final liquidation expenses.
	Retained no cash in the business.

Prepare a schedule to compute the safe installment payments made to the partners at the end of each of these three months.

LO1, LO3

28. Following is a series of *independent cases*. In each situation, indicate the cash distribution to be made at the end of the liquidation process. *Unless otherwise stated, assume that all solvent partners will reimburse the partnership for their deficit capital balances.*

Part A

The Simon, Haynes, and Jackson partnership presently reports the following accounts. Jackson is personally insolvent and can contribute only an additional $3,000 to the partnership. Simon is also insolvent and has no available funds.

Cash	$ 30,000
Liabilities	22,000
Haynes, loan	10,000
Simon, capital (40%)	16,000
Haynes, capital (20%)	(6,000)
Jackson, capital (40%)	(12,000)

Part B

Hough, Luck, and Cummings operate a local accounting firm as a partnership. After working together for several years, they have decided to liquidate the partnership's property. The partners have prepared the following balance sheet:

Cash	$ 20,000	Liabilities	$ 40,000
Hough, loan	8,000	Luck, loan	10,000
Noncash assets	162,000	Hough, capital (50%)	90,000
		Luck, capital (40%)	30,000
		Cummings, capital (10%)	20,000
Total assets	$190,000	Total liabilities and capital	$190,000

The firm sells the noncash assets for $80,000; it will use $21,000 of this amount to pay liquidation expenses. All three of these partners are personally insolvent.

Part C

Use the same information as in Part B, but assume that the profits and losses are split 2:4:4 to Hough, Luck, and Cummings, respectively, and that liquidation expenses are only $6,000.

Part D

Following the liquidation of all noncash assets, the partnership of Redmond, Ledbetter, Watson, and Sandridge has the following account balances:

Liabilities	$ 28,000
Redmond, loan	5,000
Redmond, capital (20%)	(21,000)
Ledbetter, capital (10%)	(30,000)
Watson, capital (30%)	3,000
Sandridge, capital (40%)	15,000

Redmond is personally insolvent.

LO1, LO5

29. The partnership of Frick, Wilson, and Clarke has elected to cease all operations and liquidate its business property. A balance sheet drawn up at this time shows the following account balances:

Cash	$ 48,000	Liabilities	$ 35,000
Noncash assets	177,000	Frick, capital (60%)	101,000
		Wilson, capital (20%)	28,000
		Clarke, capital (20%)	61,000
Total assets	$225,000	Total liabilities and capital	$225,000

The following transactions occur in liquidating this business:

* Distributed safe capital balances immediately to the partners. Liquidation expenses of $9,000 are estimated as a basis for this computation.
* Sold noncash assets with a book value of $80,000 for $48,000.
* Paid all liabilities.
* Distributed safe capital balances again.
* Sold remaining noncash assets for $44,000.

- Paid liquidation expenses of $7,000.
- Distributed remaining cash to the partners and closed the financial records of the business permanently.

Produce a final schedule of liquidation for this partnership.

LO2, LO5

30. **Part A**

The partnership of Wingler, Norris, Rodgers, and Guthrie was formed several years ago as a local architectural firm. Several partners have recently undergone personal financial problems and have decided to terminate operations and liquidate the business. The following balance sheet is drawn up as a guideline for this process:

Cash	$ 15,000	Liabilities	$ 74,000
Accounts receivable	82,000	Rodgers, loan	35,000
Inventory	101,000	Wingler, capital (30%)	120,000
Land	85,000	Norris, capital (10%)	88,000
Building and		Rodgers, capital (20%)	74,000
equipment (net)	168,000	Guthrie, capital (40%)	60,000
Total assets	$451,000	Total liabilities and capital	$451,000

When the liquidation commenced, expenses of $16,000 were anticipated as being necessary to dispose of all property.

Prepare a predistribution plan for this partnership.

Part B

The following transactions transpire during the liquidation of the Wingler, Norris, Rodgers, and Guthrie partnership:

- Collected 80 percent of the total accounts receivable with the rest judged to be uncollectible.
- Sold the land, building, and equipment for $150,000.
- Made safe capital distributions.
- Learned that Guthrie, who has become personally insolvent, will make no further contributions.
- Paid all liabilities.
- Sold all inventory for $71,000.
- Made safe capital distributions again.
- Paid liquidation expenses of $11,000.
- Made final cash disbursements to the partners based on the assumption that all partners other than Guthrie are personally solvent.

Prepare journal entries to record these liquidation transactions.

Develop Your Skills

RESEARCH CASE

A client of the CPA firm of Harston and Mendez is a medical practice of seven local doctors. One doctor has been sued for several million dollars as the result of a recent operation. Because of what appears to be this doctor's very poor judgment, a patient died. Although that doctor was solely involved with the patient in question, the lawsuit names the entire practice as a defendant. Originally, four of these doctors formed this business as a general partnership. However, five years ago, the partners converted the business to a limited liability partnership based on the laws of the state in which they operate.

Read the following articles as well as any other published information that is available on partner and partnership liability:

"Partners Forever? Within Andersen, Personal Liability May Bring Ruin," *The Wall Street Journal,* April 2, 2002, p. C1.

"Collapse: Speed of Andersen's Demise Amazing," *Milwaukee Journal Sentinel,* June 16, 2002, p. D1.

Required

Based on the facts presented in this case, answer these questions:

1. What liability do the other six partners in this medical practice have in connection with this lawsuit?
2. What factors will be important in determining the exact liability (if any) of these six doctors?

ANALYSIS CASE

Go to the Web site www.napico.com and click on "Partnership Financial Information—Click Here." Then click on "2008 Annual Reports" to access the annual report for National Tax Credit Investors II (NTCI II).

Read the financial statements contained in the 2008 annual report and the accompanying notes, especially any that discuss the partnership form of organization.

Assume that an investor is considering investing in this partnership and has downloaded this report for study and analysis.

Required

1. What differences between NTCI II's financial statements and those of an incorporated entity exist?
2. Assume that this potential investor is not aware of the potential implications of owning a partnership rather than a corporation. What information is available in these statements to advise this individual of the unique characteristics of this legal business form?

COMMUNICATION CASE

Read the following as well as any other published articles on the bankruptcy of the partnership of Laventhol & Horwath:

"Laventhol Says It Plans to File for Chapter 11," *The Wall Street Journal,* November 20, 1990, p. A3.

"Laventhol Partners Face Long Process That Could End in Personal Bankruptcy," *The Wall Street Journal,* November 20, 1990, p. B5.

"Laventhol Bankruptcy Filing Indicates Liabilities May Be as Much as $2 Billion," *The Wall Street Journal,* November 23, 1990, p. A4.

Required

Write a report describing the potential liabilities that the members of a partnership could incur.

EXCEL CASE

The partnership of Wilson, Cho, and Arrington has the following account information:

Partner	Capital Balance	Share of Profits and Losses
Wilson	$200,000	40%
Cho	180,000	20
Arrington	110,000	40

This partnership will be liquidated, and the partners are scheduled to receive cash equal to any ending positive capital balance. If a negative capital balance results, the partner is expected to contribute that amount.

Assume that losses of $50,000 occur during the liquidation followed later by additional and final losses of $100,000.

Required

1. Create a spreadsheet to determine the capital balances that remain for each of the three partners after these two losses are incurred.

2. Modify this spreadsheet so that it can be used for different capital balances, different allocation patterns, and different liquidation gains and losses.

Accounting for State and Local Governments (Part 1)

To even a seasoned veteran of accounting, the financial statements produced for a state or local government can appear to be written in a complex foreign language.

- The 2008 financial statements for Bismarck, North Dakota, report other financing sources and uses for its governmental funds that include $19.8 million of operating transfers-in and $18.1 million of operating transfers-out.

- The June 30, 2008, balance sheet for the governmental funds of Portland, Maine, discloses a $6.8 million fund balance reserved for encumbrances.

- The 2008 comprehensive annual financial report for Phoenix, Arizona, contains more than 245 pages of data including the dollar amounts of expenditures made in connection with public safety ($765 million), community enrichment ($227 million), and environmental services ($24 million).

- In 2008, Greensboro, North Carolina, reported two complete and distinct sets of financial statements. One disclosed that the city's governmental activities owed more than $288 million in liabilities whereas the second set indicated that, at the same point in time, the city's governmental funds reported only $46 million in liabilities.

- For the year ending June 30, 2008, Nashville and Davidson County, Tennessee, reported that operating its public library system resulted in a net financial burden of $27 million for the citizens, while its department of water and sewerage services provided a financial benefit of $69 million.

Merely a quick perusal of such information points to fundamental differences with the reporting that most people associate with the financial statements of for-profit businesses. One or more underlying causes must be responsible for the uniqueness of the financial statements of state and local governments. This chapter and the next introduce the principles and practices that underlie state and local government accounting and explain the logic behind their application.

LEARNING OBJECTIVES

After studying this chapter, you should be able to:

LO1 Explain the history of and the reasons for the unique characteristics of the financial statements produced by state and local governments.

LO2 Differentiate between the two sets of financial statements produced by state and local governments.

LO3 Understand the reason that fund accounting has traditionally been such a prominent factor in the internal recording of state and local governments.

LO4 Identify the three fund types and the individual fund categories within each.

LO5 Understand the basic structure of government-wide financial statements and fund-based financial statements (as produced for the governmental funds).

LO6 Record the passage of a budget as well as subsequent encumbrances and expenditures.

LO7 Understand the reporting of capital assets, supplies, and prepaid expenses by a state or local government.

LO8 Determine the proper timing for the recognition of revenues from non-exchange transactions.

LO9 Account for the issuance of long-term bonds and the reporting of special assessment projects.

LO10 Record the various types of monetary transfers that occur within the funds of a state or local government.

These chapters are designed not only to demonstrate reporting procedures but also to explain the evolution that has led state and local governments to produce financial statements that are markedly different in many places from those of for-profit businesses.

INTRODUCTION TO THE ACCOUNTING FOR STATE AND LOCAL GOVERNMENTS

LO1

Explain the history of and the reasons for the unique characteristics of the financial statements produced by state and local governments.

In the United States, thousands of state and local government reporting entities touch the lives of the citizenry on a daily basis. In addition to the federal and 50 state governments, 89,476 local governments existed as of 2007. Of these, 39,044 were general purpose local governments—3,033 county governments and 36,011 subcounty governments, including 19,492 municipal governments and 16,519 township governments. The remainder, which comprised more than one-half of the total, were special purpose local governments, including 14,561 school districts and school system governments and 37,381 special district governments.[1] Nearly 14.7 million people were employed by state and local governments. Income and sales taxes are collected, property taxes are assessed, schools are operated, fire departments are maintained, garbage is collected, and roads are paved. Actions of one or more governments affect every individual.

Accounting for such governments is not merely a matching of expenses with earned revenues so that net income can be determined. The setting of tax rates and allocating of limited financial resources among such worthy causes as education, police, welfare, and the environment create heated debates throughout the nation. To keep the public informed so that proper decisions are more likely to be made, government reporting has historically focused on identifying the methods used to generate financial resources and the uses made of those resources.

Indeed, this approach is appropriate for the short-term decisions necessitated by gathering and utilizing financial resources to carry out public policy. For the longer term, though, information to reflect the overall financial stability of the government is also needed. Hence, state and local governments prepare not one but two complete and distinct sets of financial statements. The need for this dual reporting system demonstrates the difficulty that governments face in satisfying a wide array of user needs. For the student, nothing is more vital than recognizing that state and local governments produce two sets of statements, each with its own unique principles and objectives.

The creation of this dual reporting system is probably the most significant step that has transpired in the evolution of the generally accepted accounting principles used by state and local governments. The American Institute of Certified Public Accountants (AICPA) and the National Council on Governmental Accounting (NCGA) made significant strides during earlier decades in establishing sound accounting principles.[2] In June 1984, the Governmental Accounting Standards Board (GASB) became the public sector counterpart of the Financial Accounting Standards Board. GASB holds the primary responsibility in the United States for setting authoritative accounting standards for state and local government units.[3] In the same manner as the Financial Accounting Standards Board, GASB is an independent body functioning under the oversight of the Financial Accounting Foundation. Thus, a formal mechanism is in place to guide the development of state and local government accounting.

---

[1] www.census.gov/govs/cog/GovOrgTab03ss.html.

[2] The NCGA was a quasi-independent agency of the Government Finance Officers Association. The NCGA held authority for state and local government accounting from 1973 through 1984. The National Committee on Municipal Accounting had this responsibility from 1934 until 1941, and the National Committee on Governmental Accounting established government accounting principles from 1949 through 1954 and again from 1967 until 1973. During several periods, no group held primary responsibility for the development of governmental accounting. For an overview of the work of the GASB, see Terry K. Patton and Robert J. Freeman, "The GASB Turns 25: A Retrospective," *Government Finance Review,* April 2009.

[3] In 1990, the Director of the Office of Management and Budget, the Secretary of the Treasury, and the Comptroller General created the Federal Accounting Standards Advisory Board (FASAB). FASAB recommends accounting principles and standards for the U.S. federal government and its agencies to use. Information about FASAB can be found at www.fasab.gov.

Governmental Accounting—User Needs

The unique aspects of any system of accounting should be a direct result of the perceived needs of financial statement users. Identification of these informational requirements is, therefore, a logical first step in the study of the accounting principles applied to state and local governments. Specific procedures utilized in the reporting process can be understood best as an outgrowth of these needs.

Often, though, user expectations are complex and even contradictory, especially for governmental entities. The taxpayer, the government employee, the bondholder, and the public official may each be seeking distinctly different types of financial information about a governmental unit.

> My own reflection on the subject leads me to the conviction that appropriate and adequate accounting for state and local governmental units involves a far more complex set of interrelationships, to be reported to a more diverse set of users with a greater variety of interests and needs, than exists in business accounting and reporting.[4]

In *Concepts Statement No. 1*, "Objectives of Financial Reporting," GASB recognized this challenge by identifying three groups of primary users of external state and local governmental financial reports: the citizenry, legislative and oversight bodies, and creditors and investors. It then described the needs and interests of each of these groups.

> **Citizenry**—Want to evaluate the likelihood of tax or service fee increases, to determine the sources and uses of resources, to forecast revenues in order to influence spending decisions, to ensure that resources were used in accordance with appropriations, to assess financial condition, and to compare budgeted to actual results.
> **Legislative and oversight bodies**—Want to assess the overall financial condition when developing budgets and program recommendations, to monitor operating results to assure compliance with mandates, to determine the reasonableness of fees and the need for tax changes, and to ascertain the ability to finance new programs and capital needs.
> **Investors and creditors**—Want to know the amount of available and likely future financial resources, to measure the debt position and the ability to service that debt, and to review operating results and cash flow data.[5]

Thus, the quest for useful governmental reporting encounters a significant obstacle: User needs are so broad that no one set of financial statements or accounting principles can possibly satisfy all expectations. How can voters, bondholders, city officials, and the other users of the financial statements provided by state and local governments receive the information that they need for decision-making purposes? How can statements that are prepared for citizens also be sufficient for the needs of creditors and investors?

LO2

Differentiate between the two sets of financial statements produced by state and local governments.

Two Sets of Financial Statements

Eventually, the desire to provide financial information that could satisfy such broad demands led GASB to require the production of two distinct sets of statements by state and local governments:

> **Fund-based financial statements** have been designed "to show restrictions on the planned use of resources or to measure, *in the short term*, the revenues and expenditures arising from certain activities."[6]
> **Government-wide financial statements** will have a longer-term focus because they will report "*all* revenues and *all* costs of providing services each year, not just those received or paid in the current year or soon after year-end."[7]

---

[4] Robert K. Mautz, "Financial Reporting: Should Government Emulate Business?" *Journal of Accountancy*, August 1981, p. 53.

[5] GASB *Concepts Statement No. 1*, "Objectives of Financial Reporting," May 1987, para. 33–37.

[6] GASB *Statement No. 34*, "Basic Financial Statements—and Management's Discussion and Analysis—for State and Local Governments," June 1999, preface p. 1.

[7] Ibid., p. 2.

Fund-Based Financial Statements. These statements report individual activities and the amount of financial resources allocated to them each period as well as the use made of those resources. They help citizens assess the government's fiscal accountability in raising and utilizing money. For example, fund-based financial statements report the amount spent on such services as public safety, education, health and sanitation, and the construction of new roads. The primary measurement focus in these statements, at least for the public service activities, is the flow and amount of *current financial resources*. The timing of recognition in most cases is based on *modified accrual accounting*. Modified accrual accounting recognizes (1) revenues when the resulting current financial resources are measurable and available to be used and (2) expenditures when they cause a reduction in current financial resources.

In applying modified accrual accounting, identifying when resources are "available" for current-period expenditures can be quite important. The term "available" means that current financial resources will be received soon enough in the future to be used in paying for current period expenditures. The determination of what is meant by "soon enough" is up to the reporting government. In 2008, the City of Norfolk, Virginia, disclosed that "the City generally considers revenues, except for grant revenues, to be available if they are collected within 45 days of the end of the fiscal year." For that reason, a 2008 revenue that was collected within the first 45 days of 2009 is still recognized by this city in 2008 because it was available to pay 2008 expenditures. However, the City of Richmond, Virginia, applies a policy of two months and the City of Raleigh, North Carolina, uses 90 days. In creating fund-based financial statements, the definition of available can vary from one government to the next. The one exception under modified accrual accounting is the recognition of property taxes where a 60-day maximum period is mandated.

Government-Wide Financial Statements. These statements report a government's financial affairs as a whole. They provide a method of assessing operational accountability, the government's ability to meet its operating objectives. This information helps users make evaluations of the financial decisions and long-term stability of the government by allowing them to:

- Determine whether the government's overall financial position improved or deteriorated.
- Evaluate whether the government's current-year revenues were sufficient to pay for current-year services.
- Understand the cost of providing services to the citizenry.
- See how the government finances its programs—through user fees and other program revenues along with general tax revenues.
- Understand the extent to which the government has invested in capital assets, including roads, bridges, and other infrastructure assets.[8]

To achieve these reporting goals, the government-wide financial statements' measurement focus is on all *economic resources* (not just current financial resources such as cash and receivables), and these statements utilize *accrual accounting* for timing purposes much like a for-profit entity. They report all assets and liabilities and recognize revenues and expenses in a way that is comparable to business-type accounting.

The Need for Two Sets of Financial Statements

One aspect of governmental reporting has remained constant over the years: the goal of making the government accountable to the public. Because of the essential role of democracy within U.S. society, the creators of accounting principles have attempted to provide a vehicle for evaluating governmental actions. Citizens should be aware of the means that officials use to raise money and allocate scarce resources. Voters must evaluate the wisdom, as well as the honesty, of the members of government. Most voters are also taxpayers; thus they naturally exhibit special interest in the results obtained from their involuntary contributions, such as taxes and tolls. Because elected and appointed officials hold authority over the public's money, governmental reporting has traditionally stressed this stewardship responsibility.

> Accountability is the cornerstone of all financial reporting in government. . . . Accountability requires governments to answer to the citizenry—to justify the raising of public resources and

[8] Ibid., p. 3.

the purposes for which they are used. Governmental accountability is based on the belief that the citizenry has a "right to know," a right to receive openly declared facts that may lead to public debate by the citizens and their elected representatives.[9]

To promote transparency for users, reporting has historically been directed toward measuring and identifying the financial resources generated and expended by each of a government's diverse activities. Fund-based statements allow readers to focus on individual governmental activities. At least in connection with public services, such as the police department and public library, the fund-based financial statements answer three relevant questions:

- How did the government generate its current financial resources?
- Where did those financial resources go?
- What amount of those financial resources is presently held?

The term *current financial resources* normally encompasses monetary assets available for officials to spend to meet the government's needs this year. Thus, when reporting current financial resources, a government is primarily monitoring cash, investments, and receivables. To stress accountability, the traditional government accounting system has focused almost exclusively on these resources as well as any current claims against them. For this reason, little reporting emphasis has been historically placed on accounts such as Buildings, Equipment, and Long-Term Debts that have no direct impact on current financial resources.

Obviously, stressing accountability by monitoring just the flow of current financial resources is an approach that cannot meet all user needs. Thus, many conventional reporting objectives were long ignored. Does the government have too much long-term debt, for example? As a result, investors and creditors were frequently sharp critics of governmental accounting. "When cities get into financial trouble, few citizens know about it until the day the interest can't be met or the teachers paid. . . . Had the books been kept like any decent corporation's that could never have happened."[10]

Consequently, GASB mandated the inclusion of government-wide financial statements to provide an additional dimension for government reporting. This second set of statements does not focus solely on current financial resources but seeks to report all assets at the disposal of government officials as well as all liabilities that must eventually be paid. Likewise, revenues and expenses are recognized according to accrual accounting and provide a completely different level of financial information.

With two sets of financial statements, each user (whether citizen or investor) can select the information considered to be the most relevant. Of course, not everyone believes that additional data will always be helpful. "One of the tougher challenges of the current information age is sorting out the information most relevant for decision making from the vast amounts of data generated by today's state-of-the-art information systems. Financial reports cannot simply keep growing in size indefinitely to encompass every new type of information that becomes available."[11]

	Fund-Based Financial Statements*	Government-Wide Financial Statements
Emphasis	Individual activities (during current period)	Government as a whole
Measurement focus	Current financial resources (cash, investments, and receivables and claims to those assets)	All economic resources (all assets and all liabilities)
General information	Inflows and outflows of current financial resources	Overall financial health
Timing of recognition	Modified accrual accounting	Accrual accounting

*The information provided here for fund-based financial statements only applies to public service activities such as public safety and education. As will be discussed shortly, other activities are reported more in keeping with government-wide financial statements.

[9] GASB *Concepts Statement No. 1,* para. 56.

[10] Richard Greene, "You Can't Fight City Hall—If You Can't Understand It," *Forbes,* March 3, 1980, p. 92.

[11] Jeffrey L. Esser, "Standard Setting—How Much Is Enough?" *Government Finance Review,* April 2005, p. 3.

LO3

Understand the reason that fund accounting has traditionally been such a prominent factor in the internal recording of state and local governments.

Internal Record Keeping—Fund Accounting

In gathering financial information, most state and local governments have always faced the challenge of reporting a diverse array of activities financed from numerous sources. Accountability and control become special concerns for governments that operate through a multitude of relatively independent departments and functions. Consequently, for internal monitoring purposes, the accounting for each government activity is maintained in separate quasi-independent bookkeeping systems referred to as *funds*. Hence, the accounting process accumulates separate data for every activity (library, school system, fire department, road construction, and the like).

The internal information gathered in this manner has then served as the foundation for fund-based financial statements. An underlying assumption of government reporting has long been that most statement users prefer to see information segregated by function in order to assess each activity individually. The internal accounting records provided that information and it could be transferred directly into fund-based financial statements for external distribution.

Because no common profit motive exists to tie all of these various functions and services together, consolidated activity balances were historically not presented. Combining operating results from the city zoo, fire department, water system, print shop, and the like would provide figures of questionable utility if accountability and control over the usage of current financial resources are the primary goals. Financial reporting was to provide information about the individual activities, not the government as a whole.

The addition of government-wide statements does not affect the use of fund accounting for control purposes. Consequently, the separate funds monitored by a state or local government still serve as the basic foundation for internal reporting. Although a single list of identifiable functions is not possible, the following frequently are included:

Public safety	Judicial system
Highway maintenance	Debt repayment
Sanitation	Bridge construction
Health	Water and sewer system
Welfare	Municipal swimming pool
Culture and recreation	Data processing center
Education	Endowment funds
Parks	Employee pensions

The actual number of funds in use depends on the extent of services that the government offers and the grouping of related activities. For example, separate funds may be set up to account for a high school and its athletic programs, or these activities may be combined into a single fund.

> The general rule is to establish the minimum number of separate funds consistent with legal specifications and operational requirements. . . . Using too many funds causes inflexibility and undue complexity . . . and is best avoided in the interest of efficient and economical financial administration.[12]

The requirement passed in 1999 for government-wide financial statements to be reported along with fund-based financial statements was radical for many reasons. However, one significant outcome for the governments was that they had to start reporting information (the total cost of roads, for example) that had never been accumulated previously. Fund accounting monitors the increases and decreases in current financial resources. As will be seen in this chapter and the next, a considerable amount of additional information was required to create financial statements that reported all of the economic resources of the government as a whole.

Fund Accounting Classifications

For internal record keeping, all funds (whether for the police department, the municipal golf course, or some other activity) are categorized into one of three distinct groups. This classification

[12] GASB Cod. Sec. 1100.108.

system provides clearer reporting of the government's various activities. Furthermore, having separate groups allows for unique accounting principles to be applied to each.

- *Governmental funds*—include all funds that account for activities a government carries out primarily to provide citizens with services that are financed primarily through taxes. The police and fire departments are reported within the governmental funds.
- *Proprietary funds*—account for a government's ongoing activities that are similar to those conducted by for-profit organizations. This fund type normally encompasses operations that assess a user charge so that determining profitability or cost recovery is important. For example, both a municipal golf course and a toll road are reported within the proprietary funds.
- *Fiduciary funds*—account for monies held by the government in a trustee or agency capacity. Such assets must be maintained for others and cannot be used by the government for its own programs. Assets held in a pension plan for government employees are monitored within the fiduciary funds.

Governmental Funds

In many state and municipal accounting systems, the governmental funds tend to dominate because a service orientation usually prevails. The internal accounting system can maintain individual funds for every distinct service function: public safety, libraries, construction of a town hall, and so on. Each of these governmental funds accumulates and expends current financial resources to achieve one or more desired public goals.

To provide better reported information and control, the governmental funds are subdivided into five categories: the General Fund, Special Revenue Funds, Capital Projects Funds, Debt Service Funds, and Permanent Funds. This classification system forms an overall structure for financial reporting purposes.

The General Fund   GASB's definition of the General Fund appears to be somewhat understated: "to account for and report all financial resources not accounted for and reported in another fund."[13] This description seems to imply that the General Fund records only miscellaneous revenues and expenditures when, in actuality, it accounts for many of a government's most important services, a broad range of ongoing functions. For example, the 2008 fund-based financial statements for the City of Baltimore, Maryland, disclosed 11 major areas of current expenditures within its General Fund:

General government	Recreation and culture
Public safety and regulations	Highways and streets
Conservation of health	Sanitation and waste removal
Social services	Public service
Education	Economic development
Public library	

Expenditures reported for these categories were in excess of $1.23 billion and made up more than 58 percent of the total for all of the city's governmental funds for the year ended June 30, 2008.

Special Revenue Funds   Special Revenue Funds account for resource inflows that are restricted or committed for a specific purpose other than debt payments or capital projects. Because of donor stipulations or legislative mandates, these financial resources must be spent in a specified fashion. Saint Paul, Minnesota, for example, reported approximately $150 million of revenues within over 30 individual Special Revenue Funds during the 2008 fiscal year. Sources were as diverse as fees charged for use of the crime laboratory, rent received from the use of Municipal Stadium, administration fees for charitable gambling, money received from solid waste and recycling programs, and parking meter fees. The Special Revenue Funds category accounts for these monies because legal or donor restrictions were attached to the revenue to require that expenditure be limited to specific operating purposes. As an example, according to Saint Paul's annual financial report, receipts from charitable gambling must be administered

---

[13] GASB *Statement No. 54,* "Fund Balance Reporting and Governmental Fund Type Definitions," March 2009, para. 29.

"in conformance with City Council action for the support of youth athletics or otherwise as legally determined." Thus, the accounting system monitors the receipt and disbursement of any financial resources from this source by including them in the Special Revenue Funds.

Capital Projects Funds   As the title implies, this fund type accounts for financial resources restricted, committed, or assigned to cover the costs incurred in acquiring or constructing government facilities such as bridges, high schools, roads, or municipal office complexes. Funding for these projects normally comes from grants, sale of bonds, or transfers from general revenue. The actual asset being obtained is not reported here; only the money to finance the purchase or construction is recorded. For example, the Lexington-Fayette Urban County Government in Kentucky reported, as of June 30, 2008, that it was holding a total of more than $19.4 million in financial resources in 19 different Capital Projects Funds to be used in projects such as acquisition or construction in connection with a cultural center, road projects, a golf course, and equipment leasing.

Debt Service Funds   These funds record financial resources accumulated to pay long-term liabilities and interest as they come due. However, this fund type does not account for a government's long-term debt. Debt Service Funds are created to monitor the monetary balances currently available to make the eventual payment to satisfy long-term liabilities. Thus, on June 30, 2008, the city of Birmingham, Alabama, reported more than $42 million of cash and investments in its debt service funds, money being held to pay long-term debt and interest. For the year then ended, this fund had made more than $16 million in principal payments and $17 million in interest payments.

Permanent Funds   The Permanent Funds category accounts for financial resources restricted by external donor, contract, or legislation with the stipulation that the principal cannot be spent but any income can be used by the government, often for a designated purpose to benefit the general citizenry. As an example, the City of Dallas, Texas, reported holding more than $9 million as of September 30, 2008, that had come almost entirely from private donations whose income was designated to maintain four different parks. Such gifts are frequently referred to as *endowments*.

Proprietary Funds

The proprietary funds category accounts for government activities, such as a bus system or subway line, that assess a user charge. Such services resemble those found in the business world. Because the user charge helps the government make a profit or, at least, recover part of its cost, the proprietary funds are reported in much the same way on both the fund-based financial statements and the government-wide financial statements. The accounting resembles that of a for-profit activity in that accrual accounting is used to recognize all assets and liabilities.

To facilitate financial reporting, the proprietary funds are broken down into two divisions:

Enterprise Funds   Any government operation that is open to the public and financed, at least in part, by user charges is likely to be classified as an Enterprise Fund. A municipality, for example, might generate revenues from the use of a public swimming pool, golf course, airport, water and sewage service, and the like. The City of Charlotte, North Carolina, earned $438 million in revenue in 2008 from several Enterprise Funds including its airport, public transit, and water and sewer services.

The number of enterprise funds has increased rather dramatically over recent years as governments have attempted to expand services without raising taxes. This situation requires those citizens utilizing a particular service to shoulder a higher percentage of its costs. "Enterprise funds have become an attractive alternative revenue source for local governments to recover all or part of the cost of goods or services from those directly benefiting from them."[14]

Enterprise Fund activities that collect direct fees from customers resemble business activities. Not surprisingly, even in the fund-based financial statements, the accounting process for these operations parallels that found in for-profit reporting. These funds use accrual basis accounting with a focus on all economic, not just current financial, resources.

A question arises, though, as to how much revenue an activity must generate before it is viewed as an Enterprise Fund. For example, if a city wants to promote mass transit and charges

[14] Jeffrey Molinari and Charlie Tyer, "Local Government Enterprise Fund Activity: Trends and Implications," *Public Administration Quarterly,* Fall 2003, p. 369.

only a nickel to ride its bus line, should that activity be viewed as part of an Enterprise Fund (a business-type activity) or within the General Fund (a governmental activity)?

Any activity that charges the public a user fee may be classified as an Enterprise Fund. However, this designation is *required* if the activity meets any one of the following criteria. At that point, the amount of revenue is viewed as significant:

- The activity generates net revenues that provide the sole security for the debts of the activity.
- Laws or regulations require recovering the activity's costs (including depreciation and debt service) through fees or charges.
- Fees and charges are set at prices intended to recover costs including depreciation and debt service.

Internal Service Funds   This second proprietary fund type accounts for any operation that provides services to another department or agency within the government on a cost-reimbursement basis. As with enterprise funds, internal service funds charge fees but perform their service for the primary benefit of parties within the government rather than for outside users. In the same manner as enterprise funds, internal service funds are accounted for much like a for-profit operation in the private sector.

The City of Lincoln, Nebraska, lists seven operations in its 2008 financial statements that are accounted for as separate internal service funds:

> *Information services fund*—to account for the cost of operating a central data processing facility.
> *Engineering revolving fund*—to account for the cost of operating a central engineering pool.
> *Insurance revolving fund*—to account for the cost of providing several types of self-insurance programs.
> *Fleet services fund*—to account for the operations of a centralized maintenance facility for city equipment.
> *Police garage fund*—to account for the operation of a maintenance facility for police and other government vehicles.
> *Communication services fund*—to account for the costs of providing graphic arts and telecommunications services.
> *Copy services fund*—to account for the cost of providing copy services.

Fiduciary Funds

The final classification, fiduciary funds, accounts for assets held in a trustee or agency capacity for external parties so that the money cannot be used to support the government's own programs. Like proprietary funds, fiduciary funds use the economic resources measurement focus and accrual accounting for the timing of revenues and expenses. Because these assets are not available for the benefit of the government, fiduciary funds are omitted from government-wide financial statements although separate statements are included within the fund-based financial statements.

Four distinct types of fiduciary funds exist:

Investment Trust Funds   The first fund type accounts for the outside portion of investment pools when the reporting government has accepted financial resources from other governments in order to have more money to invest and hopefully earn a higher return. For example, the state of Virginia held almost $3.5 billion at June 30, 2008, identified as a local government investment pool that "helps local governmental entities maximize their rate of return by commingling their resources for investment purposes."

Private-Purpose Trust Funds   The second fund type accounts for monies held in a trustee capacity when both principal and interest are for the benefit of specifically designated external parties such as individuals, private organizations, or other governments. Unclaimed property is usually recorded here, for example.

Pension Trust Funds   The third type accounts for an employee retirement system. Because of the need to provide adequate benefits for government workers, this fund type can become quite large. The City of Philadelphia, for example, reported assets of more than $5.8 billion in its pension trust fund as of June 30, 2008.

Agency Funds   The fourth type of fiduciary fund records any resources a government holds as an agent for individuals, private organizations, or other government units. For example, one government could collect taxes and tolls on behalf of another. To ensure safety and control, the Agency Fund separately maintains this money until it is transferred to the proper authority.

OVERVIEW OF STATE AND LOCAL GOVERNMENT FINANCIAL STATEMENTS

LO5

Understand the basic structure of government-wide financial statements and fund-based financial statements (as produced for the governmental funds).

Although a complete analysis of the financial statements of a state or local government is presented in the subsequent chapter, an overview of four basic financial statements will be helpful at this point to illustrate how certain events are reported. These examples are not complete but can be used to demonstrate the presentation of various transactions and accounts.

Government-Wide Financial Statements

Only two financial statements make up the government-wide financial statements: *the statement of net assets* and *the statement of activities.* These statements separate the reporting into governmental activities (all governmental funds and most internal service funds) and business-type activities (all enterprise funds and any remaining internal service funds).[15] As mentioned earlier, government-wide financial statements do not report the transactions and balances of any fiduciary funds, which are shown only in separate fund-based financial statements.

Exhibit 11.1 shows the basic structure of a statement of net assets. Under the economic resources measurement focus used in the government-wide financial statements, all assets and liabilities are reported. The final section of this statement, the net assets category, indicates (1) the amount of capital assets being reported less related debt, (2) restrictions on any net assets, and (3) the total amount of unrestricted net assets. For example, in Exhibit 11.1, the Governmental Activities holds $80 of completely unrestricted net assets and Business-Type Activities has $30 of unrestricted net assets.

The statement of activities in Exhibit 11.2 provides details about revenues and expenses, once again separated into governmental activities and business-type activities. This is a statement that is usually read horizontally first and then vertically. The statement shows direct expenses and program revenues for each government function. Program revenues include fines, fees, grants, and the like that the specific activity generates. Thus, a single net revenue or net expense is determined horizontally for each function as a way of indicating its financial burden or financial benefit to the government.

Here, for example, at Point A the public safety category shows a net cost to the government of $8,820, expenses of $9,700 that are partially offset by program revenues of $880. The amounts for all activities are summed vertically to show the total cost of operating the government, an amount that is offset by general revenues such as property taxes and sales taxes. Here, the governmental activities cost $20,720 (Point B) whereas the business-type activities generated a financial benefit of $1,940 (Point C). At Point D, the reader of the statements can see that the government generated property taxes of $20,400 to cover virtually all of the cost of providing its governmental activities.

Fund-Based Financial Statements

A state or local government produces a number of fund-based financial statements. However, at this introductory stage, only the two fundamental statements that most parallel the two

---

[15] Government-wide financial statements report internal service funds as governmental activities if their primary purpose is to serve the governmental funds. Conversely, internal service funds are included with business-type activities if they mainly exist to help one or more enterprise funds. For example, a print shop (an internal service fund) should be reported within the governmental activities if its work is primarily for the benefit of a governmental fund such as the public library. However, if its work is a service to a bus line (or some other enterprise fund), the print shop is classified within the business-type activities.

EXHIBIT 11.1
Statement of Net Assets—
Government-Wide
Financial Statements

	Governmental Activities	Business-Type Activities	Total
Assets			
Cash	$ 100	$ 130	$ 230
Investments	900	40	940
Receivables	600	400	1,000
Internal amounts due	50	(50)	–0–
Supplies and materials	30	40	70
Capital assets (net of depreciation)	2,950	2,750	5,700
Total assets	$4,630	$3,310	$7,940
Liabilities			
Accounts payable	$ 750	$ 230	$ 980
Noncurrent liabilities			
Due within one year	400	180	580
Due in more than one year	1,800	700	2,500
Total liabilities	$2,950	$1,110	$4,060
Net Assets			
Invested in capital assets, net of related debt	$1,410	$2,110	$3,520
Restricted for:			
Capital projects	50	–0–	50
Debt service	140	60	200
Unrestricted	80	30	110
Total net assets	$1,680	$2,200	$3,880

EXHIBIT 11.2   Statement of Activities—Government-Wide Financial Statements

			Net (Expense) Revenue		
Function	**Expenses**	**Program Revenues**	**Governmental Activities**	**Business-Type Activities**	**Total**
Governmental activities					
General government	$ 3,200	$ 1,400	$ (1,800)	n/a	$ (1,800)
Public safety	9,700	880	(8,820) Ⓐ	n/a	(8,820)
Public works	2,600	600	(2,000)	n/a	(2,000)
Education	8,400	300	(8,100)	n/a	(8,100)
Total governmental activities	$23,900	$ 3,180	$(20,720)	n/a	$(20,720)
Business-type activities					
Water	$ 3,600	$ 4,030	n/a	$ 430	$ 430
Sewer	4,920	5,610	n/a	690	690
Airport	2,300	3,120	n/a	820	820
Total business-type activities	$10,820	$12,760	n/a	$1,940	$ 1,940
Total government	$34,720	$15,940	$(20,720) Ⓑ	$1,940 Ⓒ	$(18,780)
General revenues:					
Property taxes			$ 20,400 Ⓓ	–0–	$ 20,400
Investment earnings			420	$ 70	490
Transfers			600	(600)	–0–
Total general revenues and transfers			$ 21,420	$ (530)	$ 20,890
Change in net assets			$ 700	$1,410	$ 2,110
Beginning net assets			980	790	1,770
Ending net assets			$ 1,680	$2,200	$ 3,880

EXHIBIT 11.3   **Balance Sheet—Governmental Funds**
Fund-Based Financial Statements

	General Fund	Library Program	Other Governmental Funds	Total Governmental Funds
Assets				
Cash	$ 40	$ 10	$ 50	$ 100
Investments	580	120	200	900
Receivables	120	200	210	530
Supplies and materials	10	10	10	30
Total assets	$750	$340	$470	$1,560
Liabilities				
Accounts payable	$230	$170	$110	$ 510
Notes payable—current	300	–0–	100	400
Total liabilities	$530	$170	$210	$ 910
Fund Balances				
Nonspendable	$ 10	$ 10	$ 10	$ 30
Restricted	100	90	60	250
Committed	30	50	100	180
Assigned	20	20	90	130
Unassigned	60	–	–	60
Total fund balances	$220	$170	$260	$ 650
Total liabilities and fund balances	$750	$340	$470	$1,560

government-wide statements are included. First, Exhibit 11.3 shows *a balance sheet* for the governmental funds and then Exhibit 11.4 presents *a statement of revenues, expenditures, and changes in fund balances* produced for the same governmental funds. The balance sheet reports the current financial resources (assets) for the various funds and the claims to those resources (liabilities). As can be seen in Exhibit 11.4, three categories are present in the second fund-based statement that will be discussed in detail throughout the remainder of this chapter and the next:

Revenues

Expenditures

Other Financing Sources (Uses)

Note that the figures for these fund-based financial statements will not be the same as those presented for the governmental activities in the government-wide statement of net assets (Exhibit 11.1) and statement of activities (Exhibit 11.2). For example, the asset total reported for the governmental activities in Exhibit 11.1 is $4,630, whereas the asset total for all governmental funds in Exhibit 11.3 is only $1,560. These differences result primarily for three reasons:

1. In the government-wide statements, internal service funds are grouped with the funds that they primarily benefit. Thus, they are included with the governmental activities if they assist governmental funds and in business-type activities if they assist enterprise funds. However, fund-based statements report all internal service funds as proprietary funds, not as governmental funds. *Totals will vary because funds are grouped differently.*

2. Governmental activities use the economic resources measurement focus whereas the governmental funds, in the fund-based statements, use the current financial resources measurement focus. *Different assets and liabilities are being reported.*

3. Governmental activities use accrual accounting in government-wide statements; modified accrual accounting is used in creating fund-based financial statements for the governmental funds. *The timing of recognition is different.*

EXHIBIT 11.4 Statement of Revenues, Expenditures, and Other Changes in Fund Balances—Governmental Funds
Fund-Based Financial Statements

	General Fund	Library Program	Other Governmental Funds	Total Governmental Funds
Revenues				
Property taxes	$17,200	$ 900	$ 2,300	$20,400
Investment earnings	100	200	180	480
Program revenues	500	100	2,500	3,100
Total revenues	$17,800	$1,200	$ 4,980	$23,980
Expenditures				
Current:				
General government	$ 3,400	–0–	$ 100	$ 3,500
Public safety	5,100	–0–	400	5,500
Education	6,700	$ 800	–0–	7,500
Debt service:				
Principal	–0–	–0–	1,000	1,000
Interest	–0–	–0–	600	600
Capital outlay	1,100	300	3,300	4,700
Total expenditures	$16,300	$1,100	$ 5,400	$22,800
Excess (deficiency) of revenues over expenditures	$ 1,500	$ 100	$ (420)	$ 1,180
Other Financing Sources (Uses)				
Bond proceeds	–0–	–0–	$ 1,000	$ 1,000
Transfers in	–0–	$ 20	580	600
Transfers out	$ (1,300)	–0–	$ (1,000)	(2,300)
Total other financing sources and uses	$ (1,300)	$ 20	$ 580	$ (700)
Change in fund balances	$ 200	$ 120	$ 160	$ 480
Fund balances—beginning	20	50	100	170
Fund balances—ending	$ 220	$ 170	$ 260	$ 650

Because of these differences, reconciliations between the totals presented in Exhibits 11.1 and 11.3 and between Exhibits 11.2 and 11.4 should be reported. Those reconciliations are discussed in detail in the following chapter.

Major Funds

In looking at both of the fund-based financial statements presented (Exhibits 11.3 and 11.4), note that the General Fund and every other individual fund that qualifies as major is shown in a separate column. The assumption here is that the Library Program (probably one of this government's special revenue funds) is the only individual fund outside the General Fund that is considered major. Information for all other funds is then grouped together. Consequently, identification of a "major" fund becomes quite important for disclosure purposes. It is defined as follows:

> The reporting government's main operating fund (the general fund or its equivalent) should always be reported as a major fund. Other individual governmental and enterprise funds should be reported in separate columns as major funds based on these criteria:
>
> a. Total assets, liabilities, revenues, or expenditures/expenses of that individual governmental or enterprise fund are at least 10 percent of the corresponding total (assets, liabilities, and so forth) for all funds of that category or type (that is, total governmental or total enterprise funds), *and*
>
> b. Total assets, liabilities, revenues, or expenditures/expenses of the individual governmental fund or enterprise fund are at least 5 percent of the corresponding total for all governmental and enterprise funds combined.

In addition to funds that meet the major fund criteria, any other governmental or enterprise fund that the government's officials believe is particularly important to financial statement users (for example, because of public interest or consistency) may be reported as a major fund.[16]

Fund Balances

One last unique aspect of the structure of fund-based financial statements for the governmental funds should be noted. As a government, the balance sheet (Exhibit 11.3) does not need a stockholders' equity section to report contributed capital, retained earnings, and the like for each separate fund. Instead, the term "fund balance" is used to indicate the amount of assets held in excess of liabilities—the net current financial resources at that time. This term has long been used in a rather generic fashion.

In February 2009, GASB issued its *Statement 54* "Fund Balance Reporting and Governmental Fund Type Definitions" to standardize the reporting of the fund balance within five categories. For example, in Exhibit 11.3, the General Fund reports assets of $750 and liabilities of $530 indicating net assets of $220. From a reporting perspective, the most significant question to be answered is: What use can be made of this $220? The purpose of the fund balance classifications, therefore, is to indicate the availability of this excess amount.

Fund-Balance—Nonspendable.   As the name implies, this amount of the assets reported in a fund cannot be spent by government officials. That typically occurs for two reasons. First, some assets such as supplies and prepaid expenses are simply not in a spendable form. Second, financial resources are occasionally received that cannot be spent because of externally imposed limitations. A gift, for example, is donated by a citizen that must be held with the stipulation that only future income can be used. This fund balance figure indicates that assets are present but not available for government spending.

Fund-Balance—Restricted.   This figure indicates the amount of assets held by the government that must be spent in a manner designated by an external party. For example, a grant from another government for a specified purpose creates an increase in this category as would a bond covenant that requires proceeds to be used in a particular manner.

Fund-Balance—Committed.   Here, the assets have been designated for a particular purpose, not by an outside party but rather by the highest level of decision-making authority in the government. For example, a state legislature might vote to set aside $100 million for road construction. On the balance sheet, that decision is disclosed by an increase in the reported amount of the "fund balance—committed" total. Of course, the legislature does have the power to reverse its decision so the commitment is not necessarily binding.

Fund-Balance—Assigned.   Frequently, in the regular operations of a government, money is designated for a specific purpose without formal action by the highest level of decision-making authority. The head of the government's finance committee might designate cash of $1 million to use in a few months to pay off the current installment of a bond. However, if necessary, that money could be switched to some other purpose if needed in the interim. To indicate that its use has been established internally but not by the highest level of authority, the fund balance is labeled as "assigned."

Fund-Balance—Unassigned.   This category is only found in the General Fund and reflects any amount of net assets where no use has been designated either externally or internally. This money is available to government officials for any purpose viewed as appropriate.

This classification system must be used in state and local government financial statements for periods beginning after June 15, 2010. To illustrate the reporting, note how each of the following transactions affects a city government's balance sheet created as part of the fund-based financial statements for the governmental funds.

• Supplies costing $30,000 that will be used in the future to beautify the local parks are bought on the last day of the fiscal year. The supplies are shown as an asset with an equal amount reported within the "fund-balance—nonspendable" for this fund.

[16] GASB *Statement 34*, para. 76.

- A citizen dies and leaves investments valued at $1 million to the city with the requirement that only the income can be spent and must be used for park beautification. Reported assets increase, as does the "fund-balance—restricted" balance for this fund.
- The highest level of decision makers for this city vote unanimously to set aside $90,000 in unassigned cash to be used to beautify the local parks. The "fund-balance—unassigned" drops by $90,000 while the "fund-balance—committed" increases.
- The director of finance for the city sets aside $12,000 in previously unassigned cash to be used to buy new benches for the city's parks. Because the decision was not made at the highest level of decision making, the "fund-balance—unassigned" goes down while the "fund-balance—assigned" rises.
- The city government receives property tax revenues of $100,000. City officials might eventually decide to use some or all of this money to complete the beautification of the city's parks, but no decision has yet been made. In the General Fund, assets increase by this amount and the "fund-balance—unassigned" increases.

ACCOUNTING FOR GOVERNMENTAL FUNDS

LO6

Record the passage of a budget as well as subsequent encumbrances and expenditures.

The remainder of this chapter presents many of the unique aspects of the accounting process utilized within the governmental funds: the General Fund, Special Revenue Funds, Capital Projects Funds, Debt Service Funds, and Permanent Funds. It is in these five funds where the distinct approach of governmental accounting can best be seen. Because of the dual nature of the reporting process, most of this accounting must be demonstrated twice, once for fund-based financial statements and a second time for the government-wide financial statements.

Much discussion has occurred as to whether governments should, for practicality, keep two separate sets of financial records (one for fund-based statements and another for government-wide statements) or merely one set that must then be adjusted rather significantly at the end of the year to create the second set of financial statements. Many governments have elected to continue maintaining only fund-based information internally that could be transformed into government-wide financial statements at year-end. However, over time, as software programs and computer systems become more sophisticated, governments will likely find that keeping two distinct sets of books is a reasonable approach. Being able to analyze complex transactions completely as they happen seems to be advantageous, and having two sets of records reduces what otherwise could be a massive amount of work at the end of each fiscal year.

Therefore, this textbook examines each transaction from both a fund-based and a government-wide perspective. Accounting for these events in two different ways seems to be an easier mental process than learning one method now and later attempting to convert that entire set of reported data into figures consistent with the second method. For each example, it is important to note the impact on the fund-based financial statements for the governmental funds (where current financial resources are measured based on modified accrual accounting) in comparison to the effect on the government-wide statements for the governmental activities (that show all economic resources based on accrual accounting).

The Importance of Budgets and the Recording of Budgetary Entries

Budgeting is an essential element of the financial planning, control, and performance evaluation processes of many governments. In contrast to commercial organizations' planning-oriented budgetary practices, governments usually adopt budgets that have the force of law, are subject to sanctions for overspending budgetary authorizations, and have extensive controls to ensure budgetary compliance.[17]

In a chronological sense, the first significant accounting procedure encountered by a state or locality is the recording of budgetary entries. To enhance accountability, government officials normally are required to adopt an annual budget for each separate activity to anticipate the

[17] American Institute of Certified Public Accountants, *Audit & Accounting Guide, State and Local Governments*, with conforming changes as of March 1, 2009, para. 11.01.

inflow of financial resources and establish approved expenditure levels. The budget serves several important purposes:

1. *Expresses public policy.* If, for example, more money is budgeted for child care and less for the environment, the citizens are made aware of the decision to allocate limited government resources in this manner.
2. *Serves as an expression of financial intent for the upcoming fiscal year.* The budget presents the financial plan for the government for the upcoming period.
3. *Provides control because it establishes spending limitations for each activity.*
4. *Offers a means of evaluating performance* by allowing a comparison of actual results with the levels found in the budget.
5. *Indicates whether the government anticipates having sufficient revenues to pay for all of the expenditures that have been approved.* In the current economic climate when many governments face declining revenues, the amount and handling of proposed deficits should be of interest to every citizen.

GASB even states that "many believe the budget is the most significant financial document produced by a government unit."[18]

Once a budget has been produced and enacted into law, formal accounting recognition is frequently required as a means of enhancing these benefits. In this way, the public has the opportunity to review the amounts of current financial resources expected to be received and expended. Reporting revenue projections and complying with spending limitations are considered essential for government accountability. Furthermore, many governments must legally maintain balanced budgets. By entering budget figures into the accounting records at the start of each fiscal year, comparisons can be made between actual and budgeted figures at any interim point during the period. At the end of the year, all budget entries are reversed and closed.

Budget information must be disclosed for the General Fund and each major fund within the Special Revenue Funds. Because of the importance of the information, governments are required to report comparisons between the original budget, the final budget, and the actual figures for the period as required supplementary information presented after the notes to its financial statements. As an allowed alternative, a separate statement can be shown within the government's fund-based financial statements.

To illustrate, assume that a city enacts a motel excise tax with the revenue to be used to promote tourism and conventions. Because the receipts are legally restricted for this specified purpose, the city must establish a separate Special Revenue Fund. Assume that for the 2010 fiscal year, the tax is expected to generate $490,000 in revenues. Based on this projection, the city council authorizes the expenditure of $400,000 (referred to as an *appropriation*) for promotional programs during the current year. Of this amount, $200,000 is designated for salaries, $30,000 for utilities, $80,000 for advertising, and $90,000 for supplies. The $90,000 difference between the anticipated revenue inflow and this appropriation is a budgeted surplus to be accumulated by the government for future use or in case the actual revenue proves to be too small to support budget plans.

To formally acknowledge the council's action, the accounting records of this fund include the following journal entry. No similar entry is needed for government-wide financial statements.

Fund-Based Financial Statements—Budgetary Entry

Special Revenue Fund—Tourism and Convention Promotions		
Estimated Revenues—Tax Levy	490,000	
Appropriations—Salaries		200,000
Appropriations—Utilities		30,000
Appropriations—Advertising		80,000
Appropriations—Supplies		90,000
Budgetary Fund Balance		90,000
To record annual budget for tourism and convention promotions funded by motel excise tax.		

[18] GASB *Concepts Statement No. 1*, para. 19

This entry indicates both an estimation of and the source of the funding (the tax levy) and the approved amount of expenditures. Each of these figures remains in the records of this Special Revenue Fund for the entire year to allow for planning, disclosure, and control. The Budgetary Fund Balance account indicates an anticipated surplus (or, in some cases, a shortage) projected for the period. Here, the size of this fund is expected to increase by $90,000 during the year.

In this way, budgetary entries also reflect a government's *interperiod equity.* This term refers to the alignment of revenues and spending for a period and the possible shift of payments to future generations. If a government projects revenues as $10 million but approves expenditures of $11 million, the extra million must be financed in some manner, usually by debt to be repaid in the future. The benefits of the additional expenditures are enjoyed today, but citizens of a later time period must bear the cost.

The original budget is not always the final appropriations budget for the year because of later amendments. For example, government officers can vote to change appropriation levels if more or less money becomes available than had been anticipated. Thus, for the year ending June 30, 2008, the City of Greensboro, North Carolina, reported that $28,983,724 had originally been appropriated for culture and recreation. That amount was later increased to $29,428,359, but only $27,794,172 was actually spent.

Assume, to illustrate, that officials in charge of tourism for this city appeal to the council during the year for an additional $50,000 to create a special advertising campaign. If approved, the original budgetary entry is adjusted:

Fund-Based Financial Statements—Budget Amendment

Special Revenue Fund—Tourism and Convention Promotions		
Budgetary Fund Balance	50,000	
Appropriations—Advertising		50,000
To record additional appropriation for advertising.		

Assume that the city actually received $488,000 in tax revenues during the year and spent $437,000 as follows:

Salaries	$196,000
Utilities	29,000
Advertising	125,000
Supplies	87,000

This information should be disclosed as follows. The Variance column is recommended but not required:

TOURISM AND CONVENTION PROMOTIONS
Year Ended December 31, 2010
Budget Comparison Schedule

	Budgeted Amounts		Actual Amounts	Variance with Final Budget—
	Original	Final	(budgetary basis)	Positive (negative)
Resources (inflows):				
Tax levy	$490,000	$490,000	$488,000	$ (2,000)
Charges to appropriations (outflows):				
Salaries	$200,000	$200,000	$196,000	$ 4,000
Utilities	30,000	30,000	29,000	1,000
Advertising	80,000	130,000	125,000	5,000
Supplies	90,000	90,000	87,000	3,000
Total charges	$400,000	$450,000	$437,000	$13,000
Change in fund balance	$ 90,000	$ 40,000	$ 51,000	$11,000

Encumbrances

One additional budgetary procedure that plays a central role in government accounting is the recording of financial commitments referred to as *encumbrances.* In contrast to for-profit accounting, purchase commitments and contracts are recorded in the governmental funds prior to becoming legal liabilities. This recording of encumbrances provides an efficient method for keeping up with financial commitments so that officials will not accidentally overspend a fund's appropriated amount. Encumbrance accounting is appropriate (although not required) within any governmental fund. At any point during the fiscal year, information on both expended and committed amounts is then available to aid government officials.

To illustrate, assume that a city's police department orders $18,000 in equipment from a vendor. As an ongoing service activity, the police department is accounted for within the General Fund. Because only an order has been placed, no entry is recorded at this point for the government-wide financial statements that tend to follow for-profit accounting. However, this amount of the General Fund's financial resources has been committed even though no formal liability will exist until the equipment is received. To guard against spending more than has been appropriated, an encumbrance is recorded any time a governmental fund enters into a purchase order, contract, or other formal commitment.

Fund-Based Financial Statements—Commitment Created

General Fund—Police Department

Encumbrances Control	18,000	
Fund Balance—Reserved for Encumbrances		18,000
To record an order placed for equipment.		

The Encumbrances account records the commitment that has been incurred. The use of a control account here simply indicates that the government's accounting system includes a subsidiary ledger that maintains more detailed information about this $18,000 amount. Without a subsidiary ledger, the debit entry should be made to Encumbrances—Equipment or a similar account.

When the police department eventually receives the equipment, a legal liability for payment replaces the commitment. Hence, the encumbrance is removed from the accounting records and an Expenditures account is recognized to show the reduction in current financial resources. Often, because of sales taxes, freight costs, or other price adjustments, the actual invoice total will differ from the original estimation. For this reason, the expenditure will not necessarily agree with the corresponding encumbrance. Note that because of the current financial resource focus of fund-based financial statements, there will not be an equipment account entry for this long-lived asset. Assume, for illustration purposes, that an invoice for $18,160 accompanies the equipment when it is received.

Fund-Based Financial Statements—Order Received

General Fund

Fund Balance—Reserved for Encumbrances	18,000	
Encumbrances Control		18,000
To remove encumbrance for equipment that has now been received.		
Expenditures—Equipment	18,160	
Vouchers Payable		18,160
To record the receipt of equipment and the accompanying liability.		

In producing government-wide financial statements, the only entry created by this ordering and receiving of equipment is an increase in the specific asset and the related liability when legal title is conveyed. As in for-profit accounting, the commitment is not recorded.

The handling of encumbrances at year-end has changed recently. Any commitments that remain outstanding are removed from the accounting records by reversing the original entry because no transaction has occurred. The recording of encumbrances is to help prevent spending more money than the amount authorized for the period.

Assuming that the commitment will be honored in the subsequent year, the accounting issue is whether any additional reporting is needed on the current balance sheet. If the fund balance has already been reclassified as restricted, committed, or assigned in recognition of this eventual expenditure, then no further change is needed. The appropriate fund balance reflects the decision to use that portion of the fund's net assets to meet this commitment. However, if no fund balance is reported as restricted, committed, or assigned, then the amount of the encumbrance should be reclassified as either committed or assigned to denote the anticipated use of the fund's assets.[19]

To illustrate, assume that the general fund of the city that ordered the $18,000 in equipment reports assets of $600,000 and liabilities of $500,000. On the balance sheet, the fund balance shows $40,000 as assigned and $60,000 as unassigned. At the end of the fiscal year, the $18,000 encumbrance is unfulfilled and removed from the records for that period. However, the government will pay for the equipment when it arrives in the following year. The reporting of the fund balance figures on the balance sheet can be affected in one of two ways.

- If the $40,000 fund balance—assigned already includes an $18,000 amount reflecting the commitment for this equipment, no change is necessary. The appropriate amount of the fund's net assets is shown as assigned.

- If the $40,000 fund balance—assigned does not include $18,000 to be spent on the equipment, then the fund balance—unassigned is reduced by that amount and fund balance—assigned (or possibly committed depending on the level of the decision to acquire the equipment) is increased. The assets and liabilities are not affected since the equipment has not been received, but the $18,000 figure is shown as assigned (or committed) to indicate that this amount of the net assets is not freely available to government officials. Per GASB, "Encumbered amounts for specific purposes for which amounts have not been previously restricted, committed, or assigned should not be classified as unassigned but, rather, should be included within committed or assigned fund balance, as appropriate."[20]

RECOGNITION OF EXPENDITURES FOR OPERATIONS AND CAPITAL ADDITIONS

LO6

Record the passage of a budget as well as subsequent encumbrances and expenditures.

Although budgetary and encumbrance entries are unique, their impact on the accounting process is somewhat limited because they do not directly affect a fund's financial results for the period. Conversely, the method by which states and localities record the receipt and disbursement of assets can significantly alter the reported data. For example, because a primary emphasis in the governmental funds is on measuring changes in current financial resources, *neither expenses nor capital assets are recorded in the fund-based financial statements.* Probably no more significant distinction exists between the fund-based statements and the government-wide statements.

As shown previously, governmental funds report an Expenditures account in the fund-based statements. This balance reflects outflows or other reductions in current financial resources caused by the acquisition of a good or service (or some other utility). The reduction of resources is recorded as an expenditure whether it is for rent, a fire truck, salaries, or a computer. In each case, a good or service is acquired. The statement of revenues, expenditures, and other changes in fund balances (Exhibit 11.4) allows the reader to see the utilization of an activity's current financial resources. Spending $1,000 for electricity for the past three months is an

---

[19] If not already reported as restricted, a fund balance cannot be internally restricted. The restricted designation is used to indicate that external parties or applicable laws created the restriction.

[20] GASB *Statement No. 54*, "Fund Balance Reporting and Governmental Fund Type Definitions," February 2009, para. 24.

expenditure of a fund's current financial resources in exactly the same way that buying a $70,000 ambulance is:

Fund-Based Financial Statements—Expenditures for Expense and Capital Asset

Expenditures—Electricity	1,000	
Vouchers (or Accounts) Payable		1,000
To record charges covering the past three months.		
Expenditures—Ambulance	70,000	
Vouchers (or Accounts) Payable		70,000
To record acquisition of ambulance.		

Within the governmental funds, the timing of the recognition of expenditures (and revenues) follows the *modified accrual basis of accounting.* For expenditures, modified accrual accounting requires recognizing a claim against current financial resources when it is created. If a claim is established in one period to be settled in the subsequent period using year-end financial resources, the expenditure and liability are recorded in the initial year. However, as discussed earlier, the maximum length of time for the change in current financial resources to occur—often 60 days into the subsequent period—should be disclosed. Thus, if equipment is received 15 days before the end of the year but payment will not be made until 75 days later, recording the expenditure is still likely to be made in the first year, depending on the recognition period utilized by the government.

The recording of expenditures rather than expenses and capital assets is one of the most distinctive characteristics of traditional governmental accounting. In fund-based statements, a governmental fund records both operating costs such as salaries and rent and the entire cost of all buildings, machines, and other capital assets as expenditures. No net income figure is calculated for these funds; thus, computing and recording subsequent depreciation is not relevant to the reporting process and is omitted entirely. It has no effect on current financial resources.

For the government-wide financial statements, all economic resources are being measured. Consequently, the previous two transactions would be recorded in this second set of statements as follows:

Government-Wide Financial Statements—Recording Expense and Capital Asset

Utilities Expense	1,000	
Voucher (or Accounts) Payable		1,000
To record electricity charges for the past three months.		
Ambulance	70,000	
Voucher (or Accounts) Payable		70,000
To record acquisition of new ambulance.		

Capital Assets and Fund-Based Financial Statements

LO7

Understand the reporting of capital assets, supplies, and prepaid expenses by a state or local government.

One interesting result of measuring and recording only expenditures within the fund-based statements of the governmental funds is that virtually no assets other than current financial resources such as cash, receivables, and investments are reported. All capital assets are recorded as expenditures at the time of purchase or construction with that balance closed out at the end of the fiscal period. Note that the statement in Exhibit 11.3 shows no buildings, schools, computers, trucks, or other equipment as assets.

With the creation of government-wide financial statements, a record of all capital assets is available in the statement of net assets (see Exhibit 11.1). Thus, recording only expenditures in the fund-based financial statements does not leave a gap in the information available to interested parties. In the initial production of government-wide financial statements, one problem was the reporting of "infrastructure" assets including roads, sidewalks, bridges, and the like that are normally stationary and can be preserved for a significant period of time. A bridge, for example, might last for more than 100 years. Traditionally, the formal recording of such infrastructure assets was optional. To save time and energy, many governments simply did not

Discussion **Question**

IS IT AN ASSET OR A LIABILITY?

During the evolution of government accounting, many scholars have discussed its unique features. In the August 1989 issue of the *Journal of Accountancy* R.K. Mautz described the reporting needs of governments and not-for-profit organizations (such as charities) in "Not-For-Profit Financial Reporting: Another View."

As an illustration of their accounting problems, Mautz examined the method by which a city should record a newly constructed high school building. Conventional business wisdom would say that such a property represents an asset of the government. Thus, the cost should be capitalized and then depreciated over an estimated useful life. However, in paragraph 26 of FASB *Concepts Statements No. 6,* an essential characteristic of an asset is "a probable future benefit . . . to contribute directly to future cash inflows."

Mautz reasoned that the school building cannot be considered an asset because it provides no net contribution to cash inflows. In truth, a high school requires the government to make significant cash outflows for maintenance, repairs, utilities, salaries, and the like. Public educational facilities (as well as many of the other properties of a government such as a fire station or municipal building) are acquired with the understanding that net cash outflows will result for years to come.

Consequently, Mautz considered whether the construction of a high school is not actually the incurrence of a liability because the government is taking on an obligation that will necessitate future cash payments. This idea also is rejected, once again based on the guidance of *Concepts Statement No. 6* (para. 36), because the cash outflow is not required at a "specified or determinable date, on occurrence of a specified event, or on demand."

Is a high school building an asset or is it a liability? If it is neither, how should the cost be recorded? How is the high school reported in fund-based financial statements? How is the high school reported in government-wide financial statements? Which of these two approaches provides the best portrayal of the decision to acquire or construct this building? Can a government possibly be accounted for in the same manner as a for-profit enterprise?

maintain a record of these assets after the original expenditure. Thus, in creating the initial set of government-wide financial statements, records were often unavailable for some or all of the infrastructure assets that were bought or constructed over the decades.

Because of the potential problem of establishing cost-based balances for all infrastructure assets, GASB made an exception in reporting for government-wide financial statements. A government must now capitalize all new infrastructure assets bought or built. However, the book value of infrastructure assets acquired before the advent of government-wide financial statements only had to be approximated. GASB suggested methods by which costs incurred for highways, curbing, sidewalks, and the like could be estimated for reporting purposes. For example, current costs for such projects could be determined and then adjusted for both inflation and usage since the dates the assets were originally obtained. However, an important limitation was placed on the need for such complex calculations. This type of historical estimation and reporting is required only for major general infrastructure assets acquired or significantly improved since June 30, 1980. Thus, a city is probably not required to determine a cost approximation for a sidewalk built in 1928.

As mentioned previously, fund-based financial statements do not recognize depreciation expense in connection with governmental funds for two reasons:

1. These funds reflect expenditures rather than expenses, and the entire cost of the asset was reported as an expenditure at the time of the original claim against current financial resources. Reporting subsequent depreciation would reflect the impact twice: once when acquired and once when depreciated.

2. These funds traditionally do not record expenses. Reporting depreciation expense (rather than an expenditure) is not consistent with measuring the change in current financial resources.

However, the government-wide financial statements (as well as fund-based statements for proprietary and fiduciary funds) list assets rather than expenditures for such costs, and therefore depreciation is appropriate. Consequently, on these statements, depreciation on all long-lived assets with finite lives should be calculated and reported each period.

Supplies and Prepaid Items

In gathering information for government-wide financial statements, the acquisition of supplies and prepaid costs such as rent or insurance is not particularly complicated. An asset is recorded at the time of acquisition and subsequently reclassified to expense as the asset's utility is consumed by use or time. However, reporting prepaid costs and supplies by the governmental funds within the fund-based financial statements is not so straightforward. These assets have a relatively short life. Should the cost incurred be reported as an asset until consumed or recorded directly as an expenditure at the time of acquisition?

Traditionally, governments have used the *purchases method,* which simply records these costs as expenditures at the point that a claim to current financial resources is created. No asset is recorded. For disclosure purposes, though, remaining supplies or prepaid items (such as insurance or rent) are then entered into the accounting records as assets just prior to production of financial statements. Mechanically, the asset is recorded along with an offsetting amount in fund balance—nonspendable to inform the reader that the fund is reporting assets that are not current financial resources available for spending in the future. Thus, the City of Philadelphia discloses that the "supplies of governmental funds are recorded as expenditures when purchased rather than capitalized as inventory."

The *purchases method* reflects modified accrual accounting because the entire cost is recognized as an expenditure when current financial resources are initially reduced. However, many governments have chosen to have their governmental funds report supplies and prepaid items using an accepted alternative known as the *consumption method.*

The consumption method parallels the process utilized in creating government-wide financial statements. Supplies or prepayments are recorded as assets when acquired. Subsequently, as the utility is consumed by usage or over time, the cost is reclassified into an expenditures account. As explained by the City of Birmingham, Alabama, "[i]nventory consists of expendable supplies held in the General Fund for consumption. The cost is recorded as an expenditure at the time individual inventory items are used (consumption method)." Under this approach, the expenditure is matched with the period of specific usage. Because these assets cannot be spent for government programs or other needs, an equal portion of the Fund Balance account should be reclassified as nonspendable as is shown in the balance sheet in Exhibit 11.3.

To illustrate, assume that a municipality purchases $20,000 in supplies for various General Fund activities. During the remainder of the fiscal period, $18,000 of this amount is consumed so that only $2,000 remains at year-end. These events could be recorded through either of the following sets of entries:

Fund-Based Financial Statements—Supplies and Prepaid Expenses

Purchases Method

Expenditures—Supplies	20,000	
Vouchers Payable		20,000
To record purchase of supplies for various ongoing activities.		
Inventory of Supplies	2,000	
Fund Balance—Nonspendable		2,000
To establish balance for supplies remaining at year's end.		

Consumption Method

Inventory of Supplies	20,000	
Vouchers Payable		20,000
To record purchase of supplies for various ongoing activities.		
Expenditures—Control	18,000	
Inventory of Supplies		18,000
To record consumption of supplies during period. Because a $2,000 asset that cannot be spent remains, an equal portion of the Fund Balance is reclassified from unassigned to nonspendable. This reclassification is normally done in creating the statements, not through a journal entry.		

LO8

Determine the proper timing for the recognition of revenues from nonexchange transactions.

Recognition of Revenues—Overview

The recognition of some revenues has always posed theoretical issues for state and local governments. For most of their revenues, such as property taxes, income taxes, and grants, no earning process exists as in a for-profit business. These revenues are referred to as nonexchange transactions. Taxes, fines, and the like are assessed or imposed on the citizens to support the government's operations rather than giving the payors a specific good or service in return for their payments.

GASB *Statement Number 33,* "Accounting and Financial Reporting for Nonexchange Transactions," provides a comprehensive system for recognizing many of these revenues. This statement does not apply to true revenues such as interest or rents for which an earning process does exist. Instead, it concentrates on "nonexchange transactions," including most taxes, fines, grants, gifts, and the like for which the government does not provide a direct and equal benefit for the amount received.

> In a nonexchange transaction, a government (including the federal government, as a provider) either gives value (benefit) to another party without directly receiving equal value in exchange or receives value (benefit) from another party without directly giving equal value in exchange.[21]

For organizational purposes, nonexchange transactions are separated into four distinct classifications, each with its own rules as to proper recognition:

- *Derived tax revenues.* A tax assessment is imposed when an underlying exchange takes place. Income taxes and sales taxes are the best examples of this type of revenue. A sale occurs, for example, and a sales tax is imposed, or income is earned and an income tax is assessed.
- *Imposed nonexchange revenues.* Property taxes and fines and penalties are viewed as imposed nonexchange revenues because the government mandates an assessment, but no underlying transaction occurs. As an example, real estate or other property is owned and a property tax is levied. The government is taxing ownership here, not a specific transaction.
- *Government-mandated nonexchange transactions.* This category includes monies, such as grants conveyed from one government to another, to help cover the costs of required programs. If a state specifies that a city must create a homeless shelter and then provides a grant of $400,000 to help defray the cost, the city records the inflow of money using these prescribed rules. The state has mandated the utilization of the grant to meet the law. City officials have no choice; the state government has required the shelter to be constructed and is providing part or all of the funding.
- *Voluntary nonexchange transactions.* In this final classification, money has been conveyed willingly to the state or local government by an individual, another government, or an organization, usually for a particular purpose. For example, a state might grant a city $900,000 to help improve reading programs in its schools. Unless the state mandated an enhancement in these reading programs, this grant is accounted for as a voluntary nonexchange transaction. The decision has been made that the money will provide an important benefit, but no separate government requirement led the state to make the conveyance.

Derived Tax Revenues Such as Income Taxes and Sales Taxes

Accounting for derived tax revenues is relatively straightforward. These revenues are normally recognized in government-wide financial statements when the underlying transaction occurs. Thus, when a taxpayer earns income, the government should record the resulting income tax revenue. Likewise, when a sale is made, the government should recognize the sales tax revenue that is created.

Assume, for example, that sales by businesses that operate within a locality amount to $10 million for the current year and a sales tax of 4 percent is assessed. In the period in which the sales are made, the following entry is required of the government. The amounts should be reported net of any estimated refunds or uncollectible balances.

---

[21] GASB *Statement 33,* "Accounting and Financial Reporting for Nonexchange Transactions," December 1998, para. 7.

Government-Wide Financial Statements—Derived Tax Revenues

Receivable—Sales Taxes	400,000	
Revenue—Sales Taxes		400,000
To recognize amount of sales tax that will be collected in connection with sales for the current period. Same entry is appropriate for the fund-based statements of the governmental fund if the money qualifies as available.		

For fund-based financial statements, the preceding rules also apply except for one additional requirement. In connection with governmental funds, the resources must be available before the revenue can be recognized. That is, the amounts must be received during the year or soon enough thereafter to satisfy claims to current financial resources. In that way, the essence of modified accrual accounting is utilized at the fund level of reporting. As mentioned previously, except in the reporting of property taxes, the government selects and must disclose the length of time that serves as the boundary for financial resources to be viewed as available. As with any revenue, if the use of the receipts is stipulated, the fund balance must be shown as restricted, committed, or assigned based on the source of the decision making.

Imposed Nonexchange Revenues Such as Property Taxes and Fines

Accounting for imposed nonexchange revenues is a bit more complicated than for derived tax revenues because no underlying transaction exists to guide the timing of the revenue recognition. Interestingly, GASB set up separate rules for recognizing the asset and the related revenue. A receivable is to be recorded when the government first has an enforceable legal claim as defined in that particular jurisdiction (or when cash is received if a prepayment is made). For the revenue side of the transaction, recognition should be made in the time period when the resulting resources are required to be used or in the first period in which use is permitted.

To illustrate, assume that officials of the City of Alban need to generate property tax revenues of at least $500,000 to finance budgeted government spending for Year 2. On October 1, Year 1, property tax assessments totaling $530,000 are mailed to the citizens. Assume that according to applicable state law, the city has no enforceable claim until January 1, Year 2 (often called the *lien date*). However, to encourage early payment, the city allows a 5 percent discount on any amount received by December 31, Year 1.

No entry is recorded on October 1, Year 1. Although the assessments have been delivered, no enforceable legal claim yet exists, and the proceeds from the tax cannot be used until Year 2. However, assume that $30,000 of the assessments is collected from citizens during the final three months of Year 1. After reduction for the 5 percent discount, the collection is $28,500.

Government-Wide Financial Statements and Fund-Based Financial Statements—Property Taxes

Year 1		
Cash	28,500	
Deferred Property Tax Revenues		28,500
To record collection of property tax prior to the start of the levy year after reduction for 5 percent discount.		

Assume that city officials expect to collect 96 percent of the remaining $500,000 in assessments, or $480,000. At the beginning of Year 2, both this receivable and the related revenue can be recognized. The receivable is reported at that time because an enforceable claim comes into existence. For government-wide statements, the remaining revenue is reported in Year 2 because that is the period in which the money can first be used. In the following journal entry, note that the revenue is reduced directly by the estimate of taxes that are expected to be uncollectible. In addition, the previously collected amount is recognized in Year 2 as revenue because, once again, this is the period for which use is allowed.

Government Wide Financial Statement—Property Taxes

January 1, Year 2		
Property Tax Receivable	500,000	
Allowance for Uncollectible Taxes		20,000
Revenues—Property Taxes		480,000
To recognize property tax assessment for Year 2.		
Deferred Property Tax Revenues	28,500	
Revenues—Property Taxes		28,500
To recognize property tax proceeds for Year 2 collected during Year 1.		

The preceding recording would be the same for the fund-based financial statements unless some portion of the future cash collection is viewed as not being available this period. Because property taxes are such a significant source of revenue for many governments, a specific 60-day maximum period for recognition has been standardized rather than allowing the government to choose.

To illustrate, assume that historical records indicate that $400,000 of this anticipated $480,000 will be collected during Year 2, another $50,000 in the first 60 days of Year 3, and the final $30,000 beyond 60 days into Year 3. This last $30,000 is not viewed as available to pay for Year 2 expenditures. Revenue recognition is not appropriate until Year 3. Only $450,000 of the financial resources are expected to be available. For the fund-based statements, this entry must conform to modified accrual accounting. Again, revenues are recorded net of estimated uncollectible taxes.

Fund-Based Financial Statements—Property Taxes

January 1, Year 2		
Property Tax Receivable	500,000	
Allowance for Uncollectible Taxes		20,000
Revenues—Property Taxes		450,000
Deferred Property Tax Revenues		30,000
To record amount of property taxes measurable and available for Year 2 expenditures. $30,000 is not expected until after 60 days into Year 3.		
Deferred Property Tax Revenues	28,500	
Revenues—Property Taxes		28,500
To recognize property tax proceeds for Year 2 collected during Year 1.		

Government-Mandated Nonexchange Transactions and Voluntary Nonexchange Transactions

Although these two sources of revenues are identified separately, the timing of accounting recognition is the same so they are logically discussed together. Governments recognize these types of revenue (often in the form of a grant) when all eligibility requirements have been met. Until eligibility has been established, the existence of some degree of uncertainty precludes recognition. Thus, revenue reporting occurs at the time of eligibility even if the money was actually received earlier.

Eligibility requirements are divided into four general classifications. Applicable requirements must all be met before revenues can be recorded for either government-mandated nonexchange transactions or voluntary nonexchange transactions.

1. *Required characteristics of the recipients.* In many programs, the government scheduled to receive funds is given standards that must be met in advance. For example, assume that a state grant has been awarded to a city to help teach all kindergarten children in its school system to read. However, as part of this program, state law has been changed to mandate that all kindergarten teachers must hold proper certification. Consequently, the state will

not convey the grant to the city until all kindergarten teachers have met this standard. The city must conform to state law first. Because of this eligibility requirement, revenue recognition of this grant is delayed until all teachers have become certified.

2. *Time requirements.* Programs can specify when money is to be used. To illustrate, assume that in April, a state provides a grant to a city to buy milk for each child during the subsequent school year starting in September. The grant should be recognized as revenue in the period of use or in the period when the use of the funds is first permitted.

3. *Reimbursement.* Many grants and other forms of similar support are designed to reimburse a government for amounts spent appropriately. These arrangements are often called *expenditure-driven programs*. Assume that a state informs a locality that it will reimburse the city government for money paid to provide milk to schoolchildren who could not otherwise afford it. In such cases, proper spending is the eligibility requirement; the city recognizes no revenue until the city's own money is spent for milk.

4. *Contingencies.* In voluntary nonexchange transactions (but not in government-mandated nonexchange transactions), revenue may be withheld until a specified procurement action has been taken. A grant might be given to buy park equipment, for example, but only after an appropriate piece of land has been acquired on which to build the park. Until a lot is obtained (or other required action is taken) a contingency exists, and the revenue should not be recognized.

LO9

Account for the issuance of long-term bonds and the reporting of special assessment projects.

Issuance of Bonds

Although not a revenue, the issuance of bonds serves as a major source of financing for many state and local governments. At the end of 2008, the total of all such long-term debt outstanding for state and local governments amounted to the almost unbelievable balance of $2.23 trillion.[22] Proceeds from these debt issuances are used for many purposes, including general financing and a wide variety of construction projects. As of June 30, 2008, the City of San Diego, California, had approximately $2.7 billion of long-term bonds outstanding. Of that amount, more than $1.3 billion had been issued by governmental activities and nearly $1.4 billion by business-type activities.

Because the proceeds of a bond issuance must be repaid, the government recognizes no revenues under either method of financial reporting. The reporting in the government-wide financial statements is hardly controversial: Both the cash and the debt are increased to reflect the issuance. Conversely, in the fund-based financial statements, recording is not so simple. Cash is received, but the debt is not a claim on current financial resources. Thus, from that perspective, the inflow of current financial resources does not create a revenue or a liability that can be reported.

Assume, for example, that the Town of Ruark sells $9 million in general obligation bonds at face value to finance the construction of a new school building. Because of the intended use of this money, the town established a Capital Projects Fund to monitor the cash. To emphasize that this inflow of money is not derived from a revenue, Ruark utilizes a special designation, *Other Financing Sources*. Note in Exhibit 11.4 the placement of Other Financing Sources (Uses) at the bottom of the statement of revenues, expenditures, and other changes in fund balance to identify changes in the amount of current financial resources created through transactions other than revenues and expenditures. Issuance of a long-term bond is a prime example.

The following journal entry is created to reflect the sale of these bonds in the fund-based statement if issued by one of the governmental funds:

Fund-Based Financial Statements—Issuance of Bonds

Capital Projects Funds—School Building		
Cash	9,000,000	
Other Financing Sources—Bond Proceeds		9,000,000
To record issuance of bonds to finance construction project.		

[22] U.S. Federal Reserve, *Federal Reserve Statistical Release,* "Flow of Funds Account of the United States," 2005–2008 (Washington, D.C.: Federal Reserve, June 11, 2009), Table L.1, p. 500.

Although an inflow of cash into this fund has taken place, no revenue has been generated. However, in the same manner as a revenue, the Other Financing Sources is a measurement account that is closed out at year-end. As the preceding entry shows, the actual $9 million liability is completely omitted from the Capital Projects Funds. Because the governmental funds stress accountability for the inflows and outflows of current financial resources, recognition of long-term debts in fund-based accounting has traditionally been considered inappropriate. For example, the balance sheet in Exhibit 11.3 shows no long-term liabilities at all for the governmental funds but only claims to current financial resources. Any reader of the financial statements who wants to see the amount of the government's long-term debts must examine the statement of net assets in the government-wide financial statements (see Exhibit 11.1).

Payment of Long-Term Liabilities

The payment of long-term liabilities again demonstrates the huge differences between the government-wide financial statements and the fund-based financial statements. For the government-wide statements, recording the payment of principal and interest is the same as the accounting used by a for-profit organization. For the fund-based statements, an expenditure account is recognized for settlement of the debt and also for the related interest (often paid for and recorded in a Debt Service Fund). Both payments reduce current financial resources.

Assume as an illustration that a government has a $500,000 bond payment coming due along with three months of interest amounting to $10,000. This example assumes that cash had been set aside previously in the Debt Service Fund to satisfy this obligation. The needed entries follow:

Government-Wide Financial Statements—Bond and Interest Payments

Bond Payable	500,000	
Interest Expense	10,000	
Cash		510,000
To record payment of bond and related interest.		

Fund-Based Financial Statements—Bond and Interest Payments

Debt Service Funds		
Expenditure—Bond Principal	500,000	
Expenditure—Interest	10,000	
Cash		510,000
To record payment of bond and related interest.		

Tax Anticipation Notes

One type of formal debt is recorded in the same manner for government-wide and fund-based financial statements. State and local governments often issue short-term debts to provide financing until revenue sources have been collected. For example, if property tax payments are expected at a particular point in time, the government might need to borrow money for operations until that date. These short-term liabilities are often referred to as *tax anticipation notes* because they are outstanding until a sufficient amount of taxes can be collected. As short-term liabilities, these debts are a claim on current financial resources. Thus, for the fund-based financial statements, the issuance is not recorded as an other financing source but as a liability in the same manner as in the government-wide financial statements. Amounts paid for interest, though, are still recorded as an expenditure in producing fund-based statements and as an expense on the government-wide financial statements.

Assume a city borrows $300,000 on a 60-day note on January 1 and agrees to pay back $305,000 on March 1. The city will repay the debt with receipts from property taxes. For both sets of financial statements, cash is increased as well as the related liability.

At repayment, however, different entries are required:

Fund-Based Financial Statements—Payment of Tax Anticipation Notes

Tax Anticipation Note Payable	300,000	
Expenditure—Interest	5,000	
Cash		305,000
To record payment of short-term debt and interest for two months.		

Government-Wide Financial Statements—Payment of Tax Anticipative Notes

Tax Anticipation Note Payable	300,000	
Interest Expense	5,000	
Cash		305,000
To record payment of short-term debt and interest for two months.		

LO9

Account for the issuance of long-term bonds and the reporting of special assessment projects.

Special Assessments

Governments occasionally provide improvements or services that directly benefit a particular property and assess the costs (in whole or part) to the owner. In many cases, the owners actually petition the government to initiate such projects to enhance property values. Paving streets, installing water and sewage lines, and constructing curbs and sidewalks are typical examples. To finance the work, the government usually issues debt and places a lien on the property being improved to ensure reimbursement. The City of Fargo, North Dakota, reported special assessment receivables of over $192 million as of December 31, 2008. That amount was explained by the following description: "As projects are finalized and closed, the majority are financed through the issuance of bonds, which are then repaid through special assessments from the benefiting property owners. As the bonds are issued and special assessments are approved, the special assessments are recorded as receivables."

Government-wide financial statements handle the debt and subsequent construction project in the manner of a for-profit enterprise. The asset is recorded at cost and assessments are made and collected. These receipts are then used to settle the debt. For example, assume that a sidewalk is to be added to a neighborhood at a cost of $20,000. The city is to sell bonds of this amount to finance the construction with repayment eventually to be made using funds collected from the owners of the property benefited. Total interest to be paid is $2,000. The assessment to the owners is set at $22,000 to cover all costs.

Government-Wide Financial Statements—Special Assessment Project

Cash	20,000	
Bond Payable—Special Assessment		20,000
To record debt issued to finance sidewalk construction.		
Infrastructure Asset—Sidewalk	20,000	
Cash		20,000
To record payment to contractor for the cost of building new sidewalk.		
Taxes Receivable—Special Assessment	22,000	
Revenue—Special Assessment		22,000
To record citizens' charges for special assessment project.		

Cash	22,000	
Taxes Receivable—Special Assessment		22,000
To record collection of money from assessment of citizens for sidewalk construction.		
Bond Payable—Special Assessment	20,000	
Interest Expense	2,000	
Cash		22,000
To record payment of debt on special assessment bonds.		

In the fund-based financial statements, this same series of transactions has a completely different appearance. Neither the infrastructure nor the long-term debt is recorded because the current financial resources measurement basis is used.

Fund-Based Financial Statements—Special Assessment Project

Capital Projects Fund—Special Assessment Project

Cash	20,000	
Other Financing Sources—Bond Proceeds		20,000
To record issuance of bonds to finance sidewalk construction with payment to be made from a special assessment levy.		
Expenditures—Special Assessment	20,000	
Cash		20,000
To record payment to contractor for the cost of constructing sidewalk.		

Debt Service Fund—Special Assessment Project

Taxes Receivable—Special Assessment	22,000	
Revenue—Special Assessment		22,000
To record assessment that will be used to pay bond principal and related interest incurred after construction.		
Cash	22,000	
Taxes Receivable—Special Assessment		22,000
To record collection of assessment paid by citizens to extinguish bond and interest incurred in construction of sidewalk.		
Expenditure—Special Assessment Bond	20,000	
Expenditure—Interest	2,000	
Cash		22,000
To record payment of bonds payable and interest incurred in construction of sidewalk.		

One other aspect of the reporting of special assessment projects should be mentioned. In some cases, the government may facilitate a project but accept no legal obligation for it. The government's role is limited to conveying funds from one party to another so that the government assumes no liability (either primary or secondary) for the debt. Normally in such cases, the money goes from citizens to the government and then directly to the contractors. The government is merely serving as a conduit.

If the government has no liability for defaults, overruns, or other related problems, recording the special assessment assets, liabilities, revenues, expenses, other financing sources, and expenditures is not really relevant to the government's resources. In that situation, all transactions are recorded in an agency fund as increases and decreases in cash, amount due from citizens, and amount due to contractors. As a fiduciary fund, no reportable impact appears within the government-wide statements.

LO10

Record the various types of monetary transfers that occur within the funds of a state or local government.

Interfund Transactions

Interfund transactions are commonly used within government units as a way to direct sufficient resources to all activities and functions. Monetary transfers made from the General Fund are especially prevalent because general tax revenues are initially accumulated in this fund. For example, the General Fund for Houston, Texas, indicated in the fund-based financial statements for the year ending June 30, 2008, that approximately $256 million had been transferred out to other funds while only $9 million had been transferred in from other funds. Because of the emphasis on resource availability in individual funds, transfers are not offset or eliminated in fund-based statements.

However, the government-wide financial statements do not report many such transfers because they frequently occur solely within the governmental activities. For example, a transfer from the General Fund to the Debt Service Fund is reported in both funds on fund-based financial statements but would create no net impact in the government-wide financial statements because they are both classified as governmental activities.

Thus, for government-wide financial reporting, the following distinctions for transfers are drawn:

- *Intra-activity transactions* occur between two governmental funds (so that net totals reported for governmental activities are not affected) or between two enterprise funds (so that totals reported for business-type activities are not affected). Transfers between governmental funds and most Internal Service Funds are usually included here because, as discussed previously, Internal Service Funds are usually reported as governmental activities in government-wide statements. Government-wide financial statements do not report intra-activity transactions because they create no overall change in either the governmental activities or the business-type activities.

- *Interactivity transactions* occur between governmental funds and enterprise funds. They impact the totals reported for both governmental activities and business-type activities. Government-wide financial statements do report interactivity transactions. In Exhibit 11.1, for example, internal amounts due ($50) are reported within the asset section of the statement of net assets and then offset to arrive at overall government totals. Likewise, in Exhibit 11.2, transfers ($600) between the two activity classifications appear at the very bottom of the general revenues section. Again, individual totals are shown and then eliminated so that no amount is reported for the government as a whole. Although most transfers are intra-activity, interactivity transactions are also common. In its June 30, 2008, government-wide financial statements, the City of St. Louis reported (and then eliminated) internal balances of $9.3 million and interactivity transfers of $8.7 million.

Consequently, in discussing interfund transactions, the reporting for government-wide statements is appropriate only when an interactivity transaction is involved.

Interfund Transfers

The most common interfund transactions are transfers within the governmental funds to ensure adequate financing of budgeted expenditures. A city council could vote to transfer $800,000 from the General Fund to the Capital Projects Funds to cover a portion of the cost of a new school building. This scenario involves recording the following entries:

Fund-Based Financial Statements—Intra-Activity Transactions

General Fund		
Other Financing Uses—Transfers Out—Capital Projects Fund	800,000	
Due to Capital Projects Fund		800,000
To record authorization transfer for school construction.		

Capital Projects Funds		
Due from General Fund	800,000	
Other Financing Sources—Transfers In—General Fund		800,000
To record transfer to be received for school construction.		

The *Other Financing Uses/Sources* designations are appropriate here; financial resources are being moved into and out of these funds although neither revenues nor expenditures have been earned or incurred. As Exhibit 11.4 shows, these balances are reported by each fund in the statement of revenues, expenditures, and other changes in fund balances. Each figure is shown but is not offset in any way. Both accounts are then closed out at the end of the current year. The *Due to/Due from* accounts are the equivalent of interfund payable and receivable balances, and each account is reported within the proper fund on its balance sheet. Again no elimination is made in arriving at total figures for the governmental funds.

Because this is an intra-activity transaction, neither of the above entries is made in creating the government-wide financial statements. Financial resources are simply being shifted within the governmental activities.

Not all monetary transfers are for normal operating purposes; nonrecurring or nonroutine transfers may also take place. For example, money might be transferred from the General Fund to create or expand an enterprise fund such as a bus or subway system. Assume that a city sets aside $1 million of unassigned money to help permanently finance a new subway system that will be open to the public. For convenience, this transaction is recorded as if cash is transferred immediately so that no receivable or payable is necessary:

Fund-Based Financial Statements—Interactivity Transactions

General Fund

Other Financing Uses—Transfers Out—Subway System	1,000,000	
Cash		1,000,000
To record transfer to help finance subway system.		

Enterprise Fund

Cash	1,000,000	
Capital Contributions		1,000,000
To record receipt of transfer from unrestricted funds.		

Because this transfer is an interactivity transaction (between governmental activities and business-type activities), entries are also made for the government-wide financial statements. This transfer reduces the assets of the governmental activities but increases the assets in the business-type activities. The balances will be offset in arriving at totals for the government as a whole.

Government-Wide Financial Statements—Interactivity Transactions

Governmental Activities

Transfers Out—Subway System	1,000,000	
Cash		1,000,000
To record transfer to help finance subway system.		

Business-Type Activities

Cash	1,000,000	
Transfers In—General Fund		1,000,000
To record receipt of transfer from unrestricted funds.		

Internal Exchange Transactions

Some transfers made within a government are actually the same as revenues and expenditures. For example, a city's payment to its own print shop (or any other Internal Service Fund or

Enterprise Fund) for services or materials is the equivalent of a transaction with an outside party. To avoid confusion in reporting, such transfers are recorded as revenues and expenditures or expenses as if the transaction had occurred with an unrelated party. No differentiation is made; these payments are not treated as transfers that are designed to shift resources from one fund to another.

The fund-based financial statements record all such internal exchange transactions. However, because Internal Service Funds are usually reported as governmental activities in the government-wide statements, exchanges between a governmental fund and one of these internal service funds normally has no net impact on the overall figures being reported and should be omitted.

To illustrate, assume that a government pays its print shop (an internal service fund) $8,000 for work done for the police department. In addition, the government pays another $1,000 to a toll road operated as an enterprise fund to allow fire department vehicles to ride on the highway without having to make individual payments. Both of these internal exchange payments are made for rendered services:

Fund-Based Financial Statements—Internal Exchange Transactions

General Fund

Expenditures—Printing	8,000	
Expenditures—Toll Road Privileges	1,000	
Cash		9,000
To record payment for printing supplies for use by police department and for use of toll road.		

Internal Service Fund—Print Shop

Cash	8,000	
Revenues		8,000
To record collection of money paid by the police department for printing supplies.		

Enterprise Fund—Toll Road

Cash	1,000	
Revenues		1,000
To record money collected from government for vehicular use of toll roads.		

The $8,000 transaction with the print shop is not reflected on government-wide financial statements if this internal service fund is classified within the governmental activities. In that case, the transfer is the equivalent of an intra-activity transaction. However, the $1,000 payment made by the police department (a governmental activity) to the enterprise fund (a business-type activity) is the same as an interactivity transfer and is reported in the following entries.

Government-Wide Financial Statements—Internal Exchange Transactions

Governmental Activities

Expenses—Toll Road Privileges	1,000	
Cash		1,000
To record payment for use of toll road by fire department's vehicles.		

Business-Type Activities

Cash	1,000	
Revenues		1,000
To record money collected from government for vehicular use of toll roads.		

Summary

1. Readers of state and local government financial statements have a wide variety of informational needs. No single set of financial statements seems capable of meeting all these user needs, a factor that influenced the requirement that two sets of statements be reported. Accountability of government officials and control over public spending have always been essential elements of traditional government accounting. GASB attempted to keep those priorities in place but to broaden the scope of the financial statements being produced.

2. A state or local government unit produces fund-based financial statements utilizing fund accounting. In this system, activities are classified into three broad categories (governmental, proprietary, and fiduciary). Governmental funds account for service activities; proprietary funds account for activities for which a user charge is assessed; and fiduciary funds account for assets that the government holds as a trustee or agent for an external party.

3. Governmental funds have several fund types: the General Fund, Special Revenue Funds, Capital Projects Funds, Debt Service Funds, and Permanent Funds. Proprietary funds are comprised of Enterprise Funds and Internal Service Funds. Fiduciary funds encompass Pension Trust Funds, Investment Trust Funds, Private-Purpose Trust Funds, and Agency Funds.

4. Government-wide financial statements present a statement of net assets and a statement of activities that are separated into governmental activities (the governmental funds and usually the Internal Service Funds) and business-type activities (Enterprise Funds and occasionally an Internal Service Fund). These statements measure all economic resources. The timing of recognition is guided by accrual accounting.

5. Fund-based financial statements include a number of financial statements. This chapter focused on the balance sheet and the statement of revenues, expenditures, and other changes in fund balances for the governmental funds. These statements must show the General Fund and any other individual major fund separately. These statements measure current financial resources. The timing of recognition is guided by modified accrual accounting.

6. To aid in control over financial resources, most governmental funds record their approved budgets each year. This initial budget as well as any final amended budget and actual figures for the period are then reported as required supplementary information along with the financial statements or as a separate statement within the fund-based financial statements.

7. Commitments for purchase orders and contracts are actually recorded in the individual governmental funds by recognizing encumbrances. These balances are recorded when the commitment is made and removed when an actual claim to current financial resources replaces them to help government officials avoid spending more than the amounts properly appropriated.

8. The fund-based financial statements recognize expenditures for capital outlay, long-term debt payment, and expense-type costs when a claim to current financial resources comes into existence. Government-wide financial statements capitalize capital outlay, reduce liabilities for debt payments, and record expenses in expense accounts.

9. Revenue recognition for nonexchange transactions such as sales taxes and property taxes is based on a classification system set up by GASB. Recognition depends on whether the revenue is a derived tax revenue, imposed nonexchange revenue, government-mandated nonexchange transaction, or voluntary nonexchange transaction.

10. The issuance of long-term bonds is recorded as an "other financing source" by the governmental funds because the resource inflow is not a revenue. It is shown as an increase in a long-term liability by the proprietary funds and in the government-wide financial statements.

11. Transfers between funds are normally reported as an "other financing source" and "other financing use" within the fund-based financial statements and are not eliminated or offset. The government-wide statements do not report such transactions unless they create an impact in overall governmental activities and business-type activities. If reported, the amounts are offset in deriving figures for the government as a whole. For internal exchange transactions in which payment is made for a good or service, the fund-based statements recognize a revenue and an expenditure. The government-wide financial statements normally do not reflect such transfers unless they occur between an enterprise fund and a governmental fund. In that case, both a revenue and an expense are increased.

Comprehensive Illustration

PROBLEM

(*Estimated Time: 50 Minutes*). The Town of Drexel has the following financial transactions.

1. The town council adopts an annual budget for the General Fund estimating general revenues of $1.7 million, approved expenditures of $1.5 million, and approved transfers out of $120,000.

2. The town levies property taxes of $1.3 million. It expects to collect all but 3 percent of these taxes during the year. Of the levied amount, $40,000 will be collected next year, after more than 60 days.

3. The town orders two new police cars at an approximate cost of $110,000.

4. A transfer of $50,000 is made from the General Fund to the Debt Service Fund.

5. The town pays a bond payable of $40,000 along with $10,000 of interest using money previously set aside.

6. The Town of Drexel issues a $2 million bond at face value to acquire a building to convert into a high school.

7. The two police cars are received with an invoice price of $112,000. The voucher has been approved for this amount but not yet been paid.

8. The town acquires the building for the high school for $2 million in cash and immediately begins renovating it.

9. Depreciation on the new police cars is computed as $30,000 for the period.

10. The town borrows $100,000 on a 30-day tax anticipation note.

11. The Town of Drexel begins a special assessment curbing project. The government sells $800,000 in notes at face value to finance this project. The town has pledged to guarantee the debt if the assessments collected do not cover the entire balance.

12. A contractor completes the curbing project and is paid $800,000.

13. The town assesses citizens $850,000 for the completed curbing project.

14. The town collects the special assessments of $850,000 in full and repays the debt plus $50,000 in interest.

15. The town receives a $10,000 cash grant to beautify a local park. The grant must be used to reimburse specific costs that the town incurs.

16. The town spends $4,000 to beautify the park.

Required

a. Prepare journal entries for the town based on the production of fund-based financial statements.

b. Prepare journal entries in anticipation of preparing government-wide financial statements.

SOLUTION

a. ***Fund-Based Financial Statements***

1.   **General Fund**

Estimated Revenues Control	1,700,000	
Appropriations Control		1,500,000
Estimated Other Financing Uses Control		120,000
Budgetary Fund Balance		80,000

2.   **General Fund**

Property Tax Receivable	1,300,000	
Allowance for Uncollectible Taxes		39,000
Deferred Revenue		40,000
Revenues—Property Taxes		1,221,000

3.   **General Fund**

Encumbrances Control	110,000	
Fund Balance—Reserved for Encumbrances		110,000

4.   **General Fund**

Other Financing Uses—Transfers Out	50,000	
Cash		50,000

Debt Service Funds

Cash	50,000	
Other Financing Sources—Transfers In		50,000

5.   **Debt Service Funds**

Expenditures—Principal	40,000	
Expenditures—Interest	10,000	
Cash		50,000

6.   **Capital Projects Funds**

Cash	2,000,000	
Other Financing Sources—Bond Proceeds		2,000,000

7.   **General Fund**

Fund Balance—Reserved for Encumbrances	110,000	
Encumbrances Control		110,000
Expenditures Control	112,000	
Vouchers Payable		112,000

8.   **Capital Projects Funds**

Expenditures—Building	2,000,000	
Cash		2,000,000

9. No entry is recorded. Expenditures rather than expenses are recorded by the governmental funds.

10.   **General Fund**

Cash	100,000	
Tax Anticipation Note Payable		100,000

11.   **Capital Projects Funds**

Cash	800,000	
Other Financing Sources—Special Assessments Note		800,000

12.   **Capital Projects Funds**

Expenditures—Curbing	800,000	
Cash		800,000

13.   **Debt Service Funds**

Taxes Receivable—Special Assessment	850,000	
Revenues—Special Assessment		850,000

14.   **Debt Service Funds**

Cash	850,000	
Taxes Receivable—Special Assessment		850,000
Expenditures—Principal	800,000	
Expenditures—Interest	50,000	
Cash		850,000

15.   **Special Revenue Funds**

Cash	10,000	
Deferred Revenues		10,000

16.   **Special Revenue Funds**

Expenditures—Park Beautification	4,000	
Cash		4,000
Deferred Revenues	4,000	
Revenues—Grants		4,000

b. ***Government-Wide Financial Statements***

1. Budgetary entries are not reported within the government-wide financial statements. They are recorded in the individual funds and are then shown as required supplementary information.

2. **Governmental Activities**

Property Tax Receivable	1,300,000	
Allowance for Uncollectible Taxes		39,000
Revenues—Property Taxes		1,261,000

3. Commitments are not reported in the government-wide financial statements.

4. This transfer was within the governmental funds and, therefore, had no net effect on the governmental activities. No journal entry is needed.

5. **Governmental Activities**

Bonds Payable	40,000	
Interest Expense	10,000	
Cash		50,000

6. **Governmental Activities**

Cash	2,000,000	
Bonds Payable		2,000,000

7. **Governmental Activities**

Police Cars (or Vehicles)	112,000	
Vouchers Payable		112,000

8. **Governmental Activities**

Building	2,000,000	
Cash		2,000,000

9. **Governmental Activities**

Depreciation Expense	30,000	
Accumulated Depreciation		30,000

10. **Governmental Activities**

Cash	100,000	
Tax Anticipation Note Payable		100,000

11. **Governmental Activities**

Cash	800,000	
Special Assessment Notes Payable		800,000

12. **Governmental Activities**

Infrastructure Assets—Curbing	800,000	
Cash		800,000

13. **Governmental Activities**

Taxes Receivable—Special Assessment	850,000	
Revenues—Special Assessment		850,000

14. **Governmental Activities**

Cash	850,000	
Taxes Receivable—Special Assessment		850,000
Special Assessment Notes Payable	800,000	
Interest Expense	50,000	
Cash		850,000

15. **Governmental Activities**

Cash	10,000	
Deferred Revenues		10,000

16. **Governmental Activities**

Expenses—Park Beautification	4,000	
Cash		4,000
Deferred Revenues	4,000	
Revenues—Grants		4,000

Questions

1. How have users' needs impacted the development of accounting principles for state and local government units?

2. Why have accountability and control been so important in the traditional accounting for state and local government units?

3. In general, how has the double system of financial statements impacted the financial reporting of state and local governments?

4. What are the basic financial statements that a state or local government now produces?

5. What measurement focus is used in fund-based financial statements for governmental funds, and what system is applied to determine the timing of revenue and expenditure recognition?

6. What measurement focus is used in government-wide financial statements, and what system is applied to determine the timing of revenue and expense recognition?

7. What assets are viewed as current financial resources?

8. In applying the current financial resources measurement focus, when are liabilities recognized?

9. What are the three classifications of funds? What funds are included in each of these three?

10. What are the five fund types within the governmental funds? What types of events does each of these report?

11. What are the two fund types within the proprietary funds? What types of events does each report?

12. What are the four fund types within the fiduciary funds? What types of events does each report?

13. What are the two major divisions reported in government-wide financial statements? What funds are *not* reported in these financial statements?

14. Fund-based financial statements have separate columns for each activity. Which activities are reported in this manner?

15. Why are budgetary entries recorded in the individual funds of a state or local government?

16. How are budget results shown in the financial reporting of a state or local government?

17. When is an encumbrance recorded? What happens to this balance? How are encumbrances reported in government-wide financial statements?

18. An encumbrance is still outstanding at the end of the fiscal year. The government anticipates that it will honor this encumbrance in the next year. How does the government report this encumbrance?

19. What costs cause a governmental fund to report an expenditure?

20. At what point in time does a governmental fund report an expenditure?

21. How do governmental funds report capital outlay in fund-based financial statements? How do government-wide financial statements report capital expenditures?

22. What are the two different ways that supplies and prepaid items can be recorded on fund-based financial statements?

23. What are the four classifications of nonexchange revenues that a state or local government can recognize? In each case, when are revenues normally recognized?

24. When is a receivable recognized for property tax assessments? When is the revenue recognized?

25. How is the issuance of a long-term bond reported on fund-based financial statements? How is the issuance of a long-term bond reported on government-wide financial statements?

26. What is a special assessment project? How are special assessment projects reported?

27. How are interfund transfers reported in fund-based financial statements?

28. In government-wide financial statements, how do an intra-activity transaction and an interactivity transaction differ? How is each reported?

29. What is an internal exchange transaction, and how is it reported?

Problems

LO4

1. Which of the following is *not* a governmental fund?
   a. Special Revenue Fund.
   b. Internal Service Fund.
   c. Capital Projects Fund.
   d. Debt Service Fund.

LO4

2. What is the purpose of a Special Revenue Fund?
   a. To account for revenues legally restricted as to expenditure.
   b. To account for ongoing activities.
   c. To account for gifts when only subsequently earned income can be expended.
   d. To account for the cost of long-lived assets bought with designated funds.

LO4

3. What is the purpose of Enterprise Funds?
   a. To account for operations that provide services to other departments within a government.
   b. To account for asset transfers.
   c. To account for ongoing activities such as the police and fire departments.
   d. To account for operations financed in whole or in part by outside user charges.

LO4

4. Which of the following statements is true?
   a. There are three different types of proprietary funds.
   b. There are three different types of fiduciary funds.
   c. There are five different types of fiduciary funds.
   d. There are five different types of governmental funds.

LO1, LO6

5. A government expects to receive revenues of $400,000 but has approved expenditures of $430,000. The anticipated shortage will have an impact on which of the following terms?
   a. Interperiod equity.
   b. Modified accrual accounting.
   c. Consumption accounting.
   d. Account groups.

LO4

6. A citizen of the City of Townsend gives it a gift of $22,000 in investments. The citizen requires that the investments be held but any resulting income must be used to help maintain the city's cemetery. In which fund should this asset be reported?
   a. Special Revenue Funds.
   b. Capital Projects Funds.
   c. Permanent Funds.
   d. General Fund.

LO2

7. Which of the following statements is correct for governmental funds?
   a. Fund-based financial statements measure economic resources.
   b. Government-wide financial statements measure only current financial resources.
   c. Fund-based financial statements measure both economic resources and current financial resources.
   d. Government-wide financial statements measure economic resources.

LO2

8. Which of the following statements is correct for governmental funds?

    a. Fund-based financial statements measure revenues and expenditures based on modified accrual accounting.

    b. Government-wide financial statements measure revenues and expenses based on modified accrual accounting.

    c. Fund-based financial statements measure revenues and expenses based on accrual accounting.

    d. Government-wide financial statements measure revenues and expenditures based on accrual accounting.

LO2, LO7

9. During the current year, a government buys land for $80,000. Which of the following is *not* true?

    a. The land could be reported as an asset by the business-type activities in the government-wide financial statements.

    b. The land could be reported as an asset by the governmental activities in the government-wide financial statements.

    c. The land could be reported as an asset by the proprietary funds in the fund-based financial statements.

    d. The land could be reported as an asset by the governmental funds in the fund-based financial statements.

LO6

10. Which of the following statements is true concerning the recording of a budget?

    a. At the beginning of the year, debit Appropriations.

    b. A debit to the Budgetary Fund Balance account indicates an expected surplus.

    c. At the beginning of the year, debit Estimated Revenues.

    d. At the end of the year, credit Appropriations.

LO1, LO2, LO7

11. The General Fund pays rent for two months. Which of the following is *not* correct?

    a. Rent expense should be reported in the government-wide financial statements.

    b. Rent expense should be reported in the General Fund.

    c. An expenditure should be reported in the fund-based financial statements.

    d. If one month of rent is in the first year with the other month in the next year, either the purchases method or the consumption method can be used in fund-based statements.

LO6, LO7

12. A purchase order for $3,000 is recorded in the General Fund for the purchase of a new computer. The computer is received at an actual cost of $3,020. Which of the following is correct?

    a. Machinery is increased in the General Fund by $3,020.

    b. An encumbrance account is reduced by $3,020.

    c. An expenditure is increased by $3,020.

    d. An expenditure is recorded for the additional $20.

LO2, LO6

13. At the end of the current year, a government reports a fund balance—assigned of $9,000 in connection with an encumbrance. What information is being conveyed?

    a. A donor has given the government $9,000 that must be used in a specified fashion.

    b. The government has made $9,000 in commitments in one year that will be honored in the subsequent year.

    c. Encumbrances exceeded expenditures by $9,000 during the current year.

    d. The government spent $9,000 less than was appropriated.

LO2, LO3, LO7

14. A government buys equipment for its police department at a cost of $54,000. Which of the following is *not* true?

    a. Equipment will increase by $54,000 in the government-wide financial statements.

    b. Depreciation in connection with this equipment will be reported in the fund-based financial statements.

    c. The equipment will not appear within the reported assets in the fund-based financial statements.

    d. An expenditure for $54,000 will be reported in the fund-based financial statements.

LO3, LO7

15. A city acquires supplies for its fire department and uses the consumption method of accounting. Which of the following statements is true for the fund-based statements?

    a. An expenditures account was debited at the time of receipt.

    b. An expense is recorded as the supplies are consumed.

    c. An inventory account is debited at the time of the acquisition.

    d. The supplies are recorded within the General Fixed Assets Account Group.

LO8

16. An income tax is an example of which of the following?

    a. Derived tax revenue.

    b. Imposed nonexchange revenue.

    c. Government-mandated nonexchange revenue.

    d. Voluntary nonexchange transaction.

LO8

17. The state government passes a law requiring localities to upgrade their water treatment facilities. The state then awards a grant of $500,000 to the Town of Midlothian to help pay for this cost. What type of revenue is this grant?

    a. Derived tax revenue.

    b. Imposed nonexchange revenue.

    c. Government-mandated nonexchange revenue.

    d. Voluntary nonexchange transaction.

LO8

18. The state awards a grant of $50,000 to the Town of Glenville. The state will pay the grant money to the town as a reimbursement for money spent on road repair. At the time of the grant, the state pays $8,000 in advance. During the first year of this program, the town spent $14,000 and applied for reimbursement. What amount of revenue should be recognized?

    a. $-0-.

    b. $8,000.

    c. $14,000.

    d. $50,000.

LO5, LO9

19. A city issues a 60-day tax anticipation note to fund operations. What recording should it make?

    a. The liability should be reported in the government-wide financial statements; an other financing source should be shown in the fund-based financial statements.

    b. A liability should be reported in the government-wide financial statements and in the fund-based financial statements.

    c. An other financing source should be shown in the government-wide financial statements and in the fund-based financial statements.

    d. An other financing source should be shown in the government-wide financial statements; a liability is reported in the fund-based financial statements.

LO5, LO9

20. A city issues five-year bonds payable to finance construction of a new school. What recording should be made?

    a. Report the liability in the government-wide financial statements; show an other financing source in the fund-based financial statements.

    b. Report a liability in the government-wide financial statements and in the fund-based financial statements.

    c. Show an other financing source in the government-wide financial statements and in the fund-based financial statements.

    d. Show an other financing source in the government-wide financial statements; report a liability in the fund-based financial statements.

LO2, LO9

21. A $110,000 payment is made on a long-term liability. Of this amount, $10,000 represents interest. Which of the following is *not* true?

    a. Reduce liabilities by $100,000 in the government-wide financial statements.

    b. Record a $110,000 expenditure in the fund-based financial statements.

    c. Reduce liabilities by $100,000 in the fund-based financial statements.

    d. Recognize $10,000 interest expense in the government-wide financial statements.

LO1, LO9

22. A city constructs a special assessment project (a sidewalk) for which it is secondarily liable. The city issues bonds of $90,000. It authorizes another $10,000 that is transferred out of the General Fund. The sidewalk is built for $100,000. The citizens are billed for $90,000. They pay this amount and the debt is paid off. Where is the $100,000 expenditure for construction recorded?

    a. It is not recorded by the city.

    b. It is recorded in the Agency Fund.

    c. It is recorded in the General Fund.

    d. It is recorded in the Capital Projects Fund.

LO4, LO9

23. A city constructs curbing in a new neighborhood and finances it as a special assessment. Under what condition should this activity be recorded in the Agency Fund?
    a. Never; the work is reported in the Capital Projects Funds.
    b. Only if the city is secondarily liable for any debt incurred to finance construction costs.
    c. Only if the city is in no way liable for the costs of the construction.
    d. In all cases.

LO10

24. Which of the following is an example of an interactivity transaction?
    a. Money is transferred from the General Fund to the Debt Service Fund.
    b. Money is transferred from the Capital Projects Fund to the General Fund.
    c. Money is transferred from the Special Revenue Fund to the Debt Service Fund.
    d. Money is transferred from the General Fund to the Enterprise Fund.

LO5, LO10

25. Cash of $60,000 is transferred from the General Fund to the Debt Service Fund. What is reported on the government-wide financial statements?
    a. No reporting is made.
    b. Other Financing Sources increase by $60,000; Other Financing Uses increase by $60,000.
    c. Revenues increase by $60,000; Expenditures increase by $60,000.
    d. Revenues increase by $60,000; Expenses increase by $60,000.

LO5, LO10

26. Cash of $60,000 is transferred from the General Fund to the Debt Service Fund. What is reported on the fund-based financial statements?
    a. No reporting is made.
    b. Other Financing Sources increase by $60,000; Other Financing Uses increase by $60,000.
    c. Revenues increase by $60,000; Expenditures increase by $60,000.
    d. Revenues increase by $60,000; Expenses increase by $60,000.

LO5, LO10

27. Cash of $20,000 is transferred from the General Fund to the Enterprise Fund to pay for work that was done. What is reported on the government-wide financial statements?
    a. No reporting is made.
    b. Other Financing Sources increase by $20,000; Other Financing Uses increase by $20,000.
    c. Revenues increase by $20,000; Expenditures increase by $20,000.
    d. Revenues increase by $20,000; Expenses increase by $20,000.

LO5, LO10

28. Cash of $20,000 is transferred from the General Fund to the Enterprise Fund to pay for work that was done. What is reported on the fund-based financial statements?
    a. No reporting is made.
    b. Other Financing Sources increase by $20,000; Other Financing Uses increase by $20,000.
    c. Revenues increase by $20,000; Expenditures increase by $20,000.
    d. Revenues increase by $20,000; Expenses increase by $20,000.

LO3, LO6

29. The board of commissioners of the City of Hartmoore adopted a General Fund budget for the year ending June 30, 2010, that included revenues of $1,000,000, bond proceeds of $400,000, appropriations of $900,000, and operating transfers out of $300,000. If this budget is formally integrated into the accounting records, what journal entry is required at the beginning of the year? What later entry is required?

LO2, LO6, LO7

30. A city orders a new computer for its General Fund at an anticipated cost of $88,000. Its actual cost when received is $89,400. Payment is subsequently made. Give all required journal entries for fund-based and government-wide financial statements. What information do the government-wide financial statements present? What information do the fund-based financial statements present?

LO1, LO2, LO7

31. Cash of $90,000 is transferred from a city's General Fund to start construction on a police station. The city issues a bond at its $1.8 million face value. The police station is built for $1.89 million. Prepare all necessary journal entries for these transactions for fund-based and government-wide financial statements. Assume that the city does not record the commitment. What information do the government-wide financial statements present? What information do the fund-based financial statements present?

LO2, LO5–LO10

e**X**cel

32. A local government has the following transactions during the current fiscal period. Prepare journal entries without dollar amounts, first for fund-based financial statements and then for government-wide financial statements.
    a. The budget for the police department, ambulance service, and other ongoing activities is passed. Funding is from property taxes, transfers, and bond proceeds. All monetary outflows will be for expenses and fixed assets. A deficit is projected.
    b. A bond is issued at face value to fund the construction of a new municipal building.

c. A computer is ordered for the tax department.

d. The computer is received.

e. The invoice for the computer is paid.

f. The city council agrees to transfer money from the General Fund as partial payment for a special assessments project but has not done so. The city will be secondarily liable for any money borrowed for this work.

g. The city council creates a motor pool to service all government vehicles. Money is transferred from the General Fund to permanently finance this facility.

h. Property taxes are levied. Although officials believe that most of these taxes should be collected during the current period, a small percentage is estimated to be uncollectible.

i. The city collects grant money from the state that must be spent as a supplement to the salaries of the police force. No entry has been recorded.

j. A portion of the grant money in (i) is properly spent.

LO2, LO4, LO7, LO8, LO10

33. Prepare journal entries for the City of Pudding's governmental funds to record the following transactions, first for fund-based financial statements and then for government-wide financial statements.

a. A new truck for the sanitation department was ordered at a cost of $94,000.

b. The city print shop did $1,200 worth of work for the school system (but has not yet been paid).

c. An $11 million bond was issued to build a new road.

d. Cash of $140,000 is transferred from the General Fund to provide permanent financing for a municipal swimming pool that will be viewed as an Enterprise Fund.

e. The truck ordered in (a) is received at an actual cost of $96,000. Payment is not made at this time.

f. Cash of $32,000 is transferred from the General Fund to the Capital Projects Fund.

g. A state grant of $30,000 is received that must be spent to promote recycling.

h. The first $5,000 of the state grant received in (g) is appropriately expended.

LO2, LO5, LO7–LO10

34. Prepare journal entries for a local government to record the following transactions, first for fund-based financial statements and then for government-wide financial statements.

a. The government sells $900,000 in bonds at face value to finance construction of a warehouse.

b. A $1.1 million contract is signed for construction of the warehouse.

c. A $130,000 transfer of unrestricted funds was made for the eventual payment of the debt in (a).

d. Equipment for the fire department is received with a cost of $12,000. When it was ordered, an anticipated cost of $11,800 had been recorded.

e. Supplies to be used in the schools are bought for $2,000 cash. The consumption method is used.

f. A state grant of $90,000 is awarded to supplement police salaries. The money will be paid to reimburse the government after the supplements have been paid to the police officers.

g. Property tax assessments are mailed to citizens of the government. The total assessment is $600,000, although officials anticipate that 4 percent will never be collected. There is an enforceable legal claim for this money and the government can use it immediately.

LO4–LO10

35. The following trial balances are for the governmental funds of the City of Copeland prepared from the current accounting records:

General Fund

	Debit	Credit
Cash	$ 19,000	
Taxes Receivable	202,000	
Allowance for Uncollectible Taxes		$ 2,000
Vouchers Payable		24,000
Due to Debt Service Fund		10,000
Deferred Revenues		16,000
Fund Balance—Reserved for Encumbrances		9,000
Fund Balance—Unassigned		103,000
Revenues Control		176,000
Expenditures Control	110,000	
Encumbrances Control	9,000	
Estimated Revenues Control	190,000	
Appropriations Control		171,000
Budgetary Fund Balance		19,000
Totals	$530,000	$530,000

Debt Service Fund

	Debit	Credit
Cash	$ 8,000	
Investments	51,000	
Taxes Receivable	11,000	
Due from General Fund	10,000	
Fund Balance—Committed		$ 45,000
Revenues Control		20,000
Other Financing Sources—Operating Transfers In		90,000
Expenditures Control	75,000	
Totals	$155,000	$155,000

Capital Projects Fund

	Debit	Credit
Cash	$ 70,000	
Special Assessments Receivable	90,000	
Contracts Payable		$ 50,000
Deferred Revenues		90,000
Fund Balance—Reserved for Encumbrances		16,000
Fund Balance—Unassigned		—0—
Other Financing Sources		150,000
Expenditures Control	130,000	
Encumbrances	16,000	
Estimated Other Financing Sources	150,000	
Appropriations		150,000
Totals	$456,000	$456,000

Special Revenue Fund

	Debit	Credit
Cash	$ 14,000	
Taxes Receivable	41,000	
Inventory of Supplies	4,000	
Vouchers Payable		$ 25,000
Deferred Revenues		3,000
Fund Balance—Nonspendable		4,000
Fund Balance—Reserved for Encumbrances		3,000
Fund Balance—Unreserved, Undesignated		19,000
Revenues Control		56,000
Expenditures Control	48,000	
Encumbrances	3,000	
Estimated Revenues	75,000	
Appropriations		60,000
Budgetary Fund Balance		15,000
Totals	$185,000	$185,000

Based on the information presented for each of these governmental funds, answer the following questions:

a. How much more money can city officials expend or commit from the General Fund during the remainder of the current year?

b. Why does the Capital Projects Fund have no construction or capital asset accounts?

c. What does the $150,000 Appropriations balance found in the Capital Projects Fund represent?

d. Several funds have balances for Encumbrances and Fund Balance—Reserved for Encumbrances. How will these amounts be accounted for at the end of the fiscal year?

e. Why does the Fund Balance—Unassigned account in the Capital Projects Fund have a zero balance?

f. What are possible explanations for the $150,000 Other Financing Sources balance found in the Capital Projects Fund?

g. What does the $75,000 balance in the Expenditures Control account of the Debt Service Fund represent?

h. What is the purpose of the Special Assessments Receivable found in the Capital Projects Fund?

i. In the Special Revenue Fund, what is the purpose of the Fund Balance—Nonspendable account?

j. Why does the Debt Service Fund not have budgetary account balances?

LO2–LO10

36. Following are descriptions of transactions and other financial events for the City of Tetris for the year ending December 2010. Not all transactions have been included here. Only the General Fund formally records a budget. No encumbrances were carried over from 2009.

Paid salary for police officers	$ 21,000
Received government grant to pay ambulance drivers	40,000
Estimated revenues	232,000
Received invoices for rent on equipment used by fire department during last four months of the year	3,000
Paid for newly constructed city hall	1,044,000
Made commitment to acquire ambulance	111,000
Received cash from bonds sold for construction purposes	300,000
Placed order for new sanitation truck	154,000
Paid salary to ambulance drivers—money derived from state government grant given for that purpose	24,000
Paid for supplies for school system	16,000
Made transfer from General Fund to eventually pay off a long-term debt	33,000
Received but did not pay for new ambulance	120,000
Levied property tax receivables for 2010. City anticipates that 95 percent ($190,000) will be collected during the year and 5 percent will be uncollectible	200,000
Acquired and paid for new school bus	40,000
Received cash from business licenses and parking meters (not previously accrued)	14,000
Made appropriations	225,000

The following questions are *independent* although each is based on the preceding information. Assume that the government is preparing information for its fund-based financial statements.

a. What is the balance in the Budgetary Fund Balance account for the budget for the year? Is it a debit or credit?

b. Assume that 60 percent of the school supplies are used during the year so that 40 percent remain. If the consumption method is being applied, how is this recorded?

c. The sanitation truck that was ordered was not received before the end of the year. The commitment will be honored in the subsequent year when the truck arrives. What reporting is made at the end of 2010?

d. Assume that the ambulance was received on December 31, 2010. Provide all necessary journal entries on that date.

e. Give all journal entries that should have been made when the $33,000 transfer was made to eventually pay off a long-term debt.

f. What amount of revenue would be recognized for the period? Explain the composition of this total.

g. What are the total expenditures? Explain the makeup of this total. Include (*b*) here.

h. What journal entry or entries were prepared when the bonds were issued?

LO2–LO10

37. Chesterfield County had the following transactions. Prepare the entries first for fund-based financial statements and then for government-wide financial statements.

a. A budget is passed for all ongoing activities. Revenue is anticipated to be $834,000 with approved spending of $540,000 and operating transfers out of $242,000.

b. A contract is signed with a construction company to build a new central office building for the government at a cost of $8 million. A budget for this project has previously been recorded.

c. Bonds are sold for $8 million (face value) to finance construction of the new office building.

d. The new building is completed. An invoice for $8 million is received and paid.

e. Previously unrestricted cash of $1 million is set aside to begin paying the bonds issued in (*c*).

f. A portion of the bonds comes due and $1 million is paid. Of this total, $100,000 represents interest. The interest had not been previously accrued.

g. Citizens' property tax levies are assessed. Total billing for this tax is $800,000. On this date, the assessment is a legally enforceable claim according to the laws of this state. The money to be received is designated for the current period and 90 percent is assumed to be collectible in this period with receipt of an additional 6 percent during subsequent periods but in time to be available to pay current period claims. The remainder is expected to be uncollectible.

h. Cash of $120,000 is received from a toll road. This money is restricted for highway maintenance.

i. The county received investments valued at $300,000 as a donation from a grateful citizen. Income from these investments must be used to beautify local parks.

LO5

eXcel

38. The following trial balance is taken from the General Fund of the City of Jennings for the year ending December 31, 2010. Prepare a condensed statement of revenues, expenditures, and other changes in fund balance and also prepare a condensed balance sheet.

	Debit	Credit
Accounts Payable		$ 90,000
Cash	$ 30,000	
Contracts Payable		90,000
Deferred Revenues		40,000
Due from Capital Projects Funds	60,000	
Due to Debt Service Funds		40,000
Expenditures	510,000	
Fund Balance—Unassigned		170,000
Investments	410,000	
Revenues		740,000
Other Financing Sources—Bond Proceeds		300,000
Other Financing Sources—Transfers In		50,000
Other Financing Uses—Transfers Out	470,000	
Taxes Receivable	220,000	
Vouchers Payable		180,000
Totals	$1,700,000	$1,700,000

LO2, LO5–LO10

39. A city has only one activity, its school system. The school system is accounted for within the General Fund. For convenience, assume that, at the start of 2010, the school system and the city have no assets. During the year, the city assessed $400,000 in property taxes. Of this amount, it collected $320,000 during the year, received $50,000 within a few weeks after the end of the year, and expected the remainder to be collected about six months later. The city makes the following payments during 2010: salary expense, $100,000; rent expense, $70,000; equipment (received on January 1 with a five-year life and no salvage value), $50,000; land, $30,000; and maintenance expense, $20,000. In addition, on the last day of the year, the city purchased a $200,000 building by signing a long-term liability. The building has a 20-year life and no salvage value, and the liability accrues interest at a 10 percent annual rate. The city also buys two computers on the last day of the year for $4,000 each. One will be paid for in 30 days and the other in 90 days. The computers should last for four years and have no salvage value. During the year, the school system charged students $3,000 for school fees and collected the entire amount. Any depreciation is recorded using the straight-line method.

a. Produce a statement of net assets and a statement of activities for this city's government-wide financial statements.

b. Produce a balance sheet and a statement of revenues, expenditures, and changes in fund balance for the fund-based financial statements. Assume that *available* is defined by the city as anything to be received within 60 days.

LO5, LO7–LO10

40. The following transactions relate to the General Fund of the city of Lost Angel for the year ending December 31, 2010. Prepare a statement of revenues, expenditures, and other changes in fund balance for the General Fund for the period to be included in the fund-based financial statements. Assume that the fund balance at the beginning of the year was $180,000. Assume also that the purchases method is applied to the supplies and that receipt within 60 days is used as the definition of available resources.

a. Collected property tax revenue of $700,000. A remaining assessment of $100,000 will be collected in the subsequent period. Half of that amount should be collected within 30 days, and the remainder will be received in about five months after the end of the year.

b. Spent $200,000 on four new police cars with 10-year lives. A price of $207,000 had been anticipated when the cars were ordered. The city calculates all depreciation using the straight-line method with no salvage value. The half-year convention is used.

   c. Transferred $90,000 to a debt service fund.

   d. Issued a long-term bond for $200,000 on July 1. Interest at a 10 percent annual rate will be paid each year starting on June 30, 2011.

   e. Ordered a new computer with a five-year life for $40,000.

   f. Paid salaries of $30,000. Another $10,000 will be owed at the end of the year but will not be paid for 30 days.

   g. Received the new computer but at a cost of $41,000; payment to be made in 45 days.

   h. Bought supplies for $10,000 in cash.

   i. Used $8,000 of the supplies in (h).

LO5, LO7–LO10

41. Use the transactions in problem 40 but prepare a statement of net assets for the government-wide financial statements. Assume that the General Fund had $180,000 in cash on the first day of the year and no other assets or liabilities. No amount was restricted, committed, or assigned.

LO1, LO6

42. Government officials of the City of Jones expect to receive General Fund revenues of $400,000 in 2010 but approve spending only $380,000. Later in the year, as they receive more information, they increase the revenue projection to $420,000. Officials approve the spending of an additional $15,000. For each of the following, indicate whether the statement is true or false and, if false, explain why.

   a. In recording this budget, appropriations should be credited initially for $380,000.

   b. The city must disclose this budgetary data within the required supplemental information section reported after the notes to the financial statements.

   c. When reporting budgetary information for the year, three figures should be reported: amended budget, initial budget, and actual figures.

   d. In making the budgetary entry, a debit must be made to some type of Fund Balance account to indicate the projected surplus.

   e. The reporting of the budget is reflected in the government-wide financial statements.

LO8

43. On December 1, 2010, a state government awards a city government a grant of $1 million to be used specifically to provide hot lunches for all schoolchildren. No money is received until June 1, 2011. For each of the following, indicate whether the statement is true or false and, if false, explain why.

   a. Because the government received no money until June 1, 2011, no amount of revenue can be recognized in 2010 on the government-wide financial statements.

   b. If this grant has no eligibility requirements and the money is properly spent in September 2011 for the hot lunches, the revenue should be recognized during that September.

   c. Because the money came from the state government and because the government specified the use, this is a government-mandated nonexchange transaction.

   d. If the government had received the money on December 1, 2010, but eligibility requirements had not been met yet, a deferred revenue of $1 million would have been recognized on the government-wide financial statements.

   e. The rules for recognition of this revenue were created by GASB *Statement 34*.

LO2, LO5, LO7–LO10

44. Indicate (i) how each of the following transactions impacts the fund balance of the General Fund, and its classifications, for fund-based financial statements and (ii) what the impact is on the net asset balance of the governmental funds for government-wide financial statements.

   a. Issue a five-year bond for $6 million to finance general operations.

   b. Pay cash of $149,000 for a truck to be used by the police department.

   c. The fire department pays $17,000 to a government motor pool that services the vehicles of only the police and fire departments.

   d. Levy property taxes of $75,000 for the current year that will not be collected until four months into the subsequent year.

   e. Receive a grant for $7,000 that must be returned unless the money is spent according to the stipulations of the conveyance.

   f. Make sales of $20 million during the current year. The government charges a 5 percent sales tax. Half of this amount is to be collected 10 days after the end of the year with the remainder to be collected 10 weeks after the end of the year. "Available" has been defined by this government as 75 days.

   g. Order a computer for the school system at an anticipated cost of $23,000.

   h. A cash transfer of $18,000 is approved from the General Fund to a Capital Projects Fund.

LO4, LO5, LO10

45. Fund A transfers $20,000 to Fund B. For each of the following, indicate whether the statement is true or false and, if false, explain why.

 a. If Fund A is the General Fund and Fund B is an Enterprise Fund, nothing will be shown for this transfer on the statement of activities within the government-wide financial statements.

 b. If Fund A is the General Fund and Fund B is a Debt Service Fund, nothing will be shown for this transfer on the statement of activities within the government-wide financial statements.

 c. If Fund A is the General Fund and Fund B is an Enterprise Fund, a $20,000 reduction will be reported on the statement of revenues, expenditures, and other changes for the governmental funds within the fund-based financial statements.

 d. If Fund A is the General Fund and Fund B is a Special Revenue Fund (which is not considered a major fund), no changes will be shown on the statement of revenues, expenditures, and other changes within the fund-based financial statements.

 e. If Fund A is the General Fund and Fund B is an Internal Service Fund and this is for work done, the General Fund will report an expense of $20,000 within the fund-based financial statements.

Use the following information for Problems 46–52:

Assume that the City of Coyote has already produced its financial statements for December 31, 2010, and the year then ended. The city's General Fund was only for education and parks. Its Capital Projects Funds worked with each of these functions at times. The city also had established an Enterprise Fund to account for its art museum.

The government-wide financial statements indicated the following figures:

- Education reported net expenses of $600,000.
- Parks reported net expenses of $100,000.
- Art museum reported net revenues of $50,000.
- General government revenues for the year were $800,000 with an overall increase in the city's net assets of $150,000.

The fund-based financial statements indicated the following for the entire year:

- The General Fund reported a $30,000 increase in its fund balance.
- The Capital Projects Fund reported a $40,000 increase in its fund balance.
- The Enterprise Fund reported a $60,000 increase in its net assets.

The CPA firm of Abernethy and Chapman has been asked to review several transactions that occurred during 2010 and indicate how to correct any erroneous reporting and the impact of each error. View each situation as *independent*.

LO2, LO5, LO9

46. During 2010, the City of Coyote contracted to build a sidewalk costing $10,000 as a special assessments project for which it collected $10,000 from affected citizens. The government had no obligation in connection with this project. Both a $10,000 revenue and a $10,000 expenditure were recorded in the Capital Projects Fund. In preparing government-wide financial statements, an asset and a general revenue were recorded for $10,000.

 a. In the general information, the Capital Projects Fund reported a $ 40,000 increase in its fund balance. What was the correct overall change in the Capital Projects Fund's balance during 2010?

 b. In the general information, a $150,000 overall increase in the city's net assets was found on the government-wide financial statements. What was the correct overall change in the city's net assets on the government-wide financial statements?

LO9

47. On December 30, 2010, the City of Coyote borrowed $20,000 for the General Fund on a 60-day note. In that fund, both Cash and Other Financing Sources were recorded. In the general information, a $30,000 overall increase was reported in the General Fund balance. What was the correct change in the General Fund's balance for 2010?

LO2, LO4, LO5

48. An art display set up for the community was recorded within the General Fund and generated revenues of $9,000 but had expenditures of $45,000 ($15,000 in expenses and $30,000 to buy land for the display). The CPA firm has determined that this program should have been recorded as an Enterprise Fund activity because it was offered in association with the art museum.

 a. What was the correct change in the General Fund's balance for 2010?

 b. What was the correct overall change in the city's net assets on the government-wide financial statements?

 c. What was the correct change in the net assets of the Enterprise Fund on the fund-based financial statements?

LO2, LO5, LO8

49. The City of Coyote mailed property tax bills for 2011 to its citizens during August 2010. Payments could be made early to receive a discount. The levy becomes legally enforceable on February 15, 2011. All money received must be spent during 2011 or later. The total assessment is $300,000; 40 percent of that amount, less a 10 percent discount, is collected in 2010. The city expects to receive all of the remaining money during 2011 with no discount. During 2010, the government increased cash as well as a revenue for the amount received. No change was made in creating the government-wide financial statements.

   a. What was the correct overall change in the city's net assets as shown on the government-wide financial statements?

   b. What was the correct change for 2010 in the fund balance reported in the General Fund?

LO2, LO5, LO8

50. The City of Coyote mailed property tax bills for 2011 to its citizens during August 2010. Payments could be made early to receive a discount. The levy becomes legally enforceable on February 15, 2011. All money received must be spent during 2011 or later. The total assessment is $300,000, and 40 percent of that amount is collected in 2010 less a 10 percent discount. The city expects to receive all the rest of the money during 2011 with no discount. During 2010, the government increased cash and a revenue for the amount received. In addition, a receivable account and a deferred revenue account for $180,000 were recognized.

   a. In the general information, an overall increase in the city's net assets of $150,000 was found on the government-wide financial statements. What was the correct overall change in the city's net assets as reported on the government-wide financial statements?

   b. In the general information, an overall increase of $30,000 was reported in the General Fund balance. What was the correct change during 2010 in the General Fund's balance?

LO2, LO5, LO7, LO8

51. In 2010, the City of Coyote received a $320,000 cash grant from the state to stop air pollution. Assume that although a special revenue fund could have been set up, the money remained in the General Fund. Cash was received immediately but had to be returned if the city had not lowered air pollution by 25 percent by 2013. On December 31, 2010, Coyote spent $210,000 of this money for a large machine to help begin to reduce pollution. The machine is expected to last for five years and was recorded as an expenditure in the General Fund and as an asset on the government-wide financial statements where it was depreciated based on the straight-line method and the half-year convention. Because the money had been received, all $320,000 was recorded as a revenue on both the fund-based and the government-wide financial statements.

   a. What was the correct change for 2010 in the General Fund's balance?

   b. What was the correct overall change in the net assets reported on the government-wide financial statements?

LO2

52. During 2010, the City of Coyote's General Fund received $10,000, which was recorded as a general revenue when it was actually a program revenue earned by its park program.

   a. What was the correct overall change for 2010 in the net assets reported on the government-wide financial statements?

   b. In the general information, the parks reported net expenses for the period of $100,000. What was the correct amount of net expenses reported by the parks?

Develop Your Skills

RESEARCH CASE 1

The City of Hampshore is currently preparing financial statements for the past fiscal year. The city manager is concerned because the city encountered some unusual transactions during the current fiscal period and is unsure as to their handling.

Required

Use a copy of GASB *Statement 34* to answer each of the following questions.

1. For government accounting, what is the definition of *extraordinary item?*

2. For government accounting, what is the definition of *special item?*

3. On government-wide financial statements, how should extraordinary items and special items be reported?

RESEARCH CASE 2

The City of Danmark is preparing financial statements. Officials are currently working on the statement of activities within the government-wide financial statements. A question has arisen as to whether a particular revenue should be identified on government-wide statements as a program revenue or a general revenue.

Required

Use a copy of GASB *Statement 34* to answer each of the following questions.

1. How is a program revenue defined?
2. What are common examples of program revenues?
3. How is a general revenue defined?
4. What are common examples of general revenues?

ANALYSIS CASE 1

Search the Internet for the official Web site of one or more state or local governments. After reviewing this Web site, determine whether the latest comprehensive annual financial report (CAFR) is available on the site. For example, the most recent comprehensive annual financial report for the City of Sacramento can be found at www.cityofsacramento.org/cafr/ and the comprehensive annual financial report for the City of Phoenix can be found at http://phoenix.gov/menu/cityfinfinance.html. Use the financial statements that you locate to answer the following questions.

Required

1. How does the audit opinion given to this city by its independent auditors differ from the audit opinion rendered on the financial statements for a for-profit business?
2. A reconciliation should be presented to explain the difference between the net changes in fund balances for the governmental funds (fund-based financial statements) and the change in net assets for the governmental activities (government-wide financial statements). What were several of the largest reasons for the difference?
3. What were the city's largest sources of general revenues?
4. What was the total amount of expenditures recorded by the General Fund during the period? How were those expenditures classified?
5. What assets are reported for the General Fund?
6. Review the notes to the financial statements and then determine the number of days the government uses to define the end-of-year financial resources that are viewed as currently available.
7. Did the size of the General Fund balance increase or decrease during the most recent year and by how much?

ANALYSIS CASE 2

Go to the Web site www.gasb.org and scroll down to the topic "Exposure Drafts." Review any exposure drafts currently being considered by the GASB.

Required

Identify the major impacts that the proposed changes would create in government accounting.

COMMUNICATION CASE 1

Go to the Web site www.gasb.org and click on "Strategic Plan" within the left column. Click on "Full Strategic Plan." Read the vision, mission, core values, and goals of GASB.

Required

Assume that a financial analyst with whom you are working is interested in knowing more about the purpose of GASB. Write a short memo explaining the work of GASB based on its vision, mission, core values, and goals.

COMMUNICATION CASE 2

Obtain a copy of GASB *Statement 34*. Read paragraphs 239 through 277.

Required

Write a report describing alternatives that the GASB considered when it created *Statement 34*. Indicate the alternative that you would have viewed as most appropriate, and describe why the GASB did not choose it.

COMMUNICATION CASE 3

Search the Internet for the official Web site of one or more state or local governments. After reviewing this Web site, determine whether the latest comprehensive annual financial report (CAFR) is available on the site. For example, a recent comprehensive annual financial report for the City of Minneapolis can be found at www.ci.minneapolis.mn.us/financial-reports/ and for the City of Tallahassee, Florida, can be found at http://www.talgov.com/dma/accounting/annualrprts.cfm. Read the Management's Discussion and Analysis (MD&A) that should be located near the beginning of the annual report.

Required

Write a memo to explain four or five of the most interesting pieces of information that the Management's Discussion and Analysis provides.

EXCEL CASE

The City of Bainland has been undergoing financial difficulties because of a decrease in its tax base caused by corporations leaving the area. On January 1, 2010, the city has a fund balance of only $400,000 in its governmental funds. In 2009, the city had revenues of $1.4 million and expenditures of $1.48 million. The city's treasurer has forecast that, unless something is done, revenues will decrease at 2 percent per year while expenditures will increase at 3 percent per year.

Required

1. Create a spreadsheet to predict in what year the government will have a zero fund balance.
2. One proposal is that the city slash its expenditures by laying off government workers. That will lead to a 3 percent decrease in expenditures each year rather than a 3 percent increase. However, because of the unemployment, the city will receive less tax revenue. Thus, instead of a 2 percent decrease in revenues, the city expects a 5 percent decrease per year. Adapt the spreadsheet created in requirement (1) to predict what year the government will have a zero fund balance if this option is taken.
3. Another proposal is to increase spending to draw new businesses to the area. This action will lead to a 7 percent increase in expenditures every year, but revenues are expected to rise by 4 percent per year. Adapt the spreadsheet created in requirement (1) to predict what year the government will have a zero fund balance under this option.

Accounting for State and Local Governments (Part 2)

The previous chapter introduced many of the unique aspects of financial reporting applicable to state and local governments. Fund accounting, encumbrances, expenditures, revenue recognition, the issuance of bonds, and the like in connection with both traditional fund-based financial statements and the newer government-wide financial statements were all presented and analyzed. This initial coverage was designed to explain the rationale underlying the accounting required of these government entities, especially the differences caused by the dual nature of the financial reporting process.

The current chapter carries this analysis further, first by delving into more complex financial situations. Many state and local government units are quite large and face numerous transactions as complicated as any a for-profit business encounters. This chapter examines issues such as capital leases, solid waste landfills, donated artworks, and the depreciation of infrastructure assets to broaden the scope of understanding of state and local government accounting.

Second, the chapter discusses the overall financial reporting model. Within this coverage, the actual composition of a government is examined. Because of the wide variety of agencies and other activities that operate in connection with a government, determining inclusion within the financial statements is not as easy as in a for-profit business where ownership of more than 50 percent of the voting stock is the primary criterion.

CAPITAL LEASES

Notes to the 2008 financial statements of the City and County of Denver, Colorado, describe the government in the role of *lessee:*

> The governmental activity capital leases are for various properties including the Wellington Webb Municipal Office Building, 2000 West Third Avenue, the Blair-Caldwell Research Library, the Buell Theatre, the 5440 Roslyn maintenance facility property, a jail dorm building, three fire stations, and portions of three parking garages. The capital leases also include certain

LEARNING OBJECTIVES

After studying this chapter, you should be able to:

LO1   Account for lease contracts where the state or local government finds itself as either lessor or lessee.

LO2   Recognize the liability caused by the eventual closure and postclosure costs of operating a solid waste landfill as well as for the compensated absences earned by government employees.

LO3   Record the donation and acquisition of works of art and historical treasures.

LO4   Explain the reporting and possible depreciation of infrastructure assets.

LO5   Understand the composition of a state or local government's comprehensive annual financial report (CAFR).

LO6   Explain the makeup of a primary government and its relationship to component units.

LO7   Understand the physical structure of a complete set of government-wide financial statements and a complete set of fund-based financial statements.

LO8   Prepare financial statements for a public college or university.

LO1

Account for lease contracts where the state or local government finds itself as either lessor or lessee.

computer and safety equipment, the Figaro simultext system, snow plows, street sweepers, and a production press. The Water Board leases are for 40 percent of the storage capacity and 40 percent of the water rights of Ritschard Dam and Wolford Mountain Reservoir, and leases of certain facilities. The City currently leases two City Park parking structures, adjacent to the Denver Museum of Nature and Sciences (DMNS) and the Denver Zoo, from Denver Capital Leasing Corporation (DCLC).

In contrast, the notes to the 2008 financial statements of the City of Dallas, Texas, describe the government as a *lessor:*

> The City is also under several lease agreements as lessor whereby it receives revenues from leasing airport terminal space, hangars, parking spaces, ramps, land, buildings, and office space to air carriers and other tenants. These revenue leases are considered for accounting purposes to be operating leases.

Obviously, state and local governments (in the same manner as for-profit businesses) sometimes lease property rather than purchasing it directly. Leasing can provide lower interest rates or reduce the risk of obsolescence and damage. Leasing is simply an efficient way that many organizations (for-profit or governmental) can acquire needed equipment, machinery, buildings, or other assets. At the same time, like the City of Dallas, a government can find itself in the position of lessor. This is particularly true when the city or state holds property that it prefers not to operate itself.

For reporting purposes, such leases must be recorded as either capital leases or operating leases. The initial accounting issue is to separate one type from another. In that regard, GASB has accepted the criteria applied by FASB [FASB ASC (Subtopic 840-30)] as the method of differentiation. A lease that meets any one of four criteria is classified as a capital lease. If none are met, it is an operating lease.

1. The lease transfers ownership of the property to the lessee by the end of the lease term.
2. The lease contains an option to purchase the leased property at a bargain price.
3. The lease term is equal to or more than 75 percent of the estimated economic life of the leased property.
4. The present value of rental or other minimum lease payments equals or exceeds 90 percent of the fair value of the leased property.

For example, assume that a city leases a truck that has a 10-year expected life and a fair value of $50,000. In each of these four sample situations, the city is required to account for the property as a capital lease:

- The lease is for six years, but the city automatically receives title to the truck at the end of that term (so that criterion 1 is met).
- The lease is for five years, but the city can buy the truck for $3,000 at the end of that time, an amount that is viewed as significantly less than the expected fair value at that point (so that criterion 2 is met).
- The lease is for eight years, after which time the truck will be returned to the lessor (so that criterion 3 is met).
- The lease is for seven years, but the present value of the minimum lease payments is equal to or more than $45,000, or 90 percent of the fair value (so that criterion 4 is met). In this last example, the lessee is viewed as paying the equivalent of the purchase price to obtain use of the asset.

Leases—Government-Wide Financial Statements

In reporting property obtained by capital lease, accounting used in constructing the government-wide financial statements is identical to that of a for-profit enterprise. The government-wide statements report both an asset and a liability, initially at the present value of the minimum lease payments, in the same manner as the accounting for a debt-financed acquisition. Assume, for example, that a police department signs an 8-year lease on January 1, Year 1, for a truck with a 10-year estimated life. Because this contract meets the third of the preceding criteria, the transaction must be recorded as a capital lease.

Assume that the lease calls for annual payments of $10,000 per year with the first payment made at the signing of the lease and that a 10 percent annual interest rate is appropriate for the city. The present value of the minimum lease payments applying a 10 percent annual interest rate to an annuity due for eight years is $58,680 (rounded). The city makes the following entries within the governmental activities because the lease relates to the police department (part of the General Fund). However, the same reporting is appropriate within the business-type activities if an enterprise fund had been involved. As indicated in the previous chapter, no accounting distinction between the two types of activities is drawn.

Government-Wide Financial Statements—Capital Lease, Government as Lessee

January 1, Year 1		
Truck—Capital Lease	58,680	
Capital Lease Obligation		58,680
To record capital lease.		
Capital Lease Obligation	10,000	
Cash		10,000
To record first payment on leased truck.		

Assuming that the straight-line method is being used, the city should recognize depreciation expense of $7,335 ($58,680/8 years) at the end of each year. However, if the title to the asset will be transferred to the city or if a bargain purchase option exists, the full 10-year life is appropriate for depreciation purposes because the lessee (the city) expects to get full use of the asset.

At the end of the first year, when the city makes the next payment, part of that $10,000 will be attributed to interest with the remainder viewed as a reduction in the liability principal. Because the first payment reduced the obligation to $48,680 and the interest rate is 10 percent, the interest recorded for the first year is $4,868. The remaining $5,132 ($10,000 less $4,868) decreases the debt to $43,548.

Government-Wide Financial Statements—Capital Lease, Year-End Entries

December 31, Year 1		
Depreciation Expense	7,335	
Accumulated Depreciation—Leased Truck		7,335
To record depreciation of leased truck for first year of use.		
Interest Expense	4,868	
Capital Lease Obligation	5,132	
Cash		10,000
To record payment on capital lease at end of first year.		

Leases—Fund-Based Financial Statements

Assume that the same truck lease is being recorded in the fund-based financial statements for the governmental funds. If a proprietary fund is involved, the handling is the same as in the preceding situation. A difference appears only for the governmental funds.

Using the same eight-year lease in connection with the truck being obtained and payments of $10,000 per year, an amount with a present value of $58,680, the General Fund (or whichever governmental fund is gaining use of the asset) records the following entry:

Fund-Based Financial Statements—Capital Lease, Government as Lessee

January 1, Year 1 **General Fund**		
Expenditures—Leased Asset	58,680	
Other Financing Sources—Capital Lease		58,680
To record signing of an eight-year lease for a truck that meets the requirements of a capital lease.		

Expenditures—Lease Principal	10,000	
Cash		10,000
To record first payment on leased truck.		

Note that the General Fund reports neither the capital asset nor the long-term liability. They are not current financial resources nor are they claims to current financial resources. At the end of this initial year, when the next payment is made, $4,868 (10 percent of the obligation after the first payment) is considered interest; the rest reduces the principal. Depreciation is ignored.

Fund-Based Financial Statements—Capital Lease, Year-End Entries

December 31, Year 1		
General Fund		
Expenditures—Interest	4,868	
Expenditures—Lease Principal	5,132	
Cash		10,000
To record payment at the end of first year on leased truck recorded as a capital lease.		

At first glance, the fund-based journal entries appear to be double counting the expenditures, once when the asset is obtained and again when the periodic payments are made. This approach, though, is consistent with government accounting. The government had an option; it could have either leased the asset or borrowed money and bought the asset. Because the overall result is the same in both cases, the reporting process should not create different pictures.

The preceding entries seek to mirror the presentation that results in the fund-based statements if the city follows the alternative strategy for acquiring the asset: (1) borrowed money on a long-term liability, (2) used the money to acquire the asset, and (3) subsequently paid the long-term liability and any accrued interest. When the city uses this borrow-and-buy approach, the recording is as follows in the fund-based statements:

1. To reflect the borrowing, the city reports an other financing source because the money received did not come from a revenue.
2. At the time of the asset's acquisition, the city reports an expenditure in keeping with the goal of presenting the changes in current financial resources.
3. For the same reason, the subsequent payment of debt and interest leads to a second recording of expenditures.

Consequently, if the city borrows money and buys the asset, one "other financing source" and two separate "expenditures" result. The preceding journal entries created for the capital lease are structured to arrive at that same reporting impact.

The radical differences between fund-based financial statements and government-wide financial statements are, once again, quite striking. At the end of this first year, the figures found in the two statements are not comparable in any way:

	Fund-Based Financial Statements	**Government-Wide Financial Statements**
Asset	Not applicable	$58,680
Accumulated depreciation	Not applicable	7,335
Liability	Not applicable	43,548
Expenditures:		
Asset acquisition	$58,680	Not applicable
Debt principal	5,132	Not applicable
Interest	4,868	Not applicable
Other financing sources	58,680	Not applicable
Depreciation expense	Not applicable	7,335
Interest expense	Not applicable	4,868

SOLID WASTE LANDFILL

LO2

Recognize the liability caused by the eventual closure and postclosure costs of operating a solid waste landfill as well as for the compensated absences earned by government employees.

The following information is disclosed in the notes to the financial statements of the City of Greensboro, North Carolina, as of June 30, 2008:

> The City owns and operates a regional landfill site located in the northeast portion of the City. State and federal laws require the City to place a final cover on its White Street landfill site and to perform certain maintenance and monitoring functions at the site for thirty years after closure. The City reports a portion of these closure and postclosure care costs as an operating expense in each period based on landfill capacity used as of each June 30. The $18,402,884 reported as landfill closure and postclosure care liability at June 30, 2008, is based on 100% use of the estimated capacity of Phase II and Phase III, Cells 1 and 2. Phase III, Cell 3, is estimated at 45% of capacity. . . .
>
> The estimated liability amounts are based on what it would cost to perform all closure and postclosure care in the current year. Actual cost may be higher due to inflation, changes in technology, or changes in regulations. At June 30, 2008, the City had expended $3,876,035 to complete closure for the White Street facility, Phase II. The balance of closure costs, estimated at $9,694,115 and estimated at $8,705,769 for postclosure care will be funded over the remaining life of the landfill.

Thousands of state and local governments operate solid waste landfills to provide a place for citizens and local companies to dispose of trash and other forms of garbage and refuse. Governments frequently report landfill operations within the enterprise funds because many of these facilities require a user fee. However, some landfills are open to the public without fee so that reporting within the General Fund is appropriate.

Regardless of the type of fund utilized, solid waste landfills can be sources of huge liabilities for these governments. The U.S. Environmental Protection Agency has strict rules on closure requirements as well as groundwater monitoring and other postclosure activities. Satisfying such requirements can be quite costly. Thus, the operation of a landfill eventually necessitates large payments to ensure that the facility is properly closed and then monitored and maintained for an extended period. Theoretically, the relevant accounting question has always been how to report these eventual costs while the landfill is still in operation.

To illustrate, assume that a city opens a landfill in Year 1 that is expected to take 10 years to fill. In the recording process each year, the city must estimate the current costs required to close the landfill. Such costs include the amount to be paid to cover the area and for all postclosure maintenance. As mentioned above by the City of Greensboro, the government uses current rather than future costs as a better measure of the present obligation. However, such amounts must then be adjusted each period for inflation as well as technology and regulation changes.

Assume, for this example, that the current cost for closure is estimated at $1 million and for postclosure maintenance at $400,000. Assume that during Year 1, the city makes an initial payment of $30,000 toward the closure costs. At the end of this first year, city engineers estimate that 16 percent of the available space has been filled.

Landfills—Government-Wide Financial Statements

Regardless of whether the city reports this solid waste landfill as a governmental activity (within the General Fund) or as a business-type activity (within an enterprise fund), it must recognize the closure and postclosure costs in the government-wide statements based on accrual accounting and the economic resources measurement basis. Because the government anticipates total cleanup costs of $1.4 million and the landfill is 16 percent filled, $224,000 should be accrued in this first year ($1.4 million $\times$ 16%).

The city also made an initial payment during the year. This payment simply reduces the liability being reported:

Government-Wide Financial Statements—Estimated Landfill Closure Costs

Year 1		
Expense—Landfill Closure	224,000	
Landfill Closure Liability		224,000
To recognize the Year 1 portion of total costs for eventual closure of landfill.		

Landfill Closure Liability	30,000	
Cash		30,000
To record first payment of costs necessitated by eventual closure of the landfill.		

To complete this example, assume that the landfill is judged to be 27 percent filled at the end of Year 2 and the city makes another $30,000 payment toward future closure costs. However, because of inflation and newly anticipated changes in technology, the city now believes that current closure costs are $1.1 million with postclosure costs amounting to $500,000.

Using this new and revised information, the city should recognize that it now has estimated total costs of $432,000 at the end of Year 2 ($1.6 million $\times$ 27%). Because it recorded $224,000 in Year 1, the city now accrues an additional $208,000 in Year 2 ($432,000 − $224,000):

Government-Wide Financial Statements—Estimated Landfill Cleanup Costs

Year 2		
Expense—Landfill Closure	208,000	
Landfill Closure Liability		208,000
To recognize Year 2 portion of costs for eventual closure of landfill.		
Landfill Closure Liability	30,000	
Cash		30,000
To record second payment of costs necessitated by eventual closure of the landfill.		

Consequently, in the Year 2 government-wide financial statements, the city reports:

Expense—Landfill closure	$208,000
Landfill closure liability ($224,000 + 208,000 − $30,000 − 30,000)	$372,000

Landfills—Fund-Based Financial Statements

If a government reports a solid waste landfill as an enterprise fund, the reporting is the same in the fund-based financial statements as just shown above for the government-wide statements. All economic resources are again measured based on accrual accounting.

However, if the landfill is recorded in the General Fund, the city reports only the change in current financial resources. Despite the huge eventual liability, the reduction in current financial resources is limited to the annual payment of $30,000. The actual liability is too far into the future to warrant reporting. Thus, the only entry required each year in this example for the fund-based financial statements is as follows:

Fund-Based Financial Statements—Payment toward Landfill Cleanup Costs

Year 1 and Year 2 **General Fund**		
Expenditures—Closure Costs	30,000	
Cash		30,000
To record annual payment toward the eventual closure costs of the city's solid waste landfill.		

COMPENSATED ABSENCES

LO2

Recognize the liability caused by the eventual closure and postclosure costs of operating a solid waste landfill as well as for the compensated absences earned by government employees.

State and local governments have numerous employees: police officers, schoolteachers, maintenance workers, and the like. As of June 30, 2008, the City of Baltimore, Maryland, reported having 15,326 full-time-equivalent employees.[1] In the same manner as the employees of a for-profit organization, government employees earn vacation days, sick leave days, and holidays, collectively known as *compensated absences,* that can amount to a significant amount of money. For example, at June 30, 2008, the City of Baltimore reported a debt of nearly $172 million for such compensated absences ($16.7 million as a current liability and $155.2 million as a long-term liability). This obligation was explained in part through footnote disclosure such as: "Employees earn one day of sick leave for each completed month of service, and there is no limitation on the number of sick days that can accumulate."

Accounting for such liabilities is much the same as was demonstrated for capital leases and solid waste landfills. In the government-wide financial statements, the city accrues the expense as incurred. Conversely in producing fund-based financial statements for the governmental funds, only actual payments and claims to current financial resources are included. For example, assume that a city reaches the end of Year 1 and owes its General Fund employees $40,000 because of compensated absences to be taken in the future for vacation days, holidays, and sick leave that have been earned. However, only $5,000 of these absences are expected to be taken early enough in Year 2 to require the use of current financial resources. Perhaps several employees are scheduled to take their vacations in the first two months of the subsequent period.

Consequently, a $40,000 liability exists at the end of Year 1 but only $5,000 of that amount is a claim on the government's current financial resources:

Government-Wide Financial Statements—Compensated Absences

Year 1		
Expenses—Compensated Absences	40,000	
Liability—Compensated Absences		40,000
To accrue amount owed at the end of Year 1 to employees for vacations, sick leave, and holidays.		

In the fund-based financial statements, reporting for the governmental funds reflects the changes in current financial resources. As the following entry shows, only the $5,000 that will be paid early in the next year is included. The remainder of the debt is not yet reported because it is not a claim to current financial resources. Again, however, if employees work in an area of the government reported as an enterprise fund, fund-based accounting is the same as in the government-wide statements.

Fund-Based Financial Statements—Compensated Absences

Year 1		
General Fund		
Expenditures—Compensated Absences	5,000	
Liability—Compensated Absences		5,000
To accrue amount of compensated absences that will be taken early in Year 2 so that it requires the use of Year 1 financial resources.		

[1] Statistical information listed at the end of a comprehensive annual financial report can provide a wide array of fascinating information about the reporting government. For example, in 2008 the City of Baltimore repaired 15,478 potholes while the police made 61,637 arrests and issued 386,099 parking citations. The city owned 473 marked patrol vehicles, 5,827 acres of parks, 39 fire station buildings, and 34 library buildings (holding 2.5 million library books).

WORKS OF ART AND HISTORICAL TREASURES

Private not-for-profit organizations have long debated the proper reporting of artworks and other museum pieces they buy or receive by gift. Governmental accounting occasionally faces the same issue. How should a government report works of art, museum artifacts, and other historical treasures in its financial statements?

Assume, for example, that a city maintains a small museum in the basement of its main office building. The museum was created to display documents, maps, and paintings and other works of art that depict the history of the city and the surrounding area. The government bought several of the displayed items, but local citizens also donated a number of them. Several of these pieces are quite valuable.

GASB *Statement 34* is clear on the handling of the items acquired for this city museum. Paragraph 27 states that, except in certain specified cases, "governments should capitalize works of art, historical treasures, and similar assets at their historical cost or fair value at date of donation." Thus, the government-wide statement of net assets will report an antique map bought for $5,000 as an asset at that cost. In the same manner, a similar map received as a gift is also recorded as a $5,000 asset.

If the city bought the map for cash, the journal entry is

Government-Wide Financial Statements—Acquisition of Historical Treasure

Museum Piece—Map	5,000	
Cash		5,000
To record acquisition of map for the city's museum.		

In producing fund-based financial statements, the museum could be viewed as an enterprise fund if an entrance fee is charged. If so, the above entry is replicated. Or, the museum could be accounted for within the Governmental Funds and the entry below is then used to indicate the decrease in current resources caused by the cash payment.

Fund-Based Financial Statements—Acquisition of Historical Treasure

General Fund		
Expenditure—Museum Piece	5,000	
Cash		5,000
To record acquisition of map for the city's museum, an activity that is being reported within the General Fund.		

Conversely, if this map had been donated to the city, capitalization of the asset for government-wide financial statements is still appropriate based on its fair value at the date of conveyance. The gift is viewed as a voluntary nonexchange transaction. A revenue will be properly recognized when all eligibility requirements have been met. Until that time, a deferred revenue is recognized.

The following entry is made in the government-wide financial statements, but no parallel entry is made in the fund-based statements for the governmental funds because no change occurs in the amount of available current financial resources.

Government-Wide Financial Statements—Donation of Historical Treasure

Museum Piece—Map	5,000	
Revenue—Donation		5,000
To record gift of map for the city's museum.		

A theoretical problem arises in the recognition of such assets in government-wide financial statements regardless of whether they were purchased or obtained by gift. Unless a user charge is assessed, items such as a map displayed for the public to see does not generate cash flows or any other direct economic benefit. Therefore, does the map actually qualify as an asset to be reported?

GASB "encouraged" the capitalization of all such artworks and historical treasures. However, if all three of the following criteria are met, recording a work of art or historical treasure as an asset is optional:

1. It is held for public exhibition, education, or research in furtherance of public service rather than for financial gain.
2. It is protected, kept unencumbered, cared for, and preserved.
3. It is subject to an organizational policy that requires the proceeds from sales of collection items to be used to acquire other items for collections.[2]

If these guidelines are met, the artwork or historical treasure will not provide any direct economic benefit to the government. Thus, although the transaction must be recorded, it does not have to be classified as an asset. Instead, in the entries previously shown for the government-wide statements, an expense rather than an asset can be recorded regardless of whether the item was obtained by purchase or gift. GASB's handling of this issue closely parallels rules established by FASB in its standards utilized by private not-for-profit organizations.

If a government capitalizes a work of art or other historical treasure, an additional theoretical question arises, this time about depreciation. Does the map on display in the museum actually depreciate in value over time? Does the *Mona Lisa* have a finite life? In connection with such assets, depreciation is required only if the asset is "exhaustible"—that is, if its utility will be used up by display, education, or research. Depreciation is not necessary if the work of art or historical treasure is viewed as being inexhaustible. For example, a bronze statue could well be viewed as an inexhaustible asset according to these guidelines so that depreciation is allowed but not required.

INFRASTRUCTURE ASSETS AND DEPRECIATION

LO4

Explain the reporting and possible depreciation of infrastructure assets.

Paragraph 19 of GASB *Statement 34* defines infrastructure assets as "long-lived capital assets that normally are stationary in nature and normally can be preserved for a significantly greater number of years than most capital assets." Examples include roads, bridges, tunnels, lighting systems, curbing, and sidewalks. As the previous chapter discussed, recording infrastructure items was historically an optional practice. Now, though, new infrastructure costs must be recorded as assets in the government-wide statements. For the governmental funds, these same costs continue to be recorded as expenditures in the fund-based statements because both acquisition and construction create a reduction in current financial resources.

Beyond simply recording new infrastructure items as assets, a state or local government also has to capitalize many infrastructure assets acquired prior to the establishment of government-wide financial statements. A major road system constructed 25 years ago, for example, must be shown as an asset in the government-wide statements. Because cost figures for these earlier acquisitions and constructions may not be readily available, estimations are allowed. In addition, because approximating the cost of all infrastructure items acquired prior to the initial creation of government-wide statements is virtually impossible, this capitalization requirement is limited to major assets that (1) were acquired in fiscal years ending after June 30, 1980, or (2) had major renovations, restorations, or improvements since that date.

For this reason, notes to the 2008 financial statements for the City of St. Louis, Missouri, disclosed:

> General infrastructure assets acquired prior to July 1, 2001, consist of the road network and other infrastructure assets that were acquired or that received substantial improvement subsequent to June 30, 1980, and are reported at estimated historical cost using deflated replacement cost.

---

[2] GASB *Statement 34*, "Basic Financial Statements—and Management's Discussion and Analysis—for State and local Governments," June 1999, para. 27.

As discussed previously, depreciation is now required for all capital assets appearing in the government-wide financial statements except for land as well as artworks and historical treasures that are deemed to be inexhaustible. The need for depreciation was debated by GASB in connection with infrastructure items: Is depreciation appropriate for this type of asset? For example, construction of the Brooklyn Bridge was finished in 1883 at a cost of about $15 million. That particular piece of infrastructure has operated now for more than 125 years and, with proper maintenance, might well continue to carry traffic for another 125 years. Much the same can be said of many roads, sidewalks, and the like built today. With appropriate repair and maintenance, such assets could have lives that are almost indefinite. What expected life should New York City use to depreciate the cost incurred in constructing a street such as Fifth Avenue?

Not surprisingly, governments tend to depreciate some of their infrastructure assets over extended periods. The City of Bismarck, North Dakota, uses lives that range from 20 to 100 years, whereas the City of Portland, Maine, depreciates these assets over periods from 30 to 67 years.

However, a unique alternative to depreciating the cost of eligible infrastructure assets such as the Brooklyn Bridge or Fifth Avenue is available. This method, known as the *modified approach*, eliminates the need for depreciating infrastructure. If specified guidelines are met, a government can choose to expense all maintenance costs each year in lieu of recording depreciation. Additions and improvements must be capitalized, but the cost of maintaining the infrastructure in proper working condition is expensed. Thus, if this method is applied, New York City will directly expense the amount spent on repair and other maintenance of Fifth Avenue so that depreciation of the street's capitalized cost is not recorded. Effectively, proper maintenance of infrastructure assets can extend their lives indefinitely.

Use of the modified approach requires the government to accumulate information about all of the infrastructure assets within either a network or a subsystem of a network. For example, all roads could be deemed a network while state roads, rural roads, and interstate highways might make up three subsystems of that network. Fifth Avenue is probably not a network or a subsystem by itself.

- For eligible assets, the government must establish a minimum acceptable condition level for the network or subsystem of the network and then maintain documentation that this minimum level is being met.
- The government must have an asset management system in place to monitor the particular network or subsystem of a network in question. This system should assess the ongoing condition of the eligible assets to ensure that they are, indeed, able to operate at the predetermined level.

The state of Texas has adopted the modified approach in connection with reporting its highway system. In its comprehensive annual financial report, the determination of a minimum acceptable condition level is explained as follows:

> The Texas Department of Transportation (TxDOT) performs yearly condition assessments through its Texas Maintenance Assessment Program (TxMAP). Under this program, visual inspections are conducted on approximately 10 percent of the interstate system and 5 percent of the non-interstate system (national, state and farm-to-market roadways). For each section of highway observed, 21 elements separated into three highway components are assessed scores from 0 to 5 (0 = NA, 1 = Failed, 2 = Poor, 3 = Fair, 4 = Good, 5 = Excellent) in order to determine the condition of the highways. Each element within a component is weighted according to importance and each component is weighted according to importance to determine the overall condition of the highways. The overall score is converted to a percentage measurement for reporting (1 = 20%, 2 = 40%, 3 = 60%, 4 = 80%, 5 = 100%). TxDOT has adopted a minimum condition level of 80 percent for the interstate system, 75 percent for the non-interstate system and 80 percent for the Central Texas Turnpike System based on TxMap assessments.

The note goes on to indicate that the minimum was met in 2008 with scores of 83.7 percent, 79.0 percent, and 91.7 percent, respectively.

The modified approach does provide a method by which governments can avoid depreciating infrastructure assets such as the Brooklyn Bridge that can have virtually an unlimited life. The issue is, How many governments will go to the trouble of creating the standards and documentation required by this approach simply to avoid recording depreciation expense? "I am beginning to see more infrastructure-heavy organizations—such as airport authorities, transportation authorities, or large states with huge road networks—select the modified approach. However, to date, I have not encountered too many general government entities that have considered using it."[3]

EXPANDED FINANCIAL REPORTING

LO5

Understand the composition of a state or local government's comprehensive annual financial report (CAFR).

The SEC has long advocated inclusion of a verbal explanation of a for-profit company's operations and financial position to accompany its financial statements. This memorandum, known generally as the *management's discussion and analysis* (MD&A), provides a wealth of vital information for the reader of the financial statements. Thus, in evaluating for-profit organizations, outside decision makers are accustomed to having a "plain English" explanation of the figures and other critical information disclosed within the statements. For example General Electric Company's 2008 financial statements contained a Management's Discussion and Analysis that covered 30 pages. Consequently, a stockholder, creditor, potential investor, or other interested party is provided with extensive details to describe and supplement the facts and figures presented within the company's financial statements.

GASB now requires state and local governments to provide a similar MD&A. Thus, the general purpose external financial statements of a state or local government are composed of three distinct sections:

1. Management's discussion and analysis.
2. Financial statements:
   a. Government-wide financial statements.
   b. Fund-based financial statements.
   c. Notes to the financial statements.
3. Required supplementary information (other than the MD&A). For example, the City of Saint Paul, Minnesota, uses this section to compare budgetary figures with actual results for each major fund although a separate statement within the fund-based financial statements could also have been used.

GASB explains its justification for requiring officials to provide readers of the government's financial statements with an MD&A:

> The basic financial statements should be preceded by MD&A, which is required supplementary information (RSI). MD&A should provide an objective and easily readable analysis of the government's financial activities based on currently known facts, decisions, or conditions. The financial managers of governments are knowledgeable about the transactions, events, and conditions that are reflected in the government's financial report and of the fiscal policies that govern its operations. MD&A provides financial managers with the opportunity to present both a short- and a long-term analysis of the government's activities. MD&A should discuss current-year results in comparison with the prior year, with emphasis on the current year. This fact-based analysis should discuss the positive and negative aspects of the comparison with the prior year. The use of charts, graphs, and tables is encouraged to enhance the understandability of the information.[4]

As an illustration, the 2008 financial statements for the City of Raleigh, North Carolina, begin with a management's discussion and analysis of 16 pages that present explanations such as the following:

- The cost of all governmental activities this year was $325.4 million. This cost was incurred in order to provide basic municipal services to the citizens of Raleigh. These services include, but are not limited to: police, fire, solid waste services, parks and recreation, streets maintenance, inspections, planning, and others.
- The amount that our taxpayers paid for these activities through property taxes was $151.7 million.
- Those who directly benefited from service-fee based programs paid $41.2 million in charges for services.

[3] E-mail from Jack Reagan, partner, KPMG, Washington, DC, August 18, 2009.
[4] GASB *Statement No. 34,* paras. 8 and 9.

The general purpose external financial statements are presented to the public as part of a comprehensive annual financial report (often referred to as a *CAFR*). The CAFR also includes other extensive information about the reporting government. For example, the 2008 CAFR for the City of Orlando, Florida, with total revenues of about $600 million, was approximately 270 pages long. In comparison, the 2008 annual report for Wal-Mart, with more than $378 billion in revenues, was only 54 pages.

The CAFR of a state or local government must include three broad sections:

1. *Introductory section*—includes a letter of transmittal from appropriate government officials, an organization chart, and a list of principal officers.

2. *Financial section*—presents the general purpose external financial statement and reproduces the auditor's report. The government also usually prepares additional supplementary information such as combining statements to present financial information for funds that do not qualify as major.

3. *Statistical section*—discloses a wide range of data about the government.

THE PRIMARY GOVERNMENT AND COMPONENT UNITS

LO6

Explain the makeup of a primary government and its relationship to component units.

Primary Government

The primary government serves as the nucleus and focus of the financial reporting entity as defined by GAAP. All state governments and general-purpose local governments automatically should be treated as primary governments.[5]

According to governmental accounting, every reporting entity should prepare a comprehensive annual financial report. The reporting entity starts with a primary government such as a town, city, county, or state. The CAFR also includes all funds, activities, organizations, agencies, offices, and departments that are not legally separate from the primary government.

However, states and localities often have difficulty determining which of these separate activities should be presented with the primary government as part of the reporting entity. Except in rare cases, a business enterprise such as IBM or Ford Motor Company simply consolidates all corporations over which it has control. A state or locality can interact with numerous separate departments, agencies, boards, institutes, commissions, and the like. Should all of these functions be included as either governmental activities or business-type activities within the government's CAFR? If not, what reporting is appropriate?

The almost unlimited number of activities that can be related to a government raises problems for officials attempting to outline the parameters of the entity being reported. Organizations such as turnpike commissions, port authorities, public housing boards, and downtown development commissions have become commonplace in recent years. The primary government may have created many of these, but they remain legally separate organizations. Such entities are designed to focus attention on specific issues or problems. They often promise better efficiency because of their corporate-style structure.

As an example, in the notes to the financial statements in its 2008 CAFR, the City of Boston, Massachusetts, lists the following separate organizations related to the government but whose financial information had *not* been included with that of the city. The mayor appoints the members of each governing body, but city authority does not extend beyond making these appointments:

- Boston Housing Authority.
- Boston Industrial Development Financing Authority.
- Boston Water and Sewer Commission.

---

[5] Stephen J. Gauthier, *Governmental Accounting, Auditing, and Financial Reporting—Using the GASB 34 Model* (Chicago: Government Finance Officers Association, 2005), p. 58.

Conversely, the City of Atlanta, Georgia, at June 30, 2008, indicated a number of activities that were legally separate from the city government but were still presented within that city's financial information because the city is financially accountable:

- Atlanta-Fulton County Recreation Authority.
- Atlanta Development Authority.
- Atlanta CoRA, Inc.

Clearly, these examples show that activities related to a government can be included in or excluded from the information produced by the primary government. Because of the extremely wide variety of possible activities, determining which functions actually comprise a state or locality is not always an easy task. According to paragraphs 2 and 8 of GASB *Statement 14,* "The Financial Reporting Entity," the major criterion for inclusion in a government's comprehensive annual financial report is financial accountability:

> Financial reporting based on accountability should enable the financial statement reader to focus on the body of organizations that are related by a common thread of accountability to the constituent citizenry. . . . Elected officials are accountable to those citizens for their public policy decisions, regardless of whether these decisions are carried out directly by the elected officials through the operations of the primary government or *by their designees through the operations of specially created organizations.* [Emphasis added.]

Component Units

Some activities are legally separate from a primary government but so closely connected that omission from the statements of that primary government cannot be justified. Because of the relationship, elected officials of the primary government are financially accountable for these separate organizations known as *component units.* That is why the City of Atlanta included the Atlanta-Fulton County Recreation Authority and the other activities mentioned above in its CAFR; they qualified as component units. They are not part of the government but are reported by the government.

Despite being legally separate, component units are included within the financial statements of the primary government to indicate that the connection is close enough to warrant being part of the reporting entity. Thus, identification of such activities can be quite important. Two sets of criteria have been established. If either is met, the activity qualifies as a component unit to be reported within the CAFR of the primary government. The parameters of the reporting entity encompass both the primary government and any component units.

Criterion 1

The separate organization (such as the Atlanta-Fulton County Recreation Authority) is viewed as a component unit if it fiscally depends on the primary government (the City of Atlanta). As defined, *fiscal dependency* means that the organization cannot do one or more of the following without approval of the primary government: adopt its own budget, levy taxes or set rates, or issue bonded debt.

Criterion 2

First, officials of the primary government must appoint a voting majority of the governing board of the separate organization. Second, either the primary government must be able to impose its will on that board or the separate organization provides a financial benefit or imposes a financial burden on the primary government.

For example, a state (the primary government) might establish a legally separate commission to oversee off-track betting. However, if the state appoints a voting majority of the board membership and the financial benefits from revenues generated by the commission accrue to the state, the commission is considered a component unit of the state for reporting purposes.

Three aspects of the second criterion should be explained further to ensure proper application.

Voting Majority of the Governing Board The authority to elect a voting majority must be substantive. If, for example, the primary government simply confirms the choices that other parties make, financial accountability is not present. In the same way, financial accountability does not result when the primary government must select the governing board from a limited slate of candidates (such as picking three individuals from an approved list of five). Thus, the primary government must have the actual responsibility of appointing a voting majority of the board before the organization meets this portion of the second criterion.

Imposition of the Primary Government's Will on the Governing Board   Such power is indicated if the government can significantly influence the programs, projects, activities, or level of services the organization provides. This degree of influence is present if the primary government can remove an appointed board member at will, modify or approve budgets, override decisions of the board, modify or approve rate or fee changes, and hire or dismiss the individuals responsible for day-to-day operations.

Financial Benefit or Financial Burden on the Primary Government   A financial connection exists between the organization and the primary government if the government is entitled to the organization's resources, the government is legally obligated to finance any deficits or provide support, or the government is responsible for the organization's debts.

Reporting Component Units

Component units are reported in one of two ways: discrete or blended presentation. Many component units are discretely presented at the far right side of the government-wide statements. For example, the June 30, 2008, Statement of Net Assets for the City of Detroit, Michigan, shows that the primary government had total assets of more than $10.7 billion whereas its discretely presented component units shown just to the right of the primary government reported total assets of $957 million.

According to the financial statements, these component units were made up of the following separate organizations:

- Detroit Brownfield Redevelopment Authority
- Detroit Public Library
- Detroit Transportation Corporation
- Downtown Development Authority
- Eastern Market Corporation
- Economic Development Corporation
- Greater Detroit Resource Recovery Authority
- Local Development Finance Authority
- Museum of African American History
- Tax Increment Finance Authority

As an alternative placement, a primary government can include component units as an actual part of the reporting government (a process referred to as *blending*). Although legally separate, the component is so intertwined with the primary government that inclusion is necessary to appropriately present the financial information. In discussing the reporting of its three component units, the City of Atlanta, Georgia, indicates that two are discretely presented while the other is blended:

> The government-wide financial statements include not only the City itself (known as the primary government), but also the legally separate Atlanta-Fulton County Recreation Authority, Atlanta CoRA Inc., and Atlanta Development Authority for which the City is financially accountable. Financial information for these *component units* is reported separately from the financial information presented for the primary government itself, except for Atlanta CoRA, Inc., whose statements are blended with the primary government.

One other aspect of the overall reporting process should be noted: the possible existence of related organizations. In such cases, the primary government is accountable because it appoints a voting majority of the outside organization's governing board. However, fiscal dependency as defined earlier is not present, and the primary government cannot impose its will on the board or gather financial benefits or burdens from the relationship. The organization does not qualify as a component unit to be included in the government's financial reporting. However, the primary government must still disclose the nature of the relationship.

IS IT PART OF THE COUNTY?

Harland County is in a financially distressed area in Missouri. In hopes of enticing business to this area, the state legislature appropriated $3 million to start an industrial development commission. The federal government provided an additional $1 million. The state appointed 15 individuals to a board to oversee the operations of this commission, and county officials named 5 members. The commission began operations by raising funds from local citizens and businesses. It received $700,000 in donations and pledges. The county provided clerical assistance and allowed the commission to use one floor of the county office building for its headquarters. The county government must approve the commission's annual operating budget.

During the current period, the commission spent $2.4 million. It achieved notable success. Several large manufacturing companies have recently begun to explore the possibility of opening plants in the county.

Harland County is presently preparing its comprehensive annual financial report. Should it include the revenues, expenditures, assets, expenses, and liabilities of the industrial development commission? Is it a fund within the county's primary government, a component unit, or a related organization?

Is the industrial development commission a component unit of the State of Missouri? How should its activities be presented in the state's comprehensive annual financial report?

Special Purpose Governments

Cities, counties, states, and the like are known as *general purpose governments.* They provide a wide range of services such as police protection, road repair, and sanitation. They are primary governments, each within its own reporting entity. However, activities that qualify as special purpose governments are also viewed as primary governments for separate reporting purposes.

Thousands of special purpose governments exist throughout the country; they carry out only a single function for the public or a limited number of functions. Common examples include public school districts, colleges and universities, utilities, hospitals, transit authorities, and library services. A note to the 2008 financial statements prepared for the University of Iowa indicates that "for financial reporting purposes, the University is considered a special-purpose government."

When reporting a single activity, such as a transit system, school system, or utility, the question arises as to whether it is (1) part of a larger government such as a city or county as either a fund or a component unit, (2) a nongovernmental not-for-profit organization, or (3) a special purpose government that produces its own financial statements according to governmental accounting principles.

An activity or function is deemed a special purpose government if it meets the following criteria:

1. Have a separately elected governing body.
2. Be legally independent, which it can demonstrate by having corporate powers such as the right to sue and be sued as well as the right to buy, sell, and lease property in its own name.
3. Be fiscally independent of other state and local governments.

For example, a school system that satisfies all three is reported as a special purpose government that produces its own financial statements. However, if that same school system fails to meet any one of these, its financial condition and operations are likely to be maintained within the General Fund or Special Revenue Funds of a city or county government.

As mentioned previously, an activity is normally considered to be fiscally independent if its leadership can determine the activity's budget without having to seek the approval of an outside party, levy taxes or set rates without having to seek outside approval, and can issue bonded debt without outside approval.

The comprehensive annual financial report for the Charlotte-Mecklenburg County, North Carolina, Board of Education shows total expenses for the year ended June 30, 2008, of more than $1.25 billion as a special purpose government. A note to these statements explains why the Board represents a primary government to be reported separately from the local general purpose government:

> The Charlotte-Mecklenburg Board of Education (Board) is a Local Education Agency empowered by State law [Chapter 115C of the North Carolina General Statutes] with the responsibility to oversee and control all activities related to public school education in Charlotte-Mecklenburg, North Carolina. The Board receives State, Local, and Federal government funding and must adhere to the legal requirements of each funding entity. Although Mecklenburg County (the County) levies all taxes, the Board determines how the school system will spend the funds generated for schools. The County cannot modify the school system's budget, nor is the County entitled to share in any surpluses or required to finance any deficits of the school system. For these reasons, the Board is not fiscally dependent on the County and therefore is recognized as a primary government.

GOVERNMENT-WIDE AND FUND-BASED FINANCIAL STATEMENTS ILLUSTRATED

LO7

Understand the physical structure of a complete set of government-wide financial statements and a complete set of fund-based financial statements.

At the core of a governmental reporting entity's comprehensive annual financial report are the general purpose financial statements. As described, these statements are made up of government-wide financial statements and fund-based financial statements. Government-wide statements present financial information for both governmental activities and business-type activities. They measure economic resources and utilize accrual accounting.

The fund-based statements separately present the governmental funds, the proprietary funds, and the fiduciary funds. The measurement focus and the timing of recognition depend on the fund in question. For governmental funds, the current financial resources measurement focus is used with modified accrual accounting. However, both proprietary funds and fiduciary funds use accrual accounting to report all economic resources.

In the previous chapter, four of these statements were outlined to introduce the basic structure of each. However, now that a deeper understanding of government accounting has been established, these same statements as well as several other fund-based statements can be examined in more detail. Having an appreciation for the end result of the accounting process helps to explain how diverse elements of government accounting fit together into a complete reporting package.[6] Hundreds, if not thousands, of actual financial statements are readily available. An Internet search will locate the home page of virtually any U.S. city or county of significant size. On that site, a search of "CAFR" or "annual financial report" should locate the latest statements. Understanding is greatly enhanced by reviewing such statements.

Statement of Net Assets—Government-Wide Financial Statements

Exhibit 12.1 presents the June 30, 2008, statement of net assets for the City of Sacramento, California. As a government-wide financial statement, it is designed to report the economic resources of the government as a whole (except for the fiduciary funds, which are not included because those assets must be used for a purpose outside the primary government).

Several aspects of this statement of net assets should be noted specifically:

- The measurement focus is the economic resources controlled by the government. Thus, all assets including capital assets are reported. Long-term liabilities are presented for the same reason.
- Capital assets other than land, land improvements, inexhaustible artworks, and construction in progress are reported net of accumulated depreciation because depreciation is required on the government-wide statements. (See Point A.) Newly acquired infrastructure assets are

---

[6] The examples presented here illustrate the government-wide financial statements and the fund-based financial statements for both governmental funds and proprietary funds. Because they are more specialized, the fund-based statements for the fiduciary funds have been omitted. Those statements can be found at www.cityofsacramento.org/cafr/.

EXHIBIT 12.1 Government-Wide Financial Statements

CITY OF SACRAMENTO
Statement of Net Assets
June 30, 2008
(in thousands)

	Primary Government			Component Units©
	Governmental Activities	Business-Type Activities	Total	
Assets				
Cash and investments	$ 420,104	$ 126,918	$ 547,022	$ 1,211
Securities lending assets	96,374	19,190	115,564	—
Receivables, net	255,201	58,393	313,594	14,901
Internal balances®	20,502	(20,502)	—	—
Inventories	3,051	3,202	6,253	98
Prepaid items	478	10	488	376
Restricted cash and investments	149,207	16,439	165,646	33,428
Deferred charges	5,169	4,672	9,841	3,052
Land and other capital assets not being depreciated	356,593	103,766	460,359	4,954
Other capital assets, net of depreciationⒶ	1,291,223	915,814	2,207,037	60,163
Total assets	2,597,902	1,227,902	3,825,804	118,183
Liabilities				
Securities lending obligations	96,374	19,190	115,564	—
Payables	83,240	27,093	110,333	8,506
Unearned revenue	21,601	2,525	24,126	17
Long-term liabilities:				
Due within one year	66,385	16,852	83,237	6,065
Due in more than one year	629,919	385,316	1,015,235	110,202
Total liabilities	897,519	450,976	1,348,495	124,790
Net Assets (Deficit)				
Invested in capital assets, net of related debt	1,411,436	656,951	2,068,387	(24,397)
Restricted for:				
Capital projects	124,919	—	124,919	—
Debt service	531	—	531	9,575
Trust and endowments:				
Expendable	6,159	—	6,159	—
Nonexpendable	1,934	—	1,934	—
Other	30,996	—	30,996	10,416
Unrestricted	124,408	119,975	244,383	(2,201)
Total net assets (deficit)	$1,700,383	$ 776,926	$2,477,309	$ (6,607)

The notes to the financial statements are an integral part of this statement.

included within the capital assets. The remaining historical cost basis of previously acquired infrastructure, if major and acquired or renovated since 1980, has been estimated and capitalized. Infrastructure depreciation is omitted if the modified approach is used. However, the City of Sacramento did not choose to use the modified approach.

- The primary government is divided into governmental activities and business-type activities. Governmental funds are reported as governmental activities whereas enterprise funds comprise most, if not all, of the business-type activities. Even though recorded within the proprietary funds, internal service funds are normally included within the governmental activities because those services are rendered primarily for the benefit of activities within the governmental funds. However, if a particular internal service fund predominantly serves an enterprise fund, that internal service fund should be included as a business-type activity.

- The internal balances shown in the asset section (Point B) come from receivables and payables between the governmental activities and the business-type activities. The internal balances reported on this statement offset, so that there is no effect on the totals shown for the primary government.

- Investments are reported at fair value rather than historical cost.

- Discretely presented component units are grouped and shown to the far right side of the statement (Point C) so that the reported amounts do not affect the primary government figures. However, blended component units are included, as appropriate, within either the governmental activities or the business-type activities as if they were individual funds. According to the notes to the City of Sacramento's financial statements, there were two discretely presented component units, the Sacramento Regional Arts Facilities Financing Authority and the Sacramento Hotel Corporation, as well as two blended component units, the Sacramento City Employee Retirement System and the Sacramento City Financing Authority.

- Because this is a statement of net assets, the format is not structured to stress that assets are equal to liabilities plus equities as is found in a typical balance sheet. Rather, the assets ($3.83 billion for the primary government) less liabilities of $1.35 billion indicated net assets of $2.48 billion.

- As the Net Assets section shows, several amounts have been restricted for capital projects, debt service, and the like. Restrictions are reported in this manner only if usage of the assets has been specified by external parties such as creditors, grantors, or other external party, or because of laws passed through constitutional provisions or enabling legislation.

- Although not restricted, the amount of net assets tied up in capital assets less any related debt is reported as a separate figure within the Net Assets section. Such amounts are not readily available.

Statement of Activities—Government-Wide Financial Statements

The statement of activities presents a wide array of information about a state or local government. As the statement for the City of Sacramento, California, shows in Exhibit 12.2, the same general classification system of governmental activities, business-type activities, and component units used in Exhibit 12.1 provides the structural basis for reporting. However, the format here is more complex and requires close analysis.

- Operating expenses are presented in the first column (Point D). They are not classified according to individual causes such as salaries, rent, depreciation, or insurance. Instead, all expenses are shown by function, which is more relevant to readers: general government, police, fire, general services, and the like. As paragraph 41 of GASB *Statement 14* states, "as a minimum, governments should report direct expenses for each function. Direct expenses are those that are specifically associated with a service, program, or department and, thus, are clearly identifiable to a particular function." Expenses are shown for governmental activities, business-type activities, and the two discretely presented component units.

- Interest expense on general long-term debt (Point E) is normally viewed as an indirect expense because it benefits many government operations. However, due to its size, informational value, and difficulty of allocation, this expense frequently is shown as in Exhibit 12.2 as a separate "function." In the second column, a portion of the expenses assigned to two governmental activities are allocated as indirect expenses to business-type activities.

- After operating and indirect expenses have been determined for each function, related program revenues are reported in the next three columns (Point F). Program revenues are those revenues derived from the function itself or from outsiders seeking to reduce the government's cost for that function. As Exhibit 12.2 shows, program revenues are classified as:

  1. *Charges for services.* For example, a monthly charge is normally assessed for water service; therefore, this first business-type activity shows more than $65.1 million in program revenues. In contrast, most government functions generate only relatively small amounts of revenue from sources such as parking meter revenues, fines for speeding tickets, concessions at parks, and the like.

2. *Operating grants and contributions.* This column reports amounts received from outside grants and similar sources that were designated for some type of operating purpose. For example, $16.2 million in operating grants and contributions is shown for the Sacramento police.

3. *Capital grants and contributions.* This column shows outside grants and similar sources when the resources were designated for capital asset additions. For the City of Sacramento, during this year, the largest amount of capital grants and contributions (by far) went to Transportation (Point G).

- After expenses have been assigned along with related program revenues, a net (expense) or revenue figure can be determined for each function. This net figure provides a measure of the financial cost (or benefit) of the various government functions. For example, in Exhibit 12.2, the police department had more than $159.2 million in operating expenses but was able to generate program revenues of only $20.4 million from charges for services and operating grants and contributions. Thus, as disclosed at Point H, the Sacramento taxpayers had to bear a financial burden of over $138.8 million for police protection. That cost is important information to citizens reading these statements. In contrast, the water system reported operating and indirect expenses of $63.4 million, but its charges, grants, and contributions totaled nearly $69 million. Thus, this business-type activity generated net revenues of approximately $5.5 million (see Point I) as a financial benefit for the government during this period.

- Net expenses and revenues can be determined in total for each category of the government. In this example, all of the governmental activities are combined to report net expenses of more than $306 million (see Point J) while the business-type activities generated net revenues of approximately $5 million (see Point K). The component units reported net expenses of over $2 million (see Point L). Notice at Point M that these totals are transferred to the second part of this statement so the impact of general revenues can be included where appropriate.

- General revenues are reported as additions to either the governmental activities, business-type activities, or component units. All taxes are general revenues because they do not reflect a charge for services; they are obtained from the population as a whole. At Point N, property taxes of nearly $138 million are shown as the largest revenue contributing to meet the cost of the governmental activities provided by the City of Sacramento. In addition, inflows such as the gain on sale of capital assets fall under this same category.

- Transfers of $12,898,000 during the year between governmental activities and business-type activities are also shown under the general revenues, but they offset, so that no impact is created on the total for the primary government (see Point O).

Balance Sheet—Governmental Funds—Fund-Based Statements

Switching now to the fund-based financial statements, Exhibit 12.3 presents the balance sheet for the governmental funds reported by the City of Sacramento. This statement measures only current financial resources and uses modified accrual accounting for timing purposes. No proprietary funds, component units, or fiduciary funds are included; this fund-based statement reflects just the governmental funds. Several parts of this statement should be noted:

- A separate column must be shown for the General Fund and any other major fund monitored within the governmental funds. The city has identified six funds as major including the Capital Projects Fund and the Special Revenue Fund associated with the Crocker Art Museum Fund. The government can classify any fund as major if officials believe it is especially important to statement users. However, as mentioned in the previous chapter, a fund is considered major and must be reported separately if it meets two criteria:

1. Total assets, liabilities, revenues, or expenses/expenditures of the fund are at least 10 percent of the corresponding total for all such funds.

2. Total assets, liabilities, revenues, or expenses/expenditures of the fund are at least 5 percent of the corresponding total for all governmental funds and enterprise funds combined.

All funds that are not considered to be major are combined and reported as "Other Governmental Funds."

EXHIBIT 12.2 Government-Wide Financial Statements

CITY OF SACRAMENTO
Statement of Activities
For the Fiscal Year Ended June 30, 2008
(in thousands)

Functions/Programs	Operating Expenses Ⓓ	Indirect Expenses Allocation	Program Revenues Ⓕ — Charges for Services	Program Revenues Ⓕ — Operating Grants and Contributions	Program Revenues Ⓕ — Capital Grants and Contributions	Net (Expense) Revenue
Primary government:						
Governmental activities:						
General government	$ 56,787	$(6,946)	$ 5,233	$ —	$ 138	$ (44,470) Ⓗ
Police	159,207	—	4,203	16,190	—	(138,814) Ⓗ
Fire	104,149	—	17,936	1,725	—	(84,488)
General services	29,196	(1,669)	10,471	3	156	(16,897)
Transportation	89,016	—	19,574	17,398	78,347 Ⓖ	26,303
Economic development	10,048	—	8,143	15	1,677	(213)
Convention, culture & leisure	21,518	—	9,425	935	28,413	17,255
Parks and recreation	60,930	—	13,343	14,652	13,764	(19,171)
Code enforcement	10,154	—	3,800	323	—	(6,031)
Development services	30,247	—	19,867	—	5,987	(4,393)
Planning	6,830	—	114	604	13,426	7,314
Neighborhood services	1,667	—	123	—	—	(1,544)
Library	9,935	—	—	—	11	(9,924)
Interest on long-term debt	31,157 Ⓔ	—	—	—	—	(31,157)
Total governmental activities	620,841	(8,615)	112,232	51,845	141,919	(306,230) Ⓙ
Business-type activities:						
Water	60,944	2,420	65,127	—	3,702	5,465 Ⓘ
Sewer	17,439	891	20,704	—	1,042	3,416
Storm drainage	36,947	1,623	33,289	410	7,201	2,330
Solid waste	46,427	2,308	52,434	760	—	4,459
Community center	19,743	764	7,556	—	—	(12,951)
Parking	16,669	485	19,626	—	—	2,472
Child development	6,604	—	5,587	654	—	(363)
Marina	1,133	124	1,378	—	—	121
Total business-type activities	205,906	8,615	205,701	1,824	11,945	4,949 Ⓚ
Total primary government	$826,747	$ —	$317,933	$53,669	$153,864	$(301,281)
Component units:						
Sacramento Hotel Corporation	$ 37,589	$ —	$ 36,093	$ —	$ —	$ (1,496)
Sacramento Regional Arts						
Facilities Financing Authority	736					(736)
Total component units	$ 38,325	$ —	$ 36,093	$ —	$ —	$ (2,232) Ⓛ

The notes to the financial statements are an integral part of this statement.

continued from page 546

CITY OF SACRAMENTO
Statement of Activities
For the Fiscal Year Ended June 30, 2008
(in thousands)

	Primary government			Component Units
	Governmental Activities	Business-type Activities	Total	
Change in net assets:				
Net (expense) revenue	$ (306,230) Ⓜ	$ 4,949	$ (301,281)	$ (2,232)
General revenues:				
Taxes:				
Property taxes	137,782 Ⓝ	—	137,782	—
Utility user taxes	57,561	—	57,561	—
Other taxes	23,865	17,538	41,403	—
Unrestricted sales taxes shared state revenue	54,821	—	54,821	—
Unrestricted in lieu sales tax	16,344	—	16,344	—
Unrestricted intergovernmental revenue	2,836	—	2,836	—
Unrestricted investment earnings	31,507	6,898	38,405	2,004
Unrestricted miscellaneous	12,149	353	12,502	—
Special item—distribution from component unit	28,088	—	28,088	—
Special item—gain on sale of capital asset	—	19,860	19,860	—
Special item—payment to redevelopment agency	(9,297)	(14,215)	(23,512)	—
Transfers	12,898	(12,898)	— Ⓞ	—
Total general revenues, special items, and transfers	368,554	17,536	386,090	2,004
Change in net assets	62,324 Ⓤ	22,485	84,809	(228)
Net assets (deficit), beginning of year	1,638,059	754,441	2,392,500	(6,379)
Net assets (deficit), end of year	$1,700,383	$776,926	$2,477,309	$ (6,607)

EXHIBIT 12.3 Fund-Based Financial Statements

CITY OF SACRAMENTO
Governmental Funds
Balance Sheet
June 30, 2008 (in thousands)

	General Fund	General Fund Projects Fund	Capital Grants Fund	Crocker Art Museum Fund	Financing Plans Fund	1997 Lease Revenue Bond Fund	Transportation and Development Fund	Other Governmental Funds	Total Governmental Funds
Assets									
Cash and investments held by City	$101,711	$ 977	$ —	$ —	$115,031	$ 2,006	$66,747	$ 94,271	$380,743
Cash and investments held by fiscal agent	—	—	—	—	—	21	—	314	335
Security lending assets	28,452	23,990	—	7,283	29,225	—	—	1,343	90,293
Receivables, net:									
Taxes	25,160	—	—	—	—	—	—	42	25,202
Accounts	9,724	—	707	—	15,384	—	1,860	2,292	29,967
Loans	1,601	—	—	—	—	70,930	—	875	73,406
Investment securities sold	2,935	2,476	—	752	3,017	—	—	—	9,180
Intergovernmental	—	—	34,818	—	—	—	8,821	69,474	113,113
Interest	942	796	—	241	969	398	—	129	3,475
Due from other funds	15	—	25	—	523	—	—	—	538
Inventories	—	—	—	—	—	—	—	1,315	1,315
Prepaid items	449	—	—	—	—	—	—	29	478
Restricted assets:									
Cash and investments held by City	—	100,605	25	26,491	8	782	—	1,372	129,283
Cash and investments held by fiscal agent	—	—	—	—	—	—	—	19,924	19,924
Advances to other funds	400	—	—	—	—	—	—	—	400
Total assets	$171,389	$128,844	$35,550	$34,767	$164,157	$74,137	$77,428	$191,380	$877,652
Liabilities:									
Securities lending obligations	$ 28,452	$ 23,990	$ —	$ 7,283	$ 29,225	$ —	$ —	$ 1,343	$ 90,293
Accounts payable	37,425	7,179	5,682	—	739	—	8,150	6,436	65,611
Due to other funds	—	—	23,696	—	—	—	5,757	2,222	31,675
Matured bonds and interest payable	—	—	—	—	—	—	—	3,043	3,043

continued from page 548

								Total
Deposits	172	—	631	—	—	—	511	630	1,944
Deferred revenue	5,988	—	38,616	—	17,203	71,328	7,001	73,922	214,058
Advances from other funds	390	—	—	—	—	—	—	7,436	7,826
Total liabilities	72,427	31,169	68,625	7,283	47,167	71,328	21,419	95,032	414,450
Fund Balances (deficit): Ⓟ									
Reserved:									
For noncurrent assets	1,604	—	—	—	—	—	—	875	2,479
For encumbrances	8,947	42,718	14,219	42,164	1,655	—	9,144	3,769	122,616
For debt services	—	531	—	—	—	803	—	21,300	22,634
For inventories and prepaids	449	—	—	—	—	—	—	1,344	1,793
For trust obligations	—	—	—	—	—	—	—	1,934	1,934
Unreserved:									
Designated for economic uncertainty	33,100	—	—	—	—	—	—	—	33,100
Designated for capital projects	28,942	42,886	—	—	30,359	—	28,664	—	130,851
Designated for SHRA—hotel sale	6,458	—	—	—	—	—	—	—	6,458
Designated for Voluntary Separation Program (VSP)	3,912	—	—	—	—	—	—	—	3,912
Designated for fiscal year 2009 results	492	—	—	—	—	—	—	—	492
Designated for subsequent year's expenditures	14,058	—	—	—	—	—	9,180	—	23,238
Undesignated	1,000	11,540	(47,294)	(14,680)	84,976	2,006	9,021	—	46,569
Unreserved, reported in:									
Special revenue funds	—	—	—	—	—	—	—	32,424	32,424
Debt service funds	—	—	—	—	—	—	—	7,194	7,194
Capital projects funds	—	—	—	—	—	—	—	23,808	23,808
Permanent funds	—	—	—	—	—	—	—	3,700	3,700
Total fund balances (deficit)	98,962	97,675	(33,075)	27,484	116,990	2,809	56,009	96,348	463,202 Ⓠ
Total liabilities and fund balances (deficit)	$171,389	$128,844	$35,550	$34,767	$164,157	$74,137	$77,428	$191,380	$877,652

- This balance sheet reports no capital assets or long-term debts because only current financial resources are being measured.

- Totals for the governmental funds appear in the final column. However, internal balances such as "due from other funds" (a receivable) and "due to other funds" (a liability) have not been offset. The governmental totals are just mathematical summations, not consolidated balances.

- The Fund Balances figures reported at Point P look significantly different than the nonspendable, restricted, committed, assigned, and unassigned categories discussed in the previous chapter. The City of Sacramento financial statements shown here were produced before the new rules for reporting the Fund Balance were issued.

- The total Fund Balances figure for the governmental funds of $463.2 million (Point Q) is significantly different from the $1.7 billion in total net assets reported for governmental activities as a whole in the statement of net assets (Exhibit 12.1). To help understand that large disparity, a reconciliation is included along with the balance sheet (titled Reconciliation of the Balance Sheet to the Statement of Net Assets—Governmental Funds). According to this reconciliation, the four largest items that formed the link between the totals shown for the governmental activities of the government-wide financial statements and those of the governmental funds of the fund-based financial statements are:

    1. Approximately $1.7 billion of capital assets reported by the governmental activities on the government-wide financial statements (Exhibit 12.1) were omitted on the comparable fund-based financial statement (Exhibit 12.3).

    2. Revenue transactions of $193 million reported on the government-wide statements had not been recognized in the fund-based statements because the resulting financial resources were not viewed as being available in the current period.

    3. The government-wide financial statements reported long-term liabilities (of approximately $638 million), but the fund-based statement did not. They did not represent claims to current financial resources.

    4. Internal service funds with net assets of $84 million were included in the governmental activities although, for fund-based financial statements, they were classified as proprietary funds rather than governmental funds.

Statement of Revenues, Expenditures, and Changes in Fund Balances—Governmental Funds—Fund-Based Statements

Exhibit 12.4 presents the statement of revenues, expenditures, and changes in fund balances for the governmental funds of the City of Sacramento. Once again, the General Fund is detailed in a separate column along with each of the major funds previously identified. Figures for all remaining nonmajor funds are then accumulated and shown together.

In examining Exhibit 12.4, note each of the following:

- Because the current financial resources measurement focus is being utilized, expenditures (Point R) rather than expenses are reported. For example, Capital Outlay is presented here as a reduction in resources rather than the acquisition of an asset. In the same way, Debt Service—Principal is reported on the statement in Exhibit 12.4 as an expenditure instead of a decrease in liabilities.

- Because the modified accrual method of accounting is used for timing purposes, reported amounts will be different than those previously shown. For example, total expenditures for interest and fiscal charges are listed on Exhibit 12.4 as $30,689,000 (Point S) whereas interest on long-term debt was disclosed in Exhibit 12.2 at Point E as $31,157,000. The first figure measures expenditures during the period using modified accrual accounting and the second figure is the amount of expense recognized according to accrual accounting.

- Exhibit 12.4 presents other financing sources and uses to reflect the issuance of long-term debt, distribution from a component unit, and transfers made between the funds. Because the fund-based statements are designed to present individual fund activities rather than government-wide figures, no elimination of the transfers is made.

- A reconciliation should be shown between the ending change in governmental fund balances (a decrease at Point T of nearly $50 million) in Exhibit 12.4 and the ending change in net assets for governmental activities in Exhibit 12.2 (an increase at Point U of $62 million). For the City of Sacramento, the major differences listed on this reconciliation involved the acquisition of capital assets ($144.5 million), the recording of depreciation ($74.7 million), the recording of revenues that did not provide current financial resources ($25.9 million), the recording of expenses that are not claims to current financial resources ($22.3 million), and the repayment of long-term debt ($19.5 million).

Statement of Net Assets—Proprietary Funds—Fund-Based Statements

The assets and liabilities of the City of Sacramento's proprietary funds, as reported in the fund-based financial statements, are presented in Exhibit 12.5. This statement shows individual information about six major enterprise funds, with a single column for the summation of all other enterprise funds. In addition, the statement provides a total for all of the enterprise funds. Specific information is available for the water fund, sewer fund, storm drainage fund, solid waste fund, community center fund, and the parking fund.

In examining Exhibit 12.5, a considerable amount of significant information should be noted:

- This fund-based statement also combines and exhibits the internal service funds (Point Z) because they are proprietary funds. However, government-wide financial statements usually report these same internal service funds as part of the governmental activities.

- Because the proprietary funds utilize accrual accounting to measure economic resources, the totals for the enterprise funds in Exhibit 12.5 agree in most ways with the total figures in Exhibit 12.1. The amount of detail, however, is more extensive in the fund-based financial statements. For example, the statement in Exhibit 12.1 uses only two accounts to describe capital assets whereas Exhibit 12.5 uses seven.

- Restricted cash and investments (Point V) of more than $16 million are listed under Noncurrent assets. An external source or specific laws must have designated the use of this money in some manner.

- Note in both the current and noncurrent liabilities that the City of Sacramento discloses amounts owed in connection with accrued compensated absences, liability for landfill closure, and capital lease obligations payable. All three were discussed earlier in this chapter.

Statement of Revenues, Expenses, and Changes in Fund Net Assets—Proprietary Funds—Fund-Based Statements

Just as the statement of net assets in Exhibit 12.5 provides individual information about specific enterprise funds (and totals for the internal service funds), the statement of revenues, expenses, and changes in fund net assets in Exhibit 12.6 gives the revenues and expenses for those same funds in detail. As an example, in Exhibit 12.2 operating and indirect expenses were listed for each of the business-type functions. Here, in Exhibit 12.6 (Point W), operating expenses are separately listed for employee services, services and supplies, depreciation, insurance premiums, and claims expenses. In addition, several nonoperating items are listed including interest expense and amortization of deferred charges. Finally, because this statement reflects all changes in the net assets of each activity, capital contributions as well as transfers in and out and special items are included at the bottom of the statement. Thus, extensive information is available about each of these funds, which is the objective of the fund-based financial statements.

Statement of Cash Flows—Proprietary Funds—Fund-Based Statements

One of the most unique aspects of the fund-based financial statements is the statement of cash flows for the proprietary funds (see Exhibit 12.7). Because a proprietary fund operates in a manner similar to a for-profit business, information about cash flows is considered as vital as it is for Intel and Coca-Cola. However, the physical structure is not entirely the same.

EXHIBIT 12.4 Fund-Based Financial Statements

CITY OF SACRAMENTO
Governmental Funds
Statement of Revenues, Expenditures and Changes in Fund Balances
For the Fiscal Year Ended June 30, 2008 (in thousands)

	General Fund	General Fund Projects Fund	Capital Grants Fund	Crocker Art Museum Fund	Financing Plans Fund	1997 Lease Revenue Bond Fund	Transportation and Development Fund	Other Governmental Funds	Total Governmental Funds
Revenues:									
Taxes	$283,822	$ —	$ —	$ —	$ —	$ —	$ 2,676	$ —	$ 286,498
Intergovernmental	16,039	—	35,324	—	—	—	40,246	45,732	137,341
Charges for services	51,626	—	—	—	—	—	5,764	5,895	63,285
Fines, forfeits and penalties	8,597	—	—	—	—	—	1,319	—	9,916
Interest, rents, and concessions	3,173	6,597	—	1,187	6,703	134	3,051	7,585	28,430
Community service fees	—	—	—	—	11,159	—	1,920	3,752	16,831
Assessment levies	—	—	—	—	—	—	—	25,894	25,894
Contributions and donations	585	—	—	15,028	—	4,762	—	11,378	31,753
Miscellaneous	246	—	—	—	—	—	—	50	296
Total revenues	364,088	6,597	35,324	16,215	17,862	4,896	54,976	100,286	600,244
Expenditures: ®									
Current:									
General government	32,946	—	—	—	—	—	—	832	33,778
Police	132,394	—	—	—	—	—	—	15,998	148,392
Fire	92,869	—	—	—	—	—	—	1,415	94,284
General services	14,138	—	—	—	—	—	—	9,060	23,198
Transportation	8,492	—	—	—	—	—	15,793	5,950	30,235
Neighborhood services	1,398	—	—	—	—	—	—	149	1,547
Convention, culture and leisure	6,158	1,275	—	—	—	—	—	8,647	16,080
Economic development	4,186	—	—	—	—	—	—	3,849	8,035
Parks and recreation	29,630	—	—	—	118	—	—	23,751	53,499

552

continued from page 552

Code enforcement	9,272	—	—	—	—	—	—	323	9,595
Development services	21,107	—	—	—	385	—	6,769	—	28,261
Planning	2,476	—	—	—	—	—	—	3,150	5,626
Library	9,366	—	—	—	—	—	—	—	9,366
Utilities	83	—	—	—	—	—	—	—	83
Nondepartmental	26,993	—	—	—	258	—	—	122	27,373
Capital outlay	16,839	34,595	41,785	—	14,308	—	28,411	17,569	153,507
Debt service:									
Principal	1,392	—	—	—	2,610	—	—	15,527	19,529
Interest and fiscal charges	344	823	—	248	2,110	4,174	—	22,990	30,689 [S]
Bond issuance costs	—	—	—	—	—	607	—	—	607
Total expenditures	410,083	36,693	41,785	248	19,789	4,781	50,973	129,332	693,684
Excess (deficiency) of revenues over (under) expenditures	(45,995)	(30,096)	(6,461)	15,967	(1,927)	115	4,003	(29,046)	(93,440)
Other financing sources (uses):									
Transfers in	24,814	—	—	—	—	—	1,948	32,227	58,989
Transfers out	(32,281)	(1,453)	—	(1,013)	(2,525)	—	(2,313)	(195)	(39,780)
Issuance of long-term debt	2,155	—	—	—	3,511	—	—	—	5,666
Special item—distribution from component unit	28,088	—	—	—	—	—	—	—	28,088
Special item—payment to redevelopment agency	(9,297)	—	—	—	—	—	—	—	(9,297)
Total other financing sources (uses)	13,479	(1,453)	—	(1,013)	986	—	(365)	32,032	43,666
Net change in fund balances	(32,516)	(31,549)	(6,461)	14,954	(941)	115	3,638	2,986	(49,774) [T]
Fund balances (deficit), beginning of year	131,478	129,224	(26,614)	12,530	117,931	2,694	52,371	93,362	512,976
Fund balances (deficit), end of year	$ 98,962	$ 97,675	$ (33,075)	$ 27,484	$ 116,990	$ 2,809	$ 56,009	$ 96,348	$ 463,202

EXHIBIT 12.5 Fund-Based Financial Statements

CITY OF SACRAMENTO
Proprietary Funds
Statement of Net Assets
June 30, 2008
(in thousands)

	Business-Type Activities—Enterprise Funds								Governmental Activities—Internal Service Funds (Z)
	Water Fund	Sewer Fund	Storm Drainage Fund	Solid Waste Fund	Community Center Fund	Parking Fund	Other Enterprise Funds	Total	
Assets									
Current assets:									
Cash and investments held by City	$ 43,688	$ 17,706	$ 19,059	$ —	$ 16,138	$ 28,373	$ 1,811	$ 126,775	$ 38,899
Cash and investments held by fiscal agent	—	—	—	—	143	—	—	143	127
Security lending assets	11,357	—	—	—	—	7,833	—	19,190	6,081
Receivables, net:									
Taxes	—	—	—	—	2,453	—	—	2,453	—
Accounts	10,637	10,035	7,809	11,617	138	563	262	41,061	28
Loans	743	110	329	—	—	—	—	1,182	—
Investment securities sold	1,172	—	—	—	—	809	—	1,981	628
Intergovernmental	690	457	200	618	—	—	—	1,965	—
Interest	414	17	60	—	113	279	—	883	202
Due from other funds	—	—	214	—	—	—	—	214	41,630
Inventories	3,044	88	70	—	—	—	—	3,202	1,736
Prepaid items	—	—	1	—	1	—	8	10	—
Total current assets	71,745	28,413	27,742	12,235	18,986	37,857	2,081	199,059	89,331
Noncurrent assets:									
Restricted assets: (V)									
Cash and investments held by City	—	—	151	2,800	105	283	740	4,079	—
Cash and investments held by fiscal agent	—	—	765	—	9,804	1,791	—	12,360	—
Advances to other funds	—	—	—	—	—	200	—	200	17,435
Loans receivable	2,759	1,519	4,557	—	33	—	—	8,868	—
Deferred charges	2,215	—	53	348	1,400	442	214	4,672	42
Capital assets:									
Land	645	1,137	10,151	1,133	21,739	6,795	3,821	45,421	6,456
Buildings and improvements	37,383	14,906	8,223	31,191	111,201	59,384	8,924	271,212	1,434
Machinery and equipment	12,039	3,439	13,827	7,135	2,729	3,492	38	42,699	—
Vehicles	—	—	—	—	—	—	—	—	109,506
Transmission and distribution system	484,857	121,634	334,561	—	—	—	—	941,052	—
Construction in progress	29,630	7,037	7,186	1,327	1,040	3,403	8,722	58,345	1,115

continued from page 554

								Total	
Less: accumulated depreciation	(126,338)	(42,917)	(84,025)	(13,303)	(43,081)	(22,421)	(7,064)	(339,149)	(70,559)
Total noncurrent assets	443,190	106,755	295,449	30,631	104,970	53,369	15,395	1,049,759	65,429
Total assets	514,935	135,168	323,191	42,866	123,956	91,226	17,476	1,248,818	154,760
Liabilities									
Current Liabilities:									
Securities lending obligations	$ 11,357	$ —	$ —	$ —	$ —	$ 7,833	$ —	$ 19,190	$ 6,081
Accounts payable and accrued expenses	4,780	8,684	2,849	2,366	1,938	1,551	2,099	24,267	8,380
Accrued compensated absences	159	25	103	69	34	17	15	422	62
Due to other funds	329	107	220	8,962	1,000	89	—	10,707	—
Interest payable	697	103	378	107	912	241	247	2,685	14
Accrued claims	—	—	—	—	—	—	—	—	15,122
Liability for landfill closure	—	—	—	760	—	—	—	760	—
Deposits	—	—	—	—	—	—	141	141	—
Unearned revenue	—	—	1	—	1,346	201	977	2,525	472
Capital lease payable, current portion	—	—	—	554	—	—	76	630	—
Revenue and other bonds payable, net, current portion	3,208	—	316	626	5,129	710	—	9,989	270
Utility district payable	305	—	—	—	—	—	—	305	—
Notes payable, current portion	—	641	3,850	—	—	—	255	4,746	—
Total current liabilities	20,835	9,560	7,717	13,444	10,359	10,642	3,810	76,367	30,401
Noncurrent liabilities:									
Accrued compensated absences	1,959	663	1,910	1,212	562	284	312	6,902	1,017
Advances from other funds	986	323	662	737	7,233	268	—	10,209	—
Water fee credits	1,988	—	—	—	—	—	—	1,988	—
OPEB liability	940	408	433	1,275	102	177	43	3,378	446
Accrued claims	—	—	—	—	—	—	—	—	34,560
Liability for landfill closure	—	—	—	12,151	—	—	—	12,151	—
Capital lease obligations payable	—	—	—	670	—	—	1,410	2,080	—
Revenue and other bonds payable, net	167,868	—	7,080	24,755	76,083	37,190	—	312,976	4,282
Notes payable	—	8,753	26,257	—	—	—	10,220	45,230	—
Utility district payable	611	—	—	—	—	—	—	611	—
Total noncurrent liabilities	174,352	10,147	36,342	40,800	83,980	37,919	11,985	395,525	40,305
Total liabilities	195,187	19,707	44,059	54,244	94,339	48,561	15,795	471,892	70,706
Net Assets (Deficit)									
Invested in capital assets, net of related debt	266,443	95,739	252,958	3,571	21,413	14,586	2,241	656,951	43,386
Unrestricted	53,305	19,722	26,174	(14,949)	8,204	28,079	(560)	119,975	40,668
Total net assets (deficit)	$319,748	$115,461	$279,132	$(11,378)	$29,617	$42,665	$1,681	$776,926	$84,054

The notes to the financial statements are an integral part of this statement.

EXHIBIT 12.6   Fund-Based Financial Statements

CITY OF SACRAMENTO
Proprietary Funds
Statement of Revenues, Expenses and Changes in Fund Net Assets
For the Fiscal Year Ended June 30, 2008
(in thousands)

| | | | Business-Type Activities—Enterprise Funds | | | | | | Governmental |
	Water Fund	Sewer Fund	Storm Drainage Fund	Solid Waste Fund	Community Center Fund	Parking Fund	Other Enterprise Funds	Total	Activities—Internal Service Funds
Operating revenues:									
Charges for services:									
User fees and charges	$ 62,305	$ 19,673	$ 33,215	$ 52,041	$ 2,643	$ 18,425	$ 6,864	$195,166	$ 68,485
Rents and concessions	—	—	—	—	4,755	1,195	—	5,950	—
Charge to Regional Sanitation District for operating and maintaining treatment plant	—	966	—	—	—	—	—	966	—
Miscellaneous	2,822	65	74	393	158	6	101	3,619	401
Total operating revenues	65,127	20,704	33,289	52,434	7,556	19,626	6,965	205,701	68,886
Operating expenses: (W)									
Employee services	21,722	7,644	20,355	16,680	6,246	4,126	5,888	82,661	11,170
Services and supplies	20,008	6,906	6,780	28,666	5,649	7,185	1,479	76,673	27,540
Depreciation	12,997	3,555	10,233	1,959	2,617	2,306	188	33,855	8,494
Insurance premiums	—	—	—	—	—	—	—	—	2,070
Claims expense	—	—	—	—	—	—	—	—	5,553
Total operating expenses	54,727	18,105	37,368	47,305	14,512	13,617	7,555	193,189	54,827
Operating income (loss)	10,400	2,599	(4,079)	5,129	(6,956)	6,009	(590)	12,512	14,059

continued from page 556

Nonoperating revenues (expenses):

Interest and investment revenue	2,580	760	1,183	(235)	1,217	1,278	115	6,898	4,207
Transient occupancy taxes	—	—	—	—	17,538	—	—	17,538	—
Revenue from other agencies	—	353	410	760	—	—	654	2,177	—
Interest expense	(8,518)	(225)	(1,198)	(1,403)	(5,863)	(2,544)	(306)	(20,057)	(365)
Amortization of deferred charges	(119)	—	(4)	(27)	(132)	(25)	—	(307)	(3)
Gain on disposition of capital assets	—	—	—	—	—	(968)	—	(968)	138
Total nonoperating revenues (expenses)	(6,057)	888	391	(905)	12,760	(2,259)	463	5,281	3,977
Income (loss) before contributions and transfers	4,343	3,487	(3,688)	4,224	5,804	3,750	(127)	17,793	18,036
Capital contributions	5,239	2,099	11,302	—	—	—	—	18,640	—
Special item—gain on sale of capital asset	—	—	—	—	—	19,860	—	19,860	—
Special item—payment to redevelopment agency	—	—	—	—	—	(14,215)	—	(14,215)	—
Transfers in	—	17	—	5	1,754	—	—	1,776	407
Transfers out	(6,670)	(2,135)	(3,624)	(5,248)	(1,552)	(1,981)	(159)	(21,369)	(23)
Changes in net assets	2,912	3,468	3,990	(1,019)	6,006	7,414	(286)	22,485	18,420
Total net assets (deficit), beginning of year	316,836	111,993	275,142	(10,359)	23,611	35,251	1,967	754,441	65,634
Total net assets (deficit), end of year	$319,748	$115,461	$279,132	$(11,378)	$29,617	$42,665	$1,681	$776,926	$84,054

EXHIBIT 12.7 Fund-Based Financial Statements

CITY OF SACRAMENTO
Proprietary Funds
Statement of Cash Flows
For the Fiscal Year Ended June 30, 2008
(in thousands)

		Business-Type Activities—Enterprise Funds							
	Water Fund	Sewer Fund	Storm Drainage Fund	Solid Waste Fund	Community Center Fund	Parking Fund	Other Enterprise Funds	Total	Governmental Activities—Internal Service Funds
Cash flows from operating activities: ⊗									
Receipts from customers and users	$ 62,964	$ 17,890	$ 31,558	$ 49,919	$ 7,709	$ 19,659	$ 7,235	$ 196,934	$ —
Receipts from interfund services provided									117,017
Payments to suppliers	(20,024)	(3,183)	(5,651)	(29,618)	(4,832)	(6,824)	(1,415)	(71,547)	(73,577)
Payments to employees	(20,287)	(7,077)	(19,545)	(15,030)	(5,951)	(3,856)	(5,622)	(77,368)	(10,503)
Claims paid	—	—	—	—	—	—	—	—	(13,582)
Net cash provided by (used for) operating activities	22,653	7,630	6,362	5,271	(3,074)	8,979	198	48,019	19,355
Cash flows from noncapital financing activities:									
Transient occupancy taxes	—	—	—	—	17,628	—	—	17,628	—
Payment to redevelopment agency	—	—	—	—	—	(14,215)	—	(14,215)	—
Transfers in from other funds	—	17	5	5	1,754	—	—	1,776	—
Transfers out to other funds	(6,670)	(2,135)	(3,624)	(5,248)	(1,552)	(1,981)	(159)	(21,369)	(23)
Proceeds from interfund borrowing	—	—	—	1,476	—	268	—	1,744	—
Collections on interfund loans	—	—	52	—	—	—	—	52	—
Loans to other funds	—	—	—	—	—	—	—	—	(2,991)
Interfund loan repayments	—	—	—	—	(1,500)	—	—	(1,500)	—
Intergovernmental revenue received	—	353	410	760	—	—	654	2,177	—
Net cash provided by (used for) noncapital financing activities	(6,670)	(1,765)	(3,162)	(3,007)	16,330	(15,928)	495	(13,707)	(3,014)

continued from page 558

Cash flows from capital and related financing activities: (Y)

Proceeds from issuance of debt	—	—	1,925	—	—	5,749	—	7,674	—
Proceeds from interfund borrowing	1,315	430	882	983	89	—	—	3,699	—
Acquisition and construction of capital assets	(13,460)	(4,997)	(8,559)	(1,267)	(2,158)	(6,821)	(234)	(37,496)	(10,266)
Proceeds from disposition of capital assets	—	—	—	—	21,683	—	—	21,683	69
Water fee credits issued	407	—	—	—	—	—	—	407	—
Principal payments on capital debt	(1,967)	(627)	(2,289)	(692)	(950)	(244)	(5,731)	(12,500)	(239)
Interest payments on capital debt	(8,318)	(232)	(1,109)	(1,339)	(1,985)	(314)	(4,627)	(17,924)	(169)
Transfers in from other funds	—	—	—	—	—	—	—	—	407
Capital contributions received	2,628	1,042	—	—	—	—	—	3,670	—
Loan repayments received	4,821	107	321	—	—	—	—	5,249	—
Net cash provided by (used for) capital and related financing activities	(14,574)	(4,277)	(8,829)	(2,315)	16,679	(1,630)	(10,592)	(25,538)	(10,198)
Cash flows from investing activities:									
Collection of interest and investment revenue	2,353	761	1,424	(235)	1,221	751	115	6,390	4,219
Investments sold with settlement after year end	(1,172)	—	—	—	—	(809)	—	(1,981)	(628)
Loan repayment received	—	—	—	—	6	—	—	6	—
Net cash provided by (used for) investing activities	1,181	761	1,424	(235)	1,227	(58)	115	4,415	3,591
Net increase (decrease) in cash and cash equivalents	2,590	2,349	(4,205)	(286)	3,891	9,672	(822)	13,189	9,734
Cash and cash equivalents, beginning of year, restated	41,098	15,357	24,180	3,086	22,299	20,775	3,373	130,168	29,292
Cash and cash equivalents, end of year	$43,688	$17,706	$19,975	$2,800	$26,190	$30,447	$2,551	$143,357	$39,026
Reconciliation of cash and cash equivalents to the Statement of Net Assets:									
Cash and investments held by City	$43,688	$17,706	$19,059	$—	$16,138	$28,373	$1,811	$126,775	$38,899
Cash and investments held by fiscal agent	—	—	—	—	143	—	—	143	127
Restricted cash and investments held by City	—	—	151	2,800	105	283	740	4,079	—
Restricted cash and investments held by fiscal agent	—	—	765	—	9,804	1,791	—	12,360	—
Total cash and cash equivalents, end of year	$43,688	$17,706	$19,975	$2,800	$26,190	$30,447	$2,551	$143,357	$39,026

One of the main differences is that the statement of cash flows shown here for the proprietary funds has four sections rather than just three:

1. Cash flows from operating activities.
2. Cash flows from noncapital financing activities.
3. Cash flows from capital and related financing activities.
4. Cash flows from investing activities.

- The presentation of cash flows from operating activities (Point X) is very similar to that prepared by a for-profit business. However, rather than being an optional method of presentation, as with for-profit accounting, the direct method of reporting operating activities is required. The indirect method that is so commonly used by businesses is not allowed.

- Cash flows from noncapital financing activities includes (1) proceeds and payments on debt *not* attributable to the acquisition or construction of capital assets and (2) grants and subsidies *not* restricted for capital purposes or operating activities.

- Cash flows from capital and related financing activities focus on the amounts spent on capital assets and the source of that funding. Exhibit 12.7 shows typical examples (Point Y): proceeds from issuance of debt, acquisition and construction of capital assets, and proceeds from disposition of capital assets.

- Cash flows from investing activities disclose amounts paid and received from investments.

REPORTING PUBLIC COLLEGES AND UNIVERSITIES

LO8

Prepare financial statements for a public college or university.

Public colleges and universities such as The Ohio State University and the University of Kansas historically have been in a somewhat awkward position in terms of financial accounting. Private schools including Harvard, Duke, and Stanford follow the FASB Accounting Standards Codification. Authoritative accounting literature on contributions and the proper form of financial statements have provided a significant amount of official reporting guidance for these private institutions. Generally accepted accounting principles developed for such not-for-profit organizations have progressed greatly over the years.

In contrast, GASB has retained primary authority over the reporting of public colleges and universities. Much of the GASB's work, however, has been directed at improving the accounting standards utilized by state and local government units. Consequently, until recently, the evolution of financial statements for public schools has lagged behind that for other types of reporting.

For decades the question of whether the financial statements prepared for public colleges and universities should resemble those of private schools has been the subject of much theoretical discussion. Generally, the operations of public colleges and universities differ in at least two important ways from private schools. First, the state or other governments directly provide a significant amount of funding (at least for qualifying students), lessening the reliance on tuition and fees. For example, information provided with the 2008 financial statements of Utah State University disclosed state grants and appropriations of $176 million and federal grants and contracts of approximately $110 million in comparison to revenues of only $67 million from tuition and fees (after scholarship allowances).

Second, because of the ability to generate money each year from the government, public schools often raise and accumulate a smaller amount of endowment funds than private schools. Private schools usually try to build a large endowment to ensure financial security; this is not always necessary at a public school backed by the state or another government. For example, at June 30, 2008, Princeton University, a private school, held investments with a fair value of approximately $15.9 billion, an amount (roughly equal to $2 million per student) that is almost beyond the comprehension of officials at most public colleges.

Do these and other differences warrant unique financial statements for public colleges and universities? In many ways, public and private schools are very much alike. They both educate students, charge tuition and other fees, conduct scholarly research, maintain libraries and sports teams, operate cafeterias and museums, and the like. What should be the measurement basis and what should be the form of the financial statements to reflect the financial activity and position of a public college or university?

Four alternatives have been suggested for properly constructing the financial statements that public colleges and universities prepare and distribute:

1. Simply adopt FASB's requirements so that all colleges and universities (public and private) prepare comparable financial statements. The private reporting model is now relatively well developed. This suggestion presents some potential problems, however, because FASB, a group that has not had to deal with the intricacies found in governmental entities, might fail to comprehend the unique aspects of public schools. The reporting needs associated with such institutions might go unnoticed. In addition, loss of authority to FASB could weaken GASB. Politically, reducing the power of this board is not a goal of the organizations that provide much of GASB's support and financing.

2. Apply a more traditional model focusing on fund-based statements and the wide variety of funds that such schools often maintain. However, both private not-for-profit organizations and governments (at least in part) have abandoned the reporting of individual funds. For public schools to continue relying on this approach seems somewhat outdated.

3. Create an entirely new set of financial statements designed specifically to meet the unique needs of a public college or university. If FASB's Accounting Standards Codification is not to be followed, the fundamental differences between private and public schools must be significant. If those differences can be identified, new statements could be developed to satisfy the informational needs of users and properly reflect the events and transactions of these public institutions. Unfortunately, the creation of a new set of financial statements would require an enormous amount of work by GASB. Would the benefit gained from tailor-made financial statements outweigh the cost of producing new standards for reporting public schools?

4. Adopt the same reporting model for public schools that has been created for state and local governments. Because a large amount of funding for public schools comes directly from governments, the financial statement format utilized by a city or county could be applied.

GASB *Statement 35,* "Basic Financial Statements—and Management's Discussion and Analysis—for Public Colleges and Universities," issued in November 1999, officially selected the fourth option. According to paragraph 25, "the objective of this Statement is to amend *Statement 34* to include public colleges and universities in the financial reporting model established by that Statement." This pronouncement creates a standard reporting model for all public colleges and universities such as the University of Florida and Michigan State University.

However, a review of public college and university financial statements shows that many do not prepare both government-wide and fund-based financial statements. Such schools can logically be viewed as large enterprise funds: They have a user charge (tuition and fees), and they are open to the public. As discussed, accounting for enterprise funds in government-wide statements and fund-based statements is very similar. For these proprietary funds, both statements report all economic resources and use accrual accounting.

Thus, having two sets of almost identical statements was viewed by the GASB as redundant. For this reason, most public schools are allowed to prepare a single set of statements. Consequently, a note to the financial statements for Middle Tennessee State University for June 30, 2008, and the year then ending provides a common rationale for the method by which the statements are structured:

> For financial statement purposes, Middle Tennessee State University is considered a special-purpose government engaged *only in business-type activities.* Accordingly, the financial statements have been prepared using the economic resources measurement focus and the accrual basis of accounting. Revenues are recorded when earned, and expenses are recorded when a liability is incurred, regardless of the timing of related cash flows. Grants and similar items are recognized as revenue as soon as all eligibility requirements imposed by the provider have been met. [Emphasis added.]

Exhibit 12.8 presents the financial statements for June 30, 2008, and the year then ended for James Madison University (a public school) for illustration purposes, although the accompanying notes have been omitted. The component unit that is reported here is identified as follows:

> The James Madison University Foundation, Inc. meets the criteria which qualify it as a component unit of the University. The Foundation is a legally separate, tax-exempt organization formed to promote the achievements and further the aims and purposes of the University.

EXHIBIT 12.8

JAMES MADISON UNIVERSITY
Statement of Net Assets
As of June 30, 2008

	2008	
	James Madison University	Component Unit
Assets		
Current assets:		
Cash and cash equivalents (Note 1 O., 2)	$ 80,934,146	$ 1,564,770
Securities lending—Cash and cash equivalents (Note 2)	4,283,467	—
Short-term investments (Note 2)	16,135,861	—
Accounts receivable (Net of allowance for doubtful accounts of $340,931) (Note 3)	5,199,574	45,074
Contributions receivable (Net of allowance for doubtful contributions of $40,321) (Note 3) ......-	—	1,975,712
Due from the Commonwealth (Note 1 O., 4)	8,675,904	—
Prepaid expenses	5,293,919	30,300
Inventory	717,916	—
Notes receivable (Net of allowance for doubtful accounts of $46,208)	524,295	—
Total current assets	121,765,082	3,615,856
Non-current assets:		
Restricted cash and cash equivalents (Note 1 O., 2) ..	31,960,868	—
Endowment investments (Note 2)	236,948	35,549,782
Other long-term investments (Note 2)	660,616	29,995,637
Contributions receivable (Net allowance for doubtful contributions of $166,792) (Note 3)	—	8,172,842
Due from the Commonwealth (Note 1 O., 4)	8,312,935	—
Notes receivable (Net of allowance for doubtful accounts of $190,109)	2,141,705	—
Capital assets, net: (Note 5)		
Non-depreciable	98,704,624	312,391
Depreciable	404,250,035	403,805
Other assets	—	8,141
Total non-current assets	546,267,731	74,442,598
Total assets	668,032,813	78,058,454
Liabilities		
Current liabilities:		
Accounts payable and accrued expenses (Note 6) ...	36,332,271	177,756
Deferred revenue	10,902,526	—
Obligations under securities lending	20,419,328	—
Deposits held in custody for others	3,375,865	—
Demand note payable	—	—
Long-term liabilities—current portion (Note 7)	18,078,562	437,588
Advance from the Treasurer of Virginia	62,500	—
Total current liabilities	89,171,052	615,344
Non-current liabilities (Note 7)	114,506,770	1,077,779
Total liabilities	203,677,822	1,693,123
Net Assets		
Invested in capital assets, Net of related debt	402,361,323	716,196
Restricted for:		
Non-expendable:		
Scholarships and fellowships	317,261	26,421,501
Research and public service	—	1,952,393
Other	—	10,527,213

(*continued*)

EXHIBIT 12.8
(continued)

	2008	
	James Madison University	**Component Unit**
Expendable:		
Scholarships and fellowships	50,743	5,262,695
Research and public service	2,167,651	879,157
Debt service	9,404	596,104
Capital projects	11,125,011	9,218,916
Loans	344,591	—
Other	—	13,148,602
Unrestricted	47,979,007	7,642,554
Total net assets	$464,354,991	$76,365,331

The accompanying notes to financial statements are an integral part of this statement.

JAMES MADISON UNIVERSITY
Statement of Revenues, Expenses, and Changes in Net Assets
For the Year Ended June 30, 2008

	2008	
	James Madison University	**Component Unit**
Operating revenues:		
Student tuition and fees (Net of scholarship allowances of $7,148,487)	$116,453,199	$ —
Gifts and contributions	—	12,143,084
Federal grants and contracts	12,588,258	—
State grants and contracts	6,848,436	—
Non-governmental grants and contracts	4,618,784	—
Auxiliary enterprises (Net of scholarship allowances of $5,731,404) (Note 10)	115,334,434	—
Other operating revenues	1,472,934	965,912
Total operating revenues	257,316,045	13,108,996
Operating expenses (Note 11):		
Instruction	111,236,644	817,037
Research	5,922,628	14,437
Public service	11,522,193	88,546
Academic support	27,607,524	358,820
Student services	12,527,005	64,339
Institutional support	21,867,048	3,240,225
Operation and maintenance—plant	28,993,421	55,437
Depreciation	20,376,369	118,996
Student aid	6,298,269	1,767,595
Auxiliary activities (Note 10)	90,314,477	828,403
Total operating expenses	336,665,578	7,353,835
Operating gain/(loss)	(79,349,533)	5,755,161
Non-operating revenues/(expenses):		
State appropriations (Note 12)	82,810,149	—
Grants and contracts (Note 1 L.)	4,363,043	—
Gifts	1,524,711	—
Investment income (Net of investment expense of $907,568 for the University and $433,601 for the Foundation)	6,627,327	(7,647,864)
In-Kind support from James Madison University	—	2,265,037

(continued)

EXHIBIT 12.8
(*continued*)

	2008	
	James Madison University	Component Unit
Interest on capital asset—related debt	(4,092,175)	(212,546)
Gain/(loss) on disposal of plant assets	(75,662)	—
Payment to the Commonwealth	(711,906)	—
Net non-operating revenues/(expenses)	90,445,487	(5,595,373)
Income before other revenues, expenses, gains or losses	11,095,954	159,788
Capital appropriations and contributions (Note 13) . . .	52,459,804	—
Capital gifts	576,821	—
Additions/(reductions) to permanent endowments	—	3,087,613
Net other revenues	53,036,625	3,087,613
Increase in net assets	64,132,579	3,247,401
Net assets—beginning of year	400,222,412	73,117,930
Net assets—end of year	$464,354,991	$76,365,331

The accompanying notes to financial statements are an integral part of this statement.

JAMES MADISON UNIVERSITY
Statement of Cash Flows
For the Year Ended June 30, 2008

	2008
Cash flows from operating activities:	
Student tuition and fees	$116,116,954
Grants and contracts (Note 1 L.)	24,127,243
Auxiliary enterprises	115,561,542
Other receipts	1,376,820
Payments to employees	(142,666,639)
Payments for fringe benefits	(45,748,857)
Payments for services and supplies	(87,550,038)
Payments for utilities	(12,727,770)
Payments for scholarships and fellowships	(6,298,269)
Payments for noncapitalized plant improvements and equipment	(18,741,433)
Loans issued to students	(590,709)
Collections of loans from students	408,572
Net cash used by operating activities	(56,732,584)
Cash flows from noncapital financing activities:	
State appropriations	82,808,646
Nonoperating grants and contracts (Note 1 L.)	4,363,043
Payment to the Commonwealth	(711,906)
Gifts and grants for other than capital purposes	1,524,711
Loans issued to students and employees	(2,100)
Collections of loans from students and employees	2,100
Agency receipts	14,599,177
Agency payments	(14,582,073)
Reductions to permanent endowment	—
Net cash provided by noncapital financing activities	88,001,598
Cash flows from capital financing activities:	
Capital appropriations and contributions (Note 1 O.)	51,735,150
Proceeds from capital debt	34,523,071

(*continued*)

EXHIBIT 12.8
(*concluded*)

	2008
Capital gifts	—
Proceeds from sale of capital assets	58,260
Purchase of capital assets	(80,793,325)
Principal paid on capital debt, leases, and installments	(18,723,060)
Interest paid on capital debt, leases, and installments	(4,927,954)
Net cash used by capital financing activities	(18,127,858)
Cash flows from investing activities:	
Interest on investments	1,425,637
Interest on cash management pools	4,692,471
Net cash provided by investing activities	6,118,108
Net increase in cash	19,259,264
Cash and cash equivalents—beginning of the year, restated	93,635,750
Cash and cash equivalents—end of the year (Note 1 O.)	$112,895,014

Note that these statements are quite similar to the fund-based financial statements presented in this chapter for the proprietary funds of the City of Sacramento, California (Exhibits 12.5, 12.6, and 12.7).

Summary

1. As with businesses, state and local governments often obtain assets through lease arrangements. Government accounting applies the same criteria for identifying a capital lease as a for-profit organization. Government-wide financial statements initially report both the resulting asset and liability at the present value of the minimum lease payments. This asset is depreciated over the time that the government expects to use it. Interest expense on the reported liability is recognized each period. Fund-based financial statements recognize an expenditure and an other financing source at this same present value when the contract is initiated. Subsequent payments on the debt and interest are also recognized as expenditures.

2. Solid waste landfills create large potential debts for a government because of closure and postclosure costs. Government-wide statements accrue this liability each period based on the latest cost estimations and the portion of the property that has been filled. Fund-based financial statements report no expenditures until a claim to current financial resources is made.

3. Government employees often have the right to future compensated absences because of holidays, vacations, sick leave, and the like. In creating government-wide statements, the debts for these absences are estimated and reported as the employees earn them. Fund-based statements do not recognize a liability until the use of current financial resources is expected.

4. A state or local government that obtains a work of art or historical treasure normally records it as a capital asset on the government-wide financial statements. However, if specified guidelines are met, an expense can replace recognition of the asset. A state or local government that receives such a work of art or historical treasure through donation must still recognize revenue according to the rules established for voluntary nonexchange transactions. In contrast, fund-based financial statements for the governmental funds report no capital assets and, therefore, do not show these items.

5. Depreciation must be recorded each period for works of art and historical treasures that are capitalized unless they are viewed as inexhaustible.

6. Infrastructure assets must be capitalized and depreciated on the government-wide financial statements. However, depreciation is not recorded if the modified approach is applied. Under this method, if a monitoring system is created to ensure that a network of infrastructure is maintained yearly at a predetermined condition, the cost of this care is expensed in lieu of recording depreciation.

7. A state or local government must include a management's discussion and analysis (MD&A) as part of its general purpose external financial reporting. As with for-profit businesses, this MD&A provides a verbal explanation of the government's operations and financial position.

8. A primary government produces a comprehensive annual financial report (CAFR). Both state and local governments as well as any special purpose government that meets certain provisions are viewed as primary governments. A component unit is any function that is legally separate from a primary government but for which financial accountability still exists. In the government-wide statements, component units can be discretely presented to the right of the primary government or can be blended within the actual funds of the primary government.

9. A statement of net assets and a statement of activities are prepared as government-wide financial statements based on the economic resources measurement focus and accrual accounting. These statements separate governmental activities from business-type activities. Internal service funds are usually included with the governmental funds in the governmental activities. The statement of activities reports expenses by function along with related program revenues to determine the net expense or revenue resulting from each function. The government then shows the amount of general revenues as its way of covering the net expenses of the various functions.

10. In fund-based financial statements reported for the governmental funds, the General Fund and any other major fund are reported in separate columns. These statements are based on measuring current financial resources using modified accrual accounting. Additional statements are presented for proprietary funds and fiduciary funds.

11. Financial statements prepared by public colleges and universities must follow the same reporting guidelines as those created for state and local government units. Those statements will differ from the statements produced by private schools that follow FASB guidelines. Many public schools view themselves as special purpose governments that are engaged only in business-type activities. Thus, they only need to present fund-based statements for a proprietary fund.

Comprehensive Illustration

PROBLEM

(*Estimated Time: 40 minutes*) The following is a series of transactions for a city. Indicate how the city reports each transaction within the government-wide financial statements and then on the fund-based financial statements. Assume that the city follows a policy of considering resources as available if they will be received within 60 days. Incurred liabilities are assumed to be claims to current resources if they will be paid within 60 days.

1. Borrowed money by issuing a 20-year bond for $3 million, its face value. This money is to be used to construct a highway around the city.

2. Transferred cash of $100,000 from the General Fund to the debt service funds to make the first payment of principal and interest on the bond in (1).

3. Paid the cash in (2) on the bond. Of this total, $70,000 represents interest; the remainder reduces the principal of the bond payable.

4. Completed construction of the highway and paid the entire $3 million.

5. The highway is expected to last for 30 years. However, the government qualifies to use the modified approach, which it has adopted for this system. A $35,000 cost is incurred during the year to maintain the highway at an appropriate, predetermined condition. Of this amount, $29,000 was paid immediately but the other $6,000 will not be paid until the sixth month of the subsequent year.

6. Received lights for the new highway donated from a local business. The lights are valued at $200,000 and should last for 20 years. The modified approach is not used for this network of infrastructure, but straight-line depreciation is applied using the half-year convention.

7. Leased a truck to maintain the new highway. The lease qualifies as a capital lease. The present value of the minimum payments is $70,000. Depreciation for this year is $10,000 and interest is $6,000. A single $11,000 payment in cash is made.

8. Recorded cash revenues of $2 million from the local subway system and made salary expense payments of $300,000 to its employees.

9. Opened a solid waste landfill at the beginning of the year that will be used for 20 years. This year an estimated 4 percent of the capacity was filled. The city anticipates closure and postclosure requirements will be $2 million based on current cost figures although no costs have been incurred to date.

SOLUTION

1. *Government-wide financial statements.* On the statement of net assets, under the Governmental Activities column, both Cash and Noncurrent Liabilities increase by $3 million.

   Fund-based financial statements. The Cash balance increases on the balance sheet by $3 million whereas Other Financing Sources increases by the same amount on the statement of revenues, expenditures, and changes in fund balances. These amounts will be shown in the Other Governmental Funds column unless this particular capital projects fund is judged to be major so that a separate column is required.

2. *Government-wide financial statements.* No recording of this transfer is shown because the amount was an intra-activity transaction entirely carried out within the governmental activities.

   Fund-based financial statements. The Cash balance of the General Fund on the balance sheet decreases while the cash listed for other governmental funds (or debt service fund) increases. On the statement of revenues, expenditures, and other changes in fund balances, the General Fund shows an Other Financing Use of $100,000 whereas the other governmental funds report an Other Financing Source. These balances will not be offset in arriving at total figures.

3. *Government-wide financial statements.* On the statement of net assets, Cash for the governmental activities decreases by $100,000 and the total reported for Noncurrent Liabilities drops by $30,000 because of the principal payment. The statement of activities then recognizes $70,000 in interest expense as a governmental activity.

   Fund-based financial statements. First, Cash decreases by $100,000 on the balance sheet under the Other Governmental Funds (or Debt Service Fund) column. Second, on the statement of revenues, expenditures, and changes in fund balances, a $30,000 principal expenditure is reported with a $70,000 interest expenditure. These amounts are shown within other governmental funds (or debt service fund).

4. *Government-wide financial statements.* Under the governmental activities listed on the statement of net assets, Cash decreases by $3 million and Capital Assets increases by the same amount. All new infrastructure costs are capitalized.

   Fund-based financial statements. On the balance sheet, cash reported for other governmental funds decreases. Again, if this particular capital projects fund qualifies as major, the effects are shown in a separate column rather than in the Other Governmental funds column. The statement of revenues, expenditures, and changes in fund balances reports a $3 million expenditure as a capital outlay.

5. *Government-wide financial statements.* The statement of net assets reports a $29,000 decrease in cash under governmental activities and a $6,000 increase in a current liability. The statement of activities includes the $35,000 expense within an appropriate function such as public works. Because the modified approach is being applied, the maintenance expense is recognized instead of depreciation expense.

   Fund-based financial statements. Because the $6,000 liability will not require the use of current financial resources (it will not be paid within 60 days), it is not recorded at this time at the fund level. Thus, the balance sheet reports only a $29,000 drop in cash, probably under the General Fund. A $29,000 expenditure is recorded on the statement of revenues, expenditures, and changes in fund balances for public works.

6. *Government-wide financial statements.* The lights do not qualify as works of art or historical treasures and must therefore be reported as capital assets on the statement of net assets at the $200,000 value. Based on a 20-year life and the half-year convention, $5,000 in accumulated depreciation must be recognized to reduce the reported net asset to $195,000. For the statement of activities, a $200,000 revenue is appropriate unless eligibility requirements for the donation have not yet been fulfilled. This revenue should be shown as a program revenue (Capital Grants and Contributions) to offset the expenses reported for public works. Depreciation of $5,000 should also be included as an expense for public works ($200,000/20 years × 0.5 year).

   Fund-based financial statements. No reporting is required because current financial resources were not affected.

7. *Government-wide financial statements.* On the statement of net assets, both the leased truck and the lease liability are reported under the governmental activities, at the present value of $70,000. Then $10,000 in accumulated depreciation reduces the truck's book value. The liability is reduced by $5,000, the amount of the $11,000 payment less $6,000 attributed to interest. The statement of activities reports interest of $6,000 and depreciation of $10,000 as expenses directly related to the public works function.

   Fund-based financial statements. The balance sheet, probably under the General Fund, reports an $11,000 reduction in cash. The statement of revenues, expenditures, and changes in fund balances records a $70,000 expenditure as a capital outlay and recognizes an Other Financing Source of the same amount. This statement also shows another $11,000 in expenditures: $6,000 as interest and $5,000 for debt reduction.

8. *Government-wide financial statements.* Cash on the statement of net assets increases under the business-type activities by $1.7 million. The statement of activities reports expenses for the

subway system as $300,000 while the related program revenues for charges for services rendered increase by $2 million so that the net revenue resulting from this business-type activity is $1.7 million.

Fund-based financial statements. The statement of net assets for the proprietary funds (see Exhibit 12.5) should include a separate column for the subway system, assuming that it qualifies as a major fund. Cash in this column increases by $1.7 million. Likewise, the statement of revenues, expenses, and changes in fund net assets for the proprietary funds (see Exhibit 12.6) reports operating revenues of $2 million for the subway system. The list of operating expenses will include personnel services of $300,000. The statement of cash flows (see Exhibit 12.7) also reports both the inflow and outflow of cash under Cash Flows from Operating Activities.

9. *Government-wide financial statements.* Because the landfill is 4 percent filled and this is its first year, that portion of the overall $2 million ($80,000) cost must be recognized to date. The statement of net assets shows this amount as a noncurrent liability. The balance is presented as either a governmental activity or a business-type activity, depending on the landfill's fund classification. Likewise, the statement of activities reports the same $80,000 expense figure.

Fund-based financial statements. This liability does not require the use of current financial resources and is not reported if the landfill is considered a governmental fund. However, if the landfill is viewed as an enterprise fund, the separate statements prepared for the proprietary funds show both the $80,000 expense and liability (see Exhibits 12.5 and 12.6).

Questions

1. What criteria does a state or local government apply to determine whether to capitalize a lease?
2. On January 1, 2010, a city signs a capital lease for new equipment for the police department. How does the city report this transaction on government-wide financial statements? On fund-based financial statements?
3. On December 31, 2010, the city in question 2 makes its first annual lease payment. How does the city report the payment on government-wide financial statements? On fund-based financial statements?
4. Why does the operation of a solid waste landfill create reporting concerns for a local government?
5. A landfill is scheduled to be filled to capacity gradually over a 10-year period. However, at the end of the first year of operations, the landfill is only 7 percent filled. How much liability for closure and postclosure costs should be recognized on government-wide financial statements? How much liability should be recognized on fund-based financial statements assuming that the landfill is recorded in an enterprise fund? How much liability should be recognized on fund-based financial statements assuming that the landfill is recorded in the General Fund?
6. A city operates a solid waste landfill. This facility is 11 percent full after the first year of operation and 24 percent after the second year. How much expense should be recognized on the government-wide financial statements in the second year for closure costs? Assuming that the landfill is reported in the General Fund, what expenditure should be recognized in the second year on the fund-based financial statements?
7. A teacher working for the City of Lights earns vacation pay of $2,000 during 2010. However, the vacation will not be taken until near the end of 2011. In the government-wide financial statements for 2010, how is this compensated absence reported? How is this compensated absence reported in the fund-based financial statements for 2010?
8. Assume in question 7 that the teacher takes the vacation late in 2011 and is paid the entire $2,000. What journal entry is reported in creating each of the two types of financial statements?
9. The City of Salem is given a painting by Picasso to display in its city hall. Under what condition will the city *not* report this painting as a capital asset on its government-wide financial statements? If it does report the painting as a capital asset, must the city report depreciation?
10. Assume in question 9 that the city does not choose to report the painting on the government-wide financial statements as a capital asset. Must the city report a revenue for the gift?
11. Under what condition is the modified approach applied?
12. What impact does the use of the modified approach have on reporting within the government-wide financial statements?
13. What does the management's discussion and analysis (MD&A) normally include? Where does a state or local government present this information?
14. What does a comprehensive annual financial report (known as the CAFR) include?

15. A primary government can be either a general purpose government or a special purpose government. What is the difference in these two? How does an activity qualify as a special purpose government?

16. The Willingham Museum qualifies as a component unit of the City of Willingham. How does an activity or function qualify to be a component unit of a primary government?

17. What is the difference between a blended component unit and a discretely presented component unit?

18. What are the two government-wide financial statements? What does each normally present?

19. What are the two fund-based financial statements for governmental funds? What information does each normally present?

20. What is the difference in program revenues and general revenues? Why is that distinction important?

21. Why does a government determine the net expenses or revenues for each of the functions within its statement of activities?

22. How are internal service funds reported on government-wide financial statements?

23. How are fiduciary funds reported on government-wide financial statements?

24. What are some of the major differences that exist between private colleges and universities and public colleges and universities that affect financial reporting?

25. What is the most common form for the financial statements of public colleges and universities?

Problems

LO1

1. A city government has obtained an asset through a capital lease. Which of the following is true for the government-wide financial statements?
   a. The accounting parallels that used in for-profit accounting.
   b. The city must report an other financing source.
   c. The city must report an expenditure.
   d. Recognition of depreciation is optional.

LO1

2. A city government has a six-year capital lease for property being used within the General Fund. Minimum lease payments total $70,000 starting next year but have a current present value of $49,000. What is the total amount of expenditures to be recognized on the fund-based financial statements over the six-year period?
   a. $–0–.
   b. $49,000.
   c. $70,000.
   d. $119,000.

LO1

3. A city government holds a six-year capital lease for property being used within the General Fund. Minimum lease payments total $70,000 starting next year but have a current present value of $49,000. What is the total amount of other financing sources to be recognized on the fund-based financial statements over this six-year period?
   a. $–0–.
   b. $49,000.
   c. $70,000.
   d. $119,000.

LO1

4. A city government has a nine-year capital lease for property being used within the General Fund. The lease was signed on January 1, 2010. Minimum lease payments total $90,000 starting at the end of the first year but have a current present value of $69,000. Annual payments are $10,000, and the interest rate being applied is 10 percent. When the first payment is made on December 31, 2010, which of the following recordings is made?

Government-Wide Statements	Fund-Based Statements
a. Interest Expense $–0–	Interest Expense $–0–
b. Interest Expense $6,900	Expenditures $6,900
c. Expenditures $10,000	Expenditures $10,000
d. Interest Expense $6,900	Expenditures $10,000

LO1

5. A city government has a nine-year capital lease for property being used within the General Fund. The lease was signed on January 1, 2010. Minimum lease payments total $90,000 starting at the end of the first year but have a current present value of $69,000. Annual payments are $10,000, and the

interest rate being applied is 10 percent. What liability is reported on the fund-based financial statements as of December 31, 2010, after the first payment has been made?

    a. $–0–.

    b. $59,000.

    c. $65,900.

    d. $80,000.

LO2

6. A city creates a solid waste landfill. It assesses every person or company that uses the landfill a charge based on the amount of materials contributed. In which of the following will the landfill probably be recorded?

    a. General Fund.

    b. Special revenues funds.

    c. Internal service funds.

    d. Enterprise funds.

Use the following information for problems 7, 8, and 9

A city starts a solid waste landfill that it expects to fill to capacity gradually over a 10-year period. At the end of the first year, it is 8 percent filled. At the end of the second year, it is 19 percent filled. Currently, the cost of closure and postclosure is estimated at $1 million. None of this amount will be paid until the landfill has reached its capacity.

LO2

7. Which of the following is true for the Year 2 government-wide financial statements?

    a. Both expense and liability will be zero.

    b. Both expense and liability will be $110,000.

    c. Expense will be $110,000 and liability will be $190,000.

    d. Expense will be $100,000 and liability will be $200,000.

LO2

8. If this landfill is judged to be a proprietary fund, what liability will be reported at the end of the second year on fund-based financial statements?

    a. $–0–.

    b. $110,000.

    c. $190,000.

    d. $200,000.

LO2

9. If this landfill is judged to be a governmental fund, what liability will be reported at the end of the second year on fund-based financial statements?

    a. $–0–.

    b. $110,000.

    c. $190,000.

    d. $200,000.

Use the following information for problems 10 and 11:

The employees of the City of Jones earn vacation time that totals $1,000 per week during the year. Of this amount, $12,000 is actually taken in Year 1 and the remainder is taken in Year 2.

LO2

10. What liability should the city report on government-wide financial statements at the end of Year 1?

    a. It depends on whether the employees work at governmental activities or business-type activities.

    b. $–0–.

    c. $40,000.

    d. $52,000.

LO2

11. What amount of liability should the city recognize on fund-based financial statements at December 31, Year 1? Assume that all remaining vacations will be taken in July.

    a. It depends on whether the employees work at governmental activities or business-type activities.

    b. $–0–.

    c. $40,000.

    d. $52,000.

LO3

12. The City of Wilson receives a large sculpture valued at $240,000 as a gift to be placed in front of the municipal building. Which of the following is true for reporting the gift on the government-wide financial statements?
    a. A capital asset of $240,000 must be reported.
    b. No capital asset will be reported.
    c. If conditions are met, recording the sculpture as a capital asset is optional.
    d. The sculpture will be recorded but only for the amount paid by the city.

LO3

13. In problem 12, which of the following statements is true about reporting a revenue?
    a. A revenue will be reported.
    b. Revenue is reported but only if the asset is reported.
    c. If the asset is not capitalized, no revenue should be recognized.
    d. As a gift, no revenue would ever be reported.

LO3

14. Assume in problem 12 that the city reports the work as a capital asset. Which of the following is true?
    a. Depreciation is not recorded because the city has no cost.
    b. Depreciation is not required if the asset is viewed as being inexhaustible.
    c. Depreciation must be recognized because the asset is capitalized.
    d. Because the property was received as a gift, recognition of depreciation is optional.

LO4

15. A city builds sidewalks throughout its various neighborhoods at a cost of $200,000. Which of the following is *not* true?
    a. Because the sidewalks qualify as infrastructure, the asset is viewed in the same way as land so that no depreciation is recorded.
    b. Depreciation is required unless the modified approach is utilized.
    c. The modified approach recognizes maintenance expense in lieu of depreciation expense for qualifying infrastructure assets.
    d. The modified approach is allowed only if the city maintains the network of sidewalks at least at a predetermined condition.

LO4

16. Which of the following is true about use of the modified approach?
    a. It can be applied to all capital assets of a state or local government.
    b. It is used to adjust depreciation expense either up or down based on conditions for the period.
    c. It is required for infrastructure assets.
    d. For qualified assets, it eliminates the recording of depreciation.

LO5

17. Which of the following is true about the management's discussion and analysis (MD&A)?
    a. It is an optional addition to the comprehensive annual financial report, but the GASB encourages its inclusion.
    b. It adds a verbal explanation for the numbers and trends presented in the financial statements.
    c. It appears at the very end of a government's comprehensive annual financial report.
    d. It replaces a portion of the fund-based financial statements traditionally presented by a state or local government.

LO6

18. Which of the following is *not* necessary for a special purpose local government to be viewed as a primary government for reporting purposes?
    a. It must have a separately elected governing body.
    b. It must have specifically defined geographic boundaries.
    c. It must be fiscally independent.
    d. It must have corporate powers to prove that it is legally independent.

LO6

19. An accountant is trying to determine whether the school system of the City of Abraham is fiscally independent. Which of the following is *not* a requirement for being deemed fiscally independent?
    a. Holding property in its own name.
    b. Issuing bonded debt without outside approval.
    c. Passing its own budget without outside approval.
    d. Setting taxes or rates without outside approval.

LO6

20. An employment agency for individuals with disabilities works closely with the City of Hanover. The employment agency is legally separate from the city but still depends on it for financial support. How should Hanover report the employment agency in its comprehensive annual financial report?

    a. Not at all because the agency is legally separate.

    b. As a part of the General Fund.

    c. As a component unit.

    d. As a related organization.

LO7

21. The City of Bacon holds cash of $820,000 that was received from the issuance of a bond and, according to the contract, must be spent for the construction of a new elementary school. The city also has $60,000 in supplies. How should the fund balance be reported?

    a. Restricted—$880,000

    b. Nonspendable—$60,000 and restricted—$820,000

    c. Nonspendable—$60,000 and committed—$820,000

    d. Nonspendable—$60,000 and assigned—$820,000

LO6

22. For component units, what is the difference in *discrete presentation* and *blending*?

    a. A blended component unit is shown to the left of the statements; a discretely presented component unit is shown to the right.

    b. A blended component unit is shown at the bottom of the statements; a discretely presented component unit is shown within the statements like a fund.

    c. A blended component unit is shown within the statements like a fund; a discretely presented component unit is shown to the right.

    d. A blended component unit is shown to the right of the statements; a discretely presented component unit is shown in completely separate statements.

LO7

23. A government reports that its public safety function had expenses of $900,000 last year and program revenues of $200,000 so that its net expenses were $700,000. On which financial statement is this information presented?

    a. Statement of activities.

    b. Statement of cash flows.

    c. Statement of revenues and expenditures.

    d. Statement of net assets.

LO7

24. Government-wide financial statements make a distinction between program revenues and general revenues. How is that difference shown?

    a. Program revenues are offset against the expenses of a specific function; general revenues are assigned to governmental activities and business-type activities in general.

    b. General revenues are shown at the top of the statement of revenues and expenditures; program revenues are shown at the bottom.

    c. General revenues are labeled as operating revenues; program revenues are shown as miscellaneous income.

    d. General revenues are broken down by type; program revenues are reported as a single figure for the government.

LO7

25. Which of the following is true about the statement of cash flows for the proprietary funds of a state or local government?

    a. The indirect method of reporting cash flows from operating activities is allowed although the direct method is recommended.

    b. The structure of the statement is virtually identical to that of a for-profit business.

    c. The statement is divided into four separate sections of cash flows.

    d. Amounts spent on capital assets are reported in a separate section from amounts raised to finance those capital assets.

LO8

26. Which of the following is most likely to be true about the financial reporting of a public college or university?

    a. It resembles the financial reporting of private colleges and universities.

    b. It will continue to use its own unique style of financial reporting.

    c. It resembles the financial reporting made by a proprietary fund within the fund-based financial statements for a state or local government.

    d. It will soon be reported using a financial statement format unique to the needs of public colleges and universities that GASB is scheduled to create.

LO1

27. On January 1, 2010, a city entered into the following leases for equipment items. Each of the leases qualifies as a capital lease. Initial payments are on December 31, 2010. An interest rate of 10 percent is viewed as appropriate. No bargain purchase options exist.

Fund	Annual Payments	Total Payments	Present Value of Total Payments
General (5-year life)	$8,000	$40,000	$33,350
Enterprise (6-year life)	6,000	36,000	28,750

a. What balances should be reported on government-wide financial statements for December 31, 2010, and the year then ended?

b. What balances should be reported on fund-based financial statements for December 31, 2010, and the year then ended?

LO1

28. On January 1, 2010, a city entered into the following leases for equipment items. Each of the leases qualifies as a capital lease. Initial payments are on December 31, 2010. An interest rate of 12 percent is viewed as appropriate. No bargain purchase options exist.

Fund	Annual Payments	Total Payments	Present Value of Total Payments
General (10-year life)	$3,000	$30,000	$19,000
Enterprise (4-year life)	9,000	36,000	30,600

a. Prepare journal entries for the year 2010 for both of these leases for government-wide financial statements.

b. Prepare journal entries for the year 2010 for both of these leases for fund-based financial statements.

LO1

29. On January 1, 2010, the City of Verga leased a large truck for five years and made the initial annual payment of $22,000 immediately. The present value of these payments based on an 8 percent interest rate is assumed to be $87,800. The truck has an expected useful life of five years.

a. Assuming that the city's fire department will use the truck, what journal entries should be made for 2010 and 2011 on the government-wide financial statements?

b. Assuming that city's fire department will use the the truck, what journal entries should be made for 2010 and 2011 on the fund-based financial statements?

c. Assuming that the airport (an enterprise fund) operated by the city will use the truck, what journal entries should be made for 2010 and 2011 on the fund-based financial statements?

LO2

30. On January 1, 2010, the City of Hastings created a solid waste landfill that it expects to reach capacity gradually over the next 20 years. If the landfill were to be closed at the current time, closure costs would be approximately $1.2 million plus an additional $700,000 for postclosure work. Of these totals, the city must pay $50,000 on December 31 of each year for preliminary closure work. At the end of 2010, the landfill reached 3 percent of capacity. At the end of 2011, the landfill reached 9 percent of capacity. Also at the end of 2011, a reassessment is made; total closure costs are determined to be $1.4 million rather than $1.2 million.

a. Assuming that the landfill is viewed as an enterprise fund, what journal entries are made in 2010 and 2011 on the government-wide financial statements?

b. Assuming that the landfill is reported within the general fund, what journal entries are made in 2010 and 2011 on the government-wide financial statements?

c. Assuming that the landfill is viewed as an enterprise fund, what journal entries are made in 2010 and 2011 on fund-based financial statements?

d. Assuming that the landfill is reported within the general fund, what journal entries are made in 2010 and 2011 on fund-based financial statements?

LO2

31. The City of Lawrence opens a solid waste landfill in 2010 that is at 54 percent of capacity on December 31, 2010. The city had initially anticipated closure costs of $2 million but later that year decided that closure costs would actually be $2.4 million. None of these costs will be incurred until 2017 when the landfill is scheduled to be closed.

a. What will appear on the government-wide financial statements for this landfill for the year ended December 31, 2010?

b. Assuming that the landfill is recorded within the General Fund, what will appear on the fund-based financial statements for this landfill for the year ended December 31, 2010?

LO2

32. Mary T. Lincoln works for the City of Columbus. She volunteered to work over the 2010 Christmas break to earn a short vacation during the first week of January 2011. She earns three vacation days and will be paid $400 per day. She takes her vacation in January and is paid for those days.

    a. Prepare the journal entries on the government-wide financial statements for 2010 and 2011 because of these events.

    b. Assume that Lincoln works in an activity reported within the General Fund. Prepare journal entries for the fund-based financial statements for 2010 and 2011 because of these events.

    c. Assume that Lincoln works in an activity reported within the General Fund but that she does not plan to take her three vacation days until near the end of 2011. What journal entries should be made for the fund-based financial statements in 2010 and 2011?

LO3

33. On January 1, 2010, a rich citizen of the Town of Ristoni donates a painting valued at $300,000 to be displayed to the public in a government building. Although this painting meets the three criteria to qualify as an artwork, town officials choose to record it as an asset. There are no eligibility requirements for the gift. The asset is judged to be inexhaustible so that depreciation will not be reported.

    a. For the year ended December 31, 2010, what will be reported on government-wide financial statements in connection with this gift?

    b. How does the answer to requirement (*a*) change if the government decides to depreciate this asset over a 10-year period using straight-line depreciation?

    c. How does the answer to requirement (*a*) change if the government decides not to capitalize the asset?

LO3

34. On January 1, 2010, a city pays $60,000 for a work of art to display in the local library. The city will take appropriate measures to protect and preserve the piece. However, if the work is ever sold, the money received will go into unrestricted funds. The work is viewed as inexhaustible, but the city has opted to depreciate this cost over 20 years (using the straight-line method).

    a. How is this work be reported on the government-wide financial statements for the year ended December 31, 2010?

    b. How is this work be reported in the fund-based financial statements for the year ended December 31, 2010?

LO4

35. A city government adds street lights within its boundaries at a total cost of $100,000. The lights should burn for at least 10 years but can last significantly longer if maintained properly. The city sets up a system to monitor these lights with the goal that 97 percent will be working at any one time. During the year, the city spends $6,300 to clean and repair the lights so that they are working according to the specified conditions. However, it spends another $9,000 to construct lights for several new streets in the city.

    Describe the various ways these costs could be reported on government-wide statements.

LO5

36. The City of Francois, Texas, has begun the process of producing its current comprehensive annual financial report (CAFR). Several organizations that operate within the city are related in some way to the primary government. The city's accountant is attempting to determine how these organizations should be included in the reporting process.

    a. What is the major criterion for inclusion in a government's CAFR?

    b. How does an activity or function qualify as a special purpose government?

    c. How is the legal separation of a special purpose government evaluated?

    d. How is the fiscal independence of a special purpose government evaluated?

    e. What is a component unit, and how is it normally reported on government-wide financial statements?

    f. How does a primary government prove that it can impose its will on a component unit?

    g. What does the blending of a component unit mean?

LO4, LO5

37. The County of Maxnell decides to create a sanitation department and offer its services to the public for a fee. As a result, county officials plan to account for this activity within the enterprise funds. Make journal entries for this operation for the following 2010 transactions as well as necessary adjusting entries at the end of the year. Assume that the information is being gathered for fund-based financial statements. Only entries for the sanitation department are required here:

    January 1—Received unrestricted funds of $90,000 from the General Fund as permanent financing.

    February 1—Borrowed an additional $130,000 from a local bank at a 12 percent annual interest rate.

    March 1—Ordered a truck at an expected cost of $108,000.

April 1—Received the truck and made full payment. The actual cost amounted to $110,000. The truck has a 10-year life and no salvage value. Straight-line depreciation is to be used.

May 1—Received a $20,000 cash grant from the state to help supplement the pay of the sanitation workers. The money must be used for that purpose.

June 1—Rented a garage for the truck at a cost of $1,000 per month and paid 12 months of rent in advance.

July 1—Charged citizens $13,000 for services. Of this amount, $11,000 has been collected.

August 1—Made a $10,000 cash payment on the 12 percent note of February 1. This payment covers both interest and principal.

September 1—Paid salaries of $18,000 using the grant received on May 1.

October 1—Paid truck maintenance costs of $1,000.

November 1—Paid additional salaries of $10,000, first using the rest of the grant money received May 1.

December 31—Sent invoices totaling $19,000 to customers for services over the past six months. Collected $3,000 cash immediately.

LO2, LO3, LO5, LO7

38. The following information pertains to the City of Williamson for 2010, its first year of legal existence. For convenience, assume that all transactions are for the General Fund, which has three separate functions: general government, public safety, and health and sanitation.

Receipts:
Property taxes $320,000
Franchise taxes 42,000
Charges for general government services 5,000
Charges for public safety services 3,000
Charges for health and sanitation services 42,000
Issued long-term note payable 200,000
Receivables at end of year:
Property taxes (90 percent estimated to be collectible) 90,000
Payments:
Salary:
General government 66,000
Public safety 39,000
Health and sanitation 22,000
Rent:
General government 11,000
Public safety 18,000
Health and sanitation 3,000
Maintenance:
General government 21,000
Public safety 5,000
Health and sanitation 9,000
Insurance:
General government 8,000
Public safety ($2,000 still prepaid at end of year) 11,000
Health and sanitation 12,000
Interest on debt 16,000
Principal payment on debt 4,000
Building 120,000
Equipment 80,000
Supplies (20 percent still held) (public safety) 15,000
Investments 90,000
Ordered but not received:
Equipment 12,000
Due in one month at end of year:
Salaries:
General government 4,000
Public safety 7,000
Health and sanitation 8,000

Compensated absences for general government workers at year-end total $13,000. These amounts will not be taken until late in the year 2011.

The city received a piece of art this year valued at $14,000 that it is using for general government purposes. There are no eligibility requirements. The city chose not to capitalize this property.

The general government uses the building that was acquired and is depreciating it over 10 years using the straight-line method with no salvage value. The city uses the equipment for health and sanitation and depreciates it using the straight-line method over five years with no salvage value.

The investments are valued at $103,000 at the end of the year.

For the equipment that has been ordered but not yet received, the City Council (the highest decision-making body in the government) has voted to honor the commitment when the equipment is received.

a. Prepare a statement of activities and a statement of net assets for governmental activities for December 31, 2010, and the year then ended.

b. Prepare a statement of revenues, expenditures, and other changes in fund balances and a balance sheet for the General Fund as of December 31, 2010, and the year then ended. Assume that the city applies the consumption method.

LO1, LO2, LO5, LO7　39. The City of Bernard starts the year of 2010 with the following unrestricted amounts in its General Fund: cash of $20,000 and investments of $70,000. In addition, it holds a building bought on January 1, 2009, for general government purposes for $300,000 and related long-term debt of $240,000. The building is being depreciated on the straight-line method over 10 years. The interest rate is 10 percent. The General Fund has four separate functions: general government, public safety, public works, and health and sanitation. Other information includes the following:

Receipts:

Property taxes	$510,000
Sales taxes	99,000
Dividend income	20,000
Charges for general government services	15,000
Charges for public safety services	8,000
Charges for public works	4,000
Charges for health and sanitation services	31,000
Charges for landfill	8,000
Grant to be used for salaries for health workers (no eligibility requirements)	25,000
Issued long-term note payable	200,000
Sold above investments	84,000

Receivables at year end:

Property taxes ($10,000 is expected to be uncollectible)	130,000

Payments:

Salary:

General government	90,000
Public safety	94,000
Public works	69,000
Health and sanitation (all from grant)	22,000

Utilities:

General government	9,000
Public safety	16,000
Public works	13,000
Health and sanitation	4,000

Insurance:

General government	25,000
Public safety	12,000
Public works (all prepaid as of the end of the year)	6,000
Health and sanitation	4,000

Miscellaneous:

General government	12,000
Public safety	10,000
Public works	9,000
Health and sanitation	7,000

(continued)

Interest on previous debt	24,000
Principal payment on previous debt	10,000
Interest on new debt	18,000
Building (public works)	210,000
Equipment (public safety)	90,000
Public works supplies (30 percent still held)	20,000
Investments	111,000
Ordered but not received:	
Equipment	24,000
Supplies	7,000
Due at end of year:	
Salaries:	
General government	14,000
Public safety	17,000
Public works	5,000

The city leased a truck on the last day of the year. The first payment will be made at the end of the next year. Total payments will amount to $90,000 but have a present value of $64,000.

The city started a landfill this year that it is recording within its General Fund. It is included as a public works function. Closure costs today would be $260,000 although the landfill is not expected to be filled for nine more years. The city has incurred no costs to date although the landfill is now 15 percent filled.

For the equipment and supplies that have been ordered but not yet received, the City Council (the highest decision-making body in the government) has voted to honor the commitment when the items are received.

The new building is being depreciated over 20 years using the straight-line method and no salvage value, whereas depreciation of the equipment is similar except that its life is only 10 years. Assume the city records a full year's depreciation in the year of acquisition.

The investments are valued at $116,000 at year-end.

a. Prepare a statement of activities and a statement of net assets for governmental activities for December 31, 2010, and the year then ended.

b. Prepare a statement of revenues, expenditures, and changes in fund balances and a balance sheet for the General Fund as of December 31, 2010, and the year then ended. Assume that the purchases method is being applied.

LO2, LO3, LO5, LO7

40. The City of Pfeiffer starts the year of 2010 with the General Fund and an enterprise fund. The General Fund has two activities: education and parks/recreation. For convenience, assume that the General Fund holds $123,000 cash and a new school building costing $1 million. The city utilizes straight-line depreciation. The building has a 20-year life and no salvage value. The enterprise fund has $62,000 cash and a new $600,000 civic auditorium with a 30-year life and no salvage value. The enterprise fund monitors just one activity, the rental of the civic auditorium for entertainment and other cultural affairs.

The following transactions for the city take place during 2010. Assume that the city's fiscal year ends on December 31.

a. Decides to build a municipal park and transfers $70,000 into a capital projects fund and immediately expends $20,000 for a piece of land. The creation of this fund and this transfer were made by the highest level of government authority.

b. Borrows $110,000 cash on a long-term bond for use in creating the new municipal park.

c. Assesses property taxes on the first day of the year. The assessment, which is immediately enforceable, totals $600,000. Of this amount, $510,000 will be collected during 2010 and another $50,000 is expected in the first month of 2011. The remainder is expected about halfway through 2011.

d. Constructs a building in the park in (b) for $80,000 cash for playing basketball and other sports. It is put into service on July 1 and should last 10 years with no salvage value.

e. Builds a sidewalk around the new park for $10,000 cash and puts it into service on July 1. It should last for 10 years, but the city plans to keep it up to a predetermined quality level so that it will last almost indefinitely.

f. Opens the park and charges an entrance fee of only a token amount so that it records the park, therefore, in the General Fund. Collections during this first year total $8,000.

g. Buys a new parking deck for $200,000, paying $20,000 cash and signing a long-term note for the rest. The parking deck, which is to go into operation on July 1, is across the street from the civic auditorium and is considered part of that activity. It has a 20-year life and no salvage value.

h. Receives a $100,000 cash grant for the city school system that must be spent for school lunches for the poor. Appropriate spending of these funds is viewed as an eligibility requirement of this grant. During the current year, $37,000 of the amount received was properly spent.

i. Charges students in the school system a total fee of $6,000 for books and the like. Of this amount, 90 percent is collected during 2010 with the remainder expected to be collected in the first few weeks of 2011.

j. Buys school supplies for $22,000 cash and uses $17,000 of them. The General Fund uses the purchases method.

k. Receives a painting by a local artist to be displayed in the local school. It qualifies as a work of art, and officials have chosen not to capitalize it. The painting has a value of $80,000. It is viewed as inexhaustible.

l. Transfers $20,000 cash from the General Fund to the Enterprise Fund as a capital contribution.

m. Orders a school bus for $99,000.

n. Receives the school bus and pays an actual cost of $102,000. The bus is put into operation on October 1 and should last for five years with no salvage value.

o. Pays salaries of $240,000 to schoolteachers. In addition, owes and will pay $30,000 during the first two weeks of 2011. Vacations worth $23,000 have also been earned but will not be taken until July 2011.

p. Pays salaries of $42,000 to city auditorium workers. In addition, owes and will pay $3,000 in the first two weeks of 2011. Vacations worth $5,000 have also been earned but will not be taken until July 2011.

q. Charges customers $130,000 for the rental of the civic auditorium. Of this balance, collected $110,000 in cash and will collect the remainder in April 2011.

r. Pays $9,000 maintenance charges for the building and sidewalk in (d) and (e).

s. Pays $14,000 on the bond in (b) on the last day of 2010: $5,000 principal and $9,000 interest.

t. Accrues interest of $13,000 on the note in (g) as of the end of 2010, an amount that it will pay in June 2011.

u. Assumes that a museum that operates within the city is a component unit that will be discretely presented. The museum reports to city officials that it had $42,000 of direct expenses this past year and $50,000 in revenues from admission charges. The only assets that it had at year-end were cash of $24,000, building (net of depreciation) of $300,000, and a long-term liability of $210,000.

Prepare the 2010 government-wide financial statements for this city. Assume the use of the modified approach.

LO2, LO3, LO5, LO7

41. Use the information in problem 40 to prepare the 2010 fund-based financial statements for the governmental funds and the proprietary funds. A statement of cash flows is not required. Assume that "available" is defined as within 60 days and that all funds are major. The General Fund is used for debt repayment.

LO1, LO2, LO5

42. For each of the following, indicate whether the statement is true or false and include a brief explanation for your answer.

a. A pension trust fund appears in the government-wide financial statements but not in the fund-based financial statements.

b. Permanent funds are included as one of the governmental funds.

c. A fire department placed orders of $20,000 for equipment. The equipment is received but at a cost of $20,800. In compliance with requirements for fund-based financial statements, an encumbrance of $20,000 was recorded when the order was placed, and an expenditure of $20,800 was recorded when the order was received.

d. The government reported a landfill as an enterprise fund. At the end of Year 1, the government estimated that the landfill will cost $800,000 to clean up when it is eventually full. Currently, it is 12 percent filled. At the end of Year 2, the estimation was changed to $860,000 when it was 20 percent filled. No payments are due for several years. Fund-based financial statements for Year 2 should report a $76,000 expense.

e. A city reports a landfill in the General Fund. At the end of Year 1, the government anticipated the landfill would cost $900,000 to clean up when it is full and reported that it was 11 percent filled.

At the end of Year 2, the estimates were changed to $850,000 and 20 percent filled. No payments are due for several years. Government-wide financial statements for Year 2 should report a $71,000 expense.

    f. A lease for a computer (that has a six-year life) is signed on January 1, Year 1, with six annual payments of $10,000. The police department will use the computer. The first payment is to be made immediately. The present value of the $60,000 in cash flows is $39,000 based on a 10 percent rate. Fund-based financial statements for Year 1 should report total expenditures of $10,000.

    g. An agency fund has neither revenues nor expenditures but reports expenses.

    h. A lease for a computer (that has a six-year life) is signed on January 1, Year 1, with six annual payments of $10,000. The computer is to be used by the police department. The first payment is to be made immediately. The present value of the $60,000 in cash flows is $39,000 based on a 10 percent rate. Government-wide financial statements for Year 1 should report expenses of $9,400.

For problems 43 through 48, use the following introductory information:
The City of Wolfe has issued its financial statements for Year 4 (assume that the city uses a calendar year). The city maintains the General Fund made up of two functions: (1) education and (2) parks. The city also utilizes capital projects funds for ongoing construction and an enterprise fund to account for its art museum. It also has one discretely presented component unit.

    The government-wide financial statements indicated the following Year 4 totals:

        Education had net expenses of $710,000.
        Parks had net expenses of $130,000.
        Art museum had net revenues of $80,000.
        General revenues were $900,000; the overall increase in net assets was $140,000.

    The fund-based financial statements issued for Year 4 indicated the following:

        The General Fund had an increase of $30,000 in its fund balance.
        The Capital Projects Fund had an increase of $40,000 in its fund balance.
        The Enterprise Fund had an increase of $60,000 in its net assets.

    Officials for Wolfe define "available" as current financial resources to be paid or collected within 60 days.

LO3

43. On the first day of Year 4, the city receives a painting as a gift that qualifies as a work of art. It has a 30-year life, is worth $15,000, and is being displayed at one of the local parks. The accountant accidentally capitalized and depreciated it although officials had wanted to use the allowed alternative. Respond to the following:

    a. According to the information provided, the General Fund reported a $30,000 increase in its fund balance. If city officials had used proper alternatives in this reporting, what would have been the correct change in the fund balance for the General Fund for the year?

    b. According to the information provided, the parks reported net expenses of $130,000. If city officials had used proper alternatives in this reporting, what was the correct net expense for parks for the year?

    c. Assume the same information except that the art was given to the art museum but not recorded at all. What should have been the overall change in net assets for Year 4 on government-wide financial statements, assuming that officials still preferred the allowed alternative?

LO1

44. On January 1, Year 4, the government leased a police car for five years at $20,000 per year with the first payment being made on December 31, Year 4. This is a capitalized lease. Assume that, at a reasonable interest rate of 10 percent, the present value of a five-year annuity due is $62,000. In the government-wide financial statements, the government recorded a $20,000 increase in expense and a $20,000 reduction in cash as its only entry. In the fund-based financial statements, the government increased Expenditures by $20,000 and reduced Cash for $20,000 as its only entry.

    a. According to the information provided, the overall increase in net assets reported was $140,000. What was the correct overall change in the net assets in the government-wide financial statements?

    b. According to the information provided, the General Fund reported an increase of $30,000 in its fund balance. What was the correct change in the fund balance for the General Fund?

LO6

45. Assume that the one component unit had program revenues of $30,000 and expenses of $42,000 and spent $10,000 for land during Year 4. However, it should have been handled as a blended component unit, not as a discretely presented component unit. According to the information provided,

the overall increase in net assets reported was $140,000. What was the correct overall change in the net assets in the government-wide financial statements?

LO2

46. At the end of Year 4, the city owed teachers $60,000 in vacation pay that had not been recorded. The assumption is that these vacations will be taken evenly over the next year. A 60-day period is used to determine available funds.

   a. What is the correct change in the fund balance of the General Fund for the year?

   b. What is the correct overall change in the net assets in the government-wide financial statements?

LO2

47. The city maintains a landfill that has been recorded within its parks. The landfill generated program revenues of $4,000 in Year 4 and cash expenses of $15,000. It also paid $3,000 cash for a piece of land. These transactions were recorded as would have been anticipated, but no other recording was made this year. The city assumes that it will have to pay $200,000 to clean up the landfill when it is closed in several years. The landfill was 18 percent filled at the end of Year 3 and is 26 percent filled at the end of Year 4. No payments will be necessary for several more years. For convenience, assume that the entries in all previous years were correctly handled regardless of the situation.

   a. The city believes that the landfill was included correctly in all previous years as one of its Enterprise Funds. According to the information provided, the overall increase in net assets reported was $140,000. What is the correct overall change in the net assets in the government-wide financial statements?

   b. The city believes that the landfill was included correctly in all previous years in one of the Enterprise Funds. According to the information provided, the Enterprise Fund reported an increase in its net assets of $60,000. What is the correct change in the net assets of the Enterprise Fund in the fund-based financial statements?

   c. The city believes that the landfill was included correctly in all previous years within the General Fund. What is the correct change in the fund balance of the General Fund?

LO4

48. On the first day of the year, the City of Wolfe bought $20,000 of equipment with a five-year life and no salvage value for its school system. It was capitalized but no other entries were ever made. The machine was monitored using the modified approach.

   a. What was the correct overall change in the net assets in the government-wide financial statements?

   b. What was the total of correct net expenses for education in the government-wide statements?

LO1

49. A police department leases a car on July 1, Year 1, with five annual payments of $20,000 each. It immediately makes the first payment, and the present value of the annuity due is $78,000 based on an assumed rate of 10 percent. The car has a five-year life. Assume that this is a capitalized lease. Indicate whether each of the following *independent* statements is true or false and briefly explain each answer.

   a. The fund-based financial statements will show a total liability of $3,900 at the end of Year 1.

   b. The government-wide financial statements will show a total liability of $58,000 at the end of Year 1.

   c. The government-wide financial statements will show total interest expense of $2,900 in Year 1.

   d. The fund-based financial statements will show total expenditures of $20,000 in Year 1.

   e. The government-wide financial statements will show a net leased asset of $70,200 at the end of Year 1.

   f. If this were an ordinary annuity so that the first payment was made in Year 2, no expenditure would be reported in the fund-based financial statements in Year 1.

   g. If the car had an eight-year useful life, this contract could not be a capitalized lease.

   h. Over the entire life of the car, the amount of expense recognized in the government-wide financial statements will be the same as the amount of expenditures recognized in the fund-based financial statements.

LO2

50. A city has a solid waste landfill that was filled 12 percent in Year 1 and 26 percent in Year 2. During those periods, the government expected that total closure costs would be $2 million. As a result, it paid $50,000 to an environmental company on July 1 of each of these two years. Such payments will continue for several years to come. Indicate whether each of the following *independent* statements is true or false and briefly explain each answer.

   a. The government-wide financial statements will show a $230,000 expense in Year 2 but only if reported in an enterprise fund.

   b. The fund-based financial statements will show a $50,000 liability in Year 2 if this landfill is reported in the General Fund.

    c. The fund-based financial statements will show a $50,000 liability at the end of Year 2 if this landfill is reported in an enterprise fund.

    d. If this landfill is reported in an enterprise fund, the government-wide financial statements and the fund-based financial statements will basically have the same reporting.

    e. The government-wide financial statements will show a $420,000 liability at the end of Year 2.

    f. Over the landfill's entire life, the amount of expense recognized in the government-wide financial statements will be the same as the amount of expenditures recognized in the fund-based financial statements.

LO2

51. Use the same information as in problem 50 except that, by the end of Year 3, the landfill is 40 percent filled. The city realizes that the total closure costs will be $3 million. Indicate whether each of the following *independent* statements is true or false and briefly explain each answer.

    a. If the city had known the costs were going to be $3 million from the beginning, the reporting on the fund-based financial statements would have been different in the past years if the landfill had been reported in an enterprise fund.

    b. If the landfill is monitored in the General Fund, a liability will be reported for the governmental activities in the government-wide financial statements at the end of Year 3.

    c. A $680,000 expense should be recognized in Year 3 in the government-wide financial statements.

    d. Because the closure costs reflect a future flow of cash, any liability reported in the government-wide financial statements must be reported at present value.

LO3

52. A city receives a copy of its original charter from the year 1799 as a gift from a citizen. The document will be put under glass and displayed in the city hall for all to see. The fair value is estimated at $10,000. Indicate whether each of the following *independent* statements is true or false and briefly explain each answer.

    a. If the city government does not have a policy for handling any proceeds if it ever sells the document, the city must report a $10,000 asset within its government-wide financial statements.

    b. Assume that this gift qualifies for optional handling and that the city chooses to report it as an asset. For the government-wide financial statements, depreciation is required.

    c. Assume this gift qualifies for optional handling and the document is deemed to be exhaustible. The city must report an immediate expense of $10,000 in the government-wide financial statements.

    d. Assume that this gift qualifies for optional handling. The city must make a decision as to whether to recognize a revenue of $10,000 in the government-wide financial statements.

    e. Assume that this gift qualifies for optional handling. The city can choose to report the gift in the statement of net activities for the government-wide financial statements in a way so that there is no overall net effect.

LO6

53. A city starts a public library that has separate incorporation and gets some of its money from the state and some from private donations. Indicate whether each of the following *independent* statements is true or false and briefly explain each answer.

    a. If the city appoints 7 of the 10 directors, it must report the library as a component unit.

    b. If the library is a component unit and its financial results are shown as part of the governmental activities of the city, it is known as a *blended component unit.*

    c. If the library appoints its own board but the city must approve its budget, the library must be reported as a blended component unit.

    d. The choice of whether a component unit is blended or reported discretely is up to the city's discretion.

Develop Your Skills

RESEARCH CASE 1

CPA *skills*

The City of Abernethy has three large bridges built in the later part of the 1980s that were not capitalized at the time. In creating government-wide financial statements, the city's accountant is interested in receiving suggestions as to how to determine a valid amount to report currently for these bridges.

Required

Use a copy of GASB *Statement 34* as the basis for writing a report to this accountant to indicate various ways to make this calculation. Use examples that will help illustrate the process.

RESEARCH CASE 2

Officials for the City of Artichoke, West Virginia, have recently formed a transit authority to create a public transportation system for the community. These same officials are now preparing the city's CAFR for the most recent year. The transit authority has already lost a considerable amount of money and the officials have become interested in its reporting and whether it qualifies as a component unit of the city.

Following are several articles written about the reporting of component units by a state or local government:

"Financial Reporting for Affiliated Organizations," *The Journal of Government Financial Management,* Winter 2003.

"How to Implement GASB Statement No. 34," *The Journal of Accountancy,* November 2001.

"Accounting for Affiliated Organizations," *Government Finance Review,* December 2002.

"Component Unit Reporting in the New Reporting Model," *The CPA Journal,* October 2001.

Required

Read one or more of the above articles and any others that you may discover about component units. Write a memo to these city officials providing as much detailed information about component units and their reporting as you can to help these individuals understand the challenges and difficulties of this reporting.

ANALYSIS CASE 1

Read the following journal article: "25 Years of State and Local Governmental Financial Reporting—An Accounting Standards Perspective," *The Government Accountants Journal,* Fall 1992.

Or, as a second possibility, do a search of books in the college library for advanced accounting textbooks or government accounting textbooks that were published prior to 2000.

Required

Accounting for state and local governments has changed considerably in just the last 10–20 years. Write a report to highlight some of the differences you noted between the process described before 2000 and that which has been presented in Chapters 11 and 12 of this textbook.

ANALYSIS CASE 2

Go to Web site www.portlandonline.com/omf/index.cfm?c=49561&a=228968 and find the 2008 comprehensive annual financial report for the City of Portland, Oregon. One of the most important additions to state and local government accounting is the required inclusion of a management's discussion and analysis. Read this section of the Portland report.

Required

Write a report indicating the types of information found in this government's MD&A that would not have previously been available in the city's financial statements.

COMMUNICATION CASE 1

Read the following articles and any other papers that are available on setting governmental accounting standards:

"The Governmental Accounting Standards Board: Factors Influencing Its Operation and Initial Technical Agenda," *The Government Accountants Journal,* Spring 2000.

"Governmental Accounting Standards Come of Age: Highlights from the First 20 Years," *Government Finance Review,* April 2005.

"GASB Re-Examines Fund Balance Reporting and Definitions of Fund Types," *Government Finance Review,* December 2006.

"A Century of Governmental Accounting and Financial Reporting Leadership," *Government Finance Review,* April 2006.

"The GASB Turns 25: A Retrospective," *Government Finance Review,* April 2009.

Required

Write a short paper discussing the evolution of governmental accounting.

COMMUNICATION CASE 2

The City of Larissa recently opened a solid waste landfill to serve the area's citizens and businesses. The city's accountant has gone to city officials for guidance as to whether to record the landfill within the General Fund or as a separate enterprise fund. Officials have asked for guidance on how to make that decision and how the answer will impact the government's financial reporting.

Required

Write a memo to the government officials describing the factors that should influence the decision as to the fund in which to report the landfill. Describe the impact that this decision will have on the city's future comprehensive annual financial reports.

EXCEL CASE

The City of Loveland previously adopted GASB *Statement 34.* Now city officials are attempting to determine reported values for major infrastructure assets that it had obtained prior to the implementation of the statement. The chief concern is determining a value for the city's hundreds of miles of roads that were built at various times over the past 20 years. Each road is assumed to last for 50 years (depreciation is 2 percent per year).

As of December 31, 2010, city engineers believed that one mile of new road would cost $2.3 million. For convenience, each road is assumed to have been acquired as of January 1 of the year in which it was put into operation. Officials have done some investigation and believe that the cost of a mile of road has increased by 8 percent each year over the past 30 years.

Required

Build a spreadsheet to determine what value should now be reported for each mile of road depending on the year it was put in operation. For example, what reported value should be disclosed in the government-wide financial statements for 10 miles of roads put into operation on January 1, 2003?

KAPLAN

CPA REVIEW

Please visit the text Web site for the online CPA Simulation.

The City of Clarksville (Clarksville) is incorporated and has a December 31 fiscal year-end. The City Council (Council) approves the budget annually. For internal reporting purposes, Clarksville uses the modified accrual basis of accounting to record its General Fund transactions. For external reporting purposes, Clarksville prepares a comprehensive annual financial report that includes both government-wide and fund-based financial statements.

The city has a policy that any financial resources to be received within 60 days are viewed as currently being available.

At the beginning of Year 1, the Council authorized the construction of a new recreation center. Its estimated cost is $25 million. Clarksville plans to finance the construction by combining bond proceeds with a state grant and making a transfer from the city's General Fund.

Topics to be covered in this simulation:

- Transfers.
- Infrastructure and modified approach.
- Statement of cash flows.
- Property taxes.
- Budgetary entries.
- Nonexchange transactions.
- Revenue and expenditure recognition.
- Encumbrances.

Index

Page numbers followed by n refer to notes.

G